PHLIP (Prentice Hall Learning on the Internet Partnership) is a content-rich multidisciplinary business Web site created by professors for professors and their students.

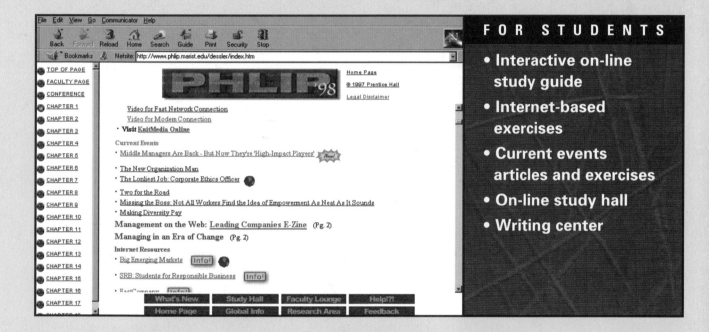

FOR STUDENTS

- Interactive on-line study guide
- Internet-based exercises
- Current events articles and exercises
- On-line study hall
- Writing center

FOR FACULTY

- Instructor's Manual and PowerPoint slides
- On-line course syllabus builder
- Faculty resource center
- CME—Course Monitor Edition for on-line course management featuring a roster, announcements, and a grade book

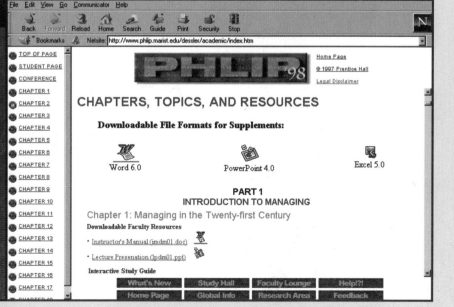

SIXTH EDITION

MANAGEMENT

STEPHEN P. ROBBINS
San Diego State University

MARY COULTER
Southwest Missouri State University

Prentice Hall
Upper Saddle River, New Jersey 07458

Senior Editor: David Shafer
Editorial Assistant: Christopher Stogdill/Shannon Sims
Editor-in-Chief: Natalie Anderson
Marketing Manager: Tamara Wederbrand
Senior Production Editor: Judith Leale
Managing Editor: Dee Josephson
Manufacturing Supervisor: Arnold Vila
Manufacturing Manager: Vincent Scelta
Formatting Supervisor: Christy Mahon
Electronic Art Supervisor: Warren Fischbach
Electronic Artist: Annie Bartell
Senior Manager of Production and Technology: Lorraine Patsco
Designer: Cheryl Asherman
Design Manager: Patricia Smythe
Interior Design: Ark Design
Photo Research Supervisor: Melinda Lee Reo
Image Permission Supervisor: Kay Dellosa
Photo Researcher: Melinda Alexander
Cover Design: Cheryl Asherman
Cover Illustration: John Bleck

Copyright ©1999, 1996 by Prentice-Hall, Inc.
A Simon & Schuster Company
Upper Saddle River, New Jersey 07458

Library of Congress Cataloging-in-Publication Data
Robbins, Stephen P.,
    Management / Stephen P. Robbins, Mary Coulter. —6th ed.
      p.   cm.
    Includes bibliographical references and index.
    ISBN 0-13-921503-4 (hardcover)
    1. Management.   I. Coulter, Mary K.   II. Title.
HD31.R5647 1998   98–10502
658—dc21   CIP

Prentice-Hall International (UK) Limited, London
Prentice-Hall of Australia Pty. Limited, Sydney
Prentice-Hall Canada, Inc., Toronto
Prentice-Hall Hispanoamericana, S.A., Mexico
Prentice-Hall of India Private Limited, New Delhi
Prentice-Hall of Japan, Inc., Tokyo
Simon & Schuster Asia Pte. Ltd., Singapore
Editora Prentice-Hall do Brasil, Ltda., Rio de Janeiro

Printed in the United States of America

10 9 8 7 6 5 4 3 2

To Laura Ospanik

—S.P.R.

To my mom and dad, Mildred
and Marion Maaks, who taught
me well!

—M.C.

Stephen P. Robbins received his Ph.D. from the University of Arizona. He previously worked for the Shell Oil Company and Reynolds Metals Company. Since completing his graduate studies, Dr. Robbins has taught at the University of Nebraska at Omaha, Concordia University in Montreal, the University of Baltimore, Southern Illinois University at Edwardsville, and San Diego State University. Dr. Robbins' research interests have focused on conflict, power, and politics in organizations, as well as the development of effective interpersonal skills. His articles on these and other topics have appeared in such journals as *Business Horizons*, the *California Management Review*, *Business and Economic Perspectives*, *International Management*, *Management Review*, *Canadian Personnel and Industrial Relations*, and the *Journal of Management Education*.

In recent years, Dr. Robbins has been spending most of his professional time writing textbooks. In addition to *Management*, sixth edition, these include *Organizational Behavior*, eighth edition (Prentice Hall, 1998); *Fundamentals of Management*, second edition, with David DeCenzo (Prentice Hall, 1998); *Supervision Today!*, second edition, with David DeCenzo (Prentice Hall, 1998); *Human Resource Management*, sixth edition, with David DeCenzo (Wiley, 1999); *Managing Today!* (Prentice Hall, 1997); *Essentials of Organizational Behavior*, fifth edition (Prentice Hall, 1997); *Training in InterPersonal Skills*, second edition, with Philip Hunsaker (Prentice Hall, 1996); and *Organization Theory*, third edition (Prentice Hall, 1990). These books are used at more than a thousand U.S. colleges and universities, as well as hundreds of schools throughout Canada, Latin America, Australia, New Zealand, Asia, Scandinavia, and Europe.

In Dr. Robbins' "other life," he participates in masters' track competition. Since turning 50 in 1993, he has set numerous indoor and outdoor world sprint records. He's also won gold medals in World Veteran Games in 100m, 200m, and 400m. In 1995, Robbins was named the year's outstanding age-40-and-over male track and field athlete by the Masters Track and Field Committee of USA Track & Field, the national governing body for athletes in the United States.

Mary Coulter received her Ph.D. in Management from the University of Arkansas in Fayetteville. Before completing her graduate work, she held different jobs including high school teacher, legal assistant, and government program planner. She has taught at Drury College, the University of Arkansas, Trinity University, and Southwest Missouri State University. Dr. Coulter's research interests have focused on competitive strategies for not-for-profit arts organizations and the use of new media in the educational process. Her research on these and other topics has appeared in such journals as *Journal of Business Strategies*, *Case Research Journal*, and *Journal of Business Research*. In addition to *Management*, Dr. Coulter has published another book with Prentice Hall, *Strategic Management in Action*, which is designed for the capstone business course in strategy. When she's not busy teaching or writing, she enjoys puttering around in her flower gardens, playing the piano, reading all different types of books, and enjoying many different activities with daughters Sarah and Katie.

Brief Contents

Contents

PART FOUR • ORGANIZING   298

CHAPTER 10

Organizational Structure and Design   298

CHAPTER 11

Human Resource Management   336

Special Features

ENTREPRENEURSHIP

MANAGING WORKFORCE DIVERSITY

Our publisher recently informed us that in its last edition this book was the world's number-one selling management textbook. We were obviously flattered to know that more than 400 colleges and universities chose our book as their introductory management text. But we have no intentions of resting on our laurels. Being the market leader also means that we have an ongoing responsibility to you, the reader, to continue the types of innovative presentations of management topics that we have had in the past.

Management is a dynamic discipline, and a textbook on the subject must constantly undergo significant changes to stay current. So we've carefully revised this sixth edition of *Management*. We've retained the basic paradigm, content, and features that have proven successful in previous editions. And importantly, we've added new topics and features that better reflect the field of management, and capture its excitement in the twenty-first century.

Retained from the Previous Edition

Adopters continually praise this book for its strong applications orientation. This is not just a book describing management theories. In addition to including extensive examples (which most other textbooks now do), we go out and talk with real managers. Then we bring their experiences to our readers. No other textbook has so successfully blended management theory with management practice. And based on feedback that we get from faculty and students, we remain confident that this new edition continues to make management concepts meaningful and to excite readers about the possibilities for careers in management. We'd like to describe some of the features we have retained in this edition.

- *Manager's Dilemma and Managers Respond.* We have continued this unique feature in this edition. Each chapter opens with a dilemma that a real-life manager is facing. The managers in these dilemmas come from a variety of organizations. From Lorenzo Zambrano, CEO of Cemex to Adam Werbach, Executive Director of the Sierra Club to Jeff Bezos, founder of the on-line bookstore Amazon.com, these managers reflect a broad and varied cross-section of situations. Each dilemma ends with the statement "What Would You Do?" providing an opportunity for student participation and active learning. Then, each chapter closes with a section titled "Managers Respond" where two real, practicing managers provide a short discussion of what they'd do if they were faced with the dilemma described at the beginning of the chapter. These managers also come from a broad and varied spectrum of types of organizations, levels in organizations, and sizes of organizations. Their responses help students link management concepts to management practice.

- *Managers Speak Out.* In each chapter, you'll find this theme box in which we interview real managers and ask them a broad range of questions. The information provided by these interviews provides a diverse perspective of managers and managerial philosophies. Again, we believe that bringing in real managers makes the text more practical and shows the relevance of this book's content to a manager's daily job. Many of these managers appear on video in a "Question and Answer" format on the accompanying CD-ROM (Look for the CD-ROM icon to identify which managers appear on the video).

- *Self-Assessment Exercises.* When the senior author first introduced self-assessment exercises in the second edition of the text, they were a novel idea in a management text. Now most books have them. Although the idea is no longer unique, you'll find that we've improved the focus and relevance of these exercises. You'll also find that several of the self-assessment exercises have been made more user-friendly; that is, we've included them on the accompanying CD-ROM where you can complete and score them.

- *For Your Immediate Action.* Each chapter has a "For Your Immediate Action" assignment in the end-of-chapter learning material. They attempt to capture the problem-solving dimensions of the manager's job by providing realistic problems related to specific chapter content. Many of these FYIAs in this edition are new— new situations, new issues, and new people.

- *Video Cases.* In this edition we offer two distinct video programs. First, we offer a traditional video case at the end of each chapter. These video cases include both ABC News video segments from the ABC News/Prentice Hall Video Library and selected segments from the *Small Business 2000* PBS series. A wide variety of situations is represented in these video cases. Second, there also are six video cases that highlight Showtime Networks Inc. These written cases about Showtime appear at the end of the textbook and integrate each part's chapter material. Each written case is accompanied by customized video segments that focus on the organizational and managerial issues that Showtime's managers are dealing with.

- *Emphasis on Workforce Diversity, Career, and Entrepreneurship Topics.* These topics are important ones to today's management students. We have chosen to continue highlighting these topics in boxed themes throughout the chapters.

- *Writing Style.* This revision continues both authors' commitment to present management concepts in a lively and conversational style. We carefully blend theories and examples. Our goal is to present chapter material in an interesting and relevant manner without oversimplifying the discussion. Of course, writing style is a subjective interpretation; only you can judge whether we've successfully achieved our goal.

New to This Edition

There are several new features and content topics that have been included in this revision. New topics to this edition include information technology, learning organizations, the "greening" of management, core competencies, project management, autonomous internal units, broadbanding compensation, skill-based pay plans, visionary leadership, team leadership, trust, customer-driven operations, ISO 9000, and numerous others. The research base for this revision has been updated, as well. Additionally, there are several new features you'll find in this revision.

- *Skills Modules.* Management students need to learn how to do management tasks as well as to learn *about* management. Today, the *how's* of being a manager have become just as important as the *what's*. To reflect the increased importance being placed on management skills, we identified 23 key skills encompassing the four management functions (planning, organizing, leading, and controlling) and developed Skills Modules that are included in a special section at the back of this book. Each Skills Module provides a short discussion about the skill, a list of suggestions or behaviors for doing this skill, a scenario that lets you practice the skill, some activities designed to help you reinforce the skill, and comments on the skill from practicing managers.

- *Testing. . . Testing. . . 1, 2, 3.* An innovation new to this edition that we're excited about is our "Testing. . . Testing. . . 1, 2, 3" feature. In multiple places throughout each chapter, you'll find a box that lists three questions addressing very specific factual information in the section you've just read. These questions were designed to help you review and assess whether you understood the material you've just read. We believe that you'll find this feature to be a convenient and useful way to review and reinforce key chapter information. Suggested responses can be found on the accompanying CD-ROM.

- *Management CD-ROM.* Each copy of *Management 6/e* includes a **free CD-ROM** containing material to help you better study and understand managers and management. Some of the features include:
  - Question and answer format video from many of the managers highlighted in the "Managers Speak Out" boxes.
  - Self-Assessment exercises that can be completed and scored for immediate feedback.
  - Accompanying video for the Showtime Networks Inc. integrative cases.
  - Suggested answers and page references to all "Testing. . . Testing. . . 1, 2, 3" boxes.
  - World Wide Web link to our companion Web site PHLIP (Prentice Hall Learning on the Internet Partnership) <http://www.phlip.com> which contains additional learning resources.

- *Thinking Critically about Ethics.* Being able to think critically about issues is important for managers. In the body of every chapter, you'll find a "Thinking Critically about Ethics" box. This feature provides material that stresses the value elements in managerial decisions.

- *Reorganized Chapter on Management History.* We've updated the history chapter! The history chapter now covers the historical development of managerial thought rather than focusing just on broad approaches to management. We added discussions of early motivation and leadership theories to this chapter rather than discussing them (as do most other management textbooks) in their respective chapters. We feel this is a better approach because it better differentiates motivation and leadership theories that set the foundation for our current knowledge from cutting-edge contemporary theories.

In-Text Learning Aids

A good textbook should teach as well as present ideas. Toward that end, we've tried to make this book an effective learning tool. We'd like to point out some specific pedagogical features that are designed to help readers better assimilate the material presented.

- *Chapter Learning Objectives.* Before you start a trip, it's valuable to know where you're headed. That way, you can minimize possible problems or detours. The same holds true in reading a text. To make your learning more efficient, each chapter opens with a list of learning objectives that describe what you should be able to do after reading the chapter. These objectives are designed to focus your attention on the major issues within each chapter.

- *Chapter Summaries.* Just as objectives clarify where you're going, chapter summaries remind you of where you've been. Each chapter concludes with a concise summary organized around the opening learning objectives.

- *Key Terms.* Every chapter highlights a number of key terms that you'll need to know. These terms are highlighted in bold print when they first appear and are defined at that time in the adjoining margin.
- *Testing. . . Testing. . . 1, 2, 3 Boxes.* Key factual material is highlighted by way of ongoing questions included in boxes throughout the chapters.
- *Thinking about Management Issues Questions.* Every chapter in the book has five questions that are designed to get you to think about management issues. These questions require you to integrate, synthesize, or apply management concepts. They allow you to demonstrate that you not only know the facts in the chapter but also can apply those facts in dealing with more complex issues.
- *Case Application and Questions.* Each chapter includes a case application and questions for analysis. A case is simply a description of a real-life managerial situation. By reading and analyzing the case and answering the questions at the end of the case, you can see if you understand and can apply the management concepts discussed in the chapter.

Supplements

Instructor's Manual. Developed by co-author Mary Coulter, it includes a chapter outline and synopsis; answers to "Testing. . . Testing. . . 1, 2, 3" questions and "Thinking about Management Issues" questions; teaching notes and suggestions for using the "Thinking Critically about Ethics" boxes, "For Your Immediate Action" exercises, chapter case applications, integrative Showtime Networks Inc. cases, and other video cases.

Computerized Instructor's Manual. The print version is available on a 3.5" IBM format.

Study Guide. Includes chapter objectives, lecture outline, key terms, and sample questions for students.

Test Item File. This test bank has over 2,500 test questions including multiple choice, true/false, scenario-based multiple choice, and discussion questions. The answer key includes page references and is annotated according to orientation (factual or applied) and level of difficulty (easy, moderate, or challenging).

Prentice Hall Test Manager. The test item file is designed for use with the Prentice Hall Test Manager, a computerized package that allows the user to custom design, save, and generate classroom tests. Available in 3.5" IBM or Mac disc, the Test Manager also permits professors to edit, add, or delete questions from the file and to export files to various word processing programs (including Corel WordPerfect and Microsoft Word).

Overhead Transparencies. 100 four-color acetates are available for classroom illustration. Many of which are from outside of the text.

Electronic Transparencies. The overhead transparencies collection is on IBM 3.5" disc for classroom use. Available through your Prentice Hall sales representative or electronically from our companion Web site.

Video Library. Nineteen video clips are included that correlate with the end-of-chapter video cases found in the text. The customized Showtime Networks Inc. videos that make up the integrative cases are also part of the video library.

***Management 6/e* CD-ROM.** Each copy of *Management 6/e* includes a **free CD-ROM**. Some of the features include:

- Comments from many of the managers highlighted in the "Managers Speak Out" boxes.
- Self-Assessment exercises that can be completed and scored for immediate feedback.
- Accompanying video for the Showtime Networks Inc. cases.
- Suggested answers and page references to all "Testing. . . Testing. . . 1, 2, 3" boxes.
- World Wide Web link to our companion Web site PHLIP (Prentice Hall Learning on the Internet Partnership) <http://www.phlip.com> which contains additional learning resources.

PHLIP. Prentice Hall Learning on the Internet Partnership offers a content-rich Web site to support both professors and students. It features:

- Bimonthly news updates that are integrated into specific chapters of the text.
- Internet resources—links to a wide variety of sites to enhance and expand the text's coverage of select topics.
- Internet exercises—developed specifically for *Management sixth edition* to help students learn how to use the Web as a management resource.
- Interactive Study Guide—on-line, real time testing program that instantly grades multiple choice, true-false, and fill-in questions; reports grades to the professor, and gives in-text page references for incorrect answers.

You can view this site at **<http://www.prenhall.com/robbinsmgt>**.

Acknowledgments

Every author relies on the comments of reviewers and ours were particularly helpful. We want to thank the following people for their comments and suggestions. June Freund, Pittsburgh State University; James Robinson, Trenton State University; Rick Moron, University of California, Berkeley; Bill Walsh, University of Illinois; Andy Kein, Keller Graduate School of Management; David Kennedy, Berkeley School of Business; Jim Jones, University of Nebraska, Omaha; and Rick Castaldi, San Francisco State University.

Regardless of how good the manuscript is that we turn in, it's only three or four floppy disks until our friends at Prentice Hall swing into action. Then PH's crack team of editors, production personnel, designers, marketing specialists, and sales representatives turn those couple of million digital characters into a bound textbook and see that it gets into faculty and students' hands. Our thanks on making this book "go" include David Shafer, Natalie Anderson, Jim Boyd, Sandy Steiner, Tami Wederbrand, Judy Leale, Christopher Stogdill, Shannon Sims, Lisamarie Brassini, and Shane Gemza.

A special thank you is extended to dt ogilvie at Rutgers, the State University of New Jersey, for developing the Showtime Networks Inc. Integrative Cases and to all the people at Showtime, Matt Blank, Mark Greenberg, Roy Langbord, Gwen Marcus, and especially to Brett McCarty who gave their time and insights. We also appreciate and thank all of those managers who so graciously gave of their time to either be part of the "Managers Speak Out" feature or the "Managers Respond" feature. Without these people, our belief in showing managers as "people, people, people" would be hard to implement.

Finally, Steve would like to acknowledge the support of his wife, Laura. Her insights and understanding make the job of textbook writing a lot more enjoyable. And her creative contributions make all his books better. Mary would like to acknowledge and thank her extremely understanding and tolerant husband, Ron, and their beautiful, talented, and remarkably well-adjusted daughters, Sarah and Katie.

Introduction

A MANAGER'S DILEMMA

A manager's job is frequently filled with challenges, big and small, as Elaine Chao would readily admit.[1] As the former director of the Peace Corps, Chao often faced unusual situations that required intelligent managerial decisions and actions. But those were nothing compared with the situation she faced when she took over as president at the national office of the United Way of America <http://www.unitedway.org>.

Just how bad was it at the over 110-year-old organization? One serious problem that Chao had to deal with in the early 1990s was increasing competition for donors' dollars from other not-for-profit agencies. At the same time, an economic recession was slowing monetary donations in general. At an organization whose very existence depended on private donations, the double whammy of new competitors and slowing contributions was a significant managerial challenge. But those weren't the worst problems Chao had to deal with. You may be asking yourself about now,

how *could* it be any worse than seeing your funding base shrinking? Well, it could be and it was! The national headquarters of the United Way was embroiled in a shocking and sordid scandal that would threaten its funding even more.

Chao's immediate predecessor (William Aramony, who served as United Way's president for 22 years) had resigned under charges that he had diverted organizational funds to finance a lavish lifestyle, including limousine transportation, trips on the Concorde supersonic jet, exotic vacations, and expensive gifts for a teenage mistress. He was convicted in 1996 of mail, wire, and tax fraud and is currently serving a seven-year prison sentence. As you can well imagine, the negative publicity surrounding this whole disastrous situation was overwhelming and had a significant impact on activities and programs at United Way headquarters. One-third of the member (local community) United Way chapters across the United States withdrew their support from the national office as funds raised by these local chapters fell 4.1 percent. Because of the accumulated shortfall of funds arising from the new competitors, the economic slowdown, and now this shocking scandal, for the first time ever, United Way's national office was unable to meet its payroll. Morale among headquarters staff plummeted. They were angry and disillusioned, and they weren't the only ones. After news of the scandal broke, the public media reported how employees at one well-known Silicon Valley company expressed their anger by boycotting United Way campaign meetings and publicly ripping up their United Way pledge cards. Other local United Way chapters across the United States had to deal with similar reactions from upset and angry donors. These

1

Introduction to Organizations and Management

local United Way chapters expressed their dissatisfaction, in turn, by withdrawing support from the national office. This situation would require exceptional managerial skills, talents, and actions.

What types of managerial skills do you think would be needed to address the pressing problems facing the United Way? Put yourself in Elaine Chao's situation. What managerial skills would you apply in tackling this situation?

WHAT WOULD YOU DO?

Elaine Chao is an excellent example of what today's successful managers are like and the skills they must have in dealing with the problems and challenges of managing. And she may not be what you might expect! Managers can be found from under age 18 to over 80. Managers run not only large corporations but also small businesses, government departments, hospitals, not-for-profit agencies, museums, schools, and even such nontraditional organizations as coalitions or cooperatives. Managers can also be found doing managerial work in every country on the globe. In addition, some managers hold positions at the top of their organizations, whereas others are near the bottom, and they are just as likely today to be women as they are men. However, although women are well represented in the lower and midlevels of management, the number in top executive positions remains low. Data collected by Catalyst, a nonprofit research group, found that only 10 percent of top jobs at the United States' 500 largest companies are held by women. That figure drops to 2.4 percent if you look only at the elite top-level jobs of chairman, president, CEO, and executive vice president. Several organizations including Motorola, Coopers & Lybrand, Dow Chemical, Avon Products, and Colgate-Palmolive are taking significant steps to attract and promote women executives.[2]

This book is about the work that Elaine Chao and the tens of millions of other managers like her do. Although the management situations you're likely to face probably will not be as serious or challenging as the one facing Elaine, the fact remains that managers and the work they do are important factors in all types and sizes of organizations. In this chapter, we introduce you to managers and management by answering, or at least beginning to answer, these questions: *What* is an organization and *how* is the concept of an organization changing? *Who* are managers; *what* is management; and *what* do managers do? Finally, we'll wrap up the chapter by discussing *why* you should spend your time studying management.

WHAT IS AN ORGANIZATION?

organization

A deliberate arrangement of people to accomplish some specific purpose.

Managers work in organizations. If there were no organizations, there would be no need for managers. What is an organization? An **organization** is a deliberate arrangement of people to accomplish some specific purpose. Your college or university is an organization; so are fraternities, government departments, churches, Microsoft Corporation, your neighborhood video store, the United Way, the New York Yankees baseball team, and the Mayo Clinic. These are all organizations because they all share three common characteristics as shown in Figure 1-1.

First, each organization has a distinct purpose. This purpose is typically expressed in terms of a goal or a set of goals that the organization hopes to accomplish. Second, each organization is composed of people. One person working alone is not an organization, and it takes people to perform the work that's necessary for the organization to achieve its goals. Third, all organizations develop some deliberate structure so that their members can do their work. That structure may be open and flexible, with no clear and precise delineations of job duties or strict adherence to any explicit job arrangements—in other words, a simple network of loose work relationships—or the structure may be more traditional, with clearly and carefully

FIGURE 1-1	Characteristics of Organizations

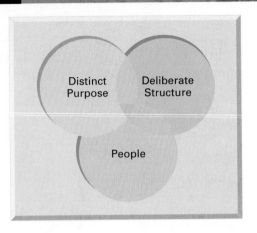

defined rules, regulations, and job descriptions and some members identified as "bosses" who have authority over other members. But no matter what type of structural arrangement an organization uses, it does require some deliberate structure so members' work relationships are clarified. In summary, the term *organization* refers to an entity that has a distinct purpose, includes people or members, and has some type of deliberate structure.

Although these three characteristics are important to our definition of *what* an organization is, the concept of an organization is changing. It's no longer appropriate to assume that all organizations are going to be structured like IBM, Exxon, or General Motors, with clearly identifiable divisions, departments, and work units. In fact, one of General Motors' independent subsidiaries, Saturn Corporation, may be more characteristic of what contemporary organizations look like, with its flexible work arrangements, employee work teams, open communication systems, and supplier alliances. Just how is the concept of an organization changing? Table 1-1 lists some differences between a traditional view and a contem-

TABLE 1-1	The Changing Organization

Traditional Organization	New Organization
• Stable	• Dynamic
• Inflexible	• Flexible
• Job-focused	• Skills-focused
• Work is defined by job positions	• Work is defined in terms of tasks to be done
• Individual-oriented	• Team-oriented
• Permanent jobs	• Temporary jobs
• Command-oriented	• Involvement-oriented
• Managers always make decisions	• Employees participate in decision making
• Rule-oriented	• Customer-oriented
• Relatively homogeneous workforce	• Diverse workforce
• Workdays defined as 9 to 5	• Workdays have no time boundaries
• Hierarchical relationships	• Lateral and networked relationships
• Work at organizational facility during specific hours	• Work anywhere, anytime

All of these organizations share three common characteristics: distinct purpose; people; and deliberate structure.

porary view of organizations. Today's organizations are becoming more open, flexible, and responsive to changes.[3]

Why are organizations changing? Because the world around them has changed. Societal, economic, global, and technological changes have created an environment in which successful organizations (those that consistently meet their goals) must embrace new ways of getting their work done. Examples include the "information explosion," increasing globalization, and changing employee workplace expectations. Even though the concept of organizations may be changing, managers and management continue to be important to organizations.

1 What are the three characteristics of organizations?

2 Why are managers important to an organization's success?

3 Why are organizations changing?

TESTING...
TESTING...
1   2   3

WHO ARE MANAGERS?

It used to be fairly simple to define who managers were: They were the organizational members who oversaw and directed the work of other members. It was easy to differentiate *managers* from *operatives;* the latter term described those organizational members who worked directly on a job or task and had no subordinates. But it isn't quite that simple anymore! The changing nature of organizations and work has, in many organizations, blurred the clear lines of distinction between managers and operatives. Many traditional workers' jobs now include managerial activities, especially on teams. For instance, team members often develop plans, make decisions, and monitor their own performance. And as these so-called operative employees assume responsibilities that traditionally were deemed as belonging to management, definitions we've used in the past no longer work.

How *do* we define who managers are? A **manager** is an organizational member who integrates and coordinates the work of others. That may mean direct responsibility for a group of people in one department, or it might mean supervising a single person. It could also involve coordinating the work activities of a team composed of people from several different departments or even people from other organizations. Keep in mind, however, that managers may have other work duties not related to integrating the work of others. For example, an insurance claims supervisor may also process claims in addition to coordinating the work activities of other claims clerks.

Is there some way to classify managers in organizations? There is, particularly for traditionally structured organizations—that is, those with deliberate work arrangements or structures shaped like a pyramid that reflects the fact that the number of employees is greater at the bottom than at the top. As shown in Figure 1-2, we typically describe managers as either first-line, middle, or top in this type of organization. Identifying exactly who the managers are in these organizations isn't difficult, although you should be aware that managers may have a variety of titles. **First-line managers** are the lowest level of management and are often called *supervisors*. In a manufacturing plant, the first-line (or lowest-level) manager may be called a *foreman*. On an athletic team the coach would be considered the first-line manager. **Middle managers** include all levels of management between the supervisory level and the top level of the organization. They may have titles such as department or agency head, project leader, plant manager, unit chief, dean, bishop, or division manager. At or near the top of the organization are the **top managers**, who are responsible for making organization-wide decisions and establishing the policies and strategies that affect the entire organization. These individuals typically have titles such as executive vice president, president, managing director, chief operating officer, chief executive

manager

An organizational member who integrates and coordinates the work of others.

first-line managers

Supervisors; the lowest level of management.

middle managers

All levels of management between the supervisory level and the top level of the organization.

top managers

Managers at or near the top of the organization who are responsible for making organization-wide decisions and establishing the policies and strategies that affect the entire organization.

FIGURE 1-2 **Organizational Levels**

Top Managers

Middle Managers

First-Line Managers

Nonmanagerial Employees

officer, or chairman of the board. In the chapter-opening Manager's Dilemma, Elaine Chao was a top-level manager. She held the title of president and was involved in implementing broad and comprehensive changes that affected the entire organization.

Throughout this book, we'll be discussing organizations and managers from this more traditional pyramidal perspective, although not all organizations have this traditional structure. But even organizations that have more flexible and loosely configured structures need individuals to fulfill the role of manager—that is, someone who integrates and coordinates the work of others.

If you choose a managerial career, you are likely to have a variety of titles and job responsibilities. Over the course of your career, these managerial jobs may take you to several organizations, both traditional and nontraditional. If you decide on a career in management, you'll find yourself in an exciting and challenging profession!

**TESTING...
TESTING...**
1 2 3

4 How are managers distinct from nonmanagerial employees?

5 Explain why it isn't always easy to determine exactly who the managers are in organizations.

6 Contrast the three different levels of management.

WHAT IS MANAGEMENT?

Just as organizations have common characteristics, so do managers. Although their titles and work responsibilities vary widely, their jobs share common characteristics—whether the manager is a $30,000 a year supervisor in the mailroom at Hershey Foods overseeing a staff of five or a $6.3 million a year chief executive officer of General Electric responsible for coordinating an organization with more than 239,000 employees and annual sales totaling over $79 billion.

management

The process of coordinating and integrating work activities so that they're completed efficiently and effectively with and through other people.

The term **management** refers to the process of coordinating and integrating work activities so that they are completed efficiently and effectively with and through other people. Let's look at some of the specific parts of this definition.

The *process* represents the ongoing functions or primary activities engaged in by managers. These functions are typically labeled planning, organizing, leading, and controlling.

We elaborate on these functions and the process of management in the next section as we look more closely at what managers do.

We know from the previous section, in which we described who managers are, that coordinating and integrating others' work is what distinguishes a managerial position from a nonmanagerial one. Through management (that is, through coordinating and integrating the work of others), organizational work activities are completed efficiently and effectively; or at least that's what management aspires to do.

Efficiency is a vital part of management. It refers to the relationship between inputs and outputs. If you can get more output from the given inputs, you have increased efficiency. Similarly, if you can get the same output from less input, you also have increased efficiency. Because managers deal with scarce input resources—mainly people, money, and equipment—they are concerned with the efficient use of those resources. Management, therefore, is concerned with minimizing resource costs. From this perspective, efficiency is often referred to as "doing things right"—that is, not wasting resources.

However, it's not enough simply to be efficient. Management is also concerned with completing activities so that organizational goals are attained; that is, management is concerned with **effectiveness**. When managers achieve their organization's goals, we say they are effective. Effectiveness is often described as "doing the right things"—that is, those work activities that will help the organization reach its goals. Whereas efficiency is concerned with the means of getting things done, effectiveness is concerned with the ends, or attainment of organizational goals (Figure 1-3).

Efficiency and effectiveness are related. It is easier to be effective if one ignores efficiency. For instance, Packard-Bell could produce expensive personal computers with significantly enhanced top-of-the-line computing features if it disregarded labor and material input costs. And some federal agencies have been criticized regularly on the grounds that they are reasonably effective but extremely inefficient; that is, they get their jobs done but at a high cost. Management is concerned, then, not only with getting activities completed and meeting organizational goals (effectiveness) but also with doing so as efficiently as possible.

Can organizations be efficient and yet not effective? Yes, by doing the wrong things well! For instance, many universities have become highly efficient in processing students. By using computer-assisted learning and Internet-based course material, long-distance

efficiency

The relationship between inputs and outputs, the goal of which is to minimize resource costs.

effectiveness

Goal attainment.

| FIGURE 1-3 | **Efficiency and Effectiveness in Management** |

Efficiency (Means)

Resource Usage

High Waste ⟶ Low Waste

Effectiveness (Ends)

Goal Attainment

High Attainment ⟵ Low Attainment

Management Strives For:
Low resource waste (high efficiency)
High goal attainment (high effectiveness)

Interview with Piki Harrelson, Regional Manager, Southwest Region, Tommy Hilfiger, USA, Dallas, Texas

Describe your job.

I work as a regional manager in the Southwest region for Tommy Hilfiger, USA. I manage a team of 14 merchandise coordinators and one district manager in Texas and Oklahoma. In addition, I serve as a liaison between department store account buyers (including Dillard's and Foley's) and our sales executives at Tommy Hilfiger. My regional manager position covers three areas of responsibility: (1) Business planning. It's all about dollars! I need to meet the company objectives but make sure to stay within budget. (2) Managing my region, which includes managing planned and unexpected projects. Projects include such activities as management reports, new product launches, in-store merchandising, visual directives, shifts in business objectives and trends, and personal appearances. (3) Training and development. I need to set clear objectives for my team. I want them to always understand what their "focus" is, but I also continue to nurture "out of the box" thinking.

Why are managers important to organizations?

Managers are important because they instill desirable (corporate-oriented) behaviors in employees to achieve Tommy Hilfiger objectives. At Tommy Hilfiger, managers are important because they monitor the pulse of what's happening in the field. What is happening in New York, where Tommy Hilfiger is headquartered and where all senior managers are, is very different from what is happening in Dallas or in Springfield or in St. Louis.

We all know that change is a constant for organizations. How do you deal with the challenges of change?

Oh yes, the changes associated with growing pains! At Tommy Hilfiger, we've restructured Retail Development (which is the official name of my department) twice since I started in July 1994. In dealing with these changes, I try to keep my focus on defining what the actual objectives are. My most common report back to corporate headquarters is, "If my team takes on *this project,* then *this other project* will not get completed." In addition, in dealing with the challenges of change, I've found that it's important to create partners. Whatever the task may be, I want to partner with my director before I present the changes to my people. ■

learning classes, large lecture classes, and heavy reliance on part-time faculty, administrators have significantly cut the cost of educating each student. Yet, students, alumni, and accrediting agencies have questioned whether students are being educated properly. Of course, in successful organizations, high efficiency and high effectiveness typically go hand in hand. Poor management is most often due to both inefficiency and ineffectiveness or to effectiveness achieved through inefficiency.

7 How is management a process?

8 Define efficiency and effectiveness and explain why they're important to management.

9 Explain how efficiency and effectiveness are related.

WHAT DO MANAGERS DO?

Describing what managers do isn't an easy or simple task! Just as no two organizations are exactly alike, no two managers' jobs are exactly alike. But even given these constraints, we have well over 100 years of formal management study to draw from and some specific categorization schemes that have been developed to describe what managers do. What are these categorization schemes? We're going to look at what managers do in terms of functions and processes, roles, skills, managing systems, and managing different and changing situations.

Management Functions and Processes

In the early part of the twentieth century, a French industrialist by the name of Henri Fayol proposed that all managers perform five management functions: They plan, organize, command, coordinate, and control.[4] In the mid-1950s, two professors at the University of California–Los Angeles drew upon Fayol's work and used the functions of planning, organizing, staffing, directing, and controlling as the framework for a management textbook that for 20 years was the most widely sold text on the subject.[5] Most management textbooks (and this one is no exception) still continue to be organized around **management functions**, though they have been condensed down to four basic functions: planning, organizing, leading, and controlling (Figure 1-4). Let's briefly define what each of these management functions encompasses.

If you have no particular destination in mind, it doesn't matter what road you take. Because organizations exist to achieve some purpose, someone must clearly define that purpose and the means for its achievement. Management is that someone. The **planning** function involves the process of defining goals, establishing a strategy for achieving those goals, and developing plans to integrate and coordinate activities.

Managers are also responsible for designing an organization's structure. We call this function **organizing**. It includes the process of determining what tasks are to be done, who

management functions

Managers' work activities of planning, organizing, leading, and controlling.

planning

Includes defining goals, establishing strategy, and developing plans to coordinate activities.

organizing

Determining what tasks are to be done, who is to do them, how the tasks are to be grouped, who reports to whom, and where decisions are to be made.

FIGURE 1-4   **Management Functions**

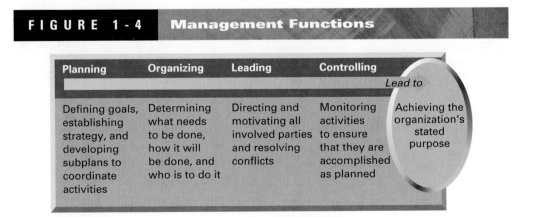

is to do them, how the tasks are to be grouped, who reports to whom, and at what level decisions are made.

leading

Includes motivating subordinates, directing others, selecting the most effective communication channels, and resolving conflicts.

As we know, every organization includes people, and management's job is to integrate and coordinate the work of those people. This is the **leading** function. When managers motivate subordinates, direct the activities of others, select the most effective communication channel, or resolve conflicts among members, they are leading.

The final management function managers perform is **controlling**. After the goals are set (planning function), the plans formulated (planning function), the structural arrangements determined (organizing function), and the people hired, trained, and motivated (leading function), something may still go wrong. To ensure that things are going as they should, managers must monitor performance. Actual performance must be compared with the previously set goals. If there are any significant deviations, it's management's job to get work performance back on track. This process of monitoring, comparing, and correcting is what we mean by the controlling function.

controlling

Monitoring activities to ensure that they are being accomplished as planned and correcting any significant deviations.

The reality of managing isn't quite as simplistic as these descriptions of the management functions might lead you to believe. In fact, it's probably more realistic to describe the functions managers perform from the perspective of a process. The **management process** is the set of ongoing decisions and work activities in which managers engage as they plan, organize, lead, and control. What this means is that as managers do their work (that is, as they "perform" the management functions), their work activities are often done in an ongoing and continuous manner—in a process. There is no simple, cut-and-dried beginning or ending point as managers plan, organize, lead, and control. As managers "manage," they often find themselves engaging in activities that involve some planning, some organizing, some leading, and some controlling, and perhaps not even in that sequential order.

management process

The set of ongoing decisions and actions in which managers engage as they plan, organize, lead, and control.

The continued popularity of the functional and process approaches to describe what managers do is a tribute to their clarity and simplicity. But do they accurately describe what managers actually do?[6] Following the functional and process approach, it's easy to answer the question "What do managers do?" They plan, organize, lead, and control through a series of ongoing and continuous decisions and work activities. But does that answer really describe what all managers do? One prominent management researcher, Henry Mintzberg, would say no, arguing that what managers do can best be described by looking at the roles they play at work.

Stephanie Streeter is a group vice president at Avery Dennison, a maker of adhesives and labels based in Pasadena, California. Her office products division contributes almost a third to Avery Dennison's $3.2 billion in annual revenues. A varsity basketball player for four years at Stanford University, Streeter has applied the concepts of teamwork, risk taking, dealing with missed shots, and taking charge of the situation to the way she plans, organizes, leads, and controls.

Management Roles

In the late 1960s, Mintzberg did a detailed study of five top managers at work.[7] What he discovered challenged several long-held notions about the manager's job. For instance, in contrast to the predominant views at the time that managers were reflective thinkers who carefully and systematically processed information before making decisions, Mintzberg found that his managers engaged in a large number of varied, unpatterned, and short-duration activities. There was little time for reflective thinking because the managers encountered constant interruptions. Half of these managers' activities lasted less than nine minutes each. In addition to these insights on what managers did, Mintzberg provided a categorization scheme for defining what managers do based on actual managers on the job.

Mintzberg concluded that managers perform 10 different but highly interrelated roles. The term **management roles** refers to specific categories of managerial behavior. (Think of the different roles you play and the different behaviors you're expected to exhibit and the different work you're expected to do in these roles: a student, a sibling, an employee, a volunteer, and so forth.) As shown in Table 1-2, Mintzberg's 10 managerial roles can be grouped as those primarily concerned with interpersonal relationships, the transfer of information, and decision making.

management roles

Specific categories of managerial behavior.

Interpersonal Roles.   All managers are required to perform duties that involve people (subordinates and persons outside the organization) and other duties that are ceremonial and symbolic in nature. These are the **interpersonal roles**. When a college president hands out diplomas at commencement or a factory supervisor gives a group of high school students a plant tour, he or she is acting in a *figurehead* role. All managers have a role as a *leader*. This role includes hiring, training, motivating, and disciplining employees. The third role within the interpersonal grouping is the *liaison* role. Mintzberg described this activity as contacting external sources who provide the manager with information. These sources are individuals or groups outside the manager's unit and may be inside or outside the organization. The sales manager who obtains information from the human resources manager in his or her same company has an internal liaison relationship. When that sales manager confers with other sales executives at a marketing trade association meeting, he or she has an outside liaison relationship.

interpersonal roles

Roles that involve figurehead, leader, and liaison activities.

Informational Roles.   All managers, to some degree, have **informational roles**: receiving, collecting, and disseminating information. Typically, if they're getting this information from outside their own organization, they do so by reading magazines and talking with others to learn of changes in the public's tastes, what competitors may be planning, and the like. Mintzberg called this the *monitor* role. Managers also act as conduits of information to organizational members. This is the *disseminator* role. When they represent the organization to outsiders, managers also perform a *spokesperson* role.

informational roles

Roles that involve monitor, disseminator, and spokesperson activities.

Decisional Roles.   Finally, Mintzberg identified four **decisional roles**, which revolve around making choices. As *entrepreneurs,* managers initiate and oversee new projects that will improve their organization's performance. As *disturbance handlers,* managers take corrective action in response to unforeseen problems. As *resource allocators,* managers are responsible for allocating human, physical, and monetary resources. Last, managers

decisional roles

Roles that involve entrepreneur, disturbance handler, resource allocator, and negotiator.

Suppose you're in a management position and you're asked to lie about information you have. Is lying always wrong, or might it be acceptable under certain circumstances? What, if any, would those circumstances be? What about simply distorting information that you have? Is that always wrong, or might it be acceptable under certain circumstances? ■

THINKING CRITICALLY

ABOUT ETHICS

TABLE 1-2   Mintzberg's Managerial Roles

Role	Description	Examples of Identifiable Activities
INTERPERSONAL		
Figurehead	Symbolic head; obliged to perform a number of routine duties of a legal or social nature	Greeting visitors; signing legal documents
Leader	Responsible for the motivation and activation of subordinates; responsible for staffing, training, and associated duties	Performing virtually all activities that involve subordinates
Liaison	Maintains self-developed network of outside contacts and informers who provide favors and information	Acknowledging mail; doing external board work; performing other activities that involve outsiders
INFORMATIONAL		
Monitor	Seeks and receives wide variety of special information (much of it current) to develop thorough understanding of organization and environment; emerges as nerve center of internal and external information about the organization	Reading periodicals and reports; maintaining personal contacts
Disseminator	Transmits information received from outsiders or from subordinates to members of the organization; some information is factual, some involves interpretation and integration of diverse value positions of organizational influencers	Holding informational meetings; making phone calls to relay information
Spokesperson	Transmits information to outsiders on organization's plans, policies, actions, results, etc.; serves as expert on organization's industry	Holding board meetings; giving information to the media
DECISIONAL		
Entrepreneur	Searches organization and its environment for opportunities and initiates "improvement projects" to bring about changes; supervises design of certain projects	Organizing strategy and review sessions to develop new programs
Disturbance handler	Responsible for corrective action when organization faces important, unexpected disturbances	Organizing strategy and review sessions that involve disturbances and crises
Resource allocator	Responsible for the allocation of organizational resources of all kinds—in effect, the making or approval of all significant organizational decisions	Scheduling; requesting authorization; performing any activity that involves budgeting and the programming of subordinates' work
Negotiator	Responsible for representing the organization at major negotiations	Participating in union contract negotiations

Source: H. Mintzberg, *The Nature of Managerial Work* (New York: Harper & Row, 1973), pp. 93–94. Copyright © 1973 by Henry Mintzberg. Reprinted by permission of Harper & Row, Publishers, Inc.

perform as *negotiators* when they discuss and bargain with other groups to gain advantages for their own units.

An Evaluation.   A number of follow-up studies have tested the validity of Mintzberg's role categories among different types of organizations and at different levels within given organizations.[8] The evidence generally supports the idea that managers—regardless of the type of organization or level in the organization—perform similar roles. However, the emphasis that managers give to the various roles seems to change with their organizational level.[9] Specifically, the roles of disseminator, figurehead, negotiator, liaison, and spokesperson are more important at the higher levels of the organization than at the lower ones. Conversely, the leader role is more important for lower-level managers than it is for either middle- or top-level managers.

Have these 10 roles, which are derived from actual observations of managerial work, invalidated the more traditional functions of planning, organizing, leading, and controlling? Definitely not!

First, the functional approach still represents the most useful way of conceptualizing the manager's job. "The classical functions provide clear and discrete methods of classifying the thousands of activities that managers carry out and the techniques they use in terms of the functions they perform for the achievement of goals."[10] Second, although Mintzberg may offer a more detailed and elaborate classification scheme of what managers do, these roles are substantially reconcilable with the four functions.[11] Many of Mintzberg's roles align smoothly with one or more of the functions. For instance, resource allocation is part of planning, as is the entrepreneurial role, and all three of the interpersonal roles are part of the leading function. Although most of the other roles fit into one or more of the four functions, not all of them do; the difference is substantially explained by Mintzberg's intermixing management activities and pure managerial work.[12]

All managers do some work that isn't purely managerial. The fact that Mintzberg's executives spent time in public relations or raising money attests to the precision of Mintzberg's observation methods, but it shows that not everything a manager does is necessarily an essential part of the manager's job. Consequently, some activities may have been included in Mintzberg's classifications that shouldn't have been.

Do the comments above mean that Mintzberg's role categories are invalid? Not at all! Mintzberg clearly offered new insights into what managers do. The attention his work has received is evidence of the importance attributed to defining management roles. But management is a relatively young discipline and still evolving. Future research comparing and integrating Mintzberg's roles with the four functions will continue to expand our understanding of the manager's job.

---

10 Briefly describe the four common functions all managers perform.

11 What is the management process, and how does it reflect what managers do?

12 Describe Mintzberg's 10 management roles and how they are used to explain what managers do.

TESTING...
TESTING...

1 **2** **3**

Management Skills

As you can see from the preceding discussion, a manager's job is varied and complex. Managers need certain skills to perform the duties and activities associated with being a manager—in other words, to do what a manager does. What types of skills does a manager

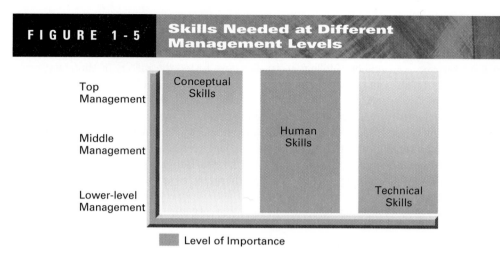

FIGURE 1-5   **Skills Needed at Different Management Levels**

Top Management

Middle Management

Lower-level Management

Conceptual Skills

Human Skills

Technical Skills

Level of Importance

need in "doing" management? Research by Robert L. Katz during the early 1970s found that managers needed three essential skills or competencies: *technical, human,* and *conceptual*.[13] He also found that the relative importance of these skills varied according to the manager's level within the organization. Figure 1-5 shows the relative importance of the different skills at the three management levels: top, middle, and lower.

technical skills

Skills that include knowledge of and proficiency in a certain specialized field.

Technical Skills.   First-line managers, as well as many middle managers, are heavily involved in technical aspects of the organization's operations. **Technical skills** include knowledge of and proficiency in a certain specialized field, such as engineering, computers, finance, or manufacturing. For example, an accounts payable manager must be proficient in accounting rules and standardized forms so that she can resolve problems and answer questions that her accounts payable clerks might encounter. Katz proposed that technical skills become less important as a manager moves into higher levels of management, but even top managers need some proficiency in the organization's specialty. Celeste Baranski, Vice President of Hardware Engineering at Eo, a manufacturer of hand-held personal digital assistants (PDAs), for instance, frequently uses her engineering skills in her position as a manager.

FIGURE 1-6   **Selected Skills* of Effective Managers**

Managing Conflict

Setting Goals

Solving Problems

Working Well in Groups

EFFECTIVE MANAGERS

Interpersonal Skills

Verbal Communication

Time Management

*These are just a few of the skills that have been identified as important to being an effective manager.

Human Skills.   The ability to work well with other people both individually and in a group is a **human skill.** Because managers deal directly with people, this skill is crucial! In fact, Katz said that human skills remained just as important at the top levels of management as they did at the lower levels. Managers with good human skills are able to get the best out of their people. They know how to communicate, motivate, lead, and inspire enthusiasm and trust. In later chapters, we will cover many of the important behavioral topics that are part of this skill area.

Conceptual Skills.   Managers also must have the ability to think and to conceptualize about abstract situations. They must be able to see the organization as a whole and the relationships among its various subunits and to visualize how the organization fits into its broader environment. Why? These abilities are essential to effective decision making, and all managers are involved in making decisions. **Conceptual skills** are needed by all managers at all levels, but Katz proposed that these skills become more important as they move into top management positions.

How relevant are these three management skills to today's managers? Katz's study served to highlight the importance of management skills in defining what managers do; more-recent studies have expanded our view of skills by looking at those needed by effective managers.[14] Some of the skills identified in these studies are shown in Figure 1-6. As you can see, most of these skills are more specific and descriptive than Katz's broad categorization. In addition, employers continue to emphasize the importance of skills as they look at hiring college graduates. What skills do employers rank as important in evaluating job candidates? Figure 1-7 shows employers' rankings of selected job-related skills.

human skills

The ability to work well with other people both individually and in a group.

conceptual skills

The ability to think and conceptualize about abstract situations, to see the organization as a whole and the relationships among its various subunits, and to visualize how the organization fits into its environment.

FIGURE 1-7   Employers' Rankings of Skills in Job Candidates

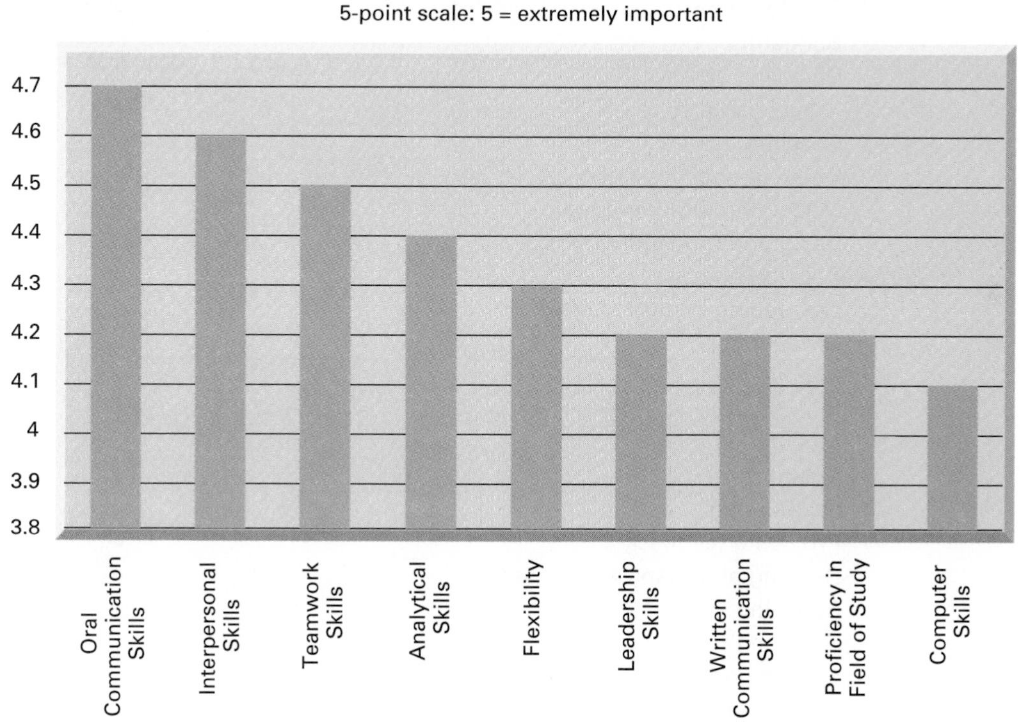

Source: Based on a survey of employers hiring new college graduates, National Association of Colleges and Employers, fall 1995.

In today's demanding and dynamic workplace, employees who are invaluable to an organization must be willing to constantly upgrade their skills and take on extra work outside their own specific job area. And there's no doubt that skills will continue to be an important way of describing what a manager does. In fact, understanding and developing management skills are so important that we've incorporated a condensed skills feature in the text. At the end of the textbook, you'll find a separate section with skill-building modules. The 23 skills we've chosen to feature in these skill-building modules reflect a broad cross section of managerial activities that we believe to be important elements of the four managerial functions. A matrix of the relationship between these skills and the four management functions is shown in Figure 1-8. Note that many of the skills are important to more than one function. As you study the management functions in more depth in later chapters of the book, you'll have the opportunity to practice (using any or all of the skill-building modules) some of the key skills that are part of doing what a manager does. Although no skill-building module can make you an instant expert in a certain area, these exercises can provide you an introductory understanding and appreciation of some of the skills you'll need to master in order to be an effective manager.

FIGURE 1-8 — Management Skills and Management Functions Matrix

Skill	Planning	Organizing	Leading	Controlling
Acquiring power		✓	✓	
Active listening			✓	✓
Assessing cross-cultural differences		✓	✓	
Budgeting	✓			✓
Choosing an effective leadership style			✓	
Coaching			✓	
Creating effective teams		✓	✓	
Delegating (empowerment)		✓	✓	
Designing motivating jobs		✓	✓	
Developing trust			✓	
Developing control charts	✓			✓
Disciplining			✓	✓
Interviewing		✓	✓	
Managing resistance to change		✓	✓	✓
Managing time	✓			✓
Mentoring			✓	
Negotiating			✓	
Providing feedback			✓	✓
Reading an organization's culture		✓	✓	
Reducing stress		✓	✓	
Scanning the environment	✓			✓
Setting goals	✓			✓
Solving problems creatively	✓			

13 Describe the three skills Katz felt were essential to managers.

14 How does the importance of the three management skills change depending on management level?

15 What other types of skills have been identified as important for managers?

TESTING...
TESTING...

1 2 3

Managing Systems

Another way to look at the manager's job is from the perspective of managing systems. But what is a system? A **system** is a set of interrelated and interdependent parts arranged in a manner that produces a unified whole. According to that definition, societies are systems and so are automobiles, animals, and human bodies. For instance, the systems perspective is used by physiologists to explain how animals maintain an equilibrium state by taking in inputs and generating outputs.

The two basic types of systems are closed and open. **Closed systems** are not influenced by and do not interact with their environment. In contrast, the concept of an **open system** recognizes the dynamic interaction of the system with its environment. Although the idea of organizations as open systems was first proposed in the 1930s by a management writer named Chester Barnard, widespread acceptance of the notion took another 30 years. Today, when we call organizations systems, we mean open systems; that is, we accept that an organization constantly interacts with its environment.

Figure 1-9 shows a diagram of an organization from an open systems perspective. For a business firm, inputs include raw materials, human resources, capital, technology, and information. The transformation process turns these inputs into finished products or services through employees' work activities, management activities, and the organization's technology and operations methods. Outputs include products and services, financial results (profits, break-even, or losses), information, and human results such as employees' levels of job satisfaction and productivity. In addition, the system's ultimate success depends on effective interactions with its environment: those groups or institutions upon which it depends. These might include suppliers, labor unions, financial institutions, government agencies, and customers. For a business organization, the sale of products and services generates revenue that can be used to pay wages and taxes, buy more inputs, repay loans, and generate profits for the owners. If revenues aren't enough to satisfy various environmental demands, the organization downsizes or dies.

How does the systems perspective add to our understanding of what managers do? Systems researchers envisioned an organization as being made up of "interdependent factors, including individuals, groups, attitudes, motives, formal structure, interactions, goals, status, and authority."[15] The job of a manager, then, is to ensure that all the interdependent parts of the organization are working together so that the organization's goals can be achieved; that is, the manager's job in an organizational "system" would be to coordinate and integrate the work activities of the various parts of the organization. How does this describe what happens in organizations? If the manager were a first-line manager, the part of the organizational system in which he or she would coordinate and integrate work activities would typically be narrow and limited to one organizational area or a few specific areas. On the other hand, if the manager were a top-level manager, the part of the organizational system that he or she would be responsible for managing would, of course, be broader and more comprehensive and would encompass numerous (if not all) organizational areas. If the manager were a middle manager, he or she would be responsible for coordinating and integrating work activities in parts of the organizational system somewhere between broad and narrow.

system

A set of interrelated and interdependent parts arranged in a manner that produces a unified whole.

closed systems

Systems that are not influenced by and do not interact with their environment.

open systems

Systems that dynamically interact with their environment.

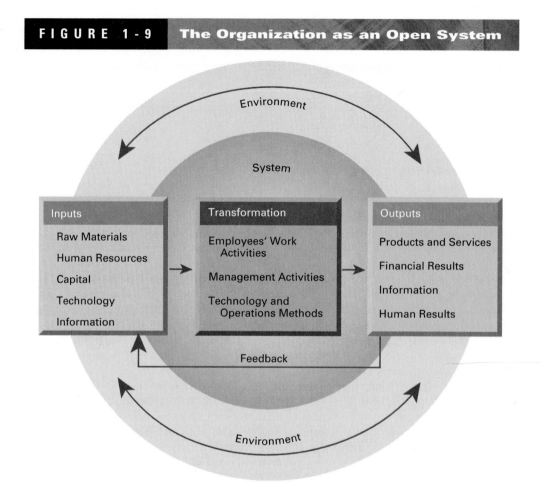

FIGURE 1-9   The Organization as an Open System

In addition, the systems view of a manager's job implies that decisions and actions taken in one organizational area will affect others and vice versa (this is known as the interdependency characteristic of systems). For instance, no matter how efficient an organization's production department might be, if its marketing department does not anticipate changes in consumer tastes and work with the product development department in creating products consumers want, the organization's overall performance will suffer. Likewise, if the purchasing department fails to acquire the right quantity and quality of inputs, the production department will not be able to do its job effectively. So the systems approach recognizes the interdependence of, and the need for, coordinating the various activities within the organization.

An open systems approach recognizes that organizations are not self-contained. They rely on their environment for essential inputs and as sources to absorb their outputs. No organization can survive for long if it ignores government regulations, supplier relations, or the varied external constituencies upon which it depends. Thus, an important part of a manager's job is recognizing and understanding the impact of the various external factors. (We'll cover many of these external environmental forces in chapter 3 when we discuss in detail how management must understand its environment and the constraints it imposes.)

Just how relevant is the systems approach for describing what a manager does? It appears to be quite relevant, particularly since a manager's job entails coordinating and integrating various work activities so that the system of interrelated and interdependent parts (the organization) meets its goals. Although the systems perspective does not provide

The concept of an organization as a open system of interrelated parts working together as a whole is easily seen at Sun Microsystems of Mountain View, California. Employees confer in informal work areas called "forum" spaces to discuss product and market issues.

specific descriptions of what managers do, it does provide a more general and broader picture than other perspectives do. Moreover, viewing the manager's job as linking the organization to its environment makes the organization more sensitive and responsive to key constituencies such as customers, suppliers, government agencies, and the community in which it operates.

Managing in Different and Changing Situations

Management, like life itself, is not based on simplistic principles. Insurance companies know that not all individuals have the same probability of being in an auto accident. Factors such as age, gender, driving record, and number of miles driven per year are *contingencies* that influence accident rates. Similarly, you cannot say that students always learn more in small classes than in large ones. Research tells us that contingency factors such as course content and the teaching style of the instructor influence the relationship between class size and learning effectiveness.

The **contingency perspective** (sometimes called the situational approach) of management underscores and emphasizes the fact that organizations are different, face different circumstances (contingencies), and thus may require different ways of managing—that is, different managerial decisions and actions. Therefore, when we describe what managers do from this perspective, we're recognizing that managers must "read" and attempt to interpret the situational contingencies facing them before deciding the best way to coordinate and integrate work activities.

A contingency approach to describing what managers do is intuitively logical. Because organizations and even units within the same organization are diverse—in size, objectives, work being done, and the like—it would be surprising to find universally applicable principles (rules) that would work in *all* situations. In other words, managing Microsoft's software design engineers would be different from managing salesclerks at Sears and would even be different from managing Microsoft's own marketing staff. But, of course, it's one thing to say "It all depends" and another to say what it depends upon. Management researchers have been working to identify these "what" variables. Table 1-3 describes four popular contingency variables. The list is not comprehensive—at least 100 different variables have been identified—but it represents those most widely used and gives you an idea of what we mean by the term *contingency variable.* As you can see from the list, the contingency variables can have a significant impact on what managers do—that is, on the way work activities are coordinated and integrated.

contingency perspective

A view that the organization recognizes and responds to situational variables as they arise.

TABLE 1-3   Popular Contingency Variables

Organization Size. The number of people in an organization is a major influence on what managers do. As size increases, so do the problems of coordination. For instance, the type of organization structure appropriate for an organization of 50,000 employees is likely to be inefficient for an organization of 50 employees.

Routineness of Task Technology. To achieve its purpose, an organization uses technology; that is, it engages in the process of transforming inputs into outputs. Routine technologies require organizational structures, leadership styles, and control systems that differ from those required by customized or nonroutine technologies.

Environmental Uncertainty. The degree of uncertainty caused by political, technological, sociocultural, and economic changes influences the management process. What works best in a stable and predictable environment may be totally inappropriate in a rapidly changing and unpredictable environment.

Individual Differences. Individuals differ in terms of their desire for growth, autonomy, tolerance of ambiguity, and expectations. These and other individual differences are particularly important when managers select motivation techniques, leadership styles, and job designs.

The primary value of the contingency approach is that it stresses that there are no simplistic or universal rules for managers to follow in doing their jobs. Instead, a manager's job involves managing different and changing situations, and managers' actions should be appropriate for the situations in which they find themselves.

**TESTING...
TESTING...**

16 Describe an organization using the systems perspective.

17 Describe how the systems perspective is used to describe what managers do.

18 What is the contingency perspective, and how is it used to describe what managers do?

Looking Back at the Multiple Perspectives on the Manager's Job

As we've shown throughout this section, a manager's job can be described from various perspectives: functions, roles, essential skills, systems, and different and changing situations. In her position as president of the national offices of the United Way, Elaine Chao (described in our opening dilemma) is a good example of the many complex and varied facets of a manager's job. For instance, in dealing with the unhappy local United Way chapters that have withdrawn their financial support, she would need to use certain skills and the management functions. In addition, she might exhibit work behaviors characteristic of the figurehead role, the monitor role, or the negotiator role. The fact that Chao is having to deal with this organization-environment relationship is a reflection of the systems perspective of her job.

Chao's position exhibits many of the job aspects we've covered, but is her situation typical? In other words, just how universal is the manager's job?

IS THE MANAGER'S JOB UNIVERSAL?

We have previously mentioned the universal need for management in organizations. So far, we have discussed management as if it were generic; that is, a manager is a manager regardless of where or what he or she manages. If management is truly a generic discipline, then what a manager does should be essentially the same regardless of whether he or she is a top-level executive or a low-level supervisor; in a business firm or a nonprofit arts organization; in a large corporation or a small business; located in Paris, France, or Paris, Texas. Let's take a closer look at the generic issue.

Organizational Level

We have already said that the breadth of a manager's job varies depending on the manager's position in the organization. But the fact that a supervisor in a research laboratory at 3M Company does not do exactly the same things that the president of 3M does should not be interpreted to mean that their jobs are inherently different. The differences are of degree and emphasis, not of function. All managers, regardless of level, make decisions. They plan, organize, lead, and control. But the amount of time they give to each function isn't necessarily the same. In addition, the content of the managerial functions changes with the manager's level. For example, as we'll discuss in chapter 10, top managers are likely to be concerned with designing the overall organization, whereas lower-level managers are more likely to focus on designing the jobs of individuals and work groups. This difference simply is a reflection of the breadth (broad to narrow) of each manager's job.

Organizational Type

Does a manager who works for the Alabama State Department of Revenue or the El Paso, Texas, public utility company do the same things that a manager at San Antonio's Pace Foods does? Put another way, is the manager's job the same in both profit and not-for-profit organizations? The answer: For the most part, yes.[16]

First, let's dispense with a few fallacies about the manager's job in public organizations.

Fallacy 1. Decisions in public organizations emphasize political priorities, whereas decisions in business organizations are rational and apolitical.

Truth. Decisions in all organizations are influenced by political considerations. We'll discuss that fact in chapter 6.

Fallacy 2. Public decision makers, in contrast to their business counterparts, are constrained by administrative procedures that limit managerial authority and autonomy.

Truth. As we'll show in chapter 3, almost all managers find that significant constraints have been placed on their managerial discretion.

Fallacy 3. It's hard to get high performance out of government employees because, compared with their business counterparts, they're lazy, more security oriented, and less motivated.

Truth. The evidence indicates that there is no significant difference in the motivational needs of public and business employees.[17]

Regardless of the type of organization a manager works in, there are commonalities to all managerial jobs. All managers make decisions, set objectives, create workable organization structures, hire and motivate employees, secure legitimacy for their organization's existence, and develop internal political support in order to implement programs.

Of course, there are some noteworthy differences. The most important is measuring performance. Profit, or "the bottom line," acts as an unambiguous measure of the effectiveness of a business organization. There is no such universal measure in not-for-profit organizations. Measuring the performance of charitable organizations, museums, schools, or government agencies is, therefore, considerably more difficult. Managers in these organizations generally do not face the market test for financial performance, although they too must be efficient and effective in order to help their organizations survive.

Our conclusion is that, although there are distinctions between the management of profit and not-for-profit organizations, the two are far more alike than they are different. Both are concerned with having managers who can effectively and efficiently plan, organize, lead, and control while managing the various parts of the organizational system and while managing the changing situations the organization faces.

Organizational Size

Is the manager's job any different in a small organization than in a large one? This question is best answered by looking at the job of managers in small business firms and comparing them with our previous discussion of managerial roles. First, however, let's define small business and the part it plays in our economic system.

There is no commonly agreed-upon definition of a small business because there are different criteria used to define *small*—for example, number of employees, annual sales, or total assets. For our purposes, we'll call a **small business** any independently owned and operated, profit-seeking enterprise that has fewer than 500 employees.

Small businesses may be little in size, but they have a very large impact on the economies of the United States and other countries. Statistics tell us that small businesses constitute about 97 percent of all nonfarm businesses in the United States; they employ more than 54 percent of the private workforce; they dominate such U.S. industries as retailing and construction; and they will generate more than half of all new U.S. jobs created during the next decade. Moreover, small businesses are where the job growth has been in recent years. Between 1990 and 1994, U.S. firms with 19 or fewer employees created a significant percentage of the new jobs.[18] The increasing importance of small businesses is a worldwide phenomenon; small businesses are becoming popular in places such as Japan, China, Korea, France, Germany, and the United Kingdom.[19]

Now to the question at hand: Is the job of managing a small business different from that of managing a large one? One study comparing the two found that the importance of roles differed significantly.[20] As illustrated in Figure 1-10, the small business manager's most

small business

An independently owned and operated profit-seeking enterprise having fewer than 500 employees.

Yla Eason, founder and CEO of Olmec Toys of Richmond, Virginia, epitomizes the growing numbers of successful women entrepreneurs. Eason, a Harvard Business School graduate, started her business selling dolls for children of color when her 3-year-old son wanted to be like He-Man but couldn't because He-Man was white. Eason founded her business in 1985. Now Olmec Toys has annual revenues in excess of $5 million and sells more than 31 dolls for children of color.

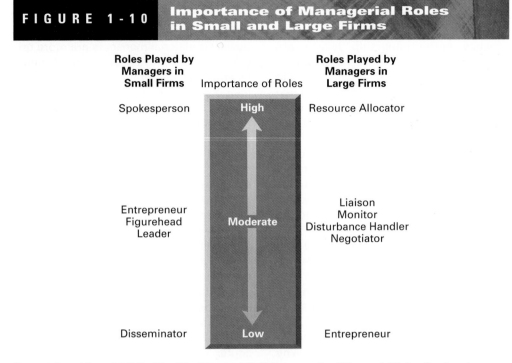

FIGURE 1-10	Importance of Managerial Roles in Small and Large Firms

Roles Played by Managers in Small Firms — Importance of Roles — **Roles Played by Managers in Large Firms**

Spokesperson — **High** — Resource Allocator

Entrepreneur / Figurehead / Leader — **Moderate** — Liaison / Monitor / Disturbance Handler / Negotiator

Disseminator — **Low** — Entrepreneur

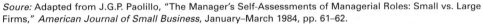

Soure: Adapted from J.G.P. Paolillo, "The Manager's Self-Assessments of Managerial Roles: Small vs. Large Firms," *American Journal of Small Business*, January–March 1984, pp. 61–62.

important role is that of spokesperson. The small business manager spends a large amount of time doing such outwardly directed activities as meeting with customers, arranging financing with bankers, searching for new opportunities, and stimulating change. In contrast, the most important concerns of a manager in a large organization are directed internally, toward deciding which organizational units get what available resources and how much of them. Also, according to this study, the entrepreneurial role—looking for business opportunities and planning activities for performance improvement—is least important to managers in large firms.

Compared with a manager in a large organization, a small business manager is more likely to be a generalist. His or her job will combine the activities of a large corporation's chief executive with many of the day-to-day activities done by a first-line supervisor. Moreover, the structure and formality that characterize a manager's job in a large organization tend to give way to informality in small firms. Planning is less likely to be a carefully orchestrated ritual. The organization's design is less complex and structured, and control in the small business relies more on direct observation than on sophisticated computerized monitoring systems.[21]

Again, as with organizational level, when we compare small and large organizations we see differences in degree and emphasis but not in function. Managers in both small and large organizations perform essentially the same activities; only how they go about them and the proportion of time they spend on each are different.

Cross-National Transferability

The last generic management issue concerns whether management concepts are transferable across national borders. If managerial concepts were completely generic, they would apply universally, regardless of economic, social, political, or cultural differences. Studies

ENTREPRENEURSHIP

entrepreneurship

A process by which people pursue opportunities, fulfilling needs and wants through innovation, without regard to the resources they currently control.

Managers versus Entrepreneurs

Because entrepreneurship issues are important to your study of management, we've included Entrepreneurship boxes in selected chapters. The first thing we need to do, however, is to define what we mean by an entrepreneur. There are about as many definitions of entrepreneur as there are authors who write about entrepreneurship. We'll define **entrepreneurship** as a process by which individuals pursue opportunities, fulfilling needs and wants through innovation, without regard to the resources they currently control.

It's also important to recognize that managing a small business is not necessarily the same as entrepreneurship. Not all small business managers are entrepreneurs. Many small business managers don't innovate. They merely operate their businesses like large, bureaucratic organizations—just on a smaller scale. Why do we make such a distinction? Because there are some key differences in the managerial styles of entrepreneurs and traditional bureaucratic managers of small or large organizations. What are some of these differences?

Entrepreneurs actively seek change by exploiting opportunities, whereas traditional managers tend to be more custodial. When searching for these opportunities, entrepreneurs often put their own personal financial security at risk. The hierarchical structure of bureaucratic organizations typically insulates managers from these financial wagers and rewards them for minimizing risks and avoiding failures. In fact, traditional managers tend to avoid risk, whereas entrepreneurs accept risk as part of the entrepreneurial process. In return, entrepreneurs are motivated by independence and the opportunity to create financial gain. Traditional managers tend to be motivated by career promotions and other traditional corporate rewards including office location and size, staff, and power. Traditional managers are more oriented toward the achievement of short-term goals; entrepreneurs are looking at their business's growth over a longer term, say five to ten years. The managerial activities that the two engage in are also different. Entrepreneurs tend to be directly involved in their organization's operational activities; traditional managers tend to delegate tasks and supervise those workers performing the tasks. Finally, traditional managers and entrepreneurs have different views toward failures and mistakes. Entrepreneurs tend to accept mistakes as a normal part of doing business; traditional managers tend to avoid putting themselves into situations in which they could fail or make a mistake.

Linda Lang is an entrepreneur! She founded Arizona Rotocraft, Inc., a helicopter engine repair shop in 1993 with $25,000. She started her company after divorcing her husband and liquidating the concrete business they had run. Some people may think that a woman is unlikely to be successful in the field of helicopter repair, but Lang has built her company to 21 employees and over $6 million in annual revenues. Although she realistically accepts that this business could fail, Lang is taking steps to see it does not. In a large company, a manager with the responsibility of managing a division or product line might not take the risks that Lang and other entrepreneurs like her take and may not be as firmly committed to seeing the venture succeed.

So, even though managers in small businesses perform essentially the same managerial activities as managers in large organizations, we do find some clear distinctions between entrepreneurs and traditional business managers.[22]

that have compared preferred managerial practices between countries have not generally supported the universality of management concepts. In chapter 4, we'll examine some specific differences between countries. At this point, it is sufficient to say that most of the concepts we'll be discussing in future chapters apply to the United States, Canada, Great Britain, Australia, and other English-speaking democracies. We have to modify these concepts if we want to apply them in India, Korea, or any other country whose economic, political, social, or cultural environment differs greatly from that of the so-called free-market democracies.[23]

19 What are the similarities and differences between managers at different organizational levels?

20 How is the job of managing a small business different from that of managing a large one?

21 Are management concepts transferable across national borders? Explain.

WHY STUDY MANAGEMENT?

The first reason for studying management is that we all have a vested interest in improving the way organizations are managed. Why? Because we interact with organizations every single day of our lives. Does it frustrate you when you have to spend three hours in a department of motor vehicles office to get your driver's license renewed? Are you irritated when none of the salespeople in a department store seem interested in helping you? Do you get annoyed when you call an airline three times and their sales representatives quote you three different prices for the same trip? Doesn't it seem as if something is wrong when a multibillion dollar telescope, purchased with taxpayers' money, won't work properly? These are all examples of problems created by poor management. Organizations that are well managed—and we'll share many examples of these throughout the text—develop a loyal

Career Opportunities in Management

What are the opportunities for a career in management? It may seem, given the continually depressing news reports of organizational downsizings, that a career in management might not exactly be a wise choice! So here you are, a student taking this management course, and you may be asking yourself about now, "What's the use? Why should I learn about management when it seems as if organizations are only continuing to downsize and all the management jobs are disappearing?"

We want to assure you that there are abundant opportunities for management jobs![24] The U.S. Bureau of Labor Statistics estimates a 17 percent growth in executive, administrative, and managerial jobs over the next 10 years. But these jobs may not be in the organizations or fields that you'd expect. Although there

may be limited demand for managers in the traditional, Fortune 500-type companies, the hot growth prospects for managers are in small and medium-sized organizations. In fact, a survey of college career services professionals showed that an overwhelming 84 percent of the respondents reported an increased number of college graduates pursuing full-time employment with small businesses. And these graduates were not only seeking positions in small businesses, they were actually securing them. A good place to land a management position can be a smaller-sized organization. In addition, there's continuing strong demand for managers in growing fields such as new media development; any information technology area including computers, software, organizational intranets, or Internet–World Wide Web content development; telecommunications; employee assistance and training; and not-for-profit agencies. ■

constituency, grow, and prosper. Those that are poorly managed find themselves with a declining customer base and reduced revenues. Eventually, the survival of poorly managed organizations becomes threatened. Just look at the number of airline and retail companies that have gone bankrupt! Companies such as Braniff and Eastern Airlines, Sizzler Steakhouses, Gimbels, and W.T. Grant were once thriving organizations, but ineffective management did them in. Today those companies no longer exist.

The second reason for studying management is the reality that for most of you, once you graduate from college and begin your career, you will either manage or be managed. For those who plan on management careers, an understanding of the management process forms the foundation upon which to build your management skills.

Of course, it would be naive to assume that everyone who studies management is planning a career in management. A course in management may only be a requirement for a degree you want; but that shouldn't make the study of management irrelevant. Assuming that you will have to work for a living and recognizing that you will almost certainly work in an organization, you will probably be a manager, have some managerial responsibilities even if you're not a manager, or work for a manager. You can gain a great deal of insight into the way your boss behaves and the internal workings of organizations by studying management. The point is that you don't have to aspire to be a manager to gain something valuable from a course in management.

••••••••••••••••••••••••••••

managers respond to "a manager's dilemma"

••••••••••••••••••••••••••••••••

MANAGER 1

Clearly, there is an urgent need to regain credibility and trust within United Way and the community at large. Action steps Elaine Chao might take include: (1) restate or redefine mission and objectives of United Way for employees: why does it exist, what results are expected, how will results be measured, and how will organization function; (2) define my beliefs and expectations: importance of the mission, ethics, employee behavior and accountability, and targets and results; (3) develop a plan for reestablishing a positive image and high level of public trust for United Way: involve some key local chapters to generate ideas, support, and key messages and communicate vision and plans to all United Way chapters across the United States; (4) communicate to the general public the content of United Way's new message; and (5) conduct periodic assessments and surveys of results and attitudes until targets have been met.

Peter Belluschi, retired Vice President of Bleach Paper Board/Newsprint Division of Weyerhaeuser and President-Chairman of the Board of the North Pacific Paper Company, Portland, Oregon

MANAGER 2

A public scandal, financial difficulties, and employee morale problems can tax the skills of even a well-seasoned manager. It would be important to use both human and management planning skills to overcome these challenges. I would first develop a financial plan to cover operating costs and increase contributions. Once the plan was completed, I would obtain funding for operating expenses by securing a bank loan or a personalized solicitation, or both, for help from past top contributors. The next task would be to execute the plans, and that requires human skills. Communication is absolutely critical to the success of United Way. This means positively influencing the opinions of three groups: the public, the local community United Way chapters, and the employees. I'd start this communication by holding frequent meetings with the employees to keep them informed of pertinent issues. I would acknowledge the need to repair the organization's reputation and ask them to join me as part of the solution. I would also discuss the new internal control policies, share the plans, and review the financial goals. Honesty and leadership are what employees will want to see during these meetings. In addition, I'd communicate much of the same information to the local United Way chapters and even try to make some regional visits to instill confidence. Finally, I would meet with the media and the press to discuss the internal controls, to demonstrate confidence in the organization, and to reflect on the many accomplishments of United Way. To summarize, managers need much more than technical knowledge. Human skills and conceptual skills are also vitally important.

Denise Radtke Currier, Senior Vice President of Administration, First Bank of America, Lockport, Illinois

for your
IMMEDIATE
action

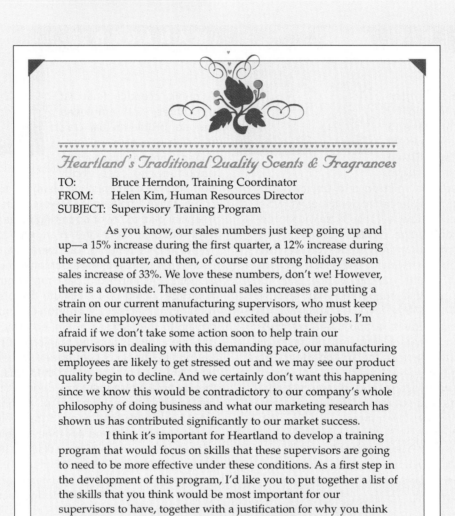

Heartland's Traditional Quality Scents & Fragrances

TO: Bruce Herndon, Training Coordinator
FROM: Helen Kim, Human Resources Director
SUBJECT: Supervisory Training Program

As you know, our sales numbers just keep going up and up—a 15% increase during the first quarter, a 12% increase during the second quarter, and then, of course our strong holiday season sales increase of 33%. We love these numbers, don't we! However, there is a downside. These continual sales increases are putting a strain on our current manufacturing supervisors, who must keep their line employees motivated and excited about their jobs. I'm afraid if we don't take some action soon to help train our supervisors in dealing with this demanding pace, our manufacturing employees are likely to get stressed out and we may see our product quality begin to decline. And we certainly don't want this happening since we know this would be contradictory to our company's whole philosophy of doing business and what our marketing research has shown us has contributed significantly to our market success.

I think it's important for Heartland to develop a training program that would focus on skills that these supervisors are going to need to be more effective under these conditions. As a first step in the development of this program, I'd like you to put together a list of the skills that you think would be most important for our supervisors to have, together with a justification for why you think these skills are important. Please keep this information under two pages typed and get it to me as soon as possible. Once we've had a chance to discuss what you come up with, we'll be ready to proceed with actually designing some skills training sessions.

This fictionalized memorandum was created for educational purposes only. It is not meant to reflect positively or negatively on management practices at Heartland's Traditional Quality Scents and Fragrances.

SUMMARY

This summary is organized by the chapter-opening objectives found on p. 2.

1. An organization is a deliberate arrangement of people to accomplish some specific purpose. Organizations are becoming more open, flexible, and responsive to changes.

2. Managers are organizational members who integrate and coordinate the work of others. They may have titles such as supervisor, department head, dean, division manager, vice president, president, and chief operating officer. The role of a manager has changed because many traditional workers' jobs now include managerial activities, especially on teams. As nonmanagerial employees have assumed responsibilities that traditionally were deemed as belonging to management, the lines of distinction between managers and nonmanagers have blurred.

3. Management refers to the process of coordinating and integrating work activities so that they're completed efficiently and effectively with and through other people.

4. Effectiveness is concerned with getting activities completed—that is, goal attainment. Efficiency is concerned with minimizing resource costs in the completion of those activities.

5. Planning involves defining an organization's goals and establishing strategies and plans to achieve those goals. Organizing includes designing a structure to carry out the plans. Leading involves integrating and coordinating the work of the organization's people. Finally, controlling includes monitoring, comparing, and correcting the organization's performance. The process of management refers to the idea that management consists of a set of ongoing decisions and actions in which managers engage as they plan, organize, lead, and control.

6. Henry Mintzberg concluded from his study of five chief executives that managers perform 10 different roles or behaviors. He classified them into three sets. One set is concerned with interpersonal relationships (figurehead, leader, liaison). The second set is related to the transfer of information (monitor, disseminator, spokesperson). The third set deals with decision making (entrepreneur, disturbance handler, resource allocator, negotiator).

7. One of the early studies on management skills, conducted by Robert Katz, identified three skills managers need: technical, human, and conceptual. He showed that the relative importance of these skills varied according to the management level within the organization. Since that study, other research has identified other skills that effective managers possess. Some of these skills include setting goals, solving problems, managing time, working well in groups, and managing conflict.

8. The systems perspective can be used to describe what a manager does because organizations are open systems with interrelated and interdependent parts. Within this "system," managers coordinate and integrate the various work activities so that the organization can meet its goals.

9. The contingency perspective (sometimes called the situational approach) is a reflection of the fact that organizations are different, face different circumstances (contingencies), and thus may require different ways of managing.

10. Management has several universal characteristics. Regardless of level in an organization, all managers perform the same four functions; however, the emphasis placed on and content of each function varies with the manager's position in the hierarchy. Similarly, for the most part, the manager's job is the same regardless of the type or size of organization he or she is in. The universal properties of management are found mainly in the world's English-speaking democracies, and it is therefore unwise to assume that they are universally transferable outside so-called free-market democracies.

11. People in all walks of life have come to recognize the important role that good management plays in our society. The study of management, for those who aspire to managerial positions, provides the body of knowledge that will help them to be more effective managers. For those who do not plan on careers in management, the study of management can give them a great deal of insight into the way their bosses behave and into the internal activities of organizations.

THINKING ABOUT MANAGEMENT ISSUES

1. Would you describe management as a profession in the same way that law or accounting is a profession? Support your position.

2. Is your college instructor a manager? Discuss in terms of both Fayol's managerial functions, Mintzberg's managerial roles, Katz's skills, the systems perspective, and the contingency perspective.

3. Why do you think skills of job candidates have become so important to employers? What are the implications for (a) managers, in general, and (b) you, personally?

4. Some so-called managers oversee only assembly-line robots or a roomful of computers. Can they really be managers if they have no subordinates?

5. Is there one best "style" of management? Why or why not?

SELF-ASSESSMENT EXERCISE

EXERCISE IN SELF-PERCEPTION

One of the most important things you can do in preparing yourself for a successful career is to get to know your own personal strengths and weaknesses. At the end of each chapter throughout this text, we have included a Self-Assessment Exercise for you to complete and score. These Self-Assessment Exercises can assist you in your own self-awareness journey.

Even though behavioral experts say we should "know ourself," most research shows that the majority of people are very poor self-evaluators. How we perceive ourselves is crucial to how we perceive and deal with others. As a manager, your approach to or style of managing will reflect you and your personal characteristics. This chapter's Self-Assessment Exercise is designed to help you begin to understand your own characteristics.

Self-Perception Rating Scale

Instructions: Each of the following paragraphs gives a description of personal characteristics that might or might not be true of you. For each statement try to determine the degree to which the statement is typical of you. Try to be as objective as you can. Rate each statement according to the following scale:

      7   The statement is very characteristic of me.
      6   The statement is somewhat characteristic of me.
      5   The statement is slightly characteristic of me.
      4   The statement is neither characteristic nor uncharacteristic of me.
      3   The statement is slightly uncharacteristic of me.
      2   The statement is somewhat uncharacteristic of me.
      1   The statement is very uncharacteristic of me.

_____ **1.** I resent suggestions, hold to my present ways, and tend to resist pressures to change.

_____ **2.** I am orderly and tend to systematize things and people.

_____ **3.** I am disorganized and live in a state of clutter.

_____ **4.** I do each day's work well but resist and resent evaluation. I am inclined to get involved in busy-work and avoid tasks that call for a lot of future planning and preparation.

_____ **5.** I tend to do a lot of dreaming and have been sometimes referred to as an "idea" person but accused of having lost a sense of proportion or perspective.

_____ **6.** I spend much of my time and energy in criticizing political parties, school, work, other people, and so on.

_____ **7.** I am a worrier. Often I worry about things that have not happened or about things that are already over.

_____ **8.** I am sarcastic, sometimes toward others in my presence and sometimes toward others who are not present.

_____ **9.** I am likely to nag if things aren't going well.

_____ **10.** I am a procrastinator, putting off decisions until I have sought out and questioned others; often it is then too late to take the best action.

_____ **11.** I am what people could call decisive. I am efficient, size things up quickly, and act so as to get results right away.

_____ **12.** I avoid becoming entangled in other people's emotional problems and usually find some excuse to get away from people who are about to "unload" on me.

_____ **13.** I consider myself an honest person. I am often quite frank even if the truth is painful to others.

_____ **14.** I am quite sensitive and often take things said very personally. I am likely to fly off the handle with little provocation.

_____ **15.** I find it very difficult to "step down in responsibility" to make room for others. Once I have gained a position with status, I find it difficult to give it up.

When you have completed the scale, transfer your rating for each paragraph to the feedback chart shown in the scoring section.

See scoring key on page SK–1.

Source: Copyright © 1981, Richard E. Dutton. Reprinted by permission.

TAKE IT TO THE NET

We invite you to visit the Robbins/Coulter companion Web site at http://www.prenhall.com/robbinsmgt for this chapter's Internet resources.

CASE APPLICATION

Reluctantly a Manager— The Unspoken Realities of Managing

For Matt Scott, the realities of a manager's job have proved to be a not-so-satisfying experience. Matt has worked since November 1994 at Fore Systems Inc., a fast-growing computer upstart company based in Pittsburgh. Fore's capabilities are in an area of technology known as asynchronous transfer mode (ATM), a computer networking system that allows vast amounts of information, including real-time video and audio, to be delivered at a far faster rate than most existing systems do. Organizations that need instantaneous access to shared information are clamoring for this type of software capability, and Fore Systems is on the cutting-edge of this technology. From the time Fore went public in 1994 with about 200 employees, it has grown to more than 1,400 employees, with annual revenues surpassing $400 million. With this rapid growth has come the need for more managers and more formal management systems.

Armed with undergraduate and graduate degrees in computer science from Western Washington University in Bellingham, Washington, Matt signed on at Fore to write long computer codes for the ATM software. Although many of us wouldn't (and couldn't) find job satisfaction in writing computer code, Matt thrived on the challenge because it gave him "the creative thrill of composing short stories with the mental challenge of solving a tough crossword puzzle." Fore Systems, like many computer software companies, offered a freewheeling, often unstructured, environment where employees could take on extra tasks if they wanted to. And Matt did. He reorganized the computer lab, took over the ordering of equipment, and organized seminars in which the company's disparate teams could share and compare notes. His work philosophy was best summed up by a sticker he had purchased from a Greenpeace booth at a rock concert: "Silence is the voice of complicity." Matt's boundless energy and enthusiasm impressed his superiors, in particular, the director of software engineering.

At the end of 1995, Matt was thrust into the leadership position of a new team that was going to work on a project code-named "Maryland." As the team's leader (which wasn't considered a "management" job), Matt hoped to assume a leadership role but still have some involvement with writing code. It wasn't long, though, before he encountered his first management challenge. One team member, Sanjaya Choudhury, strongly disagreed with him about what features should be included in the computer network design the team was working on. Team meetings often deteriorated into loud and heated arguments between the two. The other two team members sat by uncomfortably during these disagreements. Matt finally concluded that he and Mr. Choudhury would never be close or in complete agreement, but he also recognized that Mr. Choudhury was intelligent and knowledgeable about the technology. Accepting their differences, Matt chose to use Mr. Choudhury as a "check and balance" on what the team was doing. The project team suffered another complication in late spring 1996, when Fore acquired a company that required the software they had been writing to accommodate a different technology, one the team didn't know all that well. However, this unexpected frustration unified the team. One team member said, "We shared this common feeling that, 'This really sucks.' That made us more of a team." And the addition of a new team member in June 1996 further unified the team in completing its assigned task.

That June was also a milestone for Matt. He was promoted into one of four new management positions created in the software engineering division. The new job combined project team leadership with increased management responsibilities. Although Matt had enjoyed guiding a project and helping lead design, he wasn't sure about being a "real" manager. The new position had its obvious plusses (a 15 percent pay raise, more stock options, a corner cubicle office, and a portable computer to take home), but the drawbacks were the decreased amount of time to write code and increased responsibilities for doing management-type things such as making decisions and planning, organizing, and controlling. After long and serious discussions with his boss and his wife, Matt decided to accept the promotion. But he pledged to stay true to his own idea of a manager: "I wasn't going to change who I am for whatever the position is."

Meanwhile, the Maryland project team was facing its own difficulties. The original August 1996 system software ship deadline had slipped to October, which was an absolute final date because the project was to be introduced at a trade show in San Jose, California. The work pace to complete the thousands of lines of code became intense and furious. The team was working nights and weekends. When their computer systems would go down unexpectedly, team members would have to work together to get them up and running. Tempers flared frequently, and Matt found his days filled with meetings and other management chores. During the project's busiest weeks, he had to spend 60 hours preparing and distributing employee performance reviews. His frustration grew. "I'm no longer part of the team. I've become the manager." What was happening within Fore Systems itself also was adding to his frustration. The organization's growth had brought about more formal chains of command. Outside auditors roamed the building, checking to see if the proper paperwork had been kept and filed. A project now had to meet rigorous criteria to pass through each stage of product development before being released for market tests.

Despite these circumstances, the team completed its project in time to take it to the October trade show. Comparing its system with those of competitors there, the team recognized that what they had developed was way ahead of their rivals' systems. After final debugging and testing, the software was put on a CD-ROM and shipped to the first customers in late April 1997. Even given the team's ultimate accomplishments, Matt was dissatisfied. He gave up his manager's title and moved out of his corner cubicle. Instead of working "above" a team, he's now working in a hands-on role within a team on another project.

QUESTIONS

1. Analyze Matt's job as team leader and as a manager using Mintzberg's roles framework.
2. Which management skills do you think would be important in both the team leader position and the management position that Matt held? Did you identify similar or different skills for the two? Why?
3. Use both the systems and contingency perspectives to describe Matt's team leader and management positions.

4. Why do you think some individuals might find little job satisfaction in a manager's job? What do you think are the implications for both organizations and individuals?

5. What characteristics do you think might differentiate people who would find satisfaction in a management job from those who would not?

6. How might the study of management benefit a computer programming major who plans on (a) working for a large software development firm or (b) starting his or her own software development firm?

Source: M. Murray, "Who's the Boss?" *Wall Street Journal,* May 14, 1997, pp. A1+.

VIDEO CASE APPLICATION

Caring Management

Although caring may not be a word many people would normally associate with management, Cheryl Womack of Kansas City, Missouri, has built a $45 million company by caring about her customers *and* her 75 employees. She started her business—VCW Inc., which she laughingly says stands for Very Cute Women—in 1981 in the basement of her home with one telephone and call-waiting. What does VCW Inc. do? The company oversees the National Association of Independent Truckers. VCW offers cost-effective insurance coverage, retirement benefit plans, low-interest credit cards, and other benefits to approximately 8,000 (out of 300,000 total) independent truck drivers who belong to this association. In addition, many large motor carriers who hire independent drivers also are her customers.

Womack's customers are a unique breed, indeed! Independent truck drivers "move the world" as they haul across the country in their 18-wheelers most of the products we use every day. Independent truck drivers also are businessmen and must run their businesses effectively or they won't survive in this intensely competitive industry. How does VCW show that it cares about its customers—these independent truckers? It provides an answer to a problem that many of them face: where to find cost-effective insurance coverage and other types of financial coverage that other insurance companies refuse to carry. Womack subscribes to the belief that if you can help solve a customer's problem, you'll be successful. She and her employees *have* been successful at solving their customers' problems and caring about them by providing outstanding customer service. But Womack's caring management doesn't stop with her customers. It extends to her employees, as well.

Her most telling statement about her management philosophy is that "everything I do here is designed to cultivate and grow employees." From the beautifully designed offices to the formal dinners and travel experiences she provides, Womack sees her role as a mentor for employees, not as a boss. She wants her employees to not only do their jobs but also to recreate, redesign, and expand them. Employees can earn $1,000 for proposing suggestions that help them do their job better. VCW Inc. also has a profit-sharing plan that gives employees a stake in the company's ability to make a profit. Womack also recognizes that employees need more than financial caring. To that end, she implemented on-site day care for employees' children, and employees enjoy inexpensive, delicious home-cooked meals at the office prepared by an employee who started at VCW in customer service but who had always dreamed of a job cooking for others. Cheryl strongly believes in the power of such benefits to show employees that she cares about them and wants them to be committed and productive at their jobs.

QUESTIONS

1. What characteristics of the "new organization" found in Table 1-1 does Cheryl Womack's company, VCW Inc., exhibit? Explain your choices.

2. At which of the four management functions does Cheryl Womack seem to be particularly strong? Which of the management skills? Provide examples supporting your choices.

3. What can you learn about being a manager from Cheryl Womack? Be specific.

4. What do you think it means to be a mentor, not a boss?

Source: Based on *Small Business 2000, Show 110.*

A MANAGER'S DILEMMA

Workforce diversity. What does that term mean to you? More important, in what ways do you think diversity is affecting how managers do their job? The reality of workforce diversity in organizations and its impact on managers' jobs can be seen in the experiences of one manager at EDS Customer Service Technologies. In his job as Diversity Director, Gary Collier is responsible for developing employee training programs and workshops on diversity issues.[1]

What does EDS <http://www.eds.com> do? The company is a global leader in providing information services and assists other organizations in assessing, designing, and managing their information systems. EDS employs more than 98,000 men and women worldwide and has operations in more than 42 countries. Because it operates in so many countries around the globe, it is important for EDS managers and all other company employees to be sensitive to workforce differences, including cultural, religious, age, disabilities, gender, race, and social status issues.

Why has EDS made this strong commitment to diversity training? For one simple reason: To sustain the company's growth, it must hire thousands of new employees every year. For instance, during 1996, EDS increased its workforce by 16 percent (more than 13,500 employees). To sustain its growth, the company must recruit and keep the best and brightest talent from the unique cultures in each and every one of the countries in which it's doing business. In addition, EDS employees are well aware of diversity issues when dealing with the all-important customers in the various markets it serves because they need to be responsive to cultural differences. But what types of information should be included in these diversity awareness workshops? Put yourself in Collier's position. Develop a brief outline of the types of information you think would be important to include in manager training workshops on diversity awareness and sensitivity.

WHAT WOULD YOU DO?

EDS's diversity training program isn't all that unusual. Many other organizations, large and small, have made similar commitments to understanding the challenges and rewards of diversity. The practice of management has always reflected the times and societal conditions, so now we are seeing organizations developing and implementing workforce diversity awareness and training programs. Such programs are a reflection of the reality organizations face: a diverse workforce and a diverse customer base. Although the management training Gary Collier has been asked to implement may be in response to societal trends, he's discovering it's not always easy to implement new ideas. In fact, the history of management is filled with examples of evolutions and revolutions in implementing new ideas of how organizations should be managed!

The purpose of this chapter is to demonstrate that a knowledge of management history can help

CHAPTER

2

Management

Yesterday

and Today

you understand management theory and practice as they are today. We'll introduce you to the origins of many contemporary management concepts and show how they have evolved to reflect the changing needs of organizations and society as a whole. We'll also introduce important trends and issues that managers currently face in order to link the past with the future and to demonstrate that the field of management is still evolving.

HISTORICAL BACKGROUND

Organized endeavors directed by people responsible for planning, organizing, leading, and controlling activities have existed for thousands of years. The Egyptian pyramids and the Great Wall of China are tangible evidence that projects of tremendous scope, employing tens of thousands of people, were undertaken well before modern times. The pyramids are a particularly interesting example. The construction of a single pyramid occupied more than 100,000 people for 20 years.[2] Who told each worker what to do? Who ensured that there would be enough stones at the site to keep workers busy? The answer to such questions is managers. Regardless of what managers were called at the time, someone had to plan what was to be done, organize people and materials to do it, lead and direct the workers, and impose some controls to ensure that everything was done as planned.

Other early management practices can be seen during the 1400s in the city of Venice, Italy, a major economic and trade center. The Venetians developed an early form of business enterprise and engaged in many activities common to today's organizations, such as an assembly line that standardized production, a warehouse and inventory system to monitor its contents, personnel (human resource management) functions required to manage the labor force, and an accounting system that kept track of revenues and costs.[3]

These examples from the past demonstrate that organizations have been around for thousands of years and that management has been practiced for an equivalent period. However, it has been only in the past several hundred years, particularly in the twentieth century, that management has undergone systematic investigation, acquired a common body of knowledge, and become a formal discipline for study. Two significant historical events also have played a role in promoting the study of management.

The largest of the pyramids contained more than two million blocks, each weighing several tons. Someone had to design the structure, find a stone quarry, and arrange for the stones to be cut and moved—possibly over land and by water—to the construction site. Then someone had to organize the people and materials, lead and direct the workers, and impose controls to ensure that everything was completed as planned.

First, in 1776, Adam Smith published a classical economic doctrine, *The Wealth of Nations,* in which he argued the economic advantages that organizations and society would gain from the **division of labor**. Using the pin manufacturing industry as an example, Smith claimed that 10 individuals, each doing a specialized task, could produce about 48,000 pins a day among them. However, if each person was working separately and had to draw wire, straighten it, cut it, pound heads for each pin, sharpen the point, and solder the head and pin shaft, it would be quite an accomplishment to produce a meager 10 pins a day!

Smith concluded that division of labor increased productivity by increasing each worker's skill and dexterity, by saving time that is commonly lost in changing tasks, and by creating labor-saving inventions and machinery. The continued popularity of job specialization—in service jobs such as teaching and medicine as well as on assembly lines—is undoubtedly due to the economic advantages cited over 200 years ago by Adam Smith.

The second, and possibly most important, pre-twentieth-century influence on management was the **Industrial Revolution**. Starting in the eighteenth century in Great Britain, the revolution had crossed the Atlantic to America by the end of the Civil War. What did the Industrial Revolution do? Its major contribution was the substitution of machine power for human power, which, in turn, made it more economical to manufacture goods in factories rather than at home. These large efficient factories using power-driven equipment required managerial skills. Why? Managers were needed to forecast demand, ensure that enough material was on hand to make products, assign tasks to people, direct daily activities, coordinate the various tasks, ensure that the machines were kept in good working condition and work standards were maintained, find markets for the finished products, and so forth. When a factory owner had a hundred people (or more) working and a regular payroll to meet, it became important to keep workers busy. Planning, organizing, leading, and controlling became necessary.

The advent of machine power, mass production, reduced transportation costs that followed the rapid expansion of the railroads, and almost no governmental regulation also supported the development of big corporations. John D. Rockefeller (oil industry), Andrew Carnegie (steel industry), and other entrepreneurs were creating large businesses that would require formalized management practices. The need for a formal theory to guide managers in running their organizations had arrived. However, it wasn't until the early 1900s that the first major step toward developing such a theory was taken.

The development of management theories has been characterized by differing beliefs about what managers do and how they should do it. In the next sections we present the contributions of four approaches (scientific management, general administrative, quantitative, and organizational behavior). Scientific management looked at management from the perspective of improving the productivity and efficiency of operative personnel. The general administrative theorists were concerned with the overall organization and how to make it more effective. (The scientific management advocates and the general administrative theorists are frequently referred to as the **classical theorists** because their writings established the framework for many of our contemporary ideas on management and organization.) Then, there was a group who focused on developing and applying quantitative models. Finally, there's the group of researchers who emphasized human behavior in organizations, or the "people side" of management.

Keep in mind that each is concerned with the same "animal"; the differences reflect the backgrounds and interests of the writers. A relevant analogy is the classic story of the blind men and the elephant, in which each man declares the elephant to be like the part he is feeling: The first man touching the side declares that an elephant is like a wall; the second touches the trunk and says the elephant is like a snake; the third feels one of the elephant's tusks and believes the elephant to be like a spear; the fourth grabs a leg and says an elephant is like a tree; and the fifth touches the elephant's tail and concludes that the animal is like a rope. Each is encountering the same elephant, but what each observes depends on where he stands. Similarly, each of the four management per-

division of labor

The breakdown of jobs into narrow, repetitive tasks.

Industrial Revolution

The advent of machine power, mass production, and efficient transportation.

classical theorists

The term used to describe early management theorists whose writings established the framework for many of our contemporary ideas on management and organization.

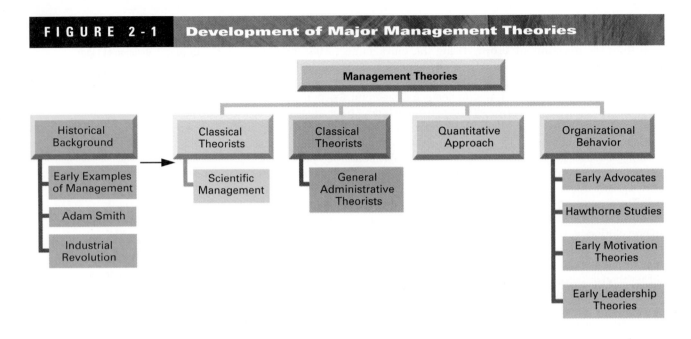

FIGURE 2-1   **Development of Major Management Theories**

spectives is correct and makes an important contribution to our overall understanding of management. However, each is also a limited view of a larger animal (Figure 2-1). We'll begin our journey into management's past by looking at the contributions of scientific management.

TESTING...
TESTING...

1 What are some early evidences of management practice?

2 Explain the advantages of using division of labor in organizations and how the Industrial Revolution increased the need for a formal theory of management.

3 What are the four major approaches to the study of management?

SCIENTIFIC MANAGEMENT

If you had to pinpoint the year modern management theory was born, 1911 would be a logical choice. That was the year Frederick Winslow Taylor's *Principles of Scientific Management* was published. Its contents would become widely accepted by managers throughout the world. The book described the theory of **scientific management**: the use of scientific methods to define the "one best way" for a job to be done. The studies conducted before and after the book's publication established Taylor as the "father" of scientific management.

scientific management

The use of the scientific method to define the "one best way" for a job to be done.

Frederick W. Taylor

Taylor did most of his work at the Midvale and Bethlehem Steel Companies in Pennsylvania. As a mechanical engineer with a Quaker and Puritan background, he was continually appalled by workers' inefficiencies. Employees used vastly different techniques to do the same job. They were inclined to "take it easy" on the job, and Taylor believed that worker output was only about one-third of what was possible. Therefore, he set out to correct the

Frederick Taylor (1856-1915) was the father of scientific management.

situation by applying the scientific method to shop floor jobs. He spent more than two decades passionately pursuing the "one best way" for each job to be done.

It's important for you to understand what Taylor saw at Midvale that aroused his determination to improve the way things were done in the plant. At the time, there were no clear concepts of worker and management responsibilities. Virtually no effective work standards existed, and workers purposely worked at a slow pace. Management decisions were "seat of the pants," based on hunch and intuition. Workers were placed on jobs with little or no concern for matching their abilities and aptitudes with the tasks they were required to do. Most important, management and workers considered themselves in continual conflict. Rather than cooperating to their mutual benefit, they perceived their relationship as a zero-sum game; any gain by one would be at the expense of the other.

Taylor sought to create a mental revolution among both the workers and managers by defining clear guidelines for improving production efficiency. He defined four principles of management (Table 2-1) and argued that following these principles would result in the prosperity of both managers and workers. Workers would earn more pay and managers would earn more profits.[4] Let's look at an example of Taylor's scientific management principles.

Probably the most widely cited example of Taylor's scientific management was the pig iron experiment. Workers loaded "pigs" of iron weighing 92 pounds onto rail cars. Their daily average output was 12.5 tons. However, Taylor believed that by scientifically analyzing the job to determine the one best way to load pig iron, the output could be increased to between 47 and 48 tons per day. After a long period of scientifically trying various combinations of procedures, techniques, and tools, Taylor succeeded in getting the level of productivity he thought possible. Taylor put the right person on the job with the correct tools and equipment, had the worker follow his instructions exactly, and motivated the worker with an economic incentive of a significantly higher daily wage from approximately $1.15 to $1.85 a day. The 48-ton objective was reached.

Using similar approaches to other jobs, Taylor was able to define the "one best way" for doing each job. He could then, after selecting the right people for the job, train them to do

TABLE 2-1	**Taylor's Four Principles of Management**

1. Develop a science for each element of an individual's work, which will replace the old rule-of-thumb method.
2. Scientifically select and then train, teach, and develop the worker. (Previously, workers chose their own work and trained themselves as best they could.)
3. Heartily cooperate with the workers so as to ensure that all work is done in accordance with the principles of the science that has been developed.
4. Divide work and responsibility almost equally between management and workers. Management takes over all work for which it is better fitted than the workers. (Previously, almost all the work and the greater part of the responsibility were thrown on the workers.)

it precisely in this one best way. To motivate workers, he favored incentive wage plans. Overall, Taylor achieved consistent improvements in productivity in the range of 200 percent or more. He affirmed the role of managers to plan and control and that of workers to perform as they were instructed. Taylor's ideas spread in the United States and also in France, Germany, Russia, and Japan. The early acceptance of scientific management techniques by U.S. manufacturing companies gave them a comparative advantage over foreign firms that made U.S. manufacturing efficiency the envy of the world—at least for 50 years or so. Taylor's ideas inspired others to study and develop methods of scientific management. His most prominent followers were Frank and Lillian Gilbreth.

Frank and Lillian Gilbreth

A construction contractor by trade, Frank Gilbreth gave up his contracting career in 1912 to study scientific management after hearing Taylor speak at a professional meeting. Frank and his wife, Lillian, a psychologist, studied work arrangements to eliminate wasteful hand-and-body motions. The Gilbreths also experimented with the design and use of the proper tools and equipment for optimizing work performance.[5]

Frank Gilbreth is probably best known for his experiments in reducing the number of motions in bricklaying. By carefully analyzing the bricklayer's job, he reduced the number of motions in the laying of exterior brick from 18 to about 5. On interior brick, the 18 motions were reduced to 2. Using Gilbreth's techniques, the bricklayer could be more productive and less fatigued at the end of the day.

The Gilbreths were among the first researchers to use motion pictures to study hand-and-body motions. They devised a microchronometer that recorded time to 1/2000 of a second, placed it in the field of study being photographed, and thus determined how long a worker spent doing each motion. Wasted motions missed by the naked eye could be identified and eliminated. The Gilbreths also devised a classification scheme to label 17 basic hand motions—such as "search," "select," "grasp," "hold"—which they called **therbligs** (Gilbreth spelled backward with the *th* transposed). This scheme allowed the Gilbreths a more precise way of analyzing the exact elements of any worker's hand movements.

therbligs

A classification scheme for labeling seventeen basic hand motions.

Putting Scientific Management into Perspective

Why did scientific management receive so much attention? Certainly, many of the guidelines Taylor and others devised for improving production efficiency appear to us today to

Frank and Lillian Gilbreth, parents of 12 children, ran their household using scientific management principles and techniques. Two of their children wrote a book *Cheaper by the Dozen* that described life with the two masters of efficiency.

be common sense. For example, we think it's obvious that managers should carefully screen, select, and train workers before putting them on a job.

However, to understand the importance of scientific management, you have to consider the times in which Taylor, the Gilbreths, and other scientific management advocates lived. The standard of living was low. Production was highly labor intensive. For example, at the turn of the century, Midvale Steel may have employed 20 or 30 workers who did nothing but load pig iron onto rail cars. Today, their entire daily tonnage could probably be done in several hours by one person with a hydraulic forklift. But they didn't have such mechanical devices. Similarly, the breakthroughs that Gilbreth achieved in bricklaying are meaningful only when you recognize that most quality buildings at that time were constructed of brick, land was cheap, and the major cost of a factory or home was the cost of the materials (bricks) and the labor cost to lay them. Scientific management was important, therefore, because it could raise the standard of living of entire countries by making workers more efficient and productive and adding to their wages. In addition, spending six months or more studying one job—as Taylor did in the pig iron experiment—made sense only for labor-intensive procedures in which workers performed the same tasks over and over. The other important thing to recognize about the scientific management approach is that many of the techniques developed by Taylor, the Gilbreths, and others are still used in organizations today. But current management practice isn't restricted to the scientific management approach. In fact, we can see theories and ideas from the next major approach we will discuss—the general administrative approach—being used as well.

4 **What relevance does scientific management have to current management practice?**

5 **What were Frederick W. Taylor's contributions to scientific management?**

6 **Explain Frank and Lillian Gilbreth's contributions to scientific management.**

**TESTING...
TESTING...**

1   2   3

GENERAL ADMINISTRATIVE THEORISTS

Another group of writers looked at the subject of management but focused on the entire organization. We call them the **general administrative theorists.** They developed more general theories of what managers do and what constituted good management practice. The most prominent of these general administrative theorists were Henri Fayol, Max Weber, and Ralph Davis.

Henri Fayol

We mentioned Henri Fayol in chapter 1 for having described management as a universal set of functions that included planning, organizing, commanding, coordinating, and controlling. Because his writings were important, let's look closer at what he had to say.[6]

Fayol wrote during the same period as Taylor. However, whereas Taylor was concerned with management at the shop level (what we call the job of a supervisor) and used the scientific method, Fayol's attention was directed at the activities of *all* managers, and he wrote from personal experience. Taylor was a scientist; Fayol, the managing director of a large French coal-mining firm, was a practitioner.

Fayol described the practice of management as something distinct from accounting, finance, production, distribution, and other typical business functions. He argued that management was an activity common to all human endeavors in business, government, and even in the home. He then proceeded to state 14 **principles of management**—fundamental or universal truths—that could be taught in schools and universities. These principles are shown in Table 2-2.

Max Weber

Max Weber (pronounced VAY-ber) was a German sociologist. Writing in the early 1900s, Weber developed a theory of authority structures and described organizational activity on the basis of authority relations.[7] He described an ideal type of organization he called a **bureaucracy**. It was a system characterized by division of labor, a clearly defined hierarchy, detailed rules and regulations, and impersonal relationships. Weber recognized that this "ideal bureaucracy" didn't exist in reality but, rather, represented a selective reconstruction of the real world. He meant it as a basis for theorizing about work and how work could be done in large groups. His theory became the model structural design for many of today's large organizations. The features of Weber's ideal bureaucratic structure are outlined in Table 2-3.

Bureaucracy, as described by Weber, is a lot like scientific management in its ideology. Both emphasize rationality, predictability, impersonality, technical competence, and authoritarianism. Although Weber's writings were less operational than Taylor's, the fact that his "ideal type" still describes many contemporary organizations attests to the importance of his work.

Ralph C. Davis

The final major contributor to the general administrative theories of management that we are going to describe is Ralph C. Davis.[8] An engineer by training, Davis developed his perspective as a result of his exposure to management at both the bottom level and executive level. His first exposure to management was through his job as an industrial engineer (a job that used scientific management techniques and principles) at the Winchester Repeating Arms Company, but Davis got a different perspective when he moved to General Motors in 1927. As the founder of the Department of Management at the General Motors Institute, Davis was exposed to the unique managerial philosophies of the legendary Alfred P. Sloan (General Motors' president, and architect of the decentralized organizational structure design that most experts believed was responsible for GM's phenomenal growth during the 1920s and 1930s). Through his work at the GM Institute and from his reading of the translated edition of Fayol's management book, Davis developed his own administrative philoso-

general administrative theorists

Writers who developed general theories of what managers do and what constitutes good management practice.

principles of management

Universal truths of management that can be taught in schools.

bureaucracy

A form of organization marked by division of labor, hierarchy, rules and regulations, and impersonal relationships.

T A B L E 2 - 2	**Fayol's Fourteen Principles of Management**

1. *Division of work.* This principle is the same as Adam Smith's division of labor. Specialization increases output by making employees more efficient.
2. *Authority.* Managers must be able to give orders. Authority gives them this right. Along with authority, however, goes responsibility. Wherever authority is exercised, responsibility arises.
3. *Discipline.* Employees must obey and respect the rules that govern the organization. Good discipline is the result of effective leadership, a clear understanding between management and workers regarding the organization's rules, and the judicious use of penalties for infractions of the rules.
4. *Unity of command.* Every employee should receive orders from only one superior.
5. *Unity of direction.* Each group of organizational activities that have the same objective should be directed by one manager using one plan.
6. *Subordination of individual interests to the general interest.* The interests of any one employee or group of employees should not take precedence over the interests of the organization as a whole.
7. *Remuneration.* Workers must be paid a fair wage for their services.
8. *Centralization.* This term refers to the degree to which subordinates are involved in decision making. Whether decision making is centralized (to management) or decentralized (to subordinates) is a question of proper proportion. The task is to find the optimum degree of centralization for each situation.
9. *Scalar chain.* The line of authority from top management to the lowest ranks is the scalar chain. Communications should follow this chain. However, if following the chain creates delays, cross-communications can be allowed if agreed to by all parties and superiors are kept informed.
10. *Order.* People and materials should be in the right place at the right time.
11. *Equity.* Managers should be kind and fair to their subordinates.
12. *Stability of tenure of personnel.* High employee turnover is inefficient. Management should provide orderly personnel planning and ensure that replacements are available to fill vacancies.
13. *Initiative.* Employees who are allowed to originate and carry out plans will exert high levels of effort.
14. *Esprit de corps.* Promoting team spirit will build harmony and unity within the organization.

T A B L E 2 - 3	**Weber's Ideal Bureaucracy**

1. *Division of labor.* Jobs are broken down into simple, routine, and well-defined tasks.
2. *Authority hierarchy.* Offices or positions are organized in a hierarchy, each lower one being controlled and supervised by a higher one.
3. *Formal selection.* All organizational members are to be selected on the basis of technical qualifications demonstrated by training, education, or formal examination.
4. *Formal rules and regulations.* To ensure uniformity and to regulate the actions of employees, managers must depend heavily on formal organizational rules.
5. *Impersonality.* Rules and controls are applied uniformly, avoiding involvement with personalities and personal preferences of employees.
6. *Career orientation.* Managers are professional officials rather than owners of the units they manage. They work for fixed salaries and pursue their careers within the organization.

phy of management. He described the "organic" functions of management as planning, organizing, and controlling and proposed that these functions are universally applicable to all types of organizations. In his book *The Fundamentals of Top Management*, published in 1951, Davis further refined the concept of management as "the function of executive leadership."[9] He also stressed the need for "professional" managers who had a keen understanding of management, especially with respect to leadership and to relations between the organization and the community. If there were still any doubts or uncertainties about the importance of management to organizations, Davis's work served to lessen them.

Putting the General Administrative Theories into Perspective

Some of our current management ideas and practices can be directly traced to the contributions of the general administrative theorists. For instance, the functional view of a manager's job can be attributed to Henri Fayol. And even though the contingency perspective of a manager's job (which we described in chapter 1) proposed that universalistic management principles for all types of organizations are not feasible, Fayol's 14 principles do serve as a frame of reference from which many current management concepts and theories have evolved.

Weber's bureaucracy was an attempt to formulate an ideal prototype for designing organizations. It was a response to the abuses that Weber saw going on within organizations of that time. Weber believed that his model could remove the ambiguity, inefficiencies, and patronage that characterized many organizations. Although many characteristics of Weber's bureaucracy are still evident in large organizations, his model is not as popular as it was a decade ago. Many managers today feel that bureaucracy's emphasis on strict division of labor, adherence to formal rules and regulations, and impersonal application of rules and controls takes away the individual employee's creativity and flexibility to respond to the dynamic and complex changes taking place in the global market.

Davis's description of executive leadership and professional managers reiterated the importance of managers and management to organizations. His writings contributed to the growing body of knowledge about management and also alerted researchers and practitioners to the need for professional management education. In addition, Davis's recognition of the relationship between organizations and their communities reflects what we today call social responsibility (an important topic we'll discuss in chapter 5).

**TESTING...
TESTING...**
1 2 3

7 **What were Fayol's principles of management and how do they compare with Taylor's?**

8 **What was Weber's contribution to the general administrative theories of management?**

9 **What did Davis contribute to our understanding of management practice?**

QUANTITATIVE APPROACH

We next will review the quantitative approach to management. This approach has also been labeled *operations research* or *management science*. It evolved out of the development of mathematical and statistical solutions to military problems during World War II.

Background

After World War II, many quantitative techniques that had been used for military problems were applied to the business sector. One group of military officers, nicknamed the Whiz Kids, joined Ford Motor Company in the mid-1940s and immediately began using statistical methods and quantitative models to improve decision making at Ford. The two of these individuals whose names are most recognizable are Robert McNamara—who went on to become president of Ford, U.S. Secretary of Defense, and head of the World Bank—and Charles "Tex" Thornton—who founded the billion dollar conglomerate Litton Industries. What is the quantitative approach that such people as McNamara and Thornton helped develop and apply?

The **quantitative approach** to management includes applications of statistics, optimization models, information models, and computer simulations. Linear programming, for instance, is a technique that managers can use to improve resource allocation decisions. Work scheduling can be more efficient as a result of critical-path scheduling analysis. Decisions on determining the optimum inventory levels a company should maintain have been significantly influenced by the economic order quantity model.

quantitative approach

The use of quantitative techniques to improve decision making.

Putting the Quantitative Approach into Perspective

The quantitative approach has contributed most directly to management decision making in planning and control. However, the quantitative approach has not influenced management practice as much as the next one we're going to discuss—organizational behavior—for a number of reasons including that many managers are unfamiliar with the quantitative tools, behavioral problems are more widespread and visible, and it is easier for most students and managers to relate to real, day-to-day people problems than to the more abstract activity of constructing quantitative models. Yet the quantitative approach and the widespread availability of sophisticated computer software programs to aid in developing models, equations, and formulas have added another dimension to the evolution of management practice and thinking. We cover many of the quantitative techniques in chapters 9 and 19.

TESTING...
TESTING...
1 2 3

10 What is the quantitative approach to management?

11 Explain what contributed to the development of the quantitative approach to management.

12 What did the quantitative approach contribute to the field of management?

TOWARD UNDERSTANDING ORGANIZATIONAL BEHAVIOR

As we know, managers get things done by working with people. This explains why some writers and researchers have chosen to look at management by focusing on the organization's human resources. The field of study concerned with the actions (behavior) of people at work is called **organizational behavior (OB)**. Much of what currently makes up the field of human resources (personnel) management, as well as contemporary views on motivation, leadership, teamwork, and conflict management have come out of organizational behavior research.

organizational behavior (OB)

The field of study concerned with the actions (behavior) of people at work.

Early Advocates

Although there were undoubtedly a number of people in the late 1800s and early 1900s who recognized the importance of the human factor to an organization's success, four individuals stand out as early advocates of the organizational behavior approach. They are Robert Owen, Hugo Munsterberg, Mary Parker Follett, and Chester Barnard.

Robert Owen was a successful Scottish businessman who bought his first factory in 1789 when he was just 18. Repulsed by the harsh practices he saw in factories across

Scotland—such as the employment of young children (many under the age of 10), 13-hour workdays, and miserable working conditions—Owen became a social reformer. He chided factory owners for treating their equipment better than they did their workers. He argued that money spent on improving labor was one of the best investments that business executives could make. He claimed that showing concern for employees was highly profitable for management and would relieve human misery. Owen proposed an idealistic workplace where work hours would be regulated, child labor would be outlawed, public education would be provided, meals at work would be furnished, and businesses would be involved in community projects.[10] As one author noted, however, Owen is remembered in management theory more for his courage and commitment to reducing the suffering of the working class than for his management successes.[11]

Hugo Munsterberg created the field of industrial psychology—the scientific study of individuals at work to maximize their productivity and adjustment. In his text *Psychology and Industrial Efficiency,* published in 1913, he argued for the scientific study of human behavior to identify general patterns and to explain individual differences.[12] He suggested the use of psychological tests to improve employee selection, the value of learning theory in the development of training methods, and the study of human behavior in order to understand what techniques are most effective for motivating workers. Interestingly, he saw a connection between scientific management and industrial psychology. Both sought increased efficiency through scientific work analyses and through better alignment of individual skills and abilities with the demands of various jobs. Much of our current knowledge of employee selection techniques, employee training, job design, and motivation is built on the work of Munsterberg.

Mary Parker Follett was one of the earliest writers to recognize that organizations could be viewed from the perspective of individual and group behavior.[13] Follett was a social philosopher in the early 1900s who proposed more people-oriented ideas, a radical change from the scientific management theories being promoted. She thought that organizations should be based on a group ethic rather than on individualism, and she argued that individual potential remains only potential until released through group association. Her concepts had clear implications for management practice. The implication was that managers and workers should view themselves as partners—as part of a common group. As such, managers should rely on their expertise and knowledge to lead subordinates rather than on the formal authority of their position. Her humanistic ideas influenced the way we look at motivation, leadership, teamwork, power, and authority.

Chester Barnard was another person whose ideas bridged the classical and organizational behavior viewpoints. Like Fayol, Barnard was a practitioner; he was president of New Jersey Bell Telephone Company. He had read and was influenced by Weber's writings. But unlike Weber, who had a mechanistic and impersonal view of organizations, Barnard saw organizations as social systems that require human cooperation. He believed that organizations are made up of people who have interacting social relationships. The manager's roles are to communicate and stimulate subordinates to high levels of effort. A major part of an organization's success, as Barnard saw it, depends on obtaining cooperation from its people. And as we discussed in chapter 1, Barnard also argued that organizations are open systems; their success depends on maintaining good relations with external groups and institutions with whom the organization regularly interacts. By recognizing the organization's dependence on investors, suppliers, customers, and other external constituencies, Barnard introduced the idea that managers have to examine the environment and then adjust the organization to maintain a state of equilibrium. He expressed his views in his book *The Functions of the Executive,* published in 1938.[14]

Hawthorne studies

A series of studies during the 1920s and 1930s that provided new insights into individual and group behavior.

The Hawthorne Studies

Without question, the most important contribution to the developing OB field came out of the **Hawthorne studies**, conducted at the Western Electric Company Works in Cicero, Illinois. These studies, started in 1924 but expanded and carried on through the early

1930s, were initially devised by Western Electric industrial engineers as a scientific management experiment. They wanted to examine the effect of various illumination levels on worker productivity. Control and experimental groups were established. The experimental group was exposed to various lighting intensities, and the control group worked under a constant intensity. The engineers had expected individual output to be directly related to the intensity of the light. They found, however, that as the level of light was increased in the experimental group, output for both groups increased. To the surprise of the engineers, as the light level was decreased in the experimental group, productivity continued to increase in both groups. In fact, a productivity decrease was observed in the experimental group only when the level of light was reduced to that of a moonlit night. The engineers concluded that illumination intensity was not directly related to group productivity, but they could not explain the results they had witnessed.

In 1927, the Western Electric engineers asked Harvard professor Elton Mayo and his associates to join the study as consultants. Thus began a relationship that would last through 1932 and encompass numerous experiments in the redesign of jobs, changes in workday and workweek length, introduction of rest periods, and individual versus group wage plans.[15] For example, one experiment was designed to evaluate the effect of a group piecework incentive pay system on group productivity. The results indicated that the incentive plan had less effect on a worker's output than did group pressure and acceptance and the accompanying security. Social norms or standards of the group, therefore, were concluded to be the key determinants of individual work behavior.

Scholars generally agree that the Hawthorne studies had a dramatic impact on the direction of management thought and the role of human behavior in organizations. Mayo concluded that behavior and sentiments are closely related, that group influences significantly affect individual behavior, that group standards establish individual worker output, and that money is less a factor in determining output than are group standards, group sentiments, and security. These conclusions led to a new emphasis on the human behavior factor in the functioning of organizations and the attainment of their goals.

The Hawthorne studies did receive criticism. Attacks were made on procedures, analyses of findings, and the conclusions.[16] From a historical standpoint, however, it's of little importance whether the studies were academically sound or their conclusions justified. What *is* important is that they stimulated an interest in human behavior in organizations. The Hawthorne studies played a significant role in changing the dominant view at the time that employees were no different from any other machines that the organization used; that is, they were there only for the purpose of helping the organization efficiently reach its goals.

These women were part of the experiments at the Hawthorne plant of Western Electric. The Hawthorne studies dramatized that a worker was not a machine and scientific management's "one best way" approach had to be modified to recognize the effects of individual and group behavior.

13 **What is organizational behavior?**

14 **Who were some of the early advocates of the OB approach to management, and what were their contributions?**

15 **Describe the Hawthorne studies and their contribution to management practice.**

---

motivation

The willingness to exert high levels of effort to reach organizational goals as conditioned by that effort's ability to satisfy some individual need.

hierarchy of needs theory

Maslow's theory that there is a hierarchy of five human needs: physiological, safety, social, esteem, and self-actualization. As each need is substantially satisfied, the next becomes dominant.

physiological needs

Basic food, drink, shelter, and sexual needs.

safety needs

A person's needs for security and protection from physical and emotional harm.

social needs

A person's needs for affection, belongingness, acceptance, and friendship.

esteem needs

Internal factors such as self-respect, autonomy, and achievement and external factors such as status, recognition, and attention.

self-actualization needs

A person's drive to become what he or she is capable of becoming.

Early Motivation Theories

A major thrust of understanding employees' work behaviors in organizations was understanding how and why employees were motivated. What is employee **motivation**? We'll define it as the willingness to exert high levels of effort to reach organizational goals as conditioned by that effort's ability to satisfy some individual need. Let's look at some of the contributions of early motivation researchers to the evolution of management theory and practice.

Maslow's Hierarchy of Needs Theory.   The best-known theory of motivation is probably Abraham Maslow's **hierarchy of needs theory**.[17] Maslow was a humanistic psychologist who proposed that within every human being is a hierarchy of five needs:

1. **Physiological needs:** food, drink, shelter, sexual satisfaction, and other physical requirements

2. **Safety needs:** security and protection from physical and emotional harm, as well as assurance that physical needs will continue to be met

3. **Social needs:** affection, belongingness, acceptance, and friendship

4. **Esteem needs:** internal esteem factors such as self-respect, autonomy, and achievement and external esteem factors such as status, recognition, and attention

5. **Self-actualization needs:** growth, achieving one's potential, and self-fulfillment; the drive to become what one is capable of becoming

Abraham Maslow (1908–1970), a humanistic psychologist, gave us one of the most widely recognized theories of motivation. Maslow proposed that people possess an innate inclination to develop their potential and seek self-actualization.

In terms of motivation, Maslow argued that each level in the hierarchy must be substantially satisfied before the next is activated and that once a need is substantially satisfied it no longer motivates behavior. In other words, as each need is substantially satisfied, the next need becomes dominant. In terms of Figure 2-2, the individual moves up the needs hierarchy. From the standpoint of motivation, Maslow's theory proposed that, although no need is ever fully satisfied, a substantially satisfied need will no longer motivate an individual. If you want to motivate someone, according to Maslow, you need to understand what level that person is on in the hierarchy and focus on satisfying needs at or above that level. Managers who accepted Maslow's hierarchy attempted to change their organizations and management practices so that employees' needs could be satisfied.

In addition, Maslow separated the five needs into higher and lower levels. Physiological and safety needs were described as *lower-order needs*; social, esteem, and self-actualization were described as *higher-order needs*. The differentiation between the two levels was made on the premise that higher-order needs are satisfied internally, and lower-order needs are predominantly satisfied externally. In fact, the natural conclusion from Maslow's classification is that, in times of economic prosperity, almost all permanently employed workers have their lower-order needs substantially met.

Maslow's need theory received wide recognition, particularly among practicing managers during the 1960s and 1970s. This recognition can be attributed to the theory's intuitive logic and ease of understanding. Unfortunately, however, research doesn't generally validate the theory. Maslow provided no empirical substantiation for his theory, and several studies that sought to validate it could not.[18]

McGregor's Theory X and Theory Y. Douglas McGregor is best known for his formulation of two sets of assumptions about human nature: Theory X and Theory Y.[19] Very simply, **Theory X** presents an essentially negative view of people. It assumes that they have little ambition, dislike work, want to avoid responsibility, and need to be closely directed to work effectively. **Theory Y** offers a positive view. It assumes that people can exercise self-direction, accept responsibility, and consider work to be as natural as rest or play. McGregor

Theory X

The assumption that employees dislike work, are lazy, seek to avoid responsibility, and must be coerced to perform.

Theory Y

The assumption that employees are creative, seek responsibility, and can exercise self-direction.

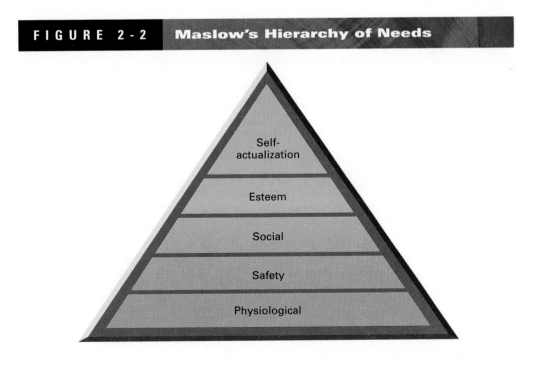

FIGURE 2-2 **Maslow's Hierarchy of Needs**

believed that Theory Y assumptions best captured the true nature of workers and should guide management practice. The assumptions of both Theory X and Theory Y are summarized in Table 2-4.

What did McGregor's analysis imply about motivation? The answer is best expressed in the framework presented by Maslow. Theory X assumed that lower-order needs dominated individuals, and Theory Y assumed that higher-order needs dominated. McGregor himself held to the belief that the assumptions of Theory Y were more valid than were those of Theory X. Therefore he proposed that participation in decision making, responsible and challenging jobs, and good group relations would maximize job motivation.

Unfortunately, there is no evidence to confirm that either set of assumptions is valid or that accepting Theory Y assumptions and altering your actions accordingly will make employees more motivated. For instance, there are very effective managers who hold Theory X assumptions. Karl-Josef Neukirchen, CEO of Germany's $15.8 billion metals and engineering conglomerate Metallgesellschaft, essentially follows Theory X. His approach to managing is strict, stern, and focused on getting results. He says, "You can't have the goal of being loved. Motivation is not kissing and being friendly to everybody. It's setting targets and achieving them."[20] Yet his reputation as a corporate "savior" of nearly bankrupt companies demonstrates the power of his "crack-the-whip" style.

motivation-hygiene theory

The theory that intrinsic factors are related to job satisfaction and motivation, whereas extrinsic factors are associated with job dissatisfaction.

Herzberg's Motivation-Hygiene Theory.   The **motivation-hygiene theory** was proposed by psychologist Frederick Herzberg in the late 1950s.[21] Believing that an individual's relation to his or her work is a basic one and that his or her attitude toward work determines success or failure, Herzberg investigated the question "What do people want from their jobs?" He asked people to describe in detail situations in which they felt exceptionally good or bad about their jobs. Their responses were tabulated and categorized, and Herzberg's findings are shown in Figure 2-3.

Herzberg concluded from his analysis of the findings that the replies people give when they feel good about their jobs are significantly different from the replies they give when they feel bad. As shown in Figure 2-3, certain characteristics were consistently related to job satisfaction (factors on the left side of the figure), and others to job dissatisfaction (the right side of the figure). Intrinsic factors such as achievement, recognition, and responsi-

TABLE 2-4	**Theory X and Theory Y Assumptions**
Theory X Employees inherently dislike work and will attempt to avoid it, whenever possible.	**Theory Y** Employees view work as being as natural as rest or play.
Employees must be coerced, controlled, or threatened with punishment to achieve desired goals.	Employees will exercise self-direction and self-control if they are committed to the objectives.
Employees will shirk responsibilities and seek formal direction whenever possible.	The average person can learn to accept, and even seek, responsibility.
Most workers place security above all other factors associated with work and will display little ambition.	The ability to make good decisions is widely dispersed throughout the population and is not necessarily the ability solely of managers.

FIGURE 2-3   Herzberg's Motivation-Hygiene Theory

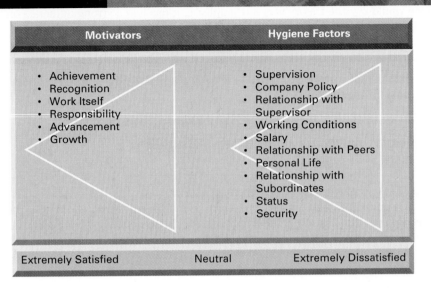

Motivators	Hygiene Factors
• Achievement • Recognition • Work Itself • Responsibility • Advancement • Growth	• Supervision • Company Policy • Relationship with Supervisor • Working Conditions • Salary • Relationship with Peers • Personal Life • Relationship with Subordinates • Status • Security

Extremely Satisfied   Neutral   Extremely Dissatisfied

bility were related to job satisfaction. When the people questioned felt good about their work, they tended to attribute these characteristics to themselves. On the other hand, when they were dissatisfied, they tended to cite extrinsic factors such as company policy and administration, supervision, interpersonal relationships, and working conditions.

In addition, Herzberg believed that the data suggested that the opposite of satisfaction was not dissatisfaction, as had traditionally been believed. Removing dissatisfying characteristics from a job would not necessarily make the job satisfying. As shown in Figure 2-4, Herzberg proposed that his findings indicated the existence of a dual continuum: The opposite of "satisfaction" is "no satisfaction," and the opposite of "dissatisfaction" is "no dissatisfaction."

According to Herzberg, the factors that lead to job satisfaction are separate and distinct from those that lead to job dissatisfaction. Therefore managers who sought to eliminate factors that created job dissatisfaction could bring about workplace harmony but not necessarily motivation. Because they don't motivate employees, the factors that create job dissatisfaction were characterized by Herzberg as **hygiene factors**. When these factors are adequate, people will not be dissatisfied, but they will not be satisfied either. To motivate people on their jobs, Herzberg suggested emphasizing **motivators**, the factors that increase job satisfaction.

hygiene factors

Factors that eliminate job dissatisfaction.

motivators

Factors that increase job satisfaction.

FIGURE 2-4   Contrasting Views of Satisfaction-Dissatisfaction

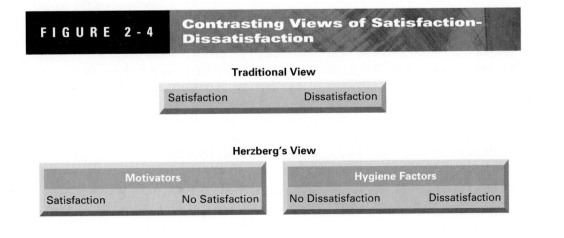

Traditional View

Satisfaction	Dissatisfaction

Herzberg's View

Motivators	Hygiene Factors
Satisfaction No Satisfaction	No Dissatisfaction Dissatisfaction

Critics of Herzberg's conclusions focused on his procedures and methodology, but Herzberg's theory enjoyed wide popularity from the mid-1960s to the early 1980s. Although today we would say the theory was too simplistic, it has had a strong influence on how we currently design jobs (which we will discuss in chapter 15).

16 **What is motivation and how is Maslow's hierarchy of needs theory a theory of motivation?**

17 **What are McGregor's Theory X and Theory Y assumptions?**

18 **Describe Herzberg's motivation-hygiene theory.**

Early Theories of Leadership

Another OB area of high interest to early management researchers was leadership. **Leadership** is defined as an influence process in which individuals, by their actions, facilitate the movement of a group toward a common or shared goal. What did researchers want to know about leadership? Mainly they were searching for an answer to the question "What is an effective leader?"

leadership

An influence process in which individuals, by their actions, facilitate the movement of a group toward a common or shared goal.

Trait Theories. Early leadership research in the 1920s and 1930s focused on leader traits—characteristics that might be used to differentiate leaders from nonleaders—but these research efforts often resulted in dead ends. It proved to be impossible to identify a set of traits that would *always* differentiate leaders from followers. However, later attempts to identify traits consistently *associated* with leadership were more successful. Six traits on which leaders were seen to differ from nonleaders were drive, the desire to lead, honesty and integrity, self-confidence, intelligence, and job-relevant knowledge.[22] These traits are briefly described in Table 2-5.

TABLE 2-5 **Six Traits That Differentiate Leaders from Nonleaders**

1. *Drive.* Leaders exhibit a high effort level. They have a relatively high desire for achievement, they are ambitious, they have a lot of energy, they are tirelessly persistent in their activities, and they show initiative.
2. *Desire to lead.* Leaders have a strong desire to influence and lead others. They demonstrate the willingness to take responsibility.
3. *Honesty and integrity.* Leaders build trusting relationships between themselves and followers by being truthful or nondeceitful and by showing high consistency between word and deed.
4. *Self-confidence.* Followers look to leaders for an absence of self-doubt. Leaders, therefore, need to show self-confidence in order to convince followers of the rightness of goals and decisions.
5. *Intelligence.* Leaders need to be intelligent enough to gather, synthesize, and interpret large amounts of information, and they need to be able to create visions, solve problems, and make correct decisions.
6. *Job-relevant knowledge.* Effective leaders have a high degree of knowledge about the company, industry, and technical matters. In-depth knowledge allows leaders to make well-informed decisions and to understand the implications of those decisions.

Source: S.A. Kirkpatrick and E.A. Locke, "Leadership: Do Traits Really Matter?" *Academy of Management Executive,* May 1991, pp. 48–60.

Yet researchers agreed that traits alone were not sufficient for explaining effective leadership. Explanations based solely on traits ignored the interactions of leaders and their subordinates as well as situational factors. Possessing the appropriate traits only made it more likely that an individual would be an effective leader. Therefore, leadership research from the late 1940s through the mid-1960s concentrated on the preferred behavioral styles that leaders demonstrated. Researchers wondered whether there was something unique in what effective leaders did—in other words, in their *behavior.*

Behavioral Theories.   Researchers hoped that the **behavioral theories** approach would not only provide more-definitive answers about the nature of leadership but, if successful, would also have practical implications quite different from those of the trait approach. If trait research had been successful, it would have provided a basis for *selecting* the "right" people to assume formal leadership positions in organizations. In contrast, if behavioral studies turned up critical behavioral determinants of leadership, people could be *trained* to be leaders. There are four main leader behavior studies we need to look at. (See Table 2-6 for a summary of the major leader behavior dimensions and the conclusions of each of these studies.)

behavioral theories

Leadership theories identifying behaviors that differentiate effective leaders from ineffective leaders.

TABLE 2-6	Behavioral Theories of Leadership	
	Behavioral Dimension	**Conclusion**
University of Iowa	*Democratic style:* involving subordinates, delegating authority, and encouraging participation *Autocratic style:* dictating work methods, centralizing decision making, and limiting participation *Laissez-faire style:* giving group freedom to make decisions and complete work	Democratic style of leadership was most effective, although later studies showed mixed results.
Ohio State	*Consideration:* being considerate of followers' ideas and feelings *Initiating structure:* structuring work and work relationship to meet job goals	High-high leader (high in consideration and high in initiating structure) achieved high subordinate performance and satisfaction, but not in all situations.
University of Michigan	*Employee oriented:* emphasized interpersonal relationships and taking care of employees' needs *Production oriented:* emphasized technical or task aspects of job	Employee-oriented leaders were associated with high group productivity and higher job satisfaction.
Managerial Grid	*Concern for people:* measured leader's concern for subordinates on a scale of 1 to 9 (low to high) *Concern for production:* measured leader's concern for getting job done on a scale of 1 to 9 (low to high)	Managers performed best with a 9,9 style (high concern for production and high concern for people).

autocratic style

Describes a leader who typically tends to centralize authority, dictate work methods, make unilateral decisions, and limit subordinate participation.

democratic style

Describes a leader who tends to involve subordinates in decision making, delegate authority, encourage participation in deciding work methods, and use feedback as an opportunity for coaching.

laissez-faire style

Describes a leader who generally gives the group complete freedom to make decisions and complete the work in whatever way it sees fit.

initiating structure

The extent to which a leader defines and structures his or her role and the roles of subordinates to attain goals.

The University of Iowa studies (conducted by Kurt Lewin and his associates) explored three leadership styles, or ways of behaving.[23] The **autocratic** style described a leader who typically tended to centralize authority, dictate work methods, make unilateral decisions, and limit subordinate participation. The **democratic** style of leadership described a leader who tended to involve subordinates in decision making, delegate authority, encourage participation in deciding work methods and goals, and use feedback as an opportunity for coaching subordinates. Finally, the **laissez-faire** style leader generally gave the group complete freedom to make decisions and complete the work in whatever way it saw fit. Lewin and his associates wondered which was the most effective. Their results seemed to indicate that the democratic style contributed to both good quantity and good quality of work. Had the answer to the question of most effective leadership behavior been found? Unfortunately, it wasn't that simple. Later studies of the autocratic and democratic styles of leadership showed mixed results. For instance, the democratic leadership style sometimes produced higher performance levels than the autocratic style, but at other times it produced group performance that was lower than or just equal to the performance produced by the autocratic leadership style. More consistent results were found, however, when a measure of subordinate satisfaction was used. Group members' satisfaction levels were generally higher under a democratic leader than under an autocratic one.[24]

Now leaders had a dilemma! Should they focus on achieving higher performance levels or on achieving higher subordinate satisfaction? This recognition of the dual nature of a leader's behavior—that is, focusing on the work to be done (the task) and focusing on the people within the group—was also a key characteristic of the other important early behavioral studies.

The Ohio State studies identified two important dimensions of leader behavior.[25] Beginning with a list of more than 1,000 behavioral dimensions, the researchers eventually narrowed it down to just two that accounted for most of the leadership behavior described by subordinates. They called these two dimensions initiating structure and consideration. **Initiating structure** referred to the extent to which a leader was likely

John Warnock (right) and Charles Geschke founded Adobe Systems Inc. in 1982 and have focused on building a company for the long term and maintaining the people-oriented culture, no matter how large the company became. Now with a "family" of over 1,700 employees, Warnock and Geschke are continuing their commitment to getting the job done but not forgetting their employees are people.

to define and structure his or her role and the roles of subordinates in the search for goal attainment. It included behavior that attempted to organize work, work relationships, and goals. **Consideration** was defined as the extent to which a person had job relationships characterized by mutual trust and respect for subordinates' ideas and feelings. A leader who was high in consideration helped subordinates with personal problems, was friendly and approachable, and treated all subordinates as equals. He or she showed concern for (was considerate of) his or her followers' comfort, well-being, status, and satisfaction.

Were these behavioral dimensions adequate descriptions of leader behavior? Research found that a leader who was high in both initiating structure and consideration (a **high-high leader**) achieved high subordinate performance and satisfaction more frequently than one who rated low on either consideration, initiating structure, or both. However, the high-high style did not always yield positive results. Enough exceptions were found to indicate that situational factors needed to be integrated into the theory.

Leadership studies completed at the University of Michigan's Survey Research Center at about the same time as those being done at Ohio State had a similar research objective: Identify behavioral characteristics of leaders that were related to performance effectiveness. The Michigan group also came up with two dimensions of leadership behavior, which they labeled employee oriented and production oriented.[26] Leaders who were *employee oriented* were described as emphasizing interpersonal relations; they took a personal interest in the needs of their subordinates and accepted individual differences among members. The *production-oriented* leaders, in contrast, tended to emphasize the technical or task aspects of the job, were concerned mainly with accomplishing their group's tasks, and regarded group members as a means to that end. The conclusions of the Michigan researchers strongly favored leaders who were employee oriented. Employee-oriented leaders were associated with high group productivity and higher job satisfaction. Production-oriented leaders were associated with low group productivity and lower worker satisfaction.

The behavioral dimensions from these early leadership studies provided the basis for the development of a two-dimensional grid for appraising leadership styles. This **managerial grid** used the behavioral dimensions "concern for people" and "concern for production" and evaluated a leader's use of these behaviors, ranking them on a scale from 1 (low) to 9 (high).[27] Although the grid, shown in Figure 2-5, had 81 potential categories into which a leader's behavioral style might fall, only five were designated as key leadership styles: impoverished management (1,1), task management (9,1), middle-of-the-road management (5,5), country club management (1,9), and team management (9,9). Of these five styles, the researchers concluded that managers performed best using a 9,9 style. Unfortunately, the grid offered no answers to the question of what made a manager an effective leader; it only provided a framework for conceptualizing leadership style. In fact, there's been little substantive evidence to support the conclusion that a 9,9 style is most effective in all situations.[28]

consideration

The extent to which a person has job relationships characterized by mutual trust, respect for subordinates' ideas, and regard for their feelings.

high-high leader

A leader high in both initiating structure and consideration.

managerial grid

A two-dimensional portrayal of leadership based on concern for people and concern for production.

19 Define *leadership*.

20 What are leadership traits, and what has leadership research shown about traits?

21 Compare and contrast the findings of (a) the University of Iowa studies; (b) the Ohio State studies; (c) the University of Michigan studies; and (d) the managerial grid.

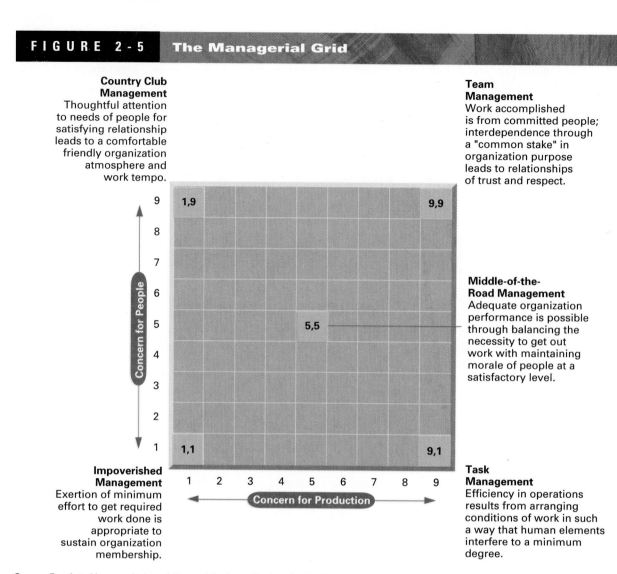

FIGURE 2-5   The Managerial Grid

Country Club Management
Thoughtful attention to needs of people for satisfying relationship leads to a comfortable friendly organization atmosphere and work tempo.

Team Management
Work accomplished is from committed people; interdependence through a "common stake" in organization purpose leads to relationships of trust and respect.

Middle-of-the-Road Management
Adequate organization performance is possible through balancing the necessity to get out work with maintaining morale of people at a satisfactory level.

Impoverished Management
Exertion of minimum effort to get required work done is appropriate to sustain organization membership.

Task Management
Efficiency in operations results from arranging conditions of work in such a way that human elements interfere to a minimum degree.

Concern for People (vertical axis, 1–9)
Concern for Production (horizontal axis, 1–9)

1,9   9,9
5,5
1,1   9,1

Source: Reprinted by permission of *Harvard Business Review*. An Exhibit from "Breakthrough in Organization Development" by Robert R. Blake, Jane S. Mouton, Louis B. Barnes, and Larry E. Greiner, November–December 1964, p. 136. Copyright © 1964 by the President and Fellows of Harvard College; all rights reserved.

Putting the Organizational Behavior Contributions into Perspective

Both scientific management advocates and the general administrative theorists viewed organizational employees as machines. Managers were the engineers. They ensured that the inputs were available and that the machine was properly maintained. Any failure by employees to generate the desired output was viewed as an engineering problem. Contributors to the organizational behavior approach forced managers in many organizations to reassess this simplistic machine-model view.

CURRENT TRENDS AND ISSUES

Where are we today? What current management concepts and practices are shaping "tomorrow's history"? In this section, we'll attempt to answer those questions by introducing several trends and issues that we believe are changing the way managers do their jobs:

Interview with Duke Rohlen, Owner and Founder of Left at Albuquerque, Palo Alto, California

Describe your job.

I'm the founder of a rapidly growing restaurant company that currently owns and operates six Southwestern-style restaurants in California. My company will open six more restaurants in 1998, bringing total revenues to $35 million and the total number of employees to over 1,000. In addition to setting the vision of the company, constantly working to maintain a strong culture, and assisting in raising money for our growth (all responsibilities I share with my partner), I have three specific responsibilities: (1) work with our real estate director to locate sites, pitch the concept to developers, and negotiate strong leases; (2) work with architects to design the restaurants and then work with our construction department to build these restaurants in a cost effective and timely manner; and (3) work with our marketing director to develop Left at Albuquerque into a strong brand with a national reputation.

What types of skills do you think tomorrow's managers will need?

I believe the success of any manager—today or in the future—depends on his or her ability to communicate well, clearly establish expectations, and then hold people to those standards—and to be fair. Additionally, managers must be able to think on their feet, delegate responsibility, think big-picture, make decisions quickly, admit fault and accept responsibility, and prioritize their time. Most important, I think managers must be willing to challenge the status quo and question conventional wisdom. Creative tension propels organizations forward.

What types of management issues have you had to deal with in your organization?

The most difficult types of management issues in our organization are communication related. As leaders, we're constantly challenged to communicate our vision, to keep our employees informed about progress and problems, to keep them motivated and challenged in their jobs, and to ensure a high level of personal job satisfaction and accountability. As we've grown in both the number of restaurants and the number of employees, it has been a major challenge to develop systems and communication lines that allow everyone to feel included.

What do you think is the most serious management issue that faces organizations?

I believe the most serious management issue facing organizations is apathy in the workplace. It's extremely challenging to keep employees motivated and excited about their jobs.

globalization, workforce diversity, information technology, continually learning and adaptive organizations, total quality management, dismantling of the hierarchy, and ethics and trust. Throughout the text we focus more closely on many of these themes in the various boxes, examples, and exercises included in the chapters.

Globalization

Organizational operations no longer stop at national borders. Coca-Cola, for instance, may be headquartered in Atlanta, Georgia, but it operates worldwide. In fact, over 67 percent of its annual revenues come from outside the United States.[29] Other United States-based companies such as Exxon, Avon, Citicorp, and IBM also generate more than 60 percent of their revenues outside the United States. Foreign auto manufacturers—Toyota, BMW, and Mercedes-Benz—make cars in the United States, while Ford, a U.S. company, makes cars in Mexico and Europe. Burger King is owned by a British company. Columbia Pictures is owned by Sony, a Japanese firm. The world has definitely become a global village!

Managers in organizations of all sizes and types around the world are faced with the opportunities and challenges of operating in a global market. Globalization is such a significant topic that we devote one complete chapter to it (see chapter 4) and integrate discussion of its impact on the various management functions throughout the text. In fact, you'll see that several of our opening manager dilemmas, end-of-chapter cases, and chapter examples feature global managers and organizations.

Workforce Diversity

workforce diversity

Employees in organizations are heterogeneous in terms of gender, race, ethnicity, or other characteristics.

America's workforce is changing. Before 1980, the workforce was made up primarily of white males working full time to support a wife who was not employed outside the home and their school-aged children. But that description no longer fits! Today's organizations are characterized by **workforce diversity**. Workers are more heterogeneous in terms of gender, race, ethnicity, age, and other characteristics that reflect differences. One report noted that by the year 2005, minorities and women will compose a significantly larger share of the workforce. The number of men, youths, blacks, and non-Hispanic whites will continue to grow, but they will constitute a smaller percentage of the workforce.[30] The implications for effectively managing such diversity are enormous. For instance, organizations must ensure that their motivational programs and techniques are appropriate for diverse age groups. Or, organizations (such as EDS Customer Service Technologies from the chapter-opening dilemma) may need to hire employees from other countries to fill job vacancies, and managers will need diversity awareness and training to do this successfully. In fact, experts predict monumental workplace changes during the first part of the next century as more women, minorities, elderly, and immigrants enter the job market. Smart managers recognize that diversity can be an asset because it brings a broad range of viewpoints and problem-solving skills to a company. An organization that uses *all* its human resources will enjoy a powerful competitive advantage.

Even managers of organizations in Japan, Australia, Germany, Italy, and other industrialized nations must deal with issues of workforce diversity. For instance, as the level of immigration rises in Italy and the number of women entering the workforce increases in Japan, managers are finding the need to effectively manage diversity.

Until 10 to 15 years ago, people took a "melting pot" approach to differences in organizations. We assumed that people who were different would somehow automatically want to assimilate. But we now recognize that employees don't set aside their cultural values and lifestyle preferences when they come to work. The challenge for managers, therefore, is to make their organizations more accommodating to diverse groups of people by addressing different lifestyles, family needs, and work styles. The melting pot assumption has been replaced by the recognition and celebration of differences.[31]

Workforce diversity has important implications for management practice.[32] Managers are having to shift their philosophy from treating everyone alike to recognizing differences and responding to those differences in ways that will ensure employee retention and greater productivity, while at the same time not discriminating. Many companies such as Shoney's, Kodak, Reebok, Ryder Systems, Baxter Healthcare, Marriott Corporation, U.S. Postal Service, and EDS have developed ongoing diversity management programs. We'll highlight many diversity-related issues and how companies are responding to those issues throughout this text in our Managing Workforce Diversity boxes.

Information Technology

Information technology has had (and continues to have) a significant impact on the way that organizations are managed. For instance, Dell Computer Corporation designed its newest factory without any space for inventory storage, and General Electric Corporation plans to save millions of dollars by buying spare parts for its facilities over the Internet. Both of those decisions and actions were made possible by information technology.[33] In addition, information technology has created the ability to circumvent the physical confines of doing work only in a specified organizational location. With notebook and desktop computers, fax machines, high-speed modems, organizational intranets, and other forms of information technology, organizational members can do their work anyplace, anytime.

What are the implications of this vast spread of information technology? One important implication is that employees' job skill requirements will increase.[34] Workers will need the ability to read and comprehend software and hardware manuals, technical journals, and detailed reports. Another implication of this spread of information technology is that it tends to level the competitive playing field. Information technology provides organizations (no matter their size or market power) with the ability to innovate, bring products to market rapidly, and respond quickly to customer requests. For example, Tommy Boy Records, a small hip hop record producer, uses information technology to control its own marketing, sales, pricing, and distribution and, thereby, to compete successfully against the most powerful global entertainment conglomerates.[35] And we can't talk about information technology without mentioning the impact of the Internet and World Wide Web. Even today's textbooks aren't considered acceptable if they don't have some type of Internet or Web presence. (Check out our Web site at <www.prenhall.com/robbinsmgt>) We will refer to other relevant Web sites in other chapters.) We will discuss more fully the role of information technology in the design of organizational structure in chapter 10.

The U.S. Army has made a significant investment in information technology. The new computer systems are designed to give soldiers far more information about where they are and where the enemy is than any fighting force in history has ever had. Using data gathered by satellites, video-equipped drones, and scouts wearing minicams, decision makers back at command headquarters can transmit this information to every vehicle and every battlefield unit.

Continually Learning and Adaptive Organizations

The organizational world that existed when Taylor, Fayol, Weber, or even Maslow were writing no longer exists. Managers now confront an environment in which change is taking place at an unprecedented rate; new competitors spring up overnight and old ones disappear through mergers, acquisitions, or by failing to keep up with the changing marketplace. Constant innovations in computer and telecommunications technologies combined with the globalization of product and financial markets have created a chaotic world. As a result, many of the past management guidelines and principles—created for a world that was far more stable and predictable—no longer apply. The successful organizations of the twenty-first century will be flexible and able to learn and respond quickly, and they will be led by managers who can challenge conventional wisdom, utilize the organization's knowledge base, and effectively enact massive and revolutionary changes.

learning organization

An organization that has developed the capacity to continuously adapt and change.

As you'll see throughout the rest of the book, organizations will need the capability to continually learn and adapt to achieve long-term success in this type of dynamic environment. A **learning organization** is one that has developed the capacity to continuously adapt and change. The need for continual change and innovation is requiring that many organizations reinvent themselves. Managers may be faced with restructuring their organizations by reducing vertical levels, redesigning jobs around teams, or reengineering work processes. **Reengineering** refers to a radical redesign of all or part of a company's work processes to improve productivity and financial performance.[36] It's a procedure in which traditional assumptions and approaches are questioned and work activities are radically changed and redesigned. The essence of reengineering asks: How would we design the structure and processes in this organization if we started from scratch?

reengineering

A radical redesign of all or part of a company's work processes to improve productivity and financial performance.

Continually learning and adapting organizations are faced with changing and improving the way work is done. Managers play an important role in planning, organizing, and leading any change efforts, and managers themselves are having to change their styles. They're transforming themselves from bosses into team leaders. Instead of telling people what to do and how to do it, an increasing number of managers are finding that they become more effective when they focus on listening, motivating, and coaching.

Total Quality Management

total quality management (TQM)

A philosophy of management that is driven by customer needs and expectations and focuses on continual improvement in work processes.

A quality revolution spread through both the business and the public sectors during the 1980s and 1990s.[37] The generic term used to describe this revolution is **total quality management,** or **TQM** for short. It was inspired by a small group of quality experts, the most prominent being an American named W. Edwards Deming.

Motorola Corp. is well known for its commitment to employee training and learning. It has many characteristics of a learning organization including strong leadership, sharing of information (as illustrated in this team training situation), an organizational strategy that stresses the search for new opportunities, and a culture that emphasizes a sense of community, caring, and trust.

In 1950, Deming went to Japan and advised many top Japanese managers on how to improve their production effectiveness. Central to his management methods was the use of statistics to analyze variability in production processes. A well-managed organization, according to Deming, is one in which statistical control reduced variability and resulted in uniform quality and predictable quantity of output. Deming developed a 14-point program for transforming organizations. (We will review the program in detail in chapter 18.)

Today, Deming's original program has expanded into TQM—a philosophy of management driven by continual improvement and responding to customer needs and expectations.[38] (See Table 2-7.) Moreover, the term *customer* in TQM has expanded beyond the traditional definition to include anyone who interacts with the organization's product or service either internally or externally. So TQM encompasses employees and suppliers as well as the people who purchase the organization's goods or services. The objective is to create an organization committed to continuous improvement.

TQM represents a counterpoint to earlier management theories that were based on the belief that low costs were the only road to increased productivity. For example, the American auto industry is often used as a classic example of what can go wrong when attention is focused solely on trying to keep costs down. Back in the late 1970s, GM, Ford, and Chrysler built products that many consumers rejected. Moreover, when the costs of rejects, repairing shoddy work, recalls, and expensive controls to identify quality problems were factored in, the U.S. manufacturers actually were less productive than many foreign competitors. The Japanese demonstrated that it was possible for the highest-quality manufacturers also to be among the lowest-cost producers. American manufacturers in the auto industry and other industries soon realized the importance of TQM and implemented many of its basic components, such as quality control groups, process improvement, teamwork, improved supplier relations, and listening to consumers' needs and wants.

TQM is important, and we'll discuss it throughout the book. For example, we'll show how TQM can be a competitive advantage (chapter 8) and is used for benchmarking competition (chapter 9); we will also discuss methods for implementing TQM (chapters 12 and 18) and the role of teams in TQM (chapter 14).

T A B L E   2 - 7   **What Is Total Quality Management?**

1. Intense focus on the *customer*. The customer includes not only outsiders who buy the organization's products or services but also internal customers (such as shipping or accounts payable personnel) who interact with and serve others in the organization.
2. Concern for *continual improvement*. TQM is a commitment to never being satisfied. "Very good" is not good enough. Quality can always be improved.
3. Improvement in the *quality of everything* the organization does. TQM uses a very broad definition of quality. It relates not only to the final product but also to how the organization handles deliveries, how rapidly it responds to complaints, how politely the phones are answered, and the like.
4. Accurate *measurement*. TQM uses statistical techniques to measure every critical variable in the organization's operations. These are compared against standards or benchmarks to identify problems, trace them to their roots, and eliminate their causes.
5. *Empowerment of employees*. TQM involves the people on the line in the improvement process. Teams are widely used in TQM programs as empowerment vehicles for finding and solving problems.

Dismantling the Hierarchy

The large corporations of the 1960s, 1970s, and 1980s sought to own and control as much of their operating activities as possible. Organizations such as General Motors, U.S. Steel, and IBM were largely self-sufficient. They owned the manufacturing plants that built their products. To maintain maximum control, they created powerful centralized departments at corporate headquarters to carefully monitor the decisions of lower-level managers throughout the company's numerous and widespread facilities. For similar control reasons, they often acquired or merged with the organizations that supplied them with raw materials. Support activities such as accounting and maintenance were done by people employed by the corporation.

This description no longer fits today's organizations. Most have aggressively dismantled their hierarchies in order to cut costs, improve efficiency and competitiveness, increase employee participation, increase flexibility, and concentrate on those work activities they can do best. These dismantling efforts have been executed through organizational actions such as downsizing, using contingent workers, and empowering individual employees and teams.

downsizing

Organizational restructuring efforts in which individuals are laid off from their jobs.

Downsizing is an organizational action that reduces the size of the workforce through extensive layoffs.[39] During the last few years, thousands of executives, managers, and professionals have been laid off from their jobs as organizations streamlined, restructured, and downsized. At 100 of the largest U.S. companies, 77 percent of all layoffs involved white-collar workers.[40] This trend of downsizing—sometimes called *rightsizing, RIFs* (reductions in force), and *restructuring*—may continue to affect managers, particularly in large corporate organizations, for a period of time. What are the implications of downsizing?

One key issue that's associated with organizational downsizing is the impact of these actions—both good and bad. On the positive side, a study of the track records of the 10 largest downsizers during 1990–1995 showed that even though these companies (such as Digital Equipment, McDonnell Douglas, General Electric, General Motors, and Sears) shed a little over 29 percent of their workers, productivity *per worker* rose by nearly 28 percent.[41] But the downside has been the toll it takes on workers and the elusive financial gains from the action. A different study of 52 corporate restructurings found that organizational downsizings had little, if any, positive impact on company earnings or stock market performance. The human costs can be high as well. For instance, a survey of 62 major U.S. companies that had downsized reported that more than 70 percent were grappling with serious problems of low morale and mistrust of management. Another study of 292 companies found that those that had downsized had seen a greater rise in disability claims than had nondownsizers.[42] Downsizing isn't an issue facing just U.S. managers. Managers in other countries including Japan, Germany, Great Britain, France, and Italy are coping with the challenges of downsizing.[43]

As corporations have downsized and shed full-time workers, many of those laid off have become part of the contingent workforce by default as they take temporary jobs. **Contingent workers** are nonpermanent workers including temporaries, part-timers, consultants, freelancers, and contract workers.[44] There are people who purposely choose the advantages offered by contingent work. Among this group are working mothers who want greater flexibility, young people still experimenting with different job options before settling down, and seniors who do not want or need a full-time position.

Estimates of the numbers of contingent workers vary widely. Some labor experts contend that contingent workers make up as little as 13 percent of the workforce; others say

contingent workers

Nonpermanent workers including temporaries, part-timers, consultants, freelancers, and contract workers.

THINKING CRITICALLY

ABOUT ETHICS

Coming up the elevator after lunch, you overhear a conversation between two managers that a good friend of yours in another department at work is about to be laid off. Would you tell your friend what you overheard? Why or why not? What are the ethical implications of telling your friend the news before he hears it from his manager? What are the ethical implications of not telling him? ■

that the figure may be as high as 30 percent. What *is* known is that the number is growing. Since 1980, the number of contingent workers has grown three times as fast as the labor force as a whole. If present growth continues, workers in "temporary" job situations could account for 50 percent of the workforce within a decade.[45]

Managing a contingent workforce has its own special set of challenges. Companies with experience in successfully managing large numbers of contingent workers say that treating these individuals fairly and flexibly is the key. Also, managers must work especially hard to make sure that contingent workers aren't treated as second-class citizens in the workplace. In fact, keeping the entire workforce motivated, creatively involved, and committed to doing a good job is the real work of today's and future managers.

Finally, as organizations dismantle their hierarchies, they're increasingly relying on empowered workers and teams. Employee empowerment is here to stay.[46] **Empowerment** involves increasing the decision-making discretion of workers.[47] It builds on ideas originally proposed by early organizational behavior theorists such as Maslow and Herzberg.

empowerment

Increasing the decision-making discretion of workers.

Throughout the first three-quarters of the twentieth century, many organizations stifled the capabilities of their workforce. They overspecialized jobs and demotivated employees by treating them like unthinking machines. As you will remember from our discussion of scientific management, Frederick Taylor argued for division of work and separating management and worker responsibilities. He wanted managers to do the planning and thinking. Workers were just to do what they were told. That approach might have been effective at that time, but today's workers are far better educated and trained than workers were in Taylor's day. In fact, because of the complexity of many jobs, today's workers are often considerably more knowledgeable than their manager about how best to do their jobs. This fact has not been ignored by management. Managers recognize that they can often improve quality, productivity, and employee commitment by redesigning jobs and letting individual workers and work teams make job-related decisions. Successful employee empowerment experiments at companies such as Birkenstock, Hallmark, W.L. Gore and Associates, Adobe Systems, Federal Express, and Motorola suggest that there are advantages to expanding the worker's role in performing job activities rather than practicing Taylor's segmentation of responsibilities. We will explore the concepts of empowerment in more detail in chapters 14, 15, and 16.

Ethics and Trust

Many observers believe that organizations are suffering from a lack of ethics and trustworthiness. Behaviors that were once thought reprehensible—lying, cheating, misrepresenting, covering up mistakes—have become, in many people's eyes, acceptable or even necessary practices. Even college students seem to have become caught up in this wave. A Rutgers University study of more than 6,000 students found that, among those anticipating careers in business, 76 percent admitted to having cheated on at least one test and 19 percent acknowledged having cheated on four or more tests.[48] Figure 2-6 shows the results of another survey of ethical issues administered to managers and students. What would your responses have been?

Concern over this perceived decline in ethical standards is being addressed at two levels. First, ethics education is being widely expanded in college curriculums. For instance, the main accrediting agency for business schools now requires all its members to integrate ethical issues throughout their business curriculum. Second, organizations themselves are creating codes of ethics, introducing ethics training programs, and hiring ethics officers. In chapter 5, we'll discuss fundamental concepts relating to managerial ethics. Moreover, we have included a Thinking Critically about Ethics box in each chapter.

psychological contracts

The unwritten commitments and perceived obligations between workers and employers.

There seems to be a feeling, particularly given the seemingly callous nature with which some organizations lay off employees or reengineer work processes, that organizations cannot be trusted. Many observers feel that the **psychological contracts**, the unwritten commitments and perceived obligations between workers and their employers, have been

---

FIGURE 2-6   **Truthfulness of Others**

	YES	NO	UNSURE

Have you ever cheated on an exam or assignment?

Undergraduate Business Students
| 29% | 69% | 2% |

Graduate Business Students
| 53% | 42% | 5% |

Is it OK to get around the law if you don't actually break it?

Inc. Readers, Business Managers
| 27% | 61% | 12% |

Undergraduate Business Students
| 23% | 51% | 26% |

Graduate Business Students
| 37% | 42% | 21% |

Do you always tell the truth?

Inc. Readers, Business Managers
| 15% | 83% | 2% |

Undergraduate Business Students
| 17% | 75% | 8% |

Graduate Business Students
| 32% | 57% | 11% |

If you could get into a movie without paying and not get caught, would you do it?

Inc. Readers, Business Managers
| 29% | 70% | 1% |

Undergraduate Business Students
| 60% | 33% | 7% |

Graduate Business Students
| 43% | 39% | 18% |

---

violated.[49] In the past, employers essentially guaranteed workers long-term job security. In return, employees responded with hard work, commitment, and loyalty. When employers broke this covenant through actions such as downsizing or reengineering, employees responded in kind. In addition, employees have lost trust in their employers as a result of such practices as failing to confront poor performers, underrewarding high performers, ignoring charges of workplace harassment, and turning promotion decisions into political contests.

There's no doubt that the workplace has changed. The old loyalty bonds between employers and employees have loosened significantly. Yet, given the dynamic global competitive environment that organizations face, the old employment relationships—that is, the old psychological contracts that were appropriate for a more stable time—probably aren't realistic. The management challenge is that the new technology-based organizational structures, structural design options, and practice of empowerment all require *increased* trust within organizations. The issue of rebuilding trust is one that managers will have to address in order to provide a work environment in which all organizational members are encouraged and allowed to contribute their best. Employees have to trust management to treat them fairly, and management has to trust workers to conscientiously fulfill their work responsibilities.

Some organizations are taking steps to create this type of environment. For example, Kodak has developed a "social contract" in which workers pledge to better understand the business and the customers, to adapt to change, and to give 100 percent effort. In return, Kodak pledges to provide extensive employee training, career development, and appraisal of managers' performance.[50] Although Kodak's actions are a good example of what organizations might do to rebuild employee trust, managers everywhere have the same challenge—understanding how current trends and issues, such as ethics and trust, affect the way they manage.

22 What is workforce diversity, and why is it an important issue for managers?

23 Describe continually learning and adaptive organizations.

24 Explain how total quality management, downsizing, contingent workers, empowerment, psychological contracts, and trust are issues managers must deal with.

managers respond to "a manager's dilemma"

MANAGER 1

If I were designing manager training workshops on diversity awareness and sensitivity, I would first of all include information on what diversity is, how it affects our organization, and why it's important to our organization's future success. During the discussion on these topics, I would ask for attendees to provide input about their perceptions and personal experiences with diversity, both good and bad. I would also ask attendees for specific ways that diversity could help our organization achieve higher levels of success.

In addition, as I designed the workshop I would consider that employees' learning abilities vary; that is, the way people learn best isn't always the same for everyone. Some people learn best through visual presentation of information, others learn best through reading material, others through discussions, and so forth. Therefore, I would use audio/visual presentations, lectures, round table discussions, and written manuals. In that way, the workshop itself is promoting and accommodating diversity awareness and sensitivity.

Finally, I would also strive to have a diversity of trainers so employees have the benefit of seeing diversity in action. I think it's important to exhibit or model the type of behavior that the workshop is designed to provide employees. By having a diverse pool of trainers, attendees will recognize that our organization is committed to understanding and embracing diversity.

Janet Weber, Director of Marketing, Empire Bank, Springfield, Missouri

MANAGER 2

Here is an outline of the types of information I think would be important to include:

1. *Introduction.* Show top management support by having at least one person from top management serve as "champion" by participating in diversity training sessions; present corporate justification and benefits for providing diversity training.
2. *Diversity awareness.* Share demographic data on diversity of employees and customers perhaps by using a world map with pins in countries showing ethnic origins of employees and customers; give managers a questionnaire to complete regarding their own experiences with diversity; describe diversity training done in other companies and the favorable results and benefits; acknowledge and celebrate existing diversity within our own workforce; provide information on gender differences, sexual harassment, and multicultural traditions (there's a calendar available with 400 events from 35 groups).
3. *Bring diversity awareness into daily life.* Establish an in-house Diversity Resource Center; offer effective gender communications seminars; institute a mentoring program; appoint a diversity advisory or steering committee; display multicultural artwork in corporate offices; sponsor a fashion show in which people dress in native costumes from a country in their ancestry; encourage travel abroad; and organize a dinner of international foods for managers or employees or both.

Dave Dayton, President, Dayton Computer Services, Inc., Grove City, Pennsylvania

for your
IMMEDIATE
action

YOUR ADVERTISING PARTNERS   •   FT. LAUDERDALE, FLORIDA

CREATIVE   SOLUTIONS

TO: Bonita Juarez, Summer Intern
FROM: Harvey Brown, Senior Partner
RE: Contingent Employees

First of all, I'd like to welcome you to Creative Solutions as our summer intern. Creative Solutions has served the advertising and marketing communications needs of organizations in the south Florida area for over 10 years. We like to think that a big part of our success is due to our ability to "sniff out" trends for our clients. This brings me to the first assignment that I'd like you to complete. We've been asked by a client of ours in the home health care industry to determine what impact the continuing trend of contingent workers is likely to have. I'd like you to do some research (please make use of our library or feel free to search the Internet) on this topic. Write up a brief (no more than one page, single-spaced) summary that answers the following questions:

- What is meant by the term *contingent employee*?
- What overall trends are forecasted for the numbers of contingent workers?
- What trends are forecasted for the health care industry as far as the numbers of contingent workers?
- What conclusions or implications could you draw from these data?

Thanks for all your help! I'm looking forward to seeing what you find on this topic.

SUMMARY

This summary is organized by the chapter-opening objectives found on p. 36.

1. Studying management history helps you to understand theory and practice as they are today. It also helps you to see how current management concepts have evolved over time. Current management concepts are the result of continual development, testing, modification, retesting, and so on.

2. Important pre-twentieth-century contributions to management included the building of the Egyptian pyramids, management practices in Venice, Adam Smith's writings on division of labor, and the Industrial Revolution. The building of the pyramids was an immense project requiring the coordination of tens of thousands of workers. Clearly, this demanded management skills. The business dealings in the city of Venice provided an important example of many management practices still in use today. Smith's writings on the manufacturing of pins vividly illustrated the dramatic economies that could be achieved through division of labor. The Industrial Revolution made it more economical to manufacture goods in factories. Factory production, in turn, significantly increased the need for applying management techniques to production processes.

3. Scientific management made possible dramatic increases—200 percent and more—in productivity. The application of its principles moved management from being a "seat-of-the-pants" practice to a serious, scientific discipline. Frederick Taylor proposed four principles of management: (a) developing a science for each element of an individual's work, (b) scientifically selecting and training workers, (c) cooperating with workers, and (d) allocating responsibility to both management and workers. The Gilbreths (Frank and Lillian) were best known for their study of work arrangements to eliminate wasteful hand-and-body motions and their design of proper tools and equipment for optimizing work performance.

4. Henri Fayol was the first to define management as a universal set of functions: planning, organizing, commanding, coordinating, and controlling. He argued that management is an activity common to all human undertakings, and he identified 14 principles of management that could be taught. Max Weber defined the ideal bureaucracy as having division of labor, a clearly defined hierarchy, detailed rules and regulations, and impersonal relationships. Ralph C. Davis's writings contributed to the growing body of knowledge about management and alerted researchers and practitioners to the need for professional management education.

5. The quantitative approach to management advocated the use of models, equations, and formulas for management decision making in planning and controlling.

6. Robert Owen, a successful Scottish businessman, proposed an idealistic workplace and claimed that showing concern for employees should be highly profitable for management. Hugo Munsterberg is best known for creating the field of industrial psychology, the scientific study of individuals at work to maximize their productivity and adjustment. Mary Parker Follett proposed that managers and workers should view themselves as partners and as part of a common group. Finally, Chester Barnard believed that organizations are made up of people who have interacting social relationships and the manager's roles are to communicate and stimulate subordinates to high levels of effort.

7. The Hawthorne studies led to a new emphasis on the human factor in the functioning of organizations and provided new insights into group norms and behavior. Management actively began to seek increased employee job satisfaction and higher morale.

8. Early motivation theories included Maslow's hierarchy of needs theory, McGregor's Theory X and Theory Y, and Herzberg's motivation-hygiene theory. Maslow's hierarchy of needs theory states that there are five needs people attempt to satisfy in a steplike progression: physiological, safety, social, esteem, and self-actualization. Theory X is basically a negative view of human nature, whereas Theory Y is basically positive. Herzberg's motivation-hygiene theory proposed that not all job factors can motivate employees. The hygiene factors simply serve to reduce dissatisfaction, whereas it is the motivation factors that produce job satisfaction.

9. Behavioral leadership theories focused on the preferred behavioral styles that leaders demonstrated. The University of Iowa studies looked at the leadership behaviors of autocratic, democratic, and laissez-faire leaders. The Ohio State studies identified two leadership behavior dimensions: initiating structure and consideration. The University of Michigan studies also identified two dimensions of leadership behavior, but called them employee oriented and production oriented. Blake and Mouton used them in a two-dimensional managerial grid that conceptualized leadership style.

10. Globalization affects all sizes and types of organizations. Workforce diversity requires managers to recognize and acknowledge employee differences. Information technology has an impact on many different aspects of managing organizations. Continually learning and adaptive organizations are faced with changing and improving the way work is done. Managers who emphasize the use of total quality management processes are committed to continuous improvement of work activities. Managers are dismantling organizational hierarchies in order to cut costs, improve efficiency and competitiveness, increase employee participation, increase flexibility, and concentrate on those work activities they do best. Finally, successful managers and organizations have to face the issue of a perceived decline in organizational ethics and trust.

THINKING ABOUT MANAGEMENT ISSUES

1. "The development of management thought has been determined by historical times and societal conditions." Do you agree or disagree with this statement? Discuss.

2. What kind of workplace would Henri Fayol create? How about Mary Parker Follett? How about Frederick Herzberg?

3. Can a mathematical (quantitative) technique help a manager solve a "people" problem such as how to motivate employees or how to distribute work equitably? Explain.

4. How might an individual's age, career stage, geographical location, and organization size affect his or her needs as described in Maslow's hierarchy?

5. What are some personal traits you think might be useful to a leader? Would these traits be more valuable in some situations than in others? Explain.

SELF-ASSESSMENT EXERCISE

IS A BUREAUCRACY FOR YOU?

Many organizations still exhibit the characteristics of a bureaucracy as described by Weber. Some people would fit in well with highly bureaucratic organizations; others would feel stifled and cramped. What is your preference? To determine your level of comfort with bureaucratic organizations, take the following self-assessment exercise.

Instructions: For each statement, check the response (either mostly agree or mostly disagree) that best represents your feelings.

	Mostly Agree	Mostly Disagree
1. I value stability in my job.	___	___
2. I like a predictable organization.	___	___
3. The best job for me would be one in which the future is uncertain.	___	___
4. The federal government would be a nice place to work.	___	___
5. Rules, policies, and procedures tend to frustrate me.	___	___
6. I would enjoy working for a company that employed 85,000 people worldwide.	___	___
7. Being self-employed would involve more risk than I'm willing to take.	___	___
8. Before accepting a job, I would like to see an exact job description.	___	___
9. I would prefer a job as a freelance house painter to one as a clerk for the Department of Motor Vehicles.	___	___
10. Seniority should be as important as performance in determining pay increases and promotion.	___	___
11. It would give me a feeling of pride to work for the largest and most successful company in its field.	___	___
12. Given a choice, I would prefer to make $40,000 a year as a vice president in a small company to $45,000 as a staff specialist in a large company.	___	___
13. I would regard wearing an employee badge with a number on it as a degrading experience.	___	___
14. Parking spaces in a company lot should be assigned on the basis of job level.	___	___
15. If an accountant works for a large organization, he or she cannot be a true professional.	___	___
16. Before accepting a job (given a choice), I would want to make sure that the company had a very fine program of employee benefits.	___	___
17. A company will probably not be successful unless it establishes a clear set of rules and procedures.	___	___
18. Regular working hours and vacations are more important to me than finding thrills on the job.	___	___
19. You should respect people according to their rank.	___	___
20. Rules are meant to be broken.	___	___

See scoring key on page SK–1.

Source: A.J. DuBrin, *Human Relations: A Job Oriented Approach* © 1978, pp. 687–88. Reprinted with permission of Reston Publishing Co., a Prentice Hall Co., 11480 Sunset Hills Road, Reston, VA 22090.

• •

TAKE IT TO THE NET

We invite you to visit the Robbins/Coulter companion Web site at
http://www.prenhall.com/robbinsmgt for this chapter's Internet resources.

CASE APPLICATION

Best Little House Builder in Texas

Doyle Wilson of Austin, Texas, has broken all the traditional beliefs about doing business in the home-building industry—an industry that's neither glamorous nor high-tech and one that many people identify with missed deadlines, cost overruns, and broken promises. By doing business differently, Wilson has built a fast company in a slow industry.

As president and CEO of Doyle Wilson Homebuilder, Inc., Wilson built his company and sold 404 homes worth more than $56 million in the Austin area during 1996. During 1997, his company sold 430 homes, generating gross revenues of almost $60 million. Wilson may not be the biggest house builder in Texas, or even the biggest in Austin, but he has proved to be one of the most innovative. What does he do differently?

One thing that distinguishes this company is that houses are actually built fast. Managers and employees are obsessed with finding ways to slice time off the construction process. For instance, during one nine-month period, the average construction time for a Wilson home was reduced 25 percent—from 165 days to 124 days—and the company is working now to bring that time down even more. Why is faster better? Faster construction translates to less expensive homes. Wilson offers homes at prices up to 10 percent less than his competitors'.

The other thing that sets the company apart is that Wilson himself takes management ideas seriously, especially quality and efficiency. He revamped and restructured his entire company around the quality principles and ideas of W. Edwards Deming and the lean manufacturing principles developed at Toyota

Motor Corporation. (Check out the company's Web site at <http://www.doylewilson.com>.) This emphasis on quality and efficiency led to the receipt of an award in 1996—the National Housing Quality Award—that for house builders is the equivalent of the Malcolm Baldridge Quality Award. The story behind Wilson's conversion to quality fanatic is interesting.

Shopping for a new car in 1991, he ended up at an Austin dealership that practiced customer satisfaction techniques based on Deming's quality principles. Wilson was so intrigued that he signed up for a seminar led by Deming himself. Not long after attending this seminar, Wilson discovered the best seller *The Machine That Changed the World,* a description of Toyota's lean-production system. Wilson realized the power of both approaches and set about reinventing his business.

At first his managers and employees thought that this obsession with speeding things up and driving out defects was crazy, but Wilson continued to lead the change program forward. His people eventually began to accept it and support it. Wilson also broadened the scope of his thinking. He understood that many construction delays happened long before the first nail was hammered, so he went to Austin's building department to identify ways to speed up the permit process. The results were more-productive relations with the city and an impressive decrease in permit-issue time—from 7–21 days to 24–48 hours. Wilson also tackled his supplier base. He reduced the number of construction-materials suppliers from more than 100 to around 40 and worked closely with them to cut lead times for the delivery of materials.

Although Wilson is pleased with the progress he and his employees have made, he knows that there's still a long way to go. He stated, "We operate under the principles of continual improvement, and continual improvement is all about continuing."

QUESTIONS

1. What examples of the use of scientific management do you see in this company? How would Taylor and the Gilbreths have addressed the goals that Wilson had—speeding things up and driving out defects?

2. Describe other historical management approaches you see in how this company is managed.

3. Using the description of TQM found in Table 2-7, explain how these ideas might be used in Wilson's company. If Wilson owned a discount stock brokerage company (or any other type of business) instead of a home-building company, would these TQM ideas still apply? Explain.

4. Do some research on the Malcolm Baldrige Quality Award. What are the criteria for winning this award? Would Doyle Wilson Homebuilder, Inc. fit these criteria? Explain.

5. What characteristics and management practices does this company exhibit that might be important for successful organizations in the next century?

Source: C. Novicki, "Meet the Best Little House Builder in Texas," *Fast Company Web Page* <http://www.fastcompany.com>, April 17, 1997.

ABCNEWS | **VIDEO CASE APPLICATION**

The Changing World of Corporate Loyalty

The list of blue chip companies handing out pink slips continues to grow. Sears announces 50,000 jobs will be eliminated; IBM says it will cut 63,000 jobs; Kodak plans to lay off 10,000 employees. And entire job categories have disappeared before our eyes. For example, between 1986 and 1994, banks eliminated 41,000 tellers, most of whom were replaced by ATMs. Increasingly, there is no such thing as job security. The following comments by Albert Dunlap, former chairman and CEO of Scott Paper Company and currently CEO of Sunbeam Corporation, although harsh, capture the essence of the new employer-employee arrangement. Dunlap, incidentally, has built a reputation for cutting jobs: hence his nickname, Chainsaw Al. He begins by defending his nickname.

"It's not offensive because I've gone into companies that have had very poor results. The company, before I joined Scott, they lost $277 million and were on credit watch, and I was forced to fire about 35 percent of the people, but 65 percent of the people had a more secure future than they've ever had before, and that's what people don't realize. I'm the doctor. I didn't create the problem.

"The reason to be in business is to make money for your shareholders. The shareholders own the company. They take all the risks. No company ever gives the shareholders their money back when they go bust, and you have an awesome responsibility to see that they get the proper return for their risk.

"The free enterprise system is very efficient when it's allowed to perform. America was becoming unproductive in global economies. American companies were failing. Because people have come in and made the tough decisions, American companies are now becoming successful. They're becoming global giants. And over time, they will create considerably more employment. And yes, some people have to lose their jobs, but as I said before, that's a lot better than everyone losing their jobs.

"The world has changed over the last 20 years. But business is not a social experiment. You exist in business to be competitive, to come out with the best products, the best facilities, and to create a future for your people, and the companies that do well must have good products, must have good employee relations, because it all figures into the future of the company.

"The business role is to provide as secure a future for its employees as it can, and within doing that, some people lose their job. That has happened since the beginning of time. And because people didn't take their responsibilities to run efficient corporations seriously, we're in the situation we are now. And the last person that should arbitrate it is the government, the largest business in America with the worst balance sheet, the poorest management, services people don't want, and a bloated cost structure."

QUESTIONS

1. Do you think Albert Dunlap is accurately describing today's business climate? Why or why not?

2. Do you believe that there's a difference between downsizing for organizational survival and downsizing for "economic reasons"? Discuss.
3. What are the implications of Dunlap's comments for managers? For employees?
4. Do you think Dunlap is a hero or a villain? Discuss.

Source: Based on "Corporate Layoffs and the Fate of American Workers," *ABC News Nightline*, aired February 14, 1996.

Defining the Manager's Terrain

A MANAGER'S DILEMMA

Can a small organization ever hope to successfully compete and prosper in the fiercely competitive automotive world as a preferred supplier? Ideal Steel and Builders' Supplies, Inc. has! The company fabricates and erects structural and miscellaneous steel used by the Big Three automakers (Ford, Chrysler, and General Motors) in their manufacturing plants; in addition, Ideal distributes and sells various building supplies and manufactures their very own Ideal Shield® Protective Guard Rail System. One of Ideal's satellite plants is located in an old General Motors Cadillac plant in Detroit along with three other companies who together make up the Hispanic Manufacturing Center. (The Hispanic Manufacturing Center was formed to encourage companies to invest and to bring back work within Southwest Detroit.) Much of Ideal Steel's success can be traced to its founder and president, Frank Venegas, Jr. As Ideal Steel's top manager, Venegas has created an organizational culture that is highly positive and optimistic, hard-working, family friendly, and yet fun.[1]

Ideal Steel began in 1979 with $12,000 in cash from the sale of a gold Cadillac that Venegas won in a drawing. After enduring serious financial setbacks in its early years, Ideal has reached over $30 million in annual sales. It has 80 employees and is an important Tier One supplier to the Big Three automakers. From Ideal's very beginnings, Venegas emphasized quality production and quality products. Ideal's strict attention to quality paid off. In fact, in 1996, Ford Motor awarded Ideal one of its distinguished Q1 quality ratings, which are given only to those select suppliers who attain outstanding quality levels. In addition, Ideal has won several customer service, business, and safety awards from various organizations. Venegas readily admits that an organizational culture that reflects pride in one's work and a positive attitude have played a critical role in his company's success.

How can the various work values Venegas believes in so strongly (such as quality, hard work, being family friendly, having pride in what you do and a positive attitude, and being fun) be conveyed to new employees so that they will be encouraged to conform to this workplace culture? Put yourself in Venegas's position. How could you ensure that Ideal Steel's new employees learn and behave in ways according to the expected organizational culture?

WHAT WOULD YOU DO?

Frank Venegas is a manager who recognizes the role that organizational culture plays in creating the type of organization he wants. Like managers everywhere, he wants to see his organization succeed. He also recognizes the challenges facing his organization from both its internal culture and the external environment. But how much actual impact does a manager like Frank Venegas have on an organization's performance? We need to explore more closely the question: Are an organization's successes or failures always directly attributable to managers?

3

Organizational Culture and Environment: The Constraints

THE MANAGER: OMNIPOTENT OR SYMBOLIC?

The dominant view in management theory and society in general is that managers are directly responsible for an organization's success or failure. We'll call this perspective the **omnipotent view of management.** In contrast, some observers have argued that managers have little influence on organizational outcomes. They propose that much of an organization's success or failure is due to forces outside management's control. This perspective has been labeled the **symbolic view of management.**[2]

In this section, we review each of these perspectives. Our reason should be obvious. The analysis will help clarify just how much credit or blame managers should receive for their organization's performance.

omnipotent view of management

The view that managers are directly responsible for an organization's success or failure.

symbolic view of management

The view that managers have only a limited effect on substantive organizational outcomes because of the large number of factors outside of management's control.

The Omnipotent View

In chapter 1, we discussed the importance of managers and management to organizations. This view reflects a dominant assumption in management theory: The quality of an organization's managers determines the quality of the organization itself. It's assumed that differences in an organization's effectiveness or efficiency are due to the decisions and actions of its managers. Good managers anticipate change, exploit opportunities, correct poor performance, and lead their organizations toward their objectives (they even change those objectives when necessary). When profits are up, management takes the credit and rewards itself with bonuses, stock options, and the like. When profits are down, the board of directors replaces top management in the belief that new management will bring improved results. For example, at the home furnishings retailer Bombay Company, Chief Executive Officer Robert Nourse was removed from his position after sales and profits declined in the mid-1990s, and a new CEO was named to replace him.

The view of managers as omnipotent is consistent with the stereotypical picture of the swashbuckling, take-charge business executive who can overcome any obstacle in carrying out the organization's objectives. This omnipotent view, of course, is not limited to business organizations. We can also use it to help explain the high turnover among college and professional coaches. Both college and professional sports coaches can be considered the "managers" of their teams. They decide which players to recruit and which players start the game, select assistant coaches, teach plays to their teams, and select every play during games. Coaches who lose more games than they win are seen as ineffective. They are fired and replaced by new coaches who, it is hoped, will correct the inadequate performance.

Regardless of extenuating circumstances, when organizations perform poorly, someone has to be held accountable. In our society, that role is played by managers. Of course, when things go well, managers get the credit—even if they had little to do with causing the positive outcome.

The Symbolic View

For more than two weeks in August 1997, a Teamsters Union strike of United Parcel Service (UPS) altered the business decisions and activities of thousands of organizations, small and large. The U.S. Postal Service, Federal Express, and other package delivery companies saw their business volume and revenues increase dramatically. Other companies, such as C.S. Cleaning Service, which had a cleaning contract with the Springfield and Branson, Missouri, locations to keep the brown trucks and the offices clean, found their business volume and revenues decrease. Were these business outcomes the result of managers' decisions and actions, or were they beyond the control of the organizations' managers?

This example represents the symbolic view of managers. The symbolic view suggests that a manager's ability to affect outcomes is constrained by external factors. In this view, it is unreasonable to expect managers to have a significant effect on an organization's performance. According to the symbolic view, an organization's results are influenced by fac-

tors outside the control of management. These factors include the economy, market (customer) changes, governmental policies, competitors' actions, the state of the particular industry, the control of proprietary technology, and decisions made by previous managers in the organization.

Following the symbolic view, managers have, at best, a limited effect on *substantive organizational outcomes*. What managers do affect are *symbolic* outcomes.[3] A manager's role is seen as creating meaning out of randomness, confusion, and ambiguity. Managers manifest an illusion of control by developing plans, making decisions, and performing other managerial duties. They do so for the benefit of stockholders, customers, employees, and the public. When things go right, we need someone to praise. Managers play that role. Similarly, when things go wrong, we need someone to blame. Managers play that role, too. According to the symbolic view, however, the actual part managers play in success or failure is minimal.

Reality Suggests a Synthesis

In reality, managers are neither helpless nor all powerful. Internal constraints that restrict a manager's decision options exist within every organization. These internal constraints arise from the organization's culture. In addition, external constraints impinge on the organization and restrict managerial freedom. The external constraints come from the organization's environment.

Figure 3-1 shows the manager as operating within constraints. The organization's culture and environment press against the manager, restricting his or her options. Yet, despite these constraints, managers are not powerless. There's still an area in which managers can exert a significant amount of influence on an organization's performance—an area in which good managers differentiate themselves from poor ones. In the remainder of this chapter, we will discuss organizational culture and environment as constraints. But, as we'll also point out later in this book, these constraints need not be regarded as fixed in all situations. As Frank Venegas at Ideal Steel recognizes, managers may be able to change and influence their culture and environment and thus expand their area of discretion.

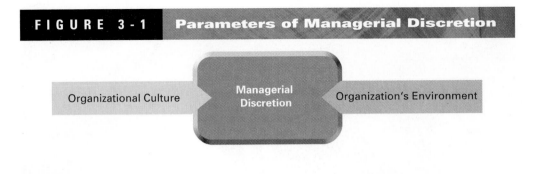

FIGURE 3-1 Parameters of Managerial Discretion

Organizational Culture → Managerial Discretion ← Organization's Environment

TESTING...
TESTING...

1 2 3

1 Why does the omnipotent view of management dominate management theory?

2 Explain the symbolic view of management.

3 Which of these views is most appropriate in reality? Explain.

THE ORGANIZATION'S CULTURE

We know that every individual has something that psychologists call "personality." An individual's personality is made up of a set of relatively permanent and stable traits. When we describe someone as warm, innovative, relaxed, or conservative, we are describing personality traits. An organization, too, has a personality, which we call its *culture*.

What Is Organizational Culture?

organizational culture

A system of shared meaning within an organization that determines, in large degree, how employees act.

What do we specifically mean by the term **organizational culture**? We use the term to refer to a system of shared meaning held by members that distinguishes the organization from other organizations. It represents a common perception held by the organization's members. Just as tribal cultures have rules and taboos that dictate how members will act toward each other and outsiders, organizations have cultures that govern how its members should behave. In every organization, there are systems or patterns of values, symbols, rituals, myths, and practices that have evolved over time.[4] These shared values determine, in large degree, what employees see and how they respond to their world.[5] When confronted with a problem, the organizational culture restricts what employees can do by suggesting the corrrect way—"the way we do things here"—to conceptualize, define, analyze, and solve the problem. Look back at the chapter-opening Manager's Dilemma. Think how Ideal Steel's culture was described by Venegas and how it would influence the way employees did their jobs.

Our definition of culture implies several things. First, culture is a perception. Individuals perceive the culture of the organization on the basis of what they see or hear within the organization. Even though individuals may have different backgrounds or work at different levels in the organization, they tend to describe the organization's culture in similar terms. That is the *shared* aspect of culture. Second, *organizational culture* is a descriptive term. It's concerned with how members perceive the organization not with whether they like it. It describes rather than evaluates.

Research suggests that there are seven dimensions that, in aggregate, capture the essence of an organization's culture.[6] These dimensions have been described as follows:

1. *Innovation and risk taking.* The degree to which employees are encouraged to be innovative and to take risks.

2. *Attention to detail.* The degree to which employees are expected to exhibit precision, analysis, and attention to detail.

At Amy's Ice Creams, employees often perform in ways that customers won't forget! They juggle with their serving spades, toss scoops of ice cream to one another behind the counter, and break-dance on top of the freezer. Whatever wacky things they do, there's one thing they're all encouraged to do: create fun for the customers.

3. *Outcome orientation.* The degree to which managers focus on results or outcomes rather than on the techniques and processes used to achieve those outcomes.

4. *People orientation.* The degree to which management decisions take into consideration the effect of outcomes on people within the organization.

5. *Team orientation.* The degree to which work activities are organized around teams rather than individuals.

6. *Aggressiveness.* The degree to which people are aggressive and competitive rather than easygoing and cooperative.

7. *Stability.* The degree to which organizational activities emphasize maintaining the status quo in contrast to growth.

As illustrated in Figure 3-2, each of these characteristics exists on a continuum from low to high. Appraising the organization on these seven dimensions, then, gives a compos-

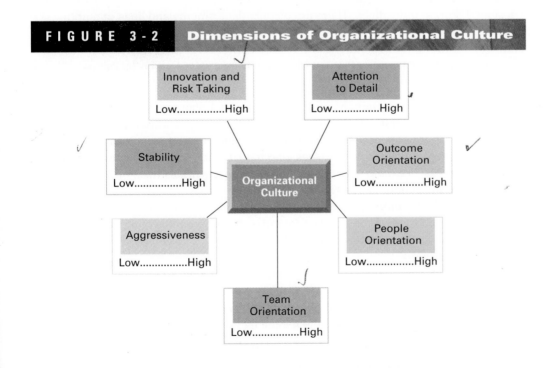

FIGURE 3-2   Dimensions of Organizational Culture

ite picture of the organization's culture. Table 3-1 demonstrates how these dimensions can be mixed to create significantly different organizations. Organizations also differ on the strength of their cultures.

Strong versus Weak Cultures

strong cultures

Organizations in which the key values are intensely held and widely shared.

Although all organizations have cultures, not all cultures have an equal impact on employees. **Strong cultures**—organizations in which the key values are intensely held and widely shared—have a greater influence on employees than do weak cultures. The more employees accept the organization's key values and the greater their commitment to those values, the stronger the culture is.

Whether an organization's culture is strong, weak, or somewhere in between depends on factors such as the size of the organization, how long it has been around, how much turnover there has been among employees, and the intensity with which the culture was originated. Some organizations do not make clear what is important and what is not; this lack of clarity is a characteristic of weak cultures. In such organizations, culture is unlikely

---

TABLE 3-1   Contrasting Organizational Cultures

Organization A

This organization is a manufacturing firm. Managers are expected to fully document all decisions, and "good managers" are those who can provide detailed data to support their recommendations. Creative decisions that incur significant change or risk are not encouraged. Because managers of failed projects are openly criticized and penalized, managers try not to implement ideas that deviate much from the status quo. One lower-level manager quoted an often-used phrase in the company: "If it ain't broke, don't fix it."

Employees are required to follow extensive rules and regulations in this firm. Managers supervise employees closely to ensure that there are no deviations. Management is concerned with high productivity, regardless of the impact on employee morale or turnover.

Work activities are designed around individuals. There are distinct departments and lines of authority, and employees are expected to minimize formal contact with other employees outside their functional area or line of command. Performance evaluations and rewards emphasize individual effort, although seniority tends to be the primary factor in the determination of pay raises and promotions.

Organization B

This organization is also a manufacturing firm. Here, however, management encourages and rewards risk taking and change. Decisions based on intuition are valued as much as those that are well rationalized. Management prides itself on its history of experimenting with new technologies and its success in regularly introducing innovative products. Managers or employees who have a good idea are encouraged to "run with it," and failures are treated as "learning experiences." The company prides itself on being market driven and rapidly responsive to the changing needs of its customers.

There are few rules and regulations for employees to follow, and supervision is loose because management believes that its employees are hardworking and trustworthy. Management is concerned with high productivity but believes that this comes through treating its people right. The company is proud of its reputation as being a good place to work.

Job activities are designed around work teams, and team members are encouraged to interact with people across functions and authority levels. Employees talk positively about the competition between teams. Individuals and teams have goals, and bonuses are based on achievement of outcomes. Employees are given considerable autonomy in choosing the means by which the goals are attained.

to strongly affect managers. Most organizations, however, have moderate to strong cultures. There is relatively high agreement on what's important, what defines "good" employee behavior, what it takes to get ahead, and so forth. In fact, one study of organizational culture found that employees in firms with strong cultures were more committed to their firm than were employees in firms with weak cultures. The firms with strong cultures also used their recruitment efforts and socialization practices to build employee commitment.[7] And an increasing body of evidence suggests that strong cultures are associated with high organizational performance.[8] What are the implications for the way managers manage? We might expect that an organization's culture will have an increasing impact on what managers do as it becomes stronger.[9]

4 **What is organizational culture?**

5 **Describe the seven dimensions of organizational culture.**

6 **Will strong or weak cultures have the greatest impact on managers? Why?**

Culture as the Organization's Personality

In many organizations, especially those with strong cultures, one cultural dimension often rises above the others and essentially shapes the organization and the way organizational members do their work. For instance, Sony Corporation stays intensely focused on product innovation. The company "lives and breathes" new product development, and employees' work decisions and actions support that goal. Let's look at how different organizations have chosen different cultural themes—that is, look at their different "personalities."

Strong Risk-Taking Personalities.   The cultures of some organizations encourage employees to take risks. For instance, employees at Physio-Control Corporation, a Redmond, Washington, maker of medical devices, know that they will be supported in taking risks and trying new and different approaches.[10] The company's philosophy is that "people will take risks only if supported by the culture." Other good examples of organizations with strong risk-taking personalities include Intel and the Virgin Group.

Strong Attention-to-Detail Personalities.   In this type of culture, the organization focuses intently on the nuts and bolts—the details—of the business. Organizations that have made quality their driving themes have attention-to-detail personalities. For example, the company featured in the chapter-opening Manager's Dilemma, Ideal Steel, had a culture with a strong focus on quality, and Ideal's strict attention to quality led to a prestigious quality designation. Another example of a strong attention-to-detail culture can be seen at Black Diamond Equipment of Salt Lake City, a manufacturer of rock-climbing equipment. Most of the company's employees are also experienced and avid rock climbers. The company's vice president of human resources says, "We breathe it (rock climbing), live it, think about it constantly, which makes the whole company a marketing and design resource. It kills complacency."[11]

Strong Outcome-Orientation Personalities.   Some organizations succeed by focusing on results or outcomes such as customer service. This type of culture can be seen, for example, at Seattle-based Nordstrom. This well-known department store chain has developed one of the strongest customer service cultures in the retailing industry. Nordstrom employees know in no uncertain terms what is expected of them, and those expectations go a long way in shaping their behavior.

Strong People-Orientation Personalities. Some organizations have made their employees a central part of their cultures. For example, at Adobe Systems Inc., the third-largest U.S. manufacturer of personal computer software, based in Mountain View, California, employees are treated as "family." One of the company's co-founders states, "Every capital asset we have at Adobe gets into an automobile and drives home at night. Without them, there is nothing of substance in this company. It is the creativity of individuals—not machines—that determines the success of this company."[12] Other examples of organizations with strong people cultures include Southwest Airlines, Hewlett-Packard, Toro Company, and Quad/Graphics.

Strong Team-Orientation Personalities. An increasing number of small organizations and divisions of large organizations are shaping their cultures around the team concept. Many law firms and other professional practices now organize their operations around teams. For instance, the largest law firm in the Pacific Northwest, Perkins Coie, has its 300-plus attorneys operating in teams organized around litigation, business, personal planning, and environmental law. Another team-oriented culture can be seen at ABB Industrial Systems Inc. of Columbus, Ohio, where employee teams manage the production process design, supplier and customer relationships, work schedules, vacations, and any other tasks typically done by a supervisor.[13] The common theme in these organizations is their commitment to teams to define the essence of their identity.

Strong Aggressiveness Personalities. Some organizations value aggressiveness above all else. For instance, Microsoft is often characterized as being superaggressive and exhibiting both the best and worst characteristics of the entrepreneurial spirit. Microsoft's aggressiveness in fighting competitiors, protecting its copyrights, and using the court system against rivals has created a long list of adversaries (including the federal government) that continue to try to rein in the software behemoth.[14] Another organization noted for its aggressive personality is Coca-Cola. It competes fiercely in every one of its global markets. Evidence of the company's fierce competitiveness and aggressiveness can be seen in a statement made by Coke's president: "What do you do when your competitor is drowning? Get a live hose and stick it in his mouth."[15]

Strong Nonstability Personalities. Finally, there are organizations that define their cultures by their overwhelming emphasis on growth. One company that exemplifies this

Employee work teams at Nortel (Northern Telecom) meet in office spaces specifically designed to encourage teamwork.

type of culture is Intel Corporation, the world's leading manufacturer of computer chips. As the demand for more sophisticated computers and software has soared, so has Intel's business. But Intel isn't content to wait for computer manufacturers and software developers to create its growth; instead it aims to be "the visionary leader of the entire computer industry."[16] The company's culture is focused on creating users and uses for its microprocessors (computer chips). Another example of this type of culture can be seen in South Korea's Daewoo Group. Kim Woo-Choong, Daewoo's chairman, is pursuing an intensive globalization strategy, particularly in the emerging markets of Asia, Eastern Europe, and Latin America.[17] His goal for the company—US$200 billion by the year 2000—seems to be pretty ambitious, particularly given the fact that sales in 1997 were only a third of this goal. But everything in this company's culture is focused on growth.

The Source of Culture

An organization's current customs, traditions, and general way of doing things are largely due to what it has done before and the degree of success it has had with those endeavors. The original source of an organization's culture usually reflects the vision or mission of the organization's founders. Because the founders have the original idea, they also may have biases on how to carry out the idea. They're not constrained by previous customs or approaches. The founders establish the early culture by projecting an image of what the organization should be. The small size of most new organizations also helps the founders instill their vision in all organizational members.

Let's look at two examples of individuals who have had immeasurable influence on shaping their organizations' cultures. One is Yvon Chouinard, the founder of the outdoor gear company Patagonia, Inc. An avid "extreme adventurer," Chouinard approached the business in a laid-back, casual manner. For instance, he hired employees not on the basis of any specific business skills but because he had climbed, fished, or surfed with them. Employees were friends, and work was treated as something fun to do. In a speech Chouinard gave a few years ago, he uttered the timeless line, "Let my people go surfing!" Although Patagonia is now a $125 million a year company with more than 500 employees, its culture still reflects Chouinard's values and philosophy. Another example of the power of the founder's vision on culture is Fred Smith at FedEx. The company's aggressiveness, willingness to take risks, focus on innovation, and emphasis on service are central themes that founder Smith has articulated since FedEx's founding.

7 What constitutes an organization's "personality"?

8 Describe the different types of personalities an organization might have.

9 What is the source of an organization's culture?

How Employees Learn Culture

Culture is transmitted to employees in a number of ways. The most instrumental are stories, rituals, material symbols, and language.

Stories.   Organizational "stories" typically contain a narrative of significant events or people including such things as the organization's founders, rule breaking, rags-to-riches successes, reductions in the workforce, relocation of employees, reactions to past mistakes, and organizational coping.[18] For instance, Hewlett-Packard has numerous stories that portray the company's unique culture, known as the HP Way. One of the most enduring values espoused by the HP Way is that innovation and flexibility are key to doing your job, even if it means ignoring orders from your supervisor. The story is told about the time that David Packard (one of the company's founders) was visiting from headquarters and spontaneously awarded a "Medal of Defiance" to an engineer by the name of Chuck House. It seems that Packard himself had told House to halt work on a new computer monitor, stating, "When I come back next year I don't want to see that project in the lab." House decided that if the project was in production, Packard sure wouldn't find it in the lab, so he pushed ahead with the project. The monitors turned out to be a huge success and created an entirely new market. That's when House received his medal. Young HP employees still look for ways to get a product or prototype completed before top managers have figured out whether they even want it.[19] Organizational stories anchor the present in the past, provide explanations and legitimacy for current practices, and exemplify what is important to the organization.[20]

Rituals.   Rituals are repetitive sequences of activities that express and reinforce the key values of the organization, what goals are most important, which people are important, and which are expendable.[21] A good example of an organizational ritual is the process college faculty members typically go through in their quest for permanent employment—tenure. Typically, the faculty member is on probation for six years. At the end of that period, the individual's colleagues must make one of two choices: Extend a tenured appointment, or issue a one-year terminal contract. What does it take to obtain tenure? It usually requires satisfactory teaching performance, service to the department and university, and scholarly activity. But, of course, what satisfies the requirements for tenure in one department at one university may be inadequate at another. The key is that the tenure decision, in essence, asks those in the department who are tenured to assess whether the candidate has demonstrated, on the basis of six years of performance, that he or she "fits in." College faculty who have been socialized properly will have proved themselves worthy of being granted tenure. When tenure is not granted, it's often because the faculty member is not doing well in those areas that the tenured faculty believe are important. The instructor fails to adapt to the norms established by the department. Although other types of profit and not-for-profit organizations may not have the tenure ritual as educational institutions do, they, too, have rituals that express and reinforce key values. For example, one of the best-known corporate rituals is Mary Kay Cosmetics' annual award meeting.[22] Looking like a cross between a circus and a Miss America pageant, the meeting takes place over a couple of days in a large auditorium, on a stage in front of a large, cheering audience, with all the participants dressed in glamorous evening clothes. Salespeople are rewarded for their success in achieving sales goals with an array of flashy gifts including gold and diamond pins, furs, and pink Cadillacs. This "show" acts as a motivator by publicly acknowledging outstanding sales performance. In addition, the ritual aspect reinforces Mary Kay's determination and optimism, which enabled her to overcome personal hardships, found her own company, and achieve material success. It conveys to her salespeople that reaching their sales goals is important and that through hard work and encouragement they too can achieve success. Your second author had the experience of being on a flight out of Dallas one year with a planeload of Mary Kay sales representatives headed home from the annual awards meeting. Their contagious enthusiasm and excitement made it obvious that this annual "ritual" played a significant role in establishing desired levels of motivation and behavioral expectations, which, after all, is what an organization's culture should do.

Material Symbols.   Did you ever notice that some corporations provide their top executives with chauffeur-driven limousines and, when they travel by air, unlimited use of the corporate jet? Executives at other organizations may not get to ride in limousines or private jets, but they still might get a car and air transportation paid for by the company. The car, however, is a Chevrolet (with no driver) and the seat is in the coach section of a commercial airliner.

The layout of an organization's facilities, dress attire, the types of automobiles top executives are provided, and the presence or absence of corporate aircraft are examples of material symbols. Others include the size of offices, the elegance of furnishings, executive "perks" (extra "goodies" such as health club memberships, country club memberships, wine or book club subscriptions, use of company-owned resort facilities, and so forth), the existence of employee lounges or on-site dining facilities, and reserved parking spaces for certain employees. These material symbols convey to employees who is important, the degree of egalitarianism desired by top management, and the kinds of behavior (for example, risk taking, conservative, authoritarian, participative, individualistic, social) that are expected and appropriate.

Language.   Many organizations and units within organizations use language as a way to identify members of a culture. By learning this language, members attest to their acceptance of the culture and, in so doing, help to preserve it. For instance, when Lou Gerstner left RJR Nabisco for the top position at IBM, he had to learn a whole new vocabulary: *the Orchard* (IBM's Armonk, New York, corporate headquarters, which was once an apple orchard); *big iron* (mainframe computers); *hypo* (a high-potential employee); *a one performer* (an employee with IBM's top performance rating); and *PROFS* (Professional Office Systems, IBM's internal electronic mail system).[23]

Over time, organizations often develop unique terms to describe equipment, key personnel, suppliers, customers, or products that are related to its business. New employees are frequently overwhelmed with acronyms and jargon that, after a short period of time, become a natural part of their language. Once assimilated, this language acts as a common denominator that unites members of a given culture.

Influence on Management Practice

Because it constrains what they can and cannot do, an organization's culture is particularly relevant to managers. These constraints are rarely explicit. They're not written down. It's unlikely that they'll even be spoken. But they're there, and all managers quickly learn what to do and not to do in their organizations. For instance, you won't find the following values written down anywhere, but each comes from a real organization.

Look busy even if you're not.

If you take risks and fail around here, you'll pay dearly for it.

Before you make a decision, run it by your boss so that he or she is never surprised.

We make our product only as good as the competition forces us to.

What made us successful in the past will make us successful in the future.

If you want to get to the top here, you have to be a team player.

The link between values such as these and managerial behavior is fairly straightforward. If an organization's culture supports the belief that profits can be increased by cost cutting and that the company's best interests are served by achieving slow but steady increases in quarterly earnings, managers throughout the organization are unlikely to pursue programs that are innovative, risky, long term, or expansionary. For organizations that value and encourage workforce diversity, the organizational culture and thus managers' decisions and actions, should be supportive of diversity efforts. (See the Managing Workforce Diversity box for more information on creating cultures supportive of diversity.) In organizations whose culture conveys a basic distrust of employees, managers are more likely to use an authoritarian leadership style than a democratic one. Why? The culture establishes for managers what is appropriate behavior. For example, at Nike Inc., distinctive, unusual, and sometimes rebellious, decisions and actions are the norm. Even though Nike's culture may appear freewheeling, it provides guidance (in effect, constrains) on what and how Nike's managers plan, organize, lead, and control.

Phil Knight, CEO of Nike, has been described as a "rebel with a cause." He built his company by following his own approaches to doing business, which usually means doing just the opposite of what "the establishment" is doing.

Creating a Supportive Culture for Diversity

We know from our discussion in chapter 2 that managing a diverse workforce is a key challenge facing today's managers. As the composition of the workforce changes, managers must take a long hard look at their organizational culture to see if the shared values and meanings that were appropriate for a more homogeneous employee base will support diverse views. How can managers create a culture that advocates and encourages diversity?[24]

The old approach to managing diversity was to expect people who were different to hide or adapt their cultural differences so that they blended into the organization's dominant culture. Now managers who accept and promote diversity as a valuable corporate asset recognize that it benefits the organization by bringing in varied perspectives on work and a broad range of problem-solving skills. An organizational culture that nourishes and celebrates diversity lets employees be themselves and encourages them to develop their own unique strengths and to present innovative ideas from their diverse perspectives. No longer do diverse employees feel as if they have to "play it safe" by hiding their differences.

Creating a culture that supports and encourages diversity is a major organizational effort. Managers throughout the organization at every level must fundamentally accept that diversity is valued and must reflect this acceptance in what they say and do. An organization that truly wants to promote diversity must shape its culture to allow diversity to flourish. One way to do this is for managers to assimilate diverse perspectives while performing the managerial functions. For example, at the Marriott Marquis Hotel in New York's Times Square, managers are taught in required diversity training classes that the best way to cope with diversity-related conflict is to focus narrowly on performance and never to define problems in terms of gender, culture, or race. At Harvard Pilgrim, a health care company, managers' annual bonuses are tied to their success rates in promoting women and minority workers and whether employees feel that the company is more supportive of diversity efforts.

Beyond the day-to-day managerial activities, organizations should consider developing ways of reinforcing employee behaviors that embrace diversity. Some suggestions include encouraging individuals to value and defend diverse views, creating traditions and ceremonies that celebrate diversity, rewarding appropriate "heroes" and "heroines" who accept and promote diversity, and communicating through formal and informal networks reports about employees who champion diversity issues. For example, at Xerox Corporation, some senior executives have been designated as "champions" and are responsible for addressing employees' concerns about diversity efforts. At Ortho Biotech, a Johnson & Johnson subsidiary, President Dennis Longstreet has made managing diversity a top priority. He meets regularly with so-called affinity groups—white males; single people; gay, lesbian, and bisexual men and women; secretaries; black males; and others—and says, "It's about listening to people, their problems and their aspirations. It's amazing how unaware you can be of the impact you have on people different from you."

Developing an organizational culture that supports diversity may be difficult but offers high potential benefits. Organizations like those described and numerous others have found ways to design policies and practices that allow diversity to prosper and thrive. These organizations see cultural or environmental changes not as constraints but as opportunities from which to profit. ■

MANAGING

WORKFORCE

DIVERSITY

An organization's culture, especially a strong one, constrains a manager's decision-making options in all management functions. As shown in Table 3-2, the major areas of a manager's job are influenced by the culture in which he or she operates.

TABLE 3-2	**Examples of Managerial Decisions Affected by Culture**

Planning

The degree of risk that plans should contain

Whether plans should be developed by individuals or teams

The degree of environmental scanning in which management will engage

Organizing

How much autonomy should be designed into employees' jobs

Whether tasks should be done by individuals or in teams

The degree to which department managers interact with each other

Leading

The degree to which managers are concerned with increasing employee job satisfaction

What leadership styles are appropriate

Whether all disagreements—even constuctive ones—should be eliminated

Controlling

Whether to impose external controls or to allow employees to control their own actions

What criteria should be emphasized in employee performance evaluations

What repercussions will occur from exceeding one's budget

TESTING... TESTING...

10 Describe how stories and rituals shape an organization's culture.

11 What role do material symbols and language play in an organization's culture?

12 How does culture affect what a manager does?

THE ENVIRONMENT

Remember from our discussion in chapter 1 that the systems approach proposed that no organization operates independently. Anyone who questions the impact of the external environment on managing should consider the following:

The Cadillac Division of General Motors has watched its faithful buyers grow silver-haired. Its average new car buyer is now over 55 years old. To counteract this demographic trend, the company's managers are looking at ways to attract a new, younger generation of buyers.

Teresa Iglesias-Soloman hoped to benefit from the burgeoning Hispanic population, which is growing five times faster than the general U.S. population. She started a mail-order company that distributes a children's catalog, *Ninos*, written in both English and Spanish. The catalog features books, videos, and other products for English-speaking children who want to learn Spanish and for Spanish-speaking children who want to learn English.

As these two examples show, there are forces in the environment that play a major role in shaping managers' actions. In this section, we'll identify some of the critical environmental forces that affect management and show how they constrain managerial discretion.

Defining the Environment

The term **environment** refers to institutions or forces that are outside the organization and potentially affect the organization's performance. As one writer described it, "Just take the universe, subtract from it the subset that represents the organization, and the remainder is environment."[25] But it's really not that simple.

General versus Specific Environment. The **general environment** includes everything outside the organization, such as economic factors, political conditions, sociocultural influences, globalization issues, and technological factors. It encompasses conditions that *may* affect the organization but whose relevance is not clear. The development of the technology to place the contents of an entire bookshelf on one small digital versatile disk (DVD) is an example of a factor in the general environment of publisher Simon & Schuster. Its long-term impact on the book industry is unclear, but it could be great. Similarly, the strength of the U.S. dollar against the pound and yen is an environmental force for U.S. companies that operate in Great Britain and Japan, but its effect is best described as only potentially relevant.

The bulk of management's attention is usually given to the organization's specific environment. The **specific environment** is the part of the environment that is directly relevant to the achievement of an organization's goals. It consists of the critical constituencies or stakeholders that can positively or negatively influence an organization's effectiveness. Each organization's specific environment is unique and changes with conditions. Typically, it will include suppliers of inputs, clients or customers, competitors, government agencies, and public pressure groups. For example, Lockheed-Martin Corporation depends heavily on defense contracts, so the U.S. Department of Defense is in its specific environment. Of course, elements in an organization's specific environment can become part of its general environment over time and vice versa. For example, Reed Elsevier's Lexis and Nexis electronic on-line databases used to be available only at libraries. Now any individual with a PC and a modem can tap into any of the on-line information services. Companies like Reed Elsevier and Dow Jones Information Services find that their customer base has broadened. Individual consumers used to be only a minor part of these organizations' general environment, but they now play a more important role in their specific environments and affect managers' decision making.

An organization's specific environment varies depending on the "niche" that the organization has carved out for itself with respect to the range of products or services it offers and the markets it serves. Timex and Rolex both make wristwatches, but their specific environments differ because they operate in distinctly different market niches. North Arkansas Community College and the University of Florida are both institutions of higher education, but they do substantially different things and appeal to different segments of the higher education market. The managers or administrators in these organizations face different constituencies in their specific environments, and the environmental factors that one is dependent on and that critically influence performance may not be relevant to the other even though they may appear to be in the same type of business.

Assessing Environmental Uncertainty. The environment is important to managers because not all environments are the same. They differ by what we call their degree of **environmental uncertainty**. Environmental uncertainty, in turn, can be divided into two dimensions: degree of change and degree of complexity.

environment

Outside institutions or forces that potentially affect an organization's performance.

general environment

Everything outside the organization.

specific environment

The part of the environment that is directly relevant to the achievement of an organization's goals.

environmental uncertainty

The degree of change and complexity in an organization's environment.

Interview with Mike Dorf, CEO, KnitMedia, Inc., New York, New York

Describe your job.

My job has changed significantly in the last few years. I used to be able to work all day in my office and interact only slightly with my staff—that is, the initial small group who all knew what their tasks were. Today I spend little time during the regular day working on my projects, but I'm more like a massage therapist, machine oiler, or psychotherapist working with each manager (now up to around 12 people) and getting them to understand how to get their tasks done, reach their goals, and delegate to the people who report to them. I have to help them understand how everyone and all the work we do fits together in our cooperative goal. Clearly, we are in a build mode. I have hired six new management-level people in the last three months. My early mornings or late nights and weekends are now my only time to get *my* work done. What does my work involve? Strategic thinking, researching who we should work with, what festivals we should build, what artists to sign, who to book in the club, and so forth. My time to be an artist/company man and to grow this organization that I envision means that I clearly have a price tag on my time.

What types of skills do you think tomorrow's managers will need?

Managers need a work ethic as if they themselves were the owners. Also, computer/Internet savvy will be important. Everything we do is about being connected to other people in the outside world and to our internal world. It's about communication. The computer has become this great and efficient communication device. Using e-mail saves time. Web demonstrations save money. Understanding this new paradigm intrinsically or as an invisible thinking cap for everything everyone does will make tomorrow's managers significantly better than those not up to speed.

How do employees at your company "learn" your organization's culture?

They learn it by observation and talking to fellow staff members. Integrating friendships early and also going to our club/bar the first week and talking usually will make them learn the culture fast!

What are the most serious external (those outside your organization) issues facing your organization?

Getting capital for growth is a big issue. We did a first round of financing and are now looking for the second round. Another issue is bandwidth growth. Why? The faster the pipeline into people's homes, the more niche content like ours we can profitably get to people. I would also say another issue is Andy Grove's (CEO of Intel Corporation) "battle of the eyeballs" in which the competitiveness of so many entertainment options might fraction the audience too much in the future. This is something that our organization is going to have to deal with. ■

If the components in an organization's environment change frequently, we call it a *dynamic* environment. If change is minimal, we call it a *stable* one. A stable environment might be one in which there are no new competitors, no new technological breakthroughs by current competitors, little activity by public pressure groups to influence the organization, and so forth. For instance, at Justin Boot Company of Fort Worth, Texas, managers are always seeking new market opportunities even though its environment is a relatively stable one in which change is infrequent. Although Justin's managers had to deal with the continuing popularity of its standard work boots for both country-western and heavy-metal grunge fanatics, the company's environment can still be considered relatively stable.

In contrast, Compaq Computer and the other computer manufacturers face an uncertain and unpredictable environment. At Compaq, based in Houston, Texas, managers experienced firsthand during the 1990s the volatility of the PC marketplace. Although the company grew explosively during the 1980s by selling desktop computers to business customers, it suffered severe setbacks when the 1990–1991 recession hit. To continue as a viable competitor in the industry, the new CEO directed company managers to begin looking more closely at the consumer market. After implementing several dramatic changes in manufacturing and marketing, Compaq began rushing a series of lower-priced and user-friendly computers to the market in early 1992. The company has been on a roll ever since and even acquired one of its competitors, Tandem Computers, in mid-1997. Compaq and the other computer manufacturers face an uncertain and unpredictable environment.

What about rapid change that is predictable? Retail department stores are a good example. They typically make one quarter to one third of their sales in December. The drop-off from December to January is significant. Does this predictable change in consumer demand make department stores' environment dynamic? No. When we talk about degree of change, we mean change that is unpredictable. If change can be accurately anticipated, it's not an uncertainty managers must confront.

The other dimension of uncertainty describes the degree of **environmental complexity**. The degree of complexity refers to the number of components in an organization's environment and the extent of the knowledge that the organization has about those components. For example, Hasbro Toy Company, the world's largest toy manufacturer, simplified its environment by acquiring many of its competitors including Kenner Toys, Parker Brothers, and Tonka Toys. The fewer competitors, customers, suppliers, and government agencies that an organization must interact with, the less uncertainty there is in its environment.

Complexity is also measured in terms of the knowledge an organization needs to have about its environment. For instance, managers at Boeing must know a great deal about their suppliers' operations if they want to ensure that the jets they build will perform flawlessly. On the other hand, managers of retail grocery stores have a minimal need for sophisticated knowledge about their suppliers.

Environmental uncertainty can be described as shown in the matrix in Figure 3-3. There are four cells, with cell 1 being lowest in environmental uncertainty and cell 4 being highest. Managers' influence on organizational outcomes is greatest in cell 1 and least in cell 4.

Because uncertainty is a threat to an organization's effectiveness, managers try to minimize it. Given a choice, managers would prefer to operate in environments like those in cell 1. But managers rarely have full control over that choice. For example, managers at organizations developing content for Internet/World Wide Web applications in the mid-1990s found themselves in cell 4. Because they chose this particular niche to operate in, they faced a highly dynamic and complex environment. Had they chosen to manufacture standard wire coat hangers, they would probably have found themselves in cell 1.

The Organization and Its Environment.   Figure 3-4 summarizes our position that an organization is an open system that interacts with and depends on its specific environment

environmental complexity

The number of components in an organization's environment and the extent of an organization's knowledge about its environmental components.

while remaining ever aware of the potential influences of its general environment. In the following sections we elaborate on the components in both the specific and general environments and show how environments can constrain the choices available to managers.

FIGURE 3-3   **Environmental Uncertainty Matrix**

Degree of Change

	Stable	**Dynamic**
Simple	**Cell 1** Stable and predictable environment Few components in environment Components are somewhat similar and remain basically the same Minimal need for sophisticated knowledge of components	**Cell 2** Dynamic and unpredictable environment Few components in environment Components are somewhat similar but are in continual process of change Minimal need for sophisticated knowledge of components
Complex	**Cell 3** Stable and predictable environment Many components in environment Components are not similar to one another and remain basically the same High need for sophisticated knowledge of components	**Cell 4** Dynamic and unpredictable environment Many components in environment Components are not similar to one another and are in continual process of change High need for sophisticated knowledge of components

Degree of Complexity

FIGURE 3-4   **The Organization and Its Environment**

Identifying Environmental Opportunities

In an uncertain environment the risks associated with starting a new business venture are high, yet individuals still pursue their dreams of being an entrepreneur. How do entrepreneurs get their ideas?[26]

An article in *Harvard Business Review* presented information about how entrepreneurs recognize trends or environmental opportunities. In a survey of 100 entrepreneurs who created some of the fastest-growing private companies in the United States, the overwhelming majority (71 percent) replicated or modified an idea gained through previous employment. For instance, Scott MacHardy and Mark Lane took a $15,000 investment and turned it into a company with over $25 million in revenue. Their company, Coed Sportswear, Inc., is renowned for its line of T-shirts with suggestive sayings. When the original holder of the Coed Naked trademark ran into financial trouble, MacHardy and Lane purchased the trademark and embarked on building a successful business.

The next largest percentage of survey respondents (20 percent) said they got their ideas for an entrepreneurial venture from a serendipitous discovery. Included in this group were comments such as: "built temporary or casual job into a business," "happened to read about the industry," "wanted product [or service] as an individual consumer," and "thought up idea during honeymoon in Italy"! Robert Plath's Travelpro Rollaboard suitcase is a good example; he developed his idea because he could have used it in his job as an airline pilot. Even though his fellow pilots laughed at his suitcase on wheels, you can now see his product in any airport around the world. Plath is having the last laugh from his idea. So far it has brought in over $30 million. Another entrepreneur, Susanne St. Amant of Ottawa, Ontario, took advantage of the vast retailing opportunities offered on the Web. She started an on-line Web site selling products emblazoned with Japanese cartoon characters from the *Sailor Moon* series after her kids begged and begged her for T-shirts, notebooks, and other licensed merchandise. She figured if her kids were that fanatical about the product, there were probably other kid "customers" just as enthusiastic.

Finally, a small percentage of survey respondents indicated that they got their ideas from the personal computer revolution (5 percent) and through systematic research for opportunities (4 percent). Scanning the environment to take advantage of trends can be a good approach for entrepreneurs to develop successful and profitable ideas.

Although entrepreneurs get their ideas in different ways, it is obvious that they are particularly alert to environmental factors and opportunities that could prove to be the beginning of a new business venture. ■

ENTREPRENEURSHIP

TESTING... TESTING...

13 Define an organization's environment, and explain the difference between its specific and its general environments.

14 What is environmental uncertainty?

15 Describe the two components of environmental uncertainty.

The Specific Environment

As previously noted, different organizations face different specific environments. For most organizations, though, suppliers, customers, competitors, governmental agencies, and special-interest pressure groups are external factors that impose uncertainty.

Suppliers.   When you think of an organization's suppliers, you typically think of firms that provide materials and equipment. For Walt Disney World in Florida, these include firms that sell soft drink syrups, computers, food, flowers and other nursery stock, concrete, and paper products. But the term *suppliers* also includes providers of financial and labor inputs. Stockholders, banks, insurance companies, pension funds, and other similar institutions are needed to ensure a continuous supply of capital. Exxon can have drilling rights to an oil field that can generate billions of dollars in profits, but the profits will remain only potential unless managers can obtain the funds necessary to drill the wells. Labor unions, occupational associations, and local labor markets are sources of employees. A lack of qualified nurses, for instance, can make it difficult for a hospital to fulfill demand and achieve its objectives.

Managers seek to ensure a steady flow of needed inputs at the lowest price possible. Because these inputs represent uncertainties—that is, their unavailability or delay can significantly reduce the organization's effectiveness—managers typically go to great efforts to ensure a steady reliable flow. As you'll see later in this book, the reason most large organizations have purchasing, finance, and human resources departments is to supply the machinery, equipment, capital, and labor inputs they need to operate.

Customers.   Organizations exist to meet the needs of customers. It's the customer or client who absorbs the organization's output. This is true even for governmental organizations. They exist to provide services, and we are reminded, especially at election time, that we indicate by our votes how satisfied we are as customers.

Customers obviously represent potential uncertainty to an organization: Their tastes can change; they can become dissatisfied with the organization's product or service. Of course, some organizations face considerably more uncertainty as a result of their customers than do others. For example, what do you think of when you think of Club Med? Club Med's image traditionally was one of care-free singles having fun in the sun in exotic locales. Club Med found, however, that as their target customers married and had children, these same individuals now were looking for family-oriented vacation resorts where they could bring the kids. Although Club Med responded to the changing demands of its customers by offering different types of vacation packages, including family-oriented ones, the company found it hard to change its original image.

Competitors.   All organizations, even monopolies, have one or more competitors. The U.S. Postal Service has a monopoly on mail service, but it competes against FedEx, United Parcel Service, and other forms of communication such as the telephone, electronic mail, and fax machines. Nike competes against Reebok, Adidas, and Fila among others. Coca-Cola competes against Pepsi and other soft drink companies. Not-for-profit organizations such as the Metropolitan Museum of Art and Girl Scouts USA also compete for dollars, volunteers, and customers.

Managers cannot afford to ignore the competition. When they do, they pay dearly! For instance, many problems incurred by the railroads from the 1940s through the 1970s have been attributed to their failure to recognize who their competitors were. They thought they were in the railroad business when, in fact, they were in the transportation business. Trucking, shipping, air, and bus and private automobile transportation are all competitors of railroads. Another example of how important it is to know the competitors can be seen in the broadcast media industry. Until the early 1980s, the three major broadcasting networks—ABC, CBS, and NBC—virtually controlled what you watched on television. The rapid expansion of the Fox, Warner, and UPN networks, cable, VCRs, syndicated programs sold to local stations, and even the Internet and World Wide Web have given viewers a much broader choice of what to watch. In fact, as technological capabilities continue to expand, the number of viewing options will provide even more competition for the broadcast networks.

These examples illustrate that competitors—in terms of pricing, services offered, new products developed, and the like—represent an important environmental force that managers must monitor and to which they must be prepared to respond.

Government.   Federal, state, and local governments influence what organizations can and cannot do. Some federal legislation has significant implications. For example, consider the following: The Sherman Anti-Trust Act of 1890 sought to stop monopoly practices that resulted in restraint of trade. The National Labor Relations Act of 1935 stipulated that employers were required to recognize a union chosen by the majority of their employees and also established procedures and rules governing collective bargaining. The Civil Rights Act of 1964 made it unlawful for an employer to discharge, refuse to hire, or discriminate in employment against an individual because of race, color, religion, sex, or national origin. The Americans with Disabilities Act of 1990 (ADA) was designed to make jobs and public facilities more accessible to people with disabilities. Table 3-3 lists other significant legislation affecting business firms.

Certain organizations, by virtue of what they do, are scrutinized closely by specific governmental agencies. Organizations in the telecommunications industry—including telephone companies and radio and television stations—are regulated by the Federal Communications Commission. If your firm manufactures pharmaceuticals, what you can sell is determined by the Food and Drug Administration. Publicly held companies must abide by the guidelines established by the Securities and Exchange Commission.

However, the federal government isn't the only source of legal regulations that govern organizations. State and local governmental regulations extend and modify many federal standards. For instance, more than a dozen cities, including Baltimore, Los Angeles, and New York, require companies doing city business to pay employees more than the minimum wage.

Organizations spend a great deal of time and money to meet governmental regulations,[27] but the effects of these regulations go beyond time and money. They also reduce managerial discretion by limiting the choices available to managers. Consider the decision to dismiss an employee.[28] Historically, employees were free to quit an organization at any time and employers had the right to fire an employee at any time with or without cause. Laws and court decisions, however, have put increasing limits on what employers may do. Employers are increasingly expected to deal with employees by following the principles of good faith and fair dealing. Employees who feel that they have been wrongfully discharged can take their case to court. Juries are increasingly deciding what is or is not "fair." This trend has made it more difficult for managers to fire poor performers or to dismiss employees for off-duty conduct. For example, IBM dismissed a female employee for dating someone who worked for a competitor. She sued IBM, arguing that her personal relationship wasn't expressly prohibited by IBM's policies and represented no conflict of interest. She won a $300,000 settlement from the company.

Pressure Groups.   Managers must recognize the special-interest groups that attempt to influence the actions of organizations. Automobile manufacturers, toy makers, and airlines have been visible targets of Ralph Nader's Center for Responsive Law. Conservative citizen action groups have successfully pressured publishers of elementary and secondary American history textbooks to change content that their group members have found offensive. And it would be an unusual week if we didn't read that environmental activists were picketing, boycotting, or threatening some organization in order to get managers to change their policies.

TABLE 3-3	Selected Significant Legislation Regulating Business Since 1970
Legislation	**Purpose**
Occupational Safety and Health Act of 1970	Requires employer to provide a working environment free from hazards to health
Consumer Product Safety Act of 1972	Sets standards on selected products; requires warning labels, and orders product recalls
Equal Employment Opportunity Act of 1972	Forbids discrimination in all areas of employer-employee relations
Employee Retirement Income Security Act of 1974	Enacted by Congress to protect an employee's right to his or her pension
Toxic Substance Control Act of 1976	Provides for the assessment and control of toxic substances
Airline Deregulation Act of 1978	Eliminated route restrictions and price controls in the airline industry
Tax Reform Act of 1986	Provided for a major restructuring of the U.S. federal income tax rate system
Worker Adjustment and Retraining Notification Act of 1988	Prohibits employers from discriminating against individuals with physical or mental disabilities or the chronically ill; also requires organizations to reasonably accommodate these individuals
Americans with Disabilities Act of 1990	Requires employers with 100 or more employees to provide 60 days' notice before a facility closing or mass layoff
Civil Rights Act of 1991	Reaffirms and tightens prohibition of discrimination; permits individuals to sue for punitive damages in cases of intentional discrimination
Women's Business Development Act of 1991	Assists the development of small business concerns owned and controlled by women through a training program and a loan program that eases access to credit through the Small Business Administration (SBA) loan program
Family and Medical Leave Act of 1993	Grants 12 weeks of unpaid leave each year to employees for the birth or adoption of a child or the care of a spouse, child, or parent with a serious health condition; covers organizations with 50 or more employees
North American Free Trade Agreement of 1993	Created a free-trade zone between the United States, Canada, and Mexico
Child Safety Protection Act of 1994	Provides for labeling requirements on certain toys that contain parts or packaging that could harm children and requires manufacturers of such toys to report any serious accidents or deaths of children to the Consumer Product Safety Commission
General Agreement on Tariffs and Trade (GATT) of 1994	Provides for the lowering of tariffs globally by roughly 40%, extending intellectual property protection worldwide, and tightening rules on investment and trade in services

As social and political movements change, so too does the power of pressure groups. For example, through their persistent efforts, groups such as MADD (Mothers Against Drunk Driving) and SADD (Students Against Drunk Driving) have not only managed to make changes in the alcoholic beverage and restaurant and bar industries but have also raised public awareness about the problem of drunk drivers.

You're the program manager for a small, but growing, FM radio station in Gainesville, Florida, that plays music from the pop charts. For the past several weeks, you've been playing a song that's near the top of the charts and is frequently requested by your listeners. One afternoon you receive a phone call from a well-respected black businessman in Gainesville who is also a spokesperson for the city's black community. He says this song is degrading to all women and, in particular, black women and asks that you stop playing it. What will you do? What guidelines might you suggest for dealing with the demands of special-interest groups that would be both ethical and good for business? ■

The General Environment

Economic, political, social, global, and technological conditions that can affect the management of organizations usually do not have as large an impact on an organization's operations as the specific environment has, but managers must take them into account. For instance, in 1997, scientists announced the discovery of a technology that made it possible to genetically reproduce (clone) adult mammals. Managers of organizations in industries including agricultural, biomedical, and pharmaceuticals recognized that this discovery had the potential to significantly affect their organizations' growth and profitability, so they carefully follow progress on this research.

Economic Conditions. Interest rates, inflation rates, changes in disposable income, stock market indexes, and the stage of the general business cycle are some of the economic factors in the general environment that can affect management practices in an organization. For example, many specialty retailers such as the Sharper Image, the Limited, and Williams-Sonoma are acutely aware of the impact the level of consumer disposable income has on their sales. When consumers' incomes fall or when their confidence about job security declines, they will postpone purchasing anything that isn't a necessity. Even charitable organizations such as the United Way (recall the chapter-opening Manager's Dilemma in chapter 1) feel the impact of economic factors. During economic downturns, they are asked to provide greater assistance while, at the same time, their contributions typically decrease.

Political Conditions. Political conditions include the general stability of the countries in which an organization operates and the specific attitudes that elected governmental officials hold toward business. In the United States, organizations have generally operated in a stable political environment. But management is a global activity. Moreover, many U.S. firms have operations in countries whose record for stability is erratic—for example, Libya, South Africa, China, and Iran. Managers should attempt to forecast major political changes in countries in which they operate. In this way, they can better anticipate political conditions, from the devaluation of a country's monetary unit to a dictator's decision to nationalize certain industries and expropriate their assets.

Social Conditions. Managers must adapt their practices to the changing expectations of the society in which they operate. As values, customs, and tastes change, managers must also change. This principle applies to both their product and service offerings and their internal operating policies. For instance, the increase in the number of working women (over 58 percent of all adult women are employed outside the home) and their changing career expectations have prompted organizations to adjust their internal organizational policies. Organizations that fail to offer child care facilities or family leave policies may find it increasingly difficult to hire competent, committed female employees. Another societal trend that is affecting organizations is the aging of the workforce.

The aging of the U.S. workforce is having a significant impact on managerial practices both inside and outside the organization.

In 1970, the median age in the United States was under 28. In the year 2000, it will have reached 35 and is forecasted to continue rising for a number of years. What are some of the implications? Organizations that cater to the needs of seniors can expect a larger market share. There is likely to be increased demand for health care and for homes in the Sunbelt states. This trend also means that organizations will have to redesign products and services for an aging market. Levi Strauss, for example, produces fuller-cut jeans designed to fit the middle-aged person's body. The aging of the workforce also has implications for managerial practices inside organizations. Managers can expect to have more employees in their fifties, sixties, and even seventies! This change is likely to translate into more experienced workers with needs that differ from those of their younger co-workers. For instance, older workers tend to place greater value on such employee benefits as health insurance and pension plans and less value on college tuition reimbursement programs and generous moving allowances.

Global.   As we discussed in chapter 2, globalization is one of the major factors affecting managers and organizations. Managers of both large and small organizations are challenged by an increasing number of global competitors and consumer markets as part of the external environment. We will cover this component of the external environment in detail in the next chapter.

Technological Conditions.   Our final consideration in the external environment is technology. We live in a time of technological change. In terms of the five components in the general environment, the most rapid changes during the past quarter-century have probably occurred in technology. Table 3-4 describes what are predicted to be the top 10 technologies for the year 2005. (Keep in mind that these predictions were made in the mid-1990s, and some of the technologies are already available.) We have automated offices, electronic meetings, robotic manufacturing, lasers, integrated circuits, microprocessors, and synthetic fuels. Companies that capitalize on technology, such as 3M, General Electric, and Motorola, prosper. In addition, many successful retailers such as Wal-Mart, Barnes and

TABLE 3-4	Top Ten Technologies for 2005

(As ranked by Batelle Technology Management Group)

1. *Genome mapping.* Including gene probes that can predict who will get what disease
2. *Supermaterials.* Used for communications, energy, transportation
3. *Compact energy sources.* Long-lasting and powerful fuel cells and batteries
4. *High-definition TV.* Sharp, crisp digital video images
5. *Hand-held electronic devices.* Phone, computer, and fax in one device
6. *Manufacturing smart systems.* Sensor-driven assembly lines
7. *Anti-aging products.* Gene research that finds ways to slow aging
8. *Targeted medical instruments.* Target ailment only and minimize side effects
9. *Hybrid-fuel vehicles.* Offer lower gas use and harmful emissions while providing better performance
10. *Edutainment.* Educational games and computerized simulations for children

Source: Based on L. Light and R. Coxeter, "Wonders of Tomorrow," *Business Week,* March 6, 1995, p. 6.

Noble, and Dillard's Department Stores use sophisticated inventory information systems to keep on top of current sales trends. Other organizations, such as Prime Trucking Inc. with its on-board truck computers, American Airlines with its Sabre Reservation System, and Amazon.com Books (check its Web site at <http://www.amazon.com>) use information as a competitive advantage and have adopted technologically advanced information systems to stay ahead of their competitors. Similarly, hospitals, universities, airports, police departments, and even military organizations that adapt to major technological advances have a competitive edge over those that do not.

Another example of how the technological environment has affected organizations is in the design of offices. Offices have become virtual communication centers. Managers can now link their computers, telephones, word processors, photocopiers, fax machines, filing storage, and other office activities into an integrated system. In fact, many organizations are using **intranets** (internal organizational communication systems that use Internet technology and are accessible only by organizational employees) for helping employees do their work effectively and efficiently. For managers of all organizations, these technological advancements mean faster and better decision-making capability.

intranets

Internal organizational communication systems that use Internet technology and are accessible only by employees.

Influence on Management Practice

As we have seen, organizations are not self-contained or self-sufficient. They interact with and are influenced by their environment. Organizations depend on their environment as a source of inputs and as a recipient of their outputs. Organizations must also abide by the laws and regulations and respond to groups that challenge the organization's actions. As such, suppliers, customers, governmental agencies, public pressure groups, and similar constituencies can exert power over an organization. This power, for instance, is unusually evident among publicly held companies whose stock is controlled by such institutional investors as insurance companies, mutual funds, and pension plans. When these institutions hold a controlling amount of stock in an organization, their interests can dictate management's interests. They have the power to control boards of directors and indirectly to fire management. The result is that managers' options are constrained to reflect the desires of these institutional investors. Even when an organization's managers do not face constraints from such groups, they must cope with other changes in the environment.

TABLE 3-5	Executives' Views on External Environmental Changes

(survey of 400 executives)

Change in their companies is rapid or extremely rapid	79%
They have a conservative or reluctant approach to change	62%
The pace of change will accelerate	61%
Their companies are very capable of coping with change	47%
Their companies have formal structures to handle change	44%
Large corporations are best equipped to manage change	32%
They could not name a company good at managing change	25%
General Electric is the best company at managing change	17%[a]

Source: K.H. Hammonds, "In Business This Week," *Business Week,* September 20, 1993, p. 44.
[a]Most-named company.

A survey of 400 chief executives from some of the largest U.S. companies indicated that they see the environment as changing even faster.[29] As shown in Table 3-5, a large majority of the executives surveyed felt that change in their companies was rapid and that this pace of change would continue to accelerate. Even more surprising was the fact that less than half of these CEOs felt that their companies were very capable of coping with the changing environmental forces.

As we have stated throughout this chapter, many of the environmental forces are dynamic and create considerable uncertainty for management. Customers' tastes and preferences change. New laws are enacted. Suppliers cannot meet contractual delivery dates. Competitors introduce new technologies, products, and services. To the degree that these environmental uncertainties cannot be anticipated, they force managers to respond in ways that they might not prefer. The greater the environmental uncertainty an organization faces, the more the environment limits managers' options and the freedom to determine their own destiny.

 **TESTING... TESTING...** 1 2 3

16 Describe the five factors in an organization's specific environment.

17 Describe the five factors in an organization's general environment.

18 How is management practice influenced by the environment?

managers respond to "a manager's dilemma"

MANAGER 1

Having employees conform to the expected values in a workplace culture is important. If I were in Mr. Venegas's position, I would make it clear to employees from their first day on the job what the expectations were, both in terms of work performance and work behavior. These expectations can be communicated to new employees through some type of ongoing orientation program at least through the first week or two on the job. Also, throughout the first month on the job, it would be important to positively reinforce these values and expectations. This would be the responsibility of the new employee's manager. Finally, I would use weekly or monthly "awards ceremonies" to recognize outstanding job performance. People like to be praised and to receive recognition for their work. These types of awards ceremonies also serve as reinforcers of what types of work behavior are necessary in order to get recognized.

Cindy Brewer, Independent Information Technology Consultant and Trainer, Rockford, Illinois

MANAGER 2

Instilling expected organizational culture values isn't going to be easy, but it can be done. I believe that the best way for Mr. Venegas to instill the work values he wants in his new employees is to pair up the new hires with employees already working there who exemplify expected types of work performance and work behaviors. This type of mentoring relationship will allow new employees to learn by watching others. My experience has been that most people learn more from watching others than by being told something. The key will be making sure that these chosen mentors have good work habits and exhibit the types of cultural values that are important to Ideal Steel. By being paired with an "oldtimer," the new hires will be able to experience firsthand what the workplace expectations are. I would require these mentor relationships for the new employees at least through their first performance appraisal period.

Matt Musick, Consultant, Anderson Consulting, Kansas City, Missouri

for your
IMMEDIATE
action

The Wild Wild West
EATERTAINMENT COMPANY

To: Rick Katzfey, Director of Research
From: Freda Rowe, VP of Operations
Subject: Competitive Intelligence

First off, I'd like to say "welcome aboard"! The other members of the management team and I are looking forward to working with you as we develop and grow our chain of restaurants. As you're well aware, themed "eatertainment" restaurants (some of our well-known competitors include Hard Rock Cafe, Planet Hollywood, and Dive!) have been extremely popular. We think our idea for a Wild Wild West theme is a sure-fire winner and one that will appeal to a broad customer base, both here in the United States and globally.

However, before we proceed further with our final business plan, we're going to need some information about our other competitors in this industry. We'd like to know the following: (1) Who are our major competitors? (2) What are their "themes"? (3) What unique and unusual activities are they doing? and (4) What are their sales and profits figures (if available)? Could you provide me with this information in a two-page report by the end of the week?

This fictionalized memorandum was created for educational purposes only. It is not meant to reflect positively or negatively on management practices at the Wild Wild West.

SUMMARY

This summary is organized by the chapter-opening objectives found on p. 76.

1. The omnipotent view is dominant in management theory and in society. It argues that managers are directly responsible for the success or failure of an organization. In contrast, the symbolic view argues that management has only a limited effect on substantive organizational outcomes because of the large number of factors outside of management's control; however, management greatly influences symbolic outcomes.

2. Organizational culture is a system of shared meaning within an organization that determines, in large degree, how employees act.

3. An organization's culture is composed of seven characteristics: innovation and risk taking, attention to detail, outcome orientation, people orientation, team orientation, aggressiveness, and stability.

4. A strong culture is one in which the key values are intensely held and widely shared. Strong cultures have a greater influence on employees than do weak cultures. In many organizations, particularly those with strong cultures, one of the seven cultural dimensions often rises above all others and shapes the organization and the way organizational members do their work.

5. The various ways that employees learn an organization's culture include stories, rituals, material symbols, and language. Organizational stories typically contain a narrative of significant events or people that portray the unique culture. Rituals are repetitive sequences of activities that express and reinforce the key values, important goals, and important people. Material symbols include things such as the layout of the facilities, dress codes, elegance of office furnishings, and other observable (tangible) items. Language refers to special and unique terms, jargon, and acronyms that are related to an organization's business.

6. Culture constrains managers because it acts as an automatic filter that biases the manager's perceptions, thoughts, and feelings. Strong cultures particularly constrain a manager's decision-making options by conveying which alternatives are acceptable and which are not.

7. The general environment encompasses forces that have the potential to affect the organization but whose relevance is not overtly clear. The specific environment is that part of the environment that is directly relevant to the achievement of the organization's goals.

8. Environmental uncertainty is determined by the degree of *change* and *complexity* in the environment. Stable and simple environments are relatively certain. The more dynamic and complex the environment, the higher the uncertainty.

9. The components of the specific environment include suppliers, customers, competitors, governmental agencies, and public pressure groups.

10. Factors in the general environment include economic, political, social, global, and technological factors.

11. High environmental uncertainty limits management's options and its freedom to determine its own destiny.

THINKING ABOUT MANAGEMENT ISSUES

1. Refer to Table 3-1. How would a first-line supervisor's job differ in these two organizations?
2. Describe an effective culture for (a) a relatively stable environment and (b) a dynamic environment.
3. Classrooms have cultures. Describe your class culture. Does it constrain your instructor? How?

4. "You can't change an organization's culture." Build an argument to support that statement; then negate your argument.
5. Managers are often characterized as "boundary spanners." What do you think this term refers to, and why do you think it might be an important description of what a manager does in relation to external environmental factors?

SELF-ASSESSMENT EXERCISE

WHAT KIND OF ORGANIZATIONAL CULTURE FITS YOU BEST?

Instructions: For each of the following statements, circle the level of agreement or disagreement that you personally feel:

SA = Strongly agree
A = Agree
U = Uncertain
D = Disagree
SD = Strongly disagree

	Strongly Agree				Strongly Disagree
1. I like being part of a team and having my performance assessed in terms of my contribution to the team.	SA	A	U	D	SD
2. No person's needs should be compromised in order for a department to achieve its goals.	SA	A	U	D	SD
3. I like the thrill and excitement from taking risks.	SA	A	U	D	SD
4. If a person's job performance is inadequate, it's irrelevant how much effort he or she made.	SA	A	U	D	SD
5. I like things to be stable and predictable.	SA	A	U	D	SD
6. I prefer managers who provide detailed and rational explanations for their decisions.	SA	A	U	D	SD
7. I like to work where there isn't a great deal of pressure and where people are essentially easygoing.	SA	A	U	D	SD

See scoring key on page SK–2.

TAKE IT TO THE NET

We invite you to visit the Robbins/Coulter companion Web site at http://www.prenhall.com/robbinsmgt for this chapter's Internet resources.

CASE APPLICATION

Cleaning Up at SOL

As one of northern Europe's most admired companies, SOL Cleaning Service, located in Helsinki, Finland, isn't what you might expect. The company's headquarters in a renovated film studio positively "explodes" with color, creativity, and chaos. Walls are painted bright red, white, and yellow, and employees wander the halls talking on yellow high-tech portable phones. When necessary, they meet in work area "neighborhoods," each with a distinct personality. For instance, one neighborhood resembles a treehouse. Another has oddly shaped tables that can be fitted together like a jigsaw puzzle. The employee training room looks like a multimedia paradise—with overhead projectors, VCRs, computers, and chalkboards—and the window shades are decorated with circus scenes. These bright and energetic surroundings might seem tailor-made for creative, artistic organizational types (such as software designers, screenwriters, or advertising executives), but SOL competes in a basic, grungy, and unglamorous business—industrial cleaning. It's a high-energy, fast-paced, knowledge-driven organization whose business is scrubbing hospital floors, making hotel beds, and sweeping grocery store aisles.

The philosophy of Liisa Joronen, SOL's chairman and owner, is: "In a service business, if you're not happy with yourself, how can you make the customer happy?" Answering that question has made Joronen's company wildly successful. As a spin-off from a fam-ily-owned business, SOL opened its doors on January 1, 1992, with 2,000 employees, 1,500 customers, and revenues of $35 million. In 1997, it had 3,500 employees, 3,000 customers, and $60 million in revenues. What does SOL do differently to "clean up" in an industry notorious for high turnover, low wages, and terrible service?

SOL is characterized by five values. First, hard work has to be fun. Joronen believes that, because few people dream of becoming a cleaner, the keys to keeping her employees satisfied on the job are fun and individual freedom. SOL's culture is built around optimism and good cheer. Cleaners wear bright red-and-yellow jumpsuits that reinforce the company's enthusiastic and fun image. SOL's logo—a yellow happy face—is plastered on everything from the company's stationery to the most important financial statements. Employees enjoy the freedom of minimal rules and regulations; there are no titles, individual offices, or set working hours; and the company has eliminated all perks and status symbols.

The second corporate value that characterizes SOL is that there are no low-skill jobs. The company invests significant amounts of time and money in training employees. There are just so many ways to polish a table or to shampoo a carpet, so SOL employees also study topics such as time management, people skills, and budgeting. Training is focused on turning cleaners into customer service specialists. Joronen says, "Our main goal is to change how cleaners work. To let them use their brains as well as their hands." By upgrading its employees, SOL is upgrading its business. In fact, some of the hospitals that employ SOL's cleaners have begun using them for "night nurse" duties; they do things such as help patients to the bathroom and notify the doctor on call about emergencies. And at many of the large grocery stores, SOL cleaners stock the shelves as well as sweep the aisles.

Another corporate value of SOL is that people who set their own targets shoot for the stars. SOL employees have significant amounts of responsibility and authority. The company's supervisors, each of whom leads a team of up to 50 cleaners, work with the teams to create their own budgets, do their own hiring, and negotiate their own deals with customers. Joronen's philosophy is that people will set targets for themselves higher than what anyone would set for them. These self-managed teams can even build their own offices. SOL has 23 "satellite studios" around Finland. However, a studio opens only when there is enough business to cover the costs of rent, equipment, and employee training. To stay in business, the studio must be profitable.

The fourth value that SOL stresses is that loose organizations need tight measures. Although Joronen believes in employee autonomy, she is a fanatic about performance measurement and accountability. The company measures performance frequently, and most of these measures focus on customer satisfaction. Says Joronen, "The more we free our people from rules, the more we need good measurements."

Finally, SOL believes that great service demands cutting-edge technology. SOL may be in a "low-end" business, but that doesn't mean it has to be low tech. In fact, laptop computers and cellular phones are standard equipment for all supervisors at SOL. Why? This investment in technology frees them up to work where they want and how they want. The company also stores all its critical budget documents and performance reports on its intranet and uses it for scheduling training, relaying company news, and informing employees about upcoming company events.

QUESTIONS

1. Using Figure 3-2, describe SOL's organizational culture.
2. Would the five values that characterize SOL's culture be as effective in other types of organizations? Why or why not?
3. Describe how you think new employees at SOL might "learn" the culture.
4. Which of the seven types of organizational personality would you characterize SOL as having? Support your choice.
5. How might SOL's culture constrain the behavior of a newly hired executive?

Source: G. Imperato, "Dirty Business, Bright Ideas," *Fast Company Web Page* <http://www.fastcompany.com>, April 16, 1997.

VIDEO CASE APPLICATION

The Bean Queen

There's the Bean Queen. There are Bean Counters. And there are Human Beans. All can be found at Buckeye Beans and Herbs in Spokane, Washington. Jill Smith is the Bean Queen. She's a self-proclaimed hippie artist turned entrepreneur who started her company in 1983 with an investment of $1,000. From that small, inauspicious beginning, Buckeye Beans now has sales revenues approaching $8 million and employs 50 people (human beans). Buckeye Beans has been innovative in expanding its product line, which started out with one product, Buckeye Bean Soup, and now includes a line of all-natural soups, chili, bread mixes, and pasta. Buckeye Beans also pioneered special-occasion-shaped pasta: that is, pasta

shaped like Christmas trees, hearts, bunnies, dolphins, leaves, grapes, baseballs, and even golf balls. But what strikes you most about Buckeye Beans isn't its unique products, it's the unusual organizational culture that melds this company together.

That unusual organizational culture is reflected in the company's simple mission statement: Make people smile. Smith's belief is that cooking should be fun and that the experience of cooking can be a fun escape, not a drudgery. That's why the first ingredient listed on all Buckeye's product packages is a cup of good wine for the cook. Buckeye's strategy, that its products go beyond just a simple bag of beans and instead serve as entertainment, is also seen in the company's HEHE principle: humor, education, health, and environment. That's what Jill Smith, husband Doug, and other Buckeye employees believe in and value.

Shared values are very important to Smith and her employees. Not only are many of Buckeye's employees family and long-time friends, but they all share like values. As Smith built Buckeye Beans, she felt it was important that her employees have the same value systems. And although she admits that her approach wouldn't work for every organization, she does think it's important for managers to identify their basic values and what they're trying to accomplish. Smith suggests asking what kinds of values are important and what kind of organization is desired. For Buckeye Beans, the approach has been to create a "different" type of company—a new model—in which the business is run and employee and customer relationships operate on the basis of trust, confidence, loy-

alty, and working hard together to get something done. As Smith so earnestly stresses, it's easier to work hard when you have a philosophy like that.

QUESTIONS

1. Using Figure 3-2 as a guide, how would you describe Buckeye Beans' organizational culture?
2. If Buckeye Beans and Herbs continues to grow in size, what challenges will it face in maintaining its organizational culture? What advice would you give Jill Smith about maintaining the culture?
3. How could Buckeye Beans use stories, rituals, material symbols, and language to transmit its culture to employees? Give specific examples.

Source: Based on *Small Business 2000, Show 203.*

A MANAGER'S DILEMMA

Global sales opportunities are alluring to both large and small organizations world-wide, even in China, where selling internationally isn't always an option for entrepreneurs. In fact, it's often discouraged by the Chinese government. But the hurdles presented by governmental rules and regulations and cultural restrictions haven't stopped Pan Yaping, a successful Chinese business owner![1]

Pan's Xingtehao Industrial Corporation has transformed itself from a maker of cheap Christmas trinkets into a $100 million consumer electronics company. His factory in Shanghai may appear to be old fashioned and relatively crude, but the workers there produce modern, sophisticated electric drills for sale in various global markets. Nearly everything produced at this Shanghai factory and at Pan's other factories is destined for sale in overseas markets, especially Europe. Power tools, home exercise equipment, lamps, battery chargers, vacuum cleaners, and back massage machines are

just a few of the many products his company manufactures that are sold outside China.

Although the European market has proved lucrative for his company, Pan wants to keep expanding his sales and is looking at moving into the U.S. market. But, even though the U.S. market is potentially huge, Pan, like any smart global manager, doesn't want to enter it blindly. What will he need to know about the political, legal, economic, and cultural environment before attempting to sell his products in the United States? Put yourself in Pan's position. What types of information would you need in order to make intelligent decisions about moving into U.S. markets?

WHAT WOULD YOU DO?

The Xingtehao Industrial Corporation example demonstrates that the global environment of business affects all types and sizes of organizations around the world. It's now a whole new ball game for managers. With the entire world as a marketplace and national borders becoming irrelevant, the potential for organizations to grow and expand increases dramatically. For instance, a study of 1,250 highly diverse American manufacturing firms found that companies that operated in multiple countries had twice the sales growth and significantly higher profitability than strictly domestic firms.[2]

As the opening dilemma also implies, however, the elimination of global borders and trade barriers can work both ways! New competitors can suddenly appear at any time, anywhere. Managers who don't closely monitor changes in their global environment or who fail to respond quickly to those changes are likely to find new competitors in their domestic markets and their organization's survival in doubt.

C H A P T E R

4

Managing

in a Global

Environment

WHO OWNS WHAT?

One way to grasp the changing nature of the global environment is to consider the country of ownership origin for some familiar products and companies. You might be surprised to find that many name brand products you thought were made by U.S. companies aren't! Take the following quiz[3] and then check your answers at the end of the book on page SK–1.

1. Where is the parent company of Braun household appliances (electric shavers, coffee makers, etc.) located?

   a. Switzerland   b. Germany   c. United States   d. Japan

2. The Bic Pen Company is:

   a. Japanese   b. British   c. American (United States)   d. French

3. The company that owns Haagen Daz ice cream is in:

   a. Germany   b. Great Britain   c. Sweden   d. Japan

4. RCA television sets are produced by a company based in:

   a. France   b. United States   c. Malaysia   d. Taiwan

5. The firm that owns Green Giant vegetables is:

   a. American (United States) b. Canadian   c. British   d. Italian

6. The owners of Godiva chocolate are:

   a. American (United States)   b. Swiss   c. Dutch   d. Swedish

7. The company that produces Vaseline is:

   a. French   b. Dutch   c. German   d. American (United States)

8. Wrangler jeans are made by a company that is:

   a. Japanese   b. Taiwanese   c. British   d. American (United States)

9. The company that owns Holiday Inns is headquartered in:

   a. Saudi Arabia   b. France   c. United States   d. Great Britain

10. Tropicana orange juice is owned by a company that is headquartered in:

    a. Mexico   b. Canada   c. United States   d. Japan

How well did you score? Were you aware of how many products we use every day that are actually made by companies not based in the United States?

To further emphasize our point about the international aspects of business today, take a look at Table 4-1. This is a partial list of U.S. companies that derive half or more of their revenues from foreign operations. As you can see, these companies represent a broad cross section of products, markets, and industries.

WHAT'S YOUR GLOBAL PERSPECTIVE?

It's not unusual for Germans and Italians to speak three or four languages. Most Japanese schoolchildren begin studying English in the early elementary grades. On the other hand, most American children study only English in school. Americans tend to think of English as the only international business language, and they don't see a need to study other languages.

Monolingualism is just one of the signs that Americans suffer from **parochialism**. That is, they view the world solely through their own eyes and perspectives.[4] People with a parochial attitude do not recognize that other people have different ways of living and working. Parochialism is an obstacle for many U.S. managers. Whereas their counterparts around the world have sought to better understand foreign customs and market differences, U.S. managers too frequently are guilty of ignoring foreign values and customs and rigidly applying an attitude of "ours is better than theirs" to foreign cultures. But this type

parochialism

A narrow view of the world; an inability to recognize differences between people.

TABLE 4-1	Selected Companies with over 60 Percent of Total Revenues from Non-U.S. Operations

Company	Percentage of Revenue from Non-U.S. Operations
Exxon	76.8
Colgate-Palmolive	71.6
Manpower	70.8
Mobil	67.2
Coca-Cola	67.1
Pharmacia & Upjohn	66.7
Avon Products	65.3
Digital Equipment	64.8
Gillette	63.1
Unisys	63.1
IBM	61.3
Citicorp	60.6
Crown Cork & Seal	60.1

Source: "Buying American," *Forbes*, July 28, 1997, pp. 218–20.

of selfish, parochialistic attitude isn't the only approach that managers might take toward international business. Managers might have one of three perspectives or attitudes toward international business.[5] These three basic attitudes are ethnocentric (home country–oriented, including parochialistic), polycentric (host country–oriented), and geocentric (world-oriented). Table 4-2 summarizes the key points about each of these global perspectives. Let's look at each more closely.

An **ethnocentric attitude** is the parochialistic belief that the best work approaches and practices are those of the home country (the country in which the company's head-

ethnocentric attitude

The parochialistic belief that the best work approaches and practices are those of the home country (the country in which the company's headquarters are located).

TABLE 4-2	Key Information about Three Global Perspectives	
	Ethnocentric	**Polycentric**	**Geocentric**
Orientation	Home Country	Host Country	World
Advantages	• Simpler structure • More tightly controlled	• Extensive knowledge of foreign market and workplace • More support from host government • Committed local managers with high morale	• Forces understanding of global issues • Balanced local and global objectives • Best people and work approaches used regardless of origin
Drawbacks	• More ineffective management • Inflexibility • Social and political backlash	• Duplication of work • Reduced efficiency • Difficult to maintain global objectives because of intense focus on local traditions	• Difficult to achieve • Managers must have both local and global knowledge

polycentric attitude

The view that the managers in the host country (the foreign country in which the organization is doing business) know the best work approaches and practices for running their operations.

geocentric attitude

A world-oriented view that focuses on using the best approaches and people from around the globe.

quarters are located). Managers with an ethnocentric attitude see people in foreign countries as inferior to people in the home country. They would not trust foreign employees with key decisions or technology. The advantages of such an attitude are that the organization can have a simpler structure and managers can exercise closer control over people and work processes. The drawbacks of this view toward global operations include the following: Managerial decisions and actions might be less effective because managers aren't taking into account the differences that characterize foreign cultures, markets, and employees; employees in foreign locations cannot be flexible in performing their work and cannot use methods or approaches that they feel would work best; and there is the potential for social and political backlash from the country in which the organization is doing business.

The **polycentric attitude** is the view that the managers in the host country (the foreign country in which the organization is doing business) know the best work approaches and practices for running their operations. Managers with a polycentric attitude view every foreign operation as different and hard to understand. Thus, these managers are likely to leave their foreign facilities alone and let foreign employees figure out how best to do things. The advantage of such an approach is that each foreign facility does have extensive knowledge of how best to manage the workplace and the market. Also, managers in the foreign operations are likely to be more committed and have higher morale than would managers imported from the home country. In addition, the host government is likely to provide more support if its own citizens are hired. However, the drawback of such a "hands-off" attitude is the duplication of work efforts around the world, particularly if an organization has several facilities in different foreign locations. Why is duplication of effort a drawback? It leads to inefficient and ineffective use of organizational resources. Finally, the last disadvantage to this approach to managing global operations is that it's difficult to maintain global (worldwide) objectives because of the intense focus on local traditions and ways of doing things.

The last type of global perspective that managers might have is the **geocentric attitude**, which is a world-oriented view focusing on using the best approaches and people from around the globe. Managers with this type of attitude believe that it's important to have a global view both at the organization's headquarters in the home country and in the various foreign work facilities. Major issues and decisions are viewed globally by looking for the best approaches and people regardless of origin. As you might well assume, one advantage of such an approach is that it forces managers to have a global understanding of issues. In addition, managers with this perspective must look at balancing both local and global objectives and must also look for the best ways of doing things. However, the desirability of having such a global perspective is also its main drawback. It's difficult for managers to have both local and global knowledge and be able to effectively and efficiently use both.

Successful global management requires enhanced sensitivity to differences in national customs and practices. Management practices that work in Chicago might not be appropriate in Shanghai or Berlin. Read through the examples in Table 4-3 of the cultural blunders that can happen when managers ignore foreign values and customs and rigidly apply their own to foreign cultures. Later in this chapter and throughout the rest of the book, you'll see how a geocentric attitude toward managing requires eliminating parochial attitudes and carefully developing an understanding of cultural differences between countries.

TESTING... TESTING... 1 2 3

1 How does a global economy create both opportunities and threats for managers?

2 What is parochialism, and how does it create problems for managers?

3 Compare and contrast the three different attitudes toward international business.

TABLE 4-3	**Examples of Cross-Cultural Blunders**

- You're in Shanghai on business. Walking down the street one day, you pass a Chinese colleague. He asks you, "Have you eaten yet?" You answer, "No, not yet." He rushes off, looking embarrassed and uncomfortable. The phrase, "Have you eaten yet?" is a common greeting—just like "Hi, how are you?" in the United States. It's the Chinese way of saying "Is your belly full today?" or "Is life treating you well?"
- A U.S. manager who had recently been transferred to Saudi Arabia successfully obtained a signature on a million dollar contract from a Saudi manufacturer. The manufacturer's representative had arrived at the meeting several hours late, but the U.S. executive considered this tardiness unimportant. The American was certainly surprised and frustrated to learn later that the Saudi had no intention of abiding by the contract. He had signed it only to be polite after showing up late for the appointment.
- A West Virginia executive visiting Germany for the first time was invited to the home of his largest customer. He decided to be a good guest and brought the hostess a bouquet of a dozen red roses. He later learned that in Germany it is bad luck to present an even number of flowers and that red roses are symbolic of a strong romantic interest.
- A U.S. executive based in Peru was viewed by Peruvian managers as cold and unworthy of trust because, in face-to-face discussions, he kept backing away. He didn't understand that in Peru and other Latin countries, the custom is to stand quite close to the person with whom you are speaking.
- The "thumbs up" gesture is considered offensive in Middle East, rude in Australia, and a sign of "OK" in France.
- It's rude to cross your arms while facing someone in Turkey.

Source: See D.A. Ricks, M.Y.C. Fu, and J.S. Arpas, *International Business Blunders* (Columbus, OH: Grid, 1974); A. Bennett, "American Culture Is Often a Puzzle for Foreign Managers in the U.S." *Wall Street Journal*, February 12, 1986, p. 29; C.F. Valentine, "Blunders Abroad," *Nation's Business*, March 1989, p. 54; R.E. Axtell (ed.), *Do's and Taboos around the World*, 3rd ed. (New York: John Wiley & Sons, 1993); B. Pachter, "When in Japan, Don't Cross Your Legs," *Business Ethics*, March–April 1996, p. 50; and V. Frazee, "Keeping Up on Chinese Culture," *Global Workforce*, October 1996, pp. 16–17.

THE CHANGING GLOBAL ENVIRONMENT

Several significant forces are reshaping the global environment that managers face. In this section, we'll discuss two important forces: regional trading alliances and the different types of global organizations.

Regional Trading Alliances

Just a few years ago, international competition could be described best in terms of country against country—the United States versus Japan, France versus Germany, Mexico versus Canada. Now, global competition has been reshaped by the creation of regional trading and cooperation agreements. The most notable of these include the 15-nation European Union and the three-nation North American Free Trade Agreement.

The European Union. The signing of the Maastricht Treaty (named for the Dutch town in which the treaty was signed) in February 1992 created the formation of a 12-nation **European Union (EU)**. This treaty united the 380 million people of Belgium, Denmark, France, Greece, Ireland, Italy, Luxembourg, the Netherlands, Portugal, Spain, the United Kingdom, and Germany. By 1995, three other countries—Austria, Finland, and Sweden—had joined the group.[6] (See Figure 4-1.) Before the creation of the EU, each of these nations had border controls, border taxes, border subsidies, nationalistic policies, and pro-

European Union (EU)

A union of 15 European nations created to eliminate national barriers to travel, employment, investment, and trade.

FIGURE 4-1   European Union Countries

tected industries. Now, the EU is a single market; there are no national barriers to travel, employment, investment, and trade. A driver hauling cargo from Amsterdam to Lisbon can clear four border crossings and five countries by showing a single piece of paper. Before the EU, that same driver needed two pounds of official documents. The ultimate goal of the EU is to have common customs duties and unified industrial and commercial policies as well as a single currency and a regional central bank. Many problems have been associated with full implementation, however, and it will undoubtedly take several more years to reach the point of full unification. For instance, there are intense negotiations and deliberations among the EU countries in establishing a single currency—the Euro, as it will be called.[7] The plan is that, by the year 2002, Euro notes and coins will replace the various national currencies over a six-month period.

The primary motivation for the union of these fifteen nations was to allow them to reassert their position against the industrial strength of the United States and Japan. Working in separate countries that created barriers against one another, European industries were unable to develop the economies of scale enjoyed by American and Japanese firms. The EU allows European firms to tap into what is now one of the world's richest markets.

The European Union is furthering global competition by encouraging European businesses to consolidate and merge operations as well as to form alliances with new partners, both within and outside Europe. In such diverse industries as telecommunications, heavy equipment, pharmaceuticals, civilian aerospace, banking, automobiles, computers, electronics, and food and beverages, U.S. firms now face vigorous challenges from their European counterparts.

MANAGERS

SPEAK

OUT

Madelyn Gengelbach, Marketing Strategist, Hallmark Cards, Inc., Kansas City, Missouri

Describe your job.

I'm a Marketing Strategist at Hallmark Cards, Inc., the world's largest maker of greeting cards and personal expression products. I'm responsible for the packaged writing paper line, which includes stationery, notes, and thank you notes. In the "four Ps" of marketing (product, pricing, promotion, place), I have control of two: pricing and product. Our company's upper management determines place (distribution channels), and promotion of Hallmark products is determined by our advertising and promotion group. My job entails writing marketing and pricing plans, performing retail and wholesale sales analysis, and constructing product offerings. I spend a lot of my time with the Creative Product Designer assigned to my products. She is the liaison between our artists and writers and the business unit. Together we develop products and identify consumer segments to target.

In what ways do global (international) issues affect your organization?

We are a worldwide company, and our products are sold in many countries. The economic health, exchange rate, trade policies, and labor and environmental regulations of these countries affect our production costs, sales, and profits.

What global issue do you see as the most challenging for your organization?

Our core products, especially greeting cards, are primarily an English-speaking cultural tradition. Our marketing skills are challenged when we sell products in a non-English-speaking culture. It takes years to carve out a presence in the consumer's mind. Product awareness isn't enough, though. The real challenge is to turn awareness into purchase intent. To grow as a global corporation, we must continue to develop our skills in adapting our marketing techniques and our products to other cultures. ■

Many of the more advanced and lesser developed countries of central and eastern Europe are seeking associate status with the EU. Even now, countries such as the Czech Republic, Hungary, and Poland have opened their markets to EU products. By the year 2000, there is likely to be a Greater European Economic Alliance encompassing more than 425 million people in at least 21 countries across Europe. With a gross domestic product in 1992 of almost $7.8 trillion, Europe is the largest economic market in the world.

North American Free Trade Agreement (NAFTA). When agreements in key matters covered under the **North American Free Trade Agreement (NAFTA)** were reached by the Mexican, Canadian, and U.S. governments on August 12, 1992, a vast market of more than 363 million consumers was opened; NAFTA created an economic bloc exceeding $7 trillion (Figure 4-2).

NAFTA went into effect on January 1, 1994, and eventually all barriers to free trade—such as tariffs, import licensing requirements, and customs user fees—among the three

North American Free Trade Agreement (NAFTA)

An agreement among the Mexican, Canadian, and U.S. governments in which all barriers to free trade will eventually be eliminated.

FIGURE 4-2   North American Free-Trade Areas

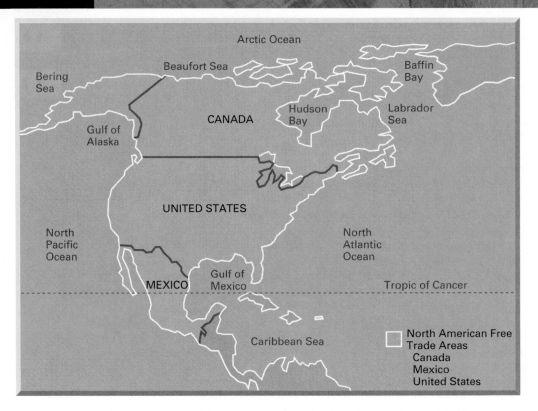

countries will be eliminated.[8] The signing of NAFTA had both critics and champions.[9] Treaty advocates emphasized the long-term benefits of job creation, market development, and increased standard of living for all three countries. Opponents warned that job loss to Mexico would devastate many U.S. industries and would increase U.S. joblessness.

Hewlett-Packard has made a major move into the growing Mexican market. Here, some of its dealers are being trained in its Mexico City training center.

Environmentalists feared increased water and air pollution and toxic dumping because of weaker standards by the Mexican government. What have been the effects now that the trade agreement has been in force for a period of time?

Studies of NAFTA's impact have shown varied results. One study reported positive effects for job employment; another said that NAFTA's effects were mainly negative.[10] Reality probably lies somewhere in between the two extremes. One analyst did stress, however, that the expansion of NAFTA would be essential to North America's future competitiveness and economic power.[11]

In addition, other Latin American nations are clamoring to become part of free-trade blocs. Colombia, Mexico, and Venezuela led the way when, in 1994, all three governments signed an economic pact eliminating import duties and tariffs. Ecuador has asked to join the group and will likely become a part of it. Eventually, these countries hope to entice others in Latin America to join and create a free-trade zone extending from Mexico to Argentina.[12] There is another free-trade bloc, known as the Southern Cone Common Market, or Mercosur.[13] (See Figure 4-3.) Its members are Chile, Brazil, Argentina, Paraguay, Uruguay,

FIGURE 4-3   Mercosur Members

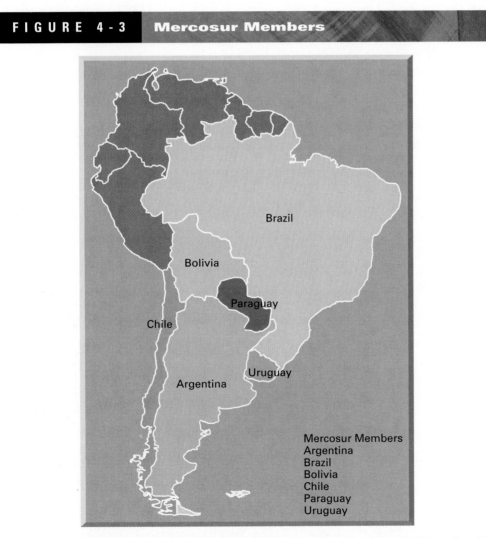

Mercosur Members
Argentina
Brazil
Bolivia
Chile
Paraguay
Uruguay

Source: Based on C. Sims, "Chile Will Enter a Big South American Free-Trade Bloc," *New York Times,* June 26, 1996, p. C2.

and Bolivia. As new trading blocs are created in this part of the globe, we are likely to see changes in how organizations, particularly those with significant business interests in these regions, are managed.

Association of Southeast Asian Nations (ASEAN) and Other Asian Developments. During the years ahead, Asia, and particularly the Southeast Asian region, promises to be one of the fastest-growing economic regions of the world. It will be an increasingly important regional economic and political alliance whose impact eventually could rival that of both NAFTA and the EU. As a trading entity, the **Association of Southeast Asian Nations (ASEAN)** currently has ten members: Brunei, Indonesia, Malaysia, the Philippines, Singapore, Thailand, Vietnam, Myanmar (formerly known as Burma), Cambodia, and Laos (Figure 4-4). The ASEAN region had an inflation-adjusted economic growth rate of approximately 7.6 percent in 1997 and is expected to have a population of approximately 500 million and an economy approaching US$1 trillion by the year 2000.[14] The potential economic power of the Asian region in the next century has some politicians and government policy makers talking about creating TAFTA (Transatlantic Free Trade Area), which would team the European Union and NAFTA countries.[15] Under a TAFTA arrangement, the 15 countries from the EU and the three countries from NAFTA would formally agree on free trade among themselves. However, talk of TAFTA for now is just that, talk.

Another significant historical and economic event in the Asian region that has the potential to affect the management of global organizations was the return of Hong Kong

Association of Southeast Asian Nations (ASEAN)

A trading alliance of ten Southeast Asian nations.

FIGURE 4-4 ASEAN Members, 1997

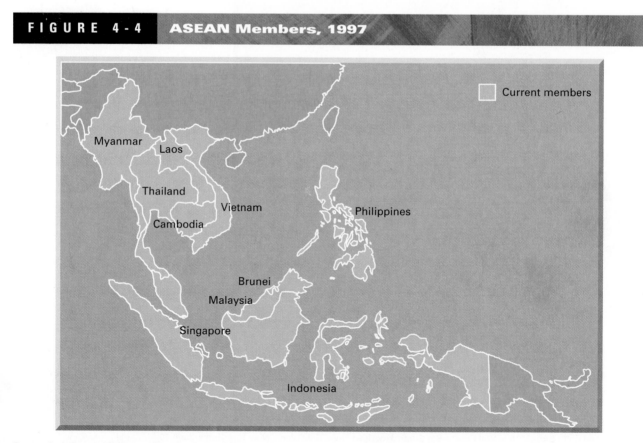

Source: Based on J. McClenahen and T. Clark, "ASEAN at Work," *IW*, May 19, 1997, p. 42.

from British rule to Chinese rule on July 1, 1997.[16] Although the long-run effects (both politically and economically) of this transfer are yet to be seen, there's no doubt that China will be an increasingly significant economic force in the future (refer to the chapter-opening Manager's Dilemma).

4 **Describe the European Union including what it is, why it was formed, and what challenges it is facing.**

5 **Describe the North American Free Trade Agreement including what it is, why it was formed, what its impact has been, and what challenges it is facing.**

6 **Describe the Association of Southeast Asian Nations and other significant Asian developments that have the potential to affect managers of global organizations.**

Global Organizations

International businesses have been around for a long time. Siemens, Remington, and Singer, for instance, were selling their products in many countries in the nineteenth century. Ford Motor Company set up its first overseas sales branch in France in 1908. By the 1920s, other companies, including Fiat, Unilever, and Royal Dutch/Shell had gone multinational. But it was not until the mid-1960s that **multinational corporations (MNCs)** became commonplace. These corporations—which maintain significant operations in two or more countries simultaneously but are based in one home country—inaugurated the rapid growth in international trade. With its focus on control from the home country, the MNC characterizes the ethnocentric attitude toward the management of an organization's global business.

The expanding global environment has extended the reach and goals of MNCs to create an even more generic global organization called the **transnational corporation (TNC)**. This type of organization does not seek to replicate its domestic successes by managing foreign operations from its home country. Rather, decision making in TNCs takes place at the local level. Nationals typically are hired to run operations in each country. The product or marketing strategies for each country are uniquely tailored to that country's culture. (This type of global organization can be described by the polycentric attitude.) Nestlé, for example, is a transnational. With operations in almost every country on the globe, it is the world's largest food company, yet its managers match the company's products to its consumers. Thus, in parts of Europe Nestlé sells products that are not available in the United States or Latin America. Another example is Frito-Lay, a division of PepsiCo, which markets a Dorito chip in the British market that differs in both taste and texture from the U.S. and Canadian version.

Many large, well-known companies are moving to more effectively globalize their management structure by breaking down internal arrangements that impose artificial geographical barriers; this global type of organization is called a **borderless organization**. The borderless organization can be said to approach global business from the geocentric perspective. For instance, IBM dropped its organizational structure based on country and reorganized into 14 industry groups. Ford merged its culturally distinct European and North American auto operations and plans to add a Latin American and an Asia-Pacific division in the future. Bristol-Myers Squibb changed its consumer business to become more aggressive in international sales and installed a new executive in charge of worldwide consumer medicines such as Bufferin and Excedrin. The move to borderless management is an attempt by organizations to increase efficiency and effectiveness in a competitive global marketplace.[17]

multinational corporation (MNC)

A company that maintains significant operations in more than one country simultaneously but manages them all from one base in a home country.

transnational corporation (TNC)

A company that maintains significant operations in more than one country simultaneously and decentralizes decision making in each operation to the local country.

borderless organization

A global type of organization in which artificial geographical barriers are eliminated so that the management structure can be more effectively globalized.

Harley Davidson motorcycles symbolize a classic American image worldwide. The company gets approximately 25% of its revenue from global sales. Harleys are a big hit in Tokyo, where waiting lists for the bikes can be up to six months long.

Although managers of multinational, transnational, and borderless organizations have become increasingly global in their perspectives and accept the reality that national borders no longer define ways of doing business efficiently and effectively, politicians and the general public in the United States have been slower to accept this fact. Many U.S. politicians and union leaders propose that the increasing sales of products from Japan, Mexico, or China are taking jobs away from Americans. They have strongly supported the "Buy American" theme. The irony is that many of these so-called foreign products that critics attack are made in the United States. For instance, excavators sold by Komatsu, a Japanese firm, are mostly made in Illinois; similar products sold under the John Deere label are built by Hitachi in Japan. American workers at the Mercedes-Benz plant in Vance, Alabama, produce the company's mass-market sport-utility vehicle. Similarly, most Sony televisions sold in the United States are made in California, and "American" manufacturer Zenith makes its televisions in Mexico. The message from these examples should be clear: A company's national origin is no longer an accurate measure of where it does business or the national origin of its employees. (Remember the quiz at the beginning of the chapter!) Such companies as Hoescht, Toyota, and Siemens employ thousands of people in the United States. At the same time, such corporations as Coca-Cola, Exxon, EDS, and Citicorp employ thousands in places such as India, Hong Kong, France, and the United Kingdom. So phrases like "Buy American" represent old stereotypes and fail to grasp the changing global environment.

TESTING... TESTING...

7 What is a multinational corporation (MNC), and which global perspective does it reflect?

8 Describe a transnational corporation (TNC) and the global perspective it reflects.

9 What is a borderless corporation, and which global perspective does it reflect?

Todd Alexander knew it wouldn't be easy starting his wine distribution business, Vendemmia Inc., based in Atlanta. But although he faced a mountain of paperwork getting it underway, he did have going for him his fluent Italian and a love of Italy he had nurtured since his days as a high-school exchange student.

HOW ORGANIZATIONS GO INTERNATIONAL

How does an organization evolve into a global organization? It typically proceeds through three stages as shown in Figure 4-5. In Stage I, managers make the first push toward going international merely by exporting the organization's products to other countries. This is a passive step toward international involvement involving minimal risk because managers make no serious efforts to tap foreign markets. Rather, the organization fills foreign orders only when it gets them. This may be the first and only international involvement many firms in the mail-order business have.

In Stage II, managers make an overt commitment to sell products in foreign countries or to have them made in foreign factories, but there is still no physical presence of company employees outside the company's home country. On the sales side, Stage II typically is done either by sending domestic employees on regular business trips to meet foreign customers

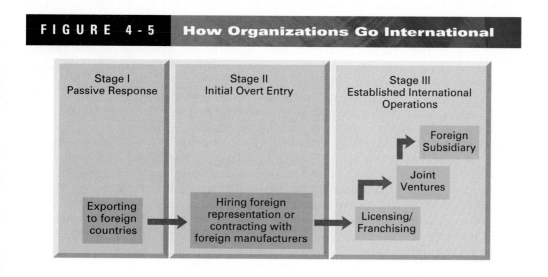

FIGURE 4-5   How Organizations Go International

Stage I Passive Response	Stage II Initial Overt Entry	Stage III Established International Operations
Exporting to foreign countries	Hiring foreign representation or contracting with foreign manufacturers	Licensing/ Franchising → Joint Ventures → Foreign Subsidiary

or by hiring foreign agents or brokers to represent the organization's product line. On the manufacturing side, managers will contract with a foreign firm to produce the organization's products.

Stage III represents a strong commitment by managers to pursue international markets aggressively. As shown in Figure 4-5, managers can do this in different ways. They can *license* or *franchise* to another firm the right to use the organization's brand name, technology, or product specifications. This approach is used widely by pharmaceutical companies and fast-food chains such as Pizza Hut. *Joint ventures* involve a larger commitment; a domestic and a foreign firm share the cost of developing new products or building production facilities in a foreign country. These are also often called *strategic alliances*. These partnerships provide a fast and less expensive way for companies to compete globally than would doing it on their own. Recent cross-border alliances include British Airways and American Airlines, Polaroid and Minolta, and Nestlé and General Mills. Managers make the greatest commitment (and assume the greatest risk) when the organization sets up a *foreign subsidiary*. As we discussed earlier in the chapter, the subsidiary can be managed as an MNC (domestic control), a TNC (foreign control), or a borderless organization (global control).

TESTING... TESTING...

10 What is the first stage of international involvement that most organizations will typically use?

11 What happens during Stage II of international involvement?

12 Describe the various approaches to Stage III of international involvement.

MANAGING IN A FOREIGN ENVIRONMENT

Assume for a moment that you're an American manager going to work for a branch of an international organization in a foreign country. You know that your environment will differ from the one at home, but how? What should you be on the lookout for?

Any manager who finds himself or herself in a strange country faces new challenges. In this section, we'll look at some challenges and offer guidelines for responding. Because most readers of this text were raised in the United States, we'll present our discussion through the eyes of a U.S. manager. Of course, our analytical framework could be used by any manager regardless of national origin who has to manage in a foreign environment.

The Legal-Political Environment

Managers in the United States are accustomed to stable legal and political systems. Changes are slow, and legal and political procedures are well established. Elections are held at regular intervals. Even changes in political parties after a presidential election do not produce any quick, radical transformations. The stability of laws governing the actions of individuals and institutions allows for accurate predictions. The same cannot be said for all nations.

Some countries have a history of unstable governments. Some South American and African countries have had six governments in as many years. With each new government have come new rules. The goal of one government may be to nationalize the country's key industries; the goal of the next may be to stimulate free enterprise. Managers of business firms in these countries face dramatically greater uncertainty as a result of political instability. Political interference is also a fact of life in many Asian countries. For example, Anoa Dussol-Perran started her passenger helicopter service in Vietnam despite seemingly endless official paperwork and red tape. Her goal is to keep expanding her business even though the wheels of government may turn slowly.

Foreign countries often have lax product-labeling laws. As a product manager for a U.S. drug company, you're responsible for the profitability of a new drug whose side effects can be serious, although not fatal. Adding this information to the label or even putting an informational insert into the package will add significantly to the product's cost, threatening profitability margins. What will you do? Why? What factors will influence your decision? ■

The legal-political environment doesn't have to be unstable or revolutionary to be of concern to managers. Just the fact that a country's social and political system differs from that of the United States is important. Managers must recognize these differences if they are to understand the constraints under which they operate and the opportunities that exist. For instance, laws differ between nations on industrial spying, restraint of trade, working conditions, payment of bribes, the rights of privacy, the rights of workers, and so forth.

The Economic Environment

The global manager has economic concerns that the manager who operates in a single country doesn't have. Three of the most obvious are fluctuating currency exchange rates, inflation rates, and diverse tax policies.

A global firm's profits can vary dramatically depending on the strength of its home currency and the currencies of the countries in which it operates. Any devaluation of a nation's currency significantly affects the level of a company's profits. The strength of a foreign nation's currency can also affect managers' decisions. For example, General Motors had imported its Geo Storm to the United States from Japan but decided to discontinue the model when the strength of the Japanese yen against the dollar made the product uneconomical.

Economic inflation rates can vary widely in different regions of the world. For example, in small nations such as Bolivia, annual inflation has reached 26,000 percent! Even in larger and more industrialized countries such as Brazil, the annual rate of inflation has sometimes reached 2,700 percent. The inflation rate influences prices paid for raw materials, labor, and other supplies. In addition, it affects the price that a company can charge for its goods or services.

Finally, diverse tax policies are a major worry for a global manager. Some host countries are more restrictive than the organization's home country. Others are far more lenient. About the only certainty is that tax rules differ from country to country. Managers need precise knowledge of the various tax rules in countries in which they operate to minimize their corporation's overall tax obligation.

13 What is the legal-political environment, and why is it relevant to understanding global management?

14 What are the primary economic factors global managers need to be aware of in global management?

15 How does a foreign country's economic environment affect managerial practice?

TESTING... TESTING...
1 **2** **3**

The Cultural Environment

The final global environmental force is the cultural differences between nations. As we know from chapter 3, organizations have different internal cultures. Countries have cultures too, as anthropologists have long been telling us. Like organizational culture,

national culture

The attitudes and perspectives shared by individuals from a specific country that shape their behavior and the way they see the world.

national culture is something that is shared by all, or most, inhabitants of a country and that shapes their behavior and the way they see the world.[18]

Does national culture override an organization's culture? For example, is an IBM facility in Germany more likely to reflect German ethnicity or IBM's corporate culture? Research indicates that national culture has a greater effect on employees than does their organization's culture.[19] German employees at an IBM facility in Munich will be influenced more by German culture than by IBM's culture. This means that as influential as organizational culture may be on managerial practice, national culture is even more influential.

Legal, political, and economic differences among countries are fairly obvious. The Japanese manager who works in the United States or his or her American counterpart in Japan can get information on their country's laws or tax policies without too much difficulty. Obtaining information about a country's cultural differences is a lot harder. The primary reason is that natives are nearly incapable of explaining their culture's unique characteristics to someone else. If you're an American raised in the United States, how would you characterize U.S. culture? In other words, what are Americans like? Think about it for a moment and then see how many of the points in Table 4-4 you identified.

The most valuable framework to help managers better understand differences between national cultures was developed by Geert Hofstede. He surveyed more than 116,000 employees in 40 countries who worked for a single international corporation. What did he find? His huge database revealed that national culture had a major impact on employees' work-related values and attitudes. In fact, it explained more of the differences than did age, sex, profes-

---

TABLE 4-4 What Are Americans Like?

Americans are very *informal*. They tend to treat people alike even when there are great differences in age or social standing.

Americans are *direct*. They don't talk around things. To some foreigners, this may appear as abrupt or even rude behavior.

Americans are *competitive*. Some foreigners may find Americans assertive or overbearing.

Americans are *achievers*. They like to keep score, whether at work or at play. They emphasize accomplishments.

Americans are *independent* and *individualistic*. They place a high value on freedom and believe that individuals can shape and control their own destiny.

Americans are *questioners*. They ask a lot of questions, even of someone they have just met. Many of these questions may seem pointless ("How ya' doin'?") or personal ("What kind of work do you do?").

Americans *dislike silence*. They would rather talk about the weather than deal with silence in a conversation.

Americans *value punctuality*. They keep appointment calendars and live according to schedules and clocks.

Americans *value cleanliness*. They often seem obsessed with bathing, eliminating body odors, and wearing clean clothes.

Source: Based on M. Ernest (ed.), *Predeparture Orientation Handbook: For Foreign Students and Scholars Planning to Study in the United States* (Washington, DC: U.S. Information Agency, Bureau of Cultural Affairs, 1984), pp. 103–05; A. Bennett, "American Culture Is Often a Puzzle for Foreign Managers in the U.S.," *Wall Street Journal*, February 12, 1986, p. 29; "Don't Think Our Way's the Only Way," *The Pryor Report*, February 1988, p. 9; and B.J. Wattenberg, "The Attitudes behind American Exceptionalism," *U.S. News & World Report*, August 7, 1989, p. 25.

sion, or position in the organization. More important, Hofstede found that managers and employees varied on four dimensions of national culture: (1) individualism versus collectivism, (2) power distance, (3) uncertainty avoidance, and (4) quantity versus quality of life.[20] We don't have the space to review the results Hofstede obtained on each of the dimensions for each of the 40 countries, although 12 examples are presented in Table 4-5.

Individualism versus Collectivism.   **Individualism** refers to a loosely knit social framework in which people are supposed to look after their own interests and those of their immediate family. They can do so because of the large amount of freedom that an individualistic society allows its citizens. The opposite is **collectivism**, which is characterized by a tight social framework in which people expect others in groups of which they are a part (such as a family or an organization) to look after them and to protect them when they are in trouble. In exchange, they feel they owe absolute loyalty to the group.

Hofstede found that the degree of individualism in a country was closely related to that country's wealth. Wealthier countries such as the United States, Great Britain, and the Netherlands are very individualistic. Poorer countries such as Colombia and Pakistan are very collectivistic.

Power Distance.   People naturally vary in terms of physical and intellectual abilities. This variation, in turn, creates differences in wealth and power. How does a society deal with these inequalities? Hofstede used the term **power distance** as a measure of the extent to which a society accepts the fact that power in institutions and organizations is distributed unequally. A high power distance society accepts wide differences in power in organizations. Employees show a great deal of respect for those in authority. Titles, rank, and status carry a lot of weight. When negotiating in high power distance countries, companies find that it helps to send representatives with titles at least as impressive as those with whom they are bargaining. Countries high in power distance include the Philippines, Venezuela, and India. In contrast, a low power distance society plays down inequalities as

individualism

A cultural dimension in which people are supposed to look after their own interests and those of their immediate family.

collectivism

A cultural dimension in which people expect others in their group to look after them and to protect them when they are in trouble.

power distance

A cultural measure of the extent to which a society accepts the unequal distribution of power in institutions and organizations.

TABLE 4-5	Examples of Hofstede's Cultural Dimensions			
Country	**Individualism/ Collectivism**	**Power Distance**	**Uncertainty Avoidance**	**Quantity of Life[a]**
Australia	Individual	Small	Moderate	Strong
Canada	Individual	Moderate	Low	Moderate
England	Individual	Small	Moderate	Strong
France	Individual	Large	High	Weak
Greece	Collective✓	Large ✓	High✓	Moderate
Italy	Individual	Moderate	High	Strong
Japan	Collective ✓	Moderate	High	Strong
Mexico	Collective ✓	Large ✓	High	Strong
Singapore	Collective ✓	Large ✓	Low	Moderate
Sweden	Individual	Small	Low	Weak
United States	Individual	Small	Low	Strong
Venezuela	Collective	Large	High	Strong

Source: Based on G. Hofstede, "Motivation, Leadership, and Organization: Do American Theories Apply Abroad?" *Organizational Dynamics,* Summer 1980, pp. 42–63.

[a] A weak quantity score is equivalent to high quality of life.

Although it is an economically rich country, Japan scores high on collectivism. This trait helps explain the popularity and success of teams in Japanese automotive factories.

much as possible. Superiors still have authority, but employees are not fearful or in awe of the boss. Denmark, the United States, Israel, and Austria are examples of countries with low power distance scores.

Uncertainty Avoidance.   We live in a world of uncertainty. The future is largely unknown and always will be. Societies respond to this uncertainty in different ways. Some socialize their members into accepting it with equanimity. People in such societies are relatively comfortable with risks. They're also relatively tolerant of behavior and opinions that differ from their own because they don't feel threatened by them. Hofstede describes such societies as having low **uncertainty avoidance**. That is, people feel quite secure. Countries that fall into this category include Singapore and Denmark.

A society that's high in uncertainty avoidance is characterized by a high level of anxiety among its people, which manifests itself in nervousness, high stress, and aggressiveness. Because people in these cultures feel threatened by uncertainty and ambiguity, mechanisms are created to provide security and to reduce risk. Organizations in these cultures are likely to have formal rules and little tolerance for unusual ideas and behaviors, and members will strive to believe in absolute truths. Not surprisingly, in organizations in countries with high uncertainty avoidance employees demonstrate relatively low job mobility, and lifetime employment is a widely practiced policy. Countries in this category include Japan, Portugal, and Greece.

Quantity versus Quality of Life.   The fourth dimension, like individualism and collectivism, is a dichotomy. Some cultures emphasize the **quantity of life** and value things such as assertiveness and the acquisition of money and material goods. Cultures that emphasize the **quality of life** value relationships and show sensitivity and concern for the welfare of others. Hofstede found that Japan and Austria scored high on the quantity dimension. In contrast, Norway, Sweden, Denmark, and Finland scored high on the quality dimension.

A Guide for U.S. Managers.   We used the United States earlier as a point of reference, so we'll conclude this section by reviewing how the United States ranked on Hofstede's four dimensions and considering how a U.S. manager working in another country might be able to use Hofstede's research findings. Comparing the 40 countries on the

uncertainty avoidance

A cultural measure of the degree to which people tolerate risk and unconventional behavior.

quantity of life

A national culture attribute describing the extent to which societal values are characterized by assertiveness and materialism.

quality of life

A national culture attribute that reflects the emphasis placed upon relationships and concern for others.

four dimensions, Hofstede found the U.S. culture to be the highest among all countries on individualism, below average on power distance, well below average on uncertainty avoidance, and well above average on quantity of life. These conclusions are consistent with how the world views the United States. That is, the United States is seen as stressing the individualistic ethic, having a representative government with democratic ideals, being relatively free from threats of uncertainty, and having a capitalistic economy that values aggressiveness and materialism. In which countries are U.S. managers likely to fit best? Which are likely to create the biggest adjustment problems? All we have to do is identify those countries that are most and least like the United States on the four dimensions. The United States is strongly individualistic but low on power distance. This same pattern was exhibited by Great Britain, Australia, Canada, the Netherlands, and New Zealand. Those least similar to the United States on these dimensions were Venezuela, Colombia, Pakistan, Singapore, and the Philippines. The United States scored low on uncertainty avoidance and high on quantity of life. This same pattern was shown by Ireland, Great Britain, the Philippines, Canada, New Zealand, Australia, India, and South Africa. Those least similar to the United States on these dimensions were Chile and Portugal. These results empirically support part of what many of us suspected—that the U.S. manager transferred to London, Toronto, Melbourne, or a similar Anglo city would have to make the fewest adjustments. In addition, the results further identify the countries in which **culture shock** (the

culture shock

The feelings of confusion, disorientation, and emotional upheaval caused by being immersed in a new culture.

Entrepreneurship around the World

What role does entrepreneurship play in other countries around the globe? Does it make important economic contributions? Do entrepreneurs the world over share the same types of traits and characteristics? Let's see if we can answer those questions.[21]

The relatively easy availability of capital for start-ups and an attitude that encourages new companies and tolerates business failures may lead you to believe that entrepreneurship in the United States is more significant here than anywhere else in the world. However, that isn't the case! In most European countries, small and medium-sized businesses have always played a more important role as job providers than do small businesses in the United States, and that role is growing in most European nations. In addition, small businesses in Europe are changing the way they do business. No longer are these small businesses content to stay small. Many are becoming growth-oriented global competitors. What about entrepreneurship in the Asian region? Although statistics on the number and importance of new and small companies in Asia are difficult to obtain, most experts believe that entrepreneurship is flourishing in this region as well. For example, in mainland China, entrepreneurial ventures are springing up at a rate that dwarfs the rate in every other country. Researchers estimate that there are approximately 20.8 million small enterprises in China. Entrepreneurship would appear to be an important activity in many global regions!

Do entrepreneurs around the world exhibit the same types of personality traits and characteristics? NO! One study found that entrepreneurs in various countries had different views about what made them successful. For example, Irish entrepreneurs specified their strengths as organizing and planning, dealing with people, and conducting business operations, in that order. Russians cited idea generation, business operations, and organizing and planning. Americans noted product innovation, dealing with people, and sales and marketing, organizing and planning. Hungarian entrepreneurs saw their strengths as dealing with people, innovation, and planning. Some of the differences shown in this study may be explained by the different national cultures of the various countries. ■

ENTREPRENEURSHIP

feelings of confusion, disorientation, and emotional upheaval caused by being immersed in a new culture) is likely to be greatest and the need to modify one's managerial style will be most critical.

16 How does national culture differ from organizational culture? How are they similar?

17 Describe Hofstede's four characteristics of national culture.

18 How can an understanding of Hofstede's four dimensions help managers be more effective in a global marketplace?

IS A GLOBAL ASSIGNMENT FOR YOU?

How do organizations decide which individuals will be sent on global assignments? Typically the decision is based on employee selection criteria that are influenced by the company's experience and commitment to global operations. Table 4-6 lists several specific criteria that have been used by global organizations from Australia, the United States, Britain, Canada, France, New Zealand, and Asia in global employee selection decisions. Obviously, technical skills are important for success in overseas assignments, but other skills such as language skills, flexibility, and family adaptability are needed as well. You can see by the list that both technical and human factors are usually considered. Organizations that don't consider both are likely to experience a failure rate in sending employees on global assignment.[22]

TABLE 4-6	**Criteria for Making Global Employee Selection Decisions**		
	Australian Managers *N = 47*	**Expatriate Managers**[a] *N = 52*	**Asian Managers** *N = 15*
1. Ability to adapt	1	1	2
2. Technical competence	2	3	1
3. Spouse and family adaptability	3	2	4
4. Human relations skill	4	4	3
5. Desire to serve overseas	5	5	5
6. Previous overseas experience	6	7	7
7. Understanding of host country culture	7	6	6
8. Academic qualifications	8	8	8
9. Knowledge of language of country	9	9	9
10. Understanding of home country culture	10	10	10

Source: R.J. Stone, "Expatriate Selection and Failure," *Human Resource Planning* 14, No. 1 (1991), p. 10. Used with permission.

[a] American, British, Canadian, French, New Zealand, or Australian managers working for a multinational corporation outside their home countries.

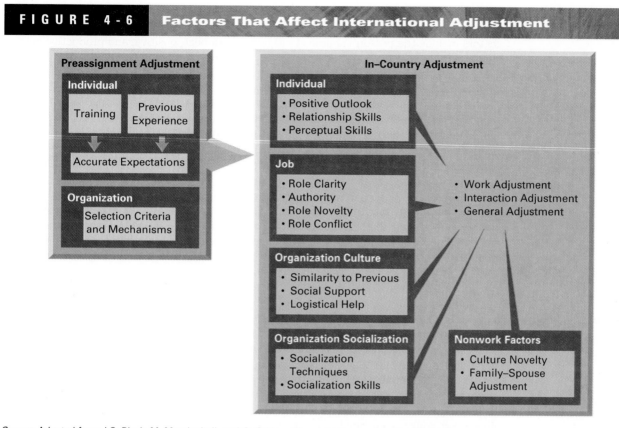

FIGURE 4-6   Factors That Affect International Adjustment

Source: Adapted from J.S. Black, M. Mendenhall, and G. Oddou, "Toward a Comprehensive Model of International Adjustment: An Integration of Multiple Theoretical Perspectives," *Academy of Management Review*, April 1991, p. 303.

Once an employee has been selected as a good candidate for a managerial position in a foreign country, there are several individual and organizational factors that determine whether he or she can effectively adjust to an overseas assignment. Figure 4–6 portrays some typical adjustment factors.

As the figure shows, there are two major types of adjustments a person makes when being transferred to another country: preassignment adjustment and in-country adjustment. The preassignment adjustment period is affected by a number of factors. For one thing, it's important that, before taking an overseas assignment, an individual have accurate expectations of the realities of the proposed position and the country to which he or she is being transferred. A person's expectations are affected by the level of predeparture training and previous experience with the assigned country or similar cultures. Predeparture training such as cross-cultural seminars or workshops that provide information about the culture and work life of the country to which a person is being transferred can help smooth the preassignment adjustment period. Also, the adjustment will be easier for a person who has had experience with the culture of the assigned country than it will be for a person who has not.

There are certain things that an organization can do to make the preassignment adjustment smoother. For instance, the organization should have appropriate selection criteria (like those shown in Table 4-6) and mechanisms in place for choosing individuals for global assignments. By carefully selecting individuals for overseas assignments, an organization can alleviate many of the transition problems.

Once the person has been transferred to the foreign location, there's a period of in-country adjustment, which also involves individual and organizational factors. Individual factors include the person's abilities to (1) remain upbeat, positive, and productive even in new situations that may be pressure packed and stressful, (2) interact effectively with host country co-workers, and (3) accurately perceive and adapt to the country's cultural values and norms.

Organizational factors that can ease the transition include the job that the person will be doing, the organization's culture, and the level of organizational socialization. We can see from Figure 4–6 that the important job factors for successful adjustment to a new country are related to the clarity of job expectations, the authority the individual has to make decisions, the newness of the work-related activities, and the amount of role conflict that exists. If these job factors are not properly considered, a person transferred to another country faces a long period of adjustment or perhaps even an unsatisfactory adjustment.

Organizational culture factors that should be considered for successful transition include how similar the organizational culture is to what the individual has experienced in the past, the social support provided by the organizational culture, and the amount of logistical help provided by the organization to make the adjustment easier. Again, if these factors are not properly addressed, a person transferred to another country may not adjust as quickly or effectively to being a productive employee.

organizational socialization

The process that employees go through to adapt to an organization's culture.

Another factor that determines the success of an individual's adjustment to an overseas assignment is his or her skills of organizational socialization. **Organizational socialization** refers to the process that employees go through to adapt to an organization's culture. The cultural transition will be easier if the individual develops effective socialization skills and quickly learns the "way things are done around here."

Finally, it's important to note that nonwork considerations also influence how effectively an individual will adjust to a foreign assignment. These include how an individual personally adjusts to the novelty of the culture and how the family and spouse adjust. The family-spouse adjustment can be a major source of problems. The realities of living in a different culture, where simple tasks such as grocery shopping, driving a car, or going to a movie can be logistical challenges, create stresses for individuals and their families. Culture shock is a real and normal reaction. Studies have shown after about four to six months, however, most people adjust to the new culture.[23]

TESTING... TESTING...

19 What selection criteria might companies use in determining which individuals to send on overseas assignments?

20 What types of preassignment adjustments does an individual going on a global assignment have to make? How can these adjustments be made easier?

21 What types of in-country adjustments does an individual going on a global assignment have to make? How can these adjustments be made easier?

managers respond to "a manager's dilemma"

MANAGER 1

The information that I'd want would fall into three specific areas. First, I'd want information that could be collected *within* the company, including an objective assessment of the company and what we do well, advice from the staff on international commerce, sales data, and advice from any foreign nationals who work within the company. Then, I'd gather information *outside* the company, including publicly available material on trade with the United States, Chinese and U.S. government information about Chinese trade with the United States, advice from other Chinese manufacturers who may have experience in the U.S. consumer market, advice from consulting firms that have experience in trade between China and the United States, and advice from a Chinese law firm that has contacts in the United States. Finally, there would be some information I'd gather through *testing and in person* such as visiting the United States and talking with manufacturers and government sources and visiting U.S. retail establishments. I'd also be sure to obtain information from religious sources about the practical implications of U.S. religious beliefs that might differ from China.

Bill Newton, *Chairman, SATEC, Solon, Ohio*

MANAGER 2

Pan Yaping's manufacturing experience and subsequent success in China should help him with what I believe will be his largest hurdle in the U.S. consumer market—the governmental regulations to which his factory must comply. Pan's knowledge of U.S. governmental factory regulations and trade practices will need to be extensive. Beyond these political challenges, Pan may encounter difficulties with U.S. environmental groups. I suggest that Pan research the various active U.S. environmental groups in order to understand their potential impact. I believe his final challenge will be establishing the distribution channel for selling his products. Hiring a U.S. public relations or marketing research firm may help him identify the retailers that will serve his company best in creating an efficient marketing system in the United States.

Kristin Feyen, *Training Manager, Executrain of San Francisco, San Francisco, California*

for your
IMMEDIATE
action

Delaney Environmental Services

To: Sandy Burk, Director of Operations
From: J. Delaney, Managing Director
Subject: Global expansion

Sandy, as we talked about last week at some length, I think it's important that DES start carefully looking at expanding its global market opportunities. We have developed a successful track record for providing environmental consulting and design services here in San Antonio, and I believe that with our experience we have a lot to offer the Latin American market, particularly in Mexico.

I would like for you to do some research into the problems we might face in moving into the Mexican market. Specifically, I would like for you to cover: (1) cultural differences we would need to consider, (2) the current currency rate of exchange and how it has changed over the last three years, and (3) any legal or political situations we need to be aware of. Since this is just an initial analysis for us to study, please keep your report to two pages or less.

SUMMARY

This summary is organized by the chapter-opening objectives found on p. 110.

1. Competitors and markets are no longer defined within national borders. New competitors can suddenly appear from anywhere in the world. New markets are opening up in countries around the world. Managers must think globally if their organizations are to succeed over the long term.

2. The three different global perspectives are ethnocentric, polycentric, and geocentric. An ethnocentric attitude is the parochialistic belief that the best work approaches and practices are those of the home country. The polycentric attitude is the view that the managers in the host country know the best work approaches and practices for running their operations. The geocentric attitude is a world-oriented view that focuses on using the best approaches and people from around the globe.

3. The European Union (EU) is a 15-nation trading alliance whose purpose is to have common customs duties and unified industrial and commercial policies. NAFTA (North American Free Trade Agreement) is a three-nation trading alliance between the United States, Mexico, and Canada. ASEAN (Association of Southeast Asian Nations) is a ten-nation trading alliance in one of the fastest-growing economic regions in the world.

4. Regional trading alliances create more-powerful economic entities. Many countries have joined these alliances in order to compete more effectively. For instance, countries joined the European Union to compete more aggressively against such economically powerful countries as the United States and Japan.

5. Multinational corporations have significant operations functioning in two or more countries simultaneously, but primary decision making and control are based in the company's home country. Transnationals also have significant operations in multiple countries, but decision making is decentralized to the local level. Borderless organizations are a global type of organization in which artificial geographical barriers are eliminated.

6. The typical stages by which organizations go international are (1) exporting to foreign countries; (2) hiring foreign representation or contracting with foreign manufacturers; and (3) establishing international operations through licensing or franchising, joint ventures or strategic alliances, and foreign subsidiaries.

7. The four primary dimensions on which nations' cultures differ are individualism versus collectivism, power distance, uncertainty avoidance, and quantity versus quality of life.

8. U.S. culture is characterized as being high on individualism, below average on power distance, well below average on uncertainty avoidance, and well above average on quantity of life.

9. A manager on global assignment faces two periods of adjustment: the time before going to a foreign country and the time while in the new country. Both individual and organizational factors influence the successful adjustment of managers to overseas assignments.

THINKING ABOUT MANAGEMENT ISSUES

1. What are the managerial implications of a borderless organization?

2. Can the Hofstede framework presented in this chapter be used to guide managers in a South Korean hospital or a government agency in Peru? Discuss.

3. Compare the advantages and drawbacks of the various approaches to going international.

4. What challenges might confront a Mexican manager transferred to the United States to manage a manufacturing plant in Tucson, Arizona?

5. In what ways do you think global factors have changed, or will change, the way organizations select and train managers?

SELF-ASSESSMENT EXERCISE

WHAT ARE YOUR CULTURAL ATTITUDES?

How well you would adapt and function in a different country depends to some extent on your cultural attitudes. If you are to succeed in the global economy, you'll need to develop a certain degree of cultural sensitivity. Take this self-assessment exercise to measure your cultural attitudes.

Instructions: Indicate the extent to which you agree or disagree with each of the following statements. Answer each statement by circling the appropriate number; for example, if you strongly agree with a particular statement, you will circle the 5 next to that statement.

    5 = Strongly agree
    4 = Agree
    3 = Neither agree nor disagree
    2 = Disagree
    1 = Strongly disagree

	Strongly Agree				Strongly Disagree
1. It is important to have job requirements and instructions spelled out so people always know what they are expected to do.	5	4	3	2	1
2. Managers expect workers to closely follow instructions and procedures.	5	4	3	2	1
3. Rules and regulations are important because they inform workers what the organization expects of them.	5	4	3	2	1
4. Standard operating procedures are helpful to workers on the job.	5	4	3	2	1
5. Instructions for operations are important for workers on the job.	5	4	3	2	1
6. Individual rewards are not as important as group welfare.	5	4	3	2	1
7. Group success is more important than individual success.	5	4	3	2	1
8. Being accepted by the group is more important than working on your own.	5	4	3	2	1
9. An individual should not pursue his or her own objectives without considering the welfare of the group.	5	4	3	2	1
10. It is important for a manager to encourage loyalty and a sense of duty to the group.	5	4	3	2	1
11. Managers should make most decisions without consulting subordinates.	5	4	3	2	1
12. It is often necessary for a supervisor to emphasize his or her authority and power when dealing with subordinates.	5	4	3	2	1
13. Managers should be careful not to ask the opinions of subordinates too frequently.	5	4	3	2	1
14. A manager should avoid socializing with his or her subordinates off the job.	5	4	3	2	1
15. Subordinates should not disagree with their manager's decisions.	5	4	3	2	1
16. Managers should not delegate difficult and important tasks to their subordinates.	5	4	3	2	1
17. Meetings are usually run more effectively when they are chaired by a man than by a woman.	5	4	3	2	1
18. It is more important for men to have a professional career than it is for women to have a professional career.	5	4	3	2	1
19. Women do not value recognition and promotion in their work as much as men do.	5	4	3	2	1
20. Women value working in a friendly atmosphere more than men do.	5	4	3	2	1
21. Men usually solve problems with logical analysis; women usually solve problems with intuition.	5	4	3	2	1

		Strongly Agree				Strongly Disagree
22.	Solving organizational problems usually requires the active, forcible approach that is typical of men.	5	4	3	2	1
23.	It is preferable to have a man in a high-level position rather than a woman.	5	4	3	2	1
24.	There are some jobs in which a man can always do better than a woman.	5	4	3	2	1
25.	Women are more concerned with social aspects of their job than they are with getting ahead.	5	4	3	2	1

See scoring key on page SK–2.

Source: This questionnaire is part of a larger instrument currently under development by Professors Peter W. Dorfman and Jon P. Howell, both of New Mexico State University. Reprinted by permission of the authors.

TAKE IT TO THE NET

We invite you to visit the Robbins/Coulter companion Web site at http://www.prenhall.com/robbinsmgt for this chapter's Internet resources.

CASE APPLICATION

Shooting for Overseas Success

The National Basketball Association (NBA) has emerged as the first truly global sports league. Basketball has sparked the interest of fans and players around the globe, and the NBA is cashing in on the game's universal appeal. Ask someone in China what the most popular basketball team is and the answer will be the "Red Oxen" from Chicago. The league is a global entertainment company, and its basketball games are televised everywhere. In conjunction with its partners, the NBA has also sold well over $500 million worth of licensed merchandise outside the United States, including basketballs, backboards, T-shirts, and caps. The transformation of a faltering domestic sport into a phenomenal global commercial success is a fascinating story of effective and efficient international management.

Although every other major U.S. sports league has tried to go global, none has been able to achieve the level of success that the NBA has achieved. The National Football League launched the European-based World Football League in 1991. But after an initial burst of interest, football's popularity faded in Europe and Japan. With losses exceeding $100 million, the World League struggled to find television audiences and sponsors. Major league baseball, on the

other hand, had so many domestic problems that team owners were never able to focus on the sport's potential global market. In addition, baseball's global expansion plans were slowed by its misplaced emphasis on Europe, where baseball isn't that popular. Other professional sports leagues haven't had the market power or appeal to attempt global expansion.

What's behind the NBA's global success story? One factor is that the league has a huge natural advantage over other sports. Basketball is played nearly everywhere around the globe, and the game itself is easily understood. Professional and amateur basketball leagues have thrived for years in Europe and Asia. In addition, basketball has been an Olympic sport since 1936. In fact, in the 1992 Barcelona Olympics, the U.S. "Dream Team" was a worldwide sensation, generating an even greater interest in pro basketball. Wherever the Dream Team players went in Barcelona, they were mobbed by adoring fans. The NBA's global push got an enormous boost from this exposure.

Other significant factors that have contributed to the NBA's global appeal can be traced to two men: David J. Stern, NBA's commissioner, and Michael Jordan, the sensational player who has parlayed his success on the court into a host of worldwide product endorsements. Stern became commissioner of the NBA in 1984, the same year that Jordan entered the league. Stern immediately recognized the impact of cable and satellite television not only domestically but throughout the world and the potential these media held for exporting the game of basketball. He recalls, "You'd think the critical change in the world of sports and entertainment was the coming of the satellite. But it was the coming of cable…which opened up the variety of programming, from the existing three networks to countless new, competing channels." The impact of cable, while remarkable in itself domestically, was even greater internationally. Some countries only had one or two television networks, which were mostly state controlled. Cable provided a lot more channels, and those new channels needed good entertainment and needed it quickly. Televised professional basketball games provided that entertainment. Stern says, "We were ready." The widespread reach of cable not only broadened the audience for programs but also extended the reach of advertising far beyond what traditional broadcasting had been able to deliver. This is where Michael Jordan and his advertising partners, particularly Nike, came in. Like the NBA, Nike wanted to attack the global market in the 1980s. Using television as the primary advertising weapon, Nike's commercials turned Jordan into a worldwide celebrity known as much for his winning personality and competitive spirit as for his basketball prowess. All of a sudden, little boys around the world wanted to "be like Mike." The combination of Jordan's own Air Nike line, his athletic ability, his fierce competitive zeal, his smile, and Nike's drive for global dominance soon made him the world's foremost athletic celebrity, helping propel the image of the NBA globally as well.

The final factor that contributed to the NBA's global success is the fact that the league didn't showcase only American talent: Hakeem Olajuwon (Houston Rockets) is from Nigeria; Toni Kukok (Chicago Bulls) is from the former Yugoslavia; and Rik Smits (Indianapolis Pacers) is from Holland. As NBA teams hire extraordinary basketball talent from around the world, the game draws even greater global interest.

With Michael's soaring popularity, the use of superior athletes from around the globe, and the mechanism for delivering global entertainment in place, the NBA was in an enviable position for its global push. And that's exactly what commissioner Stern had planned.

QUESTIONS

1. What global perspective do you think the NBA and its member teams exhibit? Explain why this attitude has or hasn't contributed to the NBA's global success.
2. What legal-political, economic, and cultural differences might be significant to an NBA team recruiting a player from a foreign country? How would you deal with these differences?
3. Suppose you were hired as a talent scout for one of the NBA's teams and assigned to Shanghai, China. What would you do to make a successful adjustment both personally and professionally?
4. How has the NBA exhibited effective and efficient international management? Be specific.

Source: D. Halberstam, "David Did It," *World Business*, January–February 1996, pp. 34–39; J. Metaxas, "NBA Shoots for Success Overseas," *CNNfn Web Page* <www.cnnfn.com>, April 23, 1996; and M. Gunther, "They All Want to Be Like Mike," *Fortune*, July 21, 1997, pp. 51–53.

Shopping the World

From his home in Tampa, Florida, Jimmy Fand shops the world . . . literally. As the owner of The Tile Connection, North America's largest ceramic tile importer, Fand scours the world for different and unique tile. He got into this business because he found such poor selections and high prices when he was shopping for ceramic tile for a home he was building for his family in Tampa. Growing up in Colombia, where tile is a common fixture in homes and offices, he knew there had to be better choices than he was finding. He decided to go into business himself and search out and import tile from foreign tile manufacturers. His global searches have led him to high-quality tile manufacturers in Spain, Portugal, Colombia, Brazil, Argentina, Japan, Turkey, and other places all around the world.

Fand's background is quite interesting, as well. He came to New York City at the age of 19 and found the city to be a truly exciting place that fulfilled his every expectation of a large cosmopolitan city. And, despite the fact that he was a high school dropout, Fand went on to complete three university degrees. It's likely that his success and confidence in being a global businessperson come from his willingness to absorb new experiences.

Fand is truly comfortable dealing with suppliers from other countries. He speaks numerous languages including Spanish, English, Italian, and Portuguese. He thinks that everyone should look at the global marketplace because of the numerous business opportu-

nities it offers, but he recognizes that many people are afraid to do business outside the United States. His advice for those who are fearful of taking the plunge into the global marketplace includes: (1) Be cautious whom you deal with. Know your business contacts. (2) Go to trade shows, domestically and internationally. Get to know others within your industry. (3) Do your homework. Know your products and know the pricing. Fand goes on to say that after you've done your research, don't be afraid to weed out unacceptable business partners. After all, your business image and reputation are at stake. You wouldn't want to jeopardize those by accepting shoddy products or service.

QUESTIONS

1. Would you describe Jimmy Fand as parochialistic? Why or why not?
2. Using the Internet and World Wide Web, get some basic information (population, economic data, geographical facts, and so forth) about one of the countries from which The Tile Connection imports products.
3. Suppose that you were looking to locate ceramic tile manufacturers in an Asian country from whom you could possibly import tile. What information would you want about the country before doing business there?
4. What do you think about Fand's advice for doing business globally? Would you add anything to his list? Be specific.

Source: Based on *Small Business 2000, Show 405.*

A MANAGER'S DILEMMA

One of the biggest fears of a food service company's owner or manager has to be the hepatitis A virus,[1] a highly contagious virus transmitted by sharing food, utensils, cigarettes, or drug paraphernalia with an infected person. Food service workers aren't any more susceptible to the illness than anyone else, but an infected employee could easily spread the virus by handling food, especially cold foods. The virus, which is rarely fatal, can cause flulike illness for several weeks. There is no cure for hepatitis A, but there is a vaccine that can prevent it. An outbreak of hepatitis A in southwestern Missouri during summer and fall of 1996 had the county and state health departments wondering what

disastrous situations awaited. But the government officials weren't the only ones sitting on pins and needles. Local food service owners and managers feared what a case of hepatitis might do to their businesses, both in the long run and in the short run. One local food service business was to find out.

Bob Mericle (see photo), owner of a Waffle House restaurant in Springfield, Missouri, faced a serious dilemma. He learned one September morning that one of the cooks in his restaurant could have exposed as many as 350 people to hepatitis A during a five-day period when he was at work. The cook was thought to have contracted the virus through an infant living in his apartment complex. Because children usually show no symptoms of the disease, they can easily pass it on to adults. Mericle had a decision to make. Should he go public with the information, or should he only report it to the health department as was required? Put yourself in Mericle's position. List reasons why you should go public with the information and reasons why you shouldn't.

WHAT WOULD YOU DO?

Dealing with a difficult dilemma such as whether to publicize an infectious disease exposure is just one example of the types of ethical and social responsibility issues managers may have to cope with as they plan, organize, lead, and control. As managers and organizations go about their business, social factors can and do influence their actions. In this chapter we'll establish a foundation for understanding social responsibility and managerial ethics. The discussion of these topics is placed at this point in the text to link them to the preceding and following subjects. Specifically, we'll show that social responsibility is a response to a changing environment (chapter 3) and that ethical considerations should be important criteria in managerial decision making (the topic of chapter 6).

CHAPTER

5

Social Responsibility and Managerial Ethics

WHAT IS SOCIAL RESPONSIBILITY?

The issue of corporate social responsibility once drew little attention, but during the 1960s social activists began to question the singular economic (profit-making) objective of business firms. Were large corporations irresponsible because they discriminated against minorities and women, as shown by the obvious absence of female and minority managers? Did Kennecott Copper ignore its social responsibilities by allowing its smelters to pollute the air over hundreds of square miles of Arizona?

Before the 1960s, few people asked such questions. But times have changed. Managers now regularly face decisions that have a dimension of social responsibility: Philanthropy, pricing, employee relations, resource conservation, product quality and safety, and operations in countries that violate human rights are some of the more obvious. To help you understand how managers make such decisions, we will begin by defining social responsibility.

Two Opposing Views

Few terms have been defined in as many different ways as *social responsibility*. Some of the more popular meanings include "profit making only," "going beyond profit making," "voluntary activities," "concern for the broader social system," and "social responsiveness."[2] Most of the debate has focused on the extremes. On one side, there's the classical—or purely economic—view that management's only social responsibility is to maximize profits. On the other side stands the socioeconomic position, which holds that management's responsibility goes well beyond making profits to include protecting and improving society's welfare.

classical view

The view that management's only social responsibility is to maximize profits.

The Classical View.   The most outspoken advocate of the **classical view** is economist and Nobel laureate Milton Friedman.[3] He argues that most managers today are professional managers, which means that they don't own the business they run. They're employees, responsible only to the stockholders. Their primary responsibility, therefore, is to operate the business in the best interests of the stockholders. What are those interests? Friedman contends that the stockholders have a single concern: financial return.

According to Friedman, when managers decide on their own to spend their organization's resources for the "social good," they undermine the market mechanism. Someone must pay for this redistribution of assets. If socially responsible actions reduce profits and dividends, stockholders lose. If wages and benefits have to be reduced to pay for social actions, employees lose. If prices are raised to pay for social actions, consumers lose. If higher prices are rejected by consumers and sales drop, the business might not survive, in which case, *all* the organization's constituencies lose. Moreover, Friedman argues that when professional managers pursue anything other than profit, they implicitly appoint themselves as nonelected policy makers. He questions whether managers of business firms have the expertise for deciding how society should be. That, Friedman says, is what we elect political representatives to decide.

Friedman's argument is probably best understood by using microeconomics. If socially responsible actions add to the cost of doing business, those costs either have to be passed on to consumers in the form of higher prices or absorbed by stockholders through a smaller profit margin. If management raises prices in a competitive market, it will lose sales. In a purely competitive market where competitors have not assumed the costs of social responsibility, prices cannot be raised without losing the entire market. In such a situation, the costs have to be absorbed by the business, and the result is lower profits.

The classical view also contends that there are pressures in a competitive market for investment funds to go where they'll get the highest return. If the socially responsible firm cannot pass on its higher social costs to consumers and has to absorb them internally, it will generate a lower rate of return. Over time, investment funds will gravitate away from socially responsible firms toward those that aren't, because the latter will provide higher rates of return. In an extreme scenario, if all the firms in a particular country—say, the United States—incurred additional social costs because management perceived doing so to be one of business's goals, the survival of entire domestic industries could be threatened by foreign competitors who chose not to incur such social costs.

The Socioeconomic View.   The socioeconomic position counters that times have changed, and with them society's expectations of business. This view is best illustrated in the legal formation of corporations. Corporations are chartered by state governments, and the same government that grants a charter can take it away. So corporations are *not* independent entities responsible only to stockholders. They also have a responsibility to the larger society that endorses their creation and supports them. One author, in supporting the **socioeconomic view**, reminds us that "maximizing profits is a company's second priority, not its first. The first is ensuring its survival."[4]

Take the case of the Manville Corporation. For over 100 years, the company was a mainstay of American industry. From its days as the leading supplier of asbestos insulation for ships and airplanes during World War II, the company prospered until the late 1970s. Then, large numbers of employees began to file lawsuits alleging that exposure to airborne asbestos had permanently scarred their lungs and contributed to mesothelioma, a fatal cancer. The knowledge about the damaging effects of asbestos wasn't a surprise to the company's decision makers. Senior managers already were aware that asbestos caused fatal lung diseases. As a matter of policy, these managers decided to conceal the information from affected employees. The reason? Profits! In court testimony, a lawyer recalled how, in the mid-1940s, he had questioned Manville's corporate counsel about the company's policy of concealing chest X-ray results from employees. The lawyer had asked, "Do you mean to tell me you would let them work until they dropped dead?" The reply was, "Yes, we save a lot of money that way."[5] That might have been true in the short run, but it certainly wasn't in the long run. The company was forced to file for bankruptcy in 1982 to protect itself against thousands of potential asbestos-related lawsuits. It emerged from bankruptcy in 1988 but with staggering asbestos-related liabilities. The claims proved to be so overwhelming—the company had to set up a personal injury settlement trust fund with $2.6 billion in cash and bonds and a pledge of a certain percentage of future profits—that on April 1, 1996, Manville Corporation went out of business permanently. Only the independent trust fund that is to continue paying out settlements to asbestos claimants retains the Manville name.[6] What happened to Manville is an example of what can happen when managers take a short-term perspective. Many workers died needlessly, stockholders lost a great deal of money, and a major corporation went out of business. Another example of why companies must act responsibly in order to ensure their survival can be seen in the continuing controversy over whether tobacco company executives knew several years ago about the dangers of smoking and secondhand smoke and how their knowledge may have affected their decisions.

A major flaw in the classicist's view, as seen by socioeconomic proponents, is their time frame. Supporters of the socioeconomic view contend that managers should be concerned with maximizing financial returns over the *long run*. To do that, they must accept some social obligations and the costs that go with them. They must protect society's welfare by not polluting, not discriminating, not engaging in deceptive advertising, and so on. They must also play an activist role in improving society by involving themselves in their communities and contributing to charitable organizations.

A final point made by proponents of the socioeconomic position is that the classical view flies in the face of reality.[7] Modern business organizations are no longer merely economic institutions. They lobby, form political action committees, and engage in other activities to influence the political process for their benefit. Society accepts and even encourages business to become involved in its social, political, and legal environment. That might not have been true 50 years ago, but it is the reality of today. In fact, a survey of business

socioeconomic view

The view that management's social responsibility goes well beyond the making of profits to include protecting and improving society's welfare.

Firms can demonstrate their responsibility to society in ways that are creative and fun. In support of an annual nonalcoholic New Year's Eve, business and community organizations in Honolulu fund a public celebration called "First Night." These Bancorp Hawaii Inc. employees and their relatives sell commemorative T-shirts to help pay for the event, championing the firm's commitment to the socioeconomic view of business.

owners reported that 68 percent would continue socially responsible practices even if they found that the activities were cutting into profits.[8]

TESTING... TESTING...

1 Describe the classical view of social responsibility.

2 Describe the socioeconomic view of social responsibility.

3 According to the socioeconomic view of social responsibility, what are the flaws in the classical view?

Arguments For and Against Social Responsibility

What are the specific arguments for and against business's assuming social responsibilities? In this section, we'll outline the major points that have been presented.[9]

Arguments For.   The major arguments supporting business's being socially responsible are:

1. *Public expectations.* Social expectations of business have increased dramatically since the 1960s. Public opinion now supports business's pursuing social as well as economic goals.

2. *Long-run profits.* Socially responsible businesses tend to have more secure long-run profits. This is the normal result of the better community relations and improved business image that responsible behavior brings.

3. *Ethical obligation.* A business firm can and should have a social conscience. Businesses should be socially responsible because responsible actions are right for their own sake.

4. *Public image.* Firms seek to enhance their public image to get increased sales, better employees, access to financing, and other benefits. Because the public considers social goals important, business can create a favorable public image by pursuing social goals.

5. *Better environment.* Business involvement can help solve difficult social problems, helping create a better quality of life and a more desirable community in which to attract and keep skilled employees.

6. *Discouragement of further governmental regulation.* Governmental regulation adds economic costs and restricts managers' decision flexibility. By becoming socially responsible, business can expect less government regulation.

7. *Balance of responsibility and power.* Business holds a large amount of power in society. An equally large amount of responsibility is required to balance against it. When power is significantly greater than responsibility, the imbalance encourages irresponsible behavior that works against the public good.

8. *Stockholder interests.* Social responsibility will improve a business's stock price in the long run. The stock market will view the socially responsible company as less risky and open to public criticism. Therefore, it will award its stock a higher price-earnings ratio.

9. *Possession of resources.* Business organizations have the financial resources, technical experts, and managerial talent to support public and charitable projects that need assistance.

10. *Superiority of prevention over cures.* Social problems must be addressed at some time. Business should act before these problems become serious and costly to correct, taking managers' energies away from accomplishing their goal of producing goods and services.

Arguments Against.   The major arguments presented against business's assuming social responsibility are:

1. *Violation of profit maximization.* This is the essence of the classical viewpoint. Business is being socially responsible when it attends strictly to its economic interests and leaves other activities to other institutions.

2. *Dilution of purpose.* The pursuit of social goals dilutes business's primary purpose: economic productivity. Society may suffer if both economic and social goals are poorly accomplished.

3. *Costs.* Many socially responsible actions do not cover their costs. Someone has to pay those costs. Business must absorb the costs or pass them on to consumers through higher prices.

4. *Too much power.* Business is already one of the most powerful sectors of our society. If it pursues social goals, it will have even more power. Society has given business enough power.

5. *Lack of skills.* The outlook and abilities of business leaders are oriented primarily toward economics. Businesspeople are poorly qualified to address social issues.

6. *Lack of accountability.* Political representatives pursue social goals and are held accountable for their actions. Such is not the case with business leaders. There are no direct lines of social accountability from the business sector to the public.

In an effort to be (or at least appear to be) socially responsible, many organizations donate dollars to philanthropic and charitable causes. In addition, many organizations ask their employees to make individual donations to these causes. Suppose you're the manager of a work team, and you know that several of your employees can't afford to pledge money right now because of various personal and financial problems. You've also been told by your supervisor that the CEO has been known to check the list of individual contributors to see who is and is not "supporting these very important causes." What would you do? What ethical guidelines might you suggest for individual and organizational contributions to philanthropic and charitable causes? ■

THINKING CRITICALLY

ABOUT ETHICS

7. *Lack of broad public support.* There is no broad mandate or outcry from society for business to become involved in social issues. The public is divided on the issue of business's social responsibility. In fact, the topic typically generates heated debate. Actions taken under such divided support are likely to fail.

From Obligations to Responsiveness

social responsibility

An obligation, beyond that required by the law and economics, for a firm to pursue long-term goals that are good for society.

Now it's time to pinpoint precisely what we mean when we talk about **social responsibility**. It is a business firm's obligation, beyond that required by the law and economics, to pursue long-term goals that are good for society.[10] Note that this definition assumes that business obeys laws and pursues economic interests. We take as a given that all business firms—those that are socially responsible and those that aren't—will obey all relevant laws that society enacts. Also note that this definition views business as a moral agent. In its effort to do good for society, it must differentiate between right and wrong.

social obligation

The obligation of a business to meet its economic and legal responsibilities.

We can understand social responsibility better if we compare it with two similar concepts: social obligation and social responsiveness.[11] As Figure 5-1 illustrates, social obligation is the foundation of business's social involvement. A business has fulfilled its **social obligation** when it meets economic and legal responsibilities and no more. It does the minimum required by law. Following an approach of social obligation, a firm pursues social goals only to the extent that they contribute to its economic goals. In contrast to social obligation, however, both social responsibility and social responsiveness go beyond merely meeting basic economic and legal standards.

Social responsibility adds an ethical imperative to do those things that make society better and not to do those that could make it worse. A socially responsible organization goes beyond what it must do by law or chooses to do only because it makes economic sense to doing what it can to help improve society because that's the right, or ethical, thing to do. As Table 5-1 describes, social responsibility requires business to determine what is right or wrong and to make ethical decisions and engage in ethical business activities. A socially responsible organization does what is right because it has an "obligation" to act that way. On the other hand, **social responsiveness** refers to the capacity of a firm to adapt to changing societal conditions. The idea of social responsiveness stresses that managers make practical decisions about the societal actions in which they engage.[12] A socially responsive organization acts the way it does because of its desire to satisfy some expressed social need. Social responsiveness is guided by social norms. The value of social norms is that they can provide managers with a meaningful guide for decision making. The following example might help make the distinction between responsibility and responsiveness clearer:

social responsiveness

The capacity of a firm to adapt to changing societal conditions.

> Suppose, for example, that a multiproduct firm's social responsibility is to produce reasonably safe products. Similarly, the same firm is responsive every

FIGURE   5-1   **Levels of Social Involvement**

Social Responsibility

Social Responsiveness

Social Obligation

TABLE 5-1	Social Responsibility versus Social Responsiveness	
	Social Responsibility	**Social Responsiveness**
Major consideration	Ethical	Pragmatic
Focus	Ends	Means
Emphasis	Obligation	Responses
Decision framework	Long term	Medium and short term

Source: Adapted from S.L. Wartick and P.L. Cochran, "The Evolution of the Corporate Social Performance Model," *Academy of Management Review*, October 1985, p. 766.

time it produces an unsafe product: it withdraws the product from the market as soon as the product is found to be unsafe. After, say, ten recalls, will the firm be recognized as socially responsible? Will the firm be recognized as socially responsive? The likely answers to these questions are "No" to the first, but "Yes" to the second.[13]

How does this example illustrate the distinction between social responsibility and social responsiveness? The organization's decision to continue producing unsafe products, even though it espoused a responsibility to produce reasonably safe products, would make it appear socially irresponsible in the eyes of the public; that is, it wasn't doing the right, or ethical, thing. However, the organization's quick action in withdrawing unsafe products from the market would make it appear socially responsive because it was responding to what the public wanted (demanded) it do.

A company that meets pollution control standards established by the federal government or does not discriminate against employees over the age of 40 in promotion decisions is meeting its social obligation and nothing more. When it provides on-site child care facil-

As CEO of her own Washington, DC, based company, Creative Associates International, Inc., Charito Kruvant believes passionately in helping the women citizens of less developed countries create a better life for themselves. Her commitment to helping women in countries ravaged by war and upheaval comes from having experienced political and civil unrest firsthand in her native Bolivia. She says, "I know the tensions it can bring to families."

Tonya Hatosyan, an employee of First National Bank in Glen Burnie, Maryland, volunteers with others to help make renovations on a house in Crofton (MD). All volunteered as part of "Christmas in April."

ities for employees, packages products in 100 percent recycled paper, or announces that it will not purchase, process, or sell any tuna caught in association with dolphins, it is being socially responsive. Why? Pressure from working parents and environmentalists make such practices pragmatic. Of course, an organization that provided child care, offered recycled packaging, or sought to protect dolphins back in the 1970s probably would have been accurately characterized as a socially responsible company.

Advocates of social responsiveness believe that the concept replaces philosophical talk with practical action. They see it as a more tangible and achievable objective than social responsibility.[14] Rather than assessing what's good for society in the long term, managers in a socially responsive organization identify the prevailing social norms and then change their social involvement to respond to changing societal conditions. For instance, several large print media companies such as Prentice Hall, McGraw-Hill, the *Los Angeles Times*, the *Washington Post*, and the *New York Times* are involved in efforts to increase literacy. At least 60 U.S. banks have created community development corporations to help improve run-down neighborhoods, and food companies such as General Mills, Grand Metropolitan, Kraft General Foods, and Sara Lee donate a portion of their product sales to local community hunger programs. These are examples of socially responsive actions for right now.

**TESTING...
TESTING...**

1   2   3

4 What are the arguments for business's being socially responsible?

5 What are some of the arguments against business involvement in social responsibility?

6 Differentiate between social obligation, social responsiveness, and social responsibility.

SOCIAL RESPONSIBILITY AND ECONOMIC PERFORMANCE

In this section, we seek to answer the question: Do socially responsible activities lower a company's economic performance? A number of studies have looked at this question.[15] All recognized the methodological limitations related to measures of "social responsibility" and "economic performance."[16] Most determined a firm's social performance by analyzing the content of annual reports, citations of social actions in articles on the company, or public perception "reputation" indexes. Such criteria certainly have drawbacks as reliable measures of social responsibility. Although measures of economic performance (such as net income, return on equity, or per share stock prices) are more objective, they are generally used to indicate only short-term financial performance. It may well be that the impact of social responsibility on a firm's profits—either positive or negative—takes a number of years to manifest itself. If there is a time lag, studies that use short-term financial data are not likely to show valid results. There is also the issue of causation. If, for example, the evidence showed that social involvement and economic performance were positively related, this relation would not necessarily mean that social involvement caused higher economic performance. It very well could be the opposite. That is, it might mean that high profits permit firms the luxury of being socially involved.[17]

Given these cautions, what do the various research studies find? The majority show a positive relationship between corporate social involvement and economic performance. One review of 13 studies found only one negative association. In that instance, the price of socially responsible firms' stocks didn't do as well as national stock indexes.[18] Another study found that firms' corporate social performance was positively associated with prior financial performance.[19] More interesting, however, was the fact that this same study found that corporate social performance was positively associated with future financial performance. In addition, a stock evaluation index known as the Domini 400 Social Index created in 1990, has, since its inception, done better overall than the Standard & Poor's 500 Index. For a five-year period ending February 28, 1997, the average annual return of the Domini 400 was 17.5 percent, whereas the S&P 500 averaged only 16.95 percent.[20] The logic behind these positive relationships appears to be that social involvement provides benefits to a firm that more than offset its cost. These benefits include a positive consumer image, a competitive advantage in attracting prospective employees, a more dedicated and motivated workforce, and less interference from regulators.[21]

There's also another way to look at this issue. A number of socially conscious mutual stock funds have been started in recent years. Table 5-2 lists the largest and most popular of these U.S. funds that describe themselves as responsible investors. Typically, these funds will not invest in companies that are involved in liquor, gambling, tobacco, nuclear power, weapons, price fixing, or fraud. These mutual funds provide a way for individual investors to support socially responsible companies in yet another way. Also, one of the largest public pension systems in the United States, CALPERS (California Public Employees' Retirement System), announced in June 1994 that it would start making investment decisions in part according to how well companies treat their employees.[22] This announcement signaled the first time that a major institutional investor had explicitly stated that a company's workplace practices would be used as part of an analysis of company performance.

What conclusion can we draw from all this? The most meaningful conclusion we can make is that there is little substantive evidence to say that a company's socially responsible actions significantly hurt its long-term economic performance. Given the current political and social pressures on business to pursue social goals, this conclusion may have great significance for managerial decision making. So the answer to our question—Do socially responsible activities lower a company's economic performance?—appears to be No!

VALUES-BASED MANAGEMENT

Values-based management is an approach to managing in which managers establish, promote, and practice an organization's shared values. An organization's values reflect what it stands for and what it believes in. As we discussed in chapter 3, the shared organizational values form the organization's culture and influence the way the organization operates and employees behave.[23] For instance, at Tom's of Maine, a manufacturer of natural personal care products, the company's shared values have become part of the overall business strategy. Every managerial decision at Tom's is evaluated in light of the values found in its

values-based management

An approach to managing in which managers establish, promote, and practice an organization's shared values.

TABLE 5-2	Representative Listing of Social and Environmental Fund Groups

Fund	Guidelines Used for Investing
Amana Income www.saturna.com	Invests according to Islamic principles
American Trust Allegiance	Invests according to Christian Science principles; screens out tobacco, liquor, gaming, pharmaceuticals and medical services
Aquinas Equity Growth	No screens but uses its shares to force change
Aquinas Equity Income	Uses its shares to force change in areas such as abortion, weapons, human rights, the environment and fair employment
Ariel Appreciation	Screens out tobacco, nuclear power, weapons, and polluters
Ariel Growth	Screens out tobacco, nuclear power, weapons, and polluters
Calvert Managed Growth www. calvertgroup.com	Screens out alcohol, tobacco, gaming, nuclear power, weapons, polluters, and discriminatory policies
Calvert Social Equity www.calvertgroup.com	Screens out alcohol, tobacco, gaming, nuclear power, weapons, polluters, and discriminatory policies
Citizens Index Fund www.efund.com	Screens out alcohol, tobacco, gaming, nuclear power, weapons, polluters, discriminatory policies, and animal testing
Cruelty-Free Value Fund www.crueltyfree.com	Screens out companies that use animal testing or are associated with any activities that harm animals
Delaware Quantum Fund	Screens out alcohol, tobacco, gaming, nuclear power, weapons, and polluters
Domini Social Equity	Screens out alcohol, tobacco, gaming, nuclear power, weapons, polluters, and discriminatory policy
Dreyfus Third Century www.Dreyfus.com	Screens out alcohol, tobacco, polluters, and discriminatory policies
Green Century Balanced	Screens out tobacco, nuclear power, nuclear weapons, and polluters
Green Century Equity Fund	Screens out alcohol, tobacco, gaming, nuclear power, weapons, polluters, and discriminatory policies
Lutheran Brotherhood www.Luthbro.com	Invests according to Lutheran principles; restricted to Lutherans
Meyers Pride Value Fund www.pridefund.com	Favors companies with established antidiscriminatory policies toward gays and lesbians
Parnassus Fund networth.galt.com/parnassus	Screens out alcohol, tobacco, gaming, nuclear power, weapons, polluters, and discriminatory policies
Women's Equity Mutual Fund www.womens-equity.com	Favors companies with progressive policies toward women

Source: Based on P. Mao, "Socially Responsible Investing," *Sky Magazine*, June 1997, p. 50.

At Tom's of Maine, CEO Tom Chappell struggled to find a way to bring his values into running the multimillion dollar business he had founded with his wife, Kate. In his autobiographical book *The Soul of a Business*, Chappell describes his self-awareness journey and states, "I confessed how confused I was about what I should be doing with the rest of my life…I had to make a real go of something I'd started. What more could I do in life except make more money? Where were the purpose and direction for the rest of my life?"

Statement of Beliefs and Mission Statement. Tom's is committed to both social responsibility and profits. For any company that believes in and practices values-based management, the shared corporate values serve many purposes.

Purposes of Shared Values

The values that organizational members share serve at least three main purposes as shown in Figure 5-2. Let's look at them more closely.

A company's shared values act as guideposts for managerial decisions and actions.[24] For example, at clothing manufacturer Blue Bell, Inc., a strong tradition of corporate values guides managers as they plan, organize, lead, and control organizational activities. Their shared values were developed through a series of participative discussions and are expressed in the acronym PRIDE: *p*rofitability through excellence, *r*espect for the individual, *i*nvolved citizenship, *d*edication to fairness and integrity, and *e*xisting for the customer. In fact, any new manager participating in Blue Bell's management training programs quickly learns that an important part of being a manager for this firm is sharing and following the beliefs expressed by PRIDE.

FIGURE 5-2   **Purposes of Shared Values**

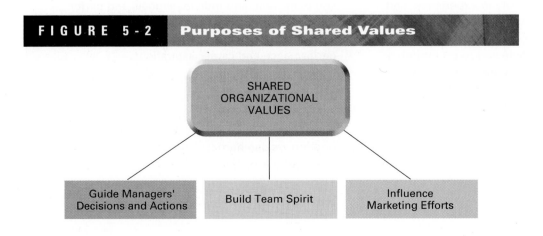

Another purpose of shared values is the impact they have on shaping employee behavior and communicating what the organization expects of its members.[25] Robert Haas, Chairman and CEO of blue-jeans maker Levi Strauss & Company, is committed to bringing social values into the way he runs the business. Haas guided the development of the Levi Strauss Aspirations Statement (Figure 5-3), a major endeavor designed to define the shared corporate values that guide both management and the company's large and diverse workforce. The document provides a clear and concise description of expectations for employee behavior.

Shared corporate values also influence marketing efforts. For example, Avon Products Inc. has made a significant commitment to educating women about breast cancer.[26] Its support for this program came about after the company asked women what their number one

---

FIGURE 5-3   **Levi Strauss Company's Aspirations Statement**

Aspirations Statement

We all want a company that our people are proud of and committed to, where all employees have an opportunity to contribute, learn, grow, and advance based on merit, not politics or background. We want our people to feel respected, treated fairly, listened to, and involved. Above all we want satisfaction from accomplishments and friendships, balanced personal and professional lives, and to have fun in our endeavors.

When we describe the kind of Levi Strauss & Co. we want in the future, what we are talking about is building on the foundation we have inherited: affirming the best of our company's traditions, closing gaps that may exist between principles and practices, and updating some of our values to reflect contemporary circumstances.

What type of leadership is necessary to make our Aspirations a Reality?

New Behaviors: Leadership that exemplifies directness, openness to influence, commitment to the success of others, willingness to acknowledge our own contributions to problems, personal accountability, teamwork, and trust. Not only must we model these behaviors but we must coach others to adopt them.

Diversity: Leadership that values a diverse workforce (age, sex, ethnic group, etc.) at all levels of the organization, diversity in experience, and diversity in perspectives. We have committed to taking full advantage of the rich backgrounds and abilities of all our people and to promoting a greater diversity in positions of influence. Differing points of view will be sought; diversity will be valued and honesty rewarded, not suppressed.

Recognition: Leadership that provides greater recognition—both financial and psychic—for individuals and teams that contribute to our success. Recognition must be given to all who contribute: those who create and innovate and also those who continually support the day-to-day business requirements.

Ethical Management Practices: Leadership that epitomizes the stated standards of ethical behavior. We must provide clarity about our expectations and must enforce these standards through the corporation.

Communications: Leadership that is clear about company, unit, and individual goals and performance. People must know what is expected of them and receive timely honest feedback on their performance and career aspirations.

Empowerment: Leadership that increases the authority and responsibility of those closest to our products and customers. By actively pushing responsibility, trust, and recognition into the organization we can harness and release the capabilities of all our people.

Source: R. Howard, "Values Make the Company: An Interview with Robert Haas," *Harvard Business Review*, September–October 1990, pp. 133–44.

health concern was and breast cancer was the answer. In response, the company created the Avon Worldwide Fund for Women's Health, an umbrella organization that has spread to 19 countries around the world. The company's biggest women's health program under this fund is its Breast Cancer Awareness Crusade. The company's salesforce of more than 440,000 educates women about the disease by bringing brochures on their sales visits. The director of the crusade says, "All of the interaction that happens with an Avon rep on something as important as breast cancer should improve customer relations and make for easier sales." Avon has found a way to link its business to a pressing social concern and to improve its marketing efforts all at the same time.

Finally, shared values are a way to build team spirit in organizations.[27] When employees embrace the stated corporate values, they develop a deeper personal commitment to their work and feel obligated to take responsibility for their actions. Because the shared values influence the way work is done, employees become more enthusiastic about doing things they support and believe in. At companies such as Tom's of Maine, Blue Bell, Avon Products, Levi Strauss, and numerous others, employees know what is expected of them on the job. They use the shared corporate values to shape the way they work. But how do organizations develop a set of shared values?

Developing Shared Values

As any company that uses values-based management will tell you, it's not easy to establish the shared corporate values. At Tom's of Maine, the process involved everyone in the company. All the employees, working in groups of four to six, took a hard look at defining "who are we" and "what are we about." But the commitment by Tom's employees to developing shared corporate values did not stop there. The company's employees realized that they were to actually use the values they helped define and develop; they realized that those shared values really mattered. They began to understand that they were part of a unique corporate culture in which values shaped the business strategy.[28] Also, training programs like those used at Blue Bell are an important way to develop employees' sense of ownership of the corporate values.

A survey of Fortune 1000 companies found that 95 percent of the respondents were convinced they would have to adopt more socially responsible business practices in coming years to preserve their competitive edge.[29] Getting employees to buy into a set of core values that emphasize a commitment to doing good requires strong corporate leadership. Corporate managers are responsible for shaping the organization so that its values, norms, and ideals appeal strongly to employees. Some specific suggestions for developing a good corporate values statement are listed in Table 5-3.

TABLE 5-3	**Suggestions for Creating a Good Corporate Values Statement**

1. Involve everyone in the company.
2. Allow customizing of the values by individual departments or units.
3. Expect and accept employee resistance.
4. Keep the statement short.
5. Avoid trivial statements.
6. Leave out religious references.
7. Challenge it.
8. Live it.

Source: Based on A. Farnham, "State Your Values: Hold the Hot Air," *Fortune,* April 19, 1993, pp. 117–24.

Companies that practice values-based management have accepted a broad perspective regarding their commitment to being socially responsible and socially responsive. One value in particular that many organizational managers are beginning to recognize as important has to do with the environmental responsibility of the organization and of individuals. This "greening" of management is what we're going to look at in the next section.

7 What have research studies found about the relationship between an organization's social involvement and its economic performance?

8 How is values-based management related to the concepts of social responsibility and social responsiveness?

9 What purposes do shared values serve, and how should shared values be developed?

THE "GREENING" OF MANAGEMENT

Until the late 1960s, people (and organizations) paid little attention to the environmental consequences of their decisions and actions.[30] Although there were some groups—mainly the Sierra Club and other environmental activist groups—that were concerned with conserving the land and its natural resources, about the only popular reference to saving the environment you would have seen at that time was the ubiquitous printed request "Please Do Not Litter." A number of highly visible ecological problems and environmental disasters brought about a new awareness and spirit of environmentalism among individuals, groups, and organizations. Increasingly, managers began to confront questions about the natural environment and its impact on organizations. This recognition of the close link between an organization's decisions and activities and its impact on the natural environment is referred to as the **greening of management**. Let's look at some issues managers may have to address as they "go green."

greening of management

The recognition of the close link between an organization's decisions and activities and its impact on the natural environment.

Global Environmental Problems

One "green" issue managers must deal with as they become more involved in preserving the natural environment is recognizing the main global environmental problems and how these problems are changing. The list of global environmental problems is long. Some of the more serious ones include natural resource depletion, global warming, pollution (air, water, and soil), industrial accidents, and toxic wastes. How did these problems occur? Much of the blame can be placed on industrial activities in developed (affluent) countries over the last half century.[31] In fact, various reports have shown that affluent societies account for more than 75 percent of the world's energy and resource consumption and also create most of the industrial, toxic, and consumer waste.[32] Another way of describing the source of global environmental problems is to look at how much land it takes to meet an average consumer's needs. For instance, it takes 12.2 acres to supply the average person's needs in the United States; in the Netherlands, it takes 8 acres; and in India, it takes 1 acre.[33] An equally disturbing aspect of these statistics is that as the world population doubles over the next 50 years and as emerging economies become more market oriented and affluent, global environmental problems can be expected to worsen.[34] However, many organizations, large and small, have accepted their responsibility to respect and protect the natural environment. What role *can* organizations play in addressing global environmental problems? In other words, how can they "go green"?

How Organizations Go Green

There are many things that managers and organizations can do to protect and preserve the natural environment. Some organizations do no more than what is required by law (that is, they fulfill their social obligation); others have made radical changes in the way they do business. Products and production processes have become cleaner. For instance, the case at the end of the chapter tells about the efforts of one individual who is developing radical ecofactories that have completely eliminated pollution in the production process. Many other companies also have made environmentally friendly changes. For example, Whirlpool won an appliance industry competition and a $30 million prize for developing a CFC-free high-efficiency refrigerator. (CFCs, short for chlorofluorocarbons, have been linked to the degradation of the ozone layer surrounding the earth.) The 3M Corporation has been a leader in waste-reduction efforts with its 3 Ps Program (Pollution Prevention Pays), and both Volkswagen and BMW are working to create recyclable automobiles. There are numerous other examples of environmentally friendly actions taken by global organizations. Although these examples may be interesting, they really don't tell us much about how organizations go green. One approach to organizational roles in environmental responsibility uses the term *shades of green* to describe different approaches that organizations may embrace.[35] What are these shades of green?

There are at least four approaches organizations can take with respect to environmental issues. As you can see in Figure 5-4, the first approach simply is doing what is required legally: the *legal approach*. Under this approach, organizations exhibit little environmental sensitivity. They will obey laws, rules, and regulations willingly and without legal challenge, and they may even try to use the law to their own advantage, but that's the extent of their being green. For example, many durable product manufacturers and oil refiners have taken the legal approach and comply with the relevant environmental laws and regulations, but they go no further. This approach is a good illustration of social obligation: These organizations simply are following their legal obligations of pollution prevention and environmental protection. As an organization becomes more aware of and sensitive to environmental issues, it may adopt the *market approach*. Under this approach, organizations respond to the environmental preferences of their customers. Whatever customers demand in terms of environmentally friendly products will be what the organization provides. The DuPont company would be a good example of the market approach as it developed a new type of herbicide that has helped farmers around the world reduce their annual use of chemicals by more than 45 million pounds. By developing this product, DuPont was responding to the demands of its customers (farmers) who wanted to minimize the use of chemicals on their crops. Under the

FIGURE 5-4   Approaches to Being Green

Source: Based on R.E. Freeman, J. Pierce, and R. Dodd, *Shades of Green: Business Ethics and the Environment* (New York: Oxford University Press, 1995).

stakeholders

Any constituency in the external environment that is affected by an organization's decisions and policies.

next approach, the *stakeholder approach*, the organization chooses to respond to multiple demands made by **stakeholders** (any group in the organization's external environment that is affected by an organization's decisions and actions). Under the stakeholder approach, the green organization will work to meet the environmental demands of groups such as employees, suppliers, investors, or the community. For example, Compaq Computer Corporation has developed corporate programs to minimize harmful emissions, to recycle, and to reduce both waste and energy consumption in response to demands by its various stakeholders. Both the market approach and the stakeholder approach are good illustrations of social responsiveness. Finally, if an organization pursues an *activist* (also called a dark green) *approach*, it looks for ways to respect and preserve the earth and its natural resources. For example, Natural Cotton Colours Inc., an Arizona-based company, grows and sells naturally colored cotton that doesn't require bleaching or dying and is naturally resistant to diseases and pests. The activist approach exhibits the highest degree of environmental sensitivity and is a good illustration of social responsibility.

A GUIDE THROUGH THE MAZE

So far, we have presented some themes related to an organization's social responsibility. Unfortunately, they don't lead us down a straight and clear path. In this section, we'll provide a modest guide through the maze to try and clarify the key issues.

The path will become easier to follow if we can identify the people to whom business managers are responsible. Classicists would say that stockholders or owners are their only legitimate concern. Progressives would respond that managers are responsible to any individual or group who is affected by the organization's decisions and policies: that is, the stakeholders.[36]

Figure 5-5 illustrates a four-stage model of the expansion of an organization's social responsibility.[37] What you do as a manager in terms of pursuing social goals depends on the person or persons to whom you believe you're responsible. A Stage 1 manager will promote the stockholders' interests by seeking to minimize costs and maximize profits. At Stage 2, managers will accept their responsibility to their employees and focus on human resource concerns. Because they'll want to get, keep, and motivate good employees, they'll improve working conditions, expand employee rights, increase job security, and the like.

At Stage 3, managers will expand their goals to include fair prices, high-quality products and services, safe products, good supplier relations, and similar practices. Stage 3 managers perceive that they can meet their responsibilities to stockholders only indirectly by meeting the needs of their other constituents.

Finally, Stage 4 characterizes the extreme socioeconomic definition of social responsibility. At this stage, managers are responsible to society as a whole. Their business is seen as a public property, and they are responsible for advancing the public good. The acceptance of such responsibility means that managers actively promote social justice, preserve the environment, and support social and cultural activities. They take these stances even if

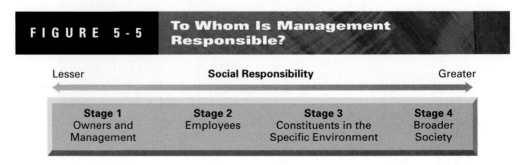

FIGURE 5-5	To Whom Is Management Responsible?

Lesser   **Social Responsibility**   Greater

Stage 1 Owners and Management	Stage 2 Employees	Stage 3 Constituents in the Specific Environment	Stage 4 Broader Society

Interview with José Legaspi, Legaspi Company, Marketing Realty Services, Montebello, California

Describe your job.

I'm president and CEO of the Legaspi Company, a full-service marketing and real estate services company, including development, asset management, property management, and brokerage.

What types of skills do you think tomorrow's managers will need?

I believe that tomorrow's managers will need the ability to hire according to changing demographics in the United States. This also means having the ability to foresee the types of employees needed to implement worldwide business development. The manager must be sensitive to multicultural characteristics and issues, including social and business norms of the persons with whom one is dealing, even if those norms are different from his or her own.

How do you stress the importance of ethics in your job?

Usually any industry is a relatively small circle of interpersonal and interorganizational relationships. Individuals who work in an industry know others who work in the industry and are aware of how they do business. As our business has expanded internationally, we find that the same also is true. Maintaining a high degree of honesty, frankness, and service has provided my company with a corresponding reputation for being ethical in all our business dealings regardless of global location. The fact that others in our industry are aware of the way we treat customers, suppliers, and each other as we carry out our business makes it important for us to manage ethically.

What values do you think are important for organizations?

The values that are important for my company include honesty; frankness; the fervor of following through with people, activities, and expectations; thoroughness; and always making ourselves available to whomever calls on us. ■

such actions negatively affect profits. For instance, Tom Chappell of Tom's of Maine, described earlier, could be considered a Stage 4 manager.

Each stage implies an increasing level of managerial discretion. As managers move to the right along the continuum in Figure 5-5, they have to make more judgment calls. At Stage 4, they are required to impose their values of right and wrong on society. For example, when is a product dangerous to society? Is RJ Reynolds doing "right" for society when it sells Kraft cheese but "wrong" when it sells cigarettes? Or is producing a product with a high fat and sodium content also wrong? Is a public utility company that operates nuclear power plants behaving irresponsibly toward society? Is it wrong for a large global company to take advantage of all legal tax loopholes if doing so means paying little or no tax on billions of dollars in profits? These are the types of judgment calls managers must make.

There's no simple right-wrong dichotomy that can help managers make socially responsible decisions. Clearly, managers of business firms have a basic responsibility to obey the laws in the communities and countries in which they operate and to make a profit. Failure to achieve either of those goals threatens the organization's survival. Beyond that, managers need to identify the people to whom they believe they're responsible. We suggest that by focusing on their stakeholders and their expectations of the organization, managers reduce the likelihood that they will ignore their responsibilities to critical constituencies or alienate them, and they can make responsible choices.

TESTING... TESTING... 1 2 3

10 What is the greening of management, and why is it important?

11 Describe how organizations can go green.

12 What are the four stages of social responsibility, and what role do stakeholders play in each stage?

MANAGERIAL ETHICS

Is it ethical for a salesperson to offer a bribe to a purchasing agent as an inducement to buy? Would it make any difference if the bribe came out of the salesperson's commission? Is it ethical for someone to understate his or her educational qualifications in order to get a job during an economic slump if that person would ordinarily be considered overqualified for the job? Is it ethical for someone to use a company car for private use? How about using the company telephone for personal long distance calls? Is it ethical to ask a company secretary to type personal letters?[38]

ethics

Rules and principles that define right and wrong conduct.

The term **ethics** commonly refers to the rules and principles that define right and wrong conduct.[39] In this section, we look at the ethical dimension of managerial decisions. Many decisions that managers make require them to consider who may be affected—in terms of the result as well as the process.[40] We'll present four different views of ethics and look at the factors that influence a manager's ethics. We'll conclude by offering some suggestions for what organizations can do to improve the ethical behavior of employees.

Levi's CEO Robert Haas has led the effort to build ethics into his company's bottom line. He insists that the "Mr. Clean Jeans" emphasis on values is not just nice behavior but smart business as well.

Four Views of Ethics

There are four perspectives on business ethics.[41] The first is the **utilitarian view of ethics**, in which decisions are made solely on the basis of their outcomes or consequences. Utilitarian theory seeks to provide a quantitative method for making ethical decisions. The goal of utilitarianism is to provide the greatest good for the greatest number. Following the utilitarian view, a manager might conclude that laying off 20 percent of the workforce in her plant is justified because it will increase the plant's profitability, improve job security for the remaining 80 percent, and be in the best interest of stockholders. On the one hand, utilitarianism encourages efficiency and productivity and is consistent with the goal of profit maximization. On the other hand, it can result in biased allocations of resources, especially when some of those affected by the decision lack representation or a voice in the decision. Utilitarianism can also result in the rights of some stakeholders being ignored.

Another ethical perspective is the **rights view of ethics**. This position is concerned with respecting and protecting individual liberties and privileges, including the rights to privacy, freedom of conscience, free speech, and due process. This would include, for example, protecting the rights of employees to free speech when they report violations of laws by their employers. The positive side of the rights perspective is that it protects individuals' freedom and privacy. But it has a negative side in organizations. It can present obstacles to high productivity and efficiency by creating a work climate that is more concerned with legally protecting individuals' rights than with getting the job done.

The next view is the **theory of justice view of ethics**. This calls for managers to impose and enforce rules fairly and impartially. A manager would be using a theory of justice perspective in deciding to pay a new entry-level employee $1.50 an hour over the minimum wage because he or she believes that the minimum wage is inadequate to allow employees to meet their basic financial obligations. Imposing standards of justice also comes with pluses and minuses. It protects the interests of those stakeholders who may be underrepresented or lack power, but it can encourage a sense of entitlement that might make employees reduce risk taking, innovation, and productivity.

The final perspective is a newer approach called the **integrative social contracts theory** view that proposes combining empirical (what is) and normative (what should be) approaches to business ethics. This view of ethics is based on the integration of two "contracts": the general social contract among economic participants that defines the ground rules for doing business and a more specific contract among specific members of a community that covers acceptable ways of behaving. For instance, in deciding what wage to pay workers in a new factory in Ciudad Juarez, Mexico, the integrative social contracts theory would say that an organization would base the decision on existing wage levels in the community. This view of business ethics differs from the other three in that it suggests that managers need to look at existing ethical norms in industries and corporations in order to determine what constitutes right and wrong decisions and actions.

Studies have shown that most businesspeople continue to hold utilitarian attitudes toward ethical behavior.[42] This finding shouldn't be a total surprise because the utilitarian view is consistent with such business goals as efficiency, productivity, and high profits. By maximizing profits, for instance, an executive can argue that he or she is gaining the greatest good for the greatest number.

Because of the changing world of management, that perspective needs to change. Utilitarianism tends to downplay the satisfaction of individual and minority interests for the benefit of the majority, and new trends toward individual rights and social justice mean that managers need ethical standards based on nonutilitarian criteria. This is an obvious challenge to today's manager because making decisions using such criteria as individual rights, social justice, and community standards involves far more ambiguities than using utilitarian criteria such as effects on efficiency and profits. The result, of course, is that managers increasingly find themselves struggling with ethical dilemmas.

utilitarian view of ethics

Decisions are made solely on the basis of their outcomes or consequences.

rights view of ethics

Decisions are concerned with respecting and protecting basic rights of individuals.

theory of justice view of ethics

Decision makers seek to impose and enforce rules fairly and impartially.

integrative social contracts theory

A view that proposes that decisions should be made on the basis of empirical (what is) and normative (what should be) factors.

13 What is ethics, and why is it important for managers to be aware of ethics?

14 Describe the four views of business ethics.

15 Which of the four views of business ethics is most popular among businesspeople? Why?

Factors That Affect Managerial Ethics

Whether a manager acts ethically or unethically is the result of a complex interaction between the manager's stage of moral development and several moderating variables including individual characteristics, the organization's structural design, the organization's culture, and the intensity of the ethical issue.[43] (See Figure 5-6.) People who lack a strong moral sense are much less likely to do the wrong things if they're constrained by rules, policies, job descriptions, or strong cultural norms that disapprove of such behaviors. Conversely, very moral individuals can be corrupted by an organizational structure and culture that permits or encourages unethical practices. Moreover, managers are more likely to make ethical decisions on issues when high moral intensity is involved. Let's look more closely at the various factors that influence whether managers behave ethically or unethically.

Stage of Moral Development.   Substantial research confirms the existence of three levels of moral development, each composed of two stages.[44] At each successive stage, an individual's moral judgment becomes less and less dependent on outside influences. The three levels and six stages are described in Table 5-4.

The first level is labeled *preconventional*. At this level, individuals respond to notions of right or wrong when there are personal consequences involved, such as physical punishment, reward, or exchange of favors. Reasoning at the *conventional* level indicates that moral values reside in maintaining the conventional order and the expectations of others. At the *principled* level, individuals make a clear effort to define moral principles apart from the authority of the groups to which they belong or society in general.

Research on these stages allows us to draw several conclusions.[45] First, people proceed through the six stages in lockstep fashion. They gradually move up a ladder, stage by stage. Second, there is no guarantee of continued moral development. Development can terminate at any stage. Third, the majority of adults are at Stage 4. They are limited to obeying

---

FIGURE 5-6   **Factors That Affect Ethical and Unethical Behavior**

TABLE 5-4	Stages of Moral Development

Level	Description of Stage
Principled	6. Following self-chosen ethical principles even if they violate the law
	5. Valuing rights of others and upholding absolute values and rights regardless of the majority's opinion
Conventional	4. Maintaining conventional order by fulfilling obligations to which you have agreed
	3. Living up to what is expected by people close to you
Preconventional	2. Following rules only when doing so is in your immediate interest
	1. Sticking to rules to avoid physical punishment

Source: Based on L. Kohlberg, "Moral Stages and Moralization: The Cognitive-Developmental Approach," in T. Lickona (ed.), *Moral Development and Behavior: Theory, Research, and Social Issues* (New York: Holt, Rinehart & Winston, 1976), pp. 34–35.

the rules and will be predisposed to behave ethically. For instance, a Stage 3 manager is likely to make decisions that will receive peer approval; a Stage 4 manager will seek to be a "good corporate citizen" by making decisions that respect the organization's rules and procedures; and a Stage 5 manager is likely to challenge organizational practices that he or she believes to be wrong. Many recent efforts by colleges to raise students' ethical awareness and standards are focused on helping them move to the principled level.

Individual Characteristics.   Every person enters an organization with a relatively entrenched set of **values**. Developed in an individual's early years—from parents, teachers, friends, and others—these values represent basic convictions about what is right and wrong. Thus, managers in an organization often possess very different personal values.[46] Note that although *values* and *stage of moral development* may seem similar they are not. The former are broad and cover a wide range of issues; the latter is specifically a measure of independence from outside influences.

Two personality variables have also been found to influence an individual's actions according to his or her beliefs about what is right or wrong: ego strength and locus of control. **Ego strength** is a personality measure of the strength of a person's convictions. People who score high on ego strength are likely to resist impulses and follow their convictions more than those who are low on ego strength. That is, individuals high in ego strength are more likely to do what they think is right. We would expect managers with high ego strength to demonstrate more consistency between moral judgment and moral action than those with low ego strength.

Locus of control is a personality attribute that measures the degree to which people believe they are masters of their own fate. People with an internal locus of control believe that they control their own destinies; those with an external locus believe that what happens to them in life is due to luck or chance. From an ethical perspective, externals are less likely to take personal responsibility for the consequences of their behavior and are more likely to rely on external forces. Internals, on the other hand, are more likely to take responsibility for consequences and rely on their own internal standards of right and wrong to guide their behavior.[47] Managers with an internal locus of control will probably demonstrate more consistency between their moral judgments and moral actions than will external managers.

values

Basic convictions about what is right and wrong.

ego strength

A personality characteristic that measures the strength of a person's convictions.

locus of control

A personality attribute that measures the degree to which people believe they are masters of their own fate.

Doug Thron is a 20-something nature photographer who is fighting a corporate raider in order to save an ancient California forest in Humboldt County from being cut down. Thron is a good example of an individual with high ego strength.

Structural Variables.   An organization's structural design helps shape the ethical behavior of managers. Some structures provide strong guidance, whereas others only create ambiguity for managers. Structural designs that minimize ambiguity and continuously remind managers of what is ethical are more likely to encourage ethical behavior.

Formal rules and regulations reduce ambiguity. Job descriptions and written codes of ethics are examples of formal guides that promote consistent behavior. Research continues to show, though, that the behavior of superiors is the strongest single influence on an individual's own ethical or unethical behavior.[48] People check to see what those in authority are doing and use that as a benchmark for acceptable practices and what is expected of them. Some performance appraisal systems focus exclusively on outcomes. Others evaluate means as well as ends. When managers are evaluated only on outcomes, there are increased pressures to do "whatever is necessary" to look good on the outcome variables. Closely associated with the appraisal system is the way rewards are allocated. The more rewards or punishment depend on specific goal outcomes, the more pressure there is on managers to do whatever they must to reach those goals and perhaps compromise their ethical standards. Structures also differ in the amount of time, competition, cost, and similar pressures placed on jobholders. The greater the pressure, the more likely it is that managers will compromise their ethical standards.

TESTING...
TESTING...

1   2   3

16 Describe the stages of moral development and how they might affect a manager's ethics.

17 What individual characteristics might affect a manager's ethics?

18 How might structural variables affect a manager's ethics?

Organization's Culture.   The content and strength of an organization's culture also influence ethical behavior.[49] An organizational culture most likely to shape high ethical standards is one that is high in risk tolerance, control, and conflict tolerance. Managers in

If it doesn't feel right, chances are there's a reason.

If it doesn't look right, chances are there's a reason.

If it doesn't smell right, chances are there's a reason.

This Boeing Company imaginative poster series reinforces the core value of ethical behavior for its employees by first engaging their interest with humor.

such a culture are encouraged to be aggressive and innovative, are aware that unethical practices will be discovered, and feel free to openly challenge demands or expectations they consider to be unrealistic or personally undesirable.

A strong culture will exert more influence on managers than a weak one. If the culture is strong and supports high ethical standards, it should have a very powerful and positive influence on a manager's ethical behavior. The Boeing Company, for example, has a strong culture that has long stressed ethical corporate dealings with customers, employees, the community, and shareholders. To reinforce the importance of ethical decisions and actions, the company developed a series of light-hearted posters (see page 163) designed to grab employees' attention and then focus on more serious ethics subjects. In a weak organizational culture, however, managers are more likely to rely on subculture norms as a behavioral guide. Work groups and departmental standards will strongly influence ethical behavior in organizations with weak overall cultures.

Issue Intensity.   A student who would never consider breaking into an instructor's office to steal an introductory accounting exam does not think twice about asking a friend who took the same accounting course from the same instructor last year what questions were on the exam. Similarly, an executive might think nothing about taking home a few office supplies yet be highly concerned about the possible embezzlement of company funds.

These examples illustrate the final factor that affects a manager's ethical behavior: the characteristics of the ethical issue itself.[50] As Figure 5-7 shows, six characteristics have been identified as relevant in determining issue intensity:[51]

1. How great a harm (or benefit) is done to victims (or beneficiaries) of the ethical act in question? *Example:* Putting 1,000 people out of work is more harmful than putting only 10 people out of work.

2. How much consensus is there that the act is evil (or good)? *Example:* More Americans agree that it is wrong to bribe a customs official in Texas than agree it is wrong to bribe a customs official in Mexico.

3. What is the probability that the act will actually take place and will actually cause the harm (or benefit) predicted? *Example:* Selling a gun to a known armed robber has greater probability of harm than selling a gun to a law-abiding citizen.

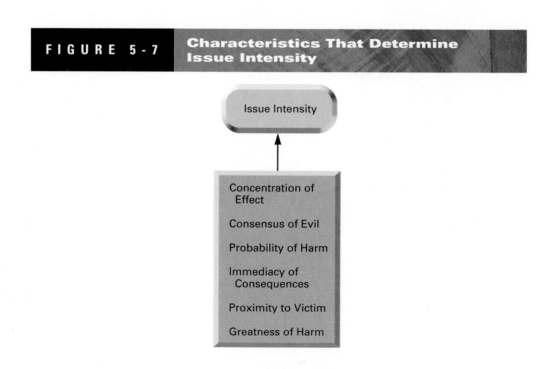

FIGURE 5-7   Characteristics That Determine Issue Intensity

Issue Intensity

Concentration of Effect

Consensus of Evil

Probability of Harm

Immediacy of Consequences

Proximity to Victim

Greatness of Harm

4. What's the length of time between the act in question and its expected consequences? *Example:* Reducing the retirement benefits of current retirees has greater immediate consequences than reducing the retirement benefits of current employees who are between the ages of 40 and 50.

5. How close do you feel (socially, psychologically, or physically) to the victims (or beneficiaries) of the evil (beneficial) act in question? *Example:* Layoffs in one's own work unit hit closer to home than do layoffs in a remote city.

6. How large is the concentrated effect of the ethical act on the people involved? *Example:* A change in the warranty policy denying coverage to 10 people with claims of $10,000 has a more concentrated effect than a change denying coverage to 10,000 people with claims of $10.

According to these guidelines, the larger the number of people harmed, the greater the consensus that an act is evil, the higher the probability that an act will take place and actually cause harm, the shorter the length of time until the consequences of the act surface, and the closer the observer feels to the victims of the act, the greater the issue intensity. In sum, these six factors determine how important an ethical issue is, and we should expect managers to behave more ethically when a moral issue is important to them than when it is not.

19 **How does an organization's culture influence ethical behavior?**

20 **Describe the type of organizational culture that's most likely to shape high ethical standards.**

21 **What determines the degree of intensity of an ethical issue?**

Ethics in an International Context

Are ethical standards universal? Hardly! Social and cultural differences between countries are important environmental factors that determine ethical and unethical behavior. For example, the manager of a Mexican firm bribes several high-ranking government officials in Mexico City to secure a profitable government contract for his firm. Such a practice would be seen as unethical, if not illegal, in the United States. But it is a standard business practice in Mexico.

Should Coca-Cola employees in Saudi Arabia adhere to U.S. ethical standards, or should they follow local standards of acceptable behavior? If Airbus (a European firm) pays a $10 million "broker's fee" to a middleman to get a major contract with a Middle Eastern airline, should Boeing be restricted from doing the same because such practices are considered improper in the United States?

In the case of payments to influence foreign officials or politicians, there is a law to guide U.S. managers. The Foreign Corrupt Practices Act, passed in 1977, makes it illegal for U.S. firms to knowingly corrupt a foreign official. Even this law does not always reduce ethical dilemmas to black and white. In some Latin American countries, for example, government bureaucrats are paid ridiculously low salaries because custom dictates that they receive small payments from those they serve. Payoffs to these bureaucrats "grease the machinery" of government and ensure that things get done. The Foreign Corrupt Practices Act does not expressly prohibit small payoffs to foreign government employees whose duties are primarily ministerial or clerical *when* such payoffs are an accepted part of a country's business practices.

Although it is important for individual managers working in foreign cultures to recognize the various social, cultural, and political and legal influences on what is appropriate and acceptable behavior, global organizations must also clarify their ethical guidelines so that employees know what is expected of them while working in a foreign location. This adds another dimension to making ethical judgments. To confirm their commitment to doing business ethically, many large global organizations, including the Chase Manhattan Corporation, Canon, Inc., Matsushita Electric Industrial Co., Ltd., and Siemens AG, are part of a group called the Caux Round Table.[52] The group's purpose is to focus attention on issues of global corporate responsibility and ethical business. It has outlined seven general principles, ranging from a general declaration of a recognition of the responsibilities of businesses toward stakeholders to respecting rules to avoiding illicit operations (Table 5-5). Why are these companies making this commitment? The members believe that the world business community plays a significant role in improving economic and social conditions.

Toward Improving Ethical Behavior

Top management can do a number of things if they're serious about reducing unethical practices in their organization. They can seek to select individuals with high ethical standards, establish codes of ethics and decision rules, lead by example, delineate job goals, and provide ethics training. Taken individually, these actions will probably not have much impact. But when all or most of them are implemented as part of a comprehensive ethics program, they have the potential to significantly improve an organization's ethical climate. The key term here, however, is *potential*. There are no guarantees that a well-designed ethics program will lead to the outcome desired. Dow Corning, for instance, was long recognized as a pioneer in corporate ethics, and its ethics program had been cited as among the most elaborate in corporate America.[53] But the company's ethics program didn't stop its managers from covering up and misrepresenting the results of studies on their silicone gel breast implants.

Selection.   Given that individuals are at different stages of moral development and possess different personal value systems and personalities, an organization's employee selection process—interviews, tests, background checks, and the like—should be used to eliminate ethically undesirable applicants. This is no easy task! Even under the best of circumstances, individuals with questionable standards of right and wrong will be hired. That outcome is to be expected and needn't pose a problem if other controls are in place.

TABLE 5-5	Principles for Business: Caux Round Table

Principle 1:	The Responsibilities of Business: Beyond Shareholders Toward Stakeholders
Principle 2:	The Economic and Social Impact of Business: Toward Innovation, Justice, and World Community
Principle 3:	Business Behavior: Beyond the Letter of Law Toward a Spirit of Trust
Principle 4:	Respect for Rules
Principle 5:	Support for Multilateral Trade
Principle 6:	Respect for the Environment
Principle 7:	Avoidance of Illicit Operations

Source: Business Ethics, May–June 1995, pp. 26–27.

But the selection process should be viewed as an opportunity to learn about an individual's level of moral development, personal values, ego strength, and locus of control.[54]

Codes of Ethics and Decision Rules.   We've already seen how ambiguity about what is and is not ethical can be a problem for employees. Codes of ethics are an increasingly popular response for reducing that ambiguity.[55] For instance, nearly 90 percent of Fortune 1000 companies have a stated code of ethics.[56]

A **code of ethics** is a formal document that states an organization's primary values and the ethical rules it expects its employees to follow. It has been suggested that codes should be specific enough to show employees the spirit in which they are supposed to do things yet loose enough to allow for freedom of judgment.[57] These suggestions seem to have been applied at Citicorp, as shown in Figure 5-8.

What do most codes of ethics look like? A survey of business ethics—including those of such varied firms as Exxon, Sara Lee, DuPont, Bank of Boston, and Wisconsin Electric Power—found that their content tended to fall into three categories: (1) Be a dependable organizational citizen; (2) do not do anything unlawful or improper that will harm the organization; and (3) be good to customers.[58] Table 5-6 lists the variables included in each of these clusters in order of their frequency of mention. However, another study of over 200 Fortune 500 corporations suggested that many codes of ethics are not as effective as they might be because they omit important issues.[59] Seventy-five percent, for example, failed to address personal character matters, product safety, product quality, environmental affairs, or civic and community affairs. In contrast, more than three-quarters mentioned issues such as relations with the U.S. government, customer and supplier relations, political con-

code of ethics

A formal statement of an organization's primary values and the ethical rules it expects its employees to follow.

FIGURE 5-8   **Code of Ethics**

Citicorp's Basic Principles of Ethical Standards and Conflict of Interest Policy— Committee on Good Corporate Practice

Citicorp has earned a reputation for excellence and integrity while achieving outstanding business success. In order to safeguard our record of integrity, we should be careful to deal with customers who also have high standards of integrity. We should not accept any business plan or individual proposition that might impair Citicorp's reputation.

Committee on Good Corporate Practice

The Committee on Good Corporate Practice is part of Citicorp's continuing program to avoid situations in which our personal interests may conflict or appear to conflict with either Citicorp's or its customers' interests.

The Committee members determine whether or not a conflict of interest exists in a given situation, and advise and assist us whenever questions arise. If we have any doubt as to whether a conflict of interest exists, or whether a situation raises a reasonable question of conflict, we should report the facts to a supervisor and seek guidance. If the supervisor is in doubt, he or she should, in turn, request the Committee's guidance. Questions should be forwarded to the Committee chairman or the Committee secretary through the Corporate Secretary's Office.

There is no wish to inquire into any individual's personal affairs beyond the point that will keep the name of Citicorp above reproach and prevent censure of its people. Each of us must do his or her part in maintaining our high standards by promptly disclosing or submitting for review any situation that could develop into a possible conflict of interest.

Source: Ethical Choices, Citicorp, p. 6.

T A B L E 5 - 6	**Clusters of Variables Found in Eighty-three Corporate Codes of Business Ethics**

Cluster 1. Be a Dependable Organizational Citizen
1. Comply with safety, health, and security regulations.
2. Demonstrate courtesy, respect, honesty, and fairness.
3. Illegal drugs and alcohol at work are prohibited.
4. Manage personal finances well.
5. Exhibit good attendance and punctuality.
6. Follow directives of supervisors.
7. Do not use abusive language.
8. Dress in business attire.
9. Firearms at work are prohibited.

Cluster 2. Do Not Do Anything Unlawful or Improper That Will Harm the Organization
1. Conduct business in compliance with all laws.
2. Payments for unlawful purposes are prohibited.
3. Bribes are prohibited.
4. Avoid outside activities that impair duties.
5. Maintain confidentiality of records.
6. Comply with all antitrust and trade regulations.
7. Comply with all accounting rules and controls.
8. Do not use company property for personal benefit.
9. Employees are personally accountable for company funds.
10. Do not propagate false or misleading information.
11. Make decisions without regard for personal gain.

Cluster 3. Be Good to Customers
1. Convey true claims in product advertisements.
2. Perform assigned duties to the best of your ability.
3. Provide products and services of the highest quality.

Source: F.R. David, "An Empirical Study of Codes of Business Ethics: A Strategic Perspective," paper presented at the 48th Annual Academy of Management Conference, Anaheim, CA, August 1988.

---

tributions, and conflicts of interest. The authors of this study concluded that "codes are really dealing with infractions against the corporation, rather than illegalities on behalf of the corporation."[60] That is, codes tended to give most attention to areas of illegal or unethical conduct that are likely to decrease a company's profits.[61]

In isolation, ethical codes are not likely to be much more than window dressing. Their effectiveness depends heavily on whether management supports them and how employees who break the codes are treated. When management considers them to be important, regularly reaffirms their content, and publicly reprimands rule breakers, ethics codes can supply a strong foundation for an effective corporate ethics program.

Another approach that uses formal written statements to guide employee behavior has been suggested by Laura Nash.[62] She proposes 12 questions to act as decision rules in guiding managers as they handle ethical dimensions in decision making. The questions are listed in Table 5-7.

TABLE 5-7	**Twelve Questions for Examining the Ethics of a Business Decision**

1. Have you defined the problem accurately?
2. How would you define the problem if you stood on the other side of the fence?
3. How did this situation occur in the first place?
4. To whom and to what do you give your loyalty as a person and as a member of the corporation?
5. What is your intention in making this decision?
6. How does this intention compare with the probable results?
7. Whom could your decision or action injure?
8. Can you discuss the problem with the affected parties before you make the decision?
9. Are you confident that your position will be as valid over a long period of time as it seems now?
10. Could you disclose without qualm your decision or action to your boss, your chief executive officer, the board of directors, your family, society as a whole?
11. What is the symbolic potential of your action if understood? If misunderstood?
12. Under what conditions would you allow exceptions to your stand?

Source: Reprinted by permission of *Harvard Business Review*. An exhibit from "Ethics without the Sermon" by L.L. Nash, November–December 1981, p. 81. Copyright © 1981 by the President and Fellows of Harvard College; all rights reserved.

22 What role might the Caux Round Table play in encouraging ethical behavior in global organizations?

23 Describe how the employee selection process might be used to encourage ethical behavior.

24 What are codes of ethics, and how can their effectiveness be improved?

Top Management's Leadership.   Codes of ethics require a commitment from top managers. Why? Because it's the top managers who set the cultural tone. They are role models in terms of both words and actions, though what they do is probably far more important than what they say. If top managers, for example, use company resources for their personal use, inflate their expense accounts, or give favored treatment to friends, they imply that such behavior is acceptable for all employees.

Top managers also set the cultural tone by their reward and punishment practices. The choice of whom and what are rewarded with pay increases and promotions sends a strong message to employees. The promotion of a manager for achieving impressive results in an ethically questionable manner indicates to everyone that those questionable ways are acceptable. When wrongdoing is uncovered, managers must not only punish the wrongdoer but also publicize the fact and make the outcome visible to everyone in the organization. This practice sends another message, "Doing wrong has a price, and it's not in your best interest to act unethically!"

Job Goals.   Employees should have tangible and realistic goals. Explicit goals can create ethical problems if they make unrealistic demands on employees. Under the stress of unrealistic goals, otherwise ethical employees will often take the attitude that "anything goes." When goals are clear and realistic, they reduce ambiguity for employees and motivate rather than punish.

Ethics Training. More and more organizations are setting up seminars, workshops, and similar ethics training programs to try to increase ethical behavior. Ethics researchers estimate that over 40 percent of U.S. companies provide some form of ethics training.[63] But these training programs aren't without controversy. The primary debate is whether you can actually teach ethics. Critics, for instance, stress that the effort is pointless because people establish their individual value systems when they are very young. Proponents, however, note that several studies have found that values can be learned after early childhood. In addition, they cite evidence that shows that teaching ethical problem solving can make an actual difference in ethical behaviors;[64] that training has increased individuals' level of moral development;[65] and that, if it does nothing else, ethics training increases awareness of ethical issues in business.[66]

How do you teach ethics? Let's look at how it's done at Nynex, which is now a part of Bell Atlantic Corporation.[67] When implementing its Code of Business Conduct in November 1995, the company didn't just distribute simple photocopied documents resembling a college term paper that would be thrown in a desk drawer and immediately forgotten. Instead, the company's code came in a three-ring notebook packaged with a 30-minute videotape featuring real-life vignettes portraying key ethics issues that employees might face in the workplace. Managers were also given the mandate of ensuring that every employee—from top to bottom of the organization—attended a code review meeting to become familiar with the information and with the support systems available for guidance. During these code review meetings, managers showed the videotape and used the detailed leader's guide to facilitate discussions on the ethics issues being presented.

Another part of the company's ethics training program is "Plays for Living: The Human Element." These 20- to 25-minute live-action dramas focusing on workplace harassment issues are presented to groups of employees and followed by a group discussion. During the presentation, the actors intermittently step out of their roles to describe their feelings at that particular moment. What this "freeze-frame" technique accomplishes is to bring to light the emotional elements of behavior that typically are not raised voluntarily by employee participants. Managers believe that both the videotape and the live-action dramas bring ethics to life for their employees and make it more relevant to their everyday workplace behaviors.

Ethics training sessions can provide a number of benefits.[68] They reinforce the organization's standards of conduct. They're a reminder that top managers want employees to consider ethical issues in making decisions. They clarify what practices are and are not permissible. Finally, when managers discuss common concerns among themselves, they are reassured that they aren't alone in facing ethical dilemmas. This reassurance can strengthen their confidence when they have to take unpopular but ethically correct stances.

Comprehensive Performance Appraisal. When performance appraisals focus only on economic outcomes, ends will begin to justify means. If an organization wants its managers to uphold high ethical standards, it must include this dimension in its appraisal process. For example, a manager's annual review might include a point-by-point evaluation of how his or her decisions measured against the company's code of ethics as well as on the more traditional economic criteria. Needless to say, if the manager looks good on the economic criteria but scores poorly on ethical conduct, appropriate action needs to be taken.

TESTING... TESTING...

25 What role does top management's leadership play in encouraging ethical behavior? In establishing job goals?

26 Describe how ethics training programs are used to encourage ethical behavior.

27 If an organization wishes to encourage ethical behavior, how should its performance appraisal program be designed?

Independent Social Audits.　An important element of unethical behavior is fear of being caught. Independent audits, which evaluate decisions and management practices in terms of the organization's code of ethics, increase the likelihood of detection. These audits can be routine evaluations, performed on a regular basis just as financial audits are, or they can occur randomly with no prior announcement. An effective ethical program should probably include both. To maintain integrity, the auditors should be responsible to the company's board of directors and present their findings directly to the board. This practice not only gives the auditors clout, but also lessens the opportunity for retaliation from those being audited.

Formal Protective Mechanisms.　Our last recommendation is for organizations to provide formal mechanisms so that employees who face ethical dilemmas can do something about them without fear of reprimand. An organization might, for instance, designate ethical counselors. When employees face a dilemma, they could go to these advisers for guidance. The ethical counselor's role would be first, a sounding board, a channel to let employees openly verbalize their ethical problem, the problem's cause, and their own options. Then, after the options are clear, the adviser might take the role of an advocate who champions the "right" alternatives. In fact, according to the director of the Center for Business Ethics at Bentley College, around 20 percent of corporations now have ethics officers. The organization might also create a special appeals process that employees could use without risk to themselves to raise ethical issues or blow the whistle on violators.[69]

A FINAL THOUGHT

It seems that current news headlines abound with stories of ethically questionable practices at large and well-known companies: Nike and Wal-Mart using overseas sweatshop labor to manufacture clothing and tennis shoes; Sears using strong-arm tactics in collecting consumer debts; sales agents at Prudential using deceptive sales practices to push policyholders to make questionable insurance choices and decisions; managers at Archer Daniels Midland (ADM) engaging in price fixing; and Bausch and Lomb using deceptive accounting principles and practices in order to meet strictly numbers-oriented performance goals. What's going on? Has ethics taken a back seat in business?

A recent survey shows that workplace pressures are leading more and more employees to consider acting unethically or illegally on the job. The study developed by the Ethics Officer Association in conjunction with the American Society of Chartered Life Underwriters and Chartered Financial Consultants surveyed a cross section of 5,000 American workers from various household income levels and occupational categories.[70] The results indicated that 56 percent of those surveyed felt pressure to act unethically or illegally on the job, with 48 percent having said they actually committed such activities. What types of unethical business activities were reported? Here is a sampling that respondents admitted to: cut corners on quality control (16 percent); covered up incidents (14 percent); abused or lied about sick days (11 percent); lied to or deceived customers (9 percent); put inappropriate pressure on others (7 percent); falsified numbers or reports (6 percent); lied to or deceived superiors on serious matters (5 percent); withheld important information (5 percent); misused or stole company property (4 percent); took credit for someone's work or idea (4 percent); and engaged in copyright or software infringement (3 percent).

Unfortunately, unethical behaviors aren't prevalent just in the workplace. On campuses across the United States, cheating on tests is rising even at campuses with honor codes. A 1996 study of 4,300 students at 31 highly selective colleges (14 of which had honor codes) reported that 30 percent of students at the schools with honor codes had cheated on a test (this percentage had risen from a previous study conducted in 1990).[71] At schools without honor codes, 45 percent reported that they had cheated on a test (this percentage had actually fallen slightly from the 1990 study). What majors cheated the most? The survey said business students, followed by engineering majors.

What are the implications for managers, current and future? Doing the right thing—that is, managing ethically—isn't always easy. However, because society's expectations of its institutions are regularly changing, managers must continually monitor those expectations. What is ethically acceptable today may be a poor guide for the future.

**TESTING...
TESTING...**

28 How could independent social audits be used to encourage ethical behavior?

29 What types of formal protective mechanisms could an organization implement to encourage ethical behavior?

30 Provide some statistics about the status of ethical behavior in the workplace. What are the implications for managers?

managers respond to "a manager's dilemma"

MANAGER 1

When an employee contracts hepatitis A, the public relations and financial effects on a restaurant may be serious. Reasons that a business might choose to withhold the information include: The announcement creates a negative image of the business, and there is a potential for lost sales and income.

Nonetheless, it's important that the restaurant owners make a public announcement of possible exposure of patrons to hepatitis A. Prompt notification may prevent additional cases by giving persons the opportunity to get treatment with immune globulin. In order to be effective, immune globulin must be administered within two weeks of exposure. Therefore, prompt public announcement of the exposure is very important. An owner in this situation should first seek the advice of the public health department and coordinate their efforts, because intensive and coordinated efforts are required for controlling hepatitis A outbreaks. Public health authorities can provide information and recommend treatment for persons exposed. The reasons why Mr. Mericle should go public include: Hepatitis A is a serious disease, and, although individuals rarely die from it, they could; the costs associated with medical care and work loss are high; preventive measures are available and can reduce the spread of the virus; the media may be the only effective way to quickly reach patrons who were exposed; and the public expects businesses to be socially responsible and to put the health and safety of their clients above their own financial interests.

Debra Barnhart, M.P.H.,Vice President, St. John's Regional Health System, Springfield, Missouri

MANAGER 2

The owner has a choice: Go public with the information and risk losing business, or tell only the health department as required by law and leave hundreds of people exposed to a serious virus. To go public would most certainly damage the business and might even be so serious as to bankrupt it. Employees would likely have their hours greatly reduced or be laid off. Such a decision would affect the lives of many more people than just the owner and his family. However, telling only the health department would have much greater consequences. Hundreds of people could contract the virus and become ill. In turn, the people they come in contact with would also be exposed. Such a turn of events could lead to an epidemic that could literally be spread around the country.

This comes down to a matter of right and wrong. The only right thing to do is to go public with the information. My company has a mission statement that very clearly identifies our shared values. We are very interested in achieving a reasonable return on our investment, but we are likewise committed to acting in a manner consistent with Christian values and ethics.

Business managers in all sizes and types of organizations have a social responsibility to the community they serve. Acting ethically may not maximize profits in the short term, but it will most likely have the largest long-term return.

Jerry Henry, Director of Research/Database, Silver Dollar City, Branson, Missouri

for your
IMMEDIATE
action

Prime
HEALTHCARE PROVIDERS

TO: Frank Flokstra, Director of Corporate Legal Affairs
FROM: Van Sifferman, CEO
SUBJECT: Protecting Whistleblowers

I'm sure you're well aware of the public embarrassment that our company has suffered over the Brenda Matheny "whistleblower" case. She argued in court that top managers had ignored her claims that several executives in our Clinic Division, where she worked, were providing false information in padding Medicare reimbursement claims in order to make profit performance goals. She said she also feared reprisal from her direct supervisors if she informed on them. That was her defense for going directly to the federal authorities with her allegations.

The loss of this case (and the $3 million settlement) makes it very clear that we have a serious problem. It's not enough that we fired the three managers involved in this scheme. We must do something immediately to change the ethical climate in our organization. No employee should need to go to outside authorities if he or she perceives wrongdoing. Employees must feel secure in knowing that we maintain high ethical standards and will protect any employee who reports unethical practices.

Although this case is now closed, we must ensure that something like this never happens again. I want you to provide me a written plan (not to exceed two pages in length) that describes specifically what we can do to (1) encourage employees to speak out if they see any wrongdoings and (2) protect them when they do so.

This organization has been disguised for obvious reasons.

SUMMARY

This summary is organized by the chapter-opening objectives found on p. 140.

1. According to the classical view, business's only social responsibility is to maximize financial returns for stockholders. The opposing socioeconomic view holds that business has a responsibility to the larger society.

2. The arguments for business's being socially responsible include public expectations, long-run profits, ethical obligation, public image, a better environment, fewer governmental regulations, balancing of responsibility and power, stockholder interests, possession of resources, and the superiority of prevention over cures. The arguments against hold that social responsibility violates the profit-maximization objective, dilutes the organization's purpose, costs too much, gives business too much power, requires skills that business does not have, lacks accountability, and lacks wide public support.

3. Social obligation is when an organization has met its economic and legal responsibilities and no more. Social responsiveness refers to the capacity of a firm to respond to social pressures and is guided by social norms. Social responsibility refers to business's pursuit of long-term goals that are good for society and requires business to determine what is right or wrong by seeking out fundamental ethical truths.

4. Most research studies show a positive relationship between corporate social involvement and economic performance. The evidence does not find that acting in a socially responsible way significantly reduces a corporation's long-term economic performance.

5. Values-based management refers to an approach to managing in which managers establish, promote, and practice the organization's shared values. The shared values make up the organization's culture and influence the way the organization operates and employees behave.

6. The greening of management is the recognition of the close link between an organization's decisions and activities and its impact on the natural environment. Organizations might go green using any of four approaches: the legal approach, the market approach, the stakeholder approach, and the activist approach.

7. A stakeholder is any constituency in an organization's environment that is affected by the organization's decisions and policies. By focusing on the organization's stakeholders and their expectations of the organization, management is not likely to ignore its responsibilities to critical constituencies.

8. *Ethics* refers to rules or principles that define right and wrong conduct.

9. The utilitarian view makes decisions on the basis of their outcomes or consequences. The rights view seeks to respect and protect basic rights of individuals. The theory of justice view seeks to impose and enforce rules fairly and impartially. The integrative social contracts view recognizes the implicit contracts between organizations and the ethical standards of the community within which they operate.

10. Whether a manager acts ethically or unethically is the result of a complex interaction between the manager's stage of moral development, his or her individual characteristics, the organization's structural design, the organization's culture, and the intensity of the ethical issue.

11. There are three levels of moral development, each comprising two stages. The first two stages are influenced exclusively by an individual's personal interests. Stages 3 and 4 are influenced by the expectations of others. Stages 5 and 6 are influenced by personal ethical principles of what is right.

12. A comprehensive ethical program would include selection to weed out ethically undesirable job applicants, a code of ethics and decision rules, a commitment by top management, clear and realistic job goals, ethics training, comprehensive performance appraisals, independent social audits, and formal protective mechanisms.

THINKING ABOUT MANAGEMENT ISSUES

1. What does social responsibility mean to you? Do you think business firms should be socially responsible? Why?

2. Do you think values-based management is just a "do-gooder" ploy? Explain your answer.

3. Find two examples of companies that fit the profile of each of the four approaches to going green. For each example, describe what specific activities the company is doing. (You will probably need to do some research at the library or on the Internet.)

4. A whistleblower is someone who reports his or her employer's unethical practices to outsiders. What are some problems that could be associated with employee whistleblowing for (a) the whistleblower and (b) the organization?

5. Describe the characteristics and behaviors of what you would consider an ethical manager.

SELF-ASSESSMENT EXERCISE

ATTITUDES TOWARD BUSINESS ETHICS QUESTIONNAIRE

Instructions: Indicate your level of agreement with these 18 statements about business ethics using the scale of 1 (strongly disagree) to 5 (strongly agree).

        5 = Strongly agree
        4 = Agree
        3 = Neither agree nor disagree
        2 = Disagree
        1 = Strongly disagree

	Strongly Agree			Strongly Disagree	
1. The only moral of business is making money.	5	4	3	2	1
2. A person who is doing well in business does not have to worry about moral problems.	5	4	3	2	1
3. Every businessperson acts according to moral principles, whether he or she is aware of it or not.	5	4	3	2	1
4. Act according to the law, and you can't go wrong morally.	5	4	3	2	1
5. Ethics in business is basically an adjustment between expectations and the ways people behave.	5	4	3	2	1
6. Business decisions involve a realistic economic attitude and not a moral philosophy.	5	4	3	2	1
7. Moral values are irrelevant to the business world.	5	4	3	2	1
8. "Business ethics" is a concept for public relations only.	5	4	3	2	1
9. Competitiveness and profitability are important values.	5	4	3	2	1
10. Conditions of a free economy will best serve the needs of society. Limiting competition can only hurt society and actually violates basic natural laws.	5	4	3	2	1
11. As a consumer, when making an auto insurance claim, I try to get as much as possible regardless of the extent of the damage.	5	4	3	2	1

	Strongly Agree				Strongly Disagree
12. While shopping at the supermarket, it is appropriate to switch price tags on packages.	5	4	3	2	1
13. As an employee, I can take home office supplies; it doesn't hurt anyone.	5	4	3	2	1
14. I view sick days as vacation days that I deserve.	5	4	3	2	1
15. Employees' wages should be determined according to the laws of supply and demand.	5	4	3	2	1
16. If you want a specific goal, you have to take the necessary steps.	5	4	3	2	1
17. The business world has its own rules.	5	4	3	2	1
18. A good businessperson is a successful businessperson.	5	4	3	2	1

Turn to page SK–3 to compare your scores with those of other management and liberal arts students.

Source: A. Reichel and Y. Neumann, *Journal of Instructional Psychology*, March 1988, pp. 25–33. Reprinted with permission of authors.

TAKE IT TO THE NET

We invite you to visit the Robbins/Coulter companion Web site at http://www.prenhall.com/robbinsmgt for this chapter's Internet resources.

CASE APPLICATION

Being Green

Gunter Pauli, a native of Belgium now living in Tokyo, represents a whole new breed of businessperson: a social entrepreneur. His philosophy is that twenty-first-century companies will have to be not only financially sustainable but socially sustainable as well. Is Pauli a radical environmental activist with unrealistic and idealistic notions or an insightful visionary?

Pauli's business background and credentials are impressive. He graduated from INSEAD (a prestigious European business school) and spent several years traveling across Europe lecturing and consulting for IBM, the global computer company. He's written eight management books and is fluent in six languages. But he considers himself more of a social crusader than a business leader. Since 1992, he has championed an ambitious program challenging how conventional companies work. He wants to create manufacturing facilities that function as closed-loop systems—that is, factories that completely eliminate waste by reusing or recycling all the raw materials

they take in. Pauli calls this approach zero-emissions manufacturing and believes it is the next big breakthrough in business productivity. Total quality management meant zero defects. Just-in-time manufacturing meant zero inventories. In zero emissions, you're striving for zero waste, you use everything. You completely eliminate waste. He says, "This is part of the drive for higher productivity. We're always pushing to do more with labor and capital. It's time to focus on the productivity of raw materials. Zero emissions sounds radical today. In 20 years it will be standard operating procedure."

This "radical" operating concept is already in effect in a few places around the globe. Pauli is the former CEO of Ecover, a small Belgian company that produces cleaning products (laundry powder, dishwashing liquid, shampoos, car wax, and other products) from natural soaps and renewable raw materials. Ecover opened a near-zero-emissions factory in October 1992 in Malle, Belgium. What is unique about this factory is that it's a "green" marvel. A huge grass roof keeps the factory cool in summer and warm in winter. The water treatment system runs on wind and solar energy. The bricks in the factory walls are made of recycled clay from coal mines. But Pauli doesn't even like the term *green* to describe Ecover's products or its factory. He says that most people assume that *green* means lousy performance at a high price. Instead, what Ecover does is develop high-technology products based on a mastery of the chemistry of renewable resources. It's in the business of pioneering sustainable economic and social development.

Pauli believed that the media sensation created by Ecover's green factory was a prime opportunity to create a global product brand by opening more factories around the world, but his lead investor and partner preferred a more cautious approach. So Pauli left Ecover and moved to Tokyo to work for the United Nations University and the Zero Emissions Research Initiative (ZERI). From there he coordinates a global network of scientists, corporate executives, and political leaders who are piecing together zero-emissions technology and documenting its performance benefits. ZERI's budget for 1995 was $2 million; for 1996, $10 million; and in 1997, Pauli was developing a $50 million investment fund (to be financed by various world governments) that would underwrite zero-emissions factories in different industries around the world. In fact, construction was completed in mid-1997 on the world's most unconventional brewery in Namibia in southern Africa. The brewery was designed as a model of what zero-emissions factories would be like. Pauli describes it as a fully integrated biosystem. Water (the brewing process wastes massive amounts of water) flows from the brewery into the ponds designed for fish farming. Mushrooms grow on piles of used grain (brewing also requires huge supplies of grain) from the fermentation process. Chickens feed on earthworms turned loose in the grain. The waste from the chickens is put into a machine called a digester, which generates methane gas that produces steam for the fermentation process. Pauli says, "Does it make sense—morally, environmentally, economically—just to waste those resources? Is there no food shortage in the world?"

QUESTIONS

1. What view of social responsibility would you call Gunter Pauli's approach, and at what stage of social responsibility would you place his activities? Explain your choices.
2. What stakeholders would be most important to ZERI? Explain your choices.
3. What do you think ZERI's Statement of Values might include? Keep it brief (one page or less). You might want to look at Levi Strauss's Aspirations Statement on p.152 for guidance.
4. What's your opinion of Gunter Pauli's crusade for zero-emissions production? Is it smart business? Do you agree? Disagree? Why? Be prepared to defend your answers in class.

Source: S. Butler, "Green Machine," *Fast Company Web Page*, <http://www.fastcompany.com>, April 16, 1997.

When You Care Enough to Send the Very Best

Although "caring enough to send the very best" may be the marketing slogan for the world's largest manufacturer of greeting cards, caring and compassion also are fitting descriptions of Judi Jacobsen's Madison Park Greeting Card Company of Seattle, Washington. The slogan, however, would have to be changed to "caring enough to *do* the very best." Jacobsen's compassion is directed at the community where her business is located and at the people she employs.

At the age of 30, Jacobsen decided to pursue her desire to paint. People who saw and bought her paintings told her that they would make good greeting cards. Taking that advice to heart, together with a partner, Jacobsen started Madison Park Greeting Card Company. Today she sells her greeting cards in more than 4,000 specialty shops around the United States. Madison Park employs 25 people and has reached the $3 million sales mark. The admirable part of this story is not just the fact that Jacobsen was able to pursue her dream but also that she had a strong commitment to helping others. Her community involvement started with her decision to locate her business in a rundown section of town and to help revitalize the area. In addition, she has a strong and specific concern for her employees.

Jacobsen's management philosophy is that one of the best things you can do for your people is to give them meaningful work. To put this philosophy into practice, she has hired Cambodian refugees who couldn't speak English but who could pack cards into boxes. She has hired hearing-impaired employees and displaced mothers for other jobs at Madison Park. Jacobsen strongly believes that people count more than the bottom line and that, although she understands that businesses must do well to be able to help others, having a balance between profits and people is important. She says, "If I had to choose people or profits, I'd put people first."

QUESTIONS

1. What types of values do you think Judi Jacobsen's Madison Park Greeting Card Company embraces?
2. Would you call Judi Jacobsen socially responsive or socially responsible? Explain your choice.
3. Using Figure 5-5, in which stage of social responsibility would you place Madison Park? Explain your choice.
4. What's your opinion of Judi's statement, "If I had to choose people or profits, I'd put people first"? What would this type of philosophy imply as far as management decisions and actions?

Source: Based on *Small Business 2000, Show 104.*

LEARNING OBJECTIVES

After reading this chapter, you should be able to

1 Outline the steps in the decision-making process

2 Explain why decision making is so pervasive in organizations

3 Describe the rational decision maker

4 Describe the perfectly rational decision-making process

5 Describe the boundedly rational decision-making process

6 Explain the role that intuition plays in the decision-making process

7 Identify the two types of decision problems and the two types of decisions that are used to solve them

8 Differentiate the decision conditions of certainty, risk, and uncertainty

9 Describe the different decision-making styles

A MANAGER'S DILEMMA

How would you like to take a managerial position in an organization whose customers complained constantly and loudly about the poor level and quality of service and in which your efforts to improve things were essentially thwarted because your budget to run the business was continually being sliced away bit by bit? That's the type of challenging situation that Shirley DeLibero faced when she took over as executive director of the New Jersey Transit Department.[1]

Before DeLibero took over this job, irate customers who used the Transit Department's trains and buses complained loudly because the equipment was frequently late. In addition, the government decision makers in charge of making budget allocations to the department were providing significantly less funding to run and maintain the transit system's equipment.

The transit system also had a long-running history of annual fare hikes and poor equipment maintenance, which led to continual breakdowns and contributed to the

problem with the transit systems' trains and buses frequently running behind schedule. Customers were paying more for the service and getting significantly less satisfactory service! No wonder they complained constantly! Also, because of these widespread organizational problems, the individuals in the transit workers' union—the people who actually drove the buses and the trains—had low morale. This was another problem for DeLibero to tackle: how to address the concerns, dissatisfactions, and anxieties of the department's drivers.

DeLibero wasn't overwhelmed by all these challenges. As the highest ranking African-American woman in the public transportation industry, she had faced challenges before in the various transportation management positions she had held. The key to straightening out the Transit Department's problems would be making good managerial decisions, and doing that begins with employee morale. How could you use the steps in the decision process to start addressing the employee morale problems that faced the Transit Department? Put yourself in DeLibero's situation. Using the steps in the managerial decision-making process, describe how you would tackle the concerns of the Transit Department's employees.

WHAT WOULD YOU DO?

Like managers everywhere around the globe, Shirley DeLibero needs to make good decisions at the New Jersey Transit Department. Making good decisions is something that every manager strives to do since the overall quality of managerial decisions goes a long way in determining organizational success or failure. In this chapter, we examine the concept of decision making and how managers make decisions.

CHAPTER

6

Decision Making:

The Essence of

the Manager's Job

THE DECISION-MAKING PROCESS

decision

A choice made from two or more alternatives.

decision-making process

A set of eight steps that include identifying a problem, selecting an alternative, and evaluating the decision's effectiveness.

problem

A discrepancy between an existing and a desired state of affairs.

Individuals at all levels and in all areas of organizations make **decisions**. That is, they make choices from two or more alternatives. For instance, top-level managers make decisions about their organization's goals, where to locate manufacturing facilities, what new markets to move into, and what products or services to offer. Middle and lower-level managers make decisions about weekly or monthly production schedules, handling problems that arise, allocating pay raises, and selecting or disciplining employees. But making decisions isn't something that just managers do. All organizational members make decisions that affect their jobs and the organization they work for. How are decisions made? What's involved with making decisions?

Although decision making is typically described as "choosing among alternatives," that view is overly simplistic. Why? Because decision making is a comprehensive process not just a simple act of choosing among alternatives.

Figure 6-1 illustrates the **decision-making process** as a set of eight steps that begins with identifying a problem and decision criteria and allocating weights to those criteria; moves to developing, analyzing, and selecting an alternative that can resolve the problem; implements the alternative; and concludes with evaluating the decision's effectiveness. This process is as relevant to your personal decision about where you will take your summer vacation as it is to a corporate action such as Frito Lay's decision to introduce a new low-sodium, low-fat snack. The process also can be used to describe both individual and group decisions. Let's take a closer look at the process in order to understand what each step involves.

Step 1: Identifying a Problem

The decision-making process begins with the existence of a **problem** or, more specifically, a discrepancy between an existing and a desired state of affairs.[2] Let's develop an example that illustrates this point and that we can use throughout this section. To keep it simple, let's make the example something most of us can relate to: the decision to buy a new notebook computer. Take the case of a sales manager whose sales representatives need new notebook computers because their old ones just don't have enough memory or aren't fast enough to handle the volume of work anymore. Again, for simplicity's sake, assume that it's not economical to add memory to the old ones and that corporate headquarters requires that the managers purchase new computers rather than lease them. Now we have a problem. There's a disparity between the need of the sales representatives to have large, fast notebooks and their having ones that are at capacity and slow. The sales manager has a decision to make.

Unfortunately, this example doesn't tell us much about how managers identify problems. In the real world, most problems don't come with neon signs in bright bold colors flashing "problem." The sales representatives' complaints about slow computers with disk drives at capacity might be a clear signal to the sales manager that she needs to get them new notebook computers, but few problems are quite that obvious. Is a 5 percent decline in sales a problem? Or are declining sales merely a symptom of another problem, such as product obsolescence or poor advertising? Also, keep in mind that one manager's problem is another manager's satisfactory state of affairs. Problem identification is subjective. Furthermore, the manager who mistakenly solves the wrong problem perfectly is likely to perform just as poorly as the manager who fails to identify the right problem and does nothing. Problem identification is neither a simple nor an insignificant step of the decision-making process.[3] Before something can be characterized as a problem, managers have to be aware of the discrepancy, they have to be under pressure to take action, and they must have the resources necessary to take action.[4] Figure 6-2 shows the characteristics of a problem.

FIGURE 6-1   The Decision-Making Process

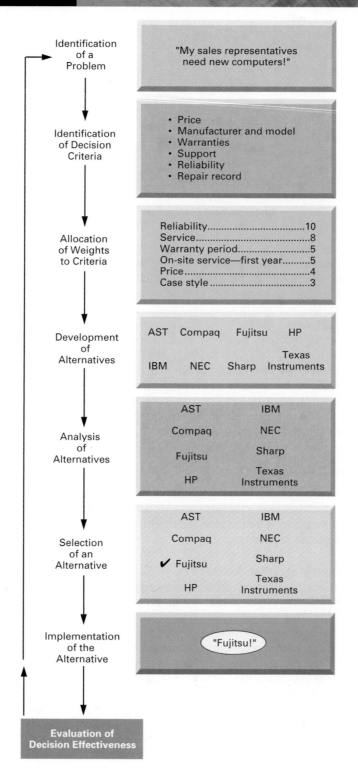

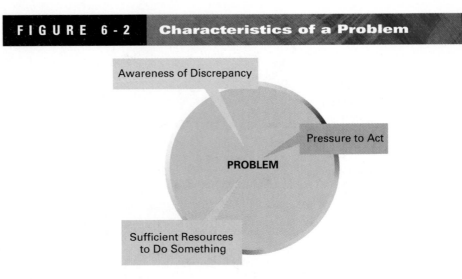

FIGURE 6-2   Characteristics of a Problem

Awareness of Discrepancy

Pressure to Act

PROBLEM

Sufficient Resources
to Do Something

How do managers become aware they have a discrepancy? They obviously have to make a comparison between their current state of affairs and some standard. What is that standard? It can be past performance, previously set goals, or the performance of some other unit within the organization or in other organizations. In our computer buying example, the standard is past performance—having computers that hold all the critical product and sales information so that the sales representatives can efficiently run the desired programs.

A discrepancy without pressure becomes a problem that can be put off to some future time. To initiate the decision process, then, the problem also must be such that it exerts some type of pressure on the manager to act. Pressure might include organizational policies, deadlines, financial crises, complaints from customers or subordinates (look at the chapter-opening case and the customer and employee complaints that Shirley DeLibero had to deal with), expectations from the boss, or an upcoming performance evaluation.

Finally, managers aren't likely to characterize something as a problem if they perceive that they don't have the authority, budget, information, or other resources necessary to act on it. When managers perceive a problem and are under pressure to act, but feel they have inadequate resources, they usually describe the situation as one in which unrealistic expectations are being placed on them.

Step 2: Identifying Decision Criteria

decision criteria

Criteria that define what is relevant in a decision.

Once a manager has identified a problem that needs attention, the **decision criteria** important to resolving the problem must be identified. That is, managers must determine what's relevant in making a decision. In our computer buying example, the sales manager has to assess what factors are relevant to her decision. These might include criteria such as price, product model and manufacturer, standard features, optional equipment, service warranties, repair record, and service support after purchase. These criteria reflect what the sales manager thinks is relevant in her decision.

Whether they are explicitly stated or not, every decision maker has criteria that guide his or her decisions. Note that, in this step in the decision-making process, what isn't identified is as important as what is. If the sales manager doesn't consider a service warranty to be a criterion, then it will not influence her final choice of computers. Thus, if a decision maker doesn't identify a particular feature as a criterion in this second step, it's treated as irrelevant.

When making decisions, as in our computer purchase example, managers must identify the criteria—model, brand, price, warranty period— that are important.

1 What is a decision, and who makes decisions in organizations?

2 In the first step of the decision-making process, how do managers know there is a problem?

3 What are decision criteria, and why are they important to the decision-making process?

TESTING... TESTING...

1 2 3

Step 3: Allocating Weights to the Criteria

The criteria listed in the previous step aren't all equally important, so the decision maker must weight the items in order to give them the correct priority in the decision. How do you weight criteria? A simple approach is merely to give the most important criterion a weight of 10 and then assign weights to the rest against that standard. Thus, in contrast to a criterion that you gave a 5, the highest factor would be twice as important. Of course, you could use 100 or 1,000 or any number you select as the highest weight. The idea is to use your personal preferences to assign a priority to the relevant criteria in your decision as well as to indicate their degree of importance by assigning a weight to each.

Table 6-1 lists the criteria and weights that our sales manager developed for her computer replacement decision. Reliability is the most important criterion in her decision, with such factors as case style and price having low weights.

TABLE 6-1	Criteria and Weights for Computer Replacement Decision

Criterion	Weight
Reliability	10[a]
Service	8
Warranty period	5
On-site service—first year	5
Price	4
Case style	3

[a]In this example, the highest rating for a criterion is 10 points.

Step 4: Developing Alternatives

The fourth step requires the decision maker to list the viable alternatives that could resolve the problem. No attempt is made in this step to evaluate these alternatives, only to list them. Let's assume that our plant manager has identified eight notebook computer models as viable choices. These are AST Ascentia A42, Compaq Armada 4100, Fujitsu LifeBook 555T, HP OmniBook 5500CT, IBM ThinkPad 760ED, NEC Versa 2435CD, Sharp WideNote W-100T, and Texas Instruments TravelMate 6050.

Step 5: Analyzing Alternatives

Once the alternatives have been identified, the decision maker must critically analyze each one. The strengths and weaknesses of each alternative become evident as they are compared with the criteria and weights established in Steps 2 and 3.

Each alternative is evaluated by appraising it against the criteria. Table 6-2 shows the assessed values that the plant manager gave each of her eight alternatives after she had talked to computer experts and read the latest information from computer magazines.

Keep in mind that the ratings given the eight computer models shown in Table 6-2 are based on the personal assessment made by the sales manager. Again, we're using a 1 to 10 scale. Some assessments can be achieved in a relatively objective fashion. For instance, the purchase price represents the best price the manager can get from local retailers, and consumer magazines report performance data from users. But the assessment of reliability is clearly a personal judgment. The point is that most decisions contain judgments. They are reflected in the criteria chosen in Step 2, the weights given to the criteria, and the evaluation of alternatives. This explains why two computer buyers with the same amount of money may look at two totally different sets of alternatives or even look at the same alternatives and rate them differently.

Table 6-2 represents only an assessment of the eight alternatives against the decision criteria. It doesn't reflect the weighting done in Step 3. If one choice had scored 10 on every criterion, you wouldn't need to consider the weights. Similarly, if the weights were all equal, you could evaluate each alternative merely by summing up the appropriate lines in Table 6-2. For instance, the AST Ascentia A42 would have a score of 34, and the IBM ThinkPad 760ED a score of 45. If you multiply each alternative assessment (Table 6-2) against its weight (Table 6-1), you get Table 6-3. The sum of these scores represents an evaluation of each alternative against the previously established criteria and weights. Notice that the weighting of the criteria has significantly changed the ranking of alternatives in our example.

TABLE 6-2	Assessed Values of Notebook Computer Alternatives against Decision Criteria					
Model	Reliability	Service	Warranty	On-site Service	Price	Case Style
AST Ascentia A42	8	3	5	10	3	5
Compaq Armada 4100	8	5	10	5	6	5
Fujitsu LifeBook 555T	10	8	5	10	3	10
HP OmniBook 5500CT	8	5	5	10	3	10
IBM ThinkPad 760ED	6	8	5	10	6	10
NEC Versa 2435CD	10	8	5	5	3	10
Sharp WideNote W-100T	2	10	5	10	10	10
Texas Instruments TravelMate 6050	4	10	5	10	10	5

TABLE 6-3	Evaluation of Notebook Computer Alternatives against Criteria and Weights						
Model	**Reliability**	**Service**	**Warranty**	**On-site Service**	**Price**	**Case Style**	**Total**
AST Ascentia A42	80	24	25	50	12	15	206
Compaq Armada 4100	80	40	50	25	24	15	234
Fujitsu LifeBook 555T	100	64	25	50	12	30	281
HP OmniBook 5500CT	80	40	25	50	12	30	237
IBM ThinkPad 760ED	60	64	25	50	24	30	253
NEC Versa 2435CD	100	64	25	25	12	30	256
Sharp WideNote W-100T	20	80	25	50	40	30	245
Texas Instruments TravelMate 6050	40	80	25	50	40	15	250

Step 6: Selecting an Alternative

The sixth step is the critical act of choosing the best alternative from among those listed and assessed. We have determined all the pertinent factors in the decision, weighted them appropriately, and identified the viable alternatives. Now we merely have to choose the alternative that generated the highest score in Step 5. In our computer purchase example (Table 6-3), the decision maker would choose the Fujitsu LifeBook 555T computer. On the basis of the criteria identified, the weights given to the criteria, and the decision maker's assessment of each computer company's ranking on the criteria, the Fujitsu computer scored highest (281 points) and thus became the "best" alternative.

Step 7: Implementing the Alternative

Although the choice process is completed in the previous step, the decision may still fail if it isn't implemented properly. Therefore, Step 7 is concerned with putting the decision into action.

Implementation includes conveying the decision to those affected and getting their commitment to it. As we will discuss in chapter 14, groups or teams can help a manager achieve commitment. If the people who must carry out a decision participate in the process, they're more likely to enthusiastically support the outcome than if they are just told what to do. For instance, if in our decision example the sales representatives had participated in the purchase decision they would be likely to enthusiastically accept the new machines and any new training necessary. (Parts Three through Five of this book detail how decisions are implemented by effective planning, organizing, and leading.)

implementation

Conveying a decision to those affected and getting their commitment to it.

Step 8: Evaluating Decision Effectiveness

The last step in the decision-making process appraises the result of the decision to see whether the problem has been resolved. Did the alternative chosen in Step 6 and implemented in Step 7 accomplish the desired result? The evaluation of results is detailed in Part Six of this book, where we look at the control function.

What would happen if, as a result of this evaluation, the problem still existed? The manager would then need to dissect carefully what went wrong. Was the problem incorrectly defined? Were errors made in the evaluation of the various alternatives? Was the right alternative selected but improperly implemented? Answers to questions like those might send the manager back to one of the earlier steps. It might even require starting the whole decision process over.

THE PERVASIVENESS OF DECISION MAKING

Everyone in organizations makes decisions, but decision making is particularly important in every aspect of a manager's job. As Table 6-4 illustrates, decision making is part of all four managerial functions. That is why managers—when they plan, organize, lead, and control—are frequently called *decision makers.* In fact, it is correct to say that *decision making* is synonymous with *managing.*[5]

The fact that almost everything a manager does involves decision making doesn't mean that decisions are always long, involved, or clearly evident to an outside observer. Much of a manager's decision-making activity is routine. Every day of the year you make a decision about the problem of when to eat lunch. It's no big deal. You've made the decision thousands of times before. It offers few problems and can usually be handled quickly. It is the type of decision you almost forget *is* a decision. Managers make dozens of these routine decisions every day. Keep in mind that even though a decision seems easy to make or has been faced by a manager a number of times before, it is a decision nonetheless.

**TESTING...
TESTING...**
1 2 3

4 Why is the allocation of weights to criteria important to decision making?

5 How do managers develop, analyze, select, and implement alternatives and then assess whether the decision was effective?

6 Why are managers typically described as decision makers?

TABLE 6-4	**Decisions in the Management Functions**

Planning
What are the organization's long-term objectives?
What strategies will best achieve those objectives?
What should the organization's short-term objectives be?
How difficult should individual goals be?

Organizing
How many subordinates should I have report directly to me?
How much centralization should there be in the organization?
How should jobs be designed?
When should the organization implement a different structure?

Leading
How do I handle employees who appear to be low in motivation?
What is the most effective leadership style in a given situation?
How will a specific change affect worker productivity?
When is the right time to stimulate conflict?

Controlling
What activities in the organization need to be controlled?
How should those activities be controlled?
When is a performance deviation significant?
What type of management information system should the organization have?

THE MANAGER AS DECISION MAKER

Although we have described the steps in the decision-making process, we still don't know much about the manager as a decision maker and how decisions are actually made in organizations. How can we best describe the decision-making situation and the person who makes the decisions? In this section we look at those issues. We'll start by looking at three perspectives on how decisions are made.

Making Decisions: Rationality, Bounded Rationality, and Intuition

Managerial decision making is assumed to be **rational**. By that we mean that managers make consistent, value-maximizing choices within specified constraints.[6] What are the underlying assumptions of rationality, and how valid are those assumptions?

Assumptions of Rationality.   A decision maker who was perfectly rational would be fully objective and logical. He or she would define a problem carefully and would have a clear and specific goal. Moreover, the steps in the decision-making process would consistently lead toward selecting the alternative that maximizes the likelihood of achieving that goal. Figure 6-3 summarizes the assumptions of rationality.

- *Problem clarity.* In rational decision making, the problem is clear and unambiguous. The decision maker is assumed to have complete information regarding the decision situation.

- *Goal orientation.* In rational decision making there is no conflict over the goal. Whether the decision involves purchasing a new notebook computer, selecting a college to attend, choosing the proper price for a new product, or picking the right job applicant to fill a vacancy, the decision maker has a single, well-defined goal that he or she is trying to reach.

- *Known options.* It is assumed that the decision maker is creative, can identify all the relevant criteria, and can list all the viable alternatives. Further, the decision maker is aware of all the possible consequences of each alternative.

- *Clear preferences.* Rationality assumes that the criteria and alternatives can be ranked according to their importance.

rational

Describes choices that are consistent and value-maximizing within specified constraints.

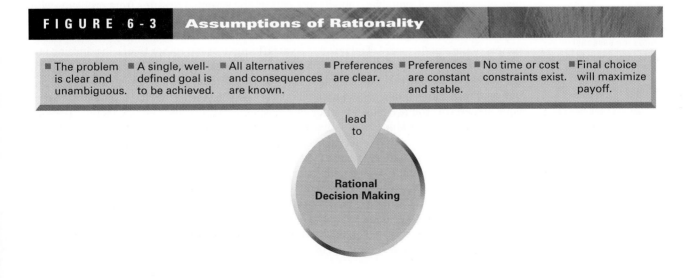

FIGURE 6-3   Assumptions of Rationality

| ■ The problem is clear and unambiguous. | ■ A single, well-defined goal is to be achieved. | ■ All alternatives and consequences are known. | ■ Preferences are clear. | ■ Preferences are constant and stable. | ■ No time or cost constraints exist. | ■ Final choice will maximize payoff. |

lead to

Rational Decision Making

■ *Constant preferences.* In addition to a clear goal and preferences, it's assumed that the specific decision criteria are constant and that the weights assigned to them are stable over time.

■ *No time or cost constraints.* The rational decision maker can obtain full information about criteria and alternatives because it's assumed that there are no time or cost constraints.

■ *Maximum payoff.* The rational decision maker always chooses the alternative that will yield the maximum payoff.

Those assumptions of rationality apply to any decision. Because we're concerned with managerial decision making in an organization, however, we need to add one further assumption. Rational managerial decision making assumes that decisions are made in the best *economic* interests of the organization. That is, the decision maker is assumed to be maximizing the organization's interests, not his or her own interests.

How realistic are these assumptions about rationality? Managerial decision making can follow rational assumptions if the following conditions are met: The manager is faced with a simple problem in which the goals are clear and the alternatives limited, in which the time pressures are minimal and the cost of seeking out and evaluating alternatives is low, for which the organizational culture supports innovation and risk taking, and in which the outcomes are relatively concrete and measurable.[7] But most decisions that managers face in the real world don't meet all those tests.[8] So how are most decisions in organizations actually made? The concept of bounded rationality can help answer that question.

Bounded Rationality. Despite the limits to perfect rationality, managers are expected to appear to follow the rational process when making decisions.[9] Managers know that "good" decision makers are supposed to do certain things: identify problems, consider alternatives, gather information, and act decisively but prudently. Managers can thus be expected to exhibit the correct decision-making behaviors. By doing so, managers signal to their superiors, peers, and subordinates that they are competent and that their decisions are the result of intelligent and rational deliberation.

Table 6-5 summarizes how the perfectly rational manager would proceed through the eight-step decision process. But we already know that this perfectly rational model of decision making isn't realistic with respect to managerial decision making. Instead, managers tend to operate under assumptions of **bounded rationality**.[10] Look again at Table 6-5 for a description of how decisions are made under bounded rationality. In bounded rationality, managers construct simplified models that extract the essential features from problems without capturing all their complexity. Then, given information-processing limitations and constraints imposed by the organization, managers attempt to behave rationally within the parameters of the simple model. The result is a **satisficing** decision rather than a maximizing one: that is, a decision in which the solution is satisfactory, or "good enough." Let's look at an example. Suppose that you're a finance major and upon graduation you want a job, preferably as a personal financial planner, with a minimum salary of $28,000 and within a hundred miles of your hometown. You accept a job offer as a business credit analyst—not exactly a personal financial planner but still in the finance field—at a bank 50 miles from home at a starting salary of $28,500. A more comprehensive job search would have revealed a job in personal financial planning at a trust company only 25 miles from your hometown and starting at a salary of $30,000. Because the first job offer was satisfactory (or "good enough"), you behaved in a boundedly rational manner by accepting it, although according to the assumptions of perfect rationality, you didn't maximize your decision by searching all possible alternatives.

The implications of bounded rationality on the manager's job must not be overlooked. In situations in which the assumptions of perfect rationality don't apply (including most of the important and far-reaching decisions a manager makes), the details of the decision-

bounded rationality

Behavior that is rational within the parameters of a simplified model that captures the essential features of a problem.

satisficing

Acceptance of solutions that are "good enough."

T A B L E 6 - 5	*Two Views of the Decision-Making Process*	

Decision-making Step	Perfect Rationality	Bounded Rationality
1. Problem formulation	An important and relevant organizational problem is identified.	A visible problem that reflects the manager's interests and background is identified.
2. Identification of decision criteria	All criteria are identified.	A limited set of criteria is identified.
3. Allocation of weights to criteria	All criteria are evaluated and rated in terms of their importance to the organization's goal.	A simple model is constructed to evaluate and rate the criteria; the decision maker's self-interest strongly influences the ratings.
4. Development of alternatives	A comprehensive list of all alternatives is developed creatively.	A limited set of similar alternatives is identified.
5. Analysis of alternatives	All alternatives are assessed against the decision criteria and weights; the consequences for each alternative are known.	Beginning with a favored solution, alternatives are assessed, one at a time, against the decision criteria.
6. Selection of an alternative	*Maximizing decision*: the one with the highest economic outcome (in terms of the organization's goal) is chosen.	*Satisficing decision*: the search continues until a solution is found that is satisfactory and sufficient, at which time the search stops.
7. Implementation of alternative	Because the decision maximizes the chance of achieving the single, well-defined goal, all organizational members will embrace the solution.	Politics and power considerations will influence the acceptance of, and commitment to, the decision.
8. Evaluation	The decision's outcome is objectively evaluated against the original problem.	Measurement of the decision's results are rarely so objective as to eliminate self-interests of the evaluator; possible escalation of resources to prior commitments despite both previous failures and strong evidence that allocation of additional resources is not warranted.

making process are strongly influenced by the organization's culture, internal politics, power considerations, and even by the decision maker's use of intuitive decision making.

Role of Intuition.   What role does intuition play in managerial decision making? Managers regularly use their intuition, and it may actually help improve their decision making.[11] What is **intuitive decision making**? It's an unconscious process of making decisions on the basis of experience and accumulated judgment. Making decisions on the basis of "gut feeling" doesn't necessarily happen independently of rational analysis; rather, the two complement each other. A manager who has had experience with a particular, or even similar,

intuitive decision making

An unconscious process of making decisions on the basis of experience and accumulated judgment.

This humorous ad for the Fujitsu Corporation acknowledges the power of intuitive decision making.

type of problem or situation often can act quickly with what appears to be limited information. Such a manager doesn't rely on a systematic and thorough analysis of the problem or identification and evaluation of alternatives but instead uses his or her experience and judgment to make a decision. How common is intuitive decision making? One survey of managers and other organizational employees revealed that almost one-third of them emphasized "gut feeling" over cognitive problem solving and decision making.[12]

Whether managers use perfect rationality, bounded rationality, or intuition in making decisions, organizational reality is that they're likely to face different types of problem situations. What are the types of problem situations a manager might face in organizational decision making? That's what we look at next.

7 Describe decision making from the rationality viewpoint.

8 Describe decision making from the bounded rationality perspective.

9 Describe the role of intuition in decision making.

Types of Problems and Decisions

Managers will be faced with different types of problems and decisions as they do their jobs: that is, as they integrate and coordinate the work of others. Depending on the nature of the problem, the manager can use different types of decisions.

Well-Structured Problems and Programmed Decisions.   Some problems are straightforward. The goal of the decision maker is clear, the problem is familiar, and information about the problem is easily defined and complete. Examples of these types of problems might include a customer's wanting to return a purchase to a retail store, a supplier's being late with an important delivery, a news team's responding to an unexpected and fast-breaking event, or a college's handling of a student's wanting to drop a class. Such situations are called **well-structured problems**. For instance, a server in a restaurant spills a drink on a customer's coat. The restaurant manager has an upset customer. What does the manager do? Because drinks are frequently spilled, there's probably some standardized routine for handling the problem. For example, if the server was at fault, if the damage was significant, and if the customer asks for a remedy, the manager will offer to have the coat cleaned at the restaurant's expense. In handling this problem situation, the manager uses a **programmed decision**.

Decisions are programmed to the extent that they are repetitive and routine and to the extent that a definite approach has been worked out for handling them. Because the problem is well structured, the manager does not have to go to the trouble and expense of working up an involved decision process. Programmed decision making is relatively simple and tends to rely heavily on previous solutions. The "develop-the-alternatives" stage in the decision-making process either doesn't exist or is given little attention. Why? Because once the structured problem is defined, its solution is usually self-evident or at least reduced to very few alternatives that are familiar and that have proved successful in the past. In many cases, programmed decision making becomes decision making by precedent. Managers simply do what they and others previously have done in the same situation. The spilled drink on the customer's coat does not require the restaurant manager to identify and weight decision criteria or to develop a long list of possible solutions. Rather, the manager falls back on a systematic procedure, rule, or policy.

A **procedure** is a series of interrelated sequential steps that a manager can use for responding to a structured problem. The only real difficulty is in identifying the problem. Once the problem is clear, so is the procedure. For instance, a purchasing manager receives a request from the sales department for 15 cellular phones for use by the company's sales representatives. The purchasing manager knows that there is a definite procedure for handling this decision. The decision-making process in this case is merely executing a simple series of sequential steps.

Information technology is being used to further simplify the development of organizational procedures. Some powerful new software programs are being designed that automate routine and complex procedures. For example, at Hewlett-Packard, a comprehensive software program has automated a quarterly wage-review process of more than 13,000 salespeople.

A **rule** is an explicit statement that tells a manager what he or she ought or ought not to do. Rules are frequently used by managers when they confront a well-structured problem because they are simple to follow and ensure consistency. For example, rules about lateness and absenteeism permit supervisors to make disciplinary decisions rapidly and with a relatively high degree of fairness.

A third guide for making programmed decisions is a **policy**. It provides guidelines to channel a manager's thinking in a specific direction. In contrast to a rule, a policy establishes parameters for the decision maker rather than specifically stating what should or should not be done. Policies typically contain an ambiguous term that leaves interpretation up to the decision maker. For instance, each of the following is a policy statement:

The customer always comes first and should always be *satisfied*.

We promote from within, *whenever possible*.

Employee wages shall be *competitive* for the community in which our plants are located.

Notice that *satisfied, whenever possible,* and *competitive* are terms that require interpretation. The policy to pay competitive wages does not tell a given plant's human

well-structured problems

Straightforward, familiar, easily defined problems.

programmed decision

A repetitive decision that can be handled by a routine approach.

procedure

A series of interrelated sequential steps that can be used to respond to a structured problem.

rule

An explicit statement that tells managers what they ought or ought not to do.

policy

A guide that establishes parameters for making decisions.

resources manager the exact amount he or she should pay, but it does give direction to the decision he or she makes.

Ill-Structured Problems and Nonprogrammed Decisions. As you can well imagine, not all problems managers face are well-structured and solvable by a programmed decision. Many organizational situations involve **ill-structured problems**, which are problems that are new or unusual. Information about such problems is ambiguous or incomplete. For example, the selection of an architect to design a new corporate headquarters building is one example of an ill-structured problem. So too is the problem of whether to invest in a new, unproven technology or whether to shut down a money-losing division. When problems are ill-structured, managers must rely on nonprogrammed decision making in order to develop unique solutions. **Nonprogrammed decisions** are unique and nonrecurring. When a manager confronts an ill-structured problem, or one that is unique, there is no cut-and-dried solution. It requires a custom-made response through nonprogrammed decision making.

Integration. Figure 6-4 describes the relationship among the types of problems, the types of decisions, and organizational level. Whereas well-structured problems are resolved with programmed decision making, ill-structured problems require nonprogrammed decision making. Because lower-level managers confront familiar and repetitive problems, they most typically rely on programmed decisions such as standard operating procedures, rules, and organizational policies. The problems confronting managers are likely to become more ill-structured as they move up the organizational hierarchy. Why? Because lower-level managers handle the routine decisions themselves and send up the chain of command only decisions that they find unusual or difficult. Similarly, higher-level managers pass along routine decisions to their subordinates so that they can deal with more difficult issues.

Keep in mind, however, that few managerial decisions in the real world are either fully programmed or nonprogrammed. These are extremes, and most decisions fall somewhere in between. Few programmed decisions are designed to eliminate individual judgment completely. At the other extreme, even a unique situation requiring a nonprogrammed decision can be helped by programmed routines. It's best to think of decisions as *mainly* programmed or *mainly* nonprogrammed, rather than as completely one or the other.

A final point on this topic is that organizational efficiency is facilitated by the use of programmed decision making, which may explain its wide popularity. Whenever possible,

ill-structured problems

New problems in which information is ambiguous or incomplete.

nonprogammed decision

A unique decision that requires a custom-made solution.

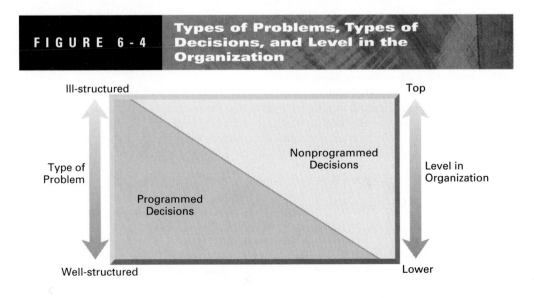

FIGURE 6-4 Types of Problems, Types of Decisions, and Level in the Organization

You're in charge of hiring a new employee to work in your area of responsibility, and one of your friends from college needs a job. You think he's qualified for the position, but you feel that you could find a better qualified and more experienced candidate if you kept looking. What will you do? Why? What factors will influence your decision? What will you tell your friend? ■

management decisions are likely to be programmed. Obviously, using programmed decisions is not too realistic at the top level of the organization because most of the problems that top managers confront are of a nonrecurring nature. But there are strong economic incentives for top managers to create standard operating procedures (SOPs), rules, and policies to guide other managers.

Programmed decisions minimize the need for managers to exercise discretion. This fact is relevant because discretion can cost money. The more nonprogrammed decision making a manager is required to do, the greater the judgment needed. Because sound judgment is an uncommon quality, it costs more to acquire the services of managers who possess it.

Some organizations try to economize by hiring less-skilled managers but do not develop programmed decision guides for them to follow. Take, for example, a small women's clothing store chain whose owner, because he chooses to pay low salaries, hires store managers with little experience and limited ability to make good judgments. This practice, by itself, might not be a problem. The trouble is that the owner provides neither training nor explicit rules and procedures to guide his store managers' decisions. The result is continuous complaints by customers about things such as promotional discounts, processing credit sales, and the handling of returns.

One of the more challenging tasks facing managers as they make decisions—programmed or nonprogrammed—is analyzing decision alternatives (Step 5 in the decision-making process). In the next section, we will look at analyzing alternatives under different conditions.

10 Describe well-structured problems and programmed decisions.

11 Differentiate between procedures, policies, and rules.

12 Describe ill-structured problems and nonprogrammed decisions.

Decision-Making Conditions

There are three conditions that managers may face as they make decisions: certainty, risk, and uncertainty. What are the characteristics of each of these decision-making conditions?

Certainty.   The ideal situation for making decisions is one of **certainty**; that is, the manager is able to make perfectly accurate decisions because the outcome of every alternative is known. For example, when Missouri's state treasurer is deciding in which bank to deposit excess state funds, he knows exactly how much interest is being offered by each bank and will be earned on the funds. He is certain about the outcomes of each alternative. As you might expect, this condition isn't characteristic of the situations in which most managerial decisions are made. It's more idealistic than realistic.

Risk.   A far more common situation is one of **risk**. By risk, we mean those conditions in which the decision maker is able to estimate the likelihood of certain alternatives or outcomes. This ability to assign probabilities to outcomes may be the result of personal expe-

certainty

A situation in which a manager can make accurate decisions because the outcome of every alternative is known.

risk

Those conditions in which the decision maker is able to estimate the likelihood of certain outcomes.

rience or secondary information. Under the conditions of risk, the manager has historical data that allow him or her to assign probabilities to different alternatives. Let's work through an example.

Suppose that you manage a ski resort in the Colorado Rockies. You're thinking about adding another lift to your current facility. Obviously, your decision will be significantly influenced by the amount of additional revenue that the new lift would generate, and additional revenue will depend on the level of snowfall. The decision is made somewhat clearer when you're reminded that you have reasonably reliable past data on snowfall levels in your area. The weather data show that during the past 10 years, you had three years of heavy snowfall, five years of normal snow, and two years of light snow. Can you use this information to determine the expected future annual revenue if the new lift is added? If you have good information on the amount of revenues for each level of snow, the answer is Yes.

You can create an expected value formulation; that is, you can compute the conditional return from each possible outcome by multiplying expected revenues by snowfall probabilities. The result is the average revenue you can expect over time if the given probabilities hold. As Table 6-6 shows, the expected revenue from adding a new ski lift is $687,500. Of course, whether that justifies a Yes or a No decision depends on the costs involved in generating that revenue—factors such as the cost of building the lift, the additional annual operating expenses for another lift, the interest rate for borrowing money, and so forth.

Uncertainty.   What happens if you have to make a decision when you're not certain about the outcomes and cannot even make reasonable probability estimates? We call such a condition **uncertainty**. Many decision-making situations managers face are ones of uncertainty. Under conditions of uncertainty, the choice of alternative is influenced by the limited amount of information available to the decision maker.

Another factor that influences choice under conditions of uncertainty is the psychological orientation of the decision maker. The optimistic manager will follow a *maximax* choice (maximizing the maximum possible payoff), the pessimist will pursue a *maximin* choice (maximizing the minimum possible payoff), and the manager who desires to minimize his maximum "regret" will opt for a *minimax* choice. Let's look at these different choice approaches using an example.

Consider the case of a marketing manager at Visa International in New York. He has determined four possible strategies (S_1, S_2, S_3, and S_4) for promoting the Visa card throughout the northeastern United States. But the marketing manager is also aware that one of his major competitors, MasterCard, has three competitive actions (CA_1, CA_2, and CA_3) of its own for promoting its own card in the same region. In this case, we'll assume that the Visa executive has no previous knowledge that would allow him to place probabilities on the suc-

uncertainty

A situation in which a decision maker has neither certainty nor reasonable probability estimates available.

| TABLE 6-6 | Expected Value for Revenues from the Addition of One Ski Lift |

Event	Expected Revenues	× Probability =	Expected Value of Each Alternative
Heavy snowfall	$850,000	0.3	$255,000
Normal snowfall	725,000	0.5	362,500
Light snowfall	350,000	0.2	70,000
			$687,500

TABLE 6-7	**Payoff Matrix**		

(in millions of dollars)

Visa Marketing Strategy	MasterCard's Response		
	CA_1	CA_2	CA_3
S_1	13	14	11
S_2	9	15	18
S_3	24	21	15
S_4	18	14	28

cess of any of his four strategies. With these facts, the Visa manager formulates the matrix in Table 6-7 to show the various Visa strategies and the resulting profit to Visa depending on the competitive action chosen by MasterCard.

In this example, if our Visa manager is an optimist he'll choose S_4, because that could produce the largest possible gain: $28 million. Note that this choice maximizes the maximum possible gain (maximax choice).

If our manager is a pessimist, he'll assume that only the worst can occur. The worst outcome for each strategy is as follows: S_1 = $11 million; S_2 = $9 million; S_3 = $15 million; S_4 = $14 million. These are the most pessimistic outcomes from each strategy. Following the maximin choice, he would maximize the minimum payoff; in other words, he'd select S_3.

In the third approach, managers recognize that once a decision is made it will not necessarily result in the most profitable payoff. There may be a regret of profits forgone (given up)—*regret* referring to the amount of money that could have been made had a different strategy been used. Managers calculate regret by subtracting all possible payoffs in each category from the maximum possible payoff for each given event, in this case for each competitive action. For our Visa manager, the highest payoff, given that MasterCard engages in CA_1, CA_2, or CA_3, is $24 million, $21 million, or $28 million, respectively (the highest number in each column). Subtracting the payoffs in Table 6-7 from those figures produces the results shown in Table 6-8.

The maximum regrets are S_1 = $17 million; S_2 = $15 million; S_3 = $13 million; and S_4 = $7 million. The minimax choice minimizes the maximum regret, so our Visa manager would choose S_4. By making this choice, he'll never have a regret of profits forgone of more than $7 million. This result contrasts, for example, with a regret of $15 million had he chosen S_2 and MasterCard had taken CA_1.

TABLE 6-8	**Regret Matrix**		

(in millions of dollars)

Visa Marketing Strategy	MasterCard's Response		
	CA_1	CA_2	CA_3
S_1	11	7	17
S_2	15	6	10
S_3	0	0	13
S_4	6	7	0

Interview with Graham Jones, Owner, G.L.A. Interiors, Toronto, Ontario, Canada

Describe your job.

I'm the owner and manager of a custom millwork and cabinetry shop that specializes in commercial office interiors. My personal responsibilities include sales, estimating costs, project management, and of course, general management of a company that has successfully doubled its sales every year for the last three years.

What kinds of skills do you think tomorrow's managers will need?

Time management! The pace of business operations definitely has increased! Tomorrow's manager must be able to think on the move and be able to make quick, effective decisions. You must be able to anticipate and avoid problems. You must be flexible enough to deal with the ever-changing conditions and circumstances any project may go through during its lifespan. The challenge is to avoid feeling pressured by the time constraints and not make hasty or ineffective decisions that will cost both time and money.

This chapter makes the point that decision making is the essence of the manager's job. What's your interpretation of this?

The group follows the leader. The ability to make effective decisions allows work to flow smoothly and be uninterrupted from start to finish, always moving forward with momentum. This results in high-quality work being done on time and within the budget.

What suggestions do you have for making effective decisions?

Information! To make effective decisions, you must know and understand the product you're selling. You must know what resources you have and the strengths and weaknesses of those resources so they may be used to their maximum potential. You must know the full status of any given project, not just your portion. Your work affects the other parts of the main project and vice versa. The most important key to effective decision making *is* information and having it as up-to-date as possible. ■

Although managers will try to analyze the numbers when possible by using payoff and regret matrixes, uncertainty often forces them to rely more on hunches, intuition, creativity, and "gut feel."

Regardless of the decision conditions, each manager is going to have his or her own style of making decisions. That's the final topic discussed in this chapter.

13 What are the characteristics of decision making under the condition of certainty?

14 Describe the characteristics of decision making under the condition of risk.

15 How might a manager deal with making decisions under conditions of uncertainty?

Decision-Making Styles

Suppose you were a new manager at the Gillette Company or at the local YMCA. How would you tackle problems that arise and that need decisions made? Managers have different styles when it comes to making decisions and solving problems. One view of decision-making styles proposes that there are three ways managers approach problems in the workplace; they're either problem avoiders, problem solvers, or problem seekers.[13] What are the characteristics of each approach?

A **problem avoider** ignores information that points to a problem. Avoiders are inactive and do not want to confront problems. A **problem solver** tries to solve problems when they come up. Solvers are reactive; they deal with problems after they occur. **Problem seekers** actively seek out problems to solve or new opportunities to pursue. They take a proactive approach by anticipating problems. Managers can, and do, use all three approaches. For example, there are times when avoiding a problem is the best response. At other times, being reactive is the only option because the problem happens so quickly. And innovative, creative organizations need managers who proactively seek opportunities and ways to do things better.

Another perspective on decision-making styles proposes that people differ along two dimensions in the way they approach decision making.[14] The first is an individual's *way of thinking*. Some of us tend to be rational and logical in the way we think or process information. A rational type looks at information in order and makes sure that it's logical and consistent before making a decision. Others of us tend to be creative and intuitive. Intuitive types don't have to process information in a certain order but are comfortable looking at it as a whole.

The other dimension describes an individual's *tolerance for ambiguity*. Again, some of us have a low tolerance for ambiguity and must have consistency and order in the way we structure information so that ambiguity is minimized. On the other hand, some of us can tolerate high levels of ambiguity and are able to process many thoughts at the same time. When we diagram these two dimensions, four decision-making styles are formed: directive, analytic, conceptual, and behavioral (Figure 6-5). Let's look more closely at each style.

■ *Directive style.* People using the **directive style** have low tolerance for ambiguity and are rational in their way of thinking. They're efficient and logical. Directive types make fast decisions and focus on the short run. Their efficiency and speed in making decisions often result in their making decisions with minimal information and assessing few alternatives.

■ *Analytic style.* Decision makers with an **analytic style** have much greater tolerance for ambiguity than do directive types. They want more information before making a decision and consider more alternatives than a directive style decision maker does. Analytic decision makers are best characterized as careful decision makers with the ability to adapt or cope with unique situations.

---

problem avoider

A person who approaches problems by avoiding or ignoring information that points to a problem.

problem solver

A person who approaches problems by trying to solve them as they come up.

problem seeker

A person who approaches problems by actively seeking out problems to solve or new opportunities to pursue.

directive style

A decision-making style that is characterized by a low tolerance for ambiguity and a rational way of thinking.

analytic style

A decision-making style that is characterized by a high tolerance for ambiguity and a rational way of thinking.

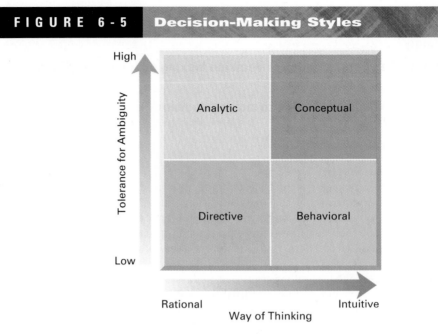

FIGURE 6-5 **Decision-Making Styles**

Source: S.P. Robbins and D.A. De Cenzo, *Supervision Today*, 2d ed. (Upper Saddle River, NJ: Prentice Hall, 1998), pp. 166.

conceptual style

A decision-making style that is characterized by a high tolerance for ambiguity and an intuitive way of thinking.

behavioral style

A decision-making style that is characterized by a low tolerance for ambiguity and an intuitive way of thinking.

■ *Conceptual style.* Individuals with a **conceptual style** tend to be very broad in their outlook and will look at many alternatives. They focus on the long run and are very good at finding creative solutions to problems.

■ *Behavioral style.* **Behavioral style** decision makers work well with others. They're concerned about the achievements of subordinates and are receptive to suggestions from others. They often use meetings to communicate, although they try to avoid conflict. Acceptance by others is important to the behavioral style decision maker.

Although these four decision-making styles are distinct, most managers have characteristics of more than one style. It's probably more realistic to think of a manager's dominant style and his or her alternate styles. Although some managers will rely almost exclusively on their dominant style, others are more flexible and can shift their style depending on the situation.

How do decision-making styles vary from country to country? For example, Huang Yantian, president of Guangdong International Trust and Investment Corporation, makes all key decisions, as do the chief executives of most Chinese companies. How does his decision-making style differ from that of Jack Welch at General Electric? The Managing Workforce Diversity box discusses some of the differences in decision-making styles in countries around the world.

TESTING...
TESTING...

16 Describe the three styles of approaching problems.

17 Compare and contrast the four decision-making styles: directive, analytic, conceptual, and behavioral.

18 How do decision-making styles differ from country to country?

Decision-Making Styles of Diverse Populations

Research shows that, to some extent, decision-making philosophies and practices differ from country to country.[15] For example, most British organizations are highly decentralized because many upper-level managers do not understand the technical details of the business. Therefore, top-level managers rely on their middle managers, who deal more closely with the day-to-day technical details, to make decisions. French firms are quite different. In France, many top managers graduated from the Grand Ecoles (universities), and many doubt that their middle managers can make good decisions. As a result, decision making tends to be centralized. In Germany, decision making tends to be fairly centralized, autocratic, and hierarchical. Managers in German businesses place a greater emphasis on productivity and quality of goods than on managing subordinates, so there is no great pressure to involve workers in decisions or even to seek out their input. Swedish companies, on the other hand, focus more on quality of work life and the importance of the individual in the organization. As you can guess, decision making tends to be decentralized and participative. The Japanese approach to decision making is different from that of any of the Europeans. In Japan, a decision-making process called *ringisei,* or decision making by consensus, is used frequently. Consensus decision making means getting agreement by everyone involved with the decision. The process is very time consuming, but it results in a high degree of commitment and acceptance by all affected parties. Although the approach combines both centralized and decentralized decision making, top-level Japanese managers still exercise a great deal of authority over what issues are examined at lower levels of the organization.

Hofstede's cultural dimensions (discussed in chapter 4) can also be used to help us understand differences in global decision-making styles. Power distance differences, for example, help explain why in high power distance cultures such as India only very-senior-level managers make decisions. In low power distance cultures such as Sweden, even low-ranking employees are expected to make most of their own decisions about day-to-day operations. Our knowledge of time orientation also helps. Managers in Egypt will make decisions at a much slower and more deliberate pace than their American counterparts, and Italians, who value the past and traditions, tend to rely on tried and proven alternatives to resolve problems. Finally, some cultures emphasize solving problems, whereas others focus on accepting situations as they are. This difference helps explain why managers in countries such as Thailand and Indonesia may take longer to identify a problem than would a U.S. manager.

As managers deal with employees from diverse cultures, they need to recognize what is common and accepted behavior when asking them to make decisions. Some individuals may not be as comfortable being closely involved in decision making as others, or they may not be willing to experiment with something radically different. Managers who accommodate the diversity in decision-making philosophies and practices can expect a high payoff: capturing the perspectives and strengths that a diverse workforce offers! ■

MANAGING

WORKFORCE

DIVERSITY

managers respond to "a manager's dilemma"

MANAGER 1

My experience at my company has been that for good communications we have to understand clearly before we can be understood. This is important for effective decision making because managers need to understand the problem before deciding what to do next. Therefore, at the New Jersey Transit Department, I would clarify perceptions from customers regarding service levels and from employees regarding morale issues. I would find out from these two groups exactly what their concerns are. Then I would promote customer and employee dialogue. I would give them an opportunity to communicate their feelings and ideas and would value their input as potential solutions. Next, I would identify costs to improve service and efficiencies. What resources are going to be necessary? Then I would develop a total strategy to get customers back and improve morale and implement that strategy. Finally, I would follow up with customers and employees in dialogue sessions to determine customer satisfaction and improved morale among employees.

Ed Crispin, Vice President Midwest Area/Area Manager, Applied Industrial Technologies, Indianapolis, Indiana

MANAGER 2

Shirley DeLibero is most definitely in a very challenging situation. She must balance the demands of several constituencies who have identified several existing problems with the Transit Department. With so many problems, Shirley must try to separate the symptoms of the problems from the problems themselves. She may, for instance, identify poor maintenance of the equipment as the main problem leading to the symptoms of late trains and buses, irate customers, frustrated workers and, therefore, low worker morale. Identifying a single problem to focus on, in this case, could help her make positive progress in this situation by keeping everyone in her organization unified on reaching a common goal.

Finally, I would caution Shirley not to think of the decision process as a "once and done" type of situation. Analyzing the successes and failures of the decision must be an ongoing process. Feedback should be continuously gathered and monitored from all parties involved. Her situation is very difficult, but with a high level of commitment from all those involved to correct the problems, improvements to the transit system should result.

Kim Scartelli, Financial Analyst, Ford Motor Company, Dearborn, Michigan

for your

IMMEDIATE action

Magic Carpet Software

We'll take you away . . .

TO: Rajiv Dutta, Research Manager
FROM: Barbara Schrenk, Vice President of Operations
RE: Software Design Decisions

For some time, I've been aware of a problem that's been brewing in our software design unit. As you're well aware, we have a diverse pool of extremely talented and skilled designers. These individuals are, undoubtedly, one of our organization's most important assets. However, I'm concerned that in the creative process, an individual designer's strong emotional attachment to software that he or she has created overshadows other important factors that should be considered in the decision whether to proceed with the new product design or not. At this point, I'm not sure how to approach this issue with the design teams. The last thing I want to do is stifle the creativity of these individuals, but if we don't come up with an action plan soon for dealing with emotional decision making I'm afraid the problem may get worse.

Please research the role of emotions in decision making. What do the "experts" say? Is it even an issue that I need to be concerned about? What's the best way to deal with emotions in decision making? Please provide me with a one-page list of the important points you find from your research. And be sure to cite your sources in case I need to do some further investigation.

SUMMARY

This summary is organized by the chapter-opening objectives found on p. 180.

1. Decision making is an eight-step process: (1) formulation of a problem, (2) identification of decision criteria, (3) allocation of weights to the criteria, (4) development of alternatives, (5) analysis of alternatives, (6) selection of an alternative, (7) implementation of the alternative, and (8) evaluation of decision effectiveness.

2. Everyone in organizations makes decisions. Decision making is particularly important in every aspect of a manager's job: that is, in planning, organizing, leading, and controlling.

3. The rational decision maker is assumed to have a clear problem, have no goal conflict, know all options, have a clear preference ordering, keep all preferences constant, have no time or cost constraints, and select a final choice that maximizes his or her payoff.

4. In the perfectly rational decision-making process: (1) the problem is identified as important and relevant; (2) all criteria are identified; (3) all criteria are evaluated; (4) a comprehensive list of alternatives is generated; (5) all alternatives are assessed against the decision criteria and weights; (6) the decision with the highest economic outcome is chosen; (7) all organizational members embrace the chosen solution; and (8) the decision's outcome is objectively evaluated against the original problem.

5. In the boundedly rational decision-making process: (1) the problem chosen is visible and reflects the manager's interests and background; (2) a limited set of criteria is identified; (3) a simple model is constructed to evaluate criteria; (4) a limited set of similar alternatives is identified; (5) alternatives are assessed one at a time; (6) the search continues until a satisfactory solution is found; (7) politics and power influence decision acceptance; and (8) the decision's outcome is evaluated against the self-interests of the evaluator.

6. Managers regularly use their intuition in making decisions. Intuitive decision making is an unconscious process of making decisions on the basis of experience and accumulated judgment.

7. Managers face well- and ill-structured problems. Well-structured problems are straightforward, familiar, easily defined, and are solved using programmed decisions. Ill-structured problems are new or unusual, involve ambiguous or incomplete information, and are solved using nonprogrammed decisions.

8. The ideal situation for making decisions occurs when the manager can make accurate decisions because he or she knows the outcome from every alternative. Such certainty, however, rarely occurs. A far more realistic situation is one of risk, in which the decision maker can estimate the likelihood of certain alternatives or outcomes. If neither certainty nor reasonable probability estimates are available, uncertainty exists, and the decision maker's choice will be influenced by intuition or hunch.

9. One description of decision-making styles says that there are problem avoiders, problem solvers, and problem seekers. Another view is that there are analytic, conceptual, directive, and behavioral decision makers.

THINKING ABOUT MANAGEMENT ISSUES

1. Why is decision making often described as the essence of a manager's job?

2. How might an organization's culture influence the way in which managers make decisions?

3. Do research (library, Internet, World Wide Web, or other sources) on developing individual creativity. What role should creativity play in decision making? Why? How could you be a more creative decision maker?

4. Would you call yourself a systematic or intuitive thinker? What are the decision-making implications of these labels? What are the implications for choosing an employer?

5. "With more and more managers using computers, they'll be able to make more-rational decisions." Do you agree or disagree with that statement? Why?

WHAT IS YOUR DECISION-MAKING STYLE?

Instructions:

1. Use the following numbers to answer each question:
   8 = when the question is MOST like you
   4 = when the question is MODERATELY like you
   2 = when the question is SLIGHTLY like you
   1 = when the question is LEAST like you
2. Rate the four answers to each question by inserting one of those numbers into each box in columns I–IV.
3. DO NOT repeat any number in a given row. For example, the numbers you might use to answer a given question could read across as 8 2 1 4, BUT NOT 8 8 1 4.
4. In answering the questions, think of how you NORMALLY act in your work situation.
5. Use the first thing that comes to your mind when answering the question. Your responses should reflect how you feel about the questions and what you prefer to do, not what you think might be the right thing to do.
6. There is no time limit in answering the questions, and there are no right or wrong answers.

	I	II	III	IV
1. My prime objective is to:	Have a position with status	Be the best in my field	Achieve recognition for my work	Feel secure in my job
2. I enjoy jobs that:	Are technical and well defined	Have considerable variety	Allow independent action	Involve people
3. I expect people working for me to be:	Productive and fast	Highly capable	Committed and responsive	Receptive to suggestions
4. In my job, I look for:	Practical results	The best solutions	New approaches or ideas	Good working environment
5. I communicate best with others:	On a direct one-to-one basis	In writing	By having a group discussion	In a formal meeting
6. In my planning, I emphasize:	Current problems	Meeting objectives	Future goals	Developing people's careers
7. When faced with solving a problem, I:	Rely on proven approaches	Apply careful analysis	Look for creative approaches	Rely on my feelings
8. When using information, I prefer:	Specific facts	Accurate and complete data	Broad coverage of many options	Limited data that are easily understood
9. When I am not sure about what to do, I:	Rely on intuition	Search for facts	Look for a possible compromise	Wait before making a decision
10. Whenever possible, I avoid:	Long debates	Incomplete work	Using numbers or formulas	Conflict with others
11. I am especially good at:	Remembering dates and facts	Solving difficult problems	Seeing many possibilities	Interacting with others

	I	II	III	IV
12. When time is important, I:	Decide and act quickly	Follow plans and priorities	Refuse to be pressured	Seek guidance or support
13. In social settings, I generally:	Speak with others	Think about what is being said	Observe what is going on	Listen to the conversation
14. I am good at remembering:	People's names	Places we met	People's faces	People's personalities
15. The work I do provides me:	The power to influence others	Challenging assignments	Achievement of my personal goals	Acceptance by the group
16. I work well with those who are:	Energetic and ambitious	Self-confident	Open-minded	Polite and trusting
17. When under stress, I:	Become anxious	Concentrate on the problem	Become frustrated	Am forgetful
18. Others consider me:	Aggressive	Disciplined	Imaginative	Supportive
19. My decisions typically are:	Realistic and direct	Systematic or abstract	Broad and flexible	Sensitive to the needs of others
20. I dislike:	Losing control	Boring work	Following rules	Being rejected

See scoring key on page SK–3. Your score reflects how you see yourself, not what you believe is correct or desirable. This assessment is related to your work situation. It covers typical decisions that you make in your work environment.

Source: A.J. Rowe, R. Mason, and K. Dickel, *Strategic Management and Business Policy* (Reading, MA: Addison-Wesley, 1982), p. 217. Reprinted by permission of Dr. Alan J. Rowe.

TAKE IT TO THE NET

We invite you to visit the Robbins/Coulter companion Web site at http://www.prenhall.com/robbinsmgt for this chapter's Internet resources.

CASE APPLICATION

Nice Pants

Levi Strauss <http://www.levi.com> is a corporate icon in the fashion industry. The privately held company with sales revenues of over $6.7 billion has led many a fashion trend—from the very first blue jeans back in the mid-1800s to the introduction in 1986 of a line of casual pants called Dockers. The Dockers brand was in the right place at the right time as the corporate world began shifting to more casual dressing. This casual trend led to Dockers' becoming a billion dollar brand. In August of 1995, Levi Strauss rolled out a new line of men's dress pants called Slates. The new pants line reflected another attempt by the company to capture a piece of the dress-pants market. Levi Strauss had previously entered this market with a line called Dress Dockers, a more sophisticated version of its very popular casual Dockers. Sales of this dressy line never took off, and it was finally discontinued. But Levi's decision makers believed that building upon the Levi Strauss name and image with a line of dress pants was important to the company's future growth and performance. And, even more important, they felt that successfully developing and marketing such a line of pants was achievable; they wanted to prove to themselves that they could compete in this market as well! Getting to this point took enormous attention to details and an incredible amount of decision making. What were some of the decisions that had to be made?

One of the first decisions Levi's managers had to make was whether the pants line would be a separate and totally new line—only the third in the company's history (Levi's and Dockers being the other two). Once they made the decision that yes, indeed, this new line would be separate from its other two lines, a name had to be chosen for the line. The new division's marketing team spent four months going through 10,000 possible names looking for one that could be trademarked globally and that could be pronounced in most languages. In addition, they wanted a name that was somewhat masculine and also a name that ended in s because the other two brand names (Levi's and Dockers) ended in s. After selecting the name Slates, the decision makers wanted to keep it as secret as possible for as long as possible. They proceeded to "test" the name by inserting the Slates name into sample news articles to evaluate how it would look in print. But these "clandestine" marketing actions became irrelevant when the decision makers learned that Microsoft was preparing to launch an on-line magazine called—wouldn't you know it—*Slate*. It was too late to choose a different name, so the managers concluded that they could trademark the name *Slates* only against use by other apparel makers, which is what they did.

With the name decision out of the way, it was time to select a logo. One initial design was a chiseled rock, which the managers eventually decided wouldn't work because they didn't want to give men the impression

that the pants came only in the color gray. The final design chosen was a sleek interwoven capital S. Then a decision had to be made about where the logo would be placed. After several months of deliberation, the managers decided that the best place was on the inside waistband above the zipper so that it would be the last thing a man saw as he put on his pants.

The next decision had to do with the actual design of the Slates pants. Based on market research, one design consideration was to have deeper pockets than those on similar pants and to have both back pockets with buttons to accommodate left-handed, as well as right-handed, males. Then the design decision turned to the belt loops. The managers debated about how many, how far apart, and how thick the belt loops should be. They ultimately decided on seven belt loops, four and a half inches apart and three-eighths inch wide. Market research also steered the decision to add sizes with odd waist measurements (that is, 31, 33, 35, and so on).

Then, it was on to production decisions. After production had already begun on the new pants and just a few months before the shipping deadline, managers halted production to change the fabric content of half the product line. The wool content was increased by 10 percent. Why? The managers said it was because they had found out that they could use better fabric without increasing the price of the pants. But the change led to several immediate production issues that had to be addressed. Production workers were getting ready to go on Christmas vacation, retailers had already placed orders based on the original fabrics, patterns no longer met specifications, dye colors were off, and to top it all off—the factories needed fabric right now to keep up production levels, and changing the fabric meant waiting for the new fabric to be delivered. Each of these issues required a series of decisions.

Decisions about marketing the new pants line also had to be made. The Slates marketing team wanted the pants to stand out in stores. They hired an architectural firm that specialized in designing luxury hotels to design a roomy, circular display. Also, the managers wanted a new hanger—something that would display the product in a unique fashion. Unfortunately, one design required too much effort to assemble; another one hid the logo; and another crumpled the pants. So the decision was made to go back to the tried-and-true approach—hangers similar to what had always been used in displaying pants. Other decisions revolved around the design of an appropriate promotion program for the new pants line.

Although little information has been released about the success of the Slates line, the story of the development process provides a good description of the managerial decisions that had to be made in several organizational areas as the new product line was launched.

QUESTIONS

1. What types of problems and decisions do you see managers dealing with in this story? Explain your choices.

2. How might each of the following be used in the decisions that had to be made in developing this new pants line: (a) perfectly rational decision making, (b) boundedly rational decision making, and (c) intuition?

3. Would you characterize the decision conditions surrounding the development of the Slates pants line as certainty, risk, or uncertainty? Explain your choice.

4. Which decision-making style might be most appropriate for each of the following decisions about the new pants line? (a) Should the new pants line be a separate and totally new line? (b) What should be the name of the new pants line? (c) What should the design of the new pants line include? Explain your choice for each decision.

Source: D. Canedy, "A Strategy of Little Left to Chance, " *New York Times*, October 9, 1996, pp. C1+.

VIDEO CASE APPLICATION

Grace under Fire

You probably wouldn't know quite what to expect from a business named Pyro Media, but you'd figure it was going to be something pretty unusual. Grace Tsjuikawa Boyd's business, Pyro Media, has pursued a pretty unusual direction, but the decision to do something different wasn't made randomly.

Boyd's Pyro Media started off as a manufacturer of huge ceramic glazed pots such as the ones you might see holding trees or plants in the lobbies of big hotels. Using her degree in art, Boyd herself initially made the high-quality glazed pots, which sold for about $1,500 each. As her business grew to the point at which it had backorders of 8 to 12 weeks, Boyd decided it was time to move to a bigger facility and invest in equipment and employees. She says, "We were in business making money and assumed that business was going to grow at the same rate it had been." Grace soon found, however, that Pyro Media's revenues didn't keep increasing by 30 percent as they

had been, but instead were dropping off. Upon investigating the situation, Boyd found out that huge corporations had begun importing and distributing terra cotta planters, essentially stealing away her business.

Boyd knew that she had to do something. She had this equipment, this 56,000-square-foot facility, and employees who knew ceramics. She called in some consultants to see what other markets her business might pursue. Their study, which took about six months, recommended that Pyro Media look into high-tech ceramic applications: in other words, using the same technology that Boyd had developed and used in making ceramic pots and applying it to a new area. On the basis of that information, Boyd hired a ceramics engineer and went after the ceramics "castables" market. The company's decision to move into this new market has been so successful that the one engineer has since been joined by seven others! Recognizing that business was falling off and analyzing the reason behind the loss of revenue were instrumental in Pyro Media's continued success. Boyd says that being able to recognize a problem is critical, especially for small businesses. Why? Because small businesses have no money to waste and no time to waste. If problems are ignored and not analyzed, the business might face quick failure.

QUESTIONS

1. A decision to move into a new market as Boyd's Pyro Media did is a major decision. How could Boyd have used the decision-making process to help her make this decision?

2. Would you call declining revenues a problem or a symptom of a problem? Why?
3. Using Figure 6-5, identify the type of decision-making style you think Boyd exhibits. Explain your choice.
4. Do you agree with Boyd's assertion that being able to recognize a problem is critical, especially for small businesses? Why or why not?

Source: Based on *Small Business 2000, Show 108.*

Planning

A MANAGER'S DILEMMA

Moscow isn't always the grim and dreary place that photographs often depict. In fact, there's a new economic vibrancy that many young people are working to take advantage of.

Three of these bright, young, and energetic individuals are James Weinstock, Paul Kuebler, and Vladimir Grumlik.[1] Weinstock (on left in photo) is a native New Yorker who has been working as a market consultant at the Moscow office of consulting firm Ernst and Young. In the summer of 1995, he teamed up with two men with whom he often worked out at a Moscow health club, Kuebler and Grumlik. Kuebler (on right in

photo) is an accountant from Riverside, California, working in Arthur Andersen's Moscow office. Grumlik is a young Russian trader of sportswear and electronics. The three men were serious about staying physically fit, but they didn't see any gym facilities in Moscow with the type of service and facility management that they thought an outstanding gym should have. The three "saw that there was a gaping hole in the market; there simply was no good Western-style health club in Moscow." So they decided to start one.

They chose a Gold's Gym franchise. The three partners found a run-down Moscow sports complex that they felt had potential to be turned into a first-rate facility. They signed a 25-year lease on it and contracted with Gold's Gym Enterprises of Venice, California, for the use of the name. But taking an idea and turning it into reality involves a lot of planning. Put yourself in the trio's position. What types of planning would Weinstock, Kuebler, and Grumlik need to do now? Describe the different plans that Jake, Paul, and Vladimir would need to turn their dream of an outstanding sports facility into reality.

WHAT WOULD YOU DO?

In this chapter we present the basics of planning. In the following pages, you'll learn the difference between formal and informal planning, why managers plan, how planning affects performance, the various types of plans that managers use, the key contingency factors that influence the types of plans that managers use in different situations, the major criticisms of planning, and the important role that objectives play in planning.

CHAPTER

7

Foundations

of Planning

THE DEFINITION OF PLANNING

planning

A process that involves defining the organization's objectives or goals, establishing an overall strategy for achieving those goals, and developing a comprehensive hierarchy of plans to integrate and coordinate activities.

What do we mean by the term **planning**? As we stated in chapter 1, planning involves defining the organization's objectives or goals, establishing an overall strategy for achieving those goals, and developing a comprehensive hierarchy of plans to integrate and coordinate activities. It is concerned with both ends (what's to be done) and means (how it's to be done).

Planning can be further defined in terms of whether it's informal or formal. All managers engage in planning, but their planning might be only informal. In informal planning, nothing is written down, and there is little or no sharing of objectives with others in the organization. This type of planning is done in many small businesses; the owner-manager has a vision of where he or she wants to go and how to get there. The planning is general and lacks continuity. Of course, informal planning exists in some large organizations as well, and some small businesses have very sophisticated formal plans.

When we use the term *planning* in this book, we mean *formal* planning. Specific objectives covering a period of years are defined. These objectives are written and made available to organizational members. Finally, specific action programs exist for the achievement of the objectives; that is, managers clearly define the path they want to take to get the organization from where it is to where they want it to be.

PURPOSES OF PLANNING

Why should managers plan? We can state at least four reasons. It gives direction, reduces the impact of change, minimizes waste and redundancy, and sets the standards used in controlling. Let's look at each of these reasons.

Planning establishes coordinated effort. It gives direction to managers and nonmanagers alike. When employees know where the organization is going and what they must contribute to reach the objective, they can coordinate their activities, cooperate with each other, and work in teams. Without planning, departments might be working at cross purposes, preventing the organization from moving efficiently toward its objectives.

Planning reduces uncertainty by forcing managers to look ahead, anticipate change, consider the impact of change, and develop appropriate responses. It also clarifies the consequences of actions managers might take in response to change.

In addition, planning reduces overlapping and wasteful activities. Coordination before the fact is likely to pinpoint waste and redundancy. Furthermore, when means and ends are clear, inefficiencies become obvious and can be corrected or eliminated.

Finally, planning establishes objectives or standards that are used in controlling. If we're unsure of what we're trying to achieve, how can we determine whether we have actually achieved it? In planning, we develop the objectives. Then, in the controlling function, we compare actual performance against the objectives, identify any significant deviations, and take the necessary corrective action. Without planning, there would be no way to control.

PLANNING AND PERFORMANCE

Do managers and organizations that plan outperform those that don't? Intuitively, you would expect the answer to be a resounding yes. Reviews of performance in organizations that plan are generally positive, but we shouldn't take that as a blanket endorsement of formal planning. We can't say that organizations that formally plan always outperform those that don't.

Numerous studies have been done to test the relationship between planning and performance.[2] On the basis of these studies, we can draw the following conclusions. First, generally speaking, formal planning is associated with higher profits, higher return on assets, and other positive financial results. Second, the quality of the planning process and the appropriate implementation of the plans probably contribute more to high performance than does the extent of planning. Finally, in those studies in which formal planning didn't lead to higher performance, the environment was the culprit. Governmental regulations, powerful labor unions, and similar environmental forces constrain managers' options and thereby reduce the impact of planning on an organization's performance. Why? Because managers will have fewer choices for planning viable alternatives. For example, planning might indicate that a manufacturing firm should produce some of its key parts in Taiwan in order to compete effectively against low-cost foreign competitors. But if the firm's labor union contract specifically forbids transferring work overseas, the firm's plan will be of no value. Dramatic shocks from the environment, such as a fire at a major customer's warehouse or a steep drop in stock prices because of inflationary fears, can also undermine an organization's best-laid plans. Given such environmental uncertainty, there's no reason to expect that firms that plan will outperform those that don't.

MISCONCEPTIONS ABOUT PLANNING

There is no shortage of misconceptions about planning. We will identify some of them and try to clear up the misunderstandings behind them.

1. *Planning that proves inaccurate is a waste of manager's time.* The end result of planning is only one of its purposes. The process itself can be valuable even if the results miss the target. Planning requires managers to think through what they want to do and how they're going to do it. This clarification can be important in and of itself. Managers who do a good job of planning will have direction and purpose, and planning is likely to minimize wasted effort. All of these benefits can occur even if the objectives being sought are missed.

2. *Planning can eliminate change.* Planning cannot eliminate change. Changes will happen no matter what managers do. Managers engage in planning in order to anticipate changes and to develop the most effective response to them.

3. *Planning reduces flexibility.* Planning implies commitment, but this is a constraint only if managers stop planning after doing it once. Planning is an ongoing activity. The fact that formal plans have been thoroughly discussed and clearly articulated can make them easier to revise than an ambiguous set of assumptions carried around in some executive's head. Also, some plans can be made more flexible than others.

1 **What are the potential benefits of formal planning?**

2 **What is the relationship between planning and organizational performance?**

3 **Identify and rebut some common misconceptions about planning.**

TYPES OF PLANS

The most popular ways to describe organizational plans are by their breadth (strategic versus operational), time frame (short term versus long term), specificity (directional versus specific), and frequency of use (single-use versus standing). Keep in mind, however, that these planning classifications aren't independent. For instance, short- and long-term plans are closely related to strategic and operational ones. And single-use plans typically are strategic, long-term, and directional. Table 7-1 lists all these types of plans according to category.

Strategic versus Operational Plans

Plans that apply to the entire organization, establish the organization's overall objectives, and seek to position the organization in terms of its environment are called **strategic plans**. Plans that specify the details of how the overall objectives are to be achieved are

strategic plans

Plans that are organization-wide, establish overall objectives, and position an organization in terms of its environment.

TABLE 7-1	**Types of Plans**		
Breadth	**Time Frame**	**Specificity**	**Frequency of Use**
Strategic	Long term	Directional	Single use
Operational	Short term	Specific	Standing

operational plans

Plans that specify details on how overall objectives are to be achieved.

called **operational plans**. How do strategic and operational plans differ? Three differences have been identified: time frame, scope, and whether they include a known set of organizational objectives.[3] Operational plans tend to cover shorter periods of time. For instance, an organization's monthly, weekly, and day-to-day plans are almost always operational. Strategic plans tend to include an extended time period—usually three years or more. They also cover a broader view of the organization and deal less with specific areas. Finally, strategic plans include the formulation of objectives, whereas operational plans assume the existence of objectives. Operational plans define ways to attain the objectives.

Short-Term versus Long-Term Plans

long-term plans

Plans that extend beyond three years.

The difference in years between short-term and long-term plans has shortened considerably. It used to be that long-term meant anything over seven years. Try to imagine what you'd like to be doing in seven years and you can begin to appreciate the difficulty that managers had in establishing plans that far in the future. As organizational environments have become more uncertain, the definition of *long term* has changed. We're going to define **long-term plans** as those with a time frame beyond three years.[4] We'll define **short-term plans** as those covering one year or less. The intermediate term is any time period in between. Although these time classifications are fairly common, an organization can designate any time frame it wants for planning purposes.

short-term plans

Plans that cover one year or less.

Specific versus Directional Plans

Intuitively, it seems right that specific plans would be preferable to directional, or loosely guided, plans. **Specific plans** have clearly defined objectives. There's no ambiguity, no problem with misunderstandings. For example, a manager who seeks to increase his or her firm's sales by 20 percent over a given 12-month period might establish specific procedures, budget allocations, and schedules of activities to reach that objective. These are specific plans.

specific plans

Plans that are clearly defined and leave no room for interpretation.

However, specific plans do have drawbacks. They require clarity and a sense of predictability that often do not exist. When uncertainty is high and management must be flexible in order to respond to unexpected changes, it is preferable to use directional plans.[5] (See Figure 7-1.)

directional plans

Flexible plans that set out general guidelines.

Directional plans identify general guidelines. They provide focus but do not lock managers into specific objectives or courses of action. Instead of detailing a specific plan to cut costs by 4 percent and increase revenues by 6 percent in the next six months, managers might formulate a directional plan for improving corporate profits by 5 to 10 percent over the next six months. The flexibility inherent in directional plans is obvious. However, this advantage must be weighed against the loss of clarity provided by specific plans. Our three managers identified in the opening dilemma would have to look at the usefulness of directional plans as opposed to more specific ones. It might be, at least at this point, more useful for them to use directional plans.

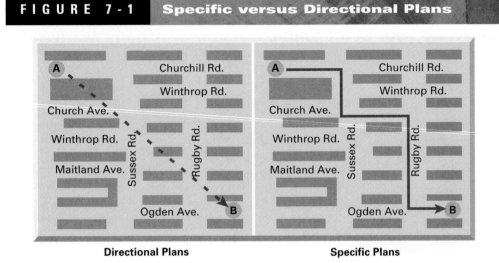

| **FIGURE 7-1** | **Specific versus Directional Plans** |

Directional Plans   Specific Plans

Frequency of Use

Some organizational plans that managers develop are ongoing; others are used only once. A **single-use plan** is a one-time plan that is specifically designed to meet the needs of a unique situation and is created in response to nonprogrammed decisions that managers make. For instance, when Charles Schwab and Company (the discount brokerage company) introduced its Internet-based transaction and information services in late 1996, top-level executives designed a single-use plan to guide the creation and implementation of the new service. In addition, in response to continued intense competitive pressures, Schwab's managers designed a single-use plan to retool the company's customer service area. Part of this plan included a study of fast-food companies such as McDonald's to see how they man-

single-use plan

A one-time plan that is specifically designed to meet the needs of a unique situation and is created in response to nonprogrammed decisions that managers make.

Michael Martin, worldwide manager for tropical corn at Advanta Seeds, has set in motion specific plans to create synergy in the production of corn seed. His success will contribute to Advanta's directional plan to achieve long-term growth in the seed market.

Interview with Geoff Gilpin, Director of Affinity Marketing, GTE Communications Corporation, Dallas, Texas

Describe your job.

As director of affinity marketing, my job is to bring in profitable revenue through working with organizations to jointly market my company's communication products to the end customer. Our goal is to decrease customer acquisition costs and increase retention. To reach these goals, I seek out organizations that have a tight relationship with their constituency or similar target markets and business objectives.

What types of skills do you think tomorrow's manager will need?

The most important skill a manager needs is flexibility. Success requires the ability to handle multiple tasks, all of a high-priority nature. Just as critical is the ability to make quick decisions, many times without all the facts. The market moves so fast that if you can't make a quick decision, you get left behind.

How do you use planning in your job?

Planning is an ongoing process. It's our road map, but the destination is constantly changing due to dynamic market conditions. In an industry like telecommunications, where things change daily, planning is critical in keeping our team informed and coordinated in our efforts. In addition, planning is an element in our continuous improvement process as we measure our actual performance against the plan and learn from the gaps.

How important are objectives to what you do? How do you establish objectives?

Objectives provide direction for our group. The focus on meeting our objectives drives results. It's critical to carefully craft objectives that fit with the business plan and to communicate them well throughout the company. In establishing objectives, I try to create easily understandable statements that will drive specific measurable behaviors that support the realization of our desired results. ■

standing plans

Ongoing plans that provide guidance for activities repeatedly performed in the organization and that are created in response to programmed decisions that managers make.

aged their franchises and how their approach might help Schwab's interaction with its branch offices.

In contrast, **standing plans** are ongoing plans that provide guidance for activities repeatedly performed in the organization. Standing plans are created in response to programmed decisions that managers make and include the policies, rules, and procedures that we defined in the previous chapter on managerial decision making. An example of a standing plan would be the sexual harassment policy developed by the University of Missouri. It provides guidance to university administrators, faculty, and staff as they perform their work activities.

CONTINGENCY FACTORS IN PLANNING

In some situations, long-term plans make sense; in others they do not. Similarly, in some instances, directional plans are more effective than specific ones. What are these situations? In this section, we describe three contingency factors that affect planning: level in the organization, degree of environmental uncertainty, and length of future commitments.[6]

Level in the Organization

Figure 7-2 shows the general relationship between a manager's level in the organization and the type of planning done. For the most part, operational planning dominates the planning activities of lower-level managers. As managers move up the hierarchy, their planning role becomes more strategy oriented. The planning effort by top executives in large organizations is mostly strategic. In a small business, of course, the owner-manager does both.

Degree of Environmental Uncertainty

The greater the environmental uncertainty, the more plans need to be directional and emphasis placed on the short term. If rapid or important technological, social, economic, legal, or other environmental changes are occurring, well-defined and precisely charted courses of action are more likely to hinder an organization's performance than help it. When environmental uncertainty is high, specific plans have to be altered to accommodate the changes—often at high cost and decreased efficiency. For example, at Continental Airlines, CEO Gordon M. Bethune and his other executives established a broad and general goal of focusing on what customers wanted most—on-time flights—to help the company become more competitive in the volatile airline industry. Because of the high level of uncertainty that's characteristic of the airline industry, the management team identified a "destination, but not a flight plan."

Also, the greater the change, the less likely it is that plans will be accurate. For example, one study found that one-year revenue plans tended to achieve 99 percent accuracy compared with 84 percent for five-year plans.[7] Therefore, if an organization faces a rapidly changing environment, managers should be flexible in planning.

We'd like to add a final thought on the importance of flexibility. Although many corporations once had large formal planning departments that generated numerous five- and ten-year plans (updated annually, of course), planning is increasingly being done by divisional or unit managers as part of their management responsibilities.[8] These plans cover shorter time periods and are more likely to consider a broader range of options. Why have we seen

FIGURE 7-2   Planning in the Hierarchy of Organizations

this changed planning approach? As we've stated before, organizations have found that the changing environment requires a more flexible and quicker response. Oftentimes, lower- and middle-level managers are the first to see the changes and thus are in the best position to plan.

In a volatile world, only the foolish would be cocky enough to believe that they could accurately forecast the future. But that fact doesn't diminish the importance of plans. Well-managed organizations are spending less time coming up with highly detailed, quantitative plans and instead are developing multiple future scenarios. For example, Southern California Edison, an electric utility in California, created 12 possible versions of the future on the basis of an economic boom, a Middle East oil crisis, expanded environmentalism efforts, and other developments. This approach to flexible planning came about after the utility's managers realized that every long-range plan they had painstakingly constructed had been rendered virtually useless by unexpected events—from the Gulf War to nuclear accidents like the one at Chernobyl to new regulatory restrictions on sulfur emissions. And of course, Southern California Edison isn't unique in facing an increasingly uncertain world. As we pointed out in chapter 3, most businesses, including for-profit and not-for-profit organizations, are finding their environments becoming more dynamic and more uncertain. These forces require managers to develop more flexible plans.

Length of Future Commitments

The other contingency factor is also related to the time frame of plans. The more that current plans affect future commitments, the longer the time frame for which managers

MANAGING WORKFORCE DIVERSITY

The Role of Planning in Developing a Productive, Diverse Workforce

We already know that the composition of the workforce is changing drastically.[9] Some of these changes are: (1) The average age of workers will rise while the pool of younger workers will shrink; (2) two-thirds of new entrants into the workforce will be women, minorities, and immigrants; (3) an increasing percentage of employees will be single parents; and (4) there will be fewer literate, skilled workers available at a time when many jobs will require a more skilled workforce. What role can planning play as organizations attempt to develop a productive and effective diverse workforce in light of these changes?

Because planning establishes coordinated organizational effort, it can provide the foundation for developing organization-wide policies, practices, and training for an organization committed to employee diversity. Planning can guide organizational activities such as employee recruitment to meet affirmative action and diversity goals, product development that encompasses diverse perspectives, and purchasing supplies and materials from diverse sources. For example, recruiting diverse employees is an important objective at Miller Brewing Company. And company managers at JP Morgan have developed a summer intern program for a diverse group of undergraduate and graduate students with the intent of attracting some of these individuals to join the company after completing their degrees. These activities were part of each organization's plan for embracing diversity.

Another way that planning can be valuable is in reducing the uncertainty associated with the changing demographics of the workforce. Labor force participation statistics already show us that the workforce is aging and more women, minorities, and immigrants are entering the workplace. As managers consider the impact of these changes, they can plan how to fully utilize the talents, skills, and abilities of their diverse employees. As part of this planning process, managers might establish short- and long-run targets or objectives for recruiting, training, and promoting diverse individuals. Also, they might develop a long-range diversity development plan that outlines the steps their organization will take to become culturally diverse. ■

should plan. This **commitment concept** means that plans should extend far enough to meet those commitments made today. Planning for too long or for too short a time period is inefficient.

Managers are not planning for future decisions. Rather, they are planning for the future impact of the decisions they are currently making. Decisions made today become a commitment to some future action or expenditure. For instance, tenure decisions in educational institutions are an excellent example of how the commitment concept should work.

When a college grants tenure to a faculty member, it's making a commitment to provide lifelong employment for that person. The tenure decision must reflect an assessment by college administrators of whether there will be a need for that individual's teaching expertise through his or her lifetime. If a college gives tenure to a 30-year-old art history professor, it should have a plan that covers at least the 40 or more years that that person could be teaching at that institution. Most important, the plan should demonstrate the need for a permanent art history professor through that time period.

To see how important the commitment concept is to planning, you need look no further than the shores of Lake Erie in Cleveland, where several distinct geometric forms are combined into an impressive building designed by I. M. Pei. The building houses the Rock and Roll Hall of Fame and Museum. In 1983, a group of record industry professionals founded the Rock and Roll Hall of Fame to honor music greats, but the Hall had no actual residence. In May 1986, the Hall of Fame board decided to build an actual hall and museum and to locate it in Cleveland because that's where local deejay Alan Freed popularized the term *rock 'n' roll* in the early 1950s. Initial plans were made, but cost estimates for building the hall and museum proved to be too low, and delays plagued the project. For instance, the ground breaking, originally scheduled for 1990, didn't take place until 1993. By that time, it wasn't feasible to back out of the project, even with the delays and higher costs. Instead, construction proceeded, and the Hall and Museum opened in September 1995. How does this example illustrate the commitment concept? The decision made back in the early 1980s became a commitment for future actions and expenditures. Once the Hall of Fame board decided to build a facility, it had to plan for the increased costs and the construction delays. The future impact of the decision to build the Rock and Roll Hall of Fame and Museum was that it committed the board to live with the decision and all its consequences, good and bad.

commitment concept

Plans should extend far enough to see through current commitments.

Cleveland's Rock and Roll Hall of Fame and Museum represents an example of the commitment concept in planning. A 1986 decision committed the governing board to a nine-year design and construction process that exceeded original time and budget estimates but could not be cut back or rescinded.

TESTING...
TESTING...
1 **2** **3**

4 How does the planning done by a top executive differ from that performed by a supervisor?

5 How does environmental uncertainty affect planning?

6 What is the commitment concept, and how does it affect planning?

CRITICISMS OF PLANNING

Formalized planning became very popular in the 1960s, and, for the most part, it still is today! It makes sense for an organization (and individuals) to establish some direction. But critics have begun to challenge some of the basic assumptions underlying planning. Let's look at the major arguments that have been directed at formal planning.

1. *Planning may create rigidity.*[10] Formal planning efforts can lock an organization into specific goals to be achieved within specific timetables. When these objectives were set, the assumption may have been that the environment wouldn't change during the time period the objectives covered. If that assumption is faulty, managers who follow a plan may have trouble. Rather than remaining flexible—and possibly throwing out the plan—managers who continue to do the things required to achieve the originally set objectives may not be able to cope with the changed environment. Forcing a course of action when the environment is fluid can be a recipe for disaster. When the Toronto-based business-form company Moore Corporation, Ltd., did that, they lost several million dollars in annual revenues.[11]

2. *Plans can't be developed for a dynamic environment.*[12] As we mentioned previously, most organizations today face dynamic environmental changes. If a basic assumption of making plans—that the environment won't change—is faulty, then how can you make plans at all? Today's business environment is often chaotic, at best. By definition, that means random and unpredictable. Managing under these conditions requires flexibility, and that may mean not being tied to formal plans.

3. *Formal plans can't replace intuition and creativity.*[13] Successful organizations are typically the result of someone's vision. But visions have a tendency to become formalized as they evolve. Formal planning efforts typically follow a methodology that includes a thorough investigation of the organization's capabilities and opportunities and a mechanistic analysis that reduces the vision to some type of programmed routine. That, again, can spell disaster for an organization. For instance, the rapid growth of Apple Computer in the late 1970s and throughout the 1980s was attributed, in part, to the creativity and anticorporate attitudes of one of its co-founders, Steven Jobs. As the company grew, Jobs felt that there was a need for more-formalized management—something he was uncomfortable doing. He hired a CEO who ultimately ousted Jobs from his own company. With Jobs's departure came increased organizational formality, including detailed planning—the same things that Jobs despised so much because he felt that they hampered creativity. By 1996, this one-time industry leader had lost much of its creativity and was struggling for survival. The situation became so bad that in 1997 Jobs was asked to return to help Apple get back on track; in fact, he was named interim CEO in September 1997.[14]

4. *Planning focuses managers' attention on today's competition not on tomorrow's survival.*[15] Formal planning has a tendency to focus on how to best capitalize on existing business opportunities within an industry. It often doesn't allow managers to consider creating or reinventing an industry. Consequently, formal plans may result in costly blunders and incur catch-up costs when others take the lead. On the other

hand, companies such as Intel and Sony have found much of their success from forging into uncharted waters, designing and developing new industries as they go.[16]

5. *Formal planning reinforces success, which may lead to failure.*[17] Success breeds success. That's an "American tradition." If it's not broken, don't fix it, right? Well, maybe not! Success may, in fact, breed failure in an uncertain environment. It's hard to change or discard previously successful plans—to leave the comfort of what works for the anxiety of the unknown. Successful plans, however, may provide a false sense of security, generating more confidence in the formal plans than is warranted. Many managers will not face the unknown until they're forced to do so by changes in the environment. By then, it may be too late!

OBJECTIVES: THE FOUNDATION OF PLANNING

Objectives are goals. We use the two terms interchangeably. What do those terms mean? They refer to desired outcomes for individuals, groups, or entire organizations.[18] They provide the direction for all management decisions and form the criterion against which actual accomplishments can be measured. That's why we call them the foundation of planning.

objectives

Desired outcomes for individuals, groups, or entire organizations.

Multiplicity of Objectives

At first glance, it might appear that organizations have a single objective: for business firms, to make a profit; for not-for-profit organizations, to efficiently provide a service. But closer analysis reveals that all organizations have multiple objectives. Businesses also seek to increase market share and satisfy employee welfare. A church provides a place for religious practices but also assists the underprivileged in its community and acts as a social gathering place for church members. No one single measure can evaluate effectively whether an organization is successful. Emphasis on one goal, such as profit, ignores other goals that must also be reached if long-term profits are to be achieved. Also, as we discussed in chapter 5, the use of a single objective (such as profit) can result in unethical practices because managers will ignore other important parts of their jobs in order to look good on that one measure.

Table 7-2 provides a sampling of both financial and strategic goals from some well-known U.S. corporations. Financial objectives are related to the financial performance of the firm; strategic objectives are related to other areas of a firm's performance. Except for

TABLE 7-2 **Stated Objectives from Large U.S. Companies**	
Financial Objectives	**Strategic Objectives**
• Faster revenue growth	• A bigger market share
• Faster earnings growth	• A higher, more secure industry rank
• Higher dividends	• Higher product quality
• Wider profit margins	• Lower costs relative to key competitors'
• Higher returns on invested capital	• Broader or more attractive product line
• Stronger bond and credit ratings	• A stronger reputation with customers
• Bigger cash flows	• Superior customer service
• A rising stock price	• Recognition as a leader in technology and/or product innovation
• Recognition as a "blue chip" company	• Increased ability to compete in international markets
• A more diversified revenue base	• Expanded growth opportunities
• Stable earnings during recessionary periods	

Source: A.A. Thompson Jr. and A.J. Strickland III, *Creating and Implementing Strategy* (Chicago: Irwin, 1995), p. 31.

a few of the financial objectives, these goals could apply to a not-for-profit organization as well. Notice, too, that, although survival isn't specifically mentioned by the firms, it's of utmost importance to all organizations. Some of the objectives listed in Table 7-2 contribute directly to profits, but, obviously, an organization must survive if other objectives are to be achieved.

7 What are the major arguments against formal planning?

8 What are objectives, and why are they considered the foundation of planning?

9 Why don't organizations have just one single objective?

Real versus Stated Objectives

stated objectives

Official statements of what an organization says—and what it wants various publics to believe—its objectives are.

Table 7-2 is a list of stated objectives. **Stated objectives** are official statements of what an organization says—and what it wants its various stakeholders to believe—its objectives are. However, stated objectives—which can be found in an organization's charter, annual report, public relations announcements or in public statements made by managers—are often conflicting and excessively influenced by what society believes organizations should do.

The conflict in stated goals exists because organizations respond to a vast array of stakeholders. Unfortunately, these stakeholders frequently evaluate the organization by different criteria. For example, when TWA was hoping for additional wage concessions from its unions, employees, who had already traded wage concessions for 30 percent of the company's equity and who had not had a raise in 10 years, weren't willing to once again postpone meaningful raises.[19] To the union's representatives, TWA's managers were saying that the company's cash position was declining and costs were soaring; the company's future was in doubt if the union didn't cooperate. At the same time, managers were trying to reassure travel agents and potential passengers by saying the company was determined to continue flying and stay in business. TWA's managers had explicitly presented themselves in one way to the union and in another way to the public. Was one goal true and the other false? No. Both were true, but they were in conflict.

Have you ever read an organization's objectives as stated in its brochures? For instance, Bass Pro Shops in Springfield, Missouri, states that it wants to provide the *Best Possible Service*.[20] One of the goals at Chili's Grill & Bar is "to enhance a high level of excellence, innovation, integrity, and ethics."[21] These types of statements are, at best, vague and are more likely to represent management's public relations skills than serve as meaningful guides to what the organization is actually seeking to accomplish. It shouldn't be surprising then to find that an organization's stated objectives are often quite irrelevant to what actually goes on in that organization.[22] For instance, one set of objectives might be issued to stockholders, another to customers, and still others to employees and the public (see Figure 7-3).

The overall objectives stated by top management should be treated for what they are: "fiction produced by an organization to account for, explain, or rationalize to particular audiences rather than as valid and reliable indications of purpose."[23] The content of objectives is substantially determined by what those audiences want to hear. Moreover, it's simpler for managers to state a set of consistent, understandable objectives than to explain a multiplicity of objectives. If you want to know what an organization's **real objectives** are, closely observe what members of the organization actually do. Actions define priorities. For example, universities that proclaim the objectives of limiting class size, facilitating close student-faculty relations, and actively involving students in the learning process and then put their students into lecture classes of 300 or more are pretty common! So, too, is the automobile

real objectives

Objectives that an organization actually pursues, as defined by the actions of its members.

FIGURE 7-3 — **Examples of Objectives for Different Stakeholders**

SBC Communications, Inc.

SBC Communications Inc. is an international leader in the telecommunications industry, serving more than 33 million access lines and 5.5 million wireless customers across the United States. Our businesses offer a wide range of innovative services, including local and long-distance telephone service, wireless communications, paging, Internet access and messaging, as well as telecommunications equipment and directory advertising and publishing.

SBC's overriding goal is to build value for its share owners. We achieve that goal by

- meeting customer needs
- creating new services
- developing businesses
- investing in growth opportunities which, over time, generate returns greater than their cost of capital

Source: Courtesy of SBC Communications, Inc.

service center that promises fast, low-cost repairs and then provides mediocre service at high prices. An awareness that real and stated objectives differ is important, if for no other reason than to understand what might otherwise seem to be management inconsistencies.

Traditional Objective Setting

The traditional role of objectives is to guide the control and direction imposed by an organization's top managers. The president of a manufacturing firm tells the production vice president what he or she expects manufacturing costs to be for the coming year. The president tells the marketing vice president what level he or she expects sales to reach for the coming year. The city mayor tells his or her chief of police how much the departmental budget will be. Then, at some later point, performance is evaluated to determine whether the assigned objectives have been achieved.

The central theme in **traditional objective setting** is that objectives are set at the top and then broken down into subgoals for each level of an organization. This traditional perspective assumes that top managers know what's best because only they can see the "big picture." Thus, the objectives that are established and passed down to each succeeding level of the organization serve to direct and guide, and in some ways to constrain, individual employees' work behaviors. Employees' work efforts at the various organizational levels are then geared to meet the objectives that have been assigned in their areas of responsibility.

In addition to being imposed from above, traditional objective setting is often largely nonoperational.[24] If the top managers define the organization's objectives in broad terms such as achieving "sufficient profits" or "market leadership," these ambiguous goals have to be made more specific as the objectives flow down through the organization. At each level, managers supply operational meaning to the goals. Specificity is achieved as each manager applies his or her own set of interpretations and biases. What often results is that objectives lose clarity and unity as they make their way down from the top of the organization to lower levels (Figure 7-4).

When the hierarchy of organizational objectives is clearly defined, it forms an integrated network of objectives, or a **means-ends chain.** Higher-level objectives, or ends, are linked to lower-level objectives, which serve as the means for their accomplishment. In

traditional objective setting

Objectives are set at the top and then broken down into subgoals for each level in an organization. The top imposes its standards on everyone below.

means-ends chain

An integrated network of organizational objectives in which higher-level objectives, or ends, are linked to lower-level objectives, which serve as the means for their accomplishment.

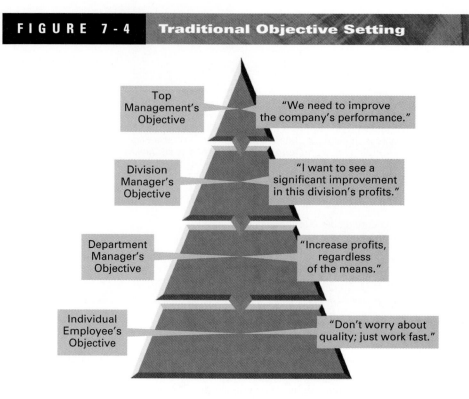

FIGURE 7-4   **Traditional Objective Setting**

Top Management's Objective — "We need to improve the company's performance."

Division Manager's Objective — "I want to see a significant improvement in this division's profits."

Department Manager's Objective — "Increase profits, regardless of the means."

Individual Employee's Objective — "Don't worry about quality; just work fast."

other words, the goals at a low level (means) must be achieved in order to reach the goals at the next level (ends). And the accomplishment of goals at that level becomes the means to achieve the goals at the next level (ends). And so forth and so on, up through the different levels of the organization.

Management by Objectives

management by objectives (MBO)

A system in which specific performance objectives are jointly determined by subordinates and their superiors, progress toward objectives is periodically reviewed, and rewards are allocated on the basis of this progress.

Instead of traditional objective setting, many organizations use **management by objectives (MBO)**. It's a management system in which specific performance objectives are jointly determined by subordinates and their superiors, progress toward objectives is periodically reviewed, and rewards are allocated on the basis of this progress. Rather than using goals only as controls, MBO uses them to motivate employees as well.

Management by objectives was first described by Peter Drucker. It consists of four elements: goal specificity, participative decision making, an explicit time period, and performance feedback.[25] Its appeal lies in its emphasis on converting overall objectives into specific objectives for organizational units and individual members. Table 7-3 lists the steps in a typical MBO program.

Do MBO programs work? Studies of actual MBO programs confirm that MBO effectively increases employee performance and organizational productivity. A review of 70 programs, for example, found organizational productivity gains in 68 of them.[26] The same review also identified top management commitment and involvement as important conditions for MBO to succeed. When top management had a high commitment to MBO and was personally involved in its implementation, the average gain in productivity was 56 percent. When commitment and involvement were low, the average gain in productivity dropped to only 6 percent.

One of the defining characteristics of management by objectives, or MBO, is that the employee's performance goals are set jointly by the employee and the manager.

TABLE 7-3	Steps in a Typical MBO Program

1. The organization's overall objectives and strategies are formulated.
2. Major objectives are allocated among divisional and departmental units.
3. Unit managers collaboratively set specific objectives for their units with their superiors.
4. Specific objectives are collaboratively set for all department members.
5. Action plans, defining how objectives are to be achieved, are specified and agreed upon by managers and subordinates.
6. The action plans are implemented.
7. Progress toward objectives is periodically reviewed, and feedback is provided.
8. Successful achievement of objectives is reinforced by performance-based rewards.

"I'm telling you. After my talk with my manager today about my work goals for the next quarter, I think our company's MBO program actually stands for 'manipulating' by objectives, not management by objectives," Pete complained to his friend Kelly. He went on, "She came in and outlined what she thought I should be working on and then asked me what I thought of it. I guess that's her way of getting me to participate in the goal setting."

Is it unethical for a manager to enter a participative goal-setting session with a pre-established set of goals that he or she wants the employee to accept? Why or why not? Is it unethical for a manager to use his or her formal position to impose specific goals on an employee? Why or why not? ■

THINKING CRITICALLY

ABOUT ETHICS

Some Final Comments on Planning and Objectives

There's no doubt that setting objectives is a vitally important part of the planning function. Without objectives to guide them, managers wouldn't know where or how to start planning, and they really wouldn't have anything *to* plan. Therefore, whether an organization chooses a more traditional approach to establishing objectives, uses some form of MBO, or has its own approach to setting goals, managers must define objectives before they can effectively and efficiently complete the rest of the planning activities. We will discuss the role of strategic management in the planning process in chapter 8 and will describe several planning tools and techniques that managers use in chapter 9.

10 How would you identify an organization's stated objectives? Its real objectives? What happens when an organization has conflicting objectives?

11 Contrast traditional objective setting and MBO.

12 What are the steps in a typical MBO program?

managers respond to "a manager's dilemma"

MANAGER 1

Building a new business from the ground up, particularly given the challenges of doing business in the Russian economy, is going to require significant planning. My experience has been that good planning can help a person achieve more effective (and efficient) work performance levels. I believe that the benefits of planning would translate to an entire organization as well. With that thought in mind, I would suggest that the trio of businessmen first establish some objectives for their business venture. For instance, how many customers do they hope to serve? What types of programs do they hope to offer? What types of revenues and profits do they want in the first year and in successive years? Although it may seem impossible to set these types of goals, they are, in fact, important to have. By setting these goals, they have some targets to aim for. Once they have identified these targets, they will need to plan how they're going to achieve their goals. This type of planning would seem to me to revolve around the various business activities they'll need to do such as marketing, human resources management, facility management, and financial management. Again, although this type of planning may seem difficult, it's important to identify not only *what* they hope to do in these areas but also *how* they are going to do it.

Ernie Collette, Casualty Claim Examiner, American Family Insurance, Springfield, Missouri

MANAGER 2

The planning activities I would use include the following: (1) Clearly define each person's goals and objectives for this venture. Are they similar and compatible? These issues need to be worked out at the beginning of any partnership agreement. In addition, developing a long-range plan of where they want the concept to go is essential. (2) Conduct some type of market research to determine if there is sufficient demand to support the planned facility. (3) Find a good location for the club. Convenience and accessibility would appear to be important in this type of facility. (4) Research the local regulatory and licensing requirements. (5) Estimate all costs associated with setting up and operating the facility, including property costs, debt service, payroll, taxes, marketing and promotional costs, and so forth. Break these costs down into monthly increments and compare with the expected number of memberships, fees, and other income to see if costs can be met and a profit made.

If the results from these planning activities were positive, then I would move to secure the property and begin developing the club.

Keith R. Smith, Manager, Geo/Hydro Services Section, Oregon Department of Transportation, Salem, Oregon

for your

IMMEDIATE action

P P²

PEOPLE POWER²

SERVING ALL YOUR HUMAN RESOURCE NEEDS

TO: **Alpha Team Members**
FROM: **Eric Smallwood, Alpha Team Leader**
SUBJECT: **Objectives for Developing the New Training Module**

Hey Alpha Team! Congratulations! We've been assigned the task of developing People Power's new Internet/World Wide Web training module. The overall objective of this new project is to design a training module for using the Internet and World Wide Web for researching information. The sales reps say we've already had several requests from our various corporate customers for this type of training program. So we're on an accelerated development schedule.

I'm asking each Alpha Team member to identify three or four specific goals for each of the three stages of the project: (1) researching customer needs, (2) researching Internet/World Wide Web for specific information sources and techniques we want to use in our training module, and (3) designing and writing specific training modules. Please have these written by next week. We'll have a team meeting to share ideas and finalize the specific objectives for this project. Then we'll be able to get to work!

This is a fictionalized account of a potentially real problem. It was written for academic purposes only.

SUMMARY

This summary is organized by the chapter-opening objectives found on p. 210.

1. Planning is the process of determining objectives and assessing the way those objectives can best be achieved.

2. Planning gives direction, reduces the impact of change, minimizes waste and redundancy, and sets the standards for use in controlling.

3. Strategic plans cover an extensive time period (typically three or more years), cover broad issues, and include the formulation of objectives. Operational plans cover shorter periods of time, focus on specifics, and assume that objectives are already known.

4. Directional plans are preferred over specific plans when uncertainty is high and when the organization is in the formative and decline stages of its life cycle.

5. A single-use plan is a one-time plan that's specifically designed to meet the needs of a unique situation and is created in response to nonprogrammed decisions that managers make. Standing plans are ongoing plans that provide guidance for activities repeatedly performed in the organization and are created in response to programmed decisions that managers make.

6. Three contingency factors in planning are a manager's level in the organization, the degree of environmental uncertainty, and the length of future commitments.

7. The commitment concept refers to the fact that a manager should plan just far enough ahead to see that the commitments that he or she makes today can be kept.

8. The major criticisms of formal planning are: (a) It may create rigidity in organizational decisions and actions; (b) plans can't be developed for a dynamic environment; (c) formal plans can't replace intuition and creativity; (d) planning focuses managers' attention on today's competition, not on tomorrow's survival; and (e) formal planning reinforces success and thereby ultimately may lead to failure.

9. Objectives are important to planning because they provide the direction for all management decisions and form the criterion against which actual accomplishments can be measured. An organization's stated objectives might not be its real objectives because management might want to tell people what they want to hear and because it is simpler to state a set of consistent, understandable objectives than to explain a multiplicity of objectives.

10. In traditional objective setting, objectives are set at the top of the organization and then are broken down into subgoals for each level of an organization. The objectives are established and passed down to each succeeding level. In MBO (management by objectives), specific performance objectives are jointly determined by subordinates and their superiors, progress toward objectives is periodically reviewed, and rewards are allocated on the basis of this progress.

THINKING ABOUT MANAGEMENT ISSUES

1. Will planning become more or less important to managers in the future? Why?

2. If planning is so crucial, why do some managers choose not to do it? What would you tell these managers?

3. Explain how planning involves making decisions today that will have an impact later.

4. How might planning in a not-for-profit organization such as the American Cancer Society differ from planning in a for-profit organization such as Coca-Cola?

5. What types of planning do you do in your personal life? Describe these plans in terms of being (a) strategic or operational, (b) short- or long-term, and (c) specific or directional.

SELF-ASSESSMENT EXERCISE

HOW WELL DO I SET GOALS?

How well do you plan in your personal life and, if you're employed, in your organizational setting? The following questions are designed to help you assess how well goal-setting processes are working in your personal and work lives. Indicate how much you agree or disagree with each statement. When you finish, review the items that received the lowest scores.

5 Strongly agree
4 Agree
3 Neither agree nor disagree
2 Disagree
1 Strongly disagree

At school and in my personal life,

_____ **1.** I am proactive rather than reactive.
_____ **2.** I set aside enough time and resources to study and complete projects.
_____ **3.** I am able to budget money to buy the things I really want without going broke.
_____ **4.** I have thought through what I want to do in school.
_____ **5.** I have a plan for completing my major.
_____ **6.** My goals for the future are realistic.

At work (complete only if you have work experience),

_____ **1.** We are proactive rather than reactive.
_____ **2.** Policies, programs, and procedures are developed in an integrated fashion.
_____ **3.** Time and resources are committed to set goals and objectives.
_____ **4.** We work on forecasting future opportunities and threats.
_____ **5.** The overall mission is clear to all.
_____ **6.** Goal-setting processes take place at the organizational unit and individual levels.
_____ **7.** There are written goals and objectives.
_____ **8.** There are long-range goals and objectives.
_____ **9.** There is short-range objective setting.
_____ **10.** Goals and objectives are realistic.
_____ **11.** Goals and objectives are challenging.
_____ **12.** Goals and objectives are reviewed and modified on a regular cycle.
_____ **13.** Accomplishment of goals and objectives is tied to a reward system.
_____ **14.** Pursuing goals and objectives is a productive activity.

See scoring key on page SK–3.

Source: R.E. Quinn, S.R. Faerman, M.P. Thompson, and M.R. McGrath, *Becoming a Master Manager: A Competency Framework* (New York: Wiley, 1990), pp. 33–34.

•
TAKE IT TO THE NET

We invite you to visit the Robbins/Coulter companion Web site at http://www.prenhall.com/robbinsmgt for this chapter's Internet resources.

CASE APPLICATION

I Can See Clearly Now

"The most important thing for any organization is to have everyone focused on the same objectives and to have the objectives clearly defined." So says Kathleen Cote, Chief Executive Officer of Computervision Corporation of Bedford, Massachusetts. Computervision Corporation <http://www.cv.com> is a leading supplier of desktop and enterprise-wide product design and development software and services. Its vision is to be the partner of choice for the most important thing its customers do—product development. The company pioneered CAD/CAM (computer-aided design/computer-aided manufacturing) hardware and software back in 1971 and was flying high during the 1980s as revenues and profits soared. Then, the once-profitable company posted losses of nearly $1.3 billion from 1991 through 1993. Cote headed the operating committee that developed the strategic plan for Computervision's turnaround and ultimate survival. Her work in that area led to her being named president and chief operating officer of the company in December 1995 and being named to the top management job in June 1996.

Cote's management style happens to be very people oriented, and she knew how she wanted to run the company. What the company had to do to become successful again and what she had to do as CEO to make that happen were crystal-clear in her mind: The company had to clearly define its objectives, and she had to make sure that everyone was focused on those objectives. Cote stated, "The top three things I am working on have to be the top three things everyone is working on. We are only going to be successful together." How did she go about making that happen?

The first thing Cote did was to have her senior managers identify where Computervision was winning business and where it was losing business. On the basis of that analysis, they decided to shift the company's focus to providing product development solutions through software and services and putting less of an emphasis on hardware. The top managers then established corporate objectives and communi-cated them down through the organization. Those objectives were then used to clearly define individual performance objectives. In addition, Cote was firmly committed to sticking to the objectives. She said, "I'm a firm believer that if you stay on course and never get off, you will have great success. There really is no surprise if you have a plan in place."

Cote isn't just focused on establishing and communicating common objectives for organizational employees. She also is strongly committed to making sure objectives are met. Managers (and all organizational employees) are held accountable for meeting their respective objectives and doing what they say they are going to do. Says Cote, "I don't like surprises. If something isn't going right, let me know what you can do about it to work through the issues and the problem." According to Cote, achieving the objectives entails showing employees how they are a part of making the plans happen and making them feel that they play an important role in helping the company meet its goals.

How has Computervision performed under Cote's leadership? The company posted a net income of $9.8 million in 1994, a profit of $22.8 million in 1995, and a profit of $26 million in the first three quarters of 1996, but it did suffer a loss of $5.9 million in the fourth quarter of 1996. That loss abruptly ended the company's string of 11 consecutive profitable quarters. But, despite the unexpected fourth-quarter loss, industry and financial analysts expect Computervision to continue its history of solid profits.

QUESTIONS

1. What's your reaction to Cote's philosophy that the most important thing for any organization is to have everyone focused on the same objectives and to have the objectives clearly defined? Do you agree? Why or why not? What would be the drawbacks of such a philosophy?
2. What role did strategic plans play in Computervision's turnaround? What role should they play in the company's future? What role should operational plans play?

3. One of the major criticisms of formal planning is that planning may create rigidity, particularly in a dynamic environment. How do you think Kathleen Cote would respond to that criticism?

4. How might the commitment concept affect planning at Computervision?

5. Would you call Computervision's approach to setting objectives a more traditional approach or more of an MBO approach? Explain your choice.

Source: M.A. Verespej, "Future Vision," *IW,* February 17, 1997, pp. 50–55.

ABCNEWS **VIDEO CASE APPLICATION**

Behind-the-Scenes Planning of the First Lunar Landing

"Houston, Tranquility Base here. The *Eagle* has landed." Even now, more than 30 years later, these words stir the imagination. For those who watched the first lunar landing on July 20, 1969, they are forever frozen in memory. Yet, what went on behind the scenes of that feat makes its successful accomplishment seem even more incredible! What looked like a smooth-sailing operation that worked perfectly and according to plan came dangerously close to disaster.

To put three astronauts in the depths of outer space and then to have two of them take a spacecraft and land it on the moon involved an unbelievable amount of detailed planning. From the countdown to the liftoff of the enormously powerful *Saturn V* rocket to the delicate maneuvering of the lunar spacecraft, each detail had been meticulously planned. Or so the technicians and controllers thought!

The first sign of something amiss was when Neil Armstrong and Buzz Aldrin began the descent toward the lunar surface in the tiny and extremely fragile *Eagle* spacecraft. An alarm—something called the 1202 ("twelve-oh-two")—went off. The person monitoring the descent of the *Eagle* from back on Earth in Mission Control recalls, "I didn't have the foggiest idea of what '1202' was." There was less than eight minutes to landing on the surface of the moon, and the only person at Mission Control who seemed to know what this 1202 alarm meant was Steve Bales, a 26-year-old technician. For what seemed like an eternity, the entire space program waited to see if Bales

would call off the moon landing. Bales finally determined that the problem simply was that the on-board computer had too much to process, but as long as it didn't shut down completely, they could still make a safe moon landing. The *Eagle* was given a "go" for landing despite the alarm.

The next problem arose when the *Eagle* was 5,000 feet off the surface of the moon and moving down at 100 feet a second. The computer swung the spacecraft into position for descent, but when Neil Armstrong looked out from the window of the *Eagle,* he saw nothing he recognized from his earlier studies of the moon's surface. The computer guidance system was taking them right into a boulder field—not at all what had been planned. The delicate lunar lander couldn't survive landing on rocks the size of Volkswagens. At 350 feet above the surface, Neil Armstrong, without saying a word to Mission Control in Houston, started to fly the spacecraft manually, searching for someplace to land. The engineers and technicians in Mission Control sat by helplessly, absolutely unable to offer any assistance. As Armstrong got closer and closer to the surface, all he could still see was large boulders.

Meanwhile, in Houston, the computers showed that the *Eagle's* landing tank was running dangerously low on fuel. One of the individuals in Mission Control that day recalls, "From then on, there was nothing we could do to help the crew. All we could do was let them know how much fuel they had left." The decision was made by Mission Control that if the *Eagle* didn't land within the next 60 seconds, the mission would be aborted. At 25 seconds, then 20 seconds, Armstrong was still 100 feet off the moon's surface, but he had found a spot that looked safe for landing *if* he could get there in time. The silence at this point in the Mission Control room was deafening. Then the very calm, cool, and collected voice of Neil Armstrong came across the communication system: "Houston, Tranquility Base here. The *Eagle* has landed." And the rest of the story is history!

QUESTIONS

1. What role would specific plans play in planning the lunar landing mission? What role would directional plans play?

2. Do you see any evidences of contingency planning in the description of this situation? Explain.
3. What do you think the stated objectives of the lunar landing space mission might have been? How about the real objectives?

Source: Based on "One Giant Leap," *ABC News Day One,* aired July 11, 1994.

A MANAGER'S DILEMMA

Few people have heard of Leonardo Del Vecchio, chairman and founder of Luxottica Group. Yet, in 1995, Del Vecchio's Luxottica Group made the largest single investment in the United States by purchasing United States Shoe Corporation for $1.4 billion.[1]

What is Luxottica, and what exactly does it do? The Italian company is a successful eyeglass frame manufacturer. But its purchase of U.S. Shoe, a conglomerate that included the huge optical retail chain LensCrafters, was part of a global strategy because it also gave Luxottica a direct retail channel. Del Vecchio's

company now not only designs and manufactures the frames but sells them as well. For any American wearing medium-priced to expensive glasses, chances are one out of five that the frames were made by Luxottica.

Luxottica has been described as the type of company that the rest of Europe desperately needs in today's globalized economy: cash rich, little debt, not afraid to take risks or to innovate, and willing to act like a predator abroad. Del Vecchio's strategy for Luxottica has been a simple one: Grow by cutting out the middleman. Over the span of three decades, Luxottica has been transformed from an eyeglass-frame parts supplier to a full-frame manufacturer to a global distributor. And now, with the acquisition of the world's biggest optical chain, Del Vecchio is taking Luxottica straight into customer retailing.

Put yourself in Del Vecchio's position. How could he use a SWOT (strengths, weaknesses, opportunities, and threats) analysis to strategically manage this ever-expanding global empire? What would a SWOT analysis show about Luxottica's situation?

WHAT WOULD YOU DO?

The importance of having a good strategy can be seen by what Leonardo Del Vecchio has been able to do with Luxottica Group. By designing strategies to help Luxottica dominate its industry, Del Vecchio has built his company into the prosperous, thriving global organization it is today. An underlying theme in this chapter is that good strategies result in high organizational performance. Yet the fact that strategic management plays a critical role in an organization's success has been widely recognized only since the early 1970s.

CHAPTER

8

Strategic

Management

THE INCREASING IMPORTANCE OF STRATEGIC MANAGEMENT

Before the early 1970s, managers who made long-range plans generally assumed that better times were ahead. Plans for the future were merely extensions of what the organization had done in the past. However, environmental shocks such as energy crises, deregulation of many industries, accelerating technological change, and increasing global competition undermined this approach to long-range planning. These changes in the "rules of the game" forced managers to develop a systematic approach to analyzing the environment, assessing their organization's strengths and weaknesses, and identifying opportunities that would give the organization a competitive advantage. The value of thinking strategically began to be recognized.[2]

Why is strategic management considered so important? Because it's involved in many of the decisions that managers make. Most of the significant current business events reported in the various business publications involve strategic management. For example, on a recent day, there were reports of the return of Steve Jobs to Apple Computer as the interim CEO, the announcement by Intel Corporation of a new chip technology, and the continuing negotiations over the alliance between American Airlines and British Airways. All are examples of managers' making strategic decisions. Also, one survey of business owners found that 69 percent had strategic plans, and among those owners, 89 percent responded that they had found their plans to be effective.[3] They stated, for example, that strategic planning gave them specific goals and provided their staffs with a unified vision. Although some management analysts proclaim that strategic planning is "dead," there are many others who emphasize the importance of strategic planning.[4] In addition, studies of the effectiveness of strategic planning and management have found that, in general, companies with formal strategic management systems had higher financial returns than did companies with no such system.[5]

Today, strategic management has moved beyond for-profit business organizations to include governmental agencies, hospitals, and other not-for-profit organizations. For instance, when the U.S. Postal Service found itself in intense competitive battles with overnight package delivery companies, electronic mail services, and private mailing facilities, the U.S. Postmaster General (the Postal Service's CEO) used strategic management to help pinpoint important strategic issues and to design appropriate strategic responses. He reorganized the agency by trimming four layers of management and developed marketing innovations such as the popular self-adhesive stamps and the Postal Service's Global Priority Mail. One strategic innovation being implemented is an Electronic Postmark that would be used to certify electronic mail messages.[6] Although strategic management in not-for-profits has not been as well researched as that in for-profit organizations, we know that it's important for these organizations as well.

LEVELS OF STRATEGY

If an organization produced a single product or service, managers could develop a single strategic plan that covered everything it did. But many organizations are in diverse lines of business. For example, General Electric is in a variety of businesses—everything from manufacturing airplane engines and light bulbs to owning the NBC television network and the financial investment group Kidder Peabody. The Gillette Company includes a diverse array of products ranging from blades and razors and toiletry items to writing instruments, stationery products, and small household and personal care appliances. Each of these different businesses typically demands a separate strategy. Moreover, these multibusiness companies also have diverse functional departments such as finance and marketing that support each of their businesses. As a result, we need to differentiate between corporate-level, business-level, and functional-level strategies (Figure 8-1).

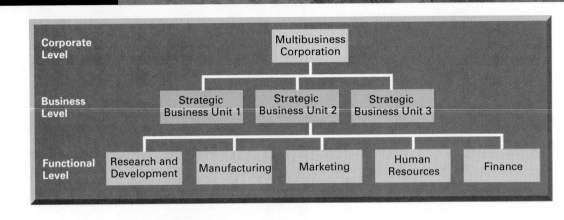

FIGURE 8-1 **Levels of Strategy**

Corporate-Level Strategy

If an organization is in more than one type of business, it will need a **corporate-level strategy**. This strategy seeks to answer the question: What business or businesses should we be in? Corporate-level strategy determines the roles that each business unit in the organization will play. At a company such as PepsiCo, for example, top management's corporate-level strategy integrates the strategies of its Pepsi, 7-Up International, and Frito-Lay divisions. PepsiCo did have a restaurant division that included Taco Bell, Pizza Hut, and KFC, but, because of intense competitive pressures in the restaurant industry, PepsiCo changed its corporate-level strategy and sold off that division to concentrate on its soda and snack food divisions.

corporate-level strategy

Seeks to determine what businesses a corporation should be in.

Business-Level Strategy

A **business-level strategy** seeks to answer the question: How should we compete in each of our businesses? For the small organization in only one line of business or the large organization that has not diversified into different products or markets, the business-level strategy typically coincides with the organization's corporate strategy. For organizations in multiple businesses, however, each division will have its own strategy that defines the products or services it will offer, the customers it wants to reach, and the like. For example, the French company LVMH-Moet Hennessy Louis Vuitton has different business-level strategies for its Christian Dior couture division, Louis Vuitton leather goods division, Guerlain perfume division, Fred Joailler jewels division, Hennessy cognac division, and its other luxury products divisions. Each has developed its own unique approach for distinguishing itself from its competitors by identifying target customers, appropriate products, and effective promotions.

When an organization is in several different businesses, planning can be facilitated by creating strategic business units. A **strategic business unit (SBU)** represents a single business or grouping of related businesses. Each SBU will have its own unique mission, competitors, and strategy. These distinguish an SBU from the other businesses of the parent organization. In a company such as General Electric, which is in many diverse lines of business, managers might create a dozen or more SBUs.

The SBU concept separates business units on the basis of the following principles:

business-level strategy

Seeks to determine how a corporation should compete in each of its businesses.

strategic business unit (SBU)

A single business or collection of businesses that is independent and formulates its own strategy.

- The organization is managed as a "portfolio" of businesses; each business unit serves a clearly defined product-market segment with a clearly defined strategy.

- Each business unit in the portfolio develops a strategy tailored to its capabilities and competitive needs but consistent with the overall organization's capabilities and needs.

France's luxury retailer LVMH-Moet Hennessy Louis Vuitton provides a prime example of successful business-level strategies. The firm's chairman, Bernard Arnault, oversees strategic business units that manufacture leather goods, perfume, jewelry, and champagne and cognac.

■ The total portfolio is managed to serve the interests of the organization as a whole: to achieve balanced growth in sales, earnings, and asset mix at an acceptable and controlled level of risk.[7]

Functional-Level Strategy

functional-level strategy

Seeks to determine how to support the business-level strategy.

A **functional-level strategy** seeks to answer the question: How do we support the business-level strategy? For organizations that have traditional functional departments such as manufacturing, marketing, human resources, research and development, and finance, these strategies need to support the business-level strategy. For example, when R.R. Donnelley & Sons Company, a Chicago-based printer, made a strategic decision to invest significant dollars in new high-tech digital printing methods, its marketing department had to develop new sales plans and promotional pieces, the production department had to incorporate the digital equipment in the printing plants, and the human resources department had to update its employee selection and training programs.

In the rest of this chapter, we focus on corporate-level and business-level strategies. This emphasis is not to diminish the importance of functional-level strategies. Rather, it reflects the emphasis that researchers and practitioners have placed on developing strategic frameworks.

TESTING... TESTING... 1 2 3

1 Why is strategic management important to organizations?

2 Differentiate between the three levels of strategy.

3 What is an SBU, and how is it distinguished from the parent corporation?

strategic management process

An eight-step process that encompasses strategic planning, implementation, and evaluation.

THE STRATEGIC MANAGEMENT PROCESS

The **strategic management process**, as illustrated in Figure 8-2, is an eight-step process that encompasses strategic planning, implementation, and evaluation. Although the first six steps describe the planning that must take place, implementation and evaluation are just as important! Even the best strategies can fail if management does not implement or evaluate

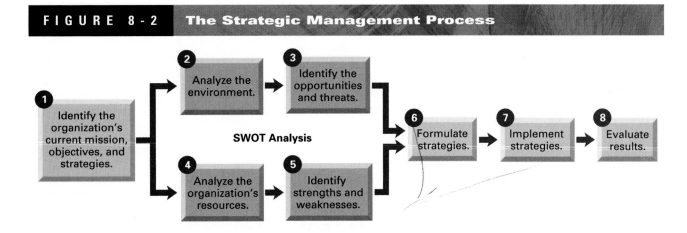

FIGURE 8-2   The Strategic Management Process

them properly. In this section we examine in detail the various steps in the strategic management process.

Step 1: Identifying the Organization's Current Mission, Objectives, and Strategies

Every organization needs a **mission** that defines its purpose and answers the question: What is our reason for being in business? Defining the organization's mission forces managers to identify the scope of its products or services carefully. For instance, the mission of Prime Trucking Inc., a transportation company headquartered in Missouri, is "to prosper while providing excellent service to our customers." At the Federal Bureau of Prisons, the mission statement reads, "The Federal Bureau of Prisons protects society by confining offenders in the controlled environments of prisons and community-based facilities that are safe, humane, and appropriately secure, and which provide work and other self-improvement opportunities to assist offenders in becoming law-abiding citizens." The mission statement of the Cherokee Nation includes the following: "to promote and sustain the self-reliance of its members." At Merix Corporation, a $140 million electronic interconnect supplier based in Forest Grove, Oregon, the mission statement is rather unusual; it's a visual mission statement. The company's philosophy is that a graphical representation of the company's mission requires organizational members to think in new, metaphoric ways about their work, and the images that emerge will be more dynamic, personal, and meaningful than mere words. (See Figure 8-3 for a further description of the typical components of mission statements.)

These statements provide clues to what these organizations see as their reason for being in business. When a company does a poor job of defining its purpose and scope of purpose, the results can be disastrous. For instance, Sears was the dominant U.S. retailer until Wal-Mart overtook them as king of the retailing industry. Why did Sears lose out to Wal-Mart? Many retail industry analysts believe that Sears's problems were the result of its inability to clearly define its mission. The one-stop shopping concept of "stocks and socks," which reflected its purchase of the Dean Witter brokerage firm in addition to its traditional clothing product lines, proved too broad to manage successfully. Sears tried to do too many things and confused its customers. Strategic managers at Sears finally recognized the problems that this confusing retailing mix had created and took significant steps (including selling the brokerage firm and eliminating its catalog division) to correct its lack of strategic mission. Since that time, the company's performance has been improving.[8]

Determining the purpose or reason for one's business is as important for not-for-profit organizations as it is for business firms. For example, is a college training students for the professions, training students for particular jobs, or educating students through a well-

mission

The purpose of an organization.

FIGURE 8-3   **Mission Statement Components**

1. Customer market	We believe our first responsibility is to the doctors, nurses and patients, to mothers and all others who use our products and services. (Johnson & Johnson)
2. Product and service	AMAX's principal products are molybdenum, coal, iron ore, copper, lead, zinc, petroleum and natural gas, potash, phosphates, nickel, tungsten, silver, gold, and magnesium. (AMAX)
3. Geographical domain	We are dedicated to the total success of Corning Glass Works as a worldwide competitor. (Corning Glass)
4. Technology	Control Data is in the business of applying microelectronics and computer technology in two general areas: computer-related hardware and computing-enhancing services, which include computation, information, education, and finance. (Control Data)
5. Concern for survival	In this respect, the company will conduct its operations prudently and will provide the profits and growth which will assure Hoover's ultimate success. (Hoover Universal)
6. Philosophy	We believe human development to be the worthiest of goals of civilization and independence to be the superior condition for nurturing growth in the capabilities of people. (Sun Company)
7. Self-concept	Hoover Universal is a diversified, multi-industry corporation with strong manufacturing capabilities, entrepreneurial policies, and individual business unit autonomy. (Hoover Universal)
8. Concern for public image	Also, we must be responsive to the broader concerns of the public, including especially the general desire for improvement in the quality of life, equal opportunity for all and the constructive use of natural resources. (Sun Company)

Source: J.A. Pearce II and F.R. David, "Corporate Mission Statements: The Bottom Line," *Academy of Management Executive*, May 1992, pp. 109–16.

---

rounded liberal education? Is it seeking students from the top 5 percent of high school graduates, students with low academic grades but high aptitude test scores, or students in the vast middle ground? When and where should education take place? Answers to questions like those clarify the organization's current purpose. For instance, many colleges are making significant investments in long-distance learning arrangements and tapping into markets that they traditionally may not have served.

It's also important for managers to identify the objectives and strategies currently being used. As we explained in chapter 7, objectives are the foundation of planning. A company's objectives provide the measurable performance targets that workers strive to reach. Knowing the company's current objectives gives managers a basis for deciding whether those objectives need to be changed. For the same reasons, it is important for managers to identify the organization's current strategies.

Step 2: Analyzing the External Environment

In chapter 3, we described the external environment as a primary constraint on a manager's actions. Analyzing that environment is a critical step in the strategy process. Why? Because an organization's environment, to a large degree, defines management's available options. A successful strategy will be one that aligns well with the environment.[9] Managers in every organization need to analyze the environment. They need to know, for instance, what the competition is doing, what pending legislation might affect the organization, and what the labor supply is like in locations where it operates.

For example, to prosper in the rough-and-tumble athletic shoe industry, a company needs to be able to "read" the external environment and sense consumer trends. George Yohn, owner of Airwalk, has built a successful company doing this. He noticed the growing interest of young adults in "extreme" sports and saw the potential for specialized shoes. Airwalk's shoes for skateboarding and other extreme sports, including snowboarding and BMX biking, were snapped up by people who were doing the extreme sports and by those who wanted to look as if they did them. To reinforce its anti-Nike image, Airwalk recruited 125 extreme athletes—including skateboarders, bike riders, and snowboarders—to do sports shows every week all across the United States.[10]

Step 2 of the strategic management process is complete when management has an accurate grasp of what is taking place in its environment and is aware of important trends that might affect its operations.

Strategy and the Entrepreneur

Strategic planning carries a "big business" bias. It implies a formalization and structure that fits well with large, established organizations that have abundant resources. Yet many strategic planning concepts can be applied directly to those who wish to pursue the entrepreneurial route in management, but with a different emphasis.[11]

Entrepreneurs approach strategy differently than typical bureaucratic managers do. This difference can be seen in the way they address key strategic questions. The typical bureaucratic manager asks strategic questions in the following order: What resources do I control? What structure determines our organization's relationship to its market? How can I minimize the impact of others on my ability to perform? What opportunity is appropriate? On the other hand, the typical entrepreneur will ask: Where is the opportunity? How do I capitalize on it? What resources do I need? How do I gain control over them? What structure is best?

The entrepreneur's strategic emphasis is driven by *perception of opportunity* rather than by *availability of resources.* The entrepreneur's inclination is to monitor the environment closely in search of opportunities. The resources at his or her disposal take a back seat to identifying an idea that can be pursued.

Once an opportunity is identified, the entrepreneur begins to look for ways to take advantage of it. Because an entrepreneur's personality characteristics typically include a willingness to work hard, self-confidence, optimism, determination, and a high energy level, the entrepreneur is confident that the opportunity can be exploited. Moreover, the entrepreneur is not afraid to risk financial security, career opportunities, family relations, or psychic well-being to get the new venture off the ground. Entrepreneurs tend to ignore the cold hard facts about a new business's chances for success. (One study found that 40 percent of new businesses fail in the first year, 60 percent fail by the end of the second year, and 90 percent fail by the end of the tenth year.) Nevertheless, the entrepreneur who sees an opportunity has the confidence and determination to believe that he or she will be one of the surviving ones.

Only after the entrepreneur has identified an opportunity and a way to exploit it does he or she begin to feel concerned about resources. The entrepreneur's priorities are first to find out what resources are needed and then to determine how they can be obtained. Entrepreneurs are often able to make imaginative and highly efficient use of very limited resources. Further, as entrepreneurship has grown in popularity, the availability of financial resources to support new ventures has increased. Finally, once the resource obstacles have been overcome, the entrepreneur will put together the organizational structure, people, marketing plan, and other components necessary to implement the overall strategy. ∎

ENTREPRENEURSHIP

opportunities

Positive external environmental factors.

threats

Negative external environmental factors.

Step 3: Identifying Opportunities and Threats

After analyzing the environment, management needs to assess what it has learned in terms of opportunities that the organization can exploit and threats it faces.[12] **Opportunities** are positive external environmental factors; **threats** are negative.

Keep in mind that the same environment can present opportunities to one organization and pose threats to another in the same industry because of their different management of resources. Southwest Airlines has prospered in a turbulent industry, but many of the larger, older airlines such as TWA and Delta have faltered. What an organization considers an opportunity or a threat depends on the resources it controls.

4 List the eight steps in the strategic management process.

5 What is a mission, and why is it important?

6 What is an external analysis? What are opportunities and threats?

Step 4: Analyzing the Organization's Resources

Now we move from looking outside the organization to looking inside. For example, what skills and abilities do the organization's employees have; what resources does the organization have; has it been successful at innovating new products; what is the organization's cash flow; how do consumers perceive the organization and the quality of its products or services? This step forces managers to recognize that every organization, no matter how large or powerful, is constrained in some way by the resources and skills it has available.

The internal analysis provides important information about an organization's specific assets, skills, and work activities. If any of these organizational skills or resources are exceptional or unique, they're called the organization's **core competencies**. The core competencies are the organization's major value-creating skills, capabilities, and resources that determine the organization's competitive weapons.[13] For example, Fingerhut Company is the second largest consumer catalog marketer in the United States (behind J.C. Penney Company) and is best known for its catalog that promotes everything from toy phones to big-screen TVs. Its target customers are low- and moderate-income customers. What is Fingerhut's core competency? It's the company's ability to sort through its 500 pieces of information on each of the more than 50 million active and potential customers to zero in on the best credit risks. Fingerhut has used this core competency to successfully compete and become a leader in the catalog shopping industry.[14]

core competencies

An organization's major value-creating skills, capabilities, and resources that determine its competitive weapons.

Step 5: Identifying Strengths and Weaknesses

The analysis in Step 4 should lead to a clear assessment of the organization's internal resources (such as capital, technical expertise, skilled workforce, experienced managers, and so forth). It should also point out the organization's capabilities in performing the different functional activities (such as marketing, production and manufacturing, research and development, financial and accounting, information systems, human resources management, and so forth). Any activities the organization does well or any resources that it has available are called **strengths**. **Weaknesses** are activities the organization does not do well or the resources it needs but does not possess. Look back at our chapter-opening Manager's Dilemma; what might Leonardo Del Vecchio look at in determining his organization's strengths and weaknesses?

An understanding of the organization's culture and the strengths and drawbacks it offers management is a crucial part of Step 5 that's often overlooked.[15] Specifically, managers should be aware that strong and weak cultures have different effects on strategy and that the content of a culture has a major effect on the chosen strategy.

strengths

Activities the firm does well or resources it controls.

weaknesses

Activities the firm doesn't do well or resources it needs but doesn't possess.

As we discussed in chapter 3, an organization's culture is its personality. It reflects the values, beliefs, attitudes, and valued behaviors that embody the "way things are done around here." In a strong culture almost all employees will have a clear understanding of what the organization is about. This clarity should make it easy for managers to convey to new employees the organization's distinctive competence. At a department store chain such as Nordstrom, which has a very strong culture of customer service and satisfaction, managers are able to instill cultural values in new employees in a much shorter time than could a competitor with a weak culture. The negative side of a strong culture, of course, is that it's more difficult to change. A strong culture may act as a significant barrier to acceptance of a change in the organization's strategies. Successful organizations with strong cultures can become prisoners of their own successes.

Cultures also differ in the degree to which they encourage risk taking, exploit innovation, and reward performance. Strategic choices encompass such factors, so cultural values influence managerial preference for certain strategies. In a risk-aversive culture, for example, managers are likely to favor strategies that are defensive, that minimize financial exposure, and that react to changes in the environment rather than try to anticipate those changes. Where risk is avoided, you should not be surprised to find strategies emphasizing cost cutting and improving established product lines. Conversely, where innovation is highly valued, managers are likely to favor new technology and product development instead of more service locations or a superior salesforce. For instance, when Electronic Data Systems (EDS) Corporation, a Dallas-based company, moved into developing interactive multimedia products for the "information superhighway," it had to change its traditionally conservative strategic emphasis on data centers and computer networks. Although this strategic shift entailed more risks, company managers were confident the company's expertise could be transferred into the new arena.

Organizational culture also can promote or hinder an organization's strategic actions. One study showed that firms with "strategically appropriate cultures" outperformed selected other corporations with less appropriate cultures.[16] Just what is a strategically appropriate culture? It's one that supports the firm's chosen strategy. For instance, at Hewlett-Packard, a high-tech company with over $38 billion in annual revenues, growth is the chosen strategy, and employees' product innovation efforts are enthusiastically supported within the corporate culture. In fact HP's culture, renowned for its openness, employee freedom, and autonomy, has played a key role in the company's successful implementation of its global growth strategies.

The informal culture cultivated at many technology firms such as Microsoft is credited with keeping alive a spirit of innovation and experimentation in which new product ideas can develop.

FIGURE 8-4   **Identifying the Organization's Opportunities**

Organization's Resources/Abilities   **Organization's Opportunities**   Opportunities in the Environment

SWOT analysis

Analysis of an organization's strengths and weaknesses and its environmental opportunities and threats.

The merging of Steps 3 and 5 results in an assessment of the organization's internal resources and abilities and opportunities in its external environment (Figure 8-4). This is frequently called **SWOT analysis** because it brings together the organization's *s*trengths, *w*eaknesses, *o*pportunities, and *t*hreats in order to identify a strategic niche that the organization might exploit. For instance, as Internet and World Wide Web usage continued to increase, strategic managers at the Seattle-based software company Microsoft, Inc. extended its exploitation of this market by acquiring and merging with companies with specialized Web expertise including, among others, UUNET Technologies, Inc.(an Internet service provider), Vermeer Technologies (maker of FrontPage, a Web page creation system), Colusa Software (maker of OmniWare, object-oriented programming software), eShop, Inc. (a leader in Internet commerce software), and Electric Gravity, Inc. (a company whose Internet Gaming Zone features multiplayer games). Although this expansion was costly, company executives knew they had to exploit this strategic niche and take advantage of the opportunity in the external environment.

In light of the SWOT analysis, managers also reevaluate the organization's current mission and objectives. Are they realistic? Do they need modification? Are we where we want to be right now? If changes are needed in the overall direction, this is where they are likely to originate. If no changes are necessary, management is ready to begin the actual formulation of strategies.

TESTING... TESTING...   1 2 3

7 What are core competencies, and what role do resources and capabilities play in an organization's core competencies?

8 What are organizational strengths and weaknesses?

9 Why is a SWOT analysis important?

Step 6: Formulating Strategies

Strategies need to be established for the corporate, business, and functional levels. The formulation of these strategies follows the decision-making process we discussed in chapter 6. Specifically, managers need to develop and evaluate strategic alternatives and then select strategies that are compatible at each level and that allow the organization to best capitalize on its strengths and environmental opportunities.

Doing a Personal SWOT Analysis

A SWOT analysis can be a useful tool for examining your own skills, abilities, career preferences, and career opportunities. Doing a personal SWOT analysis involves taking a hard look at what your individual strengths and weaknesses are and then assessing the opportunities and threats of various career paths that might interest you.[17]

Step 1: Assessing personal strengths and weaknesses. All of us have special skills, talents, and abilities. Each of us enjoys doing certain activities and not others. For example, some people hate sitting at a desk all day; others panic at the thought of having to interact with strangers. List the activities you enjoy and the things you are good at. (The self-assessment exercises at the end of every chapter can help you define some of your strengths.) Also, identify some things you don't enjoy and you're not so good at. It's important to recognize our weaknesses so that we can either try to correct them or stay away from careers in which those things would be important. List your important individual strengths and weaknesses. Highlight those you think are particularly significant.

Step 2: Identifying career opportunities and threats. We know from this chapter and chapter 3 that different industries (and the companies in those industries) face different external opportunities and threats. It's important to identify these external factors for the simple reason that your initial job offers and future career advancement can be significantly influenced by these opportunities and threats. A company that's in an industry filled with negative factors will offer few job openings or career advancement opportunities. On the other hand, job prospects will be bright in industries that have abundant

positive external factors. List two or three industries you have an interest in (for example, health care, financial services, or telecommunications) and critically evaluate the opportunities and threats facing those industries.

Step 3: Outlining five-year career objectives. Taking your SWOT assessments, list four or five career objectives that you would like to accomplish within five years of graduation. These objectives might include things such as type of job you'd like to have, how many people you might be supervising, or the type of salary you'd like to be making. Keep in mind that ideally you should try to match your individual strengths with industry opportunities.

Step 4: Outlining a five-year career action plan. Now it's time to get specific! Write a specific career action plan for accomplishing each of the career objectives you identified in the previous step. State exactly what you will do, and by when, in order to meet each objective. If you think you will need special assistance, state what it is and how you will get it. For example, your personal SWOT analysis may indicate that in order to achieve your desired career objective, you need to take more courses in management. Your career action plan should indicate when you will take those courses. Your specific career action plan will provide you with guidance for making decisions, just as an organization's plans provide direction to managers.

Doing this type of personal SWOT analysis takes effort, yet the payoff will be a coherent, realistic career strategy that you can pursue. Having a challenging, rewarding, and fun career doesn't just happen (at least to most of us). By expending some time in identifying what's personally important, you can develop a strategic plan and assure that it's implemented to your satisfaction. ■

MANAGING YOUR CAREER

Step 6 is complete when managers have developed a set of strategies that will give the organization a relative advantage over its rivals. As you'll see later in the chapter, this step requires a careful evaluation of the competitive forces within the organization's industry and an assessment of appropriate competitive strategies. Successful managers will choose strategies that give their organization the most favorable competitive edge; then they will try to sustain that advantage over time. For example, executives at Harley-Davidson formulated marketing strategies to solidify its market image and help reinforce its dominance in the fiercely competitive large motorcycle market. They have also invested in state-of-the-art manufacturing facilities and equipment in response to their commitment to efficiency, innovation, and quality. Harley's corporate, business, and functional strategies have enabled it to successfully compete in the global market.

Step 7: Implementing Strategies

The next-to-last step in the strategic management process is implementation. A strategy is only as good as its implementation. No matter how effectively a company has planned its strategies, it cannot succeed if the strategies aren't implemented properly. The rest of the chapters in this book address a number of issues related to strategy implementation. For instance, in chapter 10, we discuss the strategy-structure relationship. We show how successful strategies require a properly matched organizational structure. If an organization significantly changes its strategy, it needs to make appropriate changes in its overall structural design. In fact, we show that many of the new designs for organizational structure are ways for organizations to cope with environmental and strategic changes.

Managers might need to recruit, select, train, discipline, transfer, promote, and possibly even lay off employees to achieve the organization's strategic objectives. We discussed in chapter 2 the impact that downsizing is having on management's actions. In chapter 11, we show that if new strategies are to succeed, they often will require hiring new people with different skills, transferring some current employees to new positions, or laying off some employees. Also, since more and more organizations are using teams, the ability to build and manage effective teams is an important part of implementing strategy. Chapter 14 describes how managers can develop effective teams.

Top management leadership is a necessary ingredient in a successful strategy. So, too, is a motivated group of middle- and lower-level managers who carry out senior management's specific plans. Chapters 15 and 16 discuss ways to motivate people and offer suggestions for improving leadership effectiveness.

Step 8: Evaluating Results

The final step in the strategic management process is evaluating results. How effective have our strategies been? What adjustments, if any, are necessary? At IBM, CEO Lou Gerstner has made strategic adjustments to improve his company's competitiveness in the computer industry. These strategic actions were developed after assessing the results of previous strategies and determining that changes were needed.

In chapter 18, we review the control process. The concepts and techniques that we introduce in that chapter can be used to assess the results of strategies and to correct significant deviations.

**TESTING...
TESTING...**

10 What occurs during the strategy formulation step?

11 Why is strategy implementation important?

12 What management function does strategy evaluation encompass? Explain.

CORPORATE-LEVEL STRATEGIC FRAMEWORKS

We defined corporate-level strategy as asking the question: What business or businesses should we be in? Two popular approaches for answering that question are the grand strategies framework and the corporate portfolio matrix.

MANAGERS

SPEAK

OUT

Interview with George C. W. Gatch, Vice President, JP Morgan Investments, New York, New York

Describe your job.

I have overall responsibility for JP Morgan's U.S. mutual fund business. I manage a group of 45 individuals.

What types of skills do you think tomorrow's managers will need?

First, I think there's going to be less importance on specific technical skills. Instead, managers will need the ability to manage a diverse workforce. In the past, managers were considered the "stars." They led by example. In today's complex and dynamic environment, a good manager needs to be a player-coach. Managers need to be able to effectively get the most out of their teams of people. Motivational skills will be critical. Part of this involves the ability to directly and openly communicate with people. In addition, the manager needs the ability to build an "entrepreneurial" environment where individuals are encouraged to take risks and to take responsibility. Our company has found that the old hierarchal type of chain of command was *not* effective for a rapidly changing and competitive environment. Instead, for our organization to be nimble, flexible, and ready to seize opportunities, employees and employee teams need to be empowered and held accountable for success or lack of success. We've attempted to eliminate the bureaucracy and layers of management that tend to restrict decision making and action. We believe the key to success is building a sense of trust and ownership in employees.

Do you think it's important for an organization to have a competitive advantage? Why or why not?

It's absolutely critical. In my business, there are 8,000 mutual funds and 500 mutual fund families. To gain market share and be profitable, you have to differentiate yourself from the competition. Without a competitive advantage, it's unlikely that an organization will be successful.

How do your organization's strategies affect what you do in your job?

In my position, I do participate in the development of strategies that have a direct impact on my group. These strategies affect the level of resources and commitment my group receives. These strategies also affect my decision making.

JP Morgan has three long-term strategic plans for each of its groups. These plans cover opportunities and possible market share and anticipated return on equity. They are coordinated across our business groups by the company's top-level managers. If the top-level managers assess that an opportunity set isn't there in a particular business, that decision affects the level of resources and level of commitment to that particular group. Again, we believe that the hallmark of a successful organization is its ability to adapt its strategies to changes in the environment. And this stems back to our ability to empower individuals throughout the organization to detect those changes and to do something about them. ■

Grand Strategies

Kellogg's, Wal-Mart, and Westinghouse are successful, profitable companies, but they seem to be going in different directions. Kellogg's management is content to maintain the status quo and remain in the breakfast food industry. Wal-Mart, on the other hand, is rapidly expanding its operations and developing new businesses and retailing concepts. It's also pursuing global opportunities through alliances with foreign retailers to open Wal-Mart stores in countries such as Mexico, Argentina, and Thailand. Meanwhile, sluggish sales and an uncertain outlook in heavy industrial products and services such as turbine generators and electric and nuclear power generation have prompted Westinghouse Electric Corporation to scale back and sell some of its businesses. These different directions can be explained in terms of grand, or all-encompassing, strategies.[18] Figure 8-5 shows each of the grand strategies in relation to the SWOT analysis.

stability strategy

A corporate-level strategy characterized by an absence of significant change.

Stability.   A **stability strategy** is characterized by an absence of significant change. Examples of this strategy include continuing to serve the same clients by offering the same product or service, maintaining market share, and sustaining the organization's return-on-investment record.

When should management pursue stability? When it views the organization's performance as satisfactory and the environment appears to be stable and unchanging; that is, the firm has no valuable strengths or critical weaknesses, and there are no abundant environmental opportunities to pursue but also no critical threats to avoid.

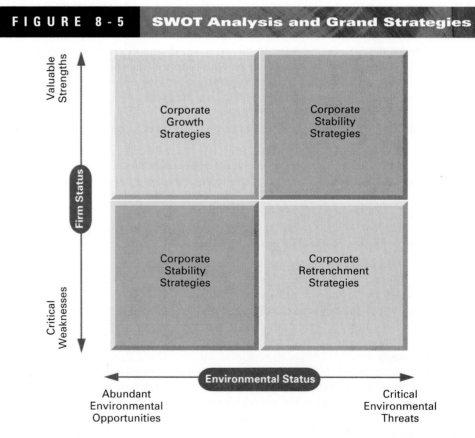

FIGURE 8-5   SWOT Analysis and Grand Strategies

Source: P. Wright, C.D. Pringle, and M.J. Kroll, *Strategic Management*, 2d ed. (Boston: Allyn and Bacon, 1994), p.82.

It's not easy to identify organizations that are pursuing a stability strategy, if for no other reason than that few top managers are willing to admit that they are doing it. In North America, growth tends to have universal appeal, and retrenchment is often accepted as a necessary evil. But managers who actively pursue stability might be considered complacent or even smug. You should be aware, however, that many *small* business owners and managers may follow a stability strategy indefinitely. Why? These individuals may feel that their business is successful enough just as it is and that it adequately meets their personal objectives.

We mentioned the Kellogg's Company as an example of a firm that uses a stability strategy. The company's continued emphasis on breakfast foods has given it a unique niche to exploit. Company managers have little interest in diversifying into other areas as many other food industry competitors have done; instead they seem to be content to maintain what they have.

Growth.   The pursuit of growth traditionally has had a magical appeal for North American firms. Supposedly, bigger is better, and biggest is best. For us, **growth strategy** means increasing the level of the organization's operations (Figure 8-5). This includes such popular measures as increasing sales revenues, number of employees, and market share. Growth can be achieved through direct expansion, merger with or acquisition of similar firms, or diversification.

Growth through direct expansion (or concentration) is achieved by internally increasing a firm's sales, production capacity, or workforce. No other firms are acquired or merged with; instead the company chooses to grow by itself through its own business operations. For instance, McDonald's has pursued a growth strategy by way of direct expansion. The company has never purchased other fast-food restaurant chains. It has grown only by granting franchises to people who are willing to be trained in the "McDonald's way" and by opening company-owned outlets.

A company might also choose to directly grow by creating (not acquiring or merging with) new businesses that operate in the same business as the original firm, in related businesses, or in unrelated businesses. For example, Brinker International is one of the United States' largest restaurant operators in the casual dining segment. Its restaurant chains include Maggiano's Little Italy, Chili's Grill & Bar, Romano's Macaroni Grill, Eatzi's, On the Border, and Cozymel's. Brinker has chosen to grow through the development of its own unique restaurant "concept" chains and not acquiring or merging with other chains.

growth strategy

A corporate-level strategy that seeks to increase the level of the organization's operations; typically includes increasing revenues, employees, or market share, or some combination.

Thai entrepreneur Sondhi Limthongkul consistently pursues a growth strategy for his firm, Asian Broadcasting Communications Network. The company has grown from a small publishing operation in 1983 to a communications empire that includes three daily newspapers, 20 other publications, and satellite broadcasting and has a net worth in the millions of dollars.

Finally, a company could directly grow by creating businesses within its own vertical channel of distribution. For instance, unlike other airlines that purchase their in-flight meals from outside suppliers, United Airlines has created its own in-flight food service business to supply itself. And Walt Disney Company not only develops its media content (cartoons, movies, and so forth) but distributes it as well through its Disney Channel, Disney stores, and the ABC television network.

Another popular way that many companies choose to grow is by merging with or acquiring *similar* firms in a strategic move known as **related diversification**. A **merger** occurs when two or more firms, usually of similar size, combine into one through an exchange of stock. For example, two large Swiss pharmaceutical companies, Ciba-Geigy and Sandoz, merged into an entity called Novartis in an attempt to compete more effectively in the intensely competitive global pharmaceuticals market. Growth can also occur by **acquisition**, which is when one company acquires another company through a payment of cash or stock or some combination of the two. Over the last several years, Johnson & Johnson, a health care products company, has acquired several companies that manufacture and market dental products, oral contraceptives, wound care products, prescription drugs, hospital products, over-the-counter drugs, diapers, feminine hygiene products, and infant products. In the aerospace industry, the Boeing Company purchased McDonnell-Douglas to form that industry's largest business. And London-based PolyGram has acquired a diverse array of entertainment-related businesses including the U.S. company Motown Record Corporation and several small independent Hollywood film producers. These are all examples of how a company can grow through acquiring related businesses.

Finally, a company can choose to grow by **unrelated diversification**, which is merging with or acquiring *unrelated* firms or firms that are not directly related to what the company does. For example, when USX (formerly known as U.S. Steel) acquired Marathon Oil Company, it moved into a different industry. As another example, Textron started as a textile company but has diversified into helicopters, chain saws, light machinery, and defense contracting. Molson Cos., Canada's largest brewer, also has business interests in cleaning products and services, retailing, and sports and entertainment. This approach was highly popular in the 1960s and 1970s. However, because of the difficulties in successfully competing in unrelated markets, the use of unrelated diversification as a means of growth has declined in popularity.

related diversification

A way that companies grow that involves merging with or acquiring *similar* firms.

merger

When two or more firms, usually of similar size, combine into one through an exchange of stock.

acquisition

When one company acquires another company through a payment of cash or by buying stock or some combination of the two.

unrelated diversification

A way that companies grow that involves merging with or acquiring *unrelated* firms or firms that are not directly related to what the company does.

An innovative diversification strategy took delivery expert Federal Express into a new but related business area. In the fall of 1996 the firm announced plans to enter the field of electronic commerce, allowing retailers and their customers to interact over the Internet via FedEx's central computer and software and to arrange for shipping via its top-ranked delivery service.

13 Why are corporate strategies described as "grand" strategies?

14 What is the stability strategy, and when might an organization use it?

15 Describe the different types of growth strategies.

Retrenchment. Until the 1980s, retrenchment was a dirty word to North American managers. No manager wanted to admit that he or she was pursuing a **retrenchment strategy**—reducing the size or diversity of organizational operations. However, during the last decade, managing decline has been actively investigated.[19] Why? Aggressive global competition, deregulation, mergers and acquisitions, and major technological break-throughs are some of the more obvious reasons.

There's no shortage of firms that have pursued a retrenchment strategy. A partial list includes some of the biggest corporate names: Mobil Oil, Procter & Gamble, AT&T, Kodak, Reebok, IBM, Chase Manhattan Bank, Toyota Motor, Pioneer Electronic, and Union Carbide. For example, at General Motors' National Car Rental System unit, a major retrenchment strategy resuscitated the faltering SBU. If the aggressive cost-cutting measures and other actions taken by company managers had not worked, GM likely would have closed down the entire operation. Retrenchment is also a strategic choice for not-for-profit organizations. For instance, changes in global politics led American military defense organizations such as the U.S. Army and Air Force to cut back by closing several military bases around the world. Also, a number of colleges and universities retrenched by eliminating certain programs, reducing the number of sections of a course being offered, or putting a freeze on hiring additional faculty and staff. These strategic actions were a response to falling student enrollments and decreased state spending on higher education.

Combination. A **combination strategy** is the simultaneous pursuit of two or more of the previous strategies. For example, one SBU in the company may be pursuing growth while another SBU is retrenching. Take, for instance, PepsiCo and the strategies its main businesses are pursuing. At its Pepsi-Cola unit, managers were following a retrenchment strategy because of strong price competition in the global soft drink industry. In addition, intense competitive pressures in the fast-food industry led managers to sell off the restaurant division, which included its Pizza Hut, KFC, and Taco Bell units. The only PepsiCo unit pursuing a strong growth strategy was its Frito-Lay division, which had a majority share of the U.S. salty-snack market.

retrenchment strategy

A corporate-level strategy that seeks to reduce the size or diversity of an organization's operations.

combination strategy

A corporate-level strategy that pursues two or more of the following strategies—stability, growth, or retrenchment—simultaneously.

THINKING CRITICALLY

ABOUT ETHICS

You're an assistant store manager for a discount store chain that's expanding rapidly, and your location in Mobile, Alabama, is just opening. There's a lot of work involved with opening a new store (ordering merchandise, checking it when it comes in, putting it on the shelves, and so forth). You're being helped by five people who were transferred from other stores in the chain. These people had been told that this was a "management training" program. The six of you work hard, and the store opens on time. One week after the store opens, your boss tells you to find a reason to let three of these five people go because there's room for only two management trainees. Do you think that it's wrong to let these people go after having told them that they were going to be part of a management training program? What ethical dilemmas do you see? How would you handle this situation? ■

BCG matrix

Strategy tool to guide resource allocation decisions on the basis of market share and growth of SBUs.

cash cows

Businesses that demonstrate low growth but have a high market share.

stars

Businesses that demonstrate high growth and have high market share.

question marks

Businesses that demonstrate high growth but have low market share.

dogs

Businesses that demonstrate low growth and have low market share.

cumulative experience curve

Assumes that when a business increases the amount of product manufactured, the per unit cost of the product will decrease.

Corporate Portfolio Matrix

It was once the most popular approach to determining corporate-level strategy—the corporate portfolio matrix.[20] The first of these matrixes was developed by the Boston Consulting Group. The **BCG matrix** introduced the idea that each of an organization's SBUs could be evaluated and plotted on a 2 × 2 matrix to identify which ones offered high potential and which were a drain on organizational resources.[21] This matrix is shown in Figure 8-6. The horizontal axis represents market share, and the vertical axis indicates anticipated market growth. *High market share* means that a business is the leader in its industry, and *high market growth* is defined as at least 10 percent annual growth in sales (after adjusting for inflation). The BCG matrix defines four business groups:

- **Cash cows** (low growth, high market share). Businesses in this category generate large amounts of cash, but their prospects for future growth are limited.
- **Stars** (high growth, high market share). These businesses are in a fast-growing market and hold a dominant share of that market but might or might not produce a positive cash flow, depending on the need for investment in new plant and equipment or product development.
- **Question marks** (high growth, low market share). These businesses are speculative and entail high risks. They are in an attractive industry, but they hold a small percent of market share.
- **Dogs** (low growth, low market share). Businesses in this category do not produce much cash, nor do they require much. These businesses hold no promise for improved performance.

It's important to understand that the BCG matrix assumes the existence of a **cumulative experience curve**. This is the assumption that if a business is producing a product and managing its production process properly, every significant *increase* in the cumulative amount of product manufactured will bring about a predictable *decrease* in the per unit cost of manufacturing the product. Specifically, the Boston Consulting Group contended that doubling manufacturing volume typically led to a 20 to 30 percent reduction in unit cost. The obvious conclusion then was that businesses with the largest market share should have the lowest costs.

Now let's turn specifically to the strategic implications of the BCG matrix. What strategy should management pursue with each group identified in the matrix? BCG's research shows that organizations that sacrifice short-run profits to gain market share yield the highest long-

FIGURE 8-6   The BCG Matrix

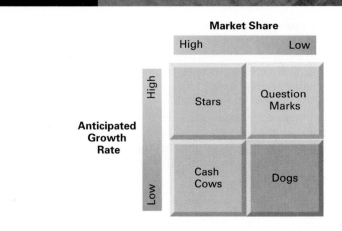

run profits. So managers should "milk" cash cows for as much as they can, limit any new investment in them to the minimal maintenance level, and use the large amounts of cash generated by them to invest in stars. Heavy investment in stars pays high dividends. The stars, of course, will eventually develop into cash cows as their markets mature and sales growth slows. The hardest decision is related to the question marks. Some should be sold off and others turned into stars. The latter requires substantial investment of resources. But question marks are risky, so managers want to have only a limited number of these speculative ventures. The dogs pose no strategic problems; they should be sold off or liquidated at the earliest opportunity. There's little to recommend keeping dogs in the corporate portfolio or allowing them to receive further company resources. Money obtained from selling off dogs can be used to buy or finance question marks. For example, the BCG matrix might indicate to Viacom management that it should sell off its video rental division because it's a dog, milk its cash cow book business, and invest in a star such as its networks division (including among others, MTV, Showtime, Nickelodeon, Comedy Channel, and VH1).

In the 1990s, the portfolio concept (and the BCG matrix in particular) lost much of its luster. Why? There are at least four reasons.[22] First, not every organization has found that increased market share leads to lower costs. To successfully move down the experience curve, managers must tightly control costs. Intel is an example of an organization that has been able to take advantage of volume and experience curve economies in its production of computer memory chips. Its sizable production volume makes it possible for Intel to invest heavily in research and development and new plant capacity and still earn huge profits. But not all organizations have been able to do that. Second, the portfolio concept assumes that an organization's businesses can be divided into a reasonable number of independent units. For large, complex organizations, doing that has been a lot easier in theory than in practice. Third, contrary to predictions, many so-called dogs have shown consistently higher levels of profitability than their growing competitors with dominant market shares. For example, according to the BCG matrix, Rolex would be considered a dog. Yet, it has been a profitable company. Finally, given the rate at which the economy has been growing in recent years and the fact that a market can have only one leader, well over half of all businesses by definition fall into the dog category. Following the corporate portfolio concept, most organizations' businesses today are cash cows and dogs, and there are few stars and question marks in which to invest.

Hewlett-Packard manufactures medical equipment, analytical instruments for the chemical and food industries, equipment for environmental monitoring, business and scientific calculators, personal computers, printers, scanners, palmtops, and printers. One way it could evaluate the operations of each of its strategic business units is to use the Boston Consulting Group matrix.

Despite these problems, the corporate portfolio matrix can be a useful strategic management tool. It provides a framework for understanding disparate businesses and establishes priorities for making resource allocation decisions. However, it has definite limitations as a device for guiding managers in establishing corporate-level strategy.

TESTING... TESTING...

16 What is a retrenchment strategy?

17 What is a combination strategy?

18 Describe the BCG matrix and why the portfolio concept is not as popular as it once was.

BUSINESS-LEVEL STRATEGIC FRAMEWORKS

Now we move to the business level, where managers decide how they want their business units to compete in the marketplace. In discussing the business-level strategies, we need to look at the role that competitive advantage plays and then at the various competitive strategies.

The Role of Competitive Advantage

competitive advantage

What sets an organization apart; its competitive edge.

Competitive advantage is a key concept in strategic management.[23] What is **competitive advantage**? It's what sets an organization apart: that is, its distinct edge. That edge might be in the form of organizational capabilities—the organization does something that others cannot do, or it does it better than others can do it. Or competitive advantage might arise from organizational assets or resources—the organization has something that its competitors do not have.

What makes some organizations more successful than others? Why do some professional basketball teams consistently win championships or draw large crowds? Why do some organizations have consistent and continuous growth in revenues and profits? Why do some colleges, universities, or departments experience continually increasing enrollments? Why do some companies consistently appear at the top of lists ranking the "best," or the "most admired," or the "most profitable"? Every organization has resources and work systems to do whatever it's in business to do, but not every organization is able to effectively exploit its resources or capabilities and to develop the core competencies that can provide it with a competitive advantage. And it's not enough for an organization simply to create a competitive advantage; it must be able to sustain it. That is, a sustainable competitive advantage enables the organization to keep its edge despite competitors' actions or evolutionary changes in the industry. One way organizations may attempt to create a sustainable competitive advantage is through total quality management.

TQM as a Competitive Advantage

If implemented properly, quality can be a way for an organization to create a sustainable competitive advantage.[24] That is why many organizations are applying total quality management (TQM) concepts to their operations in an attempt to set themselves apart from competitors.

As we first discussed in chapter 2, TQM focuses on quality and continuous improvement. To the degree that an organization can satisfy a customer's need for quality, it can differentiate itself from competitors and attract a loyal customer base. Moreover, constant improvement in the quality and reliability of an organization's products or services may result in a competitive advantage that cannot be taken away.[25] Product innovations offer little opportunity for sustained competitive advantage because they are usually copied by competitors as soon as they hit the market, but incremental improvement—an essential element of TQM—is something that might be developed into a competitive advantage. Let's look at how two very different companies are using TQM to gain competitive advantage.

At Volvo, a Swedish automobile manufacturer, maintaining world-class quality is an important goal.[26] How is the company pursuing that goal? One way is by using manufacturing operations that are designed to be efficient and economical. Rather than focusing on sheer production volume and scientific principles to attain these efficiencies, the company uses TQM principles, among other managerial innovations. Employees are encouraged to use their analytical skills and their creativity to continuously improve the organization's overall effectiveness and efficiency. Another way Volvo pursues its goal of world-class quality is through its strong corporate culture, which emphasizes building safe and reliable cars. The goal of producing safe, reliable cars is a long-standing cultural tradition that is critical to the overall way Volvo does what it's in business to do—sell cars.

At Granite Rock Company of Watsonville, California, the quality management program is just as important a strategic tool as it is at Volvo.[27] In fact, Granite Rock takes its quality program so seriously that it was awarded a Malcolm Baldridge National Quality Award. (The Baldridge Award is the United States' highest award for quality management and achievement.) What types of strategic quality innovations does Granite Rock use? The company found through numerous customer surveys that on-time delivery was its customers' highest priority. It then set about establishing standards (or benchmarks) for achieving on-time performance. It went to an unusual source for the standards: Domino's Pizza outlets, which guarantee fast, accurate delivery. From that study of Domino's, Granite Rock instituted a program in which customers simply drive up in their trucks, insert a card, and tell the machine how much of which material is needed—as you do at a bank ATM. The truck is loaded automatically, and a bill is sent to the customer later. The company's Granite Xpress is open 24 hours a day, seven days a week to meet customer needs. This strategic quality innovation and several others have helped Granite Rock remain a successful competitor in the rough-and-tumble construction materials market.

We can find numerous other examples of organizations worldwide who are using TQM as a strategic weapon. From the U.S.-based Motorola Corporation to South Korea's Daewoo Corporation, organizations are recognizing the value of TQM as a competitive advantage.

In attempting to create a competitive advantage, organizations are looking for ways to set themselves apart. How an organization chooses to do this is what the business-level strategy is all about. Let's look at some of the specific *competitive strategies* organizations might use.

Competitive Strategies

Many important ideas in strategic management have come from the work of Michael Porter of the Harvard Business School.[28] His competitive strategies framework identifies three generic strategies from which managers can choose. Success depends on selecting the right strategy—one that fits the competitive strengths (resources and capabilities) of the organization and the industry it's in. Porter's major contribution has been to carefully outline how management can create and sustain a competitive advantage that will give a company above-average profitability.

Industry Analysis.   Porter proposes that some industries are inherently more profitable (and therefore more attractive to enter or remain in) than others. For example, the pharmaceutical industry is one with historically high profit margins, and the airline industry has notoriously low ones. But a company can still make a lot of money in a "dull" industry. The key is to exploit a competitive advantage. Firms can lose money in so-called "glamor" industries such as personal computers and cable television and make it big in mundane industries such as manufacturing fire trucks and selling remanufactured auto parts.

In any industry, five competitive forces dictate the rules of competition. Together, these five forces (Figure 8-7) determine industry profitability because they directly influence the prices individual firms can charge, their cost structure, and their capital investment requirements. Managers assess an industry's attractiveness using these five factors:

1. *Threat of new entrants and barriers to entry.* Factors such as economies of scale, brand loyalty, and capital requirements determine how easy or hard it is for new competitors to enter an industry.

2. *Threat of substitutes.* Factors such as switching costs and buyer loyalty determine the degree to which customers are likely to buy a substitute product.

3. *Bargaining power of buyers.* Factors such as number of buyers in the market, buyer information, and the availability of substitutes determine the amount of influence that buyers have in an industry.

4. *Bargaining power of suppliers.* Factors such as the degree of supplier concentration and availability of substitute inputs determine the amount of power that suppliers have over firms in the industry.

5. *Existing rivalry.* Factors such as industry growth, increasing or falling demand, and product differences determine how intense the competitive rivalry will be among firms in the industry.

Selecting a Competitive Strategy.   According to Porter, no firm can successfully perform at an above-average level by trying to be all things to all people. He proposes that

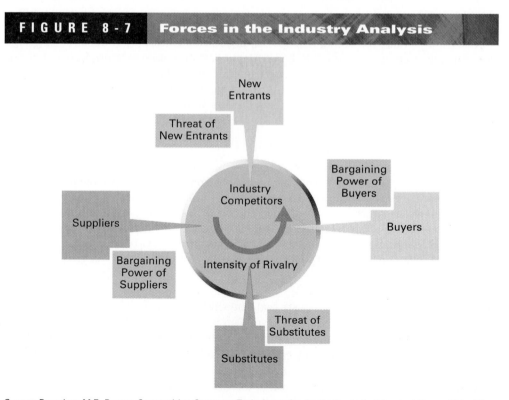

FIGURE 8-7   Forces in the Industry Analysis

Source: Based on M.E. Porter, *Competitive Strategy: Techniques for Analyzing Industries and Competitors* (New York: The Free Press, 1980).

managers select a strategy that will give the organization a competitive advantage. Porter goes on to say that a competitive advantage arises out of either having lower costs than competitors or being significantly different from competitors. On that basis, managers can choose one of three strategies: cost leadership, differentiation, or focus. Which one managers select depends on the organization's strengths and core competencies and its competitors' weaknesses (Table 8-1).

When an organization sets out to be the lowest-cost producer in its industry, it's following a **cost leadership strategy**. A low-cost leader aggressively searches out efficiencies in production, marketing, and other areas of operation. Overhead is kept to a minimum, and the firm does everything it can to cut costs. You will not find expensive art or interior decor at offices of low-cost leaders! For example, at Wal-Mart's headquarters in Bentonville, Arkansas, office furnishings are sparse and drab but functional. Although low-cost leaders do not place a lot of emphasis on "frills," the product or service being sold must be perceived as comparable to that offered by rivals or at least be acceptable to buyers. Examples of firms that have used the low-cost leader strategy include Wal-Mart, Hyundai (a Korean automobile manufacturer), Southwest Airlines, and Food Lion, Inc. (a grocery chain in the southeastern United States).

The firm that seeks to be unique in its product offering and in its industry in ways that are widely valued by customers is following a **differentiation strategy**. Sources of differ-

cost leadership strategy

The strategy an organization follows when it wants to be the lowest-cost producer in its industry.

differentiation strategy

The strategy a firm follows when it wants to be unique in its industry along dimensions widely valued by buyers.

TABLE 8-1   Common Requirements for Successfully Pursuing Porter's Competitive Strategies

Generic Strategy	Commonly Required Skills and Resources	Common Organizational Requirements
Overall cost leadership	Sustained capital investment and access to capital Process engineering skills Intense supervision of labor Products designed for ease in manufacture Low-cost distribution system	Tight cost control Frequent, detailed control reports Structured organization and responsibilities Incentives based on meeting strict quantitative targets
Differentiation	Strong marketing abilities Product engineering Creative flair Strong capability in basic research Corporate reputation for quality or technological leadership Long tradition in the industry or unique combination of skills drawn from other businesses Strong cooperation from channels	Strong coordination among functions in R&D, product development, and marketing Subjective measurement and incentives instead of quantitative measures Amenities to attract highly skilled labor, scientists, or creative people
Focus	Combination of the above policies directed at the particular strategic target	Combination of the above policies directed at the particular strategic target

Source: Reprinted from M.E. Porter, *Competitive Strategy: Techniques for Analyzing Industries and Competitors* (New York: Free Press, 1980), pp. 40–41.

Every day at Gillette's south Boston headquarters, 200 volunteers test and evaluate new razors as part of the company's ongoing product research effort. Its emphasis on innovation and quality enables Gillette to differentiate itself in the crowded personal care products market.

entiation might be high quality, extraordinary service, innovative design, technological capability, or an unusually positive brand image. The key to this strategy is that whatever product or service attribute is chosen for differentiating must set the firm apart from its competitors and be significant enough to justify a price premium that exceeds the cost of differentiating.

Practically any successful consumer product or service can be identified as an example of the differentiation strategy: Nordstrom's (customer service), Sony (reputation for quality and innovative design), Coach handbags (design and brand image), and Kimberly-Clark's Huggies Pull-Ups (product design).

The first two of Porter's strategies seek a competitive advantage in a broad range of markets and industry segments. The **focus strategy** aims at a cost advantage (cost focus) or a differentiation advantage (differentiation focus) in a narrow segment. That is, managers select a market segment or group of segments in an industry to the exclusion of others. These segments can be based on product variety, type of end buyer, distribution channel, or geographical location of buyers. For example, at Cia. Chilena de Fosforos, a large Chilean wood products manufacturer, Vice Chairman Gustavo Romero devised a focus strategy to sell chopsticks in Japan. Competitors, and even some other company managers, thought he was crazy. However, by focusing on this narrow segment, Romero's strategy managed to create more demand for his company's chopsticks than it had mature trees to make the products with.

The goal of a focus strategy is to exploit a narrow segment of a market. Of course, whether a focus strategy is feasible depends on the size of the segment and whether it can support the additional cost of focusing. Research suggests that the focus strategy may be the most effective for small business firms because they typically do not have the economies of scale or internal resources to successfully pursue one of the other two strategies.[29]

What happens if an organization is unable to develop a cost or differentiation advantage? Porter uses the term **"stuck in the middle"** to describe these organizations, which find it very difficult to achieve long-term success. When they do, it's usually a result of competing in a highly attractive industry or because all competitors are similarly stuck in the middle. Porter goes on to note that successful organizations frequently get into trouble by reaching beyond their competitive advantage and ending up stuck in the middle.

---

focus strategy

The strategy a company follows when it pursues a cost or differentiation advantage in a narrow industry segment.

stuck in the middle

Descriptive of organizations that cannot compete through cost leadership, differentiation, or focus strategies.

Originally targeted at a narrow segment of the market, cuddly Beanie Babies took off in 1996. Their cute names and low price appeal to more than just preschoolers. Ty Warner, who creates and produces Beanie Babies, profited from the biggest toy of the year as a result of his successful focus strategy.

However, a growing number of studies shows that a dual emphasis on low costs and differentiation can result in high performance.[30] To successfully follow a dual emphasis, though, an organization must be strongly committed to quality products or services, and consumers of those products or services must value quality. By providing high-quality products or services, an organization differentiates itself from its rivals. Consumers who value the high quality will purchase more of the organization's goods, and the increased demand will lead to economies of scale and lower per unit costs. For example, companies such as Anheuser-Busch, Federal Express, Intel, and Coca-Cola differentiate their products while at the same time maintaining low-cost operations.

No matter what corporate strategy, competitive advantage, or competitive strategy an organization chooses to pursue, keep in mind that all of these are part of the strategic management process, which plays a crucial role in an organization's success. Without the strategic management process to guide and direct their strategic planning decisions and actions, managers would have little chance of designing effective and efficient strategies.

19 What is competitive advantage, and why is it important to business-level strategies?

20 What does the five-forces model show?

21 Describe three possible competitive strategies.

TESTING...
TESTING...

1 2 3

managers respond to "a manager's dilemma"

MANAGER 1

As markets have become more global in nature, strategic planning has become an integral part of the ongoing developmental planning of nearly all organizations. The development of organizational strategy today must draw upon continuous informational feedback from the direct customer contact levels of the organization such as buyers, sales associates, and so forth. This information is then assimilated, analyzed, and filtered up through the management levels to the executive suite where senior executives using their experience, a methodology like the SWOT analysis, and their business instincts create the actual strategic plan. As general strategic scenarios are developed, those scenarios then should be forwarded back down through the organization, getting feedback from employees and testing the soundness of the plans.

In Mr. Del Vecchio's situation, a SWOT analysis would show the competitive advantages and disadvantages of vertically integrating his organization in the eyeglass industry. As Del Vecchio transformed his organization from an eyeglass frame parts supplier to a full eyeglass frame manufacturer and global distributor of eyewear, an ongoing SWOT analysis would have shown the advantages of eliminating the middleman and lowering his final cost to the consumer. It also would have shown that those advantages obviously outweighed any possible loss of business from competitive frame manufacturers.

Joe Lia, Regional Administrator, MVP Health Plan, Schenectady, New York

MANAGER 2

Mr. Del Vecchio can determine several things from doing a SWOT analysis. First of all, the major opportunity that stems from his purchase of Lenscrafters is that Luxottica now controls the major distribution channel for its frames. It can price its frames lower than competitors', putting the squeeze on the competition, and gaining greater market share. Or, the company may choose to maintain the current price of frames, thereby generating greater profits.

LensCrafters also serves as a source of information for Luxottica on competing framemakers. This gives Luxottica the ability to gather competitive information, sales data, and so forth, rapidly, and put this to use at LensCrafters.

There are also some threats to this strategy, however. Other framemakers may not want to sell to LensCrafters because it's now owned by a competitor. They may prefer to sell to other major optical chains such as Eyelab or Pearle Vision. In retaliation, these competing optical chains might refuse to carry Luxottica frames in their stores.

The strength that this acquisition gives Luxottica is the ability to exert greater control over the pricing and profitability of their frames. And the global nature of this new company should give them an advantage in the worldwide market.

However, one weakness is the fact that the combination of the two organizations may prove to be a real time drain for Del Vecchio and his management team. Then there's the question of culture, both organizational and regional. How will the Italian employees mix with those from the United States?

Natalie Anderson, Editor-in-Chief, B&E Publishing, Prentice Hall, Upper Saddle River, New Jersey

for your
IMMEDIATE action

BRADFORD
F I N A N C I A L   F U N D S

TO: Aletha Stamelos, Research Associate
FROM: Sandra Bradford, President
RE: New Investments

We are continually on the lookout for new additions to our technology-based fund. At a dinner meeting last night, the speaker was talking about a company called Merix Corporation. I'd like you to check out the information at its Web site <http://www.merix.com>. Then put together a list of what you feel are Merix's key strengths and potential weaknesses. Keep this list short (one page). After I've had a chance to look at it, I may have you do some more in-depth research on the company. Please get this information to me as soon as possible.

This is a fictionalized account of a potentially real problem. It was written for academic purposes only.

SUMMARY

This summary is organized by the chapter-opening objectives found on p. 234.

1. In a dynamic and uncertain environment, strategic management is important because it can provide managers with a systematic and comprehensive means for analyzing the environment, assessing their organization's strengths and weaknesses, and identifying opportunities for which they could develop and exploit a competitive advantage.

2. Corporate-level strategy seeks to determine what set of businesses the organization should be in. Business-level strategy is concerned with how the organization should compete in each of its businesses. Functional-level strategy is concerned with how functional departments can support the business-level strategy.

3. The strategic management process includes eight steps: (1) Identifying the organization's current mission, objectives, and strategies; (2) analyzing the environment; (3) identifying opportunities and threats in the environment; (4) analyzing the organization's resources; (5) identifying the organization's strengths and weaknesses; (6) formulating strategies; (7) implementing strategies; and (8) evaluating results.

4. SWOT analysis refers to analyzing the organization's internal strengths and weaknesses as well as external opportunities and threats in order to identify a niche that the organization can exploit.

5. The corporate grand strategies are stability, growth, retrenchment, and combination. A firm that's pursuing a stability strategy is not making any significant changes. A growth strategy means that the firm is increasing the level of its operations. When a firm is following a retrenchment strategy, it's reducing the size and diversity of its operations. A combination strategy is the simultaneous pursuit of two or more of the other corporate strategies.

6. The BCG matrix identifies four business groups: stars (businesses that show high growth and have high market share), cash cows (businesses that show low growth but have high market share), question marks (businesses that show high growth but have low market share), and dogs (businesses that have both low growth and low market share).

7. Competitive advantage is what sets an organization apart, its competitive edge. It comes from an organization's assets or resources and from its capabilities. It's important to organizations because without a competitive advantage they will never be able to compete successfully.

8. TQM (total quality management) can be a competitive advantage when a firm applies it as a way to set itself apart from its competitors.

9. The various competitive strategies include cost leadership, differentiation, and focus. A cost leadership strategy is the strategy an organization follows when it wants to be the lowest-cost producer in its industry. The differentiation strategy is the strategy a firm follows when it wants to be unique in its industry along dimensions widely valued by customers. The focus strategy is the strategy a company follows when it pursues a cost or differentiation advantage in a narrow industry segment.

THINKING ABOUT MANAGEMENT ISSUES

1. Perform a SWOT analysis on a local business you think you know well. What, if any, competitive advantage has this organization staked out?

2. How might the processes of strategy formulation and implementation differ for (a) large businesses, (b) small businesses, (c) not-for-profit organizations, and (d) global businesses?

3. As we have seen in previous chapters, top-, middle-, and lower-level managers make different types of decisions. How do you think this

hierarchy applies to the three levels of strategic planning?

4. Arie P. DeGues, head of planning for the Royal Dutch/Shell Group Companies, once suggested that the ability to "learn faster than competitors" may be the only sustainable competitive advantage. Do you agree? Why or why not?

5. Find five examples of what you would consider to be an SBU. For each of your examples, explain how it's an SBU.

SELF-ASSESSMENT EXERCISE

ARE YOU A RISK TAKER?

Formulating and implementing strategies typically involves taking risks. Whether the strategy is moving into a new market or divesting a "dog," there are risks involved. Not everyone is comfortable taking risks. This assessment exercise examines your level of comfort with risk taking.

Instructions: As a decision maker, do you tend to steer clear of risky situations, or do you find them tantalizing and invigorating? For example, if you had saved $20,000 would you keep it in the bank or invest it in a friend's new business venture? This quiz measures how likely you are to take risks with finances and your career. Insert T for true or F for false for each question.

_____ 1. I'd rather start my own business than work for someone else.
_____ 2. I would never take a job that requires lots of traveling.
_____ 3. If I were to gamble, I would be a high roller.
_____ 4. I like to improve on ideas.
_____ 5. I would never give up my job before I was certain I had another one.
_____ 6. I'd never invest in highly speculative stocks.
_____ 7. I'd be willing to take risks just to broaden my horizons.
_____ 8. Thinking about investing in stocks doesn't excite me.
_____ 9. I'd consider working strictly on a commission basis.
_____ 10. Knowing that any new business can fail, I'd always avoid investing in one, even if the potential payoff was high.
_____ 11. I would like to experience as much of life as possible.
_____ 12. I don't feel that I have a strong need for excitement.
_____ 13. I have a lot of energy.
_____ 14. I can easily generate lots of money-making ideas.
_____ 15. I'd never bet more money than I had at the time.
_____ 16. I enjoy proposing new ideas or concepts when the reactions of others—my boss, for example—are unknown or uncertain.
_____ 17. I have never written checks without having enough money in the bank to cover them.
_____ 18. A less secure job with a large income is more to my liking than a more secure job with an average income.
_____ 19. I'm not very independent minded.

See scoring key on page SK–4.

Source: F. Farley, 1025 West Johnson Street, University of Wisconsin, Madison, WI 53706. Copyright © 1986 by Frank Farley.

TAKE IT TO THE NET

We invite you to visit the Robbins/Coulter companion Web site at http://www.prenhall.com/robbinsmgt for this chapter's Internet resources.

CASE APPLICATION

Making Sweet Music Once Again

Gibson Guitars is a product synonymous with many rock music legends. Think, for instance, of the Les Paul models played by Keith Richards of the Rolling Stones and Paul McCartney of Beatles and Wings fame. Then, of course, there's the Flying V that the legendary Jimi Hendrix played so superbly. But strategic problems plaguing Gibson Guitar Corporation almost led to its swan song.

In 1986, the company had been virtually abandoned by its corporate owners, Norlin Industries, Inc. Equipment at the company's Nashville factory was old, and employee morale was low. The factory was turning out just 75 guitars a day and was producing none of its legendary banjos or mandolins at all. Annual revenues were a pitiful $10 million. Even among music industry experts, Gibson was believed to be "history." However, when musicians were asked what they thought of Gibson Guitars, they still thought that they were among the best you could buy. The magic of the name was still there. That's when three entrepreneurs—all business school-trained—who were looking at Gibson as a possible purchase decided to take the plunge. They bought the company in 1986 for a mere $5 million and have since engineered a dramatic rescue. The key to that turnaround lay in the changes they made in the company's strategies. The strategic emphases would be on improving efficiency, quality, and innovation and on getting the company back on a path to growth.

On taking over the company, one of the three entrepreneurs, Chairman and CEO Henry Juszkiewicz, immediately began cutting costs. For instance, a $500,000 data processing system was replaced with a $15,000 microcomputer. Thirty employees, including all top managers, were laid off. At Gibson's only other production facility, in Bozeman, Montana, computerized routers for rough-carving instruments and software for digitizing blueprints were installed. And the company's work processes were streamlined from office to factory floor. Yet, even with all these efficiency and modernization changes, Juszkiewicz wanted to maintain the founder's legendary sense of craftsmanship and quality. It wouldn't be easy, but he was determined to make it work.

If you break a guitar down into its component parts, it's nothing but a few hunks of wood, some metal, and a little plastic. But, as any skilled musician would attest, a guitar is more than the sum of its parts. The difference between perfection and mere playability is slim—about one-hundredth of an inch, about the width of a guitar string. The making of guitars is precise work. And Gibson takes its work seriously. Because the wood provides the resonance, Gibson employs brokers who scout natural woods from Maine to Cameroon. They've also diligently and carefully turned the art of guitar making into a science. From the kilns for drying raw wood to the rooms where the guitars are sprayed with lacquer, Gibson blends the craftsmanship of the 1890s with the technology of the 1990s.

A Gibson guitar is created through the help of many able hands. The early steps of the production process are mainly carpentry tasks. But as the guitar moves through the factory, the production process becomes more refined. Calipers measure veneer thickness. Frets are sawed by machine for accuracy. Necks are fitted one by one. The final product is played and sent to shipping or sent back for more work. (In the final assembly process, about 90 percent of the employees are musicians!) By the time a Gibson guitar is ready to be shipped, it's passed through the hands of at least 30 craftspeople and has spent four to six weeks on the shop floor. Despite such production precision, the company turns out about 300 guitars a day.

In addition to quality craftsmanship, the company has encouraged and valued innovation. Product changes and improvements are evaluated and implemented if judged appropriate. For instance, in 1991, the company started its Historic Collection to make copies of its old models. That way, customers who can't afford an original 1960 Les Paul Standard (which will set you back about the price of a new luxury car) can pay just $6,699 for a reissue. These innovations have contributed to Gibson's ability to keep the Gibson legend alive and profitable.

With Gibson's history and its present strategies firmly in hand, Juszkiewicz is looking toward the future. Sales have grown from $10 million in 1986 to $150 million in 1996. And he's continuing to think big. He says, "Our goal is to be the largest musical instrument company in the world." And, who knows, he just might be able to play that song, too!

QUESTIONS

1. What competitive advantage(s) do you think Gibson Guitars has? Explain your choice(s).
2. What is Gibson Guitars' competitive strategy? Explain your choice.
3. What role might TQM play in Gibson Guitars' development of a competitive advantage?

4. How could Juszkiewicz have used SWOT analysis when he first arrived at Gibson Guitars? What types of things should he have looked for in performing a SWOT analysis?
5. Describe the types of corporate (grand) strategies you see in this case.

Source: B. Watson, "How to Take on an Ailing Company and Make It Hum," *Smithsonian Magazine,* July 1996, pp. 53–61; and T. Stevens, "The Guitar Man," *IW,* June 23, 1997, pp. 12–17.

SMALL BUSINESS 2000

VIDEO CASE APPLICATION

Not Just Toying Around

The toy industry, like all others, has its good points and its bad points. One person who's trying to take advantage of the good points—that is, what he sees as the many growth opportunities in the toy industry—is Charlie Woo of Los Angeles.

Woo and his family came to the United States from Hong Kong in the late 1970s. To support the family, his mother and father initially started a restaurant but found that venture to be too time consuming. They looked to start another business and settled on the toy industry. By using their contacts in Hong Kong and by bringing their four sons into the business, the Woo family opened ABC Toys. The company's initial goal was to manufacture and distribute toys to small wholesalers who could not get products from the large toy makers because they weren't big enough customers; that is, they didn't buy in enough volume. ABC Toys had identified a specific niche and wasn't even attempting to compete with the likes of Mattel or the other large toy manufacturers. Charlie, who was just about to complete his Ph.D. in physics from UCLA, found himself making a major career switch—from physics to toys.

ABC Toys purchased several run-down warehouse buildings on a blighted corner of downtown Los Angeles. Charlie's vision was to encourage other small toy manufacturers and distributors to rent from them and together create a "toy town." He recalls that in the beginning ABC Toys was located there by itself. But Charlie reasoned that this wholesale district would enable customers to come to one location, shop comparatively, and, he hoped, end up buying more products than they would if they had to travel to separate stores. As more and more small toy companies joined ABC Toys in Toy Town, word soon spread about it and customers began coming from all over. Now there are more than 500 wholesale toy dealers within a few blocks of each other in Toy Town.

In 1989, Charlie and one other brother spun out of ABC Toys to form Megatoys. This company now employs 30 people and has hit $15 million in sales. And Charlie isn't finished yet! He believes that there is still good potential for growth in his business. Why? The changing global trade environment is opening up many potentially profitable areas. After all, in this business, if you want to be successful, you can't just toy around!

QUESTIONS

1. Charlie wants to continue Megatoys' growth. How might he use strategic management concepts to help him achieve his goals?
2. Would SWOT analysis be useful to Charlie in managing Megatoys? Why or why not? Explain your choice.
3. Charlie has asked you to make a presentation to his employees about competitive advantage. Draw up a list of the main ideas you'd want to tell them.

Source: Based on *Small Business Today, Show 107.*

A MANAGER'S DILEMMA

With product names such as Dork, Sissy, Pimp, Frigid, and Trailer Trash, Dineh Mohajer's company, Hard Candy, has shaken up the staid and conservative nail polish industry.[1] The impetus for this shakeup was the same as that for many new product ideas: dissatisfaction with what was available in the marketplace. In this instance, Mohajer was tired of the endless monotony of various shades of red nail polish that clashed gaudily with her fashionable, pastel-colored clothes. She wanted pastel-colored nail polish and proceeded to mix her own using a bit of white polish and blue dye. In the spring of 1995, she took samples of her home-made nail polishes to Fred Segal, a chain of hyper-trendy Los Angeles retail shops. The minute the product hit the shelves, customers started snapping up the bottles at $18 each. The store's owner immediately contacted Mohajer and ordered 200 more bottles. Working practically around the clock, she delivered the 200 bottles of pale yellow, blue, violet, and green nail polish two days later. Hard Candy was on its way.

With her natural feel for marketing and promotion, Mohajer created rebellious colors

and names and put her polish in bottles with cheap plastic heart-shaped rings on the cap to reinforce the company's image. She sold Hard Candy nail polishes exclusively to high-end fashion boutiques. By the fall of 1995, Hard Candy, Inc. was producing 10,000 bottles of polish a month, grossing about $70,000. But Mohajer wasn't using any management systems or formalized planning tools. All she knew was that she was paying her bills, so she assumed that her company was profitable. She had never seen a balance sheet or financial statement and kept no records of inventory, orders, sales, or invoices. Then, Mohajer found that things weren't going as smoothly as they once were. Competitors such as Krazy Kandy, Ripe, and Urban Decay entered the market. Even the cosmetics giant Revlon introduced its own line of funky, trendy colors, called Street Wear. It became obvious to Mohajer that the time was right to use more-formalized managerial planning tools and techniques.

Put yourself in Mohajer's situation. What planning tools might prove useful to Hard Candy? What benefits could be expected from each of these planning tools you might use?

WHAT WOULD YOU DO?

In this chapter we'll discuss some basic planning tools and techniques that managers like Dineh Mohajer or managers at any businesses—large or small—could use. We'll begin by looking at three planning techniques to assist managers in assessing their environment: environmental scanning, forecasting, and benchmarking. Then we'll review the most popular planning tool used by managers: budgets. We'll also look at various operational planning tools that managers might use. We'll end the chapter by looking at project management and how organizations are using it as a type of planning system. Many of the planning techniques that we discuss in this chapter are included in the skills modules at the end of the text. Check the list on p. SM–1.

Planning Tools
and Techniques

TECHNIQUES FOR ASSESSING THE ENVIRONMENT

In our last chapter, we examined the strategic management process in detail. In this section, we review several techniques that have been developed to help managers with one of the most challenging aspects of the process: assessing their organization's environment. Today's managers can accurately analyze their organization's environment by using structured techniques such as environmental scanning, forecasting, and benchmarking.

Environmental Scanning

Managers in both small and large organizations are increasingly using **environmental scanning** to anticipate and interpret changes in their environment. In fact, one study found that companies that implemented advanced environmental scanning systems increased their profits and revenue growth.[2] Companies that don't keep on top of environmental changes are likely to face just the opposite situation. For instance, managers at A.T. Cross Company, a manufacturer of luxury pens, failed to recognize that their customers' desires had changed. The company continued to produce its slender writing instruments with their distinctly "thin" profile while customers were clamoring for solid, sturdy, and "fat" luxury writing pens. Other penmakers and marketers that noticed the trends and came out with products that better fit customers' demands included Gillette Company's Waterman S.A. and Germany's Mountblanc. By sticking with its old design, Cross soon found itself pushed from the top of the luxury market to the middle. After recognizing the error of his company's ways and its failure to interpret the changing environment, CEO Russell Boss took action to attempt to restore Cross's performance.[3]

The importance of environmental scanning was first recognized (outside of national security agencies such as the CIA and the FBI) by firms in the life insurance industry in the 1970s.[4] Life insurance companies found that the demand for their product was declining although all the key environmental signals they were receiving strongly favored the sale of life insurance products. The economy and population were growing. Baby boomers were finishing school, entering the labor force, and taking on family responsibilities. The market for life insurance should have been expanding, but it wasn't. What the insurance companies had failed to recognize was a fundamental change in family structure in the United States. Young families, who represented the primary group of buyers of new insurance policies, tended to be dual-career couples who were increasingly choosing to remain childless or at least delaying the decision to have children. The life insurance needs of a family with one income, a dependent spouse, and a houseful of kids are much greater than are those of a two-income family with few, if any, children. The fact that a multibillion dollar industry could overlook such a fundamental social trend underscored the need to develop techniques for monitoring important environmental developments.

One of the fastest-growing areas of environmental scanning is **competitor intelligence**.[5] It's the process by which organizations gather information about their competitors and get answers to questions such as: Who are they? What are they doing? How will what they're doing affect us? Let's look at an example of how one organization used competitor intelligence in its planning.

Marketing managers at Monsanto Company's Nutrasweet Unit had an important decision facing them in the mid-1990s. Customers had told Nutrasweet's sales representatives that the U.S. Food and Drug Administration (FDA) was about to approve a rival sweetener from Johnson & Johnson called sucralose. To combat this competitive threat, the managers proposed a plan for a three-year, $84 million advertising campaign designed to help preserve Nutrasweet's two-thirds share of the $1.5 billion artificial sweetener market. But Nutrasweet's competitive intelligence analysts, who had carefully cultivated key contacts at the FDA and in Canada, which had already approved sucralose, reported that their analysis of the situation led them to believe that FDA approval of sucralose wasn't imminent. The conclusion was that the advertising outlay would be a waste of money, and the marketing

environmental scanning

The screening of large amounts of information to detect emerging trends and to create scenarios.

competitor intelligence

Environmental scanning activity that seeks to identify who competitors are, what they are doing, and how their actions will affect the focus organization.

plan was scrapped. The FDA still hasn't approved the use of sucralose, so the decision appears to have been a good one.[6]

Competitor intelligence experts suggest that 80 percent of what managers need to know about competitors can be found out from their own employees, suppliers, and customers.[7] Competitor intelligence doesn't necessarily have to involve organizational spying. Advertisements, promotional materials, press releases, reports filed with governmental agencies, annual reports, want ads, newspaper reports, and industry studies are examples of readily accessible sources of information. Trade shows and debriefing the salesforce can be other good sources of information on competitors. Many firms even regularly buy competitors' products and have their own engineers break them down (through a process called *reverse engineering*) to learn about new technical innovations. And the World Wide Web is opening up new sources of competitor intelligence as many corporate Web pages include new-product information and other information such as press releases.

Yet the questions and concerns that often arise about competitor intelligence pertain to the ways in which competitor information is gathered. Competitor intelligence becomes illegal corporate spying when it involves the theft of proprietary materials or trade secrets by any means. Often, there's a fine line between what's considered *legal and ethical* and what's considered *legal but unethical.* And, although the top manager at one competitive intelligence firm contends that 99.9 percent of intelligence gathering is legitimate, there's no question that some people or companies will go to any lengths to get information about competitors.[8]

Another type of environmental scanning that has become increasingly important is global scanning. The value of global scanning to managers, of course, is largely dependent on the extent of the organization's international activities. For a company that has significant international operations, global scanning can provide a wealth of information. Because world markets are complex and dynamic, managers have expanded the scope of their scanning efforts in order to gain vital information on those global forces that might affect their organizations.[9] For example, Mitsubishi Trading Company, a Japanese firm, has more than 60,000 market analysts around the world whose principal job is to identify and feed back information to the parent company.

The sources that managers have used for scanning the domestic environment are too limited for global scanning. Managers need to internationalize their perspectives and information sources. For instance, they can subscribe to information clipping services that review newspapers and business periodicals throughout the world and provide summaries. An increasing number of electronic services, including databases and the World Wide Web, can provide topic searches, and many databases even provide automatic updates in areas of special interest to managers.

Extensive environmental scanning is likely to reveal issues and concerns that could affect your organization's current or planned operations. They won't all be equally impor-

---

THINKING CRITICALLY

ABOUT ETHICS

Here are some techniques that have been suggested for gathering competitor information: (1) Get copies of lawsuits and civil suits that may have been filed against competitors. These court proceedings are public records and can expose surprising details. (2) Call the Better Business Bureau and ask if your competitors have had complaints filed against them because of fraudulent product claims or questionable business practices. (3) Pretending to be a journalist writing a story, call up competitors' offices and ask questions. (4) Get copies of your competitors' in-house newsletters and read them. (5) Buy a single share of your competitors' stock so you can get the annual report and other information the company sends out. (6) Pretend to be applying for a job at your competitor's organization and ask questions. (7) Dig through a competitor's trash.

Which, if any, of these are unethical? Defend your choices. What ethical guidelines would you suggest for competitor intelligence activities? ∎

Many firms today consider the world their marketplace and are constantly scanning at home and abroad for demographic changes and trends in customers' needs and wants.

tant, so it's usually necessary to focus in on a limited set—say, three or four—that are most important and to develop scenarios based on each of them.

scenario

A consistent view of what the future is likely to be.

A **scenario** is a consistent view of what the future is likely to be. If, for instance, scanning uncovers increasing interest by the U.S. Congress for raising the national minimum wage, managers at Shoney's Restaurants could create a multiple set of scenarios to assess the possible consequences of such an action. What would be the implications for its labor supply if the minimum wage were raised to $8.00 an hour? How about $8.50 an hour? What effect would these changes have on labor costs and on the bottom line? How might competitors respond? Different assumptions would lead to different outcomes. The intent of this exercise is not to try to predict the future but to reduce uncertainty by playing out potential situations under different specified conditions.[10] Shoney's could, for example, develop a set of scenarios ranging from optimistic to pessimistic in terms of the minimum wage issue. It would then be prepared to initiate strategic changes to get and keep a competitive advantage.

TESTING... TESTING...
1 **2** **3**

1 What is environmental scanning?

2 Describe competitor intelligence.

3 When would global scanning be an important planning tool?

Forecasting

Environmental scanning creates the foundation for forecasts. Information obtained through scanning is used to develop scenarios. These, in turn, establish premises for **forecasts,** which are predictions of outcomes.

forecasts

Predictions of outcomes.

Types of Forecasts.   Two specific outcomes managers attempt to forecast are future revenues and new technological breakthroughs. However, virtually any component in the organization's general and specific environment can be forecasted.

Quaker Oats' projected sales level for its cereals influences purchasing requirements, production goals, employment needs, inventories, and numerous other decisions. Similarly, the University of Michigan's income from tuition and state appropriations will influence course offerings, staffing needs, salary increases for faculty and staff, and the like. Both of these examples illustrate that predicting revenues—**revenue forecasting**—is a critical element of planning for both profit and not-for-profit organizations. Is revenue forecasting something that Dineh Mohajer from our chapter-opening Manager's Dilemma might want to do?

> **revenue forecasting**
>
> Predicting revenues.

Where do managers get the data for developing revenue forecasts? Typically, they begin by looking at historical revenue figures. For example, what were last year's revenues? This figure can then be adjusted for any significant trends discovered during environmental scanning. What revenue patterns have evolved over recent years? What changes in social, economic, or other factors in the general environment might alter the pattern in the future? In the specific environment, what might our competitors be doing? Answers to such questions provide the basis for revenue forecasts.

Technological forecasting attempts to predict changes in technology and the time frame in which new technologies are likely to be economically feasible. The rapid pace of technological change has brought us innovations in lasers, biotechnology, robotics, and data communications and has dramatically changed surgery techniques, pharmaceutical products, manufacturing processes used for almost every mass-produced product, and the use of computers and computer chips in products we use every day. The environmental scanning techniques discussed in the previous section can provide data on potential technological innovations.

> **technological forecasting**
>
> Predicting changes in technology and when new technologies are likely to be economically feasible.

To appreciate how important technological forecasting can be, consider what has happened in the recorded music industry. Look at the merchandise in any music store and you'll have a hard time finding vinyl, long-play record albums or eight-track tapes. Some recording companies, including Columbia and MCA, saw the market for these music mediums almost disappear during the early 1990s. Although customers still wanted to listen to music, they preferred a new technology: compact disks. The record companies that correctly forecasted this technology and foresaw its impact on their business were able to convert their production facilities, adopt the technology, and beat their competition to the music store racks. Ironically, CDs are increasingly under attack from digital tape technology. Again, those in the music recording business who accurately forecast when, or if, digital tape technology will become the preferred music medium are likely to score big in the market.

Forecasting Techniques.   Forecasting techniques fall into two categories: quantitative and qualitative. **Quantitative forecasting** applies a set of mathematical rules to a series of past data to predict outcomes. These techniques are preferred when management has sufficient "hard" data that can be used. **Qualitative forecasting**, in contrast, uses the judgment and opinions of knowledgeable experts. Qualitative techniques typically are used when precise data are limited or hard to obtain. Table 9-1 lists some of the best-known quantitative and qualitative forecasting techniques.

> **quantitative forecasting**
>
> Applies a set of mathematical rules to a series of past data to predict outcomes.
>
> **qualitative forecasting**
>
> Uses the judgment and opinions of knowledgeable individuals to predict outcomes.

One of the newest twists in forecasting uses Internet-based software and is called CFAR, which stands for collaborative forecasting and replenishment.[11] CFAR offers a standardized way for retailers and manufacturers to work together (collaborate) on forecasts by using the Internet to exchange numbers. Each organization relies on its own data about past sales trends, promotion plans, and other factors to calculate a demand forecast for a particular product. If the organizations' forecasts differ by a certain amount (say, 10 percent), the retailer and manufacturer use the Internet link to exchange more data and written comments until they arrive at a single and more accurate forecast. This mutual and collaborative forecasting helps both organizations do a better job of planning.

TABLE 9-1	Forecasting Techniques	

Technique	Description	Application
Quantitative		
Time series analysis	Fits a trend line to a mathematical equation and projects into the future by means of this equation	Predicting next quarter's sales on the basis of four years of previous sales data
Regression models	Predicts one variable on the basis of known or assumed other variables	Seeking factors that will predict a certain level of sales (for example, price, advertising expenditures)
Econometric models	Uses a set of regression equations to simulate segments of the economy	Predicting change in car sales as a result of changes in tax laws
Economic indicators	Uses one or more economic indicators to predict a future state of the economy	Using change in GDP to predict discretionary income
Substitution effect	Uses a mathematical formula to predict how, when, and under what circumstances a new product or technology will replace an existing one	Predicting the effect of microwave ovens on the sale of conventional ovens
Qualitative		
Jury of opinion	Combines and averages the opinions of experts	Polling all the company's human resouce managers to predict next year's college recruitment needs
Salesforce composition	Combines estimates from field sales personnel of customers' expected purchases	Predicting next year's sales of industrial lasers
Customer evaluation	Combines estimates from established purchases	Surveying of major dealers by a car manufacturer to determine types and quantities of products desired

Forecasting Effectiveness.   Despite the importance of forecasting to strategic planning, managers have had mixed success in forecasting trends and outcomes.[12] Forecasting techniques are most accurate when the environment is not rapidly changing. The more dynamic the environment, the more likely managers are to develop inaccurate forecasts. Forecasting also is relatively unimpressive in predicting nonseasonal events such as recessions, unusual occurrences, discontinued operations, and the actions or reactions of competitors.

Although forecasting has a mixed record, various research studies have proposed some suggestions for improving forecasting effectiveness.[13] First, use simple forecasting techniques. They tend to do as well as, and often better than, complex methods that tend to mistakenly confuse random data for meaningful information. For instance, at St. Louis-based Emerson Electric, CEO Chuck Knight found that forecasts developed as part of the company's planning process were indicating that the competition was no longer just domestic companies but international ones as well. He didn't use any complex mathematical techniques to come to this conclusion but instead relied on the information already collected as part of his company's planning process. Second, compare every forecast with "no change."

A no-change forecast is accurate approximately half the time. Third, don't rely on a single forecasting method. Make forecasts with several models and average them, especially when making long-range forecasts. Fourth, don't assume that you can accurately identify turning points in a trend. What is typically perceived as a significant turning point often turns out to be an unusual random event. And fifth, shorten the length of forecasts to improve their accuracy because accuracy decreases as the period you're trying to predict increases.

Benchmarking

A third strategic planning tool is **benchmarking**. This is the search for the best practices among competitors or noncompetitors that lead to their superior performance.[14] The basic idea behind benchmarking is that managers can improve quality by analyzing and then copying the methods of the leaders in various fields. Even small companies are finding that benchmarking can bring big benefits. As such, benchmarking is a very specific form of environmental scanning.

Xerox Corporation is widely recognized as the first U.S. company to systematically attempt benchmarking. Before 1979, Japanese firms had been aggressively copying the successes of others by traveling around the world, watching what others were doing, then applying their new knowledge to improve their products and processes. Xerox's management couldn't figure out how Japanese manufacturers could sell midsized copiers in the United States for considerably less than Xerox's production costs. So the company's head of manufacturing took a team to Japan to make a detailed study of their competitors' costs and processes. They got most of their information from Xerox's own joint venture partner, Fuji-Xerox, because it knew the competition well. What the team found was shocking. Their Japanese rivals were light-years ahead of Xerox in efficiency. Benchmarking those efficiencies marked the beginning of Xerox's turnaround in the copier industry. Today, in addition to Xerox, companies such as AT&T, DuPont, Ford, Kodak, and Motorola use benchmarking as a standard tool in their quest for performance improvement. In fact, some companies have chosen some pretty unusual benchmarking partners. Southwest Airlines, for example, studied Indy 500 pit crews, who can change a race car tire in under 15 seconds, to see how they could make their gate turnaround even faster. After all, they reasoned, you don't make money sitting on the ground; you have got to be flying passengers to the next location. IBM

benchmarking

The search for the best practices among competitors or noncompetitors that lead to their superior performance.

Benchmarking its speed at serving customers against itself keeps MBNA on its toes. The Wilmington (Delaware) credit card company posts scoreboards in its offices to let employees know how they're doing.

studied Las Vegas casinos looking for ways to discourage employee theft. Today, managers can even find benchmarking information on the Internet and the World Wide Web.

What does the benchmarking process involve? As illustrated in Figure 9-1, it typically follows four steps:

1. The organization forms a benchmarking planning team. The team's initial task is to identify what is to be benchmarked, identify comparative organizations, and determine data collection methods.

2. The team collects data internally on its own operations and externally from other organizations.

3. The data are analyzed to identify performance gaps and to determine the cause of differences.

4. An action plan is prepared and implemented that will result in meeting or exceeding the standards of others.

To illustrate the use of benchmarking, let's look at how Alcoa, one of the world's leading aluminum companies, used benchmarking to improve its manufacturing processes. The company used employee benchmarking teams to identify benchmarking opportunities throughout its worldwide facilities. These teams focused on the following criteria in identifying possible areas for benchmarking improvement: Is the topic important to our customers? Is the topic consistent with our mission, values, and milestones? Does the topic reflect an important business need? Is the topic significant in terms of costs or key nonfinancial indicators? Is the topic in an area in which additional information could influence plans and actions? Once specific benchmarking areas had been identified, an overall plan was developed that described how external and internal information was going to be gathered on the key criteria and what companies were going to be used as benchmarking targets. The teams then gathered the information and analyzed the data they collected.

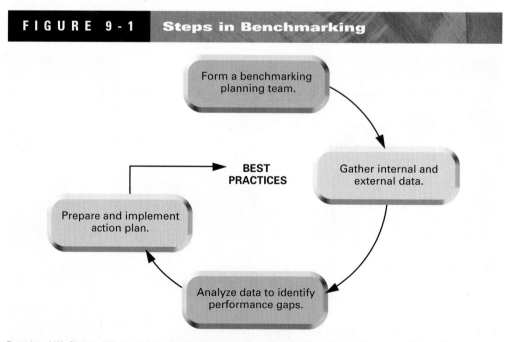

FIGURE 9-1 **Steps in Benchmarking**

Based on Y.K. Shetty, "Aiming High: Competitive Benchmarking for Superior Performance," *Long Range Planning*, February 1993, p. 42.

TABLE 9-2	**Suggestions for Improving Benchmarking Efforts**

1. Link benchmarking efforts to strategic objectives.
2. Have the right-sized team—between six and eight people is most effective.
3. Involve those individuals who will be directly affected by benchmarking efforts.
4. Focus on specific, targeted issues rather than broad, general ones.
5. Set realistic timetables.
6. Choose benchmarking targets carefully.
7. Observe proper protocol when gathering benchmarking information by dealing with the appropriate individuals.
8. Don't collect excessive, unnecessary data.
9. Look at the processes behind the numbers not just at the numbers themselves.
10. Identify benchmarking targets and then be sure to take action.

Source: Based on J.H. Sheridan, "Where Benchmarkers Go Wrong," *Industry Week*, March 15, 1993, pp. 28–34.

Performance gaps between the organization being studied and the specific Alcoa unit looking to improve its processes were quantified and studied for implications. Suggested changes were implemented, and the teams were asked what other units in the organization could benefit from the work they had done. Alcoa's corporate managers have been satisfied with the benchmarking process and the changes that came about because of it.

How can managers ensure that their benchmarking efforts are effective? Table 9-2 lists some suggestions for improving the process.

4 How effective is forecasting as a planning technique?

5 Describe the different types of forecasting.

6 What does the benchmarking process involve?

TESTING... TESTING...

1 2 3

BUDGETS

Most of us have had some experience, as limited as it might be, with budgets. We probably learned about them at a very early age when we discovered that unless we allocated our "revenues" carefully, our weekly allowance was gone before the week was half over.

A **budget** is a numerical plan for allocating resources to specific activities. Managers typically prepare budgets for revenues, expenses, and large capital expenditures such as machinery and equipment. It's not unusual, though, for budgets to be used for improving time, space, and the use of material resources. These latter types of budgets substitute non-dollar numbers for dollar amounts. Such items as person-hours, capacity utilization, or units of production can be budgeted for daily, weekly, or monthly activities. However, we'll emphasize dollar-based budgets in this section.

Why are budgets so popular? Probably because they're applicable to a wide variety of organizations and units within an organization. We live in a world in which almost everything is expressed in monetary units. Dollars, pesos, francs, yen, and the like are used as a common measuring unit within a country. It seems logical, then, that monetary budgets

budget

A numerical plan for allocating resources to specific activities.

would be a useful tool for directing activities in such diverse departments as production and marketing research or at various levels in an organization. Budgets are one planning device that most managers, regardless of organizational level, help formulate.

Types of Budgets

Budgets can be used for a number of areas or items. We're going to look at the ones managers are most likely to use.

Revenue Budgets.   The **revenue budget** is a specific type of revenue forecast. It's a budget that projects future sales. If the organization could be sure of selling everything it produced, revenue budgets would be very accurate. Managers would need only to multiply the sale price of each product by the quantity it could produce. However, such situations rarely exist. Managers must take into account their competitors' actions, planned advertising expenditures, salesforce effectiveness, and other relevant factors and make an estimate of sales volume. Also, on the basis of estimates of product demand at various prices, managers must select an appropriate sales price. Then they multiply sales volume by sales price for each product to get the revenue budget.

Expense Budgets.   Whereas revenue budgets are essentially a planning device for marketing and sales activities, expense budgets are found in all units of profit and nonprofit organizations. **Expense budgets** list the primary activities undertaken by a unit to achieve its goals and allocate a dollar amount to each. Lower expenses, when accompanied by stable quantity and quality of output, lead to greater efficiency. In times of intense competition, economic recession, or the like, managers typically look first at the expense budget as a place to make cuts and improve economic inefficiencies. Because not all expenses are linked to volume, they don't decline at the same rate when product demand drops. Managers pay particular attention to their so-called fixed expenses—those that remain relatively unchanged regardless of volume. As production levels fall, the variable expenses tend to control themselves because they decrease with volume.

Profit Budgets.   Organizational units that have easily determined revenues are often designated as profit centers and use profit budgets for planning and controlling. **Profit budgets** combine revenue and expense budgets into one. They're typically used in large organizations that have multiple facilities and divisions. Each manufacturing plant, for instance, might measure its monthly expenses (including a charge for corporate overhead) against its monthly revenues. In fact, some organizations create artificial profit centers by developing transfer prices for *intra*organizational transactions. For instance, the exploration division of Texaco produces oil only for Texaco's refining division, so the exploration unit has no "real" sales. However, Texaco turned the exploration unit into a profit center by establishing prices for each barrel of oil the division drills and then "sells" to the refining division. The internal transfers create revenue for the exploration division and allow managers in that division to formulate and be evaluated against their profit budget.

Cash Budgets.   **Cash budgets** are forecasts of how much cash the organization will have on hand and how much it will need to meet expenses. This budget can reveal potential cash flow shortages or surpluses.

Capital Expenditure Budgets.   Investments in property, buildings, and major equipment are called *capital expenditures*. These are typically substantial expenditures in terms of both magnitude and duration. For example, when Kraft decides to build a new

revenue budget
A budget that projects future sales.

expense budget
A budget that lists the primary activities undertaken by a unit and allocates a dollar amount to each.

profit budget
A budget used by separate units of an organization that combines revenue and expense budgets to determine the unit's profit contribution.

cash budget
A budget that forecasts how much cash an organization will have on hand and how much it will need to meet expenses.

Budgets are an essential planning tool in every business regardless of size.

cheese-processing production facility, that facility represents a commitment of hundreds of millions of dollars. Such a project would require an outlay of funds over several years, and it would take several years for the company to recoup its investment. The magnitude and duration of these investments justify the development of separate budgets for capital expenditures. Such **capital expenditure budgets** allow managers to forecast future capital requirements, to keep on top of important capital projects, and to ensure that adequate cash is available to meet these expenditures as they come due.

Variable or Fixed Budgets

The budgets just described are based on the assumption of a single specified volume; that is, they are **fixed budgets**. They assume a fixed sales or production volume. Most organizations, however, are not able to predict volume accurately. Moreover, some costs—such as labor, materials, and some administrative expenses—vary with volume. **Variable budgets** are designed to deal with these variations. Because plans can change, standards need to be flexible to adapt to changes. Variable budgets represent flexible standards. They can help managers better plan costs by specifying cost schedules for varying levels of volume.

capital expenditure budget

A budget that forecasts investments in property, buildings, and major equipment.

fixed budget

A budget that assumes a fixed level of sales or production.

variable budget

A budget that takes into account the costs that vary with volume.

7 Does a budget always have to be based on monetary units? Explain.

8 Describe the five types of budgets and what each is designed to do.

9 What is the difference between a variable and a fixed budget?

TESTING...
TESTING...

1 **2** **3**

MANAGERS SPEAK OUT

Interview with Lorraine Cichowski, Vice President and General Manager, *USA TODAY* Online, Arlington, Virginia

Describe your job.

I'm the vice president and general manager of the *USA TODAY* Information Network, a unit of *USA Today* created in December 1994. Our service now delivers online more than 140,000 pages of information, updated 7 days a week, 24 hours per day.

I monitor Internet trends and digital technology developments, set directions, negotiate with Web partners, have profit and loss responsibilities, address Internet conferences, and oversee an editorial operation of 55 staff members and a 35-person business staff comprised of advertising sales, marketing, business development, technology, and finance. I'm also a member of the 12-person *USA TODAY* Management committee and participate in setting direction for the *USA TODAY* brand and keep the committee informed on digital trends.

What types of skills do you think tomorrow's managers will need?

The workplace of today, and tomorrow, demands managers who are innovative, risk-takers, flexible, open to constant change, willing to work in teams, and willing to take lateral moves to build skills across disciplines. Managers and leaders of tomorrow also must be aware of global issues, sensitive to multicultural environments, and be comfortable dealing with ambiguity.

How do you monitor and assess the external changes (things outside your organization) that might affect how you do your job?

Because of the constant changes affecting the Internet, it's critical to stay informed on several levels. The most basic knowledge involves improvements to core hardware and software that power the *USA TODAY* Online Web site; my technology staff meets regularly with leaders in the industry to find out what they're developing and what we can do to test the new products. The next step is staying informed about mergers, acquisitions, and investments in the Internet industry. It's also important for me to keep up with the various futurist books dealing with the Web and the digital economy. The combination of that learning with what I call "learned intuition" in the media business and the needs of the *USA TODAY* brand, drive my business decisions.

What types of planning tools do you use?

In October of each year, I assess our business for the past year, review trends affecting the business, and set goals for the coming year. I follow a similar process about six months later as part of our annual capital budget process. As part of more regular monitoring tools, I review ad sales weekly and review revenue and expense budgets monthly. I also review monthly Web traffic numbers to determine if we need to add more Web servers and/or telecommunication lines. I ask my managers to follow the same process and encourage their supervisors to do the same. ◼

OPERATIONAL PLANNING TOOLS

Third Street Sportswear is a small, successful T-shirt manufacturer located in Ozark, Missouri. Brad and Julie Thomas, who own and run the business, spend much of their time setting up work schedules for their 38 employees, deciding how much inventory to order, and solving similar day-to-day problems. In the following pages, we'll discuss some operational planning tools that can help managers in a small business like Third Street Sportswear and also managers in larger organizations be more efficient and effective.

Scheduling

If you were to observe a group of supervisors or department managers for a few days, you would see them regularly detailing what activities have to be done, the order in which they are to be completed, who is to do each, and when they are to be completed. These managers are doing what we call **scheduling.** In this section, we'll review some useful scheduling devices.

scheduling

A list of necessary activities, their order of accomplishment, who is to do each, and the time needed to complete them.

Gantt Charts. The **Gantt chart** was developed during the early 1900s by Henry Gantt, an associate of the scientific management expert Frederick Taylor. The idea behind a Gantt chart is simple. It's essentially a bar graph, with time on the horizontal axis and the activities to be scheduled on the vertical axis. The bars show output, both planned and actual, over a period of time. The Gantt chart visually shows when tasks are supposed to be done and compares that with the actual progress on each. It's a simple but important device that lets managers detail easily what has yet to be done to complete a job or project and to assess whether an activity is ahead of, behind, or on schedule.

Gantt chart

A scheduling chart developed by Henry Gantt that shows actual and planned output over a period of time.

Figure 9-2 depicts a simplified Gantt chart that was developed for book production by a manager in a publishing firm. Time is expressed in months across the top of the chart. The major activities are listed down the left side. The planning comes in deciding what activities need to be done to get the book finished, the order in which those activities need to be

FIGURE 9-2 A Gantt Chart

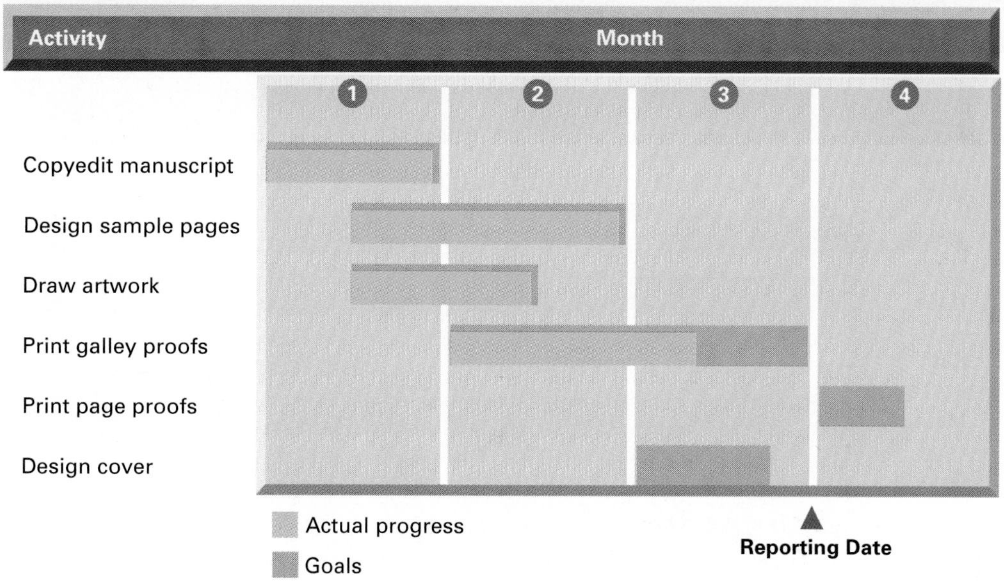

Activity
Month
1
2
3
4
Copyedit manuscript
Design sample pages
Draw artwork
Print galley proofs
Print page proofs
Design cover
Actual progress
Goals
Reporting Date

completed, and the time that should be allocated to each activity. Where a box sits within a time frame reflects its planned sequence. The shading represents actual progress. The chart becomes a control tool when the manager looks for deviations from the plan. In this example, both the design of the cover and the printing of page proofs are running behind schedule. Cover design is about three weeks behind, and page proof printing is about two weeks behind schedule. Given this information, the manager might need to take some corrective action either to make up for the two lost weeks or to ensure that no further delays will occur. At this point, the manager can expect that the book will be published at least two weeks later than planned if no corrective action is taken.

load chart

A modified Gantt chart that schedules capacity by work stations.

Load Charts. A **load chart** is a modified Gantt chart. Instead of listing activities on the vertical axis, load charts list either whole departments or specific resources. This arrangement allows managers to plan and control for capacity utilization. In other words, load charts schedule capacity by work stations.

For example, Figure 9-3 shows a load chart for six production editors at the same publishing firm. Each editor supervises the production and design of several books. By reviewing a load chart like the one shown in Figure 9-3, the executive editor, who supervises the six production editors, can see who is free to take on a new book. If everyone is fully scheduled, the executive editor might decide not to accept any new projects, to accept new projects and delay others, to make the editors work overtime, or to employ more production editors. In Figure 9-3, only Hal and Maurice are completely booked for the next six months. The other editors have some unassigned time, so they might be able to accept one or more new projects.

program evaluation and review technique (PERT)

A technique for scheduling complicated projects comprising many activities, some of which are interdependent.

PERT Network Analysis. Gantt and load charts are useful as long as the activities being scheduled are few in number and independent of each other. But what if a manager had to plan a large project such as a unit reorganization, the implementation of a cost-reduction campaign, or the development of a new product that required coordinating inputs from marketing, production, and product design personnel? Such projects require coordinating hundreds, and even thousands, of activities, some of which must be done

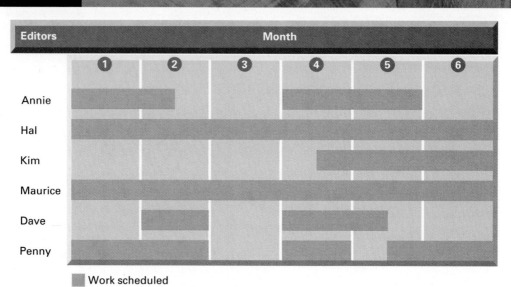

FIGURE 9-3 **A Load Chart**

Work scheduled

simultaneously and some of which cannot begin until earlier activities have been completed. If you're constructing a building, you obviously cannot start putting up the walls until the foundation is laid. How, then, can you schedule such a complex project? The Program Evaluation and Review Technique (PERT) is highly appropriate for such projects.

The **Program Evaluation and Review Technique**—usually called just **PERT** or PERT network analysis—was originally developed in the late 1950s for coordinating the more than 3,000 contractors and agencies working on the *Polaris* submarine weapon system.[15] This project was incredibly complicated, with hundreds of thousands of activities that had to be coordinated. PERT is reported to have cut two years off the completion date for the project.

A **PERT network** is a flowchartlike diagram that depicts the sequence of activities needed to complete a project and the time or costs associated with each activity. With a PERT network, a project manager must think through what has to be done, determine which events depend on one another, and identify potential trouble spots. PERT also makes it easy to compare the effects alternative actions might have on scheduling and costs. Thus, PERT allows managers to monitor a project's progress, identify possible bottlenecks, and shift resources as necessary to keep the project on schedule.

To understand how to construct a PERT network, you need to know four terms: *events, activities, slack time,* and *critical path.* Let's define these terms, outline the steps in the PERT process, and then look at an example.

Events are end points that represent the completion of major activities. **Activities** represent the time or resources required to progress from one event to another. **Slack time** is the amount of time an individual activity can be delayed without delaying the whole project. The **critical path** is the longest or most time-consuming sequence of events and activities in a PERT network. Any delay in completing events on this path would delay the completion of the entire project. In other words, activities on the critical path will have zero slack time.

Developing a PERT network requires that a manager identify all key activities needed to complete a project, rank them in order of occurrence, and estimate each activity's completion time. This process can be translated into five specific steps, which are outlined in Table 9-3.

PERT network

A flowchartlike diagram showing the sequence of activities needed to complete a project and the time or cost associated with each.

events

End points that represent the completion of major activities in a PERT network.

activities

The time or resources needed to progress from one event to another in a PERT network.

slack time

The amount of time an individual activity can be delayed without delaying the whole project.

critical path

The longest sequence of activities in a PERT network.

TABLE 9-3   Steps in Developing a PERT Network

1. *Identify every significant activity that must be achieved for a project to be completed.* The accomplishment of each activity results in a set of events or outcomes.
2. *Determine the order in which these events must be completed.*
3. *Diagram the flow of activities from start to finish, identifying each activity and its relationship to all other activities.* Use circles to indicate events and arrows to represent activities. This results in a flowchart diagram called a PERT network.
4. *Compute a time estimate for completing each activity.* This is done with a weighted average that uses an *optimistic* time estimate (t_o) of how long the activity would take under ideal conditions, a *most-likely* estimate (t_m) of the time the activity normally should take, and a *pessimistic* estimate (t_p) that represents the time that an activity should take under the worst possible conditions. The formula for calculating the expected time (t_e) is then

$$t_e = \frac{t_o + 4t_m + t_p}{6}$$

5. *Using the network diagram that contains time estimates for each activity, determine a schedule for the start and finish dates of each activity and for the entire project.* Any delays that occur along the critical path require the most attention because they can delay the whole project.

TABLE 9-4	A PERT Network for Erecting an Office Building		
Event	**Description**	**Expected Time (in weeks)**	**Preceding Event**
A	Approve design and get permits.	10	None
B	Dig subterranean garage.	6	A
C	Erect frame and siding.	14	B
D	Construct floor.	6	C
E	Install windows.	3	C
F	Put on roof.	3	C
G	Install internal wiring.	5	D, E, F
H	Install elevator.	5	G
I	Put in floor covering and paneling.	4	D
J	Put in doors and interior decorative trim.	3	I, H
K	Turn over to building management group.	1	J

As we noted at the beginning of this section, most PERT projects are complicated and may include hundreds or thousands of events. Such complicated computations are best done with a computer using specialized PERT software.[16] For our purposes, however, let's work through a simple example. Assume that you're the superintendent at a construction company. You've been assigned to oversee the construction of an office building. Because time really is money in your business, you must determine how long it will take to get the building built. You've carefully broken down the entire project into specific activities and events. Table 9-4 outlines the major events in the construction project and your estimate of the expected time required to complete each activity. Figure 9-4 shows the PERT network based on the data in Table 9-4. You've also calculated the length of time that each path of activities will take:

A-B-C-D-I-J-K (44 weeks)

A-B-C-D-G-H-J-K (50 weeks)

A-B-C-E-G-H-J-K (47 weeks)

A-B-C-F-G-H-J-K (47 weeks)

Your PERT network shows that if everything goes as planned, the total project completion time will be 50 weeks. This is calculated by tracing the project's critical path (the

FIGURE 9-4	A PERT Network for Erecting an Office Building

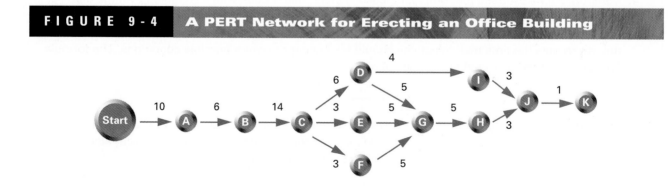

longest sequence of activities): A-B-C-D-G-H-J-K and adding up the times. You know that any delay in completing the events on this path would delay the completion of the entire project (in other words, there is no slack time—slack time is zero). Taking six weeks instead of four to put in the floor covering and paneling (Event I) would have no effect on the final completion date. Why? Because that event isn't on the critical path. But taking seven weeks instead of six to dig the subterranean garage (Event B) would likely delay the total project. A manager who needed to get back on schedule or to cut the 50-week completion time would want to concentrate on those activities along the critical path that could be completed faster. How might the manager do this? He or she could look to see if any of the other activities *not* on the critical path had slack time in which resources could be transferred to activities that *were* on the critical path.

---

10 Contrast a Gantt chart with a load chart.

11 How would PERT be used as a planning tool?

12 How would a manager construct and use a PERT network?

TESTING...
TESTING...

1 2 3

Breakeven Analysis

How many units of a product must an organization sell in order to break even—that is, to have neither profit nor loss? A manager might want to know the minimum number of units that must be sold to achieve her profit objective or whether a current product should continue to be sold or should be dropped from the organization's product line. **Breakeven analysis** is a widely used technique for helping managers make profit projections.[17]

Breakeven analysis is a simple formulation, yet it's valuable to managers because it points out the relationship between revenues, costs, and profits. To compute the breakeven point (BE), the manager needs to know the unit price of the product being sold (P), the variable cost per unit (VC), and total fixed costs (TFC).

An organization breaks even when its total revenue is just enough to equal its total costs. But total cost has two parts: a fixed component and a variable component. *Fixed costs* are expenses that do not change, regardless of volume. Examples include insurance premiums, rent, and property taxes. Fixed costs, of course, are fixed only in the short term because, in the long run, commitments terminate and could change as they are renegotiated. *Variable costs* change in proportion to output and include raw materials, labor costs, and energy costs.

The breakeven point can be computed graphically or by using the following formula:

$$BE = \frac{TFC}{P - VC}$$

This formula tells us that (1) total revenue will equal total cost when we sell enough units at a price that covers all variable unit costs and (2) the difference between price and variable costs, when multiplied by the number of units sold, equals the fixed costs.

For example, assume that Mike's Photocopying Service charges $0.10 per photocopy. If fixed costs are $27,000 a year and variable costs are $0.04 per copy, Mike can compute his breakeven point as follows: $27,000/($0.10 – $0.04) = 450,000 copies, or when annual revenues are $45,000 (450,000 copies × $0.10). This same relationship is shown graphically in Figure 9-5.

As a planning tool, breakeven analysis could help Mike set his sales objective. For example, he could determine the profit he wants and then work backward to see what sales level is needed to reach that profit. Breakeven analysis could also tell Mike how much volume has to increase to break even if he's currently running at a loss or how much volume

breakeven analysis

A technique for identifying the point at which total revenue is just sufficient to cover total costs.

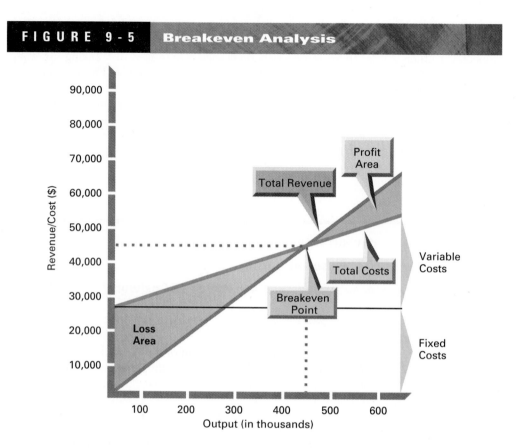

FIGURE 9-5   **Breakeven Analysis**

he can afford to lose and still break even if he's currently operating profitably. In the management of some professional sports franchises, breakeven analysis has shown the volume of ticket sales required to cover all costs to be so unrealistically high that the best action for management is to get out of the business.

Linear Programming

Dan Collier has a manufacturing plant that produces two kinds of cinnamon-scented home fragrance products: a woodchip-based potpourri sold in bags and wax candles. Business is good. He can sell all of the cinnamon-scented products he can produce. This is his problem: Given that the bags of potpourri and the wax candles go through the same production departments, how many of each type should he manufacture to maximize his profits?

A closer look at Dan's operation tells us that he can use a mathematical technique called **linear programming** to solve his resource allocation dilemma. As we'll show, linear programming is applicable to Dan's problem, but it cannot be applied to all resource allocation situations. Besides requiring limited resources and the objective of optimization, it requires that there be alternative ways of combining resources to produce a number of output mixes. There must also be a linear relationship between variables;[18] that is, a change in one variable must be accompanied by an exactly proportional change in the other. For Dan's business, that condition would be met if it took exactly twice the amount of raw materials and hours of labor to produce two of a given home fragrance product as it took to produce one.

What kinds of problems can be solved with linear programming? Some applications include selecting transportation routes that minimize shipping costs, allocating a limited advertising budget among various product brands, making the optimal assignment of personnel among projects, and determining how much of each product to make with a limited

linear programming

A mathematical technique that solves resource allocation problems.

number of resources. Let's return to Dan's problem and see how linear programming could help him solve it. Fortunately, Dan's problem is relatively simple, so we can solve it rather quickly. For complex linear programming problems, there are computer software programs designed specifically to help develop optimizing solutions.

First, we need to establish some facts about Dan's business. Dan has computed the profit margins on his home fragrance products at $10 for a bag of potpourri and $18 for a scented candle. These numbers establish the basis for Dan to be able to express his *objective function* as: maximum profit = $10P + $18S, where P is the number of bags of potpourri produced and S is the number of scented candles produced. The objective function is simply a mathematical equation that can predict the outcome of all proposed alternatives. In addition, Dan knows how much time each fragrance product must spend in each department and the monthly production capacity (1,200 hours in manufacturing and 900 hours in assembly) for the two departments (Table 9-5). The production capacity numbers act as *constraints* on his overall capacity. Now Dan can establish his constraint equations:

$$2P + 4S \leq 1,200$$
$$2P + 2S \leq 900$$

Of course, Dan can also state that $P \geq 0$ and $S \geq 0$, because neither fragrance product can be produced in a volume less than zero.

Dan has graphed his solution as shown in Figure 9-6. The shaded area represents the options that don't exceed the capacity of either department. What does this mean? Well, let's look first at the manufacturing constraint line BE. We know that total manufacturing capacity is 1,200 hours, so if Dan decides to produce all potpourri bags, the maximum he can produce is 600 (1,200 hours ÷ 2 hours required to produce a bag of potpourri). If he decides to produce all scented candles, the maximum he can produce is 300 (1,200 hours ÷ 4 hours required to produce a scented candle). The other constraint Dan faces is that of assembly, shown by line DF. If Dan decides to produce all potpourri bags, the maximum he can assemble is 450 (900 hours production capacity ÷ 2 hours required to assemble). Likewise, if Dan decides to produce all scented candles, the maximum he can assemble is also 450 because the scented candles also take 2 hours to assemble. The constraints imposed by these capacity limits establish Dan's *feasibility region.* Dan's optimal resource allocation will be defined at one of the corners within this feasibility region. Point C provides the maximum profits within the constraints stated. How do we know? At point A, profits would be 0 (no production of either potpourri bags or scented candles). At point B, profits would be $5,400 (300 scented candles × $18 profit and 0 potpourri bags produced = $5,400). At point D, profits would be $4,500 (450 potpourri bags × $10 profit and 0 scented candles produced = $4,500). At point C, however, profits would be $5,700 (150 scented candles produced × $18 profit and 300 potpourri bags produced × $10 profit = $5,700).

TABLE 9-5	Production Data for Cinnamon-Scented Products		
	Number of Hours Required (per unit)		
Department	**Potpourri Bags**	**Scented Candles**	**Monthly Production Capacity (in hours)**
Manufacturing	2	4	1,200
Assembly	2	2	900
Profit per unit	$10	$18	

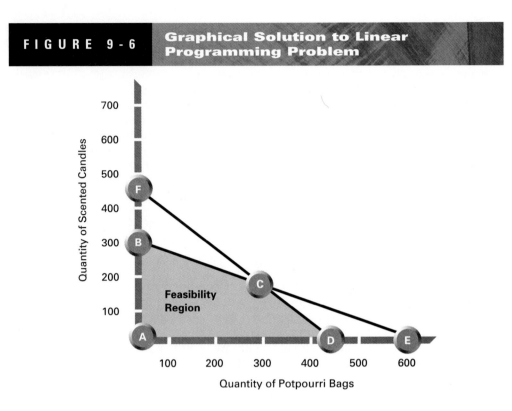

FIGURE 9-6 **Graphical Solution to Linear Programming Problem**

Queuing Theory

You're a supervisor for the San Francisco Bay Bridge Toll Authority. One of the decisions you have to make is how many of the 36 toll booths you should keep open at any given time. Queuing theory, or, as it is frequently called, *waiting-line theory*, could help you solve this problem.

A decision that involves balancing the cost of having a waiting line against the cost of service to maintain that line can be made easier with **queuing theory**. Such common situations as determining how many gas pumps are needed at gas stations, tellers at bank windows, or check-in lines at airline ticket counters are examples. In each situation, managers

queuing theory

A technique that balances the cost of having a waiting line against the cost of service to maintain that line.

A queuing model developed for promptly handling customers' calls ensures that this telemarketing representative handles customers efficiently and doesn't keep them waiting too long.

want to minimize costs by having as few stations open as possible, yet not so few as to test the patience of customers. For instance, the outdoor products firm L.L. Bean developed a queuing model for handling customers' calls that resulted in a $10 million annual savings for the company because resources in its telemarketing program were more effectively allocated. Look back at our toll booth example. During rush hours you could open all 36 booths and keep waiting time to a minimum, or you could open only one, thereby minimizing staffing costs, and risk a commuter riot.

The mathematics behind queuing theory is beyond the scope of this book. But you can see how the theory works in a simple example. Assume that you're a bank supervisor and one of your responsibilities is assigning tellers. Your bank branch has five teller windows, but you want to know whether you can get by with only one window open during an average morning. You consider 12 minutes to be the longest you would expect any customer to wait patiently in line. If it takes four minutes, on average, to serve each customer, the line should not be permitted to get longer than three deep (12 minutes ÷ 4 minutes per customer = 3 customers). If you know from experience that during the morning, people arrive at the average rate of two per minute, you can calculate the probability (P) that the line will become longer than any number (n) of customers as follows:

$$P_n = \left(1 - \frac{\text{arrival rate}}{\text{service rate}}\right) \times \left(\frac{\text{arrival rate}}{\text{service rate}}\right)^n$$

In this case, n = 3 customers, *arrival rate* = 2 per minute, and *service rate* = 4 minutes per customer. Putting these numbers into the above formula generates the following:

$$P_3 = \left(1 - \tfrac{2}{4}\right) \times \left(\tfrac{2}{4}\right)^3 = \left(\tfrac{1}{2}\right)\left(\tfrac{8}{64}\right) = \tfrac{8}{128} = 0.062$$

What does a P_3 of 0.0625 mean? It tells you that the likelihood of having more than three customers in line during the morning is one chance in 16 ($\tfrac{1}{16}$ = 0.0625). Are you willing to have four or more customers in line 6 percent of the time? If so, keeping one teller window open will be enough. If not, you'll need to open additional windows and assign personnel to staff them.

Probability Theory

With the help of **probability theory**, managers can use statistics to reduce the amount of risk in plans. By analyzing past predictable patterns, a manager can improve current and future decisions. It makes for more effective planning when, for example, the marketing manager at Porsche–North America, who is responsible for the 968-product line knows that the mean age of her customers is 35.5 years, with a standard deviation of 3.5. If she assumes a normal distribution of ages, the manager can use probability theory to calculate that 95 of every 100 customers are between 28.6 and 42.4 years of age (1.96 × standard deviation of 3.5 = 6.86; then 35.5 ± 6.86). If she were developing a new marketing program, she could use this information to target available marketing dollars effectively.

Marginal Analysis

The concept of marginal, or incremental, analysis helps decision makers optimize returns or minimize costs. **Marginal analysis** deals with the additional cost in a particular decision, rather than the average cost. For example, the commercial dry cleaner who wonders whether he should take on a new customer would consider not *total* revenue and *total* cost that would result after the order was taken, but rather what *additional* (marginal or incremental) revenue and costs would be generated by this particular order. If the incremental revenues exceeded the incremental costs, total profits would be increased by accepting the order. Managers also use marginal analysis for determining whether to add new product features. For instance, before Volvo decided to install its multilink suspension system, supplemental restraint system, and antilock braking system on its cars, managers analyzed the marginal costs and revenues generated by those product additions.

probability theory

The use of statistics to analyze past predictable patterns and to reduce risk in future plans.

marginal analysis

A planning technique that assesses the incremental costs or revenues in a decision.

These software designers at Coopers & Lybrand are perfecting a computer simulation technique called "agent-based simulation," which offers insights into real-life business decisions by allowing hundreds, thousands, or even millions of virtual humans to interact and make buying decisions. The current project simulates 50,000 imaginary CD buyers.

Simulation

simulation

A model of a real-world phenomenon that contains one or more variables that can be manipulated in order to assess their impact.

Managers are increasingly turning to simulation as a means for trying out various planning options. They use **simulation** to create a model of a real-world event and then manipulate one or more variables in the model to assess their impact. Simulation can deal with problems addressed by linear programming, but it can also deal with more complex situations.

How might a manager use simulation? Managers at the pharmaceutical manufacturer Merck used simulation as they considered acquiring Medco, a mail-order pharmacy company, for $6.6 billion. The problem Merck's managers wanted to simulate was how the company would perform in the future, with and without Medco. Managers in the finance department built a model with a vast number of variables including, among other things, information about the U.S. health care system and health care reform possibilities, profit margins, possible future changes in the mix of generic and brand-name drugs, and how the company's competitors might react to the merger. With the number of variables involved in this complex model, a simulation was used to change the variables at random and to test to see how the proposed merger would perform under different business and economic scenarios. The numerous simulations helped Merck managers decide that the Medco acquisition made sense, and they proceeded with their acquisition plan.

TESTING...
TESTING...
1   2   3

13 What is the value of breakeven analysis as a planning tool?

14 For what types of planning situations would linear programming be appropriate?

15 Describe how the following are used in planning: queuing theory, probability theory, marginal analysis, and simulation.

PROJECT MANAGEMENT

Different types of organizations, ranging from manufacturers such as Ford Motor Company to software design firms such as Purple Moon Company, are doing their work using projects. In this section, we briefly describe project management and why it has become so popular in recent years. We include project management as a planning tool and technique because it can help managers establish objectives and outline work activities.

A **project** is a one-time-only set of activities that has a definite beginning and ending point in time.[19] Projects vary in size and scope—from a NASA space shuttle launch to a sorority's holiday party. **Project management** is the task of getting the activities done on time, within budget, and according to specifications.[20]

More and more organizations are using project management. Why? Because the approach fits well with a dynamic environment and the need for flexibility and rapid response. Organizations are increasingly undertaking projects that are somewhat unusual or are unique, have specific deadlines, contain complex interrelated tasks requiring specialized skills, and are temporary in nature. These types of projects do not fit nicely and neatly into the standardized planning and operating procedures that guide an organization's other routine and ongoing work activities.

In the typical project, the work is done by a project team whose members are temporarily assigned to the project and who report to a project manager.[21] The project manager coordinates the project's activities with other departments and often reports directly to an upper-level manager. Keep in mind, however, that the project is temporary. A project team exists only long enough to complete its specific objectives. Then it disbands, and members move on to other projects, return to their permanent work departments, or leave the organization.

The essential features of the project planning process are shown in Figure 9-7. The planning process begins by clearly defining the project's objectives. This step is necessary because the manager and the team members need to know what's expected. All activities in the project and the resources needed to accomplish them must then be identified. That is, what labor and materials are needed to complete the project? This step may be time consuming and complex, particularly if the project is unique and there is none of the history or experience that typically exists in planning tasks.

Once the activities have been identified, their sequential relationship needs to be determined. What activities must be completed before others can begin? Which can be undertaken simultaneously? This step typically is done using flowchart-type diagrams.

Next, the project activities need to be scheduled. The manager estimates the time required for each activity and then uses these estimates to develop an overall project schedule and completion date. Then the project schedule is compared with the objectives, and any necessary adjustments are made. If the project time is too long, the manager might

project

A one-time-only set of activities that has a definite beginning and ending point in time.

project management

The task of getting a project's activities done on time, within budget, and according to specifications.

Members of a project management team often collaborate in meetings like this one at the San Jose *Mercury*.

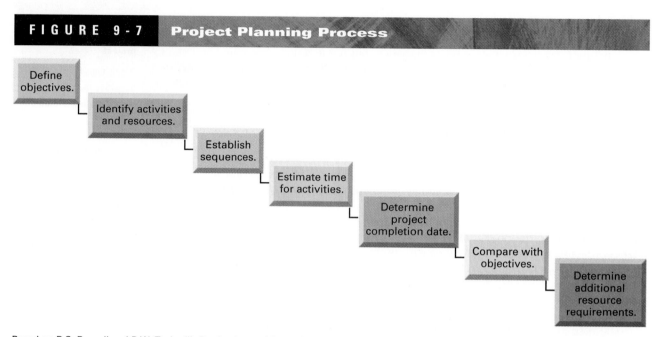

FIGURE 9-7 Project Planning Process

Based on R.S. Russell and B.W. Taylor III, *Production and Operations Management* (Upper Saddle River, NJ: Prentice Hall, 1995), p. 287.

assign more resources to critical activities so they can be completed faster. The project manager may choose to use any of the scheduling techniques that we described earlier in the chapter such as a Gantt chart, a load chart, or a PERT network.

We'll discuss other aspects of project management in other chapters. For instance, in chapter 10, we examine a project type of organizational design and, in chapter 18, we discuss project management as it is related to production and operations issues.

TESTING... TESTING...

16 What is project management?

17 What explains the growing popularity of project management?

18 List the essential steps in the project planning process.

managers respond to "a manager's dilemma"

MANAGER 1

Hard Candy needs immediate help. Ms. Mohajer needs information to find out where the business is and how it's doing. In the short term, she needs to: (1) track and evaluate the revenues and expenses; (2) determine fixed and variable costs; and (3) determine the breakeven point and do marginal analysis. These planning techniques will help her determine how the business is doing, whether and when it's making money, and eventually they will help in setting sales objectives.

Once basic accounting and financial reporting procedures are in place, various analyses of the numbers can help Ms. Mohajer get a handle on the nature of this business and guide business decisions. For example, linear programming might help her decide which nail polish colors should be produced to maximize profits.

Pete Babington, Director of Facilities, Highline Community College, Des Moines, Washington

MANAGER 2

I would first look at the environment in which Hard Candy is operating. Maybe there's been a change in consumer demand and maybe we're no longer satisfying customers. This might explain the increase in the number of new competitors. I would also use competitor intelligence to help determine what my competition is producing and perhaps even the means by which they produce it. I'd assess styles, colors, and product packaging design.

Next, Hard Candy needs a system in place to show where they stand financially. I would start by creating revenue, expense, and cash budgets. I'd use these budgets to help me plan the day-to-day company operations and to see how we stand compared with previous months. In addition, financial statements (balance sheet, income statement, and cash flow statement) will help me evaluate the company's performance over a period of time and to compare it with competitors' performance.

Finally, I would conduct a breakeven analysis on each product line and on all the lines taken as a whole. This will help me decide which products to continue and which to drop. In addition, analysis on all the product lines will tell me at what sales level I would stop just covering expenses and start making profit. I could then determine the minimum sales level in units needed for a desired profit level.

Brad Barnes, Staff Accountant; Baird, Kurtz, and Dobson; Colorado Springs, Colorado

for your

IMMEDIATE
action

FOUR MEN & A TRUCK

TO: Russell MacMillan,
           Director of Logistics

FROM: Scott Farace,
           Vice President

RE: Project "Big Move"

We've just signed a contract to coordinate the move of the People's Bank equipment, supplies, furnishings, and other materials from its old location on West College Expressway to its new location on the Pike's Road exit at Interstate 65. Russell, I'd like you to head up this project. The moving date is six weeks from now, but I'd like to see our plan of action in place as soon as possible so we can make sure we have people and resources scheduled. Would you please get together with Kathy Vega (Director of Security), Tom Forgey (Director of Operations), and Lisa Schrock (Director of Marketing) to determine: (1) the goals for this move, (2) the resources your team thinks it will need, and (3) a brief overview of the steps involved in the move.

Please type up this information in a one-page format and give it to me. Once I've had a chance to look it over, I'll schedule a project team meeting and we can decide what people and resources we'll need to have on hand.

This is a fictionalized account of a potentially real problem. It was written for academic purposes only.

SUMMARY

This summary is organized by the chapter-opening objectives found on p. 266.

1. Techniques for scanning the environment include reading newspapers, magazines, books, and trade journals; reading competitors' ads, promotional materials, and press releases; attending trade shows; debriefing sales personnel; and reverse engineering of competitors' products.

2. Quantitative forecasting applies a set of mathematical rules to a set of past data in order to predict future outcomes. Qualitative forecasting uses judgments and the opinions of knowledgeable individuals to predict outcomes.

3. Benchmarking is the search for best practices among competitors or noncompetitors that lead to their superior performance.

4. Budgets are popular planning devices because money is a universal common denominator that can be used in all types of organizations and by managers at all levels.

5. Gantt and load charts are scheduling devices. Both are bar graphs. Gantt charts monitor planned and actual activities over time; load charts focus on capacity utilization by monitoring whole departments or specific resources.

6. The five steps in developing a PERT network are: (1) identifying every significant activity that must be achieved for a project to be completed; (2) determining the order in which those activities must be completed; (3) diagramming the flow of activities in a project from start to finish; (4) estimating the time needed to complete each activity; and (5) using the network diagram to determine a schedule for the start and finish dates of each activity and for the entire project.

7. A product's breakeven point is determined by the unit price of the product, its variable cost per unit, and its total fixed costs.

8. For linear programming to be applicable, a problem must have limited resources, an objective function to optimize, alternative ways of combining resources, and a linear relationship between variables.

9. Simulation is an effective planning tool because it allows managers to simulate, on a computer, thousands of potential options at very little cost. By simulating a complex situation, managers can see how changes in variables will affect outcomes.

10. Project management involves getting a project's activities done on time, within budget, and according to specifications. A project is a one-time-only set of activities that has a definite beginning and ending point in time.

THINKING ABOUT MANAGEMENT ISSUES

1. It's a waste of time and other resources to develop a set of sophisticated scenarios for situations that may never occur. Do you agree or disagree? Support your position.

2. Do intuition and creativity have any relevance in quantitative planning tools and techniques? Explain.

3. The *Wall Street Journal* and other business periodicals often carry reports of companies that have not met their sales or profit forecasts. What are some reasons a company might not meet its forecasts? What suggestions could you make for improving the effectiveness of forecasting?

4. Assume that you manage a large fast-food restaurant in downtown Chicago and you want to know the amount of each type of sandwich to make and the number of cashiers to have working during each shift. What type of planning tool(s) do you think will be useful to you? Explain how you would use the ones you identified. What type of environmental scanning, if any, would you likely do in this management job?

5. "People can use statistics to prove whatever it is they want to prove." What do you think? What are the implications for managers and how they plan?

SELF-ASSESSMENT EXERCISE

AM I A GOOD PLANNER?

Planning is an important skill for managers. The following assessment is designed to help you understand your planning skills.

Instructions: Answer either Yes or No to each of the following questions.

	Yes	No
1. My personal objectives are clearly spelled out in writing.	___	___
2. Most of my days are hectic and disorderly.	___	___
3. I seldom make any snap decisions and usually study a problem carefully before acting.	___	___
4. I keep a desk calendar or appointment book as an aid.	___	___
5. I use "action" and "deferred action" files.	___	___
6. I generally establish starting dates and deadlines for all my projects.	___	___
7. I often ask others for advice.	___	___
8. I believe that all problems have to be solved immediately.	___	___

See scoring key on page SK–4.

Source: Copyright © 1994 by National Research Bureau, P.O. Box 1, Burlington, Iowa 52601-0001. Reprinted by permission.

TAKE IT TO THE NET

We invite you to visit the Robbins/Coulter companion Web site at http://www.prenhall.com/robbinsmgt for this chapter's Internet resources.

CASE APPLICATION

Managing Chaos

Oticon Holding A/S, a company that makes hearing aids, is hardly the type of business in which you'd expect to find radical approaches to managing. The Danish manufacturer, founded in 1905, was once an ultratraditional, hierarchical, conservative, by-the-book organization. One day, Oticon's executives realized that the marketplace had changed, technology had changed, and they were now competing with the likes of Sony, Siemens, and Phillips, large and successful global corporations. Lars Kolind, CEO, knew that in order for his company to survive and ever have a chance of being a strong, viable industry competitor, he would have to take drastic measures.

Kolind recreated Oticon into what he calls the "ultimate flexible organization." At precisely 8 A.M. on August 8, 1991, the company's revolutionary dis-organization was born. What exactly happened that day that totally transformed the company? To begin with, all organizational departments and employee job titles disappeared. Instead, all work activities became project based and were implemented by informal groupings of interested individuals. Employee "jobs" were reconfigured into unique and fluid combinations of work activities that fit each employee's own specific capabilities and needs. Today, project teams form, disband, and form again as the work requires. Project "leaders" are basically anyone in the company

with a good idea who is willing to pursue it. Project leaders compete to attract whatever resources and people they need to complete the project. Project "owners," members of Oticon's 10-person management team, provide advice and support, but they make few actual decisions.

Even the company's offices facilitate (and support) this seemingly chaotic free flow of work. All physical barriers and surroundings in the company's offices were eliminated and replaced by open spaces filled with uniform work stations on wheels that held a computer and a desk with no drawers. Individuals randomly selected desks and wheeled them together to form project work teams. Informal communication among employees replaced memos as the accepted form of communication. Coffee bars located throughout the company headquarters building are perfect for informal, stand-up meetings. Large and small "dialogue rooms" with circular sofas and a tiny table are also scattered throughout the facility.

This type of radical transformation did encounter employee resistance at first. Kolind overcame most resistance by involving employees in the process. He recruited small teams to tackle such projects as designing the tremendous electronic infrastructure that would replace the traditional reliance on pen and paper, and he put other project teams to work finding an appropriate building site and working with an architect to design the facilities.

What kind of performance has resulted from the "new" Oticon? One immediate result was the discovery that the company had already invented the first fully automatic hearing aid in the mid-1980s, but it had never made it to the market because of lack of communication between departments. Company teams immediately realized the potential of this technological breakthrough and acted quickly to introduce this new type of hearing aid. Also, Kolind estimates that there are, at any one time, approximately 100 projects of various magnitude in progress. He feels strongly that the company can respond quickly to any opportunities that emerge anywhere around the globe. In fact, Kolind says, "There's a paradox here. We're developing products twice as fast as anybody else. But when you look around, you see a very relaxed atmosphere. We're not fast on the surface; we're fast underneath."

The "ultimate flexible organization" that Lars Kolind designed is well poised to adapt to any environmental and competitive challenges sent its way. As a saying on one of the Greek-style columns found in the facility so boldly displays, "Think the unthinkable." That's exactly what this Danish company has done.

QUESTIONS

1. Given the unusual ways in which work is done at Oticon, what planning tools and techniques might be useful? Explain your choices.
2. Suppose that some organization wanted to use Oticon as a benchmark. What types of things might it learn from Oticon?
3. Compare Oticon's approach to project management with what was described in the chapter. What similarities do you see? What differences? Is one approach better than the other? Explain.

Source: P. LaBarre, "The Dis-Organization of Oticon," *Industry Week,* July 18, 1994, pp. 22–38; T. Peters, "Successful Electronic Changeovers Depend on Daring," *Springfield Business Journal,* August 8, 1994, p. 15; and LaBarre, "This Organization Is Dis-Organization," *Fast Company Web Page* <http://www.fastcompany.com>, April 16, 1997.

SMALL BUSINESS 2000

VIDEO CASE APPLICATION

Successfully Selling Bagels—in Japan

By anyone's count, 182,600 bagels a week is a lot of bagels! What's even more surprising is that that's the number currently being sold in Japan by Jerry Shapiro's company, Petrofsky's Bagels, and he predicts that sales are about to double and perhaps triple. You might not have thought there was a market in Japan for that distinct bagel taste, but Japanese consumers obviously have developed a fondness for Petrofsky's bagels.

Jerry Shapiro has been described as a modern-day explorer. It's probably fitting that Shapiro's business is based in St. Louis, Missouri, because that city was a jumping-off point for many explorers preparing to survey the western United States. Shapiro's vision, though, was more international. He believed that there was a strong potential market for his bagels in Japan. Although having a vision is important, it takes more than a vision to be successful. It takes putting the vision into action.

How did Shapiro pursue his vision? How did he get the Japanese initially to try his bagels and then get them to continue buying them? He says that getting past that initial hurdle involved several things. First and foremost was a significant amount of taste testing. Although this step was time consuming and tedious, he knew he was on the right track when a couple of elderly Japanese professors who tasted Petrofsky's bagels said the bread dough reminded them of something sweet that they had eaten when they were younger. Shapiro also says that getting his product into Japan involved several trips to that country and finding the proper trading partner. He couldn't anticipate the trends and needs of the Japanese market by sitting in his office in St. Louis. Instead Shapiro had to experience the unique characteristics of the Japanese market firsthand and had to develop a strong, long-term relationship with his company's trading partner. Although the amount of preparation and planning to get into the Japanese market may have seemed overwhelming at times, Shapiro was committed to pursuing his strategy no matter how long it took.

Having successfully implemented his vision, Shapiro gives the following advice for going into international markets: Put your plan in writing. Solicit customer participation. And finally, be prepared to do whatever it takes to build long-term relationships.

QUESTIONS

1. How could environmental scanning, particularly global scanning, have been used by Jerry Shapiro? What could scanning have shown him?
2. What other planning tools might Shapiro find necessary as he continues to do business globally? Be specific.
3. What implications do you see for managers and how they plan from the advice Shapiro gives for going into international markets?

Source: Based on *Small Business Today, Show 104.*

Organizing

After reading this chapter, you should be able to

1 Define organizational structure and organizational design

2 Explain why structure and design are important to an organization

3 Describe the six key elements of organizational structure

4 Differentiate mechanistic and organic organizational designs

5 Identify the four contingency factors that influence organizational design

6 Describe bureaucracy and its strengths

7 Explain team-based structures and why organizations are using them

8 Describe matrix organizations, project structures, and autonomous internal units

9 Identify the characteristics of a boundaryless organization and this structure's appeal

10 Explain the concept of a learning organization and how it influences organizational design

11 Describe the role that technology plays in organizational design

A MANAGER'S DILEMMA

Its Web site <http://www.amazon.com> bills it as "Earth's Biggest Bookstore." Amazon.com is the realization of Jeff Bezos's dream of retailing on the Internet.[1]

In 1994, Bezos was a successful programmer on Wall Street, but statistics on the explosive growth in use of the Internet and World Wide Web (at that time, it was growing at the rate of about 2,300% a month) kept nagging at him. He decided to quit his job and pursue his vision. Bezos drew up a list of 20 products that he figured could be sold on-line (including books, music, magazines, and PC hardware and software) and finally narrowed the list down to books or music. He settled on books for two simple reasons: There are more products to sell (more than 2 million titles in print versus 300,000 music titles), and the giant publishing companies are not as ferociously competitive as the six record companies. After pinpointing the product he would retail, Bezos piled his family's belongings into a moving van and ordered the drivers to head west. He told them he would contact them when he'd decided whether the

destination would be Colorado, Oregon, or Washington. Bezos, his wife, and their Labrador retriever headed off in the same direction.

They landed in Seattle. Why Seattle? Because it had a pool of talented computer professionals (Microsoft and numerous computer software start-ups are located there) and it was near two major book wholesalers. Bezos sold his first book from his Web site in July of 1995.

Just how does Amazon.com work? When customers log onto the company's Web site page, they can pursue their book search by title, author, or subject. Customers who are not looking for a particular title can browse through the database of over 2.5 million books to find something of interest. When customers find a book they want to buy, they use on-line forms to specify hardcover or paperback, gift wrapping, and mode of shipment. Payment is by credit card, submitted by telephone or by the Web, where the transaction is guarded by sophisticated encryption technology. With orders in hand, Amazon requests books from a distributor or publisher, and the books are delivered to the company's Seattle warehouse. The order is then packed and shipped to the customer.

The most fascinating thing about Amazon.com is that it is truly a virtual organization. It employs approximately 120 people and has no physical storefront and very little inventory. But even virtual organizations need some formal rules and regulations to be as efficient and effective as possible. Put yourself in Bezos's situation. How many and what types of formal rules and regulations could he use in his rapidly growing company?

WHAT WOULD YOU DO?

C H A P T E R

10

Organizational

Structure

and Design

Although Jeff Bezos's approach to organizational structure and design might not be right for every organization, it does illustrate how important it is for managers to design an organizational structure that helps accomplish organizational goals and objectives. In this chapter, we'll present information about designing appropriate organizational structures. We'll look at the various dimensions of organizational structure and what contingency factors influence the design. Finally, we'll look at how organizational structures evolve and at some of the newest concepts in organizational design. We'll see that Amazon.com's virtual organization may not be so unusual in the future.

DEFINING ORGANIZATIONAL STRUCTURE AND DESIGN

organizing

The process of creating an organization's structure.

organizational structure

The organization's formal framework by which job tasks are divided, grouped, and coordinated.

organizational design

The developing or changing of an organization's structure.

No other topic in management has undergone as much change in the past few years as that of organizing and organizational structure. Traditional approaches to organizing work are being questioned and reevaluated as managers search out structural designs that will best support and facilitate employees' doing the organization's work. Recall from chapter 1 that **organizing** is defined as the process of creating an organization's structure. That process is important and serves many purposes (Table 10-1). The challenge for managers is to design an organizational structure that allows employees to effectively and efficiently do their work while accomplishing organizational goals and objectives.

Just what is an organization's structure? An **organizational structure** is the formal framework by which job tasks are divided, grouped, and coordinated. Just as humans have skeletons that define their shapes, organizations have structures that define theirs. When managers develop or change an organization's structure, they are engaged in **organizational design**, a process that involves decisions about six key elements: work specialization, departmentalization, chain of command, span of control, centralization and decentralization, and formalization.[2] Let's take a closer look at each of the six elements of structure.

TESTING... TESTING...

1 Why is organizing important?

2 What is organizational structure?

3 List the six key elements used in designing an organization's structure.

TABLE 10-1	Some Purposes of Organizing

Divides work to be done into specific jobs and departments
Assigns tasks and responsibilities associated with individual jobs
Coordinates diverse organizational tasks
Clusters jobs into units
Establishes relationships among individuals, groups, and departments
Establishes formal lines of authority
Allocates and deploys organizational resources

Work Specialization

The concept of work specialization can be traced back a couple of centuries to Adam Smith's discussion of division of labor and his conclusion that it contributed to increased employee productivity. (Refer to chapter 2 if you want more information.) A well-known application of the division-of-labor concept is Henry Ford's assembly line in the early 1900s. Every Ford worker was assigned a specific, repetitive task. One person would put on the right front wheel, someone else would install the right front door, and another worker would put in the bench seat. By breaking jobs up into small standardized tasks that could be performed over and over again, Ford was able to produce cars at the rate of one every 10 seconds while using employees who had relatively limited skills.

Today we use the term **work specialization**, or division of labor, to describe the degree to which tasks in an organization are divided into separate jobs. The essence of work specialization is that an entire job is not done by one individual but instead is broken down into steps, and each step is completed by a different person. Individual employees specialize in doing part of an activity rather than the entire activity.

By the late 1940s, most manufacturing jobs in industrialized countries were being done with the use of high work specialization. Managers saw it as a way to make the most efficient use of employees' skills. How? In most organizations, some work tasks require high levels of skills and others can be performed by unskilled workers. If all workers were engaged in every step of, say, the manufacturing process, all would need the skills necessary to perform both the most demanding and the least demanding jobs. The result would be that, except when performing the most skilled or highly sophisticated work tasks, employees would be working below their skill levels. Because skilled workers are paid more than unskilled workers and their wages tend to reflect their highest level of skills, this use of organizational resources would be inefficient. Highly skilled workers would be being paid to perform simple tasks.

Managers also found that other efficiencies could be achieved through work specialization. It stands to reason that employees' skills at performing a task would improve and increase through repetition. In addition, less time would be spent in changing tasks, in putting away tools and equipment from a prior step in the work process, and in getting ready for another. Equally important, employee training for specialization is more efficient from the organization's perspective because it is easier and less costly to find and train workers to do specific, repetitive, limited tasks than to find and train workers to do all the tasks. This difference is especially true of highly sophisticated and complex operations. Could Cessna produce one Citation business jet a year if one person had to build the entire plane alone? Probably not! Finally, work specialization increases efficiency and productivity by encouraging the creation of special inventions and machinery to perform work tasks.

During the first half of the twentieth century, managers viewed work specialization as an unending source of increased productivity. And for a time it was! Because it wasn't widely practiced, its implementation in an organization almost always generated higher employee productivity. By the 1960s, however, it was becoming evident that a good thing could be carried too far. The point had been reached in some jobs at which the human diseconomies from work specialization—such as boredom, fatigue, stress, low productivity, poor quality of work, increased absenteeism, and higher job turnover—more than offset the

work specialization

The degree to which tasks in an organization are divided into separate jobs. Also known as division of labor.

Changes in technology have cut the shelf life of most employees' skills. A factory worker or clerical employee used to be able to learn one job and be reasonably sure that the skills learned to do that job would be enough for most of his or her work life. That's no longer the case. What ethical obligation do organizations have to assist workers whose skills have become obsolete? What about employees? Do they have an obligation to keep their skills from becoming obsolete? What ethical guidelines might you suggest for dealing with employee skill obsolescence? ■

The prestige of the Mayo Clinic, renowned for its expertise in every branch of medicine, is largely due to the specializations of its 1,150 physicians, 1,000 residents, and 15,000 nurses, technicians, students, and staff.

economic advantages. In such instances, worker productivity could be increased by enlarging, rather than narrowing, the scope of job activities. In addition, several organizations found that employees who were given a variety of work activities to do, allowed to do the work activities necessary to complete a whole job, and put into teams with interchangeable skills often achieved significantly higher output and were more satisfied with their jobs than were specialized workers.

Most managers today see work specialization as an important organizing mechanism but not as a source of endlessly increasing productivity. They recognize the economies it provides in certain types of jobs; they also recognize the problems it creates when it's carried to extremes. McDonald's, for example, uses high work specialization to efficiently make and sell its fast-food products, and medical personnel in most health service organizations are highly specialized. On the other hand, organizations such as Saturn Corporation and Hallmark Cards have successfully broadened the scope of jobs and reduced work specialization.

Departmentalization

departmentalization

The basis on which jobs are grouped in order to accomplish organizational goals.

functional departmentalization

Grouping jobs by functions performed.

Does your school have an educational media department? Does it have a financial aid department? If you're employed, does your organization have an advertising department or regional sales divisions? Once jobs have been divided up through work specialization they then have to be grouped back together so that common tasks can be coordinated. The basis on which jobs are grouped in order to accomplish organizational goals is called **departmentalization**. Every organization will have its own specific way of classifying and grouping work activities.

Historically, one of the most popular ways to group work activities has been by function performed, or **functional departmentalization** (Figure 10-1). For instance, a man-

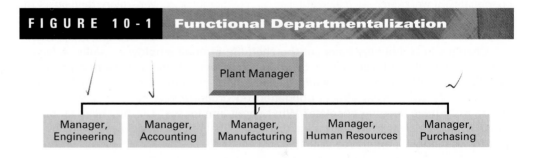

FIGURE 10-1   Functional Departmentalization

FIGURE 10-2   Product Departmentalization

Source: Bombardier Annual Report.

ufacturing manager might organize his or her plant by separating engineering, accounting, manufacturing, human resources, and purchasing specialists into common departments. A hotel might be organized around housekeeping, front desk, maintenance, restaurant operations, reservations and sales, human resources, and accounting. Of course, departmentalization by function can be used in all types of organizations, although the functions change to reflect the organization's objectives and work activities. The major advantage of this type of grouping is obtaining efficiencies from putting similar specialties and people with common skills, knowledge, and orientations together into common units.

Work activities can also be departmentalized by the type of product the organization produces—that is, by **product departmentalization**. Figure 10-2 illustrates this type of grouping as used by Bombardier Ltd., a Canadian company. Each major product area in the corporation is placed under the authority of an executive who's a specialist in, and is responsible for, everything having to do with his or her product line. Another company that uses product departmentalization is Nike. Its product structure is based on its various product lines, which include men's and women's athletic shoes for different sports and apparel and accessories. If an organization's activities were service- rather than product-related, each service would be grouped separately. For instance, an accounting firm could have departments for tax preparation, management consulting, auditing, and the like. Each department would offer an array of related services under the direction of a service manager.

Another way to departmentalize is on the basis of geography or territory—**geographical departmentalization** (Figure 10-3). The sales function, for instance, may have western, southern, midwestern, and eastern regions. Each of these regions is, in effect, a depart-

product departmentalization

Grouping jobs by product line.

geographical departmentalization

Grouping jobs on the basis of territory or geography.

FIGURE 10-3   Geographical Departmentalization

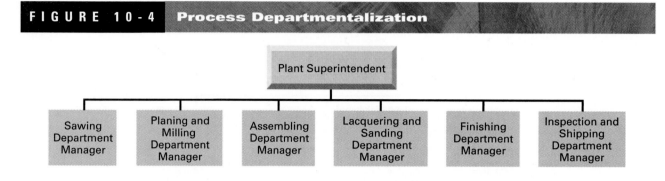

FIGURE 10-4   **Process Departmentalization**

Plant Superintendent

Sawing Department Manager | Planing and Milling Department Manager | Assembling Department Manager | Lacquering and Sanding Department Manager | Finishing Department Manager | Inspection and Shipping Department Manager

process departmentalization

Grouping jobs on the basis of product or customer flow.

ment organized around geography. If an organization's customers are scattered over a large geographical area, this form of departmentalization can be valuable.

At a wood cabinet manufacturing plant in southern Minnesota, production is organized around six departments: sawing, planing and milling, assembling, lacquering and sanding, finishing, and inspection and shipping. This is an example of **process departmentalization**, which is grouping activities on the basis of product or customer flow. Figure 10-4 illustrates the process form of departmentalization. Because each process requires particular skills, this approach offers a basis for the homogeneous categorizing of work activities. Process departmentalization can be used for processing customers as well as products. For instance, if you've ever been to a state motor vehicle office to get a driver's license, you probably went through several departments before receiving your license. In some states, applicants must go through three steps, each handled by a separate department: (1) validation, by the motor vehicle division; (2) processing, by the licensing department; and (3) payment collection, by the treasury department.

customer departmentalization

Grouping jobs on the basis of common customers.

A final means of departmentalizing is to use the particular type of customer the organization seeks to reach (Figure 10-5). This is known as **customer departmentalization**. For instance, the sales activities in an office supply firm can be broken down into three departments that service retail, wholesale, and government customers. Or a large law office might segment its staff on the basis of whether they serve corporate or individual clients. The assumption underlying customer departmentalization is that customers in each department have a common set of problems and needs that can best be met by having specialists for each.

Large organizations often combine most or all of these forms of departmentalization. For example, a major Japanese electronics firm organizes each of its divisions along functional lines and organizes its manufacturing units around processes; it departmentalizes sales around seven geographical regions; and it divides each sales region into four customer groupings.

Two general departmentalization trends seem to have taken hold during the late 1990s. First, customer departmentalization remains highly popular as an approach to departmen-

FIGURE 10-5   **Customer Departmentalization**

Director of Sales

Manager, Retail Accounts | Manager, Wholesale Accounts | Manager, Government Accounts

talizing. In order to better monitor customers' needs and to be better able to respond to changes in those needs, many organizations have emphasized customer departmentalization. For example, L.L. Bean restructured around a half-dozen customer groups on the basis of what its customers generally purchased from the company. This arrangement allowed the company to better understand its customers and to respond faster to their requirements. The second trend is that rigid functional departmentalization is being complemented by the use of cross-functional teams that cross over traditional departmental lines. In many organizations, rigid departmental divisions have been replaced by a hybrid grouping of individuals who are experts in various specialties and who work together in an organizational arrangement known as a **cross-functional team**.[3] What's unique about cross-functional teams is that they bring together diverse experts who might never cross paths in a traditional organization although their work might be highly interdependent. Today, we find cost accountants teaming up with operations managers, product designers collaborating with purchasing department employees, and marketing professionals working with research engineers.

Cross-functional teams have done everything from designing a new product and seeing that it makes it to the marketplace, to preparing a long-term corporate strategy, to creating a new layout for the factory floor. For instance, Thermos Corporation, the Schaumberg, Illinois, company known worldwide for its beverage containers and lunch boxes, replaced its old, tradition-bound functionally departmentalized structure with flexible interdisciplinary teams. One of these company teams—who called themselves the Lifestyle team—developed a new electric grill that has been very popular with consumers. The Lifestyle team, composed of individuals from engineering, marketing, and manufacturing, were involved in every aspect of bringing this winning product to market—from defining the target market, to defining the product, to working with manufacturing on a feasible design. We'll discuss the use of cross-functional teams more fully in chapter 14.

cross-functional team

A hybrid grouping of individuals who are experts in various specialties (or functions) and who work together.

---

4 **What are the advantages and drawbacks of work specialization?**

5 **Describe the ways that managers can departmentalize work activities.**

6 **What are the implications of the two recent departmentalization trends that have been observed?**

TESTING...
TESTING...
1 2 3

Chain of Command

During the 1960s and 1970s, the chain-of-command concept was a basic cornerstone of organizational design. As you'll see, it has far less importance today, but managers still need to consider its implications when they decide how best to structure their organizations.

The **chain of command** is an unbroken line of authority that extends from the upper levels of the organization down to the lowest levels and clarifies who reports to whom. It helps employees determine whom to go to if they have a problem and also to whom they are responsible.

You can't discuss the chain of command without discussing three analogous concepts: authority, responsibility, and unity of command. **Authority** refers to the rights inherent in a managerial position to give orders and to expect the orders to be obeyed.[4] To facilitate decision making and coordination, the organization provides each managerial position in the organizational structure a place in the chain of command and "grants" each manager a certain degree of authority to meet his or her responsibilities. When one is given the "right" to do something, one also assumes a corresponding obligation to perform those assigned activities. This obligation or expectation to perform is known as **responsibility**. Finally, the

chain of command

An unbroken line of authority that extends from the upper levels of the organization to the lowest levels and clarifies who reports to whom.

authority

The rights inherent in a managerial position to give orders and to expect the orders to be obeyed.

responsibility

The obligation or expectation to perform.

Although he maintains a close personal involvement in every aspect of his successful men's clothing business, Karl Kani of Karl Kani Infinity, based in Los Angeles, also sees the need to delegate some control. "It's very hard to be an expert at designing, marketing, manufacturing, and distribution,...The smartest thing to do was to enlist experts so that I could attend to the thing I do best"— designing the clothes that carry his name.

unity of command

The management principle that a subordinate should have one and only one superior to whom he or she is directly responsible.

unity of command principle (one of Henri Fayol's 14 principles of management) helps preserve the concept of an unbroken line of authority. It states that a person should have one and only one superior to whom he or she is directly responsible. If the unity of command is broken, a subordinate might have to cope with conflicting demands or priorities from several superiors.

The classical management theorists (Fayol, Weber, Taylor, and others) were enamored with the concepts of chain of command, authority, responsibility, and unity of command, but times change and so has the relevance of these basic tenets of organizational design. The concepts are substantially less relevant today because of advancements in computer technology and the trend toward empowering employees. A low-level employee today can access information in a matter of seconds that used to be available only to top managers. Similarly, computer technology increasingly allows employees anywhere in an organization to communicate with anyone else without going through formal channels: that is, through the chain of command. Moreover, the concepts of authority, responsibility, and maintaining the chain of command have become less relevant as operating employees are being empowered to make decisions that previously were reserved for management. Add the popularity of self-managed and cross-functional teams and the creation of new structural designs that include multiple bosses, and you can begin to see why the chain-of-command concept has become less relevant. Of course, many organizations still find that they are most productive by enforcing the chain of command, but their numbers are dwindling.

Span of Control

span of control

The number of subordinates a manager can supervise efficiently and effectively.

The concept of **span of control** refers to how many subordinates a manager can effectively and efficiently supervise. The question of span of control received a great deal of attention from early management writers. Although they reached no consensus on a specific ideal number, these writers favored small spans—typically no more than six—in order to maintain close control.[5] Several writers did acknowledge, however, that level in the organization was a contingency variable that could affect the number. They argued that as a manager rose in the organizational hierarchy, he or she had to deal with a greater variety of complex and ill-structured problems, so top executives should have a smaller span of control than did middle managers and, likewise, middle managers required a smaller span than did supervisors.

We now recognize and understand that the most effective and efficient span of control is increasingly determined by looking at several contingency variables. For instance, it's obvious that the more training and experience subordinates have, the less direct supervision they'll need. Therefore, managers who have well-trained and experienced employees can function quite well with a wider span. Other contingency variables that will determine the appropriate span include similarity of subordinate tasks, the complexity of those tasks, the physical proximity of subordinates, the degree to which standardized procedures are in place, the sophistication of the organization's management information system, the strength of the organization's culture, and the preferred style of the manager.[6]

Why is the span-of-control concept important? To a large degree, it determines how many levels and managers an organization will have. Other things being equal, the wider or larger the span of control, the more efficient the organizational design. Let's look at an example to illustrate the validity of that statement.

Assume that we have two organizations, and each has approximately 4,100 operative employees. As Figure 10-6 shows, if one organization has a uniform span of four and the other a span of eight, the wider span will have two fewer levels and approximately 800 fewer managers. If the average manager made $40,000 a year, the organization with the wider span would save $32 million a year in management salaries alone! Obviously, wider spans are more efficient in terms of cost. But at some point, wider spans reduce effectiveness. The contemporary view of span of control recognizes that many factors influence the appropriate number of subordinates that a manager can efficiently *and* effectively manage.

The trend in recent years has been toward larger spans of control. Wide spans of control are consistent with efforts by organizations to reduce costs, cut overhead, speed up decision making, increase flexibility, get closer to customers, and empower employees. However, to ensure that performance doesn't suffer because of these wider spans, organizations have been investing heavily in employee training. Managers recognize that they can

FIGURE 10-6 **Contrasting Spans of Control**

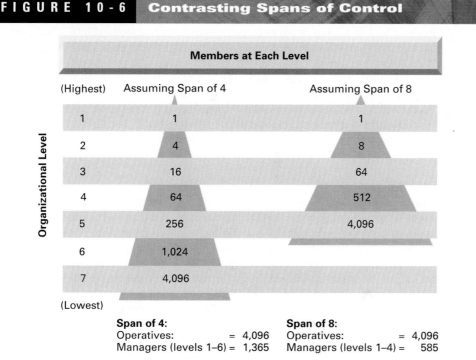

handle a wider span when employees know their jobs inside and out or can turn to their co-workers if they have questions.

Centralization and Decentralization

In some organizations, top managers make all the decisions and the lower-level managers merely carry out their directives. At the other extreme are organizations in which decision making is pushed down through the levels of management to the managers who are closest to the action. The former organizations are described as highly centralized, and the latter as decentralized.

Centralization describes the degree to which decision making is concentrated in the upper levels of the organization. If top management makes the organization's key decisions with little or no input from lower-level employees, then the organization is centralized. In contrast, the more that lower-level employees provide input or are actually given the discretion to make decisions, the more **decentralization** there is. Keep in mind that the concept of centralization-decentralization is a relative, not an absolute, one. What we mean by *relative* is that an organization is never completely centralized or decentralized. Few organizations could function effectively if all decisions were made by only a select group of top managers; nor could they function effectively if all decisions were delegated to the lowest employee levels.

Consistent with recent management efforts to make organizations more flexible and responsive, there's been a distinct trend toward decentralizing decision making. In large companies especially, lower-level managers are "closer to the action" and typically have more detailed knowledge about problems and how best to solve them than do top managers. For instance, when Interstate Bakeries Corporation of Kansas City, Missouri, purchased the Hostess and Wonder Bread brands from Ralston Purina Co., it immediately was able to revive the lagging sales of familiar brands such as Twinkies, Ding Dongs, and HoHos—something that Ralston had not been able to do. How did Interstate accomplish what Ralston could not? Whereas Ralston was structured around a bureaucracy in which nearly all decisions were made at headquarters, Interstate pushed authority down to individual plant and brand managers. They had the authority to react to local conditions in making decisions.[7] Another example of the trend toward decentralization can be found at the Bank of Montreal whose 1,164 Canadian branches have been organized into 236 "communities"—that is, a group of branches within a limited geographical area. Each community is led by a community area manager, who typically works within a 20-minute drive of the other branches. This area manager can respond faster and more intelligently to problems in his community than could some senior executive in Montreal.[8]

What determines whether an organization will move toward more centralization or more decentralization? A number of factors have been identified that tend to influence the amount of centralization or decentralization an organization has.[9] Table 10-2 lists some of them.

Formalization

Formalization refers to the degree to which jobs within the organization are standardized and the extent to which employee behavior is guided by rules and procedures. If a job is highly formalized, then the person doing that job has a minimum amount of discretion over what is to be done, when it's to be done, and how he or she should do it. Employees can be expected always to handle the same input in exactly the same way, resulting in a consistent and uniform output. In organizations with high formalization, there are explicit job descriptions, lots of organizational rules, and clearly defined procedures covering work processes. Where formalization is low, job behaviors are relatively nonstructured and employees have a great deal of freedom in how they do their work. Because an individual's discretion on the job is inversely related to the amount of behavior in that job that is preprogrammed by the organization, the greater the standardization, the less input the employee has into how his

centralization

The degree to which decision making is concentrated in the upper levels of the organization.

decentralization

The handing down of decision-making authority to lower levels in an organization.

formalization

The degree to which jobs within an organization are standardized and the extent to which employee behavior is guided by rules and procedures.

TABLE 10-2	**Factors that Influence the Amount of Centralization and Decentralization**
More Centralization	**More Decentralization**
• Environment is stable.	• Environment is complex, uncertain.
• Lower-level managers are not as capable or experienced at making decisions as upper-level managers.	• Lower-level managers are capable and experienced at making decisions.
• Lower-level managers do not want to have a say in decisions.	• Lower-level managers want a voice in decisions.
• Decisions are significant.	• Decisions are relatively minor.
• Organization is facing a crisis or the risk of company failure.	• Corporate culture is open to allowing managers to have a say in what happens.
• Company is large.	• Company is geographically dispersed.
• Effective implementation of company strategies depends on managers' retaining say over what happens.	• Effective implementation of company strategies depends on managers' having involvement and flexibility to make decisions.

or her work is to be done. Standardization not only eliminates the possibility that employees will engage in alternative behaviors, but it even removes the need for employees to consider alternatives.

The degree of formalization can vary widely between organizations and even within organizations. For instance, at an organization that publishes newspapers, news reporters often have a great deal of discretion in their job. They may be told what news topic to write about, but they have the freedom to find their own stories, research them the way they want, and write them up, usually within certain minimal guidelines. On the other hand, the compositors and typesetters who lay out the newspaper pages don't have that type of freedom. They have constraints—both time and space—that standardize how they do their work.

7 How is the chain-of-command concept used in organizing?

8 Why is span of control important to organizing decisions?

9 Describe the advantages and drawbacks of centralization and decentralization.

TESTING...
TESTING...
1 2 3

THE CONTINGENCY APPROACH TO ORGANIZATIONAL DESIGN

Organizations are not all structured in exactly the same way. That's only logical, you may be saying to yourself. After all, a company with 30 employees isn't going to look like one with 30,000 employees. But even organizations of comparable size don't necessarily have similar structures. What works for one organization may not work for another.

Structural differences among organizations aren't random or happenstance. Top managers of most organizations typically put a great deal of thought into designing an appropriate structure. What that appropriate structure is depends on four contingency variables: the organization's strategy, size, technology, and degree of environmental uncertainty. As we discovered with planning, the ideal organizational design depends on various contingency factors. In this section, we'll look at two generic models of organizational design and then look at the contingency factors that favor each.

Mechanistic and Organic Organizations

mechanistic organization

An organizational structure that's characterized by high specialization, extensive departmentalization, narrow spans of control, high formalization, a limited information network, and little participation in decision making by low-level employees.

Figure 10-7 describes two organizational forms.[10] The **mechanistic organization** is a rigid and tightly controlled structure. It's characterized by high specialization, rigid departmentalization, narrow spans of control, high formalization, a limited information network (mostly downward communication), and little participation in decision making by low-level employees.

In the mechanistic structure, work specialization creates jobs that are simple, routine, and standardized. Extensive departmentalization increases impersonality and the need for multiple layers of management to coordinate these specialized departments. There's also strict adherence to the unity-of-command principle. This ensures the existence of a formal hierarchy of authority, in which each person is supervised by one superior. Narrow spans of control, especially at increasingly higher levels of the organization, have the effect of creating tall organizational structures with many layers and levels. As the distance between the top and the bottom of the organization widens, top managers tend to impose rules and regulations to control employee behavior because they're so far removed from the lower-level activities that they cannot directly supervise and ensure the use of standard practices. Instead, they substitute high formalization.

Mechanistic types of organizational structures tend to be efficiency machines, well oiled by rules, regulations, routinization, and similar controls. This organizational design tries to minimize the impact of differing personalities, human judgments, and ambiguity because these are seen as inefficient and inconsistent. Although no pure form of the mechanistic organization exists in reality, almost all large corporations and governmental agencies tend to have many, or at least some, of these mechanistic characteristics.

organic organization

An organizational structure that's highly adaptive and flexible with little work specialization, minimal formalization, and little direct supervision of employees.

In direct contrast to the mechanistic form of organization is the **organic organization**, which is as highly adaptive and flexible a structure as the mechanistic organization is rigid and stable. Rather than having standardized jobs and regulations, the organic organization has flexibility, which allows it to change rapidly as needs require. Organic organizations have division of labor, but the jobs people do are not standardized. Employees are highly trained and empowered to handle diverse job-related problems, and organic structures frequently use employee teams. The net effect is that employees in this type of organization require minimal formal rules and little direct supervision; their high levels of skills and training and the support provided by other team members make formalization and tight managerial controls unnecessary.

FIGURE 10-7   Mechanistic versus Organic Organization

Mechanistic
- High Specialization
- Rigid Departmentalization
- Clear Chain of Command
- Narrow Spans of Control
- Centralization
- High Formalization

Organic
- Cross-Functional Teams
- Cross-Hierarchical Teams
- Free Flow of Information
- Wide Spans of Control
- Decentralization
- Low Formalization

The organic, flexible organizational structure of California ad agency TBWA Chiat/Day allows most of its 400 employees to work as informally as they want, whether they are meeting in the company dining room or working at home in their pajamas.

When is a mechanistic organizational structure preferable and when is an organic one more appropriate? Let's look at the key contingency factors that influence the structure decision.

Strategy and Structure

An organization's structure is a means to help managers achieve their objectives. Because objectives are derived from the organization's overall strategy, it's only logical that strategy and structure should be closely linked. More specifically, structure should follow strategy. If managers significantly change the organization's strategy, they will need to modify the structure to accommodate and support the change.

The initial research on the strategy-structure relationship was a study by Alfred Chandler of several large U.S. companies.[11] He traced the development of organizations such as DuPont, General Motors, Standard Oil of New Jersey, and Sears over a period of 50 years and concluded that changes in corporate strategy led to changes in an organization's structure. Specifically, Chandler found that organizations usually began with a single product or line. The simplicity of this strategy required only a simple or loose form of structure. Decisions were centralized in the hands of a single senior manager, and specialization, departmentalization, and formalization were low. As organizations grew, their strategies became more ambitious and elaborate, and the structure changed to support the chosen strategy.

Most current strategy-structure contingency frameworks tend to focus on three strategy dimensions: (1) innovation, which reflects the organization's pursuit of meaningful and unique innovations; (2) cost minimization, which reflects the organization's pursuit of tightly controlled costs; and (3) imitation, which reflects an organization's seeking to minimize risk and maximize profit opportunities by copying the market leaders. What organizational design works best with each of these strategies?[12] Innovators need the flexibility and free flow of information of the organic structure, whereas cost minimizers seek the efficiency, stability, and tight controls of the mechanistic structure. Imitators use structural characteristics from both. They use characteristics of a mechanistic structure to maintain tight controls and low costs but then will create more organic organizational subunits or divisions to pursue new directions.

Size and Structure

There's considerable historical evidence that an organization's size significantly affects its structure.[13] For instance, large organizations—those with 2,000 or more employees—tend to have more specialization, departmentalization, centralization, and rules and regulations than do small organizations. However, the relationship isn't linear. Rather, size affects structure at a decreasing rate; size becomes less important as an organization expands. Why? Essentially, once an organization has around 2,000 employees, it's already fairly mechanistic. An additional 500 employees will not have much of an impact. On the other hand, adding 500 employees to an organization that has only 300 members is likely to result in a shift toward a more mechanistic structure.

TESTING... TESTING...

10 Describe the differences between mechanistic and organic organizations.

11 Summarize the strategy-structure relationship.

12 How does the size of an organization influence its structure?

Technology and Structure

Every organization uses some form of technology to convert its inputs into outputs. To reach its objectives, the organization combines equipment, materials, knowledge, and experienced individuals into certain types and patterns of activities. For instance, the Maytag Corporation uses workers on assembly lines to build the washers, dryers, and other home appliances that it manufactures and sells. Employees at Kinkos Copies produce custom jobs for individual customers. And employees at Miles, Inc., work on a continuous-flow production line for manufacturing its vitamins. Each of these organizations represents a different type of technology.

The initial interest in technology as a determinant of structure can be traced to the work of a British scholar, Joan Woodward, in the 1960s.[14] Her research was the first major attempt to view organizational structure from a technological perspective. She demonstrated that organizational structures adapt to their technology. Although few organizational design researchers would argue today that technology is the *sole* determinant of structure, clearly it's an important contributor.[15] Let's look more closely at Woodward's research.

Woodward studied several small manufacturing firms in southern England to determine the extent to which structural design principles such as unity of command and span of con-

Technology has shaped the virtual organizational structure of VeriFone, Inc., whose terminals are used by retailers for customer credit card authorization. CEO Hatim Tyabji designed his organization's structure around four attributes: global reach, location independence, an electronic knowledge network, and time compression.

trol were related to organizational success. She was unable to derive any consistent pattern from her data until she segmented the firms into three categories based on the size of their production runs. The three categories, representing three distinct technologies, had increasing levels of complexity and sophistication. The first category, **unit production**, comprised unit or small-batch producers that manufactured custom products such as tailor-made suits or turbines for hydroelectric dams. The second category, **mass production**, included large-batch or mass-production manufacturers that made items such as refrigerators or automobiles. The third and most technically complex group, **process production**, included continuous process producers such as oil and chemical refiners.

What did Woodward find in her studies of these three groups? She found that (1) distinct relationships existed between these technology classifications and the subsequent structure of the firms and (2) the effectiveness of the organizations was related to the "fit" between technology and structure. A summary of her findings is shown in Table 10-3.

After carefully analyzing her findings, Woodward concluded that specific structures were associated with each of the three categories and that successful firms met the requirements of their technology by adopting the proper structural arrangements. She found that there was no one best way to organize a manufacturing firm. Unit and process production were most effective when matched with an organic structure, and mass production was most effective when matched with a mechanistic structure.

Since Woodward's initial work, numerous studies have been conducted on the technology-structure relationship. These studies generally demonstrate that organizational structures adapt to their technology.[16] The processes or methods that transform an organization's inputs into outputs differ by their degree of routineness. In general, the more routine the technology, the more standardized the structure can be. We would expect organizations with routine technologies to be mechanistic and organizations with nonroutine technologies to be organic.[17] Because technology has had—and continues to have—a significant impact on communication flow and organizational design, we include a separate section on those topics at the end of the chapter.

Environmental Uncertainty and Structure

In chapter 3 we introduced the organization's environment and the amount of uncertainty in that environment as constraints on managerial discretion. Why should an organization's structure be affected by its environment? Because of environmental uncertainty! Some organizations face relatively stable and simple environments; others face dynamic and complex environments. Because uncertainty threatens an organization's effectiveness, managers will try to minimize it. One way to reduce environmental uncertainty is through adjustments in the organization's structure.[18]

unit production

The production of items in units or small batches.

mass production

Large-batch manufacturing.

process production

Continuous-process production.

TABLE 10-3	Woodward's Findings on Technology, Structure, and Effectiveness		
	Unit Production	**Mass Production**	**Process Production**
Structural characteristics	Low vertical differentiation	Moderate vertical differentiation	High vertical differentiation
	Low horizontal differentiation	High horizontal differentiation	Low horizontal differentiation
	Low formalization	High formalization	Low formalization
Most effective structure	Organic	Mechanistic	Organic

There is substantial evidence relating the degree of environmental uncertainty to different structural arrangements. Essentially, the scarcer the resources and the more dynamic and complex the environment—that is, the greater the uncertainty—the greater the need for the flexibility offered by an organic design. On the other hand, in stable, simple environments with abundant resources, mechanistic designs tend to be most effective.

The evidence on the environment-structure relationship helps to explain why so many managers are restructuring their organizations to be lean, fast, and flexible. Global competition, accelerated product innovation by all competitors, and increased demands from customers for higher quality and faster deliveries are examples of dynamic environmental forces. Mechanistic organizations tend to be ill-equipped to respond to rapid environmental change and environmental uncertainty. As a result, we're seeing more managers redesigning their organizations in order to make them more organic.

TESTING... TESTING...

13 Describe Joan Woodward's findings.

14 What is the relationship between the routineness of technology and organizational structure?

15 What role does environmental uncertainty play in organizational design?

APPLICATIONS OF ORGANIZATIONAL DESIGN

What organizational designs are Ford, Toshiba, Procter & Gamble, and Amazon.com using? Let's look at various organizational designs that you might see in today's organizations.

Simple Structure

simple structure

An organizational design with low departmentalization, wide spans of control, authority centralized in a single person, and little formalization.

Most organizations start as entrepreneurial ventures with a simple structure consisting of owners and employees. A **simple structure** is defined more by what it is not than by what it is. It's not an elaborate structure.[19] If you work in or have dealt with an organization that appears to have almost no structure, it's probably a simple structure. By that we mean that it has a low degree of departmentalization, wide spans of control, authority centralized in a single person, and little formalization. It's a "flat" organization with only two or three vertical levels, an informal arrangement of employees, and one individual in whom decision-making authority is centralized.

The simple structure is most widely used by small businesses in which the owner and manager are one and the same. The strengths of the simple structure are obvious: It's fast, flexible, and inexpensive to maintain, and accountability is clear. One major weakness is that it's difficult to make it an effective structure in other than small organizations. It becomes increasingly inadequate as an organization grows because its low formalization and high centralization tend to result in information overload at the top. As the organization increases in size, decision making becomes slower and can eventually come to a standstill as the single executive tries to continue making all the decisions. If the structure isn't changed and made more elaborate, the firm is likely to lose market momentum and eventually fail. The simple structure's other weakness is that it's risky; everything depends on one person. If anything happens to that person, the organization's information and decision-making center is lost.

Bureaucracy

Many organizations do not, by choice or by design, remain simple structures. As a company increases its sales and production volume, it generally reaches a point at which it has to add employees to help cope with the additional duties and requirements of operating at that vol-

Structuring the Entrepreneurial Firm

At some point, the successful entrepreneur finds that he or she cannot do everything alone. More people are needed. The entrepreneur must then decide on the most appropriate structural arrangement for effectively carrying out the firm's activities.[20] Without some type of suitable organizational structure, the entrepreneurial firm can soon find itself in a chaotic situation.

In small firms, the organizational structure tends to evolve with very little conscious and deliberate planning on the part of the founder or owner. For the most part, it looks like a simple structure. As the entrepreneurial firm grows and the owner or founder finds it increasingly difficult to go it alone, employees are brought on board to perform certain functions or duties that the entrepreneur can't handle. These individuals tend to keep doing those same functions as the company matures. Thus is born the functional structure in which each or most of the functional aspects of the venture—such as accounting, marketing, human resources, and so on—is handled by a manager. And it's normal for this functional structure to gradually evolve rather than being created in one bold move.

With the evolution to a more deliberate structure comes a whole new set of challenges for the entrepreneur. All of a sudden, he or she must delegate authority and operating responsibility. This is typically one of the most difficult things for an entrepreneur to do—letting someone else make decisions. After all, he or she reasons, how can anyone know this business as well as I do? Also, what might have been a fairly informal, loose and flexible atmosphere that worked well when the firm was a certain size now no longer is effective. Many entrepreneurs are acutely concerned about keeping the "small company" atmosphere alive even as their organization evolves into a more structured arrangement. But having a "structured" organization doesn't necessarily mean giving up flexibility, adaptability, and freedom. In fact, many of the newest organizational designs, such as the team-based structure and the boundaryless organization, are particularly well suited to small firms. The fluidity of these contemporary structural designs may provide the entrepreneurial firm with both the openness and the rigidity it needs. ■

ume. As the number of employees rises, the organizational structure tends to become more specialized and formalized. Rules and regulations are introduced, work becomes specialized, departments are created, levels of management are added, and the organization becomes increasingly bureaucratic.

We first described the characteristics of a bureaucracy in chapter 2. Recall that it's an organizational arrangement based on order, logic, and the legitimate use of authority. When contingency factors, including growth in size, favor a bureaucratic or mechanistic design, one of two options is most likely to be used. One is a *functional structure*, in which the primary focus is on achieving the efficiencies of division of labor by grouping like specialists together in functional groupings. The other is the *divisional structure*, which creates divisions or strategic business units. Let's look at each more closely.

The **functional structure** expands the concept of functional departmentalization, which we talked about earlier, to the entire organization. Under a functional structure, management designs an organization based on grouping together similar or related occupational specialties. The strength of the functional structure lies in the cost-saving advantages that accrue from specialization. Putting similar specialties together results in economies of scale, minimizes duplication of people and equipment, and makes employees more comfortable because they are with others who "talk the same language." The biggest weakness of the functional structure is that the organization can lose sight of its best overall interests in the pursuit of functional goals. No one function is totally responsible for end results, so

functional structure

An organizational design that groups similar or related occupational specialties together.

MANAGERS

SPEAK

OUT

Interview with Sandy Steiner, President, Prentice Hall Business Publishing, Upper Saddle River, New Jersey

Describe your job.

I am the president of Prentice Hall Business Publishing, a leading publisher of college textbooks. In this role, I oversee the process to produce the books, supplements, and media tools that enable teachers and students to engage in a common language in each course. This involves production (the group that works to physically produce the book, CD-ROM, or on-line courses), editorial (the group that signs new authors to write books for us in areas of study, both established and emerging, and manages the current authors, their books, and revisions), marketing (the group that secures market feedback, disseminates the message about our books, and manages the training of our sales representatives and their sales efforts for our books), and development (the group that works one on one with the authors on the way they write, organize, and relay the content).

What types of skills do you think tomorrow's managers will need?

Tomorrow's managers will need to be very fluid in their view of their job and their ability to develop and repurpose not only their own skills but also the skills of their people to meet emerging needs. They will need to look at technology as a tool for innovation, efficiency, and expansion and not as a stumbling block. They will need to be able to engage teams of workers, sometimes those not in their direct line of authority, in the organization's goals and be clear in letting them know how each individual contributes to achieving the goals. They will need to be able to look for shortcuts to conserve energy on low-level tasks while always looking ahead to how to remain competitive in the marketplace.

How has technology affected the structure of your organization?

Technology has taken some of the more basic functions of all jobs and made them easier to master and maintain. In areas of production, it has made some processes more difficult because there is no pattern to follow for completing projects while making the most of the technology available. In addition, the explosion of the Internet has enhanced overall communication and ease of response, but this has not come without the distraction it brings to work when new messages are constantly beeping through. It also has established some unrealistic expectations for turnaround replies.

In what ways does your organization encourage employees to be open to learning new ways of doing things?

We reward all members of a group on their innovations. At quarterly meetings we publicly acknowledge and reward employees whose contributions demonstrate a "better method" for project completion or who have gone above and beyond their job description in the pursuit of better quality, timeliness, and innovation. Members of the management team are evaluated on their innovations in process and creativity in product innovation. ■

functional specialists become insulated and have little understanding of what people in other functions are doing.

The **divisional structure** is an organizational structure made up of separate units or divisions.[21] Viacom, General Motors, Daimler-Benz AG, and Carlson Companies (some of its divisions include Radisson Hotels and TGI Fridays) are examples of organizations with divisional structures. Each unit or division in a divisional structure has relatively limited autonomy, with a division manager responsible for performance and exercising strategic and operational decision-making authority over his or her unit. In divisional structures, however, a central headquarters typically acts as an external overseer to coordinate and control the various divisions, and often it provides support services, such as financial and legal, to the various units.

The strength of the divisional structure is that it focuses on results. Division executives are responsible for what happens to their products or services. The major disadvantage of this approach is the duplication of activities and resources. Because each division has its own functional departments, such as marketing, research and development, and production, the duplication of functions increases the organization's costs and reduces efficiency.

As our chapter-opening Managers' Dilemma illustrated, many contemporary organizations are finding that these traditional hierarchical organizational designs aren't appropriate for the increasingly dynamic and complex environments they face. In response to marketplace demands for being lean, flexible, and innovative, many managers are finding creative ways to structure and organize work and to make their organizations more responsive to the needs of customers, employees, and other organizational constituents.[22] In the remaining part of this chapter, we introduce you to some of the newest concepts in organizational design.

divisional structure

An organizational structure made up of semiautonomous units or divisions.

16 When would the simple structure be the preferred organizational design?

17 Why would an organization move toward the bureaucratic organizational design as it grows?

18 Contrast functional structures and divisional structures.

Team-Based Structures

In a **team-based structure**, the entire organization is made up of work groups or teams that perform the organization's work.[23] Needless to say, in a team-based structure, employee empowerment is crucial because there is no rigid line of managerial authority flowing from top to bottom. Rather, employee teams are free to design work in the way they think is best. However, the teams are also held responsible for all work activity and performance results in their respective areas. Let's look at some examples of companies that have made the transition to a team-based structure.

At Sun Life Assurance of Canada's U.S. office in Wellesley, Massachusetts, customer representatives have been reorganized into eight-person teams trained to expedite all customer requests. Now, when customers call in, they're not switched from one specialist to another but to one of the teams who takes care of every aspect of the customer's request. At Ashton Photo of Salem, Oregon, a high-volume producer of photo prints for professional photographers, employee teams of up to nine persons each are directly accountable to customers for the work they produce and package. Each of the company's three major product lines has a divisional manager who supports the teams in handling product orders and in serving as a "barrier buster" to resolve issues that come up in weekly obstacle meetings. These teams also set their own work schedules, and employee evaluations are team based.

team-based structure

An organizational structure made up of work groups or teams that perform the organization's work.

At Bayer Corporation, which operates in the health care, medical imaging, and chemical industries, self-directed work teams, empowered with decision-making authority are responsible for a wide range of tasks and responsibilities. Here, employees inspect a tank car.

An individual employee who does not have strong support from his or her team peers is unlikely to receive a raise.

The transition to organizing around teams is usually a gradual one. For example, at Birkenstock Footprint Sandals, the team-based structure grew out of the success that a company-formed "eco task force" had with developing suggestions for ways the company and its dealers could improve recycling efforts and decrease the amount of energy used in day-to-day operations. The outcomes from the 12-person task force were so popular that Birkenstock managers wanted to further tap into the creativity and enthusiasm of its employees. They decided that a team-based structure would allow them to do just that. There are many other examples of both for-profit and not-for-profit organizations that have successfully implemented a team-based structure. In chapter 14, we'll cover more thoroughly the practical details of working with teams.

Project and Matrix Structures

matrix organization

An organizational structure that assigns specialists from different functional departments to work on one or more projects being led by project managers.

During the 1960s, an unusual organizational arrangement known as the **matrix organization** was developed by companies in the U.S. aerospace industry to help them cope with the demands of efficiently and effectively managing a number of concurrent projects. A matrix organization was a structural design that assigned specialists from different functional departments to work on one or more projects being led by a project manager. Look at Figure 10-8 (an example of a matrix structure used in an aerospace firm) and you'll see along the top the familiar organizational functions of engineering, accounting, human resources, and so forth. Along the vertical dimension, however, you'll see that the various projects the aerospace firm is currently working on have been added. Each project is directed by a manager who staffs his or her project with people from each of the functional departments. The addition of this vertical dimension to the traditional horizontal functional departments, in effect, wove together elements of functional and product departmentalization—hence the term *matrix*. One other unique aspect of the matrix structure was that it created a *dual chain of command*. It explicitly violated the classical organizing principle of unity of command. Functional departmentalization was used to gain the economies from specialization, but overlying the functional departments was another set of managers responsible for specific projects within the organization.

How does the matrix work in reality? Employees in the matrix have two bosses: their functional departmental manager and their product or project manager. The project man-

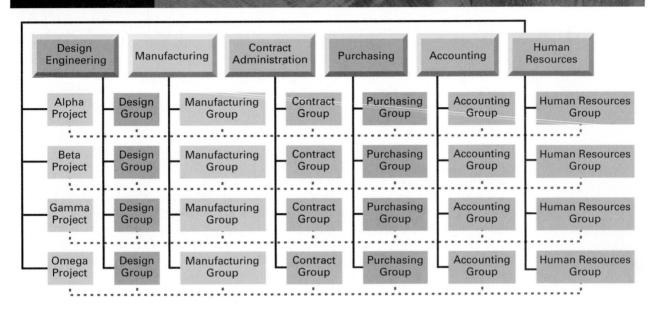

FIGURE 10-8   **A Matrix Organization in an Aerospace Firm**

agers have authority over the functional members who are part of that manager's project team. Authority is shared between the two managers. Typically, this sharing is done by giving the project manager authority over project employees relative to the project's goals. However, decisions such as promotions, salary recommendations, and annual reviews remain the functional manager's responsibility. To work effectively, project and functional managers have to communicate regularly and coordinate the demands upon the common employees.

Although the matrix structure worked well—and continues to be an effective structural design choice for many organizations—some organizations are using a more "advanced" type of **project structure**, in which employees (and the work they do) are permanently assigned to projects. Unlike the matrix structure, a project structure has no formal departments that employees return to at the completion of a project. Instead, employees take their specific skills, capabilities, and experiences to other work projects. In addition, all work activities in project structures are performed by teams of employees who become part of a project team because they have the appropriate work skills and abilities. For instance, at Oticon Holding A/S, a Danish hearing-aid manufacturer, there are no organizational departments or employee job titles. All work activities are project based, and these project teams form, disband, and form again as the work requires. Employees "join" project teams because they bring needed skills and abilities to that project. Once the project is completed, however, they move on to the next one.[24]

Project structures tend to be very fluid and flexible organizational designs. There's no departmentalization or rigid organizational hierarchy to slow down decision making or taking actions. In this type of structure, managers serve as facilitators, mentors, and coaches. They "service" the project teams by eliminating or minimizing organizational obstacles and by ensuring that the teams have the resources they need to effectively and efficiently complete their work. For example, at the Federal National Mortgage Association (Fannie Mae), which processes more than $1 billion of mortgage purchases every day, work is organized around projects. The organization's project managers don't just oversee and control the day-to-day work but instead guide project teams in defining how the work is done.[25]

project structure

An organizational structure in which employees are permanently assigned to projects.

Autonomous Internal Units

autonomous internal units

An organizational structure composed of autonomous decentralized business units, each with its own products, clients, competitors, and profit goals.

Some large organizations with numerous business units or divisions have adopted an organizational structure that's nothing more than a collection of autonomous internal units. What are **autonomous internal units**? They're separate decentralized business units, each with its own products, clients, competitors, and profit goals. Through a market-oriented infrastructure of performance measures, financial incentives, and communication systems, top-level managers evaluate these units as if they were free-standing companies.[26] Although this may sound very similar to the divisional structure that we discussed earlier under bureaucratic organizational design, the key difference is that these business units are *autonomous*. There is neither the centralized control nor the resource allocation that you would find in the divisional structure arrangement. It has been estimated that about 15 percent of large corporations have moved to this structural form.[27] Some of these companies include ABB (Asea Brown Boveri), Magna International, Thermo Electron Corporation, and Dover Corporation. Let's take a closer look at what two of these organizations do.

ABB is an enormous global organization with annual revenues exceeding $34 billion. It makes electric power generation and transmission equipment, high-speed trains, automation and robotics, and environmental-control systems. The company has more than 210,000 employees, yet its typical profit center has only 50 people! How does it do this? ABB is actually 1,300 companies divided into almost 5,000 profit centers located in 140 countries around the globe. The whole operation is strategically managed by just eight top executives based in Zurich, Switzerland. This structural arrangement allows ABB remarkable flexibility to acquire new businesses, respond to competitors, and exploit market opportunities.[28]

Thermo Electron is another large company that has perfected the ability to create autonomous internal units.[29] This high-tech firm—it makes a diverse set of products from sophisticated instruments, to bomb detectors, to artificial hearts—is actually 15 distinct companies. When a manager or engineer invents something or finds a new market for a technology, Thermo often creates a whole new autonomous company to pursue the opportunity. But Thermo always retains a majority of equity in the new company. This structural arrangement has allowed Thermo to keep the "entrepreneurial spirit" alive in its employees while accelerating the growth of new businesses.

TESTING...
TESTING...
1   2   3

19 Describe a team-based structure.

20 Compare and contrast a matrix structure and a project structure.

21 What are autonomous internal units, and when might an organization use this design?

The Boundaryless Organization

boundaryless organization

An organization whose design is not defined by, or limited to, the horizontal, vertical, or external boundaries imposed by a predefined structure.

Another approach to current organizational designs is the idea of the boundaryless organization. The term **boundaryless organization** was coined by General Electric's chairman, Jack Welch, to describe an organization whose design is not defined by, or limited to, the boundaries imposed by a predefined structure.[30] Despite GE's enormous size, Welch wanted to eliminate vertical and horizontal boundaries within GE and break down external barriers between the company and its customers and suppliers. This idea may sound odd, yet many of today's most successful organizations are finding that they can most effectively operate in today's environment by remaining flexible and *un*structured: that the ideal structure for them is *not* having a rigid, predefined structure. Instead, the boundaryless organization seeks to eliminate the chain of command, to have limitless spans of control, and to replace departments with empowered teams.[31]

A boundaryless organization can function efficiently and effectively by breaking down the artificial boundaries created by a fixed structural design. What do we mean by "boundaries"? Think of the horizontal boundaries imposed by work specialization and departmentalization, the vertical boundaries that separate employees into organizational levels and hierarchies, and the external boundaries that separate the organization from its all-important suppliers, customers, and other stakeholders. By removing vertical boundaries, management flattens the hierarchy. Cross-hierarchical teams (which include top-level managers, middle managers, supervisors, and employees) and participative decision-making practices are some of the ways that organizations are eliminating those vertical barriers. We've already discussed the use of cross-functional teams as a way to remove the horizontal organizational boundaries, as is organizing work activities around work processes instead of around functional departments. And in the case of external boundaries, organizations are using strategic alliances, telecommuting, and customer-organization linkages to minimize or eliminate the barriers. Ideally, by minimizing or eliminating these artificial boundaries, the boundaryless organization streamlines its work activities so that it can respond quickly to the tumultuous and fast-moving marketplace.

What factors have contributed to the rise of the boundaryless organization?[32] Undoubtedly, the increasing globalization of markets and competitors is a significant factor. The need to respond to complex, rapidly changing, and highly competitive global environments has created the necessity for an organization that can adapt quickly in order to take advantage of opportunities that arise anywhere in the world. Organizations are finding that the elimination of artificial structural barriers enhances their ability to adapt and respond. In effect, therefore, we find organizations moving to a fluid, flexible structure that is custom-designed as situations arise. For instance, Debi Coleman, chief executive officer of Merix Corporation, an electronic-interconnect supplier based in Forest Grove, Oregon, says, "We have people who work here that I thought were Merix employees. They have our badges and I see them every day, but it turns out that they really work for our suppliers."[33] And organizations such as NEC Corporation, Ameritech, and Boeing have formed strategic alliances with other organizations to share information and pursue market opportunities.

Another factor that has contributed to the rise in the number of boundaryless organizations is the rapidly changing technology that permits the boundaryless organization to work. Without computer network systems, software, and telecommunications capabilities, the boundaryless organization could not exist. For instance, VeriFone, the world leader in credit card authorization systems, has no corporate headquarters, no secretaries, and no paper mail. CEO Hatim Tyabji describes his organizational structure as the "blueberry pancake model, very flat, with all blueberries equal."[34] Even without a rigid, defined structure,

Taking a big step toward the concept of a boundaryless organization, Mercedes-Benz U.S. International's president and CEO Andreas Renschler wants to let employees in the firm's new Alabama plant operate "in a kind of empowerment zone" where management will "set the frame, set the goals, and let people work."

VeriFone employees have fast information at their fingertips through the company's electronic mail network. This type of organizational arrangement would not be possible without the advanced technology that's the backbone of the company's information network.

Finally, the need for rapid innovation has contributed to the evolution and development of the boundaryless organization. Rapidly changing marketplace needs and brief "windows" of opportunity demand that organizations be able to respond quickly and effectively to these situations. A boundaryless organization with its flexible structure, which might include employee teams or outside contracts with other "specialist" organizations or sophisticated electronic information networks, can respond with the rapid innovation that the global marketplace requires.

MANAGING WORKFORCE DIVERSITY

The Feminine Organization: Myth or Reality?

Research studies have generally concluded that men and women do manage differently and do use different styles of leadership. But do men and women also have different approaches to organizational design?

An organizational sociologist who has studied this area proposes that gender differences in values and moral principles often lead women to prefer an organizational form that's very different from the traditional, hierarchically rigid bureaucratic structure.[35] What does this "feminine" model of organization look like? We can identify six characteristics:

1. *It values organizational members as individual human beings.* People are treated as individuals, with individual values and needs, rather than as just someone doing a job or filling a position. In fact, a survey of women-owned businesses by the National Foundation for Women Business Owners found that these firms are likely to provide flexible work schedules, tuition reimbursement, and job-sharing arrangements.

2. *It is nonopportunistic.* Organizational relationships are seen as being valuable in and of themselves and not just as a formal means to achieve organizational objectives.

3. *Careers are defined in terms of service to others.* In the bureaucratic model, organizational members define career success in terms of promotions, amount of power acquired, and salary increases. In the feminine model, organizational members measure success in terms of service to others.

4. *There is a commitment to employee growth.* Feminine organizations create extensive personal growth opportunities for their members. Rather than emphasizing specialization and the development of a narrow range of expertise, these organizations expand members' skills and broaden employee competencies by offering new learning experiences.

5. *A caring community is fostered.* Organizational members become closely bound in a "community" sense, and they learn to trust and care for each other much as neighbors in a small town do.

6. *There is a sharing of power.* In the traditional bureaucratic organization, information and decision-making authority are highly coveted and hierarchically allocated. In the feminine organization, information is generously shared. All members who might be affected by a decision are given the opportunity to participate in the making of that decision.

This feminine model obviously might be effective and the organizational design of choice in organizations that are essentially managed by and for women, such as battered women's shelters, rape crisis centers, women's health care clinics, and entrepreneurial firms that sell products directly to the female market. But with the organizational design trends toward collaboration, teamwork, and information sharing, more and more organizations of all types may resemble the feminine organization. ◼

The Learning Organization

We first introduced the concept of a learning organization back in chapter 2 as we looked at some of the current trends and issues facing managers. The concept of a learning organization doesn't involve a specific organization design per se but instead describes an organizational mind-set or philosophy that has significant design implications. What is a **learning organization**? It is an organization that has developed the capacity to continuously adapt and change because all members take an active role in identifying and resolving work-related issues.[36] In a learning organization, employees are continually acquiring and sharing new knowledge and are willing to apply that knowledge in making decisions or performing their work. Some organizational design theorists even go so far as to say that an organization's ability to do this—that is, to learn and to apply that learning as they perform the organization's work—may be the only sustainable source of competitive advantage.[37]

What would a learning organization look like? As you can see in Figure 10-9, the important characteristics of a learning organization revolve around organizational design, information sharing, leadership, and culture. Let's take a closer look at each.

What types of organizational design elements would be necessary for organizational learning to take place? In a learning organization, it's critical for members to share information and collaborate on work activities throughout the entire organization—across different specialties and even at different organizational levels. How best to do this? By eliminating, or at the very least, minimizing, the existing structural and physical boundaries in the organization. In this type of boundaryless environment, employees are free to work together and collaborate in doing the organization's work the best way they can and to learn

learning organization

An organization that has developed the continuous capacity to adapt and change because all members take an active role in identifying and resolving work-related issues.

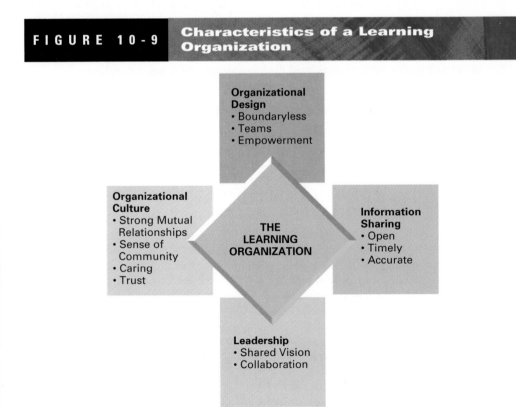

FIGURE 10-9   **Characteristics of a Learning Organization**

Based on P.M. Senge, *The Fifth Discipline: The Art and Practice of Learning Organizations* (New York: Doubleday, 1990); and R.M. Hodgetts, F. Luthans, and S.M. Lee, "New Paradigm Organizations: From Total Quality to Learning to World Class," *Organizational Dynamics*, Winter 1994, pp. 4–19.

from each other. Because of this need to cross-share and collaborate, teams also tend to be an important feature of a learning organization's structural design. Employees work in teams on whatever activities need to be done, and these employee teams are empowered to make decisions about doing their work or resolving issues. With empowered employees and teams in place, there's little need for "bosses" to control and direct. Instead, managers serve as facilitators, supporters, and advocates for employee teams.

Learning can't take place without information. For a learning organization to "learn," information must be shared among members. This means sharing it openly, in a timely manner, and in as accurate a form as possible. Because there are few structural and physical barriers in a learning organization, the environment is conducive to open communication and extensive information sharing.

Leadership plays an important role as an organization moves to become a learning organization. What should leaders in a learning organization do? One of their most important functions is facilitating the creation of a shared vision for the organization's future and then keeping organizational members aligned with that vision. In addition, leaders should support and encourage the collaborative environment that's critical to learning. Without strong and committed leadership throughout the organization, it would be extremely difficult to be a learning organization.

Finally, the organizational culture is an important aspect of being a learning organization. A learning organization's culture is one in which everyone agrees on a shared vision and everyone recognizes the inherent interrelationships between all the organization's processes, activities, functions, and external environmental interactions. There is a strong sense of community, caring for each other, and trust. In a learning organization, organizational members feel free to openly communicate, share, experiment, and learn without fear of criticism or punishment.

22 **What are some advantages and disadvantages of a boundaryless organization?**

23 **What factors have contributed to the rise in the number of boundaryless organizations?**

24 **Describe the characteristics of a learning organization.**

TECHNOLOGY, COMMUNICATIONS, AND ORGANIZATIONAL DESIGN

The 1990s have been a time of profound changes for organizations. Managers have been challenged to keep their organizations functioning smoothly while continually improving their operations and staying competitive even though both their organizations and the environment are changing rapidly. And things are not likely to get any easier for managers in the next decade! Although changing technology obviously contributed to much of the environmental uncertainty facing organizations, these same technological advances have enabled managers to organize the organization's work in new ways to become more efficient and effective. How has technology affected organizations? We will discuss two aspects: its effect on the way information is communicated in organizations and its effect on the way organizations are structured.

How Technology Affects Communications

Technology, and more specifically information technology, has radically changed the way organizational members communicate. For example, it has significantly improved a manager's ability to monitor individual or team performance, and it has allowed employees to

Away from a keyboard since his high school typing class, Louie Pokrywka is now learning to use elaborate computer schematics in his job at Kimberly-Clark's paper products mill in Connecticut. Computer technology is transforming his work and the way he communicates with other employees.

have more complete information to make faster decisions. Two developments in information technology seem to have had the most impact on organizational communication: networked computer systems and wireless capabilities.[38]

Networked Computer Systems. In a networked computer system, an organization links its computers together through compatible hardware and software, creating an organizational network. Organizational members can then communicate with each other and tap into information whether they're down the hall, across town, or halfway across the world. Although we won't want to get into the mechanics of how a network system works, we will address some of its communication applications for organizations. These include electronic mail, voice mail, facsimile mail (fax), videoconferencing and teleconferencing, electronic data interchange, and intranets.

Electronic mail, or **e-mail**, is the instantaneous transmission of written messages on computers that are linked together. Messages wait at the receiver's computer and are read at the receiver's convenience. Electronic mail is fast and cheap and can be used to send the same message to numerous people at the same time. It is a quick and convenient way for organizational members to share information and communicate.

A **voice-mail** system, on the other hand, digitizes a spoken message, transmits it over the network, and stores the message on disk for the receiver to retrieve later.[39] This capability allows information to be transmitted even though a receiver may not be physically present to take the information. Receivers can choose to save the message for future use, delete it, or route it to other parties.

Facsimile (fax) machines allow the transmission of documents containing both text and graphics over ordinary telephone lines. A sending fax machine scans and digitizes the document. A receiving fax machine reads the scanned information and reproduces it in hard copy form. Information that is best viewed in printed form can be easily and quickly shared by organizational members.

electronic mail (e-mail)

The instantaneous transmission of written messages on computers that are linked together.

voice-mail

A communication system that digitizes a spoken message, transmits it over a computer network, and stores the message on disk for the receiver to retrieve later.

facsimile (fax)

A communication system that allows the transmission of documents containing both text and graphics.

Meetings—one-on-one, team, divisional, or organization-wide—have always been one way to share information. The limitations of technology used to dictate that meetings take place among people in the same physical location, but that's no longer the case! **Teleconferencing** allows a group of people to confer simultaneously using telephone or e-mail group communication software. If meeting participants can see each other over video screens, the simultaneous conference is called **videoconferencing**. Work groups, large and small, that might be in different locations can use these communication network tools to collaborate and share information.

Electronic data interchange (EDI) is a way for organizations to exchange standard business transaction documents, such as invoices or purchase orders, using direct computer-to-computer networks. Organizations often use EDI with vendors, suppliers, and customers because it saves time and money. How? Transactions are transmitted from one organization's information system to another through a telecommunications network. The printing and handling of paper documents at one organization are eliminated as is the inputting of data at the other organization.

Finally, networked computer systems have allowed the development of organizational **intranets**—that is, internal organizational communication systems that use Internet technology and are accessible only by organizational employees. An intranet is not only an effective way to share information; it is also proving to be a convenient way for employees to collaborate on documents and projects from different locations.[40]

Wireless Capabilities.   Whereas networked computer systems require organizations to be connected by wiring, wireless communication depends on signals sent through air or space without any physical connection using things such as microwave signals, satellites, radio waves and radio antennas, or infrared light rays. Wireless products—such as personal pagers, cellular telephones, and specially equipped laptop computers—are making it possible for people in organizations to be fully accessible to each other, at any time or any place. Employees don't have to be at their desks with their computers plugged in and turned on in order to communicate with others in the organization. In fact, some people believe that the next century will be the "wireless century."[41] As technology continues to improve in this area, we are likely to see organizational members using wireless communication more and more as a way to collaborate and share information.

How Communications Affect Organizational Design

As we said at the beginning of the chapter, the challenge for managers in organizing is designing an organizational structure that allows employees to effectively and efficiently do their work while accomplishing organizational goals and objectives. Employees—teams or individuals— need information to make decisions and do their work. After describing the communications capabilities managers have at their disposal, we think it's safe to say that technology *can* significantly affect the way that organizational members communicate, share information, and do their work.

Communications and the exchange of information among organizational members are no longer constrained by geography or time. And the elimination of these physical and time constraints means that organizations no longer need to be structured solely to support and facilitate information flows and work activities horizontally or vertically. What are the implications for organizational design?

Several of the contemporary organizational designs—for instance, team-based, boundaryless, project, and learning—would not be feasible without the availability and accessibility of information made possible by technology. Collaborative work efforts among widely dispersed individuals and teams, sharing of information, and integration of decisions and work throughout an entire organization have the potential to increase the efficiency and

teleconferencing

A communication system that allows a group of people to confer simultaneously using telephone or e-mail.

videoconferencing

A communication system that allows a group of people to confer simultaneously and see each other over video screens.

electronic data interchange (EDI)

A communication system that allows organizations to exchange standard business transaction documents.

intranets

Internal organizational communication systems that use Internet technology and are accessible only by organizational employees.

Software developer Chandra Pikes wonders why she didn't try telecommuting sooner. Working at home, for the Texas Department of Human Services, has increased her productivity, and, she says, "I love it."

effectiveness of organizations. In addition, such work design options as **telecommuting**, in which employees do their work at home on a computer that is linked to the office, and **virtual workplaces**, which are offices characterized by open spaces, movable furniture, portable phones, laptop computers, and electronic files, are possible only because of information technology.

No matter what structural option managers choose for their organizations, it should help employees do their work in the best, that is, the most efficient and most effective, way they can. The structure needs to help, not hinder, organizational members as they carry out the organization's work. After all, an organization's structure is simply a means to an end.

telecommuting

A work design option in which workers are linked to the workplace by computers and modems.

virtual workplaces

Offices that are characterized by open spaces, movable furniture, portable phones, laptop computers, and electronic files.

25 How has technology affected communications?

26 Describe how organizations might use the different types of communication applications made possible by networked computer systems.

27 How has communications technology affected organizational design?

TESTING...
TESTING...

1 **2** **3**

managers respond to "a manager's dilemma"

MANAGER 1

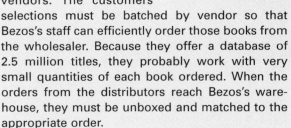

Bezos enjoys several things that help to simplify his operation. Specifically, he is dealing with one product (books) and two primary vendors. The customers' selections must be batched by vendor so that Bezos's staff can efficiently order those books from the wholesaler. Because they offer a database of 2.5 million titles, they probably work with very small quantities of each book ordered. When the orders from the distributors reach Bezos's warehouse, they must be unboxed and matched to the appropriate order.

I feel that the key to the long-term success of this business is customer service. From the time the order is placed, how long does it take to get the product into the right customer's hands and in good condition? I would combine two types of structure for this type of organization. Using functional departmentalization, you could organize those groups not specifically involved in delivering the product, such as accounting, human resources, and marketing. By using process departmentalization from order inception to follow-up customer service, you could achieve efficiency by shorter process time. I do feel that some formalization is the key to their efficiency. Bezos's structure is a simple one with few possible contingencies. He's probably heard all of the questions from consumers or at least knows the most frequently asked questions. He should allow his individual departments to take appropriate actions based on company policies he is comfortable with. If contingencies do occur that are not covered by policy, I would err on the side of expedient customer service and would allow the departments significant autonomy in decision making.

Becky Runyon, *Owner, Decorator Outlet, Jefferson City, Missouri*

MANAGER 2

Amazon.com faces the enormous challenge of managing a database of 2.5 million books and shipping to customers the exact book (or books) they ordered within a reasonable period of time, and doing all this efficiently and effectively so the business can make a profit. The other challenge the business faces is that it is also rapidly growing. Even though the business may indeed be a "virtual" organization, it is going to need *some* formalization if it hopes to be successful. What kinds of formalization might Jeff Bezos want to use? In our business we have found that it's important to have some company policies (that is, general guidelines) for the different areas of business operation. I would suggest this approach for Jeff. My feeling is that Jeff would not want a lot of specific rules and regulations, but instead would want to operate Amazon.com more like an organic organization, with flexibility and adaptability being the keys. However, even with flexibility and adaptability, there needs to be some guidance and direction for the 120 employees as they deal with the problems that arise in doing their jobs. What I would suggest is having some formalization, but not overly rigid amounts because I believe that would limit employee flexibility and adaptability to respond in the rapidly changing environment in which Amazon.com competes.

Lizzi Carol Jones, *President, An Ultimate Image, Toronto, Ontario, Canada*

for your

IMMEDIATE

action

ONTARIO   ELECTRONICS   LIMITED

To: Claude Fortier, Special Assistant to the President
From: Ian Campbell, President
Re: Learning Organizations

As you know, last week I attended the Canadian Electronics Manufacturers Industry Association annual meeting. Our luncheon speaker on the final day talked about how important it is for organizations to be responsive to customer and marketplace needs. One of the approaches for accomplishing this critical need that she described in her speech was becoming a learning organization. I came away from this talk convinced that our company's future may well depend on how well we're able to "learn."

Please find some current information on learning organizations. Although I'm sure you will be able to find numerous articles about it, limit your report to five of what you consider to be the best possible sources of information on the topic. Write a one-paragraph summary for each of these five articles, being sure to note all the bibliographic information in case we need to refer to the article later.

I would like for the executive team to move on this fairly quickly, so please have your report back to me by the end of the week.

This is a fictionalized account of a potentially real management issue and is meant for academic purposes only.

SUMMARY

This summary is organized by the chapter-opening objectives found on p. 298.

1. An organizational structure is the organization's formal framework by which job tasks are divided, grouped, and coordinated. When managers develop or change an organization's structure, they are engaged in organizational design.

2. Structure and design are important to an organization because they clarify expectations of what is to be done; divide work to avoid duplication, wasted effort, conflict, and misuse of resources; provide for logical flow of work activities; establish communication channels; provide coordinating mechanisms; focus work efforts on accomplishing objectives; and enhance planning and controlling.

3. The six key elements of organizational structure are work specialization, departmentalization, chain of command, span of control, centralization and decentralization, and formalization. Work specialization describes the degree to which tasks in the organization are divided into separate jobs. Departmentalization describes the way in which jobs are grouped in order to accomplish organizational goals. The chain of command is an unbroken line of authority that extends from the upper levels of the organization down to the lowest levels and clarifies who reports to whom. Span of control refers to how many subordinates a manager can effectively and efficiently supervise. Centralization describes the degree to which decision making is concentrated in the upper levels of the organization. Decentralization is when lower-level employees provide input or are actually given the discretion to make decisions. Formalization refers to the degree to which jobs within the organization are standardized and the extent to which employee behavior is guided by rules and procedures.

4. Mechanistic organizations are rigid and tightly controlled structures. They are characterized by high specialization, extensive departmentalization, narrow spans of control, high formalization, a limited information network (mostly downward), and little participation in decision making by lower-level employees. On the other hand, organic organizations are highly adaptive and flexible. There is division of labor, but jobs are not highly standardized. Formalization and tight managerial controls are unnecessary because employees are highly trained.

5. The four contingency factors that influence an organization's design are strategy, size, technology, and environment.

6. A bureaucracy is an organizational design with high levels of work specialization, hierarchical levels, and formalization. One of its strengths is that it helps an organization cope with increasing size. In addition, it is based on order, logic, and legitimate use of authority.

7. In a team-based structure, the entire organization is made up of work groups or teams that perform the organization's work. More and more organizations are using teams because it breaks down departmental barriers and decentralizes decision making to the level of the work team.

8. A matrix organization is a structural design that assigns specialists from different functional departments to work on one or more projects being led by a project manager. A project structure is a design in which employees are permanently assigned to projects. Autonomous internal units are autonomous decentralized business units, each with its own products, clients, competitors, and profit goals.

9. The boundaryless organization is an organizational design in which the structure is not defined by, or limited to, the boundaries imposed by traditional structures. It is a structure that is flexible and adaptable to environmental conditions. This structure is appealing because it allows organizations to respond efficiently and effectively to global markets and competition, technology advancements, and the need for rapid innovation.

10. A learning organization is an organization that has developed the capacity to continuously adapt and change because all members take an active role in making decisions or performing their work. It influences organizational design because an organization's ability to learn is

enhanced (or hindered) by its structural and physical boundaries and the amount of collaborative work efforts.

11. Technology plays an important role in organizational design because it influences how organizational employees communicate, share information, and collaborate on work.

THINKING ABOUT MANAGEMENT ISSUES

1. Can an organization's structure be changed quickly? Why or why not?

2. Would you rather work in a mechanistic or an organic organization? Why?

3. What types of skills would a manager need to effectively work in a project structure? In a boundaryless organization? In a learning organization?

4. The boundaryless organization has the potential to create a major shift in our living and working patterns. Do you agree or disagree? Explain.

5. With the availability of advanced information technology that allows an organization's work to be done anywhere at anytime, is organizing still an important managerial function? Why or why not?

SELF-ASSESSMENT EXERCISE

HOW WILLING ARE YOU TO DELEGATE?

As a manager, you must be willing to delegate work. This self-assessment will help you determine your willingness to delegate work to others.

Instructions: This instrument is designed to help you understand the assumptions you make about people and human nature. Ten pairs of statements follow. Assign a weight from 0 to 10 to each statement to show the relative strength of your belief in the statement. The total points assigned for each pair must always be 10. Be as honest with yourself as you can and resist the tendency to respond as you would like to think things are. This instrument is not a test: There are no right or wrong answers. It is designed to stimulate personal reflection and discussion.

1. _____ a. It's only human nature for people to do as little work as they can get away with.
   _____ b. When people avoid work, it's usually because their work has no meaning.

2. _____ c. If employees have access to any information they want they tend to have better attitudes and behave more responsibly.
   _____ d. If employees have access to more information than they need to do their immediate tasks, they will usually misuse it.

3. _____ e. One problem in asking for the ideas of employees is that their perspective is too limited for their suggestions to be of much practical value.
   _____ f. Asking employees for their ideas broadens their perspectives and results in the development of useful suggestions.

4. _____ g. If people don't use much imagination and ingenuity on the job, it's probably because relatively few people have much of either.
   _____ h. Most people are imaginative and creative but may not show it because of limitations imposed by supervision and the job.

5. _____ i. People tend to raise their standards if they are accountable for their own behavior and for correcting their own mistakes.
   _____ j. People tend to lower their standards if they are not punished for their misbehavior and mistakes.

6. _____ k. It's better to give people both good and bad news because most employees want the whole story, no matter how painful.

_____ l. It's better to withhold unfavorable news about business because most employees really want to hear only the good news.

7. _____ m. Because a supervisor is entitled to more respect than those below her in the organization, it weakens her prestige to admit that a subordinate was right and she was wrong.

_____ n. Because people at all levels are entitled to equal respect, a supervisor's prestige is increased when he supports this principle by admitting that a subordinate was right and he was wrong.

8. _____ o. If you give people enough money, they are less likely to be concerned with such intangibles as responsibility and recognition.

_____ p. If you give people interesting and challenging work, they are less likely to complain about such things as pay and supplemental benefits.

9. _____ q. If people are allowed to set their own goals and standards of performance, they tend to set them higher than the boss would.

_____ r. If people are allowed to set their own goals and standards of performance, they tend to set them lower than the boss would.

10. _____ s. The more knowledge and freedom a person has regarding her job, the more controls are needed to keep her in line.

_____ t. The more knowledge and freedom a person has regarding her job, the fewer controls are needed to ensure satisfactory job performance.

See the scoring key on page SK–4.

Source: D.A. Whetten and K.S. Cameron, *Developing Management Skills* (Glenview, IL: Scott, Foresman, 1984), pp. 351–352.

TAKE IT TO THE NET

We invite you to visit the Robbins/Coulter companion Web site at http://www.prenhall.com/robbinsmgt for this chapter's Internet resources.

CASE APPLICATION

A Laboratory in Organizational Design

Buckman Laboratories International (<http://knetix@buckman.com> or <http://www.buckman.com>), headquartered in Memphis, Tennessee, manufactures more than 1,000 specialty chemicals. The company employs over 1,200 people in 80 countries and its annual revenues exceed $300 million. Although this small, privately held company depends on its research laboratories for the products that bring in its revenues, the whole company itself is a laboratory in contemporary organizational design.

What is it about Buckman Labs that attracts executives from AT&T, 3M, Champion International, US West, and other Fortune 500 companies, who trek to Memphis to see and learn? They're coming to see

how the company stays so fast, global, and interactive. Bob Buckman, Buckman Lab's fiftyish CEO, recognized the power of knowledge and information long before others did. Buckman and his employees began treating knowledge as the company's most important corporate asset back in 1992. They believed that being (and remaining) competitive in a knowledge-intensive global environment required three things: (1) closing the gap between the organization and the customer; (2) staying in touch with each other; and (3) bringing *all* of the company's brainpower together to serve each customer. What were the organizational design implications of these commitments? Buckman described the real design questions as, "How do we stay connected? How do we share knowledge? How do we function anytime, anywhere—no matter what?"

Buckman Labs has organized its employees and their work around its knowledge network—K'Netix. This knowledge transfer system resulted from Buckman's being confined to bed after rupturing his back. Lying there, unable to stand or even to sit up, Buckman felt isolated and uninformed about what was happening in the company while he was flat on his back. He started thinking about how important information and knowledge were—not just to him, but to all of Buckman Labs' employees. What he needed and what his employees needed was a steady stream of information about products, markets, and customers. And this information needed to be easily accessible and easily shared. As an ardent reader of business and management writing, Buckman had read a comment from a well-known and well-respected CEO (Scandinavian Airlines' former CEO, Jan Carlzon) that stuck in his mind, "An individual without information cannot take responsibility; an individual who is given information cannot help but take responsibility."

Buckman realized that the way to maximize each of his individual employee's power was to connect each employee to the world. He wrote down what his ideal knowledge transfer system would do. Here's what he wrote: (1) It would be possible for people to talk to each other directly to minimize distortion. (2) It would give everyone access to the company's knowledge base. (3) It would allow each individual in the company to enter knowledge into the system. (4) It would be available 24 hours a day, seven days a week. (5) It would be easy to use. (6) It would communicate in whatever language was best for the user. (7) It would be updated automatically, capturing questions and answers as a future knowledge base. Such a system would require a total cultural transformation—literally turning the organization upside down by getting employees to be deeply involved with collaborating and sharing knowledge. And that's what Bob Buckman set out to do. However, transforming the company from an old pyramidal, bureaucratic, command-and-control structure to a structure in which everyone in the organization would have complete access to information and in which no one would be telling employees what to do all the time wasn't easy!

To make the knowledge organization and the actual knowledge network system a reality, Buckman first created a Knowledge Transfer Department and put Victor Baillargeon in charge. With a doctorate in organic chemistry, Baillargeon may have seemed a questionable choice for such a position. But as Buckman's assistant, Baillargeon had spent a year researching the concept of knowledge transfer. In addition, since he wasn't an information technology expert, he didn't have a vested interest in one network systems approach to the exclusion of all others. He was open to what was best for Buckman Labs.

Baillargeon's first challenge was building a network system that both encompassed the entire organization and was easy to access from anywhere in the world. His solution was to have the company's entire worldwide network put on CompuServe, a public on-line service. CompuServe offered e-mail access to 35 public network services and the ability to create private bulletin boards for intracompany use and accessible only to company employees. It took just 30 days to make the move to CompuServe. Each and every Buckman salesperson around the globe was given an IBM Thinkpad with a modem. For a basic cost of $75,000 a month in access charges, all Buckman employees could now make a simple phone call to headquarters and immediately have access to all of CompuServe's global information services. From that platform, Baillargeon then built K'Netix, Buckman Labs' global knowledge transfer network, and established seven technical forums to organize the company's on-line interactive conversations.

Getting the physical hardware and software in place was only half the battle, though. Getting employees to use the knowledge base *and* contribute to it were also important. After all, a knowledge-based company is successful only if knowledge is shared among organizational members. What was particularly difficult about this type of cultural transformation was that employees in traditional organizations had always been rewarded on their ability to hoard knowledge and thus gain power. This is how the situation at Buckman Labs was described: "There were people whose file cabinets were filled with everything they knew, and that was the source of their power." But that philosophy had to change if the knowledge system was going to work. Not long after K'Netix went on-line, Buckman made his expectations clear: "Those of you who have something intelligent to say now have a forum in which to say it. Those of you who will not or cannot contribute also become obvious. If you are not willing to contribute or participate, then you should understand that the many opportunities offered to you in the past will no longer be available." What ultimately emerged at Buckman Labs has been a mixture of visible incentives and invisible pressure to use K'Netix, especially after it was first implemented. Now, teamwork and knowledge reciprocity are part and parcel of the organizational design.

Because Buckman Labs competes in a variety of businesses, often against competitors three to five times its size, its commitment to knowledge takes on a new urgency. Salespeople need the right answer for each customer and they need it fast. K'Netix has made getting answers simple. But the company's commitment to speed, employee interactivity and knowledge sharing, and globalization would not be possible without a structural design that supported those organizational values.

QUESTIONS

1. On the basis of the case information, describe what decisions you think Buckman Labs has made regarding the six key elements of organizational design. Be as specific as possible.

2. Would you describe Buckman Labs as more of a mechanistic or an organic organization? Explain.

3. Do you think Buckman Labs could be characterized as a learning organization? Why or why not?

4. How have technology and communications affected Buckman Labs' organizational design?

5. Think about the approach to organizational design that Buckman Labs has taken. What do you think the advantages of such an approach might be? What are the drawbacks?

Source: G. Rifkin, "Buckman Labs Is Nothing But Net," *Fast Company Web Page* <http://www.fastcompany.com>, April 17, 1997; and A. Bruzzese, "Sharing Knowledge Breaks Hierarchy," *Springfield News Leader,* October 27, 1997, p. 7A.

ABCNEWS **VIDEO CASE APPLICATION**

Rules, Regulations, and You Say What?

Rules and regulations often help to keep order in an organization by establishing the parameters in which organizational members operate. In most organizations, rules and regulations help members plan, organize, control, and make decisions. And, depending on the size of the organization, these same rules and regulations can help to coordinate activities by keeping employees' work focused on goal attainment. But sometimes, rules become unwieldy and end up creating an amazing and inefficient runaround. Let's look at two such situations involving the Environmental Protection Agency (EPA) and the Department of Transportation (DOT).

The concern in the EPA situation revolved around testing for clean water at a site in Phoenix, Arizona. To do this testing, the EPA places flathead minnows and waterfleas into stormwater drains. These small creatures are then tracked as they float in the stormwater making its way into streams and rivers. When the stormwater reaches its destination, if the minnows and waterfleas are alive, the water is considered to be not contaminated. If, however, the animals die en route, the water is considered to be polluted. Simple enough, right? Well, maybe not!

The problem in Phoenix is that the riverbed being tested is dry; there's absolutely no water in it,

and there hasn't been any for years. The EPA spends about $500,000 annually on this aquatic life test—in a riverbed where no aquatic life exists. The EPA defends its actions on the grounds that they're charged with protecting the groundwater, which will ultimately become drinking water for citizens in the general vicinity. Although no one says that this goal isn't important, the EPA regulations, ironically, don't focus on drinking water, just on protecting aquatic life. So the test they're performing in Phoenix is worthless.

If you think testing a dry riverbed for aquatic life is counterproductive, just look at the rule imposed by the Department of Transportation and the Occupational Safety and Health Administration. These two government agencies require lumber companies to have specially designed gas cans to hold the fuel used in chainsaws. Each gas container (they usually hold five gallons of gasoline) is required to have "a double roll bar on top, double-walled steel sides, and a screw filter on top, and it must be vented." A gas can that meets these regulations costs about $230. And, if the extra costs aren't enough, there are also the maddening results. The filler neck on the government-approved gas can won't fit into the chainsaw, so about half of the gas poured spills out on the ground. But then, when it contaminates the ground it's not really the DOT's responsibility. That would fall under the jurisdiction of the EPA.

QUESTIONS

1. How would you describe the rules and regulations at such government agencies as the EPA and the DOT?

2. For rules and regulations to be effective, they must be enforced. At times, however, they are not applicable, as in the case of the dry riverbed in Phoenix. Can an organization have contingencies built into its rules and regulations and still effectively coordinate and control member actions? Explain your position.

3. Build an argument in support of a government agency's requirement that organizations abide by its rules and regulations. Now build an argument against it. Which of the two arguments do you feel is stronger? Discuss.

Source: "Rules, Regs, and Runaround," *ABC Primetime,* June 7, 1995.

A MANAGER'S DILEMMA

The widely publicized federal sexual harassment suit filed in 1996 against Mitsubishi Motors Corporation's U.S. unit in Normal, Illinois, served as a loud and clear warning to foreign companies operating in the United States that illegal human resource actions and practices would not be tolerated. Since the mid-1980s, the United States has become home to a number of manufacturing facilities owned by foreign companies. Many of these companies are Japanese. Some of the practices alleged in the Mitsubishi case—for instance, lewd pictures in bathrooms and continual teasing of females—wouldn't even raise an eyebrow in Japan. It's not uncommon for Japanese businessmen to openly skim through pornographic material at work or drink at hostess

bars with clients. And typically they know very few business and professional women because Japanese cultural tradition encourages women to stay at home. However, recognizing the fact that practices tolerated in Japan would be illegal in the United States, managers in many of these Japanese companies are looking for ways to ensure that they are not violating the laws.[1]

Yukio Sadamori is one of those managers. He's a manager at Mitsui and Company, Ltd., a Japanese company that does business in many industries including general trading and financing of iron and steel, machinery, chemicals, crude oil, and foodstuffs. Sadamori is in charge of Mitsui and Company's international personnel division and is responsible for training the company's Japanese employees who are headed to management positions in the United States. He has been asked to develop a training program on sexual harassment for these managers that will prepare them for the realities of managing in a U.S. workplace. Put yourself in Sadamori's position. Prepare an outline of what you might include in this sexual harassment training program.

WHAT WOULD YOU DO?

The challenge facing Yukio Sadamori of designing a sexual harassment training program for company employees reflects only a small aspect of the human resource management challenges facing managers everywhere. If an organization doesn't take its human resource management responsibilities seriously, work performance and goal accomplishment may suffer. The quality of an organization is, to a large degree, merely the summation of the quality of people it hires and keeps. Getting and keeping competent employees are critical to the success of every organization, whether the organization is just starting or has been in business for years. Therefore, part of every manager's job in the organizing function is filling job positions—that is, putting the right person into the right job.

CHAPTER

11

Human

Resource

Management

MANAGERS AND HUMAN RESOURCE DEPARTMENTS

Some readers may be thinking, "Sure, human resource decisions are important, but aren't they made by people in human resource departments? These aren't decisions that *all* managers are involved in."

It's true that, in large organizations, a number of the activities grouped under the label *human resource management* (HRM) often are done by specialists in personnel or human resources. However, not all managers work in organizations that have formal human resource departments, and those who do still must engage in some human resource activities. For instance, small-business managers are one example of individuals who frequently must do their hiring without the assistance of a human resource department. Even managers in billion-dollar corporations are involved in recruiting employee candidates, reviewing application forms, interviewing applicants, orienting new employees, appraising employee performance, making decisions about employee training, and providing career advice to subordinates. Whether or not an organization has a formal human resources department, *every* manager is involved with human resource decisions in his or her area. In addition, many organizations have begun to recognize the important role that employees play in organizational success and have committed themselves to strong HRM departments responsible for developing effective HRM practices. The HRM departments in these organizations are moving away from their traditional responsibilities of simple personnel administration to a more central role in establishing and implementing organizational strategy.[2] The strategic importance of the human resource management function is becoming evident.

STRATEGIC HUMAN RESOURCE MANAGEMENT

"Our people are our *most* important asset." How often have you heard or read this assertion by managers? Can HRM be an important strategic tool? Can HRM help establish an organization's sustainable competitive advantage? The answers seem to be yes, HRM can be an important strategic tool, and yes, it can contribute to the development of a sustainable competitive advantage. Various studies have concluded that an organization's human resources—that is, its people—can be a significant source of competitive advantage.[3] Achieving competitive success through people requires a fundamental change in how managers think about an organization's workforce and how they view the work relationship. It also involves working with and through people and seeing them as partners, not just as costs to be minimized or avoided. That's what numerous organizations, such as Adobe Systems, Southwest Airlines, and GE Fanuc, are doing. These organizations have good reasons for making strong commitments to strategically managing their human resources. In addition to their potential importance as part of organizational strategy and their possible

At SAS Institute, Inc., the largest privately held software company in the United States, a distinctly close-knit environment prevails. SAS gives every employee an office, downplays formal titles, and supports employees' pursuit of individual interests. Employees, in turn, are emphatically loyal.

Strengthening employees' broad management skills and building their commitment to their firm's mission are two of the goals of such off-site training programs as the Well Team Course. A firm can reap many benefits and even develop its competitive advantage when its human resource management includes such a strong focus on its people.

contribution to the organization's competitive advantage, an organization's HRM practices have been found to have a significant impact on organizational performance.

Studies that have looked at the link between HRM policies and practices and organizational performance have found that certain HRM policies and practices have a positive impact on performance.[4] What type of positive impact? One study reported that if an average company implemented these work practices, it could expect annually (per employee) $27,044 more in sales, $3,814 more in profits, and $18,641 in market value.[5] The term used to describe the "certain" types of HRM policies and practices that lead to such results is **high-performance work practices**. High-performance work practices can lead to both high individual and high organizational performance. Table 11-1 lists examples of high-performance work practices. The common thread in high-performance work practices seems to be a commitment to improving the knowledge, skills, and abilities of an organization's current and poten-

high-performance work practices

Human resource policies and practices that lead to high levels of performance.

TABLE 11-1	**Examples of High-Performance Work Practices**

- Self-directed work teams
- Job rotation
- High levels of skills training
- Problem-solving groups
- Total quality management procedures and processes
- Encouragement of innovative and creative behavior
- Extensive employee involvement and training

- Implementation of employee suggestions
- Contingent pay based on performance
- Coaching and mentoring
- Significant amounts of information sharing
- Use of employee attitude surveys
- Cross-functional integration
- Comprehensive employee recruitment and selection procedures

Source: Based on M. Huselid, "The Impact of Human Resource Management Practices on Turnover, Productivity, and Corporate Financial Performance," *Academy of Management Journal*, June 1995, p. 635; and B. Becker and B. Gerhart, "The Impact of Human Resource Management on Organizational Performance: Progress and Prospects," *Academy of Management Journal*, August 1996, p. 785.

tial employees, increasing their motivation, reducing loafing on the job, and enhancing the retention of quality employees while encouraging nonperformers to leave the organization.

Whether an organization chooses to implement high-performance work practices or not, there still are certain HRM activities that must be completed in order to ensure that the organization has qualified people to perform the work that needs to be done. These activities constitute the human resource management process.

THE HUMAN RESOURCE MANAGEMENT PROCESS

human resource management process

Activities necessary for staffing the organization and sustaining high employee performance.

Figure 11-1 introduces the key components of an organization's **human resource management process**. It consists of eight activities, or steps, that, if properly done, will staff an organization with competent, high-performing employees who are capable of sustaining their performance level over the long term.

The first four steps represent *human resource planning:* the addition of staff through *recruitment,* the reduction of staff through *decruitment,* and *selection,* resulting in the identification and selection of competent, skilled employees. Once you have competent people, you need to help them adapt to the organization, ensure that their job skills and knowledge are kept current, develop appropriate career development activities, and provide an efficient and effective reward system. You do this through *orientation, training, career development,* and *compensation and benefits.* The last step in the HRM process is designed to identify performance problems and correct them. This activity is called *performance appraisal;* because it's part of the manager's controlling activities, we'll cover it in chapter 19.

Notice in Figure 11-1 that the entire HRM process is influenced by the external environment. In chapter 3 we elaborated on the constraints that the environment puts on management. These constraints are probably severest in the management of human resources.

FIGURE 11-1   **The Human Resource Management Process**

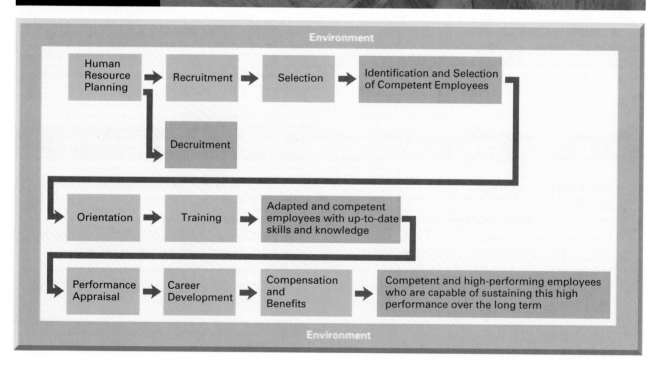

Before we review the steps in the HRM process, therefore, let's briefly examine how environmental forces influence it.

IMPORTANT ENVIRONMENTAL CONSIDERATIONS

Numerous environmental factors affect an organization's human resource management activities. The main ones that managers must deal with, however, are employee labor unions and governmental laws and regulations.

A **labor union** represents workers and seeks to protect and promote its members' interests through collective bargaining. In unionized organizations, many key personnel decisions are regulated by the terms of collective bargaining agreements. These agreements usually define such things as recruitment sources; criteria for hiring, promotions, and lay-offs; training eligibility; and disciplinary practices. For many managers in unionized organizations, good **labor-management relations** are important. The development of good labor-management relations can produce positive outcomes for management during contract negotiations: for instance, work rules that do not place unreasonable constraints on managerial decision options and reduce threats of costly strikes and work stoppages.[6] In the United States, only about 14.5 percent of the workforce is unionized.[7] Globally, however, the numbers are considerably higher. In Japan and Germany, respectively, 24.1 percent and 37.2 percent of the labor force belongs to a union. And in Mexico an estimated 30 percent of workers belong to a union.[8] Although labor unions can significantly affect an organization's HRM practices, no environmental constraint can match the influence of governmental laws and regulations, especially in North America.

Since the mid-1960s, the U.S. federal government has greatly expanded its influence over HRM decisions by enacting new laws and regulations. (See Table 11-2.) As a result of this legislation, employers today must ensure that equal employment opportunities exist for job applicants and current employees. Decisions regarding who will be hired, for example, or which employees will be chosen for a management training program must be made without regard to race, sex, religion, age, color, or national origin. Exceptions can occur only for requirements that are **bona fide occupational qualifications (BFOQs)**. The effect of legislation explains why, for instance, airlines today have flight attendants of both sexes and of varying ages. In the early 1960s, airlines hired almost exclusively flight attendants who were young, attractive females. But age, beauty, and gender are not BFOQs for this job, so those criteria had to be dropped. However, in hiring models for a men's clothing catalog, a mail-order firm can legitimately limit the job to males. Keep in mind that there are very few legitimate BFOQs that an organization can use in hiring or promoting.

Many U.S. organizations have **affirmative action programs** to ensure that decisions and practices enhance the employment, upgrading, and retention of members from protected groups, such as minorities and females. That is, the organization not only refrains from discriminating but actively seeks to enhance the status of members from protected groups. Why are organizations taking this affirmative stance? On the ethical side, they have a social responsibility to improve the status of protected group members. On the economic side, the cost of defending the organization against charges of discrimination can be enormous. For instance, Texaco Inc. paid $176.1 million to settle a race discrimination lawsuit filed by six black officials in the company's finance department who claimed that white males in Texaco's "good old boy network" received desirable promotions and the biggest raises and treated blacks derisively.[9]

Workplace safety is another area in which violations of laws and regulations can be expensive. In the mid-1990s, the U.S. Occupational Safety and Health Administration (OSHA) dramatically increased the minimum recommended penalty for willful, serious violations of workplace safety rules. For example, the minimum penalty for small businesses (those with 25 or fewer employees) increased from $5,000 to $25,000. The fines for large and medium-sized companies dramatically increased as well.[10]

labor union

An organization that represents workers and seeks to protect their interests through collective bargaining.

labor-management relations

The formal interactions between unions and an organization's management.

bona fide occupational qualification (BFOQ)

A criterion such as sex, age, or national origin that may be used as a basis for hiring if it can be clearly demonstrated to be job related.

affirmative action programs

Programs that enhance the organizational status of members of protected groups.

T A B L E 1 1 - 2	**Major U.S. Federal Laws and Regulations Related to Human Resource Management**

Year	Law or Regulation	Description
1963	Equal Pay Act	Prohibits pay differences based on sex for equal work
1964	Civil Rights Act, Title VII (amended in 1972)	Prohibits discrimination based on race, color, religion, national origin, or sex
1967	Age Discrimination in Employment Act	Prohibits age discrimination against employees between 40 and 65 years of age
1973	Vocational Rehabilitation Act	Prohibits discrimination on the basis of physical or mental disabilities
1974	Privacy Act	Gives employees the legal right to examine personnel files and letters of reference concerning them
1978	Mandatory Retirement Act	Prohibits the forced retirement of most employees before the age of 70; upper limit on age was removed in 1986
1986	Immigration Reform and Control Act	Prohibits unlawful employment of aliens and unfair immigration-related employment practices
1988	Polygraph Protection Act	Limits an employer's ability to use lie detectors
1988	Worker Adjustment and Retraining Notification Act	Requires employers with 100 or more employees to provide 60 days' notice before a facility closing or mass layoff
1990	Americans with Disabilities Act	Prohibits employers from discriminating against individuals with physical or mental disabilities or the chronically ill; also requires organizations to reasonably accommodate these individuals
1991	Civil Rights Act of 1991	Reaffirms and tightens prohibition of discrimination; permits individuals to sue for punitive damages in cases of intentional discrimination
1993	Family and Medical Leave Act of 1993	Grants 12 weeks of unpaid leave each year to employees for the birth or adoption of a child or the care of a spouse, child, or parent with a serious health condition; covers organizations with 50 or more employees

Organizations in other countries also face environmental constraints that affect managers' decisional discretion in the area of human resource management and labor relations. For example, in Germany, unions are quite powerful, although unions and management have had a more cooperative relationship than in the United States. In Denmark, Danish workers participate in the management of their firms, both directly and indirectly. They are actively involved in making workplace decisions. In China, however, worker participation in decision making is less open, and the number of employees who participate in workplace decisions is not very high. Because the laws and regulations governing human resources vary by country, managers of global companies have to familiarize themselves with the relevant information for the countries in which they operate.

Our conclusion is that managers aren't completely free to choose whom they hire, promote, or lay off; nor are they free to operate their workplace any way they want. Although governmental regulations have significantly helped to reduce discrimination, unfair employment practices, and unsafe workplaces, they have, at the same time, also reduced managers' discretion over human resource decisions.

1 **How does HRM affect all managers?**

2 **What strategic importance does HRM have for organizations?**

3 **List the eight steps in the human resource management process and how the external environment affects it.**

HUMAN RESOURCE PLANNING

Human resource planning is the process by which managers ensure that they have the right number and kinds of people in the right places, and at the right times, who are capable of effectively and efficiently completing those tasks that will help the organization achieve its overall objectives. In other words, human resource planning translates the organization's objectives into terms of the workers needed to meet those objectives.[11] Human resource planning can be condensed into three steps: (1) assessing current human resources, (2) assessing future human resource needs, and (3) developing a program to meet future human resource needs.

Current Assessment

Managers begin HR planning by reviewing the organization's current human resource status. This review is typically done by generating a *human resource inventory*. Because of the availability of sophisticated computer information systems, it's not difficult for most organizations to generate a human resource inventory report. The input for this report is derived from forms completed by employees. Such reports might include name, education, training, prior employment, languages spoken, special capabilities, and specialized skills of each employee in the organization. This inventory lets managers assess what talents and skills are currently available.

Another part of the current assessment is the **job analysis**. Whereas the human resource inventory is concerned with telling management what individual employees can do, job analysis is more fundamental. It defines the jobs within the organization and the behaviors that are necessary to perform those jobs. For instance, what are the duties of a purchasing specialist, grade 3, who works for Boise Cascade? What minimal knowledge, skills, and abilities are necessary to be able to adequately perform this job? How do the requirements for a purchasing specialist, grade 3, compare with those for a purchasing specialist, grade 2, or for a purchasing analyst? These are questions that job analysis can answer.

How is information gathered in a job analysis? There are several methods. One is the observation method, in which employees are either watched directly or filmed on the job. Another method is interviewing employees individually or in a group. A third method is the use of structured questionnaires, on which employees check or rate the items they perform in their jobs from a long list of possible task duties. Another method is the use of a technical conference, at which "experts"—usually supervisors with extensive knowledge of a job—identify a job's specific characteristics. A final method is to have employees record their daily activities in a diary or notebook, which can then be reviewed and structured into job activities.

A job analysis seeks to determine the kind of person needed to fill each job and provides information for preparing job descriptions and job specifications. A **job description** is a written statement of what a jobholder does, how it's done, and why it's done. It typically describes job content, environment, and conditions of employment. It focuses on the *job*. In contrast, a **job specification** focuses on the *person*. It states the minimum acceptable qualifications that a jobholder must possess to perform a given job successfully. The job specification identifies the knowledge, skills, and abilities needed to do the job effectively.

---

human resource planning

The process by which managers ensure that they have the right personnel, who are capable of completing those tasks that help the organization reach its objectives.

job analysis

An assessment that defines jobs and the behaviors necessary to perform them.

job description

A written statement of what a jobholder does, how it is done, and why it is done.

job specification

A statement of the minimum acceptable qualifications that an incumbent must possess to perform a given job successfully.

Human resource planning took center stage at Papa John's, a Kentucky-based pizza chain with more than 750 outlets in the United States. Once established, the human resource department standardized the corporate culture of the far-flung chain, which includes more than 500 franchise operations, and instituted needed benefits programs and recruitment strategies.

The job description and job specification are important documents when managers begin recruiting and selecting. The job description can be used to describe the job to potential candidates. The job specification keeps the manager's attention on the qualifications necessary for a person to be able to perform this job and assists in determining whether candidates are qualified.

Future Human Resource Need Assessment

Future human resource needs are determined by the organization's objectives and strategies. Demand for human resources (i.e., employees) is a result of demand for the organization's products or services. Managers can attempt to establish the number and mix of human resources needed to reach their estimate of total revenue. In some cases, the situation may be reversed. For example, in a tax consulting firm that has more business opportunities than it can handle, the only limiting factor in building revenues might be the firm's ability to find and hire staff with the needed qualifications to satisfy its clients. In most cases, however, the overall organizational goals and the resulting revenue forecast provide the major input for determining the organization's future human resource requirements.

Developing a Future Program

After they have assessed both current capabilities and future needs, managers are able to estimate shortages—both in number and in type—and to highlight areas in which the organization will be overstaffed. A program can then be developed to match these estimates with forecasts of future labor supply. So human resource planning not only provides information to guide current staffing needs but also provides projections of future human resource needs and availability.

RECRUITMENT AND DECRUITMENT

recruitment

The process of locating, identifying, and attracting capable applicants.

Once managers know their current human resource status (whether they are understaffed or overstaffed), they can begin to do something about it. If one or more vacancies exist, they can use the information gathered through job analysis to guide them in **recruitment**—that is, the process of locating, identifying, and attracting capable applicants.[12] On the other hand, if human resource planning indicates a surplus of employees, management may want to reduce the the organization's labor force. This activity is called **decruitment.**[13]

decruitment

Techniques for reducing the labor supply within an organization.

Where can a manager recruit potential job candidates? Table 11-3 offers some guidance. The source that's used should reflect the local labor market, the type or level of position, and the size of the organization.

No matter the type of position or its attractiveness, it's generally easier to recruit in large labor markets than in small ones. If for no other reasons, large labor markets such as New York or Los Angeles have a greater supply of workers. Of course, this generalization needs to be moderated by unemployment levels, wage rates, needed skills, and other factors. But, in large markets, recruitment efforts can be directed locally—to newspapers, employment agencies, colleges, or referrals by current employees.

The type or level of a position influences recruitment methods. The greater the skill required in the the job or the higher the position in the organization's hierarchy, the more the recruitment process will expand to become a regional or national search.

The scope of recruitment and the amount of effort devoted to it will also be influenced by the size of the organization. In general, the larger the organization, the easier it is to recruit job applicants. Larger organizations have a larger pool of internal candidates to choose from to fill positions above the lowest level. Larger organizations also have more visibility and, typically, more prestige. In addition, larger organizations may be perceived as offering greater opportunities for job promotions and increased responsibility.

Are certain recruiting sources better than others? More specifically, do certain recruiting sources produce superior candidates? The answer is yes. The majority of studies find that cur-

TABLE 11-3　Major Sources of Potential Job Candidates

Source	Advantages	Disadvantages
Internal search	Low cost; builds employee morale; candidates are familiar with organization	Limited supply; may not increase proportion of employees from protected groups
Advertisements	Wide distribution; can be targeted to specific groups	Generates many unqualified candidates
Employee referrals	Knowledge about the organization provided by current employee; can generate strong candidates because a good referral reflects on the recommender	May not increase the diversity and mix of employees
Public employment agencies	Free or nominal cost	Candidates tend to be unskilled or minimally trained
Private employment agencies	Wide contacts; careful screening; short-term guarantees often given	High cost
School placement	Large, centralized body of candidates	Limited to entry-level positions
Temporary help services	Fills temporary needs	Expensive; may have limited understanding of organization's overall goals and activities
Employee leasing and independent contractors	Fills temporary needs, but usually for more-specific, longer-term projects	Little commitment to organization other than current project

Recruitment isn't always easy when particular skills are required to fill certain jobs. California software maker Sybase Inc. offers its employees prizes, from the extravagant (a TV set or barbecue) to the silly (candy bars), for leads that generate successful job candidates.

rent employee referrals prove to be superior.[14] The explanation is intuitively logical. First, applicants referred by current employees are prescreened by these employees. Because the recommenders know both the job and the person being recommended, they tend to refer applicants who are well qualified for the position. Also, because current employees often feel that their reputation in the organization is at stake with a referral, they tend to refer others only when they are reasonably confident that the referral will not make them look bad.

The other approach to controlling labor supply is the process of decruitment. In the past decade, many large U.S. corporations, governmental agencies, and even small businesses have been forced to shrink the size of their workforce or restructure their skill composition.[15] These employee cutbacks can be traced to market changes, foreign competition, mergers, and the overall decline in many manufacturing industries.

Decruitment is not a pleasant task for any manager. What are a manager's decruitment options? Obviously, people can't be fired indiscriminately. But firing is not the only means of decruitment, and other choices may be more beneficial to the organization or the employee or both.[16] Table 11-4 summarizes the major options.

TABLE 11-4	Decruitment Options
Option	**Description**
Firing	Permanent involuntary termination
Layoffs	Temporary involuntary termination; may last only a few days or extend to years
Attrition	Not filling openings created by voluntary resignations or normal retirements
Transfers	Moving employees either laterally or downward; usually does not reduce costs but can reduce intraorganizational supply-demand imbalances
Reduced workweeks	Having employees work fewer hours per week, share jobs, or perform their jobs on a part-time basis
Early retirements	Providing incentives to older and more senior employees for retiring before their normal retirement date
Job sharing	Having employees share one full-time position

4 Why is a job analysis important for the job description and job specification?

5 What are possible recruitment sources?

6 What is decruitment?

SELECTION

A new college graduate with a degree in accounting walked into the human resources office of a medium-sized corporation not long ago in search of a job. Immediately, she was face to face with two doors, one of which displayed the sign "Applicants With College Degree," and the other, "Applicants Without College Degree." She opened the first door. As soon as she did so, she found two more doors. The first said, "Applicants With Grade Point Average of 3.0 or Greater," and the other, "Applicants With Grade Point Average of Less Than 3.0." She had a 3.6 average, so she again chose the first door and was once again facing two doors. One read, "Applicants With Management Majors," and the other, "Applicants With Nonmanagement Majors." Having an accounting degree, she opened the second of these doors—and found herself out in the street.[17]

Although this story is fictitious, it does convey the essence of the selection process. When human resource planning identifies a human resource shortage and develops a pool of applicants, managers need some method for screening the applicants to ensure that the most appropriate candidate is hired. That screening method is the **selection process**.

selection process

The process of screening job applicants to ensure that the most appropriate candidates are hired.

What Is Selection?

Selection is an exercise in prediction. It seeks to predict which applicants will be successful if hired. Successful in this case means performing well on the criteria the organization uses to evaluate employees. In filling a sales position, for example, the selection process should be able to predict which applicants will generate a high volume of sales; for a position as a high school teacher, it should predict which applicants will be effective educators.

Prediction.   Consider, for a moment, that any selection decision can result in four possible outcomes. As shown in Figure 11-2, two of these outcomes would be correct decisions, but two would be errors.

FIGURE 11-2   Selection Decision Outcomes

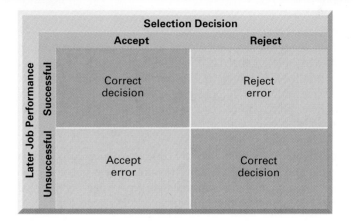

A decision is correct when the applicant was predicted to be successful and later proved to be successful on the job or when the applicant was predicted to be unsuccessful and would perform accordingly if hired. In the first case, we have successfully accepted; in the second case, we have successfully rejected.

Problems arise when we make errors by rejecting candidates who would later perform successfully on the job (reject errors) or accepting those who subsequently perform poorly (accept errors). These problems are, unfortunately, far from insignificant. Before governmental hiring laws and regulations, reject errors meant only that the costs of selection would be increased because more candidates would have to be screened. Today, however, selection techniques that result in reject errors can open the organization to charges of discrimination, especially if applicants from protected groups are disproportionately rejected. Accept errors, on the other hand, have very obvious costs to the organization, including the cost of training the employee, the costs generated or profits lost because of the employee's incompetence, and the cost of severance and the subsequent costs of further recruiting and selection screening. The major thrust of any selection activity should be to reduce the probability of making reject errors or accept errors while increasing the probability of making correct decisions.

Validity.   Any selection device that a manager uses—such as application forms, tests, interviews, or background investigations—must demonstrate **validity**. That is, there must be a proven relationship between the selection device and some relevant criterion. For example, the law prohibits managers from using a test score as a selection device unless there is clear evidence that, once on the job, individuals with high scores on this test outperform individuals with low test scores.

The burden is on managers to support that any selection device they use to differentiate applicants is related to job performance. Managers can give applicants an intelligence test and use the results to help make selection decisions, but they must be prepared to show, if challenged, that this intelligence test is a valid measure. That is, the scores on the test must be shown to be positively related to later job performance.

Reliability.   In addition to being valid, a selection device must also demonstrate reliability. **Reliability** indicates whether the device measures the same thing consistently. For example, if a test is reliable, any single individual's score should remain fairly consistent over time, assuming that the characteristics the test is measuring are also stable.

The importance of reliability should be evident. Using a selection device that is not reliable is equivalent to weighing yourself every day on an erratic scale. If the scale is unreliable—randomly fluctuating, say, 10 to 15 pounds every time you step on it—the results will not mean much. To be effective predictors, selection devices must possess an acceptable level of consistency.

Selection Devices

Managers can use a number of selection devices to reduce accept and reject errors. The best-known devices include an analysis of the job candidate's completed application form, written and performance-simulation tests, interviews, background investigations, and in some cases, a physical examination. Let's briefly review each of these devices, paying particular attention to the validity of each in predicting job performance. After we review the devices, we'll discuss when each should be used.

The Application Form.   Almost all organizations require job candidates to fill out an application. It may be only a form on which the person gives his or her name, address, and telephone number. Or it might be a comprehensive personal history profile, detailing the person's activities, skills, and accomplishments.

validity

The proven relationship that exists between a selection device and some relevant criterion.

reliability

The ability of a selection device to measure the same thing consistently.

Interview with Coleman Peterson, Senior Vice President, People Division, Wal-Mart, Bentonville, Arkansas

Describe your job.

I'm a senior vice president in the People Division (Human Resources) at Wal-Mart Inc., headquarters in Bentonville, Arkansas.

What types of skills do you think tomorrow's managers will need?

I believe that tomorrow's managers will need several key skills. One is openness to new ideas and new ways of doing things. Another is flexibility, or adaptability, since change is a constant within organizations. Another important skill would be the ability to focus on the key issues. It will also be important to have the ability to do things quickly. Finally, I think tomorrow's managers will need the ability to make things simple.

What are the important issues facing human resource managers?

One of the most important issues facing human resource managers has to be change. Organizations continually face changing conditions and must be prepared to cope with those changes. In addition, the selection issue is one that organizations must deal with. Getting, keeping, and motivating a diverse workforce to high performance levels is a challenge that begins with the selection process. Finally, I think that employee development and training is a significant issue that HR managers must deal with. People have been, and continue to be, critical to our organization's success, and we provide development and training opportunities for our employees.

How does your organization encourage employees to manage their careers?

There are numerous opportunities for employees in our organization to have a say in the direction they want their careers to go. However, this is an area in which we could do a better job. ■

Relevant biographical data and facts that can be verified—for example, rank in high school graduating class or college grade point average—have been shown to be valid performance measures for some jobs.[18] In addition, when application form items have been appropriately weighted to reflect job relatedness, this selection device has proved a valid predictor for such diverse groups as salesclerks, engineers, factory workers, district managers, clerical employees, and technicians.[19] But typically only a couple of items on the application form prove to be valid predictors of job performance, and then only for a specific job. Use of weighted applications for selection purposes is difficult and expensive because the weights have to be validated for each specific job and must be continually reviewed and updated to reflect changes in job relatedness over time.

Written Tests.   Typical types of written tests include tests of intelligence, aptitude, ability, and interest. Such tests have been used for years, although their popularity tends to run

Prospective employees commonly provide a résumé, summarizing background, education, work experiences, and accomplishments. Should it be 100 percent truthful? Is it wrong to embellish a résumé? For instance, Tammy P. made $2,700 a month when she left her previous job. On her résumé, she stated that she was making $2,900. Doug E. left a job for which his job title was "credit clerk." When looking for a new position, he described his previous title as "credit analyst" because he thought it sounded more impressive. Are these "creative enhancements" wrong? What deviations from the truth, if any, might be acceptable when writing a résumé? ■

in cycles. Written tests were widely used for a couple of decades after World War II. Beginning in the late 1960s, however, the use of tests fell out of favor. Written tests were frequently characterized as discriminatory, and many organizations could not validate that their written tests were job related.[20] But since the late 1980s, written tests have made a comeback.[21] Managers have become increasingly aware that poor hiring decisions are costly and that properly designed tests could reduce the likelihood of poor decisions' occurring. In addition, the cost of developing and validating a set of written tests for a specific job has decreased significantly. What used to take six months and cost $100,000 now takes only a couple of weeks and costs around $6,000.[22]

A review of research in this area shows that tests of intellectual ability, spatial and mechanical ability, perceptual accuracy, and motor ability are moderately valid predictors for many semiskilled and unskilled operative jobs in industrial organizations.[23] And intelligence tests are reasonably good predictors for supervisory positions.[24] However, an enduring criticism of written tests is that intelligence, and other tested characteristics, can be somewhat removed from the actual performance of a job. For example, a high score on an intelligence test is not necessarily a good indicator that an applicant will perform well as a computer programmer. This criticism has led to an increased use of performance-simulation tests.

Performance-Simulation Tests.   What better way is there to find out whether an applicant for a technical writing position at Siemens can write technical manuals than by having him or her do it? The logic of this question has led to an expanding interest in performance-simulation tests as selection devices. Undoubtedly, the enthusiasm for these tests is the fact that they are based on job analysis data, and therefore, should more easily meet the requirement of job relatedness than do written tests. Performance-simulation tests are made up of actual job behaviors rather than surrogates. The best-known performance-simulation tests are work sampling and assessment centers. The former is appropriate for routine jobs, and the latter for selecting people for managerial positions.

Work sampling involves presenting applicants with a miniature model of a job and having them perform a task or set of tasks that are central to it. Applicants demonstrate that they have the necessary skills and abilities by actually doing the tasks. By carefully devising work samples based on job analysis data, managers can determine the knowledge, skills, and abilities needed for each job. Each work sample element is then matched with a corresponding job performance element. For instance, a work sample for a job that involves computing figures on a calculator would require applicants to make similar computations. Work sample experiments generally have yielded impressive results. They have almost always yielded validity scores that are superior to those of written aptitude, personality, or intelligence tests.[25]

A more elaborate set of performance-simulation tests, specifically designed to measure a job candidate's managerial potential, is administered in **assessment centers**. In assessment centers, line executives, supervisors, or trained psychologists evaluate candidates as they go through two to four days of exercises that simulate real problems they would confront on the

work sampling

A personnel selection device in which job applicants are presented with a miniature replica of a job and are asked to perform tasks central to that job.

assessment centers

Places in which job candidates undergo performance-simulation tests that evaluate managerial potential.

job. Based on a list of descriptive dimensions that the actual job incumbent has to meet, activities might include interviews, in-basket problem-solving exercises, group discussions, and business decision games. The evidence on the effectiveness of assessment centers as a selection device is extremely impressive. Assessment centers have consistently demonstrated results that predict later job performance in managerial positions.[26] Although they're not cheap to administer, the selection of an ineffective manager can be significantly more costly.

The Interview.   The interview, along with the application form, is an almost universal selection device.[27] Not many of us have ever gotten a job without one or more interviews. Ironically, the value of the interview as a selection device has been the subject of considerable debate.[28]

Interviews can be valid and reliable selection tools, but too often they're not. When interviews are structured and well organized, and when interviewers are held to common questioning, interviews are effective predictors.[29] But most interviews don't meet those conditions. The typical interview—in which applicants are asked a varying set of essentially random questions in an informal setting—usually provide little in the way of valuable information.

All kinds of potential biases can creep into interviews if they're not well structured and standardized. To illustrate, a review of the research on interviews leads us to the following conclusions:

1. Prior knowledge about the applicant will bias the interviewer's evaluation.

2. The interviewer tends to hold a stereotype of what represents a "good" applicant.

3. The interviewer tends to favor applicants who share his or her own attitudes.

4. The order in which applicants are interviewed will influence evaluations.

5. The order in which information is elicited during the interview will influence evaluations.

6. Negative information is given unduly high weight.

7. The interviewer often makes a decision concerning the applicant's suitability within the first four or five minutes of the interview.

8. The interviewer forgets much of the interview's content within minutes after its conclusion.

9. The interview is most valid in determining an applicant's intelligence, level of motivation, and interpersonal skills.

10. A "cold" interviewer (i.e., one who's extremely formal and serious) can have a devastating effect on the verbal and nonverbal behaviors of applicants with low self-esteem.[30]

What can managers do to make interviews more valid and reliable? Table 11-5 lists some specific suggestions.

Another important factor to consider in interviewing job applicants is the legality of certain interview questions. Employment law attorneys caution managers to be extremely cautious in the types of questions they ask candidates. Table 11-6 lists some examples of typical interview questions that managers *shouldn't* ask because they could expose an organization to lawsuits by job applicants.

Background Investigations.   Background investigations are of two types: verifications of application data and reference checks. The first type has proved to be a valuable source of selection information; the latter is essentially worthless as a selection tool. Let's briefly review each.

TABLE 11-5   **Suggestions for Interviewing**

1. Structure a *fixed set of questions* for all applicants.
2. Have *detailed information about the job* for which applicants are interviewing.
3. *Minimize any prior knowledge* of applicants' background, experience, interests, test scores, or other characteristics.
4. *Ask behavioral questions* that require applicants to give detailed accounts of actual job behaviors.
5. Use a *standardized evaluation form.*
6. *Take notes* during the interview.
7. *Avoid short interviews* that encourage premature decision making.

Source: Based on D.A. DeCenzo and S.P. Robbins, *Human Resource Management*, 4th ed. (New York: Wiley, 1994), pp. 208–09.

TABLE 11-6   **Examples of Interview Questions Managers Shouldn't Ask**

- What is your date of birth?
- Have you ever filed a workers' compensation claim?
- What is your place of birth?
- Do you own a home?
- What is your native language?
- Do you have children? Plan to have children? Have child care?
- Do you have a physical or mental disability that would prevent you from doing this job?
- What religion do you practice?

Source: Based on J.S. Pauliot, "Topics to Avoid with Applicants," *Nation's Business*, July 1992, pp. 57–58; and L.M. Litvan, "Thorny Issues in Hiring," *Nation's Business*, April 1996, pp. 34–36.

Several studies indicate that verifying "facts" given on the application form is worthwhile. A significant percentage of job applicants—upwards of 33 percent—exaggerate or misrepresent dates of employment, job titles, past salaries, or reasons for leaving a prior position.[31] Many organizations also must consider the liability that potential employees may create and get as much depth in background information as necessary.[32]

The reference check is used by many organizations but is extremely difficult to justify. Whether they are work related or personal, references provide little valid information for the selection decision.[33] Employers are frequently reluctant to give candid evaluations of a former employee's job performance for fear of legal repercussions. In fact, a survey found that only 55 percent of human resource executives would "always" provide accurate references to a prospective employer. Moreover, 7 percent said they would never give an accurate reference.[34] Personal likes and dislikes also heavily influence the type of recommendation given. Personal references are likely to provide biased information. Doesn't each of us have three or four friends who will speak in glowing terms about our integrity, work habits, positive attitudes, knowledge, and skills?

Physical Examination.   For jobs with certain physical requirements, the physical examination has some validity. However, this group includes a very small number of jobs today. In almost all cases, the physical examination is done for insurance purposes. Organizations want to be sure new hires will not submit insurance claims for injuries or illnesses that they contracted before being hired.

Managers must be careful to ensure that physical requirements are job related and do not discriminate. Some physical requirements may exclude certain disabled persons, when, in fact, such requirements do not affect job performance.

What Works Best and When?

Many selection devices are of limited value to managers in making selection decisions. An understanding of the strengths and weaknesses of each will help you determine when each should be used. We offer the following advice to guide your choices.

Because the validity of selection devices varies for different types of jobs, you should use only those devices that predict for a given job. (See Table 11-7.) The application form offers limited information. Traditional written tests are reasonably effective devices for routine jobs. Work samples, however, are clearly preferable to written tests. For managerial selection, the assessment center is strongly recommended. If the interview has a place in the selection decision, it is most likely among less-routine jobs, particularly middle- and upper-level managerial positions. The interview is a reasonably good device for discerning intelligence and interpersonal skills.[35] These are most likely to be related to job performance in nonroutine activities, especially in senior managerial positions. Verification of application data is valuable for all jobs. Conversely, reference checks are generally worthless for all jobs. Finally, physical exams rarely provide any valid selection information.

7 What is the major intent of any selection activity?

8 Why are validity and reliability important in selection?

9 Describe the advantages and disadvantages of the various selection devices.

TESTING...
TESTING...

1 **2** **3**

TABLE 11-7   Quality of Selection Devices as Predictors

Selection Device	Position			
	Senior Management	Middle and Lower Management	Complex Nonmanagerial	Routine Operative
Application form	2	2	2	2
Written tests	1	1	2	3
Work samples	—	—	4	4
Assessment center	5	5	—	—
Interviews	4	3	2	2
Verification of application data	3	3	3	3
Reference checks	1	1	1	1
Physical exam	1	1	1	2

Note: Validity is measured on a scale from 5 (highest) to 1 (lowest). A dash means "not applicable."

ORIENTATION

Did you participate in some type of organized "introduction to college life" when you started school? If you did, you may have been told about your school's rules and regulations, the procedures for activities such as applying for financial aid or cashing a check or registering for classes, and you were probably introduced to some of the college administrators. A person starting a new job needs the same type of introduction to his or her job and the organization. This introduction is called **orientation**.

orientation

The introduction of a new employee into his or her job and the organization.

The major objectives of orientation are to reduce the initial anxiety all new employees feel as they begin a new job; to familiarize new employees with the job, the work unit, and the organization as a whole; and to facilitate the outsider-insider transition. Job orientation expands on the information the employee received during the recruitment and selection stages. The new employee's specific duties and responsibilities are clarified, as is the method of performance evaluation used for the job. This is also the time to resolve any unrealistic expectations new employees might hold about the job. Work unit orientation familiarizes the employee with the goals of the work unit, clarifies how his or her job contributes to the unit's goals, and includes an introduction to his or her new co-workers. Organization orientation informs the new employee about the organization's objectives, history, philosophy, procedures, and rules. This should include relevant human resource policies and benefits such as work hours, pay procedures, overtime requirements, and fringe benefits. In addition, a tour of the organization's work facilities is often part of the organization orientation.

Many organizations, particularly large ones, have formal orientation programs. Such a program might include a tour of the offices or plant, a film describing the history of the organization, and a short discussion with a representative of the human resources department who describes the organization's benefit programs. Other organizations use a more informal orientation program in which, for instance, the manager assigns the new employee to a senior member of the unit, who introduces the new employee to immediate co-workers and shows him or her the locations of the copy room, coffee machine, rest rooms, cafeteria, and the like. For example, in-house mentoring programs, during which new employees are paired up with a mentor, at Avon Products Inc. and MTV are designed to make new employees feel comfortable.[36]

Managers have an obligation to make the integration of the new employee into the organization as smooth and as free of anxiety as possible. They need to openly discuss employee beliefs regarding mutual obligations of the organization and the employee.[37] It is in the organization's, and the new employee's, best interests to get the person up and running in the job as soon as possible. Successful orientation, whether formal or informal, results in an outsider-insider transition that makes the new member feel comfortable and fairly well adjusted, lowers the likelihood of poor work performance, and reduces the probability of a surprise resignation by the new employee only a week or two into the job.

EMPLOYEE TRAINING

On the whole, planes don't cause airline accidents, people do. Most collisions, crashes, and other mishaps result from errors made by the pilot or air traffic controller or from inadequate maintenance. Weather and structural failures cause only a small percentage of accidents.[38] We point out this fact to illustrate the importance of employee training in the airline industry. Maintenance and human errors could be significantly reduced, if not prevented, by better employee training.

As job demands change, employee skills have to be altered and updated. It's been estimated, for instance, that U.S. business firms spend an astounding $59 billion on formal courses and training programs to build workers' skills.[39] Managers, of course, are responsible for deciding when subordinates need training and what form that training should take.

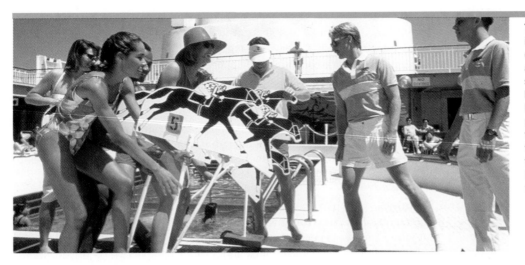

Training is a major factor in the development of cruise ship personnel. In addition to learning specific job skills, on-board staff get coaching in how to cope with the particular stresses they face, such as being away from home for weeks at a time and being on call 24 hours a day, seven days a week.

Skill Categories

We can group employee skills into three categories: technical, interpersonal, and problem solving. Most employee training activities seek to modify an employee's skills in one or more of those categories.

Technical.   Most training is directed at upgrading and improving an employee's technical skills, including basic skills—the ability to read, write, and perform math computations—as well as job-specific competencies.[40] The majority of jobs today have become more complex than they were a decade ago. Computerized factories and offices, digitally controlled machines, and other types of sophisticated technology require that employees have math, reading, and computer skills. How, for example, can employees master statistical process control or the careful measurement and self-inspection needed for tool changes in flexible manufacturing systems if they can't make basic math calculations or read detailed operating manuals? Or how can clerical personnel do their jobs effectively without the ability to understand word processing programs and electronic mail systems? For example, company officials at XEL Corporation in Aurora, Colorado, wanted to make the organization a premier producer of communications equipment. Unfortunately, many XEL employees lacked the necessary skills to work with new technologies or even to accept the autonomy managers wanted to give them. Rather than replace its entire workforce, XEL contracted with a local community college to provide training programs that would correct employees' skills deficiencies.[41]

Interpersonal.   Almost every employee belongs to a work unit. To some degree, work performance depends on an employee's ability to interact effectively with his or her co-workers and boss. Some employees have excellent interpersonal skills. Others require training to improve theirs. This includes learning how to be a better listener, how to communicate ideas more clearly, and how to reduce conflict. For instance, at Big Y Foods Inc., of Springfield, Massachusetts, employees learn to develop cooperation, teamwork, and trust through an experience-based learning program that takes place at the company's "Big Y Training Camp."[42]

Problem Solving.   Many employees have to solve problems on their job, particularly in jobs that are nonroutine. When the problem-solving skills of employees are deficient, managers might want to improve them through training. This would include participation in activities to sharpen logic, reasoning, and skills at defining problems; assessing causation; developing alternatives and building creativity; analyzing alternatives; and selecting solutions. For example, the New York-based fabric supplier F. Schumacher uses teachers from a local community college to train its managers in problem solving and conflict resolution.[43]

Training Methods

Most training takes place on the job because this approach is simple to implement and is usually inexpensive. However, on-the-job training can disrupt the workplace and result in an increase in errors while learning takes place. Also, some skill training is too complex to learn on the job. In such cases, it should take place outside the work setting.

job rotation

On-the-job training that involves lateral transfers in which employees get to work at different jobs.

On-the-Job Training. Popular on-the-job training methods include job rotation and understudy assignments. **Job rotation** involves lateral transfers that enable employees to work at different jobs. Employees get to learn a wide variety of jobs while gaining increased insights into the interdependency between jobs and a wider perspective on organizational activities. New employees frequently learn their jobs by studying under a seasoned veteran. In the trades, this arrangement is called an *apprenticeship.* In white-collar jobs, it's called a *coaching,* or *mentor*, relationship. In each, the understudy works under the observation of an experienced worker, who acts as a model whom the understudy attempts to emulate.

MANAGING YOUR CAREER

mentor

A person who sponsors or supports another employee who is lower in the organization.

Getting the Most Out of a Mentor Relationship

Acquiring a mentor who provides advice, assistance, and support might be one of the smartest career moves a young manager can make. A **mentor** is someone in the organization who is usually older, more experienced, and higher up in the organization and who can help another person achieve his or her career goals. A mentor is someone from whom you can learn and who can encourage and help you and who serves as adviser, coach, counselor, and guide. One study of managers and professionals in Belgium who were in the early stages of their careers found that career mentoring was positively related to early career promotions, general satisfaction with work, and overall satisfaction with career choice. Because there are positive benefits to be gained from having a mentor, how can you get the most out of a mentor relationship?[44]

If your organization has no formal mentoring program, you'll need to find your own mentor—someone in the organization whom you trust, respect, and like. Ask this person if he or she would be willing to serve as your mentor. Building a strong partnership with your mentor is like building any interpersonal relationship. First, honest and open communication by both of you is absolutely essential. If you're going to benefit from your mentor's accumulated years of experience and knowledge, he or she must be willing to level with you in "telling it like it is." And, as the protégé, you must exhibit a willingness to listen and learn, which also implies a willingness to ask questions and challenge your mentor. Also, treat your mentor with respect. After all, he or she has more years of experience as a manager than you and has, undoubtedly, learned much in those years. And, of course, effective work performance is absolutely essential. Having an excellent mentor is no substitute for good work performance; nor is it an excuse for poor work performance. Finally, when you get to a point in your career at which you have experience and insights to offer younger organizational members, consider becoming a mentor yourself. Mentoring helps the organization develop its managerial talent. And there can be a great deal of personal satisfaction in helping develop others. ■

Both job rotation and understudy assignments apply to the learning of technical skills. Interpersonal and problem-solving skills are acquired more effectively by training that takes place off the job.

Off-the-Job Training.   Of the off-the-job training methods available to managers, the most popular are classroom lectures, films, and simulation exercises. *Classroom lectures* are well suited for conveying specific information. They can be used effectively for developing technical and problem-solving skills. *Films* and *videos* can also be used to explicitly demonstrate technical skills that aren't easily presented by other methods. Interpersonal and problem-solving skills may best be learned through *simulation exercises* such as case analyses, experiential exercises, role playing, and group interaction sessions. Complex computer models, such as those used by airlines in pilot training, are another kind of simulation exercise, which in this case is used to teach technical skills. So, too, is **vestibule training**, in which employees learn their jobs on the same equipment they'll be using, only the training is conducted in a simulated work environment and not in the actual work setting. Many airplane maintenance trainees learn to repair engines and correct maintenance problems in specially created vestibule labs containing actual aircraft that simulate real working conditions. This method provides for careful control of learning experiences; it allows trainees to deal with every conceivable problem while minimizing interference with an airline's actual ongoing maintenance operations.

vestibule training

Training in which employees learn on the same equipment they will be using but in a simulated work environment.

---

10 What is the goal of orientation?

11 Identify three skill categories for which organizations do employee training.

12 Describe on-the-job training and off-the-job training methods.

CAREER DEVELOPMENT

The term *career* has several meanings. In popular usage, it can mean advancement ("she is on a career track"), a profession ("he has chosen a career in accounting"), or a lifelong sequence of jobs ("his career has included 12 jobs in six organizations"). For our purposes, we define a **career** as the sequence of positions held by a person during his or her lifetime.[45] By this definition, it's apparent that we all have, or will have, a career. Moreover, the concept is as relevant to transient, unskilled laborers as it is to software designers or physicians. But individual career development isn't what it used to be![46]

career

The sequence of positions occupied by a person during his or her lifetime.

The Way It Was

Although career development has been an important topic in management-related courses for the past three decades, we've witnessed some dramatic changes in the concept of career development over the years. As recently as 15 years ago, career development programs were typically designed by organizations to help employees advance their work lives within a specific organization. The focus of such programs was to provide the information, assessment, and training needed to help employees realize their career goals. Career development was also a way for the organization to attract and retain highly talented people. Those purposes are all but disappearing in today's workplace. Widespread internal changes in organizations have led to uncertainty and chaos as far as the concepts of a traditional organizational career. Downsizing, delayering, restructuring, reengineering, and other organizational adjustments have brought us to one significant conclusion about career development: The individual—not the organization—is responsible for his or her own career! You, therefore, must be prepared to do what is necessary to advance your career. You must take responsibility for designing, guiding, and developing your own career. Your career will be managed by you, not by the organization.[47] Both organizations and individuals are gradually adjusting to the notion that organizational members have to look out for themselves and become more self-reliant.

You and Your Career Today

This idea of increased personal responsibility for one's career has been described as *a boundaryless career* in which individuals rather than organizations define career progression, organizational loyalty, important skills, and marketplace value.[48] The challenge for individuals is that there are no norms and few rules to guide them in these new circumstances. Instead, individuals assume primary responsibility for career planning, career goal setting, and education and training.[49]

One of the first career decisions you have to make is career choice. The optimum career choice is one that offers the best match between what you want out of life and your interests, abilities, and market opportunities. Good career choice outcomes should result in a series of positions that give you an opportunity to be a good performer, make you want to maintain your commitment to your career, lead to highly satisfying work, and give you the proper balance between work and personal life. A good career match, then, is one in which you are able to develop a positive self-concept, to do work that you think is important, and to lead the kind of life you desire.[50] Table 11-8 provides the results from a survey of college graduates regarding what is important to them in their first jobs. How would you have ranked these items?

Once you have identified a career choice, it's time to initiate the job search. We aren't going to get into the specifics of job hunting (see Managing Your Career: Job Hunting on the Web, page 360), writing a résumé, or interviewing successfully, although those career actions are important. Let's fast forward through all that and assume that your job search was successful. It's time to go to work! How do you survive and excel in an organization?

Steps to a Successful Management Career

There are certain steps you can take that will lead to success in a career in management (Figure 11-3). The following discussion provides suggestions based on proven tactics that managers have used to advance their careers.[51]

TABLE 11-8	**Top Ten Important Job Factors for College Graduates**

(ranked in order of importance)

1. Enjoying what they do
2. Opportunity to use skills and abilities
3. Opportunity for personal development
4. Feeling what they do matters
5. Benefits
6. Recognition for good performance
7. Friendly co-workers
8. Job location
9. Lots of money
10. Working in teams

Source: Based on V. Frazee, "What's Important to College Grads in Their First Jobs?" *Personnel Journal,* July 1996, p. 21.

FIGURE 11-3 Steps to a Successful Management Career

Select your first job judiciously. Not all first jobs are alike. Where managers begin in the organization has an important effect on their career progress. Specifically, the evidence suggests that, if you have a choice, you should select a powerful department as the place to start your management career.[52] A powerful department is one in which crucial and important organizational decisions are made. Managers who start out in departments that are high in power within the organization are more likely to advance rapidly throughout their careers than are managers who start in a low-power department.

Do good work. Good work performance is a necessary (but not sufficient) condition for managerial success. The marginal performer may be rewarded in the short term, but his or her weaknesses are bound to surface eventually and cut off career advancement. Good work performance is no guarantee of success, but, without it, the probability of having a successful management career is low.

Present the right image. Assuming that your work performance is in line with that of other managers who are successful in the organization, the ability to align your image with that sought by the organization is certain to be interpreted positively. The manager should evaluate the organization's culture so that he or she understands what the organization wants and values from its managers. Then the manager is equipped to project the appro-

MANAGING

YOUR

CAREER

Job Hunting on the Web

Finding a job has gone high-tech![53] No longer must you limit your job search to newspaper classified ads, employment agencies, or any of the other traditional job sources. A growing number of organizations are using the Web to recruit candidates for job openings, and job seekers are using it to apply for jobs. In fact, one survey of HR professionals found that 47 percent used the Internet to recruit. How can you use the Internet to search for a job?

One way to find a job on the Internet is to log onto specific company sites, especially if there is a particular company in which you're interested. Many companies—Fidelity Investments, Merix Inc., United Parcel Service, and Rite Aid, to name a few—are posting job openings on their own Web sites. Usually at these company sites, you'll find a general description of the types of job openings and instructions on how to submit a résumé. In many instances, your résumé can be submitted electronically.

Another way to use the Internet to search for a job is through the major job or career sites that are devoted specifically to job listings. Some of the most popular ones are Monster Board <http://www.monster.com>, Career Mosaic <http://www.careermosaic.com>, and CareerPath <http://www.careerpath.com>. These sites will let you search by location, job title, or other criteria. One other fun site, which claims to list the "coolest jobs on the Internet," can be found at <http://www.cooljobs.com>. You could even log onto *Career* magazine's site <http://www.careermag.com> to ask for and give advice on job searches. ■

priate image in terms of style of dress; organizational relationships that one should and should not cultivate; whether one should project a risk-taking or risk-aversive stance; the organization's preferred leadership style; whether conflict should be avoided, tolerated, or encouraged; the importance attributed to getting along well with others; and so forth.

Learn the power structure. The authority relationships defined by the organization's formal structure and shown by the organizational chart explain only part of the influence patterns within an organization. It's of equal or greater importance to know and understand the organization's power structure. The effective manager needs to learn "who's really in charge, who has the goods on whom, what are the major debts and dependencies"—all things that will not be reflected in the neat boxes on the organizational chart. Once a manager has this knowledge, he or she can work within the power structure with skill and ease.[54]

Gain control of organizational resources. The control of scarce and important organizational resources is a source of power. Knowledge and expertise are particularly effective resources to control. They make you valuable to the organization and therefore likely to gain job security and advancement. For example, individuals with high-quality technical skills are in high demand in diverse industries ranging from medical fields to circuitboard manufacturing.[55]

Stay visible. Because the evaluation of managerial effectiveness can be very subjective, it's important that your boss and those in power in the organization be made aware of your contribution. If you're fortunate enough to have a job that brings your accomplishments to the attention of others, taking direct measures to increase your visibility might not be needed. But your job may require you to handle activities that are low in visibility, or your specific contribution may be indistinguishable because you are part of a group endeavor. In such cases, you will want to call attention to yourself, without creating the image of a braggart, by giving progress reports to your boss and others. Other tactics include being seen at social functions, being active in your professional associations, and developing powerful allies who speak positively about you.

Don't stay too long in your first job. The evidence indicates that, if you have a choice between staying in your first management job until you have "really made a difference" or accepting an early transfer to a new job assignment, you should go for the early transfer.[56]

By moving quickly through different jobs, you signal to others that you're on the fast track. This, then, often becomes a self-fulfilling prophecy. The message to aspiring managers is to start fast by seeking early transfers or promotions from the first management job.

Find a Mentor. As we described earlier in the chapter's first Managing Your Career box, a mentor is someone from whom you can learn and who can encourage and help you. The evidence indicates that finding a sponsor who is part of the organization's power core is essential for managers who want to make it to the top levels of management.[57]

Support your boss. Your immediate future is in the hands of your current boss. He or she evaluates your performance, and few young managers are powerful enough to successfully challenge their boss. You should make the effort to help your boss succeed, be supportive if your boss is under siege from other organizational units, and find out what criteria he or she will be using to assess your work effectiveness. Do not undermine your boss. Do not speak negatively of your boss to others. If your boss is competent and visible and possesses a power base, he or she is likely to be on the way up in the organization. By being perceived as supportive, you might find yourself being pulled along. Even if you're not promoted along with your boss, you'll have established an ally higher up in the organization. If your boss's performance is poor and his or her power is low, you should use your mentor (if you have one) to arrange a transfer. If you don't have a mentor, you should do the best job you can and look for the earliest opportunity to move to another position within the organization. It's hard to have your competence recognized or your positive performance evaluation taken seriously if your boss is perceived as incompetent.

Stay mobile. Managers are likely to move upward rapidly if they indicate a willingness to move to different geographical locations and across functional lines within the organization. Career advancement may also be facilitated by a willingness to change organizations. In slow-growth, stagnant, or declining organizations, career mobility should be especially important to the ambitious manager.

The appearance of maintaining interorganizational mobility, when coupled with control of organizational resources, can be particularly effective. If senior management needs what you have and is fearful that you might leave, they are not likely to ignore your needs. One fast-rising manager was very competent and possessed some unique skills but also made a serious effort to keep himself visible in his industry. He made a habit of regularly mentioning to those in the powerful inner circle of his firm that he received a steady stream of job offers from competitors (which was true) but that, as long as he continued to receive increasingly responsible positions and large salary increases, he had no intention of leaving

Mastech recruiter Sushma Rajagopalan faces the challenge of finding qualified software programmers in a tight job market. One of her strategies is to look for people who are interested in expanding their career opportunities but are stymied at home. She sees future hiring opportunities for her firm in Colombia and Hong Kong, for example.

his firm. This strategy has been successful for this manager. He has received three job promotions in five years, and his salary has increased fourfold.

Think laterally. This suggestion acknowledges the changing world of management in the early twenty-first century. Because of organizational restructurings and downsizings, there are fewer rungs on the promotional ladder in many large organizations. If you want to survive in this environment, it's a good idea to think in terms of lateral career moves.[58]

In the 1960s and 1970s, people who made lateral moves were assumed to be mediocre performers. Not anymore. Lateral shifts are now a viable career consideration. They give individuals a wider range of experiences, which enhances long-term mobility. In addition, these moves help energize people by making work more interesting and satisfying. So, if you are not moving ahead in your organization, consider a lateral move internally or a lateral shift to another organization.

Think of your career in terms of skills you are acquiring, and continue upgrading those skills. Organizations need employees who can readily adapt to the demands of the rapidly changing marketplace. By focusing on skills that you currently have and continuing to learn new skills, you can establish your value to the organization. It's employees who don't add value to an organization whose jobs (and careers) are in jeopardy.

Work harder than ever at developing a network. Our final suggestion is based on the recognition that having a network of friends, colleagues, neighbors, customers, suppliers, and so on can be a useful tool for career development. If you spend some time cultivating relationships and contacts throughout your industry and community, you will be prepared if worse comes to worst and your current job is eliminated. Even if your job is in no danger of being cut, having a network can prove beneficial in getting things done.

COMPENSATION AND BENEFITS

Would you work 40 hours a week (or more) for an organization for no pay and no benefits? Although we might consider doing so for some "cause" organizations, most of us expect to receive some form of reward or compensation from our employer. Developing an effective and efficient compensation system is an important part of the human resource management process.[59]

The purpose of designing an effective and appropriate compensation system is to attract and retain competent and talented individuals who can help the organization accomplish its mission and goals. In addition, an organization's compensation system has been shown to have an impact on its strategic performance.[60]

Managers must develop compensation systems that reflect the changing nature of work and the workplace in order to keep people motivated. Organizational compensation can include many different types of rewards and benefits. Table 11-9 provides a brief description of the typical compensation components an organization can provide.

How do managers determine who receives $9.00 an hour and who receives $350,000 a year? Several factors influence the differences in compensation and benefit packages for

TABLE 11-9	**Components of a Compensation System**

- Base wages and salaries
- Wage and salary add-ons
- Incentive payments
- Benefits and services

Source: Based on R.I. Henderson, *Compensation Management,* 6th ed. (Upper Saddle River, NJ: Prentice Hall, 1994), p. 16.

different employees. These include the kind of job performed, the kind of business the organization is in, whether the organization is unionized, whether the organization is labor- or capital-intensive, management's pay philosophy, the organization's geographical location, the organization's level of profitability, the size of the organization, and employee's tenure and performance. (See Figure 11-4.) Let's take a closer look at these.

The primary determinant of rate of pay is the *kind of job an employee performs.* Different jobs require different kinds and levels of skills, and these skills have varying levels of value to the organization. Typically, the higher the skill level, the higher the pay.

Because employees' levels of skills tend to affect work efficiency and effectiveness, many organizations have implemented **skill-based pay** systems, which reward employees for the job skills and competencies they can demonstrate. In a skill-based pay system, an employee's job title doesn't define his or her pay category; skills do.[61] For example, new employees at a Quaker Oats pet food plant in Topeka, Kansas, start at $8.75 an hour but can reach a top pay rate of $14.50 when they master 10 to 12 skills such as operating lift trucks and using factory computer controls.[62] Skill-based pay systems seem to mesh nicely with the changing nature of jobs and the new world of work. As one expert noted, "Slowly, but surely, we're becoming a skill-based society where your market value is tied to what you can do and what your skill set is. In this new world where skills and knowledge are what really count, it doesn't make sense to treat people as jobholders. It makes sense to treat them as people with specific skills and to pay them for those skills."[63]

Another factor that influences an employee's pay is the *kind of business the organization is in.* Private sector jobs typically provide higher rates of pay than public sector or not-for-profit jobs, especially for managerial and professional positions. The nature of the business and its impact on compensation also apply to different industries. For example, restaurants and other retail businesses have notoriously low salaries for operative employees and first-line managers.

Whether an organization or particular business unit is *unionized* can influence an employee's pay. The wages of unionized workers tend to be higher than those of nonunionized employees for comparable jobs, but this difference holds mainly in heavy manufactur-

skill-based pay

A pay system that rewards employees for the job skills and competencies they can demonstrate.

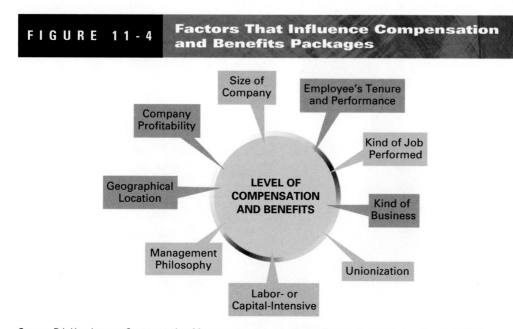

FIGURE 11-4 **Factors That Influence Compensation and Benefits Packages**

Source: R.I. Henderson, *Compensation Management*, 6th ed. (Upper Saddle River, NJ: Prentice Hall, 1994), pp. 3–24; and A. Murray, "Mom, Apple Pie, and Small Business," *Wall Street Journal*, August 15, 1994, p. A1.

ing industries (for example, steel, mining, and oil). Because the economics of global competition have forced organizations to look for ways to reduce their labor costs, unionization does not affect pay levels as it once did.

Another industry characteristic that influences the rate of pay is whether the business is *labor-* or *capital-intensive.* As businesses have become more capital-intensive, it does not take as many workers to do the organization's work, but these employees need higher levels of knowledge and skills. And highly skilled employees usually demand higher rates of pay.

Another factor that influences pay levels is *management's philosophy.* Some organizations have the philosophy that "we don't pay employees any more than we absolutely have to," whereas others are committed to a philosophy of paying their employees at or above area standards in order to attract and retain the best pool of talent.

Geographical location is another of the factors that influences pay. Usually, the geographical regions where the cost of living is highest offer the highest wages. Also, the supply and demand for labor and the prevailing unemployment rate in a particular area of a country affect the level of pay that must be offered to attract and retain competent employees.

The *profitability of the company* also influences employee pay levels. If a company is experiencing declining profits, its ability to offer high levels of pay and benefits will be affected. If the company is profitable, however, it may be able to provide higher pay levels or some type of profit-sharing system.

Studies also show that the *size of a company* affects pay levels. The hourly pay of workers at companies with more than 500 employees tends to be greater than the hourly pay of workers at smaller companies.[64]

The final factor that affects pay is an *employee's tenure and performance* at his or her job. In most cases, an employee's rate of pay increases with each year worked at an organization. But we also find that organizations may reward employees who have achieved high levels of performance by increasing their pay through some type of merit or pay-for-performance system.

Although the above factors are important influences on the design of an organization's compensation system, flexibility is becoming a key consideration. The traditional approach to paying people for their work reflected a time of job stability when an employee's pay was largely determined by seniority and job level. Given the dynamic environments that many

Some of the many factors that influence employee compensation are the kind of business, its size, and the level of skill required. Equally important are the individual's tenure, job performance, and level of skill attained.

organizations face, in which the employee skills that are absolutely critical to organizational success can change in a matter of months, the trend is to make pay systems more flexible and to reduce the number of pay levels. One way to make pay systems more flexible is through an approach called **broadbanding compensation**, which reduces the number of job levels or salary grades into a few wide bands.[65] For example, broadbanding might reduce eight pay grades, with a range of $200 a month in each, to three, with a $700 range within each. This arrangement allows managers considerably more flexibility in linking compensation to individual skills and contributions. Whatever approach they take, managers must establish a fair, equitable, and motivating compensation system that allows the organization to recruit and keep a productive workforce.

broadbanding compensation

An approach to pay systems that reduces the number of job levels or salary grades into a few wide bands.

13 How has the concept of career development changed over the last few years?

14 Why is it important for an organization to have an effective compensation system?

15 Describe the various factors that influence what pay employees receive.

TESTING... TESTING... 1 2 3

CURRENT ISSUES IN HUMAN RESOURCE MANAGEMENT

We conclude this chapter by looking at some contemporary human resource issues facing today's managers. These include managing workforce diversity, sexual harassment, family concerns, and AIDS in the workplace.

Managing Workforce Diversity

We've discussed the changing makeup of the U.S. workforce in several places throughout the book. Let's now look at how workforce diversity affects such basic HRM concerns as recruitment, selection, and orientation and training.

Recruitment.   To improve workforce diversity, managers need to widen their recruiting net. For example, the popular practice of relying on current employee referrals as a source of new job applicants tends to produce candidates who are similar to present employees. However, some organizations, such as Exabyte, a manufacturer of computer storage tape drives located in Boulder, Colorado, have been able to recruit and hire diverse individuals by relying on their current employees. Exabyte hired its first deaf employee in 1989 and found this individual to have excellent organizational skills and work habits. On the basis of that positive experience, Exabyte has since hired more nonhearing employees through employee referrals. But not every organization has the employee resources needed to achieve workforce diversity through employee referrals. So managers have to look for job applicants in places where they might not have looked before.

Some nontraditional recruitment sources managers might contact are women's job networks, over-fifty clubs, urban job banks, disabled individuals' training centers, ethnic newspapers, and gay-rights organizations. This type of outreach should enable the organization to broaden its pool of diverse applicants.

Selection.   Once a diverse set of applicants exists, efforts must be made to ensure that the selection process does not discriminate. Moreover, applicants need to be made comfortable with the organization and any interview or testing situation. They also need to be

Rockwell International is committed to achieving the benefits of diversity. It also encourages employees to support their communities. These employees from southern California are participating in a fund-raising walk for juvenile diabetes research.

made aware of management's desire to accommodate their needs. For instance, only a small number of women apply for Microsoft's technical jobs, but the company makes every effort to hire a high percentage of the female applicants and strives to make sure that these women have a successful experience once they are on the job.[66]

Orientation and Training.   The outsider-insider transition is often more challenging for women and minorities than for white males. Many organizations provide special workshops to raise diversity awareness among current employees and programs for new employees that focus on diversity issues. For example, at a Kraft cheese manufacturing plant in Missouri, managers put together an ambitious diversity program reflecting the increased value the organization had placed on incorporating diverse perspectives. One thing they did was to reward "diversity champions," individual employees who supported and promoted the benefits of diversity. They also added diversity goals to employee evaluations, encouraged nontraditional promotions, sponsored six ethnic meal days, and trained over half of the plant's employees in diversity issues.[67] The 1,700 employees of the Marriott Marquis Hotel in New York represent every race, come from 70 countries, and speak 47 languages. The hotel's managers view such diversity as a competitive advantage, particularly since the hotel serves a diverse customer base. Managing such diversity, however, has been a challenge. One thing the hotel has done is to require all its managers to take diversity classes, during which they are introduced to cross-cultural norms such as body language, eye contact, touching, and religious customs.[68]

Sexual Harassment

Sexual harassment is no longer a secret in corporate America. It was brought into the open in 1991 during the widely publicized allegations of sexual harassment by Anita Hill against Clarence Thomas when he was being considered for his U.S. Supreme Court Justice position. How widespread is the problem? Complaints to the EEOC (Equal Employment Opportunity Commission) jumped to over 14,000 in 1994 and to over 15,000 in 1995.[69] And a survey of human resource managers found that 84 percent of them had dealt with sexual harassment complaints.[70]

Until 1986, the U.S. Supreme Court didn't even recognize sexual harassment as a form of sex discrimination. In that year, the court held that employees have the right to work in an environment free from discriminatory conduct and insult.[71] **Sexual harassment** generally encompasses sexually suggestive remarks, unwanted touching and sexual advances,

sexual harassment

Behavior marked by sexually aggressive remarks, unwanted touching and sexual advances, requests for sexual favors, or other verbal or physical conduct of a sexual nature.

requests for sexual favors, and other verbal and physical conduct of a sexual nature. It's considered illegal, a violation of the federal Civil Rights Act.[72]

From management's standpoint, sexual harassment is a concern because it intimidates employees, interferes with job performance, and exposes the organization to legal liability. On this last point, the courts have ruled that if the employee who is guilty of sexual harassment is a supervisor or agent for an organization, the organization can also be found liable for sexual harassment unless it has: (1) developed a policy on sexual harassment; (2) educated employees on that policy; (3) created a procedure that employees are to follow if they feel they've been victims of sexual harassment; and (4) investigated any complaints or allegations of sexual harassment. For instance, a California jury awarded a former secretary at the nation's largest law firm $7.1 million for emotional trauma after finding that her former employer had failed to stop one of its partners from harassing the woman. The person who harassed the woman had to pay $250,000 of that award.[73] It's not only business organizations that face sexual harassment charges. The Central Intelligence Agency was the target of two legal actions brought against it by a former female employee and more than 100 women who worked in the agency's secret spy unit. The women alleged a widespread practice of discrimination and harassment.[74] Also, sexual harassment isn't just a U.S. phenomena; it's a worldwide issue.[75] Sexual harassment charges have been filed by employees in such countries as Japan, Australia, the Netherlands, Belgium, New Zealand, Sweden, and Ireland.[76] And, as the chapter-opening Manager's Dilemma pointed out, Japanese corporations with manufacturing facilities in the United States are taking their responsibilities for training managers about sexual harassment issues seriously.

Once again, to avoid liability, organizations must establish a clear and strong policy against sexual harassment.[77] That policy should then be reinforced by regular education and discussion sessions in which managers are reminded of the rule and carefully instructed that even the slightest sexual overture to another employee will not be tolerated. Studies have shown that the best training on sexual harassment gives participants a chance to talk to each other instead of just listening to a lecture or watching a film on the subject.[78] Organizations also need to have in place a procedure that employees follow if they feel they've been sexually harassed. Finally, organizations must investigate complaints or allegations of sexual harassment.

Family Concerns

What kinds of family issues can arise that might affect an employee's job performance? Here are some examples:

- Is it OK for someone to bring his baby to work because of an emergency crisis with normal child care arrangements?

- Should a boss praise an employee for flying to Japan on business the day after the employee's wife gives birth? Should a boss discipline an employee who refuses to go for the same reason?

- A manager has an assignment to give out that requires a lot of travel. In deciding whom to give it to, should she consider which workers have small children?

- Is it OK for a worker to cover his work area with pictures of his newborn baby or drawings scrawled by his young children?

- A 7½ month pregnant worker is completing an important assignment. The culmination of the project—a formal contract signing—requires a three-hour plane trip. Her doctor would prefer that she not go, but says it's up to her. The woman wants to see the assignment to its completion. The manager could easily send someone else, but he knows the project means a lot to the pregnant woman. What should he do?[79]

Organizations are beginning to recognize that employees can't (and don't) just leave their families and personal lives behind when they walk into work. An organization hires a person who has feelings, a personal life outside the office, personal problems, and family commitments. Although we're not trying to imply that an organization should be sympathetic with each and every detail of an employee's family life, we *are* seeing organizations become more attuned to the fact that employees have sick children, elderly parents who need care, and other family issues that may require special arrangements. For instance, summer can be a particularly difficult time for many working parents who need to find care for their children, so at Johnson & Johnson, employees can bring children to work, where they're picked up and dropped off for camp during the summer. At Mattel Inc. in El Segundo, California, the entire operation shuts down every Friday afternoon in order to give employees more time to spend with their children. Atlantic Richfield Company set up a toll-free line and staffed it with counselors to provide nationwide referrals to employees seeking care for elderly relatives.[80] Other companies have started on-site child care centers or implemented flexible working hours and job-sharing arrangements to try and help employees find an acceptable balance between the demands of work and family. For example, at Eddie Bauer Inc., a retailer based in Redmond, Washington, work-life programs have been designed to help employees lead more productive and balanced lives. These work-life programs include such things as on-site mammography exams, emergency child care services, and referral programs for employees experiencing problems with family relationships. Why did the company decide to provide these programs? It wanted to create a flexible work environment and an exceptional benefits package to attract top-notch employees to Eddie Bauer.[81] Other organizations, including First Tennessee Bank, Motorola, Eli Lilly, and Merrill Lynch, have experienced positive effects on productivity, employee loyalty, job satisfaction, and other performance measures when they instituted work-family strategies and programs.[82]

dual-career couples

Couples in which both partners have a professional, managerial, or administrative occupation.

Another family concern that arises is the large number of **dual-career couples**—couples in which both partners have a professional, managerial, or administrative occupation.[83] An organization's HRM policies need to reflect the special problems this situation creates for couples. Special attention needs to be given to the organization's policies regarding nepotism, relocations and transfers, and conflicts of interest.[84]

Andersen Consulting is a firm that has gone the extra mile in easing the lives of its employees. Among the many services it offers its people are ways to get household chores like dry cleaning done while employees are at work.

AIDS in the Workplace

AIDS is an issue in human resource management because of the profound impact it can have on the workplace and on employees.[85] Although many don't want to confront it, managers need to be prepared for dealing with HIV/AIDS-related issues in the workplace.[86]

Although the overall business community worldwide has been relatively slow in responding to the AIDS crisis, several U.S. companies have implemented HIV/AIDS policies and employee training and education programs. For example, Honeywell, Inc., has a well-publicized corporate policy on dealing with HIV/AIDS in the workplace and uses a number of educational forums to inform employees about HIV/AIDS issues. Another company that's been at the forefront of dealing with AIDS-related issues in the workplace is Levi Strauss & Company. Since 1987, it has sponsored AIDS awareness programs for employees. Other companies that have implemented AIDS programs include Polaroid Corporation, the Prudential Company, First Union National Bank, and Teradyne, Inc.

The goal of any workplace AIDS program should be to create an environment in which HIV-positive employees are not afraid to reveal their condition; where these individuals can continue to lead useful and productive lives; and where co-workers can ask questions, express concerns, and overcome their fear of working with individuals who are HIV-positive. What should a comprehensive AIDS program include? Experts suggest that it have the following components: (1) a workplace policy that includes adherence to applicable laws and regulations as well as provides guidelines for dealing with employees who may be HIV-positive; (2) training for managers, supervisors, and union leaders who may have HIV-positive employees within their work group; (3) employee education on AIDS-related issues; (4) family education programs and materials on AIDS and AIDS prevention; and (5) community involvement in AIDS education. In addition, any type of AIDS program requires the full commitment and support of top-level management in order to be effective.

---

16 **Why is managing workforce diversity an important HRM issue?**

17 **What is sexual harassment, and how can companies minimize the occurrences of sexual harassment at work?**

18 **How can organizations make their HRM programs and practices family friendly?**

managers respond to "a manager's dilemma"

MANAGER 1

In developing a sexual harassment prevention training program, it is important for Mr. Sadamori to incorporate and implement detailed actions to address several different areas of concern.

A complete program in harassment prevention should not be limited to sexual harassment, but must also include avoiding harassment related to race, religion, marital status, and physical or mental disabilities. The program must be designed to create awareness of what constitutes harassment and that the company maintains a zero-tolerance position on harassment. Employees must be trained in recognizing and reporting incidents that they deem may constitute harassment and that the same standards of the program apply to executives, managers, supervisors, and co-workers.

All employees should be required to complete the training as a condition of employment and sign documentation that they have received training, understand the policies, and agree to report any instances of harassment that they observe or are aware of. Investigations and interviews should be conducted in a timely manner once a complaint is made. Many times, companies that have suffered damages due to harassment claims do so not so much because an incident has occurred but more because no actions were taken to prevent or respond to the incident. Mr. Sadamori needs to make the seriousness of this harassment training clear to the managers.

Dennis Alexander, *General Manager, Sunrise Company dba Indian Ridge Country Club, Palm Desert, California*

MANAGER 2

First of all, I would introduce the group to American culture. The intent here is to demonstrate how an issue that they may consider trivial can be very serious in the United States. Then I would give them a package that would include information about the civil rights movement and other rights movements. The next phase would be a video about sexual harassment. The video should include definitions and examples of sexual harassment. The video should point out that sexual harassment is determined through the "eyes of the beholder." The third phase would include actual role playing. I would have the managers act out "do's" and "don'ts" of sexual harassment while the group critiques the actions. Finally, I would go over the company's sexual harassment policy—which should be one of zero tolerance. If the company doesn't have one, I would have the group create one.

T. J. Owens, *Ed.D., Dean of Student Services, Gavilan College, Gilroy, California*

for your
IMMEDIATE
action

WWC
WESTERN WASHINGTON CABLE

TO: Devon Miller, Director of Human Resources
FROM: Taylor Gillioz, President
SUBJECT: Company Sexual Harassment Policy

It has come to my attention that some of our employees don't have a clear understanding of what practices or actions constitute sexual harassment. As I'm sure you're well aware, this is an area where there can be no ambiguity. We need to take immediate action to remedy this situation.

I'd like for you to develop a one-page handout that describes what sexual harassment is, what constitutes acceptable and unacceptable behavior and talk, and any other information you think is pertinent to educating employees about sexual harassment. Please also develop a brief (one page or less) description of an appropriate procedure that employees could follow if they believe that they've been the victims of sexual harassment.

Please have this material to me by the end of the week.

This is a fictionalized account of a potentially real problem. It was written for academic purposes only.

SUMMARY

This summary is organized by the chapter-opening objectives found on p. 336.

1. Strategic human resource management is important because various studies have concluded that an organization's human resources—that is, its people—can be a significant source of competitive advantage. Achieving competitive success through people requires a fundamental change in how managers think about an organization's workforce and how they view the work relationship. It also means working with and through people and seeing them as partners, not just as costs to be minimized or avoided.

2. The human resource management process seeks to staff the organization and sustain high employee performance through human resource planning, recruitment or decruitment, selection, orientation, training, career development, compensation and benefits, and performance appraisal.

3. A job description is a written statement of what a jobholder does, how it is done, and why it is done. A job specification states the minimum acceptable qualifications that a jobholder must possess to perform a given job successfully.

4. Recruitment seeks to develop a pool of potential job candidates. Typical sources include an internal search, advertisements, employee referrals, employment agencies, school placement centers, and temporary help services. Decruitment reduces the labor supply within an organization through options such as firing, layoffs, attrition, transfers, reduced workweeks, and early retirements.

5. The quality of a selection device is determined by its validity and reliability. If a device is not valid, then no proven relationship exists between it and relevant job criteria. If a selection device is not reliable, it cannot be assumed to be a consistent measure.

6. Selection devices must match the job in question. Work samples work best with low-level jobs. Assessment centers work best for managerial positions. The validity of the interview as a selection device increases for progressively higher levels of management.

7. Employee training can be on the job or off the job. Popular on-the-job methods include job rotation, understudying, and apprenticeships. The more popular off-the-job methods are classroom lectures, films, and simulation exercises.

8. The main challenge of managing your personal career is recognizing the fact that you—not the organization—are responsible for your career! You have to prepare to do whatever is necessary to advance your career. You will take responsibility for designing, guiding, and developing your career. Your career will be driven by you, not by the organization.

9. HRM practices can facilitate workforce diversity by widening the recruitment net, eliminating any discriminatory selection practices, communicating to applicants the company's willingness to accommodate their needs, and providing employee training and education programs that focus on diversity.

10. Sexual harassment is a growing concern for management because it intimidates employees, interferes with job performance, and exposes the organization to liability.

THINKING ABOUT MANAGEMENT ISSUES

1. Are there moral limits on how far a prospective employer should delve into an applicant's personal life by means of interviews or tests? Explain.

2. Assume that you're the director of new product research for a company that has 75 employees and is expanding rapidly. What specific practices would you implement to recruit diverse individuals?

3. Should an employer have the right to choose employees without governmental interference? Support your conclusion.

4. A survey by the Human Resource Institute at Eckerd College in St. Petersburg, Florida, identi-
fied the following HR concerns for the year 2005: skill level of the workforce; managing change; information technology; aging of the workforce; quality of education; work ethic, values, and attitudes of workers; managing diversity; improving productivity; and employee communications.[87] Explain what role HRM might play in addressing each of these concerns.

5. Studies show that women's salaries still lag behind men's, and even with equal opportunity laws and regulations, women are paid about 72 percent of what men are paid. How would you design a compensation system that would address this issue?

SELF-ASSESSMENT EXERCISE

DIVERSITY QUESTIONNAIRE

Instructions: Place a number next to each question that best describes your own actions and beliefs.

1 = Almost always
2 = Frequently
3 = Sometimes
4 = Seldom
5 = Almost never

_____ 1. Do you recognize and challenge the perceptions, assumptions, and biases that affect your thinking?

_____ 2. Do you think about the impact of what you say or how you act before you speak or act?

_____ 3. Do you do everything you can to prevent the reinforcement of prejudices, including avoiding using negative stereotypes when you speak?

_____ 4. Do you demonstrate your respect for people who are not from the dominant culture by doing things that show you feel they are as competent and skilled as others, including handing them responsibility as often as you do others?

_____ 5. Do you encourage people who are not from the dominant culture to speak out on their concerns and respect those issues?

_____ 6. Do you speak up when someone is making racial, sexual, or other derogatory remarks or is humiliating another person?

_____ 7. Do you apologize when you realize you might have offended someone by inappropriate behavior or comments?

_____ 8. Do you try to know people as individuals not as representatives of specific groups and include different types of people in your peer group?

_____ 9. Do you accept the notion that people from all backgrounds need to socialize with and reinforce one another?

_____ 10. Do you do everything that you can to understand your own background and try to educate yourself about other backgrounds, including different communication styles?

See scoring key on page SK–4.

Source: Based on W. Sonnenschein, _The Practical Executive and Workforce Diversity_, (Lincolnwood, IL: NTC Business Books, 1997).

TAKE IT TO THE NET

We invite you to visit the Robbins/Coulter companion Web site at http://www.prenhall.com/robbinsmgt for this chapter's Internet resources.

CASE APPLICATION

Dream Team

Would you agree that an organization is nothing without its employees? If you do, then it would seem that the only sustainable competitive advantage an organization would have for the future would be its employees, right? That type of HRM philosophy has worked quite well for Rhino Foods Inc., a small specialty-dessert manufacturer in Burlington, Vermont.

Rhino Foods is not a giant corporation, but it has developed a strong competitive advantage that has enabled it to succeed despite continuing intense competition and other types of external challenges. Although the company has had its ups and downs, most of its financial and other types of organizational performance have been above average. What is the source of its competitive advantage? Rhino's founder and its other managers point to the company's 83-member workforce—its very own dream team! What does Rhino do differently? What types of HRM programs has Rhino implemented? Let's take a closer look.

The first place to look is at the company's purpose statement:

> The employees and families of Rhino Foods are its greatest assets. The company's relationship with its employees is founded on a climate of mutual trust and respect within an environment for listening and personal expression. Rhino Foods declares that it is a vehicle for people to get what they want.

The words that make up the purpose statement were chosen very carefully as a reflection of founder Ted Castle's philosophy about both the role of the organization and the role of the employee. For instance, the inclusion of "families" in the first sentence is a recognition that employees do lead lives outside the organization and that there is a mutual influence between an employee's home life and an employee's work life. Castle explained, "To try to say that one doesn't affect the other is putting blinders on." The next sentence in the company's purpose statement emphasizes the mutual trust and respect that the company feels are important. Management research has shown that this type of trusting relationship is important for high individual performance levels, which, in turn, lead to high organizational performance levels. If individuals aren't performing at their absolute best, it's extremely difficult, if not impossible, for an organization to perform at its absolute best. And finally, the last statement in the purpose reflects the belief that people who are good at getting what they want will be good at getting results, both at work and in their personal lives.

An HRM practice that symbolizes Rhino's belief about its employees' being the source of its competitive advantage is the strong use of employee empowerment—letting employees have significant control and say over what jobs they do and how they do them. In Rhino's case, the extent of the belief in the power of employee empowerment can be seen in the way managers handled a potential layoff in the mid-1990s. Instead of making an across-the-board decision about who would stay and who would be let go and announcing their decision to employees, the managers chose to let the employees decide how to handle it. What the employees came up with was truly an innovative solution. They chose to partner with local businesses that needed extra help at that time. Some employees went to Ben & Jerry's Homemade Inc. (a major customer of Rhino, which makes the chocolate chip cookie dough that goes into Ben & Jerry's ice cream). Others went to jobs at a local gardening products catalog firm. Castle promised the employees who "volunteered" to leave that their jobs would be waiting for them when they returned to Rhino, as long as they had fulfilled their duties to the best of their abilities at their temporary employers. What a unique idea! And it worked! When Rhino's sales picked up, the employees returned with a renewed sense of commitment to the organization because it hadn't just thoughtlessly and callously laid off its people. From that time, when Rhino employed only around 40 people, sales have grown enough to require its current staff of 83 people.

Finally, Rhino uses an unusual approach to challenging its employees. The company's philosophy is that "employees who challenge themselves personally see a difference professionally too." A unique program—called the "wants" program—has been in effect at Rhino for a few years to help employees challenge themselves. Employees are encouraged to set and achieve goals—no matter how intimidating those goals might be. In this program, a group of eight employees from all areas and levels in the company have been trained as wants coordinators. An employee can meet for an hour, one on one, with a wants coordinator on company time once every three months to set goals and discuss how to work on achieving those goals. The wants (goals) don't have to be work related. For instance, employees have dreamed about reuniting with a family member or learning to skydive. The point of the program is to challenge employees and show them that they can make things happen on their own. The wants coordinators have been carefully trained by the company's director of human resources, Marlene Dailey, to "coach" employees and not just give them answers. Dailey explains, "The more they (the employees) understand that they create their own world, whether it's here or at home, the more confidence they have in their abilities." The only problem with this program is that the company's increasing size has made it much more difficult to handle logistically. In fact, the company is beginning to look at developing a better way to meet the needs of its growing workforce. If Rhino's past developments are any indication, it will undoubtedly be a program that champions and supports its "dream team"!

QUESTIONS

1. What do you think Rhino's philosophy might be regarding the role of strategic human resource management? Explain.

2. On the basis of information included in the case, create a recruitment advertisement for a production line position that Rhino Foods might use.
3. How is Rhino Foods dealing with work-family issues?
4. Would Rhino Foods' approach to human resource management work in a company with 20,000 employees? Why or why not?

Source: T.H. Naylor, W.H. Willimon, and R. Osterberg, "The Search for Community in the Workplace," *Business and Society Review,* Spring 1995, pp. 42–47; and G. Flynn, "Why Rhino Won't Wait 'Til Tomorrow," *Personnel Journal,* July 1996, pp. 36–43.

VIDEO CASE APPLICATION

The Fine Art of Managing People

Every business has three basic components, or the three *P*s: the *product,* or service being provided; the *process,* or the way the product or service is being delivered; and the *people.* Of those three components, the most crucial is the people. Successful business owners are likely to say that the single most important factor in their business's success is the people. Although there's some science behind managing people, there's a lot of art as well. What do some successful businesspeople have to say about the fine art of managing people? Let's take a look!

Jeff Gordon, owner of an ad agency in Washington, D.C., says that recruitment is the single most important task of any business leader. He recruits full time, and he may have to sift through 150–300 people to get that one outstanding person. However, in his

business, he has to put that kind of effort into recruiting to identify the "gems" who are so critical to his company's success.

Jill and Doug Smith approached people management somewhat differently than what experts advise. They have developed their business, Buckeye Beans and Herbs of Spokane, Washington, using friends and family. And as Jill says, this approach can be either a tremendous negative or a tremendous positive. It's been a tremendous positive for their business because they all share similar values. In fact, she describes her business as a value-added people company.

When Dale Crownover, owner of Texas Name-Plate of Dallas, Texas, implemented a quality improvement program, he found that his employees wanted more communication opportunities. At the company's monthly meetings, regular employees (not just managers) get involved. Crownover says it's really all about sharing and communicating; letting employees know the goals, the plans, why we're doing what we're doing, and how we're doing. Very simply, he's found that employees want to be part of something.

Finally, Greg Thurman of Hartford Communication in Priest River, Idaho, says he doesn't tell people what to do but asks them what they think they should do to solve a problem. His goal was to create an environment in which people didn't feel stifled. As Thurman says, "I don't know every job as well as the people doing the job." Therefore, instead of telling them how to do their jobs, he encourages employees to look for answers and then together they "polish" a solution.

QUESTIONS

1. What "people" advice did each of the four business owners profiled give?
2. What's your opinion of the advice these business owners gave?
3. How could the advice that each of these business owners described help in the design of an organization's HRM programs and actions? Be specific.

Source: Based on *Small Business 2000, Show 413.*

A MANAGER'S DILEMMA

Change. It's a fact of life for organizations in today's fast-moving, competitive environment. One of the major types of change an organization might face is a merger with another organization. Merging two different organizational cultures and coping with the resulting changes can present interesting, and often difficult, managerial challenges.

In the dynamic telecommunications industry, for instance, forces for change are arising both externally and internally. When Southwestern Bell and Pacific Telesis Group merged in March 1997 (the new company goes by the name SBC Communications, Inc.), two companies whose cultures were more alike than not were brought together.[1] Both companies brought a strong commitment to a diverse workforce to the "marriage" since both served a widely diverse customer base in the two largest states in

their markets: Texas and California. In fact, SBC's combined workforce has a greater percentage of minority workers than the percentage in the national workforce. But even with similar organizational cultures, there was some uncertainty on the part of employees about the change and what it would mean to them. For instance, how would their job duties change? What would the performance appraisal system be like in the newly merged company? Would the same behaviors be rewarded? These were just a few of the change issues that SBC managers had to deal with.

Heriberto Guerra Jr. and Norma Martinez, two high-ranking managers at SBC, had to develop effective ways of managing changes associated with the merger. Guerra is managing director of corporate development and Martinez serves as vice president of diversity marketing. The most critical changes they had to cope with involved the expansion of employees' work duties that typically occur during mergers. Both managers wondered how they could use education and communication to reduce employees' resistance to change brought about by the merger. Put yourself in their situation. How would you educate your subordinates and communicate to them the importance and necessity of the impending changes in their work duties?

WHAT WOULD YOU DO?

The managerial challenges faced by Guerra and Martinez in preparing their employees for the changes brought about by their company's merger are certainly not unique. Big companies, small businesses, universities and colleges, state and city governments, and even the military are being forced to significantly change the way they do things. Although change has always been a part of the manager's job, it has become even more important in recent years. We'll describe why in this chapter. We'll also discuss ways in which managers can stimulate innovation and increase their organization's adaptability.

Managing Change and Innovation

WHAT IS CHANGE?

change

An alteration in people, structure, or technology.

If it weren't for **change**—that is, any alterations in people, structure, or technology—the manager's job would be relatively easy. Planning would be simple because tomorrow would be no different from today. The issue of effective organizational design would also be solved because the environment would be free from uncertainty and there would be no need to adapt. Similarly, decision making would be dramatically streamlined because the outcome of each alternative could be predicted with almost certain accuracy. It would, indeed, simplify the manager's job if, for example, competitors did not introduce new products or services, if customers didn't demand new and improved products, if governmental regulations were never modified, or if employees' needs never changed. But that's not the way it is. Change is an organizational reality. Handling change is an integral part of every manager's job. In this chapter, we address the key issues related to managing change.

FORCES FOR CHANGE

In chapter 3, we pointed out that there are both external and internal forces that constrain managers. These same forces also bring about the need for change. Let's briefly look at the factors that can create the need for change.

External Forces

The external forces that create the need for change come from various sources. In recent years, the *marketplace* has affected firms such as Dell Computer as competition from Gateway, Packard Bell, and Acer intensified in the battle for consumers' personal computer purchases. These companies constantly adapt to changing consumer desires as they develop new PCs and improve marketing strategies. *Governmental laws and regulations* are a frequent impetus for change. For example, the passage of the Americans with Disabilities Act required thousands of organizations (profit and not-for-profit) to reconfigure restrooms, add ramps, widen doorways, and take other actions to improve accommodations for persons with disabilities. Likewise, any national health care reform legislation that ultimately may be enacted by the U.S. Congress will, undoubtedly, bring changes in human resource management policies.

During the tenure of its late CEO Jerry Junkins, Texas Instruments had already begun a series of fundamental changes to cope with a disastrous fall in the price of its signature product, a specialized computer chip. Unexpectedly appointed CEO after Junkins's sudden death, Tom Engibous, pictured here, inherited a situation already in flux and determined that the best course was to speed up the changes. Says a market researcher in the industry, "Tom is bold....He's making things happen."

Market conditions, a major external force for change, almost caused a disaster at Pinnacle Brands, a company that gets 65 percent of its business from baseball trading cards. When baseball players went on strike, management asked employees to come up with new ideas to make and save money. The employees' ideas were worth $40 million in revenue.

Technology also creates the need for change. For example, recent developments in sophisticated and extremely expensive diagnostic equipment have created significant economies of scale for hospitals and medical centers. Assembly-line technology in other industries is undergoing dramatic changes as organizations replace human labor with robots. Even in the greeting card industry, the proliferation of electronic mail and the World Wide Web have influenced the way people send greeting cards. The fluctuation in *labor markets* forces managers to change. For instance, the demand for health care technicians and specialists has made it necessary for organizations that need those kinds of employees to change their human resource management activities to attract and retain skilled employees in the areas of greatest need.

Economic changes, of course, affect almost all organizations. For instance, recessionary pressures force organizations to become more cost efficient. But even in a robust economy, uncertainties about interest rates, federal budget deficits, and foreign trade create conditions that may force organizations to change.

Internal Forces

In addition to the external forces we described above, internal forces can also stimulate the need for change. These internal forces tend to originate primarily from the internal operations of the organization or from the impact of external changes.

A redefinition or modification of an organization's *strategy* often introduces a host of changes. For instance, when Harley-Davidson, the United States' major domestic motorcycle manufacturer, was forced to implement a turnaround strategy in order to survive, it made numerous changes in production, such as using strict product quality control processes and drastically modernizing its factories. In addition, an organization's *workforce* is rarely static. Its composition changes in terms of age, education, sex, and so forth. In a stable organization with an increasing number of older executives, for instance, there might be a need to restructure jobs in order to retain younger managers who occupy lower ranks. The compensation and benefits system might also need to be adapted to reflect the needs

Since it was founded in 1951, the Nature Conservancy has devoted its resources to buying and setting aside land to preserve threatened habitats and species around the world. CEO John Sawhill, a believer in change, has spearheaded major shifts in the company's mission since 1990. During that time, the group has had the fastest growth rate of any of its peers.

of an older workforce. The introduction of new *equipment* represents another internal force for change. Employees may have their jobs redesigned, need to undergo training on how to operate the new equipment, or be required to establish new interaction patterns within their work group. *Employee attitudes* such as increased job dissatisfaction may lead to increased absenteeism, more voluntary resignations, and even labor strikes. Such events will, in turn, often lead to changes in management policies and practices.

The Manager as Change Agent

Changes within an organization need a catalyst. People who act as catalysts and assume the responsibility for managing the change process are called **change agents.**

Any manager can be a change agent. As we review the information on change, we assume that it's initiated and carried out by a manager within the organization. However, the change agent could be a nonmanager—for example, an internal staff specialist or outside consultant whose expertise is in change implementation. For major systemwide changes, an organization will often hire outside consultants to provide advice and assistance. Because they're from the outside, they can offer an objective perspective that insiders may lack. However, outside consultants are usually at a disadvantage because they have an inadequate understanding of the organization's history, culture, operating procedures, and people. Outside consultants are also prone to initiate more drastic change than insiders would (which can be either a benefit or a disadvantage) because they don't have to live with the repercussions after the change is implemented. In contrast, internal managers who act as change agents may be more thoughtful (and possibly overly cautious) because they must live with the consequences of their decisions.

change agents

People who act as catalysts and manage the change process.

TESTING...
TESTING...

1 Why is handling change an integral part of every manager's job?

2 What internal and external forces create the need for organizations to change?

3 Who are change agents, and what role do they play in the change process?

The Entrepreneur as Change Agent

Of the many hats that the entrepreneur wears, the change agent hat is one of the most important.[2] When changes are needed in the entrepreneurial organization, it is the entrepreneur who first recognizes the need for change and acts as the catalyst, cheerleader, and chief change consultant.

Change isn't easy in any organization, but it can be particularly difficult for small, entrepreneurial organizations. Even if a person is comfortable with taking risks, as entrepreneurs usually are, change can be hard. That's why it's important for the entrepreneur to recognize the critical role he or she plays in implementing change.

As a change agent, the entrepreneur is, first and foremost, a catalyst for change. He or she should be alert to the signs that change is needed. Both external and internal forces can act upon the entrepreneurial organization, just as they do on other organizations. The complex and uncertain environment can create the need to change. And, often, the entrepreneur is the person who recognizes the need for change and directs it. For instance, at MRM Inc., a Detroit-based distributor of pneumatic components, Tony Rigato, the company's president, made some radical changes in the company's approach to selling products after one of the company's major suppliers began trying to dictate the prices MRM quoted to its customers. Rigato decided he needed to "reinvent" MRM and set about developing a new logo and slogan, retraining sales representatives, and redesigning a compensation program.

The entrepreneur also must act as cheerleader and coach while implementing change. Overcoming any resistance to change requires intense interpersonal efforts and support. The entrepreneurial organization may have a flexible and loose structure, so the entrepreneur may want to overcome employee resistance to change by using the behaviorally oriented techniques such as education and communication, participation, and facilitation and support. These approaches may work better than coercion, manipulation, and negotiation, which tend to pit sides against each other.

Finally, the entrepreneur acts as chief change consultant. Because the fees for outside consultants can be costly, an entrepreneur may need to facilitate and direct organizational change efforts. The advantage is that because of his or her intimate knowledge of the situation, any change efforts can be accurately designed. However, intimate knowledge of and close ties to his or her company may make the entrepreneur reluctant to enact broad sweeping changes, even if they are desperately needed. The entrepreneur wants to avoid being overly cautious in developing appropriate change efforts. ■

ENTREPRENEURSHIP

TWO VIEWS OF THE CHANGE PROCESS

We can use two very different metaphors to describe the change process.[3] One metaphor envisions the organization as a large ship crossing a calm sea. The ship's captain and crew know exactly where they're going because they've made the trip many times before. Change comes in the form of an occasional storm, a brief distraction in an otherwise calm and predictable trip. In the other metaphor, the organization is seen as a small raft navigating a raging river with uninterrupted white-water rapids. Aboard the raft are half-a-dozen people who have never worked together before, who are totally unfamiliar with the river, who are unsure of their eventual destination, and who, as if things weren't bad enough, are traveling in pitch-dark night. In the white-water rapids metaphor, change is a natural state, and managing change is a continual process. These two metaphors present very different approaches to understanding and responding to change. Let's take a closer look at each one.

The Calm Waters Metaphor

Until very recently, the calm waters metaphor dominated the thinking of academics and practicing managers. It's best illustrated by Kurt Lewin's three-step description of the change process.[4] (See Figure 12-1.)

According to Lewin, successful change requires *unfreezing* the status quo, *changing* to a new state, and *refreezing* to make the change permanent. The status quo can be considered an equilibrium state. To move from this equilibrium, unfreezing is necessary. It can be achieved in one of three ways:

1. Increase the *driving forces,* which direct behavior away from the status quo.

2. Decrease the *restraining forces,* which hinder behavior away from the status quo.

3. Combine the two approaches.

Once unfreezing has been accomplished, the change itself can be implemented. However, the mere introduction of change doesn't ensure that the change will take hold. The new situation needs to be *refrozen* so that it can be sustained over time. Unless this last step is done, there's a very strong chance that the change will be short lived and employees will revert to the original equilibrium state. The objective of refreezing, then, is to stabilize the new situation by balancing the driving and restraining forces.

Note how Lewin's three-step process treats change simply as a break in the organization's equilibrium state. The status quo has been disturbed, and change is necessary to establish a new equilibrium state. This view was probably appropriate to the relatively calm environment that most organizations faced from the 1950s to the 1970s. However, this calm waters metaphor is obsolete as a way to describe the kind of seas that managers in today's organizations have to navigate.

The White-Water Rapids Metaphor

The white-water rapids metaphor is consistent with our discussion of uncertain and dynamic environments in chapter 3. It's consistent with Mintzberg's observation, discussed in chapter 1, that the manager's job is one of constant interruptions. It's also consistent with the dynamics that are characteristic of going from an industrial society to a world dominated by information and ideas.

To get a feeling for what managing change might be like when you have to continually maneuver in uninterrupted rapids, consider attending a college that had the following rules: Courses vary in length. Unfortunately, when you sign up, you don't know how long a course will run. It might go for two weeks or 30 weeks. Furthermore, the instructor can end a course any time he or she wants, with no prior warning. If that isn't bad enough, the length of the class changes each time it meets: sometimes the class lasts 20 minutes; other times

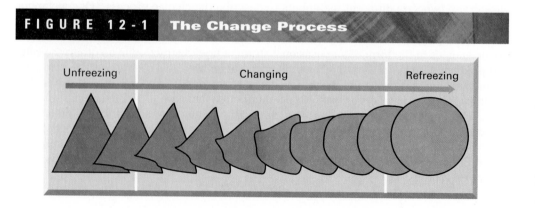

FIGURE 12-1   The Change Process

Unfreezing   Changing   Refreezing

Constant improvement defines the business condition of white-water change at Herman Miller's SQA Division. Management has created 30 percent annual growth by making enormous changes in the division's mission, physical surroundings, and work environment. Michael Volkema, CEO, presides over the white-water-rapids environment at SQA, which stands for "Simple, Quick, and Affordable."

it runs for three hours. And the time of the next class meeting is set by the instructor during this class. And there's one more thing. All exams are unannounced, so you have to be ready for a test at any time. To succeed in this college, you would have to be incredibly flexible and able to respond quickly to every changing condition. Students who were overly structured, "slow" to respond, or uncomfortable with change would not survive.

A growing number of managers is coming to accept that their job is much like what a student would face in such a college. The stability and predictability of the calm water metaphor do not exist. Disruptions in the status quo are not occasional and temporary, and they are not followed by a return to calm waters. Many managers never get out of the rapids. They face constant change, bordering on chaos. These managers are being forced to play a game they have never played before, and the game is governed by rules that are created as the game progresses.[5]

Is the white-water rapids metaphor an exaggeration? No! Take the case of Converse Inc., of North Reading, Massachusetts.[6] In the intensely competitive athletic shoe business, a company has to be prepared for any possibility. Kids (a major target market for athletic shoes) are no longer content with updated sneaker styles every few years. They want new and unique styles more often. Large megaretailers who sell the shoes are demanding more from manufacturers such as holding more inventory, replenishing supplies faster, and helping find ways to sell more shoes. And competition is hot! Industry leaders Nike and Reebok are meters ahead of other industry competitors. Converse knew that if it wanted to remain in business and be successful, it had to change. Company managers decided on a series of changes ranging from reviving its once-popular Chuck Taylor line of canvas basketball shoes to signing new spokespersons to implementing a companywide TQM program. These types of significant organizational changes were essential for Converse to survive the white-water rapids environment in which it operates.

Putting the Two Views in Perspective

Does *every* manager face a world of constant and chaotic change? No, but the number of managers who don't is dwindling rapidly. Managers in such businesses as computer software and women's high-fashion clothing have long confronted a world of white-water rapids. These managers used to look enviously at their counterparts in industries such as auto manufacturing, oil exploration, banking, publishing, and air transportation, who historically faced a stable and predictable environment. There might have been cause for their envy in the 1960s, but there certainly isn't today!

Today, an organization that treats change as the occasional disturbance in an otherwise calm and stable world is running a great risk. Too much is changing too fast for any organization or its managers to be complacent. Most competitive advantages last only a short time—often less than 18 months. People Express Airlines—a no-frills, no-reservations-needed company—is a good example. It was once described in the business news as the model "new look" firm; it went bankrupt a short time later. As Tom Peters has aptly noted, the old saying "If it ain't broke, don't fix it" no longer applies. In its place, he suggests, "If it ain't broke, you just haven't looked hard enough. Fix it anyway."[7]

ORGANIZATIONAL INERTIA AND RESISTANCE TO CHANGE

As change agents, managers should be motivated to initiate change because they are committed to improving their organization's effectiveness. However, change can be a threat to managers. Of course, change can be a threat to nonmanagerial people as well. Organizations can build up inertia that motivates people to resist changing their status quo, even though change might be beneficial. In this section, we will review why people in organizations resist change and what can be done to lessen their resistance.

Resistance to Change

It has been said that most people hate any change that doesn't jingle in their pockets. This resistance to change is well documented.[8] Why do people resist change? An individual is likely to resist change for three reasons: uncertainty, concern over personal loss, and the belief that the change is not in the organization's best interest.[9]

Changes replace the known with ambiguity and uncertainty. Regardless of how much you may dislike attending college, at least you know what to do. You know what's expected of you. When you leave college for the world of full-time employment, regardless of how eager you are to get out of college, you'll trade the known for the unknown. Employees in organizations are faced with similar uncertainty. For example, when quality control methods based on sophisticated statistical models are introduced into manufacturing plants, many quality control inspectors will have to learn the new methods. Some inspectors may fear that they will be unable to do so. They may, therefore, develop a negative attitude toward statistical control techniques or behave dysfunctionally if required to use them.

The second cause of resistance is the fear of losing something already possessed. Change threatens the investment you've already made in the status quo. The more people have invested in the current system, the more they resist change. Why? They fear the loss of status, money, authority, friendships, personal convenience, or other benefits that they value. This explains why older employees tend to resist change more than younger ones. Older employees have generally invested more in the current system and therefore have more to lose by changing.

A final cause of resistance is a person's belief that the change is incompatible with the goals and best interests of the organization. An employee who believes that a new job procedure proposed by a change agent will reduce productivity or product quality can be expected to resist the change. If the employee expresses his or her resistance positively (perhaps by clearly expressing it to the change agent, along with substantiation), the resistance can be beneficial to the organization.

Techniques for Reducing Resistance

When managers see resistance to change as dysfunctional, what actions can they take? Six tactics have been suggested for use by managers or other change agents in dealing with resistance to change.[10]

Interview with Larry Lim, Executive Director, Lynton Consulting Services, Singapore

Describe your job.

I'm chief executive of Lynton Consulting Services and am responsible for the total performance of the company. This includes all aspects of planning, directing, and reporting and any accountability to the board of directors.

What types of skills do you think tomorrow's managers will need?

There are three that I think will be important. First, total human relationship and public relations skills. Next, cross-cultural management techniques will be important, particularly with the increased globalization of business. Finally, I think the ability to change mind-sets—creativity and originality in generating ideas—will be important.

How do you manage the significant changes that face your organization?

1. Initiate "learning company concept"—that is, a commitment to embrace change through education and training.
2. Empower staff members to make decisions and be responsible for what they have decided.
3. Form "fast track" teams.
4. Place staff members as owners and members of the organization and not as mere employees on fixed pay scales getting the usual benefits and bonuses.

How do you try to be innovative and creative in your job?

I believe in organic organizational structures, which facilitate the flexibility and free flow of ideas among staffers. In addition, I have tried to build an innovative culture in which successes and failures are rewarded and tolerated and mistakes are celebrated. Finally, I think it's important to build and foster the "learning company" concept, in which members learn and relearn all the time to remain current, relevant, competitive, and be fit for tomorrow's world. ■

Education and Communication.   Resistance can be reduced by communicating with employees to help them see the logic of a change. This tactic assumes that the source of resistance stems from misinformation or poor communication: If employees receive the full facts and have any misunderstandings clarified, they will no longer resist the change. Employees can be educated through one-on-one discussions, memos, group meetings, or reports. Does this tactic work? It does, provided that the source of resistance is inadequate communication and that management-employee relations are characterized by mutual trust and credibility. If those conditions don't exist, the tactic is unlikely to succeed. Moreover, the time and effort that this approach requires must be weighed against its advantages, particularly when the change affects a large number of people.

Participation.   It's difficult for individuals to resist a change decision in which they participated. Before a change is made, those who are opposed can be brought into the decision process. Assuming that the participants have the expertise to make a meaningful contribution, their involvement can reduce resistance, obtain commitment to seeing the change succeed, and increase the quality of the change decision. However, this technique has its disadvantages: the possibility of a poor solution and the amount of time it takes.

Facilitation and Support.   Change agents can offer a range of supportive efforts to reduce resistance. When employees' fears and anxiety are high, employee counseling and therapy, new skills training, or a short paid leave of absence might facilitate adjustment. The drawback of this tactic, as in the others we've just discussed, is that it's time consuming. Furthermore, it's expensive, and its implementation offers no assurance of success.

Negotiation.   Another way for the change agent to deal with potential resistance to change is to exchange something of value for a reduction in the resistance. For instance, if the resistance is centered in a few powerful individuals, a specific reward package can be negotiated that will meet their individual needs. Negotiation as a tactic may be necessary when resistance comes from a powerful source, such as a union. Yet you cannot ignore its potentially high costs. There's also the risk that a change agent who has once negotiated in exchange for lessened resistance is open to the possibility of being blackmailed by others with power.

Manipulation and Cooptation.   *Manipulation* refers to covert attempts to influence. Twisting and distorting facts to make them appear more attractive, withholding damaging information, and creating false rumors to get employees to accept a change are all examples of manipulation. For instance, if managers threaten to close a particular manufacturing plant if the employees don't accept an across-the-board pay cut, when they actually have no intention of doing so, they're using manipulation. *Cooptation* is a form of both manipulation and participation. It seeks to "buy off" the leaders of a resistance group by giving them a key role in the change decision. The leaders' advice is sought, not to arrive at a better decision but to get their endorsement. Both manipulation and cooptation are relatively inexpensive and easy ways to gain the support of adversaries, but the tactics can fail miserably if the targets become aware that they're being tricked or used. Once the deception has been discovered, the change agent's credibility may drop to zero.

Coercion.   Last on the list of tactics is *coercion*—that is, using direct threats or force on the resisters. Managers who are really determined to close a manufacturing plant if employees don't agree to a pay cut are using coercion. Other examples of coercion include threats of transfer, loss of promotions, negative performance evaluations, or a poor letter of recommendation. The advantages of coercion are approximately the same as those of manipulation and cooptation. The major disadvantage of this method is that coercion very often is illegal. Even legal coercion tends to be seen as bullying and can completely undermine a change agent's credibility.

TESTING... TESTING...
1 **2** **3**

4 Contrast the calm-waters metaphor and the white-water rapids metaphor of change.

5 Why do people resist change?

6 Describe the techniques for reducing resistance to change.

TECHNIQUES FOR MANAGING CHANGE

What *can* a manager change? The manager's options for change essentially fall into three categories: structure, technology, and people (Figure 12-2). Changing *structure* includes any alteration in authority relations, coordination mechanisms, degree of centralization, job redesign, or similar structural variables. Changing *technology* encompasses modifications in the way work is performed or the methods and equipment that are used. Changing *people* refers to changes in employee attitudes, expectations, perceptions, and behavior.

Changing Structure

In chapter 10, we discussed structural issues. Managers were described as having responsibility for such organizing activities as choosing the organization's formal design, allocating authority, and determining the degree of decentralization that would prevail. Once those structural decisions have been made, however, they aren't set in concrete. Changing conditions demand changes in the structure. As a result, the manager, in his or her role as change agent, might need to modify the structure.

What options does the manager have for changing structure? Essentially the same ones we introduced in our discussion of structure and design. A few examples should make these options clearer. Recall from chapter 10 that an organization's structure is defined in terms of work specialization, departmentalization, chain of command, span of control, centralization and decentralization, and formalization. Managers can alter one or more of these *structural components*. For instance, departmental responsibilities can be combined, vertical layers removed, and spans of control widened to make the organization flatter and less bureaucratic. Or more rules and procedures could be implemented to increase standardization. An increase in decentralization can be used to speed up the decision-making process. For instance, AT&T's top management eliminated a fourth of the company's pay-

FIGURE 12-2   Three Categories of Change

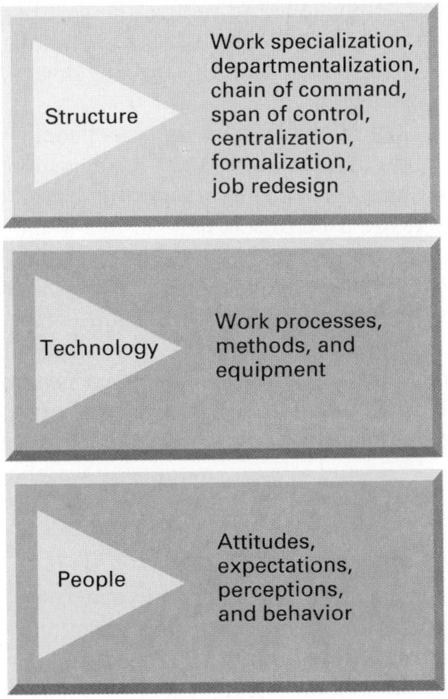

Structure — Work specialization, departmentalization, chain of command, span of control, centralization, formalization, job redesign

Technology — Work processes, methods, and equipment

People — Attitudes, expectations, perceptions, and behavior

roll, cut several levels out of the hierarchy, widened spans, and decentralized decision making into new operating units. Organizational downsizing efforts involve changes in structure, and we will discuss the challenges of managing downsizing later in this chapter.

Another option would be to introduce major changes in the actual *structural design.* For instance, the merger between Southwestern Bell and Pacific Telesis Group described in the chapter-opening Manager's Dilemma involved structural design changes. Or structural design changes might include a shift from a functional to a product structure or the creation of a project structure design. Polaroid Corporation, for example, replaced its traditional functional structure with a new design that arranged work around cross-functional teams. Semco S/A, a Brazilian manufacturing company that specializes in marine and food-service equipment, implemented an even more radical change in its structural design.[11] In the company's manufacturing plants, some workers are full-time Semco employees, some work for Semco part-time, some work for themselves and supply Semco with components or services, some work for themselves under contract to outside companies, and some work for each other. The employees bid on contracts for doing work. What's the benefit for the company? It's able to respond more efficiently and effectively to rapid and uncertain changes in the marketplace. The benefit for employees: Many avoided being laid off, and now, by essentially being private "entrepreneurs," they have a chance to earn significantly more money.

Changing Technology

Managers can also change the technology used to convert inputs into outputs. Most early studies in management—such as the work of Taylor and the Gilbreths—dealt with efforts aimed at technological change. If you recall, scientific management sought to implement changes that would increase production efficiency based on time-and-motion studies. Today, major technological changes usually involve the introduction of new equipment, tools, or methods; automation; or computerization.

Competitive factors or new innovations within an industry often require managers to introduce *new equipment, tools,* or *operating methods.* For example, U.S. aluminum companies such as Alcoa and Reynolds have significantly modernized their plants to compete more effectively against foreign manufacturers. More efficient handling equipment, furnaces, and presses have been installed to reduce the cost of manufacturing aluminum. Even the U.S. Army applied updated technology to its operations, including such advancements as a simulated three-dimensional shootout training device and electronic mail capability among troops on the battlefield.[12]

Automation is a technological change that replaces people with machines. It began in the Industrial Revolution and continues today as a management option. Automation has been introduced (and sometimes resisted) in organizations such as the U.S. Postal Service where automatic mail sorters are used to sort mail, or in automobile assembly lines, where robots do jobs that blue-collar workers used to perform.

Probably the most visible technological changes in recent years, though, have come through managers' efforts to expand *computerization.* Most organizations now have sophisticated information systems. For instance, grocery stores and numerous other retailers use scanners linked to computers that provide instant inventory information. Also, it's very uncommon to find an office today that is not computerized. For example, Benetton Group SpA uses computers to link together its manufacturing plants outside Treviso, Italy, with the company's sales outlets and a highly automated warehouse that employs only 19 people to handle 30,000 boxes a day.[13]

organizational development (OD)

Techniques to change people and the quality of interpersonal work relationships.

Changing People

Since the 1960s, academic researchers and practicing managers have become increasingly interested in helping individuals and groups within organizations work together more effectively. The term **organizational development (OD)**, though occasionally referring to all types of change, essentially focuses on techniques or programs to change people and the

New technology has made truckers, formerly independent, some of the most closely watched U.S. employees. Satellites enable managers to track trucks continuously, and electronic engines can be regulated not to exceed set speed limits. Says Robert Low, president of QUALCOMM Inc., "The successful carriers of the future are going to think of better ways to provide total services to the shipper and receiver through this type of technology."

nature and quality of interpersonal work relationships.[14] The most popular OD techniques are shown in Figure 12-3. The common thread in these techniques is that each seeks to bring about changes in or among the organization's human resources.

FIGURE 12-3   **Organizational Development Techniques**

sensitivity training

A method of changing behavior through unstructured group interaction.

Sensitivity training is a method of changing behavior through unstructured group interaction. The group is made up of a professional behavioral scientist and a set of participants. There's no specified agenda. The professional, who isn't to function as the group leader, merely creates the opportunity for participants to express their ideas and feelings. The discussion is free and open. Participants can bring up any topic they like. What evolves is a discussion that focuses on the individual participants and their interactive processes.

The research evidence on the effectiveness of sensitivity training as a change technique shows mixed results. On the positive side, sensitivity training appears to stimulate short-term improvement in communication skills, to improve perceptual accuracy, and to increase a person's willingness to use participation.[15] The impact of these changes on job performance, however, is not known,[16] and the technique is not immune from psychological risks.[17]

survey feedback

A technique for assessing attitudes and perceptions, identifying discrepancies in these attitudes and perceptions, and resolving the differences by using survey information in feedback groups.

Survey feedback is a technique for assessing the attitudes and perceptions of organizational members, identifying discrepancies in those attitudes and perceptions, and resolving the differences by communicating survey information in feedback groups. A questionnaire is typically completed by all members of an organization or work unit. It asks members for their perceptions and attitudes on a broad range of topics such as decision-making practices, communication effectiveness, coordination between units, and satisfaction with the organization, job, peers, and immediate manager. Data from the questionnaire are tabulated and distributed to the relevant employees, and the information obtained becomes a catalyst for identifying problems and clarifying issues that may be creating difficulties for people.

process consultation

Help given by an outside consultant to a manager in perceiving, understanding, and acting upon process events.

In **process consultation**, an outside consultant helps the manager to "perceive, understand, and act upon process events" with which he or she must deal.[18] These might include, for example, work flows, informal relationships among unit members, and formal communication channels. The consultant gives the manager insight into what's going on. The consultant isn't there to solve the manager's problem. Rather, the consultant acts as a coach to help the manager diagnose which interpersonal processes need improvement. If the manager, with the help of the consultant, can't solve the problem, the consultant will help the manager locate an expert who has the appropriate knowledge.

team building

Interaction among members of work teams to learn how each member thinks and works.

In **team building**, work team members interact to learn how each member thinks and works. Through high interaction, team members learn to increase trust and openness. Activities that might be included in a team-building program include group goal setting, development of positive interpersonal relations among team members, role analysis to clarify each member's role and responsibilities, and team process analysis. This process has become particularly important in organizations that have moved to a team-based structure.

intergroup development

Changing the attitudes, stereotypes, and perceptions that work groups have about each other.

The attempt to change the attitudes, stereotypes, and perceptions that members of work groups have about each other is called **intergroup development**. For example, if two groups have a history of strained work relationships, they can meet independently to develop lists of their perceptions of themselves, of the other group, and of how they believe the other group perceives them. The groups then share their lists and discuss similarities and differences. Differences are clearly articulated, the groups look for the causes of the differences, and efforts are made to develop solutions that will improve relations between the groups.

TESTING... TESTING...

7 What options does a manager have for changing an organization's structure?

8 How has changing technology influenced organizational change?

9 Describe the different OD techniques.

Preparing for a Changing Workplace

Face it: The only constant thing about change is that it's constant. These days, you don't have the luxury of dealing with change only once in a while. No, in fact, the workplace seems to change almost continuously. How can you cope with and take advantage of what seems to a hopelessly chaotic situation? Before you throw your hands up in frustration, let's look at some ways you can deal with the demands of a constantly changing workplace.[19]

Being prepared is not a credo just for the Boy Scouts; it should be your motto for dealing with a workplace that is constantly changing. What do we mean by "being prepared"? It means taking the initiative and being responsible for your own personal career development. Rather than depending on your organization to provide you with career development and training opportunities, do it yourself. Take advantage of continuing education or graduate courses at local colleges. Sign up for workshops and seminars that can help you enhance your skills. Upgrading your skills to keep them current is one of the most important things you can do to cope with a changing workplace.

It is also important for you to be a positive force when faced with workplace changes. We don't mean that you should automatically accept any change that's being implemented. If you think that a proposed change isn't appropriate or won't be effective, voice your opposition in a constructive manner. Being constructive may mean providing an alternative to what is being suggested. However, if you feel that the change is beneficial, support it.

The changes that an organization makes in response to a dynamic environment can be overwhelming and stressful. But you can contend with a changing workplace by being prepared and by being a positive force for change. ■

MANAGING YOUR CAREER

CONTEMPORARY ISSUES IN MANAGING CHANGE

Today's change issues—altering organizational cultures, implementing TQM, reengineering, managing downsizing, and handling employee stress—will continue to be critical concerns for managers during the early years of the twenty-first century.

- What can managers do to change an organizational culture when that culture no longer supports the organization's mission?

- How do managers implement a continuous change program such as TQM?

- What implications for changing structure, technology, and people are associated with reengineering and downsizing efforts?

- What can managers do to help employees handle the stress created by today's competitive environment?

In this section, we'll look at each of these issues and discuss what actions managers should consider for dealing with them.

Changing Organizational Cultures

The fact that an organization's culture is made up of relatively stable and permanent characteristics (see chapter 3) tends to make that culture very resistant to change.[20] A culture takes a long time to form, and once established it tends to become entrenched. Strong cultures, such as IBM or Sears, are particularly resistant to change because employees have become so committed to them. For instance, when Arthur Martinez was brought in as Sears's CEO, he had a difficult time changing the ingrained Sears culture. He described it as a "very uptight, self-absorbed, role-conscious, and title-conscious imperial system."[21] However, he continued to make cultural changes slowly, yet deliberately. If, over time, a certain culture

becomes inappropriate to an organization and a handicap to management, there might be little a manager can do to change it, especially in the short run. Even under the most favorable
conditions, cultural changes have to be viewed in years, not weeks or months.

Understanding the Situational Factors.   What "favorable conditions" might facilitate cultural change? The evidence suggests that cultural change is most likely to take place
when most or all of the following conditions exist:

- *A dramatic crisis occurs.* This can be the shock that undermines the status quo and
  calls into question the relevance of the current culture. Examples are a surprising
  financial setback, the loss of a major customer, or a dramatic technological innovation
  by a competitor.

- *Leadership changes hands.* New top leadership, who can provide an alternative set
  of key values, may be perceived as more capable of responding to the crisis than the
  old leaders were. Top leadership includes the organization's chief executive but might
  include all senior management positions.

- *The organization is young and small.* The younger the organization, the less
  entrenched its culture. Similarly, it is easier for management to communicate new values in a small organization than in a large one.

- *The culture is weak.* The more widely held a culture and the higher the agreement
  among members on its overall values, the more difficult it will be to change.
  Conversely, weak cultures are more receptive to change than are strong ones.[22]

These situational factors help to explain why a company such as Sears had difficulty
reshaping its culture. For the most part, employees didn't perceive their company's day-to-
day problems as critical. "New" leadership had in the past been more in name than in substance. Top managers at Sears had been long-term veterans of the company, steeped in the
organization's established culture. And finally, Sears is neither young nor small, and it's definitely not a weak culture.

How Can Cultural Change Be Accomplished?   Now we ask the question: If conditions are right, how do managers go about enacting a cultural change? The challenge is to
unfreeze the current culture. No single action is likely to have the impact necessary to
unfreeze something that's so ingrained and highly valued. Thus, there needs to be a comprehensive and coordinated strategy for managing cultural change, as shown in Table 12-1.

The best place to begin is with a cultural analysis.[23] This would include a cultural audit
to assess the current culture, a comparison of the present culture with the culture that is

TABLE 12-1   The Road to Cultural Change

- Conduct a cultural analysis to identify cultural elements needing change.
- Make it clear to employees that the organization's survival is legitimately
  threatened if change is not forthcoming.
- Appoint new leadership with a new vision.
- Initiate a reorganization.
- Introduce new stories and rituals to convey the new vision.
- Change the selection and socialization processes and the evaluation and
  reward systems to support the new values.

desired, and an analysis of the "gap" to identify what cultural elements specifically need changing.

We've discussed the importance of a dramatic crisis as a means to unfreeze an entrenched culture. Unfortunately, crises aren't always evident to all members of the organization. It might be necessary for managers to make the crisis more visible. It's important that everyone throughout the organization recognize that survival is at stake. If employees don't see the urgency for change, it's unlikely that a strong culture will respond to change efforts.

The appointment of a new top executive is likely to dramatize that major changes are going to take place. He or she can serve as a new role model and offer new standards of behavior. However, this executive needs to introduce his or her new vision of the organization quickly and to fill key management positions with individuals who are loyal to that vision.

Along with a shakeup of key management personnel, it also makes sense to initiate a reorganization. The creation of new units, the combination of some, and the elimination of others conveys, in very visible terms, that managers are determined to move the organization in new directions. For instance, Oy Nokia, a Finnish company best known for its toilet paper and galoshes, has become a leading player in the global cellular phone market. This transformation required a major shakeup of its corporate culture to change from an old "smokestack" company to a high-tech telecommunications superpower.[24] The CEO ousted "old guard" managers and brought in a new group of younger managers who were more in favor of change. In addition, entrepreneurial, risk-seeking new product ventures by employees were encouraged and rewarded throughout the company. Without these drastic cultural changes, it's unlikely that Nokia could have become even a strong competitor in a dynamic, high-tech industry.

New leaders brought into an organization will want to move quickly also to create new stories and rituals to replace those that were previously used to convey to employees the organization's dominant values. Delays will allow the old culture to become associated with the new leadership, thus closing the window of opportunity for change. Finally, managers will want to change the selection and socialization processes and the evaluation and reward systems to support employees who embrace the new values that are sought.

The preceding suggestions, of course, provide no guarantee that change efforts will succeed. Organizational members don't quickly let go of values that they understand and that have worked well for them in the past. Managers must, therefore, be patient. Change, if it comes, will be slow. And managers must keep constantly alert to protect against any

Successfully coping with a rapidly changing environment demands managers who aren't afraid to make changes. Many managers at Chrysler Corporation represent a new breed of auto industry managers: people with advanced degrees, technical know-how, and humanistic management techniques.

MANAGING WORKFORCE DIVERSITY

The Paradox of Diversity

When organizations bring diverse individuals into an organization and socialize them into the culture, a paradox is created.[25] Managers want these new employees to accept the organization's core cultural values. Otherwise, the employees may have a difficult time fitting in or being accepted. At the same time, managers want to openly acknowledge, embrace, and show support for the diverse perspectives and ideas that these employees bring to the workplace.

Strong organizational cultures put considerable pressure on employees to conform, and the range of acceptable values and styles of behavior is limited. Therein lies the paradox. Organizations hire diverse individuals because of their unique strengths, yet their diverse behaviors and strengths are likely to diminish in strong cultures as people attempt to fit in.

A manager's challenge in this paradox of diversity is to balance two conflicting goals: to encourage employees to accept the organization's dominant values and to encourage employees to accept differences. When changes are made in the organization's culture, managers need to remember the importance of keeping diversity alive. ■

return to old, familiar practices and traditions. For instance, Nissan Motor Corporation USA set out to change the way it sold cars.[26] For years, the company's culture had been manufacturer-driven, producing whatever it wanted. Then it became dealer-driven; dealers played a key role in deciding how things would be done. However, given the realities of the marketplace and the many ways that customers can now buy cars (for example, over the Internet, through a broker, or through megadealers such as CarMax), Nissan saw a need to change its culture toward being more customer focused. It initiated the cultural change process by offering monetary incentives to dealers who got positive reviews on customer satisfaction surveys. But company managers felt that this tactic did not give the new culture a big enough push. Now the company is giving its best dealers a larger territory and helping them meet customers' needs better through services such as faster loan processing. All in all, the cultural change at Nissan has taken time to implement. Yet, CEO Bob Thomas is committed to a successful cultural change, however long it takes.

Implementing TQM

Total quality management (TQM) is essentially a continuous, incremental change program. It is compatible with the calm waters metaphor because TQM recognizes that organizations must continuously find ways to navigate the problems that arise as they strive to improve. In this section, we draw on our knowledge of change processes to consider how managers can effectively implement TQM.

First, let's briefly review the key components of TQM. You'll remember that it focuses on customer needs, emphasizes participation and teamwork, and seeks to create a culture in which all employees strive to continuously improve such activities and outputs as the quality of the organization's products or services, customer response time, or work processes. It might be helpful to look at TQM in terms of the three areas toward which managers can direct change efforts: structure, technology, and people (Figure 12-4).

Focusing the Change Effort.   The *structure* of an organization that expects to implement TQM successfully will need to be decentralized; will have minimal organizational levels, wide spans of control, and limited work specialization; and will support cross-functional teams. These structural design options give employees the authority and means to implement process improvements. For instance, the creation of work teams that cut across departmental lines allows the people who are closest to a problem and who understand it best to solve that problem. In addition, cross-functional teams encourage cooperative problem solving rather than "us-versus-them" finger pointing.

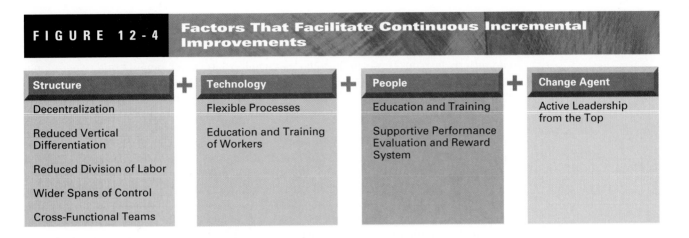

FIGURE 12-4 **Factors That Facilitate Continuous Incremental Improvements**

Structure		Technology		People		Change Agent
Decentralization	+	Flexible Processes	+	Education and Training	+	Active Leadership from the Top
Reduced Vertical Differentiation		Education and Training of Workers		Supportive Performance Evaluation and Reward System		
Reduced Division of Labor						
Wider Spans of Control						
Cross-Functional Teams						

The primary emphasis of *technology* change in TQM is directed at developing flexible processes to support continuous improvement. Employees committed to TQM are constantly looking for things to fix. Thus, work processes must be adaptable to continual change and fine tuning. To achieve this goal, TQM requires an extensive commitment to educating and training workers. The organization must provide employees with training in skills such as problem solving, decision making, negotiation, statistical analysis, and team building.[27] For example, employees need to be able to analyze and interpret data. An organization with a TQM program should provide work teams with quality data such as failure rates, reject rates, and scrap rates. It should provide feedback data on customer satisfaction. It should give the teams the necessary information to create and monitor process control charts. And, of course, the structure should empower the work teams to make continual improvements in the operations on the basis of process control data.

The *people* dimension of TQM requires a workforce committed to the organization's objectives of quality and continual improvement. This goal, too, necessitates proper education and training. It also demands a performance evaluation and reward system that supports and encourages TQM objectives. In addition, successful programs put quality objectives into bonus plans for executives and incentives for operating employees.[28] For instance, the implementation of L.L. Bean's TQM program was totally focused on employee development, the development of new roles for managers, and the creation of a system for communicating that role. Since the introduction of the TQM system, the company has improved its profitability, boosted customer satisfaction, enhanced safety, and reduced order backlogs.[29]

Role of the Change Agent.   Studies of successful TQM programs consistently demonstrate that these programs require active and strong leadership from the CEO.[30] It's that person who sets the vision and continually conveys the message. For instance, Larry Bossidy, CEO of AlliedSignal, Inc., says that he continually reminds his employees of the importance of customer satisfaction, continuous improvement, and employee involvement, the core elements of the company's TQM program.[31]

10 What situational factors might facilitate cultural change in an organization?

11 How can cultural change be implemented?

12 What change efforts might be associated with implementing a TQM program?

TESTING...
TESTING...

1 2 3

Reengineering

The historical role of change agents in organizations was to fix and improve things bit by bit. When the environment changed slowly, organizations could respond to those changes in an orderly fashion. However, in today's dynamic white-water rapids world, where long-term marketplace success increasingly belongs to the flexible and adaptive organization, there's a need for a new kind of change agent: someone who can throw out the conventional wisdom about how things "have always been done" and initiate radical change.[32]

Turbulent times require revolutionary, not orderly, change. For instance, PointCast's approach to news delivery is characteristic of a revolutionary change. Nobody knew for certain whether the company's news "push" format would work, yet Chris Hassett, CEO and co-founder of the company along with brother Greg, did know that major environmental changes were occurring: lifestyle changes as people worked longer, often with more unpredictable work hours, and who had less interest in and less time for reading a daily newspaper or watching a news broadcast; changes in technology and the availability of that technology, including the Internet, World Wide Web, and computer screen savers; and changes in the news broadcast industry. All these factors pointed to a need for a change in the way news was delivered: from news delivery at specific times, to a personalized news-on-demand delivery system right on your computer screen. Thus PointCast was born.[33] And the need for revolutionary change is just as vital for organizations around the globe as it is for U.S. companies. For instance, in Japan, the uncertain environment has caused some maverick firms to radically change the old, traditional ways of doing business. Kenji Asao, a credit union executive in Tsu, Japan, proudly boasts about the drastic innovations he pioneered that lowered operating costs and allowed his company to offer borrowers the lowest interest rates of all credit unions in Japan.[34] Organizations worldwide are increasingly looking for managers who can introduce and successfully implement revolutionary change—managers who can direct reengineering efforts.

We introduced the concept of reengineering in chapter 2.[35] Recall that it's a radical redesign of all or part of a company's work processes. In reengineering, a company drastically changes its structure, technology, and people by starting from scratch in reexamining the way the organization's work is done. During reengineering efforts, managers continually ask themselves "How could this process be improved?" or "What's a better way of performing this activity?" For instance, Eaton Corporation reengineered its new-product-development process to help the company reach aggressive growth goals. The managers' and workers' redesign of the product innovation process led to a doubling of revenues during a five-year period from 1992 to 1996 and an increase in earnings from Eaton's historical 3 percent to 6 percent. At Agway, a giant farm supply cooperative in the northeastern United States, managers reengineered by splitting up the retail and commercial farming divisions. The result was better service to farmers and the elimination of a whole layer of costs. At Sweden's ICA Handlarnas, reengineering of work processes resulted in the linking of all the company's 3,350 retail stores to a single mainframe database so that inventory information was instantly available to managers. Other European companies that have reengineered work processes include Ciba-Geigy, Rolls-Royce Motor Cars, and Siemens.

How is the concept of reengineering related to the other change topics we've talked about? It's not a replacement for any change efforts that the organization may be implementing. Instead, for many companies, it's the first step in changing. Reengineering provides the framework for making changes. Whether it's market changes, changes in the economic climate, or changes in organizational strategy that are creating the need to change, organizations that decide to reengineer must look first at the way people work and interact within the organization. Once these work processes have been identified and critically evaluated, then managers and subordinates can look for ways to "do it better." Doing it better might involve total quality initiatives, changes in organizational culture, or any other types of changes that we have discussed in this chapter. However, the point of reengineering is

Siemens Business Communications Systems, Inc., used reengineering not only to return to financial stability but also to boost employee confidence, with new employee contracts and by transforming itself into a learning organization.

that the organization peels away its old way of doing things to discover what types of changes to implement.

You might be asking yourself by now whether reengineering is just another term for TQM. The answer is definitely no! Although both are focused on organizational change, the goals and means they use are clearly different. (See Table 12-2.) TQM is a commitment to continuous, incremental change. It's about continually improving organizational activities that are basically OK. TQM works from the bottom up in the organization, emphasizing participative decision making in both planning and implementing the TQM program. On the other hand, reengineering is about dramatic and radical shifts in the way the organization performs its work. It's focused on quantum changes and starting over in redesigning the way work is done. Reengineering is initiated by top management, although, once the process is complete, the workplace tends to be largely self-managed.

Managing the Downsized Workplace

Downsizing was a dominant structural change strategy of organizations during the 1990s. Labor market analysts reported that companies shed some 14 million workers from 1990 to 1996.[36] Another study of 1,200 companies surveyed by the American Management Association reported that nearly 40 percent of them had cut jobs in three or more years since 1990.[37] Why *did* so many companies downsize during that time? Mainly to increase productivity! Organizations were bombarded by economic, global, technological, and market forces that created an environment in which they had to become more competitive to

TABLE 12-2	TQM versus Reengineering
TQM	**Reengineering**
• Continuous, incremental change	• Radical change
• Fixing and improving	• Redesigning—starting over
• Mostly "as is"	• Mostly "what can be"
• Works from bottom up in organization	• Initiated by top management

succeed, and in some cases even to survive. Managers had little choice but to look for ways to increase worker productivity and thus competitiveness.

Did downsizing lead to the anticipated productivity gains? Among the top 10 corporate job cutters from 1990 to 1995 (which included, among others, Digital Equipment, McDonnell-Douglas, General Electric, IBM, and Sears), productivity increased an average of 27.9 percent.[38] Although these gains are impressive, not all downsizing organizations had similar experiences.

Downsizing has had a dark side as well. A study of 62 major U.S. companies that downsized during the 1990s found that 70 percent of them were struggling with serious problems of low employee morale and mistrust of management.[39] Other surveys have found that many downsizing organizations showed little improvement in profits and productivity after all.[40]

How can managers best manage a downsized workplace? There are no easy ways to downsize. There will be disruptions in the workplace and in employees' personal lives. Stress, frustration, anxiety, and anger are typical reactions of both individuals who are being laid off and the survivors. Are there actions that managers can take to make the adjustment as painless as possible? Experts who have studied numerous organizational downsizings say that there are.[41]

Open and honest communication is critical. Individuals who are being let go need to be informed as soon as possible. Survivors need to know the company's new goals and expectations, how their jobs might change, and what the near future holds for them. Managers who have been through downsizing efforts point out the importance of communicating openly and as soon as information is available.

In providing assistance to employees who are being "let go," many organizations offer some form of severance pay or benefits for a specified period of time. Some offer both. Managers want to be sure they're following any laws and regulations that might affect the length of time pay and benefits must be offered and the types of pay and benefits that must be provided. Also, many organizations provide job search assistance. This assistance might be provided directly by the organization or by a job search firm that has been hired specifically to help laid-off employees find new jobs.

For some "downsized" individuals, however, the trauma associated with job loss leads to serious repercussions, particularly for those whose job is their whole life. Because their job is viewed as such a major part of their identity, they may view the layoff as an attack on their self-esteem. At the extreme, these individuals may resort to acts of workplace violence. And violence aimed at employers or former employers is the fastest-growing category of workplace violence.[42] The problem has become so serious that the National Institute for Occupational Safety and Health has issued recommendations designed to prevent workplace violence.

Downsizing can be just as stressful for survivors. They often fear being the next to lose their jobs. Or they may find that their job responsibilities have increased because the orga-

Downsizing has become an international phenomenon, as Kazuhiko Tashiro of Japan well knows. He left Sumitomo Corporation when his transfer to a lesser position was made permanent. He now sells socks and T-shirts door to door.

nization's work demands typically remain unchanged while the number of people available declines. To ease the pain on survivors, managers may want to provide opportunities for them to talk to counselors about their guilt, anger, and anxieties. Group discussions can also provide an opportunity for survivors to vent their feelings. Other organizations have used downsizing efforts to implement increased employee participation programs such as empowerment, self-managed work teams, and mentoring.

Handling Employee Stress

For many employees, change creates stress. A dynamic and uncertain environment characterized by mergers, restructurings, reengineering efforts, forced retirements, and downsizing has created a large number of employees who are overworked and stressed out.[43] In this section, we review what specifically is meant by the term *stress*, what causes it, how to identify it, and what managers can do to reduce it.

What Is Stress?   **Stress** is a dynamic condition in which an individual is confronted with an opportunity, constraint, or demand related to what he or she desires and for which the outcome is perceived to be both uncertain and important.[44] That is a complicated definition, so let's look at its components more closely.

> **stress**
>
> A dynamic condition in which an individual is confronted with an opportunity, constraint, or demand related to what he or she desires and for which the outcome is perceived to be both uncertain and important.

Stress is not necessarily bad in and of itself. Although stress is often discussed in a negative context, it also has a positive value, particularly when it offers a potential gain. Functional stress allows an athlete or stage performer to perform at his or her highest level in crucial situations.

However, stress is more often associated with constraints and demands. A constraint prevents you from doing what you desire; demands refer to the loss of something desired. When you take a test at school or undergo your annual performance review at work, you feel stress because you confront opportunity, constraints, and demands. A good performance review may lead to a promotion, greater responsibilities, and a higher salary. But a poor review may keep you from getting the promotion. An extremely poor review might lead to your being fired.

Just because the conditions are right for stress to surface does not always mean it will. Two conditions are necessary for *potential* stress to become *actual* stress.[45] There must be uncertainty over the outcome, and the outcome must be important. Regardless of the conditions, a stressful condition exists only when there is doubt or uncertainty regarding whether the opportunity will be seized, whether the constraint will be removed, or whether the loss will be avoided. That is, stress is highest for individuals who are uncertain whether they will win or lose and lowest for individuals who think that winning or losing is a certainty. The importance of the outcome is also a critical factor. If winning or losing is unimportant, there is no stress. An employee who feels that keeping a job or earning a promotion is unimportant will experience no stress before a performance review.

Causes of Stress.   As illustrated in Figure 12-5, the causes of stress can be found in issues related to the organization or in personal factors that evolve out of the employee's private life. Clearly, change of any kind has the potential to cause stress. It can present opportunities, constraints, or demands. Moreover, changes are frequently created in a climate of uncertainty and around issues that are important to employees. It's not surprising, then, that change is a major stressor.

An employee's job and the organization's structure are also pervasive causes of stress. Excessive workloads create stress, as do pressures to maintain a machine-regulated pace. At the other extreme, job boredom can also create stress. Individuals with challenging jobs have less anxiety, depression, and physical illness than do those with jobs that are not challenging.[46] Role conflict and ambiguity over job expectations also create stress.[47] The former imposes contradictory demands on the employee, and the latter creates uncertainty about what to do. A classic structural source of stress is when unity of command is broken

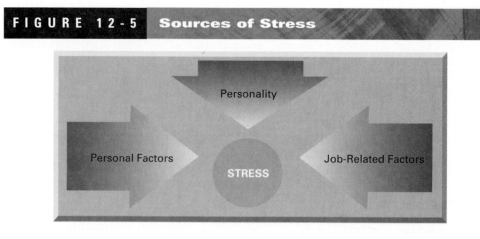

FIGURE 12-5   Sources of Stress

Personality

Personal Factors

STRESS

Job-Related Factors

and employees must deal with more than one boss. Additional organizational factors that cause employee stress include excessive rules and regulations, an unresponsive and unsupportive boss, ambiguous communications, and unpleasant working conditions such as extreme temperatures, poor lighting, or distracting noises.

Personal factors that can create stress include the death of a family member, a divorce, and personal financial difficulties.[48] Because employees bring their personal problems with them to work, a full understanding of employee stress requires consideration of personal factors.

There's evidence that an employee's personality acts as a moderator to strengthen or diminish the impact of both organizational and personal stressors.[49] The most commonly used description is what is called the Type A–Type B dichotomy.[50] Individuals exhibiting **Type A behavior** are characterized by a chronic sense of time urgency and an excessive competitive drive. They're impatient, do everything quickly, and have great difficulty coping with leisure time. **Type B behavior** is just the opposite: relaxed, easygoing, and noncompetitive. Type As live with moderate to high levels of stress; they are more susceptible to heart disease than are Type Bs. From a manager's perspective, Type As are more likely to show symptoms of stress, even if organizational and personal stressors are low.

Signs of Stress.   What signs indicate that an employee's stress level might be too high? Stress shows itself in a number of ways. For instance, an employee who is experiencing a high level of stress may become depressed, accident prone, or argumentative; may have difficulty making routine decisions; may be easily distracted, and so on. These symptoms can be grouped under three general categories: physiological, psychological, and behavioral.[51] (See Figure 12-6.)

Most of the early concern over stress was directed at physiological symptoms, primarily because the topic was researched by specialists in the health and medical sciences. Their research led to the conclusion that stress could create changes in metabolism, increase heart and breathing rates, raise blood pressure, bring on headaches, and induce heart attacks.

The link between stress and certain physiological symptoms is not entirely clear. There are few, if any, consistent relationships.[52] This inconsistency is attributed to the complexity of the symptoms and the difficulty in measuring them objectively. But physiological symptoms, although important, have the least direct relevance to managers.

Of greater importance are the psychological symptoms. Stress can cause dissatisfaction. Job-related stress can cause job-related dissatisfaction. Job dissatisfaction, in fact, is "the simplest and most obvious psychological effect" of stress.[53] But stress has other psychological indications: for instance, tension, anxiety, irritability, boredom, and procrastination. Behavioral symptoms of stress include changes in productivity, absenteeism, and job

Type A behavior

Behavior marked by a chronic sense of time urgency and an excessive competitive drive.

Type B behavior

Behavior that is relaxed, easygoing, and noncompetitive.

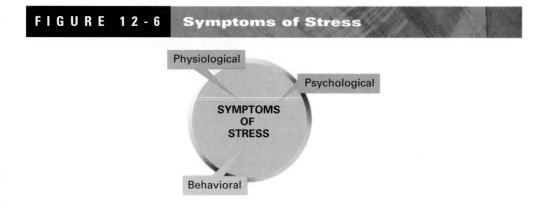

FIGURE 12-6   Symptoms of Stress

turnover as well as changes in eating habits, increased smoking or consumption of alcohol, rapid speech, fidgeting, and sleep disorders.

Reducing Stress.   As we mentioned earlier, not all stress is dysfunctional. Moreover, realistically, stress can never be totally eliminated from a person's life, either off the job or on. As we review stress reduction techniques, keep in mind that our concern is with reducing the kind of stress that leads to dysfunctional behavior.

In terms of organizational factors, any attempt to lower stress levels has to begin with employee *selection.* Management needs to make sure that an employee's abilities match the requirements of the job. When employees are in over their heads, their stress levels typically will be high. A realistic job preview during the selection process will also minimize stress by reducing ambiguity over job expectations. Improved organizational communications will keep ambiguity-induced stress to a minimum. Similarly, a performance planning program such as MBO will clarify job responsibilities, provide clear performance objectives, and reduce ambiguity through feedback. Job redesign is also a way to reduce stress. If stress can be traced directly to boredom or to work overload, jobs should be redesigned to increase challenge or to reduce the workload. Redesigns that increase opportunities for employees to participate in decisions and to gain social support have also been found to lessen stress.[54]

Stress that arises from an employee's personal life raises two problems. First, it's difficult for the manager to control directly. Second, there are ethical considerations. Specifically, does the manager have the right to intrude—even in the most subtle ways—in the employee's personal life? If a manager believes it's ethical and the employee is receptive, there are a few approaches the manager can consider. Employee *counseling* can provide stress relief. Employees often want to talk to someone about their problems, and the organization—through its managers, in-house human resource counselors, or free or low-cost outside professional help—can meet that need. Companies such as Citicorp, AT&T, and Johnson & Johnson provide extensive counseling services for their employees. A *time management program* offered to employees whose personal lives suffer from a lack of planning

Although numerous organizations are providing stress reduction programs, many employees choose not to participate. Why? Many employees are reluctant to ask for help, especially if a major source of that stress is job insecurity. After all, there's still a stigma associated with stress. Employees don't want to be perceived as being unable to cope effectively with the demands of their job or to handle their job duties. Although they may need stress management now more than ever, few employees want to admit that they're stressed. What can be done about this paradox? Do organizations even *have* an ethical responsibility to help employees deal with stress? ▪

THINKING CRITICALLY

ABOUT ETHICS

and organization that, in turn, creates stress may help them sort out their priorities.[55] For instance, Honeywell provides such a service. Still another approach is organizationally sponsored *physical activity programs*.[56] Mutual of Omaha, for example, has a Wellness Center in its Omaha offices. Other companies such as Coors Brewing Company in Golden, Colorado, the Quaker Oats Company in Chicago, and Home Box Office in New York have set up on-site exercise centers for employees.[57] And at Philadelphia-based Cigna Corporation, employees can take a 5-, 10-, or 15-minute stress break when and where they need it. The company's philosophy is that "a few minutes of stretching or deep breathing can enhance personal health as well as attitudes, work performance, and overall teamwork."[58]

13 Contrast reengineering and TQM as change efforts.

14 How can managers best manage a downsized workplace?

15 What signs might indicate to a manager that an employee's stress level is too high?

STIMULATING INNOVATION

"Innovate or lose!" That has increasingly become the rallying cry of today's managers. In the dynamic, chaotic world of global competition, organizations must create new products and services and adopt state-of-the-art technology if they are to compete successfully. Coors, for instance, has long been known for its technical innovations; it was the first beer company to use aluminum cans for packaging its products and it was also the first to produce cold-filtered beer. However, company president W. Leo Kiely III says that the beer industry has become so intensely competitive that Coors needs even more marketing and technological innovations if it is going to be a viable competitor.[59]

The standard of innovation toward which many organizations strive is that achieved by the 3M Company.[60] 3M has developed a reputation for innovation over a long period of time. One of its stated objectives is that 25 percent of each division's profits are to come from products less than five years old. To meet this goal, 3M typically launches more than 200 new products each year. Yet another company well known for its continual innovation is Intel, the computer chip maker. Continual advancements in chip designs and new product introductions have been instrumental to Intel's success and its industry position as a market leader.

What's the secret to 3M's and Intel's success? What, if anything, can other managers do to make their organizations more innovative? In the following pages, we'll try to answer those questions as we discuss the factors behind innovation.

Creativity versus Innovation

creativity

The ability to combine ideas in a unique way or to make unusual associations between ideas.

Creativity refers to the ability to combine ideas in a unique way or to make unusual associations between ideas.[61] An organization that stimulates creativity develops novel approaches to doing the work or unique solutions to problems. **Innovation** is the process of taking a creative idea and turning it into a useful product, service, or method of operation. Thus, the innovative organization is characterized by its ability to channel creativity into useful outcomes. When managers talk about changing an organization to make it more creative, they usually mean they want to stimulate innovation. Intel and 3M are aptly described as innovative because they take novel ideas and turn them into profitable products. For example, look at 3M's cellophane tape, Scotch-Guard protective coatings, Post-It note pads, and diapers with elastic waistbands. And Intel leads all chip manufacturers worldwide in miniaturization and has had enormous success in developing smaller and faster technology. Intel is committed to staying ahead of its competition by continually introducing a stream of new and more powerful products.

innovation

The process of taking a creative idea and turning it into a useful product, service, or method of operation.

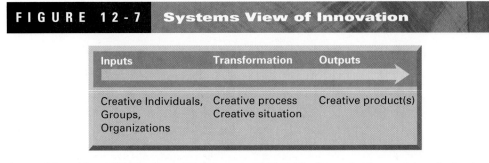

FIGURE 12-7   Systems View of Innovation

Inputs	Transformation	Outputs
Creative Individuals, Groups, Organizations	Creative process Creative situation	Creative product(s)

Source: Adapted from R.W. Woodman, J.E. Sawyer, and R.W. Griffin, "Toward a Theory of Organizational Creativity," *Academy of Management Review*, April 1993, p. 309.

Fostering Innovation

By using the systems model we introduced in chapter 1, we can better understand how organizations become more innovative.[62] (See Figure 12-7.) We see from the model that to get our desired output (i.e., creative products), we have to look at the inputs and the transformation of those inputs. Inputs include creative people and groups within the organization. But just having creative people isn't enough. It takes the right environment for the innovation process to take hold and prosper, just as a flower requires the proper soil, watering, and light levels to grow. What does this "right" environment look like? We've identified three sets of variables that have been found to stimulate innovation: the organization's structure, culture, and human resource practices (Figure 12-8).

Structural Variables.   On the basis of extensive research, we can conclude three things about the effect of structural variables on innovation.[63] First, organic structures positively influence innovation. Because this type of organization is relatively low in formalization, centralization, and work specialization, organic structures facilitate the flexibility, adaptability, and cross-fertilization that facilitate the adoption of innovations. Second, the easy availability of plentiful resources provides a key building block for innovation. With an abundance of resources, management can afford to purchase innovations, can afford the cost of instituting innovations, and can absorb failures. Finally, frequent interunit communication helps to break down barriers to innovation.[64] Cross-functional teams, task forces, and other such organizational designs facilitate interaction across departmental lines and are widely used in innovative organizations. 3M, for instance, is highly decentralized and takes on many of the characteristics of small, organic organizations. The company also has the "deep pockets" needed to support its policy of allowing scientists and engineers to use up to 15 percent of their time on projects of their own choosing.

Cultural Variables.   Innovative organizations tend to have similar cultures.[65] They encourage experimentation; reward both successes and failures; and celebrate mistakes. An innovative culture is likely to have the following characteristics:

- *Acceptance of ambiguity.* Too much emphasis on objectivity and specificity constrains creativity.

- *Tolerance of the impractical.* Individuals who offer impractical, even foolish, answers to what-if questions are not stifled. What at first seems impractical might lead to innovative solutions.

- *Low external controls.* Rules, regulations, policies, and similar controls are kept to a minimum.

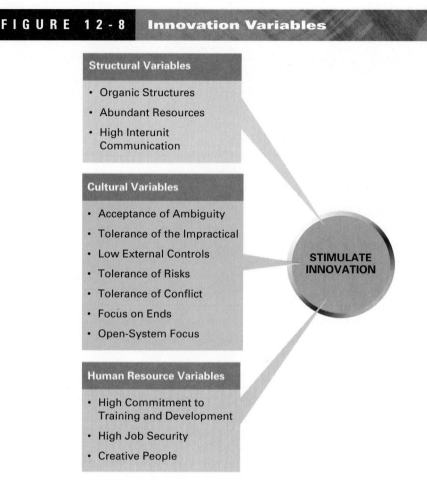

FIGURE 12-8   Innovation Variables

Structural Variables

- Organic Structures
- Abundant Resources
- High Interunit Communication

Cultural Variables

- Acceptance of Ambiguity
- Tolerance of the Impractical
- Low External Controls
- Tolerance of Risks
- Tolerance of Conflict
- Focus on Ends
- Open-System Focus

STIMULATE INNOVATION

Human Resource Variables

- High Commitment to Training and Development
- High Job Security
- Creative People

■ *Tolerance of risk.* Employees are encouraged to experiment without fear of consequences should they fail. Mistakes are treated as learning opportunities.

■ *Tolerance of conflict.* Diversity of opinions is encouraged. Harmony and agreement between individuals or units are *not* assumed to be evidence of high performance.

■ *Focus on ends rather than means.* Goals are made clear, and individuals are encouraged to consider alternative routes toward meeting the goals. Focusing on ends suggests that there might be several right answers to any given problem.

■ *Open-system focus.* The organization closely monitors the environment and responds rapidly to changes as they occur.

Human Resource Variables

idea champions

Individuals who actively and enthusiastically support a new idea, build support, overcome resistance, and ensure that the innovation is implemented.

Within the *human resources* category, we find that innovative organizations actively promote the training and development of their members so that their knowledge remains current; offer their employees high job security to reduce the fear of getting fired for making mistakes; and encourage individuals to become "champions" of change. **Idea champions** actively and enthusiastically support a new idea, build support, overcome resistance, and ensure that the innovation is implemented. Recent research finds that champions have common personality characteristics: extremely high self-confidence, persistence, energy,

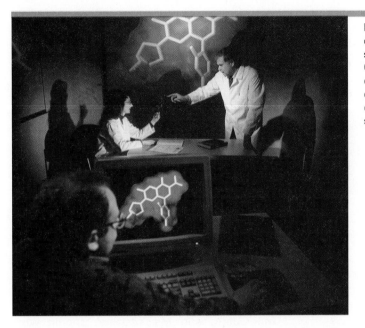

Innovation, such as the computer modeling of drugs shown here at Pfizer Corporation, thrives when creativity is encouraged and channeled into practical outcomes. The molecules shown here are an antibiotic.

and a tendency toward risk taking. Champions also display characteristics associated with dynamic leadership. They inspire and energize others with their vision of the potential of an innovation and through their strong personal conviction in their mission. They're also good at gaining the commitment of others to support their mission. In addition, champions have jobs that provide considerable decison-making discretion. This autonomy helps them introduce and implement innovations in organizations.[66] For instance, the tiny self-powered, self-guided rover vehicle named *Sojourner* that scientists (and the rest of us) watched in amazement as it explored the surface of the planet Mars never would have been built had it not been for an idea champion by the name of Donna L. Shirley. As the head of Mars exploration at NASA's Jet Propulsion Laboratory in Pasadena, California, Shirley had been working since the early 1980s on the idea of putting roving vehicles on Mars. Despite ongoing funding and support problems, she continued to champion the idea until it was approved in the early 1990s. The successful Mars Pathfinder mission and *Sojourner*'s primetime debut attest to the power of an idea champion.[67]

16 Differentiate between creativity and innovation.

17 How can the systems model be used to help organizations become more innovative?

18 Describe the specific structural, cultural, and human resource variables associated with innovation.

managers respond to "a manager's dilemma"

MANAGER 1

The change situation that Mr. Guerra and Ms. Martinez are facing is one that many managers face in today's organizations. Mergers, acquisitions, and even downsizings are common in many different types of organizations. These two SBC managers want to use education and communication to reduce employees' resistance to change brought about by the merger of their company with another telecommunications company. In my job as an independent technology consultant and trainer, I continually work with people who are facing change in the way they do their jobs. I have found that what works best is informing employees ahead of time about the impending changes and the impact that the proposed changes might have on them. Many people resist change because they fear the unknown. By keeping the lines of communication open, Guerra and Martinez can have a head start on managing any resistance to the change. Even if they don't have complete and full information about all the potential implications of the change, they can communicate what they do know with their employees. In addition, as I train people in using new technology, I have found that giving them an opportunity to participate in how they implement the change is helpful. In this way, employees feel as if they have some control over what is happening.

Cindy Brewer, Independent Information Technology Consultant and Trainer, Rockford, Illinois

MANAGER 2

I'd look at this situation as an opportunity—an opportunity to help the affected people realize their value to SBC and to look at how to increase that value. In addition, it's an opportunity for SBC to establish some clear two-way communication and lay the groundwork for developing a true team atmosphere.

Mr. Guerra and Ms. Martinez should work toward helping the individuals who report to them to understand how valuable they are to the company now. People are much more open to change, in this case change in work duties, when they feel they're wanted, appreciated, and important. To do this, I would sit down with those who would be most affected by the changes to their work duties and discuss, one on one, with each one how his or her contributions are valuable to the new organization. Then I would also work at fostering a team approach by discussing with these individuals how their contributions were important to the work team. In addition, Mr. Guerra and Ms. Martinez will need to stress the importance to employees that full participation is essential for the merger to be successful. By helping these people realize their importance and value to SBC, they can help lay the foundation for a successful transition. Finally, organizational communication needs to be open in both directions. Employees need to feel that they can go to their manager and be heard without the risk of repercussions for providing honest feedback. All of these suggestions were ones that our organization used when it went through a merger in the mid-1990s.

Tom Zimmerman, Sales Manager, The Office Furniture Store, Cincinnati, Ohio

for your
IMMEDIATE
action

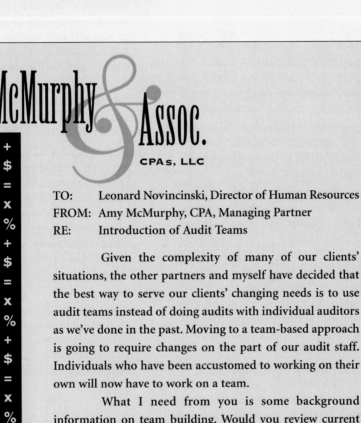

McMurphy & Assoc.
CPAs, LLC

TO: Leonard Novincinski, Director of Human Resources
FROM: Amy McMurphy, CPA, Managing Partner
RE: Introduction of Audit Teams

Given the complexity of many of our clients' situations, the other partners and myself have decided that the best way to serve our clients' changing needs is to use audit teams instead of doing audits with individual auditors as we've done in the past. Moving to a team-based approach is going to require changes on the part of our audit staff. Individuals who have been accustomed to working on their own will now have to work on a team.

What I need from you is some background information on team building. Would you review current literature on team building and provide me with a one-page, single-spaced list of the most important ideas about what an effective team is and what it takes to build an effective team? I will then share these ideas with the other partners. Once we've had a chance to digest the information, I'll meet with you to begin preparing our approach to implementing this change.

This is a fictionalized account of a potentially real problem. It was written for academic purposes only.

SUMMARY

This summary is organized by the chapter-opening objectives found on page 378.

1. The calm waters metaphor views change as a break in the organization's equilibrium state. Organizations are seen as stable and predictable, disturbed by an occasional crisis. The white-water rapids metaphor views change as continual and unpredictable. Managers must deal with ongoing and almost chaotic change.

2. Change is often resisted because of the uncertainty it creates, concern for personal loss, and a belief that it might not be in the organization's best interest.

3. Six tactics reduce resistance to change: education and communication, participation, facilitation and support, negotiation, manipulation and cooptation, and coercion.

4. Managers can change the organization's *structure* by altering structural components such as work specialization, departmentalization, chain of command, span of control, centralization and decentralization, and formalization; change the organization's *technology* by altering work processes, methods, and equipment; or change the organization's *people* by altering attitudes, expectations, perceptions, or behavior.

5. Dramatic crises and changes in top leadership facilitate cultural change by providing major shocks to employees and the status quo. Having a small or young organization and a weak culture facilitates cultural change by providing a more impressionable base to work with.

6. Managers can implement TQM by providing the right structure, technology, and human resources. The structure should be decentral-ized; should have minimal organizational levels, wide spans of control, and limited work specialization; and should support cross-functional teams. The technology must be flexible to support continuous improvement. The workforce must be committed to the objectives of quality and continual improvement.

7. Reengineering involves radically redesigning an organization's work processes. These activities involve changes in structure, technology, and human resources.

8. Managing a downsized workplace involves recognizing that there will be disruptions in the workplace and in employees' personal lives. Some things that managers can do include communicating openly and honestly, deciding how best to provide assistance to the downsized employees, and easing the frustrations and stress of the individuals remaining in the organization.

9. Techniques for reducing employee stress include carefully matching applicants with jobs in the selection process, having clear performance objectives, redesigning jobs to increase challenge and reduce the workload, counseling employees, providing time management programs, and sponsoring physical activity programs.

10. Organizations can stimulate innovation by having structures that are flexible, having easy access to resources, and having fluid communication. Innovation is also stimulated in a culture that is relaxed, is supportive of new ideas, encourages monitoring of the environment, and has creative people who are well trained, current in their fields, and secure in their jobs.

THINKING ABOUT MANAGEMENT ISSUES

1. Can a low-level employee be a change agent? Explain your answer.

2. Contrast management practices in these two retail electronics stores: In one, managers followed the calm-waters view of change; in the other, managers followed the white-water rapids view.

3. How can an innovative culture make an organization more effective? Could such an innovative culture make an organization less effective? Explain.

4. Do you think a TQM program could be developed that consisted of continual revolutionary change as opposed to continual gradual change? Discuss.

5. Organizations typically have limits to how much change they can absorb. As a manager, what signs would you look for that might suggest that your organization has exceeded its capacity to change?

SELF-ASSESSMENT EXERCISE

HOW INNOVATIVE ARE YOU?

Organizations need innovative people to lead the way in making changes. In fact, much of the TQM movement is about innovation and change. And we know that quantum changes require innovative, risk-seeking personalities. Are you one of those innovative people? This self-assessment exercise will help you find out.

Instructions: To find out how innovative you are, react to the following 18 statements. Remember, there are no right or wrong answers. Rather, we are interested in exploring your attitudes. Answer using the following scale.

   SA = Strongly agree
    A = Agree
    ? = Undecided
    D = Disagree
   SD = Strongly disagree

	Strongly Agree				Strongly Disagree
1. I try new ideas and new approaches to problems.	SA	A	?	D	SD
2. I take things or situations apart to find a new use for existing methods or existing equipment.	SA	A	?	D	SD
3. I can be counted on by my friends to find a new use for existing methods or existing equipment.	SA	A	?	D	SD

4. Among my friends, I'm usually the first person to try out a new idea or method. SA   A   ?   D   SD
5. I demonstrate originality. SA   A   ?   D   SD
6. I like to work on a problem that has caused others great difficulty. SA   A   ?   D   SD
7. I plan on developing contacts with experts in my field located in different companies or departments. SA   A   ?   D   SD
8. I plan on budgeting time and money for the pursuit of novel ideas. SA   A   ?   D   SD
9. I make comments at meetings on new ways of doing things. SA   A   ?   D   SD
10. If my friends were asked, they would say I'm a wit. SA   A   ?   D   SD
11. I seldom stick to the rules or follow protocol. SA   A   ?   D   SD
12. I discourage formal meetings to discuss ideas. SA   A   ?   D   SD
13. I usually support a friend's suggestion on new ways to do things. SA   A   ?   D   SD
14. I probably will not turn down ambiguous job assignments. SA   A   ?   D   SD
15. People who depart from the accepted organizational routine should not be punished. SA   A   ?   D   SD
16. I hope to be known for the quantity of my work rather than the quality of my work when starting a new project. SA   A   ?   D   SD
17. I must be able to find enough variety of experience on my job or I will leave it. SA   A   ?   D   SD
18. I am going to leave a job that doesn't challenge me. SA   A   ?   D   SD

See scoring key on page SK–4.

Source: J.E. Ettlie and R.D. O'Keefe, "Innovative Attitudes, Values, and Intentions in Organizations," *Journal of Management Studies,* 19, 1982, p. 176.

TAKE IT TO THE NET

We invite you to visit the Robbins/Coulter companion Web site at http://www.prenhall.com/robbinsmgt for this chapter's Internet resources.

CASE APPLICATION

Flying High

1995 and 1996 were great years for Continental Airlines! The company had its most profitable years ever and soared from worst to first in several key performance areas related to customer service (such as on-time performance, baggage handling, and cus-tomer complaints). And, according to *Business Week* magazine, in 1995, Continental had the best-performing stock on the New York Stock Exchange. (It sky-rocketed from $6.50 a share in January 1995 to close at the end of December at $42.25.) Continental Airlines might be flying high now, but not that long ago it was floundering under bankruptcy protection.

The company was forced into the bankruptcy filing in 1991 by an unmanageable debt load and fuel prices that were skyrocketing because of the Gulf War. What happened to prompt such a remarkable turnaround, particularly in an industry that is widely regarded as one of the most uncertain?

Gordon M. Bethune, Continental's CEO, was a key factor. Bethune came to Continental in late 1994 from the Boeing Company. Faced with tremendous external and internal pressures, he quickly revamped Continental's operations to make it more efficient. But probably his most important action was to rally the airline's extremely unhappy workforce around a common goal. Continental employees' unhappiness and distrust of management were long-running carry-overs from the 1980s.

During the tumultuous 1980s, the airline's then-owner, Frank Lorenzo, tried to create a mega-airline by splicing together several weak airlines including Continental, Texas International, People Express, and New York Air. He even bought the floundering Eastern Airlines and brought it into the fold. Then Lorenzo used the protection offered by bankruptcy to nullify union contracts. Needless to say, Continental's union members despised him. He also slashed costs and funneled the cash to other enterprises in which he was involved. Eventually, the U.S. Department of Transportation declared Lorenzo "unfit" to own a U.S. airline, and he was forced out. But the Lorenzo era left deep internal organizational wounds. Here was an organization with serious internal problems facing a turbulent external environment. Another person might have thrown in the towel, but Bethune was not intimidated by the seemingly insurmountable problems.

Bethune knew that to persuade informed and demanding customers that Continental *was* a different airline, he had first to persuade his own employees. Some of his initial actions were to repaint the company's fleet of airplanes, remove surveillance cameras from the executive suite, and order airplane cockpits be thoroughly cleaned every 30 days instead of every 90 days. He also eliminated one-third of Continental's 60 vice presidents and replaced another third.

Bethune also acted quickly to get employees focused on specific targets. Rather than emphasizing generic cost-cutting efforts or zeroing in on simplistic reactions to competitors' actions, he put everyone on notice that they would be measured together on what mattered most to customers—on-time flights. To emphasize his commitment, he let employees know he would be using the Department of Transportation's monthly rankings as the company's new performance yardstick. To make sure employees were motivated to meet these new performance targets, Bethune promised to pay every employee a separate $65 check in any month the airline finished in the top half of the federal rankings. To make the impact of these "bonus" checks even more obvious, he had the checks mailed directly to employees' homes, banned direct deposit of them in bank accounts, and withheld the extra income taxes from regular paychecks not from the bonus checks. Although $65 may not seem like a lot of money, the checks symbolized to Continental's employees that management was now willing to pay rewards instead of constantly asking for givebacks. By March 1995, the second month of Bethune's $65 offer, Continental had moved from last to first in the government's on-time rankings. As the airline began to run more smoothly, costs dropped and high-fare business passengers began returning. Continental now pays each worker $65 for finishing only second or third in the rankings; if they finish first, the check goes up to $100.

One other important thing Bethune did was provide Continental with a vision. A friend (and competitor), Southwest Airlines' CEO Herb Kelleher, says, "A chief executive can do a lot of things on paper and with a calculator, but the most important thing is unifying people and giving them a vision. I think Gordon has been positively inspirational." One of Bethune's favorite remarks in reference to Continental's miserable history is, "You can make a pizza so cheap no one will eat it." The new Continental's vision is best depicted in the four points of its Go Forward Plan, which is Continental's blueprint for success: Fly to Win, Fund the Future, Make Reliability a Reality, and

Work Together. The evolving four-point plan has helped the company define and communicate its goals. For a company that once was in a serious tailspin, Continental seems to be flying high!

QUESTIONS

1. Explain what external and internal forces were creating the need for Continental to change. Would you describe this change situation as calm-waters or white-water rapids? Why?
2. How did Bethune effect cultural change at Continental? What could this situation teach you about changing organizational cultures?
3. Airline employees experience significant levels of on-the-job stress. If you were asked to create a

stress management program for flight crews, what types of things would you include?
4. What impact do you think each of the four points in the company's Go Forward Plan might have on creativity and innovation efforts by employees?

Source: S. McCartney, "Continental Air Posts Record Earnings," *Wall Street Journal*, January 24, 1996, p. B4; McCartney, "Continental Air's First Period Sets Record, Aided by High Fares," *Wall Street Journal*, April 23, 1996, p. B4; McCartney, "Back on Course," *Wall Street Journal*, May 15, 1996, pp. A1+; G. Flynn, "A Flight Plan for Success," *Workforce*, July 1997, pp. 72–78; and Continental Airlines' Web page, <http://www.flycontinental.com>.

ABCNEWS **V I D E O   C A S E   A P P L I C A T I O N**

Slam Dunk!

Sex sells. Just as promoters of men's sports aim to do, women's sports promoters are looking to get sports fans to spend dollars, and lots of them. Savvy marketers have long known that sex appeal gets attention in an overcrowded marketplace, and until the summer of 1997, sex appeal was often used to promote women's sports. Starting with the initial season of the WNBA, the Women's National Basketball Association, that approach is changing. But getting people to see women sports stars as more than just sexy athletes won't be easy!

The 1990s boom in figure skating provides a lesson about the good things that can happen when people get interested in a sport. As televised figure skating events became more and more popular, fans of the sport flocked to ice rinks around the country. From group lessons to private lessons, from purchasing new skating equipment to repairing broken equipment, the dollars spent on ice skating took off. However, as a sport, figure skating features lithe, slender females in short, skimpy, and often sexy, cos-

tumes. And even though the sport hasn't been actively promoted with sex appeal, it would appear to be the underlying aura surrounding figure skating. With the debut of the WNBA, this approach to women's sports changed.

After watching the first promotions for the WNBA, Jeff Jensen of *Advertising Age* concluded that a three-cornered women's sports industrial complex was being built. Its components included performers, presenters, and producers of equipment. He said, "You need all of those things working in unison and concert for…something like women's sports to really take off. And that's exactly what we're seeing right now." Val Ackerman, the WNBA president, knows that changing the perception of women's sports isn't going to be easy. Yet she says that her league's survival depends on their ability to deliver an audience: actually, three primary target audiences. One is existing basketball fans, who are probably predominantly male. The second is active women 18 to 34 who have some connection to sports. The third is younger women who are just starting to play sports. There's a feeling among the supporters of the WNBA that the new professional women's basketball league will send a signal that women athletes can take themselves more seriously. That attitude helps legitimize all women's sports whether it's roller blading, swimming, or mountain climbing. Even some businesses are pushing for the changed attitude toward women's sports. For instance, Nike aims to increase its sales to women. Nike spokeswoman Sue Levin says, "This is an opportunity where what's good for Nike's business is also the right thing to do because we really believe strongly as a company that sports are good for girls and women."

QUESTIONS

1. Would you characterize this situation as more like the calm waters metaphor of change or the white-water rapids metaphor? Explain.

2. Describe some other organizations that might be affected by the changing view of women's sports and how they might be affected.

3. Of the three primary target audiences for the WNBA, whose attitudes do you think will be the most difficult to change? Why? How would you suggest tackling this challenge?

4. What implications for change management do you see from the statement that the new professional women's basketball league will send a signal that women athletes can take themselves more seriously and will help legitimize *all* women's sports?

Source: Based on "The WNBA and the Changing Role of Women's Sports," *ABC Nightline*, June 24, 1997.

Leading

A MANAGER'S DILEMMA

The new president of the Sierra Club <www.sierraclub.org> doesn't mind being called a kid. Although the organization he heads is well over 100 years old, Adam Werbach is just in his mid-twenties. Werbach, who was elected president of the Sierra Club in May 1996, is discovering that his age is both an asset and a liability in dealing with the various stakeholders of the Sierra Club.[1]

The Sierra Club, founded in 1892 by the naturalist John Muir, is the United States' oldest and largest grassroots environmental organization. It has around 600,000 members and an annual budget in excess of $44 million. The club's president is responsible for supervising the professional staff and a network of 5,000 volunteers, leading the 15-member board meetings, acting as general spokesperson, and administering the organization's budget. But Werbach brings more to the position. His knack for attracting press attention—something he's always been good at—has raised the public profile of the Sierra Club since he was first elected to the position.

Werbach has had a longstanding interest in environmental issues. As a second grader, he organized a petition drive calling for the dismissal of U.S. Interior Secretary James Watt,

an arch enemy of the environmental movement. During his teen years, Werbach founded a youth division of the Sierra Club that now has over 30,000 members and organized a one-time distribution of black snow cones to high school and college students around the country to dramatize the risk of opening up the Alaska National Wildlife Refuge to oil drilling. His supporters say that his talents and enthusiasm outweigh his young age and shortage of experience, and that enthusiasm will go a long way in attracting Werbach's generation—a largely untapped constituency—to the Sierra Club. However, Werbach's style hasn't appealed to everyone. Early in his tenure as president, Werbach quipped that he didn't want the Sierra Club to be thought of as "an organization of aging hippies." This remark didn't set too well with the club's substantial ex-hippie membership. Although Werbach has worked hard to improve his relationship with the club's baby boomer members, he's had limited success.

How might he use an understanding of attitudes and their effect on behavior to help him develop a stronger working relationship with Sierra's board of directors, which has several baby boomers on it? Put yourself in Werbach's situation. How would you use what you know about attitudes and their effect on behavior in working with the board of directors to develop future plans, programs, and activities for the Sierra Club?

WHAT WOULD YOU DO?

You probably are already aware of the fact that people differ in their attitudes and behavior. For instance, you regularly have to deal with people who have different types of personalities. And haven't you seen family members or friends engage in behaviors that prompted you to wonder: Why did they do that? As the opening dilemma illustrates, effective managers need to understand behavior. This chapter looks at several psychological factors that influence employee behavior and then considers the implications of each for management practice.

CHAPTER

13

Foundations

of Behavior

TOWARD EXPLAINING AND PREDICTING BEHAVIOR

behavior

The actions of people.

organizational behavior

The study of the actions of
people at work.

The material in this and the next three chapters draws heavily on the field of study that is
known as *organizational behavior (OB)*. Although it's concerned with the subject of
behavior—that is, the actions of people—**organizational behavior** is concerned more
specifically with the actions of people at work.

One of the challenges in understanding organizational behavior is that it addresses
issues that aren't obvious. Like an iceberg, organizational behavior has a small visible
dimension and a much larger hidden portion. (See Figure 13-1.) What we see when we look
at organizations is their formal aspects: strategies, objectives, policies and procedures,
structure, technology, formal authority, and chains of command. But under the surface are
other elements that managers need to understand. As we'll show, OB provides managers
with considerable insights into these important, but hidden, aspects of the organization.

Focus of Organizational Behavior

Organizational behavior focuses primarily on two major areas. First, OB looks at *individual behavior*. Based predominantly on contributions from psychologists, this area includes
such topics as attitudes, personality, perception, learning, and motivation. Second, OB is
concerned with *group behavior,* which includes norms, roles, team building, and conflict.
Our knowledge about groups comes basically from the work of sociologists and social psychologists. Unfortunately, the behavior of a group of employees cannot be understood by
merely summing up the actions of the individuals in the group because individuals in a
group setting behave differently from individuals acting alone. You see this characteristic at
its extreme, for instance, when a street gang harasses innocent citizens. The gang members, acting individually, might never engage in such behavior. Therefore, because employees in an organization are both individuals and members of groups, we need to study them
at two levels. In this chapter, we'll provide the foundation for understanding individual
behavior. Then, in the next chapter, we'll introduce basic concepts related to understanding group behavior.

FIGURE 13-1   **The Organization as an Iceberg**

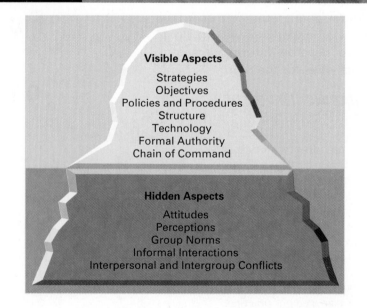

Visible Aspects

Strategies
Objectives
Policies and Procedures
Structure
Technology
Formal Authority
Chain of Command

Hidden Aspects

Attitudes
Perceptions
Group Norms
Informal Interactions
Interpersonal and Intergroup Conflicts

Willis T. White is president of West Coast Valet Service, a California commercial laundry and dry cleaner. When it comes to employees' emotions, he says, "Give them a high priority, because they affect productivity." White's attitude reflects the same focus as the field of organizational behavior—the psychological aspects of human behavior at work.

Goals of Organizational Behavior

The goals of OB are to *explain* and to *predict behavior*. Why do managers need this skill? Simply, in order to manage their employees' behavior. We know that a manager's success depends on getting things done through people. To do this, the manager needs to be able to explain why employees engage in some behaviors rather than others and to predict how employees will respond to various actions the manager might take.

What employee behaviors are we specifically concerned about explaining and predicting? We'll emphasize employee productivity, absenteeism, and turnover. We'll also look at job satisfaction. Although job satisfaction is an attitude rather than a behavior, it is an outcome that concerns many managers. In the following pages, we'll address how an understanding of employee attitudes, personality, perception, and learning can help us predict and explain employee productivity, absence and turnover rates, and job satisfaction.

ATTITUDES

Attitudes are evaluative statements—either favorable or unfavorable—concerning objects, people, or events. They reflect how an individual feels about something. When a person says, "I like my job," he or she is expressing an attitude about work.

To better understand the concept of attitudes, we should look at an attitude as being made up of three components: cognition, affect, and behavior.[2] The **cognitive component** of an attitude is made up of the beliefs, opinions, knowledge, or information held by a person. The belief that "discrimination is wrong" illustrates a cognition. The **affective component** of an attitude is the emotional or feeling part of an attitude. Using our example, this component would be reflected by the statement "I don't like Jon because he discriminates against minorities." Finally, affect can lead to behavioral outcomes. The **behavioral component** of an attitude refers to an intention to behave in a certain way toward someone or something. To continue our example, I might choose to avoid Jon because of my feelings about him. Looking at attitudes as being made up of three components—cognition, affect, and behavior—helps to show the complexity of attitudes. But for the sake of clarity, keep in mind that the term *attitude* usually refers only to the affective component.

Naturally, managers aren't interested in every attitude an employee might hold. They're specifically interested in job-related attitudes. The three most popular of these are job satisfaction, job involvement, and organizational commitment.[3] **Job satisfaction** is an employee's general attitude toward his or her job. When people speak of employee atti-

attitudes

Evaluative statements concerning objects, people, or events.

cognitive component of an attitude

The beliefs, opinions, knowledge, or information held by a person.

affective component of an attitude

The emotional or feeling segment of an attitude.

behavioral component of an attitude

An intention to behave in a certain way toward someone or something.

job satisfaction

A person's general attitude toward his or her job.

tudes, they usually are referring to job satisfaction. **Job involvement** is the degree to which an employee identifies with his or her job, actively participates in it, and considers his or her job performance to be important to his or her self-worth. Finally, **organizational commitment** represents an employee's orientation toward the organization in terms of his or her loyalty to, identification with, and involvement in the organization. In recent years, these have been popular topics for organizational researchers.[4]

TESTING... TESTING...

1 How does organizational behavior help resolve the problems that arise because the organization is like an iceberg?

2 What are the three components of an attitude?

3 Describe the three job-related attitudes.

job involvement

The degree to which an employee identifies with his or her job, actively participates in it, and considers his or her job performance important to his or her self-worth.

organizational commitment

An employee's orientation toward the organization in terms of his or her loyalty to, identification with, and involvement in the organization.

Attitudes and Consistency

Did you ever notice that people change what they say so it doesn't contradict what they do? Perhaps a friend of yours has continually argued that American cars are poorly built and that he'd never own anything but a foreign car. Then his dad gives him a late-model American-made car, and suddenly they're not so bad. Or, when going through sorority rush, a new freshman believes that sororities are good and that pledging a sorority is important. However, if she isn't asked to join one, she may say that sorority life isn't all that great anyway.

Research has generally concluded that people seek consistency among their attitudes and between their attitudes and behavior.[5] This means that individuals try to reconcile differing attitudes and align their attitudes and behavior so they appear rational and consistent. When there is an inconsistency, individuals will take steps to correct it either by altering the attitudes or the behavior or by developing a rationalization for the inconsistency.

For example, a campus recruiter for XYZ Company who visits college campuses, identifies qualified job candidates, and sells them on the advantages of XYZ as a good place to work would be in conflict if he personally believed that XYZ had poor working conditions and few opportunities for recent college graduates. This recruiter could, over time, find his attitudes toward XYZ becoming more positive. He may, in effect, convince himself by continually articulating the merits of working for the company. Another alternative would be for the recruiter to become overtly negative about XYZ and the opportunities within the firm for prospective candidates. The original enthusiasm that the recruiter might have shown would dwindle, probably to be replaced by open cynicism toward the company. Finally, the recruiter might acknowledge that XYZ is an undesirable place to work, but as a professional recruiter, his obligation is to present the positive aspects of working for the company. He might further rationalize that no work place is perfect and that his job isn't to present both sides of the issue but to present a favorable picture of the company.

Cognitive Dissonance Theory

Can we assume from this consistency principle that an individual's behavior can always be predicted if we know his or her attitude on a subject? The answer, unfortunately, is more complex than merely Yes or No.

cognitive dissonance

Any incompatibility between two or more attitudes or between behavior and attitudes.

Leon Festinger, in the late 1950s, proposed the theory of **cognitive dissonance**.[6] This theory sought to explain the relationship between attitudes and behavior. Dissonance in this case means inconsistency. Cognitive dissonance refers to any inconsistency that an individual might perceive between two or more of his or her attitudes, or between his or her behavior and attitudes. Festinger argued that any form of inconsistency is uncomfortable and that individuals will try to reduce the dissonance and thus, the discomfort. In other words, individuals seek a stable state with a minimum of dissonance.

Of course, no one can completely avoid dissonance. You know that cheating on your income tax is wrong, but you "fudge" the numbers a bit every year and hope you won't be audited. Or you tell your children to brush their teeth after every meal, but you don't do it yourself. How do people cope with cognitive dissonance? Festinger proposed that the desire to reduce dissonance is determined by the *importance* of the factors creating the dissonance, the degree of *influence* the individual believes he or she has over those factors, and the *rewards* that may be involved in dissonance.

If the factors creating the dissonance are relatively unimportant, the pressure to correct the imbalance will be low. However, say that a corporate manager—Mrs. Lopez—believes strongly that no company should pollute. Unfortunately, Mrs. Lopez, because of job requirements, is placed in the position of having to make decisions that would trade off her company's profitability against her attitudes on pollution. She knows that dumping the company's wastewater into a local river (for this example, we'll assume that dumping is legal) is in her company's best economic interest. What will she do? Clearly, Mrs. Lopez will be experiencing a high degree of cognitive dissonance. Because of the importance of the elements in this example, we can't expect Mrs. Lopez to ignore the inconsistency, but there are several paths that she can follow to deal with her dilemma. She can change her behavior (use her authority to order that the dumping stop). Or she can reduce dissonance by concluding that the dissonant behavior isn't so important after all ("I've got to have a job,

How fast am I? Well, I caught a jackrabbit when I was 6, and in 1988, I clocked in at 23.5 mph in the 100-meter. Sure, some of that's natural, but I do train hard and drink milk. 2%. It's loaded with nutrients like calcium and vitamin D, so I drink lots of it. Nice and slow.

MILK
Where's *your* mustache?®

By deliberately creating cognitive dissonance between the image of celebrities and a mundane product, the National Fluid Milk Processor Promotion Board hoped to raise public awareness of milk's nutritional benefits. The campaign succeeded and became an advertising classic.

and in my role as a corporate decision maker, I often have to place the good of my company above that of the environment or society"). A third alternative would be for Mrs. Lopez to change her attitude ("There's nothing wrong with dumping wastewater into the river"). Still another choice would be for her to identify compatible factors that outweigh the dissonant ones ("The benefits to society from our manufacturing our product more than offset the cost to society of the resulting water pollution").

The degree of influence that individuals believe they have over the factors will affect their reaction to the dissonance. If they perceive the dissonance to be an uncontrollable result—something about which they have no choice—they are unlikely to be receptive to attitude change or to feel a need for it. If, for example, the dissonance-producing behavior was required as a result of a boss's order, the pressure to reduce dissonance would be less than if the behavior had been performed voluntarily. Although dissonance would exist, it could be rationalized and justified by the need to follow the boss's orders—that is, by the lack of individual choice and control.

Rewards also influence the degree to which individuals are motivated to reduce dissonance. Coupling high dissonance with high rewards tends to reduce the tension inherent in the dissonance, by motivating the individual to believe that there is consistency.

These moderating factors suggest that just because individuals experience dissonance, they will not necessarily move directly toward consistency: that is, reducing the dissonance. If the issues contributing to the dissonance are of minimal importance, if an individual perceives that the dissonance is externally imposed and is substantially uncontrollable by him or her, or if rewards are significant enough to offset the dissonance, the individual will not be under great tension to reduce the dissonance.

Attitude Surveys

attitude surveys

Eliciting responses from employees through questionnaires about how they feel about their jobs, work groups, supervisors, or the organization.

Many organizations regularly survey their employees about their attitudes. Figure 13-2 shows what an attitude survey might look like. Typically, **attitude surveys** present the employee with a set of statements or questions. Ideally, the items will be designed to obtain the specific information that management desires. An attitude score is achieved by summing up responses to individual questionnaire items. These scores can then be averaged for job groups, departments, divisions, or the organization as a whole. For instance, at First Union Bank in Charlotte, North Carolina, employee surveys are viewed as a report card about the company from employees.

The Satisfaction-Productivity Controversy

From the 1930s to the mid-1960s, it was widely believed that happy workers were productive workers. As a result of the Hawthorne studies (discussed in chapter 2), managers generalized that if their employees were satisfied with their jobs, that satisfaction would be translated into high productivity. Many of the paternalistic actions by managers in the 1930s, 1940s, and 1950s—things such as forming company bowling teams and credit unions, having company picnics, and training supervisors to be sensitive to the concerns of subordinates—were supposed to make workers happy. But belief in the happy worker idea was based more on wishful thinking than on hard evidence.

A careful review of research indicates that if satisfaction does have a positive effect on productivity, it's quite small.[7] However, looking at situational contingency variables has improved the relationship.[8] For example, the relationship is strongest when the employee's behavior isn't constrained or controlled by outside factors. An employee's productivity on machine-paced jobs, for instance, is going to be more heavily influenced by the speed of the machine than by his or her level of satisfaction. Another important contingency variable seems to be job level. The satisfaction-performance correlations are strongest for higher-level employees. Thus, we might expect the relationship to be more relevant for individuals in professional, supervisory, and managerial positions than for operatives.

FIGURE 13-2   **Sample Attitude Survey**

Please answer each of the following statements using the following rating scale:

$$5 = \text{Strongly agree}$$
$$4 = \text{Agree}$$
$$3 = \text{Undecided}$$
$$2 = \text{Disagree}$$
$$1 = \text{Strongly disagree}$$

Statement   **Rating**

1. This company is a pretty good place to work.   _____
2. I can get ahead in this company if I make the effort.   _____
3. This company's wage rates are competitive with those of other
   companies.   _____
4. Employee promotion decisions are handled fairly.   _____
5. I understand the various fringe benefits the company offers.   _____
6. My job makes the best use of my abilities.   _____
7. My workload is challenging but not burdensome.   _____
8. I have trust and confidence in my boss.   _____
9. I feel free to tell my boss what I think.   _____
10. I know what my boss expects of me.   _____

Source: Based on T. Lammers, "The Essential Employee Survey," *Inc.*, December 1992, pp. 159–61.

Unfortunately, most studies on the relationship between satisfaction and productivity used research designs that could not prove cause and effect. Studies that controlled for a causal relation indicate that a more valid conclusion is that productivity leads to satisfaction rather than the other way around.[9] If you do a good job, you intrinsically feel good about it. In addition, assuming that the organization rewards productivity, your higher productivity should increase verbal recognition, your pay level, and promotion opportunities. These rewards, in turn, increase your level of satisfaction with the job.

Implications for Managers

We know that employees will try to reduce dissonance. And, not surprisingly, there's relatively strong evidence that committed and satisfied employees have low rates of turnover and absenteeism.[10] Because most managers want to minimize the number of resignations and absences—especially among their most productive employees—they should do those things that will generate positive job attitudes. For instance, dissonance can be managed. If employees are required to do things that appear inconsistent to them or that are at odds with their attitudes, managers should remember that pressure to reduce the dissonance is minimized when the employee perceives that the dissonance is externally imposed and uncontrollable. The pressure is also decreased if rewards are significant enough to offset the dissonance. So the manager might point to external forces such as competitors, customers, or other factors when explaining the need to perform some work activity the individual may have some dissonance about. Or the manager can provide rewards that an individual desires in order to decrease his or her attempts to eliminate the dissonance.

The findings about the satisfaction-productivity relationships have important implications for managers. They suggest that the goal of making employees happy on the assumption that their being happy will lead to high productivity is probably misdirected. Managers who follow this strategy could end up with a very happy, but very unproductive, group of employees. Managers would get better results by directing their attention primarily to what will help employees become more productive. Then, successful job performance should lead to feelings of accomplishment, increased pay, promotions, and other rewards—all desirable outcomes—which then lead to job satisfaction.

TESTING...
TESTING...

4 **Explain how individuals reconcile inconsistencies between attitudes and behaviors.**

5 **What are attitude surveys, and how might they help managers?**

6 **Describe the relationship between job satisfaction and productivity.**

PERSONALITY

Some people are quiet and passive; others are loud and aggressive. When we describe people in terms such as *quiet, passive, loud, aggressive, ambitious, extroverted, loyal, tense,* or *sociable,* we're categorizing them in terms of *personality traits.* An individual's **personality** is the unique combination of the psychological traits we use to describe that person.

personality

A combination of psychological traits that describes a person.

Personality Traits

How would you describe your personality? There are dozens of personality traits. For instance, aggressive, shy, ambitious, loyal, and lazy. Over the years, researchers have attempted to focus specifically on which traits would lead to identifying one's personality. Two of these most widely recognized efforts include the Myers-Briggs Type Indicator and the five-factor model of personality.

Myers-Briggs Type Indicator. Personality assessment tests are commonly used to reveal an individual's personality traits. One of the most popular personality tests is the Myers-Briggs Type Indicator (or MBTI, as it's often called). It consists of more than a hundred questions that ask people how they usually act or feel in different situations.[11] The way you respond to these questions puts you at one end or another of four dimensions:

1. *Social interaction.*   extrovert or introvert (E or I)   An extrovert is someone who is outgoing, dominant, and often aggressive and who wants to change the world. Extroverts need a work environment that is varied and action oriented, that lets them be with others, and that gives them a variety of experiences. An individual who's shy and withdrawn and focuses on understanding the world is described as an introvert. Introverts prefer a work environment that is quiet and concentrated, that lets them be alone, and that gives them a chance to explore in depth a limited set of experiences.

2. *Preference for gathering data.*   sensing or intuitive (S or N)   Sensing types dislike new problems unless there are standard ways to solve them; they like an established routine, have a high need for closure, show patience with routine details, and tend to be good at precise work. On the other hand, intuitive types are individuals who like solving new problems, dislike doing the same thing over and over again, jump to conclusions, are impatient with routine details, and dislike taking time for precision.

3. *Preference for decision making.*   feeling or thinking (F or T)   Individuals who are feeling types are aware of other people and their feelings, like harmony, need occasional praise, dislike telling people unpleasant things, tend to be sympathetic, and relate well to most people. Thinking types are unemotional and uninterested in peo-

ple's feelings, like analysis and putting things into logical order, are able to reprimand people and fire them when necessary, may seem hard-hearted, and tend to relate well only to other thinking types.

4. *Style of making decisions.*   perceptive or judgmental (P or J)   Perceptive types are curious, spontaneous, flexible, adaptable, and tolerant. They focus on starting a task, postpone decisions, and want to find out all about the task before starting it. Judgmental types are decisive, good planners, purposeful, and exacting. They focus on completing a task, make decisions quickly, and want only the information necessary to get a task done.

Combining these preferences provides descriptions of 16 personality types. Table 13-1 summarizes a few of them.

   How could the MBTI help managers? Proponents of the test believe that it's important to know these personality types because they influence the way people interact and solve problems. For instance, if your boss is an intuitor and you're a sensor, you'll gather information in different ways. An intuitor prefers gut reactions, whereas a sensor prefers facts. To work well with your boss, you would have to present more than just facts about a situation and bring out how you feel about it. The MBTI has been used to help managers select employees who are well matched to certain types of jobs. All in all, the MBTI can be a useful tool for understanding personality and predicting people's behavior.

The Big-Five Model of Personality.   Although the MBTI is very popular, it suffers from one major criticism. It lacks evidence to support its validity. That same criticism can't be applied to the five-factor model of personality, more often called the **big-five model.**[12] The big five personality traits are:

big-five model

Five-factor model of personality that includes extraversion, agreeableness, conscientiousness, emotional stability, and openness to experience.

TABLE 13-1	**Examples of MBTI Personality Types**
Type	**Description**
INFJ (introvert, intuitive, feeling, judgmental)	Quietly forceful, conscientious, and concerned for others. Such people succeed by perseverance, originality, and the desire to do whatever is needed or wanted. They are often highly respected for their uncompromising principles.
ESTP (extrovert, sensing, thinking, perceptive)	Blunt and sometimes insensitive. Such people are matter-of-fact and do not worry or hurry. They enjoy whatever comes along. They work best with real things that can be assembled or disassembled.
ISFP (introvert, sensing, feeling, perceptive)	Sensitive, kind, modest, shy, and quietly friendly. Such people strongly dislike disagreements and will avoid them. They are loyal followers and quite often are relaxed about getting things done.
ENTJ (extrovert, intuitive, thinking, judgmental)	Warm, friendly, candid, and decisive; also usually skilled in anything that requires reasoning and intelligent talk, but may sometimes overestimate what they are capable of doing.

Source: Based on I. Briggs-Myers, *Introduction to Type* (Palo Alto, CA: Consulting Psychologists Press, 1980), pp. 7–8.

1. *Extraversion.* A personality dimension that describes the degree to which someone is sociable, talkative, and assertive.

2. *Agreeableness.* A personality dimension that describes the degree to which someone is good-natured, cooperative, and trusting.

3. *Conscientiousness.* A personality dimension that describes the degree to which someone is responsible, dependable, persistent, and achievement oriented.

4. *Emotional stability.* A personality dimension that describes the degree to which someone is calm, enthusiastic, and secure (positive) or tense, nervous, depressed, and insecure (negative).

5. *Openness to experience.* A personality dimension that describes the degree to which someone is imaginative, artistically sensitive, and intellectual.

The big five provide more than just a personality framework. Research has shown that important relationships exist between these personality dimensions and job performance. For example, one study examined five categories of occupations: *professionals* (such as engineers, architects, attorneys), *police, managers, salespeople,* and *semiskilled and skilled employees.*[13] Job performance was defined in terms of employee performance ratings, training competency, and personnel data such as salary level. The results of the study showed that conscientiousness predicted job performance for all five occupational groups. Predictions for the other personality dimensions depended on the situation and on the occupational group. For example, extraversion predicted performance in managerial and sales positions—occupations in which high social interaction is necessary. Openness to experience was found to be important in predicting training competency. Ironically, emotional security wasn't positively related to job performance. Although one might expect calm and secure workers to perform better than nervous ones, that wasn't the case. Perhaps that result is a function of the likelihood that emotionally stable workers often keep their jobs and emotionally unstable workers often do not. Given that all the people who participated in the study were employed, the variance on that dimension was small and nonsignificant.

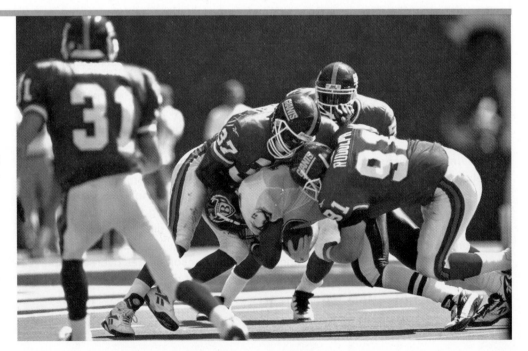

The use of psychological tests has become popular among NFL teams such as the New York Giants, pictured here. The tests measure traits such as aggressiveness and competitiveness, predict players' reactions in hypothetical situations, and even predict how well a new draft pick will fit in.

Predicting Behavior from Personality Traits

Five specific personality traits have proved to be the most powerful in explaining individual behavior in organizations. They are *locus of control, Machiavellianism, self-esteem, self-monitoring,* and *risk propensity.*

Locus of Control.   Some people believe that they control their own fate. Others see themselves as pawns, believing that what happens to them in their lives is due to luck or chance. The **locus of control** in the first case is *internal*; these people believe that they control their own destiny. The locus of control in the second case is *external*; these people believe that their lives are controlled by outside forces.[14] Research evidence indicates that employees who rate high on externality are less satisfied with their jobs, more alienated from the work setting, and less involved in their jobs than are those who rate high on internality.[15] A manager might also expect externals to blame a poor performance evaluation on their boss's prejudice, their co-workers, or other events outside their control; internals would explain the same evaluation in terms of their own actions.

locus of control

The degree to which people believe they are masters of their own fate.

Machiavellianism.   The second characteristic is called **Machiavellianism** (Mach), named after Niccolo Machiavelli, who wrote in the sixteenth century on how to gain and manipulate power. An individual who is high in Machiavellianism—in contrast to someone who is low—is pragmatic, maintains emotional distance, and believes that ends can justify means.[16] "If it works, use it" is consistent with a high Mach perspective. Do high Machs make good employees? That answer depends on the type of job and whether you consider ethical implications in evaluating performance. In jobs that require bargaining skills (such as labor negotiator or purchasing manager) or that have substantial rewards for winning (such as a commissioned salesperson), high Machs are productive. In jobs in which ends do not justify the means or that lack absolute measures of performance, it's difficult to predict the performance of high Machs.

Machiavellianism

A measure of the degree to which people are pragmatic, maintain emotional distance, and believe that ends can justify means.

Self-Esteem.   People differ in the degree to which they like or dislike themselves. This trait is called **self-esteem**.[17] The research on self-esteem (SE) offers some interesting insights into organizational behavior. For example, self-esteem is directly related to expectations for success. High SEs believe that they possess the ability they need in order to succeed at work. Individuals with high SEs will take more risks in job selection and are more likely to choose unconventional jobs than are people with low SEs.

self-esteem

An individual's degree of like or dislike for himself or herself.

The most common finding on self-esteem is that low SEs are more susceptible to external influence than are high SEs. Low SEs are dependent on receiving positive evaluations from others. As a result, they're more likely to seek approval from others and are more prone to conform to the beliefs and behaviors of those they respect than are high SEs. In managerial positions, low SEs will tend to be concerned with pleasing others and, therefore, will be less likely to take unpopular stands than are high SEs.

Not surprisingly, self-esteem has also been found to be related to job satisfaction. A number of studies confirm that high SEs are more satisfied with their jobs than are low SEs.

Self-Monitoring.   Another personality trait that has received increasing attention is called **self-monitoring**.[18] It refers to an individual's ability to adjust his or her behavior to external, situational factors. Individuals high in self-monitoring show considerable adaptability in adjusting their behavior to external, situational factors. They're highly sensitive to external cues and can behave differently in different situations. High self-monitors are capable of presenting striking contradictions between their public persona and their private selves. Low self-monitors cannot adjust their behavior. They tend to display their true dispositions and attitudes in every situation, and there's high behavioral consistency between who they are and what they do.

self-monitoring

A personality trait that measures an individual's ability to adjust his or her behavior to external situational factors.

Research on self-monitoring is fairly new, thus predictions are hard to make. However, preliminary evidence suggests that high self-monitors pay closer attention to the behavior of others and are more flexible than are low self-monitors.[19] We might also hypothesize that high self-monitors will be successful in managerial positions that require them to play multiple, and even contradictory, roles. The high self-monitor is capable of putting on different "faces" for different audiences.

Risk Taking.   People differ in their willingness to take chances. Differences in the propensity to assume or to avoid risk have been shown to affect how long it takes managers to make a decision and how much information they require before making their choice. For instance, in one study, a group of managers worked on simulated personnel exercises that required them to make hiring decisions. High risk-taking managers took less time to make decisions and used less information in making their choices than did the low risk-taking managers. Interestingly, the decision accuracy was the same for the two groups. To maximize organizational effectiveness, managers should try to align employee risk-taking propensity with specific job demands.[20] For instance, a high risk-taking propensity may lead to effective performance for a commodities trader in a brokerage firm because this type of job demands rapid decision making. On the other hand, a high risk-taking propensity might prove a major obstacle to accountants auditing financial statements.

Personality Types in Different National Cultures

We know that there are certainly no common personality types for a given country. You can, for instance, find high risk takers and low risk takers in almost any culture. Yet a country's culture can influence *dominant* personality characteristics of its people. We can see this effect of national culture by looking at one of the personality traits we have just discussed: locus of control.

ENTREPRENEURSHIP

The Entrepreneurial Personality

One of the most researched topics in entrepreneurship has been the search to determine what, if any, psychological characteristics entrepreneurs have in common.[21] A number of characteristics have been identified, including a willingness to work hard, self-confidence, optimism, determination, and a high energy level. But three factors are regularly at the top of most lists profiling the entrepreneurial personality. Entrepreneurs have a high need for achievement, believe strongly that they can control their own destinies, and take only moderate risks.

The research allows us to draw a general description of entrepreneurs. They tend to be independent types who prefer to be personally responsible for solving problems, for setting goals, and for reaching those goals. They value independence and particularly don't like being controlled by others. They're not afraid to take chances, but they're not wild risk takers either. They prefer to take calculated risks in which they feel that they can have some control over the outcome.

The evidence on entrepreneurial personalities leads us to two obvious conclusions. First, people with this personality makeup aren't likely to be contented, productive employees in the typical large corporation or governmental agency. The rules, regulations, and controls that these bureaucracies impose on their members frustrate entrepreneurs. Second, the challenges and conditions inherent in starting one's own business mesh well with the entrepreneurial personality. Starting a new venture that they control appeals to their willingness to take risks and determine their own destinies. But the risk that they perceive as moderate, because they believe that their future is fully in their own hands, is often seen as high by non-entrepreneurs. ■

National cultures differ in terms of the degree to which people believe they control their environment. For instance, North Americans believe that they can dominate their environment; other societies, such as those in Middle Eastern countries, believe that life is essentially preordained or predetermined. Notice how closely this distinction parallels the concept of internal and external locus of control. On the basis of this particular cultural characteristic, we should expect a larger proportion of internals in the U.S. and Canadian workforces than in the workforces of Saudi Arabia or Iran.

As we have seen throughout this section, personality traits influence employees' behavior. For global managers, understanding how personality traits differ takes on added significance when looking at it from the perspective of national culture.

Matching Personalities and Jobs

Individual personalities differ. So, too, do jobs. Following this logic, theorists have tried to determine which types of personalities match which types of job. The best-documented personality-job fit theory has been developed by psychologist John Holland.[22] His theory states that an employee's satisfaction with his or her job, as well as his or her likelihood of leaving that job, depends on the degree to which the individual's personality matches the occupational environment. Holland identified six basic personality types. Table 13-2 describes each of the six types, their personality characteristics, and sample occupations.

TABLE 13-2	Holland's Typology of Personality and Sample Occupations	
Type	**Personality Characteristics**	**Sample Occupations**
Realistic. Prefers physical activities that require skill, strength, and coordination	Shy, genuine, persistent, stable, conforming, practical	Mechanic, drill press operator, assembly-line worker, farmer
Investigative. Prefers activities involving thinking, organizing, and understanding	Analytical, original, curious, independent	Biologist, economist, mathematician, news reporter
Social. Prefers activities that involve helping and developing others	Sociable, friendly, cooperative, understanding	Social worker, teacher, counselor, clinical psychologist
Conventional. Prefers rule-regulated, orderly, and unambiguous activities	Conforming, efficient, practical, unimaginative, inflexible	Accountant, corporate manager, bank teller, file clerk
Enterprising. Prefers verbal activities in which there are opportunities to influence others and attain power	Self-confident, ambitious, energetic, domineering	Lawyer, real estate agent, public relations specialist, small business manager
Artistic. Prefers ambiguous and unsystematic activities that allow creative expression	Imaginative, disorderly, idealistic, emotional, impractical	Painter, musician, writer, interior decorator

Source: Based on J.L. Holland, *Making Vocational Choices: A Theory of Vocational Personalities and Work Environments*, 2d ed. (Upper Saddle River, NJ: Prentice Hall, 1985).

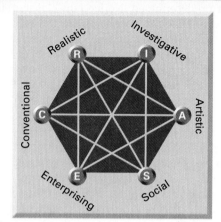

FIGURE 13-3   **Relationships among Occupational Personality Types**

Source: J.L. Holland, *Making Vocational Choices: A Theory of Vocational Personalities and Work Environments,* 2d ed. (Upper Saddle River, NJ: Prentice Hall, 1985). Used by permission. This model originally appeared in J.L. Holland et al., "An Empirical Occupational Classification Derived from a Theory of Personality and Intended for Practice and Research," ACT Research Report No. 29 (Iowa City: The American College Testing Program, 1969).

Holland's research strongly supports the hexagonal diagram in Figure 13-3.[23] This figure illustrates that the closer two fields or orientations are in the hexagon, the more compatible they are. Adjacent categories are quite similar; those diagonally opposite are highly dissimilar.

What does all this mean? The theory proposes that satisfaction is highest and turnover lowest when personality and occupation are compatible. Social individuals should be in "people" type jobs, and so forth. A realistic person in a realistic job is in a more congruent situation than is a realistic person in an investigative job. A realistic person in a social job is in the most incongruent situation possible. The key points of this model are that (1) there do appear to be intrinsic differences in personality among individuals; (2) there are differ-

Sometimes the only way an entrepreneurial spirit can find a job that matches his personality is to create it. That's what Douglas Dunbebin did when he founded his own graphic design firm in Beltsville, Maryland, and started working with clients whose missions, such as the rights of women and migrant farm workers, matched issues that concern him. Here Dunbebin (left) presents Habitat's president, Millard Fuller, with a check for $30,000 he raised for the group through a T-shirt project.

ent types of jobs, and (3) people in job environments compatible with their personality types should be more satisfied and less likely to resign voluntarily than should people in incongruent jobs.

Implications for Managers

The major value of a manager's understanding personality differences probably lies in employee selection. Managers are likely to have higher-performing and more-satisfied employees if consideration is given to matching personality types with jobs. In addition, there may be other benefits. By recognizing that people approach problem solving, decision making, and job interactions differently, a manager can better understand why, for instance, a subordinate is uncomfortable with making quick decisions or why an employee insists on gathering as much information as possible before addressing a problem. Or, for instance, managers can expect that individuals with an external locus of control may be less satisfied with their jobs than internals and also that they may be less willing to accept responsibility for their actions.

7 Contrast the MBTI and the big-five models in terms of understanding personality.

8 Describe the five personality traits that have proved to be the most powerful in explaining individual behavior in organizations.

9 How can we use our knowledge of personality to match people to jobs?

TESTING...
TESTING...

1 2 3

PERCEPTION

Perception is a process by which individuals organize and interpret their sensory impressions in order to give meaning to their environment. Research on perception consistently demonstrates that individuals may look at the same thing yet perceive it differently. One manager, for instance, can interpret the fact that her assistant regularly takes several days to make important decisions as evidence that the assistant is slow, disorganized, and afraid to make decisions. Another manager, with the same assistant, might interpret the same tendency as evidence that the assistant is thoughtful, thorough, and deliberate. The first manager would probably evaluate her assistant negatively; the second manager would probably evaluate the person positively. The point is that none of us sees reality. We interpret what we see and call it reality. And, of course, as the example shows, we act according to our perceptions.

perception

The process of organizing and interpreting sensory impressions in order to give meaning to the environment.

Factors That Influence Perception

How do we explain the fact that people can perceive the same thing differently? A number of factors operate to shape and sometimes distort perception. These factors can reside in the *perceiver;* in the object, or *target,* being perceived; or in the context of the *situation* in which the perception occurs.

The Perceiver.   When an individual looks at a target and attempts to interpret what he or she sees, the individual's personal characteristics will heavily influence the interpretation. These personal characteristics include attitudes, personality, motives, interests, experiences, and expectations.

The Target.   The characteristics of the target being observed can also affect what's perceived. Loud people are more likely than quiet people to be noticed in a group. So, too, are extremely attractive or unattractive individuals. Because targets aren't looked at in isolation,

FIGURE 13-4   **Perception Challenges: What Do You See?**

Old woman or young woman?   Two faces or an urn?   A knight on a horse?

the relationship of a target to its background also influences perception (see Figure 13-4 for some examples), as does our tendency to group close things and similar things together.

The Situation.   The context in which we see objects or events is also important. The time at which an object or event is seen can influence attention, as can location, light, heat, color, and any number of other situational factors.

Attribution Theory

Much of the research on perception is directed at inanimate objects. Managers, though, are more concerned with people. So our discussion of perception should focus on person perception.

Our perceptions of people differ from our perceptions of inanimate objects such as desks, machines, or buildings, because we make inferences about the actions of people that we don't make about objects. Objects don't have beliefs, motives, or intentions; people do. The result is that, when we observe people, we try to develop explanations of why they behave in certain ways. Our perception and judgment of a person's actions, therefore, will be significantly influenced by the assumptions we make about the person's internal state.

attribution theory

A theory used to develop explanations of how we judge people differently depending on the meaning we attribute to a given behavior.

Attribution theory has been developed to explain how we judge people differently depending on what meaning we attribute to a given behavior.[24] Basically, the theory suggests that when we observe an individual's behavior, we attempt to determine whether it was internally or externally caused. Internally caused behaviors are those that are believed to be under the personal control of the individual. Externally caused behavior results from outside factors; that is, the person is forced into the behavior by the situation. That determination, however, depends on three factors: distinctiveness, consensus, and consistency.

Distinctiveness refers to whether an individual displays a behavior in many situations or whether it's particular to one situation. Is the employee who arrived late today the same person that some employees are complaining is a "goof-off"? What we want to know is whether this behavior is unusual. If it's unusual, the observer is likely to attribute the behavior to external forces. However, if the action isn't unusual, it will probably be judged as internal.

If everyone who's faced with a similar situation responds in the same way, we can say the behavior shows *consensus*. A tardy employee's behavior would meet this criterion if all employees who took the same route to work were also late. From an attribution perspective, if consensus is high you are likely to give an external attribution to the employee's tar-

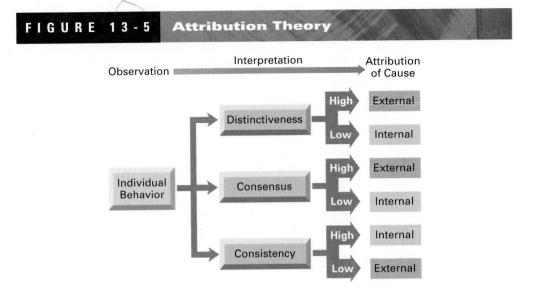

FIGURE 13-5   **Attribution Theory**

diness; but if other employees who took the same route made it to work on time, you would conclude that the cause was internal.

Finally, an observer looks for *consistency* in a person's actions. Does the person engage in the behaviors regularly and consistently? Does the person respond the same way over time? Coming in 10 minutes late for work isn't perceived in the same way if, for one employee, it represents an unusual case (she hasn't been late in months), while for another it's part of a routine pattern (she's late two or three times every week). The more consistent the behavior, the more the observer is inclined to attribute it to internal causes.

Figure 13-5 summarizes the key elements of attribution theory. It would tell us, for instance, that if an employee—let's call him Mr. Liu—generally performs at or about the same level on other related tasks as he does on his current task (low distinctiveness), if other employees frequently perform differently (better or worse) than Mr. Liu does on that current task (low consensus), and if Mr. Liu's performance on this current task is consistent over time (high consistency), his manager or anyone else who is judging Mr. Liu's work is likely to hold him primarily responsible for his task performance (internal attribution).

One of the most interesting findings drawn from attribution theory is that there are errors or biases that distort attributions. For instance, there's substantial evidence to support the fact that, when we make judgments about the behavior of other people, we have a tendency to underestimate the influence of external factors and to overestimate the influence of internal or personal factors.[25] This tendency is called the **fundamental attribution error** and can explain why a sales manager may be prone to attribute the poor performance of her sales representatives to laziness rather than to the innovative product line introduced by a competitor. There's also a tendency for individuals to attribute their own successes to internal factors such as ability or effort while putting the blame for personal failure on external factors such as luck. This tendency is called the **self-serving bias** and suggests that feedback provided to employees in performance reviews will be predictably distorted by them depending on whether it's positive or negative.

Shortcuts Frequently Used in Judging Others

We use a number of shortcuts when we judge others. Perceiving and interpreting what others do is a lot of work. As a result, individuals develop techniques for making the task more manageable. These techniques are frequently valuable; they let us make accurate perceptions rapidly and provide valid data for making predictions. However, they are not foolproof.

fundamental attribution error

The tendency to underestimate the influence of external factors and overestimate the influence of internal factors when making judgments about the behavior of others.

self-serving bias

The tendency for individuals to attribute their own successes to internal factors while putting the blame for failures on external factors.

selectivity

The process by which people assimilate certain bits and pieces of what they observe, depending on their interests, background, and attitudes.

assumed similarity

The belief that others are like oneself.

stereotyping

Judging a person on the basis of one's perception of a group to which he or she belongs.

halo effect

A general impression of an individual based on a single characteristic.

They can and do get us into trouble. An understanding of these shortcuts can be helpful for recognizing when they can result in significant distortions.

Individuals cannot assimilate all they observe, so they engage in **selectivity.** They take in bits and pieces of the vast amounts of stimuli bombarding their senses. These bits and pieces aren't chosen randomly; they are selectively chosen depending on the interests, background, experience, and attitudes of the observer. Selective perception allows us to "speed read" others, but not without the risk of drawing an inaccurate picture.

It's easy to judge others if we assume that they're similar to us. In **assumed similarity,** or the "like me" effect, the observer's perception of others is influenced more by the observer's own characteristics than by those of the person observed. For example, if you want challenges and responsibility in your job, you'll assume that others want the same. People who assume that others are like them can, of course, be right, but most of the time they're wrong.

When we judge someone on the basis of our perception of a group he or she is part of, we're using the shortcut called **stereotyping.** "Married people are more stable employees than single persons" and "union people expect something for nothing" are examples of stereotyping. To the degree that a stereotype is based on fact, it may produce accurate judgments. However, many stereotypes have no foundation in fact. In such cases, stereotypes distort judgments.[26]

When we form a general impression about a person on the basis of a single characteristic, such as intelligence, sociability, or appearance, we're being influenced by the **halo effect.** This effect frequently occurs when students evaluate their classroom instructor. Students may isolate a single trait such as enthusiasm and allow their entire evaluation to be slanted by their perception of this one trait. An instructor might be quiet, assured, knowledgeable, and highly qualified, but if his classroom teaching style lacks zest, he might be rated lower on a number of other characteristics.

Implications for Managers

Managers need to recognize that their employees react to perceptions, not to reality. So whether a manager's appraisal of an employee is actually objective and unbiased or whether the organization's wage levels are actually among the highest in the industry is less relevant than what employees perceive them to be. If individuals perceive appraisals to be biased or wage levels as low, they'll behave as if those conditions actually exist. Employees organize and interpret what they see, so there is always the potential for perceptual distortion.

The message to managers should be clear: Pay close attention to how employees perceive both their jobs and management practices. Remember, the valuable employee who

Andrew Busey (front), president of Ichat at 25, is one member of the so-called Generation X who belies the stereotype of young people as "slackers." His company, which he founded after working for both IBM and Microcom, makes software that allows Web surfers to electronically "chat" while visiting interactive sites.

Challenging the Stereotypes of Women and Older Workers

What's your perception of women and older workers? Is it something like this: Women show less initiative on the job than men do. They are less committed to their career and organization. And if you ask them to relocate, forget it. They probably won't, especially if they have children. And older workers! Older workers have high absentee rates because they're so often sick. That comes with age, you know. They're also slower, more accident prone, tend to complain more, and cost employers more than younger workers.

Well, if that's your perception, you're wrong![27] As long as these types of perceptions prevail, they hurt women and older workers and they hurt the organizations that need their skills. The stereotype of women as uncommitted employees who won't stay with an organization or who won't relocate is just plain not true. The primary reason female professionals resign their jobs is not home or childrearing responsibilities. It's frustration with career progress. In fact, one study reported that 73 percent of women who quit large companies moved to

another company, whereas only 7 percent resigned to stay home.

Many young people's perceptions of older workers are also way off base. They stereotype by describing workers over 55 in terms such as incompetent, or past their prime, or slow to respond. The evidence suggests that they are, in reality, reliable, trained, and experienced. The facts confirm that older workers almost always display significantly lower absenteeism than younger workers, have about half the accident rate of younger workers, and consistently score higher on job satisfaction. Moreover, there is no research evidence that age negatively affects job productivity or costs employers more.

Negative gender and ageist stereotypes not only adversely affect women and older workers but also are likely to be a major handicap for organizations in the future. Because of the projected shortage of skilled workers in North America and much of Western Europe beginning in the early years of the next decade organizations will be desperately searching for employees who have skills and experience. Organizations that refuse to recognize that both women and older workers are a valuable labor resource will lose a large part of an increasingly smaller talent pool. ■

MANAGING WORKFORCE DIVERSITY

quits because of an inaccurate perception is just as great a loss to an organization as the valuable employee who quits for a valid reason.

10 How can an understanding of perception help managers better understand individual behavior?

11 What role does attribution theory play in perception?

12 Name four shortcuts used in judging others. What effect does each have on perception?

TESTING... TESTING... **1 2 3**

LEARNING

The last individual behavior concept we are going to introduce in this chapter is learning. It is included for the obvious reason that almost all complex behavior is learned. If we want to explain and predict behavior, we need to understand how people learn.

What is learning? A psychologist's definition is considerably broader than the average person's view that "it's what we did when we went to school." In actuality, each of us is continually going to school. Learning occurs all the time. We continuously learn from our experiences. A workable definition of **learning** is, therefore, any relatively permanent change in behavior that occurs as a result of experience.

Operant Conditioning

Operant conditioning argues that behavior is a function of its consequences. People learn to behave to get something they want or to avoid something they don't want. Operant behavior describes voluntary or learned behavior in contrast to reflexive or unlearned behavior. The tendency to repeat such behavior is influenced by the reinforcement or lack of reinforcement that happens as a result of the behavior. Reinforcement, therefore, strengthens a behavior and increases the likelihood that it will be repeated.

Building on earlier work in the field, B. F. Skinner's research has widely expanded our knowledge of operant conditioning.[28] Even his most outspoken critics, a sizable group, admit that his operant concepts work.

Behavior is assumed to be determined from without—that is, learned—rather than from within—reflexive or unlearned. Skinner argued that creating pleasing and desirable consequences to follow some specific behavior would increase the frequency of that behavior. People will most likely engage in desired behaviors if they are positively reinforced for doing so, and rewards are most effective if they immediately follow the desired response. In addition, behavior that isn't rewarded, or is punished, is less likely to be done again.

You see examples of operant conditioning everywhere. Any situation in which it's either explicitly stated or implicitly suggested that reinforcements (rewards) are contingent on some action on your part is an example of operant conditioning. Your instructor says that if you want a high grade in the course, you must give correct answers on the tests. A salesperson working on commission knows that earning a sizable income is contingent upon generating high sales in his or her territory. Of course, the linkage between behavior and reinforcement can also work to teach the individual to engage in behaviors that work against the best interests of the organization. Assume that your boss tells you that if you'll work overtime during the next three-week busy season, you'll be compensated for it at the next performance appraisal. Then, when performance appraisal time comes, you are given no positive reinforcement (such as praise for pitching in and helping out when needed). What will you do the next time your boss asks you to work overtime? You'll probably refuse. Your behavior can be explained by operant conditioning: If a behavior isn't positively reinforced, the probability that the behavior will be repeated declines.

Social Learning

Individuals can learn by observing what happens to other people and just by being told about something as well as by direct experiences. So, for example, much of what we have learned comes from watching models—parents, teachers, peers, television and movie performers, bosses, and so forth. This view that we can learn both through observation and direct experience has been called **social learning theory.**

Although social learning theory is an extension of operant conditioning—that is, it assumes that behavior is a function of consequences—it also acknowledges the existence of observational learning and the importance of perception in learning. People respond to how they perceive and define consequences not to the specific consequences themselves.

The influence of models is central to the social learning viewpoint. The amount of influence that a model will have on an individual is determined by four processes:

1. *Attentional processes.* People learn from a model only when they recognize and pay attention to its critical features. We tend to be most influenced by models who are attractive, repeatedly available, we think are important, or we see as similar to us.

2. *Retention processes.* A model's influence will depend on how well the individual remembers the model's action, even after the model is no longer readily available.

learning

Any relatively permanent change in behavior that occurs as a result of experience.

operant conditioning

A type of conditioning in which desired voluntary behavior leads to a reward or prevents a punishment.

social learning theory

People can learn through observation and direct experience.

Interview with Samuel W. (Bill) France, Director for Technical Support, ServiceMaster Management Services Group, Downers Grove, Illinois

Describe your job.

I work as the head of a team of eight engineers whose job is to provide four types of support to our executive-level and on-site management teams. We provide survey support for new sales, start-up project management to new accounts, ongoing support to existing customers, and special work as required. We have five housekeeping experts and three plant operations and maintenance experts on the team. My job is to orchestrate this effort by coordinating and communicating with the sales executives, the operations directors, the account managers, and the company officers. When I'm in the home office, I spend about 50 percent of my time talking on the phone or writing e-mail responses and directions, about 30 percent writing plans or documents for the future, and 20 percent working directly with my engineers, the executive-level leaders, on-site managers, or my peers who are the directors of operations. I travel about two weeks out of four, on average.

What types of skills do you think tomorrow's managers will need?

The primary function all managers need is people skills. This means the ability to communicate effectively using both written and spoken media. You need the ability to understand how people think and act. You must be sensitive to who people are and why they are working. In addition, managers will need well-honed computer skills, at least one foreign language (I strongly recommend Spanish), and good functional math skills. Also, managers need to have leadership skills.

Does your organization do employee attitude surveys? Can you describe what you do?

Yes, in fact I just completed one in the summer of 1997. ServiceMaster employed a consultant to prepare and mail out the written survey. For myself, I find out what employees are thinking by knowing them and talking with them frequently. "Management by Walking Around" is an often-heard phrase now for a very important function—get to know your people so they know you. You can't do this if you don't get out and watch, *listen,* and talk to them.

What do you think is the most effective way of dealing with employees who have "poor" interpersonal skills?

You must be honest with them in a tactful way so they know what they are doing wrong. Don't avoid the problem by trying to ignore the person's lack of skill. It doesn't work. The problem gets worse until the bad result is to let the person go. I saw this happen to a good plant engineer who had a hot temper. Confront the person in an honest way. The golden rule applies here: Do unto others as you would have them do unto you. Approach the person in a way that gets his attention but earns his trust so he knows you're trying to help him solve a problem. Very often the weakness that you're seeing is a hidden strength—it's a skill being misapplied. ■

MANAGING

YOUR

CAREER

Learning to Get Along with Difficult People

We've all been around people who are, to put it mildly, difficult to get along with. These people might be chronic complainers, they might be meddlers who think they know everything about everyone else's job and don't hesitate to tell you so, or they might exhibit any number of other unpleasant interpersonal characteristics. They can make your job as a manager extremely hard and your work day very stressful if you don't know how to deal with them. Being around difficult people tends to bring out the worst in all of us. What can you do? How do you learn to get along with these difficult people?[29]

Getting along with difficult people takes a little bit of patience, planning, and preparation. What you need is an approach that helps you diffuse a lot of the negative aspects of dealing with these individuals. For instance, it helps to write down a detailed description of the person's behavior. Describe what this person does that bothers you. Then, try to understand her behavior. Put yourself in her shoes and see what she's seeing—see things from her perspective. Doing these things initially might help you better understand and predict her behavior.

Unfortunately, trying to understand the person usually isn't enough for getting along. You'll also need some specific strategies for coping with different types of difficult personalities. Here are some of the most common types of difficult people you'll meet and some strategies for dealing with them.

The Hostile, Aggressive Types. With this type, you need to: stand up for yourself; give them time to run down; don't worry about being polite, just jump in if you need to; get their attention carefully; get them to sit down; speak from your own point of view; avoid a head-on fight; and be ready to be friendly.

The Complainers. With the complainers, you need to: listen attentively; acknowledge their concerns; be prepared to interrupt their litany of complaints; don't agree, but do acknowledge what they're saying; state facts without comment and apology; and switch them to problem solving.

The Silent or Nonresponsive Types. With this type, you need to: ask open-ended questions; use the friendly, silent stare; don't fill the silent pauses for them in conversations; comment on what's happening; and help break the tension by making them feel more at ease.

The Know-It-All Experts. The keys to dealing with this type are: be on top of things; listen and acknowledge their comments; question firmly, but don't confront; avoid being a counterexpert; and work with them to channel their energy in positive directions. ■

3. *Motor reproduction processes.* After a person has seen a new behavior by observing the model, the watching must be converted to doing. This process then demonstrates that the individual can perform the modeled activities.

4. *Reinforcement processes.* Individuals will be motivated to exhibit the modeled behavior if positive incentives or rewards are provided. Behaviors that are reinforced will be given more attention, learned better, and performed more often.

Shaping: A Managerial Tool

Because learning takes place on the job as well as prior to it, managers will be concerned with how they can teach employees to behave in ways that most benefit the organization. Thus, managers will often attempt to "mold" individuals by guiding their learning in graduated steps. This process is called **shaping behavior**.

Consider the situation in which an employee's behavior is significantly different from that sought by management. If management reinforced the individual only when he or she showed desirable responses, there might be very little reinforcement taking place. In such a case, shaping offers a logical approach toward achieving the desired behavior.

shaping behavior

Systematically reinforcing each successive step that moves an individual closer to the desired response.

We shape behavior by systematically reinforcing each successive step that moves the individual closer to the desired response. If an employee who has chronically been a half-hour late for work comes in only 20 minutes late, we can reinforce the improvement. Reinforcement would increase as responses more closely reached the desired behavior.

There are four ways to shape behavior: positive reinforcement, negative reinforcement, punishment, or extinction. When a behavior is followed with something pleasant, such as when a manager praises an employee for a job well done, it's called *positive reinforcement.* Rewarding a response with the elimination or withdrawal of something unpleasant is called *negative reinforcement.* Managers who habitually criticize their subordinates for taking extended coffee breaks are using negative reinforcement. The only way these employees stop the criticism is to shorten their breaks. *Punishment* penalizes undesirable behavior. Suspending an employee for two days without pay for showing up at work drunk is an example of punishment. Eliminating any reinforcement that's maintaining a behavior is called *extinction.* When a behavior isn't reinforced, gradually it disappears. In meetings, managers who wish to discourage employees from continually asking irrelevant or distracting questions can eliminate this behavior by ignoring those employees when they raise their hands to speak. Soon this behavior will disappear.

Both positive and negative reinforcement result in learning. They strengthen a desired response and increase the probability that a behavior will be repeated. Both punishment and extinction also result in learning; however, they weaken behavior and tend to decrease its frequency.

Implications for Managers

Employees are going to learn on the job. The only issue then is whether managers are going to manage their learning through the rewards they allocate and the examples they set or allow it to occur haphazardly. If marginal employees are rewarded with pay raises and promotions, they will have little reason to change their behavior. In fact, productive employees, seeing that marginal performance gets rewarded, might change their behavior. If managers want behavior A but reward behavior B, they should not be surprised to find employees' learning to engage in behavior B. Similarly, managers should expect that employees will look to them as models. Managers who are consistently late to work, or take two hours for lunch, or help themselves to company office supplies for personal use should expect employees to read the message they are sending and model their behavior accordingly.

13 How could operant conditioning help a manager understand and predict behavior?

14 What is social learning theory, and what are its implications for managing people at work?

15 How can managers "shape" employees' behavior?

**TESTING...
TESTING...**

1   2   3

Is shaping behavior a form of manipulative control? Animal trainers use rewards to get dogs, porpoises, and whales to perform extraordinary stunts. Behavioral psychologists have put rats through thousands of experiments by manipulating their food supply. Trainers and researchers shape the behavior of animals by controlling consequences. Such learning techniques may be appropriate for animals performing in zoos, circuses, or laboratories, but are they appropriate for managing the behavior of people at work? Suppose an employee does something that the organization judges to be wrong but that was motivated by a manager's control of rewards. Say, for instance, the employee fudges a sales report because bonuses are based on sales volume. Is that employee any less responsible for his or her actions than if such rewards had not been involved? Explain your position. ■

THINKING CRITICALLY

ABOUT ETHICS

managers respond to "a manager's dilemma"

MANAGER 1

Adam has encountered a dilemma familiar to most managers: how to win the support of both fellow decision makers and employees who may come from different generations, lifestyles, or economic situations. I'd suggest that he can gain the support of his older and more experienced board of directors by (1) acknowledging the benefits of their vast experience and knowledge of history; (2) showing an understanding of their personal philosophies; (3) acknowledging the great successes of past Sierra Club activities and how important this history is to determining the future plans and activities; (4) acknowledging his own shortcomings, such as his inexperience due to his youthful age; (5) constantly soliciting input from the board to make them feel valuable and well utilized; and (6) placing board members who may be particularly important and well respected by the group in positions of responsibility and authority.

Bill Johnston, Director of Public Relations, San Diego Chargers, San Diego, California

MANAGER 2

Although this might seem like a difficult situation to Adam, for the good of the organization, he's going to have to learn to deal with individuals who hold different attitudes than he does. Actually, Adam's not alone in this; it's difficult for most people to work with or be around people who have different attitudes than they do. However, by understanding something about attitudes and how they shape behavior, Adam can learn to draw upon the best that all of his board members have to offer. I have found when I have to deal with people who don't have the same attitudes that I do, it's best to focus on something other than our differences. Find a common area of interest or agreement that all parties can focus their energies on. In this way, you draw attention away from the negatives and focus on the positives.

Ernie Collette, Casualty Claim Examiner, American Family Insurance, Springfield, Missouri

for your **IMMEDIATE** action

TO: ☞ Michelle DePriest, Executive Vice President, Finance
FR: ✌ Aaron Sigler, President
RE: ☞ Hiring a Corporate Controller

As we discussed last Friday, our revenues, and consequently our manufacturing operations, have grown to the point where we need to hire a person for a newly created position, Corporate Controller. This person will be responsible for establishing needed operational and financial standards (such as number of labor hours and other standard costs to manufacture an entertainment center or any of our other wood furniture) for our various work units. This person will be working with financial and manufacturing statistics to establish these standards, so he or she should have a background in accounting, finance, or operations management.

I recall something from my management class in college that certain personality types fit best with certain types of jobs. Would you do some research on this for me and write up a short (no more than a page) report describing the type of personality you think might be an appropriate match for this position and why? Get this in to me by the end of the week.

This is a fictionalized account of a potentially real problem. It was written for academic purposes only.

SUMMARY

This summary is organized by the chapter-opening learning objectives found on p. 416.

1. The field of organizational behavior is concerned with the actions of people—managers and operatives alike—in organizations. By focusing on individual- and group-level concepts, OB seeks to explain and predict behavior. Because they get things done through other people, managers will be more effective leaders if they have an understanding of behavior.

2. The three components of an attitude are cognitive, affective, and behavioral. The cognitive component consists of the beliefs, opinions, knowledge, or information held by a person. The affective component is the emotional or feeling segment of an attitude. Finally, the behavioral component is an intention to behave in a certain way toward someone or something.

3. People seek consistency among their attitudes and their behavior. They seek to reconcile divergent attitudes and to align their attitudes and behavior so they appear rational and consistent.

4. The correlation between satisfaction and productivity tends to be low. The best evidence suggests that productivity leads to satisfaction rather than, as was popularly believed, the other way around.

5. The Myers-Briggs Type Indicator (or MBTI) is a personality assessment test that asks people how they usually act or feel in different situations. The way a person responds to the questions are combined into one of 16 personality types. The MBTI can help managers understand and predict people's behavior.

6. The big-five model of personality proposes that there are five personality factors: extraversion, agreeableness, conscientiousness, emotional stability, and openness to experience. Research has shown that important relationships exist between these personality dimensions and job performance.

7. Holland identified six basic personality types and six sets of congruent occupations. He found that when individuals were properly matched with occupations that were consistent with their personality types, they experienced high job satisfaction and exhibited low turnover rates.

8. Attribution theory can help explain how we judge people differently depending on what meaning we attribute to a given behavior. When we observe an individual's behavior, we attempt to determine whether it was internally or externally caused. That determination is based on three factors: distinctiveness, consensus, and consistency.

9. There are four shortcuts managers use in judging others. Selectivity is the process by which people assimilate selected bits and pieces of what they observe, depending on their interests, background, and attitudes. Assumed similarity is the belief that others are like oneself. Stereotyping is judging a person on the basis of a group to which he or she belongs. The halo effect is a general impression of an individual based on a single characteristic.

10. Managers can shape or mold employee behavior by systematically reinforcing each successive step that moves the employee closer to the desired behavior.

THINKING ABOUT MANAGEMENT ISSUES

1. How could you use personality traits to improve employee selection?

2. When we use shortcuts to judge others, are the consequences always negative? Explain.

3. What behavioral predictions might you make if you knew that an employee had (a) an external locus of control? (b) a low Mach score? (c) low self-esteem? (d) high self-monitoring tendencies?

4. "Managers should never use discipline with a problem employee." Do you agree or disagree? Discuss.

5. How important do you think knowledge of OB is to low-, middle-, and upper-level managers? What type of OB knowledge do you think is most important to each? Why?

SELF-ASSESSMENT EXERCISE

WHAT'S YOUR PERSONALITY TYPE?

Here's a short, modified version of the MBTI. Mark your responses to the following questionnaire on a separate sheet of paper. Keep in mind that there are no right or wrong answers to any of these items.

Part 1. Circle the response that comes closest to how you usually feel or act.

1. I am more careful about
   a. People's feelings.
   b. Their rights.

2. I usually get on better with
   a. Imaginative people.
   b. Realistic people.

3. It is a higher compliment to be called
   a. A person of real feeling.
   b. A consistently reasonable person.

4. In doing something with many people, it appeals more to me
   a. To do it in the accepted way.
   b. To invent a way of my own.

5. I get more annoyed at
   a. Fancy theories.
   b. People who do not like theories.

6. It is higher praise to call someone
   a. A person of vision.
   b. A person of common sense.

7. I more often let
   a. My heart rule my head.
   b. My head rule my heart.

8. I think it is a worse fault
   a. To show too much warmth.
   b. To be unsympathetic.

9. If I were a teacher, I would rather teach
   a. Courses involving theory.
   b. Fact courses.

Part II. Which word in the following pair appeals to you more? Circle a or b.

10. a. Compassion   b. Foresight
11. a. Justice   b. Mercy
12. a. Production   b. Design
13. a. Gentle   b. Firm
14. a. Uncritical   b. Critical
15. a. Literal   b. Figurative
16. a. Imaginative   b. Matter-of-fact

See Scoring Key on page SK–4.

Source: Adapted from the Myers-Briggs Type Indicator, I. Myers, *The Myers-Briggs Type Indicator* (Princeton, NJ: Educational Testing Service, 1962), cited in D. Hellriegel, J.W. Slocum Jr., and R.W. Woodman, *Organizational Behavior*, 3rd ed. (St. Paul, MN: West, 1983), pp. 128–43.

TAKE IT TO THE NET

We invite you to visit the Robbins/Coulter companion Web site at
http://www.prenhall.com/robbinsmgt for this chapter's Internet resources.

CASE APPLICATION

Teaching an Old Dog New Tricks—A Success Story from Eastern Europe

In Keckskemet, Hungary, at the Petofi Printing & Packaging Company, employees are learning that doing things the way they have always been done is no way to compete in a global marketplace that is extremely demanding about product quality standards. Eastern European companies have discovered that the shoddy merchandise they traditionally produced will not sell. What it took to get employees at the Petofi plant to produce at the new levels of quality provides an eye-opening lesson in organizational behavior.

Petofi Printing & Packaging Company manufactures cardboard boxes, wrappers, and other types of containers. Only a few years ago, Petofi's production line employees saw nothing unusual about drinking alcoholic beverages at work throughout the workday. In fact, managers would open the schnapps in the morning and usually by 11 o'clock, according to one source, "everyone was in the bag." It's no wonder product quality was so pitiful! Flies would buzz in through open windows and get stuck in the paint on the cardboard. Containers were delivered to customers in the wrong colors and sizes. If a customer provided a sample box to use as a prototype model for an order, employees would make something similar to it, but there was no concerted effort to precisely meet the customer's specifications. Workers had high absenteeism rates, and managers stressed "no wasting of materials" even if it meant shipping out junk products. How did this company turn itself around to the point where it has won awards from the World Packaging Association and achieved quality levels that meet the highest global standards?

The first thing that happened at Petofi was that new top managers were brought in to lead the company. Then, with $35 million in additional cash inflows provided by various investors, new state-of-the-art production equipment was installed. The company now has 40 new machines, including computer-controlled laser equipment to make prototypes, offset printers, computerized color analyzers, ultraviolet varnishing, and cameras to check for printing imperfections. But operating this sophisticated equipment requires a sober workforce that takes pride in producing a quality product. And this has been the hardest change for Petofi.

The workforce was whipped into shape by a combination of inducements and threats. The new managers offered workers huge incentives to improve their performance—a 40 percent pay raise (to an average of $600 a month), year-end bonuses, and better working conditions. They also brought in customers to the shop floor and took employees to trade shows to teach them about the importance of quality. If workers still didn't get the quality message, managers reminded them. If a customer rejected a product shipment, the mistake was traced back to the workers responsible and their wages were docked. If a worker was caught drinking alcohol on the job, a third of his or her monthly salary was deducted. If an offense was serious enough, the worker was fired; being fired is a strong deterrent in a city with double-digit unemployment. Needless to say, because workers wanted to keep their jobs and perform them well, only a few of them have actually been disciplined.

The tactics have worked. Most of Petofi's products are now exported. Some of its customers include such well-known transnationals as Unilever NV of the Netherlands, Sara Lee Corporation's Douwe Egberts unit of Budapest, and General Electric Company and Philip Morris Companies of the United States. Apparently, old dogs can be taught new tricks, but it takes a real understanding of employee behavior to make it work.

QUESTIONS

1. What do you think caused the original sloppy behavior described at Petofi?
2. How have Petofi's managers used the process of shaping behavior?
3. Can you see any use of social learning theory in this case? Discuss.
4. Would you expect employees to exhibit higher or lower job satisfaction after the changes than before?

Source: D. Milbank, "East Europe's Industry Is Raising Its Quality and Taking on West," *Wall Street Journal*, September 21, 1994, pp. A1+.

Age and Attitudes

Did you know that U.S. federal laws consider anyone 40 years of age or more as an older worker? You probably know that, because of laws against age discrimination, no organization has the right to discriminate against older workers. Despite the law, however, as companies continue to downsize and millions of 40+ workers look for work, examples of age discrimination are happening every day in every profession across the United States. Statistics show that it takes older job seekers 64 percent longer to find work than younger ones. Even though age discrimination is illegal, it appears to be such an ingrained part of our culture that we may not even recognize it and when we're doing it.

Think about your perception of older workers. Would you say they're sick more often, they can't work as hard, and they don't stay with a company as long as younger workers do? Well, if that is what you think, you're wrong! A study by Days Inn Corporation, which deliberately recruits older workers, found that older workers stay with the company longer, take fewer sick days, and are just as productive as their younger counterparts. In fact, the president of Days Inn says that older workers are actually *less* expensive than the average U.S. worker.

Do these attitudes we may subconsciously have about older workers affect the way we behave? Yes. They often have subtle influences on the way we treat older persons. For instance, in job interviews, differences can be seen in the treatment of younger and older applicants. In several staged interviews with pairs of applicants—one older woman and one younger woman—the younger women were accommodated more by the interviewer. The older women were subtly discouraged. In fact, in one-third of these 24 staged interviews, a startling difference in the way older and younger job applicants were treated could be seen. In another staged interview situation, one individual was made up to look young one time and older another in interviews at the same company. His "younger" self was offered a job at a brokerage firm even though this "person" had less job experience than his "older" self and didn't follow up on the interview with a letter or phone call. Although the interviewers didn't appear to purposely discriminate (after all, it *is* illegal) against the older job applicants in the way they acted and in the questions they asked, differences could still be seen. Attitudes that we have about elderly people in general, and older workers in particular, appear to influence the way we react and act.

QUESTIONS

1. Describe the three components of an attitude—cognitive, affective, and behavioral—in relation to the attitudes often held about older workers as shown in this video clip.
2. What role do you think perception plays in the way we subtly behave toward older persons?
3. Is stereotyping part of the problem with attitudes about age? Explain.

Source: "Age and Attitudes," *ABC News Primetime*, June 9, 1994.

A MANAGER'S DILEMMA

Even well-managed organizations don't always work as efficiently and effectively as possible. At Hewlett-Packard's North American distribution facility in Bridgewater, New Jersey, billions of dollars in products, from PCs to toner cartridges, are handled from order to delivery.[1] But there was a major problem with work processes at the facility; it took an average of 26 days for a product to reach the customer after an order had been received. Employees used some 70 different computer systems to transfer and track order information. What's interesting is that these inefficient work processes were taking place at a facility of one of the leaders in the high-tech industry <http://www.hp.com>!

One characteristic that distinguishes an outstanding organization is its ability to know when problems need to be addressed and then proceeds to do something about it. The job of reengineering the inefficient work processes at this distribution facility fell to two managers: Mei-Lin Cheng (standing on top of the boxes, second from the left) and Julie Anderson (sitting on top of the boxes, in the middle). Given their assignment of totally revamping the work processes, these two

managers decided to go out on a limb. They bargained for complete freedom from their bosses at HP headquarters to tackle this job by agreeing to achieve significant and measurable improvements in customer satisfaction in less than nine months. No, Cheng and Anderson weren't crazy or inept! They felt that to tackle and succeed at a major process redesign and improvement project like this would take the combined input, experience, and cooperation of many employees. They wanted full autonomy so they could create and design a team that could handle the massive reengineering effort.

Cheng and Anderson assembled a team of 35 people from HP and two other companies (Andersen Consulting, a management consulting firm, and Menlo Logistics, HP's transportation and distribution partner) to work on the work process redesign. They explained the ground rules regarding the goals and constraints of the project. Then Cheng and Anderson stood back and let the team come up with the answers. But even given the team's autonomy and freedom to approach the work process redesign in the way they felt was best, the inevitable conflicts had to be managed.

What types of conflicts did the team face? Some conflicts initially arose over whether to tackle the work process problems from a total perspective or piece by piece. Other conflicts arose as the team became accustomed to the concept that no one individual was going to have the best idea, but the best ideas would come from the collective intelligence of the team. And there were other conflicts along the way as the team tackled its assignment.

Put yourself in Cheng and Anderson's situation. How should they manage the conflicts that arose as this reengineering team did its work?

WHAT WOULD YOU DO?

CHAPTER

14

Understanding

Groups

and Teams

The responsibilities that Mei-Lin Cheng and Julie Anderson had for managing a team whose goal was reengineering the distribution processes at the Hewlett-Packard North American distribution center aren't unusual in organizations. Thousands of organizations have made the move to restructure work around groups rather than individuals. Why? What do these teams look like? How can interested managers build effective teams? These are some of the types of questions we will be answering in this chapter. First, however, let's begin by developing our understanding of group behavior.

UNDERSTANDING GROUP BEHAVIOR

The behavior of a group is not merely the sum total of the behaviors of all the individuals in the group. Why? Because individuals act differently in groups than they do when they are alone. Therefore, if we want to understand organizational behavior more fully, we need to study groups.

What Is a Group?

group

Two or more interacting and interdependent individuals who come together to achieve particular objectives.

A **group** is defined as two or more interacting and interdependent individuals who come together to achieve particular objectives. Groups can be either formal or informal. *Formal groups* are work groups established by the organization that have designated work assignments and specific tasks. In formal groups, appropriate behaviors are stipulated by and directed toward organizational goals. Table 14-1 provides some examples of different types of formal groups used in organizations today.

In contrast, *informal groups* are of a social nature. These groups occur naturally in the work environment in response to the need for social contact. Informal groups tend to form around friendships and common interests.

Stages of Group Development

Group development is a dynamic process. Most groups are in a continual state of change. Even though groups probably never reach complete stability, there's a general pattern that describes how most groups evolve. Research on groups shows that groups pass through a

---

TABLE 14-1	**Examples of Formal Groups**

Command groups. These are the basic, traditional work groups determined by formal authority relationships and depicted on the organizational chart. They typically include a manager and those subordinates who report directly to him or her.

Cross-functional teams. These bring together the knowledge and skills of individuals from various work areas in order to come up with solutions to operational problems. Cross-functional teams also include groups whose members have been trained to do each other's jobs.

Self-managed teams. These are essentially independent groups that, in addition to doing their operating jobs, take on traditional management responsibilities such as hiring, planning and scheduling, and performance evaluations.

Task forces. These are temporary groups created to accomplish a specific task. Once the task is complete, the group is disbanded.

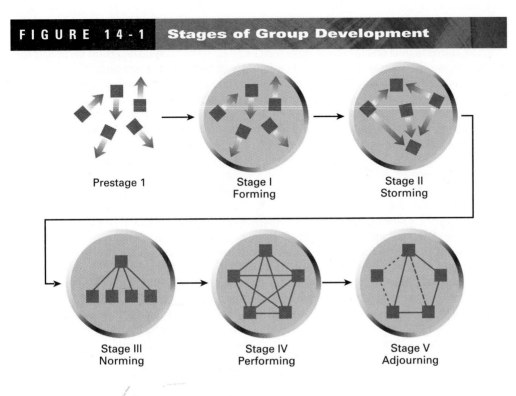

FIGURE 14-1   **Stages of Group Development**

Prestage 1

Stage I
Forming

Stage II
Storming

Stage III
Norming

Stage IV
Performing

Stage V
Adjourning

standard sequence of five stages.[2] As shown in Figure 14-1, these five stages are: *forming, storming, norming, performing,* and *adjourning.*

The first stage, **forming**, has two aspects. In the first, people are joining the group, either because of a work assignment, in the case of a formal group, or because of some other benefit desired, in the case of an informal group. Figure 14-2 depicts some reasons why people join groups.

Once the group's membership is in place, the second part of the forming stage begins: the task of defining the group's purpose, structure, and leadership. This phase is characterized by a great deal of uncertainty. Members are "testing the waters" to determine what types of behavior are acceptable. This stage is complete when members begin to think of themselves as part of a group.

The **storming** stage is one of intragroup conflict. Members accept the existence of the group but resist the control that the group imposes on individuality. Further, there is con-

forming

The first stage in group development, during which people join the group and then define the group's purpose, structure, and leadership; characterized by uncertainty.

storming

The second stage of group development, characterized by intragroup conflict.

FIGURE 14-2   **Why People Join Groups**

Security

Status

Goal Achievement

GROUP

Self-Esteem

Power

Affiliation

norming

The third stage of group development, characterized by close relationships and cohesiveness.

performing

The fourth stage in group development, when the group is fully functional.

adjourning

The final stage in group development for temporary groups, characterized by concern with wrapping up activities rather than task performance.

flict over who will control the group. When this stage is complete, there will be a relatively clear hierarchy of leadership within the group and agreement on the group's direction.

The third stage is one in which close relationships develop and the group demonstrates cohesiveness. There's now a strong sense of group identity and camaraderie. This **norming** stage is complete when the group structure solidifies and the group has assimilated a common set of expectations of what defines correct member behavior.

The fourth stage is **performing**. The group structure at this point is fully functional and accepted. Group energy has moved from getting to know and understand each other to performing the task at hand.

Performing is the last stage in the development of permanent work groups. Temporary groups—committees, task forces, teams, and similar groups—that have a limited task to perform have a fifth stage, **adjourning**. In this stage, the group prepares to disband. High levels of task performance are no longer the group's top priority. Instead, attention is directed toward wrapping-up activities. Responses of group members vary at this stage. Some are upbeat, basking in the group's accomplishments. Others may be saddened by the loss of camaraderie and friendships gained during the work group's life.

Most of you have probably experienced each of these stages in a group project for a class. Group members are selected and then meet for the first time. There's a "feeling out" period to assess what the group is going to do and how it's going to do it. This is usually rapidly followed by a battle for control: Who's going to be in charge? Once this issue is resolved and a "hierarchy" is agreed on, the group identifies specific aspects of the task, who's going to do them, and dates by which the assigned work needs to be completed. General expectations are established and agreed upon for each member. These decisions form the foundation for what you hope will be a coordinated group effort culminating in a job well done. Once the group project is complete and turned in, the group breaks up. Of course, some groups don't get much beyond the first or second stage; these groups typically turn in disappointing projects and and get lower grades.

Should you assume from the preceding discussion that a group becomes more effective as it progresses through the first four stages? Some researchers argue that effectiveness of work groups increases at advanced stages, but it's not that simple.[3] That assumption may be generally true, but what makes a group effective is a complex issue. Under some conditions, high levels of conflict are conducive to high levels of group performance. We might expect to find situations in which groups in Stage II outperform those in Stages III or IV. Similarly, groups don't always proceed clearly from one stage to the next. Sometimes, in fact, several stages may be going on simultaneously, as when groups are storming and performing at the

The organizing committee for the 1998 Olympic Winter Games held in Nagano, Japan, had a great deal of responsibility and needed to build cohesiveness quickly. Invitations to participate in the games were sent out in February 1997, shortly after this photo was made.

same time. Groups even occasionally regress to previous stages. Therefore, one shouldn't always assume that all groups precisely follow this developmental process or that Stage IV is always the most preferable. It's better to think of this model as a general framework. It reminds you that groups are dynamic entities and can help you better understand the problems and issues that are most likely to surface during a group's life. Is it likely that the group described in our chapter-opening Manager's Dilemma proceeded through the various stages of group development as they performed their task? The answer, of course, is yes!

1 Contrast formal and informal groups.

2 What are some types of formal groups in organizations?

3 Describe the five stages of group development.

TESTING...
TESTING...
1 2 3

Basic Group Concepts

In this section we introduce several concepts to help you begin to understand group behavior. These are *roles, norms, conformity, status systems, group size, group cohesiveness, conflict management,* and *informal communication.*

Roles.   We introduced the concept of roles in chapter 1 when we discussed what managers do. (Do you remember Mintzberg's managerial roles?) Of course, managers are not the only individuals in an organization who have roles. The concept of roles applies to all employees in organizations and to their life outside the organization as well.

A **role** refers to a set of expected behavior patterns attributed to someone who occupies a given position in a social unit. Individuals play multiple roles, adjusting their roles to the group to which they belong at the time. In an organization, employees attempt to determine what behaviors are expected of them. They read their job descriptions, get suggestions from their boss, and watch what their co-workers do. An individual who is confronted by divergent role expectations experiences *role conflict.* Employees in organizations often face role conflicts. The credit manager expects her credit analysts to process a minimum of 30 applications a week, but the work group pressures members to restrict output to 20 applications a week so that everyone has work to do and no one gets laid off. A young college instructor's colleagues want him to give very few high grades in order to maintain the department's reputation for having tough standards, but students want him to give out lots of high grades to enhance their grade point averages. To the degree that the instructor sincerely seeks to satisfy the expectations of both his colleagues and his students, he faces role conflict.

role

A set of behavior patterns expected of someone occupying a given position in a social unit.

Norms and Conformity.   All groups have established **norms**, or acceptable standards that are shared by the group's members. Norms dictate things such as output levels, absenteeism rates, promptness, and the amount of socializing allowed on the job.

Norms, for example, dictate the "arrival ritual" among scheduling clerks at one National Steel plant. The workday begins at 8 A.M. Most employees typically arrive a few minutes before and put their jacket, purse, lunch bag, and other personal items on their chair or desk to prove they're "at work." They then go down to the company cafeteria to get coffee and chat. Employees who violate this norm by starting work sharply at 8 o'clock are teased and pressured until their behavior conforms to the group's standard.

Although each group will have its own unique set of norms, there are common classes of norms that appear in most organizations. These focus on effort and performance, dress, and loyalty. Probably the most widespread norms are related to levels of effort and performance. Work groups typically provide their members with explicit cues on how hard to

norms

Acceptable standards shared by a group's members.

work, what level of output to have, when to look busy, when it's acceptable to goof off, and the like. These norms are extremely powerful in affecting an individual employee's performance. They're so powerful that performance predictions that are based solely on an employee's ability and level of personal motivation often prove to be wrong.

Some organizations have formal dress codes. Even in their absence, however, norms frequently develop that dictate the kind of clothing that should be worn to work. College seniors, interviewing for their first postgraduate job, discover this norm very quickly. Every semester on college campuses, students who are interviewing for jobs can usually be spotted; they're the ones walking around in the dark gray or blue pinstriped suits. They're following the dress norms that they have learned are expected in professional positions. Of course, what's acceptable dress in one organization may be very different from what is acceptable in another.

Few managers appreciate employees who belittle the organization. Similarly, professional employees and those in executive positions recognize that most employers view unfavorably those who actively look for another job while still employed at the current organization. If such people are unhappy, they know to keep their job searches secret. These examples demonstrate that loyalty norms are widespread in organizations. This concern for demonstrating loyalty, by the way, often explains why ambitious individuals who aspire to top management positions willingly take work home at night, come in on weekends, and accept transfers to cities where they would otherwise prefer not to live.

Because individuals desire acceptance by the groups to which they belong, they're susceptible to conformity pressures. The impact that group pressures for conformity can have on an individual member's judgment and attitudes was demonstrated in research by Solomon Asch.[4] Asch formed groups of seven or eight people who sat in a classroom and were asked to compare two cards held by the experimenter. One card had one line, the other had three lines of different length. As shown in Figure 14-3, one of the lines on the three-line card was identical to the line on the one-line card. Also, as shown in Figure 14-3, the difference in line length was quite obvious. The object was to announce aloud which of the three lines matched the single line. Under ordinary conditions, the error rate was less than 1 percent. But Asch wanted to know what would happen if all the members in the group began to give incorrect answers. Would the pressures to conform cause the unsuspecting subject (USS) to alter his or her answers to align with those of the others? Asch arranged the group so that only the USS was unaware that the experiment was "fixed." The seating was prearranged so that the USS was the last to announce his or her decision.

The experiment began with several sets of matching exercises in which all the subjects gave the right answers. On the third set, however, the first subject gave an obviously

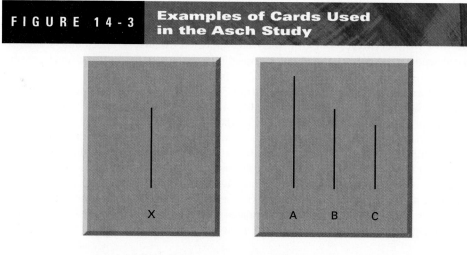

FIGURE 14-3   **Examples of Cards Used in the Asch Study**

You have been hired as a summer intern in the auditing section of an accounting firm in Dallas. After working there about a month, you conclude that the attitude in the office is "anything goes." Employees know that supervisors won't discipline them for ignoring company rules. For example, employees have to turn in expense accounts, but the process is a joke; nobody submits receipts to verify reimbursement, and nothing is ever said. In fact, when you tried to turn in your receipts with your expense report, you were told, "Nobody else turns in receipts and you don't really need to, either." You believe that because you know that no expense check has ever been denied because of failure to turn in a receipt, even though the employee handbook says receipts are required. Also, your co-workers use company phones for personal long-distance calls even though that is prohibited by the employee handbook. And one permanent employee told you to "help yourself" to any paper, pens, or pencils you might need here or at home.

What are the norms of this group? Suppose that you were the supervisor in this area. How would you go about changing the norms? ■

wrong answer—for example, saying "C" in Figure 14-3. The next subject gave the same wrong answer, and so did the others until it was the USS's turn. He knew that B was the same length as X, yet everyone had said "C." The decision confronting the USS was this: Should I state a perception publicly that differs from the preannounced position of the other group members? Or should I give an answer that I strongly believe is incorrect in order to be in agreement with the other group members? Over many experiments and many trials, subjects conformed in about 35 percent of the trials; that is, the USS gave answers he or she knew were wrong but that were consistent with the replies of other group members.

What can we conclude from this study? The results suggest that there are group norms that press us toward conformity. We desire to be one of the group and to avoid being visibly different. We can generalize further to say that when an individual's opinion of objective data differs significantly from that of others in the group, he or she feels extensive pressure to align his or her opinion to conform with the opinions of the others.

Status Systems.   **Status** is a prestige grading, position, or rank within a group. As far back as researchers have been able to trace human groups, they have found status hierarchies. Status systems are an important factor in understanding behavior. Status is a significant motivator and has behavioral consequences when individuals see a disparity between what they perceive their status to be and what others perceive it to be.

Status may be informally conferred by characteristics such as education, age, skill, or experience. Anything can have status value if others in the group evaluate it that way. Of course, just because status is informal doesn't mean that it's unimportant or that it is hard to determine who has it or who does not. Members of groups have no problem placing people into status categories, and they usually agree closely about who has high status, low status, or middle-ranking status.

It's important for employees to believe that the organization's formal status system is congruent. That is, there should be equity between the perceived ranking of an individual and the status symbols he or she is given by the organization. For instance, status incongruence occurs when a supervisor is earning less than his or her subordinates, a desirable office is occupied by a person in a low-ranking position, or paid country club membership is provided by the company for division managers but not for vice presidents. Employees expect the "things" an individual has and receives to be congruent with his or her status. When they're not, employees are likely to reject the authority of their superiors. In addition, the motivational potential of promotions decreases, and the general pattern of order and consistency in the organization is disturbed.

status

A prestige grading, position, or rank within a group.

4 What is the influence of role on group behavior?

5 How can group norms both help and hurt an organization?

6 How might status issues influence group behavior?

Group Size.   Does the size of a group affect the group's overall behavior? The answer is a definite yes, but the effect depends on which outcomes you're focusing on.[5] The evidence indicates, for instance, that small groups are faster at completing tasks than are larger ones. However, if the group is engaged in problem solving, large groups consistently get better marks than smaller ones. Translating these results into specific numbers is a bit more troublesome, but we can offer some guidelines. Large groups—those with a dozen or more members—are good for gaining diverse input. Thus, if the goal of the group is to find facts, a larger group should be more effective. On the other hand, smaller groups are better at doing something productive with those facts. Groups of approximately seven members tend to be more effective for taking action.

One of the more disturbing findings related to group size is that, as groups get incrementally larger, the contribution of individual members often tends to decrease.[6] That is, although the total productivity of a group of four is generally greater than that of a group of three, the individual productivity of each group member declines as the group expands. Thus, a group of four will tend to produce at a level less than four times the average of individual performance. The best explanation for this reduction of effort is a phenomenon known as the **free rider tendency**. The dispersion of responsibility within a group encourages individuals to slack off. When the results of the group can't be attributed to any one person, the relationship between an individual's input and the group's output is clouded. In such situations, individuals may be tempted to become "free riders" and coast on the group's efforts. In other words, there will be a reduction in efficiency when individuals think that their contributions can't be measured. The obvious conclusion from this finding is that when managers use work teams they should also provide means for identifying individual efforts.

free rider tendency

The reduction of effort that individual members contribute to the group as it increases in size.

Group Cohesiveness.   Intuitively, it makes sense that groups in which there's a lot of internal disagreement and lack of cooperation are less effective in completing their tasks than are groups in which members generally agree, cooperate, and like each other. Research in this area has focused on **group cohesiveness**, or the degree to which members are attracted to one another and share the group's goals. The more the members are attracted to one another and the more the group's goals align with their individual goals, the greater the group's cohesiveness.

group cohesiveness

The degree to which members are attracted to one another and share the group's goals.

Research has generally shown that highly cohesive groups are more effective than are those with less cohesiveness,[7] but the relationship between cohesiveness and effectiveness is more complex. A key moderating variable is the degree to which the group's attitude aligns with its formal goals or with those of the larger organization of which it is a part.[8] The more cohesive a group is, the more its members will follow its goals. If the goals are desirable (for instance, high output, quality work, cooperation with individuals outside the group), a cohesive group is more productive than a less cohesive group. But if cohesiveness is high and attitudes are unfavorable, productivity decreases. If cohesiveness is low and goals are supported, productivity increases but not as much as when both cohesiveness and support are high. When cohesiveness is low and goals are not supported, cohesiveness has no significant effect on productivity. These conclusions are summarized in Figure 14-4.

conflict

Perceived incompatible differences that result in interference or opposition.

Conflict Management.   As a group performs its assigned tasks, disagreements or conflicts inevitably will arise. When we use the term **conflict**, we're referring to *perceived*

FIGURE 14-4   The Relationship between Cohesiveness and Productivity

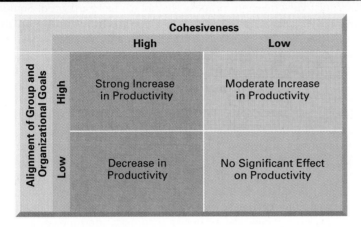

		Cohesiveness	
		High	**Low**
Alignment of Group and Organizational Goals	**High**	Strong Increase in Productivity	Moderate Increase in Productivity
	Low	Decrease in Productivity	No Significant Effect on Productivity

incompatible differences resulting in some form of interference or opposition. Whether the differences are real or not is irrelevant. If people in a group perceive that differences exist, then a conflict state exists. In addition, our definition includes the extremes, from subtle, indirect, and highly controlled forms of interference to overt acts such as strikes, riots, and wars.

Over the years, three different views have evolved regarding conflict.[9] One view argues that conflict must be avoided, that it indicates a malfunctioning or problem within the group. We call this the **traditional view of conflict**. A second view, the **human relations view of conflict**, argues that conflict is a natural and inevitable outcome in any group and that it need not be negative but, rather, has the potential to be a positive force in contributing to a work group's performance. The third and most recent perspective proposes

traditional view of conflict

The view that all conflict is bad and must be avoided.

human relations view of conflict

The view that conflict is a natural and inevitable outcome in any group.

Their musical talent is undisputed. Combine it with extraordinary cohesiveness and you get the Tokyo String Quartet, one of the world's foremost musical ensembles. (Left to right: violinists Peter Oundjian and Kikuei Ikeda, cellist Sadao Harada, and violist Kazuhide Isomura.)

not only that conflict can be a positive force in a group but also that some conflict is *absolutely necessary* for a group to perform effectively. We label this third approach the **interactionist view of conflict**.

The interactionist view does not propose that all conflicts are good. Some conflicts are seen as supporting the goals of the work group; these are **functional conflicts** of a constructive nature. Other conflicts prevent a group from achieving its goals; these are **dysfunctional conflicts** and are destructive forms.

Of course, it's one thing to argue that conflict can be valuable, but how does a manager tell whether group conflict is functional or dysfunctional? Unfortunately, the differentiation isn't clear or precise. No one level of conflict can be adopted as acceptable or unacceptable under all conditions. The type and level of conflict that will promote a healthy and positive involvement toward one group's goals may, in another group or in the same group at another time, be highly dysfunctional. Functionality or dysfunctionality, therefore, is a matter of judgment. Figure 14-5 illustrates the challenge facing managers. They want to create an environment in which group conflict is healthy but not allowed to run to extremes. Neither too little nor too much conflict is desirable. Managers should stimulate conflict to gain the full benefits of its functional properties yet reduce its level when it becomes a disruptive force.[10] Because we have yet to devise a sophisticated measuring instrument for assessing whether a given conflict level is functional or dysfunctional, the manager must

interactionist view of conflict

The view that some conflict is necessary for a group to perform effectively.

functional conflicts

Conflicts that support a group's goals.

dysfunctional conflicts

Conflicts that prevent a group from achieving its goals.

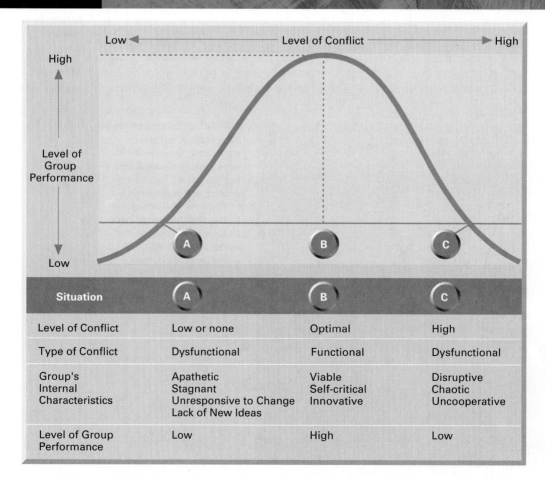

FIGURE 14-5 **Conflict and Group Performance**

Situation	A	B	C
Level of Conflict	Low or none	Optimal	High
Type of Conflict	Dysfunctional	Functional	Dysfunctional
Group's Internal Characteristics	Apathetic Stagnant Unresponsive to Change Lack of New Ideas	Viable Self-critical Innovative	Disruptive Chaotic Uncooperative
Level of Group Performance	Low	High	Low

make intelligent judgments concerning whether conflict levels in work groups are optimal, too high, or too low.

What resolution tools or techniques can a manager call upon to reduce conflict when it's too high? Managers essentially can draw upon five conflict-resolution options: avoidance, accommodation, forcing, compromise, and collaboration.[11] (See Figure 14-6.) Each has particular strengths and weaknesses, and no one option is ideal for every situation. You should consider each one a "tool" in your conflict-management "tool chest." Although you might be better at using some tools than others, the skilled manager knows what each tool can do and when each is likely to be most effective.

Not every conflict requires an assertive action. Sometimes **avoidance**—just withdrawing from or suppressing the conflict—is the best solution. When is avoidance a desirable strategy? It's most appropriate when the conflict is trivial, when emotions are running high and time is needed for the conflicting parties to cool down, or when the potential disruption from an assertive action outweighs the benefits of resolution.

The goal of **accommodation** is to maintain harmonious relationships by placing another's needs and concerns above your own. You might, for example, yield to another person's position on an issue. This option is most viable when the issue under dispute isn't that important to you or when you want to "build up credits" for later issues.

In **forcing**, you attempt to satisfy your own needs at the expense of the other party. In organizations, this is most often illustrated when a manager uses his or her formal authority to resolve a dispute. Forcing works well when you need a quick resolution on important

avoidance

Withdrawal from or suppression of conflict.

accommodation

Resolving conflicts by placing another's needs and concerns above one's own.

forcing

Satisfying one's own needs at the expense of another's.

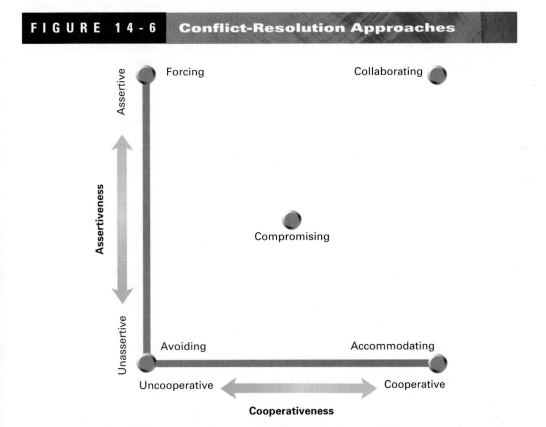

FIGURE 14-6 **Conflict-Resolution Approaches**

Source: Adapted from K.W. Thomas, "Conflict and Negotiation Processes in Organizations," in M.D. Dunnette and L.M. Hough (eds.), *Handbook of Industrial and Organizational Psychology*, vol. 3, 2d ed. (Palo Alto, CA: Consulting Psychologists Press, 1992), p. 668. With permission.

issues for which unpopular actions must be taken and when commitment by others to your solution isn't critical.

A **compromise** requires each party to give up something of value. Typically this is the approach taken by management and labor in negotiating a new labor contract. Compromise can be an optimal strategy when conflicting parties are about equal in power, when it's desirable to achieve a temporary solution to a complex issue, or when time pressures demand an expedient solution.

Finally, **collaboration** offers the ultimate win-win solution. All parties to the conflict seek to satisfy their interests. Collaboration is typically characterized by open and honest discussion among the parties, active listening to understand differences, and careful deliberation over a full range of alternatives to find a solution that's advantageous to all. When is collaboration the best conflict option? When time pressures are minimal, when all parties seriously want a win-win solution, and when the issue is too important to be compromised.

Informal Communication.   How do work groups get the information they need to perform their tasks, and how do work groups communicate both within the group and with other work groups? Although there are formal communication channels that work groups may use, many times **informal communication**—that is, communication that exists outside the organization's formally authorized communication channels—is preferred. Informal communication serves two purposes for groups: (1) Employees can satisfy their need for social interaction, and (2) group performance can be improved through these alternative, and frequently faster and more efficient, communication channels.

The informal communication network is better known by the name **grapevine**, and the grapevine is active in almost every organization. Information, both within a work group and between work groups, will flow along the grapevine. Managers often find the grapevine valuable for identifying issues that employees consider important and that are creating anxiety among them. The grapevine also can serve as both a filter and feedback mechanism for managers by highlighting issues that employees consider relevant and by planting messages that managers want employees to hear.

compromise

A solution to conflict in which each party gives up something of value.

collaboration

Resolving conflict by seeking a solution advantageous to all parties.

informal communication

Communication that exists outside the organization's formally authorized communication channels.

grapevine

The informal communication network.

7 What is the most effective size for a group?

8 Describe the relationship between group cohesiveness and productivity.

9 How do conflict management and informal communication influence group behavior?

Toward Understanding Work Group Behavior

Why are some groups more successful than others? The answer to that is complex, but it includes variables such as the abilities of the group's members, the size of the group, the level of conflict, and the internal pressures on members to conform to the group's norms. Figure 14-7 presents the major components that determine group performance and satisfaction.[12] It can help you sort out the key variables and their interrelationships.

External Conditions Imposed on the Group.   To begin understanding the behavior of a formal work group, we need to view it as a subsystem of a larger system.[13] When we accept that formal groups are subsets of a larger organizational system, we can extract part of the explanation of the group's behavior from an explanation of the organization. For instance, a product quality control team at a Kraft cheese plant in Missouri must live within the rules and policies dictated from the division's headquarters in Chicago and Philip Morris

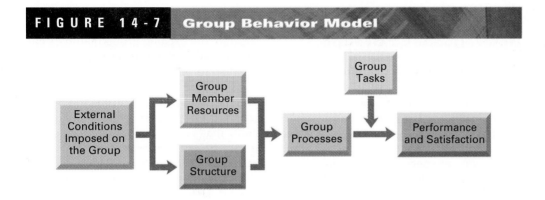

FIGURE 14-7   **Group Behavior Model**

corporate offices in Richmond, Virginia. Every work group is influenced by external conditions imposed from outside.

What are some of these external conditions? They include the organization's overall strategy, authority structures, formal regulations, the availability or absence of organization-wide resources, employee selection criteria, the organization's performance evaluation and reward system, the organization's culture, and the general physical layout of the group's work space set by the organization's industrial engineers and office designers.

Group Member Resources.   A group's potential level of performance depends to a large extent on the resources that its members individually bring to the group. These would include members' abilities and personality characteristics.

Part of a group's performance can be predicted by assessing the task-relevant and intellectual abilities of its individual members. We do occasionally read about an athletic team composed of mediocre players who, because of excellent coaching, determination, and precision teamwork, beat a far more talented group of players. Such cases make the news precisely because they are aberrations. Group performance isn't merely the summation of its individual members' abilities. However, these abilities set parameters for what members can do and how effectively they will perform in a group.

There has been a great deal of research on the relationship between personality traits and group attitudes and behaviors. The general conclusion is that attributes that tend to have a positive connotation in our culture tend to be positively related to group productivity and morale. These include traits such as sociability, self-reliance, and independence. In contrast, negative characteristics such as authoritarianism, dominance, and unconventionality tend to be negatively related to productivity and morale.[14] These personality traits affect group performance by strongly influencing how the individual will interact with other group members.

Understanding the relationship between group performance and group member resources is made more challenging in global organizations in which cross-cultural groups are prevalent. Given these conditions, managers need to establish a firm understanding of the cultural characteristics of the groups and the group members they manage.[15]

Group Structure.   Work groups aren't unorganized crowds. They have a structure that shapes members' behavior and makes it possible to explain and predict a large portion of individual behavior within the group as well as the performance of the group itself. These structure variables include roles, norms, status, group size, and leadership. We have already discussed the first four variables in this chapter and leadership will be covered in chapter 16, so we need not elaborate here. Just keep in mind that every work group has an internal structure that defines member roles, norms, status, group size, and formal leadership positions.

MANAGING
WORKFORCE
DIVERSITY

The Challenge of Coordinating Heterogeneous Groups

Understanding and managing groups that are composed of people who are similar can be a difficult undertaking in and of itself. Add in diversity and managing groups can be even more of a challenge, but the benefits to be gained from the diverse perspectives, skills, and abilities more than offset the extra effort.[16]

How can you meet the challenge of coordinating a heterogeneous (diverse) work group? It's important in managing a diverse group to stress four critical interpersonal behaviors: understanding, empathy, tolerance, and communication.

You know that people aren't the same, yet they need to be treated fairly and equitably. And cultural differences can cause people to behave in different ways. Group leaders need to understand and accept these differences. Each and every group member should be encouraged to do the same.

Empathy is closely related to understanding. As a group leader, you should try to understand others' perspectives. Put yourself in their shoes, and encourage group members to empathize as well. For instance, suppose a Japanese woman joins a group made up of Caucasian and Hispanic men. They can make her feel more welcome and comfortable in the group by identifying with how she might feel. Is she disappointed or excited about her new work assignment? Has she had any experience in working with male colleagues? By putting themselves in her position, the existing group members can enhance their ability to work together as an effective group.

Tolerance is another important interpersonal behavior in coordinating heterogeneous groups. Just because you understand that people are different and you empathize with them, doesn't mean that it's any easier to accept different perspectives or behaviors. But it's important in dealing with diverse ages, gender, cultural behaviors, or any of the other dimensions of diversity to be tolerant—to allow group members the freedom to be themselves. Part of being tolerant is being open-minded about different values, attitudes, and behaviors.

Finally, open communication is important to coordinating a diverse team. Diversity problems may intensify if people are afraid or unwilling to openly discuss issues that concern them. And for communication to work within a diverse group, it needs to be two-way. If a person wants to know whether a certain behavior is offensive to someone else, it's best to just ask. Likewise, a person who is offended by a certain behavior of another person should explain his or her concerns and ask that person to stop. As long as these communication exchanges are handled in a nonthreatening, low-key, and friendly way, they generally will have a positive outcome. And it helps to have an atmosphere within the group that supports and celebrates diversity. ■

Group Processes.   The next component in our group behavior model concerns the processes that go on within a work group—the communication patterns used by members to exchange information, group decision processes, leader behavior, power dynamics, conflict interactions, and the like. Why are processes important to understanding work group behavior? Because in groups, one and one don't necessarily add up to two. Every group begins with a potential defined by its constraints, resources, and structure. Then you add in the positive and negative process factors created within the group itself. For instance, four people on a research team may be able to generate far more ideas as a group than the members could produce individually. This synergy is a positive process factor. However, the group may also have negative process factors such as high levels of conflict or poor communication, which may hinder group effectiveness.

Group Tasks.   The final box in our model points out that the impact of group processes on the group's performance and member satisfaction depends on the task that the group is doing. More specifically, the *complexity* and *interdependence* of tasks influence the group's effectiveness.[17]

Tasks can be generalized as being either simple or complex. Simple tasks are routine and standardized. Complex tasks are ones that tend to be novel or nonroutine. We would hypothesize that the more complex the task, the more the group will benefit from discussion among group members about alternative work methods. If the task is simple, group members don't need to discuss such alternatives. They can rely on standardized operating procedures. Similarly, if there's a high degree of interdependence among the tasks that group members must perform, they'll need to interact more. Effective communication and controlled levels of conflict should, therefore, be most relevant to group performance when tasks are interdependent.

Group Decision Making

Many organizational decisions are made by groups. It's a rare organization that doesn't at some time use committees, task forces, review panels, study teams, or similar groups as vehicles for making decisions. In addition, studies tell us that managers spend up to 40 percent of their time in group meetings.[18] Undoubtedly, a large portion of that time is spent formulating problems, arriving at solutions to those problems, and determining the means for implementing the solutions. It's possible, in fact, for groups to be assigned any of the eight steps in the decision-making process. (Refer to chapter 6 for a review of the steps in the decision-making process.)

In this section, we'll look at the advantages and disadvantages of group decision making, identify when groups should be preferred, and review the more popular techniques for improving group decision making.

Advantages and Disadvantages.   What are the advantages that group decisions have over individual decisions?

1. *Provide more complete information.* There is often truth to the saying that two heads are better than one. A group brings a diversity of experience and perspectives to the decision process that an individual, acting alone, cannot.

2. *Generate more alternatives.* Because groups have a greater amount and diversity of information, they can identify more alternatives than an individual. This advantage is particularly evident when group members represent different specialties. For instance, a team made up of representatives from engineering, accounting, production, marketing, and personnel will generate alternatives that reflect their diverse specialties. Such a multiplicity of "world views" often yields a greater array of alternatives than any one of those specialists could have alone.

3. *Increase acceptance of a solution.* Many decisions fail after the final choice has been made because people do not accept the solution. However, if the people who will be affected by a certain solution and who will help implement it get to participate in the process itself, they will be likely to accept it and to encourage others to accept it as well. Group members are reluctant to fight or undermine a decision they have helped develop.

4. *Increase legitimacy.* The group decision-making process is consistent with democratic ideals, and therefore decisions made by groups may be perceived as more legitimate than decisions made by one person. The fact that the individual decision maker has complete power and has not consulted others can create a perception that a decision was made autocratically and arbitrarily.

If groups are so good at making decisions, how did the phrase "A camel is a horse put together by a committee" become so popular? The answer, of course, is that group decisions also have disadvantages.

1. *Time consuming.* It takes time to assemble a group, and the interaction that takes place once the group is in place is frequently inefficient. The result is that groups almost always take more time to reach a solution than it would take an individual making the decision alone.

2. *Minority domination.* Members of a group are never perfectly equal. They may differ in rank in the organization, experience, knowledge about the problem, influence with other members, verbal skills, assertiveness, and the like. This inequality creates the opportunity for one or more members to use their advantages to dominate others in the group. A dominant minority frequently can have an excessive influence on the final decision.

3. *Pressures to conform.* There are social pressures to conform in groups that can lead to a phenomenon called **groupthink**.[19] This is a form of conformity in which group members withhold deviant, minority, or unpopular views in order to give the appearance of agreement. Groupthink undermines critical thinking in the group and eventually harms the quality of the final decision.

4. *Ambiguous responsibility.* Group members share responsibility, but who is actually responsible for the final outcome? In an individual decision, it is clear who is responsible. In a group decision, the responsibility of any single member is diluted.

groupthink

The withholding by group members of different views in order to appear in agreement.

Effectiveness and Efficiency of Group Decision Making.   Determining whether groups are effective at making decisions depends on the criteria you use for defining effectiveness. Group decisions tend to be more *accurate.* The evidence indicates that, on average, groups make better decisions than individuals. This doesn't mean, of course, that *all* groups outperform *every* individual. But group decisions are almost always superior to those made by individuals alone.[20] If decision effectiveness is defined in terms of *speed,* individuals are superior. Group decision processes are characterized by give and take, which consumes time. Effectiveness may mean the degree to which a solution demonstrates *creativity.* If creativity is important, groups tend to be more effective than individuals.[21] There is a caveat, however; the forces that encourage groupthink must be constrained. The final criterion for effectiveness is the degree of *acceptance* that the final decision achieves. As we previously noted, because group decisions have input from more people, they are likely to result in solutions that will be more widely accepted.

The effectiveness of group decision making is also influenced by the size of the group. The larger the group, the greater the opportunity for heterogeneous representation. On the other hand, a larger group requires more coordination and more time to allow all members to contribute. So groups probably should not be too large: a minimum of five to a maximum of about 15. Evidence indicates, in fact, that groups of five, and to a lesser extent seven, are the most effective.[22] Because five and seven are odd numbers, deadlocks are avoided. These groups are large enough for members to shift roles and withdraw from unfavorable positions but still small enough for quieter members to participate actively in discussions.

However, group effectiveness shouldn't be considered without also assessing efficiency. Groups almost always come in a poor second in efficiency to an individual decision maker. With few exceptions, group decision making consumes more work time than does individual decision making. Exceptions occur when, to achieve comparable quantities of diverse input, the individual decision maker must spend a great deal of time reviewing files and talking to people. Because groups can include members from different areas, they can spend less time searching for information. However, as we noted, such decisions tend to be

Group decision making was a major tool in the genesis of Zima, a clear malt beverage marketed to so-called Generation Xers. To launch the new product, Coors put together a committee from production, marketing, public relations, and the ad agency Foote, Cone and Belding. Some of the problems inherent in group processes may have contributed to Zima's slow takeoff in the marketplace.

the exception. In general, groups are less efficient than individuals. In deciding whether to use groups, then, primary consideration must be given to assessing whether increases in effectiveness are enough to offset the losses in efficiency.

Techniques for Improving Group Decision Making.   When members of a group meet face to face and interact with one another, they create the potential for groupthink. They can censor themselves and pressure other group members into agreement. Four ways of making group decisions more creative have been suggested: brainstorming, the nominal group and Delphi techniques, and electronic meetings.

1. **Brainstorming** is a relatively simple technique for overcoming pressures for conformity that hinder the development of creative alternatives.[23] It does this by utilizing an idea-generating process that specifically encourages any and all alternatives while withholding any criticism of those alternatives. In a typical brainstorming session, a group of 6 to 12 people sit around a table. The group leader states the problem in a clear manner that is understood by all participants. Members then "free-wheel" as many alternatives as they can in a given time. No criticism is allowed, and all the alternatives are recorded for later discussion and analysis.

   brainstorming

   An idea-generating process that encourages alternatives while withholding criticism.

2. **Nominal group technique (NGT)** is a group decision-making technique in which discussion is restricted during the decision-making process. Although group members must be present, they are required to operate independently. How are group decisions made using NGT? Members meet as a group and are presented with a problem. Before any discussion takes place, each member independently writes down his or her ideas on the problem. After this silent period, each member presents one idea to the group. Each member goes in turn around the table, presenting one idea at a time until all ideas have been presented and recorded (typically on a flip chart or chalkboard). No discussion takes place until all ideas have been recorded. The group now discusses the ideas for clarity and evaluates them. Each group member silently and independently ranks the ideas. The final decision is determined by the idea with the highest aggregate ranking.

   nominal group technique (NGT)

   A group decision-making technique in which group members are physically present but operate independently.

Delphi technique

A group decision-making technique in which members never meet face to face.

3. The **Delphi technique** is similar to NGT except that it does not allow group members to meet face to face and therefore does not require the physical presence of the group members. How does the Delphi technique work? The problem is identified, and members are asked to provide possible solutions through a series of carefully designed questionnaires. Each member anonymously and independently completes the first questionnaire. Results of the first questionnaire are compiled at a central location, transcribed, and copied. Each member receives a copy of the results. After viewing the results, members are again asked for their solutions. The initial results typically trigger new solutions or cause changes in the original position. This process goes on until a consensus is reached.

electronic meetings

Decision-making groups that interact by using linked computers.

4. **Electronic meetings** are the most recent approach to group decision making and they blend NGT with sophisticated computer technology.[24] Once the technology for the meeting is in place, the concept is simple. Up to 50 people sit around a horseshoe-shaped table outfitted with computer terminals. Issues are presented to participants and they type their responses onto their computer screens. Individual comments, as well as aggregate votes, are displayed on a projection screen in the room. Experts claim that electronic meetings are as much as 55 percent faster than traditional face-to-face meetings.[25]

TESTING...
TESTING...

1 0 Why are some groups more successful than others? (Hint: Use the group behavior model.)

1 1 What are the advantages and disadvantages of group decision making?

1 2 When would groups be the best choice for making decisions?

TURNING GROUPS INTO EFFECTIVE TEAMS

A survey of 1,811 companies in the United States found that 68 percent were using formal teams to perform work activities.[26] Many smaller organizations are also using teams to perform organizational tasks and solve problems. Teams are popular and likely to continue being used. In this section, we'll discuss what a work team is, the different types of teams that organizations might use, why organizations are increasingly designing work around teams rather than individuals, and how to develop and manage work teams.

What Is a Team?

Most of us are already familiar with the idea of a team especially if we have ever participated in or watched any type of organized sports activity. Although a sports team has many of the same characteristics as a work team, work teams *are* different and have their own unique traits. Just what are **work teams**? They are formal groups, made up of interdependent individuals, responsible for the attainment of a goal.[27] Thus all work teams are groups, but only formal groups can be work teams.

work teams

Formal groups made up of interdependent individuals, responsible for the attainment of a goal.

Types of Teams

Although there are many ways to categorize teams, one convenient way is to look at teams in terms of four characteristics: purpose, duration, membership, and structure.[28] (See Figure 14-8.) Let's explain these characteristics in more detail.

Teams can vary in their purpose or goal. A team might be involved in product development, problem solving, as part of a reengineering effort, or for any other number of work-related activities. For instance, at Motorola's Austin manufacturing plant, teams are used in work process optimization projects throughout the facility. And at Case Swayne Company,

Whole Foods Market, Inc.,
the largest natural foods
grocer in the United
States, has been growing
for 18 years by building a
business model that
depends entirely on
teamwork and autonomy.
Even hiring is done by a
vote, and the company's
financials are open to all
employees.

Inc., a producer of specialty food products based in Corona, California, a work team guided
the company through the rigorous global quality standard registration process known as
ISO 9001.[29] (We will discuss ISO 9000, an earlier version of ISO 9001, in chapter 18.)

A team is either permanent or temporary. Functional department teams and others that
are part of the organization's formal structure are types of permanent teams. Temporary
teams include task forces, project teams, problem-solving teams, and any other type of
short-term team created to develop, analyze, or study a business or work-related issue.

FIGURE 14-8   **Categories of Teams**

Purpose

- Product Development
- Problem Solving
- Reengineering
- Any Other Organizational
  Purposes Desired

Structure

- Supervised
- Self-Managed

Membership

- Functional
- Cross-Functional

Duration

- Permanent
- Temporary

Team membership can either be functional or cross-functional. A departmental team is functional because it pulls its members from a specific area. However, as we have already discussed in chapter 10, many organizations are using cross-functional teams as a way to foster innovation, cooperation, and commitment. The cross-functional team has members from various functional areas and organizational levels.

Finally, teams can be either supervised or self-managed. A supervised team will be under the direction of a manager who is responsible for guiding the team in setting goals, in performing the necessary work activities, and in evaluating performance. On the other hand, a self-managed team assumes the responsibilities for managing itself.

Given these four characteristics, what are some of the popular types of teams being used in organizations today? The three best-known are functional teams, self-directed or self-managed teams, and cross-functional teams.[30]

Functional teams are composed of a manager and his or her direct subordinates from a particular functional area. Within this functional team, issues such as authority, decision making, leadership, and interactions are relatively simple and clear. Functional teams are often involved in efforts to improve work activities or to solve specific problems within their particular functional area. For example, at the California headquarters of Birkenstock Footprint Sandals, employees in sales, credit, production, warehousing, and other functional areas now work in independent teams to complete tasks and solve customer problems.[31]

Another type of team commonly being used in organizations is the self-directed or self-managed team. A **self-directed**, or **self-managed**, **team** is a formal group of employees who operate without a manager and are responsible for a complete work process or segment that delivers a product or service to an external or internal customer. The self-directed work team is responsible for getting the work done *and* for managing themselves. For instance, the Parks Operations Department of the City of Hampton, Virginia, reorganized into self-directed work teams who are responsible for ensuring whole projects are done (such as maintaining the grounds around the city's library) rather than just doing one piece of the project (such as mowing the grass). Supervisors who used to drive around in their trucks checking on the workers relinquished control to the teams.[32] Other organizations such as Federal Express and IDS Financial Services use self-managed teams in deciding how best to do the work.

The last type of team we want to discuss is the **cross-functional team**, which we introduced back in chapter 10 and defined as a hybrid grouping of individuals who are experts in various specialties and who come together across departmental lines to work on various organizational tasks. Many organizations are using cross-functional teams. For instance, at Modicon Inc., a Massachusetts-based subsidiary of Germany's Daimler-Benz that makes automation control equipment, most of the employees are involved in teams that span several functions and departments. These teams are involved in various functional activities from production to engineering to marketing.[33] At Hallmark Cards in Kansas City, editors, writers, artists, and production specialists join with employees from manufacturing, graphic arts, sales, and distribution to work on everything from developing new product ideas to improving customer deliveries.[34] Our chapter-opening Manager's Dilemma portrayed another cross-functional team—the team used in reengineering processes at Hewlett-Packard's distribution facility.

Why Use Teams?

There's no single explanation for the recent increased popularity of teams. Here are some reasons that we think are important.

Creates Esprit de Corps.   Team members expect and demand a lot from each other. In so doing, they facilitate cooperation and improve employee morale. We find that team norms tend to encourage members to excel and, at the same time, create a climate that increases job satisfaction.

functional team

A type of work team that is composed of a manager and his or her subordinates from a particular functional area.

self-directed or self-managed team

A type of work team that operates without a manager and is responsible for a complete work process or segment that delivers a product or service to an external or internal customer.

cross-functional team

A type of work team in which individuals who are experts in various specialties (or functions) work together on various organizational tasks.

MANAGERS

SPEAK

OUT

Interview with James Fripp, Field Staffing Manager, Taco Bell Corporation, Omaha, Nebraska

Describe your job.

My job as field staffing manager is to ensure that we have the proper number of salaried managers on board in the 178 units I'm responsible for staffing. In this role, I am counted on to source/recruit, interview, and determine whether an individual should move on in our interview process. This role requires me to evaluate staffing needs, analyze turnover, make the necessary recommendations when issues are noticed or observed, and do all types of recruiting events.

What types of skills do you think tomorrow's managers will need?

I believe that the managers of tomorrow, more than anything, will need to possess outstanding people (soft) skills! Computer skills will be needed as well as expertise in their field. However, even with the proliferation of computers and other amazing technologies, the most successful managers will be those who can create an environment in which people feel as if they are very important to the success of the company and are recognized for their contributions by their managers.

What do you think is important in managing an effective team?

First and foremost is ensuring that everyone on the team clearly knows and understands what the goals and expectations are. Second, is that everyone knows and understands what their specific role is on the team. Third, allowing input from the team members (whenever possible) on how to achieve the goal. Allowing input fosters ownership, which is crucial when trying to work with a team. Last, but by no means least, ensuring that all team members understand they will be held accountable for the outcome of the team.

How do you effectively manage conflicts that arise among your employees?

I establish some very basic ground rules that are communicated on day one and reiterated as frequently as needed. My main rule is that, no matter what, we always treat each other with respect and dignity. Believe it or not, this applies to both younger employees as well as adult employees and co-workers. Once this is established, I bring both individuals together and let each one share his or her side of the issue. This is important, as typically you will get a more factual account of the issue. In addition, as the individuals are giving their accounts of the issue, I will usually see them start to understand the other person's perspective and be a bit more willing to be flexible. At the end of their conversations, I will ask them for their input in resolving the conflict. The individuals involved usually find resolution. However, when they can't, I will resolve the issue by dealing with it as fairly as possible. ■

Allows Management to Think Strategically.   The use of teams, especially self-managed ones, frees up managers to do more strategic planning. When jobs are designed around individuals, managers often spend an inordinate amount of their time supervising their people and "putting out fires." They're too busy to do much strategic thinking. By using work teams, managers can redirect their energy toward bigger issues such as long-term plans.

Increases Flexibility.   Moving decision making vertically down to teams allows the organization greater flexibility. Team members frequently know more about work-related problems than do managers. Moreover, team members are closer to those problems. And on those decisions where considerable input is needed from different perspectives, teams are more flexible and can be faster because the people with the information are there and accessible.

Takes Advantage of Workforce Diversity.   Groups made up of individuals from different backgrounds and with different experiences often see things that homogeneous groups do not. Therefore, the use of diverse teams may result in more innovative ideas and better decisions than might arise if individuals alone made the decision.

Increases Performance.   Finally, all the above factors can combine to make team performance higher than might be achieved by the same individuals working alone. Organizations as varied as Burlington Northern, Knight-Ridder, Hewlett-Packard, and the Girl Scouts have found that teams eliminate waste, slash bureaucratic overhead, stimulate ideas for improvements, and generate more output per worker-hour than do more traditional individual-focused work designs.[35]

**TESTING...
TESTING...
1   2   3**

13 Compare groups and teams.

14 Contrast functional, self-directed or self-managed, and cross-functional teams.

15 Why have teams become so popular in organizations?

DEVELOPING AND MANAGING EFFECTIVE TEAMS

Teams are not automatic productivity enhancers. They can also be disappointments for management. We need to look more closely at how managers can develop and manage effective teams and how teams are used in TQM initiatives. But first, let's look at what characterizes an effective team.

Characteristics of Effective Teams

Recent research provides insights into the primary characteristics associated with effective teams.[36] Let's look at these characteristics as summarized in Figure 14-9.

Clear Goals.   High-performance teams have both a clear understanding of the goal to be achieved and a belief that the goal embodies a worthwhile or important result. Moreover, the importance of these goals encourages individuals to redirect personal concerns to these team goals. In effective teams, members are committed to the team's goals, know what they're expected to accomplish, and understand how they will work together to achieve those goals.

Relevant Skills.   Effective teams are composed of competent individuals. They have the necessary technical skills and abilities to achieve the desired goals and the personal char-

Work teams have gone international, and the best of them can boast spectacular results. Maxus Energy, the U.S. subsidiary of Argentine corporation YPF, formed a team with fellow subsidiary Maxus-Southeast Sumatra. Its members, from the United States, Holland, Great Britain, and Indonesia, had little in common but their problem: to prevent an anticipated 15 percent drop in oil production from a new field. They succeeded by pooling their expertise and even added oil reserves to their stockpiles in the process.

acteristics required to achieve excellence while working well with others. This second point is important and often overlooked. Not everyone who is technically competent has the skills to work well as a team member. High-performing teams have members who possess both technical and interpersonal skills.

FIGURE 14-9   Characteristics of Effective Teams

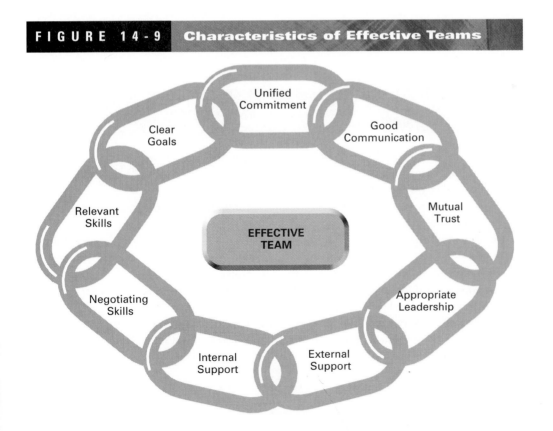

Mutual Trust. Effective teams are characterized by high mutual trust among members. That is, members believe in the integrity, character, and ability of one another. But as you probably know from personal relationships, trust is fragile. It takes a long time to build and can be easily destroyed. Also, because trust begets trust and distrust begets distrust, maintaining trust requires careful attention by management.

The climate of trust within a group tends to be strongly influenced by the organization's culture and the actions of management. Organizations that value openness, honesty, and collaborative processes and that encourage employee involvement and autonomy are likely to create trusting cultures. Table 14-2 lists six recommended actions that can help managers build and maintain trust.

Unified Commitment. Members of an effective team exhibit intense loyalty and dedication to the team. They're willing to do anything that has to be done to help their team succeed. We call this loyalty and dedication *unified commitment.*

Studies of successful teams have found that members identify with their teams.[37] Members redefine themselves to include membership in the team as an important aspect of the self. Unified commitment, then, is characterized by dedication to the team's goals and a willingness to expend extraordinary amounts of energy to achieve them.

Good Communication. Not surprisingly, effective teams are characterized by good communication. Members are able to convey messages between each other in a form that is readily and clearly understood. This includes nonverbal as well as spoken messages. Good communication is also characterized by a healthy dose of feedback from team members and managers. Feedback helps to guide team members and to correct misunderstandings. Like a couple who has been together for many years, members on high-performing teams are able to quickly and efficiently share ideas and feelings.

Negotiating Skills. When jobs are designed around individuals, their job descriptions, the organization's rules and procedures, and other types of formalized documentation clar-

TABLE 14-2	**Six Suggestions for Helping Managers Build Trust**

1. *Communicate.* Keep team members and subordinates informed by explaining decisions and policies and providing accurate feedback. Be candid about your own problems and limitations.
2. *Be supportive.* Be available and approachable. Encourage and support team members' ideas.
3. *Be respectful.* Delegate real authority to team members and listen to their ideas.
4. *Be fair.* Give credit where it's due, be objective and impartial in performance evaluations, and be generous with your praise.
5. *Be predictable.* Be consistent in your daily affairs. Make good on your explicit and implied promises.
6. *Demonstrate competence.* Develop the admiration and respect of team members by demonstrating technical and professional ability and good business sense.

Source: Adapted from F. Bartolome, "Nobody Trusts the Boss Completely—Now What?" *Harvard Business Review,* March–April 1989, pp. 135–42.

ify employee roles. Effective teams, on the other hand, tend to be flexible and are continually making adjustments. This flexibility requires team members to possess adequate negotiating skills. Problems and relationships are regularly changing in teams, requiring members to confront and reconcile differences.

Appropriate Leadership.   Effective leaders can motivate a team to follow them through the most difficult situations. How? They help clarify goals. They demonstrate that change is possible by overcoming inertia. And they increase the self-confidence of team members, helping members to realize their potential more fully. It is important to note that the best leaders aren't necessarily directive or controlling. Increasingly, effective team leaders are taking the role of coach and facilitator. They help guide and support the team, but they don't control it. This condition obviously applies to self-managed teams but also increasingly applies to task forces and cross-functional teams in which the members themselves are empowered. For some traditional managers, changing their role from boss to facilitator—from giving orders to working for the team—is a difficult transition. Although most managers relish the new-found shared authority or come to understand its advantages through leadership training, some hard-nosed dictatorial managers are just ill suited to the team concept and must be transferred or replaced.

Internal and External Support.   The final condition necessary for an effective team is a supportive climate. Internally, the team should be provided with a sound infrastructure. This includes proper training, an understandable measurement system that team members can use to evaluate their overall performance, an incentive program that recognizes and rewards team activities, and a supportive human resource system. The right infrastructure should support

The success of NASA's recent *Pathfinder* mission is a tribute to the effectiveness of its earth-bound team. The team exhibits many of the characteristics of effective teams.

members and reinforce behaviors that lead to high levels of performance. Externally, management should provide the team with the resources needed to get the job done.

Managing Teams

What's involved in managing a team? We can look at the task of managing a team using the four basic management functions: planning, organizing, leading, and controlling.[38]

Planning.   Goal determination is an important part of the planning process. As we have pointed out previously, effective teams have clear goals. It's important that team members understand and accept the team's goals.[39] Whether these goals are provided for the team, as in the case of the reengineering team in our opening dilemma that was given the task of redesigning work processes, or whether the team develops its own goals, every team member needs to know what the goals are. One easy way to check on their understanding of the goals is to have each team member write down the team's goals, then collect and analyze their statements for accuracy and consistency. If there are misconceptions about the team's goals, a team meeting can be called to clear them up.

Organizing.   Organizing tasks involved with managing a team include clarification of authority and structural issues. One of the key questions for any team is "How much authority do we have?" If the team is a self-directed or self-managed team, it has already been empowered with the authority to make certain decisions and perform specific work activities. However, even if the team is not a self-managed team, questions about what it can and cannot do often come up. If the organizational culture is supportive of employee involvement and autonomy, then its work teams are likely to have authority over what they do and how they do it. But it's important that these authority issues be addressed early so that a team knows its parameters and constraints. Structural issues also need to be resolved within the team itself. Has a leader been appointed, or will the team designate one? What tasks need to be done in order to accomplish the team's goals? What are the most effective and efficient ways to do the work? Who's going to be assigned to the various tasks, and how will the assignments be made? These are the types of structural questions that teams must answer.

Leading.   Important issues in leading that a team must address include, among others, what role the leader will play, how conflict will be handled, and what communication processes will be used. The team leader plays an important role in directing the efforts of the team. However, as we described in the section on effective teams, team leaders are increasingly becoming more of a facilitator and a coach than a "person in charge." Leading a team typically requires having sufficient technical knowledge to understand the team's work duties *and* having strong interpersonal skills so you can facilitate individual participation, motivate outstanding performance, resolve conflicts, and gain consensus on key issues. Dealing with the human dynamics of the team is often the most difficult part of managing a team. Table 14-3 lists some people skills that are important in leading a team.

Controlling.   Two of the most important controlling issues in relation to managing teams are: How will the team's performance be evaluated, and what type of reward system will be used? As organizations begin to use teams more and more, their employee appraisal and reward systems will have to change. What types of changes can we expect?

Performance criteria need to be modified to incorporate teamwork behaviors in employee evaluations.[40] Not only should individual performance be evaluated, but factors that indicate how well the individual works in the team context should also be considered. For instance, at Ideo, an industrial design firm, performance appraisals now include comments from team peers as well as from managers.[41]

Changes in the appraisal process to incorporate team efforts is only half the story. We also need to look at how teams are rewarded for their efforts and performance levels. As organizations use teams more frequently, we are beginning to see an increased use of group incentive plans. One of the most popular approaches to group incentives is **gainsharing**, an incentive program that shares the gains of the efforts of employees with those employees. In gainsharing, rewards are directly related to performance. If the team succeeds, team members will be rewarded. Team-based organizations also use rewards such as one-time bonuses, team incentive systems, employee-based recognition programs, and informal team recognition. At the head office of Aid Association for Lutherans (AAL) insurance company, for instance, team members get pay increments as they acquire and use new skills. But at Dial Corporation, which uses regional teams consisting of a marketing person, a financial specialist, a customer service representative, and the salesperson, individuals are rewarded on the basis of individual performance as measured by results against goals and on team results as measured by sales volume, sales forecasting accuracy, and improved profitability.[42] Whatever approach is used, the team itself should be the primary force in deciding what types of rewards and recognition are important.[43]

gainsharing

A group incentive program that shares the gains of the efforts of group members with those group members.

Teams and TQM

One of the central characteristics of total quality management is the use of teams. But why teams? The essence of TQM is process improvement, and employee participation is the cornerstone of process improvement. In other words, TQM requires managers to give employees the encouragement to share ideas and to act on what they suggest. Problem-solving teams provide the natural vehicle for employees to share ideas and to implement improvements. As stated by Gil Mosard, a TQM specialist at Boeing–McDonnell-Douglas, "When your measurement system tells you your process is out of control, you need teamwork for structured problem solving. Not everyone needs to know how to do all kinds of fancy control charts for performance tracking, but everybody does need to know where their process stands so they can judge if it is improving."[44]

TABLE 14-3	**Types of Interpersonal Skills Used in Managing Teams**

- Ask appropriate questions to bring out ideas and stimulate discussion.
- Listen closely and intently to members' ideas and concerns.
- Manage group discussions to encourage shy team members to participate.
- Establish an informal and nonthreatening climate so members feel free to candidly speak their thoughts.
- Use the consensus method to reach decisions on key team issues.
- Involve team members in setting goals.
- Implement meeting guidelines to minimize wasted time in group meetings.
- Encourage respect for each other so each member knows that his or her contributions are valued.
- Identify and deal with dysfunctional behaviors immediately.
- Celebrate the achievement of milestones and other team accomplishments.
- Use recognition, task assignments, and other techniques to motivate team members.

Source: Based on G.M. Parker, *Cross-Functional Teams* (San Francisco: Jossey-Bass, 1994), pp. 57–58.

At Coca-Cola Fountain Manufacturing Baltimore Syrup Operation, a dramatic turnaround has been taking place. Absenteeism, aging equipment, and outmoded management systems are being replaced by a commitment to quality, supported by employee involvement, willingness to change, and the introduction of teams.

quality circles

Work groups that meet regularly to discuss, investigate, and correct quality problems.

One team application to TQM is **quality circles**.[45] These are work groups of eight to ten employees and supervisors who share an area of responsibility. They meet regularly (typically once a week on company time and on company premises) to discuss their quality problems, investigate causes of the problems, recommend solutions, and take corrective actions. They assume responsibility for solving quality problems, and they generate and evaluate their own feedback. However, management usually makes the final decision about the implementation of recommended solutions. Figure 14-10 describes a typical quality circle process.

Finally, examples from GE Fanuc Automation North America Inc. and Amana illustrate how teams are being used in TQM programs. GE Fanuc (a joint venture between General Electric Company and FANUC Ltd. of Japan) created a program it called HIWF (Highly Involved Workforce) in which cross-functional employee teams meet for brainstorming and problem-solving sessions. In addition, these teams work together on a daily and long-term basis looking for ways to continually improve the business and specific functions.[46]

At Amana, task forces made up of people from different levels within the company deal with quality problems that cut across various functional areas. Each of the various task forces has a unique area of problem-solving responsibility. For instance, one handles in-plant products, another deals with items that arise outside the production facility, and still another focuses specifically on supplier problems. Amana claims that the use of these task forces has improved vertical and horizontal communication within the company and has substantially reduced the number of units that do not meet company specifications and the number of service problems in the field.[47]

FIGURE 14-10	How a Typical Quality Circle Operates

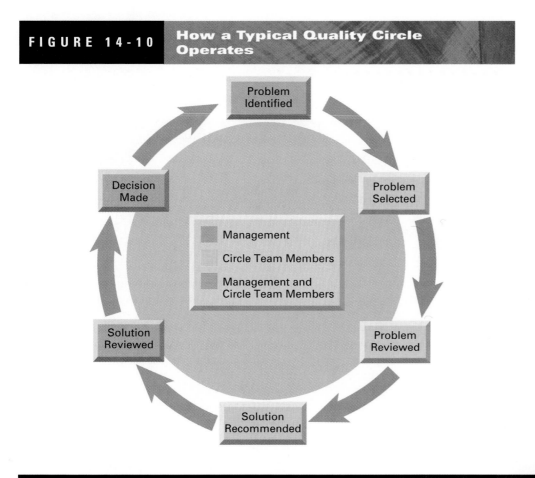

16 What characteristics do effective teams exhibit?

17 What types of issues must be addressed when managing a team?

18 How are teams used in TQM programs?

TESTING...
TESTING...

1 2 3

managers respond to "a manager's dilemma"

MANAGER 1

Because conflicts in a group are unavoidable, I would first keep everyone in the group focused on the end result of the group's task and continually reinforce to the group that there is an overriding objective—reengineering the work processes. I would also provide ample opportunities for group members to express their ideas. If team members feel like they have input and that their input is valued, they may be less likely to have conflicts because everyone recognizes that they will have a chance to express their ideas. Finally, if I were in Cheng's and Anderson's positions, I would make sure that the team members have time for socializing. The time spent doing this would not be "wasted" but would instead solidify the bonds between the team members. As part of this idea, I would suggest that as the team accomplishes steps along the way toward the overall goal of reengineering the work processes, they should celebrate these accomplishments.

Brad Barnes, Staff Accountant, Baird, Kurtz, and Dobson, Colorado Springs, Colorado

MANAGER 2

Cheng and Anderson have assembled a large group that is facing the complex task of reorganizing the work processes at this facility. I feel that they will avoid many conflicts by clearly defining the outcomes HP expects from this group. The team members must recognize these goals as valid as well as important to the continued success of the company. Cohesiveness must be promoted, possibly by creating some social occasions for members to get to know each other. It is important to keep in mind that some team members are paid to be a part of this team and some are required by their employment to participate. This situation could have some bearing on their willingness to participate, especially if it creates additional workload for the HP employees. A reward system might be considered for these individuals so that everyone is motivated to participate fully.

Cheng and Anderson should consider structuring electronic meetings for this project. HP obviously has the technology, and with a group this large it could help cut down on unnecessary dialogue at their meetings. This method creates anonymity for idea generation and will enable members to brainstorm and offer even radical ideas for consideration. This type of meeting would keep the communication more task specific and will control potential for disproportionate levels of conflict.

Becky Runyon, Owner, Decorator Outlet, Jefferson City, Missouri

for your
IMMEDIATE action

Colorado State High School Sports Association

TO: Eric Gershman, Manager,
Program Infractions
Investigations

FR: Audrey Costa, Director of
Association Services

RE: Conflicts on Investigation Teams

We've got a potentially big problem on our hands. It's come to my attention, from complaints I've been receiving, that the five-person investigation teams we're sending out into the high schools across the state to investigate allegations of rule infractions are having conflicts among team members. Because the team members have to work closely together in interviewing people, interpreting the rules, and writing up a report, I'm worried that this dissension may be hurting the quality of the team's investigation process. We've got to address this problem now in order to preserve our reputation for fair, reasonable, and high-quality investigations.

Please write up a list describing how you intend to address this problem and get it to me as soon as possible. Once I've had a chance to look it over, we'll get together to discuss it.

This is a fictionalized account of a potentially real problem. It was written for academic purposes only.

SUMMARY

This summary is organized by the chapter-opening objectives found on p. 446.

1. People join groups because of their needs for security, status, self-esteem, affiliation, power, or achievement.

2. The five stages of group development are forming, storming, norming, performing, and adjourning. Forming is the stage in which people join the group and define the group's purpose, structure, and leadership. Storming is a stage of intragroup conflict over control issues. During the norming stage, close relationships develop and the group demonstrates cohesiveness. Performing is the stage at which the group is doing the task at hand. Finally, adjourning is the stage when temporary committees, task forces, and teams with a limited task to perform prepare for disbandment.

3. A role refers to a set of behavior patterns expected of someone occupying a given position in a social unit. At any given time, employees adjust their role behaviors to the group of which they are a part. Norms are standards shared by group members. They informally convey to employees which behaviors are acceptable and which are unacceptable.

4. There are five variables in the group behavior model that, in aggregate, explain the group's performance and satisfaction. First, a group is influenced by the larger organization of which it is a part. Second, a group's potential level of performance depends to a large extent on the resources that its members individually bring to the group. Third, there is a group structure that shapes the behavior of members. Fourth, there are internal processes within the group that aid or hinder interaction and the ability of the group to perform. Finally, the impact of group processes on the group's performance and member satisfaction depends on the task that the group is doing.

5. The advantages of group decision making are: more-complete information, more alternatives, increased acceptance of a solution, and greater legitimacy. The disadvantages include the amount of time it takes, the likelihood of being dominated by a minority, the pressure to conform, and the clouding of responsibility.

6. Four ways of improving group decision making are brainstorming, the nominal group technique (NGT), the Delphi technique, and electronic meetings.

7. Teams have become increasingly popular in organizations because they build esprit de corps, free up management to do more strategic thinking, permit more flexible decision making, utilize workforce diversity, and usually increase performance.

8. Effective work teams are characterized by clear goals, members with relevant skills, mutual trust among members, unified commitment, good communication, adequate negotiating skills, and appropriate leadership.

9. Managers can build trust by communicating openly; supporting team members' ideas; being respectful, fair, and predictable; and demonstrating competence.

10. Problem-solving teams provide a natural vehicle for employees to share ideas and to implement improvements as part of the TQM process. Teams are particularly effective for resolving complex problems.

THINKING ABOUT MANAGEMENT ISSUES

1. Think of a group to which you belong (or have belonged). Trace its development through the stages of group development shown in Figure 14-1. Think of specific examples or instances describing each stage.

2. How do you think scientific management theorists would react to the increased reliance on teams in organizations? How would the behavioral science theorists react?

3. How do you explain the popularity of work teams in the United States when American culture places such high value on individualism?

4. Why might a manager want to stimulate conflict in a group or team? How could conflict be stimulated?

5. Do you think that everyone should be expected to be a team player, given the trends that we're seeing in the use of teams? Discuss.

SELF-ASSESSMENT EXERCISE

ARE YOU A TEAM PLAYER?

Instructions: This self-assessment exercise asks you to examine your behavior as a team member. For each pair of items, place a checkmark in the space in the column that best defines your behavior in class project groups, in clubs or student groups, and in work groups (if you're employed).

	Very like me	Somewhat like me	Both describe me	Somewhat like me	Very like me	
1. Flexible in own ideas	✓					Set in my own ideas
2. Open to new ideas	✓					Avoid new ideas
3. Listen well to others	✓					Tune out others
4. Trusting of others		✓				Not trusting of others
5. Readily contribute to group meetings	✓					Hold back from contributing in meetings
6. Concerned for what happens to others		✓				Not concerned for what happens to others
7. Fully committed to tasks	✓					Have little commitment to tasks
8. Share leadership with group		✓				Maintain full control of group
9. Encourage others to participate	✓					Expect others to participate without encouragement
10. Group needs come before my individual needs	✓					My individual needs come before group needs

See scoring key on page SK–5.

Source: Adapted from training materials for income maintenance supervisors, Special Topics Workshop: "Motivation, Teambuilding, and Enhancing Morale," Professional Development Program, Rockefeller College of Public Affairs and Policy, University at Albany, State University of New York. Used with permission.

TAKE IT TO THE NET

We invite you to visit the Robbins/Coulter companion Web site at http://www.prenhall.com/robbinsmgt for this chapter's Internet resources.

CASE APPLICATION

Team Adventures at Evart Glass Plant

One exercise involves team members' randomly throwing and catching various objects (such as tennis balls, hackey sacs, or koosh balls) and attempting to juggle the objects simultaneously. Another involves passing a bicycle inner tube around a circle of people who are holding hands without either breaking the circle or letting the tube touch the ground. You might think we're describing activities at a summer camp for 10-year-olds, but these are exercises being used to show one company's work teams what it means to be a team player. The company is Evart Glass Plant, in Evart, Michigan.

The Evart Glass Plant, an automobile glass manufacturer, is a division of Chrysler Corporation and the primary supplier of windows for the Chrysler Jeep Grand Cherokee. In 1994, as a result of an employee survey, Chrysler challenged each of its plants to improve organizational culture and climate. Evart Glass's culture committee decided to focus on improving interactions between employees on work teams and between work teams. As many U.S. organizations have done, the Evart Glass Plant had moved to a team-based operation. Bert Burtolozzi, the Evart Glass plant manager stated, "As we move toward a team-focused approach in our operation, team effort is what counts." However, getting employees to function effectively and efficiently as team members and getting teams to high levels of performance doesn't just happen. That's why the decision was made to send the company's 257 employees through a team-building and team-training program.

The team-training experiences were made more challenging by combining the employees into cross-functional teams, not their normal work groups. For instance, one team consisting of a forklift driver, a maintenance person, a shift supervisor, and a receptionist had to share ideas about how to move each member of the team from one side of an "electric" fence to the other side without touching the fence. The team lesson to be learned from that exercise was: Support and trust are vital parts of teamwork because sometimes team members have to be willing to open up and ask for help in order to do their jobs successfully. After a full day of completing different types of team adventures, team members gathered together to discuss the experience and to compare it with the workplace challenges they faced. The company's human resources manager said that this experience allowed everyone to "get to know the people in different work areas and to feel more comfortable about going to each other to talk and solve a work-related problem and share information."

Employees weren't immediately enamored of the idea of team-building exercises. Some workers, primarily union members, initially resisted the mandatory team training. To ease the uncertainty over what the training was all about, the company provided information to workers well in advance of the training. In addition, the actual team-building program followed a "challenge by choice" philosophy, meaning that workers were not required to participate in activities that made them uncomfortable, but they would be expected to take an active support role and cheer on their fellow team members as they completed the activity. In the end, a follow-up survey of reactions to the training was positive; many employees stated that they would like to do it again with their own work groups. In addition, employees from all levels of the organization commented that they noticed changes in attitude; for instance, people now went out of their way to help others and were making more of a concerted effort to include everyone's opinions in discussions. One person from the company's finance department summed up the whole experience by stating, "I saw the whole concept of teamwork being played out, showing you have to work together rather than just taking it all on yourself."

QUESTIONS

1. "You can't train people to be team players." Build an argument to support this statement. Then negate that argument.
2. Describe the advantages and disadvantages of using cross-functional team training rather than using the actual work teams employees were part of.
3. How might the team-building exercises such as the ones briefly described contribute to making a team more effective?
4. It's your chance to be creative! Think of a team-building exercise that would help a team meet one of the characteristics of an effective team. (See Figure 14-9.) Describe which characteristic you chose and then describe the exercise you'd use to help a team practice or enhance that characteristic.

Source: H. Campbell, "Adventures in Teamland," *Personnel Journal,* May 1996, pp. 56–62.

Group Pressures inside the FAA

Gregory May was a man with influence and power. He had a $1.5 million contract to provide diversity training for the Federal Aviation Administration. Approximately 4,000 people, including hundreds from management, had taken his course. He was perceived to be very close to senior FAA managers and was believed to share personal information with those managers about FAA employees. More important, doing well in May's training program was required to get ahead in the organization. If you didn't get May's approval for completing the course in good standing, your career could be derailed, and if you objected to some of the things in May's course, you might even get fired.

Given the importance of this course to FAA employees, you'd assume that the course would have been well thought out and professionally conducted. Well, that assumption would have been wrong! Air traffic controllers, for instance, were subjected to sessions in which they were forced to share their innermost sexual secrets. People would be expected to share details of painful experiences from their youth, which often brought them to the point of being in tears. They had to undergo weird rituals. For instance, May would bark out orders such as "sit down," "stand up," "sit down," for hours on end. He wanted complete obedience from participants. In another exercise, he would tie individuals of the same sex together and make them go to the bathroom and shower together. When one complained that the exercise embarrassed him, May tossed it off and said, "Learn from it." In still another exercise, May made male air traffic controllers run a gauntlet of women who were told to grope the men's private parts. All of this was in the name of teaching diversity.

Did anyone complain? A few did. Did they disobey? Not many. One former FAA employee said, "I was a single parent with two small children, and they're 100 percent dependent on me, and my income. And there was no way I was going to give up a 12-year career working with the FAA." So they did what they were told for fear of losing their jobs.

May is no longer doing diversity training for the FAA. A government investigation was undertaken to find out what went on and to ensure it wouldn't happen again. But, meanwhile, thousands of FAA employees spent several years being tormented by Gregory May under the guise of sensitizing workers to diversity issues.

QUESTIONS

1. What does this case say about group pressures to conform?
2. Can you make any argument favoring this type of diversity training done in a group setting? Explain your position.
3. What, if anything, does this case say about group influences on training effectiveness?

Source: Based on "A Cult and Its Influence within the FAA," *ABC Nightline*, February 21, 1995.

A MANAGER'S DILEMMA

Bill Gross (on top in photo) has always been motivated by the challenge of something new.[1] He has been starting companies since 1975, when he was just 16 years old. To help pay his way through Cal Tech, Gross built and sold plans for a solar heating device, started a successful stereo equipment company, and then sold a major software upgrade to Lotus. In 1991, he started Knowledge Adventure, a company that designed and created educational software. He sold the company in early 1997 to CUC International for a cool $100 million. Gross's newest business venture is a factory unlike any factory you've ever seen. It's an *idea* factory!

Gross's idealab! <http://www.idealab.com> is a start-up factory based in Pasadena, California. It's devoted to helping conceive and fund new companies that are designing products and services for use on the Internet and World Wide Web. His goal by the end of the decade is to build 10 companies worth an average of $100 million each that can go public or be sold. In fact, one of the compa-

nies that has already bloomed out of the fertile soil of idealab! is CitySearch <http://www.citysearch.com>, which creates on-line information services for urban communities. CitySearch is going head to head with Microsoft and America Online and so far has been able to successfully compete. How does Idealab! work?

Many of idealab!'s talented employees are entrepreneurial computer whizzes from nearby Cal Tech. Gross has a pool of 20 programmers and Web site graphic designers who are on call for the start-up companies. The members of this talent pool can be quickly assembled into what Gross calls "Internet startups in a box." This arrangement enables Gross to move very quickly from idea to execution—a capability that's critical in the fast-changing world of the Internet and Web. It also gives young and talented individuals a shot at running their own show. In fact, Gross says, "I think people are motivated the most when they have unbelievable control of their destiny."

Put yourself in Gross's situation. What else can he do to keep these talented programmers and designers motivated to continually create and innovate? How would you motivate your young, talented programmers and designers?

WHAT WOULD YOU DO?

Motivating and rewarding employees is one of the most important, and one of the most challenging, activities that managers perform. Successful managers, like Bill Gross in our chapter-opening Manager's Dilemma, understand that what motivates them personally may have little or no effect on others. Just because *you're* motivated by being part of a cohesive work team, don't assume everyone else is. Effective managers who want their employees to make a maximum effort recognize that they need to tailor their motivational practices to satisfy the needs and wants of those employees.

Motivating

Employees

WHAT IS MOTIVATION?

To understand what motivation is, let's begin by pointing out what motivation is not. Why? Because many people incorrectly view motivation as a personal trait—that is, a trait that some have and others don't. In practice, for example, a manager might label a certain employee as unmotivated. Our knowledge of motivation, though, tells us that we can't label people that way. What we know is that motivation is the result of the interaction between the individual and the situation. Certainly, individuals differ in motivational drive, but overall motivation varies from situation to situation. As we analyze the concept of motivation, keep in mind that level of motivation varies both between individuals and within individuals at different times.

As you will recall, we defined **motivation** in chapter 2 as the willingness to exert high levels of effort to reach organizational goals, conditioned by the effort's ability to satisfy some individual need. Although, in general, motivation refers to effort toward any goal, here it will refer to organizational goals because our focus is on work-related behavior. The three key elements in our definition are effort, organizational goals, and needs.

The *effort* element is a measure of intensity or drive. A motivated person tries hard. But high levels of effort are unlikely to lead to favorable job performance outcomes unless the effort is channeled in a direction that benefits the organization.[2] Therefore, we must consider the quality of the effort as well as its intensity. Effort that is directed toward, and consistent with, the organization's goals is the kind of effort that we should be seeking. Finally, we will treat motivation as a need-satisfying process, as depicted in Figure 15-1.

A **need**, in our terminology, means some internal state that makes certain outcomes appear attractive. An unsatisfied need creates tension that stimulates drives within an individual. These drives generate a search behavior to find particular goals that, if attained, will satisfy the need and reduce the tension.

We can say that motivated employees are in a state of tension. To relieve this tension, they exert effort. The greater the tension, the higher the effort level. If this effort leads to the satisfaction of the need, it reduces tension. Because we are interested in work behavior, this tension-reduction effort must also be directed toward organizational goals. Therefore, inherent in our definition of motivation is the requirement that the individual's needs be compatible and consistent with the organization's goals. When the two do not coincide, individuals may exert high levels of effort that run counter to the interests of the organization. Incidentally, that isn't so unusual. Some employees regularly spend a lot of time talking with friends at work in order to satisfy their social needs. There's a high level of effort, but it's unproductively directed.

Motivating high levels of employee performance is such an important organizational consideration that both academic researchers and practicing managers have been trying to understand and explain employee motivation for years. The earliest attempts at explaining motivation (remember our discussion of these theories in chapter 2, including Maslow's hierarchy of needs, McGregor's Theories X and Y, and Herzberg's two-factor theory) focused on pinpointing what motivated individuals. However, these theories were not able to effectively explain why employees' motivation levels differed; that is, there was no recognition that what motivated individuals was different for each person. That lack brought

motivation

The willingness to exert high levels of effort to reach organizational goals, conditioned by the effort's ability to satisfy some individual need.

need

An internal state that makes certain outcomes appear attractive.

FIGURE 15-1   The Motivation Process

Unsatisfied Need → Tension → Drives → Search Behavior → Satisfied Need → Reduction of Tension

about efforts to understand motivation from the perspective of how it happens. How *does* employee motivation take place? Perhaps if we can understand the process of motivation—that is, how it occurs—we can design effective employee motivation and reward systems that will bring about high employee work performance levels.

CONCEPTUAL FRAMEWORKS FOR UNDERSTANDING MOTIVATION

The theories and approaches we're going to look at represent the current state-of-the-art explanations of employee motivation. Although they may not be as well known as Maslow's needs hierarchy or McGregor's Theory X and Theory Y, they do have a reasonable degree of valid supporting documentation. What are these contemporary motivation approaches? We're going to look at six: three-needs theory, goal-setting theory, reinforcement theory, designing motivating jobs, equity theory, and expectancy theory.

Three-Needs Theory

David McClelland and others have proposed the **three-needs theory**—that there are three major motives or needs in work situations:

1. **Need for achievement (nAch):** the drive to excel, to achieve in relation to a set of standards, to strive to succeed

2. **Need for power (nPow):** the need to make others behave in a way that they would not have behaved otherwise

3. **Need for affiliation (nAff):** the desire for friendly and close interpersonal relationships.[3]

Some people have a compelling drive to succeed, but they're striving for personal achievement rather than for the trappings and rewards of success. They have a desire to do something better or more efficiently than it has been done before. This drive is the need for achievement. From research concerning the achievement need, McClelland found that high achievers differentiate themselves from others by their desire to do things better.[4] They seek situations in which they can take personal responsibility for finding solutions to problems, in which they can receive rapid and unambiguous feedback on their performance in order to tell whether they're improving, and in which they can set moderately challenging goals (Figure 15-2). High achievers aren't gamblers; they dislike succeeding by chance. They prefer the challenge of working at a problem and accepting the personal responsibility for success or failure rather than leaving the outcome to chance or the actions of others. An important point is that they avoid what they perceive to be very easy or very difficult tasks.

High achievers perform best when they perceive their probability of success as 50-50. They dislike gambling when the odds are high because they get no achievement satisfaction from accidental success. Similarly, they dislike low odds (high probability of success)

three-needs theory

The needs for achievement, power, and affiliation are major motives in work.

need for achievement

The drive to excel, to achieve in relation to a set of standards, to strive to succeed.

need for power

The need to make others behave in a way that they would not have behaved otherwise.

need for affiliation

The desire for friendly and close interpersonal relationships.

FIGURE 15-2   Matching Achievers and Jobs

Achievers prefer jobs that offer:
- Personal Responsibility
- Feedback
- Moderate Risk

because then there's no challenge to their skills. They like to set goals that require stretching themselves a bit. When there's an approximately equal chance of success or failure, then there's the optimal opportunity to experience feelings of successful accomplishment and satisfaction from their efforts.

The need for power is the desire to have impact and to be influential. Individuals high in nPow enjoy being in charge, strive for influence over others, and prefer to be in competitive and status-oriented situations.

The third need isolated by McClelland is affiliation, which is the desire to be liked and accepted by others. This need has received the least attention from researchers. Individuals with high nAff strive for friendships, prefer cooperative situations rather than competitive ones, and desire relationships involving a high degree of mutual understanding.

How do you find out your levels of each of these three needs? All three motives typically are measured by a projective test in which respondents react to a set of pictures. Each picture is briefly shown to a subject, who then writes a story based on the picture. (See Figure 15-3 for some examples of these pictures.) Trained interpreters then determine an individual's levels of nAch, nPow, and nAff from the stories written.

On the basis of extensive research, we can make some reasonably well-supported predictions about the relationship between the achievement need and job performance. Though less research has been done on power and affiliation needs, there are consistent findings in those areas too. First, individuals with a high need to achieve prefer and are strongly motivated in job situations with personal responsibility, feedback, and an intermediate degree of risk. The evidence consistently demonstrates, for instance, that high achievers are successful in entrepreneurial activities such as running their own business, managing a self-contained division or unit within a large organization, and many sales positions.[5] Second, a high need to achieve does not necessarily lead to being a good manager, especially in large organizations. A high nAch salesperson at Pfizer does not necessarily make a good sales manager, and good managers in large organizations such as Exxon, AT&T, or Sears do not necessarily have a high need to achieve.[6] Third, the needs for affiliation and power are closely related to managerial success.[7] The best managers are high in the need for power and low in the need for affiliation. Last, employees can be trained to stimulate their achievement need.[8] If a job calls for a high achiever, management can select a person with a high nAch or develop its own candidate through achievement training.

Telephone sales reps at SeaBear Specialty Seafoods were able to fulfill their needs for achievement, power, and affiliation when new CEO Mike Mondello gave them a free hand to redesign their crowded, noisy work area. Although they had no budget, the group used their own labor and donated or bartered materials and services to create a new and larger space during their weekend hours.

Source: D.C. McClelland and R.S. Steele, *Motivation Workshops* (New York: General Learning Press, 1972), pp. 3, 11, 15, and 19.

Goal-Setting Theory

Before a big assignment or a major class project presentation, has a teacher ever said to you "Just do your best"? What does that vague statement, "do your best" mean? Would your performance on a class project have been higher if that teacher had said to you that you needed to score a 93 percent to keep your A in the class? Might you have done better in high school English if your parents had said, "You should strive for 85 percent or higher on all your work in English class" rather than telling you to do your best? The research on goal-setting theory addresses these issues, and the findings, as you will see, are impressive in terms of the effect that goal specificity, challenge, and feedback have on performance.

In chapter 7, in our discussion of management by objectives (MBO), we stated that there was substantial support for the proposition that specific goals increase performance and that difficult goals, when accepted, result in higher performance than do easy goals. This proposition has been labeled **goal-setting theory**. It's not necessary to review the evidence again, but the results are important, so let's summarize what we know about goals as motivators.

Intention to work toward a goal is a major source of job motivation. Studies on goal setting have demonstrated the superiority of specific and challenging goals as motivating forces.[9] Specific hard goals produce a higher level of output than does the generalized goal of "do your best." The specificity of the goal itself acts as an internal stimulus. For instance, when a truck driver commits to making 12 round-trip hauls between Toronto and Buffalo, New York, each week, this intention gives him a specific objective to try to attain. We can say that, all things being equal, the trucker with a specific goal will outperform his or her counterpart operating with no goals or the generalized goal of "do your best."

You may have noticed what appears to be a contradiction between the research findings on achievement motivation and goal setting. Is it a contradiction that achievement motivation is stimulated by moderately challenging goals, whereas goal-setting theory says that motivation is maximized by difficult goals? No, and our explanation is twofold.[10] First, goal-setting theory deals with people in general. The conclusions on achievement motivation are based only on people who have a high nAch. Given the probability that no more than 10 to 20 percent of North Americans are naturally high achievers and that proportion is undoubtedly far lower in underdeveloped countries, difficult goals are still recommended for the majority of employees. Second, the conclusions of goal-setting theory apply to those who accept and are committed to the goals. Difficult goals will lead to higher performance only if they are accepted.

What about participation in the setting of goals? Will employees try harder if they have the opportunity to participate? Although we cannot say that having employees participate in the goal-setting process is *always* desirable, participation is probably preferable to assigning goals when you expect resistance to accepting difficult challenges.[11] In some cases, participatively set goals elicited superior performance; in other cases, individuals performed best when their boss assigned goals. But a major advantage may be in increasing acceptance of the goal itself as a desirable one to work toward.

Finally, people will do better when they get feedback on how well they're progressing toward their goals because feedback helps to identify discrepancies between what they have done and what they want to do; that is, feedback acts to guide behavior. But all feedback is not equally effective. Self-generated feedback—where the employee is able to monitor his or her own progress—has been shown to be a more powerful motivator than externally generated feedback.[12]

Are there any contingencies in goal-setting theory, or can we take it as a universal truth that difficult and specific goals will always lead to higher performance? In addition to feedback, three other factors have been found to influence the goals-performance relationship. These are goal commitment, adequate self-efficacy, and national culture. Goal-setting theory presupposes that an individual is committed to the goal: that is, is determined not to lower or abandon the goal. Commitment is most likely to occur when goals are made public, when the individual has an internal locus of control, and when the goals are self-set rather than assigned.[13] **Self-efficacy** refers to an individual's belief that he or she is capable of per-

goal-setting theory

The proposition that specific goals increase performance and that difficult goals, when accepted, result in higher performance than easy goals.

self-efficacy

An individual's belief that he or she is capable of performing a task.

Greg Matusky (center), CEO of Gregory Communications, a public relations firm in Pennsylvania, has found that participatory goal setting works best for his tiny company. When he needs to set goals with his seven employees, he finds that "they'll give their all if you make them part of the mission."

forming a task.[14] The higher your self-efficacy, the more confidence you have in your ability to succeed in a task. So, in difficult situations, we find that people with low self-efficacy are likely to lessen their effort or give up altogether, whereas those with high self-efficacy will try harder to master the challenge.[15] In addition, individuals high in self-efficacy seem to respond to negative feedback with increased effort and motivation, whereas those low in self-efficacy are likely to lessen their effort when given negative feedback.[16] Finally, goal-setting theory is culture bound. It is well adapted to countries like the United States and Canada because its key components align reasonably well with North American cultures. It assumes that subordinates will be reasonably independent (not too high a score on power distance), that managers and subordinates will seek challenging goals (low in uncertainty avoidance), and that performance is considered important by both managers and subordinates (high in quantity of life). So don't expect goal setting to necessarily lead to higher employee performance in countries such as Portugal or Chile, where the opposite conditions exist.

Our overall conclusion from goal-setting theory is that intentions—as articulated in terms of hard and specific goals—are a powerful motivating force. Under the proper conditions, they can lead to higher performance. However, there is no evidence that such goals are associated with increased job satisfaction.[17]

Reinforcement Theory

A counterpoint to goal-setting theory is **reinforcement theory**. Goal-setting theory proposes that an individual's purpose directs his or her actions. Reinforcement theory argues that behavior is externally caused. What controls behavior are **reinforcers**, consequences that, when immediately following a response, increase the probability that the behavior will be repeated. Hence, reinforcement theorists argue that behavior is a function of its consequences.

The key to reinforcement theory is that it ignores factors such as goals, expectations, and needs. Instead, it focuses solely on what happens to a person when he or she takes some action. This idea helps explain why publishers such as Simon & Schuster provide incentive clauses in their authors' contracts. If every time an author submits a completed

reinforcement theory

Behavior is a function of its consequences.

reinforcer

Any consequence immediately following a response that increases the probability that the behavior will be repeated.

chapter, the company sends an advance check against future royalties, the person is motivated to keep working and submitting chapters.

In chapter 13 we showed how reinforcers shape behavior and help people to learn. But the concept of reinforcement is also widely believed to explain motivation. According to B. F. Skinner, reinforcement theory can be explained as follows: People will most likely engage in desired behavior if they are rewarded for doing so; these rewards are most effective if they immediately follow a desired response, and behavior that isn't rewarded, or is punished, is less likely to be repeated.[18]

Following reinforcement theory, managers can influence employees' behavior by reinforcing acts they deem favorable. However, because the emphasis is on positive reinforcement, not punishment, managers should ignore, not punish, unfavorable behavior. Even though punishment eliminates undesired behavior faster than nonreinforcement does, its effect is often only temporary and may later have unpleasant side effects including dysfunctional behavior such as workplace conflicts, absenteeism, and turnover.

The evidence indicates that reinforcement is undoubtedly an important influence on work behavior. But reinforcement isn't the only explanation for differences in employee motivation.[19] Goals also affect motivation, as do levels of achievement needs, job design, inequities in rewards, and expectations.

**TESTING...
TESTING...**

1 Briefly describe the concept of motivation and the motivation process.

2 What are the three needs McClelland proposed that are in work situations?

3 Describe how goal-setting theory and reinforcement theory explain employee motivation.

Designing Motivating Jobs

Because managers are primarily interested in how to motivate individuals on the job, we need to look at ways to design motivating jobs. If you look closely at what an organization is and how it works, you'll find that it's composed of thousands, maybe even millions, of tasks. These tasks, in turn, are aggregated into jobs.[20] We use the term **job design** to refer to the way tasks are combined to form complete jobs. The jobs that people perform in organizations should not evolve by chance. Managers should design jobs deliberately and thoughtfully to reflect the demands of the changing environment as well as the organization's technology, skills, and abilities and the preferences of its employees.[21] When jobs are designed with those things in mind, employees are motivated to reach their full productive capabilities. Let's take a closer look at how managers can design motivating jobs.

Job Enlargement. As we saw earlier in chapters 2 and 10, job design historically has concentrated on making jobs smaller and more specialized. Yet, when jobs are narrow in focus and highly specialized, motivating employees is a real challenge. Thus, many organizations have looked at other job design options. One of the earliest efforts at overcoming the drawbacks of specialization involved the horizontal expansion of a job through increasing **job scope**—the number of different tasks required in a job and the frequency with which these tasks are repeated. For instance, a mail sorter's job could be enlarged to include physically delivering the mail to the various departments or running outgoing letters through the postage meter as well as sorting the mail. This type of job design option is called **job enlargement**.

Efforts at job enlargement that focused solely on task enlargement have had less-than-exciting results. As one employee who experienced such a redesign said, "Before I had one lousy job. Now, thanks to job enlargement, I have three lousy jobs!" However, one study that

job design

The way tasks are combined to form complete jobs.

job scope

The number of different tasks required in a job and the frequency with which those tasks are repeated.

job enlargement

The horizontal expansion of a job; an increase in job scope.

job enrichment

Vertical expansion of a job by adding planning and evaluating responsibilities.

looked at how knowledge enlargement activities (expanding the scope of knowledge used in a job) affected workers found benefits such as more satisfaction, enhanced customer service, and fewer errors.[22] Even so, most job enlargement efforts provided few challenges and little meaning to a worker's activities, although they addressed the lack of diversity in over-specialized jobs.

Job Enrichment.   Another approach to designing motivating jobs is through the vertical expansion of a job by adding planning and evaluating responsibilities—**job enrichment**. Job enrichment increases **job depth**, which is the degree of control employees have over their work. In other words, employees are empowered to assume some of the tasks typically done by their supervisors. Thus, the tasks in an enriched job should allow workers to do a complete activity with increased freedom, independence, and responsibility. These tasks should also provide feedback so that individuals can assess and correct their own performance. Although job enrichment can improve the quality of work output, employee motivation, and satisfaction, the research evidence on the use of job enrichment programs has been inconclusive.[23]

Job Characteristics Model.   Even though many organizations have implemented job enlargement and job enrichment programs and experienced mixed results, neither of these job design approaches provided a conceptual framework for analyzing jobs or for guiding managers in designing motivating jobs. The **job characteristics model (JCM)** does offer such a framework.[24] It identifies five primary job characteristics, their interrelationships, and their impact on employee productivity, motivation, and satisfaction.

According to the JCM, any job can be described in terms of five core dimensions, defined as follows:

- **Skill variety**, the degree to which a job requires a variety of activities so that an employee can use a number of different skills and talents

- **Task identity**, the degree to which a job requires completion of a whole and identifiable piece of work

- **Task significance**, the degree to which a job has a substantial impact on the lives or work of other people

- **Autonomy**, the degree to which a job provides substantial freedom, independence, and discretion to the individual in scheduling the work and determining the procedures to be used in carrying it out

- **Feedback**, the degree to which carrying out the work activities required by a job results in the individual's obtaining direct and clear information about the effectiveness of his or her performance

Figure 15-4 presents the model. Notice how the first three dimensions—skill variety, task identity, and task significance—combine to create meaningful work. What we mean is that if these three characteristics exist in a job, we can predict that the person will view his or her job as being important, valuable, and worthwhile. Notice, too, that jobs that possess autonomy give the job incumbent a feeling of personal responsibility for the results and that, if a job provides feedback, the employee will know how effectively he or she is performing.

From a motivational standpoint, the JCM suggests that intrinsic (internal) rewards are obtained when an employee *learns* (knowledge of results through feedback) that he or she *personally* (experienced responsibility through autonomy of work) has performed well on a task that he or she *cares about* (experienced meaningfulness through skill variety, task identity, and/or task significance).[25] The more these three conditions characterize a job, the

job depth

The degree of control employees have over their work.

job characteristics model (JCM)

A framework for analyzing and designing jobs; identifies five primary job characteristics, their interrelationships, and their impact on outcome variables.

skill variety

The degree to which a job requires a variety of activities so that an employee can use a number of different skills and talents.

task identity

The degree to which a job requires completion of a whole and identifiable piece of work.

task significance

The degree to which a job has a substantial impact on the lives or work of other people.

autonomy

The degree to which a job provides substantial freedom, independence, and discretion to an individual in scheduling and carrying out his or her work.

feedback

The degree to which carrying out the work activities required by a job results in an individual's obtaining direct and clear information about the effectiveness of his or her performance.

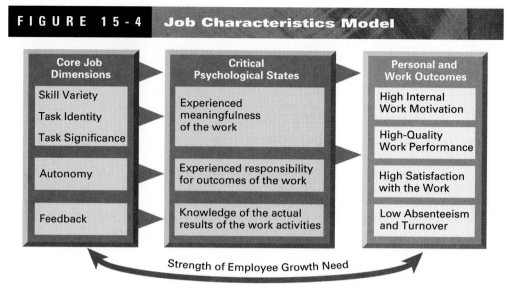

Source: J.R. Hackman and J.L. Suttle (eds.), *Improving Life at Work* (Glenview, IL: Scott, Foresman, 1977). With permission of the authors.

greater the employee's motivation, performance, and satisfaction and the lower his or her absenteeism and likelihood of resigning. As the model shows, the links between the job dimensions and the outcomes are moderated by the strength of the individual's growth need (the person's desire for self-esteem and self-actualization). This means that individuals with a high growth need are more likely to experience the psychological states and respond positively when their jobs include the core dimensions than are low-growth need individuals.

The core dimensions can be combined into a single index as shown in Figure 15-5. To score high on motivating potential, jobs must be high on at least one of the three factors that lead to experiencing meaningfulness; they must also be high on both autonomy and feedback. If jobs score high on motivating potential, the model predicts that motivation, performance, and satisfaction will be positively affected and the likelihood of absence and turnover will be diminished.[26]

The JCM provides specific guidance to managers for job design (Figure 15-6). The following suggestions, which are based on the JCM, specify the types of changes in jobs that are most likely to lead to improvement in each of the five core job dimensions. You'll notice that two of these suggestions from the JCM incorporate the earlier job design concepts we

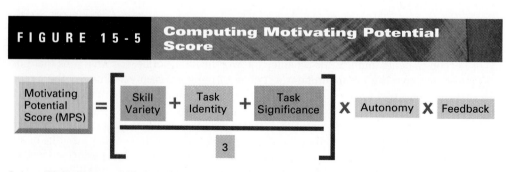

Source: J.R. Hackman and J.L. Suttle (eds.), *Improving Life at Work* (Glenview, IL: Scott, Foresman, 1977). With permission of the authors.

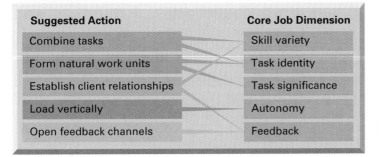

FIGURE 15-6   **Guidelines for Job Redesign**

Suggested Action	Core Job Dimension
Combine tasks	Skill variety
Form natural work units	Task identity
Establish client relationships	Task significance
Load vertically	Autonomy
Open feedback channels	Feedback

Source: J.R. Hackman and J.L. Suttle (eds.), *Improving Life at Work* (Glenview, IL: Scott, Foresman, 1977). With permission of the authors.

discussed (job enlargement and job enrichment), although the other suggestions also involve more than vertically and horizontally expanding jobs.

1. *Combine tasks.* Managers should put existing fragmented tasks back together to form a new, larger module of work (job enlargement) to increase skill variety and task identity.

2. *Create natural work units.* Managers should design tasks that form an identifiable and meaningful whole to increase employee "ownership" of the work and encourage employees to view their work as meaningful and important rather than as irrelevant and boring.

3. *Establish client relationships.* The client is the user of the product or service that the employee works on, and the client could be an internal organizational unit or person as well as an external customer. Whenever possible, managers should establish direct relationships between workers and their clients to increase skill variety, auton-

When jobs demand innovation and creativity *and* pay well, they are clearly motivating. These young motion picture animators derive great personal satisfaction from their work as well as financial reward.

omy, and feedback for the employee. For instance, at San Francisco's Park Lane Hotels International, guests nominate their favorite staffers for awards, which include Sony televisions and free nights at the hotel.[27]

4. *Expand jobs vertically.* Vertical expansion (job enrichment) gives employees responsibilities and controls that were formerly reserved for management. It partially closes the gap between the "doing" and the "controlling" aspects of the job and increases employee autonomy.

5. *Open feedback channels.* Feedback lets employees know not only how well they are performing their jobs but also whether their performances are improving, deteriorating, or remaining at a constant level. Ideally, employees should receive performance feedback directly as they do their jobs rather than from management on an occasional basis. For example, frequent fliers at Continental Airlines bestow Pride in Performance certificates to employees who have been helpful. Employees can then redeem the coupons for valuable merchandise.[28]

Equity Theory

Are you ever curious about what kind of grade the person sitting next to you in class makes on a test or on a major class project? Most of us are! Being human, we tend to compare ourselves with others. If someone offered you $50,000 a year on your first job after graduating from college, you'd probably jump at the offer and report to work enthusiastic, ready to tackle whatever needed to be done, and certainly satisfied with your pay. How would you react, though, if you found out a month or so into the job that a co-worker—another recent graduate, your age, with comparable grades from a comparable school, and with comparable work experience—was getting $55,000 a year? You'd probably be upset! Even though, in absolute terms, $50,000 is a lot of money for a new graduate to make (and you know it!), that suddenly isn't the issue. You see the issue now as relative rewards and what you believe is fair—what is equitable. The term *equity* is related to the concept of fairness and equal treatment compared with others who behave in similar ways. There's considerable evidence that employees compare their job inputs and outcomes relative to others' and that inequities influence the degree of effort that employees exert.[29]

equity theory

The theory that an employee compares his job's inputs-outcomes ratio with that of relevant others and then corrects any inequity.

Equity theory, developed by J. Stacey Adams, proposes that employees perceive what they get from a job situation (outcomes) in relation to what they put into it (inputs) and then compare their inputs-outcomes ratio with the inputs-outcomes ratios of relevant others (Table 15-1). If an employee perceives her ratio to be equal to those of relevant oth-

TABLE 15-1	**Equity Theory**
Perceived Ratio Comparison[a]	**Employee's Assessment**
$\dfrac{\text{Outcomes A}}{\text{Inputs A}} < \dfrac{\text{Outcomes B}}{\text{Inputs B}}$	Inequity (underrewarded)
$\dfrac{\text{Outcomes A}}{\text{Inputs A}} = \dfrac{\text{Outcomes B}}{\text{Inputs B}}$	Equity
$\dfrac{\text{Outcomes A}}{\text{Inputs A}} > \dfrac{\text{Outcomes B}}{\text{Inputs B}}$	Inequity (overrewarded)

[a]Person A is the employee, and person B is a relevant other or referent.

ers, a state of equity exists. In other words, she perceives that her situation is fair—that justice prevails. However, if the ratio is unequal, inequity exists and she views herself as underrewarded or overrewarded. When inequities occur, employees attempt to do something about it. What will employees do when they perceive an inequity? Let's look more closely at their probable behavioral responses.

Equity theory proposes that employees might (1) distort either their own or others' inputs or outcomes, (2) behave in some way to induce others to change their inputs or outcomes, (3) behave in some way to change their own inputs or outcomes, (4) choose a different comparison person, or (5) quit their job. When it's specifically pay that's perceived to be inequitable, the theory suggests that employees who are either underrewarded or overrewarded will react in certain ways depending on whether their wages are based on time factors or quantity of output (Figure 15-7). These types of employee reactions have generally proved to be correct,[30] and a review of the research consistently confirms the equity thesis: Employee motivation is influenced significantly by relative rewards as well as by absolute rewards. Whenever employees perceive inequity, they'll act to correct the situation.[31] The result might be lower or higher productivity, improved or reduced quality of output, increased absenteeism, or voluntary resignation.

The other aspect we need to examine in equity theory is who are these "others" against whom people compare themselves? The **referent** is an important variable in equity theory.[32] Three referent categories have been defined: other, system, and self. The "other" category includes other individuals with similar jobs in the same organization and also includes friends, neighbors, or professional associates. On the basis of what they hear at work or read about in newspapers or trade journals, employees compare their pay with that of others. The "system" category includes organizational pay policies and procedures and the administration of the system. Whatever precedents have been established by the organization regarding pay allocation are major elements of this category. The "self" category refers to inputs-outcomes ratios that are unique to the individual. It reflects past personal experiences and contacts and is influenced by criteria such as past jobs or family commitments. The choice of a particular set of referents is related to the information available about the referents as well as to their perceived relevance.

referents

The persons, systems, or selves against which individuals compare themselves to assess equity.

FIGURE 15-7	**Reactions to Perceptions of Inequitable Pay**

1 **Given payment by time, overrewarded employees will produce more than equitably paid employees.** Hourly and salaried employees will generate a high quantity or quality of production in order to increase the input side of the ratio and bring it above equity.

2 **Given payment by quantity of production, overrewarded employees will produce fewer but higher-quality units than equitably paid employees.** Individuals paid on a piece-rate basis will increase their effort to achieve equity, which can result in greater quality or quantity. However, increases in quantity will only increase inequity, because every unit produced results in further overpayment. Therefore, effort is directed toward increasing quality rather than quantity.

3 **Given payment by time, underrewarded employees will produce less or poorer-quality output.** Effort will be decreased, which will bring about lower productivity or poorer-quality output than is produced by equitably paid employees.

4 **Given payment by quantity of production, underrewarded employees will produce a large number of low-quality units in comparison with equitably paid employees.** Employees on piece-rate pay plans can bring about equity because trading off quality of output for quantity will result in an increase in rewards with little or no increase in contributions.

However applicable it might be to understanding employee motivation, we should not conclude that equity theory is flawless. The theory leaves some key issues still unclear.[33] For instance, how do employees define inputs and outcomes? How do they combine and weigh their inputs and outcomes to arrive at totals? When and how do the factors change over time? Despite these problems, equity theory does have an impressive amount of research support and offers us some important insights into employee motivation.

TESTING...
TESTING...

4 Define job enlargement and job enrichment.

5 Describe the job characteristics model as a way to design motivating jobs.

6 What are the motivation implications of equity theory?

Expectancy Theory

expectancy theory

The theory that an individual tends to act in a certain way based on the expectation that the act will be followed by a given outcome and on the attractiveness of that outcome to the individual.

The most comprehensive explanation of motivation to date is Victor Vroom's **expectancy theory**.[34] Although the theory has its critics,[35] most research evidence supports it.[36]

Expectancy theory states that an individual tends to act in a certain way based on the expectation that the act will be followed by a given outcome and on the attractiveness of that outcome to the individual. It includes three variables or relationships (see Figure 15-8):

1. *Expectancy* or *effort-performance linkage* is the probability perceived by the individual that exerting a given amount of effort will lead to a certain level of performance.

2. *Instrumentality* or *performance-reward linkage* is the degree to which the individual believes that performing at a particular level is instrumental in leading to the attainment of a desired outcome.

3. *Valence* or *attractiveness of reward* is the importance that the individual places on the potential outcome or reward that can be achieved on the job. Valence considers both the goals and needs of the individual.

This explanation of motivation might sound complex, but it really isn't that difficult to visualize. It can be summed up in the questions: How hard do I have to work to achieve a certain level of performance, and can I actually achieve that level? What reward will performing at that level of performance get me? How attractive is the reward to me, and does it help me achieve my goals? Whether you are motivated to put forth effort (i.e., to produce) at any given time depends on your particular goals and your perception of whether

FIGURE 15-8   Simplified Expectancy Model

Individual Effort → **A** → Individual Performance → **B** → Organizational Rewards → **C** → Individual Goals

A = Effort–performance linkage
B = Performance–reward linkage
C = Attractiveness

a certain level of performance is necessary to attain those goals. Let's look at the features inherent in the theory and attempt to apply it.

First, what perceived outcomes does the job offer the employee? Outcomes (rewards) may be positive—things such as pay, security, companionship, trust, fringe benefits, a chance to use talents or skills, or congenial relationships. Or the employee may view the outcomes as negative—fatigue, boredom, frustration, anxiety, harsh supervision, or threat of dismissal. Keep in mind that reality isn't relevant here. The critical issue is what the individual *perceives* the outcome to be, regardless of whether the perceptions are accurate.

Second, how attractive are the outcomes or rewards to employees? Are they valued positively, negatively, or neutrally? This obviously is a personal and internal issue that depends on the individual's attitudes, personality, and needs. A person who finds a particular reward attractive—that is, values it positively—would rather attain it than not attain it. Others may find it negative and therefore prefer not getting it. And others may be neutral about the outcome.

Third, what kind of behavior must the employee exhibit in order to achieve these rewards? The rewards aren't likely to have any effect on any individual employee's performance unless he or she knows, clearly and unambiguously, what must be done to achieve them. For example, what is "doing well" in terms of performance appraisal? What criteria will be used to judge the employee's performance?

Finally, how does the employee view his or her chances of doing what is asked? After an employee has considered his or her own skills and ability to control those variables that lead to success, what's the likelihood that he or she can successfully perform at the necessary level?[37]

Let's look at the classroom organization for an example of how you can use the expectancy theory of motivation. Most students prefer that their instructor tell them what the course expectations are. They want to know what the assignments and exams will be like, when they're going to be due or given, and how much weight each carries in the final determination of the grade. They also like to think that the amount of effort exerted in attending classes, taking notes, and studying outside class will be reasonably related to the grade they'll make in the course. Let's assume that you feel this way. Consider that five weeks into a class you're really enjoying (we'll call it MGT 301), a test is returned to you. You studied hard for this examination and put in several hours of reading the chapters and going over your notes. In the past, you've consistently made As and Bs on tests in other courses in which you expended this kind of effort. The reason you work so hard is to make top grades, which you believe are important for getting a good job after graduation. Also, you're not sure, but you might want to go on to graduate school, and you think good grades are important for getting into a good graduate program.

Well, the results of that five-week test are in. The class median was 72. Ten percent of the class scored an 85 or higher and got an A. Your grade was 46; the minimum passing mark was 50. You're angry. You're frustrated. Even more, you can't understand it. How could you possibly have done so poorly on the test when you usually score in the top range in other classes by preparing as you did for this one?

Several interesting things might happen to your behavior now. Suddenly, you will no longer be interested in attending MGT 301 regularly. You will not study for the course either. When you do attend class, you will daydream a lot—and will have an empty notebook instead of several pages of notes. "Lacking in motivation" would probably be an apt description at this point. Why did your motivation level change? You know and we know. But let's explain it by using expectancy theory.

If we use Figure 15-8 to understand this situation, we might say the following: You study and prepare for MGT 301 (put forth effort) in order to correctly answer the questions on the test (performance). Your correct answers will produce a high grade (reward), which will lead, in turn, to the security, prestige, and other benefits that come from obtaining a good job (individual goal).

The attractiveness of the outcome, which in this case is a good grade, is high. But what about the performance-reward linkage? Do you feel that the grade you received truly reflects your knowledge of the material? In other words, did the test fairly measure what you knew? If the answer is yes, then this linkage is strong. If the answer is no, then at least part of the reason for your reduced motivational level is your belief that the test wasn't a fair measure of your performance.

Another possible demotivating force may be the effort-performance relationship. If, after you took the test, you believed that you couldn't have passed it even with the amount of preparation you had done, then your motivation to study would drop. Because a low value had been placed on all the hard work and study efforts that you thought would lead you to answer the test questions correctly, your motivational level and level of effort would decrease.

The key to expectancy theory is understanding an individual's goal—and the linkage between effort and performance, between performance and rewards, and, finally, between rewards and individual goal satisfaction. As a contingency model, expectancy theory recognizes that there is no universal principle for explaining each person's motivation. In addition, knowing what needs a person seeks to satisfy does not ensure that the individual will perceive that high performance will necessarily lead to satisfying those needs.

Let's summarize some of the issues surrounding expectancy theory. First, it emphasizes payoffs, or rewards. As a result, we have to believe that the rewards an organization is offering align with what the individual wants. It's a theory based on self-interest, because each individual seeks to maximize his or her expected satisfaction of needs. Second, expectancy theory stresses that managers understand why employees view certain outcomes as attractive or unattractive. We want to reward individuals with those things they value positively. Third, expectancy theory emphasizes expected behaviors. Do employees know what's expected of them and how they'll be evaluated? Finally, the theory is concerned with perceptions. Reality is irrelevant. An individual's own perceptions of performance, reward, and goal satisfaction outcomes, not the outcomes themselves, will determine his or her level of effort.

Integrating Contemporary Theories of Motivation

We have presented six motivation theories in this chapter. You might be tempted to view them independently, but doing so would be a mistake. Many of the ideas underlying the theories are complementary, and you will better understand how to motivate people when you see how the theories fit together.[38] Figure 15-9 presents a model that integrates much of what we know about motivation. Its basic foundation is the simplified expectancy model shown in Figure 15-8. Let's work through this model, beginning at the left.

The individual effort box has an arrow leading into it. This arrow flows from the individual's goals. Consistent with goal-setting theory, this goals-effort link is meant to illustrate that goals direct behavior. Expectancy theory predicts that an employee will exert a high level of effort if he or she perceives that there is a strong relationship between effort and performance, performance and rewards, and rewards and satisfaction of personal goals. Each of these relationships, in turn, is influenced by certain factors. You can see from the model that the level of individual performance is determined not only by the level of individual effort but also by the individual's ability to perform and by whether the organization has a fair and objective performance evaluation system. The performance-reward relationship will be strong if the individual perceives that it is performance (rather than seniority, personal favorites, or some other criterion) that is rewarded. The final link in expectancy theory is the rewards-goal relationship. Need theories come into play at this point. Motivation would be high to the degree that the rewards an individual achieved for his or her high performance satisfied the dominant needs consistent with his or her individual goals.

Interview with Ted V. Schaefer, Principal, Computer Assurance Services, Coopers & Lybrand L.L.P, Denver, Colorado

Describe your job.

I am a principal with Coopers & Lybrand's Computer Assurance Services (CAS) group. Coopers & Lybrand is a worldwide professional services firm with over 70,000 employees. I am responsible for providing CAS services to clients in the northern Rocky Mountain states.

What types of skills do you think tomorrow's managers will need?

The business world has become complex, ever-changing, competitive, political, ambiguous, and fast moving. To work in this environment, quality managers need competency in a wide range of areas to successfully attract and motivate talented staff, fulfill their service mission, react to the marketplace, and maintain their professional expertise. Managers must manage their career and the environment they work in, have interpersonal skills to relate to others, and have knowledge management skills to deal with information.

To manage their career and the work environment, managers must be able to set and achieve goals and they must be self-motivated, competitive, creative, willing to try many new things, and attuned to the needs of the organization and the external marketplace.

Interpersonal skills are important for attracting and motivating staff and dealing with people in and out of the organization. Managers need to have strong communication skills, to continually mentor and train staff, to build and utilize people networks, and to understand what motivates employees. They also must have integrity, the willingness and ability to adapt to ever-changing events, and a sense of humor and must be loyal and trustworthy.

Finally, managers need to have knowledge-management skills to stay abreast of internal and external trends, maintain personal expertise, be able to sort through information to find patterns, have the ability to quickly understand situations by synthesizing information in a systematic way, and apply their knowledge and experiences to daily decision making.

How hard is it to motivate your employees? What have you found that works best?

Motivating employees can be difficult because everyone has different skills, needs, experiences, and backgrounds. Motivating employees requires custom approaches to meet an employee's individual needs. An effective method to motivate an employee is communicating with the person on a timely and consistent basis and instituting a mentor program. As part of this mentoring program, setting goals is necessary so the employee has specific and measurable goals to achieve. These goals should be directed to the person's professional career development and to the needs of the organization. Motivating factors that I have observed include a professional and ethical environment, ability to stay current in industry or technical trends, client assignments, working in a team environment, training, peer competition, clear career path and advancement, and reasonable control over work-life balance. ■

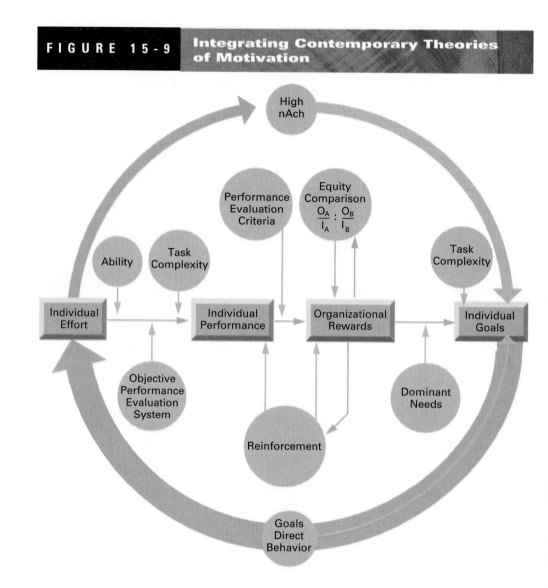

FIGURE 15-9   **Integrating Contemporary Theories of Motivation**

A closer look at the model also shows that it considers the achievement-need, reinforcement, equity, and JCM theories. The high achiever isn't motivated by the organization's assessment of his or her performance or organizational rewards: hence the jump from effort to individual goals for those with a high nAch. Remember that high achievers are internally driven as long as the jobs they're doing provide them with personal responsibility, feedback, and moderate risks. They're not concerned with the effort–performance, performance–rewards, or rewards–goal linkages.

Reinforcement theory is seen in the model by recognizing that the organization's rewards reinforce the individual's performance. If management has designed a reward system that is seen by employees as "paying off" for good performance, the rewards will reinforce and encourage continued good performance. Rewards also play a key part in equity theory. Individuals will compare the rewards (outcomes) they have received from the inputs or efforts they made with the inputs–outcomes ratio of relevant others. If inequities exist, the effort expended may be influenced.

Finally, we can see the JCM in this integrative model. Task characteristics (job design) influence job motivation at two places. First, jobs that score high in motivating potential are likely to lead to higher actual job performance because the individual's motivation will be stimulated by the job itself. So jobs that are high in complexity (motivating potential) increase the linkage between effort and performance. Second, jobs that score high in motivating potential also increase an employee's control over key elements in his or her work. Therefore, jobs that offer autonomy, feedback, and similar complex task characteristics help to satisfy the individual goals of employees who desire greater control over their work.

7 **Describe the three key linkages in expectancy theory.**

8 **What role does perception play in expectancy theory?**

9 **How might the contemporary motivation theories be integrated to explain employee motivation?**

TESTING...
TESTING...
1 2 3

CURRENT ISSUES IN MOTIVATION

So far, we have covered a lot of the theoretical bases of employee motivation. Understanding and predicting employee motivation continues to be one of the most popular areas in management research. However, even current studies of employee motivation are influenced by several significant workplace issues—issues such as motivating a diverse workforce, pay-for-performance programs, open-book management, employee stock ownership plans (ESOPs), and motivating the "new workforce." Let's take a closer look at each of these issues.

Motivating a Diverse Workforce

To maximize motivation among today's diverse workforce, managers need to think in terms of *flexibility.* For instance, studies tell us that men place more importance on having autonomy in their jobs than do women. In contrast, the opportunity to learn, convenient work hours, and good interpersonal relations are more important to women.[39] Managers need to recognize that what motivates a single mother who has two dependent children and is working full time to support her family may be very different from the needs of a young, single part-time employee or an older employee who is working only to supplement his or her retirement income. Employees have different personal needs and goals that they are

Some employees have particular personal needs. People who love to be with their dogs can bring them to work at software developer Autodesk in California. Here they are shown enjoying their lunch break.

hoping to satisfy through their job. Various types of rewards are needed to motivate employees with such diverse needs.

Many of the so-called family-friendly programs (as we discussed in chapter 11) and flexible working schedules that organizations have developed are a response to the varied needs of a diverse workforce. For instance, a job for most people in North America means leaving home and going to a place of work, arriving at 8:00 or 9:00 in the morning, putting in a fixed set of hours, and doing this routine five days a week. Yet, it doesn't have to be that way. Depending on labor market conditions, the type of work that has to be done, and employee preferences, managers might consider implementing a compressed workweek, flexible work hours, job sharing, or telecommuting.

compressed workweek

A workweek consisting of four 10-hour days.

A **compressed workweek** is a workweek consisting of four 10-hour days (a 4-40 program). Proponents claim that 4-40 programs have a favorable effect on employee absenteeism, job satisfaction, and productivity.[40] A new twist to compressed workweeks is a 9-80 schedule, which started as a way to limit pollution from commuters' cars. For example, at Texaco's headquarters in Harrison, New York, employees work nine hours every Monday through Thursday, eight hours on a Friday, and zero hours the next Friday. The flexible schedule provides employees with time off for running errands, pursuing hobbies, or taking care of family problems.[41] Studies of organizations that use compressed workweeks, however, have shown that there are also drawbacks such as a decrease in workers' productivity near the end of the longer workday, a decrease in service to customers or clients, an unwillingness to work longer days if a deadline needs to be met, and underutilization of equipment.[42] Because the compressed workweek does have its problems for employees and managers, many organizations have tried a different approach to giving workers increased freedom—flexible work hours.

flexible work hours (flextime)

A scheduling system in which employees are required to work a certain number of hours a week, but are free, within limits, to vary the hours of work.

Flexible work hours (also popularly known as **flextime**) is a scheduling system in which employees are required to work a specific number of hours a week but are free to vary those hours within certain limits. In a flextime schedule, there are certain common core hours when all employees are required to be on the job, but starting, ending, and lunch-hour times are flexible. How widespread is flextime? In the early 1970s, few companies offered this scheduling option. By the mid-1990s, however, about 85 percent of major companies offered some type of flextime option.[43] How well does flextime work? Most of the evidence shows that it tends to reduce absenteeism, improve morale, and improve worker productivity.[44] Because flextime allows employees to schedule their work hours to better align with personal demands, it can have a motivating effect. However, flextime does have its drawbacks, particularly for managers: It creates difficulties in directing subordinates outside the common core times; it causes confusion in shift work; it increases difficulties when someone with a particular skill or knowledge is not available; and it makes planning and controlling more cumbersome and costly. And flextime is just not feasible for some jobs because of the interdependence of tasks—jobs such as assembly-line operator, salesperson in a department store, and office receptionist, in which the jobholder depends on others inside or outside the organization.

job sharing

The practice of having two or more people split a 40-hour-a-week job.

Another job scheduling option that can be effective in motivating a diverse workforce is job sharing. **Job sharing** is the practice of having two or more people split a 40-hour-a-week job. This type of job schedule might be attractive, for example, to individuals with school-age children or retirees, who want to work but do not want the demands and hassles of a full-time position. The individual benefits by having a job that meets his or her needs, and the organization benefits by having the talents of more than one individual in a given job and acquiring skilled workers who might not want to work at all if they had to work full-time. In addition, job sharing can enhance productivity. Job sharers typically have better attendance records than regular, full-time employees.[45]

telecommuting

The linking by computer and modem of workers at home with co-workers and management at an office.

Computer technology has opened still another alternative for managers in the way they design motivating jobs for a diverse workforce. That alternative is to allow employees to perform their work at home by **telecommuting**.[46] Many white-collar occupations can now be carried out at home—at least technically. Modems and computers allow employees who work at home to be linked electronically to their co-workers and managers at the office.

In the United States, approximately 11 million people now telecommute, doing such things as taking orders over the phone, filling out reports and other forms, and processing or analyzing information.[47] Some of the major companies who now offer telecommuting as a job option include Levi Strauss, Pacific Bell, AT&T, IBM, Johnson & Johnson, American Express, and J.C. Penney.

For employees, the two big advantages of telecommuting are the decrease in the time and stress of commuting in urban areas and the increase in flexibility in coping with family demands. But it may have some potential drawbacks as well. For example, will telecommuters miss the regular social contact that a formal office provides? Will they be less likely to be considered for salary increases and promotions? Is being out of sight equivalent to being out of mind? Will they be able to separate their work and home roles? Answers to questions such as these are central in determining whether telecommuting will continue to expand in the future.

Managing a diverse workforce also means that managers must be flexible by being aware of cultural differences. The theories of motivation that we have been studying were developed largely by U.S. psychologists and were validated with American workers. These theories may need to be modified for different cultures.[48]

For instance, the self-interest concept is consistent with capitalism and the extremely high value placed on individualism in the United States. Because almost all of the motivation theories presented in this chapter are based on the self-interest motive, they should be applicable to organizations in such countries as Great Britain and Australia, where capitalism and individualism are highly valued. However, in more collectivist countries—such as Venezuela, Singapore, Japan, and Mexico—the link to the organization is the individual's loyalty to the organization or society rather than his or her self-interest. Employees in collectivistic cultures should be more receptive to team-based job design, group goals, and group performance evaluations. Reliance on the fear of being fired in such cultures is also likely to be less effective, even if laws allow managers to fire employees, because of the belief that the fired person will be "taken care of" by extended family, friends, or community.

The need achievement concept provides another example of a motivation theory with a U.S. bias. The view that a high need for achievement acts as an internal motivator presupposes the existence of two cultural characteristics: a willingness to accept a moderate degree of risk and a concern with performance. These characteristics would exclude countries with high uncertainty avoidance scores and high quality-of-life ratings. The included countries are almost exclusively Anglo-American countries such as New Zealand, South Africa, Ireland, the United States, and Canada.

Yet, the results of some recent studies of managers in countries other than the United States indicate that some aspects of motivation theory are transferrable.[49] For instance, the various reinforcement techniques were shown to be effective in changing performance-related behaviors of Russian textile mill workers. However, we should not automatically assume that what works with U.S. workers will have the same results with workers from different cultures.

Also, keep in mind that changing motivational techniques to fit a culture works both ways. Motivational techniques that work well in China, for example, may be inappropriate in North America. For example, a large department store in Xian, China, selects its 40 *worst* salesclerks each year.[50] These clerks write self-criticisms and analyze their shortcomings. Managers then hang a plaque over their work stations, complete with picture, proclaiming them as members of the "Forty Worst." This approach was a response to the generally poor service that managers felt the clerks were giving customers and the fact that lifetime employment is guaranteed for Chinese employees. The store's managers have found that those employees selected for the Forty Worst awards are strongly motivated to improve their performances and to get the plaques removed from their work areas. Motivation through humiliation might be acceptable and effective in China, but it isn't likely to work in North America.

Pay for Performance

Why do most people work? Although there may be many reasons why people work, most of us work because it pays us an amount of money that allows us to satisfy our needs and wants. Because pay is an important variable in motivation as one type of reward, we need to look at how we can use pay to motivate high levels of employee performance. The relation between pay and motivation explains the intent and logic behind pay-for-performance programs.

pay-for-performance programs

Compensation plans that pay employees on the basis of some performance measure.

Pay-for-performance programs are compensation plans that pay employees on the basis of some performance measure.[51] Piece-rate pay plans, wage incentive plans, profit-sharing, and lump-sum bonuses are examples. What differentiates these forms of pay from more traditional compensation plans is that instead of paying a person for time on the job, pay is adjusted to reflect some performance measure. These performance measures might include such things as individual productivity, team or work group productivity, departmental productivity, or the overall organization's profit performance. For instance, employee teams at Mobil Corporation are eligible for team-performance–based incentives of as much as 30 percent of base pay. And the six employees at Comfort Shoe Specialists, a retail store located in a shopping center outside St. Louis, each get a weekly $50 bonus if sales for the week exceed those of the previous week.[52]

Performance-based compensation is probably most compatible with expectancy theory. Specifically, individuals should perceive a strong relationship between their performance and the rewards they receive if motivation is to be maximized. If rewards are allocated only on nonperformance factors—such as seniority, job title, or across-the-board pay raises—then employees are likely to reduce their efforts.

Pay-for-performance programs are gaining in popularity. One survey of businesses found that 61 percent of the respondents were practicing some form of pay for performance for employees.[53] The popularity can be explained in terms of both motivation and cost control. From a motivation perspective, making some or all of a worker's pay conditional on some performance measure focuses his or her attention and effort toward that measure, then reinforces the continuation of the effort with a reward. If the employee, team, or organization's performance declines, so does the reward. Thus, there's an incentive to keep efforts and motivation strong. Also, performance-based bonuses and other incentive rewards avoid the fixed expense of permanent salary increases and so save money.

THINKING CRITICALLY ABOUT ETHICS

You have been hired as a telephone sales representative at World Adventures Travel Agency in Dover, Delaware. In this job, when customers call to book travel vacations, you look up airline flights, times, and fares on the computer and help customers choose what works best for them and their needs. Customers also often want help in reserving a rental car or finding a hotel room, and you're glad to help them.

Most car rental firms and hotels run contests for the sales representative who books the most cars or most hotel rooms. The contest winners receive very attractive rewards! For instance, if you book just 50 clients for one car rental chain, your name is put in a drawing for $2,500. If you book 100 clients, the drawing is for $5,000. And if you book 200 clients, you receive an all-expenses-paid, one-week Caribbean vacation. So the incentives are attractive enough to encourage you to "steer" customers toward one of those companies even though it might not be the best or cheapest for them. Your supervisor doesn't discourage participation in these programs.

Do you see anything wrong with this situation? Explain. What ethical issues do you see for (a) the employee, (b) the organization, and (c) the customer? How could an organization design performance incentive programs that encourage high levels of performance without compromising ethics? ■

But do pay-for-performance programs work? Studies seem to indicate that, yes, they do. For instance, one study found that companies that used performance management programs performed better financially than those that did not.[54] Another study showed that outcome-based incentives had a positive impact on sales, customer satisfaction, and profits.[55]

Open-Book Management

Many organizations of various sizes are involving their employees in workplace decisions by opening up the financial statements (the "books"). They share that information so that employees will be motivated to make better decisions about their work and better able to understand the implications of what they do, how they do it, and the ultimate impact on the bottom line. This approach is called **open-book management**.[56] According to a study by Ernst & Young LLP, workers who are treated as business "partners" are most likely to be more productive and more motivated to contribute to their company's profitability.[57]

The goal of open-book management is to get employees to think like an owner by seeing the impact their decisions and actions have on financial results. But most employees will not have the knowledge or background to understand the financials, so they have to be taught how to read and understand the organization's financial statements. And once employees have this knowledge, managers need to share the numbers regularly and routinely with them.

Some organizations take open-book management a step further. For instance, at Springfield Remanufacturing Company (SRC) in Springfield, Missouri, employees not only get financial information but also receive bonuses and incentive pay based on profit improvements.[58] Through this type of sharing arrangement, employees begin to see the link between their efforts, level of performance, and operational results. At Allstate's Business Insurance Group, open-book management is credited for a boost in return on equity from 2.9 percent to 16.5 percent in just three years. Employees were trained to understand the importance of key financial measures and then were provided with the information on a regular basis. The unit's president said, "It got employees involved and committed, and it gave them some ownership. They understood they had an impact on the bottom line."[59]

open-book management

A motivational approach in which an organization's financial statements (the "books") are opened to and shared with all employees.

As part of his practice of open-book management, Arnold Henning, director of financial projects at Navistar, here meets with a group of employees to discuss return on equity.

TESTING...
TESTING...

1 2 3

10 What are some options for motivating a diverse workforce?

11 How is performance-based compensation compatible with expectancy theory?

12 Describe open-book management and its use in motivation.

Employee Stock Ownership Plans (ESOPs)

employee stock ownership plan (ESOP)

A compensation program in which employees become part owners of the organization by receiving stock as a performance incentive.

Many companies are using ESOPs as an incentive for improving and motivating employee performance. According to the National Center for Employee Ownership in Oakland, California, about 10,000 companies have ESOPs.[60] An **employee stock ownership plan (ESOP)** is a compensation program in which employees become part owners of the organization by receiving stock as a performance incentive. Many ESOPs also allow employees to purchase additional stock at attractive, below-market prices. Under an ESOP, employees often are motivated to work hard because it makes them owners who will share in any gains and losses. The fruits of their labors are no longer just going into the pockets of some unknown owner—they are the owner!

Do ESOPs affect productivity and employee satisfaction? Yes, they do! The research on ESOPs indicates that they increase employee satisfaction and frequently result in higher performance. For instance, one study compared 45 ESOPs against 238 conventional companies. The ESOPs outperformed the conventional firms in terms of both employment and sales growth.[61] Other studies show that productivity in organizations with ESOPs increases but the impact is greater the longer the ESOP has been in existence.[62] So organizations should not expect immediate increases in employee motivation and productivity if an ESOP is implemented. But over the long run, employee productivity and satisfaction are likely to go up.

Employee stock ownership plans have the potential to increase employee satisfaction and work motivation, but that potential will be realized only if employees psychologically experience ownership.[63] What we mean is that, in addition to merely having a financial stake in the organization, employees need to be regularly informed about the status of the business and to have the opportunity to exercise influence over the business. When these conditions are met, "employees will be more satisfied with their jobs, more satisfied with

The employees of United Airlines are also its owners under the terms of the carrier's ESOP plan.

their organizational identification, motivated to come to work, and motivated to perform well while at work."[64]

Motivating the "New Workforce"

Special groups present unique challenges in terms of motivation. In this section we look at some of the unique problems faced in trying to motivate professional employees, contingent workers, and low-skilled, minimum-wage employees.

Motivating Professionals.   In contrast to a generation ago, the typical employee today is more likely to be a highly trained professional with a college degree than a blue-collar factory worker. These professionals receive a great deal of intrinsic satisfaction from their work. They tend to be well paid. What, if any, special concerns should managers be aware of when trying to motivate a team of engineers at Intel, a software designer at Corel, or a group of CPAs at Price Waterhouse?

Professionals are typically different from nonprofessionals.[65] They have a strong and long-term commitment to their field of expertise. Their loyalty is more often to their profession than to their employer. To keep current in their field, they need to regularly update their knowledge, and because of their commitment to their profession they rarely define their workweek as 8 A.M. to 5 P.M. five days a week.

What motivates professionals? Money and promotions typically are low on their priority list. Why? They tend to be well paid and they enjoy what they do. In contrast, job challenge tends to be ranked high. They like to tackle problems and find solutions. Their chief reward in their job is the work itself. Professionals also value support. They want others to think that what they are working on is important. That may be true for all employees, but professionals tend to be focused on their work as their central life interest, whereas nonprofessionals typically have other interests outside of work that can compensate for needs not met on the job.

The preceding description implies a few guidelines to keep in mind when motivating professionals. Provide them with ongoing challenging projects. Give them autonomy to follow their interests, and allow them to structure their work in ways they find productive. Reward them with educational opportunities—training, workshops, attending conferences—that allow them to keep current in their field. Also reward them with recognition, and ask questions and use other actions that demonstrate to them that you're sincerely interested in what they're doing and value it.

Professionals who derive intrinsic satisfaction from their work are driven by loyalty to their profession. Motivating them often means simply giving them the means and opportunity to do what they do best. This Price Waterhouse employee is using a laptop to work at home.

Motivating Contingent Workers.   As we mentioned in chapter 2, there's an increasing number of temporary or contingent workers in the workforce. The elimination of millions of jobs through downsizing has increased the number of openings for part-time, contract, and other forms of temporary workers. Contingent workers don't have the security or stability that permanent employees have, and they don't identify with the organization or display the commitment that other employees do. Temporary workers also are typically provided with little or no health care, pensions, or similar benefits.[66]

There's no simple solution for motivating contingent employees. For that small set of temps who prefer the freedom of their temporary status—some students, working mothers, seniors—the lack of stability may not be an issue. In addition, temporariness might be preferred by highly compensated physicians, engineers, accountants, or financial planners who don't want the demands of a stable job. But these are the exceptions. For the most part, temporary employees are not temporary by choice.

What will motivate involuntarily temporary employees? An obvious answer is the opportunity for permanent status. In cases in which permanent employees are selected from a pool of temporaries, temps will often work hard in hopes of becoming permanent. A less obvious answer is the opportunity for training. The ability of a temporary employee to find a new job is largely dependent on his or her skills. If the employee sees that the job he or she is doing can help develop marketable skills, then motivation is increased. From an equity standpoint, you should also consider the repercussions of mixing permanent and temporary workers when pay differentials are significant. When temps work alongside permanent employees who earn more, and get benefits, too, for doing the same job, the performance of temps is likely to suffer. Separating such employees or perhaps converting all employees to a variable-pay or skill-based pay plan might help minimize the problem.

Motivating Low-Skilled, Minimum-Wage Employees.   Suppose that in your first managerial position after graduating, you're responsible for managing a work group composed of low-skilled, minimum-wage employees. Offering more pay to these employees for high levels of performance is out of the question; your company just can't afford it. In addition, these employees have limited education and skills. What are your motivational options at this point? One of the toughest motivational challenges a manager faces is how to achieve and keep high performance levels among these types of workers.[67]

One trap we often fall into is thinking that people are motivated only by money. Although money is important as a motivator, it's not the only reward that people seek and that managers can use. In motivating minimum-wage employees, managers should look at other types of rewards that help motivate employee performance. What are some other types of rewards that managers can use? One that many companies use is employee recognition programs such as employee of the month, quarterly employee performance awards ceremonies, or other celebrations of employees' accomplishments. For instance, at many fast-food restaurants or retail stores, you will often see plaques hanging in prominent places that feature the "Employee of the Month." These types of programs serve the purpose of highlighting employees whose work performance has been of the type and level the organization wants to encourage in all its employees. Many managers also recognize the power of praise. However, you need to be sure that these "pats on the back" are sincere and are given for the right reasons. What else can managers do to motivate high levels of performance from minimum-wage employees?

Again, we can look to job design and expectancy theories for some answers. In service industries such as travel and hospitality, retail sales, child care, and maintenance in which pay for front-line employees generally does not get above the minimum wage level, successful companies are empowering these front-line employees with more authority to address customers' problems. If we use the JCM to examine this change, we can see that this type of job redesign provides enhanced motivating potential because employees now

At his Subway shop in Colorado, manager Steve Lauer (second from left) motivates employees by providing training in the first few weeks on the job, evaluating new employees often, and celebrating employees' one-year anniversaries with parties and picnics, a week of paid vacation, service pins, company sweatshirts, and a new uniform in a different color.

experience increased skill variety, task identity, task significance, autonomy, and feedback. For instance, almost every job in Marriott International hotels is being redesigned to place more workers in contact with more guests more of the time.[68] These employees are now able to take care of customer complaints and requests that formerly were referred to a supervisor or another department. In addition, employees have at least part of their pay tied to customer satisfaction, so there's a clear link between level of performance and reward (instrumentality linkage from expectancy theory). So, even though motivating minimum-wage workers may be a challenge, we can still use what we know about employee motivation to help us find some answers.

FROM THEORY TO PRACTICE: SUGGESTIONS FOR MOTIVATING EMPLOYEES

In this chapter, we've covered a lot of information about motivation. If you're a manager concerned with motivating your employees, what specific recommendations can you draw from the theories and issues presented in this chapter? Although there's no simple, all-encompassing set of guidelines, the suggestions outlined in Table 15-2 draw on the essence of what we know about motivating employees. Let's look at them more closely.

Recognize Individual Differences.   Almost every contemporary motivation theory recognizes that employees aren't homogeneous. They have different needs. They also differ in terms of attitudes, personality, and other important individual variables. For instance,

TABLE 15-2   **Suggestions for Motivating Employees**
• Recognize individual differences.
• Match people to jobs.
• Use goals.
• Ensure that goals are perceived as attainable.
• Individualize rewards.
• Link rewards to performance.
• Check the system for equity.
• Don't ignore money.

expectancy predictions are more accurate with individuals who have an internal rather than external locus of control.[69] Why? The belief of the former that events in their lives are largely under their own control is consistent with the expectancy theory's self-interest assumptions.

Match People to Jobs.   There's a great deal of evidence showing the motivational benefits of carefully matching people to jobs. For example, high achievers should be sought for a job of running a small business or an autonomous unit within a larger business. However, if the job to be filled is a managerial slot in a large bureaucratic organization, a candidate high in nPow and low in nAff should be selected. Along these same lines, don't put a high achiever into a job that's inconsistent with his or her needs. Achievers will do best in jobs that provide opportunities to participate in setting moderately challenging goals and that involve autonomy and feedback. Keep in mind that not everybody is motivated by jobs that are high in autonomy, variety, and responsibility. Such jobs are most attractive and motivating to employees with a high growth need.

Use Goals.   The literature on goal-setting theory suggests that managers should ensure that employees have hard, specific goals and feedback on how well they're doing in pursuit of those goals. For those with high achievement needs, typically a minority in any organization, the existence of external goals is less important because high achievers are already internally motivated.

Should the goals be assigned by a manager, or should employees participate in setting goals? The answer depends on your perception of goal acceptance and the organization's culture. If you expect resistance to goals, the use of participation should increase acceptance. If participation is inconsistent with the culture, use assigned goals. When participation and the culture are incongruous, employees are likely to perceive the participative process as manipulative and be turned off by it.

Ensure That Goals Are Perceived as Attainable.   Regardless of whether goals are actually attainable, employees who see goals as unattainable will reduce their effort—their feeling being "why bother." Managers must be sure, therefore, that employees feel confident that increased efforts *can* lead to achieving performance goals. For managers, this means that employees must be capable of doing the job and must perceive the performance appraisal process as both reliable and valid.

Individualize Rewards.   Because employees have different needs, what acts as a reinforcer for one may not for another. Managers should use their knowledge of employee differences to individualize the rewards over which they have control. Some of the more obvious rewards that managers allocate include pay, promotions, autonomy, and the opportunity to participate in goal setting and decision making.

Link Rewards to Performance.   Managers need to make rewards contingent on performance. Rewarding factors other than performance will only reinforce those other factors. Key rewards such as pay increases and promotions should be given for the attainment of the employee's specific goals. Managers should also look for ways to increase the visibility of rewards. Eliminating the secrecy surrounding pay by openly communicating everyone's compensation, publicizing performance bonuses, and allocating annual salary increases in a lump sum rather than spreading them out over the entire year are examples of actions that will make rewards more visible and potentially more motivating.

Check the System for Equity.   Employees should perceive that rewards or outcomes are equal to the inputs given. On a simplistic level, experience, ability, effort, and other obvious inputs should explain differences in pay, responsibility, and other obvious outcomes. The problem, however, is complicated by the existence of dozens of both inputs and outcomes and by the fact that employee groups place different degrees of importance on them. For instance, a study comparing clerical and production workers identified nearly 20 inputs and outcomes.[70] The clerical workers considered factors such as quality of work performed and job knowledge near the top of their input list, but these factors were at the bottom of the production workers' list. Similarly, production workers thought the most important inputs were intelligence and personal involvement with the task to be accomplished, two factors that were quite low in the clerks' importance ratings. There were also important, though less dramatic, differences on the outcome side. For example, production workers rated advancement very high, whereas clerical workers rated advancement in the lower third on their list. Such findings suggest that one person's equity is another's inequity, so an ideal reward system should probably weigh inputs differently in arriving at the proper rewards for each job.

Don't Ignore Money.   It's easy to get so caught up in setting goals, creating interesting jobs, and providing opportunities for participation that one forgets that money is a major reason why most people work. Thus, the allocation of performance-based wage increases, piecework bonuses, and other pay incentives is important in determining employee motivation. A review of 80 studies evaluating motivational methods and their impact on employee productivity supports this point.[71] Goal setting alone produced, on average, a 16 percent increase in productivity; redesign efforts to enrich jobs yielded 8 to 16 percent increases; employee participation in decision making produced a median increase of less than 1 percent; and monetary incentives led to an average increase of 30 percent. We are not saying that management should focus solely on money. Rather, we're simply stating the obvious—that is, if money is removed as an incentive, people aren't going to show up for work. The same cannot be said for removing goals, enriched work, or participation.

13 How can ESOPs be used to motivate employees?

14 What are some special challenges in motivating (a) professionals, (b) contingent workers, and (c) low-skilled, minimum-wage workers?

15 List some practical suggestions for motivating employees.

TESTING...
TESTING...
1 2 3

managers respond to "a manager's dilemma"

MANAGER 1

To motivate these individuals, I would ask what key motivators are important to them and then try to provide those things. Also, I would involve them in decisions that affect them, the design and direction of their work, and the growth of the business. Whenever possible, I also would provide a clear vision or mission, specific objectives, meaningful rewards, and equity positions or stock options to engender a meaningful and tangible connection between company prosperity and personal wealth. I also think it's important in motivating employees to say "yes" whenever possible. This lets people know that you're behind them and value their contributions. Finally, I would foster a work environment that establishes trust; encourages and rewards *hard* work; celebrates and rewards *smart* work; promotes learning, growth, and collaboration; makes the contributions of stellar performers visible; and is energizing, uplifting, and fun while ensuring that all employees always keep their "eye on the ball."

Debra A. Dinnocenzo, President, AL*Learn*atives®, Wexford, Pennsylvania

MANAGER 2

Bill has to come up with ways to motivate bright, young, creative professionals. Some may share his desire for "unbelievable control of their destiny" and may be comparably driven by personal goals. Offering them a piece of the action via equity options or a voice in management decisions, or both, will likely increase their level of motivation.

Bill likely realizes that there are individuals who don't share his world view but have skills that are critical to this venture's success. Providing these folks with the ability to work at, and push, the edge of their technical expertise; access to the latest tools (hardware, software, ancillary devices); and contact with a unique set of clients and colleagues may be effective motivational options.

The ability to share learning among their peers may be a source of motivation as well as a way to benefit the efforts of other projects. Sharing learning may provide a way to build a sense of the lab as more than the sum of its individual projects. It also provides a way to create a working peer community while safeguarding the venture's proprietary, intellectual capital.

A final observation: Creative folks tend to be a pretty quirky bunch. Creating an atmosphere and work environment that spawns expression of their creativity may be the overriding challenge. This would likely include being highly tolerant of ideas that may initially seem outlandish and expressing an appreciation of the creative risks Bill expects them to take.

Dave Panco, Program Manager, Analytical and Environmental Sciences, Corporate Research and Development, Weyerhaeuser Corporation, Portland, Oregon

for your
IMMEDIATE
action

LA MEXICAN KITCHEN

TO: Carla Bustamante,
Operations Manager
FROM: Brett Behrends, Shift Supervisor
SUBJECT: Turnover Rates of Servers

Carla, I need your help. As you know, we're having a difficult time keeping food servers for any period of time. In the past six months, our employee turnover rate has exceeded 60 percent. It seems like I just get them trained and then they leave. I know we both agree that our servers are important to our company's commitment to excellent customer service. We can have the best food in town, yet if our servers aren't motivated to provide excellent service, we won't have any customers.

Although these positions pay minimum wage, you and I both know that a motivated server can make another $30 to $60 a night from customer tips. But even that doesn't seem to be enough to motivate them. What would you recommend I do? Do you have any ideas about how I can better motivate our food servers? I'd appreciate your jotting down some ideas (keep it under two pages, please) and getting them to me as soon as possible. Thanks for your input!

This is a fictionalized account of a potentially real problem. It was written for academic purposes only.

SUMMARY

This summary is organized by the chapter-opening objectives found on p. 482.

1. Motivation is the willingness to exert high levels of effort toward organizational goals, conditioned by the effort's ability to satisfy some individual need. The motivation process begins with an unsatisfied need, which creates tension and drives an individual to search for goals that, if attained, will satisfy the need and reduce the tension.

2. High achievers prefer jobs that offer personal responsibility, feedback, and moderate risks.

3. Goals motivate employees by providing specific and challenging benchmarks to guide and stimulate performance.

4. Reinforcement theory emphasizes the pattern in which rewards are administered. It states that only positive, not negative, reinforcement be used, and then only to reward desired behavior. The theory assumes that behavior is environmentally caused. Goal-setting theory views motivation as coming from an individual's internal statements of purpose.

5. Organizations have attempted to design motivating jobs by using job enlargement, job enrichment, and the job characteristics model (JCM). Job enlargement is the horizontal expansion of a job that increases job scope, the number of different tasks required in a job, and the frequency with which those tasks are repeated. Job enrichment is the vertical expansion of a job that increases job depth, which is the degree of control employees have over their work. The JCM proposes that jobs have five core job dimensions—skill variety, task identity, task significance, autonomy, and feedback—that can be combined to create more-motivating jobs.

6. In equity theory, individuals compare their job's inputs-outcomes ratio with those of relevant others. If they perceive that they are being underrewarded, their work motivation declines. When individuals perceive that they are being overrewarded, they often are motivated to work harder in order to justify their pay.

7. The expectancy theory states that an individual tends to act in a certain way based on the expectation that the act will be followed by a given outcome and on the attractiveness of that outcome to the individual. Its prime components are the relationships between effort and performance, performance and rewards, and rewards and individual goals.

8. The current motivation issues facing managers include motivating a diverse workforce, designing appropriate pay-for-performance programs, using open-book management, using employee stock ownership plans (ESOPs), and motivating the new workforce (contingent workers, professionals, and low-skilled, minimum-wage employees).

9. Management practices that are likely to lead to more motivated employees include recognizing individual differences, matching people to jobs, using goals, ensuring that employees perceive goals as attainable, individualizing rewards, linking rewards to performance, checking the reward system for equity, and realizing that money is an important incentive.

THINKING ABOUT MANAGEMENT ISSUES

1. Most of us have to work for a living, and a job is a central part of our lives. So why do managers have to worry so much about employee motivation issues?

2. Describe a task you have done recently for which you exerted a high level of effort. Explain your behavior by using any of the motivation approaches described in the chapter.

3. If you had to develop an incentive system for a small manufacturing company, which elements from which motivation approaches or theories would you use? Why? Would your choice be the same if it was a medical research lab? Explain.

4. Could managers use any of the motivation theories or approaches to encourage and support workforce diversity efforts? Explain.

5. List five criteria (for example: pay, recognition, challenging work, friendships, status, the opportunity to do new things, and so forth) that would be most important to you in a job. Rank them by order of importance. Break into small groups and compare your responses. What patterns, if any, did you find?

SELF-ASSESSMENT EXERCISE

WHAT MOTIVATES YOU?

Circle the number that most closely agrees with how you feel (1 = strongly disagree; 5 = strongly agree). Consider your answers in the context of your current job or past work experience.

1. I try very hard to improve on my past performance at work.	1	2	3	4	5
2. I enjoy competition and winning.	1	2	3	4	5
3. I often find myself talking to those around me about nonwork matters.	1	2	3	4	5
4. I enjoy a difficult challenge.	1	2	3	4	5
5. I enjoy being in charge.	1	2	3	4	5
6. I want to be liked by others.	1	2	3	4	5
7. I want to know how I am progressing as I complete tasks.	1	2	3	4	5
8. I confront people who do things I disagree with.	1	2	3	4	5
9. I tend to build close relationships with co-workers.	1	2	3	4	5
10. I enjoy setting and achieving realistic goals.	1	2	3	4	5
11. I enjoy influencing other people to get my way.	1	2	3	4	5
12. I enjoy belonging to groups and organizations.	1	2	3	4	5
13. I enjoy the satisfaction of completing a difficult task.	1	2	3	4	5
14. I often work to gain more control over the events around me.	1	2	3	4	5
15. I enjoy working with others more than working alone.	1	2	3	4	5

See scoring key on page SK–5.

Source: Based on R. Steers and D. Braunstein, "A Behaviorally Based Measure of Manifest Needs in Work Settings," *Journal of Vocational Behavior*, October 1976, p. 254; and R.N. Lussier, *Human Relations in Organizations: A Skill Building Approach* (Homewood, IL: Richard D. Irwin, 1990), p. 120.

TAKE IT TO THE NET

We invite you to visit the Robbins/Coulter companion Web site at http://www.prenhall.com/robbinsmgt for this chapter's Internet resources.

CASE APPLICATION

Striking Gold

Shamee Samad and Jamie Sokalsky have struck gold. They work for Barrick Gold Corporation of Toronto, but they aren't miners. As members of the world's most profitable and third-largest gold-mining operation, all Barrick employees are enjoying generous benefits from the company's stock-option program.

Barrick introduced the idea of supplementing regular paychecks with stock in 1984. At the time, the company was strapped for cash, so management decided to use stock options as a way to attract and motivate its employees. But, in contrast to most stock-option plans, Barrick's plan covers *all* the company's employees (5,000 of them), not just upper-level managers. So far, the program appears to be a winner for both employees and the company.

Samad, for example, has been an accounts payable clerk with the company for 10 years. She joined Barrick as a 19-year-old, fresh out of high school. In her first year with the company, she earned stock options worth $11,000. That was in addition to her $24,000 salary. In the decade that she has been with Barrick, Samad has cashed in $51,000 from options she's been granted and still holds another $64,000 worth of stock. Sokalsky, meanwhile, has been with the company for only two years. As corporate treasurer, however, he has already racked up $320,000 worth of stock options. Not bad considering that his annual salary is just over $100,000.

Do stock options motivate? Ask Samad, and she'll say she thinks they do. "If I have to come in early or stay late, I do it. No questions asked." And the company has come a long way from the days when it was strapped for money. A share of Barrick bought in 1983 for $1.75 is now worth more than $42. The company has consistently outperformed other gold producers even during some very lean years in the gold business. A fall in gold prices to a three-year low in 1989, for example, hardly left a dent; Barrick's earnings were up 21 percent and its share price rose 94 percent. The following year, earnings were up 73 percent and the price of Barrick shares climbed another 38 percent, even as the Toronto Stock Exchange's Gold and Silver Index declined more than 20 percent.

QUESTIONS

1. How are stock options at Barrick motivating employees? (Use Figure 15-8 for your answer.)
2. What might be some drawbacks of a stock option incentive program for (a) the individual and (b) the organization?
3. Would stock options be effective motivators for employees at a gold producer (a) in South Africa? (b) In Peru? Defend your position.

Source: P. Simao, "Eureka!" *Canadian Business*, June 1996, pp. 66–69.

ABCNEWS VIDEO CASE APPLICATION

Pedaling Your Way to Fame

Three weeks of constant pain and punishment that demands extreme levels of courage, endurance, and motivation. This is how participants in the Tour de France describe what they go through. It's called the greatest bicycle race in the world. It's a race in which every participant must be incredibly strong, have a significant amount of courage, and possess a phenomenal endurance level.

The cyclists who race in the Tour belong to teams sponsored by commercial companies. These teams exist, however, to help their "star" win the race. Usually only one or two members of a team are capa-

ble of winning. The other riders are there to help them. They push the leaders to pick up the pace and support each other to keep going. Not surprisingly, the winner of the Tour traditionally donates the $400,000 prize to his teammates. However, the winner doesn't go home empty handed! Corporate sponsors pay their star athletes million dollar salaries, and a winner of the Tour stands to earn millions more in commercial endorsements.

What sets the Tour de France apart as one of the greatest sporting spectacles in the world and as a test of individual motivation and endurance? First of all, there's the speed. These bicyclists on two thin wheels can reach speeds of more than 60 miles an hour. One racer says that's the ultimate thrill—going fast. But, there's also the danger of a crash. The uncertainty and potential danger associated with speed and equipment failure give participants the thrill of "living on the edge." However, what really sets the Tour apart is its almost inhuman test of endurance. For three weeks, the Tour rolls on and on through cities and small villages. The riders push themselves to the limit and sometimes beyond—through a race course that covers a total of 2,500 miles. Racers pedal up to 150 miles each day, six hours a day, until they reach the finish line in Paris. Some describe the experience to be like running a marathon, then getting up and having to run it again the next day, and the next, and so on. It takes enormous levels of athletic skill and stamina, as well as mental discipline and experience. It also takes knowing yourself very well. Successful racers must know their bodies, their state of mind, and what they can and cannot do. It's a challenge that those who participate in the race gladly take.

QUESTIONS

1. In this situation, what role does the team play in motivating extraordinary levels of performance from individuals? What implications can you see for managing?
2. Use expectancy theory to explain an individual's motivation to compete in the Tour de France.
3. On what level of Maslow's hierarchy of needs do you think participants in the Tour de France would be? Discuss.

Source: Based on "Test of Courage—Tour de France," *ABC News Nightline,* July 21, 1994.

A MANAGER'S DILEMMA

More and more individual employees and teams of employees are being empowered to make key operating decisions that directly affect their work. Although employee empowerment programs may seem like an ideal way to foster employee involvement and initiative, their success depends on creating a workplace environment that nurtures and encourages individual initiative. Philip Berry, the director of human resources for Colgate-Palmolive Corporation's division in Central Europe, the Middle East, and Africa, discovered how important an empowering environment was when his company began opening manufacturing plants in Central Europe (in the Czech Republic, Slovakia, Romania, and Poland) in the mid-1990s.[1]

The workforce that Berry encountered was a long way from being empowered. Because the previous (communist) "management" style had been strictly authoritarian, employees were used to doing what they were told to do, no questions asked. Creativity and innovation were not encour-

aged. Employees were seen simply as bodies performing tasks, not as minds who could think and create. The dominant managerial philosophy had been that any thinking that had to be done would be done by managers. That, however, was *not* the way that Berry or Colgate-Palmolive wanted to operate.

Colgate-Palmolive's organizational culture had always stressed and fostered employee involvement and empowerment. And Berry was convinced that these Central European employees could learn to contribute and be as involved and committed as the company's other global employees. He chose to implement a leadership style that was consistently practiced in Colgate's various global facilities—one that encouraged employees to share their ideas about how to run the business and then rewarded them for doing so.

Put yourself in Berry's situation. How could you create that empowering environment in manufacturing facilities whose workers had always been treated as mindless and who had no experience in empowered decision making?

WHAT WOULD YOU DO?

Philip Berry is facing a big leadership challenge! To make this empowerment approach work with these employees, he is going to have to provide effective leadership. Why is leadership so important? Because it is the leaders in organizations who make things happen. If leadership is so important, it's only natural to ask: What differentiates leaders from nonleaders? What's the most appropriate style of leadership? And what can you do if you want to be seen as a leader? In this chapter, we'll try to answer those and other questions about leaders.

Leadership

MANAGERS VERSUS LEADERS

Let's begin by clarifying the distinction between managers and leaders. Authors and practitioners often equate the two, although they're not necessarily the same. Managers are appointed. Their ability to influence is based on the formal authority inherent in their positions. In contrast, leaders may either be appointed or emerge from within a group. Leaders can influence others to perform beyond the actions dictated by formal authority.

Should all managers be leaders? Conversely, should all leaders be managers? Because no one yet has been able to demonstrate either through research or logical argument that leadership ability is a handicap to a manager, we can state that all managers should *ideally* be leaders. However, not all leaders necessarily have the capabilities or skills needed in other managerial functions, and thus, not all should hold managerial positions. The fact that an individual can influence others does not tell whether he or she can also plan, organize, and control. Given (even if only ideally) that all managers should be leaders, we'll pursue the subject from a managerial perspective. Therefore, the definition of **leaders** in this chapter refers to persons who are able to influence others *and* who possess managerial authority. What is **leadership** then? It's the ability to influence a group toward the achievement of goals.

Leadership, like motivation, is an organizational behavior topic that has been heavily researched, and practically all the research has been aimed at answering the question: What is an effective leader? We can clearly see an evolution in our understanding of the leadership process in the various theories proposed to understand and explain it.

Recall from our discussion of the early origins of organizational behavior in chapter 2 that initial leadership studies focused on identifying specific traits that might be used to differentiate leaders from nonleaders. Researchers were unable to identify certain traits that always differentiated leaders, so they instead began examining the interactions of leaders and followers to determine if there was a particular behavioral style that characterized effective leaders. These behavioral theories also proved to be a dead end because they failed to recognize situational differences.

It became increasingly clear to those studying leadership that predicting leadership success involved something more complex than isolating a few leader traits or preferable

leaders

Persons who are able to influence others and who possess managerial authority.

leadership

The ability to influence a group toward the achievement of goals.

A manager who clearly possesses leadership skills is Roy Roberts, now head of Pontiac-GMC, the second largest division at General Motors. As general manager of GMC, he racked up record-breaking sales and promoted the highest level of customer service. In his new position, he'll continue to rely on the marketing, salesmanship, and people skills observers admire.

behaviors. The failure to attain consistent results led to this new focus on situational influences. The relationship between leadership style and effectiveness suggested that under condition a, leadership style x would be appropriate, whereas style y would be more suitable for condition b, and style z for condition c. But what were the conditions a, b, c, and so forth? It was one thing to say that leadership effectiveness depended on the situation and another to be able to isolate those situational conditions or contingencies.

Numerous studies have attempted to isolate critical contingency factors that affected leadership effectiveness. One author reviewing the literature on the topic found that the task being performed (that is, the complexity, type, technology, and size of the project) was a significant contingency variable, but he also uncovered studies that isolated situational factors such as style of the leader's immediate supervisor, group norms, span of control, external threats and stress, and organizational culture.[2] What's our current state of knowledge of contingency variables in leadership, and what are the most current views of leadership in organizations?

CONTEMPORARY THEORIES OF LEADERSHIP

In this section we examine various contemporary theories of leadership and look at the most up-to-date information regarding what we know about leadership in organizations. Three of these theories—Fiedler's, path-goal, and leader participation—are described as contingency theories of leadership; the others reflect more-applied views of leadership.

The Fiedler Model

The first comprehensive contingency model for leadership was developed by Fred Fiedler.[3] The **Fiedler contingency model** proposed that effective group performance depended upon the proper match between the leader's style of interacting with his or her subordinates and the degree to which the situation allowed the leader to control and influence. The model was based on the premise that a certain leadership style would be most effective in different types of situations. The key was to define those leadership styles and the different types of situations, and then to identify the appropriate combinations of style and situation. In order to understand Fiedler's model, let's look at the first of these variables—leadership style.

Fiedler proposed that a key factor in leadership success was an individual's basic leadership style. He further suggested that a person's style was one of two types: task oriented or relationship oriented. To measure a leader's style, Fiedler developed the **least-preferred co-worker (LPC) questionnaire**. As shown in Figure 16-1, it contained 16 pairs of contrasting adjectives. Respondents were asked to think of all the co-workers they had ever had and to describe the one person they *least enjoyed* working with by rating him or her on a scale of 1 to 8 for each of the 16 sets of adjectives. Fiedler believed that you could determine a person's basic leadership style on the basis of the responses to the LPC questionnaire. What were his descriptions of these styles?

Fiedler believed that if the least preferred co-worker was described in relatively positive terms (in other words, a "high" LPC score), then the respondent was primarily interested in good personal relations with co-workers. That is, if you described the person that you would least be able to work with in favorable terms, you would be labeled *relationship oriented*. In contrast, if you saw the least preferred co-worker in relatively unfavorable terms (a low LPC score), you were primarily interested in productivity and getting the job done; thus, you'd be labeled *task oriented*. Fiedler did acknowledge that there was a small group of people who fell in between those two extremes and who did not have a cut-and-dried personality sketch. One other point we need to make is that Fiedler assumed that a person's leadership style was fixed regardless of the situation. In other words, if you were a relationship-oriented leader, you'd always be one, and the same for task oriented.

After an individual's basic leadership style had been assessed through the LPC, it was necessary to evaluate the situation in order to match the leader with the situation. Fiedler's

Fiedler contingency model

The theory that effective groups depend on a proper match between a leader's style of interacting with subordinates and the degree to which the situation gives control and influence to the leader.

least-preferred co-worker (LPC) questionnaire

A questionnaire that measures whether a person is task or relationship oriented.

FIGURE 16-1   Fiedler's LPC Scale

	8	7	6	5	4	3	2	1	
Pleasant	8	7	6	5	4	3	2	1	Unpleasant
Friendly	8	7	6	5	4	3	2	1	Unfriendly
Rejecting	1	2	3	4	5	6	7	8	Accepting
Helpful	8	7	6	5	4	3	2	1	Frustrating
Unenthusiastic	1	2	3	4	5	6	7	8	Enthusiastic
Tense	1	2	3	4	5	6	7	8	Relaxed
Distant	1	2	3	4	5	6	7	8	Close
Cold	1	2	3	4	5	6	7	8	Warm
Cooperative	8	7	6	5	4	3	2	1	Uncooperative
Supportive	8	7	6	5	4	3	2	1	Hostile
Boring	1	2	3	4	5	6	7	8	Interesting
Quarrelsome	1	2	3	4	5	6	7	8	Harmonious
Self-Assured	8	7	6	5	4	3	2	1	Hesitant
Efficient	8	7	6	5	4	3	2	1	Inefficient
Gloomy	1	2	3	4	5	6	7	8	Cheerful
Open	8	7	6	5	4	3	2	1	Guarded

Source: From F.E. Fiedler and M.M. Chemers, *Leadership and Effective Management* (Glenview, IL: Scott, Foresman, 1974). Reprinted by permission of the authors.

leader-member relations

The degree of confidence, trust, and respect subordinates have in their leader.

task structure

The degree to which the job assignments are procedurized.

position power

The degree of influence a leader has over power variables such as hiring, firing, discipline, promotions, and salary increases.

research uncovered three contingency dimensions that defined the key situational factors for determining leader effectiveness. These were:

1. **Leader-member relations:** the degree of confidence, trust, and respect subordinates had for their leader; rated as either good or poor

2. **Task structure:** the degree to which the job assignments were formalized and procedurized; rated as either high or low

3. **Position power:** the degree of influence a leader had over power-based activities such as hiring, firing, discipline, promotions, and salary increases; rated as either strong or weak

Each leadership situation was evaluated in terms of these three contingency variables. Mixing these variables produces eight possible situations in which a leader can find him- or herself (bottom chart in Figure 16-2). Fiedler further classified these eight situations as being *very favorable, moderately favorable,* or *very unfavorable* for the leader. As shown in Figure 16-2, Situations I, II, and III were classified as very favorable. Situations IV, V, and VI were moderately favorable. And finally, Situations VII and VIII were described as very unfavorable.

In order to define the specific contingencies for leadership effectiveness, Fiedler studied 1,200 groups in which he compared relationship-oriented versus task-oriented leadership styles in each of the eight situational categories. He concluded that task-oriented leaders tended to perform better in situations that were very favorable to them and in situations that were very unfavorable. On the other hand, relationship-oriented leaders seemed to perform better in moderately favorable situations.

Remember that Fiedler treated an individual's leadership style as fixed. Therefore, there were really only two ways to improve leader effectiveness. First, you could bring in a new leader who better fit the situation. For instance, if the group situation rated as highly unfavorable but was led by a relationship-oriented leader, the group's performance could be improved by replacing that person with a task-oriented leader. The second alternative was to change the situation to fit the leader. This could be done by restructuring tasks or increasing or decreasing the power that the leader had over factors such as salary increases, promotions, and disciplinary actions.

Reviews of the major studies undertaken to test the overall validity of the Fiedler model led to a generally positive conclusion. That is, there has been considerable evidence to support the model.[4] However, it wasn't without shortcomings. For instance, additional variables were probably needed to fill in some gaps in the model. Moreover, there were problems with

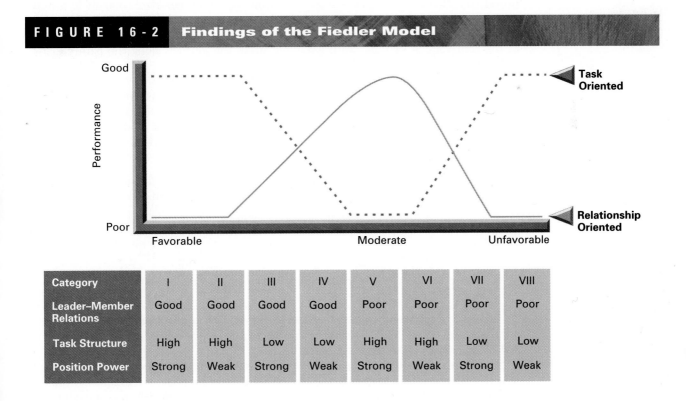

FIGURE 16-2   Findings of the Fiedler Model

Category	I	II	III	IV	V	VI	VII	VIII
Leader–Member Relations	Good	Good	Good	Good	Poor	Poor	Poor	Poor
Task Structure	High	High	Low	Low	High	High	Low	Low
Position Power	Strong	Weak	Strong	Weak	Strong	Weak	Strong	Weak

the LPC, and the practicality of it needed to be addressed. For instance, the logic underlying the LPC wasn't well understood, and studies have shown that respondents' LPC scores aren't stable over time.[5] In addition, it's probably unrealistic to assume that a person can't change his or her leadership style to fit the situation. Effective leaders can, and do, change their styles to meet the needs of a particular situation. Finally, the contingency variables were complex and difficult for practitioners to assess. It was often difficult in practice to determine how good the leader-member relations were, how structured the task was, and how much position power the leader had.[6] Despite its shortcomings, the Fiedler model provided evidence that effective leadership style and situation could be determined.

TESTING...
TESTING...
1 2 3

1 Explain how someone can be a manager but not a leader, a leader but not a manager, and both a manager and a leader.

2 What are the situational factors in Fiedler's contingency model?

3 According to Fiedler's model, (a) when are task-oriented leaders more effective, and (b) when are relationship-oriented leaders more effective?

Path-Goal Theory

path-goal theory

The theory that a leader's behavior is acceptable to subordinates insofar as they view it as a source of either immediate or future satisfaction.

Currently, one of the most respected approaches to understanding leadership is **path-goal theory**. Developed by Robert House, path-goal theory is a contingency model of leadership that extracts key elements from the expectancy theory of motivation.[7] The essence of the theory is that it's the leader's job to assist his or her followers in attaining their goals and to provide the direction or support needed to ensure that their goals are compatible with the overall objectives of the group or organization. The term *path-goal* is derived from the belief that effective leaders clarify the path to help their followers get from where they are to the achievement of their work goals and make the journey along the path easier by reducing roadblocks and pitfalls.

According to path-goal theory, a leader's behavior is *acceptable* to subordinates to the degree that they view it as an immediate source of satisfaction or as a means of future satisfaction. A leader's behavior is *motivational* to the extent that it (1) makes the satisfaction of subordinates' needs contingent on effective performance and (2) provides the coaching, guidance, support, and rewards that are necessary for effective performance. To test these statements, House identified four leadership behaviors:

- *Directive leader:* lets subordinates know what's expected of them, schedules work to be done, and gives specific guidance as to how to accomplish tasks

- *Supportive leader:* is friendly and shows concern for the needs of subordinates

- *Participative leader:* consults with subordinates and uses their suggestions before making a decision

- *Achievement-oriented leader:* sets challenging goals and expects subordinates to perform at their highest level

In contrast to Fiedler's view of a leader's behavior, House assumes that leaders are flexible. Path-goal theory implies that the same leader can display any or all of these leadership styles depending on the situation.

As Figure 16-3 illustrates, path-goal theory proposes two classes of situational or contingency variables that moderate the leadership behavior–outcome relationship: those in the *environment* that are outside the control of the subordinate (factors including task

FIGURE 16-3   Path-Goal Theory

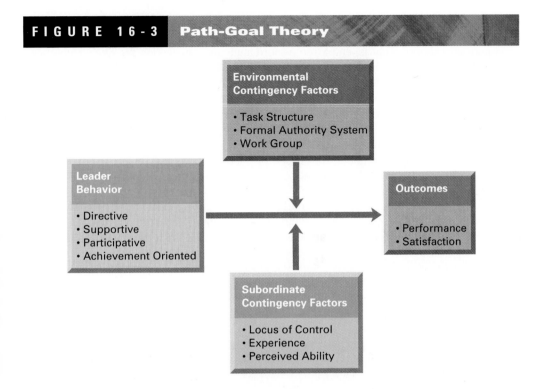

structure, the formal authority system, and the work group) and those that are part of the personal characteristics of the *subordinate* (locus of control, experience, and perceived ability). Environmental factors determine the type of leader behavior required if subordinate outcomes are to be maximized; personal characteristics of the subordinate determine how the environment and leader behavior are interpreted. The theory proposes that leader behavior will be ineffective when it's redundant with sources of environmental structure or incongruent with subordinate characteristics.

The following are some examples of hypotheses that have evolved out of path-goal theory:

■ Directive leadership leads to greater satisfaction when tasks are ambiguous or stressful than when they are highly structured and well laid out.

■ Supportive leadership results in high employee performance and satisfaction when subordinates are performing structured tasks.

■ Directive leadership is likely to be perceived as redundant among subordinates with high perceived ability or with considerable experience.

■ The clearer and more bureaucratic the formal authority relationships, the more leaders should exhibit supportive behavior and deemphasize directive behavior.

■ Directive leadership will lead to higher employee satisfaction when there is substantive conflict within a work group.

■ Subordinates with an internal locus of control (those who believe they control their own destiny) will be more satisfied with a participative style.

■ Subordinates with an external locus of control will be more satisfied with a directive style.

■ Achievement-oriented leadership will increase subordinates' expectancies that effort will lead to high performance when tasks are ambiguously structured.

Research to validate hypotheses such as these is generally encouraging. Although not every study has found positive support,[8] the majority of the evidence supports the logic underlying path-goal theory. That is, employee performance and satisfaction are likely to be positively influenced when the leader compensates for shortcomings in either the employee or the work setting. However, if the leader spends time explaining tasks when those tasks are already clear or when the employee has the ability and experience to handle them without interference, the employee is likely to see such directive behavior as redundant or even insulting.

Leader Participation Model

leader participation model

A leadership theory that provides a set of rules to determine the form and amount of participative decision making in different situations.

Another early contingency model, developed by Victor Vroom and Phillip Yetton, was the **leader participation model**, which related leadership behavior and participation to decision making.[9] Developed in the early 1970s, the model argues that leader behavior must adjust to reflect the task structure—whether it was routine, nonroutine, or anywhere in between. Vroom and Yetton's model is what we call a *normative* one, because it provided a sequential set of rules (norms) that the leader should follow in determining the form and amount of participation in decision making, as determined by the different types of situations. The model was set up as a decision tree incorporating seven contingencies about task structure (whose relevance could be identified by making "yes" or "no" choices) and five alternative leadership styles. These leadership styles are described in Table 16-1.

TABLE 16-1	**Possible Leadership Styles in the Vroom-Yetton Leader Participation Model**
Autocratic I (AI):	You solve the problem or make a decision yourself using information available to you at that time.
Autocratic II (AII):	You obtain the necessary information from subordinates and then decide on the solution to the problem yourself. You may or may not tell subordinates what the problem is in getting information from them. The role of your subordinates in making the decision is clearly one of providing the necessary information to you rather than generating or evaluating alternative solutions.
Consultative I (CI):	You share the problem with relevant subordinates individually, getting their ideas and suggestions without bringing them together as a group. Then you make the decision, which may or may not reflect your subordinates' influence.
Consultative II (CII):	You share the problem with your subordinates as a group, collectively obtaining their ideas and suggestions. Then you make the decision, which may or may not reflect your subordinates' influence.
Group II (GII):	You share the problem with your subordinates as a group. Together you generate and evaluate alternatives and attempt to reach an agreement (consensus) on a solution.

Source: V.H. Vroom and P.W. Yetton, *Leadership and Decision-Making* (Pittsburgh: University of Pittsburgh Press, 1973).

Vroom and Arthur Jago have since revised the model.[10] The new model retains the same five alternative leadership styles but expands the contingency variables to 12, including factors such as importance of technical quality of the decision, importance of subordinate commitment to the decision, level of leader information about the decision, and likelihood of subordinate conflict over preferred solutions. Vroom and Jago have developed a computer program that cuts through the complexity of the new model. But managers can still use decision trees to select their leadership style, assuming that there are no shades of gray (that is, when the status of a variable is a clear-cut "yes" or "no"), that there are no critically severe time constraints, and that subordinates are not geographically dispersed. Figure 16-4 illustrates one of these decision trees.

Research testing the original leader participation model was very encouraging.[11] But the revised model, which is a direct extension of the early version, is also consistent with

---

FIGURE 16-4 | *The Revised Leader Participation Model*

(time-driven decision tree—group problems)

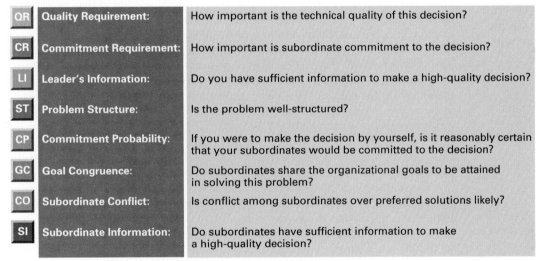

QR	**Quality Requirement:**	How important is the technical quality of this decision?
CR	**Commitment Requirement:**	How important is subordinate commitment to the decision?
LI	**Leader's Information:**	Do you have sufficient information to make a high-quality decision?
ST	**Problem Structure:**	Is the problem well-structured?
CP	**Commitment Probability:**	If you were to make the decision by yourself, is it reasonably certain that your subordinates would be committed to the decision?
GC	**Goal Congruence:**	Do subordinates share the organizational goals to be attained in solving this problem?
CO	**Subordinate Conflict:**	Is conflict among subordinates over preferred solutions likely?
SI	**Subordinate Information:**	Do subordinates have sufficient information to make a high-quality decision?

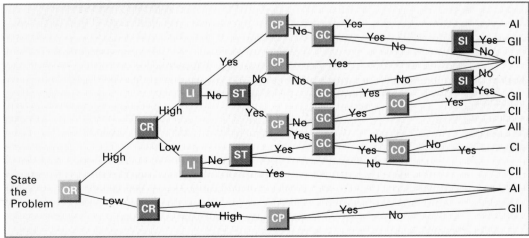

Source: V.H. Vroom and A.G. Jago, *The New Leadership: Managing Participation in Organizations* (Upper Saddle River, NJ: Prentice Hall, 1988), p. 184. With permission.

our current knowledge on the benefits and costs of participation. So, at this time, we have every reason to believe that the revised model provides an excellent guide to help managers choose the most appropriate leadership style in different situations.

TESTING... TESTING... 1 2 3

4 Explain the meaning of *path* and *goal* to the path-goal theory.

5 How does path-goal theory explain leadership?

6 Describe the leader participation model.

Attribution Theory of Leadership

attribution theory of leadership

Proposes that leadership is merely an attribution that people make about other individuals.

In chapter 13, we discussed attribution theory in relation to perception. Attribution theory has also been used to help explain the perception of leadership. Attribution theory, as you remember, deals with trying to make sense out of cause-effect relationships. When an event happens, people want to attribute it to a certain cause. The **attribution theory of leadership** says that leadership is merely an attribution that people make about other individuals.[12] Using the attribution framework, researchers have found that people tend to characterize leaders as having traits such as intelligence, outgoing personality, strong verbal skills, aggressiveness, understanding, and industriousness.[13] Similarly, the high-high leader (that is, *high* in initiating structure and *high* in consideration) has been found to be consistent with people's attributions of what makes a good leader.[14] Regardless of the situation, a high-high leadership style tends to be perceived as best. At the organizational level, the attribution framework explains why people are prone to attribute either the extremely negative or the extremely positive performance of an organization to its leadership.[15] It also helps explain the vulnerability of CEOs when their organizations suffer major financial setbacks, regardless of whether they had much to do with it. It also clarifies why these CEOs tend to be given credit for extremely positive financial results, again regardless of how much or how little they contributed.

One of the more interesting themes in the attribution theory of leadership literature is the perception that effective leaders are generally considered to be consistent or unwavering in their decisions. One explanation of why Lee Iacocca (former CEO of Chrysler) and Michael Dell (founder and CEO of Dell Computer) were perceived as leaders was that they were fully committed, steadfast, and consistent in the decisions they made and the goals they set. Evidence indicates that a "heroic" leader is perceived as being someone who takes up a difficult or unpopular cause but, through determination and persistence, ultimately succeeds.[16]

Charismatic Leadership Theory

charismatic leadership

Followers make attributions of heroic or extraordinary leadership abilities when they observe certain behaviors.

Charismatic leadership theory is an extension of attribution theory. It says that followers make attributions of heroic or extraordinary leadership abilities when they observe certain behaviors.[17] Studies of charismatic leadership have, for the most part, been directed at identifying those behaviors that differentiate charismatic leaders from their noncharismatic counterparts.

Several authors have attempted to identify personal characteristics of the charismatic leader. Robert House (of path-goal theory fame) has identified three: extremely high confidence, dominance, and strong convictions in his or her beliefs.[18] Warren Bennis, after studying 90 of the most effective and successful leaders in the United States, found that they had four common competencies: They had a compelling vision or sense of purpose; they could communicate that vision in clear terms that their followers could readily identify with; they demonstrated consistency and focus in the pursuit of their vision; and they knew their own strengths and capitalized on them.[19] The most comprehensive analysis, however, was completed by Jay Conger and Rabindra Kanungo at McGill University.[20] Among their conclusions, they proposed that charismatic leaders have an idealized goal they want to achieve and a strong personal commitment to that goal, are perceived as unconventional, are assertive and self-confident, and are perceived as agents of radical change rather than managers of the status quo. Table 16-2 summarizes the key characteristics that appear to differentiate charismatic leaders from noncharismatic ones.

What can we say about the charismatic leader's effect on his or her followers? There's an increasing body of research that shows impressive correlations between charismatic leadership and high performance and satisfaction among followers.[21] People working for charismatic leaders are motivated to exert extra work effort and, because they like their leader, express greater satisfaction.

If charisma is desirable, can people learn to be charismatic leaders? Or are charismatic leaders born with their qualities? Although a small number of experts still think that charisma can't be learned, most believe that individuals can be trained to exhibit charismatic behaviors.[22] For example, researchers have succeeded in scripting undergraduate business students to "be" charismatic.[23] The students were taught to articulate an overarching goal, communicate high performance expectations, exhibit confidence in the ability of subordinates to meet those expectations, and empathize with the needs of their subordinates; they learned to project a powerful, confident, and dynamic presence; and they practiced using a captivating and engaging voice tone. To further capture the dynamics and energy of charisma, the researchers trained the leaders to use charismatic nonverbal behaviors. The leaders alternated between pacing and sitting on the edge of

---

TABLE 16-2   Key Characteristics of Charismatic Leaders

1. *Self-confidence.* Charismatic leaders have complete confidence in their judgment and ability.

2. *Vision.* They have an idealized goal that proposes a future better than the status quo. The greater the disparity between this idealized goal and the status quo, the more likely that followers will attribute extraordinary vision to the leader.

3. *Ability to articulate the vision.* They are able to clarify and state the vision in terms that are understandable to others. This articulation demonstrates an understanding of the followers' needs and, hence, acts as a motivating force.

4. *Strong convictions about the vision.* Charismatic leaders are perceived as being strongly committed and willing to take on high personal risk, incur high costs, and engage in self-sacrifice to achieve their vision.

5. *Behavior that is out of the ordinary.* They engage in behavior that is perceived as being novel, unconventional, and counter to norms. When successful, these behaviors evoke surprise and admiration in followers.

6. *Appearance as a change agent.* Charismatic leaders are perceived as agents of radical change rather than as caretakers of the status quo.

7. *Environment sensitivity.* They are able to make realistic assessments of the environmental constraints and resources needed to bring about change.

Source: Based on J.A. Conger and R.N. Kanungo, "Behavioral Dimensions of Charismatic Leadership," in Conger, Kanungo, et al., *Charismatic Leadership* (San Francisco: Jossey-Bass, 1988), p. 91.

Orit Gadiesh is chairwoman of the consulting firm Bain & Co. One of her clients describes her particular charisma: She "makes you feel you're the most important person in the room."

their desk, leaned toward the subordinate, maintained direct eye contact, and had a relaxed posture and animated facial expressions. These students learned how to project charisma. Moreover, their subordinates had higher task performance, higher task adjustment, and better adjustment to the leader and to the group than did subordinates who worked in groups led by noncharismatic leaders.

One last point on this topic: Charismatic leadership may not always be needed to achieve high levels of employee performance. It may be most appropriate when the follower's task has an ideological component.[24] This may explain why charismatic leaders are most likely to surface in politics, religion, or a business firm that's introducing a radically new product or facing a life-threatening crisis. For instance, Franklin D. Roosevelt offered a vision to lead the country out of the Great Depression; Martin Luther King Jr. was unyielding in his desire to bring about social equality through peaceful means; and Steve Jobs achieved unwavering loyalty and commitment from the technical staff he oversaw at Apple Computer during the late 1970s and early 1980s by articulating a vision of personal computers that would dramatically change the way people lived. Charismatic leaders, in fact, may become a liability to an organization once a crisis and need for dramatic change subside.[25] Why? Because the charismatic leader's overwhelming self-confidence often becomes a problem. He or she is unable to listen to others, becomes uncomfortable when challenged by aggressive subordinates, and begins to hold an unjustifiable belief in his or her "rightness" on issues.

Visionary Leadership

visionary leadership

The ability to create and articulate a realistic, credible, attractive vision of the future for an organization or organizational unit that grows out of and improves upon the present.

Although the term *vision* is often linked with charismatic leadership, **visionary leadership** goes beyond charisma since it's the ability to create and articulate a realistic, credible, and attractive vision of the future for an organization or organizational unit that grows out of and improves upon the present situation.[26] This vision, if properly selected and implemented, is so energizing that it "in effect jump-starts the future by calling forth the skills, talents, and resources to make it happen."[27]

A review of various definitions finds that *a vision* differs from other forms of organizational direction (such as *mission* or *purpose*) in several ways. "A vision has clear and compelling imagery that offers an innovative way to improve, which recognizes and draws on traditions, and connects to actions that people can take to realize change. Vision taps people's emotions and energy. Properly articulated, a vision creates the enthusiasm that people have for sporting events and other leisure time activities, bringing the energy and commitment to the workplace."[28]

Many writers have made the case for visionary leadership. For instance, one said, "The twenty-first-century organization virtually demands visionary leadership. It cannot function without it, for an organization driven by accelerating technological change, staffed by a diverse, multicultural mix of highly intelligent knowledge workers, facing global complexity, a vast kaleidoscope of individual customer needs, and the incessant demands of multiple constituencies would simply self-destruct without a common sense of direction."[29] Another argues that vision is "the glue that binds individuals into a group with a common goal. . . . When shared by employees, [it] can keep an entire company moving forward in face of difficulties, enabling and inspiring leaders and employees alike."[30]

A survey of 1,500 senior leaders from 20 countries attests to the growing importance of visionary leadership.[31] These leaders were asked to describe the key traits or talents desirable for a CEO in the year 2000. The dominant characteristic most frequently mentioned (by 98 percent of the respondents) was the ability to convey a "strong sense of vision." Another study contrasted 18 visionary companies with 18 comparable nonvisionary firms over a 65-year period.[32] The visionary companies were found to have outperformed the comparison group by six times on standard financial criteria, and their stocks outperformed the general market by 15 times.

The key properties of a vision seem to be inspirational possibilities that are value centered, are realizable, have superior imagery, and are well articulated.[33] Visions should be able to generate possibilities that are inspirational and unique and that offer a new way of doing things and will lead to organizational distinction. A vision is likely to fail if it does not offer a view of the future that is clearly and demonstrably better for the organization and its members. Desirable visions fit the times and circumstances and reflect the uniqueness of the organization. People in the organization must also believe that the vision is attainable. The vision should be perceived as challenging yet doable. Visions that are clearly articulated and have powerful imagery are easily grasped and accepted. For example, Bill Gates's simple vision for Microsoft of "a computer on every desktop and in every home" is clear and

Visionary leadership describes the skills of Bob Wright, longtime CEO of NBC, who is credited with transforming the firm into the star of the TV business. Some of Wright's turnaround strategies were counter to what critics advised, yet they proved to be successful.

easy to visualize. And Scandinavian Airlines CEO, Jan Carlzon, used the phrase "50,000 daily moments of truth" to depict the emphasis employees were to place on customer service. Carlzon wanted every employee to ensure that each and every "moment of truth"—those moments when customers came into contact with employees—would be positive experiences.

What skills do visionary leaders exhibit? Once the vision is identified, these leaders appear to have three qualities that are related to effectiveness in their visionary roles.[34] First is *the ability to explain the vision to others.* The leader needs to make the vision clear in terms of required goals and actions through clear oral and written communication. Even the best vision is not likely to be effective if the leader isn't a strong communicator. The second skill needed is *the ability to express the vision not just verbally but through behavior.* This skill requires behaving in ways that continually convey and reinforce the vision. For example, Herb Kelleher, CEO of Southwest Airlines, lives and breathes his commitment to customer service. He's famous within the company for his boundless energy and for jumping in, when needed, to help check in passengers, load baggage, fill in for flight attendants or do anything else to make the customers' experiences more pleasant. The third skill visionary leaders need is *the ability to extend or apply the vision to different leadership contexts.* For instance, the vision has to be as meaningful to the people in accounting as to those in production, to employees in Cleveland as to those in Prague. Think back to our chapter-opening dilemma as Philip Berry attempted to involve and empower employees in Central Europe and the role that visionary leadership might play.

TESTING... TESTING...

1 2 3

7 What is the attribution theory of leadership?

8 Describe characteristics of charismatic leaders.

9 How is visionary leadership different from charismatic leadership?

Team Leadership

Leadership is increasingly taking place within a team context. As the usage of teams grows in popularity, the role of the leader in guiding team members becomes increasingly important.[35] The role of team leader *is* different from the traditional leadership role performed by first-line supervisors, as J. D. Bryant, a supervisor at Texas Instruments' Forest Lane plant in Dallas, discovered.[36] One day he was happily overseeing a staff of 15 circuitboard assemblers. The next day he was informed that the company was moving to the use of employee teams and he was to become a "facilitator." He said, "I'm supposed to teach the teams everything I know and then let them make their own decisions." But, confused about his new role, he admitted, "There was no clear plan on what I was supposed to do." What is involved in being a team leader?

Many leaders are not equipped to handle the change to employee teams. As one consultant noted, "Even the most capable managers have trouble making the transition because all the command-and-control type things they were encouraged to do before are no longer appropriate. There's no reason to have any skill or sense of this."[37] This same consultant estimated that "probably 15 percent of managers are natural team leaders; another 15 percent could never lead a team because it runs counter to their personality. [That is, they're unable to sublimate their dominating style for the good of the team.] Then there's that huge group in the middle: Team leadership doesn't come naturally to them, but they can learn it."[38]

The challenge for most managers is learning how to become an effective team leader. They have to learn skills such as having the patience to share information, being able to trust others and to give up authority, and understanding when to intervene. Effective lead-

According to Chicago Bulls coach Phil Jackson, conferring here with Michael Jordan, *not* fighting is sometimes the way to win. Jackson's ability to support the Bulls with such unusual insights on the battlefield of pro basketball is the key to his successful team leadership.

ers have mastered the difficult balancing act of knowing when to leave their teams alone and when to get involved. New team leaders may try to retain too much control at a time when team members need more autonomy, or they may abandon their teams at times when the teams need support and help.[39]

One study of organizations that had reorganized themselves around employee teams found certain common responsibilities that all leaders had to assume. These included coaching, facilitating, handling disciplinary problems, reviewing team and individual performance, training, and communication.[40] You would probably agree that many of these responsibilities apply to managers' jobs in general. However, a more meaningful way to describe the team leader's job is to focus on two priorities: (1) managing the team's external boundary and (2) facilitating the team process.[41] These priorities can be broken down into four specific leadership roles.

First, team leaders are *liaisons with external constituencies*. These may include upper management, other internal teams, customers, or suppliers. The leader represents the team to other constituencies, secures needed resources, clarifies others' expectations of the team, gathers information from the outside, and shares that information with team members.

Next, team leaders are *troubleshooters*. When the team has problems and asks for assistance, team leaders sit in on meetings and try to help resolve the problems. Troubleshooting rarely involves technical or operational issues because the team members typically know more about the tasks being done than does the team leader. The leader is most likely to contribute by asking penetrating questions, helping the team talk through problems, and getting needed resources from external constituencies.

Third, team leaders are *conflict managers*. When disagreements arise, they help process the conflict. They help identify issues such as the source of the conflict, who's involved, the issues, the resolution options available, and the advantages and disadvantages of each. By getting team members to address questions such as these, the leader minimizes the disruptive aspects of intrateam conflicts.

Finally, team leaders are *coaches*. They clarify expectations and roles, teach, offer support, cheerlead, and do whatever else is necessary to help team members keep their work performance levels high.

Transactional versus Transformational Leadership

The final branch of research we'll touch on is the difference between transformational leaders and transactional leaders.[42] As you'll see, because transformational leaders are also charismatic, there is some overlap between this topic and our previous discussion of charismatic leadership.

Most of the leadership theories presented in this chapter—for instance, Fiedler's model, path-goal theory, and the leader participation model—have been addressing **transactional leaders**. These leaders guide or motivate their followers in the direction of established goals by clarifying role and task requirements. But there's another type of leader who inspires followers to transcend their own self-interests for the good of the organization and is capable of having a profound and extraordinary effect on his or her followers. These are **transformational leaders**, and examples include Leslie Wexner of The Limited retail chain and Jack Welch of General Electric. They pay attention to the concerns and developmental needs of individual followers; they change followers' awareness of issues by helping those followers to look at old problems in new ways; and they are able to excite, arouse, and inspire followers to put out extra effort to achieve group goals.

Transactional and transformational leadership shouldn't be viewed as opposing approaches to getting things done.[43] Transformational leadership is built on top of transactional leadership. Transformational leadership produces levels of subordinate effort and performance that go beyond what would occur with a transactional approach alone. Moreover, transformational leadership is more than charisma. "The purely charismatic (leader) may want followers to adopt the charismatic's world view and go no further; the transformational leader will attempt to instill in followers the ability to question not only established views but eventually those established by the leader."[44]

The evidence supporting the superiority of transformational leadership over the transactional variety is overwhelmingly impressive. For instance, a number of studies of U.S., Canadian, and German military officers found, at every level, that transformational leaders were evaluated as being more effective than their transactional counterparts.[45] And managers at Federal Express who were rated by their followers as exhibiting more transformational leadership were evaluated by their immediate supervisors as higher performers and more promotable.[46] In summary, the overall evidence indicates that transformational, as compared with transactional, leadership is more strongly correlated with lower turnover rates, higher productivity, and higher employee satisfaction.[47]

transactional leaders

Leaders who guide or motivate their followers in the direction of established goals by clarifying role and task requirements.

transformational leaders

Leaders who provide individualized consideration, intellectual stimulation, and possess charisma.

TESTING...
TESTING...
1 2 3

10 How is the role of team leader different from the traditional leadership role performed by first-line supervisors?

11 Describe the four specific leadership roles that team leaders play.

12 What are the differences between transactional and transformational leaders?

CONTEMPORARY ISSUES IN LEADERSHIP

As you can tell from the preceding discussion on the various theories and models of leadership, the concept of "effective leadership" is continually being refined as researchers continue to study leadership in organizations and discover more about it. Let's take a closer look at some of the contemporary issues affecting leadership.

Leaders and Power

We alluded to the concept of power in chapter 10 when we discussed authority relationships in the organizational structure. **Power** is the capacity of a leader to influence work actions or decisions. Because leadership is about the process of influence, we need to look at how leaders acquire power. John French and Bertram Raven identified five sources of power: legitimate, coercive, reward, expert, and referent.[48]

Legitimate power and authority are one and the same. Legitimate power represents the power a person has as a result of his or her position in the formal organizational hierarchy. Positions of authority also are likely to have reward and coercive power, but legitimate power is broader than the power to coerce and reward. Specifically, it includes acceptance by members of an organization of the authority of a position. When school principals, bank presidents, or army captains speak (assuming that their directives are viewed to be within the authority of their positions), teachers, tellers, and first lieutenants listen and usually comply.

Coercive power is defined by French and Raven as being dependent on fear. You react to this power out of fear of the negative results that might occur if you did not comply. It rests on the application, or the threat of application, of physical sanctions such as the infliction of pain; the arousal of frustration through restriction of movement; or the controlling by force of basic physiological or safety needs. If you're a manager, typically you have some coercive power. You may be able to suspend or demote employees. You may be able to assign them work activities they find unpleasant. You may even have the option of dismissing employees. These all represent coercive actions. But you don't have to be a manager to hold coercive power. For instance, a subordinate who is in a position to embarrass his or her boss in public and who successfully uses that power to gain advantage is using coercion.

power

The capacity of a leader to influence work actions or decisions.

legitimate power

The power a person has as a result of his or her position in the formal organizational hierarchy; also called authority.

coercive power

Power that rests on the application, or the threat of application, of physical sanctions such as the infliction of pain; the arousal of frustration through restriction of movement; or the controlling by force of basic physiological or safety needs.

"We had some of the smartest scientists in the world," says CEO Mary Ann Byrnes of the engineering staff of Corsair Communications, Inc. "My job was to make them productive, to help them perfect in a short time what they had not been able to deliver before." Reward power was the basis of this MBA's influence over her scientist employees. She devoted most of her first two years with the firm to creating a new corporate culture in which a sense of community and personal commitment predominates.

reward power

Power that produces positive benefits or rewards.

expert power

Influence that results from expertise, special skill, or knowledge.

referent power

Power that arises from identification with a person who has desirable resources or personal traits.

The opposite of coercive power is **reward power**. People comply with the wishes or directives of another because it produces positive benefits; therefore, one who can distribute rewards that others view as valuable will have power over them. These rewards can be anything that another person values. In an organizational context, we think of money, favorable performance appraisals, promotions, interesting work assignments, friendly colleagues, and preferred work shifts or sales territories.

Coercive and reward power are actually counterparts of each other. If you can remove something of positive value from another or inflict something of negative value upon him or her, you have coercive power over that person. If you can give someone something of positive value or remove something of negative value, you have reward power over that person. Again, as with coercive power, you don't need to be a manager to be able to exert influence through rewards. Rewards such as friendliness, acceptance, and praise are available to everyone in the organization. To the degree that an individual seeks such rewards, your ability to give or withhold them gives you power over that individual.

Expert power is influence wielded by dint of expertise, special skill, or knowledge. In recent years, as a result of the explosion in technical knowledge, expert power has become an increasingly potent power source in organizations. As jobs have become more specialized, managers have become increasingly dependent on staff "experts" to achieve the organization's goals. As an employee increases his or her knowledge of information that is critical to the operation of a work group, and to the degree that this knowledge isn't possessed by others, expert power is enhanced. To illustrate this point, if a computer system is critical to a unit's work, and if one employee, say Chris, knows how to repair it and no one else in the office does, then the unit is dependent on Chris. If the system breaks down, Chris can use her expertise to obtain ends that she could never achieve through her position's authority alone. In such a situation, you should expect the unit's manager to try to have others trained in the workings of the computer system or to hire someone with this knowledge in order to reduce Chris's power. As others become capable of duplicating Chris's specialized activities, her expert power diminishes.

The last category of influence that French and Raven identified was **referent power**. It refers to a person who has power because of desirable resources or personal traits. If I admire and identify with you, you can exercise power over me because I want to please you. Referent power develops out of admiration of another and a desire to be like that person. You might consider the person you identify with as having what we discussed earlier, *charisma*. If you admire someone to the point of modeling your behavior and attitudes after him or her, that person possesses referent power over you. In organizations, the charismatic individual—manager or otherwise—can influence superiors, peers, and subordinates.

As we mentioned at the beginning of this section, leadership is about the power—process of influence—that leaders have over their followers and how they use that power to affect the behavior and performance of their followers. Most effective leaders rely on several different bases of power. For instance, a manager may need to use both legitimate power and referent power to influence subordinates to accept a planned organizational change. For example, Olin Pool Products, a division of Olin Chemicals, which makes chemicals used in swimming pools, went through a disastrous fire at one of its production facilities at the same time that it was going through a major organizational restructuring. Doug Cahill, the general manager, had to address employees' uncertainties over "what happens now." Cahill used both his authority and his charisma to lead his employees through this trying time.[49]

Creating a Culture of Trust

An important consideration for leaders is building credibility and trust. Followers want leaders who are credible and whom they can trust. But what do the terms *credibility* and *trust* mean?

The most dominant component of credibility is honesty. Surveys have found that honesty is consistently singled out as the number one characteristic of admired leaders.

Your boss is not satisfied with the way one of your colleagues is handling a project and she reassigns the project to you. She tells you to work with this person to find out what he has done already and to discuss any other necessary information that he might have. She wants your project report by the end of the month. This person is pretty upset and angry over the reassignment and won't give you the information you need to even start, much less complete, the project. You won't be able to meet your deadline unless you get this information.

What type of power does your colleague appear to be using? What type of influence could you possibly use to gain his cooperation? If you were involved in this situation, what could you do to resolve it successfully, yet ethically? ■

"Honesty is absolutely essential to leadership. If people are going to follow someone willingly, whether it be into battle or into the boardroom, they first want to assure themselves that the person is worthy of their trust." In addition to being honest, credible leaders have been found to be competent and inspiring.[50] They are personally able to communicate effectively their confidence and enthusiasm. Thus, followers judge a leader's **credibility** in terms of his or her honesty, competence, and ability to inspire.

Trust is closely entwined with the concept of credibility, and, in fact, the terms are often used interchangeably. **Trust** is defined as the belief in the integrity, character, and ability of a leader. Followers who trust a leader are willing to be vulnerable to the leader's actions because they are confident that their rights and interests will not be abused.[51] Research has identified five dimensions that make up the concept of trust:[52]

- *Integrity:* honesty and truthfulness
- *Competence:* technical and interpersonal knowledge and skills
- *Consistency:* reliability, predictability, and good judgment in handling situations
- *Loyalty:* willingness to protect and save face for a person
- *Openness:* willingness to share ideas and information freely

credibility

The degree to which followers perceive someone as honest, competent, and able to inspire.

trust

The belief in the integrity, character, and ability of a leader.

Consistent with the work on credibility, integrity and competence are the most critical characteristics that an individual looks for in determining another's trustworthiness. Integrity seems to be rated highest because "without a perception of the other's 'moral' character and 'basic honesty,' other dimensions of trust [are] meaningless."[53] The top rating of honesty as an identifying characteristic of admired leaders indicates the importance of credibility and trust to leadership effectiveness. Although these qualities have probably always been important, changes in the workplace have redirected the focus of leaders toward building trust.

The trend toward empowering individuals and creating self-managed work teams has reduced or removed many of the traditional control mechanisms used to monitor employees. For instance, if an employee work team is free to schedule its own work, evaluate its own performance, and even make its own hiring decisions, trust becomes critical. Employees have to trust managers to treat them fairly, and managers have to trust workers to conscientiously fulfill their responsibilities. And the trend toward expanding nonauthority relationships within and between organizations widens the need for interpersonal trust. Leaders have to increasingly lead others who may not be in their direct line of authority—members of cross-functional teams, individuals who work for suppliers or customers, and perhaps even people who represent other organizations through strategic alliances. These situations do not allow leaders the luxury of falling back on their formal positions for influence power. Many of these relationships, in fact, are fluid and fleeting. So the ability to quickly develop trust may be crucial to the success of the relationship. How crucial? One study of managers divided into high- and low-credibility groups based on scores on a credibility questionnaire found that employees who perceived their manager as having high credibility felt significantly more positive about and attached to their work and organizations than did those employees who perceived their managers as low in credibility.[54] In another study, individuals who reported that their manager was honest, competent, and inspiring were significantly more likely to feel a strong sense of teamwork and commitment to their organization than were those who reported their managers as not honest, competent, or inspiring.

Given the importance of trust to leadership, how should leaders seek to build trust? Here are some suggestions.[55]

- *Practice openness.* Mistrust comes as much from what people do not know as from what they do know. Openness leads to confidence and trust. Keep people informed, make the criteria on how decisions are made overtly clear, explain the rationale for your decisions, be candid about problems, and fully disclose relevant information.

- *Be fair.* Before making decisions or taking actions, consider how others will perceive them in terms of objectivity and fairness. Give credit where credit is due, be objective and impartial in performance appraisals, and pay attention to equity perceptions in reward distributions.

- *Speak your feelings.* Leaders who convey only hard facts come across as cold, distant, and uncaring. If you share your feelings, others will see you as real and human. They will know who you are, and their respect for you will increase.

- *Tell the truth.* If honesty is critical to credibility, you must be perceived as someone who tells the truth. People are generally more tolerant of learning something negative than of finding out that their leader lied to them.

- *Show consistency.* People want predictability. Mistrust comes from not knowing what to expect. Take the time to think about your values and beliefs. Then let them consistently guide your decisions and actions.

- *Fulfill your promises.* Trust requires that people believe you are dependable. Keep your word. Promises made must be promises kept.

- *Maintain confidences.* You trust people who are discreet and upon whom you can rely. If people make themselves vulnerable by telling you something in confidence, they need to feel assured that you will not discuss it with others or betray that confidence.

- *Demonstrate competence.* Develop the admiration and respect of others by demonstrating technical and professional ability. Pay particular attention to developing and practicing effective communication, negotiation, and other interpersonal skills.

TESTING...
TESTING...

13 What are the various sources of power that a leader might use?

14 Why is a culture of trust so important in the workplace?

15 How can leaders build trust?

Leading through Empowerment

As we've described in different sections throughout the text, managers are increasingly leading by empowering their employees. Millions of individual employees and teams of employees are making the key operating decisions that directly affect their work. They're

Empowerment takes on special meaning in the Staples, Inc. division managed by Jane Biering in Massachusetts. At regular staff meetings that include employees at all levels, Biering encourages people to "sound off" about ways to increase their sense of ownership. A sign outside her door reads, "Let the people who are closest to the work improve the way things work."

developing budgets, scheduling workloads, controlling inventories, solving quality problems, and engaging in similar activities that until very recently were viewed exclusively as part of the manager's job.[56]

The increased use of empowerment is being driven by two forces. First is the need for quick decisions by those people who are most knowledgeable about the issues. That requires moving decisions to lower levels. If organizations are to successfully compete in a dynamic global economy, they have to be able to make decisions and implement changes quickly. Second is the reality that the downsizing of organizations during the last two decades left many managers with considerably larger spans of control than they had had earlier. In order to cope with the demands of an increased load, managers had to empower their people.

Is the empowerment movement inconsistent with the contingency perspective on leadership? Yes and no! Empowerment is being touted, in some circles, as a universal panacea. This universal perspective—that is, that empowerment will work anywhere—is an anticontingency approach to leadership. On the other hand, when a workforce has the knowledge, skills, and experience to do their jobs competently and when employees seek autonomy and possess an internal locus of control, empowering people through delegation and participation would be consistent with contingency theories such as situational leadership and path-goal. For instance, it's not a coincidence that empowerment efforts are almost always coupled with extensive training. By giving employees enhanced skills, abilities, and confidence, management increases the likelihood that empowerment will succeed.

Gender and Leadership

There was a time when the question Do males and females lead differently? could be accurately characterized as a purely academic issue—interesting but not very relevant. That time has certainly passed! Millions of women are now in management positions. Millions more will continue to join the management ranks. Misconceptions about the leadership-gender relation can adversely affect hiring, performance evaluation, promotion, and other human resource decisions for both men and women. So this topic needs to be addressed. First, however, a warning: This topic tends to raise controversy.[57] If male and female styles differ, is one inferior? Moreover, if there is a difference, does labeling leadership styles by gender encourage stereotyping? These questions cannot be easily dismissed, and they should be considered. We'll come back to them later in this section.

MANAGING WORKFORCE DIVERSITY

The Communication Styles of Men and Women

"You don't understand what I'm saying and you never listen!" "You're making a big deal out of nothing." Have you ever heard these statements uttered (usually in emotionally charged voices) by friends of the opposite sex? Most of us probably have! Research shows us that men and women tend to have different styles when it comes to communicating. And these different styles can lead to significant misunderstandings and misperceptions.[58] Let's look more closely at the communication styles of men and women and the problems that can arise because of these varying styles and try to suggest some ways to minimize the barriers that spring up.

Deborah Tannen has studied the ways that men and women communicate and has found some interesting differences. The essence of her research is that men use talk to emphasize status, whereas women use it to create connection. She states that communication between the sexes can be a continual balancing act of trying to juggle our conflicting needs for intimacy and independence. Intimacy suggests closeness and commonalities; independence emphasizes separateness and differences. So how do communication problems arise? Women speak and hear a language of connection and intimacy. Men hear and speak a language of status and independence. For many men, conversations are merely a mechanism to preserve independence and maintain status in a hierarchical social order. Yet, for many women, conversations are negotiations for closeness in which people try to seek and give confirmation and support. Let's look at a few examples of what Tannen is suggesting.

Men frequently complain that women talk on and on about their problems. Women criticize men for not listening. What's happening is that when a man hears a woman talking about a problem, he frequently asserts his desire for independence and control by providing solutions. Many women, on the other hand, view conversing about a problem as a means to promote closeness. The woman presents the problem to gain support and connection, not to get the male's advice.

Here's another example. Men are often more direct than women in conversation. A man might say, "I think you're wrong on that point." A woman might say, "Have you looked at the marketing department's research report on that point?" The implication in the woman's comment is that the report will show the error. Men frequently see women's indirectness as "covert" or "sneaky," but women aren't as concerned as men with the status and one-upmanship that directness often creates.

Finally, men often criticize women for seeming to apologize all the time. Men tend to see the phrase "I'm sorry" as a sign of weakness because they interpret the phrase to mean the woman is accepting blame, when he knows she's not to blame. The woman also knows she isn't at fault. She typically uses "I'm sorry" to express regret: "I know you must feel bad about this and I do, too."

Effective communication between the sexes is important in all organizations for meeting organizational goals. How can we manage these differences in communication style? To keep gender differences from becoming persistent barriers to effective communication requires acceptance, understanding, and a commitment to communicate adaptively with each other. Both men and women need to acknowledge that there are differences in communication styles, that one style isn't better than the other, and that it takes real effort to talk with each other successfully. ∎

The Evidence. A number of studies that have focused on gender and leadership style have been conducted in recent years. Their general conclusion is that males and females do use different styles. Specifically, women tend to adopt a more democratic or participative style and a less autocratic or directive style than do men. Women are more likely to encourage participation, share power and information, and attempt to enhance followers' self-worth. They lead through inclusion and rely on their charisma, expertise, contacts, and interpersonal skills to influence others. Women tend to use transformational leadership, motivating others by transforming their self-interest into the goals of the organization. Men are more likely to use a directive, command-and-control style. They rely on the formal authority of their position for their influence base. Men use transactional leadership, handing out rewards for good work and punishment for bad.[59]

There is an interesting qualifier to the above findings. This tendency for female leaders to be more democratic than males declines when women are in male-dominated jobs. Apparently, group norms and stereotypes of male roles override personal preferences so that women abandon their natural styles in such jobs and act more autocratically.

Is Different Better?　　Given that males have historically held the majority of leadership positions in organizations, it may be tempting to assume that the existence of differences between males and females would automatically favor males. Not necessarily! In today's organizations, flexibility, teamwork, trust, and information sharing are rapidly replacing rigid structures, competitive individualism, control, and secrecy. The best managers listen, motivate, and provide support to their people. They inspire and influence rather than control. And, generally speaking, women seem to do those things better than men. As a specific example, the expanded use of cross-functional teams in organizations means that effective managers must become skillful negotiators. Women's leadership style makes them better at negotiating. They don't focus on wins, losses, and competition as men do. Women treat negotiations in the context of a continuing relationship—trying hard to make the other party a winner in its own and others' eyes.[60]

A Few Concluding Thoughts.　　The research evidence we have presented suggests a general relationship between gender and leadership style. But certainly gender does not imply destiny. Not all female leaders prefer a democratic style. And many men use transformational leadership. Thus we need to show caution in labeling leadership styles by gender. To refer to a "feminine style of leadership," for example, may create more confusion than clarity. In addition, the research we have reviewed has looked at leadership *styles*, not at leadership *effectiveness*. Which style is effective will depend on the situation. So even if men and women differ in their leadership styles, we should be careful not to assume that one is always preferable to the other. There are, for instance, organizations that have inexperienced and unmotivated workers performing ambiguous tasks in which directive leadership is likely to be most effective. In addition, both genders should be looking for a leadership style that synergistically combines the best of both masculine and feminine approaches.[61]

One last point. Some people are more flexible in adjusting their leadership behaviors to different situations than are others.[62] That said, it's probably best to think of gender as providing a behavioral *tendency* in leadership. A person may, for instance, tend toward a participative style but use an autocratic one because the situation requires the latter.

Leadership Styles and Different Cultures

One general conclusion that surfaces from the leadership literature is that effective leaders do not use any single style. They adjust their style to the situation. Although not mentioned explicitly, national culture is certainly an important situational variable in determining which leadership style will be most effective. For instance, one study of Asian leadership styles revealed that Asian managers preferred leaders who were competent decision makers, effective communicators, and supportive of employees.[63]

National culture of subordinates *can* affect leadership style. A leader cannot choose his or her style at will. "What is feasible depends to a large extent on the cultural conditioning

Interview with Betsy Reifsnider, Executive Director, Friends of the River, Sacramento, California

Describe your job.

My job revolves around a variety of tasks and responsibilities. I work closely with our program directors (conservation, development, and administration) to manage the many projects of Friends of the River. I coordinate these projects with both our paid professional staff and scores of volunteers who provide our grassroots support. I work closely with our development director to determine which major donors I need to solicit and the direction of our fundraising appeals and campaigns. Although our associate director has primary responsibility for our budget, I have ultimate responsibility for setting the budget and ensuring that we meet it. In consultation with our conservation director, I also have final responsibility for the conservation programs that Friends of the River undertakes. Often, I'm the primary spokesperson for Friends of the River. Finally, as executive director, I work with the board of directors to activate board committees, develop the strategic plan, and facilitate the board's work in setting policy.

What skills do you think tomorrow's managers will need?

I believe that tomorrow's managers need to be generalists. We need to be able to adapt to a constantly changing world and to assist our organizations and our employees in embracing that change. While technical expertise is helpful, a manager needs to respond to issues and situations that could not have been foreseen five years ago or even five months ago. To be able to respond effectively, managers need some background in a variety of areas. They also need the people skills to help people feel comfortable about change and ready to meet the various challenges of their jobs.

What leadership skills do you use in your job? What works best?

I'm a low-key manager who likes to provide the staff a great deal of autonomy and encouragement. I believe this contributes to morale, productivity, and creativity. I take a directive attitude only when necessary. Because I use my powers of authority so seldom, the staff knows when I am serious and require specific actions to be taken. In addition, I do not make decisions in a vacuum. I meet weekly with my management team to discuss budget, personnel, and management issues. I'm able to take advantage of the wealth of knowledge and experience of this team and to consider issues from a variety of perspectives.

How have you created a culture of trust?

The staff at Friends of the River works as a team, and I try to reinforce the notion that everyone's job is equally important to the organization. I encourage people to come to me with problems, and I do not violate their confidences. I also wander about the office often during the day, stopping at cubicles and chatting with people about what they're working on. It helps me stay up to date on various projects and also to sense how happy or frustrated people are feeling about their jobs. ■

of a leader's subordinates."[64] For example, a manipulative, autocratic, or directive style is compatible with high power distance, and we find high power distance scores in Arab, Far Eastern, and Latin countries. Power distance rankings should also be good indicators of employee willingness to accept participative leadership. Participation is likely to be most effective in low power distance cultures such as those in Norway, Finland, Denmark, and Sweden. And an achievement-oriented style that is focused on setting challenging goals and expects employees to perform at their highest level is likely to be most effective in cultures where uncertainty avoidance is low such as Canada, Sweden, and the United States.[65]

Sometimes Leadership Is Irrelevant!

The belief that some leadership style will always be effective regardless of the situation may not be true. Leadership may not always be important! Data from numerous studies indicate that, in many situations, any behaviors a leader exhibits are irrelevant. In other words, certain individual, job, and organizational variables can act as "substitutes for leadership," negating the influence of the leader.[66]

For instance, characteristics of subordinates such as experience, training, "professional" orientation, or need for independence can neutralize the effect of leadership. These characteristics can replace the subordinate's need for a leader's support or ability to create structure and reduce task ambiguity. Similarly, jobs that are inherently unambiguous and routine or that are intrinsically satisfying may place fewer demands on the leadership variable. Finally, such organizational characteristics as explicit formalized goals, rigid rules and procedures, or cohesive work groups can act in the place of formal leadership.

16 How is empowerment related to leadership?

17 Describe the relationship between gender and leadership style.

18 Why might leadership not even be necessary in certain organizational situations?

managers respond to "a manager's dilemma"

MANAGER 1

Mr. Berry needs to recognize that implementing these new ideas would begin with enlisting the energies of the supervisors. He should have a mandatory meeting with plant supervisors but hold it in an informal setting and with informal dress. The purpose of this meeting would be to introduce the vision of the new leadership style and to solicit ideas from supervisors on how to implement changes. In addition, Mr. Berry should establish guidelines for full dialogue between supervisors and employees allowing free and open discussion of all issues. He needs to assure existing managers that the past management style was a success due to their involvement; however, that success was limited without the full empowerment of all employees. To "model" the desired type of leadership style, Mr. Berry should acknowledge that he doesn't have the ability to answer all issues that will arise, but that he would rely on the input and full participation of all employees to ensure that the best solutions were developed. His communication style should be open, friendly, and encouraging. He should subtly encourage this new approach by placing posters around the plant that reaffirm that each person is vital to the success of the company. Mr. Berry should establish himself as a solid supporter of employee empowerment by giving the supervisors the tools and freedom to act upon their own ideas.

Carrie Hodges, Correctional Case Records Manager, Deuel Vocational Institution Reception Center, Tracy, California

MANAGER 2

Empowering employees who are used to being told what to do is certainly going to be a challenge for Mr. Berry. I think he is first going to have to create a culture of trust. As the chapter points out, followers want leaders who are credible and whom they can trust. So Mr. Berry's first challenge is creating this climate of trust. How should he go about doing that? First, he should be honest and truthful with the employees. In addition, he should be open with the employees. Keep them informed about what's expected. Make sure they understand the rationale for decisions and be candid about any problems that might arise. Mr. Berry should also be fair. My experience in dealing with employees (and with clients) is that people like to be treated fairly. In addition, I believe that part of being fair is being consistent. Finally, I think it's important for Mr. Berry to fulfill any promises that he makes to these employees. People need to know that their leaders are dependable. Once Mr. Berry has established this climate of trust, he should be able to implement the type of empowering environment that he envisions for these employees.

Lizzi Carol Jones, President, An Ultimate Image, Toronto, Ontario, Canada

for your
IMMEDIATE action

Preferred
Bank Card, Inc.

TO: Patrick Muenks, Vice President of Employee Relations
FR: Ray Plemmons, Director of Customer Service Operations
RE: Leadership Training for Customer Service Team Leaders

I agree completely with your recommendation that we
need a leadership training program for our customer
service team leaders. I think these individuals
could benefit from such a program. Our team leaders
continually struggle with keeping our customer
service representatives focused on our departmental
goal of providing timely, accurate, and friendly
service to our bank card holders who call in with
questions or complaints.

     I'd like you to put together a two-page
proposal that describes what leadership topics you
think should be covered. Plan on the program's
being 10 hours long. Also, develop some suggestions
for presenting the information in a way that would
be appealing to the participants. If we plan on
implementing this program later this year, we'll
need to get started immediately. Therefore, could
you have this report to me by the end of next week?

This is a fictionalized account of a potentially real problem. It was written for academic purposes
only.

SUMMARY

This summary is organized by the chapter-opening objectives found on p. 518.

1. Managers are appointed. Their ability to influence is based on the formal authority inherent in their positions. In contrast, leaders may either be appointed or emerge from within a group. Leaders can influence others to perform beyond the actions dictated by formal authority.

2. Fiedler's contingency model identifies three situational variables: leader-member relations, task structure, and position power. In situations that are highly favorable or highly unfavorable, task-oriented leaders tend to perform best. In moderately favorable or unfavorable situations, relationship-oriented leaders are preferred.

3. The path-goal model proposes two classes of contingency variables: those in the environment and those that are part of the personal characteristics of the subordinate. Leaders select a specific type of behavior—directive, supportive, participative, or achievement-oriented—that is congruent with the demands of the environment and the characteristics of the subordinate.

4. The attribution theory of leadership proposes that leadership is merely an attribution that people make about other individuals. Using the attribution framework, researchers have found that people tend to characterize leaders as having traits such as intelligence, outgoing personality, strong verbal skills, aggressiveness, understanding, and industriousness.

5. Charismatic leaders are self-confident, possess a vision of a better future, have a strong belief in that vision, engage in unconventional behaviors, and are perceived as agents of radical change.

6. The main skills of visionary leaders include the ability to explain the vision to others, the ability to express the vision verbally and through behavior, and the ability to extend or apply the vision to different leadership contexts.

7. Transactional leaders guide their followers in the direction of established goals by clarifying role and task requirements. Transformational leaders inspire followers to transcend their own self-interests for the good of the organization and are capable of having a profound and extraordinary effect on their followers.

8. French and Raven identified five sources or bases of power that a leader might possess: legitimate, coercive, reward, expert, and referent.

9. Leaders can create a culture of trust by practicing openness, being fair, sharing feelings, telling the truth, showing consistency, fulfilling promises, maintaining confidences, and demonstrating competence.

10. Research finds that women tend to adopt a democratic or participative style of leadership, whereas men are more likely to use a directive, command-and-control style. National culture of subordinates will also affect choice of effective leadership style. For instance, a manipulative or autocratic style would be best suited for cultures with high power distance such as Arab, Far Eastern, and Latin countries. Along these same lines, participation is likely to be most effective in low power distance cultures such as Norway, Sweden, Finland, and Denmark.

THINKING ABOUT MANAGEMENT ISSUES

1. What types of power are available to you? Which ones do you use most? Why?

2. Do you think that most managers in real life use a contingency approach to increase their leadership effectiveness? Discuss.

3. When average people on the street are asked to explain why a given individual is a leader, they tend to describe the person in terms such as *competent, consistent, self-assured, inspiring a shared vision, envoking enthusiasm for goal attainment,* and *supportive of his or her follow-*ers. How do these descriptions fit in with leadership concepts presented in the chapter?

4. What kinds of campus activities could a full-time college student do that might lead to the perception that he or she is a charismatic leader? In pursuing those activities, what might the student do to enhance this perception of being charismatic?

5. Do you think successful leaders of both genders in specific organizations tend to have similar leadership styles? Discuss.

SELF-ASSESSMENT EXERCISE

ARE YOU A CHARISMATIC LEADER?

You know from reading the chapter that a charismatic leader has certain characteristics, including self-confidence, vision, ability to articulate the vision, strong convictions about the vision, behavior that's out of the ordinary, appearance as a change agent, and environmental sensitivity. This self-assessment exercise measures your charismatic potential.

Instructions: The following statements refer to the possible ways in which you might behave toward others when you are in a leadership role. Please read each statement carefully and decide to what extent it applies to you. Then circle the appropriate number.

5 = To a very great extent
4 = To a considerable extent
3 = To a moderate extent
2 = To a slight extent
1 = To little or no extent

You...

1. Pay close attention to what others say when they are talking	1	2	3	4	5
2. Communicate clearly	1	2	3	4	5
3. Are trustworthy	1	2	3	4	5

4. Care about other people	1	2	3	4	5
5. Do not put excessive energy into avoiding failure	1	2	3	4	5
6. Make the work of others more meaningful	1	2	3	4	5
7. Seem to focus on the key issues in a situation	1	2	3	4	5
8. Get across your meaning effectively, often in unusual ways	1	2	3	4	5
9. Can be relied on to follow through on commitments	1	2	3	4	5
10. Have a great deal of self-respect	1	2	3	4	5
11. Enjoy taking carefully calculated risks	1	2	3	4	5
12. Help others feel competent in what they do	1	2	3	4	5
13. Have a clear set of priorities	1	2	3	4	5
14. Are in touch with how others feel	1	2	3	4	5
15. Rarely change once you have taken a clear position	1	2	3	4	5
16. Focus on strengths, of yourself and of others	1	2	3	4	5
17. Seem most alive when deeply involved in some project	1	2	3	4	5
18. Show others that they are all part of the same group	1	2	3	4	5
19. Get others to focus on the issues you see as important	1	2	3	4	5
20. Communicate feelings as well as ideas	1	2	3	4	5
21. Let others know where you stand	1	2	3	4	5
22. Seem to know just how you "fit" into a group	1	2	3	4	5
23. Learn from mistakes; treat errors not as disasters but as learning experiences	1	2	3	4	5
24. Are fun to be around	1	2	3	4	5

See scoring key on page SK–5.

Source: M. Sashkin and W.C. Morris, *Experiencing Management,* © 1987 by Addison-Wesley Publishing Company, Inc. Reprinted with permission of the publisher.

TAKE IT TO THE NET

We invite you to visit the Robbins/Coulter companion Web site at http://www.prenhall.com/robbinsmgt for this chapter's Internet resources.

CASE APPLICATION

Tribal Leadership

Wire harnesses for Ford and Navistar; telephones for AT&T; audio speakers for Chrysler, Harley-Davidson, and Boeing: These are just a select few of the many goods produced in Choctaw factories around Neshoba County, Mississippi. The economic revival of the Choctaw Nation is a story of the effect one person's leadership can have on an organization, in this case, an entire tribe.

What you see today around Philadelphia, Mississippi, isn't the way it always was for the Choctaws. The 8,000-member tribe was once a textbook example of the futility, poverty, and depressed conditions associated with life on an Indian reservation. As recently as 1980, 80 percent of the tribe was unemployed, with average household incomes well below the poverty line. Now, however, the quality of life for the great majority of the Choctaws has improved considerably. The average annual income for a family of four is about $22,000, with many Choctaws earning higher incomes in technical and intellectual jobs. Brick ranch houses have largely replaced the dilapidated government-built bungalows that Choctaws used to call home. The tribe has achieved virtually full employment for its members, and the tribe's numerous businesses provide employment for nontribe people in and around Philadelphia. Nearly half of the employees in the Choctaw business enterprises are white or black Mississippians. The businesses these employees work at range from factories that assemble various types of goods, to one of the South's largest printing plants, to a greeting card plant, and even a gambling casino.

The story of the Choctaw turnaround is intricately linked to that of Phillip Martin, the chairman of the Choctaw Tribal Council, who has guided the tribe's renewal since he was first elected to the position in the mid-1960s. Martin provided the vision and leadership and was the guiding force behind the revitalization of the Choctaw Tribe into the economic force that it is today. How did he do it?

Martin's first experience in the "larger" world came when he served in the Air Force in Europe in 1946. He was surprised to see starving French and Germans digging in garbage cans for food. Martin realized for the first time that white people could be as helpless and poverty-stricken as Indians. But he was also profoundly impressed by their refusal to behave like defeated people and by their determination to rebuild their lives and nations. Why couldn't the Choctaws do the same, he wondered? Upon

returning home to Mississippi after the war, Martin set about to change the course of the Choctaws. However, his vision wasn't achieved overnight. It took many years of planning, organizing, and leading to bring the Choctaw tribe to where it is today.

One key aspect of the tribe's turnaround was Martin's recognition of the economic opportunities offered by corporate investment. He realized that the driving force behind economic development was getting companies to invest in a community; it wasn't relying on government programs and public assistance. He further understood that corporations were looking for and wanted cheap and reliable labor, low taxes, and honest and cooperative government. With a grant from the federal Economic Development Administration in 1973, the tribe installed water, electricity, and sewer lines in a 20-acre industrial park on their reservation in order to entice corporations to build factories there. However, even with Martin's strong beliefs and vision about the economic desirability of an industrial park, the site sat vacant for five years. But he didn't give up. He began writing to U.S. manufacturers and kept on writing until one, Packard Electric, a division of General Motors, offered to train Choctaws to assemble wired parts for its cars and trucks. However, after one year, the Choctaw business had a debt of $1 million and was nearly bankrupt. Why? The problems could be traced primarily to the fact that most of the Choctaw employees had no conception of what it meant to be employed. Workers would take a day off for a family function and then not show up for a week. Others drank on the job. Many were unmarried women who had small children and no reliable way to get to the job, so they just skipped work.

Martin wasn't about to give up on his vision for his people, though. He brought in Lester Dalme, who at the time was a general supervisor at a General Motors' assembly plant. Dalme recalls those first days on the job: "They had no idea how a business was run, that loans had to be paid. None of them, none of their fathers, and none of their grandfathers had ever worked in a factory before. They had no idea what quality control or on-time delivery was. They thought there was a big funnel up there somewhere that money came down through. They thought profit meant some kind of plunder, something someone was stealing." Dalme set about to educate the workers that "profit" wasn't a dirty word—that the only way you stay in business and create jobs is to make a profit. Then, he was able to implement needed changes in the organization's functional departments and begin developing the capabilities needed for a competitive advantage. For example, in the production and operations area, changes were made so that the amount of resource and material waste was reduced. Also, supervisors were put to work on the assembly line so that they would know how to handle problems that arose. One critical change in the human resources management area was that the company invested in some old buses that were sent out to pick up workers who didn't have transportation. That solved the problem of workers' not having a reliable way to get to work. Dalme also told employees that alcohol or hangovers in the plant would no longer be tolerated. After about seven months, all these changes had had a definite impact, and the Choctaw tribe was on its way!

Once the tribe had established a track record with lenders, financing for several more assembly plants and a shopping center followed. In 1994, the Choctaws opened Mississippi's first inland casino as part of a resort complex that also included a golf course and a 520-room hotel. The Choctaw's strategies now include searching for "profit centers," says William Richardson, a former venture capitalist hired by Martin to put together business deals for the tribe. And to think that all of these successful business ventures started with one person's vision of how things *could* be and the determination to make that vision come true!

QUESTIONS

1. Does Martin exhibit any characteristics of a charismatic leader? Explain.
2. Would you describe Phillip Martin as a visionary leader? Why or why not?
3. Describe Martin's leadership style using path-goal theory.
4. How could Martin create a climate of trust to implement the changes he wanted?

Source: F.M. Bordewich, "How to Succeed in Business: Follow the Choctaw's Lead," *Smithsonian*, September 1996, pp. 70–81.

VIDEO CASE APPLICATION

Casting a Long Shadow

"All companies are shadows of their leader." This is a statement made by Tom Velez of CTA, who has proven to have a huge shadow indeed. He has provided the strong leadership that guided his company as it grew from nothing to $150 million in sales revenues. What can Velez teach us about leadership?

The Velez family emigrated from Ecuador to the United States, and both of Tom's parents were uneducated. However, his father strongly believed in edu-

cation and also believed in music. With these family values, it's not surprising that Velez attended the Juilliard School of Music. However, he soon realized that, although he was a good violinist, he would never be great. He began to look at other possibilities. At the time, there weren't many opportunities for Hispanics, but Velez knew that mathematics was easy for him and this self-knowledge guided him in his job search. He eventually ended up in a job at the National Aeronautics and Space Administration (NASA) and went on to get his Ph.D. in mathematics at Georgetown

University. Mathematics was a core skill that NASA needed in writing computer programs and understanding the physical phenomena coming from the data being gathered from space exploration, so Velez's skills seemed tailor made. However, in addition to his study of mathematics, Velez had studied philosophy. One of the philosophical ideas he took to heart was the idea of the creative genius—that is, a person who makes things happen. Because of NASA's mission and reputation, he expected to find many creative geniuses there; instead, he found that it was only a few people who made the biggest difference. From NASA, Velez went on to work at Martin Marietta, a large defense contractor.

Velez soon left Martin Marietta to form CTA with a partner. What does CTA do? It provides information systems and resource management capabilities to the U.S. government. How has Velez encouraged in his organization the type of creative genius he considers so important to success? His leadership approach has been based on the belief that people aren't always attracted to paychecks. Instead, they're attracted to

challenge, to opportunities, and to culture. He advises finding a way to build a team incrementally and to be a leader. As a leader, admit you're not the best. Admit you need their help and then reward those creative geniuses. How? Give them ownership in the business; give them freedom. And, he says, remember that creating the culture you want your business to have is a day-by-day, month-by-month, year-by-year process.

QUESTIONS

1. What role do you think Velez's pursuit of creative genius plays in the way he leads CTA? Explain.
2. At NASA, what types of power do you think Velez might have had? Explain.
3. Do you agree with Velez's philosophy that people aren't always attracted to paychecks? Discuss.
4. What can you learn about leadership from Tom Velez?

Source: **Based on** *Small Business Today, Show 107.*

Controlling

A MANAGER'S DILEMMA

Digital dillydallying. Cyberloafers. As more and more organizations look to provide employees with the latest in technology and on-line access, the potential for workplace abuse of the newest tools, and the time that it takes away from doing a job, grows. More than any other recent technological advancement, the Internet and World Wide Web have created opportunities for on-the-job loafing.[1] From the work loafer's point of view, the Internet is a perfect substitute for work because an employee can appear busy and actually be doing anything but work! After all, Web searches and e-mail can look like serious business. Although not every log-on to e-mail or visit to a Web site involves an employee's goofing off, many

organizations are recognizing that they need to establish some controls for these new technologies.

At Western Digital Corporation, based in Irvine, California, managers weighed the pros and cons of providing Internet access to its 10,000 employees worldwide. Western is a global company with employees in far-flung locations, and its managers knew that its communication system and customer service could benefit from employees' having access to the Internet. Yet, these managers were also aware that they would need some guidelines for controlling Internet access. Pam Burdi, director of human resources for Western Digital, was involved in that decision. She was asked to develop these guidelines for the company.

Put yourself in Burdi's situation. What should an organization's policy guidelines for Internet access and use include? Develop a set of guidelines that could be used to address the control issues of access to and use of the Internet and World Wide Web at work.

WHAT WOULD YOU DO?

Employee job behavior is just one aspect of what managers try to control. If an organization has inadequate controls, it may face skyrocketing costs or it may find that it is not achieving its goals. Regardless of the thoroughness of the planning, a program or decision still may be poorly or improperly implemented without a satisfactory control system. Effective management, therefore, needs to consider the benefits of a well-designed organizational control system.

Foundations

of Control

WHAT IS CONTROL?

control

The process of monitoring activities to ensure that they are being accomplished as planned and of correcting any significant deviations.

Control can be defined as the process of monitoring activities to ensure that they are being accomplished as planned and of correcting any significant deviations. All managers should be involved in the control function even if their units are performing as planned. Managers cannot really know whether their units are performing properly until they've evaluated what activities have been done and have compared the actual performance with the desired standard.[2] An effective control system ensures that activities are completed in ways that lead to the attainment of the organization's goals. The criterion that determines the effectiveness of a control system is how well it facilitates goal achievement. The more it helps managers achieve their organization's goals, the better the control system.[3]

Ideally, every organization would like to efficiently and effectively reach its goals. Does this mean, however, that the control systems organizations use are identical? In other words, would Microsoft, Matsushita, and British Petroleum have the same types of control systems? Probably not. William G. Ouchi suggests that there are three different approaches to designing control systems: market, bureaucratic, and clan.[4] (See Table 17-1.)

market control

An approach to designing control systems that emphasizes the use of external market mechanisms to establish the standards used in the control system.

Market control is an approach to control that emphasizes the use of external market mechanisms, such as price competition and relative market share, to establish the standards used in the control system. This approach is typically used by organizations in which the firm's products or services are clearly specified and distinct and where there's considerable marketplace competition. Under such conditions, the divisions of a company often are turned into profit centers and are evaluated by the percentage of total corporate profits each generates. For instance, at Matsushita, the various divisions (such as video, audio, home appliances, and information and industrial equipment) are evaluated according to the profits each contributes to the company's total profits. On the basis of these measures, corporate managers make decisions about future resource allocation, strategic changes, and other work activities that may need attention.

TABLE 17-1	Characteristics of Three Approaches to Control Systems
Type of Control	**Characteristics**
Market	Uses external market mechanisms, such as price competition and relative market share, to establish standards used in system. Typically used by organizations whose products or services are clearly specified and distinct and who face considerable marketplace competition.
Bureaucratic	Emphasizes organizational authority. Relies on administrative and hierarchical mechanisms, such as rules, regulations, procedures, policies, standardization of activities, well-defined job descriptions, and budgets, to ensure that employees exhibit appropriate behaviors and meet performance standards.
Clan	Regulates employee behavior by the shared values, norms, traditions, rituals, beliefs, and other aspects of the organization's culture. Often used by organizations in which teams are common and technology is changing rapidly.

In a classic illustration of the control process in action, Robin Field measured Filofax's performance and compared it with industry standards. Then the new CEO instituted a series of managerial actions designed to pull the company back from the brink. He reduced overhead by 40 percent, cut prices to reach a broader market, and acquired eight companies in related businesses. The stock price has soared.

Another approach to a control system is **bureaucratic control**, which emphasizes organizational authority and relies on administrative rules, regulations, procedures, and policies. This type of control depends on standardization of activities, well-defined job descriptions, and other administrative mechanisms, such as budgets, to ensure that employees exhibit appropriate behaviors and meet performance standards. British Petroleum provides a good example of bureaucratic control. Although managers at BP's various divisions are allowed considerable autonomy and freedom to run their units as they see fit, they're expected to adhere closely to their budgets and stay within corporate guidelines.

Under **clan control**, employee behaviors are regulated by the shared values, norms, traditions, rituals, beliefs, and other aspects of the organization's culture. For instance, corporate rituals, such as annual employee performance award dinners or holiday bonuses, play a significant part in establishing control. Whereas bureaucratic control is based on strict organizational hierarchical mechanisms, clan control is dependent upon the individual and the group (or clan) to identify appropriate and expected behaviors and performance measures. Because clan controls arise from the shared values and norms of the group, this type of control system is often found in organizations in which teams are commonly used for work activities and where technologies are changing often. For instance, at Microsoft, individuals are well aware of the expectations regarding appropriate work behavior and performance standards. The organizational culture—through the shared values, norms, and stories about the company's legendary founder, Bill Gates—conveys to individual employees "what's important around here" and "what's not important." Rather than relying on prescribed administrative controls, Microsoft's employees are guided and controlled by the clan's culture.

Most organizations don't rely totally on just one of these approaches to designing an appropriate control system. Instead, the organization may choose to emphasize either bureaucratic or clan control, in addition to using some market control measures. The key is designing an appropriate control system that helps the organization effectively and efficiently reach its goals.

THE IMPORTANCE OF CONTROL

Why is control so important? Planning can be done, an organizational structure can be created to efficiently facilitate the achievement of objectives, and employees can be directed and motivated. Still, there's no assurance that activities are going as planned and that the

bureaucratic control

An approach to designing control systems that emphasizes organizational authority and relies on administrative rules, regulations, procedures, policies, standardization of activities, and other administrative mechanisms to ensure that employees exhibit appropriate behaviors and meet performance standards.

clan control

An approach to designing control systems in which employee behaviors are regulated by the shared values, norms, traditions, rituals, beliefs, and other aspects of the organization's culture.

goals managers are seeking are, in fact, being attained. Control is important, therefore, because it's the final link in the functional chain of management activities. It's the only way managers know whether organizational goals are being met and why they are or are not. The specific value of the control function, however, lies in its relation to planning and delegating activities.

In chapter 7, we described objectives as the foundation of planning. Objectives give specific direction to managers. However, just stating objectives or having subordinates accept your objectives is no guarantee that the necessary actions to accomplish those objectives have been taken. As the old saying goes, "The best-laid plans of mice and men oft go awry." The effective manager needs to follow up to ensure that what others are supposed to do is, in fact, being done and that their objectives are, in fact, being achieved. In reality, management is an ongoing process, and controlling activities provide the critical link back to planning (Figure 17-1). If managers didn't control, they would have no way of knowing whether their objectives and plans were on target and what future actions to take.

The other area in which controlling is important is delegation. Many managers are reluctant to delegate because they fear that subordinates will do something wrong for which the manager would be held responsible. Thus, many managers are tempted to do things themselves and avoid delegating. This reluctance to delegate, however, can be reduced if managers develop an effective control system. Such a control system can provide information and feedback on the performance of subordinates to whom they've dele-

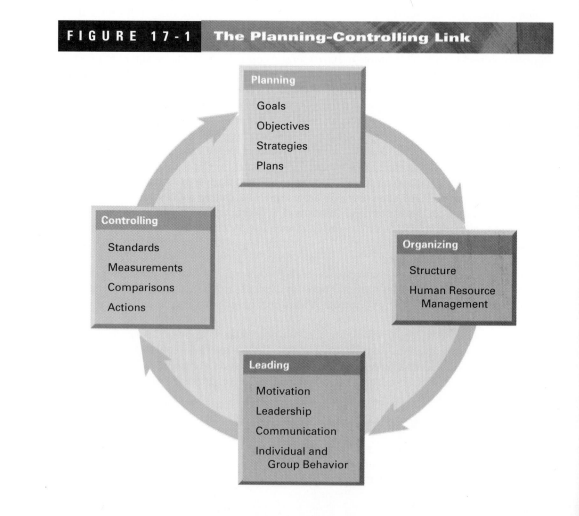

FIGURE 17-1 **The Planning-Controlling Link**

Planning
- Goals
- Objectives
- Strategies
- Plans

Organizing
- Structure
- Human Resource Management

Leading
- Motivation
- Leadership
- Communication
- Individual and Group Behavior

Controlling
- Standards
- Measurements
- Comparisons
- Actions

gated authority. An effective control system is important, therefore, because managers need to delegate authority. But because they're held ultimately responsible for the decisions that their subordinates make, managers also need a feedback mechanism, which the control system provides.

1 **What is the role of control in management?**

2 **Contrast market, bureaucratic, and clan control.**

3 **How are planning and controlling linked?**

THE CONTROL PROCESS

The **control process** consists of three separate and distinct steps: (1) *measuring* actual performance, (2) *comparing* actual performance against a standard, and (3) taking *managerial action* to correct deviations or inadequate standards (Figure 17-2). Before we consider each step in detail, you should be aware that the control process assumes that standards of performance already exist. These standards are the specific objectives against which progress can be measured. They are created during the planning process. If managers use MBO, then objectives are, by definition, tangible, verifiable, and measurable. In such instances, these objectives are the standards against which performance is measured and compared. However, even if MBO is not used, standards are the specific performance indicators that management uses. Our point is that these standards are developed in the planning process; planning must precede control.

control process

The process of measuring actual performance, comparing it against a standard, and taking managerial action to correct deviations or inadequate standards.

Measuring

To determine what actual performance is, a manager must acquire information about it. The first step in control, then, is measuring. Let's consider how we measure and what we measure.

How We Measure.   Four common sources of information frequently used by managers to measure actual performance are personal observation, statistical reports, oral reports, and written reports. Each has particular strengths and weaknesses; however, a combination

FIGURE 17-2   The Control Process

Measuring Actual Performance

GOALS AND OBJECTIVES

Organizational Divisional Departmental Individual

Comparing Actual Performance against Standard

Taking Managerial Action

of information sources increases both the number of input sources and the probability of receiving reliable information.

To get firsthand, intimate knowledge of actual activities, managers might use *personal observation*. This measuring approach provides information that isn't filtered through others. It also permits intensive coverage because minor as well as major performance activities can be observed, and it provides opportunities for a manager to "read between the lines." Management by walking around (see Entrepreneurship: Management by Walking Around, later in this chapter for more information on this topic) can pick up factual omissions, facial expressions, and tones of voice that may be missed by other sources. Unfortunately, in a time when quantitative information suggests objectivity, personal observation is often considered an inferior information source. It's subject to personal biases; what one manager sees, another might not. Personal observation also consumes a good deal of time. As companies continue to reengineer and managers' spans of control increase, this can be a significant drawback. Finally, this method suffers from obtrusiveness. Employees might interpret a manager's overt observation as a sign of a lack of confidence in them or of mistrust.

The current wide use of computers in organizations has led managers to rely increasingly on *statistical reports* for measuring actual performance. This measuring device, however, isn't limited to computer outputs. It also includes graphs, bar charts, and numerical displays of any form that managers may use to assess performance. Although statistical data are easy to visualize and effective for showing relationships, they provide limited information about an activity. Statistics report on only a few key areas that can be measured numerically and often ignore other important, often subjective, factors.

Information can also be acquired through *oral reports*—that is, through conferences, meetings, one-to-one conversations, or telephone calls. The advantages and disadvantages of this method of measuring performance are similar to those of personal observation. Although the information is filtered, it's fast, allows for feedback, and permits language expression and tone of voice, as well as words themselves, to convey meaning. Historically, one of the major drawbacks of oral reports was the problem of documenting information for later references. However, technological capabilities have progressed to the point where oral reports can be efficiently recorded and become as permanent as if they were written.

Actual performance may also be measured by *written reports*. Like statistical reports, they are slower yet more formal than first- or secondhand reports. This formality also often makes them more comprehensive and concise than oral reports. In addition, written reports are usually easy to file and reference.

Given the varied advantages and disadvantages of each of these four measurement techniques, comprehensive control efforts by managers should use all four.

What We Measure. What we measure is probably more critical to the control process than how we measure. The selection of the wrong criteria can result in serious dysfunctional consequences. Besides, what we measure determines, to a great extent, what people in the organization will attempt to excel at.[5]

Some control criteria are applicable to any management situation. For instance, because all managers, by definition, direct the activities of others, criteria such as employee satisfaction or turnover and absenteeism rates can be measured. Most managers also have budgets for their area of responsibility set in dollar costs. Keeping costs within budget is therefore a fairly common control measure. However, any comprehensive control system needs to recognize the diversity of activities among managers. For instance, a production manager in a manufacturing plant might use measures of the quantity of units produced per day, units produced per labor-hour, scrap per unit of output, or percent of rejects returned by customers. On the other hand, the manager of an administrative unit in a governmental agency might use number of document pages typed per day, number of orders processed per hour, or average time required to process paperwork. Marketing managers often use measures such as percent of market held, average dollar value per sale, or number of customer visits per salesperson.

As you might imagine, the performance of some activities is difficult to measure in quantifiable terms. It's more difficult, for instance, for an administrator to measure the performance of a research chemist or an elementary school counselor than of a person who sells life insurance. But most activities can be grouped into some objective segments that allow for measurement. The manager needs to determine what value a person, department, or unit contributes to the organization and then convert the contribution into measurable standards.

Most jobs and activities can be expressed in tangible and measurable terms. When a performance indicator can't be stated in quantifiable terms, managers should look for and use subjective measures. Certainly, subjective measures have significant limitations. Still, they're better than having no standards at all and ignoring the control function. If an activity is important, the excuse that it's difficult to measure is unacceptable. In such cases, managers should use subjective performance criteria. Of course, any analysis or decisions based on subjective criteria should recognize the limitations of such information.

Comparing

The comparing step determines the degree of variation between actual performance and the standard. Some variation in performance can be expected in all activities. It's critical, therefore, to determine the acceptable **range of variation** (Figure 17-3). Deviations that exceed this range become significant and need the manager's attention. In the comparison stage, managers are particularly concerned with the size and direction of the variation. An example should make this concept clearer.

Chris Tanner is sales manager for Eastern States Distributors. The firm distributes imported beers in several states on the U.S. East Coast. Chris prepares a report during the

range of variation

The acceptable parameters of variance between actual performance and the standard.

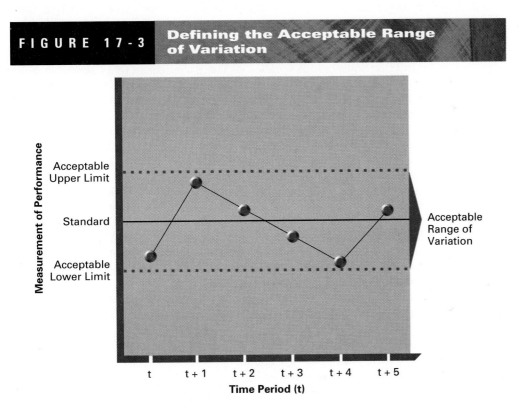

FIGURE 17-3 Defining the Acceptable Range of Variation

TABLE 17-2	Sales Performance Figures for July, Eastern States Distributors		
		(hundreds of cases)	
Brand	**Standard**	**Actual**	**Over (under)**
Heineken	1,075	913	(162)
Molson	630	634	4
Beck's	800	912	112
Moosehead	620	622	2
Labatt's	540	672	132
Corona	160	140	(20)
Amstel Light	225	220	(5)
Dos Equis	80	65	(15)
Tecate	170	286	116
Total cases	4,300	4,464	164

first week of each month that describes sales for the previous month, classified by brand name. Table 17-2 displays both the standard and actual figures for the month of July.

Should Chris be concerned about the July performance? Sales were a bit higher than originally targeted, but does that mean there were no significant deviations? Even though overall performance was generally quite favorable, several brands might need to be examined more closely by the sales manager. However, the number of brands that deserve attention depends on what Chris believes to be *significant*. How much variation should Chris allow before corrective action is taken?

The deviation on several brands (such as Molson, Moosehead, and Amstel Light) is very small and undoubtedly not worthy of special attention. On the other hand, are the shortages for Corona and Dos Equis brands significant? That's a judgment that Chris must make. Heineken sales were 15 percent below Chris's goal. This is a significant deviation and needs attention. Chris should look for a cause. In this instance, Chris attributes the loss to aggressive advertising and promotion programs by the big domestic producers, Anheuser Busch and Miller. Because Heineken is his company's number one selling import, it's most vulnerable to the promotion clout of the big domestic producers. If the decline in Heineken is more than a temporary slump (that is, if it happens again next month), then Chris will need to reduce sales orders with the brewery and lower inventory stock.

An error in understating sales can be as troublesome as an overstatement. For instance, is the surprising popularity of Tecate a one-month aberration, or is this brand increasing its market share? If the brand is increasing its market share, Chris will want to order more product from the brewery to meet consumer demand and not run short and risk losing customers. Again, Chris will have to interpret the information and make a decision. Our Eastern States' example illustrates that both overvariance and undervariance in any comparisons of measures require managerial attention.

Taking Managerial Action

The third and final step in the control process is taking managerial action. Managers can choose among three possible courses of action: They can do nothing; they can correct the actual performance; or they can revise the standards. Because "doing nothing" is fairly self-explanatory, let's look more closely at the other two.

Correct Actual Performance.   If the source of the variation in actual performance has been deficient work activities or actions, the manager will want to take corrective action. Examples of such corrective action might include changes in strategy, structure, compensation practices, or training programs; job redesign; or the replacement of personnel.

A manager who decides to correct actual performance has to make another decision: Should immediate or basic corrective action be taken? **Immediate corrective action** corrects problems at once and gets performance back on track. **Basic corrective action** asks how and why performance has deviated and then proceeds to correct the source of deviation. It's not unusual for managers to rationalize that they don't have time to take basic corrective action and therefore must be content to perpetually "put out fires" with immediate corrective action. Effective managers, however, analyze deviations and, when the benefits justify it, take the time to permanently correct significant variances between standard and actual performance.

To return to our example of Eastern States Distributors, Chris Tanner might take basic corrective action on the negative variance for Heineken by increasing promotional efforts, increasing the advertising budget for this brand, or reducing future orders with the manufacturer. The action Chris takes will depend on the assessment of each brand's potential effectiveness.

immediate corrective action

Correcting an activity at once in order to get performance back on track.

basic corrective action

Determining how and why performance has deviated and correcting the source of deviation.

Revise the Standard.   It's possible that the variance was a result of an unrealistic standard; that is, the goal may have been too high or too low. In such cases, it is the standard that needs corrective attention, not the performance. In our example, Chris might need to raise the standard for Tecate to reflect its growing popularity. This type of upward adjustment of standard frequently happens in sports when athletes adjust their performance goals upward during a season if they achieve their season goal early.

The more troublesome problem is the revision of a performance standard downward. If an employee or unit falls significantly short of reaching its target, the natural response is to shift the blame for the variance to the standard. For instance, students who make a low grade on a test often attack the grade cutoff points as too high. Rather than accept the fact that their performance was inadequate, students argue that the standards are unreasonable. Similarly, salespeople who fail to meet their monthly quota may attribute the failure to an unrealistic quota. It may be true that standards are too high, resulting in a significant variance and acting to demotivate those employees being measured against it. But keep in mind that if employees or managers don't meet the standard, the first thing they're likely to attack is the standard itself. If you believe that the standard is realistic, hold your ground. Explain your position, reaffirm to the employee or manager that you expect future performance to improve, and then take the necessary corrective action to turn that expectation into reality.

Summary of Managerial Decisions

Figure 17-4 on page 563 summarizes the manager's decisions in the control process. Although standards evolve out of objectives, the objectives are developed during planning and are considered tangential to the control process. The control process is essentially a continuous flow between measuring, comparing, and managerial action. Depending on the results of the comparing stage, a manager's decisions about what course of action to take might be do nothing, revise the standard, or correct the performance.

At this point, we must reiterate the importance of information to the whole control process. Without some organized system for collecting and disseminating information, it would be impossible for a manager to control work activities and performance. We will cover aspects of information and its relationship to control in more detail in chapter 19.

MANAGERS

SPEAK

OUT

Interview with Thomas Dunham, Vice President and General Manager, G.E. Medical Systems, Waukesha, Wisconsin

Describe your job.

I'm the vice president and general manager of GE Medical Systems. I'm responsible for a unit that has approximately 4,000 people and $1 billion in revenue. Our unit is responsible for selling and servicing GE medical equipment and we also service non-GE biomedical equipment. Sales of our products account for around 60 percent of our revenue, and 40 percent comes from the services side.

What types of skills do you think tomorrow's managers will need?

The number one skill I think managers will need is the ability to communicate in all forms. I estimate that 95 percent of the problems that happen in my organization are communication related. Second is the ability to manage information. Because of the vast amount of information that managers deal with, the ability to manage that information will be crucial for managers. Another skill I think will be important for managers is problem solving. Managers are constantly having to solve problems. Next, I think people skills, such as the ability to energize people and to lead, will be critical. Managers need the ability to get people excited about what they're doing and to take them in a direction they wouldn't otherwise go. Another skill I think will be important is the ability to communicate in at least two languages whether that second languages is a foreign language or a computer language. This is simply a reflection of the fact that organizations are global and technologically based. Finally, I think managers will need the ability to handle diversity. There are so many advantages to be gained from diversity, but if not managed effectively, the diversity can become dysfunctional. One last comment I'd like to make about skills. Technical skills are necessary and will get you in the door, but to be a successful manager in tomorrow's organization is going to take more than technical skills.

Why are controls important in your organization?

Control implies measurement and a spread of behavior. If you can't measure, you can't control. In our organization particularly, where we're dealing with equipment that has the potential to significantly affect a person's life, we're extremely conscious of our need to limit the spread of behavior. Not only do we have this obligation to our customers, we have the FDA (Food and Drug Administration) to answer to.

In our geographically dispersed organization (we have sales and service representatives around the world), it's important to measure and control because there is no "line-of-sight" management. We also like to take the "best" practices from throughout our organization and diffuse them to the rest of the organization.

In addition, in our organization we're trying to get away from simply the monetary controls and looking at more behavioral controls. What we would like to do is prevent problems (be proactive) and then if problems arise, fix them as fast as possible (be reactive). ■

FIGURE 17-4   **Managerial Decisions in the Control Process**

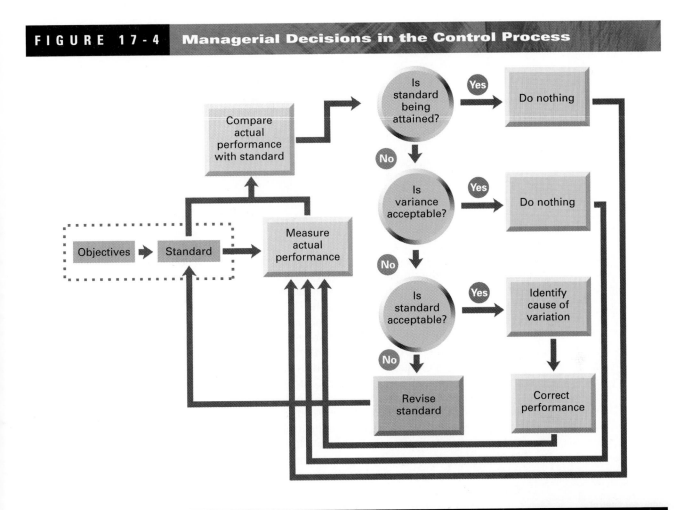

4 **What are the three steps in the control process?**

5 **Name four methods managers can use to acquire information about actual performance.**

6 **Contrast the managerial actions of correcting actual performance and revising standards.**

TYPES OF CONTROL

Managers can implement controls before an activity begins, while the activity is going on, or after the activity has been completed. The first type is called *feedforward control,* the second is *concurrent control,* and the last is *feedback control* (Figure 17-5).

Feedforward Control

The most desirable type of control—**feedforward control**—prevents anticipated problems. It's called feedforward control because it takes place in advance of the actual activity. It's future directed.[6] Let's look at some examples of feedforward control.

When McDonald's opened its first restaurant in Moscow, it sent company quality control experts to help Russian farmers learn techniques for growing high-quality potatoes and bak-

feedforward control

Control that prevents anticipated problems.

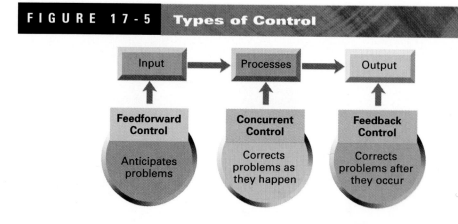

FIGURE 17-5   Types of Control

ers to learn processes for baking high-quality breads. Why? Because McDonald's strongly emphasizes product quality no matter what the geographical location. They want a cheeseburger in Moscow to taste exactly like one in Omaha. Another example of feedforward control is the move by the most prestigious U.S. accounting firms to dump potentially high-risk clients. The fear of costly litigation and damaged reputations led to decisions by high-level executives in the Big Six accounting firms to drop certain publicly traded companies as audit clients.[7] Still another example of feedforward control is the scheduled preventive maintenance programs on aircraft performed by the major airlines. These are designed to detect and, it is hoped, to prevent structural damage that might lead to an accident.

The key to feedforward controls, therefore, is taking managerial action before a problem occurs. Feedforward controls are desirable because they allow management to prevent problems rather than having to cure them later. Unfortunately, these controls require timely and accurate information that often is difficult to develop. As a result, managers frequently have to rely on the other two types of controls.

Concurrent Control

concurrent control

Control that occurs while an activity is in progress.

Concurrent control, as its name implies, takes place while an activity is in progress. When control is enacted while the work is being performed, management can correct problems before they become too costly.

The best-known form of concurrent control is direct supervision. When a manager directly oversees the actions of a subordinate, the manager can concurrently monitor the employee's actions and correct problems as they occur. Although, obviously, there's some delay between the activity and the manager's corrective response, the delay is minimal. Technical equipment can be designed to include concurrent controls. Most computers, for instance, are programmed to provide operators with immediate response if an error is made. If you input the wrong command, the program's concurrent controls reject your command and may even tell you why it's wrong. Word processing programs now alert you to potentially misspelled words. Also, many organizational quality programs rely on concurrent controls to inform workers if their performance output and levels are of sufficient quality and to ensure that quality standards are being met.

Feedback Control

feedback control

Control imposed after an action has occurred.

The most popular type of control relies on feedback. The control takes place after the activity is done. The control report that Chris Tanner used for assessing beer sales is an example of a **feedback control**.

The major drawback of this type of control is that by the time the manager has the information, the damage is already done. It's analogous to "closing the barn door after the

Many forms of concurrent control operate to ensure the on-time take-off of airplanes. In the hour before departure, most airlines' flight and ground crews run through a series of interconnecting checks and reports that link ticket attendants, baggage crews, flight attendants, deck crew, gate agent, and ramp and runway personnel in a constant stream of crucial communications.

horse has been stolen." But for many activities, feedback is the only viable type of control available. For instance, financial statements are an example of feedback controls. If, for example, the income statement shows that sales revenues are declining, the decline has already occurred. So at this point, the manager's only option is to try to determine why sales fell and to correct the situation.

Management by Walking Around

Entrepreneurs often fall into the trap of thinking that just because their business is small, they don't really need a comprehensive system of organizational controls. They may rationalize that designing an effective organizational control system is beyond their capabilities because of their limited knowledge about methods of effective control, because it's too expensive, and because they really don't have the time to implement and monitor the controls even if they did have such a system. However, entrepreneurs have at their disposal one of the most effective and inexpensive controlling techniques—something called management by walking around.[8]

Management by walking around (MBWA) is a control technique in which an entrepreneur or manager is out in the work area, interacting directly with employees and exchanging information about what's going on. By practicing MBWA, entrepreneurs can find out what's happening in their workplace by talking directly and informally with their employ-

ees. The entrepreneur is out of his or her office, "wandering around," and seeing for himself or herself what's happening. There is no need for formal, lengthy reports when MBWA is used. In fact, the informality of the process often reveals a richness of information that employees might not be willing to explain in a formal, written report. Take, for instance, Douglas Stickney, CEO of Quantum Health Resources, a company that sells drugs and services to patients with rare chronic disorders such as hemophilia. He finds that management by walking around is an extremely easy and useful way to find out what employees are thinking and what problems they're facing. On the basis of their informal information exchange, Stickney can take whatever action is necessary to deal with employees' concerns or act on ideas that they have expressed to him during his wanderings.

An organizational control system doesn't have to be complex or cumbersome to be effective. A simple technique like MBWA can be useful to an entrepreneur or even to a manager of a single department within a large, hierarchical organization. ■

Feedback has two advantages over feedforward and concurrent control.[9] First, feedback provides managers with meaningful information on how effective its planning effort was. Feedback that indicates little variance between standard and actual performance is evidence that planning was generally on target. If the deviation is great, a manager can use that information when formulating new plans to make them more effective. Second, feedback control can enhance employee motivation. People want information on how well they have performed. Feedback control provides that information.

QUALITIES OF AN EFFECTIVE CONTROL SYSTEM

Effective control systems tend to have certain characteristics in common.[10] The importance of these qualities varies with the situation, but we can generalize that the following characteristics should make a control system effective (Figure 17-6).

1. *Accuracy.* A control system that generates inaccurate information can result in management's neglecting to take action when it should or responding to a problem that does not exist. An accurate control system is reliable and produces valid data.

2. *Timeliness.* Controls should call managers' attention to variations in time to prevent serious effects on a unit's performance. The best information has little value if it is dated. Therefore, an effective control system must provide timely information.

3. *Economy.* A control system must be economical to operate. Any system of control should justify the benefits it gives in relation to the costs it incurs. To minimize costs, managers should try to impose the least amount of control that is necessary to produce the desired results.

4. *Flexibility.* Effective controls must be flexible enough to adjust to adverse change or to take advantage of new opportunities. Few organizations face environments that are so stable that there is no need for flexibility. Even highly mechanistic structures require controls that can be adjusted as times and conditions change.

5. *Understandability.* Controls that can't be understood by users have no value. It is sometimes necessary, therefore, to substitute less complex controls for sophisticated

FIGURE 17-6   **Qualities of an Effective Control System**

Corrective Action

Accuracy

Multiple Criteria

Timeliness

EFFECTIVE CONTROL SYSTEM

Economy

Emphasis on Exceptions

Flexibility

Strategic Placement

Understandability

Reasonable Criteria

An exacting control system ensures the accuracy of software written by developers at NASA's shuttle group. Billy Tate is a member of the team, which plans every new piece of code in minute detail before a single line is written. After all, its accuracy is a matter of life or death to the shuttle crews.

devices. A control system that's difficult to understand can cause unnecessary mistakes, frustrate employees, and eventually be ignored.

6. *Reasonable criteria.* Control standards must be reasonable and attainable. If they're too high or unreasonable, they no longer motivate. Because most employees don't want to risk being labeled as incompetent by accusing superiors of asking too much, employees may resort to unethical or illegal shortcuts just to meet the standards. Controls should enforce standards that challenge and "stretch" people to reach higher performance levels but that are not demotivating and do not encourage deception.

7. *Strategic placement.* Managers can't control everything that goes on in an organization. Even if they could, the benefits would not justify the costs. As a result, managers should place controls on those factors that are strategic to the organization's performance. Controls should cover the critical activities, operations, and events within the organization. They should focus on places where variations from standards are most likely to occur or where a variation would do the greatest harm. For instance, in a department whose labor costs are $20,000 a month and postage costs are $50 a month, a 5 percent cost overrun in the former is more critical than a 20 percent overrun in the latter. Hence, managers should establish controls for labor and a critical dollar allocation because postage expenses would not be that critical.

8. *Emphasis on the exception.* Because managers cannot control all activities, they should place their strategic control devices where those devices can call attention only to the exceptions. This type of "exception system" ensures that a manager is not overwhelmed by information on variations from standard. For example, an organization might have a policy that gives supervisors the authority to give annual employee raises up to $200 a month, approve individual expenses up to $500, and make capital expenditures up to $5,000. Then, only deviations above those amounts would require approval from higher levels of management. These checkpoints become controls that are part of the structural authority constraints and free management from reviewing routine expenditures.

9. *Multiple criteria.* Managers and employees alike will seek to "look good" on the criteria that are controlled. If management controls by using a single measure such as unit profit, work efforts will be focused only on looking good on that standard. Multiple measures of performance decrease this narrow focus.

Multiple criteria have a dual positive effect. Because they're more difficult to manipulate than a single measure, they can discourage efforts to merely look good. Also, because performance can rarely be objectively evaluated from a single indicator, multiple criteria make possible more accurate work performance assessments.

10. *Corrective action.* An effective control system not only indicates when a significant deviation from standard occurs but also suggests what action should be taken to correct the deviation. That is, it ought to both point out the problem and specify a solution. This is frequently done by establishing *if-then guidelines.* For instance, *if* unit revenues drop more than 5 percent, *then* unit costs should be reduced by a similar amount.

7 Why is feedforward control the most desirable type of control?

8 Contrast the advantages and disadvantages of concurrent and feedback control.

9 What qualities will an effective control system have?

THE DYSFUNCTIONAL SIDE OF CONTROLS

Have you ever noticed that the people who work in the college registrar's or records office often do not seem to care very much about a student's problem? They become so fixated on making sure that every rule is followed to the letter that they lose sight of the fact that their job is to serve students not to hassle them!

At United Parcel Service of America, long a model of corporate efficiency, managers pushed employees to get even more productive.[11] When it rolled out several new products and services—including computerized tracking systems, bulk discounts on large shipments, higher limits on package weights, and earlier and earlier "guaranteed arrival" times—employees were required to haul more packages, move heavier loads, spend more time on complicated deliveries, *and* do all that without sacrificing their productivity. Although customers loved the changes, the company's highly unionized workers did not. This example illustrates what can happen when controls are inflexible or control standards are unreasonable. People lose sight of the organization's overall goals.[12] Instead of the organization's running the controls, sometimes the controls run the organization.

Because any control system has imperfections, problems occur when individuals or organizational units attempt to look good exclusively in terms of the control devices. The result is dysfunctional in terms of the organization's goals. More often than not, this dysfunctionality is caused by incomplete measures of performance. If the control system evaluates only the quantity of output, people will ignore quality. Similarly, if the system measures activities rather than results, people will spend their time attempting to look good on the activity measures.

To avoid being reprimanded by managers because of the control system, people can engage in behaviors that are designed solely to influence the information system's data output during a given control period. Rather than actually performing well, employees can manipulate measures to give the appearance that they are performing well. The manipulation of control is not a random phenomenon. It depends on the importance of the activity. Organizationally important activities are likely to make a difference in a person's rewards, so there is a great incentive to look good on those particular measures.[13] When rewards are at stake, individuals tend to manipulate data to appear in a favorable light by, for instance, distorting actual figures, emphasizing successes, and suppressing evidence of failures. On the other hand, only random errors occur when the distribution of rewards is not affected.[14]

How much control is too much? The Japanese firm that controls 7-Eleven uses automated cash registers not only to record sales and monitor inventory but also to schedule tasks for store managers and to track their use of the built-in analytical graphs and forecasts. If they don't use them enough, managers are told to increase their activities.

What's our conclusion? It's important to recognize that controls have both an up side and a down side. Failure to design flexibility into an organizational control system can create problems more severe than those the controls were designed to prevent.

ADJUSTING CONTROLS FOR NATIONAL DIFFERENCES

The concepts of control that we have been discussing are appropriate for an organization whose units are not geographically distant or culturally distinct. But what about organizations that operate in a few or many locations worldwide? Would control systems be different, and what should managers know about adjusting controls for national differences?

Methods of controlling people and operations can be quite different in foreign countries. The differences we see in organizational control systems of multinational organizations are primarily in the measurement and corrective action steps of the control process. For the multinational corporation, managers of foreign operations tend to be less closely controlled by the home office, if for no other reason than that distance keeps them from having direct controls. The home office of a multinational must rely on extensive formal reports to maintain control. But collecting data that are comparable between countries can also create problems. For instance, a company's factory in Mexico might produce the same products as its factory in the United States. However, the Mexican factory might be much more labor intensive than its U.S. counterpart (to take strategic advantage of lower labor costs in Mexico). If headquarters' executives were to control costs by, for example, calculating labor costs per unit or output per worker, the figures would not be comparable.

Eric McKenzie owns and runs a political consulting business in Madison, Wisconsin. He has 14 employees. A few years ago he devised a workplace policy that any employee who takes home more than $3 of office supplies in a week must report the incident to the supervisor. His philosophy is that office supplies are fairly inexpensive at wholesale prices, so the impact on the bottom line ordinarily is not significant. Eric guesses that the average employee takes home about $25 a year in supplies, so he loses about $350 a year—about the same amount he'd lose if his company had a more restrictive policy. The main difference, he believes, is that employees feel grateful rather than guilty.

What do you think about such a policy? Does it encourage other potentially unethical behavior? Would such a policy work in all types and sizes of organizations? Why or why not? ■

THINKING CRITICALLY

ABOUT ETHICS

Therefore, distance creates a tendency to formalize controls, and technological differences can make control data uncomparable.

Technology's impact on control is most evident when comparing technologically advanced nations with less technologically advanced countries. Organizations in technologically advanced nations such as the United States, Japan, Canada, Great Britain, Germany, and Australia use indirect control devices—particularly computer-related reports and analyses—in addition to standardized rules and direct supervision to ensure that activities are going as planned. In less technologically advanced countries, managers tend to rely more on direct supervision and highly centralized decision making as the basic means of control. Constraints on managerial corrective action may also affect managers in foreign countries because laws in some countries do not allow management the option of closing plants, laying off employees, taking money out of the country, or bringing in a new management team from outside the country.

ETHICAL ISSUES IN CONTROL

Even though we know how important control is in organizations and the significant role it plays in the management process, ethical issues can and do arise as managers design efficient and effective control systems. Technological advances in computer hardware and software, for example, have made the process of controlling much easier, but these advances have brought with them difficult questions regarding what managers have the right to know about employees and how far they can go in controlling employee behavior, both on and off the job. In this section we look at three ethical issues in employee control: employee workplace privacy, computer monitoring of employee's work, and control of employee's off-the-job behavior.

Employee Workplace Privacy

If you work, do you think you have a right to privacy at your workplace? What can your employer find out about you and your work? You might be surprised by the answers! Employers can, among other things: read your e-mail (even those marked "personal or confidential"), tap your telephone, monitor your work by computer, store and review computer files, and monitor you in the employee bathroom or dressing room. A survey of employees' concerns about workplace privacy showed an all-time high as more than half of the respondents said they were "very concerned" about threats to their privacy at the workplace.[15]

One area that has been a hot topic of debate over employee workplace privacy is e-mail communications. The use of e-mail is flourishing throughout U.S. organizations and employees are concerned about whether they can be fired or disciplined for things they have written and sent. Many companies can, and do, monitor these electronic transmissions. For instance, a survey of more than 500 executives showed that 36 percent had reviewed employees' electronic files and mail.[16]

Ethical questions arise over the use and misuse of the information that is communicated through electronic mail networks. For instance, is the e-mail system strictly for business use? Is it OK for an employee who e-mails work information to a co-worker to also throw in some personal chit-chat? What is the appropriate use of the system? Who owns the information that flows along the network? These are tough questions to which there are no easy answers. To minimize employee concerns, managers have to develop policies regarding e-mail usage and to communicate those policies to all system users. But e-mail communications is just one aspect of the concern over the ethics of employee workplace privacy. Computer monitoring is another area in controlling workplace behavior in which ethical questions arise.

Computer Monitoring

Closely related to the issue of employee privacy at the workplace is the practice of computer monitoring of employee work performance and behavior on the job. Computer monitoring can be an excellent control mechanism. For instance, at AT&T, computer monitoring technology is being used by self-managed work teams in operating telephone call centers.[17] Computer monitoring systems can be used to collect, process, and provide performance feedback information about employees' work that can help managers with performance improvement suggestions and with employee development.[18] It has also been used to help managers identify employee work practices that might be unethical or costly. For instance, many hospitals and other health care organizations use computer monitoring to control costs of medical procedures and access to controlled medications. Likewise, many business organizations use computer monitoring systems for controlling costs, employee work behavior, and any number of other areas of organizational activities. Telemarketing organizations often monitor telephone calls of their service operators. For instance, managers at National Telecommunications Services Inc., of Washington, D.C., a telemarketing firm, randomly monitor telemarketing employees throughout a week. They do it to help employees be better at their jobs and to identify skill areas in which employees may need more training.[19] Other organizations monitor employees who deal with customer complaints to make sure the complaints are being handled appropriately. Unfortunately, computer monitoring has a questionable reputation because of instances of overuse and abuse.

Many people perceive computer monitoring as nothing more than a technologically sophisticated form of eavesdropping or a surveillance technique to catch people at slacking off on the job. Critics also claim that these techniques lead to an increase in stress-related complaints from employees who feel pressured by being under constant surveillance.[20] Supporters argue, however, that computer monitoring can be an effective employee training device and a way to improve work performance levels.

Computer monitoring techniques are so sophisticated they have created an issue of workplace privacy. To what extent should managers be able to electronically eavesdrop? When does performance appraisal become an invasion of privacy?

What about monitoring to control an employee's computer usage? As the chapter-opening dilemma pointed out, the availability of non-business-related Internet material and even the availability of computer games creates a situation in which managers may need to exercise more control. For example, an analysis of computer logs found that employees at IBM, Apple, and AT&T together visited *Penthouse* magazine's World Wide Web site 12,823 times in a single month.[21] The impact that "cyberloafing" may have on employee productivity is leading companies such as Boeing, Marathon Oil, Compaq Computer, United Technologies, and Marriott International to keep tabs on employees' computer usage. Although the federal Electronic Communications Privacy Act makes it a crime in the United States to eavesdrop or to access private communications sent via phone, voice mail, electronic mail, or the Internet, companies are usually exempt from this regulation. In most circumstances, they can monitor workers because they pay for employees' Internet access.[22]

How can organizations benefit from the control information provided by a computer monitoring system and yet minimize the potential behavioral and legal drawbacks? Experts suggest that organizations do the following: (1) Tell employees, both current and new, that they may be monitored. (2) Have a written company policy on monitoring that is posted where employees will see it and that is distributed to each employee and to have all employees acknowledge in writing that they have received a copy of the policy and that they understand it. (3) Monitor only those situations in which a legitimate business purpose is at stake, such as training or evaluating workers or controlling costs.[23] When used in this manner, computer monitoring can be an effective—and ethical—managerial control tool.

Off-the-Job Behavior

The last area we will look at in terms of the ethical issues associated with control is that concerning employees' off-the-job behavior. Just how much control should a company have over the private lives of its employees? Where should an employer's rules and controls end? Does the boss have the right to dictate what you do on your own free time and in your own home?

Invasion of employee privacy off the job is not a modern-day phenomenon. For instance, many nineteenth-century business owners made sure their employees attended church regularly. And in the early 1900s, Ford Motor Company would send social workers to employees' homes to determine whether their off-the-job habits and finances qualified them as deserving of year-end bonuses. Today, concerns about safety and costs—mostly in the areas of drug use and health care—are the forces most responsible for organizations' delving more into employees' privacy off the job.

Because of upward spiraling costs associated with health care and the problems of employee drug use (and abuse), companies are becoming more and more concerned about these issues as they affect employees, both on and off the job. Managers are taking steps to ensure that they have controls in place to minimize the problems. For instance, one study found that close to 90 percent of the workplaces surveyed tested their workers for illegal drug use.[24]

To control health care costs, many organizations are beginning to use proactive measures such as providing financial incentives to employees who live a healthy lifestyle (e.g., wearing seat belts, not smoking, not participating in dangerous recreational activities, drinking moderately or not at all, and controlling weight and blood pressure) and punishing those who do not. For example, employees at Butterworth Hospital of Grand Rapids, Michigan, who adhere to a healthy lifestyle find up to $25 extra in each biweekly paycheck. Those who do poorly on health assessment tests or who refuse to cooperate find their biweekly paycheck docked up to $25.[25] At a real estate company in Atlanta, employees are forbidden from engaging in any dangerous activity including specifically skydiving, mountain climbing, motorcycle riding, and driving a race car.[26] This policy came about after an employee had a motorcycle accident and the company's health insurance premiums went up 18 percent. And at Ford Meter Box in Wabash, Indiana, an employee was fired for smoking at home, away from the job. The company's explanation for not allowing smoking on or off the job was "skyrocketing insurance costs."

Although these examples of controlling employees' off-the-job behavior may seem unfair or unjust, nothing in the U.S. Constitution gives employees the right to privacy from their employers. The legal principle that allows employers to establish rules about all kinds of off-duty behaviors is the "employment at will" doctrine. According to this legal doctrine, if employees do not like an employer's rules, they have the option of quitting. Do you think it is unethical for a company to tell its employees that they cannot ride a motorcycle or smoke in their own home? That is, even if companies have the legal right to make such demands on their employees, do you think they should?

10 What can managers do to reduce the dysfunctionality of controls?

11 Describe what ethical issues can arise in the controlling process.

12 What can organizations do to ensure that their control systems are ethical as well as effective?

managers respond to "a manager's dilemma"

MANAGER 1

The Internet and World Wide Web have opened up significant opportunities for employees to be more productive in their work. However, the flip side is that convenient access to the Internet and World Wide Web has also presented opportunities for employees to "cyberloaf." I would suggest that Burdi ask the following questions in establishing policies for the use of the Internet for Western Digital employees. What employees might benefit most from access to the Internet and World Wide Web? How might these employees use the Internet to do their jobs more effectively and efficiently? What consequences would be appropriate for employees who misuse or abuse their company access to the Internet? How will violations of computer security be handled? What type of training will be provided to employees regarding the use of the Internet as a business tool?

Answering these questions up front will allow Burdi to design Internet use guidelines that are reasonable yet comprehensive. In addition, I would also caution her to be flexible as to the design of these guidelines. If she finds that the initial guidelines she develops are not having the intended effect, she should redesign them.

Matt Musick, *Management Consultant, Anderson Consulting, Kansas City, Missouri*

MANAGER 2

If the employees of Western Digital have hours to spend cruising the Internet, then the company has a far more serious problem than a written policy will solve! Each employee should be aware of the vision and strategy of his or her business unit and should be provided with a set of challenging objectives that contribute to the fulfillment of the business plan.

It's the job of managers at every level to communicate the plan and write clear objectives with measurable performance standards for their people. The continuing task of the managers is then to regularly interact with each person reporting directly to them to gauge progress and help each person achieve the written objectives. There are many ways to do this, but I like to (1) schedule regular weekly or monthly one-on-one formal meetings to discuss progress being made and (2) interact daily, using management by wandering around. Challenged and committed people who have regular interaction with their supervisor won't have time to waste cruising the Internet.

Ms. Burdi should draft a simple policy stating the positive benefits of using the Internet and stating that its purpose is for business only, not for personal use. Enforcement of the policy should then be up to individual managers.

Anthony Mack, *Production Manager, Satec Systems, Inc., Grove City, Pennsylvania*

for your
IMMEDIATE
action

COLLINS STATE COLLEGE

SCHOOL OF ACCOUNTANCY

TO: Dr. Matt Worobeck,
         Chair of Committee on Student Ethics
FROM: Dr. Rebecca Rodriguez, Director
RE: Minimizing Student Cheating

As you may have heard, several faculty members have expressed an interest in developing some specific controls to minimize opportunities for our students to cheat on homework assignments and exams. Since this topic falls under your committee's area of responsibility, I'd like you to get together with them and develop some suggestions.

As you look at this topic, please address your suggestions from the perspective of controlling possible student cheating (1) before it happens, (2) while in-class exams or assignments are being completed, and (3) after it has happened.

Please keep your committee's report brief (no more than 2 pages). I'd also like to have it by the end of the month so I have an opportunity to look at it before presenting it to the entire faculty at our next scheduled meeting.

SUMMARY

This summary is organized by the chapter-opening objectives found on p. 552.

1. Control is the process of monitoring activities to ensure that they are being accomplished as planned and of correcting any significant deviations.

2. The three approaches to control are market control, bureaucratic control, and clan control. Market control is an approach that emphasizes the use of external market mechanisms, such as price competition and relative market share, to establish the standards used in the control system. Bureaucratic control emphasizes organizational authority and relies on administrative rules, regulations, procedures, and policies. Under clan control systems, employee behaviors are regulated by the shared values, norms, traditions, rituals, beliefs, and other aspects of the organizational culture.

3. Control is important because it monitors whether objectives are being accomplished as planned and delegated authority is being abused.

4. In the control process, management must first have standards of performance, which arise from the objectives formed in the planning stage. Then, management must measure actual performance and compare that performance against the standards. If a variance exists between standards and actual performance, management must either adjust performance, adjust the standards, or do nothing, according to the situation.

5. The three types of control are as follows: Feedback control is future-directed and prevents anticipated problems. Concurrent control takes place while an activity is in progress. Feedback control takes place after the activity.

6. An effective control system is accurate, timely, economical, flexible, and understandable. It uses reasonable criteria, has strategic placement, emphasizes the exception, uses multiple criteria, and suggests corrective action.

7. Controls can become dysfunctional when they redirect behavior away from an organization's goals. This outcome can occur as a result of inflexibility or unreasonable standards. In addition, when rewards are at stake, individuals are likely to manipulate data so that their performance will be perceived positively.

8. Current ethical issues in control are employee workplace privacy, computer monitoring of employees' work, and control of employees' off-the-job behavior. These ethical issues are interrelated and concern the rights of employees versus the rights of employers. Employees are concerned about protecting their workplace privacy, the stress of being under constant computer surveillance, and their employer's intrusion into their personal lives. Employers, on the other hand, are primarily concerned with controlling employee health care costs, employee drug use and abuse, and employee work practices that might be potentially unethical or costly.

THINKING ABOUT MANAGEMENT ISSUES

1. What would an organization have to do to change its dominant control approach from bureaucratic to clan? From clan to bureaucratic?

2. In chapter 12 we discussed the white-water rapids view of change. Do you think it is possible to establish and maintain effective standards and controls in this type of atmosphere? Explain.

3. How could you use the concepts of control in your own personal life? Be specific. (Think in terms of feedforward, concurrent, and feedback controls as well as controls for the different areas of your life.)

4. When do electronic surveillance devices such as computers, video cameras, and telephone mon-

itoring step over the line from "effective management controls" to "intrusions on employee rights"?

5. "Every individual employee in the organization plays a role in controlling work activities." Do you agree, or do you think that control is something that only managers are responsible for? Explain.

SELF-ASSESSMENT EXERCISE

WHO CONTROLS YOUR LIFE?

Instructions: Read each of the following statements and indicate whether you agree more with choice A or choice B.

A	B
1. Making a lot of money is largely a matter of getting the right breaks.	1. Promotions are earned through hard work and persistence. _____
2. I have noticed that there is usually a direct connection between how hard I study and the grades I get.	2. Many times, the reactions of teachers seem haphazard to me. _____
3. The number of divorces indicates that more and more people are not trying to make their marriages work.	3. Marriage is largely a gamble. _____
4. It is silly to think that one can really change another person's basic attitudes.	4. When I am right, I can convince others. _____
5. Getting promoted is really a matter of being a little luckier than the next person.	5. In our society, a person's future earning power depends on his or her ability. _____
6. If one knows how to deal with people, they are really quite easily led.	6. I have little influence over the way other people behave. _____
7. The grades I make are the result of my own efforts; luck has little or nothing to do with it.	7. Sometimes I feel that I have little to do with the grades I get. _____
8. People like me can change the course of world affairs if we make ourselves heard.	8. It is only wishful thinking to believe that one can really influence what happens in our society at large. _____
9. A great deal that happens to me is probably a matter of chance.	9. I am the master of my fate. _____
10. Getting along with people is a skill that must be practiced.	10. It is almost impossible to figure out how to please some people. _____

Turn to page SK–6 for scoring directions and key.

Source: Adapted from J.B. Rotter, "External Control and Internal Control," *Psychology Today*, June 1971, p. 42. Copyright 1971 by the American Psychological Association. Adapted with permission.

TAKE IT TO THE NET

We invite you to visit the Robbins/Coulter companion Web site at http://www.prenhall.com/robbinsmgt for this chapter's Internet resources.

CASE APPLICATION

Royal Success

What do Queen Elizabeth, Prince Charles, and Swaine, Adney, and Brigg (S.A.B.) have in common? Each is highly regarded as a symbol of aristocracy in England. For S.A.B., this recognition stems from its production of leather goods, such as riding gear and buggy whips, and umbrellas. In fact, S.A.B.'s products proudly display a "lion propping up a large gold crest, the equivalent of knighthood for inanimate objects." By all accounts, it's a symbol of "royal success."

S.A.B. has been a tradition for over 250 years in England. Founded in the 1750s, it had been a family-owned business started by the Adney family. Back then, the company primarily focused on serving the monarchy—providing kings and queens, princes and princesses with top-quality products. For most of S.A.B.'s existence, the company was on top of the world, exceptionally successful and profitable. It had an elite address on Piccadilly Street in London and catered to a distinguished clientele. In fact, its customer list read like a *Who's Who* in the world; nearly every head of state of industrialized nations and the British aristocracy displayed some S.A.B. product. The kings and queens of England were so proud of the S.A.B. tradition that they continued to rent the property on Piccadilly Street for a small fraction of its true market value. Unfortunately, the good times didn't last.

S.A.B. managers assumed that the growth they were experiencing in the 1980s would be sustainable indefinitely. So they decided to expand their facilities; they built new factories and consolidated all manufacturing operations under one roof. These same executives also decided to significantly expand their firm's retail space, even opening a site in San Francisco to process mail orders coming from the United States. With this expansion came increased costs. The most notable was leaving the famed Piccadilly Street location (and its low rent) for a facility a few blocks away at a cost nearly 100 times the previous expense!

The late 1980s ushered in significant changes that brought the decade of growth to an unexpected halt. The British pound weakened against the dollar, virtually halving S.A.B.'s revenues in their mail-order business. Furthermore, consumers were beginning to change their taste and preferences for purchased goods. Luxury items—which made up a significant portion of what S.A.B. produced—were no longer in demand. The events of the late 1980s led S.A.B. to the brink of financial disaster as annual losses soon exceeded £3 million. In 1990, the Adney family, which had controlled S.A.B. for 240 years, sold out its interest to other investors, leaving England's pride and joy to be run by an impersonal corporation. For the next four years, S.A.B. languished. Then John de Bruyne came along and bought the company.

What de Bruyne found when he took over the helm of S.A.B. in June 1994 was nothing short of chaos. Few, if any, control mechanisms were in place. No one really knew what was going on or how well plans were being met. He concluded that it was doubtful that standards were being set at all. De Bruyne knew he had to make some major changes if S.A.B. was to survive.

One of the first things de Bruyne did was to focus on the firm's core business, making upscale leather goods, to recapture the firm's competitive advantage. He also reduced costs by eliminating jobs and moving the main production facility to one that had much lower rent. He implemented production controls to help increase output while simultaneously increasing the quality of each item produced. De Bruyne also implemented procedures to address current customer concerns. And he established plans and monitoring systems for capturing new business in such locations as Paris, New York, Moscow, and Hamburg.

What John de Bruyne did for S.A.B. was remarkable. In just over a year, he turned the firm completely around. In 1995, the company earned more than £2 million in profit. That translated to a more than £5 million turnaround in just 18 months!

QUESTIONS

1. How could John de Bruyne have used the steps in the control process to help him address the problems plaguing S.A.B.?
2. What types of feedforward, concurrent, and feedback controls might de Bruyne have used at S.A.B.? Be as specific as possible.
3. Mr. de Bruyne has asked you to create a control system for S.A.B. Your first task is to provide him with a description of the three major approaches to control systems and how S.A.B. might use each.
4. Given the fact that S.A.B. operates in different global locations, would the company's control system have to be different as well? Explain.

Source: G. Lesser, "A Hard Rain's Gonna Fall," *Sky,* August 1996, pp. 22–27.

VIDEO CASE APPLICATION

Keeping the Coffee Coming

At the Port of New Orleans, the largest coffee port in the United States, one company is handling an old-fashioned product in a new-fashioned way. Frederico Pacorini's SiloCaf, a fully computerized bulk coffee storage, handling, and processing facility, is a place where tradition meets technology.

SiloCaf was founded in 1933 as a forwarding company: in other words, a company that takes any type of product and moves it from any location to any other location. Today, the company specializes in forwarding commodities, primarily coffee, and the way it handles coffee is about as high-tech as it can get. Why has SiloCaf invested in technology for such a seemingly simple product? The main reason is that consumers want the same flavor from each and every can of coffee they buy. Coffee, however, is a natural product, with impurities and defects, and coffee crops are never the same, so getting a consistent flavor is difficult without some way to control the coffee blend. SiloCaf is addressing this challenge by using information systems technology and computer technology.

Mossimo Toma is SiloCaf's systems and resources manager. He is responsible for overseeing the coffee-blending process. Coffee beans come into SiloCaf's warehouse from all over the world. Each week 10 million pounds of coffee are blended (about 4 million bags per year). The coffee never stays in SiloCaf's plant more than one week. Once it's been processed and blended, it's loaded into bags or in bulk and shipped to a coffee roasting company. At any one time, SiloCaf has from 35 million to 40 million pounds of coffee in its facility for processing. If you consider the price of a pound of coffee, SiloCaf has an extremely valuable resource in its possession. Actually, SiloCaf never owns the coffee; it's owned by the roasting company or the dealer who delivers the coffee to the roasting company.

All the mechanical parts in SiloCaf's New Orleans facility have been brought from Italy, which is where the company first developed the technology. Frederico Pacorini, the son of the founder and the manager of the New Orleans facility, says that technology in a business like theirs is important because it allows them to make all the blends they need for their customers (coffee roasters), to optimize the way they do blends, and to control blends. SiloCaf's employees receive continual statistical reports for each one of the scales used to blend the coffee. The reports enable them to check the consistency of the scale's performance, which is important for achieving the consistency of the product that the end user (consumer) wants.

You'd think that all this high-tech control would be expensive, but it's not. The nice thing about SiloCaf's solution to the blend consistency challenge is that the technology they're using is relatively simple. In fact, the company's investment was a mere 1 percent of all plant investment dollars spent.

QUESTIONS

1. What types of controls do you see in this example? Be specific.
2. Given the nature of the product that SiloCaf processes, would feedforward controls be feasible? Why or why not? How about concurrent controls? Explain.
3. SiloCaf never owns the coffee it blends. Considering this fact, why would controls be important?
4. Do controls have to be expensive to be effective? Explain.

Source: Based on *Small Business 2000, Show 109.*

A MANAGER'S DILEMMA

Cement is cement—a simple, basic commodity product—or so most people think! However, Lorenzo Zambrano, CEO of Cemex, a cement company based in Monterrey, Mexico, has a very different perspective on cement <http://www.cemex.com>.[1] His approach to managing his company has helped transform it into the world's third-largest cement manufacturer with revenues of $3.3 billion and operations in 22 countries. What explains Zambrano's success?

One of his views is that the company's prime resource is its people. Although this perspective on the importance of human resources is espoused frequently by managers everywhere, it is still unusual to hear it in reference to employees in an industry like cement making, which has mostly unskilled labor and in a country where the labor supply is plentiful. Yet Zambrano believed that if Cemex was to reach its goal of becoming a globally competitive cement maker, it would have to convince its employees that they had to improve their work performance consistently and continuously. To do that, Cemex employees would have to be equipped with the necessary tools and resources, and they

would need significant levels of continual job training in order to cope with workplace demands and expectations.

Another factor contributing to Cemex's success is Zambrano's commitment to technology. Even though cement manufacturing involves producing a commodity product, Cemex has made a significant investment in high-tech information systems. Sitting in his office, Zambrano can pull up a bar chart plotting the previous day's performance at one of the company's kilns in Venezuela or a graph of kiln downtime at a facility in New Braunfels, Texas. This type of timely and comprehensive information is crucial if Cemex is to get maximum performance out of its widespread operations and to hold operating costs down as low as possible.

Yet, there's always more that Cemex's managers need to do to remain competitive in an ever-changing global market. Although product quality has always been important to Cemex, a formal TQM program has not been implemented. Zambrano believes such a formal program could help bring about continual improvements in product quality.

Put yourself in Zambrano's position. What can you do to successfully implement a TQM program in your company's various operations?

WHAT WOULD YOU DO?

T his chapter focuses on the importance of efficiency, productivity, and quality in the operations side of the organization. As our opening Manager's Dilemma points out, it is important for managers everywhere to have well-thought-out and well-designed operating systems, organizational control systems, and quality control programs to survive in the increasingly competitive global economy. If managers like Lorenzo Zambrano have these, they will be able to produce high-quality products and services at prices that meet or beat those of their rivals.

CHAPTER

18

Operations

Management

OPERATIONS MANAGEMENT AND THE TRANSFORMATION PROCESS

operations management

The design, operation, and control of the transformation process that converts resources into finished goods and services.

The term **operations management** refers to the design, operation, and control of the transformation process that converts such resources as labor and raw materials into finished goods and services. Remember, every organization produces something. Unfortunately, this fact is often overlooked except in obvious cases such as in the manufacturing of automobiles, telephones, or cement. But hospitals produce medical services, airlines produce transportation services that move people from one location to another, the military forces produce defense capabilities, and the list goes on and on. Take a university as a specific example. University administrators bring together professors, books, academic journals, audio-visual materials, computers, classrooms, and similar resources to transform "unenlightened" students into educated and skilled individuals.

Figure 18-1 portrays, in a very simplified fashion, the fact that every organization has an operations system that creates value by transforming inputs into outputs. The system takes inputs—people, capital, equipment, materials—and transforms them through an operations system into desired finished goods and services. Thus, the transformation process is just as relevant to service organizations as to those in manufacturing.

Just as every organization produces something, every unit in an organization also produces something. Marketing, finance, research and development, human resources, and accounting convert inputs into outputs such as sales, increased market share, high rates of return on capital, new and innovative products, productive and satisfied employees, and accounting reports. As a manager, you need to be familiar with operations management concepts, regardless of the area in which you manage, in order to achieve your objectives efficiently.

MANAGING PRODUCTIVITY

productivity

The overall output of goods and services produced divided by the inputs needed to generate that output.

Improving productivity has become a major goal in virtually every organization. By **productivity,** we mean the overall output of goods or services produced divided by the inputs needed to generate that output. For countries, high productivity generates "costless growth."[2] Employees can receive higher wages and company profits can increase without causing inflation. For individual organizations, increased productivity gives them a more competitive cost structure and the ability to offer more competitive prices.

Increasing productivity is a key to global competitiveness. For instance, a great deal of Japan's prosperity in the 1980s can be explained in terms of its growth in manufacturing pro-

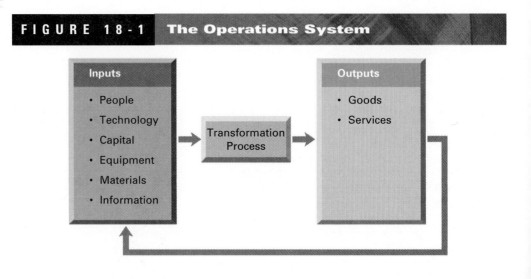

FIGURE 18-1   The Operations System

Inputs
- People
- Technology
- Capital
- Equipment
- Materials
- Information

→ Transformation Process →

Outputs
- Goods
- Services

The transformation process at the heart of operations management is what now goes on at Kent Electronics Corporation, which recently turned from simply reselling manufactured wire, cable, and resistors to assembling electronic components for major computer makers.

ductivity. Between 1979 and 1986, Japan's productivity increased at an annual rate of 5.5 percent. During the same period, U.S. productivity gained only 2.8 percent annually.[3] Firms in the United States responded by making dramatic improvements to increase their efficiency. For example, at Caterpillar, investments in productivity enhancements of both its workforce and its technology resulted in higher customer satisfaction, an increasing market share, and 27 percent greater sales with 29 percent fewer employees.[4] Chrysler Corporation found that making simple changes such as having assembly-line workers take coffee breaks in shifts rather than all at once increased worker productivity by 10 to 12 percent in just two years.[5] Another company that approached productivity improvement from a simplicity point of view was Toyota Motor Corporation. Mikio Kitano, the company's top production whiz, instituted subtle, incremental changes to improve manufacturing efficiency. He said, "The key to productivity is simplicity. Men control machines, not the other way around."[6] Productivity improvements can have dramatic results for small companies as well. For example, when Bayside Controls Inc., a small gear-parts manufacturer in Queens, New York, made changes in its production system, its average production time for a gearhead shrank from six weeks to two days.[7]

Accurately measuring national productivity in the United States has become more difficult as the economy has converted to being service and information oriented instead of manufacturing oriented. Economists and government analysts admit that increases in output value stemming from computers, software, and other information technology are not as easy to measure as increases in output stemming from tractors, ball bearings, or automobiles. Even with the new revised economic measures implemented in 1996, there's still a productivity measurement problem.[8]

However difficult it may be to accurately measure productivity, the United States is still considered among the most productive nations in the world. Even in the automobile industry, in which the Japanese have had the highest levels of productivity, U.S. workers are narrowing the gap. The time it takes U.S. workers to produce a vehicle has been reduced from 24.1 hours to 20.0 hours, a 17 percent productivity improvement.[9] In other industries, U.S. workers are more productive than workers in other countries. For instance, in general merchandise retailing, Japanese productivity is only 44 percent that of U.S. workers, and Japanese factory workers overall produce only 80 percent as much as Americans on an hourly basis.[10] Of course, this isn't a static contest between the United States and Japan. Managers in all countries are striving to improve the productivity of their employees and organizations. In this competitive climate, organizations have no choice but to look for ways to significantly improve productivity.

How can organizations improve their productivity? Productivity is a composite of people and operations variables. To improve productivity, managers must focus on both. On the people side, techniques discussed in previous chapters should be considered. Participative decision making, management by objectives, team-based work groups, and equitable pay systems are examples of people-oriented approaches toward productivity improvement. For instance, the U.S. military found that nonstop training and security operations around the globe were taking their toll on the troops. To address the serious impact on troop morale and fitness for duty, Pentagon officials decided to invest $2.7 billion in improving the military's quality of life for its "employees."[11] At Sony Corporation's plant in Kohda, Japan, the straight conveyor belt assembly line was dismantled to form a spiral line in which teams of four people assembled an entire video camcorder themselves, doing everything from soldering to testing. Output per worker on this experimental line was 10 percent higher than on a conventional assembly line.[12]

W. Edwards Deming, a management consultant and quality expert, believed that managers, not workers, were the primary source of increased productivity. He outlined 14 points for improving management's productivity. They are listed in Table 18-1.

A close look at this table reveals Deming's understanding of the interplay between people and operations. High productivity can't come solely from good "people management." The truly effective organization will maximize productivity by successfully integrating people into the overall operations system. For instance, field engineers for GE Medical Systems, a division of General Electric, used to haul around a trunkful of service and repair manuals weighing about 200 pounds on service calls to repair the company's huge imaging machines that were installed at hospitals and clinics around the world. If the technician didn't have the right manual on hand while working on the equipment, a trip to the car trunk was necessary to get the right one. The engineers estimated that they wasted as much as 15 per-

TABLE 18-1	**Deming's Fourteen Points for Improving Management's Productivity**

1. Plan for the long-term future, not for next month or next year.
2. Never be complacent concerning the quality of your product.
3. Establish statistical control over your production processes and require your suppliers to do so as well.
4. Deal with the fewest number of suppliers—the best ones, of course.
5. Find out whether your problems are confined to particular parts of the production process or stem from the overall process itself.
6. Train workers for the job that you are asking them to perform.
7. Raise the quality of your line supervisors.
8. Drive out fear.
9. Encourage departments to work closely together rather than to concentrate on departmental or divisional distinctions.
10. Do not be sucked into adopting strictly numerical goals, including the widely popular formula of "zero defect."
11. Require your workers to do quality work, not just to be at their stations from 9 to 5.
12. Train your employees to understand statistical methods.
13. Train your employees in new skills as the need arises.
14. Make top managers responsible for implementing these principles.

Source: W.E. Deming, "Improvement of Quality and Productivity through Action by Management," *National Productivity Review,* Winter 1981–1982, pp. 12–22. With permission. Copyright 1981 by Executive Enterprises, Inc., 22 West 21st St., New York, NY 10010-6904. All rights reserved.

cent of their time during a service call going back and forth to their cars. The company solved the problem by equipping its field engineers (around 2,500 in the United States alone) with laptop computers that held all the information the technician might ever need. Although this outlay of funds was a major capital expenditure, the company found that its field engineers' productivity rose by 9 percent. The company recognized the important interplay between people and the operations system.[13] The interplay between people and the operations system can also explain, for instance, why in one recent year alone, U.S. companies spent $251 billion on information technology.[14] These increased capital investments in information technology and in facilities are attempts to make organizations more modern and efficient. It also explains why so many organizations have downsized and laid off employees in recent years. These organizations hope to get more output per labor-hour—that is, to increase their productivity.

In this chapter, we'll show that factors such as size and layout of operating facilities, capacity utilization, inventory usage, and maintenance controls are important determinants of an organization's overall productivity performance.

1 **Define operations management.**

2 **Explain what the operations system is.**

3 **Why is productivity important for operations management?**

TESTING...
TESTING...

1 **2** **3**

OPERATIONS MANAGEMENT INCLUDES BOTH MANUFACTURING AND SERVICES

For the first half of this century, **manufacturing organizations**—that is, organizations that produce physical goods such as steel, automobiles, textiles, and farm machinery—dominated most advanced industrialized nations. Today, however, in the United States, Canada, Australia, and Western Europe, **service organizations** dominate. Service organizations produce nonphysical outputs such as educational, medical, retail, food, and transportation services. Figure 18-2 illustrates the characteristics of services.

manufacturing organizations

Organizations that produce physical goods such as steel, automobiles, textiles, and farm machinery.

service organizations

Organizations that produce nonphysical outputs such as educational, medical, and transportation services that are intangible, cannot be stored in inventory, and incorporate the customer or client into the actual production process.

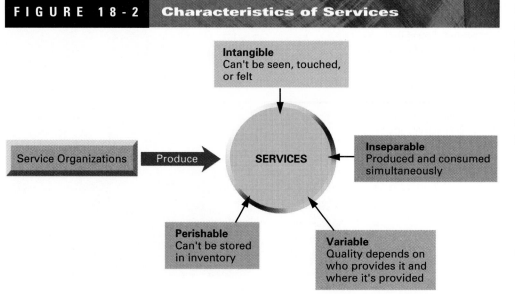

FIGURE 18-2 **Characteristics of Services**

deindustrialization

The conversion of an economy from dominance by manufacturing to dominance by service-oriented businesses.

In advanced global economies, a process called **deindustrialization** has taken place. Blue-collar jobs in manufacturing have been replaced by jobs in the service sector. Surviving manufacturing firms are becoming smaller and leaner. The bulk of new jobs is being created in services—from janitors, fast-food cooks, and servers, to computer technicians and programmers, to accountants and health care technicians. In fact, in the United States, service employment now accounts for approximately 75 percent of the workforce, whereas manufacturing employment accounts for only about 24 percent.[15]

A major challenge for managers in a deindustrialized society will be increasing productivity in the service sectors. Many managers and administrators in colleges, hospitals, airlines, governmental agencies, and similar service sector organizations are responding to the challenge by transferring concepts and techniques that worked in manufacturing to services.

For example, state and local governments are increasingly using operations management techniques.[16] The city of Madison, Wisconsin, used statistical process control and employee empowerment to improve the efficiency of its garbage collection operations. The Arkansas Department of Human Services cut the error rate on its nightly computer runs by 68 percent after a quality team figured out which programs were causing the problems and why. In Phoenix, Arizona, quality teams and operations management techniques were used to cut the costs of the city's emergency ambulance service by 25 percent while, at the same time, cutting average response time from 19 to just five minutes. At the New York State Department of Motor Vehicles, employee suggestions about service improvements have cut the wait time for a new driver's license at the Manhattan office from 60 minutes to 11 minutes.[17]

CUSTOMER-DRIVEN OPERATIONS

Organizations—profit and not-for-profit—exist to meet the needs of customers. We have alluded to the importance of customers at different times throughout this textbook. For instance, we described the role that customers play as part of an organization's specific environment in chapter 3, and our descriptions of TQM in chapters 2, 8, 9, and 12 emphasized the importance of meeting and exceeding customer needs and expectations. Customers *are* important to organizations. Without customers, there's no one to absorb the organization's outputs. But it's not enough for managers to simply recognize that customers exist. The revenues earned from customers whose needs are thoroughly and completely satisfied are the lifeblood of any organization.[18] However, it's only through *complete and total* satisfaction of their needs that customers keep coming back.[19] This type of customer

Michael Dell, CEO of Dell Computer, has built an empire selling computers direct to customers by mail and now through the Internet. Eliminating the middleman, as Dell has done, is just one way to focus on customer-driven operations.

loyalty can reap big rewards for organizations. In fact, one estimate is that "raising customer retention rates by 5 percentage points increases the value of an average customer by 25 percent to 100 percent."[20] Customer loyalty is valuable! But how can organizations capture that value? We believe that an important part of the answer is having an operations system that's customer driven.

What is a **customer-driven operations system**? It's an operations system designed around meeting and exceeding customers' needs. Successful organizations in the late 1990s and into the twenty-first century (1) think continuously about who their customers are, (2) maintain close and frequent contact with their customers, (3) determine how to provide products in a way that competitors cannot imitate, and (4) determine how to satisfy customers' current, anticipated, and even unanticipated needs.[21] In addition, their operations systems support the people and work processes to meet those needs. For instance, managers at Canadian Pacific Hotels—its 27 properties can be found from Toronto to Vancouver—looked for ways to make good on the company's promise of personalized service to customers. They examined the products and services offered and the processes used to deliver them to customers. They found that they had excellent systems in place for serving groups of customers, but the systems were not adequate or appropriate for providing personalized individual service. So the hotels' operations systems had to change. The managers appointed a "champion" at each hotel and gave that person broad cross-functional authority to see that the products and services provided to individual customers were personalized to each customer's desires. Changing to customer-driven operations wasn't easy, but it worked. The company's share of Canadian business travel jumped 16 percent in one year even though the market as a whole increased only 3 percent.[22]

customer-driven operations system

An operations system that is designed around meeting and exceeding customers' needs.

REENGINEERING WORK PROCESSES

We discussed the concept of reengineering earlier in the text and pointed out the dramatic improvements in work efficiency and effectiveness that are possible when a company radically changes and redesigns its work processes. For instance, when Union Carbide reengineered, it eliminated $400 million of fixed costs.[23] Just what does reengineering involve? How *are* work processes changed and redesigned?

Reengineering is about totally redesigning a company's operations—whether it's a manufacturing or a service organization. Believe it or not, reengineering's primary tool is a clean sheet of paper. Reengineering involves starting from scratch in rethinking and rearranging the way work is done—that is, the work processes. In effect, managers who guide reengineering efforts should ask, "If this were a new company or department, how would we do things?" The longstanding, familiar ways of approaching work are completely axed. In other words, the transformation process (the operations system) in Figure 18-1 is completely erased as those in charge of the reengineering effort start anew in designing the way the organization's product or service will be produced and delivered. Work processes and critical operations processes are boldly attacked with no regard to "that's the way it's always been done." In fact, the "way it's always been done" will not, and should not, even provide a starting point for the reengineering effort. As we described in chapter 12 on managing change, reengineering is a radical, quantum change that will shake the very foundations of the organization. Yet, for all the enormously stressful uncertainty placed on employees, the payoffs from reengineering can be powerful. For instance, GTE, a giant communications company with more than $21 billion in annual revenues, identified and eliminated several operations inefficiencies in its reengineering efforts. The radical changes in work processes resulted in almost a 30 percent increase in employee productivity.[24] A reengineering of Cigna Corporation's property and casualty claims unit and its system unit resulted in a 1,200 percent improvement in transaction processing time and a 42 percent reduction in costs.[25]

As you might guess, reengineering isn't easy. For example, when managers at ABB Daimler-Benz Transportation, a joint venture of Switzerland's ABB Asea Brown Boveri Ltd.

and Germany's Daimler-Benz, wanted to shorten the time between customer order and product delivery, the change involved completely rethinking the process from square one. Employee teams examined every step of the order process, from who needed to sign what form, to the organization of the production area, to the flow of materials from supplier to customer. This was an enormous undertaking.[26] Any organization that has made a commitment to reengineering its work operations should recognize the extensive and intensive nature of the path it's pursuing, but as the global environment becomes more dynamic and competitive, a complete overhaul of organizational operations may be the only feasible route to surviving and prospering.

TESTING...
TESTING...

4 What impact is deindustrialization having on operations management?

5 Explain why customer-driven operations are important.

6 How is reengineering related to the operations system?

STRATEGIC OPERATIONS MANAGEMENT

The era of modern manufacturing originated over 90 years ago in the United States, primarily in Detroit's automobile factories. The success that U.S. manufacturers experienced during World War II led executives of manufacturing firms to believe that troublesome production problems had been conquered. These executives focused on other functional areas such as finance and marketing. From the late 1940s through the mid-1970s, manufacturing activities were taken for granted, and to some extent, slighted. With only the occasional exception (such as the aerospace industry), top managers gave manufacturing little attention, managers "on the way up the corporate ladder" avoided it, and market leadership dwindled.

Meanwhile, as U.S. executives neglected the production side of their businesses, managers in Japan, Germany, and other countries took the opportunity to develop modern, computer-assisted facilities that fully integrated manufacturing operations into strategic planning decisions. The competition's success realigned world manufacturing leadership. For example, U.S. manufacturers soon discovered that foreign goods were being made not only less expensively but also better. Finally, by the late 1970s, U.S. manufacturers recognized that they were facing a true crisis, and they responded.[27] They invested heavily in improving manufacturing technology, increased the authority of manufacturing executives, and began incorporating existing and future production requirements into the organization's overall strategic plan. Today, successful manufacturers are taking a top-down approach to operations and are implementing comprehensive manufacturing planning systems.[28]

Wickham Skinner, a Harvard University professor, has been urging, for more than three decades, a "manufacturing focus" to strategy.[29] Skinner argues that too many important production decisions have been relegated to lower-level managers. Production needs to be managed from the top down rather than from the bottom up. Also, the organization's overall strategy needs to directly reflect its manufacturing capabilities and limitations and include operations objectives and strategies. Each organization's operations strategy needs to be unique and reflect the inherent trade-offs in any production process. Cost reduction and quality enhancement often work against each other. So, too, do short delivery times and limited inventory levels. Because there's no single "most efficient way" to produce things, top managers need to identify and emphasize the organization's competitive advantage in operations. Some organizations are competing on the more traditional basis of low prices achieved through cost reduction. Others are competing on the basis of quality, reliable delivery, warranties, short lead times, customer service, rapid product introduction, or flex-

Toyota led the auto industry in efficiency and productivity in the 1970s and 1980s, and despite being overtaken by Detroit in the 1990s it may easily return to the forefront with its trademark strategic operations management.

ible capacity. Even some of today's best-known corporate chief executives are extolling the importance of the operations side of the business. For example, General Electric's CEO, Jack Welch, communicated to his subordinates that the 1990s were the decade of manufacturing. And Hewlett-Packard's CEO, Lew Platt, called manufacturing and distribution "core competencies" of his company.[30]

These appeals for a strategic perspective to operations management have been heard. The organizations that expect to compete successfully in global markets are incorporating operations decisions in their strategic plans and are returning manufacturing executives to a place of prominence in the organization's power structure.[31] For instance, Compaq Computer of Houston, Texas, made significant investments in production and operations and developed a manufacturing system that allowed quick response to the needs of retailers and businesses rather than just selling whatever computers it happened to have in inventory.[32] Also, looking back at our chapter-opening Manager's Dilemma, Lorenzo Zambrano discovered that manufacturing excellence is critical. He closely examined the operations of his cement factories and made needed changes in order to ensure his company's long-run success.

PROJECT MANAGEMENT REVISITED

We discussed the concept of project management in chapter 9. We are revisiting it briefly in this chapter because an organization's operations system needs to support and reinforce the project organizational structure.

In a project organization, the operations system should provide an effective and efficient means of pooling the people and physical resources needed to complete the specific project or goal within the specified time period. In the illustration of the operations system shown in Figure 18-1, the inputs would now encompass the project teams and the resources needed by those teams. The transformation process would include the various activities involved with project planning, project scheduling, and project controlling used by the project teams to produce the specific outputs of the project.[33]

Operations management is just as important to project organizations as it is to those that do not use projects. As an organization makes the move to projects, its operations system must adapt to reflect the changed inputs and transformation processes. Why? To make sure that projects are completed effectively and efficiently within the time frame allotted. In fact, many of the operations planning and controlling tools and techniques that we are going to discuss next are appropriate for project teams as well as for other types of organizations.

7 Why did U.S. managers ignore the operations side of the business for so long?

8 What role should operations management play in an organization's strategy?

9 How does an organization's use of projects affect its operations system?

PLANNING OPERATIONS

As we have noted in several places throughout this book, planning must precede control. Therefore, before we can introduce operations management control techniques, we need to review a few of the more important decisions related to planning operations.

Four key decisions—capacity, location, process, and layout—provide the long-term strategic direction for operations planning. They determine the proper size of an operating system, where the physical facilities should be located, the best methods for transforming inputs into outputs, and the most efficient layout of equipment and work stations. Once these decisions have been made, three short-term decisions—the aggregate plan, the master schedule, and a materials requirements plan—need to be established. These provide the tactical plans for the operating system. In this section, we'll review these seven types of planning decisions (Figure 18-3).

Capacity Planning

Assume that you've decided to go into the boat-building business. On the basis of your analysis of the market and other environmental factors (see chapter 8), you believe that there's a market for a premium quality 28-foot sailboat. You know *what* you want to produce. What's your next step? You need to determine *how many* boats you expect to build. This decision, in turn, will determine the proper size of your plant and other facility-planning issues. When managers assess their operating system's capabilities for producing a desired number of output units for each type of product anticipated during a given time period, they're engaged in **capacity planning**.

Capacity planning begins by converting the sales demand forecasts (see chapter 9) into capacity requirements. If you produce only one type of boat, plan to sell the boats for an average of $50,000 each, and anticipate generating sales of $2.5 million during the first year, you will need to be able to handle 50 boats ($50,000 × 50 = $2,500,000). That is your physical capacity requirements. This calculation is obviously much more complex if you are producing dozens of different products.

If your organization is already established, you compare the sales demand forecast against your production capacity. Then you can determine whether you'll need to add to or subtract from your existing capacity. Keep in mind that you don't have to be in a manufacturing business to use capacity planning. It is just as relevant for determining the number of beds needed in a hospital or the maximum number of sandwiches that a Blimpies can serve during the lunch rush hour.

Once you've converted the forecast into physical capacity requirements, you'll be able to develop a set of alternative capacity plans that will meet the requirements. You often will have to make some modifications; that is, you will have to expand or reduce capacity. In the long term, you can alter the size of your operation significantly and permanently by buying new equipment or by selling off existing facilities. In the short term, however, you will be forced to make more temporary modifications. You can add an extra work shift, increase overtime, or reduce employee work hours; you can temporarily shut down operations or subcontract work out to other organizations. If you manufacture a product that can be

capacity planning

Assessing an operating system's ability to produce a desired number of output units for each type of product during a given time period.

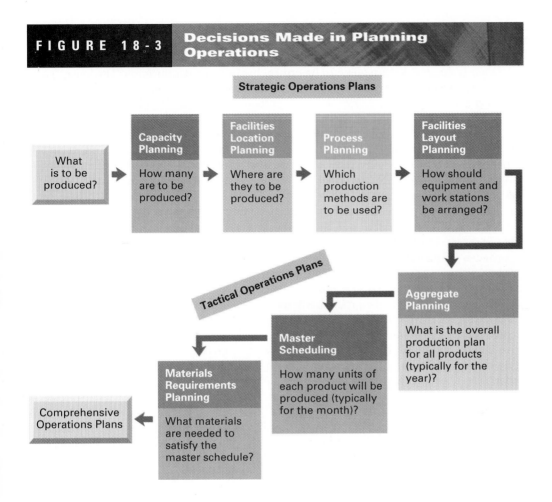

FIGURE 18-3   Decisions Made in Planning Operations

Strategic Operations Plans

What is to be produced?

Capacity Planning
How many are to be produced?

Facilities Location Planning
Where are they to be produced?

Process Planning
Which production methods are to be used?

Facilities Layout Planning
How should equipment and work stations be arranged?

Tactical Operations Plans

Aggregate Planning
What is the overall production plan for all products (typically for the year)?

Master Scheduling
How many units of each product will be produced (typically for the month)?

Materials Requirements Planning
What materials are needed to satisfy the master schedule?

Comprehensive Operations Plans

stored (like sailboats), you can build inventories during slack periods to be used when demand exceeds capacity.

Facilities Location Planning

When you determine the need for additional capacity, you must design and choose a facility. This process is called **facilities location planning.** Where you choose to locate will depend on which factors have the greatest impact on total production and distribution costs. These include availability of needed labor skills, labor costs, energy costs, proximity to suppliers or customers, and the like. Rarely are all these factors of equal importance. The kind of business you're in dictates your critical contingencies, which then dictate—to a large degree—the optimal location.

For example, the need for skilled technical specialists has led an increasing number of high-tech firms to locate in the Boston area. The area's high concentration of colleges and universities makes it easy for firms that require employees with computer, engineering, and research skills to find and hold onto such people. Similarly, it's not by chance that many manufacturers whose transformation processes are labor intensive have moved their manufacturing facilities overseas to places such as Taiwan and Malaysia. When labor costs are a critical contingency, organizations will locate their facilities where labor wage rates are low. For instance, the U.S. women's shoemaker Nine West Group Inc. does all its production in the region of Val do Sinos, Brazil, because of the low labor costs.[34] Tire manufacturers chose their original locations in northern Ohio in order to be close to their major customers,

facilities location planning

The design and location of an operations facility.

Detroit's automobile manufacturers. When customer convenience is critical, as it is for many retail stores, the location decision is often dictated by concerns such as proximity to a highway or pedestrian traffic.

What contingencies are going to be critical in your sailboat business? Obviously, you'll need employees with boat-building skills, and they're most likely to be plentiful in coastal areas such as New England, Florida, and southern California. Shipping costs of the final product are likely to be a major expenditure. So, to keep your prices competitive, you might want to locate close to your customers. That again suggests the East, West, or Gulf coast, or possibly the Great Lakes region. Weather might be an additional factor. It might be less expensive to build boats outside in warm-weather climates than indoors during winter in the northeastern United States. If labor availability, shipping costs, and weather are your critical contingencies, you still have a great deal of latitude in your location decision. After you choose a region, you still must select a community and a specific site.

Process Planning

process planning

Determining how a product or service will be produced.

In **process planning**, management determines how a product or service will be produced. Process planning encompasses evaluating the available production methods and selecting those that will best achieve the operating objectives.

For any given production process, whether in manufacturing or the service sector, there are always alternative conversion methods. Designing a restaurant, for instance, allows for a number of process choices: Should we inventory fast food (as McDonald's does); Should we have limited-option fast food (as Burger King and Wendy's do); Should we have cafeteria-style delivery, drive-in, take-out, a no-option fixed menu, or complex meals prepared to order? Key questions that ultimately determine how an organization's products or services will be produced include: Will the technology be routine or nonroutine? What degree of automation will be utilized? Should the system be developed to maximize efficiency or flexibility? How should the product or service flow through the operations systems?[35]

In our sailboat manufacturing example, the boats could be made by an assembly-line process. If you decide to keep them highly standardized, you might find a routine transformation process to be most cost efficient. But if you want each boat to be made to a customer's order, you'll require a different technology and a different set of production methods.

A good deal of process planning is going on at McDonald's these days. The fast-food giant is preparing to battle flat sales with projected improvements in everything from soft drink dispensers to french fry makers to customized sandwiches. Adding to the challenge, the firm plans to increase the speed of service.

Process planning is complex. Deciding on the best combinations of processes in terms of costs, quality, labor efficiency, and similar considerations is difficult because the decisions are interrelated. A change in one element of the production process often has spillover effects on a number of other elements. As a result, the detailed planning is usually left to production and industrial engineers under the overall guidance of top managers.

10 Why is capacity planning important in operations management?

11 What contingencies affect facilities location planning?

12 What role does process planning play in operations management?

Facilities Layout Planning

The final strategic decision in operations planning is to assess and select among alternative layout options for equipment and work stations. This step is called **facilities layout planning**. The objective of layout planning is to find a physical arrangement that will best facilitate production efficiency and that will also be appealing to employees and customers.

Layout planning begins by assessing space needs. Space has to be provided for work areas, tools and equipment, storage, maintenance facilities, rest rooms, offices, lunch areas and cafeterias, waiting rooms, and even parking lots. Then, on the basis of the previously decided process plans, various layout configurations can be evaluated to determine how efficient each is for handling the work flow. A number of layout-planning devices are available to help make these decisions; they range from simple, scaled-to-size paper cutouts to sophisticated computer software programs that can manipulate hundreds of variables and print out alternative layout designs.[36]

There are basically three work-flow layouts.[37] The **process layout** arranges components (such as work centers, equipment, or departments) together according to similarity of function. Figure 18-4 illustrates the process layout at a medical clinic. In **product layout**, the components are arranged according to the progressive steps by which the product is made. Figure 18-5 illustrates a product layout in a plant that manufactures aluminum tubing. The third approach, the **fixed-position layout**, is used when, because of its size or bulk, the product remains at one location. The product stays in place, and tools, equipment, and human skills are brought to it. Movie lot sound stages and the manufacturing of airplanes and cruise ships illustrate the fixed-position layout. The building of your 28-foot sailboats is likely to use either a product or a fixed-position layout.

Aggregate Planning

Once the strategic decisions have been made, we move to the tactical operations decisions. The first of these deals with planning the overall production activities and the operating resources needed to do them. This is called **aggregate planning** and often deals with a time frame of up to a year.

The aggregate plan provides a "big picture." On the basis of the sales demand forecast and capacity plan, the aggregate plan establishes inventory levels and production rates and estimates the size of the total operation's labor force on a monthly basis for approximately the next 12 months. The focus is on *generalities,* not specifics. Categories of products, not individual items, are considered. A paint company's aggregate plan would look at the total number of gallons of house paint to be manufactured but would avoid decisions about color or size of container. As such, the aggregate plan is particularly valuable to large operations that have a varied product line. As you will see in the next section, for the small, one-product firm, such as our sailboat manufacturing operation, the aggregate plan will look like the master schedule, only it covers a longer time frame. When completed, the aggregate plan

facilities layout planning

Assessing and selecting among alternative layout options for equipment and work stations.

process layout

Arranging manufacturing components together according to similarity of function.

product layout

Arranging manufacturing components according to the progressive steps by which a product is made.

fixed-position layout

A manufacturing layout in which the product stays in place while tools, equipment, and human skills are brought to it.

aggregate planning

Planning overall production activities and their associated operating resources.

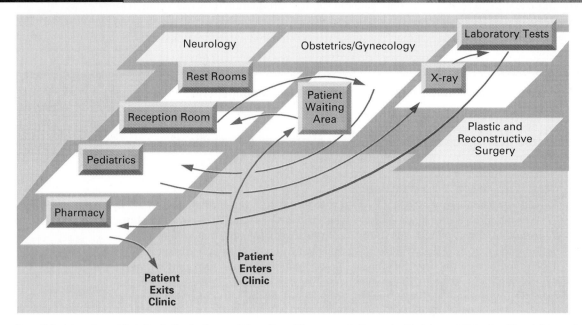

FIGURE 18-4   A Process Layout at a Medical Clinic

Source: From E.E. Adam Jr. and R.J. Ebert, *Production and Operations Management: Concepts, Models, and Behavior*, 5th ed. (Upper Saddle River, NJ: Prentice Hall, 1992), p. 254. With permission.

FIGURE 18-5   A Product Layout at an Aluminum-Tubing Plant

often points out two basic decisions: the best overall production rate to adopt and the overall number of workers to be employed during each period in the planning time frame.[38]

Master Scheduling

The **master schedule** is derived from the aggregate plan. It specifies the following: quantity and type of each item to be produced; how, when, and where they should be produced for the next day, week, or month; labor force levels; and inventory.

The first requirement of master scheduling is *disaggregation*: that is, breaking the aggregate plan down into detailed operational plans for each of the products or services the organization produces.[39] After that, these plans need to be scheduled against one another in a master schedule.

master schedule

A schedule that specifies quantity and type of items to be produced; how, when, and where they should be produced; labor force levels; and inventory.

Figure 18-6 shows a master schedule for a manufacturer of automobile transmissions. The top portion of the figure informs lower-level managers (through the aggregate plan) that top managers have authorized the capacity, inventory, and people to produce 100 heavy-duty transmissions in July, 125 in August, and so forth. The lower part of the figure illustrates a master schedule. For example, it shows how lower-level managers consider the July production for 100 heavy-duty transmissions and determine which models to make. They not only determine what specific models to make each week; they also state how many. During the first week of July, for instance, 10 units of Model 1179 and 15 units of Model 1180 will be assembled.

Material Requirements Planning

After the specific products have been determined, each should be analyzed to determine the precise materials and parts that it requires. **Material requirements planning (MRP)** is a system that uses these data for purchasing, inventorying, and priority planning purposes.

material requirements planning (MRP)

A system that dissects products into the materials and parts necessary for purchasing, inventorying, and priority planning purposes.

FIGURE 18-6 — **Developing a Master Schedule from an Aggregate Plan**

From the Aggregate Plan (units per month)

Month	July	August	September	October	November
Heavy-Duty Transmission	100	125	120	130	120
Standard Transmission	75	80	70	100	100
Economy Transmission	75	45	60	70	80
Total	250	250	250	300	300

Master Schedule for Heavy-Duty Transmission (units)

	July				August			
Week	1	2	3	4	5	6	7	8
1176	0	10	0	15	0	0	20	0
1177	0	10	0	10	0	5	10	0
1178	0	5	10	0	0	15	0	10
1179	10	0	5	0	10	15	0	0
1180	15	0	10	0	20	0	0	20
	Total 100				Total 125			

Heavy-Duty Model

Using a computer, managers can analyze product design specifications to pinpoint all the materials and parts necessary to produce the product. By merging this information with computerized inventory records, management will know the quantities of each part in inventory and when each is likely to be used up. When lead times and safety stock requirements are established and entered into the computer, MRP ensures that the right materials are available when needed.

Newly enhanced MRP software is offering production planners and schedulers even more decision support. This "constraint-based" scheduling software takes into account such factors as equipment shutdowns, labor shortages, production bottlenecks, and raw materials shortfalls in determining when and where resources should be allocated.[40]

TESTING... TESTING...

13 Contrast process, product, and fixed-position layouts.

14 How are the aggregate plan and the master schedule related?

15 What role does MRP play in operations management?

CONTROLLING OPERATIONS

Once the operating system has been designed and implemented, its key elements must be monitored. In the following sections, we discuss ways to control costs, purchasing, maintenance, and quality.

Cost Control

An automobile industry analyst once compared the U.S. and Japanese approaches to cost control: "The Japanese regard cost control as something you wake up every morning and do. Americans have always thought of it as a project. You cut costs 20 percent and say: 'Whew! That's over.' We can't afford to think that way anymore."[41]

Managers in the United States have often treated cost control as an occasional corporate crusade that is initiated and controlled by the accounting staff. Accountants establish cost standards per unit, and if deviations occur, managers look for the cause. Have material costs increased? Is labor being used efficiently? Do employees need additional training to cut waste and scrap? However, as the previous quotation implies, cost control needs to play a central part in the design of an operations system, and it needs to be a continuing concern of every manager.

cost center

A unit in which managers are held responsible for all associated costs.

direct costs

Costs incurred in proportion to the output of a particular good or service.

indirect costs

Costs that are largely unaffected by changes in output.

Many organizations have adopted the cost-center approach to controlling costs. Work areas, departments, or entire manufacturing plants are identified as distinct **cost centers**, and their managers are held responsible for the cost performance of their unit. Any unit's total costs are made up of two types of costs: direct and indirect. **Direct costs** are costs incurred in proportion to the output of a particular good or service. Labor and materials typically fall into this category. On the other hand, **indirect costs** are largely unaffected by changes in output. Even if output is zero, these costs are still incurred. Insurance expenses and the salaries of staff employees are examples of typical indirect costs. This direct-indirect distinction is important. Cost-center managers are held responsible for all direct costs in their units, but indirect costs are not necessarily within their control. However, because all costs are controllable at some level in the organization, top managers should identify where the control lies and should hold lower-level managers accountable for costs under their control.[42]

Purchasing Control

It's been said that humans are what they eat. Metaphorically, the same applies to organizations. Their processes and outputs depend on the inputs they "eat." It's difficult to make quality products out of inferior inputs. Highly skilled leather workers need quality cowhides

Controlling operations at the venerable New England Confectionery Company, makers of the famous Necco candies, has meant introducing automation and modernizing equipment to reduce labor costs and other expenses. But CEO Domenic Antonellis recognizes that "what gets to the customer, you can't change as far as I'm concerned. . . . Basically it's the same piece of candy that you as a kid used to take to the show."

if they're going to produce high-quality wallets. Gas station operators depend on a regular and dependable inflow of certain octane-rated gasolines from their suppliers in order to meet their customers' demands. If the gas isn't there, they can't sell it. If the gasoline is below the specified octane rating, customers may become dissatisfied and take their business elsewhere. Managers must therefore monitor the delivery, performance, quality, quantity, and price of inputs from suppliers. Purchasing control seeks to ensure availability, acceptable quality, continued reliable sources, and at the same time, reduced costs.

What can managers do to facilitate control of inputs? They need to gather information on the dates and conditions of arriving supplies. They need to gather data about the quality of supplies and the compatibility of those supplies with operations processes. Finally, they need to obtain data on supplier price performance. Are the prices of delivered goods the same as those quoted when the order was placed?

This information can be used to rate suppliers, identify problem suppliers, and guide managers in choosing future suppliers. Trends can be detected. Suppliers can be evaluated, for instance, on responsiveness, service, reliability, and competitiveness.

Building Close Links with Suppliers.   Many manufacturers have made suppliers their partners.[43] Instead of using 10 or more vendors and forcing them to compete against each other to gain the company's business, manufacturers are using only two or three vendors and working closely with them to improve efficiency and quality.

For instance, Motorola sends its design-and-manufacturing engineers to suppliers to help with any problems.[44] Other companies now routinely send inspection teams to rate suppliers' operations. They're assessing suppliers' manufacturing and delivery techniques, statistical process controls used to identify causes of defects, and ability to handle data electronically. Companies in the United States and around the world are doing what has long been a corporate tradition in Japan—developing long-term relationships with suppliers. As collaborators and partners, rather than adversaries, companies are finding that they can achieve better quality of inputs, fewer defects, and lower costs. Furthermore, when problems arise with suppliers, open communication channels facilitate quick resolutions.

Inventory Ordering Systems.   In many personal checkbooks, you'll find a reorder form among the remaining checks after you've used about 95 percent of them. It reminds you that it's time to reorder. This is an example of a **fixed-point reordering system**. The system is designed to "flag" or alert users at some preestablished point in the operations process to the fact that the inventory needs to be replenished. The flag is triggered when the inventory reaches a certain point or level.

The goals of a fixed-point reordering system are to minimize inventory carrying costs and to ensure a reasonable level of customer service (limiting the probability that an item will run out—a *stockout*). Therefore, the reorder point should be established to equate the time remaining before a stockout and the lead time to receive delivery of the reordered quantity. Ideally, in such cases, the newly ordered items would arrive at the same time as the last item in inventory was used up. More realistically, managers do not usually allow the inventory to fall below some safety stock level (Figure 18-7). By using certain statistical procedures, decision makers can set a reorder point at a level that gives an organization enough inventory to get through the lead-time period and some reasonable insurance against a stockout. This buffer, or safety stock, gives protection against greater usage than expected during the lead time or an unexpected delay in receiving new stock.

As a simple example, to determine a personal check reorder point, let's assume that the order lead time averages three weeks and that we write about 20 checks a week. We would need 60 checks to get us through a "normal" reordering lead time. If we feel, on the basis of history of use, that a one-week safety stock would be sufficient to get us through most

fixed-point reordering system

A system that "flags" the fact that inventory needs to be replenished when it reaches a certain level.

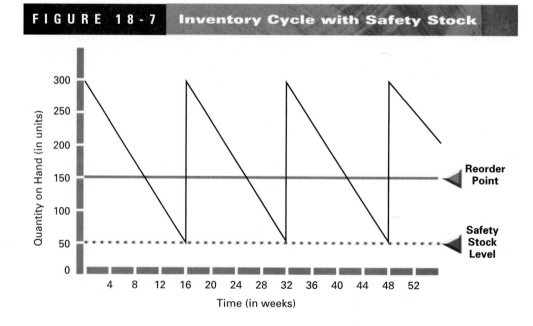

FIGURE 18-7   Inventory Cycle with Safety Stock

lead-time periods, the order should be placed when there are 80 (60 + 20) checks left in the checkbook. This is the reorder point. Another word of caution: The more safety stock, the less the risk of stockout. But the additional inventory will add to the carrying costs. Thus we again face a cost-benefit decision. At times it may be more prudent (cost-wise) to run out of stock.

One of the most primitive, but certainly effective, manual uses of the fixed-point reordering system is to keep the item—for example, pens and copy paper in an office or boxes of shoes in a retail shoe store—in two separate containers. Inventory is drawn from one until it's empty. At that point, a reorder is placed, and items are drawn from the second container. If demand for an item has been estimated properly, the replacement order to replenish the stock should arrive before the second container is used up.

Another version of the fixed-point reorder system relies on computer control. Sales are automatically recorded by a central computer that's been programmed to initiate a purchase order for an item when its inventory reaches some critical fixed point. Many retail stores use such systems. The cash registers are actually computers, and when each product's bar code is scanned at the time a customer checks out, the store's inventory record is automatically adjusted. When the inventory of an item hits the critical point, the computer tells managers to reorder or, in some systems, actually prints out the purchase order requisition.

Another common inventory system is the **fixed-interval reordering system**. The fixed-interval system uses *time* as the determining factor for inventory control. At a predetermined time—say once a week or every 90 days—the inventory is counted, and an order is placed for the number of items necessary to bring the inventory back to the desired level. The desired level is established so that if demand and ordering lead time are average, consumption will draw the inventory down to zero (or some safety lead time can be added) just as the next order arrives. This system may have some transportation economies and quantity discount economies over the fixed-point system. For example, it might allow the organization to consolidate orders from one supplier if all the items purchased from this source are reviewed at the same time. This savings is not possible with the fixed-point system.

One other popular mathematical technique for determining appropriate levels of inventory is the economic order quantity model. We'll discuss this widely used model more fully in the next chapter as we look at different controlling tools and techniques that managers can use.

Maintenance Control

Delivering goods or services in an efficient and effective manner requires operating systems with high equipment utilization and a minimum amount of downtime. Therefore managers need to be concerned with maintenance control. The importance of maintenance control, however, depends on the process technology used. A breakdown in a standardized assembly-line process can affect hundreds of employees. On an automobile or refrigerator assembly line, it's not unusual for a serious breakdown on one machine to bring an entire manu-

fixed-interval reordering system

A system that uses time as the determining factor for reviewing and reordering inventory items.

You work in the office of a company that distributes repair parts for heavy machinery throughout western Idaho. When someone calls (sometimes desperately) for a part, you look up its stock number, price, and inventory level on the computer. Your supervisor has instructed you to *always* say that the part is in stock even if the computer indicates that it's not. His rationale is that we can get the part from our own supplier in a day or two, and a short delay isn't going to hurt anyone. Then, if the customer calls back wanting to know where the part is, we can always blame a late delivery on the mail or delivery service. This situation happens at least once a day, and you're uncomfortable with it.

What can you do? How could this situation hurt (a) your customer and (b) your company? What types of ethical guidelines might you suggest for a company that wanted an effective, efficient, and ethical inventory system? ■

facturing plant to a halt. In contrast, most systems using more general-purpose and redundant processes have less interdependency between activities; therefore, a machine breakdown is likely to have less of an impact. Nevertheless, an equipment breakdown—like an inventory stockout—may mean higher costs, delayed deliveries, or lost sales.

There are three approaches to maintenance control.[45] **Preventive maintenance** is performed before a breakdown occurs. **Remedial maintenance** is a complete overhaul, replacement, or repair of the equipment when it breaks down. **Conditional maintenance** refers to overhaul or repair in response to an inspection and measurement of the equipment's state. For instance, when American Airlines tears down its jet engines every 1,000 hours, it is engaging in preventive maintenance. When it inspects the plane's tires every 24 hours and changes them when conditions warrant, it is performing conditional maintenance. Finally, if American Airlines' operations policy is to repair window shades or seat pockets on its planes only after the equipment breaks, then it is using remedial maintenance practices.

The American Airlines example points out that the type of maintenance control depends on the costs of a breakdown. The greater the cost in terms of money, time, liability, and customer goodwill, the greater the benefits from preventive maintenance. That is, the benefits can easily justify the costs.

Maintenance control should also be considered in the design of equipment. If downtime is highly inconvenient or costly, reliability can be increased by designing redundancy into the equipment. Nuclear power plants, for example, have elaborate backup systems built in. Similarly, equipment can be designed to facilitate fast or low-cost maintenance. Equipment that has fewer parts has fewer things to go wrong. High-failure items can also be placed in locations that are easily accessible or in independent modular units that can be quickly removed and replaced. Cable television operators follow these guidelines. Breakdowns infuriate customers, so when they occur, managers want to be able to correct them quickly. Speed is facilitated by centralizing equipment in easy-access locations and making extensive use of modular units. If a piece of equipment fails, the whole module of which it is a part can be pulled or replaced in just a few minutes. Television service is resumed rapidly, and the pulled modular unit can be repaired without time pressures.

Quality Control

We've discussed the concept of total quality management throughout this book. We've described it as a comprehensive, customer-focused program to continuously improve the quality of the organization's processes, products, and services. In this section, we present

preventive maintenance

Maintenance performed before a breakdown occurs.

remedial maintenance

Maintenance that calls for the overhaul, replacement, or repair of equipment when it breaks down.

conditional maintenance

Maintenance that calls for an overhaul or repair in response to an inspection.

It might surprise New York City subway riders to learn that the average distance subway cars traveled between breakdowns increased from 8,000 miles in 1984 to 58,000 miles in 1995. The Transit Authority credits such maintenance control procedures as improved maintenance shops, more-rigorous performance of routine maintenance tasks, and better management of maintenance workers.

the more limited and traditional approach to quality by focusing on its control. Whereas TQM emphasizes actions to prevent mistakes, quality control emphasizes identifying mistakes that may have already occurred.

What do we mean by *quality control*? It refers to monitoring quality—weight, strength, consistency, color, taste, reliability, finish, or any one of myriad characteristics—to ensure that the product or service meets some preestablished standard. Quality control will probably be needed at one or more points beginning with the receipt of inputs. It will continue with work in process and steps up to the final product. Assessments at intermediate stages of the transformation process typically are part of quality control. Early detection of a defective part or process can save the cost of further work on the item.

Before implementing any quality control measures, managers need to ask whether they expect to examine 100 percent of the items produced or whether a sample can be used. The inspection of every item makes sense if the cost of continuous evaluation is very low or if the consequences of a statistical error are very high (as in the manufacturing of a drug used in open-heart surgery). Statistical samples are usually less costly, and sometimes they're the only viable option. For example, if the quality test destroys the product—as happens with flash bulbs or fireworks or home pregnancy test kits—then sampling has to be utilized.

There are two categories of statistical quality control procedures: acceptance sampling and process control. **Acceptance sampling** refers to the evaluation of purchased or manufactured materials or products that already exist; it is a form of feedforward and feedback control. A sample is taken; then the decision to accept or reject the whole lot is based on a statistical calculation of sample risk error and whether the sample meets acceptable quality levels. **Process control** refers to statistically sampling items during the transformation process—a form of concurrent control—to see whether the transformation process itself is under control. For example, a process control procedure at a Coca-Cola bottling plant would be able to detect if a bottling machine was out of adjustment because it was filling 26-ounce bottles with only 23 ounces of Cherry Coke. Managers could then stop the process and readjust the machine. Statistical tests would also be used in process control to determine if the variations were outside the range of acceptable quality level. Because most production processes are not perfectly adjusted and have some innate variations, these tests would indicate serious problems within the production process itself—quality problems that should be addressed immediately.

A final consideration in quality control is related to whether the test is done by examining attributes or variables. The inspection and classification of items as acceptable or unacceptable is called **attribute sampling**. This is the way that products such as paint color, fabric used to make boxer shorts, or potato chips are evaluated. An inspector compares the items against some standard and rates their quality as acceptable or not acceptable. In contrast, **variable sampling** involves taking a measurement to determine how much an item varies from the standard. It involves a range rather than a dichotomy. Managers typically identify the standard and an acceptable deviation. Any sample that measures within the range is accepted, and those outside are rejected. For instance, Nucor Steel might test some steel bar to see whether the average breaking strength is between 120 and 140 pounds per square inch. If it's not, the cause is investigated and corrective action is initiated.

acceptance sampling

A quality control procedure in which a sample is taken and a decision to accept or reject a complete lot is based on a calculation of sample risk error.

process control

A quality control procedure in which sampling is done during the transformation process to determine whether the process itself is under control.

attribute sampling

A quality control technique that classifies items as acceptable or unacceptable on the basis of a comparison with a standard.

variable sampling

A quality control technique in which a measurement is taken to determine how much an item varies from the standard.

16 Why are cost controls and purchasing controls important parts of operations management?

17 What types of maintenance controls might a manager implement?

18 How could quality control be designed into an organization's operations system?

MANAGERS

SPEAK

OUT

Interview with James Sierk, Vice President of Quality and Productivity, AlliedSignal Corporation, Morristown, New Jersey

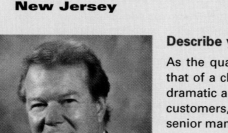

Describe your job.

As the quality officer for the company, my job is basically that of a change agent. AlliedSignal is dedicated to making dramatic and sustained improvements for the benefit of our customers, shareholders, and our people. My job is to help senior managers lead that change. I also have corporate staff responsibility for our centralized Business Services, Information Services, Materials Management, manufacturing and technical excellence organizations.

What types of skills do you think tomorrow's managers will need?

It is important to talk about both skills and values. Tomorrow's managers must know their business, technology, and the capabilities of their people. They must be agile, able to truly be leaders as well as managers, and have a high degree of self-confidence.

More important, they must have and believe in a set of values. The seven that our company espouses are good for any manager: integrity, speed, teamwork, performance, people, innovation, and, above all, a focus on the customer.

Why is quality important to organizations?

Our customers define quality for us. Meeting their needs, delighting them, has to be the first priority of our organization. At the end of the day, successful organizations will do this extremely well and, as a result, they will grow and have excellent business results. We intend to be a successful organization.

Describe how your organization instills in employees the importance of quality.

The basic motivation is already there; people want to do good things for their customers. Of course, they have to have the knowledge, skills, tools, and work environment to allow them to improve processes and to satisfy customers. It's the job of leadership to provide the means for people to gain skills, tools, and to improve how their work is done. But, more important, they must set the goals in place so people know that the first priority is to satisfy customers. ■

CURRENT ISSUES IN OPERATIONS MANAGEMENT

Capitalize on new technology! Successfully implement TQM! Achieve ISO 9000 certification! Reduce inventories! Develop outsourcing partnerships! Utilize flexibility and speed as competitive advantages! These strategies currently head up managers' lists for improving operations productivity. Because managers consider them to be essential for making products and services competitive in world markets, we'll review each of them in this section.

Technology and Product Development

Today's competitive marketplace has put tremendous pressure on manufacturers to deliver products with high quality and low cost and to significantly reduce time to market. Even if you have built the "best mousetrap," customers won't be beating a path to your door if your competitor develops a mousetrap that's almost as good but is in stores a year or two ahead of yours. Two key ingredients to successfully accelerating the product development process are organizational commitment to improving the development cycle and investment in the technology to make it happen.

One of the most effective tools that manufacturers have in meeting the time-to-market challenge is **computer-integrated manufacturing (CIM)**. This brings together the organization's strategic business plan and manufacturing plan with state-of-the-art computer applications.[46] The technologies of computer-aided design (CAD) and computer-aided manufacturing (CAM) typically are the basis for CIM. Computer-aided design essentially has made manual drafting obsolete. Using computers to visually display graphics, engineers can develop new product designs in about half the time required for manual drafting. Eagle Engine Manufacturing, for instance, used its CAD system to design a new race-car engine in nine months instead of the traditional two-plus years.[47] Computer-aided manufacturing relies on computers to guide and control the manufacturing process. Numerically controlled programs can direct machines to cut patterns, shape parts, assemble units, and perform other complicated tasks.

As technology continues to improve, CIM will support the entire manufacturing process as a continuum. Every step—from order entry to order shipping—will be expressed as data and computerized. It will allow managers to respond rapidly to changing markets. It will give companies the ability to test hundreds of design changes in hours rather than months and the flexibility to produce multiple variations of products efficiently in lot sizes as small as one or two items. When manufacturing is computer integrated, it is not necessary to stop the assembly line and spend valuable time changing dies or equipment in order to produce a new standard or nonstandard product. A single change in the computer program—which can be done in seconds—immediately realigns the manufacturing process.

computer-integrated manufacturing (CIM)

Combines the organization's strategic business plan and manufacturing plan with state-of-the-art computer applications.

A sophisticated computer program designs the molds for the Pflatzgraff Company's new dinnerware lines. The precision of this CAD technology has saved the company time and raw materials.

Implementing TQM Successfully

The list of companies that have implemented TQM programs is long and impressive. It includes such firms as Motorola, Xerox, and General Electric. But total quality improvement is important to service firms and small businesses as well. For instance, the Hard Rock Cafe in Orlando uses a system of "double checking" customers' orders as part of its total quality program.[48] At Gilbarco of Greensboro, North Carolina, a small manufacturer of gasoline dispensers and control systems, its CRISP (continuous rapid improvement in the system of production) program has helped reduce the product development cycle by 70 percent and has increased reliability by 65 percent.[49]

In addition, public sector organizations have gotten the TQM message. Henry Ford Community College of Dearborn, Michigan, was the first school to offer a guarantee for its graduates back in 1986. The school offers additional skills training of up to 16 semester hours if an employer feels that an HFCC graduate lacks the technical job skills expected for an entry-level employee.[50] The governor of Ohio has created a statewide quality council to put TQM concepts to work throughout all that state's agencies.[51] Even the U.S. federal government has implemented TQM.[52] A General Accounting Office study reported that 68 percent of the government's 2,800 installations now use TQM.

Unfortunately, not all TQM efforts are successful. Empirical studies have not shown that TQM firms consistently outperform non-TQM firms.[53] However, a study of 584 companies in the United States, Canada, Germany, and Japan provided some important insights into factors that may hinder TQM effectiveness.[54] Consistent with the contingency approach to management, the survey found that the successful application of certain TQM concepts—including teams, benchmarking, training efforts, and empowering employees—depends on the company's current performance. The following suggestions highlight the study's recommendations for lower-, medium-, and higher-performing organizations:[55]

- *For lower-performing firms.* Increase training of all types. Emphasize teams across and within departments. The formation of teams to help identify and solve small problems can help lower-performing companies as they begin their quality improvement efforts. But teams lose their value and can distract from broader strategic issues once corporate performance improves. Don't use benchmarking because it tends to create unreasonable goals and thus can frustrate quality efforts. And don't empower employees yet because they usually don't have the training to make empowerment work.

- *For medium-performing firms.* Simplify corporate processes such as design, and focus employee training on problem-solving skills.

- *For higher-performing firms.* Use benchmarking to identify new processes, products, and services. Encourage companywide quality meetings. Actively disburse decision-making power by empowering employees. Don't increase departmental teams because this tends to inhibit cooperation across functions.

The above contingency suggestions provide important limitations for the implementation of TQM, but the survey also found some practices that tended to be universally effective. These included explaining the organization's strategy to all employees, customers, and suppliers; improving and simplifying operations and development processes; and reducing the amount of time it takes from the design to the delivery of a product.

ISO 9000

ISO 9000

Quality management standards established by the International Organization for Standardization adhered to by companies around the world.

To publicly demonstrate their quality commitment, many organizations have pursued quality certification, such as **ISO 9000**. What is ISO 9000? It's a series of quality management standards being embraced by organizations around the world.[56] These standards cover everything from contract review to product design to product delivery. The ISO 9000 standards were established by the International Organization for Standardization and are

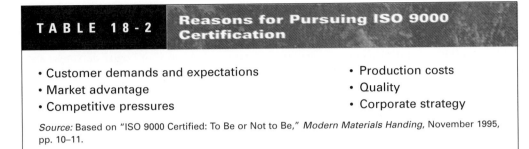

TABLE 18-2	Reasons for Pursuing ISO 9000 Certification
• Customer demands and expectations • Market advantage • Competitive pressures	• Production costs • Quality • Corporate strategy

Source: Based on "ISO 9000 Certified: To Be or Not to Be," *Modern Materials Handing,* November 1995, pp. 10–11.

becoming the internationally recognized standard for evaluating and comparing firms in the global marketplace. Gaining ISO 9000 certification provides proof that a quality operations system is in place. Table 18-2 lists some reasons why companies pursue ISO 9000 registration. In fact, this type of certification is rapidly becoming a prerequisite for doing business globally.

The number of ISO 9000 registered sites worldwide exceeded 95,000 by March of 1995. In the United States, there were more than 8,400 registered sites by the end of 1995.[57] Companies such as Alcoa, AT&T, Caterpillar, John Deere, Exxon, Federal Express, Texas Instruments, 3M, and Xerox are some of the certified manufacturers included in this number. However, ISO 9000 standards do not apply only to large manufacturers. Distribution services, consulting services, software developers, public utilities, and even some financial and educational institutions have successfully pursued certification.

It's important for managers to recognize, however, that although many positive benefits can accrue from obtaining ISO 9000 certification, the key benefit to organizations comes from the quality improvement journey itself.[58] In other words, the goal of ISO 9000 certification should be having work processes and an operations system in place that enable employees throughout the organization to perform their jobs in a consistently high-quality way.

TESTING... TESTING...

19 What role has computer-integrated manufacturing played in operations management?

20 How can TQM be implemented successfully?

21 Why might managers want to pursue ISO 9000 certification?

Reducing Inventories

A major portion of many companies' assets is tied up in inventories. For instance, Dow Chemical recently reported its inventory assets at $2.5 billion; Hewlett-Packard's were $3.7 billion; and Boeing's inventory exceeded $10.5 billion.[59] Firms that can significantly cut their inventories of raw materials and of in-process and finished goods can reduce costs and improve their efficiency.

This fact has not been lost on managers. In recent years, U.S. managers have been seeking ways to manage inventories better. On the output side, managers have been improving the information link between internal manufacturing schedules and forecasted customer demand. Marketing managers increasingly are asked to provide accurate, up-to-date information on future sales. This information is then coordinated with operating systems data to get a better match between what is produced and what the customers want. Manufacturing resource planning systems are particularly well suited to this function. On the input side, they have been experimenting with another technique widely used in Japan:

the **just-in-time (JIT) inventory system**.[60] This is a system in which inventory items arrive when they're needed in the production process instead of being stored in stock.

In Japan, JIT systems are called **kanban**. The derivation of the word gets to the essence of the just-in-time concept. *Kanban* is Japanese for "card" or "sign." Japanese suppliers ship parts to manufacturers in containers. Each container has a card, or kanban, slipped into a side pocket. When a production worker opens a container, he or she takes out the card and sends it back to the supplier. That initiates the shipping of a second container of parts that, ideally, reaches the production worker just as the last part in the first container is being used up. The ultimate goal of a JIT inventory system is to eliminate raw materials inventories by coordinating production and supply deliveries precisely. When the system works as designed, it results in a number of positive benefits for a manufacturer: reduced inventories, reduced setup time, better work flow, shorter manufacturing time, less space usage, and even higher quality. Of course, suppliers who can be depended on to deliver quality materials on time must be found. Because there are no inventories, there's no slack in the system to absorb defective materials or delays in shipment.

An illustration of JIT's benefits can be seen at the Swedish bearing maker AB SKF. Since the introduction of its JIT system, inventories have declined from around 33 percent of sales to around 24 percent. Reduction of inventory has not only saved money; it has also increased SKF's manufacturing flexibility and ability to meet its customers' demands.[61] Compaq Computer borrowed an inventory strategy used very successfully by Wal-Mart Stores Inc. In order to keep up with its needs for supplies and parts, seven of Compaq's sheet-metal and plastics suppliers from throughout the Midwest moved satellite operations or warehouse operations to Houston. One of Compaq's suppliers, Phelps Tool & Die of Kansas City, opened a 60,000-square-foot assembly plant in Houston to assemble computer casings. Now, instead of a two-day truck haul to Houston, Phelps can deliver the casings to Compaq in 15 minutes.[62]

A JIT system isn't for every manufacturer.[63] It requires that suppliers be located close to the manufacturer's production facility and that suppliers be capable of providing consistently defect-free materials. Such a system also requires reliable transportation links between suppliers and manufacturer; efficient receiving, handling, and distribution of materials; and precisely tuned production planning. When these conditions can be met, JIT can help managers reduce inventory costs.

Computer technology powers the scanners that help Bon-Ton Stores, a Pennsylvania retailer, to log merchandise and track sales. With these data the firm plans to better control its inventories in order to increase profitability.

Outsourcing and Other Supplier Partnerships

One of the biggest changes in operations management today is the steady evolution toward stronger partnerships between manufacturers and suppliers.[64] These newly forged relationships often involve outsourcing of production, in which manufacturers lower their high labor costs by shifting production to suppliers who can do it more cheaply.

What we see happening today with many manufacturers and suppliers is a closer-knit association between them. Suppliers are becoming more heavily involved with a manufacturer's *total* production process. Many of the tasks that were once performed only by the manufacturer are now being shared with key suppliers or outsourced to them. The manufacturer's role is becoming more of an orchestrator and coordinator of various suppliers' work. For instance, Whirlpool Corporation's latest model of gas range was developed without its own design engineers. Rather, the design work was performed by Eaton Corporation, one of the company's suppliers that already made gas valves and regulators for other appliance manufacturers. Whirlpool capitalized on this supplier's expertise and got its new product to market much sooner than it could have alone.[65] And at Volkswagen's new truck plant in Resende, Brazil, major suppliers actually have been assigned space in the plant. These suppliers provide their own workers, who add components to trucks coming down the assembly line. Volkswagen's employees, a minority in the plant, supervise the work and inspect finished trucks.[66] These types of strong and close-knit manufacturer-supplier partnerships are likely to continue as manufacturers look for ways to develop and sustain competitive advantages in the global marketplace.

Flexibility as a Competitive Advantage

In today's changing world of business, companies that cannot adjust rapidly will not survive. This reality puts a premium on being able to develop manufacturing flexibility.[67] As a result, many organizations are developing flexible manufacturing systems.[68]

Today's factories look like something out of a science fiction movie in which remote-controlled carts deliver a basic casting to a computerized machining center. With robots positioning and repositioning the casting, the machining center calls upon its hundreds of tools to perform various operations that turn the casting into a finished part. Completed parts, each a bit different from the others, are finished at a rate of one every 90 seconds. Neither skilled machinists nor conventional machine tools are used. Nor are there any costly delays for changing dies or tools in this factory. A single machine can make dozens or even hundreds of different parts in any order management wants. For instance, at Engineering Concepts Unlimited of Fishers, Indiana, it takes only three employees and four robots to manufacture the company's entire output of electronic engine controls.[69] At Caterpillar's assembly plant in Aurora, Illinois, unmanned vehicles, each the size of an office desk, move from one milling machine to another, delivering and picking up parts. These vehicles move around the factory floor guided by a cup-sized range finder that bounces laser beams off barcoded panels on the factory walls and tells the vehicle where it is. Computer-directed radio signals from a control center direct the vehicles' pickups and deliveries.[70]

The unique characteristic of **flexible manufacturing systems** is that, by integrating computer-aided design, engineering, and manufacturing, they can produce low-volume, custom products at a cost comparable to what had been possible only through mass production. Flexible manufacturing systems are replacing the laws of economies of scale with the laws of economies of scope. Organizations no longer have to mass-produce thousands of identical products to achieve low per unit production costs. With a flexible manufacturing system, when managers want to produce a new part, they don't change machines—they just change the computer program.

Some automated plants can build a wide variety of flawless products and switch from one product to another on cue from a central computer. John Deere, for instance, has a $1.5 billion automated factory that can turn out 10 basic tractor models with as many as 3,000

flexible manufacturing systems

Systems in which custom-made products can be mass-produced by means of computer-aided design, engineering, and manufacturing.

Speed is the hallmark of many successful manufacturers today. Specially designed software from such firms as Manugistics Group, a developer in Maryland, helps firms streamline production processes and better manage inventories, creating a competitive advantage above and beyond the strengths of the product being made.

options without plant shutdowns for retooling. In one corner of a mammoth IBM plant in Charlotte, North Carolina, 40 workers on an assembly line can build 12 different products at once, ranging from hand-held bar-code scanners to portable medical computers to satellite communications devices for truckers. The assembly line was designed to simultaneously make as many as 27 different products.[71] National Bicycle Industrial Company, which sells its bikes under the Panasonic brand, uses flexible manufacturing to produce any of 11,231,862 variations on 18 models of racing, road, and mountain bikes in 199 color patterns and an almost unlimited number of sizes.[72] These new flexible factories are also proving to be cost effective. For instance, at Sony's Digital Audio Disc Corporation in Terre Haute, Indiana, the manufacturing look is a little different. Here, workers wear dust-prevention garb from head to toe and are blasted with a high-pressure air shower before they enter the sealed room, where 300,000 CD-ROM disks are produced every 15 hours. From start to finish, the disk is untouched by human hands. Instead, robots do the work. The automation keeps the division's costs down to about 60 cents a disk on large runs. Considering that the company charges close to a dollar per disk, profit margins are quite healthy![73]

Speed as a Competitive Advantage

For years we've heard that, on the highway, speed kills. Managers are now learning that the same principle applies in business: Speed kills—only in this case, it's your competitors' speed.[74] By quickly developing, making, and distributing products and services, organizations can gain a powerful competitive advantage. Just as customers may select one organization over another because its products or services are less expensive, uniquely designed, or of superior quality, customers also choose organizations because they can get the product or service they want *fast*. For example, Domino's Pizza created a billion dollar business using speed as a competitive advantage by stressing quick delivery of its pizzas. Payless ShoeSource also uses speed to market as a competitive advantage. An automated warehouse in Topeka that covers 17 acres can restock half of Payless's stores on as little as one day's notice.[75] And Gillette Company has increased the pace at which new products are rolled out by reducing the three-year product development cycle to under two years.[76]

Other companies also have made incredible improvements in the time it takes to design and produce products. AT&T used to need two years to design a new phone. Now it does the job in less than a year. General Electric used to take three weeks after an order to deliver a custom-made industrial circuitbreaker box. They have cut that down to three days. Ross Operating Valve Company of Troy, Michigan, invested in sophisticated CAD systems and automated production equipment that have enabled the company to produce customized valves practically overnight.[77] Liz Claiborne, a women's fashion company, is benefiting from heavy investments in CAD technology and a sophisticated inventory management system that lets stores track hot items and replenish them while they are still in season.[78] And at the Boynton Beach, Florida, plant where Motorola makes pagers, orders flow in from retailers and Motorola sales representatives. The order data are digitized and sent to the assembly line, where robots and humans complete the order, often within 80 minutes after it is received. Depending on where the customer lives, the pagers can be delivered that same day or the day after.[79]

These organizations and many others worldwide are cutting red tape; flattening their organizational structures; adding cross-functional teams; redesigning their distribution chains; and using JIT, CIM, and flexible manufacturing systems to speed up their operations and put increased pressure on their competitors.

22 How is JIT a dynamic inventory system?

23 What benefits and drawbacks might outsourcing have for a manufacturer?

24 Why are flexibility and speed important competitive advantages today?

managers respond to "a manager's dilemma"

MANAGER 1

Mr. Zambrano has already made significant changes in his company's operations to make it more efficient. However, there are some things that I'd recommend he do to successfully implement a TQM program. First, I would suggest that he create a strategy for implementing TQM throughout the company's various operations. Once he has developed an overall strategy, communicate it to all employees and get their input and feedback on the proposed changes. Then he should emphasize to all Cemex's employees that they will be expected to find ways to improve and simplify the operations in the areas they're involved in. Finally, Mr. Zambrano should appoint a quality control team in the different locations to examine ways, perhaps through benchmarking other organizations, that the entire operations process can be made more efficient.

Brad Barnes, Staff Accountant, Baird, Kurtz, & Dobson, Colorado Springs, Colorado

MANAGER 2

TQM programs are quite common in today's organizations, so what Mr. Zambrano wants to do is not unusual. My experience with quality programs has been that employees need to have some input into what the quality program will look like. This is what I would suggest he do first in implementing such a program. Go personally to each of the company's widespread facilities and talk with the employees there about ways that quality can be improved. On the basis of these discussions, Mr. Zambrano may find that he needs to commit company dollars to additional employee training in specific areas. If he's intent on implementing a formal program of quality improvement, these resources are probably well spent on training. Once he has visited the company's various locations, he should ask for a specific outline of the types of quality improvement actions that will be implemented. I also think it's important that he stress the importance of each facility's being responsible for monitoring quality improvements. By making each location responsible for the outcomes of its own quality improvement program, Mr. Zambrano can show that he's serious about employee involvement and participation in quality. I'd also like to stress that I think that Mr. Zambrano's leadership during the development and implementation of this program is critical. At all times, he should be supportive of employees' involvement and participation in quality discussions at the company's various locations.

Ernie Collette, Casualty Claim Examiner, American Family Insurance, Springfield, Missouri

for your
IMMEDIATE
action

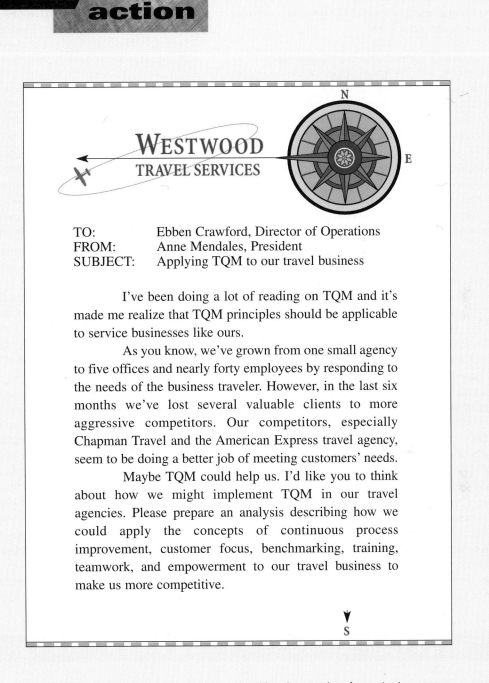

WESTWOOD
TRAVEL SERVICES

TO: Ebben Crawford, Director of Operations
FROM: Anne Mendales, President
SUBJECT: Applying TQM to our travel business

I've been doing a lot of reading on TQM and it's made me realize that TQM principles should be applicable to service businesses like ours.

As you know, we've grown from one small agency to five offices and nearly forty employees by responding to the needs of the business traveler. However, in the last six months we've lost several valuable clients to more aggressive competitors. Our competitors, especially Chapman Travel and the American Express travel agency, seem to be doing a better job of meeting customers' needs.

Maybe TQM could help us. I'd like you to think about how we might implement TQM in our travel agencies. Please prepare an analysis describing how we could apply the concepts of continuous process improvement, customer focus, benchmarking, training, teamwork, and empowerment to our travel business to make us more competitive.

This is a fictionalized account of a potentially real problem. It was written for academic purposes only.

SUMMARY

This summary is organized by the chapter-opening objectives found on p. 580.

1. The transformation process is the essence of operations management. Operations management takes inputs, including people and materials, and acts on them by transforming them into finished goods and services. This applies in service organizations as well as in manufacturing companies.

2. Customer-driven operations are important because organizations exist to meet the needs of customers. It's important that the operations system be designed around meeting and exceeding customers' expectations.

3. Reengineering of work processes involves totally redesigning a company's operations. It means starting from scratch in rethinking and rearranging the way work is done in the organization. In the operations system, the inputs and transformation process are completely redesigned as managers redefine the organization's work processes.

4. A manufacturing focus added to strategy pushes important production decisions to the top of the organization. It recognizes that an organization's overall strategy should directly reflect its manufacturing capabilities and limitations and should include operations objectives and strategies.

5. Four key decisions—capacity, location, process, and layout—provide the long-term strategic direction for operations planning. They determine the proper size of an operating system, the location of physical facilities, the best methods for transforming inputs into outputs, and the most efficient layout of equipment and work stations.

6. The three decisions that make up the tactical operations plan are the aggregate plan, the master schedule, and the material requirements plan. The aggregate plan determines the overall production plan, the master schedule determines how many units of each product will be produced, and the material requirements plan determines what materials are needed to satisfy the master schedule.

7. The three types of maintenance control are preventive, remedial, and conditional. Preventive maintenance is performed before a breakdown occurs. Remedial maintenance is performed when the equipment breaks down. Conditional maintenance is a response to an inspection.

8. Evidence demonstrates that the application of certain TQM concepts should reflect whether the organization is a low, medium, or high performer. Low-performing companies, for instance, should emphasize team creation and downplay benchmarking and empowerment. High-performing companies, on the other hand, should encourage benchmarking and empowerment and deemphasize departmental teams.

9. Just-in-time inventory systems seek to reduce inventories, reduce setup time, improve work flow, cut manufacturing time, reduce space consumption, and raise the quality of production by coordinating the arrival of inventory items with their demand in the production process. However, they require precise coordination; if this is lacking, they can threaten the smooth, continuous operation of a production system.

10. A flexible manufacturing system can give an organization a competitive advantage by allowing it to produce a wider variety of products, at a lower cost, and in considerably less time than the competition.

THINKING ABOUT MANAGEMENT ISSUES

1. Do you think that manufacturing or service organizations have the greater need for operations management? Explain.

2. How might operations management apply to other managerial functions besides control?

3. How could you use operations management concepts in your everyday life?

4. Which is more critical for success in organizations: continuous improvement or quality control? Support your position.

5. Choose some large organization that you are interested in studying. Research this company to find out what types of operations management techniques it is using. What is it doing in the area of operations management that's unusual or effective or both? Describe.

SELF-ASSESSMENT EXERCISE

HOW CUSTOMER-FOCUSED ARE YOU?

Instructions: Read through the statements and circle the answer that best describes your situation.

 1 = Strongly disagree
 2 = Disagree
 3 = Uncertain
 4 = Agree
 5 = Strongly agree

	1	2	3	4	5
1. I know who our organization's customers are.	1	2	3	4	5
2. I know how my work affects our customers' results.	1	2	3	4	5
3. My work creates value for our customers.	1	2	3	4	5
4. I'm rewarded for delivering superior results to our customers.	1	2	3	4	5
5. I use measures of customer satisfaction in my job.	1	2	3	4	5
6. I act as the customers' advocate in my job.	1	2	3	4	5
7. I know what our customers want.	1	2	3	4	5
8. I regularly ask my customers about their future plans.	1	2	3	4	5

See scoring key on page SK–6.

Source: Based on M. Treacy and F. Wiersema, *The Discipline of Market Leaders* (Reading, MA: Addison-Wesley, 1995); and Wiersema, *Customer Intimacy* (Santa Monica, CA: Knowledge Exchange, 1996).

• •

TAKE IT TO THE NET

We invite you to visit the Robbins/Coulter companion Web site at http://www.prenhall.com/robbinsmgt for this chapter's Internet resources.

CASE APPLICATION

Mercedes-Benz at Home in Alabama

Deep down in the heart of rural Dixie may seem an unlikely home for a product that's long been a symbol of European elegance, luxury, and sophistication. Yet Vance, Alabama (population 400), is where you'll find a sleek ultramodern Mercedes-Benz (MB) factory, where the company's all-activity sport-utility vehicles roll off the assembly line. The Mercedez-Benz plant here in the Deep South is being described as an exemplary model of how to set up a truly global operation.

The story began back in 1992 when Andreas Renschler, an assistant to Helmut Werner, the then-deputy president of Mercedes-Benz AG, spearheaded a project to evaluate the feasibility of MB's producing a four-wheel-drive passenger vehicle in a market outside its home market, Germany. By 1993, Renschler had been named president and CEO of Mercedes-Benz U.S. International (MBUSI) and was put in charge of managing the design, development, manufacturing, and marketing of Mercedes' new all-activity sport-utility vehicle. Renschler seemed to be the perfect choice for MB's new U.S. plant, which was slated to be a radical experiment in manufacturing and engineering techniques. He's tall (6´6´´), lanky, young, creative, and likes to shake things up. Renschler had free rein in bringing the Vance factory on-line. Unlike the Japanese automakers who impose their processes and cultures on their U.S. plants, Mercedes didn't want to create just another cookie-cutter manufacturing transplant in Alabama. Instead, the company wanted to use its $1 billion Alabama investment to position itself as a cost-competitive global manufacturer. It was to be a laboratory, and, as one of MB's managing directors said, "It has to be very successful."

One of the factors that influenced the decision to locate in the rural southern United States was labor costs, which in Germany were about 50 percent higher. In addition, MB felt that locating in the United States was important to being perceived as an established competitor in the U.S. market. The company's top managers chose Vance after considering 150 sites in 30 states. Alabama pledged $250 million in tax abatements and other incentives. In addition, Alabama business leaders presented a single bank check in the amount of $11 million to Mercedes officials. But the financial incentives, as impressive as they were, weren't what sold MB on Alabama. No, it was the plan that Alabama government officials presented to MB managers. It described how the Alabama government would help the families of German workers adjust to living in a different country and cope with a different culture.

Once the site for the new factory had been selected, Renschler set out to create a new corporate culture, deliberately separate and distinct from MB headquarters. The first thing he did was to put together a team of top managers who had a broad range of experience—four Germans and four Americans, some of whom came from other U.S. automakers and some who had worked for Japanese factories in the United States. His hope was that those with Japanese transplant experience could provide insights on how to best go about setting up shop in the United States. But the wealth of automaking experience also led to the first managerial challenge. They all spoke different "languages"—GM-ese, Nissan-ese, Mercedes-ese, and so forth. Decisions about things such as how to configure the assembly line sparked heated and intense debates. If it weren't for the one unchanging directive from MB's headquarters

in Stuttgart that Renschler had no control over—the very rigid time frame—progress would not have been possible. But faced with the tight deadline, the management team had no choice but to come up with blueprints for a factory and plans for hiring a workforce. What they came up with caught the attention of the entire auto industry!

The plant configuration (a sleek E-shaped design) itself is radically different. The major sections include a body shop where the metal stampings are assembled; an environmentally safe paint shop that's slightly pressurized to keep out the fine red clay of Alabama soil; and an assembly shop where the painted body is made into the M-class sport-utility vehicle. In addition, the administrative offices are smack dab in the middle of the manufacturing area. Vehicles being delivered from the paint shop to the assembly shop pass right through the middle of the glassed-in administrative offices. The factory layout was designed this way to keep everyone focused on the company's purpose—building Mercedes-Benz automobiles. This plant configuration was also designed to enhance communication and employee participation.

Another manufacturing operations element that distinguished this MB plant was the "modular construction techniques." Automotive components, such as the entire cockpit or dash assembly normally provided by automotive suppliers, are delivered as one unit by just one primary supplier. Only about 65 "first-tier" automotive components suppliers are involved, and only about one dozen of them are connected by file-transfer protocol (a faster version of electronic data interchange) to the Vance factory. This arrangement had several benefits. First, MB didn't have to build as large a building because they were relying on suppliers to supply these components in one unit. The chosen suppliers are the experts in designing and engineering the components. In addition, MB was able to use just-in-time inventory delivery requirements with its limited number of suppliers, which, in turn, reduced the need for warehousing materials.

Although Renschler was free to experiment with a new approach to manufacturing at the Alabama factory, Mercedes does have an exacting precise way of building cars. There's a certain level of quality engineering that customers expect from products with the name *Mercedes* on them. And at the Alabama plant, workers are expected to maintain high-quality work performance levels. Therefore, all factory-floor jobs are done in accordance with standard methods and procedures (SMPs) that spell out the exact, proper, and single way to do every task. These SMPs have been drawn up by German engineers and are posted at every work station for easy reference by the American employees. Employees must follow precise directions, and they need permission to make even the slightest alteration in their work methods.

QUESTIONS
1. Describe the factors that went into the factory location decision. Which factor do you think was most important to Mercedes' top managers? Why?
2. What advantages and drawbacks do you see in the use of standard methods and procedures for performing the assembly-line jobs at the MB factory?

3. In designing the MB factory, Renschler stated that he wanted the design to enhance employee participation. How can employee participation be encouraged in a workplace where every job is done in accordance with standard methods and procedures?
4. Do you think MB's experience at the Alabama factory is a model of how to set up a global operation? Why or why not?

Source: D. Woodruff and K.L. Miller, "Mercedes' Maverick in Alabama," *Business Week*, September 11, 1995, pp. 64–65; B.S. Moskal, "Not the Same Old Mercedes," *IW*, October 7, 1996, pp. 12–21; and J. Martin, "Mercedes: Made in Alabama," *Fortune*, July 7, 1997, pp. 150–58.

VIDEO CASE APPLICATION

Wizards of Wheels

Bicycling is a booming industry! Enthusiasts point to its appeal as a great family sport that can be enjoyed at low cost and that can be done in a variety of locations, particularly since bicycles are easily transported from one place to another—easily transported, that is, if the bicyclists have a reliable, safe, and easy-to-use bicycle rack on their vehicle. Some of the world's best bicycle racks are made by Sara and Chris Fortune's company, Graber Products of Madison, Wisconsin.

Chris Fortune says that consumers want products that are user-friendly and so do dealers. Graber Products is striving to supply that product. He says that whenever Graber develops a new product, three very simple and very basic "musts" need to be met: (1) The bicycle racks must stay on the car; (2) the bikes must stay on the rack; and (3) the racks must not scratch or mar the owner's vehicle. These three "musts" guide product innovation and development at Graber.

Innovation is one of the top business issues that faces Graber Products. Through its product innovation process, Graber wants to go beyond what's already on the market. They don't want to merely copy what other industry competitors have already done because doing that would make it extremely difficult for the company to gain market recognition. And it isn't just Chris and Sara who recognize the importance of innovation to Graber's long-term success. *Everyone* at Graber talks about innovation. For instance, the company's talented toolmakers, who bend and mold the pieces of steel into the simple yet

functional bicycle racks, are constantly innovating. They have to, and they are given the freedom to do so by the company's cellular manufacturing system. Cellular manufacturing is similar to assembly-line production, but assembly lines use some parts that are made elsewhere, whereas all parts used in cellular manufacturing are processed right in the plant. Employees can design and produce tools or processes that make them more efficient and help them achieve higher product quality levels. The cellular manufacturing system has led to two important results at Graber. First, it has improved the quality of parts because employees now are dealing with a much smaller production run. Second, it has improved efficiency by almost 25 percent.

QUESTIONS
1. What role do you think innovation plays at Graber Products?
2. Do you think there's a connection between innovativeness in *producing* a product and in *developing* a product? Explain.
3. How do you think the three product development "musts" that Chris Fortune describes might affect the innovation process at Graber Products?
4. Pretend that Sara and Chris Fortune have asked you to come to their plant in Madison, Wisconsin, to consult with them about ways to encourage innovation. Make a list of the important points you'd want to tell them.

Source: Based on *Small Business 2000, Show 410.*

A MANAGER'S DILEMMA

Managed care. Those words describe what hospitals must do well in order to succeed in today's dynamic and intensely competitive health care market. Hospitals used to make money through a charge-based system in which patients (usually through their insurance companies) paid a fee for every service provided. Under a managed care system, however, fees are fixed for certain procedures.[1] So, for instance, a hospital receives X amount of dollars for performing an appendectomy, a set amount for performing a gallbladder operation, and so forth. Hospitals receive these fixed fees for the services provided to each patient regardless of how much it actually costs them to perform the procedures. Under this type of payment system, a hospital makes money only if it can provide a service for a total cost that is less than the fixed fee. That means that hospitals are faced with the need to reduce expenses and yet maintain quality service levels.

For Kevin E. Lofton, CEO and executive director of the University of Alabama Hos-

pital, coping with and profiting in a managed care–type environment isn't an easy task even given the fact that the University of Alabama Hospital was considered one of the best in the nation even before managed care. Why isn't it easy? Because the state of Alabama had yet to embrace the managed care concept, and the sentiment at the hospital was that even if managed care became a reality, the organization's reputation would protect it from this particular health care revolution. People would come for the hospital's excellent care even if its costs were high. But Lofton knew that changes—particularly in the areas of cost and quality controls—were necessary if the hospital wanted to maintain its reputation and profitability.

Information is a critical link in creating an efficient managed care system. Lofton wants to design an information system that will help control costs and quality.

Put yourself in Lofton's situation. What should this information system look like? How could an information system help in the implementation of the cost and quality controls that would be necessary under this type of arrangement? How would you go about designing the hospital's information system?

WHAT WOULD YOU DO?

In the process of controlling the different areas of the organization, managers have various tools and techniques to help them. The sophisticated information system that Kevin Lofton is looking to implement and the performance appraisal methods that another organization uses to control employee performance and behavior are just two examples of the different types of control tools that managers have available. In this chapter, we look at the wide range of tools and techniques managers can use in controlling four distinct organizational areas: information, finances, operations, and employee behavior.

CHAPTER

19

Control Tools and Techniques

INFORMATION CONTROLS

As we saw in the chapter-opening Manager's Dilemma, controlling information can be vital to an organization's success. Managers like Kevin Lofton use information in every activity they perform, and every decision they make requires information. To be effective and efficient, however, managers need the right information at the right time and in the right amount. Inaccurate, incomplete, excessive, or delayed information will seriously impede their performance. How can managers use information for control, and how can information be controlled through management information systems?

What Is a Management Information System?

management information system (MIS)

A system that provides management with needed information on a regular basis.

Although there is no universally agreed-upon definition of a **management information system (MIS)**, we'll define it as a system used to provide management with needed information on a regular basis.[2] In theory, this system can be manual or computer based, although all current discussions, including ours, focus on computer-supported applications. The term *system* in MIS implies order, arrangement, and purpose. Further, an MIS focuses specifically on providing managers with *information,* not merely *data.* These two points are important and require elaboration.

A library provides a good analogy. Although it can contain millions of volumes, a library doesn't do users much good if they can't find what they want quickly. That's why libraries spend a great deal of time cataloging their collections and ensuring that volumes are returned to their proper locations. Organizations today are like well-stocked libraries. There's no lack of data. There is, however, a lack of ability to process those data so that the right information is available to the right person when he or she needs it.[3] Likewise, a library is almost useless if it has the book that you need immediately, but either you can't find it or the library takes a week to retrieve it from storage. An MIS, on the other hand, has organized data in some meaningful way and can access the information in a reasonable amount of time. **Data** are raw, unanalyzed facts, such as numbers, names, or quantities. But raw, unanalyzed facts are relatively useless to managers.[4] When data are analyzed and processed, they become **information**. For example, in our chapter-opening dilemma, Kevin Lofton wants an information system that provides him and other decision makers with usable information. Other companies have also recognized the value of information. For example, one of American Express Company's most "valuable" possessions is the 500 million bytes of data it has on how its customers have used their over 35 million green, gold, and platinum American Express charge cards.[5] However, until these data are organized in some meaningful way, they are useless. An MIS collects data and turns them into relevant information for managers to use. Figure 19-1 summarizes these observations.

data

Raw, unanalyzed facts.

information

Analyzed and processed data.

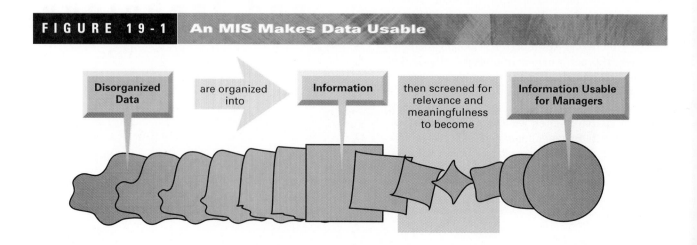

FIGURE 19-1 **An MIS Makes Data Usable**

Disorganized Data → are organized into → Information → then screened for relevance and meaningfulness to become → Information Usable for Managers

How Are Information Systems Used in Controlling?

Managers need information to control the various organizational areas efficiently and effectively. Without information, they would find it difficult to perform the activities that we discussed in chapter 17 as part of the controlling process. For instance, in measuring actual performance, managers need information about what is, in fact, happening within their area of responsibility. Also, they need information about what the standards are in order to be able to compare actual performance with the standard. In addition, managers need information to help them determine acceptable ranges of variation within these comparisons. Finally, they rely on information to help them develop appropriate courses of action if there are or are not significant deviations between actual and standard. As you can see, information plays a vital role in the controlling process. But how does a manager get the information he or she needs?

Designing the MIS

Just as there's no universal definition of what an MIS is, there's no universal approach to designing one. However, the following steps represent the key elements in putting an MIS together (Figure 19-2).

1. *Analyze the decision system.* The decisions that managers make should drive the design of any MIS. Therefore, the first step is to identify all the management decisions for which information is needed. This step should encompass all the functions within the organization and every management level from first-level supervisor to the chief executive officer.

    This step should also consider whether each decision is being made by the right person. Is it being made at the right level? By the right department? Failure to ask these questions can misdirect the design of the entire MIS. If the wrong people are making the decision and this problem isn't corrected before a sophisticated information system is put in place, these people will continue to make the decision erroneously, only faster.

2. *Analyze information requirements.* Once the decisions that will have to be made are isolated, we need to know the exact information required to effectively make them. Information needs differ according to managerial function in the organization. The information that a marketing manager needs differs from that required by a financial manager. Thus, the MIS has to be tailored to meet the varying needs of different functional managers.

    As Figure 19-3 illustrates, managers' information needs also vary by organizational level. Top-level managers are looking for environmental data and summary reports. At the other extreme, lower-level supervisors want detailed reports of operating problems. An MIS must consider these diverse requirements if it's to satisfy the varied needs of managers.

3. *Aggregate the decisions.* After each functional area and manager's needs have been identified, those that have the same or largely overlapping information requirements should be located. Even though needs vary up and down and across the organization, redundancies often occur. Both sales and production executives, for example, may

FIGURE 19-2   Steps in Designing an MIS

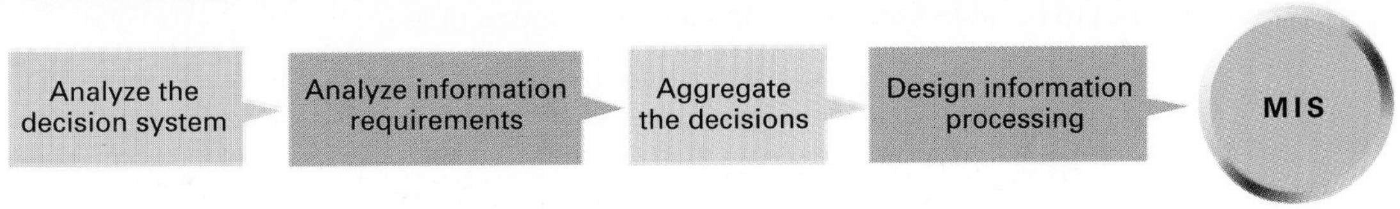

Analyze the decision system → Analyze information requirements → Aggregate the decisions → Design information processing → **MIS**

FIGURE 19-3   **Matching Information Requirements with Managerial Level**

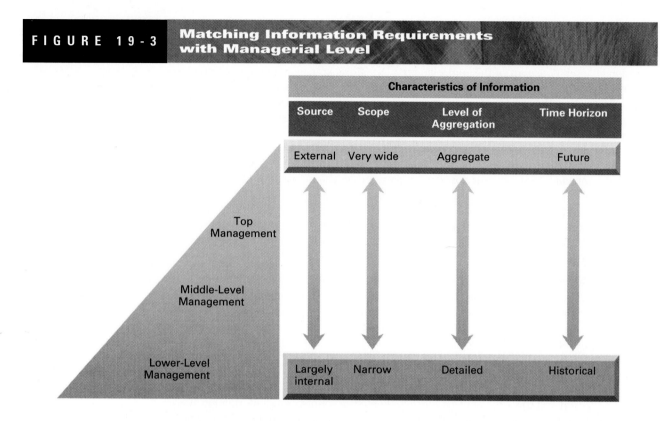

want feedback data on a given product's quality level. One executive, however, wants the feedback to ensure customer satisfaction; the other wants it to control for variances in the production processes. By identifying these redundancies, management can create systems that contain the least amount of duplication and that group together similar decisions under a single manager.

4. *Design information processing.* In this step, internal technical specialists or outside consultants develop the actual system for collecting, storing, transmitting, and retrieving information. A detailed flowchart of the desired system will be drawn up. It will include, among other things, sources and types of data, locations of users, and storage requirements. The precise hardware and software requirements will also be determined.

   Before the system is implemented, it's carefully evaluated to ensure that it will do what management wants it to do. That is, the bottom-line test of the system's effectiveness is its ability to meet each manager's information needs. A design that meets all of most managers' needs or most of all managers' needs will not provide the optimal quantity or quality of information for the organization as a whole.

Implementing the MIS

Once the MIS design has been resolved, the system needs to be implemented. The implementation phase should begin with pretesting the system, and it should conclude with building in regular evaluations in the system. The following points highlight concerns that need to be addressed during the implementation phase.

1. *Test the system before installation.* Flaws found before an information system is installed are much easier and less costly to fix than those found when the system is in place and people are depending on it. If a full pretest isn't feasible, then managers should consider introducing the new system in parallel with the old. Running the two systems

side by side for a short period of time enables managers to identify and correct bugs or omissions in the new system with minimal disturbances to the organization's operations.

2. *Prepare users with proper training.* No matter how well a system is designed, if users aren't aware of its full capabilities and don't know how to obtain those capabilities, it will never achieve its full potential. Therefore, the budget of any new MIS installation must cover time and money for training users. Even the brightest and most competent managers will require some training if they're going to be able to make full use of a new information system.

3. *Prepare for resistance.* As we discussed in the chapter on change, people tend to resist changes that appear threatening to them. A sizable body of research indicates that the introduction of computer-based information systems can be highly threatening.[6] Some people have difficulty adapting to the introduction of any new technology. Some are afraid that they will not be able to learn the new system. Others may be threatened by the new system's potential for reducing their power and status in the organization, changing interpersonal relationships, or reducing their job security.

4. *Get users involved.* One of the most effective ways of neutralizing resistance to an MIS is to have those who will be affected by the system participate fully in its design and implementation.[7] Participation will familiarize users with the system before they have to use it, increase their commitment to it because they were involved in its creation, and lessen the likelihood that their needs will be overlooked.

5. *Check for security.* As information systems become decentralized, there's a critical need to ensure that unauthorized individuals don't gain access to valuable or privileged information. When information was centralized at a single source, only a few people could tap into important databases such as production schedules, customer records, inventory accounts, credit data, and employee files. Today, however, such databases are much more vulnerable to unauthorized access. The solution is to ensure that adequate security measures are included in the system. For instance, access to the place where hardware is located should be controlled. Software should be locked up when not in use. A system should also use impossible-to-guess passwords or codes for gaining access that are changed frequently, require users to identify themselves once into the system, and impose strict controls over telephone access.

EDS's Information Management Center in Plano, Texas, is the command site from which the information services company manages its global communications in more than 42 countries. This is MIS on a very grand scale.

6. *Build in regular reviews.* The information that a manager needed last year isn't necessarily the same that he or she needs today. As customers, suppliers, governmental regulations, and other environmental factors change, so too will the information needs of managers. Implementation should be viewed as the beginning of an ongoing process. If an information system is to be valuable to managers over time, it must be regularly evaluated and modified to adapt to the changing needs of its users.

How MISs Are Changing the Manager's Job

No discussion of management information systems would be complete without assessing their impact on the manager's job. In this section, we'll touch on four key areas that are changing as a result of computer-based MIS.

Hands-On Involvement.   A few years ago, managers could avoid computers by claiming, "I don't have to know how to use computers. I can hire people to do that for me." Those days are long gone.[8] Today's managers, exposed to computers in college, and even in elementary and high school, feel at home in front of a keyboard. If anything, they've swung to the other extreme: They've become dependent on their computers and feel threatened when access is limited. Managers who fail to fully learn their systems and take advantage of their MIS capabilities will find it increasingly difficult to perform as effectively as their peers.

How will hands-on use change what managers do? Among other things, managers will spend less time on the phone, traveling to conferences, and waiting for subordinates to provide progress reports. They'll use networks for electronic mail, videoconferencing, and closely monitoring organizational activities.

Decision-Making Capability.   Because managers rely on information to make decisions and because a sophisticated MIS significantly alters the quantity and quality of information, as well as the speed with which it can be obtained, we can naturally conclude that an effective MIS will improve managers' decision-making capabilities.[9]

The effect will be seen in establishing the need for a decision, in the development and evaluation of alternatives, and in the final selection of the best alternative. On-line, real-time systems allow managers to identify problems almost as they occur. Gone are the long delays between the appearance of a serious discrepancy and a manager's ability to find out about it. For instance, Wal-Mart Stores' $600 million investment in inventory management equipment and other computerized technology allows it to track inventory and handle accounting and payments. Any problems with slow-moving inventory or not making vendor payments to take advantage of discount terms can be pinpointed immediately by managers. Database management programs allow managers to look things up or to get to the facts without going to other people or digging through piles of paper. This capability reduces a manager's dependence on others for data and makes fact gathering far more efficient. Today's manager can identify alternatives quickly, evaluate those alternatives by using a spreadsheet program and posing a series of what-if questions based on financial data, and finally select the best alternative on the basis of answers to those questions. For instance, Taco Bell's CEO, John Martin, is a fanatic about collecting customer information. His company's management information system allows him to pull up real-time sales updates from any of Taco Bell's almost 3,000 company stores in just 15 minutes. With this information, Martin can make decisions about product mix, marketing, employee training, or whatever else might be critical at that moment.[10]

Organizational Design.   Sophisticated information systems are reshaping organizations. For instance, traditional departmental boundaries will be less confining as networks cut across departments, divisions, geographical locations, and levels in the organization. The most evident change is probably that MIS is making organizations flatter and more organic.[11]

Duplicating software for friends and co-workers is a widespread practice, but software is protected by copyright law. Copying it is punishable by fines of up to $100,000 and five years in jail.

Is reproducing copyrighted software ever an acceptable practice? Explain. Is it wrong for employees of a corporation to pirate software but permissible for struggling college students who can't afford to buy their own software? As a manager, what types of ethical guidelines could you establish for software use? ■

Managers can now handle more subordinates. Why? Because computer control substitutes for personal supervision. As a result, there are wider spans of control and fewer levels in the organization. The need for staff support is also reduced with an MIS. As was noted previously, hands-on involvement allows managers to tap information directly, thus making large staff support groups, which traditionally compiled, tabulated, and analyzed data—redundant.[12] Both conditions—wider spans and reduced staff—lead to flatter organizations.

One of the more interesting phenomena created by sophisticated information systems is that they have enabled managers to lessen formalization and decentralized the organization—thus making the organizational structure more organic without any loss in control.[13] Many managers tend to prefer bureaucracy because bureaucracy facilitates control,[14] but there is more than one way to maintain control. An MIS substitutes computer control for rules and limited decision discretion. Because of computer technology, managers can be rapidly apprised of the consequences of any decision and take corrective action if necessary. There's the appearance of decentralization without any commensurate loss of control.

Power.   Information is power. Anything that changes the access to scarce and important information is going to change power relationships within an organization.[15] An MIS changes the status hierarchy in an organization. Middle managers have less status because they carry less clout. They no longer serve as the vital link between operations and the executive suite. Similarly, staff units have less prestige because senior managers no longer depend on them for evaluation and advice.

Centralized computer departments, which were extremely influential units in organizations during the 1970s, have had their role modified and their power reduced.[16] Now organized as information support centers, they no longer have exclusive control over access to databases.

In aggregate, probably the most important effect that computer-based control systems have had on the power structure has been to enable top managers to tighten the reins on their organization. In earlier years, top managers regularly depended on lower-level managers to feed information upward. Because information was filtered and "enhanced," managers knew only what their subordinates wanted them to know. Now these top managers have the power of information at their fingertips because they have direct access to data.

1 How can an MIS assist a manager in the control function?

2 What are the steps in implementing an MIS?

3 How are MISs changing the manager's job?

FINANCIAL CONTROLS

One of the primary purposes of every business firm is to earn a profit. In pursuit of this objective, managers need financial controls. Managers might, for instance, carefully analyze quarterly income statements for excessive expenses. They might also perform several financial

MANAGERS

SPEAK

OUT

Interview with Barbara Whittaker, Director, Metallic/Car Platforms, Worldwide Purchasing, General Motors, Warren, Michigan

Describe your job.

I'm involved in developing strategies for how General Motors purchases specific productive materials for the manufacture of cars worldwide. This includes managing a global team's efforts in evaluating and negotiating business deals that will deliver the right quality, service, and price.

What skills do you think tomorrow's managers will need?

As the world continues to shrink with respect to how business is conducted due to the advantages in technology for communication, transportation, and so forth, it will become increasingly important that tomorrow's managers be skilled in the ability to manage diverse groups. The ability to motivate people to accomplish the task required will be critical. I believe communication and team-building skills are the basis for managing people. This will require that managers understand the subtle differences in people. That understanding enables them to use those differences as strengths.

What types of management control tools do you use in your job?

Some of the control tools I use to understand the pulse of the organization are employee enthusiasm surveys, diagonal slice meetings with groups of people, customer evaluations, and one-on-one meetings with employees. For overall business control, I use a business plan that tracks the critical metrics for the organization—performance to budget, quality, sourcing process, and people.

How do you use information as a control tool?

Each of these tools focuses on getting data about the health of the organization and how effectively it is running. The surveys are used to understand the effect of the process and management on the people who must execute the process. What we learn from these tools is used to continuously improve the process and management. The business plan is reviewed weekly to keep focused on the key metrics to make sure that proper adjustments can be made to keep the organization on course to meet its business objectives. ▪

ratio tests to ensure that sufficient cash is available to pay ongoing expenses, that debt has not become too large and burdensome, or that assets are being used productively. In addition, they might look at budgets to see if cash, employees, or units of production are going according to plan. These are examples of how financial controls can be used to reduce costs and make the best use of an organization's financial resources. Two specific financial control tools that a wide range of managers need to understand are budgets and ratio analysis.

Budgets Revisited

In chapter 9, we discussed budgets as a planning tool. When the budget is formulated, it's a planning tool because it gives direction. It indicates what activities are important and how much resources should be allocated to each activity. As we noted, however, budgets are used for both planning and control.

Budgets also provide managers with quantitative standards against which to measure and compare resource consumption. By pointing out deviations between standard and actual consumption, they become control tools. If the deviations are judged to be significant enough to require action, the manager will want to examine what has happened and try to uncover the reasons behind the deviations. With this information, he or she can take whatever action is necessary. For example, if you use a personal budget for controlling your monthly expenses, you might find one month that your miscellaneous expenses were higher than you had budgeted for. At that point, you might cut back spending in another area, work extra hours to try to get more income, or call home for additional money.

Ratio Analysis

Table 19-1 summarizes some of the most popular financial ratios used in organizations. Taken from the organization's primary financial statements (the balance sheet and income statement), they compare two significant figures and express them as a percentage, or

TABLE 19-1	**Popular Financial Ratios**		
Objective	**Ratio**	**Calculation**	**Meaning**
Liquidity test	Current ratio	$\dfrac{\text{Current assets}}{\text{Current liabilities}}$	Tests the organization's ability to meet short-term obligations
	Acid test	$\dfrac{\text{Current assets less inventories}}{\text{Current liabilities}}$	Tests liquidity more accurately when inventories turn over slowly or are difficult to sell
Leverage test	Debt-to-assets	$\dfrac{\text{Total debt}}{\text{Total assets}}$	The higher the ratio, the more leveraged the organization
	Times-interest-earned	$\dfrac{\text{Profits before interest and taxes}}{\text{Total interest charges}}$	Measures how far profits can decline before the organization is unable to meet its interest expenses
Operations test	Inventory turnover	$\dfrac{\text{Sales}}{\text{Inventory}}$	The higher the ratio, the more efficiently inventory assets are being used
	Total asset turnover	$\dfrac{\text{Sales}}{\text{Total assets}}$	The fewer assets used to achieve a given level of sales, the more efficiently management is using the organization's total assets
Profitability	Profit margin-on-sales	$\dfrac{\text{Net profit after taxes}}{\text{Total sales}}$	Identifies the profits that various products are generating
	Return-on-investment	$\dfrac{\text{Net profit after taxes}}{\text{Total assets}}$	Measures the efficiency of assets to generate profits

ratio. Because you've undoubtedly encountered these ratios in introductory accounting and finance courses, or you will in the near future, we aren't going to elaborate on how they're calculated.

What do these ratios mean? The liquidity ratios measure an organization's ability to meet its current debt obligations. Leverage ratios examine the organization's use of debt to finance its assets and whether it's able to meet the interest payments on the debt. The operations ratios measure how efficiently the firm is using its assets. Finally, the profitability ratios measure how efficiently and effectively the firm is using its assets to generate profits. We mention these ratios only briefly here to remind you that managers use such ratios as internal control devices for monitoring how efficiently and profitably the organization uses its assets, debt, inventories, and the like.

OPERATIONS CONTROLS

The success of an organization depends to a large extent on its ability to produce goods and services effectively and efficiently. Operations control techniques are designed to assess how effective and efficient an organization's transformation processes are.

Operations control typically encompasses monitoring production activities to ensure that they're on schedule; assessing purchasing's ability to provide the proper quantity and quality of supplies needed at the lowest possible cost; monitoring the quality of the organization's products or services to ensure that they meet preestablished standards; and making sure that equipment is well maintained. We covered many of these operations activities in the preceding chapter on operations management. However, two important operations control tools deserve elaboration: TQM control charts and the EOQ model.

TQM Control Charts

We discussed the general concept of quality control in the chapter on operations management. But effective quality control involves more than just expressing a desire to have quality products. Managers must control all the various aspects of the operations system in order to achieve total quality in both products and processes. One tool they use in doing this is TQM control charts.

control chart

A management control tool that shows results of measurements over a period of time, with statistically determined upper and lower limits.

A **control chart** is an operations control tool that shows the result of measurements over a period of time, with statistically determined upper and lower limits. Control charts provide a visual means of determining whether a specific process is staying within predefined limits. For instance, employees at Ralston Purina sample the weight of dry dog food bags after they have been filled to determine the exact number of pounds in each bag and then plot the data on a control chart. This sampling alerts managers to whether the filling equipment needs adjustment. As long as the process variables fall within the acceptable range, the system is said to be "in control" (Figure 19-4). When a measurement falls outside the limits set, then the variation is unacceptable. Improvements in quality should, over time, result in a narrowing of the range between the upper and lower limits through elimination of common causes of variation. But just what do managers have to do to construct a control chart?

First, in developing a control chart, managers must recognize that there are two possible sources of process variability. One is chance, which includes variations caused by randomness in the process. These variations are found in every process and are impossible to control unless the process is fundamentally changed. The other source of variation is assignable causes. Nonchance variations can be identified and controlled. Control charts are used to identify these assignable causes of variation.

Control charts are put together with the help of some basic statistical concepts. You have probably covered in an introductory statistics class the ideas of a normal distribution (the concept that variations are assumed to follow a bell-shaped distribution curve) and standard deviation (a measure of variability in a group of numerical values). In the devel-

FIGURE 19-4 | **Sample Control Chart**

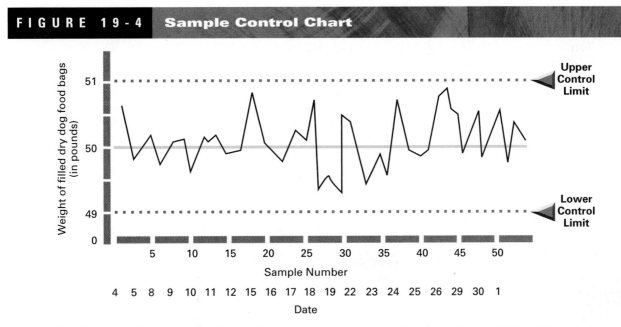

Source: M. Sashkin and K.J. Kiser, *Putting Total Quality Management to Work* (San Francisco: Berrett-Koehler, 1993), p. 170.

opment of a control chart, the upper and lower limits are defined by the degree of deviation you are willing to accept. In a normal distribution, approximately 68 percent of a set of values will fall between +1 and –1 standard deviations from the mean. (A sampling distribution becomes more like a normal distribution as the size of the sample increases.) Ninety-five percent will fall in the range of +2 and –2 standard deviations. In a typical operations setting, the limits are set at three standard deviations, which means that 99.7 percent of the mean (or average) values should lie between the control limits (Figure 19-5). What should

FIGURE 19-5 | **Control Chart Using Three Standard Deviations as Limits**

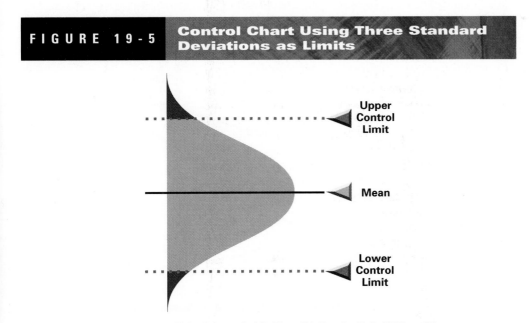

Source: S.P. Robbins, *Supervision Today!* (Upper Saddle River, NJ: Prentice Hall, 1995), p. 152.

a manager do when variations occur? When a sample average falls outside these limits—that is, above the upper control limit or below the lower limit—the process is very likely out of control. The manager should then initiate a search for the cause of the problem.

The EOQ Model

As we pointed out in the last chapter, controlling inventory is one of the important managerial tasks associated with operations control. Because an organization typically has a large dollar investment in inventory, managers want to know the appropriate amount of inventory to order and how often to order. That's what the EOQ model does.

One of the best-known techniques for mathematically deriving the optimal quantity for a purchase order is the **economic order quantity model (EOQ)**. The EOQ model seeks to balance four costs associated with ordering and carrying inventory: the *purchase costs* (purchase price plus delivery charges minus any discounts); the *ordering costs* (paperwork, follow-up, inspection upon arrival, and other processing costs); *carrying costs* (money tied up in inventory, storage, insurance, taxes, and so forth); and *stockout costs* (profits forgone from orders lost because the product wasn't available, the cost of reestablishing goodwill, and additional expenses incurred to expedite late shipments).

The objective of the EOQ model, as shown in Figure 19-6, is to minimize the total of two of these four costs: carrying costs and ordering costs. As the amount ordered gets larger and larger, average inventory increases and so do carrying costs. But placing larger orders means placing fewer orders and thus reduces ordering costs. For example, if annual demand for an inventory item is 26,000 units, and we order 500 each time, we will place 52 (26,000/500) orders a year and will have an average inventory of 250 (500/2) units. If we increase the order quantity to 2,000 units, we will place fewer orders, 13 (26,000/2,000), but our average inventory on hand will increase to 1,000 (2,000/2) units. Thus, as holding costs go up, ordering costs go down, and vice versa. As shown in Figure 19-6, the lowest total cost—and thus the most economic order quantity—is reached at the lowest point on the total cost curve. That's the point at which ordering costs equal carrying costs—the *economic order quantity*.

economic order quantity model (EOQ)

A technique for balancing purchase, ordering, carrying, and stockout costs to derive the optimal quantity for a purchase order.

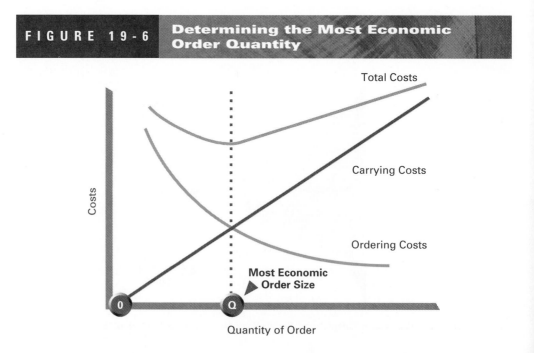

FIGURE 19-6   **Determining the Most Economic Order Quantity**

To compute this optimal order quantity, you need the following data: forecasted demand for the item during the period (D), the cost of placing each order (OC), the value or purchase price of the item (V), and the carrying cost of maintaining the total inventory expressed as a percentage (CC). We can now present the standard EOQ formula and demonstrate its use:

$$EOQ = \sqrt{\frac{2 \times D \times OC}{V \times CC}}$$

Let's work through an example. Playback Electronics, a retailer of high-quality sound and video equipment, is trying to determine its economic order quantities. The item in question is a Yamaha compact sound system. The company forecasts sales of 4,000 units a year. The purchasing manager believes that the cost of each system will be $500. The accountants estimate the cost of placing an order for the sound system at $75 per order and annual insurance, taxes, and other carrying costs at 20 percent of the system's value. Using the EOQ formula and the information above, we find:

$$EOQ = \sqrt{\frac{2 \times 4,000 \times 75}{500 \times 0.20}}$$

$$EOQ = \sqrt{6,000}$$

$$EOQ = 77.45 \text{ units} \cong 78 \text{ units}$$

The inventory model suggests to Playback's management that it's most economic to order in quantities or lots of approximately 78 units. Stated differently, they should order about 52 (4,000/78) times a year.

What would happen if a supplier, Yamaha, for example, offered Playback a 5 percent discount on purchases if Playback buys in minimum quantities of 120 units? Should Playback's management now purchase in quantities of 78 or 120? Without the discount, and therefore ordering 78 each time, Playback's annual costs for this sound system would be as follows:

Purchase cost:	$500 × 4,000 =	$2,000,000
Carrying cost (average inventory units × value of item × percentage):	78/2 × $500 × 0.20 =	3,900
Ordering cost (number of orders × cost to place order):	52 × 75 =	3,900
Total cost:	=	$2,007,800

With the 5 percent discount for ordering 120 units, the item cost would be $475. The annual inventory costs would be as follows:

Purchase cost:	$475 × 4,000 =	$1,900,000
Carrying cost:	120/2 × 475 × 0.20 =	5,700
Ordering cost:	4,000/120 × 75 =	2,500
Total cost:	=	$1,908,200

These computations tell Playback's managers that they should take the 5 percent discount. Even though they now have to stock larger quantities, the annual savings amount to almost $100,000.

A word of caution should be added. The EOQ model assumes that demand and lead time are known and constant. If those conditions cannot be met, the model shouldn't be used. For example, it generally should not be used for manufactured component inventory because the components are taken out of stock all at once or in lumps or odd lots rather

Ken Thuerbach spent two years studying every aspect of the production processes performed by the bankrupt log-home builder he acquired in the early 1970s. Only then was he able to institute new operations controls that ranged from custom-designed tools to the layout of the lumberyard and prefabricated patterns for assembling homes at the building site. Today the firm, Alpine Log Homes, is worth millions.

than at a constant rate. Does this mean that the EOQ model is useless when demand is variable? No. The model can still be of some use in demonstrating trade-offs in costs and the need to control lot sizes, but there are more-sophisticated lot-sizing models for handling "lumpy" demand and special situations.

TESTING... TESTING...

4 Why are financial controls important?

5 How can managers use TQM control charts?

6 Describe the important variables in EOQ and how it is calculated.

BEHAVIORAL CONTROLS

Managers accomplish goals by working with other people. To achieve their unit goals, managers need and depend on their employees. It's important, therefore, for managers to ensure that employees are performing as they're supposed to. Table 19-2 lists several behavioral control devices that managers have at their disposal. However, the most explicit ways managers control employee behavior are by direct supervision, performance appraisals, and discipline. Let's look closer at each of these behavioral control techniques.

Direct Supervision

On a day-to-day basis, managers oversee employees' work and correct problems as they occur. For instance, the supervisor who spots an employee taking an unnecessary risk when operating his or her equipment may point out the correct way to perform the task and tell the employee to do it the correct way in the future.

We introduced the concept of MBWA (management by walking around) in chapter 17 as a simple control technique that entrepreneurs could use. However, managers at every level of any organization can engage in MBWA to detect problems that employees might be having or to monitor employee work activities. Many practicing managers admit that they learn a lot more by getting out of their office and into the workplace than by sitting and reading subordinates' reports or by having formal meetings. The close direct contact

TABLE 19-2	**Behavioral Control Techniques**

Selection. Identify and hire people whose values, attitudes, and personality fit with what management desires.

Goals. When employees accept specific goals, the goals then direct and limit behavior.

Job design. The way jobs are designed determines, to a large degree, the tasks that a person does, the pace of the work, the people with whom he or she interacts, and similar activities.

Orientation. New-employee orientation defines which behaviors are acceptable and which are not.

Direct supervision. The physical presence of supervisors acts to constrain employee behavior and allows for rapid detection of deviant behavior.

Training. Formal training programs teach employees desired work practices.

Mentoring. Informal and formal mentoring activities by senior employees convey to junior employees "the ropes to skip and the ropes to know."

Formalization. Formal rules, policies, job descriptions, and other regulations define acceptable practices and constrain behavior.

Performance appraisals. Employees will behave in ways so as to look good on the criteria by which they will be appraised.

Organizational rewards. Rewards act as reinforcers to encourage desired behaviors and to extinguish undesirable ones.

Organizational culture. Through stories, rituals, and top management practices, culture conveys what constitutes proper behavior.

Discipline. Actions taken by managers that enforce the organization's standards and regulations.

between supervisor and subordinates that's possible with MBWA can prevent many minor behavior problems from becoming serious.

Performance Appraisal

Managers also assess their employees' work in a more formal way by means of systematic performance appraisals. **Performance appraisal** is a process of evaluating individuals in order to arrive at objective human resource decisions. Although organizations use formal employee performance appraisals for a number of reasons, one of its most important func-

performance appraisal

The evaluation of an individual's work performance in order to arrive at objective personnel decisions.

Close contact between employee and supervisor is one of the biggest advantages of MBWA, management by walking around.

tions is to control employee behavior. Because performance appraisals play such a significant role in behavior control, we need to look at the different methods managers can use. The following discussion reviews the major performance appraisal methods and looks at how feedback should be provided in the appraisal review.[17]

written essay

A performance appraisal technique in which an evaluator writes out a description of an employee's strengths, weaknesses, past performance, and potential, and then makes suggestions for improvement.

Written Essays.   Probably the simplest method of appraisal is to write a narrative describing an employee's strengths, weaknesses, past performance, and potential and then to provide suggestions for improvement. The **written essay** requires no complex forms or extensive training to complete. However, a "good" or "bad" appraisal may be determined as much by the evaluator's writing skill as by the employee's actual level of performance.

critical incidents

A performance appraisal technique in which an evaluator lists key behaviors that separate effective from ineffective job performance.

Critical Incidents.   The use of **critical incidents** focuses the evaluator's attention on those critical or key behaviors that separate effective from ineffective job performance. The appraiser writes down little anecdotes that describe what the employee did that was especially effective or ineffective. The key here is that only specific behaviors, not vaguely defined personality traits are cited. A list of critical incidents for a given employee provides a rich set of examples that the manager can use to point out desirable and undesirable behaviors to the employee.

graphic rating scales

A performance appraisal technique in which an evaluator rates a set of performance factors on an incremental scale.

Graphic Rating Scales.   One of the oldest and most popular methods of appraisal is **graphic rating scales**. This method lists a set of performance factors such as quantity and quality of work, job knowledge, cooperation, loyalty, attendance, honesty, and initiative. The evaluator then goes down the list and rates each on an incremental scale. The scales typically specify five points; for instance, a factor such as job knowledge might be rated from 1 ("poorly informed about work duties") to 5 ("has complete mastery of all phases of the job").

Why are graphic rating scales so popular? Although they don't provide the depth of information that essays or critical incidents do, they're less time consuming to develop and administer. They also allow for quantitative analysis and comparison.

behaviorally anchored rating scales (BARS)

A performance appraisal technique in which an evaluator rates employees on specific job behaviors derived from performance dimensions.

Behaviorally Anchored Rating Scales.   An approach that has received a great deal of attention in recent years involves **behaviorally anchored rating scales (BARS)**.[18] These scales combine major elements from the critical incident and graphic rating scale approaches. The appraiser rates an employee according to items along a numerical scale, but the items are examples of actual behavior on a given job rather than general descriptions or traits.

Behaviorally anchored rating scales focus on specific and measurable job *behaviors*. Key elements of jobs are broken down into performance dimensions, and then specific illustrations of effective and ineffective behaviors are identified for each performance dimension. The result is behavioral descriptions such as "anticipates," "plans," "executes," "solves immediate problems," "carries out orders," and "handles emergency situations." So, for example, a manager might rate one of her subordinate supervisors on a five-point scale of 0 (almost never) to 4 (almost always) for statements such as: "Distributes overtime equally taking seniority into account" or "Tells workers that if they have questions or problems to feel free to come and talk to him or her."

multiperson comparisons

A performance appraisal technique in which individuals are compared.

Multiperson Comparison.   **Multiperson comparisons** compare one individual's performance with that of one or more others. It's a relative, not an absolute, measuring device. The three most popular uses of this method are group order rankings, individual rankings, and paired comparisons.

group order ranking

A performance appraisal approach that groups employees into ordered classifications.

The **group order ranking** requires the evaluator to place employees into a particular classification such as "top one-fifth" or "second one-fifth." This method is often used in recommending a student for graduate school admission. Evaluators are asked to rank the student in the top 5 percent, the next 5 percent, the next 15 percent, and so on. When this method is used to appraise employees, managers rank all their subordinates. If a rater has 20 subordinates, only four can be in the top fifth, and, of course, four must be assigned to the bottom fifth.

The **individual ranking** approach requires the evaluator merely to list the employees in order from highest to lowest. Only one can be "best" or "number one." In an appraisal of 30 employees, the difference between the first and second employee is assumed to be the same as that between the twenty-first and twenty-second. Even though some employees may be closely grouped with respect to their performance levels, there can be no ties.

In the **paired comparison** approach, each employee is compared with every other employee in the comparison group and rated as either the superior or weaker member of the pair. After all paired comparisons are made, each employee is assigned a summary ranking based on the number of superior scores he or she received. Although this approach ensures that each employee is compared against every other, it can become cumbersome when large numbers of employees are being assessed.

Multiperson comparisons can be combined with other methods to yield a blend of the best from both absolute and relative standards. For example, a college could use the graphic rating scale and the individual ranking methods to provide more accurate information about its students' performance levels. An absolute grade (A, B, C, D, or F) could be assigned, and a student's relative rank in a class ascertained. A prospective employer or graduate school admissions committee could then look at two students who each got a B in financial accounting and draw considerably different conclusions about each when next to one grade it says "ranked fourth out of twenty-six" and next to the other it says "ranked seventeenth out of thirty."

Objectives.   We previously introduced management by objectives (MBO) in our discussion on planning. Management by objectives is also a mechanism for appraising performance. In fact, it's the preferred method for assessing managers and professional employees.[19]

With MBO, employees are evaluated by how well they accomplish a specific set of objectives that have been determined to be critical in the successful completion of their jobs. As you'll remember from our discussion in chapter 7, these objectives need to be tangible, verifiable, and measurable.

The popularity of MBO for assessing managers is probably due to its focus on end goals. Managers tend to emphasize such results-oriented outcomes as profit, sales, and costs. This emphasis aligns with MBO's concern with quantitative measures of performance. Because MBO emphasizes ends rather than means, this appraisal method gives managers the discretion to choose the best ways to achieve their goals.

New Approaches to Performance Appraisal.   Some companies are experimenting with different approaches to appraising employees' performance.[20] For instance, at Hoffmann-La Roche Inc., a Swiss pharmaceutical maker, all managers and subordinates sit down in January and negotiate a performance plan that's tied to the company's strategic priorities. Then managers are required to hold a formal performance review with their subordinates twice a year and to hold informal "coaching" sessions every quarter. Other companies, such as Ceridian Corporation and Wisconsin Power & Light Company, are dropping routine performance appraisals for everyone except poor performers.

Another type of performance appraisal is something called **360 degree feedback**, which is a performance appraisal review that utilizes feedback from supervisors, subordinates, and co-workers. In other words, this type of review utilizes information from the full circle of people with whom the manager interacts. Companies such as Alcoa, Pitney Bowes, AT&T, Nestlé's Perrier division, Chase Manhattan Bank, DuPont, Levi Strauss, and UPS are using this innovative approach. But users of this approach caution that, although it's effec-

individual ranking

A performance appraisal approach that ranks employees in order from highest to lowest.

paired comparison

A performance appraisal approach in which each employee is compared with every other employee and rated as either the superior or weaker member of the pair.

360 degree feedback

A performance appraisal review that utilizes feedback from supervisors, subordinates, and co-workers—the full circle of people with whom the manager interacts.

tive for career coaching and helping a manager recognize his or her strengths and weaknesses, it's not appropriate for determining pay, promotions, or terminations.

What are the benefits and drawbacks of these full-circle reviews?[21] One advantage is that they provide a more comprehensive perspective of an employee's performance. Soliciting information from all the individuals a person interacts with in his or her normal work activities enables managers to obtain a broader and more complete picture of that person's performance than could be obtained by other means. This information, in turn, increases the credibility of an employee's performance appraisal because it's less likely to be biased either positively or negatively; lack of bias is another benefit. Last, an advantage of 360 degree appraisal is that the feedback provided can enhance an employee's individual self-development. It permits an employee to compare his or her own perceptions with the perceptions that others have of his or her skills, styles, and performance.

But there are drawbacks to the process, also. It's very time consuming and complex to administer. Collecting and compiling information from a number of sources takes more time than having only one person do the evaluation. Also, some employees are not comfortable providing feedback on their supervisors. Overcoming some of those fears and the reluctance to change may require extensive employee training and change efforts within organizations that are moving to 360 degree feedback techniques.

Providing Feedback in the Appraisal Review. Many managers are reluctant to give a formal performance appraisal review for each employee. Why? Probably the two main reasons are (1) they lack complete confidence in the appraisal method used, and (2) they fear a confrontation with the employee or an unpleasant reaction from him or her if the results aren't overwhelmingly positive. Nevertheless, managers should conduct such reviews because they're the primary means by which employees get feedback on their performance and from which they can then make adjustments in their work methods or habits.

An effective review—in which the employee perceives the appraisal as fair, the manager as sincere, and the climate as constructive—is likely to result in the employee's leaving the interview in an enthusiastic mood, informed about the performance areas in which he or she needs to improve, and determined to correct the deficiencies. Unfortunately, this isn't the way it usually happens.

The problem is that performance appraisal reviews have a built-in barrier. Statistically speaking, half of all employees must be below-average performers. But evidence shows us that the *average* employee's estimate of his or her own performance level generally falls around the seventy-fifth percentile.[22] In other words, employees tend to have inflated assessments of their own performances. The good news the manager does convey may be perceived as not good enough. Six specific suggestions for providing effective feedback are: focus on specific behaviors, keep the feedback impersonal, keep the feedback goal-oriented, make the feedback well timed, ensure understanding, and direct negative feedback toward behavior that the recipient can control.

Performance Appraisal in Other Countries. Formal performance appraisals, particularly of managers, are quite common around the globe,[23] but there are some exceptions. For instance, in Sweden and China, formal performance appraisal systems are not commonly used. In countries where performance appraisal *is* an accepted practice, a wide variety of techniques are used. In Germany, for example, organizations prefer to use quantitative instruments. In countries such as Japan, China, and South Korea, where saving face is an important cultural value, more informal or indirect ways are used to provide feedback. Like managers in the United States, Israeli managers use several techniques, including trait, behavioral, and MBO systems. However, in countries such as Poland and the Commonwealth of Independent States, where organizations have recently adapted a free-market philosophy, performance appraisal still tends to be tied to personal traits and bureaucratic measures.

7 What behavioral controls can a manager use?

8 How could a manager use direct supervision as a way to control behavior?

9 Contrast the advantages and disadvantages of the following performance appraisal techniques: written essays, critical incidents, graphic rating scales, BARS, multiperson comparisons, MBO, and 360 degree feedback.

Discipline

When an employee's performance regularly isn't up to par or if an employee consistently ignores the organization's standards and regulations, the manager may have to use discipline as a way to control behavior. What specifically do we mean when we use the term **discipline**? It refers to actions taken by a manager to enforce the organization's standards and regulations. Table 19-3 lists the most common types of behavior problems that discipline is used to control and correct.

discipline

Actions taken by a manager to enforce the organization's standards and regulations.

The Hot Stove Rule of Discipline.   The **hot stove rule** is a frequently cited set of principles that can guide managers in effectively disciplining an employee.[24] The name comes from the similarities between touching a hot stove and being disciplined. Both are painful, but the analogy goes further. When you touch a hot stove, you get an *immediate* response. The burn you receive is instantaneous, leaving no doubt in your mind about the relation between cause and effect. You have ample *warning*. You know what happens if you touch a hot stove. Furthermore, the result is *consistent*. Every time you touch a hot stove, you get the same result; you get burned. Finally, the result is *impersonal*. Regardless of who you are, if you touch a hot stove, you will get burned. The analogy with discipline should be apparent, but let's briefly expand on each of those four points, because they are central ideas in disciplining effectively.

hot stove rule

Discipline should immediately follow an infraction, provide ample warning, and be consistent and impersonal.

1. *Immediacy.* The effectiveness of a disciplinary action will be reduced as the time between the infraction and the penalty lengthens. The more quickly the discipline follows the offense, the more likely it is that the employee will associate the discipline with the offense rather than with you as the dispenser of the discipline. Therefore, it's best to begin the disciplinary process as soon as possible after you notice a violation. Of course, the immediacy requirement shouldn't result in undue haste. Fair and objective treatment shouldn't be compromised for expediency.

TABLE 19-3	Types of Discipline Problems and Examples of Each
Attendance	Absenteeism, tardiness, abuse of sick leave
On-the-job behaviors	Insubordination, failure to use safety devices, alcohol or drug abuse
Dishonesty	Theft, lying to superiors, falsifying information on employment applications
Outside activities	Working for a competing organization, criminal activities, unauthorized strike activities

2. *Warning.* As a manager, you have an obligation to give warning before initiating disciplinary action. This means that the employee *must* be aware of the organization's rules and accept its standards of behavior. Disciplinary action is more likely to be interpreted by employees as fair when they've received clear warning that a given violation will lead to discipline and when they know what that discipline will be.

3. *Consistency.* Fair treatment of employees demands that disciplinary action be consistent. If you enforce rule violations in an inconsistent manner, the rules will lose their impact, morale will decline, and employees will question your competence. Productivity will suffer as a result of employee insecurity and anxiety. Your employees will want to know the limits of permissible behavior, and they'll look to your actions for guidance. Consistency, by the way, need not result in treating everyone exactly alike because that ignores mitigating circumstances. It does, however, put the responsibility on you to clearly justify disciplinary actions that might appear inconsistent to employees.

4. *Impersonal nature.* The last guideline that flows from the hot stove rule is to keep the discipline impersonal. Penalties should be connected with a given violation not with the personality of the individual violator. That is, discipline should be directed at what the employee has done, not at the employee. You're penalizing the rule violation, not the individual. Once the penalty has been imposed, you must make every effort to forget the incident and attempt to treat the employee just as you did before the problem.

More Serious Employee Behavior Problems.   As a manager, you may find at some point in your career that you have to deal with more-serious employee behavior problems, such as alcohol and drug abuse. Employee substance abuse problems can have significant negative consequences for both the organization and the individuals involved. For instance, one survey found that U.S. businesses lose around $60 billion to $90 billion annually because of employee substance abuse.[25] What are companies doing to minimize the workplace disruptions and job performance problems that result when employees abuse alcohol or drugs?

Effective discipline punishes the violation, not the employee, and skilled managers are able to administer appropriate discipline and move on, without allowing uncomfortable feelings to linger in the work relationship.

One tactic that many companies are using is drug tests of both current employees and job candidates. For instance, one study found that close to 90 percent of the workplaces surveyed tested their workers for drug use.[26] However, as Burlington Northern Railroad managers discovered, a drug testing program by itself is not enough to reduce problems of employee drug abuse. Burlington Northern has been a pioneer in campaigning for drug- and alcohol-free workplaces and has promoted that idea since 1952.[27] Its comprehensive substance abuse program includes, in addition to a drug testing program, supervisory training, an employee assistance program, and community safety awareness programs. An employee drug testing program cannot be implemented indiscriminately, however. Legal experts caution organizations that do employee drug testing to plan the program carefully, implement it consistently, and enforce it uniformly. Otherwise, the organization could be a target for employee lawsuits.[28]

Another approach to dealing with serious employee behavior problems that's becoming quite popular is the use of **employee assistance programs (EAPs)**. These are company-sponsored programs whose goal is to help employees adjust to and overcome personal problems that are adversely affecting their workplace performance.[29] Usually these programs are designed so that supervisors can refer workers to company EAP counselors or outside counselors who help employees pinpoint problems and arrange for help. But in most EAPs, employees can also contact the counselors themselves. Although alcohol and drug abuse are the major problems that EAP counselors deal with, many also provide assistance for a broad range of employee problems such as stress management, weight control, financial counseling, legal counseling, smoking cessation, or any other personal issues that create difficulties for employees. These programs are one more way in which organizations are investing in their most important resource—their employees.

employee assistance programs (EAPs)

Company-sponsored programs whose goal is to help employees adjust to and overcome personal problems that are adversely affecting their workplace performance.

Substitutes for Direct Control

Although managers can, and do, use the direct forms of behavioral control that we have just described (direct supervision, performance appraisal, and discipline) to ensure that their employees' actual work performance meets some performance standard, there are other organizational factors that act as substitutes for these direct controls. These subtle but powerful indirect organizational control mechanisms include the selection process, organizational culture, degree of formalization, and employee training.[30]

Selection Process. As we discussed in chapter 11, managers don't choose employees at random. Job applicants are processed through a series of selection devices to differentiate those individuals who are likely to be successful job performers from those who aren't likely to be successful. An effective selection process should be designed to determine if job candidates "fit" into the organization. The term *fit* in this situation implies not only the ability to do the job but also the personality, values, work habits, and attitudes that the organization desires. The selection process, therefore, screens out people who don't have the ability to do the job and prevents employment of "misfits." As such, selection is one of the most widely used techniques by which management can indirectly control employee behavior.

Organizational Culture. The more that employees accept and are committed to the values and norms of the organization's culture, the greater the likelihood that their behavior will conform to that which management desires. Organizational culture, to the degree that it's accepted by employees, acts to constrain and control their behavior. Because employees who don't accept the organization's culture aren't likely to stay employed there long, culture plays a significant role in controlling and influencing the behavior of all continuing employees. Thus, managers can indirectly control employee behavior through the culture it creates and supports.

Degree of Formalization. Managers provide most employees with a job description to clarify what their job encompasses, who they're responsible to, and what is and is not within their authority. This document formalizes behavior and, of course, also controls behavior. Because employees modify their behavior to align with the job description, it acts as a control device. Furthermore, because managers develop and define each individual job description, they can assert indirect behavioral control through it. But the job description isn't the only dimension of formalization that acts as a constraint on employee behavior. An organization's rules, procedures, and policies are other formalized controls. Each serves to guide, direct, and control an employee's work activities.

Employee Training. When managers train employees, the intention is to instill preferred work behaviors and attitudes. This intent is probably most obvious during new employee orientation, which is a type of training. During orientation, employees are often exposed to the organization's history, objectives, philosophy, and rules. In many cases, this introduction is then followed by specific job training. Although this training helps the employee adjust more readily to his or her new job, it also serves to mold and indirectly control the employee's behavior.

10 Describe the hot stove rule of discipline.

11 Why might an organization need employee assistance programs?

12 How do managers use indirect behavioral controls?

managers respond to "a manager's dilemma"

MANAGER 1

In attempting to design an information system that would help control costs and service quality by the hospital, I would suggest that Mr. Lofton first ensure that the hospital's communication network is well established and that the computer systems they have in place are properly tracking all inventory flows as well as the volume and type of patient care provided. In order to stay competitive, they must keep overall fixed and variable costs low to achieve a more efficient delivery system and to more closely match the payments received by the insurance carriers and HMOs in which their patients are enrolled. A thorough analysis should be conducted to review the rates charged versus the amounts deemed customary by the insurance providers. Mr. Lofton might also look at outside sources for controlling costs such as third-party administrators for all billing and collection services. Then, to ensure high-quality care, it's essential that the hospital's credentialing and peer review activities be as thorough as possible. Once all of these activities have been reviewed, the information system for collecting data must be well monitored and properly staffed. Again, Mr. Lofton might consider utilizing outside services for assistance with establishing the proper computer networks, accounting systems, quality assurance controls, and other crucial controls.

Calvin C. Reno, CEO, MDM Insurance Associates, Los Angeles, California

MANAGER 2

The first step I'd take would be *planning.* The goals of controlling costs and maintaining quality must be considered at all times during design. Then I'd conduct an *analysis* of the current information system to see what it is and is not doing. Next, the *design* of the system should be approached with the goals in mind. For instance, since one of the system's main goals is to help control costs, the fixed fees for each medical procedure should be used as a gauge for costs. Each procedure also could be broken down into smaller procedures, and a cost determined for each smaller procedure. By totaling the cost data of the smaller procedures that constitute a large one, the system could provide information that would help managers pinpoint cost-inefficient procedures. For the other information system objective, quality must first be defined. The system should incorporate not only the hospital's definition of quality but also patients' views of quality. Patient interviews and statistical outcomes could provide the information that would be used in controlling quality. In addition, the system could incorporate managed care procedure quality requirements. Whatever quality assessment measures the hospital desires from its information system, those measures could be compared internally as well as externally with industrywide norms. Once Mr. Lofton has determined the design of the system, it needs to be *constructed.* After thorough testing, it could be *implemented.* Finally, after the system is in use, it should be evaluated regularly to ensure it's still providing the correct information.

Drew Clippard, Programmer/Analyst, Cerner Corporation, Kansas City, Missouri

for your
IMMEDIATE
action

COMPTON
HILLS
CLASSICS

*Specializing in Quality
Historical and Classical
Literature*

HARTFORD
NEW JERSEY

TO:　　Maria Manganella
　　　　Director of Human Resources

FROM:　Daniel Tran
　　　　Vice President of Administration

　　　　As we've discussed several times, the rapid growth of our company has brought benefits as well as some areas of concern. One of the things I'm most concerned about is whether we're doing all we can, as a socially responsible employer, to assist our employees with personal problems that might be negatively affecting their work performance.

　　　　While I was catching up on my reading last night, I ran across a reference to something called employee assistance programs (EAP). Maybe there's something in this topic that we can develop for our employees. I'd like you to research EAP and write up a report that you can present at our next Executive Council meeting. Keep your report short—under two pages typed. Focus on the most current references you can find and address these points:

(1) What are employee assistance programs?
(2) What are the advantages and disadvantages of these types of programs?
(3) What do we need to know to implement one successfully?

This is a fictionalized account of a potentially real problem. It was written for academic purposes only.

SUMMARY

This summary is organized by the chapter-opening objectives found on p. 616.

1. The purpose of a management information system is to provide managers with accurate and current information for decision making and control.

2. Data are raw, unanalyzed facts. Information is data that have been organized into a usable form.

3. The key elements in designing an MIS include: analyzing the decision system, analyzing information requirements, aggregating the decisions, and developing the actual information-processing capability.

4. An MIS changes the manager's job in the following ways: Managers have more hands-on involvement; their decision-making capability is improved; organizational structures are becoming flatter and more organic; and the power that's inherent in having access to information is shifting.

5. Budgets provide managers with quantitative standards against which to measure and compare resource consumption. By pointing out deviations between standard and actual consumption, they serve as control tools.

6. TQM control charts are management control tools that show results of measurements over a period of time with statistically determined upper and lower limits. They provide a visual means of determining whether a specific process is staying within predefined limits.

7. The economic order quantity model balances the costs of ordering and carrying inventory. To calculate the optimal order quantity, you need to know the forecasted demand for an item during a specific period, the cost of placing each order, the value or purchase price of the item, and the carrying cost of maintaining the total inventory.

8. Six performance appraisal methods are: (1) written essays—written descriptions of an employee's strengths, weaknesses, past performance, potential, and areas in need of improvement; (2) critical incidents—lists of key behaviors that separate effective from ineffective job performance; (3) graphic rating scales—ratings of performance factors on an incremental scale; (4) BARS—ratings of employees on specific job behaviors derived from performance dimensions of the job; (5) multiperson comparisons—comparisons of individual employees against one another; and (6) objectives—evaluation of employees against tangible, verifiable, and measurable objectives.

9. The central ideas in the hot stove rule of discipline involve immediacy (discipline should immediately follow an infraction), advance warning (discipline should provide ample warning), consistency (discipline should be consistent), and impersonal nature (discipline should be impersonal).

10. Four organizational factors that serve as indirect behavioral controls are the employee selection process, the organizational culture, the degree of organizational formalization, and employee training.

THINKING ABOUT MANAGEMENT ISSUES

1. In what ways might the functional area in which a manager works (for example, production, sales, or accounting) affect the emphasis he or she places on each of the following types of controls: (a) information, (b) operations, (c) financial, and (d) behavioral controls?

2. Describe how you might design a performance evaluation system that would minimize the dysfunctional aspects of the behavioral control devices.

3. In what ways is information a unique resource for organizations? Give examples.

4. How does the design of an MIS affect power distribution within an organization?

5. Which do you think is more crucial for success in organizations—quality controls or total quality management? Support your position.

SELF-ASSESSMENT EXERCISE

HOW INTERNET LITERATE ARE YOU?

The increasing use of the Internet by businesses and by individuals has spawned a whole new terminology. For instance, in 'Net lingo, "flame" has nothing to do with fire and a "server" is not someone who brings you food in a restaurant. Just how Internet literate are you? This self-assessment exercise tests your knowledge of Internet terminology. Match the terms with their correct definitions.

Internet Terms:

a. Browser	f. Emoticon	k. Netiquette
b. Bookmark	g. FAQ	l. Newsgroup
c. Domain	h. Flame	m. ROTFL
d. Dot	i. Home page	n. Spam
e. Download	j. HTTP	o. WWW

_____ 1. Specific ways to act with people over the Internet; common-sense guidelines people follow in order not to disrupt or annoy other users.

_____ 2. Often referred to as a period, this is what separates parts of an Internet address.

_____ 3. Ranting and raving at someone who said something offensive.

_____ 4. Messages sent out over the Internet to try and sell products or to get people's attention; also known as electronic junk mail.

_____ 5. Stands for hypertext transfer protocol; the way Web pages are passed to the browser.

_____ 6. Otherwise known as the World Wide Web.

_____ 7. The last part of an address, such as .com or .edu.

_____ 8. The first page of a Web site and a starting point for Web users.

_____ 9. An abbreviation often used in e-mail messages and chat rooms when someone says something humorous.

_____ 10. A way to show your feelings about something someone wrote. For instance, :-).

_____ **11.** A Usenet conference or discussion forum.
_____ **12.** Many server providers have these files posted for beginners to answer commonly asked questions.
_____ **13.** A browser function that allows a user to save frequently used Web sites so they are easier to locate at a later time.
_____ **14.** Copying a host file to a personal computer to view it.
_____ **15.** A program used to view the World Wide Web.
For scoring, turn to page SK–6.

TAKE IT TO THE NET

We invite you to visit the Robbins/Coulter companion Web site at http://www.prenhall.com/robbinsmgt for this chapter's Internet resources.

CASE APPLICATION

It's Not Kids' Play Anymore

Kids are immediately attracted—like magnets to steel—by the brightly colored blue, red, and yellow tubes, mazes, slides, and towering mounds of balls. There's something about the anticipation of climbing, bouncing, jumping, and exploring that brings out the "fun-loving kid," even in those who haven't been one in years. Yet managers at Discovery Zone, a company operating indoor playgrounds across the United States, are discovering that running a successful organization isn't kids' play.

The business was started in 1989 by Ronald Matsch, a Kansas City, Missouri, gymnastics coach. His vision was that stressed-out parents would gladly pay to take their energetic kids to a clean, safe indoor play area filled with games, climbing areas, and mazes—particularly on rainy days. Matsch initially chose to franchise Discovery Zones, and by 1992, there were two company-owned units and 37 franchisees. That same year, Matsch sold the company to Donald Flynn, a major Blockbuster video stores franchiser. Flynn became CEO and brought in Wayne Huizenga (the legendary founder of Blockbuster Video, a chain of video rental stores; Waste Manage-

ment, a trash company; and Auto Nation, an automobile retailer) as a 20 percent investor.

The new owners' growth strategy was simple: Apply the Blockbuster approach to indoor playgrounds. What did that involve? Rapidly opening new units, which cost about $600,000 apiece to equip, and purchasing competitors to become the biggest player in the industry. Flynn opened new Zones as fast as he could sign his name on the real estate deals. He also began buying back franchises in order to tighten control. By the end of 1995, there were more than 300 Discovery Zone indoor playgrounds across the United States.

However, the owners soon found that managing Discovery Zones was a lot tougher than running a video store. Indoor playgrounds—filled with energetic, sweaty, and very active kids—get a lot dirtier a lot faster than video stores. They require significantly more maintenance and service. In location after location, other problems cropped up. Broken games stayed broken for days, frustrating kids. Many locations stopped selling candy because most of it wound up being stolen because of lax controls. Poor supervision by employees resulted in some kids' wandering away by themselves off the premises. By 1994, Discovery

Zone had so many basic operational problems that it ended up losing $21 million on revenues of $163 million. Mounting losses during 1995 led to the company's default on $100 million in bank debt. Eventually the company filed for Chapter 11 bankruptcy protection in March of 1996.

At that time, Donna Moore, who had launched and managed Walt Disney Company's chain of retail stores in the 1980s, was brought in as chief executive officer. She immediately recognized that the company's basic operations had to be fixed in order to fix the financial problems. She says, "When you're dealing with children, you learn that the experience can never be fixed afterward. We cannot redo a birthday party. You can refund it, but the parents will never forgive you, nor will the child. This is about getting it right the first time."

QUESTIONS

1. What types of information might the following managers at Discovery Zone need: (a) the CEO, Donna Moore, (b) the manager of a local Discovery Zone, and (c) the company's vice president of marketing?

2. What would a companywide management information system for Discovery Zone need to include? What are the implications for designing an appropriate MIS?

3. What types of behavioral controls would be needed at a local Discovery Zone? Support your choices.

4. Too rapid growth has caused many companies to stumble. What types of controls would be important for a company that is growing rapidly? Explain.

Source: L. Gubernick, "Disaster Zone," *Forbes*, June 17, 1996, pp. 66–75; and company information obtained from Compustat.

VIDEO CASE APPLICATION

Drawing the Perfect Inventory System

George Granoff, owner of The Art Store, a retail art supply store with five locations in California, has put together an inventory control system that allows him to efficiently and effectively keep his stores stocked with 17,000 art supply items. Granoff, who had no background or experience in art or in art supplies, used his extensive retailing experience and knowledge of product scanning, bar coding, just-in-time inventory, and other retail inventory control techniques to bring The Art Store on-line.

The Art Store operates with and maintains its enormous level of in-store inventory with no "back room." (In retailing language, this means there's no product being stored in a back room; all inventory owned is out on the floor.) As Granoff readily admits, it's an enormous challenge to stay in stock day in and day out with that number of items and no back room

and no warehouse. He says he's been able to do it because of organization and technology.

One area that was most important to Granoff was installing point-of-sale scanning at the front end (check-out counters) of the store and bar coding all 17,000 items. When a customer takes her merchandise to a cash register to check out, the cashier scans the bar-coded products and the encoded information is recorded and compiled. In addition, when an employee out in the store runs across empty product space—that is, an empty shelf, bin, or rack—he scans the bar code information and a written order for that item is automatically initiated. The order information is immediately transmitted over the phone lines to the manufacturer. In most cases, the ordered item is at the store within two days.

Granoff admits that his computer system is the company's workhorse. It handles the merchandising function as well as all of the company's other important business functions, such as payroll, budgeting, and so forth. Without the technology, it would have been impossible for The Art Store to grow or even to keep in stock and on hand the products its customers want. After all, being a successful retailer means having the products that customers want when they want them. If you can't do that, you won't be around very long!

QUESTIONS

1. George Granoff didn't need a background in art supplies to design his organization's inventory control system. Why not? Does Granoff's experience mean that control tools and techniques are universally applicable? Explain.

2. What are some advantages of the type of computerized inventory control system that The Art Store uses? What are some disadvantages?

3. What other control tools and techniques might Granoff find useful in managing his organization? Describe your choices.

4. What do you think Granoff meant when he said that it is organization and technology that have enabled him to monitor 17,000 inventory items?

Source: Based on *Small Business 2000, Show 303.*

skill-building modules

In this section of the textbook, you will have the opportunity to learn about, practice, and reinforce specific management skills. We have included 23 skills that encompass the four functions of management: planning, organizing, leading, and controlling. (See the matrix that follows.)

For each of the skills included in these modules, we provide the following. (1) A short introduction discusses some basic facts about the skill and defines it, if necessary. (2) A section called "Learning About" describes the suggested behaviors for doing that skill. These behaviors are presented in numbered lists in order to illustrate the specific actions associated with that skill. (3) A section entitled "Practice" presents a short scenario designed to provide you with an opportunity to practice the behaviors associated with the skill. Your professor may have you do different things with the practice scenarios. (4) A section entitled "Reinforcement" is designed to present additional activities that you could do to practice and reinforce the behaviors associated with the skill.

Management Skills and Management Functions Matrix

Skill	Planning	Organizing	Leading	Controlling
Acquiring power (SM-2)		x	x	
Active listening (SM-4)			x	x
Assessing cross-cultural differences (SM-5)		x	x	
Budgeting (SM-7)	x			x
Choosing an effective leadership style (SM-9)			x	
Coaching (SM-11)			x	
Creating effective teams (SM-13)		x	x	
Delegating (empowerment) (SM-15)		x	x	
Designing motivating jobs (SM-17)		x	x	
Developing control charts (SM-18)	x			x
Developing trust (SM-20)			x	
Disciplining (SM-21)			x	x
Interviewing (SM-23)		x	x	
Managing resistance to change (SM-25)		x	x	x
Managing time (SM-27)	x			x
Mentoring (SM-29)			x	
Negotiating (SM-30)			x	
Providing feedback (SM-32)			x	x
Reading an organization's culture (SM-34)		x	x	
Reducing stress (SM-36)		x	x	
Scanning the environment (SM-37)	x			x
Setting goals (SM-38)	x			x
Solving problems creatively (SM-40)	x			

ACQUIRING POWER

Power is a natural process in any group or organization, and to perform their jobs effectively, managers need to know how to acquire and use **power.** We discussed the concept of power earlier in chapter 16 and defined it as the capacity for a leader to influence work actions or decisions. Why is having power important? Because power makes you less dependent on others. When a manager has power, he is not as dependent on others for critical resources. And if the resources the manager controls are important, scarce, and nonsubstitutable, his power will increase because others will be more dependent on him for those resources.

Learning about Acquiring Power

You can be more effective at acquiring and using power if you use the following eight behaviors.

1. **Frame arguments in terms of organizational goals.** To be effective at acquiring power means camouflaging your self-interests. Discussions over who controls what resources should be framed in terms of the benefits that will accrue to the organization; do not point out how you personally will benefit.

MANAGING IN THE REAL WORLD

"By providing others with the information from several perspectives surrounding an issue, it allows for the ultimate opportunity to influence. The information, when presented appropriately, allows others to see things your way through realizing your logic."

Geoff Gilpin, Director of New
Business Initiatives
GTE - Long Distance
Dallas, Texas

---

2. **Develop the right image.** If you know your organization's culture, you already understand what the organization wants and values from its employees in terms of dress, associates to cultivate and those to avoid, whether to appear risk taking or risk aversive, the preferred leadership style, the importance placed on getting along well with others, and so forth. With this knowledge, you're equipped to project the appropriate image. Because the assessment of your performance isn't always a fully objective process, you need to pay attention to style as well as substance.

3. **Gain control of organizational resources.** Controlling organizational resources that are scarce and important is a source of power. Knowledge and expertise are particularly effective resources to control. They make you more valuable to the organization and, therefore, more likely to have job security, chances for advancement, and a receptive audience for your ideas.

MANAGING IN THE REAL WORLD

"I use power and influence in my job to obtain resources needed to service my clients. My position allows me to gain the attention of colleagues and clients which aids in marketing and delivering services."

Ted V. Schaefer, Principal
Coopers & Lybrand, L. L. P.
Denver, Colorado

---

4. **Make yourself appear indispensable.** Because we're dealing with appearances rather than objective facts, you can enhance your power by appearing to be indispensable. You don't really have to be indispensable as long as key people in the organization believe that you are.

5. **Be visible**. If you have a job that brings your accomplishments to the attention of others, that's great. However, if you don't have such a job, you'll want to find ways to let others in the organization know what you're doing, such as highlighting successes in routine reports, having satisfied customers relay their appreciation to senior executives in your organization, being seen at social functions, being active in your professional associations, and developing powerful allies who speak positively about your accomplishments. Of course, you'll want to be on the lookout for those projects that will increase your visibility.

6. **Develop powerful allies**. To get power, it helps to have powerful people on your side. Cultivate contacts with potentially influential people above you, at your own level, and at lower organizational levels. These allies often can provide you with information that's otherwise not readily available. In addition, having allies can provide you with a coalition of support if and when you need it.

7. **Avoid "tainted" members**. In almost every organization, there are fringe members whose status is questionable. Their performance and/or loyalty may be suspect. Keep your distance from such individuals.

8. **Support your boss**. Your immediate future is in the hands of your current boss. Because he or she evaluates your performance, you will typically want to do whatever is necessary to have your boss on your side. You should make every effort to help your boss succeed, make her look good, support her if she is under siege, and spend the time to find out the criteria she will be using to assess your effectiveness. Don't undermine your boss. And don't speak negatively of her to others.

Based on H. Mintzberg, *Power In and Around Organizations* (Upper Saddle River, NJ: Prentice Hall, 1983), p. 24; and S.P. Robbins and P.L. Hunsaker, *Training in InterPersonal Skills: TIPS for Managing People at Work*, 2nd ed. (Upper Saddle River, NJ: Prentice Hall, 1996), pp. 131–34.

Practice: Acquiring Power

Read through the following scenario. Write down some notes about how you would handle the situation described. Be sure to refer to the eight behaviors described for acquiring power. Your professor will then tell you what to do next.

You used to be the star supervisor of marketing for Hilton Electronics Corporation. But for the past year, you've been outpaced again and again by Conor whose hot new design department has been delivering everything expected of her and more. Meanwhile your best efforts to do your job well have been sabotaged and undercut by Leonila, your own manager. For example, prior to last year's international consumer electronics show, Leonila moved thousands of dollars from your budget to Conor's. Despite your best efforts, your marketing team couldn't complete all the marketing materials normally provided for a new product. Leonila has chipped away at your staff and budget ever since. Although you proved able to meet most of your objectives with less staff and budget, Leonila continued to slice away at your group. Last week she eliminated three more positions in your group to make room for a new designer and some extra equipment for Conor. Leonila is clearly taking away your resources while giving Conor whatever she wants and more. You think it's time to do something or soon you won't have any team or resources left.

Reinforcement: Acquiring Power Skills

The following suggestions are activities you can do to practice and reinforce the behavior associated with acquiring power.

1. Keep a one-week journal of your behavior describing incidences when you tried to influence others around you. Assess each incident by asking: Were you successful at these attempts to influence them? Why or why not? What could you have done differently?

2. Review six recent issues of a business periodical (such as *Business Week, Fortune, Forbes, Fast Company*, or the *Wall Street Journal*). Look for articles on reorganizations, promotions, or departures from management positions. Find at least two articles where you believe power issues are involved. Relate the content of the articles to the concepts introduced in this skill module. ■

ACTIVE LISTENING

The ability to be an effective listener is often taken for granted. Hearing is often confused with listening, but hearing is merely picking up sound vibrations. Listening is making sense of what we hear and requires paying attention, interpreting, and remembering. Effective listening is active rather than passive. Active listening is hard work and requires you to "get inside" the speaker's head in order to understand the communication from his or her point of view.

Learning about Active Listening

We can identify eight specific behaviors that effective listeners demonstrate. You can be more effective at active listening if you use these behaviors.

1. **Make eye contact.** Making eye contact with the speaker focuses your attention, reduces the likelihood that you'll be distracted, and encourages the speaker.

2. **Exhibit affirmative nods and appropriate facial expressions.** The effective listener shows interest in what's being said through nonverbal signals. Affirmative nods and appropriate facial expressions that signal interest in what's being said, when added to eye contact, convey to the speaker that you're really listening.

3. **Avoid distracting actions or gestures.** The other side of showing interest is avoiding actions that suggest your mind is elsewhere. When listening, don't look at your watch, shuffle papers, play with your pencil, or engage in similar distractions.

4. **Ask questions.** The serious listener analyzes what he or she hears and asks questions. This behavior provides clarification, ensures understanding, and assures the speaker you're really listening.

5. **Paraphrase.** Restate in *your own words* what the speaker has said. The effective listener uses phrases such as "What I hear you saying is…" or "Do you mean…?". Paraphrasing is an excellent control device to check whether or not you're listening carefully and is also a control for accuracy of understanding.

6. **Avoid interrupting the speaker.** Let the speaker complete his or her thoughts before you try to respond. Don't try to second-guess where the speaker's thoughts are going. When the speaker is finished, you'll know it.

7. **Don't overtalk.** Most of us would rather speak our own ideas than listen to what others say. While talking might be more fun and silence might be uncomfortable, you can't talk and listen at the same time. The good listener recognizes this fact and doesn't overtalk.

8. **Make smooth transitions between the roles of speaker and listener.** In most work situations you're continually shifting back and forth between the roles of speaker and listener. The effective listener makes transitions smoothly from speaker to listener and back to speaker. From a listening perspective, this means concentrating on what a speaker has to say and practicing *not* thinking about what you're going to say as soon as you get a chance.

Based on C.R. Rogers and R.E. Farson, *Active Listening* (Chicago, IL: Industrial Relations Center of the University of Chicago, 1976); and S.P. Robbins and P.L. Hunsaker, *Training in InterPersonal Skills: TIPS for Managing People at Work*, 2nd ed. (Upper Saddle River, NJ: Prentice Hall, 1996), chapter 3.

Practice: Active Listening

Read through the following scenario. Write down some notes about how you would handle the situation described. Be sure to refer to the eight behaviors described for active listening. Your professor will tell you what to do next.

Ben Lummis has always been one of the most reliable technicians at the car stereo shop you manage. Even on days when the frantic pace stressed most other employees, Ben was calm and finished his work efficiently and effectively. You didn't know much about his personal life except that he liked to read books about model railroading during his lunch break and he asked to listen to his favorite light jazz station on the shop radio for part of the day. Because his work was always top-notch, you were happy to let him maintain his somewhat aloof attitude. But over the past month, you wish you knew Ben better. He's been averaging about an absence a week and he no longer spends his lunch break reading in the break room. When he returns from wherever it is he goes, he seems even more remote than when he left. You strongly suspect that something is wrong. Even his normally reliable work is changed. Several irate customers have returned with sound systems he installed improperly. At the time of these complaints, you reviewed each problem with him carefully and each time he promised to be more careful. In addition, you checked the absence policy and found that Ben has enough time saved up to take seven more sick days this year. But things don't seem to be improving. Just this week Ben took another suspicious sick day and another angry customer has demanded that his improperly installed system be fixed.

Reinforcement: Active Listening Skills

The following suggestions are activities you can do to practice and reinforce the active listening behaviors.

1. In another lecture-format class, practice active listening for one day. Then ask yourself: Was this harder for me than a normal lecture? Did it affect my note taking? Did I ask more questions? Did it improve my understanding of the lecture's content?

2. For one week, practice active listening behaviors during phone conversations that you have with others. Keep a journal of whether listening actively was easy or difficult, what distractions there were, how you dealt with those distractions, and your assessment of whether or not active listening allowed you to get more out of the conversation. ■

ASSESSING CROSS-CULTURAL DIFFERENCES

Diverse is a realistic description of today's workforce, and workforce diversity is a major issue for managers in many organizations. The diversity that exists in the workforce today demands that managers become more sensitive to the differences that each cultural group brings to the workplace. How can managers develop this type of sensitivity? It starts with the ability to assess cross-cultural differences.

Learning about Assessing Cross-Cultural Differences

You can be more effective at assessing cross-cultural differences if you use the following six behaviors.

1. **Shift your philosophy from treating everyone alike to recognizing individual differences.** The first step for managers in assessing cross-cultural differences is often the hardest one: changing your belief that everyone is alike and must be treated alike. However, once you can

get beyond this, you can begin to appreciate the challenges and rewards of diversity.

MANAGING IN THE REAL WORLD

"It is important to research and get to know intimately the culture of the persons with whom one is dealing."

José Legaspi, Owner
Legaspi Company
Montebello, California

---

2. **Assume differences until similarity is proven.** Most of us have the tendency to assume that others are more similar to us than they really are. You're less likely to misunderstand, miscommunicate, or misperceive if you assume others are different rather than similar.

3. **When communicating, emphasize description rather than interpretation or evaluation.** Interpreting or evaluating what someone has said or done tends to be based more on the observer's culture and background than on the observed situation. Therefore, you should concentrate on describing until you've had sufficient time to observe and interpret situations from the differing perspectives of all cultures involved.

4. **Practice empathy.** Put yourself in the other's shoes. What are her or his values, experiences, and frames of reference? What do you know about his or her education, upbringing, or background that can give you added insight? Try to see the other person as he or she really is.

5. **Respond to differences in ways that will encourage desired behaviors.** Value and defend diverse views. Accept that culturally diverse employees are going to have different values, beliefs, and ways of doing things, and as long as these dif-

ferences do not detract from the organization's goals, they should be encouraged.

MANAGING IN THE REAL WORLD

"I try to make sure that everyone understands the expectations of their jobs and my expectations and give them as much freedom as I can to achieve those goals their way. It doesn't always work; misunderstandings occasionally occur, but we all try the best we can to communicate as openly as we can."

Lorraine Cichowski, Vice
President and General
Manager
USA TODAY Information
Network
Arlington, Virginia

---

6. **Avoid any practices that could be interpreted as sexist, racist, or offensive to any minorities.** Although it's important for you to not treat everyone alike, you don't want to discriminate against diverse groups under the guise of being sensitive to differences.

Based on N. Adler, *International Dimensions of Organizational Behavior*, 2nd ed. (Boston: PWS-Kent, 1991), pp. 83–84; T. Cox, "The Multicultural Organization," *Academy of Management Executive*, May 1991, pp. 34–47; and W. Sonnenschein, *The Practical Executive and Workforce Diversity* (Lincolnwood, IL: NTC Business Books, 1997), pp. 39–40.

Practice: Assessing Cross-Cultural Differences

Read through the following scenario. Write down some notes about how you would handle the situation described. Be sure to refer to the six behaviors described for assessing cross-cultural differences. Your professor will then tell you what to do next.

June Chavez is the manager of a large downtown bank in San Diego. She believes strongly in having her employees offer friendly and helpful service to the bank's customers, but she wonders how she's going to deal with the language conflicts going on in the bank. Over half of June's employees speak Spanish, which is a tremendous asset to the bank's many Spanish-speaking customers. However, at the last few meetings June holds weekly with her supervisors, the concern keeps being raised about language. The supervisors have raised the issue that some employees who speak only English resent it when their colleagues converse in a language they can't understand. In fact, the teller supervisor said at the last meeting, "On the one hand, I have people who say this is America and people should speak English, and on the other, I've got people who say that there is freedom of speech here." The other supervisors all chimed in and agreed that they were having the same types of problems. June knows that if she doesn't take action soon, she's going to have a real problem on her hands.

Reinforcement: Assessing Cross-Cultural Differences

The following suggestions are activities you can do to practice and reinforce the behaviors associated with assessing cross-cultural differences.

BUDGETING

Managers do not have unlimited resources to do their jobs. Most managers will have to deal with a **budget,** a numerical plan for allocating resources to specific activities. As planning tools, they indicate what activities are important and how many resources should be allocated to each activity. However, budgets aren't just used in planning. They're also used in controlling. As control tools, budgets provide managers with quantitative standards against which to measure and compare resource consumption. By pointing out deviations between standard and actual consumption, managers can use the budget for control purposes.

Learning about Budgeting

You can develop your skills at budgeting if you use the following seven suggestions.

1. Talk to people from a different country. If you don't know any, check with the office at your school that is responsible for coordinating international students for some possible names. Interview at least three people and get responses to the following questions: (a) What country do you come from? (b) What is your first language? (c) Describe your country's culture in terms of the role of women in the workforce, the benefits provided to employees, how managers treat their employees, and general management practices. (d) What were the greatest difficulties you had in adapting to your new culture? (e) What advice would you give me if I were in a management position in your country?

2. Review six recent issues of a business periodical (such as *Business Week, Fortune, Forbes, Fast Company,* or the *Wall Street Journal*). Find two articles on international business and evaluate them by asking: What types of cross-cultural differences might arise in these situations? How might managers deal with those cross-cultural differences? ■

1. **Determine which work activities are going to be pursued during the coming time period.** An organization's work activities are a result of the goals that have been established. Your control over which work activities your unit will be pursuing during the coming time period will depend on how much control you normally exercise over the work that must be done in order to meet those goals. In addition, the amount of control you have often depends on your level in the organizational hierarchy.

2. **Decide which resources will be necessary to accomplish the desired work activities, that is, those that will ensure goals are met.** Although there are different types of budgets used for allocating resources, the most common ones involve monetary resources. However, you also may have to budget time, space, material resources,

human resources, capacity utilization, or units of production.

you may need to determine why and take corrective action.

MANAGING IN THE REAL WORLD

"I have various budgets that I am accountable for. Each year we have a forecasted profitability statement and I must stay within those parameters. I also have a travel budget. In essence, the budgets are used to meet corporate profitability goals for my product line."

Madelyn Gengelbach,
Marketing Strategist
Hallmark Cards
Kansas City, Missouri

---

3. **Gather cost information.** You'll need accurate cost estimates of those resources you need. Old budgets may be of some help, but you'll also want to talk with your immediate manager, colleagues, and key subordinates, and to use other contacts you have developed inside and outside your organization.

4. **Once you know which resources will be available to you, assign the resources as needed to accomplish the desired work activities.** In many organizations, managers are given a monthly, quarterly, or annual budget to work with. The budget will detail which resources are available during the time period. As the manager, you have to assign the resources in an efficient and effective manner to ensure that the unit goals are met.

5. **It's wise to review the budget periodically.** Don't wait until the end of the time period to monitor whether you're over or under budget.

6. **Take action if you find that you're not staying within your budget.** Remember that a budget also serves as a control tool. If resources are being consumed more quickly than budgeted,

---

MANAGING IN THE REAL WORLD

"In my job as owner and manager of a custom millwork and cabinetry shop, I am required to competitively bid on each project when they are presented from the general contractors. When we are the successful bidder and are awarded the project, we are bound by our original quotation of what we thought it would take to do the job."

Graham Jones, Owner and
Manager
G.L.A. Interiors
Toronto, Ontario, Canada

---

7. **Use past experience as a guide when developing your budget for the next time period.** Although every budgeted time period will be different, it is possible to use past experience to pinpoint trends and potential problems. This knowledge can help you prepare for any circumstances that may arise.

Based on R.N. Anthony, J. Dearden, and N.M. Bedford, *Management Control Systems*, 5th ed. (Homewood, IL: Irwin, 1984), chapters 5–7.

Practice: Budgeting

Read through the following scenario and complete the assigned questions. Be sure to refer to the seven behaviors described for budgeting. Your professor will tell you what to do next.

You have recently been appointed as advertising manager for a new monthly health and diet magazine, *Fitness for All,* being developed by the Magazine Division at the Hearst Corporation. You were previously an advertising manager on one of the company's established magazines. In this new position, you will report to the new magazine's publisher, Molly Tymon.

Estimates of first-year subscription sales for *Fitness for All* are 125,000. Newsstand sales should add another 40,000 a month to that number, but your concern is with developing advertising revenue for the magazine.

You and Molly have set a goal of selling advertising space totaling $6 million during *Fitness for All*'s first year. You think you can do this with a staff of 10 people. Because this is a completely new publication, there is no previous budget for your advertising group. You've been asked by Molly to submit a preliminary budget for your group.

Write up a report (no longer than three pages in length) that describes in detail how you would go about fulfilling this request by Molly. For example, where would you get budget categories? Whom would you contact? Present your best effort at creating this budget for your department.

Reinforcement: Budgeting Skills

The following suggestions are activities you can do to practice and reinforce the budgeting skill behaviors.

1. Create a personal budget for the next month. Be sure to identify sources of income and planned expenditures. At the end of the month, answer the following questions: (a) Did your budget help you plan what you could and could not do this month? (b) Did unexpected situations arise that weren't included in the budget? How did you handle those? (c) How is a personal budget similar to and different from a budget that a manager might be responsible for?

2. Interview three managers from different organizations. Ask them about their budgeting responsibilities and the "lessons" they have learned about budgeting. ◼

CHOOSING AN EFFECTIVE LEADERSHIP STYLE

Effective leaders are skillful at helping the groups they lead be successful as the group goes through various stages of development. There is no leadership style that is consistently effective. Situational factors, including follower characteristics, must be taken into consideration in the selection of an effective leadership style. The key situational factors that determine leadership effectiveness include stage of group development, task structure, position power, leader-member relations, the work group, subordinate characteristics, organizational culture, and national culture.

Learning about Choosing an Effective Leadership Style

You can be more effective at choosing an effective leadership style if you use the following six suggestions.

1. **Determine the stage in which your group or team is operating: forming, storming, norming,** or performing. Because each team stage involves specific and different issues and behaviors, it's important to know in which stage your team is. **Forming** is the first stage of group development during which people join a group and then help define the group's purpose, structure, and leadership. **Storming** is the second stage of group development characterized by intragroup conflict. **Norming** is the third stage group of development characterized by close relationships and cohesiveness. **Performing** is the fourth stage in group development when the group is fully functional.

2. **If your team is in the forming stage, there are certain leader behaviors you want to exhibit.** These include making certain that all team members are introduced to one another, answering member questions, working to establish a foundation of trust and openness, modeling the behaviors you expect from the team members, and clarifying the team goals, procedures, and expectations.

MANAGING IN THE REAL WORLD

"One thing that's important in leading an effective team is ensuring that EVERYONE on the team clearly knows and understands what the goals and expectations are."

James Fripp, Field Staffing Manager
Taco Bell Corporation
Omaha, Nebraska

---

3. **If your team is in the storming stage, there are certain leader behaviors you want to exhibit.** These behaviors include identifying sources of conflict and adopting a mediator role, encouraging a win-win philosophy, restating the team's vision and its core values and goals, encouraging open discussion, encouraging an analysis of team processes in order to identify ways to improve, enhancing team cohesion and commitment, and providing recognition to individual team members as well as the team.

4. **If your team is in the norming stage, there are certain leader behaviors you want to exhibit.** These include clarifying the team's goals and expectations, providing performance feedback to individual team members and the team, encouraging the team to articulate a vision for the future, and finding ways to publicly and openly communicate the team's vision.

5. **If your team is in the performing stage, there are certain leader behaviors you want to exhibit.** These behaviors include providing regular and ongoing performance feedback, fostering innovation and innovative behavior, encouraging the team to capitalize on its strengths, celebrating achievements (large and small), and providing the team whatever support it needs to continue doing its work.

6. **Monitor the group you're leading for changes in behaviors and adjust your leadership style accordingly.** Because a group is not a static entity, it will go through up periods and down periods. You should adjust your leadership style to the needs of the situation. If the group appears to need more direction from you, provide it. If it appears to be functioning at a high level on its own, provide whatever support is necessary to keep it functioning at that level.

MANAGING IN THE REAL WORLD

"As you succeed or fail in a given job, adjust and improve your leadership skills."

James Sierk, Senior Vice President of Quality and Productivity
AlliedSignal Corporation
Morristown, New Jersey

Based on D.A. Whetten and K.S. Cameron, *Developing Management Skills*, 3rd ed. (New York: HarperCollins College Publishers, 1995), chapter 9.

Practice: Choosing an Effective Leadership Style

Read through the following scenario. Write down some notes about how you would handle the situation described. Be sure to refer to the six suggestions described for choosing an effective leadership style. Your professor will then tell you what to do next.

You've been put in charge of a three-person team working on the implementation of a central accounting function for all training done by your *Fortune* 500 company. This project is new and your position is a new one. Two team members, Tony and Maria, used to be supervisors themselves but, due to an ongoing corporate reorganization, now find themselves reporting to you. You feel like the only way to get them to do anything is to stay on them all the time. The other team member, Corbett, typically has very good ideas but he's becoming quite reluctant to share them, particularly because Tony and Maria glare at him if he says anything. This situation is proving to be a real test of your leadership skills, but you've got a six-month deadline to complete this project, and one month is already over. You've got to figure out a way to lead this team to a successful completion of the project.

Reinforcement: Choosing an Effective Leadership Style Skills

The following suggestions are activities you can do to practice and reinforce the behaviors in choosing an effective leadership style.

1. Think of a group or team to which you currently belong or of which you have been a part. What type of leadership style did the leader of this group appear to exhibit? Give some specific examples of the types of leadership behaviors he or she used. Evaluate the leadership style. Was it appropriate for the group? Why or why not? What would you have done differently? Why?

2. Observe a sports team (either college or professional) that you consider extremely successful and one that you would consider not successful. What leadership styles appear to be used in these teams? Give some specific examples of the types of leadership behaviors you observe. How would you evaluate the leadership style? Was it appropriate for the group? Why or why not? To what degree do you think leadership style influenced the team's outcomes?

3. Interview three different managers about the leadership styles they use. Ask for specific examples of how they use their leadership style. Ask the managers how they chose the style they're using and how they know if they need to change their style. ■

· ·

COACHING

Effective managers are increasingly being described as *coaches* rather than as *bosses.* Just like coaches, they're expected to provide instruction, guidance, advice, and encouragement to help employees improve their job performance.

Learning about Coaching

There are three general skills that managers should exhibit if they are to help their employees generate performance breakthroughs. You can be more effective at coaching if you use those skills and practice the following specific behaviors associated with each.

1. **Analyze ways to improve an employee's performance and capabilities.** A coach looks for opportunities for an employee to expand his or her capabilities and improve performance. How? By using the following behaviors: Observe your employee's behavior on a day-to-day basis. Ask questions of the employee: Why do you do a task this way? Can it be improved? What other approaches might be used? Show genuine interest in the employee as an individual, not merely as an employee. Respect his or her individuality. Listen to the employee.

2. **Create a supportive climate.** It's the coach's responsibility to reduce barriers to development and to facilitate a climate that encourages personal performance improvement. How? By using the following behaviors: Create a climate that contributes to a free and open exchange of ideas. Offer help and assistance. Give guidance and advice when asked. Encourage your employees. Be positive and upbeat. Don't use threats. Focus on mistakes as learning opportunities. Ask: "What did we learn from this that can help us in the future?" Reduce obstacles. Express to the employee that you value his or her contribution to the unit's goals. Take personal responsibility for the outcome, but don't rob employees of their full responsibility. Validate the employees' efforts when they succeed. Point to what was missing when they fail. Never blame the employees for poor results.

MANAGING IN THE REAL WORLD

"It is not only important to get team members motivated at the onset of a project but it is equally as important to keep them moving through the steps of completion without losing heart or interest."

Sandy Steiner, President
Prentice Hall Business
Publishing
Upper Saddle River,
New Jersey

3. **Influence employees to change their behavior.** The ultimate test of coaching effectiveness is whether or not an employee's performance improves. The concern is with ongoing growth and development. How can you do this? By using the following behaviors: Encourage continual improvement. Recognize and reward small improvements and treat coaching as a way of helping employees to continually work toward improvement. Use a collaborative style by allowing employees to participate in identifying and choosing among improvement ideas. Break difficult tasks down into simpler ones. Model the qualities that you expect from your employees. If you want openness, dedication, commitment, and responsibility from your employees, you must demonstrate these qualities yourself.

Based on C.D. Orth, H.E. Wilkinson, and R.C. Benfari, "The Manager's Role as Coach and Mentor," *Organizational Dynamics,* Spring 1987, p. 67.

MANAGING IN THE REAL WORLD

"In our office 'coaching' skills take the form of quarterly written performance evaluations where the supervisor and employee sit down together and review job performance."

Betsy Reifsnider, Executive
Director
Friends of the River
Sacramento, California

Practice: Coaching

Read through the following scenario. Write down some notes about how you would handle the situation described. Be sure to refer to the three general coaching skills and the specific behaviors associated with each. Your professor will then tell you what to do next.

Store manager Ian McCormick was thrilled with Barbara Kim's work. She was simply the best assistant department manager he had ever seen. Barbara made friends with everyone who came into the store and customers would often bring their items over to her and wait in line just for a chance to visit with her. When a supervisory position became open, Ian was glad to give Barbara the promotion. And Barbara was even happier with the promotion. She told Ian, "I can't tell you how much this means to me. I'll do anything to make this work."

As a department supervisor, Barbara was just as friendly as ever—too friendly, in fact. She seemed incapable of saying "no" to her former co-workers. She let them off nearly every time they asked, throwing the personnel schedule into disarray and leaving checkout lines open. Customers who were once happy about Barbara were now complaining. Transaction error rates also increased. Ian brought this to Barbara's attention several times, and each time Barbara said she would talk to the clerks about being more careful. But mistakes continued. Ian knows that Barbara has potential but he's not sure what to do about this situation now. Something definitely needs to be done.

Reinforcement: Coaching Skills

The following suggestions are activities you can do to practice and reinforce the coaching behaviors.

1. Talk to several instructors about ways that they deal with a student whose performance is not at the level it should be. What kinds of techniques do they use? Which, if any, of the coaching behaviors described do the instructors use?

2. Most of us are first aware of coaches and what they do in an athletic team setting. Observe different coaches (on television or firsthand) and how they deal with individuals on their team. What types of behaviors do they exhibit? Based on what you see, what coaching advice could you use as a manager? ■

CREATING EFFECTIVE TEAMS

What differentiates a *team* from a group is that members are committed to a common purpose, have a set of specific performance goals, and hold themselves mutually accountable for the team's results. Teams can produce outputs that are greater than the sum of their individual contributions. The primary force that makes a work group an effective team—that is, a real high-performing team—is its emphasis on performance.

Learning about Creating Effective Teams

Managers and team leaders have a significant impact on a team's effectiveness. As a result, they need to be able to create effective teams. You can be more effective at creating effective teams if you use the following nine behaviors.

1. **Establish a common purpose.** An effective team needs a common purpose to which all members aspire. This purpose is a vision. It's broader than any specific goals. This common purpose provides direction, momentum, and commitment for team members.

2. **Assess team strengths and weaknesses.** Team members will have different strengths and weaknesses. Knowing these strengths and weaknesses can help the team leader build upon the strengths and compensate for the weaknesses.

3. **Develop specific individual goals.** Specific individual goals help lead team members to achieve higher performance. In addition, specific goals facilitate clear communication and help maintain the focus on getting results.

4. **Get agreement on a common approach for achieving goals.** Goals are the ends a team strives to attain. Defining and agreeing upon a common approach ensure that the team is unified on the *means* for achieving those ends.

5. **Encourage acceptance of accountability for both individual and team performance.** Successful teams make members individually and jointly accountable for the team's purpose,

goals, and approach. Members understand what they are individually responsible for and what they are jointly responsible for.

6. **Build mutual trust among members.** When there is *trust,* team members believe in the integrity, character, and ability of each other. When trust is lacking, members are unable to depend on each other. Teams that lack trust tend to be short-lived.

MANAGING IN THE REAL WORLD

"At Friends of the River we also take time to have fun outside the office, usually down the rivers which are close to our office. That's a great way to build team spirit."

**Betsy Reifsnider,
Executive Director
Friends of the River
Sacramento, California**

----

7. **Maintain an appropriate mix of team member skills and personalities.** Team members come to the team with different skills and personalities. To perform effectively, teams need three types of skills. First, teams need people with technical expertise. Next, they need people with problem-solving and decision-making skills to identify problems, generate alternatives, evaluate those alternatives, and make competent choices. Finally, teams need people with good interpersonal skills.

8. **Provide needed training and resources.** Team leaders need to make sure that their teams have both the training and resources they need to accomplish their goals.

9. **Create opportunities for small achievements.** Building an effective team takes time. Team

members have to learn to think and work as a team. New teams can't be expected to hit home runs right at the beginning, every time they come to bat. Instead, team members should be encouraged to try for small achievements at the beginning.

Based on S.P. Robbins and P.L. Hunsaker, *Training in InterPersonal Skills: TIPS for Managing People at Work,* 2nd ed. (Upper Saddle River, NJ: Prentice Hall, 1996), chapter 11.

Practice: Creating Effective Teams

Read through the following scenario. Write down some notes about how you would handle the situation described. Be sure to refer to the nine behaviors described for creating effective teams. Your professor will then tell you what to do next.

You're the supervisor of a five-member project group that's been assigned the task of moving your engineering firm into the new booming area of high-speed rail construction. You and your team members have been researching the field, identifying specific business opportunities, negotiating alliances with equipment vendors, and evaluating high-speed rail experts and consultants from around the world. Throughout the process, Tonya, a highly qualified and respected engineer, has challenged everything you say during group meetings and in the workplace. For example, at a meeting two weeks ago, you presented the team with a list of 10 possible high-speed rail projects that had been identified by the team and started evaluating your organization's ability to compete for them. Tonya contradicted virtually all your comments, questioned your figures, and was quite pessimistic about the possibility of contracts. After this latest display of displeasure, two other group members, Liam and Ahmed, came to you and complained that Tonya was damaging the group's effectiveness. You originally put Tonya on the team for her expertise and insight. You'd like to find a way to reach her and get the team on the right track to its fullest potential.

Reinforcement: Creating Effective Teams Skills

The following suggestions are activities you can do to practice and reinforce the skills in creating effective teams.

1. Interview three managers at different organizations. Ask them about their experiences in managing teams. What behaviors have they found that work? What about those behaviors that have not been successful in creating an effective team?

2. After completing a team project for one of your classes, assess the effectiveness of your team by answering the following questions: Did everyone on the team know exactly why the team did what it did? Did team members have a significant amount of say or influence on decisions that affected them? Did team members have open, honest, timely, and two-way communications? Did everyone on the team know and understand the team's priorities? Did the team members work together to resolve destructive conflicts? Was everyone on the team working toward accomplishing the same thing? Did team members understand the team's unwritten rules of how to behave within the group? ■

DELEGATING

Managers get things done through other people. Because there are limits to any manager's time and knowledge, effective managers need to understand how to delegate. **Delegation** is the assignment of authority to another person to carry out specific duties. It allows a subordinate to make decisions. Delegation should not be confused with participation. In participative decision making, there's a sharing of authority. In delegation, subordinates make decisions on their own.

Learning about Delegating

A number of actions differentiate the effective delegator from the ineffective delegator. There are five behaviors that effective delegators will use.

1. **Clarify the assignment.** Determine *what* is to be delegated and *to whom.* You need to identify the person who's most capable of doing the task and then determine whether or not he or she has the time and motivation to do the task. If you have a willing and able subordinate, it's your responsibility to provide clear information on what is being delegated, the results you expect, and any time or performance expectations you may have. Unless there's an overriding need to adhere to specific methods, you should delegate only the results. Get agreement on what is to be done and the results expected, but let the subordinate decide the means.

2. **Specify the subordinate's range of discretion.** Every act of delegation comes with constraints. Although you're delegating authority to act, you're not delegating unlimited authority. You are delegating authority to act on certain issues within certain parameters. You need to specify what those parameters are so that subordinates know, in no uncertain terms, the range of their discretion.

3. **Allow the subordinate to participate.** One of the best ways to decide how much authority will be necessary to accomplish a task is to allow the subordinate who will be held accountable for that task to participate in that decision. Be aware, however, that allowing subordinates to participate can present its own set of potential problems as a result of subordinates' self-interests and biases in evaluating their own abilities.

- -

MANAGING IN THE REAL WORLD

"We empower our employees by delegating responsibility to them. We give them decision-making powers and then hold them accountable for the outcome."

Duke Rohlen, Owner
Left at Albuquerque
Restaurants
Palo Alto, California

- -

4. **Inform others that delegation has occurred.** Delegation shouldn't take place in a vacuum. Not only do the manager and subordinate need to know specifically what has been delegated and how much authority has been granted, but so does anyone else who's likely to be affected by the delegation. This includes people inside and outside the organization, if necessary. Essentially, you need to convey what has been delegated (the task and amount of authority) and to whom.

5. **Establish feedback channels.** To delegate without establishing feedback controls is inviting problems. The establishment of controls to monitor the subordinate's progress increases the likelihood that important problems will be identified and that the task will be completed on time and to the desired specifications. Ideally, these controls should be determined at the time of the initial assignment. Agree on a specific time for the completion of the task and then set progress dates when the subordinate will report back on how well he or she is doing and any major problems that may have arisen. These controls can be supplemented with periodic spot checks to ensure that authority guidelines aren't being abused, organization policies are being followed, proper procedures are being met, and the like.

MANAGING IN THE REAL WORLD

"I let my staff know that I have confidence in them, I check with them in a nonthreatening way about their projects, and I try to foster an atmosphere where they can be creative without having to worry too much about being risk takers."

Betsy Reifsnider,
Executive Director
Friends of the River
Sacramento, California

Based on S.P. Robbins and P.L. Hunsaker, *Training in InterPersonal Skills: TIPS for Managing People at Work*, 2nd ed. (Upper Saddle River, NJ: Prentice Hall, 1996), pp. 93–95; R.T. Noel, "What You Say to Your Employees When You Delegate," *Supervisory Management*, December 1993, p. 13; and S. Caudron, "Delegate for Results," *Industry Week*, February 6, 1995, pp. 27–30.

Practice: Delegating

Read through the following scenario. Write down some notes about how you would handle the situation described. Be sure to refer to the five behaviors described for delegating. Your professor will then tell you what to do next.

Ricky Lee is the supervisor of the contracts group of a large regional office supply distributor. His boss, Anne Zumwalt, has asked him to prepare by the end of the month the department's new procedures manual that will outline the steps followed in negotiating contracts with office products manufacturers who supply the organization's products. Because Ricky has another major project he's working on, he went to Anne and asked her if it would be possible to assign the rewriting of the procedures manual to Bill Harmon, one of his subordinates who's worked in the contracts group for about three years. Anne said she had no problems with Ricky reassigning the project as long as Bill knew the parameters and the expectations for the completion of the project. Ricky is preparing for his meeting in the morning with Bill regarding this assignment.

Reinforcement: Delegating Skills

The following suggestions are activities you can do to practice and reinforce the behaviors in delegating.

1. Interview a manager regarding his or her delegation skills. What activities doesn't he or she delegate? Why?

2. Teach someone else how to delegate effectively. Be sure to identify to this person the behaviors needed in delegating effectively as well as explaining why these behaviors are important. ■

DESIGNING MOTIVATING JOBS

As a manager, you're likely to be required to design jobs. How will you ensure that these jobs are motivating? What can you do regarding job design that will maximize your employees' performance? The job characteristics model, which defines five task characteristics (skill variety, task identity, task significance, autonomy, and feedback) and their relationships to employee motivation, provides a basis for designing motivating jobs.

Learning about Designing Motivating Jobs

The following five suggestions, based on the job characteristics model, specify the types of changes in jobs that are most likely to lead to improving the motivating potential for employees.

1. **Combine tasks.** As a manager, you should put existing specialized and fractionalized tasks back together to form a new, larger module of work. This step will increase skill variety and task identity.

2. **Create natural work units.** You should design tasks that form an identifiable and meaningful whole. This step will increase "ownership" of the work and will encourage employees to view their work as meaningful and important rather than as irrelevant and boring.

MANAGING IN THE REAL WORLD

"When a person is doing work they are meant to do, then it is fun and effortless. Workers become your greatest asset when you involve them in the decision processes that affect the work they do."

**Samuel W. (Bill) France,
Director for Technical Support
ServiceMaster Management
Services Group
Downers Grove, Illinois**

3. **Establish client relationships.** The client is the user of the product or service that is the basis of your employees' work. Whenever possible, you should establish direct relationships between your workers and your clients. This step increases skill variety, autonomy, and feedback for the employees.

MANAGING IN THE REAL WORLD

"I believe people remain motivated in their jobs if they are challenged, if they feel like they are growing as individuals and learning new things, and if they are given the opportunity to have an impact and make a difference."

**Duke Rohlen, Owner
Left at Albuquerque
Restaurants
Palo Alto, California**

4. **Expand jobs vertically.** Vertical expansion means giving employees responsibilities and controls that were formerly reserved for the manager. It partially closes the gap between the "doing" and "controlling" aspects of the job. This step increases employee autonomy.

5. **Open feedback channels.** By increasing feedback, employees not only learn how well they are performing their jobs but also whether their performance is improving, deteriorating, or remaining at a constant level. Ideally, this feedback should be received directly as the employee does the job, rather than from his or her manager on an occasional basis.

Based on J.R. Hackman, "Work Design," in J.R. Hackman and J.L. Suttle (eds.), *Improving Life at Work* (Santa Monica, CA: Goodyear, 1977), pp. 132–33.

Practice: Designing Motivating Jobs

Read through the following scenario. Write down some notes about how you would handle the situation described. Be sure to refer to the five suggestions described for designing motivating jobs. Your professor will then tell you what to do next.

You work for Sunrise Deliveries, a freight transportation company that makes local deliveries of products for your customers. In your position, you supervise Sunrise's six delivery drivers. Each morning your drivers drive their preloaded trucks to their destinations and wait for the products to be unloaded. There's a high turnover rate in the job. In fact, most of your drivers don't stay longer than six months. Not only is this employee turnover getting expensive, it's been hard to develop a quality customer service program when you've constantly got new faces. You've also heard complaints from the drivers that "all they do is drive." You know that you're going to have to do something to solve this problem.

Reinforcement: Designing Motivating Jobs Skills

The following suggestions are activities you can do to practice and reinforce the behaviors associated with designing motivating jobs.

1. Think of the worst job you have ever had. Analyze the job according to the five dimensions identified in the job characteristics model. Redesign the job in order to make it more satisfying and appealing.

2. Interview people in two different positions on your campus. Ask them questions about their jobs using the job characteristics model as a guide. Using the information provided, list recommendations for making the jobs more motivating. ■

DEVELOPING CONTROL CHARTS

One tool that managers can use to control all the various aspects of the operations system in order to achieve total quality in both products and processes is the **control chart**. Control charts are a management control tool that shows results of measurements over a period of time with statistically determined upper and lower limits. They provide a visual means of determining whether or not a specific process is staying within predefined limits. When a measurement falls outside the limits set, then the variation is unacceptable. Improvements in quality should, over time, result in a narrowing of the range between the upper and lower limits through eliminating common causes of variation.

Learning about Developing Control Charts

You can be more effective at developing control charts if you follow these five steps.

1. **Gather historical data**. A control chart is constructed from historical data on whatever performance criterion you're examining; future performance is compared with past performance. To do this, you need two distinctly different data sets, one to construct the control chart and a second one to reflect the most recent performance.

MANAGING IN THE REAL WORLD

"We use an approach called process mapping in our organization to help establish controls. These process maps help us get to the critical things (processes) we want to monitor."

**Thomas Dunham, Vice President and General Manager
GE Medical Systems
Waukesha, Wisconsin**

2. **Calculate a process average and upper and lower control limits**. You do this by using the historical data in the control chart construction. The control limits are based on the desired sampling distribution, that is, the degree of deviation you're willing to accept. In a typical operations setting, the limits are ordinarily set at three standard deviations, which means that 99.7 percent of the mean (or average) values should fall between the control limits.

3. **Draw the control chart**. Place the variable measurement on one axis and the sequence of samples on the other axis.

4. **Plot the current or most recent sample average on the chart**. By doing this, you will have an indication of where current performance stands in relation to historical performance.

5. **Interpret the chart**. What you should be able to determine from the chart: (a) Is the process in control and no managerial action required? (b) Is the process out of control and a cause should be sought? (c) Is the process in control but trends occurring that should alert you to possible nonrandom conditions?

Based on R.S. Russell and B.W. Taylor III, *Production and Operations Management* (Upper Saddle River, NJ: Prentice Hall, 1995).

- -

MANAGING IN THE REAL WORLD

"One area that's absolutely critical to continually control is costs because if a project runs over budget, you need to make adjustments to bring things back on track."

Graham Jones, Owner
G.L.A. Interiors
Toronto, Ontario, Canada

- -

Practice: Developing Control Charts

Read through the following scenario. Write down some notes about how you would handle the situation described. Be sure to refer to the steps for developing a control chart. Your professor will then tell you what to do next.

Lou Benson is quality control supervisor at Super Sack Manufacturing Corporation in Reed, Georgia. The 30 employees at Super Sack produce an average of 5,000 dog food bags per week. The bags they produce are used by major dog food manufacturers to package dry dog food sold at farm products stores in the southern United States. Lou has noticed that the reject rate for the bags produced has been creeping up slowly over the last six weeks. What can he do about this potential quality problem? Be specific about the information he would need and how he would go about using a control chart to plot this information.

Reinforcement: Developing Control Charts Skills

The following suggestions are activities you can do to practice and reinforce the steps in developing control charts.

1. Interview three managers at different organizations. Ask them if they use control charts in managing their units. (If they're not familiar with the concept, be prepared to describe it to them.) What do these control charts look like? Evaluate the control charts. Could they be improved? If so, how?

2. Select a business you're familiar with either through working there or through being a frequent customer. Choose an area that you think might benefit from the use of control charts. Describe how you would go about creating these control charts. Be as specific as possible in describing the data you would need and how you would gather the data. ∎

DEVELOPING TRUST

Trust plays an important role in the manager's relationship with his or her employees. Given the importance of trust, today's managers should actively seek to develop it within their work group.

Learning about Developing Trust

You can be more effective at developing trust among your employees if you use the following eight suggestions.

1. **Practice openness.** Mistrust comes as much from what people don't know as from what they do. Being open with employees leads to confidence and trust. Keep people informed. Make clear the criteria you use in making decisions. Explain the rationale for your decisions. Be forthright and candid about problems. Fully disclose all relevant information.

2. **Be fair.** Before making decisions or taking actions, consider how others will perceive them in terms of objectivity and fairness. Give credit where credit is due. Be objective and impartial in performance appraisals. Pay attention to equity perceptions in distributing rewards.

3. **Speak your feelings.** Managers who convey only hard facts come across as cold, distant, and unfeeling. When you share your feelings, others will see that you are real and human. They will know you for who you are and their respect for you is likely to increase.

4. **Tell the truth.** Being trustworthy means being credible. If honesty is critical to credibility, then you must be perceived as someone who tells the truth. Employees are more tolerant of hearing something "they don't want to hear" than of finding out that their manager lied to them.

5. **Be consistent.** People want predictability. Mistrust comes from not knowing what to expect. Take the time to think about your values and beliefs and let those values and beliefs consistently guide your decisions. When you know your central purpose, your actions will follow, and you will project a consistency that earns trust.

MANAGING IN THE REAL WORLD

"To get people to trust you, be true to your word. If you say you are going to do something, do it!"

James Fripp, Field Staffing Manager
Taco Bell Corporation
Omaha, Nebraska

6. **Fulfill your promises.** Trust requires that people believe that you are dependable. You need to ensure that you keep your word. Promises made must be promises kept.

7. **Maintain confidences.** You trust those whom you believe to be discreet and those on whom you can rely. If people open up to you and make themselves vulnerable by telling you something in confidence, they need to feel assured you won't discuss it with others or betray that confidence. If people perceive you as someone who leaks personal confidences or someone who can't be depended on, you've lost their trust.

8. **Demonstrate competence.** Develop the admiration and respect of others by demonstrating technical and professional ability. Pay particular attention to developing and displaying your communication, negotiation, and other interpersonal skills.

Based on F. Bartolome, "Nobody Trusts the Boss Completely— Now What?" *Harvard Business Review*, March–April 1989, pp. 135–42; and J.K. Butler Jr., "Toward Understanding and Measuring Conditions of Trust: Evolution of a Condition of Trust Inventory," *Journal of Management*, September 1991, pp. 643–63.

Practice: Developing Trust

Read through the following scenario. Write down some notes about how you would handle the situation described. Be sure to refer to the eight behaviors described for developing trust. Your professor will then tell you what to do next.

Donna Romines is the shipping department manager at Tastefully Tempting, a gourmet candy company based in Phoenix. Orders for the company's candy pour in from around the world. Your six-member team processes these orders. Needless to say, the three months before Christmas are quite hectic. Everybody counts the days until December 24 when the phones finally stop ringing off the wall, at least for a couple of days. You and all of your team members breathe a sigh of relief as the last box of candy is sent on its way out the door.

When the company was first founded five years ago, after the holiday rush, the owners would shut down Tastefully Tempting for two weeks after Christmas. However, as the business has grown, that practice has become too costly. There's too much business to do to be able to afford that luxury. And the rush for Valentine's Day orders start pouring in the week after Christmas. Although the two-week postholiday companywide shutdown has been phased out formally, some departments have found it difficult to get employees to gear up once again after the Christmas break. The employees who come to work after Christmas usually accomplish little.

This year, though, things have got to change. You know that the cultural "tradition" won't be easy to overcome, but your shipping team needs to be ready to tackle the orders that have piled up. After all, Tastefully Tempting's customers want their orders filled correctly and promptly!

Reinforcement: Developing Trust Skills

The following suggestions are activities you can do to practice and reinforce the behaviors associated with developing trust.

1. Keep a one-week log describing ways that your daily decisions and actions encouraged people to trust you and to not trust you. What things did you do that led to trust? What things did you do that may have led to distrust? How could you have changed your behavior so that the situations of potential distrust could have been situations of trust?

2. Review six recent issues of a business periodical (such as *Business Week, Fortune, Forbes, Fast Company*, or *Wall Street Journal*) for articles where trust (or lack of trust) may have played a role. Find two articles and describe the situation. Explain how the person(s) involved might have used skills at developing trust to handle the situation. ◼

DISCIPLINING

If an employee's performance regularly isn't up to par or if an employee consistently ignores the organization's standards and regulations, the manager may have to use discipline as a way to control behavior. What exactly is **discipline?** It's actions taken by a manager to enforce the organization's standards and regulations. The most common types of discipline problems managers have to deal with include attendance (absenteeism, tardiness, abuse of sick leave), on-the-job behaviors (failure to meet performance goals, disobedience, failure to use safety devices, alcohol or drug abuse), and dishonesty (theft, lying to supervisors).

Learning about Discipline

You can be more effective at disciplining employees if you use the following eight behaviors.

1. **Respond immediately.** The more quickly a disciplinary action follows an offense, the more likely it is that the employee will associate the discipline with the offense rather than with you as the disciplinarian. It's best to begin the disciplinary process as soon as possible after you notice a violation.

2. **Provide a warning.** You have an obligation to give a warning before initiating disciplinary action. This means that the employee must be aware of the organization's rules and accept its standards of behavior and performance. Disciplinary action is more likely to be seen as fair when employees have received a warning that a given violation will lead to discipline and when they know what that discipline will be.

3. **State the problem specifically.** Give the date, time, place, individuals involved, and any

extenuating circumstances surrounding the problem behavior. Be sure to define the problem in exact terms instead of just reciting company regulations or terms from a union contract. Explain why the behavior can't be continued by showing how it specifically affects the employee's job performance, the unit's effectiveness, and the employee's colleagues.

MANAGING IN THE REAL WORLD

"I've found that the most effective way to discipline employees is to confront them openly when they have done something which you disapprove of. If a manager is doing his (or her) job correctly and clearly communicating expectations, employees will know where they stand and when they've messed up."

**Duke Rohlen, Owner
Left at Albuquerque
Restaurants
Palo Alto, California**

4. **Allow the employee to explain his or her position.** Regardless of the facts you've uncovered, due process demands that you give the employee an opportunity to explain his or her position. From the employee's perspective, what happened? Why did it happen? What was his or her perception of the expectations, rules, regulations, and circumstances?
5. **Keep discussion impersonal.** Make sure that the discipline is directed at what the employee has done (or failed to do) and not at the employee personally.
6. **Be consistent.** Fair treatment of employees demands that disciplinary action be consistent. This doesn't mean, however, treating everyone exactly alike. Be sure to clearly justify disciplinary actions that might appear inconsistent to employees.

7. **Take progressive action.** Choose a disciplinary action that's appropriate to the infraction. Penalties should get progressively stronger if, or when, the problem is repeated. For example, you may start with an oral warning, then move progressively to a written warning, a suspension, and then dismissal.

MANAGING IN THE REAL WORLD

"The most effective way to discipline employees is to be positive, be instructive, and give employees another chance."

**Coleman Peterson, Senior Vice
President, People Division
Wal-Mart Stores
Bentonville, Arkansas**

8. **Obtain agreement on change.** Disciplining should include guidance and direction for correcting the problem. Let the employee state what he or she plans to do in the future to ensure that the problem won't be repeated.

Based on A. Belohlav, *The Art of Disciplining Your Employees* (Upper Saddle River, NJ: Prentice Hall, 1985); and R.H. Lussier, "A Discipline Model for Increasing Performance," *Supervisory Management,* August 1990, pp. 6–7.

Practice: Disciplining

Read through the following scenario. Write down some notes about how you would handle the disciplinary problem described. Be sure to refer to the eight behaviors described for effective disciplining. Your professor will then tell you what to do next.

You're a team leader in the customer services department at Mountain View Microbrewery. Carla is the newest member of your 10-person team having been there only six weeks. She came to Mountain View with good recommendations from her previous job as a customer support representative at a car dealership. However, not long after joining your team, she was late in issuing an important purchasing order. When you talked to her about it, she said it was "lost." But you discovered it in her in-box where it had been properly placed. Then, just last week, she failed to make an immediate return call to an unhappy customer who could easily have been satisfied at that point. Instead the customer worked himself into a rage and vented his unhappiness in a letter to the company's CEO. Now the latest incident with Carla came up just yesterday. As part of your company's quality control program, your team members prepare periodic reports on the service they provide to each customer and turn these reports over to an upper management group that evaluates them. Carla didn't meet her deadline for getting her report into this evaluation group and you received a call wanting to know where this report was. Because Carla is still on pro-

bation for another six weeks, it appears that the time has come for you to talk to her about her failure to meet expected work performance goals.

Reinforcement: Disciplining Skills

The following suggestions are activities you can do to practice and reinforce the disciplining behaviors.

1. Talk with three managers at three different organizations. Ask them what guidance they've received from their organizations in disciplining employees. Have them describe specific employee discipline problems they've faced and how they handled them.

2. Interview three of your current or past instructors. Ask them about their approaches to discipline. How do they handle late papers, cheating, excessive absenteeism, or other disciplinary problems? ∎

INTERVIEWING

The interview is used almost universally as part of the employee selection process. Not many of us have ever gotten a job without having gone through one or more interviews. Interviews can be valid and reliable selection tools, but they need to be structured and well organized.

Learning about Interviewing

You can be an effective interviewer if you use the following seven suggestions for interviewing job candidates.

1. **Review the job description and job specification.** Be sure that prior to the interview, you have reviewed pertinent information about the job. Why? Because this will provide you with valuable information on which to assess the job candidate. Furthermore, knowing the relevant job requirements will help eliminate interview bias.

2. **Prepare a structured set of questions you want to ask all job applicants.** By having a set of prepared questions, you ensure that the information you wish to elicit is obtainable. Further-

more, by asking similar questions, you are able to better compare all candidates' answers against a common base.

3. **Before meeting a candidate, review his or her application form and résumé.** By doing this you'll be able to create a complete picture of the candidate in terms of what is represented on the résumé or application and what the job requires. You can also begin to identify areas to explore during the interview. That is, areas that are not clearly defined on the résumé or application but that are essential to the job can become a focal point in your discussion with the candidate.

4. **Open the interview by putting the applicant at ease and by providing a brief preview of the topics to be discussed.** Interviews are stressful for job candidates. Opening the discussion with small talk, such as the weather, can give the candidate time to adjust to the interview setting. By providing a preview of topics to come, you are giving the candidate an agenda. This helps the candidate begin framing what he or she will say in response to your questions.

MANAGING IN THE REAL WORLD

"I have found that the most effective way to interview employees is by having the interview in a one-on-one setting and letting the candidate know how the interview is going to be carried out."

James Fripp, Field Staffing
Manager
Taco Bell Corporation
Omaha, Nebraska

5. **Ask your questions and listen carefully to the candidate's answers.** Select follow-up questions that flow naturally from the answers given. Focus on the responses as they relate to information you need to ensure that the candidate meets your job requirements. If you still have uncertainty, use a follow-up question to further probe for information.

MANAGING IN THE REAL WORLD

"The most effective way to interview employees involves learning about the whole person, focusing on their track record (where they've been), focusing on the future (where they want to go), and clarifying actual things they've done and accomplished."

Coleman Peterson, Senior Vice
President, People Division
Wal-Mart Stores, Inc.
Bentonville, Arkansas

6. **Close the interview by telling the applicant what is going to happen next.** Applicants are anxious about the status of your hiring decision. Be up-front with candidates regarding others who will be interviewed and the remaining steps in the hiring process. Let the candidate know your time frame for making a decision. In addition, tell the applicant how you will notify him or her about your decision.

7. **Write your evaluation of the applicant while the interview is still fresh in your mind.** Don't wait until the end of the day, after interviewing several candidates, to write your analysis of each candidate. Memory can (and often will) fail you! The sooner you complete your write-up after an interview, the better chance you have of accurately recording what occurred in the interview and your perceptions of the candidate.

Based on S.P. Robbins and D.A. DeCenzo, *Fundamentals of Management*, 2nd ed. (Upper Saddle River, NJ: Prentice Hall, 1998), p. 242.

Practice: Interviewing

Read through the following list and do the actions that are requested. Be sure to refer to the seven suggestions for conducting effective interviews. Your professor will then tell you what to do next.

1. Break into groups of three.

2. Take up to 10 minutes to compose five challenging job interview questions that you think should be relevant in the hiring of new college graduates for a sales-management training program at Kraft General Foods Corporation. Each hiree will spend 18 to 24 months as a sales representative calling on retail grocers. After this training period, successful candidates can be expected to be promoted to the position of district sales supervisor.

3. Exchange your five questions with another group.

4. Each group should allocate one of the following roles to their three members: interviewer, applicant, and observer. The person playing the applicant should rough out a brief résumé of his or her background and experience and then give it to the interviewer.

5. Role play a job interview. The interviewer should include, but not be limited to, the questions provided by the other group.

6. After the interview, the observer should evaluate the interviewer's behaviors in terms of the effective interview suggestions.

Reinforcement: Interviewing Skills

The following suggestions are activities you can do to practice and reinforce the interviewing skills.

1. On your campus, there's probably a job placement service provided for graduating seniors. If possible, talk to two or three graduating seniors who have been interviewed by organizations through this campus service. Ask them to share what happened during their interviews. Then write a brief report describing what you found out and comparing the students' experiences with the suggestions for effective interviewing.

2. Interview a manager about the interview process he or she uses in hiring new employees. What types of information does the manager try to get during an interview? (Be sure that as you interview this manager that you use the suggestions for good interviewing. Although you're not "hiring" this person, you are looking for information, which is what you're looking for during a job interview.) ■

MANAGING RESISTANCE TO CHANGE

Managers play an important role in organizational change—that is, they serve as change agents. However, managers often find that change is resisted by employees. Change represents ambiguity and uncertainty, or it threatens the status quo. How can this resistance to change be effectively managed?

Learning about Managing Resistance to Change

You can be more effective at managing resistance to change if you use the following suggestions.

1. **Assess the climate for change.** One major factor why some change programs succeed and others fail is the readiness for change. Assessing the climate for change involves answering several questions. The more affirmative answers you get, the more likely it is that change efforts will succeed.

   - Is the sponsor of the change high enough in the hierarchy to have power to effectively deal with resistance?
   - Is senior management supportive of the change and committed to it?
   - Is there a strong sense of urgency from senior managers about the need for change and is this feeling shared by the rest of the organization?
   - Do managers have a clear vision of how the future will look differently from the present?

   - Are there objective measures in place to evaluate the change effort and have reward systems been explicitly designed to reinforce them?
   - Is the specific change effort consistent with other changes going on in the organization?
   - Are unit managers willing to sacrifice their personal self-interests for the good of the organization as a whole?

MANAGING IN THE REAL WORLD

"Employees must have real opportunities to change, but if they refuse to change, they would be better to move on. It's not in their best interests or the company's to leave them in positions where they can't succeed."

James Sierk, Senior Vice President of Quality and Productivity
AlliedSignal Corporation
Morristown, New Jersey

- Do managers pride themselves on closely monitoring changes and actions by competitors?
- Are managers and employees rewarded for taking risks, being innovative, and looking for new solutions?
- Is the organizational structure flexible?
- Does communication flow both down *and* up the organizational hierarchy?
- Has the organization successfully implemented major changes in the recent past?
- Are employee satisfaction and trust in management high?
- Is there a high degree of interaction and cooperation between organizational units?
- Are decisions made quickly and do decisions take into account a wide variety of suggestions?

2. **Choose an appropriate approach for managing the resistance to change.** There are six tactics that have been suggested in dealing with resistance to change. Each is designed to be appropriate for different conditions of resistance. These include *education and communication* (used when resistance comes from lack of information or inaccurate information), *participation* (used when resistance stems from people not having all the information they need or when they have the power to resist), *facilitation and support* (used when resistance stems from people having adjustment problems), *negotiation* (used when those with power will lose out in a change), *manipulation and cooptation* (used when any other tactic will not work or is too expensive), and *coercion* (used when speed is essential and change agents possess considerable power). Which one of these approaches will be most effective depends on the source of the resistance to the change.

3. **During the time the change is being implemented and after the change is completed, communicate with employees regarding what support you may be able to provide.** Your employees need to know that you are there to support them during change efforts. Be prepared to offer the assistance that may be necessary to help your employees enact the change.

MANAGING IN THE REAL WORLD

"It's important when dealing with employees who resist change that is necessary to focus on clear goals and results."

**Larry Lim, Executive Director
Lynton Consulting Services
Singapore, China**

Based on J.P. Kotter and L.A. Schlesinger, "Choosing Strategies for Change," *Harvard Business Review*, March–April 1979, pp. 106–14; and T.A. Stewart, "Rate Your Readiness to Change," *Fortune*, February 7, 1994, pp. 106–10.

Practice: Managing Resistance to Change

Read through the following scenario. Write down some notes about how you would handle the situation described. Be sure to refer to the three suggestions described for managing resistance to change. Your professor will then tell you what to do next.

You're the nursing supervisor at a community hospital employing both emergency room and floor nurses. Each of these teams of nurses tends to work almost exclusively with others doing the same job. In your professional reading, you've come across the concept of cross-training nursing teams and giving them more varied responsibilities, which in turn has been shown to improve patient care while lowering costs. You call the two team leaders, Sue and Scott, into your office to explain that you want the nursing teams to move to this approach. To your surprise, they're both opposed to the idea. Sue says she and the other emergency room nurses feel they're needed in the ER where they fill the most vital role in the hospital. They work special hours when needed, do whatever tasks are required, and often work in difficult and stressful circumstances. They think the floor nurses have relatively easy jobs for the pay they receive. Scott, leader of the floor nurse team, tells you that his group believes the ER nurses lack the special training and extra experience that the floor nurses bring to the hospital. The floor nurses claim they have the heaviest responsibilities and do the most exacting work. Because they have ongoing contact with patients and families, they believe they shouldn't be called away from vital floor duties to help the ER nurses complete their tasks.

Reinforcement: Managing Resistance to Change Skills

The following suggestions are activities you can do to practice and reinforce the behaviors associated with effectively managing resistance to change.

1. Think about changes (major and minor) that you have dealt with over the last year. Perhaps these changes involved other people and perhaps they were personal. Did you resist the change? Did others resist the change? How did you overcome your resistance or the resistance of others to the change?

2. Interview three managers at different organizations about changes they have implemented. What was their experience in implementing the change? How did they manage resistance to the change? ■

MANAGING TIME

Time is a unique resource in that if it's wasted, it can never be replaced. Managers who use their time effectively know which activities they want to accomplish, the best order in which to do those activities, and when they want to complete those activities. **Time management** is a personal form of scheduling time effectively. The essence of time management is to use your time effectively.

Learning about Managing Time

You can be more effective at managing your time if you use the following five suggestions.

1. **Identify your objectives**. What are the specific objectives that have you set for yourself or for your unit? If you work in an organization that uses a form of MBO (management by objectives) or some other goal-setting method, these objectives may already exist.

2. **Prioritize your objectives**. Not all objectives you have are equally important. Given limitations that exist on your time, you want to give the highest priority to the objectives that are most important.

3. **List the activities that must be done to accomplish your objectives**. Planning really is the key here. You must identify the specific actions you

need to take to achieve your goals. Record these activities on a sheet of paper, an index card, or even a computer-generated schedule. These activities become your "to-do" list. Your to-do list should cover, at a minimum, those things that need to be done over the next few days. The list should be reviewed throughout the day and updated when necessary. As items are completed, they should be crossed off the list.

MANAGING IN THE REAL WORLD

"Remaining highly focused on what tasks MUST be completed in order for me to complete my most significant tasks enables me to option out or delegate lesser tasks to others."

Sandy Steiner, President, Prentice Hall Business Publishing Upper Saddle River, New Jersey

4. **Prioritize your to-do list**. This steps involves imposing a second set of priorities. Here you need to emphasize both importance and urgency. If the activity is not important, you should consider delegating it to someone else. If it's not urgent, it can usually wait. Completing this step will help you identify activities you *must* do, activities you *should* do, activities you'll do *when you can,* and activities that you can *get others to do for you.*

MANAGING IN THE REAL WORLD

"I have found that you must be dedicated to keeping your calendar and to-do list up-to-date. No matter what type of scheduling tool you use, don't worry about how it looks as long as it's effective."

**Madelyn Gengelbach,
Marketing Strategist
Hallmark Cards
Kansas City, Missouri**

5. **Schedule your day**. After prioritizing your activities, develop a daily plan. Each morning (or the night before) identify what you want to accomplish during the day. This list should identify five to seven specific things you must do during the day. Follow with those you should do, and so forth. But be realistic in your schedule. Depending on the nature of your activities, you may not be able to complete everything. Be realistic in what you can accomplish. The key is to concentrate on the "must-do's," making sure they do get done. Don't make the mistake of working on the "when you can" activities just because they are easier to accomplish. You'll be spending time on activities that really won't add to your effectiveness.

Based on R.A. Mackenzie, *The Time Trap* (New York: McGraw-Hill, 1975); R.A. Webber, *Time Is Money* (New York: The Free Press, 1980); M.E. Haynes, *Practical Time Management: How to Make the Most of Your Most Perishable Resource* (Tulsa, OK: Penn Well Books, 1985); and A. Deutschman, "The CEO's Secret of Managing Time," *Fortune*, June 1, 1992, pp. 135–46.

Practice: Managing Time

Have you ever thought about how you spend your time in a typical week? Do you know who or what "wastes" your time? For this exercise, you are to keep a time log for each day for the next week. Starting at midnight and in 15-minute increments, list what you do and who you interact with for 24 hours. To get the most accurate information, fill in each time period as it ends (except when you're asleep). Don't wait until later and attempt to complete it by memory. When you have tracked these data for a week, review the time log.

Answer the following questions. Can you identify times when you were most productive? How about those when you wasted time? Are there consistencies in the time wasters? That is, do they tend to occur at the same time, in the same place, or with the same individual(s)?

Finally, share your information with a partner in class. Look for similarities between your lists. Each of you should make two recommendations that would help the other person become a better time manager.

Reinforcement: Managing Time Skills

The following suggestions are activities you can do to practice and reinforce the behaviors associated with managing your time.

1. Interview two of your professors regarding how they effectively manage their time. What similarities do you see in their responses? How do their responses fit in with the suggestions given for this skill?

2. Use your contacts to identify two individuals—one who has a long record of personal or professional accomplishments; the other, a modest record. Interview each to learn how they manage their time. Now write a short paper analyzing to what degree their time management skills may have contributed to or hindered their record of accomplishments. ∎

MENTORING

A mentor is someone in the organization, usually older, more experienced, and in a higher-level position, who sponsors or supports another employee (a protégé) who is lower in the organization. A mentor can teach, guide, and encourage. Some organizations have formal mentoring programs, but even if your organization does not, mentoring should be an important skill for you to develop.

Learning about Mentoring

You can be more effective at mentoring if you use the following six suggestions as you mentor another person.

1. **Communicate honestly and openly with your protégé.** If your protégé is going to learn from you and benefit from your experience and knowledge, you're going to have to be open and honest as you talk about what you've done. Bring up the failures as well as the successes. Remember that mentoring is a learning process and in order for learning to take place, you're going to have to be open and honest in "telling it like it is."

MANAGING IN THE REAL WORLD

"Managers can be effective mentors by providing an insight into the institutional memory of the company, by empowering the employee to question and comment, and by providing avenues of access to the company's decision makers."

José Legaspi, Owner
The Legaspi Company
Montebello, California

---

2. **Encourage honest and open communication from your protégé.** You need to know as the mentor what your protégé hopes to gain from this relationship. You should encourage the protégé to ask for information and to be specific about what he or she wants to gain.

3. **Treat the relationship with the protégé as a learning opportunity.** Don't pretend to have all the answers and all the knowledge, but do share what you've learned through your experiences. And in your conversations and interactions with your protégé, you may be able to learn as much from that person as he or she does from you. So be open to listening to what your protégé is saying.

4. **Take the time to get to know your protégé.** As a mentor, you should be willing to take the time to get to know your protégé and his or her interests. If you're not willing to spend that extra time, you should probably not embark on a mentoring relationship.

MANAGING IN THE REAL WORLD

"Mentoring is the highest management skill to understand and apply. Managers can become good mentors by finding the best skill in each employee they manage and helping that person hone that skill."

Samuel W. (Bill) France,
Director for Technical Support
ServiceMaster Management
Services Company
Downers Grove, Illinois

---

5. **Remind your protégé that there is no substitute for effective work performance.** In any job, effective work performance is absolutely essen-

tial. It doesn't matter how much information, advice, coaching, or encouragement you provide as a mentor if the protégé isn't willing to be an effective performer.

6. **Know when it's time to let go.** Successful mentors know when it's time to let the protégé begin standing on his or her own. If the mentoring relationship has been effective, the protégé will be comfortable and confident in handling new and increasing work responsibilities. And just because the mentoring relationship is over doesn't mean that you never have contact with your protégé. It just means that the relationship becomes one of equals, not one of teacher and student.

Based on H. Rothman, "The Boss as Mentor," *Nation's Business*, April 1993, pp. 66–67; J.B. Cunningham and T. Eberle, "Characteristics of the Mentoring Experience: A Qualitative Study," *Personnel Review*, June 1993, pp. 54–66; S. Crandell, "The Joys of Mentoring," *Executive Female*, March–April 1994, pp. 38–42; and W. Heery, "Corporate Mentoring Can Break the Glass Ceiling," *HR Focus*, May 1994, pp. 17–18.

Practice: Mentoring

Read through the following scenario. Write down some notes about how you would handle the situation described. Be sure to refer to the six behaviors described for mentoring. Your professor will then tell you what to do next.

Lora Slovinsky has worked for your department in a software design firm longer than any of your other employees. You value her skills and commitment and you frequently ask her judgment on difficult issues. Very often, her ideas have been better than yours and you've let her know through both praise and pay increases how much you appreciate her contributions. Recently, though, you've begun to question Lora's judgment. The fundamental problem

is in the distinct difference in the ways you both approach your work. Your strengths lie in getting things done, on time, and under budget. Although Lora is aware of these constraints, her creativity and perfectionism sometimes make her prolong projects. On her most recent assignment, Lora seemed more intent than ever on doing things her way. Despite what you felt were clear guidelines, she was two weeks late in meeting an important customer deadline. And while her product quality was high, as always, the software design was far more elaborate than what was needed at this stage of development. Looking over her work in your office, you feel more than a little frustrated and certain that you need to address matters with Lora.

Reinforcement: Mentoring Skills

The following suggestions are activities you can do to practice and reinforce the behaviors needed in mentoring.

1. If there are individuals on your campus who act as mentors (or advisors) to first-time students, make an appointment to talk to one of these mentors. These mentors may be upper-division students or they may be professors or college staff employees. Ask them about their role as a mentor and the skills they think it takes to be an effective mentor. How do the skills they mention relate to the behaviors listed here?

2. Athletic coaches often act as mentors to their younger, assistant coaches. Interview a coach about her or his role as a mentor. What types of things do coaches do to instruct, teach, advise, and encourage their assistant coaches? Could any of these activities be transferred to an organizational setting? Explain. ■

NEGOTIATING

Negotiating is another interpersonal skill that managers use. For instance, they may have to negotiate salaries for incoming employees, cut deals with superiors, work out differences with associates, or resolve conflicts with subordinates. **Negotiation** is a process of bargaining in which two or more parties who have different preferences must make joint decisions and come to an agreement.

Learning about Negotiating

You can be more effective at negotiating if you use the following six recommended behaviors.

1. **Research your opponent.** Acquire as much information as you can about your opponent's

interests and goals. Understanding your opponent's position will help you to better understand his or her behavior, predict his or her responses to your offers, and frame solutions in terms of his or her interests.

2. **Begin with a positive overture.** Research shows that concessions tend to be reciprocated and lead to agreements. Therefore, begin bargaining with a positive overture and then reciprocate your opponent's concessions.

MANAGING IN THE REAL WORLD

"Negotiation skills are important in my job particularly in negotiating problems between employees. Negotiation skills are just sales skills if I'm just getting the question right."

Mike Dorf, CEO
KnitMedia
New York, New York

---

3. **Address problems, not personalities.** Concentrate on the negotiation issues, not on the personal characteristics of your opponent. When negotiations get tough, avoid the tendency to attack your opponent. Remember it's your opponent's ideas or position that you disagree with, not him or her personally.

4. **Pay little attention to initial offers.** Treat an initial offer as merely a point of departure. Everyone must have an initial position. Such positions tend to be extreme and idealistic. Treat them as such.

5. **Emphasize win-win solutions.** If conditions are supportive, look for an integrative solution. Frame options in terms of your opponent's interests and

look for solutions that can allow your opponent, as well as yourself, to declare a victory.

MANAGING IN THE REAL WORLD

"It's important for managers to have their people feel like they're receiving something in exchange for what you're negotiating for."

George Gatch, Vice President
J.P. Morgan and Company
New York, New York

---

6. **Create an open and trusting climate.** Skilled negotiators are better listeners, ask more questions, focus their arguments more directly, are less defensive, and have learned to avoid words or phrases that can irritate an opponent (such as "generous offer," "fair price," or "reasonable arrangement"). In other words, they are better at creating the open and trusting climate that is necessary for reaching a win-win settlement.

Based on M.H. Bazerman and M.A. Neale, *Negotiating Rationally* (New York: Free Press, 1992); and J.A. Wall, Jr. and M.W. Blum, "Negotiations," *Journal of Management*, June 1991, pp. 278–82.

Practice: Negotiating

Read through the following scenario. Write down some notes about how you would handle the situation described. Be sure to refer to the six behaviors described for negotiating. Your professor will then tell you what to do next.

As marketing director for Done Right, a regional home repair chain, you've come up with a plan you believe has a lot of potential for future sales. Your plan involves a customer information service designed to help people make their homes more environmentally sensitive. Then based upon homeowners' assessments of their homes' environmental impact, your firm will be prepared to help them deal with problems or concerns they may uncover. You're really excited about the potential of this new service. You envision pamphlets, in-store appearances by environment experts, as well as contests for consumers and school kids. After several weeks of preparations, you make your pitch to your boss, Tommy Wong. You point out how the market for environmentally sensitive home products is growing and how this growing demand represents the perfect opportunity for Done Right. Tommy seems impressed by your presentation, but he's expressed one major concern. He thinks your workload is already too high. He doesn't see how you're going to have enough time to start this new service and still be able to look after all of your other assigned duties.

PROVIDING FEEDBACK

Ask a manager about the feedback he or she gives subordinates and you're likely to get a qualified answer. If the feedback is positive, it's likely to be given promptly and enthusiastically. However, negative feedback is often treated very differently. Like most of us, managers don't particularly enjoy communicating bad news. They fear offending or having to deal with the recipient's defensiveness. The result is that negative feedback is often avoided, delayed, or substantially distorted. However, it is important for managers to provide both positive and negative feedback.

Learning about Providing Feedback

You can be more effective at providing feedback if you use the following six specific suggestions.

1. **Focus on specific behaviors.** Feedback should be specific rather than general. Avoid such statements as "You have a bad attitude" or "I'm really impressed with the good job you did." They're vague and although they provide information, they don't tell the recipient enough to correct the "bad attitude" or on what basis you

Reinforcement: Negotiating Skills

The following suggestions are activities you can do to practice and reinforce the negotiating behaviors.

1. Find three people who have recently purchased new or used cars. Interview each to learn which tactics, if any, they used to get a lower price. Write a short paper comparing your findings and relating it to the negotiating behaviors presented in this section.

2. Research current business periodicals for two examples of negotiations. The negotiations might be labor-management negotiations or they might be negotiations over buying and selling real estate or a business. What did the article say about the negotiation process? Write down specific questions that each party to the negotiation might have had. Pretend that you were a consultant to one of the parties in the negotiation. What recommendations would you have made? ■

concluded that "a good job" had been done so the person knows what behaviors to repeat.

MANAGING IN THE REAL WORLD

"I rarely ever will criticize an employee because for every negative you give a person, it takes about ten or more positive comments to overcome that critical remark."

Samuel W. (Bill) France,
Director for Technical Support
ServiceMaster Management
Services Company
Downers Grove, Illinois

2. **Keep feedback impersonal.** Feedback, particularly the negative kind, should be descriptive rather than judgmental or evaluative. No mat-

ter how upset you are, keep the feedback focused on job-related behaviors and never criticize someone personally because of an inappropriate action.

3. **Keep feedback goal oriented.** Feedback should not be given primarily to "unload" on another person. If you have to say something negative, make sure it's directed toward the recipient's goals. Ask yourself whom the feedback is supposed to help. If the answer is *you,* bite your tongue and hold the comment. Such feedback undermines your credibility and lessens the meaning and influence of future feedback.

4. **Make feedback well timed.** Feedback is most meaningful to a recipient when there's a very short interval between his or her behavior and the receipt of feedback about that behavior. Moreover, if you're particularly concerned with changing behavior, delays in providing feedback on the undesirable actions lessen the likelihood that the feedback will be effective in bringing about the desired change. Of course, making feedback prompt merely for the sake of promptness can backfire if you have insufficient information, if you're angry, or if you're otherwise emotionally upset. In such instances, "well timed" could mean "somewhat delayed."

- - - - - - - - - - - - - - - - - - - -

MANAGING IN THE REAL WORLD

"The most effective way I have found to provide feedback to my employees is by one-on-one coaching."

Thomas Dunham, Vice President and General Manager GE Medical Systems Waukesha, Wisconsin

- - - - - - - - - - - - - - - - - - - -

5. **Ensure understanding.** Make sure your feedback is concise and complete so that the recip-

ient clearly and fully understands your communication. It may help to have the recipient rephrase the content of your feedback to find out whether or not it fully captured the meaning you intended.

6. **Direct negative feedback toward behavior that the recipient can control.** There's little value in reminding a person of some shortcoming over which he or she has no control. Negative feedback should be directed at behavior that the recipient can do something about. In addition, when negative feedback is given concerning something that the recipient can control, it might be a good idea to indicate specifically what can be done to improve the situation.

Based on S.P. Robbins and P.L. Hunsaker, *Training in InterPersonal Skills: TIPS for Managing People at Work,* 2nd ed. (Upper Saddle River, NJ: Prentice Hall, 1996), chapter 5.

Practice: Providing Feedback

Read through the following scenario. Write down some notes about how you would handle the situation described. Be sure to refer to the six behaviors described for providing feedback. Your professor will then tell you what to do next.

Craig is an excellent employee whose expertise and productivity have always met or exceeded your expectations. But recently he's been making work difficult for other members of your advertising team. Like his co-workers, Craig researches and computes the costs of media buys for your agency's clients. The work requires laboriously leafing through several large reference books to find the correct base price and add-on charges for each radio or television station and time slot, calculating each actual cost, and compiling the results in a computerized spreadsheet. To make things more efficient and convenient, you've always allowed your team to bring the reference books they're using to their desks while they're using them. Lately, however, Craig has been piling books around him for days and sometimes weeks at a time. The books interfere with the flow of traffic past his desk and other people are having to go out of their way to retrieve the books from Craig's pile. It's time for you to have a talk with Craig.

Reinforcement: Providing Feedback Skills

The following suggestions are activities you can do to practice and reinforce the behaviors in providing feedback.

1. Think of three things that a friend or relative did well recently. Did you praise the person at the time? If not, why? The next time someone close to you does something well, give him or her positive feedback.

2. You have a good friend who has a mannerism (speech, body movement, style of dress, or the like) that you think is inappropriate and detracts from the overall impression that he or she makes. Come up with a plan for talking with this person. What will you say? When will you talk with your friend? How will you handle his or her reaction? ■

READING AN ORGANIZATION'S CULTURE

The ability to read an organization's culture can be a valuable skill. If you're looking for a job, you'll want to choose an employer whose culture is compatible with your values and in which you'll feel comfortable. If you can accurately assess a potential employer's culture before you make your job decision, you may be able to save yourself a lot of anxiety and reduce the likelihood of making a poor choice. Similarly, you'll undoubtedly have business transactions with numerous organizations during your professional career, such as selling a product or service, negotiating a contract, arranging a joint venture, or merely seeking out who controls certain decisions in an organization. The ability to assess another organization's culture can be a definite plus in successfully performing those pursuits.

Learning about Reading an Organization's Culture

You can be more effective at reading an organization's culture if you use the following behaviors. For the sake of simplicity, we're going to look at this skill from the perspective of a job applicant. We'll assume that you're interviewing for a job, although these skills are generalizable to many situations. Here's a list of things you can do to help learn about an organization's culture.

1. **Observe the physical surroundings.** Pay attention to signs, pictures, style of dress, length of hair, degree of openness between offices, and office furnishings and arrangements.

2. **Make note of those with whom you met.** Was it the person who would be your immediate super-

visor? Or did you meet with potential colleagues, managers from other departments, or senior executives? Based on what they revealed, to what degree do people other than the immediate supervisor have input into the hiring decision?

3. **How would you characterize the style of the people you met?** Would you characterize them as formal? Casual? Serious? Jovial?

MANAGING IN THE REAL WORLD

"I was able to determine the culture at Tommy Hilfiger USA by observing the attitude from the top down. Tommy always says he has achieved everything by surrounding himself with the best people. It's true!"

Piki Harrelson,
Regional Manager
Tommy Hilfiger, USA
Dallas, Texas

4. **Look at the organization's personnel manual.** Are formal rules and regulations printed there? If so, how detailed are these policies?

5. **Ask questions of the people with whom you meet.** The most valid and reliable information tends to come from asking the same questions

of many people (to see how closely their responses align) and by talking with individuals whose jobs link them to the outside environment. Questions that will give you insights into organizational processes and practices might include: What is the background of the founders? What is the background of current senior managers? What are their functional specialties? Were they promoted from within or hired from outside? How does the organization integrate new employees? Is there an orientation program? Is there a training program? How does your boss define his or her job success? How would you define fairness in terms of reward allocations? Can you identify some people here who are on the "fast track"? What do you think has put them on the fast track? Can you identify someone in the organization who seems to be considered an oddball or deviant? How has the organization responded to this person? Can you describe a decision that someone made that was well received? Can you describe a decision that didn't work out well? What were the consequences for the decision maker? Could you describe a crisis or critical event that has occurred recently in the organization? How did top management respond? What was learned from this experience?

MANAGING IN THE REAL WORLD

"Our company's philosophy is that we don't have work without people."

**Samuel W. (Bill) France,
Director for Technical Support
ServiceMaster Management
Services Company
Downers Grove, Illinois**

Based on S.P. Robbins, *Organizational Behavior*, 8th ed. (Upper Saddle River, NJ: Prentice Hall, 1998), p. 599.

Practice: Reading an Organization's Culture

Read through the following scenario. Write down some notes about how you would handle the situation described. Be sure to refer to the suggested behaviors described for reading an organization's culture. Your professor will then tell you what to do next.

After spending your first three years after college as a freelance graphic designer, you're looking at pursuing a job as an account executive at a graphic design firm. You feel that the scope of assignments and potential for technical training far exceed what you'd be able to do on your own and you're looking to expand your skills and meet a brand-new set of challenges. However, you want to make sure you "fit" into the organization where you're going to be spending eight hours or more every day. What's the best way for you to find a place where you'll be happy and where your style and personality will be appreciated?

Reinforcement: Reading an Organization's Culture Skills

The following suggestions are activities you can do to practice and reinforce the behaviors associated with reading an organization's culture.

1. If you're taking more than one course, assess the culture of the various classrooms in which you're enrolled. How do the cultures differ? Which culture(s) do you seem to prefer? Why?

2. Do some comparisons of the atmosphere, or feeling you have, at various organizations. Because of the number and wide variety that you'll find, it will probably be easiest for you to do this exercise using restaurants, retail stores, or banks. Based on the atmosphere that you observe, what type of organizational culture do you think these organizations might have? On what did you base your decision? Which type of culture do you prefer? Why? If you can, interview three employees at this organization for their descriptions of the organization's culture. Did their descriptions support your interpretation? Why or why not? ■

REDUCING STRESS

A dynamic and uncertain environment creates stress for many employees in today's organizations. However, the causes of stress are found not only in issues related to the organization but in factors that evolve out of an employee's personal life. Although some stress has been found as important in maintaining optimal levels of performance, too much stress can create physical, behavioral, and psychological problems.

Learning about Reducing Stress

You can be more effective at reducing stress that is leading to dysfunctional results if you use the following behaviors.

1. **Make sure that you know the requirements of a job.** Making sure that you're not "in over your head" is an important first step in reducing stress. Also be sure to clarify job responsibilities, get clear performance objectives, and get feedback on ambiguous expectations.

2. **Examine the layout of your work space.** Can you rearrange your work space to cut down on the amount of noise, interference, or general disruptions that can keep you from focusing on the work that needs to be done?

3. **Take a break when you feel overwhelmed.** Oftentimes, just taking a break away from the demands of a job can help control stress symptoms.

4. **Use management skills that can help you be a more productive worker.** Skills such as time management, problem solving, goal setting, decision making, and conflict resolution can help you address stressful situations that arise.

5. **Communicate your concerns to your supervisor.** If you're stressed out because you're not getting the support you need or don't have the resources you need to do your job efficiently and effectively, communicate this information to your boss.

MANAGING IN THE REAL WORLD

"I really try to keep issues of my job that cause stress in perspective. I can only do the best that I can given the allotted time frame and after that effort I move onto the next thing. Also, I've found that having fun at work helps to lessen my stress and the stress of others as well."

Geoff Gilpin, Director of New Business Initiatives
GTE - Long Distance
Dallas, Texas

6. **If you're the manager, be alert to signs that your employees may be under too much stress.** Watch for changes in behavior, short tempers, and general dissatisfaction with the work.

MANAGING IN THE REAL WORLD

"In dealing with people it is important not to forget that we are all only human; therefore, we should treat everyone with respect and some level of understanding."

Barbara L. Whittaker, Director,
Metallic/Car Platforms,
Worldwide Purchasing
General Motors
Warren, Michigan

Based on A.P. Brief, R.S. Schuler, and M. Van Sell, *Managing Job Stress* (Boston: Little, Brown, 1981), pp. 94–98.

Practice: Reducing Stress

Read through the following scenario. Write down some notes about how you would handle the situation described. Be sure to refer to the suggested behaviors for reducing stress. Your professor will then tell you what to do next.

You're a design supervisor at Creative Clothes, a fast-growing women's apparel maker. Six weeks ago, your boss, Sergio Autrey, transferred to another region and you were asked to fill his position. Now you're wondering whether or not you made the right decision. You're overseeing three design units instead of the one that you used to supervise. Although the people you work with are quite competent, there are a lot of creative disputes that you must resolve. In addition, there are always the tight time schedules you have in order to meet customer deadlines. You're working 12- to 14-hour days and that's just the time you put in at the office. You love the excitement of your field, but at the rate you're going, you're beginning to question whether or not you're cut out for this type of work.

Reinforcement: Reducing Stress Skills

The following suggestions are activities you can do to practice and reinforce the behaviors associated with reducing stress.

1. Examine your life. Are you experiencing undue amounts of stress? How can you reduce the stress you're facing?

2. Research the topic of stress management programs in business organizations. What types of programs are organizations implementing in order to reduce the amount of stress that employees are under? Do you think these types of programs will be successful? Why or why not? ■

SCANNING THE ENVIRONMENT

Anticipating and interpreting changes that are taking place in the environment is an important skill that managers need. Information that comes from scanning the environment can be used in making decisions and taking actions. And managers at all levels of an organization need to know how to scan the environment for important information and trends.

Learning about Scanning the Environment

You can be more effective at scanning the environment if you use the following suggestions.

1. **Decide which type of environmental information is important to your work.** Perhaps you need to know changes in customers' needs and wants or perhaps you need to know what your competitors are doing. Once you know the type of information that you'd like to have, you can look at the best ways to get that information.

2. **Regularly read and monitor pertinent information sources.** There is no scarcity of information to scan, but what you need to do is read those information sources that are pertinent. How do you know information sources are pertinent? They're pertinent if they provide you with the information that you identified as important.

MANAGING IN THE REAL WORLD

"I scan the environment by reading the financial press news and various trade magazines. In addition, I think it's important to talk to people outside the financial services industry to get their perspective."

George W. Gatch,
Vice President
J.P. Morgan and Company
New York, New York

3. **Incorporate the information that you get from environmental scanning into your decisions and actions.** Unless you use the information, you're wasting your time getting it. Also the more that you find you're using information from your environmental scanning, the more likely it is that you'll want to continue to invest time and other resources into gathering it. You'll see that this information is important to your being able to manage effectively and efficiently.

4. **Regularly review your environmental scanning activities.** If you find that you're spending too much time getting nonuseful information or if you're not using the pertinent information that you've gathered, you need to make some adjustments.

MANAGING IN THE REAL WORLD

"I use a variety of sources to stay abreast of the environment including colleagues, on-the-job training, formal training, clients, local and national news, professional groups and periodicals, the Internet, and professional databases."

**Ted V. Schaefer, Principal
Coopers & Lybrand, L. L. P.
Denver, Colorado**

----

5. **Encourage your subordinates to be alert to information that is important.** Your work unit can be your "eyes and ears" as well. Emphasize to them the importance of gathering and sharing information that may affect your unit's work performance.

Based on L.M. Fuld, *Monitoring the Competition* (New York: Wiley, 1988); E.H. Burack and N.J. Mathys, "Environmental Scanning Improves Strategic Planning," *Personnel Administrator*, 1989, pp. 82–87; and R. Subramanian, N. Fernandes, and E. Harper, "Environmental Scanning in U.S. Companies: Their Nature and Their Relationship to Performance," *Management International Review*, July 1993, pp. 271–86.

Practice: Scanning the Environment

Read through the following scenario. Write down some notes about how you would handle the situation described. Be sure to refer to the suggestions for scanning the environment. Your professor will then tell you what to do next.

You're the assistant to the president at your college. You've been asked to prepare a report outlining the external information that you think is important for her to monitor. Think of the types of information that the president would need in order to do an effective job of managing the college right now and in the next three to five years. Be as specific as you can in describing this information. Also identify where this information could be found.

Reinforcement: Scanning the Environment Skills

The following suggestions are activities you can do to practice and reinforce the behaviors associated with scanning the environment.

1. Select an organization with which you're familiar, either as an employee or perhaps as a frequent customer. Assume that you're the top manager in this organization. What types of information from environmental scanning do you think would be important to you? Where would you find this information? Now assume that you're a first-level supervisor in this organization. Would the types of information from environmental scanning that you'd want change? Explain.

2. Assume you're a regional manager for a large bookstore chain. Using the Internet, what sources of environmental and competitive information were you able to identify? For each source, what information did you find that might help you do your job better? ▪

SETTING GOALS

Employees should have a clear understanding of what they're attempting to accomplish. In addition, managers have the responsibility for seeing that this is done by helping employees set work goals. Setting goals is a skill every manager needs to develop.

Learning about Setting Goals

You can be more effective at setting goals if you use the following eight suggestions.

1. **Identify an employee's key job tasks.** Goal setting begins by defining what it is that you want your employees to accomplish. The best source for this information is each employee's job description.

2. **Establish specific and challenging goals for each key task.** Identify the level of performance expected of each employee. Specify the target toward which the employee is working.

MANAGING IN THE REAL WORLD

"In setting goals, I review past goals, the overall goals of the organization, staff goals, local goals, what is happening in the organization and in the marketplace to develop an overall framework. I try to develop goals that 'stretch' my abilities yet are attainable, timely, specific, and measurable."

Ted V. Schaefer, Principal
Coopers & Lybrand, L. L. P.
Denver, Colorado

----

3. **Specify the deadlines for each goal.** Putting deadlines on each goal reduces ambiguity. Deadlines, however, should not be set arbitrar-

ily. Rather, they need to be realistic given the tasks to be completed.

4. **Allow the employee to actively participate.** When employees participate in goal setting, they're more likely to accept the goals. However, it must be sincere participation. That is, employees must perceive that you are truly seeking their input, not just going through the motions.

MANAGING IN THE REAL WORLD

"In setting goals, I involve people all the time. I empower them and have full trust and confidence in their decision making and performance."

Larry Lim, Executive Director
Lynton Consulting Services
Singapaore, China

----

5. **Prioritize goals.** When you give someone more than one goal, it's important for you to rank the goals in order of importance. The purpose of prioritizing is to encourage the employee to take action and expend effort on each goal in proportion to its importance.

6. **Rate goals for difficulty and importance.** Goal setting should not encourage people to choose easy goals. Instead, goals should be rated for their difficulty and importance. When goals are rated, individuals can be given credit for trying difficult goals, even if they don't fully achieve them.

7. **Build in feedback mechanisms to assess goal progress.** Feedback lets employees know whether their level of effort is sufficient to attain the goal. Feedback should be both self-generated and supervisor generated. In either case, feedback should be frequent and recurring.

MANAGING IN THE REAL WORLD

"I find that it's important to review my established goals often."

Piki Harrelson,
Regional Manager
Tommy Hilfiger, USA
Dallas, Texas

8. Link rewards to goal attainment. It's natural for employees to ask, "What's in it for me?" Linking rewards to the achievement of goals will help answer that question.

Based on S.P. Robbins and D.A. DeCenzo, *Fundamentals of Management*, 2nd ed. (Upper Saddle River, NJ: Prentice Hall, 1998), p. 80.

Practice: Setting Goals

Read through the following scenario. Write down some notes about how you would handle the situation described. Be sure to refer to the eight suggestions for setting goals. Your professor will then tell you what to do next.

You worked your way through college while holding down a part-time job bagging groceries at a Food Town supermarket. When you graduated, you decided to accept a job with Food Town as a management trainee. Five years have passed and you've gained wide experience in operating a large supermarket. Sixteen months ago,

you became an assistant store manager. Last week, you received a promotion to store manager at another location. One of the things you liked about the Food Town chain is that it gave managers a great deal of autonomy in running their stores. The company provided very general policies to guide its managers. The concern was with the bottom line; for the most part, how you got there was your own business. You want to establish an MBO-type program in your store. You like the idea that everyone should have clear goals to work toward and then is evaluated against those goals.

Your store employs 90 people, although except for the managers, most work only 20 to 30 hours a week. You have five people reporting to you: an assistant manager, and grocery, produce, meat, and bakery managers. The only highly skilled jobs belong to the butchers. Other less skilled jobs include cashier, shelf stocker, cleanup, and grocery bagger.

Specifically describe how you would go about setting objectives in your new position including examples of objectives for jobs such as cashier and bakery manager.

Reinforcement: Setting Goals Skills

The following suggestions are activities you can do to practice and reinforce the behaviors in setting goals.

1. Where do you want to be in five years? Do you have specific five-year goals? Establish three goals you want to achieve. Make sure those goals are specific, challenging, and measurable.

2. Set personal and academic goals you want to achieve by the end of this college term. Prioritize and rate them for difficulty. ■

SOLVING PROBLEMS CREATIVELY

In a global business environment, where changes are fast and furious, organizations desperately need creative people. The uniqueness and variety of problems that managers face demand that they be

able to solve problems creatively. Creativity is a frame of mind. You need to expand your mind's capabilities—that is, open up your mind to new ideas. Every individual has the ability to improve his or her creativity, but many people simply don't try to develop that ability.

Learning about Solving Problems Creatively

You can be more effective at solving problems creatively if you use the following 10 suggestions.

1. **Think of yourself as creative.** Although this may be a simple suggestion, research shows that if you think you can't be creative, you won't be. Believing in your ability to be creative is the first step in becoming more creative.

2. **Pay attention to your intuition.** Every individual has a subconscious mind that works well. Sometimes answers will come to you when you least expect them. Listen to that "voice." In fact, most creative people will keep a notepad near their bed and write down ideas when the thoughts come to them. That way, they don't forget them.

3. **Move away from your comfort zone.** Every individual has a comfort zone in which certainty exists. But creativity and the known often do not mix. To be creative, you need to move away from the status quo and focus your mind on something new.

4. **Determine what you want to do.** This includes such things as taking time to understand a problem before beginning to try to resolve it, getting all the facts in mind, and trying to identify the most important facts.

5. **Look for ways to tackle the problem.** This can be accomplished by setting aside a block of time to focus on it; working out a plan for attacking it; establishing subgoals; imagining or actually using analogies wherever possible (for example, could you approach your problem like a fish out of water and look at what the fish does to cope? Or can you use the things you have to do to find your way when it's foggy to help you solve your problem?); using different problem-solving strategies such as verbal, visual, mathematical, theatrical (for instance, you might draw a diagram of the decision or problem to help you visualize it better or you might talk to yourself out loud about the problem telling it as you would tell a story to someone); trusting your intuition; and playing with possible ideas and approaches (for example, look at your problem from a different perspective or ask yourself what someone else, like your grandmother, might do if faced with the same situation).

MANAGING IN THE REAL WORLD

"I use the 'King Solomon' approach—look at each variable and find the best balance."

Mike Dorf, CEO
KnitMedia
New York, New York

---

6. **Look for ways to do things better.** This may involve trying consciously to be original, not worrying about looking foolish, eliminating cultural taboos (like gender stereotypes) that might influence your possible solutions, keeping an open mind, being alert to odd or puzzling facts, thinking of unconventional ways to use objects and the environment (for instance, thinking about how you could use newspaper or magazine headlines to help you be a better problem solver), discarding usual or habitual ways of doing things, and striving for objectivity by being as critical of your own ideas as you would those of someone else.

7. **Find several right answers.** Being creative means continuing to look for other solutions even when you think you have solved the problem. A better, more creative solution just might be found.

8. **Believe in finding a workable solution.** Like believing in yourself, you also need to believe in your ideas. If you don't think you can find a solution, you probably won't.

9. **Brainstorm with others.** Creativity is not an isolated activity. Bouncing ideas off others creates a synergistic effect.

MANAGING IN THE REAL WORLD

"One technique we use is what we call a 'work-out' which is getting people together in one room who are involved with the problem. This group looks at how we can become better and examines the process in detail."

Thomas Dunham, Vice President and General Manager GE Medical Systems Waukesha, Wisconsin

---

10. **Turn creative ideas into action.** Coming up with creative ideas is only part of the process. Once the ideas are generated, they must be implemented. Keeping great ideas in your mind, or on papers that no one will read, does little to expand your creative abilities.

Based on J. Calano and J. Salzman, "Ten Ways to Fire Up Your Creativity," *Working Woman*, July 1989, p. 94; J.V. Anderson, "Mind Mapping: A Tool for Creative Thinking," *Business Horizons*, January–February 1993, pp. 42–46; M. Loeb, "Ten Commandments for Managing Creative People," *Fortune*, January 16, 1995, pp. 135–36; and M. Henricks, "Good Thinking," *Entrepreneur*, May 1996, pp. 70–73.

Practice: Solving Problems Creatively

Read through the following scenario. Write down some notes about how you would handle the situation described. Be sure to refer to the 10 suggestions for solving problems creatively. Your professor will then tell you what to do next.

> Every time the phone rings, your stomach clenches and your palms start to sweat. And it's no wonder! As sales manager for Brinkers, a machine tool parts manufacturer, you're being besieged by customers who are calling to complain about late delivery. Your boss, Carter Hererra, acts as both production manager and scheduler. Every time your sales representatives negotiate a sale, it's up to Carter to determine whether or not production can actually meet the delivery date the customer specifies. And Carter invariably says, "No problem." The good thing about this is that you make a lot of initial sales. The bad news is that production hardly ever meets the shipment dates that Carter authorizes. And he doesn't seem to be all that concerned about the aftermath of late deliveries. He says, "Our customers know they're getting outstanding quality at a great price. Just let them try to match that anywhere. It can't be done. So even if they have to wait a couple of extra days, they're still getting the best deal they can." Somehow the customers don't see it that way. And they let you know about their unhappiness. Then it's up to you to try to soothe the relationship. You know this problem has to be taken care of, but what possible solutions are there? After all, how are you going to keep from making your boss mad or making the customers mad?

Reinforcement: Solving Problems Creatively

The following suggestions are activities you can do to practice and reinforce the behaviors associated with solving problems creatively.

1. Take out a couple of sheets of paper. You have 20 minutes to list as many medical or health care related jobs as you can that begin with the letter *r* (for example, radiologist, registered nurse). If you run out of listings before time is up, it's OK to quit early.

2. List on a piece of paper some common terms that apply to both *water* and *finance*. How many were you able to come up with? ∎

INTEGRATIVE VIDEO CASE 1

SHOWTIME

It's Showtime

This is the first of six cases in this book. These cases explore a variety of management-related issues at Showtime Networks Inc., a premium television network company. This installment is designed to be a general introduction. You may want to refer to it when you are studying the cases that follow.

The Company

Showtime Networks Inc. (SNI) is a wholly owned subsidiary of Viacom Inc., a giant media conglomerate, and operates the premium television networks Showtime, The Movie Channel (TMC), Flix, Showtime *en Español* (a separate audio feed of Showtime for its Spanish-speaking audience), and Showtime Extreme, an action-oriented channel that SNI plans to launch in the Spring of 1998. It also operates and manages the premium television network Sundance Channel, a joint venture with Robert Redford and PolyGram Filmed Entertainment. Finally, the company also has a distinct pay-per-view distribution service that creates, markets, and distributes sports and entertainment events.

SNI's parent, Viacom, also owns Simon & Schuster, Paramount Pictures, Blockbuster Video, MTV, Nickelodeon, and VH1. SNI has exclusive movie distribution contracts with Paramount and other top movie studios such as Metro-Goldwyn-Mayer (MGM) and PolyGram.

Showtime, SNI's leading brand, is an award-winning and critically acclaimed network, having won Oscar, Emmy, and Cable ACE awards for its original programs. Together SHO and TMC account for almost 99 percent of SNI's premium-service revenues.

SNI's major competitor is Home Box Office Inc. (HBO), the category leader. HBO, which also includes Cinemax, has approximately 40 million subscribers to SNI's approximately 18 million (for Showtime and The Movie Channel).

The Industry

Above the basic level of cable or satellite service is **premium**, a cable- or satellite-delivered service that generally features uncut, commercial-free programming to consumers for which cable or satellite distributors typically charge a monthly incremental fee. The largest outlet for premium television networks is the cable industry, which has about 65 million subscribers for basic services in the United States. Cable operators sell one or more premium services as an additional purchase over and above the basic level of service. Premium services are also delivered via other technologies such as wireless cable, backyard dishes, and the newer Direct Broadcast Satellite (DBS) business, which utilizes smaller backyard satellite dishes.

All SNI's business operations, including programming, sales, and marketing, face competitive pressures. One of the most significant factors facing SNI is that it is not affiliated with any cable operator, whereas HBO and Encore Media Group, a new entrant in the premium service category, are affiliated with the two largest cable operators, Time Warner and TCI, respectively.

It was thus against a complex and constantly changing backdrop that Matt Blank, new chairman of SNI, developed fresh and aggressive goals for the firm. To accomplish these goals he reorganized the company and made major strategic shifts. The reorganization included the executive ranks, since Matt knew he needed a group of talented and aggressive executives on his top management team.

The Top Management Team

Matt Blank became chairman of SNI in February 1995. A television industry veteran who has made an indelible mark on the cable industry, Matt joined SNI in 1988 after holding several senior executive positions at HBO. He has served as executive vice president, marketing at Showtime, and later as president and chief operating officer as well as president and chief executive officer. As chairman of SNI Matt began to carry out a new vision for the firm.

Gwen Marcus was promoted to executive vice president, general counsel and administration, in January 1996. In her new position she added responsibility for the human resources and administration departments to her existing position of general counsel. After beginning her legal career as an entertainment lawyer at a major New York law firm, Gwen joined SNI in 1984 as assistant counsel and has moved up the ranks since then to her present position.

Jerry Cooper, executive vice president, finance and operations, is responsible for the company's financial activities, information services, operations, and corporate development. He was formerly chief financial officer for Young Broadcasting, and before that he spent 16 years at Viacom where, among other positions, he served as senior vice president and general manager of Lifetime.

Len Fogge was hired in April 1996 as executive vice president, creative/marketing services. He had been president of Franklin Spier, Inc., the leading advertising agency for publishing, and earlier, as president of Grey Entertainment, he helped build that company into the largest entertainment advertising agency in the United States.

Mark Greenberg was promoted to executive vice president, corporate marketing and communications in January 1996, from his position as senior vice president of marketing. His responsibilities include overseeing the company's marketing strategy and planning activities, its marketing campaigns and promotions, the corporate communications department, the new sports and event programming group, and all market research. The sports and event programming group is a major operating group responsible for putting on premier boxing events, such as the two historic Holyfield vs. Tyson matches, and major concerts, such as the Spice Girls and, in years past, the Rolling Stones and the Grateful Dead. In June 1996 Mark assumed additional responsibilities for leading SNI's efforts to evaluate its strategic priorities and identify its competitive advantages. Before joining the firm in 1989 he held several sales and marketing positions at HBO.

Jerry Offsay, president of programming for SNI, is responsible for all the programming functions of the company. Because he deals with movie studios and gen-erates a massive amount of original programming, his offices are in California to give him ready access to the film industry. Jerry was previously executive vice president of ABC Productions and has been an executive producer of several films. He started his career as an entertainment attorney.

As executive vice president, sales and affiliate marketing, Showtime Networks sales and marketing, **Jeff Wade** is responsible for sales activities and affiliate marketing efforts throughout the company. Before coming to SNI as South Central regional director in 1981, he was executive vice president for affiliate relations at QVC. He serves on the board of the Sundance Channel.

We will learn more about other key managers in the cases that follow.

QUESTIONS

1. How would you characterize SNI's industry environment? What types of management skills would you expect to be most useful in that environment?
2. Given the information in this case, how would you evaluate SNI's management strengths?
3. What do you think are the implications of the fact that some of SNI's managers are former employees of HBO? What do you think in general of having former competitors in management positions within a firm? What are likely to be the strengths and weaknesses they bring to their new employer?

Source: This case was prepared by Prof. dt ogilvie of Rutgers University for purposes of class discussion. It is based on interviews and materials provided by SNI and information from the Pay TV Newsletter (Dec. 1996) and Showtime's Web site at <http//www.showtimeonline.com>.

INTEGRATIVE VIDEO CASE 2

Showtime's Terrain

This is the second case in this book that explores a variety of management-related issues at Showtime Networks Inc., a premium television network company. The first installment is a general introduction. You may want to refer to it when you are studying the case that follows.

The External Environment: Showtime's Competitive Arena

Showtime's environment is highly competitive. Rivalry between SNI and HBO is particularly fierce. HBO benefited from being first in the category and also benefits from being owned by Time Warner, which owns a leading cable operator, and it used these advantages to gain and maintain a majority share of the premium cable business. The cable industry, which provides the largest source of revenue for premium networks, is maturing and growth is slow, forecast to continue at about 1 percent per year, although about 25 percent of households with TVs do not subscribe to cable. Share in the premium cable category therefore tends to be gained at the expense of rivals, not through growth in the category. Another limiting factor on the growth of each firm's category share is the recent arrival of Starz! from Encore Media Group.

The premium services are positioned between customer firms—cable operators—and supplier firms—movie studios—that both have great bargaining power.

The principal customers of premium services are cable operators, who are typically the only distributors of wired cable television service in their local communities. Of course, because they control marketing, pricing, and distribution systems in their franchise areas, cable operators can and do play the premium networks against each other. Packaging to the final consumer, for instance, is a key competitive factor for the premium networks. When a consumer subscribes to SNI services, a local distributor will package those services as it wishes and pay SNI a licensing fee. The way the distributor packages the product and sets its retail prices could place one network at a disadvantage compared to another. If, for example, HBO is less expensive to the consumer, or if SNI product such as Showtime is only offered if the customer also purchases HBO, then SNI is at a competitive disadvantage.

On the opposite end of the supply chain, premium services are supplied primarily by a small group of movie studios and distributors, which own many of the movies licensed to the premium networks. Bidding for product is intense; each service wants exclusive programming. The recent entry of Encore Media Group has raised prices for these products.

SNI has maintained its share in the face of increasing competitive pressures, in part because of its multi-premium marketing campaigns, subscriber acquisition campaigns run principally with HBO that offer customers more than one premium service, which can be from any program supplier. The firm has also focused on working with distributors to package SNI products favorably, either together (bundling Showtime with The Movie Channel for one low price, or adding Flix and/or Sundance Channel to a Showtime subscription for a low incremental price), or with HBO and MAX at an attractive price.

Entering the Global Environment

Besides embracing the dynamic competitive environment within the United States, SNI has made a modest investment in exploring the global pay-television marketplace. The international marketplace offers an interesting challenge to create a global presence for Showtime, although SNI is not devoting significant capital or resources to international ventures at this time.

One reason for its limited interest is that distribution problems make it difficult to replicate the U.S. model of premium cable service abroad. Each country has its own governmental regulations and its own ways of handling business decisions. Some governments expect to be more deeply involved in the business equation than others.

As for telecast rights, according to Judy Pless, senior vice president, business development, "rights issues make it difficult to globalize." This means that because SNI does not control the international rights to any of the studio movies it broadcasts at home, it must buy rights separately for foreign distribution. But in many cases the foreign rights have already been disposed of. When Showtime develops its own programming, the advance sale of foreign exhibition rights to these productions is frequently done on a country-by-country basis, in order to help finance SNI's original movies as they are being made.

Judy, a seasoned executive with international experience, is responsible for evaluating and developing new international and domestic channel launches (the creation of new channels) and for negotiating international alliances for SNI. She is currently exploring the launch of an action-oriented version of Showtime, known as Showtime Extreme, in the European market.

A final international hurdle is the need to understand many different cultures' codes of ethical business conduct and ways of handling financial transactions. These can vary widely from one country to another and often differ from what is considered standard in the United States.

The Internal Environment: Showtime's Corporate Culture

SNI has a driving culture whose core behaviors are collaboration and teamwork. Its people tend to feel they have a sense of ownership in the company, a responsibility to make it work. Working hard creates a sense of community, yet individuality is maintained in an atmosphere where creativity is encouraged. As Ray Gutierrez, senior vice president, human resources and administration,

says, "To stay in the forefront of business we have to be creative everywhere."

Nat Fuchs, vice president, human resources development, says, "Our culture is dynamic, aggressive, changing. People are extremely proud of what they're doing; we have an edgy humor and value flexibility."

At the same time, as CEO Matt Blank notes, "We reward creativity when we see it, but in a competitive industry in which every mistake can be said to affect the bottom line, there is little room for failure."

QUESTIONS

1. Identify the key uncertainties SNI faces in its external environment. How do you think these uncertainties constrain management decision making?
2. Do you think business practices that are acceptable in another country but not at home should prevent U.S. companies such as SNI from conducting business abroad? When should management place ethical considerations above stockholder interests?
3. How do you think its corporate culture affects decision making at SNI? What positive and negative aspects of its culture can you identify?

Source: This case was prepared by Prof. dt ogilvie of Rutgers University for purposes of class discussion. It is based on interviews and materials provided by Showtime Networks Inc.

INTEGRATIVE VIDEO CASE 3

Strategic Planning at SNI

This is the third case in this book that explores a variety of management-related issues at Showtime Networks Inc., a premium television network company. The first installment is a general introduction. You may want to refer to it when you are studying the case that follows.

One of the first tasks Matt Blank attacked when he was appointed chairman and CEO of Showtime Networks Inc. (SNI) was a strategic restructuring of the company. To strengthen SNI's competitive position, he focused on a new set of goals and a strategic shift for the firm.

Building the Strategy

Matt developed a three-point strategy to focus on (1) original programming, (2) brand awareness, and (3) sales force management. He reasoned that Showtime had to operate under a certain set of constraints: It was the second entrant in the premium category, behind HBO which had used its timing advantage to gain the dominant position in the category. SNI therefore existed in a highly competitive environment characterized by slow growth, an entrenched leader, and limited opportunities to either raise prices or cut costs.

Matt began by setting new goals for SNI and restructuring the organization in the service of those goals. The executive area was reengineered, overhead was reduced, marginal businesses (including an entire ancillary business devoted to retail sales of SNI and third-party program services to the home satellite dish marketplace) were jettisoned, and a new strategic review process was put in place to reexamine strategy every 1 1/2 to 2 years. Selling solely to its wholesale customers was to be SNI's core competency.

Although the company has deliberately not hired anyone to work full-time on strategic planning, Mark Greenberg, executive vice president, marketing and communications, was responsible for leading SNI's efforts to make the new goals operational, evaluate SNI's strategic priorities, and determine its competitive advantages. Senior managers all participated and were held accountable. As Mark remembers, "We collected lots of data, looking at everything: ratings, pricing, packaging, competition, product costs, overhead, growth, and so on. We're a participatory organization, but we needed to take an overview at 40,000 feet, where there are fewer barriers between groups. We used a 'strategy in action'

approach taught at Columbia University's business school by Prof. Boris Yavitz to initiate our overall strategy" in relation to competitors both new and old.

The executives brainstormed on issues of pricing, distribution, programming, and operating efficiencies and determined that programming was one of SNI's major competitive advantages. "Programming is key to everything," says Judy Pless, senior vice president, business development.

Programming

One critical strategic shift that took place was a plan to create more original movies. SNI now produces more original movies than any other premium network and hopes that this volume of fresh, unseen new product will help it grow. Since theatrical films shown on premium networks tend to be much more heavily exposed after they leave the theaters (through pay per view and video rentals) than they were 10 or 12 years ago, SNI is counting on viewers being attracted to its own brand-new fare instead.

One remaining consideration, however, is the difference between HBO's and SNI's programming strategies. Where HBO will make only 10 to 12 original movies in a given year, compared to SNI's approximately 40 films, HBO will budget three to five times the amount for producing them than SNI. That means that HBO can afford to pay more for every aspect of its movies, from production values to talent. So while SNI has more original movies, HBO typically has movies with bigger stars and budgets.

Branding

With fresh programming plans in place, SNI had the tool it needed to refocus its branding strategy. Matt Blank remembers a corporate culture that lacked a strong sense of identity: "We took a critical lens to the company and found we were undefined as to product. We get hurt when the customer doesn't know where he saw a movie and attributes it to HBO. We needed to change that."

One of Matt's first steps was to hire Len Fogge, executive vice president, marketing/creative services. Len audited existing production and communications and found that while SNI had a strong product, differentiated from that of other channels, brand awareness was not very strong. Information came from many different areas in the company and there was no centralized marketing communications function. Marketing and advertising information was not presented distinctively, and it wasn't clear what kind of image SNI was trying to create when it communicated with its various constituencies (cable operators, viewers, and so on).

Len set out to create a corporate identity for SNI and began by reorganizing the marketing services area, uniting consumer and trade advertising and creative services under one umbrella. The next was to develop an ongoing focus on research that is constantly being updated. The task Len set for himself was to identify viewers' "drivers," or motives—what were the benefits viewers sought from watching? "We found that emotions were the driving force," he says. "Different categories of viewers sought different emotions."

From this research, Len developed a branding strategy that played on the great promise of a premium network—programs that viewers could not get anywhere else. SNI is now moving to build brand recognition around the idea that "with premium TV like SNI, you'll get a 'no-limits' experience that you won't get elsewhere; you'll stay in the moment for uninterrupted hours of uncut movies, sports, series, and great events."

Sales Force Management

The sales force plays a crucial role in the success of any product or service. At SNI, Jeff Wade, executive vice president, sales and affiliate marketing, resolved to enhance client relationships as a way to improve the overall sales operation and meet its revenue goals.

Jeff began by empowering the field general managers to make decisions on the local level and made them accountable for revenue, expenses, and profitability. The field managers began to hire area managers with strong financial as well as sales and marketing skills. Continuing down the chain of command, he allowed the sales force

itself to help clients find solutions to problems, instead of just "selling in" the various marketing plans and campaigns. Sales reps were asked to focus on improving the client's cash flow using Showtime's brands, thus putting them in the position of problem solver for the customer.

To emphasize the goal of working with the customer on the customer's goals, some of the area managers moved "in market" to be closer to their clients. SNI believed that having area managers live in the territories serviced would foster a greater commitment to the community as well as allow social relationships with clients to reinforce business relationships. New "point of sale" (POS) managers were hired to train customer contact staff at cable and satellite distributor call centers. The new POS managers were hired based on exceptional ability to present Showtime's products, a demonstrated high level of creativity, and a sincere enthusiasm for movies and related entertainment.

Client relations soon began to improve with the new focus on customer needs. Sales positions were enriched with additional responsibilities and rewards, with positive results.

QUESTIONS

1. Describe SNI's strategic planning process. What are the strengths and weaknesses of the planning process?
2. Do you think SNI is pursuing the best possible strategy given its internal resources and the actions of its competitors? Why or why not?
3. Describe the planning tools and techniques SNI managers might have found useful as they strategically restructured the company and why these might have been useful.
4. How well do the specific changes in sales management fit with the overall strategic plan? What elements do you think have made the change in sales focus successful for SNI?

Source: This case was prepared by Prof. dt ogilvie of Rutgers University for the purposes of class discussion. It is based on interviews and materials provided by Showtime Networks Inc.

Reorganizing Communication and Advertising

This is the fourth case in this book that explores a variety of management-related issues at Showtime Networks Inc., a premium television network company. The first installment is a general introduction. You may want to refer to it when you are studying the case that follows.

As part of his general reorganization of Showtime Networks Inc. (SNI), chairman and CEO Matt Blank sought to foster more creativity within the firm by reorganizing the advertising and creative services departments. Among the steps he took to accomplish this was to hire Len Fogge as the company's executive vice president of creative/marketing services, and to consolidate advertising and on-air promotions under Len's direction.

After auditing the departments reporting to him, Len concluded that SNI had a strong product offering, distinct from other channels, but that it lacked a comparably strong branding function. Consumer and trade advertising and promotional materials were not issued from a centralized office, various people had input into what was being said, and, while the resulting marketing messages were factually correct, they represented a kind of consensus decision making that did not accurately represent what SNI's distinctive strengths were or what the Showtime brand was all about.

Len identified three key messages that he wanted SNI's marketing to convey:

1. SNI provides programs different from anything shown on network TV.
2. SNI makes films that move people because they are about something important.
3. SNI makes "thrill-ride" viewing with programs like *Showtime Championship Boxing* and original series inspired by hit movies like *Stargate* and *Total Recall*.

Len's goal was to make sure people understood "they get an experience from Showtime they can't get anywhere else."

Conducting the Agency Review

A common occurrence in the advertising business is the agency review, in which the client firm (in this case, SNI) reviews the qualifications of several advertising agencies

that are invited to bid for the opportunity to work with the firm (or, in advertising jargon, to "pitch the account"). The firm's current ad agency may or may not be invited to participate.

Len's newly consolidated department soon conducted an agency review that included quite a few major national and international advertising agencies—and one candidate that asked to pitch the account, the in-house group that had been responsible for SNI on-air and print promotions in the past. Prepared to be impressed, Len was nevertheless "blown away" by what he characterized as this group's "total communication of the product, a demonstrable understanding of the issues, and a brand concept that reflected Showtime." The in-house team, which came to be formalized as an in-house agency known as the Red Group, easily won the account.

The Red Group brainstormed around its winning concept that there are "no limits" to what Showtime can offer viewers who seek challenge, escape, and entertainment. The resulting campaign stressed as its theme the "no-limits viewing experience," in which the viewer would find no emotional or experiential limits to Showtime's dynamic programming.

Managing On-Air Time

In the past Showtime had filled the time between shows, known as interstitial time, with miscellaneous promotions for its upcoming programs. In keeping with his strategy to unify SNI's branding messages, however, Len added to the Red Group a media group to analyze the content that went into these interstitial spots. This group's responsibility was to integrate promotional communication with the adjacent programming, so that viewers of particular programs would see between-show spots for other shows that might appeal to the same audience.

"Our interstitial time is worth $100 million," said Len. "In the past, we would schedule but not plan it. Now we analyze and plan it, tying together promos with programs."

Managing Creative People

When creative people are rewarded for their work by being given promotions into administrative work, their creativity sometimes suffers as a result. And when pure administrators can make or veto creative decisions, the results are sometimes less than optimal. Len changed the practice at SNI by giving administrative duties to administrators in his group and allowing the "creatives" to concentrate on what they did best. An added advantage of the change is that while managers, directors, vice presidents, and other strategic people have input to creative decisions, the final results now rest with the writers, producers, and art directors whose work is on the line.

To offer creatives a place to gather in a relaxed and playful atmosphere, Len also designed "the Quad," a large open office area flanked by windows and filled with comfortable furniture and golf and basketball paraphernalia. Here members of the Red Group collect to talk, play, or just look out the windows and think. Away from their offices, they can refresh their creativity or get new perspective on a problem, alone or with colleagues. The Quad is a good example of the way in which Len views his role as a "facilitator" whose job is to allow people the freedom to do what they enjoy and do best.

Encouraging Risk Taking

A final step in Len's effort to integrate a consistent message for SNI was to create an environment in which creative people could thrive on the challenge of risk taking.

"They must push the envelope," he said. "I encourage risk and I have only two responses, which are both visceral—'This is great,' or 'This is terrible.' Whichever it is, I tell people, 'You risked something; you took a step. It's not mediocre, which is the most important thing.' And they always come back with better stuff."

QUESTIONS

1. What are some of the less obvious advantages for management of the newly centralized creative/marketing services operation at SNI? Can you think of any potential disadvantages?

2. If the various creative groups reporting to Len Fogge differed about how best to convey SNI's unified branding message, how might such conflict be resolved?

3. Assess the decision to free the creative group from administrative duties. What might be some of the advantages and disadvantages of this decision for the careers of the creative people? Of the administrative personnel? What steps would you recommend SNI take to ensure the two groups work together smoothly?

Source: This case was prepared by Prof. dt ogilvie of Rutgers University for purposes of class discussion and is based on interviews and materials provided by Showtime Networks Inc.

Leading a Motivated Workforce

This is the fifth case in this book that explores a variety of management-related issues at Showtime Networks Inc., a premium television network company. The first installment is a general introduction. You may want to refer to it when you are studying the case that follows.

One of the biggest challenges of leadership, at SNI as anywhere, is attracting, retaining, and motivating a committed workforce. As demographic changes that began in the 1980s continue into the next century, managers at all levels find they must address not only the traditional motivation issues of advancement and compensation, but also new "work and family" issues that arise where employees' personal lives and their work lives intersect. Such intersections are becoming increasingly common as diversities of age, race, gender, and lifestyle become more widespread and even sought after in the workplace.

Even recruitment has changed; for example, visitors to Showtime's Web site <www.showtimeonline.com> find an opportunity there to explore job opportunities.

A company that is more attractive to work for will attract and keep better-qualified employees, as SNI knows. Here is a look at how SNI uses the newest tools of motivation.

Embracing Diversity

More and more executives today realize that having a diverse workforce is not only the right thing to do; it is also a tremendous competitive advantage. Diversity of opinion, best obtained in a diverse workforce, is also a strong defense against groupthink.

Nat Fuchs, SNI's vice president of human resource development, sought to define exactly what diversity meant to the firm. SNI put together a committee of employees who were "impassioned" about diversity and who were influential leaders in their respective areas within the firm. Together they looked first at visible diversity, a concept they later expanded to include differences in both visible and invisible factors such as race, age, gender, sexual orientation, physical challenge, and composition of family. Their goal was to encourage all departments to seek diversity, in staffing and even in programming.

Gwen Marcus, executive vice president, general counsel and administration, recalls that at first diversity in staffing raised red flags among people who thought it meant nothing more than "hiring people of color." Over time, however, that misperception was erased as people realized that SNI's commitment to diversity is not intended to promote preferential hiring on the basis of factors such as race, but rather that it addresses broader issues such as offering employee benefits programs like telecommuting, flexible work schedules, and similar work and family initiatives to accommodate the needs of a workforce with diverse backgrounds and lifestyles.

"We were the first in the industry to offer same-sex life partner insurance programs," said Nat. SNI was eventually recognized for its commitment to diverse lifestyles when it received the GLAAD (Gay Lesbian Alliance Against Defamation) Fairness Award in 1997.

The company also took a pioneering stand in favor of alternative work arrangements, which were designed to ease the difficulties faced not only by working parents but also by those caring for elderly parents or pursuing personal commitments outside SNI. As an example, said Gwen, "one of my most talented staff members is our paralegal by day and a novelist by night. He came to a point where he needed either to work a compressed work week or to quit SNI entirely. To retain the talents of a person like this, we accepted the change in hours, and it works great." Nat comments, "Nowadays, we don't even ask why you want it."

The alternative work arrangements SNI now offers weren't incorporated so easily at first. Some skepticism accompanied the initial three-month trial, but SNI imposed some conditions to increase the chances of success. Arrangements like job sharing, flextime, staggered work hours, compressed workweeks, and telecommuting were offered only where they were consistent with the workload and work flow of the affected employees and departments. Success eventually followed, and one way in which SNI was recognized for its achievements in accommodating diversity in lifestyle was in being nominated for the Women in Cable Award for Work Environment.

Another telling commendation is the high proportion of new hires who are referred by current employees.

The concept of diversity continues to expand at SNI, according to Ray Gutierrez, senior vice president of human resources and administration: "We keep expanding diversity as it plays into our business needs, continuing to define it. We have 700 full-time regular employees, plus consultants, freelancers, and temps; therefore, we work around their needs. We guide managers to help employees deal with diversity with in-house workshops and training programs, sometimes facilitated with outside consultants."

The rewards have been tangible. Nat Fuchs explains, "Our general business successes were identified with our diversity process, and so we became a model for the industry. Showtime is now seen as a leader; it has a genuine commitment and a business philosophy that encourages diversity in all aspects of its business, not a set of bureaucratic formulas or programs sitting on a shelf."

Rewarding Achievement

With the right people in place, SNI seeks to retain employees not only by addressing their varying needs but also by recognizing and rewarding their skills and achievement.

As in any company, promotions are motivating, and SNI has sought to make them highly prized. The practice of promoting people in order to enhance their credibility with outsiders is discouraged; promotions are earned. That said, about 90% of jobs at SNI are filled from within.

Performance measurement is critical since the firm is performance driven, and SNI has streamlined its appraisal process from six different systems to one. "We do upward feedback, which was initiated by employees, not management, and in some areas 360° feedback," said Ray. "We also do climate surveys asking how our employees want to be managed." Merit reviews are conducted once a year.

Awards and bonuses are many and varied, and they are not confined to the executive levels. Spot bonuses are awarded for exceptional achievements; field sales people are given incentive awards, and long-term incentives are awarded according to the overall performance of Showtime or of its parent company, Viacom. Individual employees are recognized in various ways, including the Chairman's Award, which is given by the chairman of Viacom, and the Unsung Hero Award. Both these annual awards are designated for nonmanagerial employees who are compensated below a specified salary cap, in recognition of the fact that critical support people provide invaluable service to the firm. Awards are also given for long-term tenure, and in team-based merit reviews SNI's work teams determine the level (although not the amount) of raises given to team members. At every level SNI tries to offer employees the opportunity to be recognized and rewarded.

QUESTIONS

1. How would you describe SNI's definition of diversity to a new employee of the firm? What other kinds of "invisible" diversity do you think might be identified, and how could a firm ensure that they were considered appropriately, that is, in light of its business needs?
2. If some employees do not qualify for "work and family" benefits, do you think there would be a negative backlash to such innovations, and how would you handle them to ensure fairness to all?
3. What might a firm like SNI do to prepare its employees for promotions that depend on having business and management skills?
4. How do SNI's focus on diversity of all kinds and its efforts to reward performance at all levels of the firm reinforce each other as motivational tools for management?

Source: This case was prepared by Prof. dt ogilvie of Rutgers University for purposes of class discussion. It is based on interviews and material provided by Showtime Networks Inc.

SHOWTIME.

INTEGRATIVE VIDEO CASE 6

Reengineering the Finance Department for Control

This is the sixth case in this book that explores a variety of management-related issues at Showtime Networks Inc., a premium television network company. The first installment is a general introduction. You may want to refer to it when you are studying the case that follows.

The Problem

The contracts that cover the distribution of SNI's program services to local cable systems are unique and complex. One of the disadvantages of their complexity was an inefficient billing process, which relied on cable operators to interpret the terms of their contracts themselves and determine what they thought they owed SNI. SNI, in turn, based its bills on these estimates, which often underreported the amount of money to SNI. Because the audit department could audit only about 30 percent of its 10,000 member cable systems a year, some operators owed SNI large sums of money by the time billing errors were discovered and corrected.

Confronting cable operators with corrected bills was, of course, a painful control procedure that sometimes resulted in angry customers, difficult situations for SNI salespeople, who were simultaneously trying to sell these same customers new services, and uncollectable fees that sometimes cost SNI millions of dollars in revenue a year.

The Solution

When Jerry Cooper, executive vice president of finance and operations, decided to reengineer the finance department, his goal was to devise a way for SNI to get paid correctly and on time, without audits, by putting the controls at the front end of the billing procedure. True to the spirit of the reengineering process, Jerry began with "a blank sheet of paper." In essence, he turned the organization on its side, eliminating the traditional accounting areas of accounts receivable, accounts payable, billing, travel and entertainment (T&E), and so on and replacing them with cross-functional, self-directed teams he called "rings." Each ring was designed to serve a particular area of SNI, beginning with sales.

The sales department was put first because it was the biggest and most complex area served by the finance department, and because the field sales reps worked directly with SNI's customers to administer the problematic contracts. As Jerry Scro, senior vice president and CFO, recalled, "There was a compelling business reason to begin on the sales side."

When the reengineering had been completed, each ring consisted of a small group of finance people, who came to be called financial business analysts or FBAs, and a team leader. These employees worked exclusively with the sales department *and* the customer to build a payment template with the terms and conditions of the contract. Rather than having to depend on estimates for revenue collection, SNI was now able to have the customer input the number of subscribers in the template, and the template then supplied the amount due. Billing became objective and automatic, customers were saved a great deal of work, and SNI began to realize the appropriate amounts of revenue from sales. In time the rings were actually moved out of headquarters and relocated to the regional offices, to be closer to the customers and field reps with whom they worked.

The change in structure was so successful that it was eventually expanded to the rest of the finance department and even to other departments, where informal rings work with their own particular in-house customers in creative and design services, marketing, law, and human resources. But however successful, change is never easy. Jerry Cooper estimates that it took six to nine months just to begin the reengineering process and two years to complete it, and before it was over the dedication and resolve of those committed to improving SNI's revenue controls had been repeatedly tested. "Radical change creates conflict and dissension," notes Jerry. "It was necessary to find people in the organization who understood that changes were coming in job descriptions, information systems, compensation and incentives, and the corporate culture."

The Process

The first concrete step was to look carefully at the existing finance group, which had 60 or 70 employees. Many had individual ways of doing things that made the prospect of working in teams challenging. To ensure that they could work together well, and to reinforce the new mandate that rings would select, hire, and succeed or fail as teams, management allowed the rings to choose their own members, with the understanding that new competencies and capabilities would be required of all. Everyone was given an opportunity to retrain in an internal facility, set up to cover not only basic accounting procedures but also analysis and planning skills.

Said Jerry Cooper, "A different culture was created that led to team initiatives, conflict resolution training, 360° feedback, and so on. We let go of simple clerical functions and kept raising the bar." Although some employees left the firm in this early phase of the reengineering, SNI was confident that those who remained would become new leaders in the organization.

Among the many changes that took place in finance department job descriptions were the addition of revenue-generating responsibility and the opportunity and responsibility for finance people to deal well with customers. Finance people had never dealt with customers before and had never been considered part of a revenue-generating unit. Team members in the rings also had to learn to understand the sales function, and salespeople learned how to use their rings as partners and resources in serving the customers' needs.

"This is the right way to work," said Jerry Cooper. "People are happier; they have greater job satisfaction and the ability to enhance their own careers. We put a customer focus in everything we do now, and morale is great." And, no small point, revenues are up.

QUESTIONS

1. Compare the effectiveness of SNI's past and present billing processes in terms of control. In what other business processes that you have studied can controls be built into the early stages or procedures?
2. Why might some finance employees resist the kinds of changes introduced by Jerry Cooper? In what ways do you think SNI could have reduced resistance?
3. List some controls SNI might use to ensure that the reengineering of its finance department is working in the best interests of its employees as well as generating revenue earned.

Source: This case was prepared by Prof. dt ogilvie of Rutgers University for purposes of class discussion. It is based on interviews and materials provided by Showtime Networks Inc.

Answers to Chapter 4 Quiz on page 112.

1. c. United States. Gillette owns the Braun company.
2. d. French. Societe Bic S.A. is a French company.
3. b. Great Britain. Grand Metropolitan PLC owns Haagen Daz.
4. a. France. Thomson S.A. of France produces RCA televisions.
5. c. British. Grand Metropolitan PLC in Great Britain owns Green Giant.
6. a. American (United States). Godiva chocolate is owned by Campbell Soup.
7. b. Dutch. Vaseline is produced by Unilever PLC, the Netherlands.
8. d. American (United States). Wrangler jeans are made by the VF Corporation.
9. d. Great Britain. Holiday Inn is owned by Bass PLC, England.
10. b. Canada. Tropicana orange juice is owned by Seagram Co. Ltd.

Chapter 1: Self-Perception Rating Scale

Complete Your Feedback Chart

This chart is easier to complete if you draw a horizontal line across it at the neutral value (4). Then plot your individual values. The chart is for your own information and will not be given to the instructor.

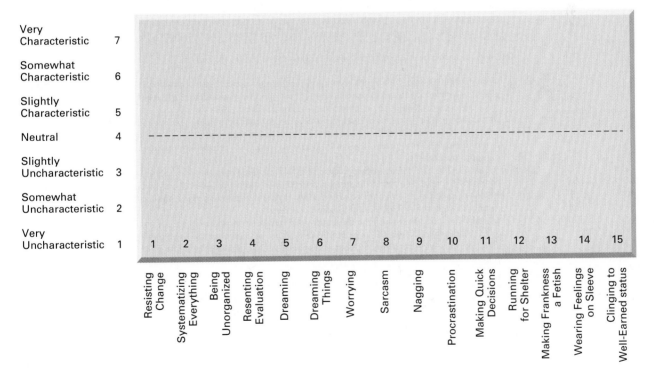

Chapter 2: Is a Bureaucracy for You?

Give yourself one point for each statement for which you responded in the bureaucratic direction:

1. Mostly agree	5. Mostly disagree	9. Mostly disagree	13. Mostly disagree	17. Mostly disagree
2. Mostly agree	6. Mostly disagree	10. Mostly agree	14. Mostly agree	18. Mostly agree
3. Mostly disagree	7. Mostly agree	11. Mostly agree	15. Mostly disagree	19. Mostly agree
4. Mostly agree	8. Mostly agree	12. Mostly disagree	16. Mostly agree	20. Mostly disagree

A very high score (15 or over) suggests that you would enjoy working in a bureaucracy. A very low score (5 or lower) suggests that you would be frustrated by working in a bureaucracy, especially a large one.

Do you think your score is representative of most college students in your major? Discuss.

Chapter 3: What Kind of Organizational Culture Fits You Best?

For items 5 and 6, score as follows:

$$
\begin{aligned}
\text{Strongly agree} &= +2 \\
\text{Agree} &= +1 \\
\text{Uncertain} &= 0 \\
\text{Disagree} &= -1 \\
\text{Strongly disagree} &= -2
\end{aligned}
$$

For items 1, 2, 3, 4, and 7, reverse the score (Strongly agree = –2, and so on). Add up your total. Your score will fall somewhere between +14 and –14.

What does your score mean? The higher your score (positive), the more comfortable you'll be in a formal, stable, rule-oriented, and structured culture. This type of culture is often associated with large corporations and governmental agencies. Negative scores indicate a preference for informal, humanistic, flexible, and innovative cultures that are more likely to be found in research units, advertising firms, high-tech companies, and small businesses.

Chapter 4: What Are Your Cultural Attitudes?

Instructions:

Sum up items 1 through 5 and divide by 5. This is your mean *uncertainty avoidance* score.
Sum up items 6 through 10 and divide by 5. This is your mean *individualism-collectivism* score.
Sum up items 11 through 16 and divide by 6. This is your mean *power distance* score.
Sum up items 17 through 25 and divide by 9. This is your mean *masculinity-femininity* score.

The exercise should be interpreted on the basis of the mean scores, as follows:

1. *Uncertainty avoidance.* Defines the extent to which people in a culture feel threatened by uncertainty and ambiguous situations and try to avoid such situations. The higher the mean score (5 is the maximum mean score), the more likely the manager is to feel threatened in new cultures.
2. *Individualism-collectivism.* Individualism implies a loosely knit social framework in which people are supposed to take care of themselves (as opposed to collectivist cultures, characterized by "individual groups" that are expected to take care of their members). The higher the mean score, the more likely a manager will be productive in a team or group environment.
3. *Power distance.* Defines the extent to which the less powerful person in a society accepts inequality in power and considers it normal. The higher the mean score, the more likely that a person will be power oriented and may have difficulty working in an environment where power is distributed among many individuals or groups. This type of person may even be manipulative and overemphasize control.
4. *Masculinity-femininity.* Defines the extent to which the dominant values of society are "masculine" (e.g., assertive and competitive) or "feminine" (e.g., less assertive and less competitive). The higher the mean score, the more likely that masculine traits are dominant. In a country such as present-day Japan, a feminine type may have trouble coping.

You can compare your scores with a sample of U.S. and Mexican students to see how well you would embrace their cultures. The closer your mean score is to their mean scores, the greater the likelihood that you would mesh with their culture.

Dimension	U.S. Students	Mexican Students
Uncertainty avoidance	3.41	4.15
Individualism-collectivism	2.19	3.33
Power distance	1.86	2.22
Masculinity-femininity	2.78	2.75

Chapter 5: Attitudes toward Business Ethics Questionnaire

Scoring Key and a Summary of the Differences between Management and Liberal Arts Students

Item	Liberal Arts Students (N = 286) Mean	Management Students (N = 243) Mean
1	2.90	3.09
2	1.76	1.88
3	2.50	2.60
4	2.62	2.54
5	3.18	3.41
6	3.75	3.88
7	2.42	2.53
8	2.67	2.88
9	3.41	3.62
10	3.58	3.79
11	3.06	3.44
12	1.50	1.33
13	1.66	1.58
14	2.29	2.31
15	3.15	3.36
16	2.61	2.78
17	3.69	3.79
18	3.52	3.38

Scoring Directions

Compare your scores on each statement against the mean (average) scores of both liberal arts and management students. Which group were you closest to on the statements? Five of the 18 statements (5, 8, 11, 12, and 18) were the most significant in terms of showing differences between the two groups of students. Why do you think the two groups of students differed significantly on these five statements?

Chapter 6: What Is Your Decision-Making Style?

Scoring the decision-style inventory:

1. Add the points in each of the four columns—I, II, III, IV.
2. The sum of the four columns should be 300 points. If your sum does not equal 300 points, check your addition and your answers.
3. Place your score for each column—I, II, III, IV—into the box of the corresponding number.

Analytic II	Conceptual III
___	___
Directive I	**Behavioral IV**
___	___

4. The box with the highest score reflects your dominant style. The closer the distribution is to a score of 75 in each category, the greater flexibility you show.

Chapter 7: How Well Do I Set Goals?

The goal-setting assessment helps you focus on basic aspects of goal-setting processes in your personal and professional or school life. The intent of this brief assessment is to get you to think about goal setting as it is related to your school, personal life, and work.

   In the first part of the assessment, we focus on whether your personal goal setting is *passive* or *active*. Question 1 examines your general tendency around "action," and Questions 4 and 5 show a specific example of proaction versus reaction (having a plan for completing your major). Questions 2 and 3 concern the *allocation of resources*. Finally, Question 6 focuses on a cornerstone of effective goal setting—creating goals that are *challenging yet attainable*. If your score on any of these questions is 3 or less, you need to gain a better understanding of the importance of goal setting and what is involved in setting goals.

In the second part of the assessment, we focus on the goal-setting processes of an organizational unit that you may work in or have knowledge about. Questions 1, 6, and 12 focus on the extent to which goal setting is an *integral part* of a work unit's operation (planning is proactive, is completed at all organizational levels, is predictable, and is done at periodic intervals). Questions 2, 3, and 13 examine the extent to which goal-setting processes are *supported by other organizational factors*. The *comprehensiveness* of organizational goal setting is addressed in Questions 4, 5, 7, 8, and 9. Finally, Questions 10, 11, and 14 address the *appropriateness* of goals. If the organizational unit you assessed scored low in any of these areas, you may want to examine more closely the planning processes being used and try to identify ways in which they could be improved.

Chapter 8: Are You a Risk Taker?

Give yourself one point for each true answer for items 1, 3, 4, 7, 9, 11, 13, 14, 16, and 18. Give yourself one point for each false answer for items 2, 5, 6, 8, 10, 12, 15, 17, and 19.

The more points you have, the more willing you are to take risks with your money and career.

Chapter 9: Am I a Good Planner?

According to the author of this questionnaire, the perfect planner would have answered:
1. Yes; 2. No; 3. Yes; 4. Yes; 5. Yes; 6. Yes; 7. Yes; 8. No

Chapter 10: How Willing Are You to Delegate?

Scoring: To determine your scores, add up the points you assigned as follows:

Sum of a, d, e, g, j, l, m, o, r, and s = (X)
Sum of b, c, f, h, i, k, n, p, q, and t = (Y)

Interpretation: The higher one's X scores, the less inclined one is to delegate tasks. Theory X assumes that people are not motivated to take responsibility unless pressured. Theory Y assumes that people seek additional responsibility and the delegated tasks will be accepted. (See chapter 2 to review McGregor's Theory X and Theory Y.)

Chapter 11: Diversity Questionnaire

The lower your score, the better you communicate and improve the climate in your diverse organization and the community at large.

Chapter 12: How Innovative Are You?

Scoring: Give yourself the following points for each circled response:

SA = 5 points
A = 4 points
? = 3 points
D = 2 points
SD = 1 point

Total your points to get your score.
Interpretation: The higher the score, the more willing you are to be innovative. Your attitude toward innovation is more positive than that of people who score low. A score of 72 or greater is high; a score of 45 or less is low. People who are not innovators have a tendency to maintain the status quo. Innovative people are entrepreneurs and ones who like to create changes in their organizations.

Chapter 13: What's Your Personality Type?

Mark each of your responses on the following scales. Then use the point value column to arrive at your score. For example, if you answered *a* to the first question, you would check *1a* in the feeling column. This response receives zero points when you add up the point value column. Instructions for classifying your scores are indicated below the scales.

Sensation	Point Value	Intuition	Point Value	Thinking	Point Value	Feeling	Point Value
2b _____	1	2a _____	2	1b _____	1	1a _____	0
4a _____	1	4b _____	1	3b _____	2	3a _____	1
5a _____	1	5b _____	1	7b _____	1	7a _____	1
6b _____	1	6a _____	0	8a _____	0	8b _____	1
9b _____	2	9a _____	2	10b _____	2	10a _____	1
12a _____	1	12b _____	0	11a _____	2	11b _____	1
15a _____	1	15b _____	1	13b _____	1	13a _____	1
16b _____	2	16a _____	0	14b _____	0	14a _____	1
(Maximum) Point Value	(10)		(7)		(9)		(7)

Classifying Total Scores

- Write *intuition* if your intuition score is equal to or greater than your sensation score.
- Write *sensation* if your sensation score is greater than your intuition score.
- Write *feeling* if your feeling score is greater than your thinking score.
- Write *thinking* if your thinking score is greater than your feeling score.

Chapter 14: Are You a Team Player?

If you answered more than half of the questions with "Very like me" or "Somewhat like me," you are likely to be a good team member. However, you might also want to ask yourself the following questions to explore further your feelings about being a team player.

1. Do these self-assessment items agree with your concept of team membership? Why or why not?
2. On the basis of your responses, what do you think your strengths are as far as working on a team? What are your weaknesses?
3. On the basis of your responses, how would you evaluate yourself as a team member?

Chapter 15: What Motivates You?

To determine your dominant needs—and what motivates you—place the number 1 through 5 that you circled for each statement next to the number for that statement.

	Achievement	Power	Affiliation
	1. _____	2. _____	3. _____
	4. _____	5. _____	6. _____
	7. _____	8. _____	9. _____
	10. _____	11. _____	12. _____
	13. _____	14. _____	15. _____
Total:	_____	_____	_____

Total each column. The sum in each column will be between 5 and 25 points. The column with the highest score tells you your dominant need.

Chapter 16: Are You a Charismatic Leader?

The questionnaire measures each of the six basic behavior leader patterns as well as a set of emotional responses. Your score can range from 4 to 20. Each question is stated as a measure of the extent to which you engage in the behavior or elicit the feelings. The higher your score, the more you demonstrate charismatic leader behaviors.

Index 1: Management of Attention (1, 7, 13, 19). Your score _____ . You pay especially close attention to people with whom you are communicating. You are also "focused in" on the key issues under discussion and help others to see clearly these key points. They have clear ideas about the relative importance or priorities of different issues under discussion.

Index 2: Management of Meaning (2, 8, 14, 20). Your score _____ . This set of items centers on your communication skills, specifically your ability to get the meaning of a message across, even if this means devising some innovative approach.

Index 3: Management of Trust (3, 9, 15, 21). Your score _____ . The key factor is your perceived trustworthiness as shown by your willingness to follow through on promises, avoidance of "flip-flop" shifts in position, and willingness to take clear positions.

Index 4: Management of Self (4, 10, 16, 22). Your score ——— . This index concerns your general attitudes toward yourself and others; that is, your overall concern for others and their feelings, as well as for "taking care of" feelings about yourself in a positive sense (e.g., self-regard).

Index 5: Management of Risk (5, 11, 17, 23). Your score ——— . Effective charismatic leaders are deeply involved in what they do and do not spend excessive amounts of time or energy on plans to "protect" themselves against failure. These leaders are willing to take risks, not on a hit-or-miss basis, but after careful estimation of the odds of success or failure.

Index 6: Management of Feelings (6, 12, 18, 24). Your score ——— . Charismatic leaders seem to consistently generate a set of feelings in others. Others feel that their work becomes more meaningful and that they are the "masters" of their own behavior; that is, they feel competent. They feel a sense of community, a "we-ness" with their colleagues and co-workers.

Chapter 17: Who Controls Your Life?

This exercise is designed to measure your locus of control. Give yourself 1 point for each of the following selections: 1B, 2A, 3A, 4B, 5B, 6A, 7A, 8A, 9B, and 10A. Scores can be interpreted as follows:

8–10	=	High internal locus of control
6–7	=	Moderate internal locus of control
5	=	Mixed
3–4	=	Moderate external locus of control
1–2	=	High external locus of control

The higher your internal score, the more you believe that you control your own destiny. The higher your external score, the more you believe that what happens to you in your life is due to luck or chance.

Chapter 18: How Customer Focused Are You?

Add your points and refer to the following scoring key.

32–40	You are highly customer focused.
24–31	You have good knowledge of the customer but could become more focused.
Less than 24	You need to become more customer focused.

Chapter 19: How Internet Literate Are You?

Scoring: (1) k; (2) d; (3) h; (4) n; (5) j; (6) o; (7) c; (8) i; (9) m; (10) f; (11) l; (12) g; (13) b; (14) e; (15) a

14–15 correct	You're a real Web wizard!
10–13 correct	You know a lot about the Web but aren't quite qualified as a Web expert yet!
7–9 correct	You qualify as a Web novice!
Under 7 correct:	You need to get out of your Model T and get on the Information Superhighway! :-)

Chapter 1

1. N.K. Austin, "Back from the Brink," *Working Woman,* January 1997, pp. 47–50.

2. L. Himelstein and S.A. Forest, "Breaking Through," *Business Week,* February 17, 1997, pp. 64–70; J.B. White and C. Hymowitz, "Watershed Generation of Women Executives Is Rising to the Top," *Wall Street Journal,* February 10, 1997, pp. A1+; A. Crittenden, "Up the Corporate Ladder: A Progress Report," *Working Woman,* May 1996, p. 22; and B. Worton, "Women at Work," *Fortune,* March 4, 1996, pp. 13–19.

3. T.A. Stewart, "Brain Power: Who Owns It. . . How They Profit from It," *Fortune,* March 17, 1997, pp. 105–10; G.P. Zachary, "The Right Mix," *Wall Street Journal,* March 13, 1997, pp. A1+; W.H. Miller, "Leadership at a Crossoads," *IW,* August 19, 1996, pp. 42–56; M. Scott, "Interview with Dee Hock," *Business Ethics,* May/June 1996, pp. 37–41; and J.O'C. Hamilton, S. Baker, and B. Vlasic, "The New Workplace," *Business Week,* April 29, 1996, pp. 106–17.

4. H. Fayol, *Industrial and General Administration* (Paris: Dunod, 1916).

5. H. Koontz and C. O'Donnell, *Principles of Management: An Analysis of Managerial Functions* (New York: McGraw-Hill, 1955).

6. For a comprehensive review of this question, see C.P. Hales, "What Do Managers Do? A Critical Review of the Evidence," *Journal of Management,* January 1986, pp. 88–115.

7. H. Mintzberg, *The Nature of Managerial Work* (New York: Harper & Row, 1973).

8. See, for example, L.D. Alexander, "The Effect Level in the Hierarchy and Functional Area Have on the Extent Mintzberg's Roles Are Required by Managerial Jobs," *Academy of Management Proceedings* (San Francisco, 1979), pp. 186–89; A.W. Lau and C.M. Pavett, "The Nature of Managerial Work: A Comparison of Public and Private Sector Managers," *Group and Organization Studies,* December 1980, pp. 453–66; M.W. McCall Jr. and C.A. Segrist, *In Pursuit of the Manager's Job: Building on Mintzberg,* Technical Report No. 14 (Greensboro, NC: Center for Creative Leadership, 1980); C.M. Pavett and A.W. Lau, "Managerial Work: The Influence of Hierarchical Level and Functional Specialty," *Academy of Management Journal,* March 1983, pp. 170–77; Hales, "What Do Managers Do?" A.I. Kraut, P.R. Pedigo, D.D. McKenna, and M.D. Dunnette, "The Role of the Manager: What's Really Important in Different Management Jobs," *Academy of Management Executive,* November 1989, pp. 286–93; and M.J. Martinko and W.L. Gardner, "Structured Observation of Managerial Work: A Replication and Synthesis," *Journal of Management Studies,* May 1990, pp. 330–57.

9. Pavett and Lau, "Managerial Work."

10. S.J. Carroll and D.A. Gillen, "Are the Classical Management Functions Useful in Describing Managerial Work?" *Academy of Management Review,* January 1987, p. 48.

11. See, for example, H. Koontz, "Commentary on the Management Theory Jungle—Nearly Two Decades Later," in H. Koontz, C. O'Donnell, and H. Weihrich (eds.), *Management: A Book of Readings,* 6th ed. (New York: McGraw-Hill, 1984), pp. 10–14; and Carroll and Gillen, "Are the Classical Management Functions Useful in Describing Managerial Work?" pp. 38–51.

12. Koontz, "Commentary on the Management Theory Jungle—Nearly Two Decades Later;" Carroll and Gillen, "Are the Classical Management Functions Useful in Describing Managerial Work?"; and P. Allan, "Managers at Work: A Large-Scale Study of the Managerial Job in New York City Government," *Academy of Management Journal,* September 1981, pp. 613–19.

13. R.L. Katz, "Skills of an Effective Administrator," *Harvard Business Review,* September–October 1974, pp. 90–102.

14. D.A. Whetten and K.S. Cameron, *Developing Management Skills,* 4th ed. (New York: HarperCollins, 1998); D.B. Curtis, J.L. Winsor, and R.D. Stephens, "National Preferences in Business and Communication Education," *Communication Education* 38, 1989, pp. 6–15; K. Cameron and M. Tschirhart, *Managerial Competencies and Organizational Effectiveness,* Working Paper, School of Business Administration, University of Michigan, 1988; F. Luthans, S.A. Rosenkrantz, and H.W. Hennessey, "What Do Successful Managers Really Do? An Observation Study of Managerial Activities," *Journal of Applied Behavioral Science,* Vol. 21, 1985, pp. 255–70; M.C. Prentice, "An Empirical Search for a Relevant Management Curriculum," *Collegiate News and Views,* Winter 1984, pp. 25–29; and G. Benson, "How Well Do Business Schools Prepare Graduates for the Business World?" *Personnel* 60 (1983) pp. 61–65.

15. K.B. DeGreene, *Sociotechnical Systems: Factors in Analysis, Design, and Management* (Upper Saddle River, NJ: Prentice Hall, 1973), p. 13.

16. See, for example, J.W. Driscoll, G. Cowger, and R. Egan, "Private Managers and Public Myths—Public Managers and Private Myths," *Sloan Management Review,* Fall 1979, pp. 53–57; D. Rogers, "Managing in the Public and Private Sectors: Similarities and Differences," *Management Review,* May 1981, pp. 48–54; G. Allison, "Public and Private Management: Are They Fundamentally Alike in All Unimportant Respects?" in F.S. Lane (ed.), *Current Issues in Public Administration,* 2nd ed. (New York: St. Martin's Press, 1982); D. Yates Jr., *The Politics of Management* (San Francisco: Jossey-Bass, 1985), pp. 12–39; J.N. Baldwin, "Public vs. Private: Not That Different, Not That Consequential," *Public Personnel Management,* Summer 1987, pp. 181–91; and H.G. Rainey, "Public Management: Recent Research on the Political Context and Managerial Roles, Structures, and Behaviors," *Journal of Management,* June 1989, pp. 229–50.

17. See, for example, W.A. Nowlin, "Factors That Motivate Public and Private Sector Managers: A Comparison," *Public Personnel Management Journal,* Fall 1982, pp. 224–27.

18. F. Katayama, "Small Business Fuels Economic Growth," *CNNfn World Wide Web Page,* March 25, 1996; J. Chun and C.E. Griffin, "The Mouse That Roared: The True State of Small Business," *Entrepreneur,* September 1996, pp. 118–22; and G. Koretz, "Startups: Still a Job Engine," *Business Week,* March 24, 1997, p. 26.

19. W. Sengenberger, G. Loveman, and M.J. Piore (eds.), *The Re-Emergence of Small Enterprises: Industrial Restructuring in Industrial Countries* (Geneva: International Institute for Labour Studies, 1990); "Entrepreneurs Pop Up in China," *Wall Street Journal,* April 7, 1994, p. A10; and J. Case, "Is America Really Different?" *State of Small Business, INC.,* 1996, pp. 108–09.

20. J.G.P. Paolillo, "The Manager's Self-Assessments of Managerial Roles: Small vs. Large Firms," *American Journal of Small Business,* January–March 1984, pp. 58–64.

21. See, for example, G. D'Amboise and M. Muldowney, "Management Theory for Small Business: Attempts and Requirements," *Academy of Management Review,* April 1988, pp. 226–40.

22. This box is based on the following: T.M. Begley and D.P. Boyd, "A Comparison of Entrepreneurs and Managers of Small Business Firms," *Journal of Management,* Spring 1987, pp. 99–108; H.H. Stevenson, M.J. Roberts, and H.I. Grousbeck, *New Business Ventures and the Entrepreneur* (Homewood, IL: Irwin, 1989); R.D. Hisrich, "Entrepreneurship/Intrapreneurship," *American Psychologist,* February 1990, p. 218; M. Warshaw, "The Entrepreneurial Mind," *Success,* April 1994, pp. 48–51; and E. Schine, "This Woman's Place Is in the Hangar," Enterprise Special Report, *Business Week,* May 13, 1996, pp. ENT 16–ENT18.

23. See, for example, D.H.B. Welsh, F. Luthans, and S.M. Sommer, "Managing Russian Factory Workers: The Impact of U.S.-Based Behavioral and Participative Techniques," *Academy of Management Journal,* February 1993, pp. 58–79; G. Hofstede, "Cultural Constraints in Management Theories," *Academy of Management Executive,* February 1993, pp. 81–94; A. Shama, "Management under Fire: The Transformation of Managers in the Soviet Union and Eastern Europe," *Academy of Management Executive,* February 1993, pp. 22–35; O.O. Sawyerr, "Environmental Uncertainty and Environmental Scanning Activities of Nigerian Manufacturing Executives: A Comparative Analysis," *Strategic Management Journal* 14 (1993), pp. 287–99; R.G. Linowes, "The Japanese Manager's Traumatic Entry into the United States: Understanding the American-Japanese Cultural Divide," *Academy of Management Executive,* November 1993, pp. 21–40; M. Cakrt, "Management Education in Eastern Europe: Toward Mutual Understanding," *Academy of Management Executive,* November 1993, pp.

63–68; M.E. de Forest, "Thinking of a Plant in Mexico," *Academy of Management Executive,* February 1994, pp. 33–40; S.M. Puffer, "Understanding the Bear: A Portrait of Russian Business Leaders," *Academy of Management Executive,* February 1994, pp. 41–61; and R. Calori and B. Dufour, "Management European Style," *Academy of Management Executive,* August 1995, pp. 61–73.

24. This box is based on the following: R. Tagiuri, "Managing People: Ten Essential Behaviors," *Harvard Business Review,* January–February 1995, pp. 10–11; "Occupational Projections and Training Data, 1996 Edition," *Bureau of Labor Statistics,* January 1996, Bulletin 2471; C. Hayes, "Cutting through the Chaos," *Black Enterprise,* February 1996, pp. 83–88; M. Jones and M. Andrews, "25 Hottest Careers for Women," *Working Woman,* July–August 1996, pp. 7–8; M.A. Frohman, "Unleash Urgency and Action," *IW,* November 4, 1996, pp. 13–16; T. Teal, "The Human Side of Management," *Harvard Business Review,* November–December 1996, pp. 35–44; "Look to Small Employers for Big Opportunities," *Job Choices: 1997,* pp. E75–E77; J. Mariotti, "The Problem with 'Management,'" *IW,* March 17, 1997, p. 72; and S. Nelton, "Leadership for the New Age," *Nation's Business,* May, 1997, pp. 18–27; J.S. McClenahen, "The Workforce in 2006," *IW,* January 5, 1998, p. 15.

Chapter 2

1. "Diversity: Making the Business Case," Special Advertising Section, *Business Week,* December 9, 1996; and phone conversation with EDS headquarters, June 23, 1997.

2. C.S. George Jr., *The History of Management Thought,* 2d ed. (Upper Saddle River, NJ: Prentice Hall, 1972), p. 4.

3. Ibid., pp. 35–41.

4. F.W. Taylor, *Principles of Scientific Management* (New York: Harper, 1911), p. 44. For other information on F.W. Taylor, see M. Banta, *Taylored Lives: Narrative Productions in the Age of Taylor, Veblen, and Ford* (Chicago: University of Chicago Press, 1993); and R. Kanigel, *The One Best Way: Frederick Winslow Taylor and the Enigma of Efficiency* (New York: Viking, 1997).

5. See for example, F.B. Gilbreth, *Motion Study* (New York: Van Nostrand, 1911); and F.B. Gilbreth and L.M. Gilbreth, *Fatigue Study* (New York: Sturgis and Walton, 1916).

6. H. Fayol, *Industrial and General Administration* (Paris: Dunod, 1916).

7. M. Weber, *The Theory of Social and Economic Organizations,* ed. T. Parsons, trans. A.M. Henderson and T. Parsons (New York: Free Press, 1947).

8. George, *The History of Management Thought,* pp. 361–63.

9. R.C. Davis, *The Fundamentals of Top Management* (New York: Harper & Row, 1951).

10. R.A. Owen, *A New View of Society* (New York: Bliss and White, 1825).

11. W.J. Duncan, *Great Ideas in Management* (San Francisco: Jossey-Bass, 1989), p. 137.

12. H. Munsterberg, *Psychology and Industrial Efficiency,* 6th ed. (Boston: Houghton Mifflin, 1913).

13. M.P. Follett, *The New State: Group Organization the Solution of Popular Government* (London: Longmans, Green and Co., 1918); and D.W. Linden, "The Mother of Them All," *Forbes,* January 16, 1995, pp. 75–76.

14. C. Barnard, *The Functions of the Executive* (Cambridge, MA: Harvard University Press, 1938).

15. E. Mayo, *The Human Problems of an Industrial Civilization* (New York: Macmillan, 1933); and F.J. Roethlisberger and W.J. Dickson, *Management and the Worker* (Cambridge, MA: Harvard University Press, 1939).

16. See for example, A. Carey, "The Hawthorne Studies: A Radical Criticism," *American Sociological Review,* June 1967, pp. 403–16; R.H. Franke and J. Kaul, "The Hawthorne Experiments: First Statistical Interpretations," *American Sociological Review,* October 1978, pp. 623–43; B. Rice, "The Hawthorne Defect: Persistence of a Flawed Theory," *Psychology Today,* February 1982, pp. 70–74; J.A. Sonnenfeld, "Shedding Light on the Hawthorne Studies," *Journal of Occupational Behavior,* April 1985, pp. 111–30; and S.R.G. Jones, "Worker Interdependence and Output: The Hawthorne Studies Reevaluated," *American Sociological Review,* April 1990, pp. 176–90; S.R. Jones, "Was There a Hawthorne Effect?" *American Sociological Review,* November 1992, pp. 451–68; and G.W. Yunker, "An Explanation of Positive and Negative Hawthorne Effects: Evidence from the Relay Assembly Test Room and Bank Wiring Observation Room Studies," paper presented, Academy of Management Annual Meeting, August 1993, Atlanta, Georgia.

17. A. Maslow, *Motivation and Personality* (New York: McGraw-Hill, 1954).

18. See, for example, D.T. Hall and K.E. Nongaim, "An Examination of Maslow's Need Hierarchy in an Organizational Setting," *Organizational Behavior and Human Performance,* February

1968, pp. 12–35; and E.E. Lawler III and J.L. Suttle, "A Causal Correlational Test of the Need Hierarchy Concept," *Organizational Behavior and Human Performance,* April 1972, pp. 265–87.

19. D. McGregor, *The Human Side of Enterprise* (New York: McGraw-Hill, 1960).

20. K.L. Miller, "I Came, I Saw, I Conquered," *Business Week,* July 4, 1994, pp. 58–60.

21. F. Herzberg, B. Mausner, and B. Snyderman, *The Motivation to Work* (New York: John Wiley, 1959); and F. Herzberg, *The Managerial Choice: To Be Effective or to Be Human,* rev. ed. (Salt Lake City, Olympus, 1982).

22. See S.A. Kirkpatrick and E.A. Locke, "Leadership: Do Traits Matter?" *Academy of Management Executive,* May 1991, pp. 48–60.

23. K. Lewin and R. Lippitt, "An Experimental Approach to the Study of Autocracy and Democracy: A Preliminary Note," *Sociometry* 1 (1938), pp. 292–300; Lewin, "Field Theory and Experiment in Social Psychology: Concepts and Methods," *American Journal of Sociology* 44 (1939), pp. 868–96; Lewin, Lippitt, and R.K. White, "Patterns of Aggressive Behavior in Experimentally Created Social Climates," *Journal of Social Psychology* 10 (1939), pp. 271–301; and Lippitt, "An Experimental Study of the Effect of Democratic and Authoritarian Group Atmospheres," *University of Iowa Studies in Child Welfare* 16 (1940), pp. 43–95.

24. B.M. Bass, *Stogdill's Handbook of Leadership* (New York: Free Press, 1981), pp. 289–99.

25. R.M. Stogdill and A.E. Coons (eds.), *Leader Behavior: Its Description and Measurement,* Research Monograph No. 88 (Columbus: Ohio State University, Bureau of Business Research, 1951). For an updated literature review of Ohio State research, see S. Kerr, C.A. Schriesheim, C.J. Murphy, and R.M. Stogdill, "Toward a Contingency Theory of Leadership Based upon the Consideration and Initiating Structure Literature," *Organizational Behavior and Human Performance,* August 1974, pp. 62–82; and B.M. Fisher, "Consideration and Initiating Structure and Their Relationships with Leader Effectiveness: A Meta-Analysis," in F. Hoy (ed.), *Proceedings of the 48th Annual Academy of Management Conference,* Anaheim, California, 1988, pp. 201–05.

26. R. Kahn and D. Katz, "Leadership Practices in Relation to Productivity and Morale," in D. Cartwright and A. Zander (eds.), *Group Dynamics: Research and Theory,* 2d ed. (Elmsford, NY: Row, Paterson, 1960).

27. R.R. Blake and J.S. Mouton, *The Managerial Grid III* (Houston: Gulf Publishing, 1984).

28. L.L. Larson, J.G. Hunt, and R.N. Osborn, "The Great Hi-Hi Leader Behavior Myth: A Lesson from Occam's Razor," *Academy of Management Journal,* December 1976, pp. 628–41; and P.C. Nystrom, "Managers and the Hi-Hi Leader Myth," *Academy of Management Journal,* June 1978, pp. 325–31.

29. "Buying American," *Forbes,* July 28, 1997, pp. 218–20.

30. K. Anderson and C. Hayes, "The Changing Labor Force," *Black Enterprise,* February 1997, p. 86.

31. G.W. Loveman and J.J. Gabarro, "The Managerial Implications of Changing Work Force Demographics: A Scoping Study," *Human Resource Management,* Spring 1991, pp. 7–29.

32. See for example, P.A. Galagan, "Navigating the Differences," *Training and Development,* April 1993, pp. 28–33; D.T. Hall and V.A. Parker, "The Role of Workplace Flexibility in Managing Diversity," *Organizational Dynamics,* Summer 1993, pp. 5–18; D. Elmuti, "Managing Diversity in the Work Place: An Immense Challenge for Both Managers and Workers," *Industrial Management,* July–August 1993, pp. 19–22; "The Challenge of Managing Diversity in the Workplace: Corporate America Is Responding to the Changing Demographics of the Work Force with a Wide Variety of Diversity Management Programs," *Black Enterprise,* July 1993, pp. 79+.

33. L. Zuckerman, "Do Computers Lift Productivity? It's Unclear, But Business Is Sold," *New York Times,* January 2, 1997, p. C15.

34. V. Frazee, "ASTD Identifies Workplace Trends," *Workforce,* March 1997, pp. 25–28.

35. B. Tucker, "Tommy Boy Can CD Future," *Fast Company Web Page,* <http://www.fastcompany.com> 4/17/97.

36. M. Hammer and J. Champy, *Reengineering the Corporation* (New York: HarperBusiness, 1993).

37. See for example, B. Krone, "Total Quality Management: An American Odyssey," *The Bureaucrat,* Fall 1990, pp. 35–38; A. Gabor, *The Man Who Discovered Quality* (New York: Random House, 1990); J. Clemmer, "How Total Is Your Quality Management?" *Canadian Business Review,* Spring 1991, pp. 38–41; M. Sashkin and K.J. Kiser, *Total Quality Management* (Seabrook, MD: Ducochon Press, 1991); J.W. Dean Jr. and D.E. Bowen, "Management Theory and Total Quality: Improving Research and Practice through Theory Development," *Academy of Management Review,* July 1994, pp. 392–418; C.A. Reeves and D.A. Bednar, "Defining Quality: Alternatives and Implications," *Academy of Management Review,* July 1994, pp. 419–45; R.K. Reger, L.T. Gustafson, S.M. Demarie, and J.V. Mullane, "Reframing the Organization: Why Implementing Total Quality Is Easier Said Than Done," *Academy of Management Review,* July 1994, pp. 565–84; T.C. Powell, "Total Quality Management as Competitive Advantage: A Review and Empirical Study," *Strategic Management Journal,* January 1995, pp. 15–37; and J.R. Hackman and R. Wageman, "Total Quality Management: Empirical, Conceptual, and Practical Issues," *Administrative Science Quarterly,* June 1995, pp. 309–42.

38. A.C. Hyde, "Rescuing Quality Management from TQM," *The Bureaucrat,* Winter 1990–1991, p. 16.

39. J.A. Byrnes, "The Pain of Downsizing," *Business Week,* May 9, 1994, pp. 60–61.

40. D. Anfuso, "Save Jobs: Strategies to Stop the Layoffs," *Personnel Journal,* June 1996, pp. 66–69.

41. G. Koretz, "Big Payoffs from Layoffs," *Business Week,* February 24, 1997, p. 30.

42. G. Koretz, "The Downside of Downsizing," *Business Week,* April 28, 1997, p. 26.

43. S. WuDunn, "When Lifetime Jobs Die Prematurely," *New York Times,* June 12, 1996, pp. C1+; and J. Tagliabue, "In Europe, a Wave of Layoffs Stuns White-Collar Workers," *New York Times,* June 20, 1996, pp. A1+.

44. B. Ettorre, "The Contingent Workforce Moves Mainstream," *Management Review,* February 1994, pp. 11–16.

45. V. Frazee, "Short-Timers Are the Employees of the Future," *Personnel Journal,* April 1996, p. 32.

46. "Employee Empowerment Is Here to Stay," *Personnel Journal,* December 1995, p. 16.

47. See K.W. Thomas and B.A. Velthouse, "Cognitive Elements of Empowerment: An 'Interpretive' Model of Intrinsic Task Motivation," *Academy of Management Review,* October 1990, pp. 66–81.

48. R. Tetzeli, "Business Students Cheat Most," *Fortune,* July 1, 1991, p. 14.

49. "The Gap between Workers and Managers Is Working," *Personnel Journal,* August 1995, p. 22; D.M. Rousseau, "Changing the Deal While Keeping the People," *Academy of Management Executive,* February 1996, pp. 50–61; M.V. Roehling, "The Origins and Early Development of the Psychological

Contract Construct," *Academy of Management Proceedings on Disk,* August 1996, pp. 1–5; and E.W. Morrison and S.L. Robinson, "When Employees Feel Betrayed: A Model of How Psychological Contract Violation Develops," *Academy of Management Review,* January 1997, pp. 226–56.

50. L. Grant, "Can Fisher Focus Kodak?" *Fortune,* January 13, 1997, pp. 76–79.

Chapter 3

1. D. Sorter, "Pride and Positive Atmosphere Catapult Small Firm," *Minority Business News USA,* February 15–March 15, 1997, p. 36.

2. For insights into the symbolic view, see J. Pfeffer, "Management as Symbolic Action: The Creation and Maintenance of Organizational Paradigms," in L.L. Cummings and B.M. Staw (eds.), *Research in Organizational Behavior,* vol. 3 (Greenwich, CT: JAI Press, 1981), pp. 1–52; D.C. Hambrick and S. Finkelstein, "Managerial Discretion: A Bridge between Polar Views of Organizational Outcomes," in L.L. Cummings and B.M. Staw (eds.), *Research in Organizational Behavior,* vol. 9 (Greenwich, CT: JAI Press, 1987), pp. 369–406; J.A. Byrne, "The Limits of Power," *Business Week,* October 23, 1987, pp. 33–35; J.R. Meindl and S.B. Ehrlich, "The Romance of Leadership and the Evaluation of Organizational Performance," *Academy of Management Journal,* March 1987, pp. 91–109; C.R. Schwenk, "Illusions of Management Control? Effects of Self-Serving Attributions on Resource Commitments and Confidence in Management," *Human Relations,* April 1990, pp. 333–47; and S.M. Puffer and J.B. Weintrop, "Corporate Performance and CEO Turnover: The Role of Performance Expectations," *Administrative Science Quarterly,* March 1991, pp. 1–19.

3. Pfeffer, "Management as Symbolic Action."

4. L. Smircich, "Concepts of Culture and Organizational Analysis," *Administrative Science Quarterly,* September 1983, p. 339; D.R. Denison, "What Is the Difference between Organizational Culture and Organizational Climate? A Native's Point of View on a Decade of Paradigm Wars," paper presented at Academy of Management Annual Meeting, 1993, Atlanta, GA; and M.J. Hatch, "The Dynamics of Organizational Culture," *Academy of Management Review,* October 1993, pp. 657–93.

5. A.M. Sapienza, "Believing Is Seeing: How Culture Influences the Decisions Top Managers Make," in R.H. Kilmann et al. (eds.), *Gaining Control of the Corporate Culture* (San Francisco: Jossey-Bass, 1985), p. 68.

6. C.A. O'Reilly III, J. Chatman, and D.F. Caldwell, "People and Organizational Culture: A Profile Comparison Approach to Assessing Person-Organization Fit," *Academy of Management Journal,* September 1991, pp. 487–516; and J.A. Chatman and K.A. Jehn, "Assessing the Relationship between Industry Characteristics and Organizational Culture: How Different Can You Be?" *Academy of Management Journal,* June 1994, pp. 522–53.

7. C. Orphen, "The Effect of Organizational Cultural Norms on the Relationships between Personnel Practices and Employee Commitment," *Journal of Psychology,* September 1993, pp. 577–79.

8. See, for example, D.R. Denison, *Corporate Culture and Organizational Effectiveness* (New York: Wiley, 1990); G.G. Gordon and N. DiTomaso, "Predicting Corporate Performance from Organizational Culture," *Journal of Management Studies,* November 1992, pp. 793–98; J.P. Kotter and J.L. Heskett, *Corporate Culture and Performance* (New York: Free Press, 1992), pp. 15–27; J.C. Collins and J.I. Porras, *Built to Last* (New York: HarperBusiness, 1994); Collins and Porras, "Building Your Company's Vision," *Harvard Business Review,* September–October 1996, pp. 65–77; and R. Goffee and G. Jones, "What Holds the Modern Company Together?" *Harvard Business Review,* November–December 1996, pp. 133–48.

9. E.H. Schien, *Organizational Culture and Leadership* (San Francisco: Jossey-Bass, 1985), pp. 314–15.

10. J.H. Sheridan, "Culture Change Lessons," *IW,* February 17, 1997, pp. 20–34.

11. J. Case, "Corporate Culture," *Inc.,* November 1996, pp. 42–53.

12. M.A. Verespej, "Empire without Emperors," *IW,* February 5, 1996, pp. 13–16.

13. Sheridan, "Culture Change Lessons."

14. See, for example, K. Rebello, "Inside Microsoft," *Business Week,* July 15, 1996, pp. 56–67; J. Markoff, "Tomorrow, the World Wide Web," *New York Times,* July 16, 1996, pp. C1+; J. Cooper Ramo, "Winner Take All," *Time,* September 16, 1996, pp. 56–64; B. Schendler, "Software Hardball," *Fortune,* September 30, 1996, pp. 106–16; S. Levy, "The Microsoft Century," *Newsweek,* December 2, 1996, pp. 56–61; and Rebello, "Bill's Quiet Shopping Spree," *Business Week,* January 13, 1997, pp. 34–35.

15. P. Sellers, "How Coke Is Kicking Pepsi's Can," *Fortune,* October 28, 1996, pp. 70–84.

16. D. Kirkpatrick, "Intel's Amazing Profit Machine," *Fortune,* February 17, 1997, p. 62.

17. L. Nakarmi, "Solo Success?" *IW,* June 23, 1997, pp. 20–24.

18. D.M. Boje, "The Storytelling Organization: A Study of Story Performance in an Office-Supply Firm," *Administrative Science Quarterly,* March 1991, pp. 106–26; and C.H. Deutsch, "The Parables of Corporate Culture," *New York Times,* October 13, 1991, p. F25.

19. N.K. Austin, "Managing by Parable," *Working Woman,* September 1995, pp. 14–16.

20. A.M. Pettigrew, "On Studying Organizational Cultures," *Administrative Science Quarterly,* December 1979, p. 576.

21. Ibid.

22. Cited in J.M. Beyer and H.M. Trice, "How an Organization's Rites Reveal Its Culture," *Organizational Dynamics,* Spring 1987, p. 15.

23. "LOB Anyone?" *Business Week,* October 4, 1993, p. 94.

24. This box is based on T.H. Cox Jr., "The Multicultural Organization," *Academy of Management Executive,* April 1991, pp. 34–47; Cox and S. Blake, "Managing Cultural Diversity: Implications for Organizational Competitiveness," *Academy of Management Executive,* August 1991, pp. 45–46; "The Challenge of Managing Diversity in the Workplace," *Black Enterprise,* July 1993, pp. 79–90; D.A. Thomas and R.J. Ely, "Making Differences Matter: A New Paradigm for Managing Diversity," *Harvard Business Review,* September–October 1996, pp. 79–90; C.A. Deutsch, "Corporate Diversity in Practice," *New York Times,* November 20, 1996, pp. C1+; and A. Markels, "How One Hotel Manages Staff's Diversity," *Wall Street Journal,* November 20, 1996, pp. B1+.

25. R.H. Miles, *Macro Organizational Behavior* (Santa Monica, CA: Goodyear Publishing, 1980), p. 195.

26. This box is based on Z. Block and I.C. MacMillan, "Size 'Em Up: How to Evaluate New Business Opportunities," *Success,* March 1994, p. 80; A. Bhide, "How Entrepreneurs Craft Strategies That Work," *Harvard Business Review,* March–April 1994, pp. 150–61; I. Abramovitch, "Revenge of the Wimp," *Success,* April 1994, p. 21; Z.J. Acs, "Where New Things Come From," *Inc.,* May 1994, p. 29; T. Stein, "Scoring with Sportswear," *Success,* September 1995, p. 31; and E. Updike, "The Novice Who Tamed the Web,"

Business Week Enterprise, June 9, 1997, pp. ENT 24–ENT 26.

27. T.S. Mescon and G.S. Vozikis, "Federal Regulation—What Are the Costs?" *Business,* January–March 1982, pp. 33–39.

28. See, for instance, A.S. Hayes, "Layoffs Take Careful Planning to Avoid Losing the Suits That Are Apt to Follow," *Wall Street Journal,* November 2, 1990, p. B1.

29. K.H. Hammonds, "In Business This Week," *Business Week,* September 20, 1993, p. 44.

Chapter 4

1. J. Kahn, "Chinese Electronics Entrepreneur Thrives," *Wall Street Journal,* April 11, 1996, p. A16.

2. G. Koretz, "Things Go Better with Multinationals—Except Jobs," *Business Week,* May 2, 1994, p. 20.

3. R.M. Hodgetts and F. Luthans, *International Management,* 2d ed. (New York: McGraw-Hill, 1994).

4. N. Adler, *International Dimensions of Organizational Behavior,* 2d ed. (Boston: PSW-Kent, 1991), p. 11.

5. H.V. Perlmutter, "The Tortuous Evolution of the Multinational Corporation," *Columbia Journal of World Business,* January–February 1969, pp. 9–18.

6. See, for instance, M. Maremont and R.A. Melcher, "Tearing Down Even More Fences in Europe," *Business Week,* November 4, 1991, pp. 50–52; S. Hammes, "Europe's Growing Market," *Fortune,* December 2, 1991, pp. 144–45; M.M. Nelson, "EC Is Swamped by Would-Be Members," *Wall Street Journal,* May 13, 1992, p. A12; and A. Bernstein, "Nordic Eyes on Europe's Big Trading Bloc," *U.S. News & World Report,* June 27, 1994, p. 12.

7. J. Marks, "Arrivederci, Lira, Au Revoir, Franc," *U.S. News & World Report,* December 16, 1996, p. 49; M. Elliott, "Hey, Can You Spare a 'Euro'?," *Newsweek,* February 17, 1997, pp. 48–49; J. Tagliabue, "A Continental Divide," *New York Times,* April 10, 1997, pp. C1+; and M. Marshall and D. Wessel, "One Currency, One Central Bank, One Big Question," *Wall Street Journal,* May 2, 1997, p. A10.

8. "The Language of Trade," *Business America,* July 1994, p. 5.

9. A. Borrus, "A Free-Trade Milestone, with Many More Miles to Go," *Business Week,* August 24, 1992, pp. 30—31; P. LaBarre, "Pace Varies, But Direction Is Right," *Industry Week,* June 6, 1994, pp. 36–38; B. Davis, "Growth of Trade Binds Nations, But It Also Can Spur Separatism," *Wall Street Journal,*

June 20, 1994, pp. A1+; N. Banerjee, "Canada's Recovery Is Expected to Cross Border and Boost Business in the U.S.," *Wall Street Journal,* June 20, 1994, p. A2; N. Templin, "Mexican Industrial Belt Is Beginning to Form as Car Makers Expand," *Wall Street Journal,* June 29, 1994, pp. A1+; and G. Smith, "NAFTA: A Green Light for Red Tape," *Business Week,* July 25, 1994.

10. R.W. Stevenson, "Nafta's Impact on Jobs Has Been Slight, Study Says," *New York Times,* December 19, 1996, pp. C1+; R.W. Stevenson, "U.S. to Report to Congress NAFTA Benefits Are Modest," *New York Times,* July 11, 1997, pp. C1+; and R.S. Greenberger, "NAFTA Is Good for U.S., Clinton Study Says," *Wall Street Journal,* July 11, 1997, p. A2.

11. R.S. Greenberger, "NAFTA Is Good for U.S., Clinton Study Says," *Wall Street Journal,* p. A2.

12. J. Brooke, "In Latin America, a Free Trade Rush," *New York Times,* June 13, 1994, pp. C1+.

13. C. Sims, "Chile Will Enter a Big South American Free-Trade Bloc," *New York Times,* June 26, 1996, p. C2.

14. J.S. McClenahen and T. Clark, "ASEAN at Work," *IW,* May 19, 1997, pp. 42–48.

15. P. Brimelow, "TAFTA?" *Forbes,* July 1, 1996, pp. 52–53.

16. S. WuDunn, "The Tail That Wags the Dragon," *New York Times,* June 27, 1997, pp. C1+.

17. J.A. Byrne et al., "Borderless Management," *Business Week,* May 23, 1994, pp. 24–26.

18. See, for example, G. Hofstede, *Culture's Consequences: International Differences in Work-Related Values* (Beverly Hills, CA: Sage Publications, 1980), pp. 25–26.

19. G. Hofstede, *Culture's Consequences;* and Hofstede, "The Cultural Relativity of Organizational Practices and Theories," *Journal of International Business Studies,* Fall 1983, pp. 75–89.

20. Hofstede called this last dimension "masculinity versus femininity," but we have changed it because of the strong sexist connotation in his choice of terms.

21. This box is based on A. Bianchi, "Entrepreneurial Traits by Nationality," *Inc.,* May 1994, p. 33; and J. Case, "Is America Really Different?," *Inc., The State of Small Business,* 1996, pp. 108–09.

22. R.L. Tung, "Human Resources Planning in Japanese Multinationals: A Model for U.S. Firms?" *Journal of International Business Studies,* Fall 1984, p. 146.

23. J.T. Gullahorn and J.E. Gullahorn, "An Extension of the U-Curve Hypothesis,"

Journal of Social Sciences, January 1963, pp. 34–47.

Chapter 5

1. R. Sylvester, "Restaurant Reports Hepatitis Case," *Springfield News Leader,* September 9, 1996, pp. 1A+; and T. Kallaos, "Restaurants Pay to Protect Workers' Health," *Springfield News Leader,* January 27, 1997, pp. 1A+.

2. A.B. Carroll, "A Three-Dimensional Conceptual Model of Corporate Performance," *Academy of Management Review,* October 1979, p. 499.

3. M. Friedman, *Capitalism and Freedom* (Chicago: University of Chicago Press, 1962); and Friedman, "The Social Responsibility of Business Is to Increase Profits," *New York Times Magazine,* September 13, 1970, p. 33.

4. S.W. Gellerman, "Why 'Good' Managers Make Bad Ethical Choices," *Harvard Business Review,* July–August 1986, p. 89.

5. Ibid., p. 86.

6. R.M. Rao, "End of the Line: Manville Is No More," *Fortune,* April 29, 1996, p. 42.

7. S.L. Wartick and P.L. Cochran, "The Evolution of the Corporate Social Performance Model," *Academy of Management Review,* October 1985, p. 760.

8. C. Caggiano, "Is Social Responsibility a Crock?" *Inc.,* May 1993, p. 15.

9. This section is based on R.J. Monsen Jr., "The Social Attitudes of Management," in J.M. McGuire (ed.), *Contemporary Management: Issues and Views* (Upper Saddle River, N.J.: Prentice Hall, 1974), p. 616; and K. Davis and W.C. Frederick, *Business and Society: Management, Public Policy, Ethics,* 5th ed. (New York: McGraw-Hill, 1984), pp. 28–41.

10. See, for example, R.A. Buccholz, *Essentials of Public Policy for Management,* 2d ed. (Upper Saddle River, NJ: Prentice Hall, 1990).

11. See S.P. Sethi, "A Conceptual Framework for Environmental Analysis of Social Issues and Evaluation of Business Response Patterns," *Academy of Management Review,* January 1979, pp. 68–74.

12. See, for example, D.J. Wood, "Corporate Social Performance Revisited," *Academy of Management Review,* October 1991, pp. 703–08.

13. Wartick and Cochran, "The Evolution of the Corporate Social Performance Model," p. 763.

14. Ibid., p. 762.

15. See, for instance, P. Cochran and R.A. Wood, "Corporate Social Responsibil-

ity and Financial Performance," *Academy of Management Journal*, March 1984, pp. 42–56; K. Aupperle, A.B. Carroll, and J.D. Hatfield, "An Empirical Examination of the Relationship between Corporate Social Responsibility and Profitability," *Academy of Management Journal*, June 1985, pp. 446–63; J.B. McGuire, A. Sundgren, and T. Schneeweis, "Corporate Social Responsibility and Firm Financial Performance," *Academy of Management Journal*, December 1988, pp. 854–72; D.M. Georgoff and J. Ross, "Corporate Social Responsibility and Management Performance," paper presented at the National Academy of Management Conference, Miami, August 1991; S.A. Zahra, B.M. Oviatt, and K. Minyard, "Effects of Corporate Ownership and Board Structure on Corporate Social Responsibility and Financial Performance," paper presented at the National Academy of Management Conference, Atlanta, August 1993; "Social Responsibility and the Bottom Line," *Business Ethics*, July–August, 1994, p. 11; D.B. Turban and D.W. Greening, "Corporate Social Performance and Organizational Attractiveness to Prospective Employees," *Academy of Management Journal*, June 1996, pp. 658–72; and S.A. Waddock and S.B. Graves, "The Corporate Social Performance–Financial Performance Link," *Strategic Management Journal*, April 1997, pp. 303–19.

16. See A.A. Ullmann, "Data in Search of a Theory: A Critical Examination of the Relationships among Social Performance, Social Disclosure, and Economic Performance of U.S. Firms," *Academy of Management Review*, July 1985, pp. 540–57; R.E. Wokutch and B.A. Spencer, "Corporate Saints and Sinners: The Effects of Philanthropic and Illegal Activity on Organizational Performance," *California Management Review*, Winter 1987, pp. 62–77; K.E. Aupperle, "The Use of Forced Choice Survey Procedures in Assessing Corporate Social Orientation," pp. 269–80; R.P. Gephart Jr., "Multiple Methods for Tracking Corporate Social Performance: Insights from a Study of Major Industrial Accidents," pp. 359–85; R. Wolfe and K. Aupperle, "Introduction to Corporate Social Performance: Methods for Evaluating an Elusive Construct," pp. 265–68, in J.E. Post (ed.), *Research in Corporate Social Performance and Policy*, vol. 12, 1991; and D.J. Wood and R.E. Jones, "Stakeholder Mismatching: A Theoretical Problem in Empirical Research on Corporate Social Performance," *International Journal of Organizational Analysis* (1995), pp. 229–67.

17. McGuire, Sundgren, and Schneeweis, "Corporate Social Responsibility and Firm Financial Performance."

18. Cochran and Wood, "Corporate Social Responsibility and Financial Performance."

19. Wood and Jones, "Stakeholder Mismatching."

20. P. Mao, "Socially Responsible Investing," *Sky Magazine*, June 1997, pp. 49–53.

21. Georgoff and Ross, "Corporate Social Responsibility and Management Performance" and Turban and Greening, "Corporate Social Performance and Organizational Attractiveness to Prospective Employees."

22. A.Q. Nomani, "Calpers Says Its Investment Decisions Will Reflect How Firms Treat Workers," *Wall Street Journal*, June 16, 1994, p. A5.

23. G.P. Alexander, "Establishing Shared Values through Management Training Programs," *Training and Development Journal*, February 1987, pp. 45–47.

24. Ibid.; J.L. Badaracco Jr. and R.R. Ellsworth, *Leadership and the Quest for Integrity* (Boston: Harvard Business School Press, 1989).

25. Same as note 24.

26. D. Kurschner, "5 Ways Ethical Business Creates Fatter Profits," *Business Ethics*, March–April 1996, pp. 20–23.

27. R. Kamen, "Values: For Show or For Real?" *Working Woman*, August 1993, p. 10.

28. Badaracco and Ellsworth, *Leadership and the Quest for Integrity*.

29. J. Bamford, "Changing Business as Usual," *Working Woman*, November 1993, pp. 62+.

30. This section is based on P. Shrivastava, "Environmental Technologies and Competitive Advantage," *Strategic Management Journal*, Summer 1995, pp. 183–200; S.L. Hart, "A Natural-Resource-Based View of the Firm," *Academy of Management Review*, December 1995, pp. 986–1014; and S.L. Hart, "Beyond Greening: Strategies for a Sustainable World," *Harvard Business Review*, January–February 1997, pp. 66–76.

31. P. Shrivastava, "Environmental Technologies and Competitive Advantage," p. 183.

32. S.L. Hart, "Beyond Greening," p. 68.

33. D. Meadows, "Our 'Footprints' Are Treading Too Much Earth," *Charleston (South Carolina) Gazette*, April 1, 1996.

34. L. Brown and Staff of the Worldwatch Institute, *State of the World* (New York: Norton, 1987–1996).

35. The concept of shades of green can be found in R.E. Freeman, J. Pierce, and R. Dodd, *Shades of Green: Business Ethics and the Environment* (New York: Oxford University Press, 1995).

36. See, for example, A.B. Carroll, "The Pyramid of Corporate Social Responsibility: toward the Moral Management of Organizational Stakeholders," *Business Horizons*, July–August 1991, pp. 39–48.

37. This section has been influenced by K.B. Boal and N. Peery, "The Cognitive Structure of Social Responsibility," *Journal of Management*, Fall–Winter 1985, pp. 71–82.

38. A.B. Carroll, *Social Responsibility of Management* (Chicago: Science Research Associates, 1984), p. 13.

39. K. Davis and W.C. Frederick, *Business and Society*, p. 76.

40. F.D. Sturdivant, *Business and Society: A Managerial Approach*, 3rd ed. (Homewood, IL: Richard D. Irwin, 1985), p. 128.

41. G.F. Cavanagh, D.J. Moberg, and M. Valasquez, "The Ethics of Organizational Politics," *Academy of Management Journal*, June 1981, pp. 363–74. See F.N. Brady, "Rules for Making Exceptions to Rules," *Academy of Management Review*, July 1987, pp. 436–44 for an argument that the theory of justice is redundant with the prior two theories. See T. Donaldson and T.W. Dunfee, "Toward a Unified Conception of Business Ethics: Integrative Social Contracts Theory," *Academy of Management Review*, April 1994, pp. 252–84 for a discussion of integrative social contracts theory.

42. D.J. Fritzsche and H. Becker, "Linking Management Behavior to Ethical Philosophy—An Empirical Investigation," *Academy of Management Journal*, March 1984, pp. 166–75.

43. B. Dumaine, "Exporting Jobs and Ethics," *Fortune*, October 5, 1992, p. 10.

44. L. Kohlberg, *Essays in Moral Development: The Philosophy of Moral Development*, vol. 1 (New York: Harper & Row, 1981); and L. Kohlberg, *Essays in Moral Development: The Psychology of Moral Development*, vol. 2 (New York: Harper & Row, 1984).

45. See, for example, J. Weber, "Managers' Moral Reasoning: Assessing Their Responses to Three Moral Dilemmas," *Human Relations*, July 1990, pp. 687–702.

46. J.H. Barnett and M.J. Karson, "Personal Values and Business Decisions: An Exploratory Investigation," *Journal of Business Ethics*, July 1987, pp. 371–82; and W.C. Frederick and J. Weber, "The Value of Corporate Managers and Their Critics: An Empirical Description and Normative Implications," in W.C. Frederick and L.E. Preston (eds.) *Business Ethics: Research Issues and Empirical Studies* (Greenwich, CT: JAI Press, 1990), pp. 123–44.

47. L.K. Trevino and S.A. Youngblood, "Bad Apples in Bad Barrels: A Causal Analysis of Ethical Decision-Making Behavior," *Journal of Applied Psychology*, August 1990, pp. 378–85; and M.E. Baehr, J.W. Jones, and A.J. Nerad, "Psychological Correlates of Business Ethics Orientation in Executives," *Journal of Business and Psychology*, Spring 1993, pp. 291–308.

48. B.Z. Posner and W.H. Schmidt, "Values and the American Manager: An Update," *California Management Review*, Spring 1984, pp. 202–16; and R.B. Morgan, "Self- and Co-Worker Perceptions of Ethics and Their Relationships to Leadership and Salary," *Academy of Management Journal*, February 1993, pp. 200–14.

49. B. Victor and J.B. Cullen, "The Organizational Bases of Ethical Work Climates," *Administrative Science Quarterly*, March 1988, pp. 101–25; J.B. Cullen, B. Victor, and C. Stephens, "An Ethical Weather Report: Assessing the Organization's Ethical Climate," *Organizational Dynamics*, Autumn 1989, pp. 50–62; Victor and Cullen, "A Theory and Measure of Ethical Climate in Organizations," in Frederick and Preston (eds.) *Business Ethics*, pp. 77–97; and R.R. Sims, "The Challenge of Ethical Behavior in Organizations," *Journal of Business Ethics*, July 1992, pp. 505–13.

50. T.M. Jones, "Ethical Decision Making by Individuals in Organizations: An Issue-Contingent Model," *Academy of Management Review*, April 1991, pp. 366–95.

51. Ibid., pp. 374–78.

52. C.M. Solomon, "Put Your Ethics to a Global Test," *Personnel Journal*, January 1996, pp. 66–74.

53. J.A. Byrne, "The Best-Laid Ethics Programs..." *Business Week*, March 9, 1992, pp. 67–68.

54. Trevino and Youngblood, "Bad Apples in Bad Barrels," p. 384.

55. See, for example, M.C. Matthews, "Codes of Ethics: Organizational Behavior and Misbehavior," in Frederick and Preston (eds.), *Business Ethics*, pp. 99–122.

56. Cited in C. Fredman, "Nationwide Examination of Corporate Consciences," *Working Woman*, December 1991, p. 39.

57. P. Richter, "Big Business Puts Ethics in Spotlight," *Los Angeles Times*, June 19, 1986, p. 29.

58. F.R. David, "An Empirical Study of Codes of Business Ethics: A Strategic Perspective," paper presented at the 48th Annual Academy of Management Conference; Anaheim, California, August 1988.

59. R. Wartzman, "Nature or Nurture? Study Blames Ethical Lapses on Corporate Goals," *Wall Street Journal*, October 9, 1987, p. 27.

60. Ibid.

61. D.R. Cressey and C.A. Moore, "Managerial Values and Corporate Codes of Ethics," *California Management Review*, Summer 1983, p. 71.

62. L. Nash, "Ethics without the Sermon," *Harvard Business Review*, November–December 1981, p. 81.

63. Associated Press, "Cheating Rampant in Workplace, Study Says," *Springfield News Leader*, April 5, 1997, p. A5.

64. T.A. Gavin, "Ethics Education," *Internal Auditor*, April 1989, pp. 54–57.

65. W. Penn and B.D. Collier, "Current Research in Moral Development as a Decision Support System," *Journal of Business Ethics*, January 1985, pp. 131–36.

66. J. Weber, "Measuring the Impact of Teaching Ethics to Future Managers: A Review, Assessment, and Recommendations," *Journal of Business Ethics*, April 1990, pp. 182–90.

67. "Ideas Worth Sharing," *Ethics Today*, Summer 1996, p. 8.

68. See, for instance, S.J. Harrington, "What Corporate America Is Teaching about Ethics"; and P.F. Miller and W.T. Coady, "Teaching Work Ethics," *Education Digest*, February 1990, pp. 54–55.

69. See, for example, A. Stark, "What's the Matter with Business Ethics?" *Harvard Business Review*, May–June 1993, pp. 38–48; "More Big Businesses Set Up Ethics Offices," *Wall Street Journal*, May 10, 1993, p. B1; W.D. Hall, *Making the Right Decision: Ethics for Managers* (New York: John Wiley & Sons, 1993); S. Gaines, "Handing Out Halos," *Business Ethics*, March–April 1994, pp. 20–24; and L.S. Paine, "Managing for Organizational Integrity," *Harvard Business Review*, March–April 1994, pp. 106–17.

70. Associated Press, "Cheating Rampant in Workplace, Study Says" *Springfield News Leader*, April 5, 1997, p. A5; and H. Fountain, "Of White Lies and Yellow Pads," *New York Times*, July 6, 1997, p. F7.

71. D. Kelly, "Cheating Up on Campuses with Honor Codes," *USA Today*, March 11, 1996, p. D1.

Chapter 6

1. P.M. White, "Wonder Women," *Black Enterprise*, April 1997, pp. 115–16.

2. W. Pounds, "The Process of Problem Finding," *Industrial Management Review*, Fall 1969, pp. 1–19.

3. R.J. Volkema, "Problem Formulation: Its Portrayal in the Texts," *Organizational Behavior Teaching Review*, 11, No. 3 (1986–87), pp. 113–26.

4. M.W. McCall Jr. and Robert E. Kaplan, *Whatever It Takes: Decision Makers at Work* (Upper Saddle River, NJ: Prentice Hall, 1985), pp. 36–38.

5. H.A. Simon, *The New Science of Management Decision* (New York: Harper & Row, 1960), p. 1.

6. See H.A. Simon, "Rationality in Psychology and Economics," *Journal of Business,* October 1986, pp. 209–24; and A. Langley, "In Search of Rationality: The Purposes behind the Use of Formal Analysis in Organizations," *Administrative Science Quarterly,* December 1989, pp. 598–631.

7. F.A. Shull Jr., A.L. Delbecq, and L.L. Cummings, *Organizational Decision Making* (New York: McGraw-Hill, 1970), p. 151.

8. See, for example, J.G. March, *A Primer on Decision Making* (New York: Free Press, 1994), pp. 8–25; and A. Langley, H. Mintzberg, P. Pitcher, E. Posada, and J. Saint-Macary, "Opening Up Decision Making: The View from the Black Stool," *Organization Science,* May–June 1995, pp. 260–79.

9. J.G. March, "Decision-Making Perspective: Decisions in Organizations and Theories of Choice," in A.H. Van de Ven and W.F. Joyce (eds.), *Perspectives on Organization Design and Behavior* (New York: Wiley-Interscience, 1981), pp. 232–33.

10. See N.McK. Agnew and J.L. Brown, "Bounded Rationality: Fallible Decisions in Unbounded Decision Space," *Behavioral Science,* July 1986, pp. 148–61; B.E. Kaufman, "A New Theory of Satisficing," *Journal of Behavioral Economics,* Spring 1990, pp. 35–51; and D.R.A. Skidd, "Revisiting Bounded Rationality," *Journal of Management Inquiry,* December 1992, pp. 343–47.

11. See K.R. Hammond, R.M. Hamm, J. Grassia, and T. Pearson, "Direct Comparison of the Efficacy of Intuitive and Analytical Cognition in Expert Judgment," *IEEE Transactions on Systems, Man, and Cybernetics* SMC-17, (1987), pp. 753–70; W.H. Agor (ed.), *Intuition in Organizations* (Newbury Park, CA: Sage Publications, 1989); and O. Behling and N.L. Eckel, "Making Sense Out of Intuition," *The Executive,* February 1991, pp. 46–47.

12. V. Pospisil, "Gut Feeling or Skilled Reasoning?" *IW,* March 3, 1997, p. 12.

13. J.R. Schermerhorn Jr., *Management for Productivity,* 4th ed. (New York: John Wiley & Sons, 1993), p. 150.

14. A.J. Rowe, James D. Boulgarides, and Michael R. McGrath, *Managerial Decision Making,* Modules in Management Series (Chicago: SRA, 1984), pp. 18–22.

15. This box is based on E.F. Jackofsky, J.W. Slocum Jr., and S.J. McQuaid,

"Cultural Values and the CEO: Alluring Companions?" *Academy of Management Executive,* February 1988, pp. 39–49; N. Sumihara, "A Case Study of Cross-Cultural Interaction in a Japanese Multinational Corporation Operating in the United States: Decision-Making Processes and Practices," in R.R. Sims and R.F. Dennehy (eds.), *Diversity and Differences in Organizations: An Agenda for Answers and Questions* (Westport, CT: Quorum Books, 1993), pp. 135–47; S.J. Vitell, S.L. Nwachukwu, and J.H. Barnes, "The Effects of Culture on Ethical Decision-Making: An Application of Hofstede's Typology," *Journal of Business Ethics,* October 1993, pp. 753–60; R.M. Hodgetts and F. Luthans, *International Management,* 2d ed. (New York: McGraw-Hill, 1994), pp. 214–15; and S.P. Robbins, *Organizational Behavior: Concepts, Controversies, and Applications,* 8th ed. (Upper Saddle River, NJ: Prentice Hall, 1998), pp. 116–17.

Chapter 7

1. P. Klebnikov, "Moscow Cowboys," *Forbes,* December 16, 1996, pp. 78–85; and J. Vitullo-Martin, "Moscow Entrepreneurs Seize Golden Opportunity," *Wall Street Journal,* January 20, 1997, p. A14.
2. See, for example, J.A. Pearce II, K.K. Robbins, and R.B. Robinson, Jr., "The Impact of Grand Strategy and Planning Formality on Financial Performance," *Strategic Management Journal,* March–April 1987, pp. 125–34; L.C. Rhyne, "Contrasting Planning Systems in High, Medium, and Low Performance Companies," *Journal of Management Studies,* July 1987, pp. 363–85; J.A. Pearce II, E.B. Freeman, and R.B. Robinson Jr., "The Tenuous Link between Formal Strategic Planning and Financial Performance," *Academy of Management Review,* October 1987, pp. 658–75; D.K. Sinha, "The Contribution of Formal Planning to Decisions," *Strategic Management Journal,* October 1990, pp. 479–92; N. Capon, J.U. Farley, and J.M. Hulbert, "Strategic Planning and Financial Performance: More Evidence," *Journal of Management Studies,* January 1994, pp. 22–38; and C.C. Miller and L.B. Cardinal, "Strategic Planning and Firm Performance: A Synthesis of More Than Two Decades of Research," *Academy of Management Journal,* March 1994, pp. 1649–85.
3. R. Ackoff, "A Concept of Corporate Planning," *Long Range Planning,* September 1970, p. 3.
4. J.D. Hunger and T.L. Wheelen, *Strategic Management,* 5th ed. (Reading, MA: Addison-Wesley, 1996), p. 143.
5. M.B. McCaskey, "A Contingency Approach to Planning: Planning with Goals and Planning without Goals," *Academy of Management Journal,* June 1974, pp. 281–91.
6. Several of these factors were suggested by J.S. Armstrong, "The Value of Formal Planning for Strategic Decisions: Review of Empirical Research," *Strategic Management Journal,* July–September 1982, pp. 197–211; and R.K. Bresser and R.C. Bishop, "Dysfunctional Effects of Formal Planning: Two Theoretical Explanations," *Academy of Management Review,* October 1983, pp. 588–99.
7. R.F. Vancil, "The Accuracy of Long-Range Planning," *Harvard Business Review,* September–October 1970, p. 99.
8. Based on R. Henkoff, "How to Plan for 1995," *Fortune,* December 31, 1990, pp. 70–77.
9. Based on E.E. Spragins, "The Diverse Work Force," *Inc.,* January 1993, p. 33; "The Challenge of Managing Diversity in the Workplace," *Black Enterprise,* July 1993, pp. 79+; D. Elmuti, "Managing Diversity in the Workplace: An Immense Challenge for Both Managers and Workers," *Industrial Management,* July–August 1993, pp. 19–22; B. Jorgensen, "Diversity: Managing a Multicultural Work Force," *Electronic Business Buyer,* September 1993, pp. 70–76; L. Harrington, "Why Managing Diversity Is So Important," *Distribution,* November 1993, pp. 88–92; B. Smith, "Recruitment Insights for Strategic Workforce Diversity," *HR Focus,* January 1994, p. 7; and F. Rice, "How to Make Diversity Pay," *Fortune,* August 8, 1994, pp. 78–86.
10. H. Mintzberg, *The Rise and Fall of Strategic Planning* (New York: Free Press, 1994).
11. S. McKay, "A Paper Tiger in the Paperless World," *Canadian Business,* April 1996, pp. 25–26.
12. Mintzberg, *The Rise and Fall of Strategic Planning.*
13. Ibid.
14. K. Rebello and P. Burrows, "The Fall of an American Icon," *Business Week,* February 5, 1996, pp. 34–42; and "Jobs Assumes Interim CEO Role," *Springfield News Leader,* September 17, 1997, p. A6.
15. G. Hamel and C.K. Prahalad, *Competing for the Future* (Boston: Harvard Business School Press, 1994).
16. J. Moore, "The Death of Competition," *Fortune,* April 15, 1996, pp. 142–43.
17. D. Miller, "The Architecture of Simplicity," *Academy of Management Review,* January 1993, pp. 116–38.
18. R. Molz, "'How Leaders Use Goals," *Long Range Planning,* October 1987, p. 91.
19. S. Chandler, "TWA Is Carrying Some Heavy Baggage," *Business Week,* April 7, 1997, p. 40.
20. Statement found on shipping order form, June 1994.
21. List of goals found in Chili's 1995 annual report, p. 4.
22. See, for instance, C.K. Warriner, "The Problem of Organizational Purpose," *Sociological Quarterly,* Spring 1965, pp. 139–46; and J. Pfeffer, *Organizational Design* (Arlington Heights, IL: AHM Publishing, 1978), pp. 5–12.
23. Ibid.
24. F.D. Tuggle, *Organizational Processes* (Arlington Heights, IL: AHM Publishing, 1978), p. 108.
25. A.W. Schrader and G.T. Seward, "MBO Makes Dollar Sense," *Personnel Journal,* July 1989, pp. 32–37.
26. R. Rodgers and J.E. Hunter, "Impact of Management by Objectives on Organizational Productivity," *Journal of Applied Psychology,* April 1991, pp. 322–36.

Chapter 8

1. J. Kandell, "Italy's Gem of a Giant," *World Business,* September–October 1996, pp. 34–39.
2. See, for example, L.J. Rosenberg and C.D. Schewe, "Strategic Planning: Fulfilling the Promise," *Business Horizons,* July–August 1985, pp. 54–62; W. Kiechel III, "Corporate Strategy for the 1990s," *Fortune,* February 29, 1988, pp. 34–42; A.D. Meyer, "What Is Strategy's Distinctive Competence?" *Journal of Management* 17, No. 4 (1991), pp. 821–33; A. Hiam, "Strategic Planning Unbound," *Journal of Business Strategy,* March–April 1993, pp. 46–52; N. Rajagopalan, A.M.A. Rasheed, and D.K. Datta, "Strategic Decision Processes: Critical Review and Future Directions," *Journal of Management,* Summer 1993, pp. 349–84; and S. Hart and C. Banbury, "How Strategy Making Processes Can Make a Difference," *Strategic Management Journal,* May 1994, pp. 251–69.
3. "A Solid Strategy Helps Companies' Growth," *Nation's Business,* October 1990, p. 10.
4. See, for example, H. Mintzberg, *The Rise and Fall of Strategic Planning* (New York: Free Press, 1994); S.J. Wall and S.R. Wall, "The Evolution (Not the Death) of Strategy," *Organizational Dynamics,* Autumn 1995, pp. 7–19; and J.A. Byrne, "Strategic Planning: It's Back!" *Business Week,* August 26, 1996, pp. 46–52.
5. L.C. Rhyne, "The Relationship of Strategic Planning to Financial Perfor-

mance," *Strategic Management Journal,* 1986, pp. 423–36; E. Mosakowski, "A Resource-Based Perspective on the Dynamic Strategy-Performance Relationship: An Empirical Examination of the Focus and Differentiation Strategies in Entrepreneurial Firms," *Journal of Management,* Winter 1993, pp. 819–39; N. Capon, J.U. Farley, and J.M. Hulbert, "Strategic Planning and Financial Performance: More Evidence," *Journal of Management Studies,* January 1994, pp. 22–38; and C.C. Miller and L.B. Cardinal, "Strategic Planning and Firm Performance: A Synthesis of More Than Two Decades of Research," *Academy of Management Journal,* December 1994, pp. 1649–65.

6. W.H. Miller, "Runyon Delivers a Turnaround," *IW,* February 3, 1997, pp. 44–49; and "E-Stamps Replace Sticking with Clicking," *Springfield News-Leader,* April 1, 1998, p. 12A.

7. W.K. Hall, "SBUs: Hot, New Topic in Management of Diversification," *Business Horizons,* February 1978, p. 17.

8. L. Grant, "Corporate Connections," *U.S. News and World Report,* August 2, 1993, pp. 46–48; and "A Blurred Mission at Sears," in P. Wright, C.D. Pringle, and M.J. Kroll, *Strategic Management* (Boston: Allyn and Bacon, 1994), p. 51.

9. See, for example, M. Li and R.J. Litschert, "Linking Strategy-Making Process and Environment: A Theory," paper presented at the 1993 Academy of Management Meeting, Atlanta, Georgia; D. Marline, B.T. Lamont, and J.J. Hoffman, "Choice Situation, Strategy, and Performance: A Reexamination," *Strategic Management Journal,* March 1994, pp. 229–39; and D. Miller, T.K. Lanta, F.J. Milliken, and H.J. Korn, "The Evolution of Strategic Simplicity: Exploring Two Models of Organizational Adaption," *Journal of Management,* 22, No. 3 (1996), pp. 863–87.

10. C. Brown, "For Cool Old Dudes Only," *Forbes,* August 12, 1996, pp. 81–83.

11. Based on A.C. Cooper et al., *New Business in America: The Firms and Their Owners* (Washington, DC: The NFIB Foundation, 1990), p. 1; J.A. Timmons, *New Venture Creation: Entrepreneurship in the 1990s* (Homewood, IL: Richard D. Irwin, 1990), p. 9; R.H. Brockhaus Sr., "The Psychology of the Entrepreneur," in C.A. Kent, D.L. Sexton, and K.H. Vesper (eds.), *Encyclopedia of Entrepreneurship* (Upper Saddle River, NJ: Prentice Hall, 1982), pp. 41–49; H.H. Stevenson and D.E. Gumpert, "The Heart of Entrepreneurship," *Harvard Business Review,* March–April 1985, pp. 85–94; R.L. Osborne, "Second Phase Entrepreneurship: Breaking Through the

Growth Wall," *Business Horizons,* January–February 1994, pp. 80–86; and B. O'Reilly, "The New Face of Small Business," *Fortune,* May 2, 1994, pp. 82–88.

12. See S.E. Jackson and J.E. Dutton, "Discerning Threats and Opportunities," *Administrative Science Quarterly,* September 1988, pp. 370–87.

13. C.K. Prahalad and G. Hamel, "The Core Competence of the Corporation," *Harvard Business Review,* May–June 1990, pp. 79–91.

14. S. Chandler, "Data Is Power: Just Ask Fingerhut," *Business Week,* June 3, 1996, p. 69.

15. See, for example, J.B. Barney, "Organizational Culture: Can It Be a Source of Sustained Competitive Advantage?" *Academy of Management Review,* July 1986, pp. 656–65; C. Scholz, "Corporate Culture and Strategy—The Problem of Strategic Fit," *Long Range Planning,* August 1987, pp. 78–87; S. Green, "Understanding Corporate Culture and Its Relation to Strategy," *International Studies of Management and Organization,* Summer 1988, pp. 6–28; T. Kono, "Corporate Culture and Long-Range Planning," *Long Range Planning,* August 1990, pp. 9–19; and C.M. Fiol, "Managing Culture as a Competitive Resource: An Identity-Based View of Sustainable Competitive Advantage," *Journal of Management,* March 1991, pp. 191–211.

16. J.P. Kotter and J.L. Heskett, *Corporate Culture and Performance* (New York: Free Press, 1992).

17. Box based on R.J. Lewicki, D.D. Bowen, D.T. Hall, and F.S. Hall, *Experiences in Management and Organizational Behavior,* 3rd ed. (New York: John Wiley & Sons, 1988), pp. 261–67; A. Williams, "Career Planning: Build on Strengths, Strengthen Weaknesses," *The Black Collegian,* September–October 1993, pp. 78–86; C.C. Campbell-Rock, "Career Planning Strategies That Really Work," *The Black Collegian,* September–October 1993, pp. 88–93; B. Kaye, "Career Development—Anytime, Anyplace," *Training and Development,* December 1993, pp. 46–49; W. Wooten, "Using Knowledge, Skill, and Ability (KSA) Data to Identify Career Pathing Oportunities," *Public Personnel Management,* Winter 1993, pp. 551–63; C. Mossop, "Values Assessment: Key to Managing Careers," *CMA—The Management Accounting Magazine,* March 1994, p. 33; and A.D. Pinkney, "Winning in the Workplace," *Essence,* March 1994, pp. 79–80.

18. See W. F. Glueck, *Business Policy: Strategy Formulation and Management Action,* 2d ed. (New York: McGraw-Hill, 1976), pp. 120–47; J.A.

Pearce II, "Selecting among Alternative Grand Strategies," *California Management Review,* Spring 1982, pp. 23–31; and T.T. Herbert and H. Deresky, "Generic Strategies: An Empirical Investigation of Typology Validity and Strategy Content," *Strategic Management Journal,* March–April 1987, pp. 135–47.

19. See, for example, K.R. Harrigan, *Strategies for Declining Businesses* (Lexington, MA: Lexington, 1980); K.S. Cameron, M.U. Kim, and D.A. Whetten, "Organizational Effects of Decline and Turbulence," *Administrative Science Quarterly,* June 1987, pp. 222–40; "Downsizing Record Set by Firms in Year: 56% Report Job Cuts," *Wall Street Journal,* August 12, 1991, p. A2; and K.S. Cameron, S.J. Freeman, and A.K. Mishra, "Best Practices in White-Collar Downsizing: Managing Contradictions," *Academy of Management Executive,* August 1991, pp. 57–73; C.M. Daily, "CEO and Director Turnover in Failing Firms: The Illusion of Change," paper presented at the 1993 Academy of Management Annual Meeting, Atlanta, Georgia; and J.L. Morrow Jr. and L. Busenitz, "Turnaround and Retrenchment in Mature and Growth Industries," paper presented at the 1993 Academy of Management Annual Meeting, Atlanta, Georgia.

20. P. Haspeslagh, "Portfolio Planning: Uses and Limits," *Harvard Business Review,* January–February 1982, pp. 58–73.

21. *Perspective on Experience* (Boston: Boston Consulting Group, 1970).

22. See, for example, D.C. Hambrick, I.C. Macmillan, and D.L. Day, "Strategic Attributes and Performance in the BCG Matrix: A PIMS-Based Analysis of Industrial Product Businesses," *Academy of Management Journal,* September 1982, pp. 510–31. H.K. Christensen, A.C. Cooper, and C.A. DeKluyver, "The Dog Business: A Re-Examination," *Business Horizons,* November–December 1982, pp. 12–18; W. Baldwin, "The Market Share Myth," *Forbes,* March 14, 1983, pp. 109–15; R.A. Bettis and W.K. Hall, "The Business Portfolio Approach—Where It Falls Down in Practice," *Long Range Planning,* April 1983, pp. 95–104; and J. Fierman, "How to Make Money in Mature Markets," *Fortune,* November 25, 1985, pp. 47–53.

23. R. Rumelt, "Towards a Strategic Theory of the Firm," in R. Lamb (ed.), *Competitive Strategic Management* (Upper Saddle River, NJ: Prentice Hall, 1984), pp. 556–70; M.E. Porter, *Competitive Advantage: Creating and Sustaining Superior Performance* (New

York: Free Press, 1985); J. Barney, "Firm Resources and Sustained Competitive Advantage," *Journal of Management* 17, No. 1 (1991), pp. 99–120; M.A. Peteraf, "The Cornerstones of Competitive Advantage: A Resource-Based View," *Strategic Management Journal,* March 1993, pp. 179–91; and J.B. Barney, "Looking Inside for Competitive Advantage," *Academy of Management Executive,* November 1995, pp. 49–61.

24. T.C. Powell, "Total Quality Management as Competitive Advantage: A Review and Empirical Study," *Strategic Management Journal,* January 1995, pp. 15–37.

25. See R.J. Schonenberger, "Is Strategy Strategic? Impact of Total Quality Management on Strategy," *Academy of Management Executive,* August 1992, pp. 80–87; C.A. Barclay, "Quality Strategy and TQM Policies: Empirical Evidence," *Management International Review,* Special Issue 1993, pp. 87–98; T.E. Benson, "A Business Strategy Comes of Age," *Industry Week,* May 3, 1993, pp. 40–44; R. Jacob, "TQM: More Than a Dying Fad?" *Fortune,* October 18, 1993, pp. 66–72; R. Krishnan, A.B. Shani, R.M. Grant, and R. Baer, "In Search of Quality Improvement Problems of Design and Implementation," *Academy of Management Executive,* November 1993, pp. 7–20; B. Voss, "Quality's Second Coming," *Journal of Business Strategy,* March–April 1994, pp. 42–46; M. Barrier, "Raising TQM Consciousness," *Nation's Business,* April 1994, pp. 62–64; and special issue of *Academy of Management Review* devoted to TQM, July 1994, pp. 390–584.

26. "Quality Happens through People," *Fortune,* 11th Annual Quality Section, September 18, 1995, pp. S5–S6.

27. M. Barrier, "Learning the Meaning of Measurement," *Nation's Business,* June 1994, pp. 72–74.

28. See, for example, M.E. Porter, *Competitive Strategy: Techniques for Analyzing Industries and Competitors* (New York: Free Press, 1980); Porter, *Competitive Advantage: Creating and Sustaining Superior Performance*; G.G. Dess and P.S. Davis, "Porter's (1980) Generic Strategies as Determinants of Strategic Group Membership and Organizational Performance," *Academy of Management Journal,* September 1984, pp. 467–88; Dess and Davis, "Porter's (1980) Generic Strategies and Performance: An Empirical Examination with American Data—Part I: Testing Porter," *Organization Studies,* No. 1 (1986), pp. 37–55; Dess and Davis, "Porter's (1980) Generic Strategies and Performance: An Empirical

Examination with American Data—Part II: Performance Implications," *Organization Studies,* No. 3 (1986), pp. 255–61; M.E. Porter, "From Competitive Advantage to Corporate Strategy," *Harvard Business Review,* May–June 1987, pp. 43–59; A.I. Murray, "A Contingency View of Porter's 'Generic Strategies,'" *Academy of Management Review,* July 1988, pp. 390–400; C.W.L. Hill, "Differentiation versus Low Cost or Differentiation and Low Cost: A Contingency Framework," *Academy of Management Review,* July 1988, pp. 401–12; I. Bamberger, "Developing Competitive Advantage in Small and Medium-Sized Firms," *Long Range Planning,* October 1989, pp. 80–88; and D.F. Jennings and J.R. Lumpkin, "Insights between Environmental Scanning Activities and Porter's Generic Strategies: An Empirical Analysis," *Strategic Management Journal,* 18, No. 4 (1992), pp. 791–803.

29. D. Miller and J. Toulouse, "Strategy, Structure, CEO Personality, and Performance in Small Firms," *American Journal of Small Business,* Winter 1986, pp. 47–62.

30. Hill, "Differentiation versus Low Cost or Differentiation and Low Cost"; R.E. White, "Organizing to Make Business Unit Strategies Work," in H.E. Glass (ed.), *Handbook of Business Strategy,* 2d ed. (Boston: Warren Gorham and Lamont, 1991), pp. 24.1–24.14; D. Miller, "The Generic Strategy Trap," *Journal of Business Strategy,* January–February 1991, pp. 37–41; and S. Cappel, P. Wright, M. Kroll, and D. Wyld, "Competitive Strategies and Business Performance: An Empirical Study of Select Service Businesses," *International Journal of Management,* March 1992, pp. 1–11.

C h a p t e r   9

1. S. Sansoni, "Fashion Renegade," *Forbes,* March 10, 1997, p. 72.

2. S.C. Jain, "Environmental Scanning in U.S. Corporations," *Long Range Planning,* April 1984, pp. 117–28; see also L.M. Fuld, *Monitoring the Competition* (New York: John Wiley & Sons, 1988); E.H. Burack and N.J. Mathys, "Environmental Scanning Improves Strategic Planning," *Personnel Administrator,* April 1989, pp. 82–87; J.B. Thomas, S.M. Clark, and D.A. Gioia, "Strategic Sensemaking and Organizational Performance: Linkages among Scanning, Interpretation, Action, and Outcomes," *Academy of Management Journal,* April 1993, pp. 239–70; R. Subramanian, N. Fernandes, and E. Harper, "Environmental Scanning in U.S. Companies: Their Nature and

Their Relationship to Performance," *Management International Review,* July 1993, pp. 271–86; and B.K. Boyd and J. Fulk, "Executive Scanning and Perceived Uncertainty: A Multidimensional Model," *Journal of Management,* 22 No. 1 (1996) pp. 1–21.

3. M. Schuman, "Thin Is Out, Fat Is In," *Forbes,* May 9, 1994, pp. 92–94.

4. W.L. Renfro and J.L. Morrison, "Detecting Signals of Change," *The Futurist,* August 1984, p. 49.

5. B. Gilad, "The Role of Organized Competitive Intelligence in Corporate Strategy," *Columbia Journal of World Business,* Winter 1989, pp. 29–35; B.D. Gelb, M. J. Saxton, G.M. Zinkhan, and N.D. Albers, "Competitive Intelligence Insights from Executives," *Business Horizons,* January–February 1991, pp. 43–47; L. Fuld, "A Recipe for Business Intelligence," *Journal of Business Strategy,* January–February 1991, pp. 12–17; G.B. Roush, "A Program for Sharing Corporate Intelligence," *Journal of Business Strategy,* January–February 1991, pp. 4–7; J.P. Herring, "The Role of Intelligence in Formulating Strategy," *Journal of Business Strategy,* September–October 1992, pp. 54–60; R.S. Teitelbaum, "The New Role for Intelligence," *Fortune,* November 2, 1992, pp. 104–07; and K. Western, "Ethical Spying," *Business Ethics,* September–October 1995, pp. 22–23.

6. S. Crock, G. Smith, J. Weber, R. Melcher, and L. Himelstein, "They Snoop to Conquer," *Business Week,* October 28, 1996, pp. 172–76.

7. B. Ettore, "Managing Competitive Intelligence," *Management Review,* October 1995, pp. 15–19.

8. Western, "Ethical Spying."

9. W.H. Davidson, "The Role of Global Scanning in Business Planning," *Organizational Dynamics,* Winter 1991, pp. 5–16.

10. M. Werner, "Planning for Uncertain Futures: Building Commitment through Scenario Planning," *Business Horizons,* May–June 1990, pp. 55–58.

11. J.W. Verity, "Clearing the Cobwebs from the Stockroom," *Business Week,* October 21, 1996, p. 140.

12. See J.K. Glassman, "The Year of Gazing Dangerously," *Business Month,* March 1990, pp. 13–14; A.B. Fisher, "Is Long-Range Planning Worth It?" *Fortune,* April 23, 1990, pp. 281–84; J.A. Fraser, "On Target," *Inc.,* April 1991, pp. 113–14; P. Schwartz, *The Art of the Long View* (New York: Doubleday/Currency, 1991); S. Davis, "Twenty Tips for Developing 20/20 Vision for Business," *Journal of Management Development,* September 1993, pp. 15–20; and G. Hamel and C.K. Praha-

lad, "Competing for the Future," *Harvard Business Review,* July–August 1994, pp. 122–28.

13. P.N. Pant and W.H. Starbuck, "Innocents in the Forest: Forecasting and Research Methods," *Journal of Management,* June 1990, pp. 433–60.

14. This section is based on A. Weimer, "Benchmarking Maps the Route to Quality," *Industry Week,* July 20, 1992, pp. 54–55; J. Main, "How to Steal the Best Ideas Around," *Fortune,* October 19, 1992, pp. 102–06; H. Rothman, "You Need Not Be Big to Benchmark," *Nation's Business,* December 1992, pp. 64–65; Y.K. Shetty, "Benchmarking for Superior Performance," *Long Range Planning* 1, (April 1993) pp. 39–44; G.H. Watson, "How Process Benchmarking Supports Corporate Strategy," *Planning Review,* January–February 1993, pp. 12–15; N. Banerjee, "Firms Analyze Rivals to Help Fix Themselves," *Wall Street Journal,* May 3, 1994, p. B1+; S. George and A. Weimerskirch, *Total Quality Management: Strategies and Techniques Proven at Today's Most Successful Companies* (New York: John Wiley & Sons, 1994), pp. 207–21; S. Greengard, "Discover Best Practices," *Personnel Journal,* November 1995, pp. 62–73; and J. Martin, "Are You as Good as You Think You Are?" *Fortune,* September 30, 1996, pp. 142–52.

15. See H.E. Fearon, W.A. Ruch, V.G. Reuter, C.D. Wieters, and R.R. Reck, *Fundamentals of Production/Operations Management,* 3rd ed. (St. Paul, MN: West Publishing, 1986), p. 97.

16. For a discussion of software and application to a project for restructuring a large retail chain, see P.A. Strassman, "The Best-Laid Plans," *Inc.,* October 1988, pp. 135–88; also see, D.L. Kimbler, "Operational Planning: Going Beyond PERT with TQM Tools," *Industrial Management,* September–October 1993, pp. 26–29.

17. See, for example, S. Stiansen, "Breaking Even," *Success,* November 1988, p. 16.

18. S.E. Barndt and D.W. Carvey, *Essentials of Operations Management* (Upper Saddle River, NJ: Prentice Hall, 1982), p. 134.

19. E.E. Adam Jr. and R.J. Ebert, *Production and Operations Management,* 5th ed. (Upper Saddle River, NJ: Prentice Hall, 1992), p. 333.

20. See, for instance, J.W. Weiss and R.K. Wysocki, *5-Phase Project Management* (Reading, MA: Addison-Wesley, 1992), p. 3.

21. This discussion is based on R.S. Russell and B.W. Taylor III, *Production and Operations Management* (Upper Saddle River, NJ: Prentice Hall, 1995), p. 827.

Chapter 10

1. G.B. Knight, "How Wall Street Whiz Found a Niche Selling Books on the Internet," *Wall Street Journal,* May 16, 1996, pp. A1+; K. Rebello, "A Literary Hangout—Without the Latte," *Business Week,* September 23, 1996, p. 106; M.H. Martin, "The Next Big Thing: A Bookstore?" *Fortune,* December 9, 1996, pp. 168–70; M. Slovan, "Bound for the Internet," *Nation's Business,* March 1997, pp. 34–35; and M. Krantz, "Amazonian Challenge," *Time,* April 14, 1997, p. 71.

2. See, for example, R.L. Daft, *Organization Theory and Design,* 6th ed. (St. Paul, MN: West Publishing, 1998).

3. This section based on J.A. Byrne, "The McKinsey Mystique," *Business Week,* September 20, 1993, p. 70; B. Dumaine, "Payoff from the New Management," *Fortune,* December 13, 1993, pp. 103–10; Byrne, "The Horizontal Corporation," *Business Week,* December 20, 1993, pp. 76–81; R. Semler, "Why My Former Employees Still Work for Me," *Harvard Business Review,* January–February 1994, pp. 64–74; R.A. Lutz, "Implementing Technological Change with Cross-Functional Teams," *Research-Technology Management,* March–April 1994, pp. 14–18; and G.M. Parker, *Cross-Functional Teams* (San Francisco: Jossey-Bass, 1994).

4. For a discussion of authority, see W.A. Kahn and K.E. Kram, "Authority at Work: Internal Models and Their Organizational Consequences," *Academy of Management Review,* January 1994, pp. 17–50.

5. L. Urwick, *The Elements of Administration* (New York: Harper & Row, 1944), pp. 52–53.

6. D. Van Fleet, "Span of Management Research and Issues," *Academy of Management Journal,* September 1983, pp. 546–52.

7. R. Gibson, "Interstate Bakeries Is Able to Mine Profit from a Golden Cake," *Wall Street Journal,* January 31, 1997, pp. A1+.

8. A. Ross, "BMO's Big Bang," *Canadian Business,* January 1994, pp. 58–63.

9. See, for example, H. Mintzberg, *Power In and Around Organizations* (Upper Saddle River, NJ: Prentice Hall, 1983); J. Child, *Organization: A Guide to Problems and Practices* (London: Kaiser & Row, 1984).

10. T. Burns and G.M. Stalker, *The Management of Innovation* (London: Tavistock, 1961); and D.A. Morand, "The Role of Behavioral Formality and Informality in the Enactment of Bureaucratic versus Organic Organizations," *Academy of Management Review,* October 1995, pp. 831–72.

11. A.D. Chandler, Jr., *Strategy and Structure: Chapters in the History of the Industrial Enterprise* (Cambridge, MA: MIT Press, 1962).

12. See, for instance, R.E. Miles and C.C. Snow, *Organizational Strategy, Structure, and Process* (New York: McGraw-Hill, 1978); D. Miller, "The Structural and Environmental Correlates of Business Strategy," *Strategic Management Journal,* January–February 1987, pp. 55–76; H.L. Boschken, "Strategy and Structure: Reconceiving the Relationship," *Journal of Management,* March 1990, pp. 135–50; H.A. Simon, "Strategy and Organizational Evolution," *Strategic Management Journal,* January 1993, pp. 131–42; R. Parthasarthy and S.P. Sethi, "Relating Strategy and Structure to Flexible Automation: A Test of Fit and Performance Implications," *Strategic Management Journal,* 14, no. 6 (1993), pp. 529–49; D.C. Galunic and K.M. Eisenhardt, "Renewing the Strategy-Structure-Performance Paradigm," in B.M. Staw and L.L. Cummings, (eds.) *Research in Organizational Behavior,* vol. 16 (Greenwich, CT: JAI Press, 1994), pp. 215–55; and D. Jennings and S. Seaman, "High and Low Levels of Organizational Adaptation: An Empirical Analysis of Strategy, Structure, and Performance," *Strategic Management Journal,* July 1994, pp. 459–75.

13. See, for instance, P.M. Blau and R.A. Schoenherr, *The Structure of Organizations* (New York: Basic Books, 1971); D.S. Pugh, "The Aston Program of Research: Retrospect and Prospect," in A.H. Van de Ven and W.F. Joyce (eds.), *Perspectives on Organization Design and Behavior* (New York: John Wiley, 1981), pp. 135–66; and R.Z. Gooding and J.A. Wagner III, "A Meta-Analytic Review of the Relationship between Size and Performance: The Productivity and Efficiency of Organizations and Their Subunits," *Administrative Science Quarterly,* December 1985, pp. 462–81.

14. J. Woodward, *Industrial Organization: Theory and Practice* (London: Oxford University Press, 1965).

15. C.C. Miller, W.H. Glick, Y.-D. Wang, and G. Huber, "Understanding Technology-Structure Relationships: Theory Development and Meta-Analytic Theory Testing," *Academy of Management Journal,* June 1991, pp. 370–99.

16. See, for instance, C. Perrow, "A Framework for the Comparative Analysis of Organizations," *American Sociological Review,* April 1967, pp. 194–208; J.D. Thompson, *Organizations in Action* (New York: McGraw-Hill, 1967); J. Hage and M. Aiken,

"Routine Technology, Social Structure, and Organizational Goals," *Administrative Science Quarterly*, September 1969, pp. 366–77; and Miller et al., "Understanding Technology-Structure Relationships."

17. D. Gerwin, "Relationships between Structure and Technology," in P.C. Nystrom and W.H. Starbuck (eds.), *Handbook of Organizational Design*, vol. 2 (New York: Oxford University Press, 1981), pp. 3–38; and D.M. Rousseau and R.A. Cooke, "Technology and Structure: The Concrete, Abstract, and Activity Systems of Organizations," *Journal of Management*, Fall–Winter 1984, pp. 345–61.

18. F.E. Emery and E. Trist, "The Causal Texture of Organizational Environments," *Human Relations*, February 1965, pp. 21–32; P. Lawrence and J.W. Lorsch, *Organization and Environment: Managing Differentiation and Integration* (Boston: Harvard Business School, Division of Research, 1967); and M. Yasai-Ardekani, "Structural Adaptations to Environments," *Academy of Management Review*, January 1986, pp. 9–21.

19. H. Mintzberg, *Structure in Fives: Designing Effective Organizations* (Upper Saddle River, NJ: Prentice Hall, 1983), p. 157.

20. Based on F.L. Fry, *Entrepreneurship: A Planning Approach* (Minneapolis–St. Paul: West Publishing, 1993), pp. 319–40; R.L. Osborne, "Second Phase Entrepreneurship: Breaking through the Growth Wall," *Business Horizons*, January–February 1994, pp. 80–86; R. Cammarano, "The Four Stages of Growth," *Nation's Business*, June 1994, pp. 64–65; and J.G. Longenecker, C.W. Moore, and J.W. Petty, *Small Business Management* (Cincinnati: South-Western Publishing, 1994), pp. 421–25.

21. R.J. Williams, J.J. Hoffman, and B.T. Lamont, "The Influence of Top Management Team Characteristics on M-Form Implementation Time," *Journal of Managerial Issues*, Winter 1995, pp. 466–80.

22. See, for example, R.E. Hoskisson, C.W.L. Hill, and H. Kim, "The Multidivisional Structure: Organizational Fossil or Source of Value?" *Journal of Management* 19, No. 2 (1993) pp. 269–98; I.I. Mitroff, R.O. Mason, and C.M. Pearson, "Radical Surgery: What Will Tomorrow's Organizations Look Like?" *Academy of Management Executive*, February 1994, pp. 11–21; T. Clancy, "Radical Surgery: A View from the Operating Theater," *Academy of Management Executive*, February 1994, pp. 73–78; E. Pinchot and G. Pinchot, *The End of Bureaucracy and the Rise*

of the Intelligent Organization (San Francisco: Berrett-Koehler Publishers, 1994); T. Peters, "Crazy Times Call for Crazy Organizations," *Success*, July–August 1994, pp. 24A+; and T.H. Davenport and J.E.K. Delano, "On Tomorrow's Organizations: Moving Forward, or A Step Backwards?", *Academy of Management Executive*, August 1994, pp. 93–98.

23. See, for example, H. Rothman, "The Power of Empowerment," *Nation's Business*, June 1993, pp. 49–52; B. Dumaine, "Payoff from the New Management"; J.A. Byrne, "The Horizontal Corporation," and J.R. Katzenbach and D.K. Smith, in *The Wisdom of Teams* (Boston: Harvard Business School Press, 1993); L. Grant, "New Jewel in the Crown," *U.S. News & World Report*, February 28, 1994, pp. 55–57; D. Ray and H. Bronstein, *Teaming Up: Making the Transition to a Self-Directed Team-Based Organization* (New York: McGraw Hill, 1995); and D.R. Denison, S.L. Hart, and J.A. Kahn, "From Chimneys to Cross-Functional Teams: Developing and Validating a Diagnostic Model," *Academy of Management Journal*, December 1996, pp. 1005–23.

24. P. LaBarre, "This Organization Is Dis-Organization," *Fast Company Web Page* <http://www.fastcompany.com>, April 16, 1997.

25. T.A. Stewart, "The Corporate Jungle Spawns a New Species: The Project Manager," *Fortune*, July 10, 1995, pp. 179–80.

26. W.E. Halal, "From Hierarchy to Enterprise: Internal Markets Are the New Foundation of Management," *Academy of Management Executive*, November 1994, pp. 69–83; and J.S. DeMott, "Managing Bigness," *World Business*, September–October 1996, pp. 30–33.

27. Cited in *At Work*, May–June 1993, p. 3.

28. M.F.R. Kets deVries, "Making a Giant Dance," *Across the Board*, October 1994, pp. 27–32.

29. H. Kahalas and K. Suchon, "Managing a Perpetual Idea Machine: Inside the Creator's Mind," *The Executive*, May 1995, pp. 57–66; and N. Alster, "Making the Kids Stand on Their Own," *Forbes*, October 9, 1995, pp. 49–56.

30. See, for example, G.G. Dess, A.M.A. Rasheed, K.J. McLaughlin, and R.L. Priem, "The New Corporate Architecture," *Academy of Management Executive*, August, 1995, pp. 7–20.

31. For additional readings on boundaryless organizations, see "The Boundaryless Organization: Break the Chains of Organizational Structures," *HR Focus*, April 1996, p. 21; R.M. Hodgetts, "A Conversation with Steve Kerr," *Organizational*

Dynamics, Spring 1996, pp. 68–79; and J. Gebhardt, "The Boundaryless Organization," *Sloan Management Review*, Winter 1996, pp. 117–19. For another view of boundaryless organizations, see B. Victor, "The Dark Side of the New Organizational Forms: An Editorial Essay," *Organization Science*, November 1994, pp. 479–82.

32. R.W. Keidel, "Rethinking Organizational Design," *Academy of Management Executive*, November 1994, pp. 12–27; R. Ashkenas, D. Ulrich, T. Jick, and S. Kerr, *The Boundaryless Organization: Breaking the Chains of Organization Structure* (San Francisco: Jossey–Bass, 1995); P. LaBarre, "The Seamless Enterprise," *IW*, June 19, 1995, pp. 22–34; G.G. Dess and others, *Academy of Management Executive*, August 1995; D. Ulrich and S. Kerr, "Creating the Boundaryless Organization: The Radical Reconstruction of Organization Capabilities," *Planning Review*, September–October 1995, pp. 41–45; and A. Majchrzak and Q. Wang, "Breaking the Functional Mind-Set in Process Organizations," *Harvard Business Review*, September–October 1996, pp. 93–99.

33. Labarre, "The Seamless Enterprise," p. 22.

34. T. Peters, "Successful Electronic Changeovers Depend on Daring," *Springfield Business Journal*, August 8, 1994, p. 15; and W. C. Taylor, "At Verifone It's a Dog's Life (and They Love It!)," *Fast Company Web Page* <http://www.fastcompany.com>, April 16, 1997.

35. Based on J.A. Fraser, "Women, Power, and the New GE," *Working Woman*, December 1992, pp. 58+; S.P. Robbins, *Organizational Behavior: Concepts, Controversies, and Applications*, 7th ed. (Upper Saddle River, N.J.: Prentice Hall, 1996), pp. 567–68; "Mother Nurture," *Wall Street Journal*, August 23, 1994, p. A1; and M. Maier, "Confronting the (F)laws of the Pyramid: The Enduring Legacy of the Space Shuttle *Challenger* Disaster," *Academy of Management Proceedings on Disk*, 1996.

36. P.M. Senge, *The Fifth Discipline: The Art and Practice of Learning Organizations* (New York: Doubleday, 1990).

37. J.M. Liedtka, "Collaborating across Lines of Business for Competitive Advantage," *Academy of Management Executive*, April 1996, pp. 20–37; and G. Szulanski, "Exploring Internal Stickiness: Impediments to the Transfer of Best Practice within the Firm," *Strategic Management Journal*, Winter Special Issue, 1996, pp. 27–43.

38. See, for example, R. Hotch, "Communications Revolution," *Nation's Busi-*

ness, May 1993, pp. 20–28; and L. Rout (ed.), "The Corporate Connection," *Wall Street Journal Special Reports*, November 18, 1996, pp. R1–R34.

39. K.C. Laudon and J.P. Laudon, *Essentials of Management Information Systems* (Upper Saddle River, NJ: Prentice Hall, 1995), p. 234.

40. See, for example, A.L. Sprout, "The Internet inside Your Company," *Fortune*, November 27, 1995, pp. 161–68; A. Cortese, "Here Comes the Intranet," *Business Week*, February 26, 1996, pp. 76–84; G. Taninecz, "The Web Within," *IW*, March 4, 1996, pp. 45–51; Rout (ed.), *Wall Street Journal Special Reports*; and M.J. Cronin, "Intranets Reach the Factory Floor," *Fortune*, August 18, 1997, p. 208.

41. B. Ziegler, "Building a Wireless Future," *Business Week*, April 5, 1993, p. 57.

Chapter 11

1. V. Reitman, "Cramming for the Exotic U.S. Workplace," *Wall Street Journal*, July 9, 1996, p. A14.

2. K. Brennan and V. Pospisil, "Changing Role for HR," *IW*, February 3, 1997, p. 12.

3. P.M. Wright and G.C. McMahan, "Theoretical Perspectives for Strategic Human Resource Management," *Journal of Management* 18, No. 1 (1992), pp. 295–320; A.A. Lado and M.C. Wilson, "Human Resource Systems and Sustained Competitive Advantage," *Academy of Management Review*, October 1994, pp. 699–727; and J. Pfeffer, *Competitive Advantage Through People* (Boston: Harvard Business School Press, 1994).

4. J.B. Arthur, "Effects of Human Resource Systems on Manufacturing Performance and Turnover," *Academy of Management Journal*, June 1994, pp. 670–87; M.A. Huselid, "The Impact of Human Resource Management Practices on Turnover, Productivity, and Corporate Financial Performance," *Academy of Management Journal*, June 1995, pp. 635–72; M.J. Koch and R.G. McGrath, "Improving Labor Productivity: Human Resource Management Policies Do Matter," *Strategic Management Journal*, May 1996, pp. 335–54; B. Becker and B. Gerhart, "The Impact of Human Resource Management on Organizational Performance: Progress and Prospects," *Academy of Management Journal*, August 1996, pp. 779–801; M.A. Youndt, S.A. Snell, J.W. Dean, Jr., and D.P. Lepak, "Human Resource Management, Manufacturing Strategy, and Firm Performance," *Academy of Management Journal*, August 1996, pp. 836–66; J.T. Delaney and M.A. Huselid, "The Impact of Human Resource Management Practices on Perceptions of Organizational Performance," *Academy of Management Journal*, August 1996, pp. 949–69; and M.A. Huselid, S.E. Jackson, and R.S. Schuler, "Technical and Strategic Human Resource Management Effectiveness as Determinants of Firm Performance," *Academy of Management Journal*, January 1997, pp. 171–88.

5. Huselid, "The Impact of Human Resource Management Practices on Turnover, Productivity, and Corporate Financial Performance."

6. See, for example, M.A. Verespej, "Partnership in the Trenches," *Industry Week*, October 17, 1988, pp. 56–64; "Unions and Management Are in a Family Way," *U.S. News & World Report*, June 12, 1989, p. 24; T.A. Kochan, "Toward a Mutual Gains Paradigm for Labor-Management Relations," *Labor Law Journal*, August 1993, pp. 454–64; and A. Bernstein, "Why America Needs Unions, But Not the Kind It Has Now," *Business Week*, May 23, 1994, pp. 70–82.

7. J. Worsham, "Labor's New Assault," *Nation's Business*, June 1997, pp. 16–23.

8. "Foreign Labor Trends—Germany," U.S. Department of Labor, 1994–1995; "Foreign Labor Trends—Japan," U.S. Department of Labor, 1994–1995; and "Foreign Labor Trends—Mexico," U.S. Department of Labor, 1995–1996.

9. P. Fritsch, A. Sullivan, and R. Sharpe, "Texaco to Pay $176.1 Million in Bias Suit," *Wall Street Journal*, November 18, 1996, p. A3+.

10. L.M. Litvan, "OSHA Sharply Increases Fines for Serious Safety Violations," *Nation's Business*, September 1994, p. 8.

11. E.H. Burack, "Corporate Business and Human Resource Planning Practices: Strategic Issues and Concerns," *Organizational Dynamics*, Summer 1986, pp. 73–87.

12. T.J. Bergmann and M.S. Taylor, "College Recruitment: What Attracts Students to Organizations?" *Personnel*, May–June 1984, pp. 34–46; and A.S. Bargerstock and G. Swanson, "Four Ways to Build Cooperative Recruitment Alliances," *HRMagazine*, March 1991, p. 49.

13. J.R. Gordon, *Human Resource Management: A Practical Approach* (Boston: Allyn and Bacon, 1986), p. 170.

14. See, for example, J.P. Kirnan, J.E. Farley, and K.F. Geisinger, "The Relationship between Recruiting Source, Applicant Quality, and Hire Performance: An Analysis by Sex, Ethnicity, and Age," *Personnel Psychology*, Summer 1989, pp. 293–308.

15. J. Spiers, "Upper Middle Class Woes," *Fortune*, December 27, 1993, p. 80; and M. London, "Redeployment and Continuous Learning in the 21st Century: Hard Lessons and Positive Examples from the Downsizing Era," *Academy of Management Executive*, November 1996, pp. 67–79.

16. See, for example, L. Greenhalgh, A.T. Lawrence, and R.I. Sutton, "Determinants of Work Force Reduction Strategies in Declining Organizations," *Academy of Management Review*, April 1988, pp. 241–54.

17. This story was directly influenced by a similar example in A. Sloane, *Personnel: Managing Human Resources* (Upper Saddle River, NJ: Prentice Hall, 1983), p. 127.

18. J.J. Asher, "The Biographical Item: Can It Be Improved?" *Personnel Psychology*, Summer 1972, p. 266.

19. G.W. England, *Development and Use of Weighted Application Blanks*, rev. ed. (Minneapolis: Industrial Relations Center, University of Minnesota, 1971).

20. J. Aberth, "Pre-Employment Testing Is Losing Favor," *Personnel Journal*, September 1986, pp. 96–104.

21. C. Lee, "Testing Makes a Comeback," *Training*, December 1988, pp. 49–59.

22. Ibid., p. 50.

23. E.E. Ghiselli, "The Validity of Aptitude Tests in Personnel Selection," *Personnel Psychology*, Winter 1973, p. 475.

24. G. Grimsley and H.F. Jarrett, "The Relation of Managerial Achievement to Test Measures Obtained in the Employment Situation: Methodology and Results," *Personnel Psychology*, Spring 1973, pp. 31–48; and A.K. Korman, "The Prediction of Managerial Performance: A Review," *Personnel Psychology*, Summer 1986, pp. 295–322.

25. I.T. Robertson and R.S. Kandola, "Work Sample Tests: Validity, Adverse Impact, and Applicant Reaction," *Journal of Occupational Psychology*, 55, No. 3 (1982), pp. 171–83.

26. G.C. Thornton, *Assessment Centers in Human Resource Management* (Reading, MA: Addison-Wesley, 1992).

27. R.L. Dipboye, *Selection Interviews: Process Perspectives* (Cincinnati: South-Western Publishing, 1992), p. 6.

28. See, for instance, R.D. Arveny and J.E. Campion, "The Employment Interview: A Summary and Review of Recent Research," *Personnel Psychology*, Summer 1982, pp. 281–322; and M.M. Harris, "Reconsidering the Employment Interview: A Review of Recent Literature and Suggestions for

Future Research," *Personnel Psychology*, Winter 1989, pp. 691–726.

29. Dipboye, *Selection Interviews*, p. 180.

30. See, for instance, Arveny and Campion, "The Employment Interview"; M.D. Hakel, "Employment Interview," in K.M. Rowland and G.R. Ferris (eds.), *Personnel Management: New Perspectives* (Boston: Allyn and Bacon, 1982), pp. 192–255; E.C. Webster, *The Employment Interview: A Social Judgment Process* (Schomberg, ON: S.I.P. Publications, 1982); Harris, "Reconsidering the Employment Interview"; A.P. Phillips and R.L. Dipboye, "Correlational Tests of Predictions from a Process Model of the Interview," *Journal of Applied Psychology*, February 1989, pp. 41–52; H.G. Baker and M.S. Spier, "The Employment Interview: Guaranteed Improvement in Reliability," *Public Personnel Management*, Spring 1990, pp. 85–87; and R.C. Liden, C.L. Martin, and C.K. Parsons, "Interviewer and Applicant Behavior in Employment Interviews," *Academy of Management Journal*, April 1993, pp. 372–86.

31. *Human Resource Management: Ideas and Trends* (Commerce Clearing House, May 17, 1992), p. 85.

32. N.D. Bates, "Understanding the Liability of Negligent Hiring," *Security Management Supplement*, July 1990, p. 7A.

33. P.M. Muchinsky, "The Use of Reference Reports in Personnel Selection: A Review and Evaluation," *Journal of Occupational Psychology*, April 1979, pp. 187–97; R.R. Reilly and G.T. Chao, "Validity and Fairness of Some Alternative Employee Selection Procedures," *Personnel Psychology*, Spring 1982, pp. 1–62; and S. Adler, "Verifying a Job Candidate's Background: The State of Practice in a Vital Human Resources Activity," *Review of Business*, Winter 1993, pp. 3–8.

34. Cited in "If You Can't Say Something Nice…," *Wall Street Journal*, March 4, 1988, p. 25.

35. E.C. Mayfield and N. Schmitt, "Social and Situational Determinants of Interview Decisions: Implications for Employment Interviews," *Personnel Psychology*, Spring 1976, p. 81.

36. V. Meyer, "Welcoming New Hires with a Buddy System," *Business Ethics*, May–June 1996, p. 56.

37. S.L. Robinson, M.S. Kraatz, and D.M. Rousseau, "Changing Obligations and the Psychological Contract: A Longitudinal Study," *Academy of Management Journal*, February 1994, pp. 137–52.

38. Cited in "The Five Factors That Make for Airline Accidents," *Fortune*, May 22, 1989, p. 80.

39. 16th Annual Survey, *Training*, October 1997, p. 36.

40. See, for example, J.C. Szabo, "Boosting Workers' Basic Skills," *Nation's Business*, January 1992, pp. 38–40; and R. Henkoff, "Companies That Train Best," *Fortune*, March 22, 1993, pp. 20–25.

41. M.P. Cronin, "Training: Asking Workers What They Want," *Inc.*, August 1994, p. 103.

42. J. Misitano, "They Have Fun Too," *Progressive Grocer*, May 1994, pp. 135–39.

43. L. Therrien, "Retooling American Workers," *Business Week*, September 27, 1993, pp. 76–81.

44. Based on V.A. Parker and K.E. Kram, "Women Mentoring Women: Creating Conditions for Connection," *Business Horizons*, March–April 1993, pp. 42–51; H. Rothman, "The Boss as Mentor," *Nation's Business*, April 1993, pp. 66–67; J.B. Cunningham and T. Eberle, "Characteristics of the Mentoring Experience: A Qualitative Study," *Personnel Review*, June 1993, pp. 54–66; W.T. Whitely and P. Coetsier, "The Relationship of Career Mentoring to Early Career Outcomes," *Organization Studies*, Summer 1993, pp. 419–41; S. Crandell, "The Joys of Mentoring," *Executive Female*, March–April 1994, pp. 38–42; and W. Heery, "Corporate Mentoring Can Break the Glass Ceiling," *HR Focus*, May 1994, pp. 17–18.

45. D.E. Super and D.T. Hall, "Career Development: Exploration and Planning," in M.R. Rosenzweig and L.W. Porter (eds.), *Annual Review of Psychology*, vol. 29 (Palo Alto, CA: Annual Reviews, 1978), p. 334.

46. D.T. Hall, "Protean Careers of the 21st Century," *Academy of Management Executive*, November 1996, pp. 8–16; M.B. Arthur and D.M. Rousseau, "A Career Lexicon for the 21st Century," *Academy of Management Executive*, November 1996, pp. 28–39; N. Nicholson, "Career Systems in Crisis: Change and Opportunity in the Information Age," *Academy of Management Executive*, November 1996, pp. 40–51; and K.R. Brousseau, M.J. Driver, K. Enertoh, and R. Larsson, "Career Pandemonium: Realigning Organizations and Individuals," *Academy of Management Executive*, November 1996, pp. 52–66.

47. Hall, "Protean Careers of the 21st Century."

48. M.B. Arthur and D.M. Rousseau, *The Boundaryless Career: A New Employment Principle for a New Organizational Era* (New York: Oxford University Press, 1996).

49. M. Cianni and D. Wnuck, "Individual Growth and Team Enhancement: Moving toward a New Model of Career Development," *Academy of Management Executive*, February 1997, pp. 105–15.

50. D.E. Super, "A Life-Span Life Space Approach to Career Development," *Journal of Vocational Behavior*, Spring 1980, pp. 282–98; see also E.P. Cook and M. Arthur, *Career Theory Handbook* (Upper Saddle River, NJ: Prentice Hall, 1991), pp. 99–131; and L.S. Richman, "The New Worker Elite," *Fortune*, August 22, 1994, pp. 56–66.

51. R. Henkoff, "Winning the New Career Game," *Fortune*, July 12, 1993, pp. 46–49; "10 Tips for Managing Your Career," *Personnel Journal*, October 1995, p. 106; and A. Fisher, "Six Ways to Supercharge Your Career," *Fortune*, January 13, 1997, pp. 46–48.

52. J.E. Sheridan, J.W. Slocum, Jr., R. Buda, and R.C. Thompson, "Effects of Corporate Sponsorship and Departmental Power on Career Tournaments," *Academy of Management Journal*, September 1990, pp. 578–602.

53. Based on C. Hayes and N.Z. Sabir, "Taking Your Job Search Online," *Black Enterprise*, January 1996, pp. 70–74; and K. Rothmyer, "Working the Net," *Working Woman*, June 1997, pp. 53–56.

54. C. Perrow, *Complex Organizations: A Critical Essay* (Glenwood, IL: Scott, Foresman, 1972), p. 43.

55. L.S. Richman, "The New Worker Elite," *Fortune*, August 22, 1994, pp. 56–66.

56. Sheridan et al., "Effects of Corporate Sponsorship and Departmental Power on Career Tournaments."

57. S.C. Bushardt, R.N. Moore, and S.C. Debnath, "Picking the Right Person for Your Mentor," *S.A.M. Advanced Management Journal*, Summer 1982, pp. 46–51; E.A. Fagenson, "The Power of a Mentor," *Group and Organization Studies*, June 1988, pp. 182–94; and G.F. Dreher and R.A. Ash, "A Comparative Study of Mentoring among Men and Women in Managerial, Professional, and Technical Positions," *Journal of Applied Psychology*, October 1990, pp. 539–46.

58. See, for example, D. Kirkpatrick, "Is Your Career on Track?" *Fortune*, June 2, 1990, pp. 38–48; A. Saltzman, "Side-stepping Your Way to the Top," *U.S. News & World Report*, September 17, 1990, pp. 60–61; and B. Nussbaum, "I'm Worried about My Job," *Business Week*, October 7, 1991, pp. 94–97.

59. This section based on R.I. Henderson, *Compensation Management*, 6th ed.

(Upper Saddle River, NJ: Prentice Hall, 1994), pp. 3–24.

60. L.R. Gomez-Mejia, "Structure and Process of Diversification, Compensation Strategy, and Firm Performance," *Strategic Management Journal* 13 (1992), pp. 381–97; and E. Montemayor, "Congruence between Pay Policy and Competitive Strategy in High-Performing Firms," *Journal of Management* 22, No. 6 (1996), pp. 889–908.

61. E.E. Lawler III, G.E. Ledford Jr., and L. Chang, "Who Uses Skill-Based Pay and Why," *Compensation and Benefits Review*, March–April 1993, p. 22; and Ledford, "Paying for the Skills, Knowledge and Competencies of Knowledge Workers," *Compensation and Benefits Review*, July–August 1995, pp. 55–62.

62. L. Wiener, "No New Skills? No Raise," *U.S. News & World Report*, October 26, 1992, p. 78.

63. M. Rowland, "It's What You Can Do That Counts," *New York Times*, June 6, 1993, p. F17.

64. A. Murray, "Mom, Apple Pie, and Small Business," *Wall Street Journal*, August 15, 1994, p. A1.

65. S. Haslett, "Broadbanding: A Strategic Tool for Organizational Change," *Compensation & Benefits Review*, November–December 1995, pp. 40–46.

66. Interview with Bill Gates, "Bill Gates on Rewiring the Power Structure," *Working Woman*, April 1994, p. 62; F. Moody, "Wonder Women in the Rude Boys' Paradise," *Fast Company Web Page* <http://www.fastcompany.com>, April 17, 1997.

67. R. Leger, "Linked by Differences," *Springfield News–Leader*, December 31, 1993, pp. B6+.

68. A. Markels, "How One Hotel Manages Staff's Diversity," *Wall Street Journal*, November 20, 1996, pp. B1+.

69. E. Janice, "I'm Not Going to Take It Any More," *Black Enterprise*, February 1996, p. 65.

70. "Sexual Harassment: A Result of On-the-Job Stress?" *Workforce*, March 1997, p. 16.

71. S. Nayyar and S. Miller, "Making It Easier to Strike Back," *Newsweek*, September 12, 1994, p. 50.

72. See D.E. Terpstra and D.D. Baker, "Outcomes of Federal Court Decisions on Sexual Harassment," *Academy of Management Journal*, March 1992, pp. 181–90; B. Jorgensen, "Warning: Sexual Harassment Can Be Dangerous to Your Company's Health," *Electronic Business*, May 1993, pp. 53–56; J. Waldroup, "Sex, Laws, and Video Training," *American Demographics*, April 1994, pp. 14–15; M.M. Gallagher, "EEOC Speaks Plainly about Sexual Harassment," *HR Focus*, May 1994, p. 19; and "Sexual Harassment: A Primer," *Time*, June 6, 1994.

73. Nayyar and Miller, "Making It Easier to Strike Back."

74. J.J. Fialka, "CIA Is Charged in Two Legal Actions with Abuse toward Women, Toleration of Heavy Drinking," *Wall Street Journal*, September 9, 1994, p. A16.

75. "U.S. Leads Way in Sex Harassment Laws, Study Says," *Evening Sun*, November 30, 1992, pp. A1+; and W. Hardman and J. Heidelberg, "When Sexual Harassment Is a Foreign Affair," *Personnel Journal*, April 1996, pp. 91–97.

76. S. Webb, *The Webb Report: A Newsletter on Sexual Harassment* (Seattle: Premier Publishing, January 1994), pp. 4–7, and (April 1994), pp. 2–5.

77. See T. Segal, "Getting Serious about Sexual Harassment," *Business Week*, November 9, 1992, pp. 78–82; S.J. Bresler and R. Thacker, "Four-Point Plan Helps Solve Harassment Problems," *HRMagazine*, May 1993, pp. 117–21; "Sexual Harassment in the Workplace: It's against the Law," pamphlet from Justice Management Division of Equal Employment Opportunity Commission, June 29, 1993; S.F. Bovet, "Sexual Harassment: What's Happening and How to Deal with It," *Public Relations Journal*, November 1993, pp. 26–29; R.L. Anderson and J.W. Robinson, "The Rest of the Story in Sexual Harassment Cases," *Review of Business*, Winter 1993, pp. 13–16; R.A. Thacker, "Innovative Steps to Take in Sexual Harassment Prevention," *Business Horizons*, January–February 1994, pp. 29–32; and T.R. Haggard and M.G. Alexander Jr., "Tips on Drafting and Enforcing a Policy against Sexual Harassment," *Industrial Management*, January–February 1994, pp. 2–5.

78. A.B. Fisher, "Sexual Harassment: What to Do," *Fortune*, August 23, 1993, p. 85.

79. These examples are excerpted from S. Shellenbarger, "Work & Family," special section of the *Wall Street Journal*, June 21, 1993, pp. R1–R14.

80. These three examples excerpted from the *Wall Street Journal*, January 11, 1994, p. A1.

81. L. Faught, "At Eddie Bauer, You Can Work and Have a Life," *Workforce*, April 1997, pp. 83–90.

82. J. Lawlor, "The Bottom Line on Work-Family Programs," *Working Woman*, July–August 1996, pp. 54+; K.H. Hammonds, "Balancing Work and Family," *Business Week*, September 16, 1996, pp. 74–80; and A. Saltzman, "Companies in a Family Way," *U.S. News & World Report*, May 12, 1997, pp. 64–73.

83. K.E. Newgren, C.E. Kellogg, and W. Gardner, "Corporate Responses to Dual-Career Couples: A Decade of Transformation," *Akron Business and Economic Review*, Summer 1988, p. 85.

84. Newgren et al., "Corporate Responses to Dual-Career Couples"; and C. Reynolds and R. Bennett, "The Career Couple Challenge," *Personnel Journal New Product News*, supplement to the September 1995 issue, pp. 1–7.

85. N.L. Breuer, "Emerging Trends for Managing AIDS in the Workplace," *Personnel Journal*, June 1995, pp. 125–34.

86. This section is based on J.P. Kohl and A.N. Miller, "U.S. Organizations' Response to AIDS in the Workplace: A Review and Suggestions for Managers," *Management Decision*, July 1994, pp. 43–51; R.A. Stone, "AIDS in the Workplace: An Executive Update," *Academy of Management Executive*, August 1994, pp. 52–64; and Breuer, "Emerging Trends for Managing AIDS in the Workplace."

87. J.J. Laabs, "Eyeing Future HR Concerns," *Personnel Journal*, January 1996, p. 30.

Chapter 12

1. C. Cardwell, "Merging Cultures," *Hispanic Business*, September 1996, pp. 23–26.

2. Based on, G. Fuchsberg, "Small Firms Struggle with Latest Management Trends," *Wall Street Journal*, August 26, 1993, p. B2; M. Barrier, "Re-engineering Your Company," *Nation's Business*, February 1994, pp. 16–22; J. Weiss, "Reengineering the Small Business," *Small Business Reports*, May 1994, pp. 37–43; and K. Dunlap Godsey, "Back on Track," *Success*, May 1997, pp. 52–54.

3. The idea for these metaphors came from P.B. Vaill, *Managing as a Performing Art: New Ideas for a World of Chaotic Change* (San Francisco: Jossey-Bass, 1989).

4. K. Lewin, *Field Theory in Social Science* (New York: Harper & Row, 1951).

5. See, for instance, T. Peters, *Thriving on Chaos* (New York: Alfred A. Knopf, 1987); and T. Peters, "Thriving in Chaos," *Working Woman*, September 1993, pp. 42+.

6. M. Davids, "Wanted: Strategic Planners," *Journal of Business Strategy*, May–June 1995, pp. 30–38.

7. Peters, *Thriving on Chaos*, p. 3ff.

8. See, for example, B.M. Staw, "Counterforces to Change," in P.S. Goodman and Associates (eds.), *Change in Organizations* (San Francisco: Jossey-Bass, 1982), pp. 87–121.

9. J.P. Kotter and L.A. Schlesinger, "Choosing Strategies for Change," *Harvard Business Review*, March–April 1979, pp. 107–09; P. Strebel, "Why Do Employees Resist Change?" *Harvard Business Review*, May–June 1996, pp. 86–92; J. Mariotti, "Troubled by Resistance to Change," *IW*, October 7, 1996, p. 30; and A. Reichers, J.P. Wanous, and J.T. Austin, "Understanding and Managing Cynicism about Organizational Change," *Academy of Management Executive*, February 1997, pp. 48–57.

10. Kotter and Schlesinger, "Choosing Strategies for Change," pp. 106–11; K. Matejka and R. Julian, "Resistance to Change Is Natural," *Supervisory Management*, October 1993, p. 10; C. O'Connor, "Resistance: The Repercussions of Change," *Leadership & Organization Development Journal*, October 1993, pp. 30–36; J. Landau, "Organizational Change and Barriers to Innovation: A Case Study in the Italian Public Sector," *Human Relations*, December 1993, pp. 1411–29; A. Sagie and M. Koslowsky, "Organizational Attitudes and Behaviors as a Function of Participation in Strategic and Tactical Change Decisions: An Application of Path-Goal Theory," *Journal of Organizational Behavior*, January 1994, pp. 37–47; V.D. Miller, J.R. Johnson, and J. Grau, "Antecedents to Willingness to Participate in a Planned Organizational Change," *Journal of Applied Communication Research*, February 1994, pp. 59–80; P. Pritchett and R. Pound, *The Employee Handbook for Organizational Change* (Dallas: Pritchett Publishing, 1994); and R. Maurer, *Beyond the Wall of Resistance: Unconventional Strategies That Build Support for Change* (Austin: Bard Books, 1996).

11. R. Semler, "Why My Former Employees Still Work for Me," *Harvard Business Review*, January–February 1994, pp. 64–74.

12. L. Smith, "New Ideas from the Army (Really)," *Fortune*, September 19, 1994, pp. 203–12.

13. D. Lavin, "European Business Rushes to Automate," *Wall Street Journal*, July 23, 1997, p. A14.

14. See, for example, W.L. French and C.H. Bell Jr., *Organization Development: Behavioral Science Interventions for Organization Improvement*, 4th ed. (Upper Saddle River, NJ: Prentice Hall, 1990); C.L. Walck, "Organization Development in the USSR: An Overview and a Case Sample," *Journal of Managerial Psychology*, March 1993, pp. 10–17; T.C. Head and P.F. Sorensen, "Cultural Values and Organizational Development: A Seven-Country Study," *Leadership & Organization Development Journal*, March 1993, pp. 3–7; M.P. O'Driscoll, and J.L. Eubanks, "Behavioral Competencies, Goal Setting, and OD Practitioner Effectiveness," *Group & Organization Management*, September 1993, pp. 308–26; and A.H. Church, W.W. Burke, and D.F. Van Eynde, "Values, Motives, and Interventions of Organization Development Practitioners," *Group & Organization Management*, March 1994, pp. 5–50.

15. P.B. Smith, "Controlled Studies of the Outcome of Sensitivity Training," *Psychological Bulletin*, July 1975, pp. 597–622.

16. J.P. Campbell and M.D. Dunnette, "Effectiveness of T-Group Experience in Managerial Training and Development," *Psychological Bulletin*, August 1968, pp. 73–104.

17. M.A. Lieberman, I.D. Yalom, and M.B. Miles, *Encounter Groups: First Facts* (New York: Basic Books, 1973); and C.A. Bramlette and J.H. Tucker, "Encounter Groups: Positive Change or Deterioration? More Data and a Partial Replication," *Human Relations*, April 1981, pp. 303–14.

18. E.H. Schien, *Process Consultation: Its Role in Organizational Development* (Reading, MA: Addison-Wesley, 1969), p. 9.

19. Based on B. Kaye, "Career Development—Anytime, Anyplace," *Training & Development*, December 1993, pp. 46–49; A.D. Pinkney, "Winning in the Workplace," *Essence*, March 1994, pp. 79–80; C.B. Bardwell, "Career Planning & Job Search Guide 1994," *The Black Collegian*, March–April 1994, pp. 59–64; and W. Kiechel III, "A Manager's Career in the New Economy," *Fortune*, April 4, 1994, pp. 68–72.

20. See T.H. Fitzgerald, "Can Change in Organizational Culture Really Be Managed?" *Organizational Dynamics*, Autumn 1988, pp. 5–15; B. Dumaine, "Creating a New Company Culture," *Fortune*, January 15, 1990, pp. 127–31; P.F. Drucker, "Don't Change Corporate Culture—Use It!" *Wall Street Journal*, March 28, 1991, p. A14; J. Martin, *Cultures in Organizations: Three Perspectives* (New York: Oxford University Press, 1992); D.C. Pheysey, *Organizational Cultures: Types and Transformations* (London: Routledge, 1993); C.G. Smith and R.P. Vecchio, "Organizational Culture and Strategic Management: Issues in the Strategic Management of Change," *Journal of Managerial Issues*, Spring 1993, pp. 53–70; P. Bate, *Strategies for Cultural Change* (Boston: Butterworth-Heinemann, 1994); and P. Anthony, *Managing Culture* (Philadelphia: Open University Press, 1994).

21. J. Greenwald, "Reinventing Sears," *Time*, December 23, 1996, pp. 53–55.

22. See, for example, R.H. Kilmann, M.J. Saxton, and R. Serpa (eds.), *Gaining Control of the Corporate Culture* (San Francisco: Jossey-Bass, 1985); and D.C. Hambrick and S. Finkelstein, "Managerial Discretion: A Bridge between Polar Views of Organizational Outcomes," in L.L. Cummings and B.M. Staw (eds.), *Research in Organizational Behavior*, vol. 9 (Greenwich, CT: JAI Press, 1987), p. 384.

23. M. Albert, "Assessing Cultural Change Needs," *Training and Development Journal*, May 1985, pp. 94–98; A.A. Armenakis, S.G. Harris, and K.W. Mossholder, "Creating Readiness for Organizational Change," *Human Relations*, June 1993, pp. 681–703; and D. Nicoll, "Corporate Change Programmes: A False Panacea?" *Management Decision*, September 1993, pp. 4–9.

24. K. Pope, "Nokia Sheds Some Old Businesses for a New Calling," *Wall Street Journal*, August 19, 1994, p. B3.

25. Based on C. Lindsay, "Paradoxes of Organizational Diversity: Living within the Paradoxes," in L.R. Jauch and J.L. Wall (eds.), *Proceedings of the 50th Academy of Management Conference*, San Francisco, 1990, pp. 374–78.

26. "To Meet the Future, Nissan Looks to Its Past," *Business Ethics*, November–December 1996, p. 7.

27. D. Ciampa, *Total Quality: A User's Guide for Implementation* (Reading, MA: Addison-Wesley, 1992), pp. 100–04; M.K. Allio, "3M's Sophisticated Formula for Teamwork," *Planning Review*, November–December 1993, pp. 19–21; J. Clemmer, "Making Change Work: Integrating Focus, Effort, and Direction," *Canadian Business Review*, Winter 1993, pp. 29–31; and M. Shandler and M. Egan, "Leadership for Quality," *Journal for Quality and Participation*, March 1994, pp. 66–71.

28. K.H. Hammonds, "Where Did We Go Wrong?" *Business Week*, Quality 1991 Special Issue, p. 38; R.J. Jeszenka, "Breaking through the Resistance: Achieving TQM in Maintenance," *Plant Engineering*, January 14, 1993, pp. 132–33; A. McLeod, "Make It Happen," *The Quill*, April 1993, pp. 27–28; K.A. Smith, "Total Quality Management in the Public Sector: The Nuts and Bolts of a TQM Effort," *Quality Progress*, July 1993, pp. 57–62; S. Cau-

dron, "How HR Drives TQM," *Personnel Journal*, August 1993, pp. 48A–59A; S. Caudron, "Change Keeps TQM Programs Thriving," *Personnel Journal*, October 1993, pp. 104–09; K. Bright and C.L. Cooper, "Organizational Culture and the Management of Quality: Towards a New Framework," *Journal of Managerial Psychology*, November 1993, pp. 21–27; and M. Rigg, "Organization Change and Individual Behavior," *Industrial Engineering*, December 1993, pp. 12–13.

29. D. Anfuso, "At L.L. Bean, Quality Starts with People," *Personnel Journal*, January 1994, p. 60.

30. Ciampa, *Total Quality*, pp. 113–52; D.A. Waldman, "A Theoretical Consideration of Leadership and Total Quality Management," *Leadership Quarterly* 4, No. 1 (1993), pp. 65–79; J.P. West, E.M. Berman, and M.E. Milakovich, "Implementing TQM in Local Government: The Leadership Challenge," *Public Productivity and Management Review*, Winter 1993, pp. 175–89; R.G. McGrath, "Regaining Competitive Advantage through Leadership," *Quality Progress*, December 1993, pp. 109–10; M.J. Whalen and M.A. Rahim, "Common Barriers to Implementation and Development of a TQM Program," *Industrial Management*, March–April 1994, pp. 19–21; and C. Miller, "TQM Out: 'Continuous Process Improvement' In," *Marketing News*, May 9, 1994, pp. 5–6.

31. J.S. McClenahen, "52 Fiefdoms No More," *IW*, January 20, 1997, pp. 58–63.

32. J. Huey, "Nothing Is Impossible," *Fortune*, September 23, 1991, pp. 134–40; J.H. Want, "Managing Radical Change," *Journal of Business Strategy*, May–June 1993, pp. 20–28; W.H. Hegarty, "Organizational Survival Means Embracing Change," *Business Horizons*, November–December 1993, pp. 1–4; T. Goss, R. Pascale, and A. Athos, "The Reinvention Roller Coaster: Risking the Present for a Powerful Future," *Harvard Business Review*, November–December 1993, pp. 97–108; B. Voss, J. Vitiello, C. Johnson, and C.D. Winslow, "Setting a Course for Radical Change," *Journal of Business Strategy*, November–December 1993, pp. 52–57; S. Sherman, "A Master Class in Radical Change," *Fortune*, December 13, 1993, pp. 82–90; R.M. Hodgetts, F. Luthans, and S.M. Lee, "New Paradigm Organizations: From Total Quality to Learning to World-Class," *Organizational Dynamics*, Winter 1994, pp. 4–19; B.T. Lamont, R.J. Williams, and J.J. Hoffman, "Performance During 'M-Form' Reorganization and Recovery Time: The Effects of Prior Strategy and Implementation Speed," *Academy of Management Journal*, February 1994, pp. 153–66; M.J. Wheatley, "Can the US Army Become a Learning Organization?" *Journal for Quality and Participation*, March 1994, pp. 50–55; and S. Rothwell, "Culture and Change," *Journal of General Management*, Spring 1994, pp. M22–M35.

33. R.E. Stross, "No Escaping the News Now," *U.S. News & World Report*, October 7, 1996, pp. 54–56; and K. Dunlap Godsey, "The Next Big Thing," *Success*, April 1997, pp. 41–48.

34. M. Williams and M. Kanabayashi, "Trashing Tradition," *Wall Street Journal*, April 29, 1994, pp. A1+.

35. This section is based on M. Hammer and J. Champy, *Reengineering the Corporation: A Manifesto for Business Revolution* (New York: HarperBusiness, 1993); H. Gleckman, J. Carey, R. Mitchell, T. Smart, and C. Rouch, "The Technology Payoff," *Business Week*, June 14, 1993, pp. 56–68; T.A. Stewart, "Reengineering: The Hot New Managing Tool," *Fortune*, August 23, 1993, pp. 40–48; G. Fuchsberg, "Small Firms Struggle with Latest Management Trends," *Wall Street Journal*, August 26, 1993, p. B2; M. Barrier, "Re-engineering Your Company," *Nation's Business*, February 1994, pp. 16–22; and J.P. Womack and D.T. Jones, "From Lean Production to the Lean Enterprise," *Harvard Business Review*, March–April 1994, pp. 93–103.

36. J. Worsham, "The Flip Side of Downsizing," *Nation's Business*, October 1996, pp. 18–25.

37. Associated Press, "Downsizing Waning, Survey Says," *Springfield News Leader*, October 22, 1997, p. 12A.

38. G. Koretz, "Big Payoffs from Layoffs," *Business Week*, February 24, 1997, p. 30.

39. G. Koretz, "The Downside of Downsizing," *Business Week*, April 28, 1997, p. 26.

40. Koretz, "Big Payoffs from Layoffs."

41. See, for instance, R.C. Ford and P.L. Perrewe, "After the Layoff: Closing the Barn Door before All the Horses Are Gone," *Business Horizons*, July–August 1993, pp. 34–40; S. Greengard, "Don't Rush Downsizing: Plan, Plan, Plan," *Personnel Journal*, November 1993, pp. 64–72; J.P. Emshoff, "How to Increase Employee Loyalty While You Downsize," *Business Horizons*, March–April 1994, pp. 49–57; J.A. Byrne, "The Pain of Downsizing," *Business Week*, May 9, 1994, pp. 60–69; S. Caminiti, "What Happens to Laid-Off Managers," *Fortune*, June 13, 1994, pp. 68–78; N. Bennett, C.L. Martin, R.J. Bies, and J. Brockner, "Coping with a Layoff: A Longitudinal Study of Victims," *Journal of Management* 21, No. 6 (1995), pp. 1025–40; J.C. Latack, A.J. Kinicki, and G.E. Prussia, "An Integrative Process Model of Coping with Job Loss," *Academy of Management Review*, April 1995, pp. 311–42; S. Caudron, "Teach Downsizing Survivors How to Thrive," *Personnel Journal*, January 1996, pp. 38–48; and G.D. Bruton, J.K. Keels, and C.L. Shook, "Downsizing the Firm: Answering the Strategic Questions," *Academy of Management Executive*, May 1996, pp. 38–45.

42. A. Toufexis, "Workers Who Fight Firing with Fire," *Time*, April 25, 1994, p. 36.

43. "Workplace Stress Is Rampant, Especially with the Recession," *Wall Street Journal*, May 5, 1992, p. A1; V.M. Gibson, "Stress in the Workplace: A Hidden Cost Factor," *HR Focus*, January 1993, p. 15; J. Iacovini, "The Human Side of Organization Change," *Training and Development*, January 1993, pp. 65–68; R. Waxler and T. Higginson, "Discovering Methods to Reduce Workplace Stress," *Industrial Engineering*, June 1993, pp. 19–21; and C.L. Cordes and T.W. Dougherty, "A Review and an Integration of Research on Job Burnout," *Academy of Management Review*, October 1993, pp. 621–56.

44. Adapted from R.S. Schuler, "Definition and Conceptualization of Stress in Organizations," *Organizational Behavior and Human Performance*, April 1980, p. 189.

45. Ibid., p. 191.

46. "Stress and Boredom," *Behavior Today*, August 1975, pp. 22–25.

47. R.L. Kahn, B.N. Wolfe, R.P. Quinn, and J.D. Snock, *Organizational Stress: Studies in Role Conflict and Ambiguity* (New York: John Wiley, 1964); and C.S. Smith and J. Tisak, "Discrepancy Measures of Role Stress Revisited: New Perspectives on Old Issues," *Organizational Behavior & Human Decision Processes*, November 1993, pp. 285–307.

48. T.H. Holmes and M. Masuda, "Life Change and Illness Susceptibility," in J.P. Scott and E.C. Senay (eds.), *Separation and Depression*, Publication No. 94 (Washington, DC: American Association for the Advancement of Science, 1973), pp. 176–79.

49. A.P. Brief, R.S. Schuler, and M. Van Sell, *Managing Job Stress* (Boston: Little, Brown, 1981), pp. 94–98.

50. See, for instance, M. Friedman and R.H. Rosenman, *Type A Behavior and Your Heart* (New York: Knopf, 1974); and M. Jamal, "Type A Behavior and Job Performance: Some Suggestive Findings," *Journal of Human Stress*, Summer 1985, pp. 60–68.

51. Schuler, "Definition and Conceptualization of Stress in Organizations," pp. 200–05.

52. T.A. Beehr and J.E. Newman, "Job Stress, Employee Health, and Organizational Effectiveness: A Facet Analysis, Model, and Literature Review," *Personnel Psychology*, Winter 1978, pp. 665–99.

53. Ibid, p. 687.

54. S.E. Jackson, "Participation in Decision Making as a Strategy for Reducing Job-Related Strain," *Journal of Applied Psychology*, February 1983, pp. 3–19; C.D. Fisher, "Boredom at Work: A Neglected Concept," *Human Relations*, March 1993, pp. 395–417; C.A. Heaney, et al., "Industrial Relations, Worksite Stress Reduction and Employee Well-Being: A Participatory Action Research Investigation," *Journal of Organizational Behavior*, September 1993, pp. 495–510; P. Froiland, "What Cures Job Stress?" *Training*, December 1993, pp. 32–36; C.L. Cooper and S. Cartwright, "Healthy Mind, Healthy Organization—A Proactive Approach to Occupational Stress," *Human Relations*, April 1994, pp. 455–71; and A.A. Brott, "New Approaches to Job Stress," *Nation's Business*, May 1994, pp. 81–82.

55. See R.S. Schuler, "Time Management: A Stress Management Technique," *Personnel Journal*, December 1979, pp. 851–55; and M.E. Haynes, *Practical Time Management: How to Make the Most of Your Most Perishable Resource* (Tulsa: Penn Well Books, 1985).

56. N.S. Bruning and D.R. Frew, "Effects of Exercise, Relaxation, and Management Skills Training on Physiological Stress Indicators: A Field Experiment," *Journal of Applied Psychology*, November 1987, pp. 515–21; and P. Buhler, "Stress Management," *Supervision*, May 1993, pp. 17–19.

57. M. Marriott, "The Workout Ethic Gets Taken to Work," *New York Times*, March 20, 1996, p. B1+.

58. "Take Five," *Personnel Journal*, September 1996, p. 24.

59. P. Sellers, "A Whole New Ball Game in Beer," *Fortune*, September 19, 1994, pp. 79–86.

60. See, for example, R. Mitchell, "Masters of Innovation," *Business Week*, April 10, 1989, p. 58; K. Kelly, "3M Run Scared? Forget about It," *Business Week*, September 16, 1991, pp. 59–62; and J.C. Collins and J.I. Porras, *Built to Last* (New York: HarperBusiness, 1994).

61. These definitions are based on T.M. Amabile, "A Model of Creativity and Innovation in Organizations," in B.M. Staw and L.L. Cummings (eds.), *Research in Organizational Behavior*, vol. 10 (Greenwich, CT: JAI Press, 1988), p. 126.

62. R.W. Woodman, J.E. Sawyer, and R.W. Griffin, "Toward a Theory of Organizational Creativity," *Academy of Management Review*, April 1993, pp. 293–321.

63. F. Damanpour, "Organizational Innovation: A Meta-Analysis of Effects of Determinants and Moderators," *Academy of Management Journal*, September 1991, pp. 555–90; S.D. Saleh and C.K. Wang, "The Management of Innovation: Strategy, Structure, and Organizational Climate," *IEEE Transactions on Engineering Management*, February 1993, pp. 14–22; J.F. Coates and J. Jarratt, "Workplace Creativity," *Employment Relations Today*, Spring 1994, pp. 11–22; G.R. Oldham and A. Cummings, "Employee Creativity: Personal and Contextual Factors at Work," *Academy of Management Journal*, June 1996, pp. 607–34.

64. P.R. Monge, M.D. Cozzens, and N.S. Contractor, "Communication and Motivational Predictors of the Dynamics of Organizational Innovations," *Organization Science*, May 1992, pp. 250–74.

65. See, for instance, Amabile, "A Model of Creativity and Innovation in Organizations," p. 147; M. Tushman and D. Nadler, "Organizing for Innovation," *California Management Review*, Spring 1986, pp. 74–92; R. Moss Kanter, "When a Thousand Flowers Bloom: Structural, Collective, and Social Conditions for Innovation in Organization," in Staw and Cummings, (eds.), *Research in Organizational Behavior*, vol. 10, pp. 169–211; G. Morgan, "Endangered Species: New Ideas," *Business Month*, April 1989, pp. 75–77; S.G. Scott and R.A. Bruce, "Determinants of Innovative People: A Path Model of Individual Innovation in the Workplace," *Academy of Management Journal*, June 1994, pp. 580–607; T.M. Amabile, R. Conti, H. Coon, J. Lazenby, and M. Herron, "Assessing the Work Environment for Creativity," *Academy of Management Journal*, October 1996, pp. 1154–84; and A. deGues, "The Living Company," *Harvard Business Review*, March–April 1997, pp. 51–59.

66. J.M. Howell and C.A. Higgins, "Champions of Change," *Business Quarterly*, Spring 1990, pp. 31–32; P.A. Carrow-Moffett, "Change Agent Skills: Creating Leadership for School Renewal," *NASSP Bulletin*, April 1993, pp. 57–62; T. Stjernberg and A. Philips, "Organizational Innovations in a Long-Term Perspective: Legitimacy and Souls-of-Fire as Critical Factors of Change and Viability," *Human Relations*, October 1993, pp. 1193–2023; and J. Ramos, "Producing Change That Lasts," *Across the Board*, March 1994, pp. 29–33.

67. W.J. Broad, "A Tiny Rover, Built on the Cheap, Is Ready to Explore Distant Mars," *New York Times*, July 5, 1997, p. 9.

Chapter 13

1. C. Goldberg, "Sierra Club Gets a Young New Face," *New York Times*, June 2, 1996, p. Y9; P.A. King, "A Sprout for Sierra," *Newsweek*, June 17, 1996, p. 71; and J. Chetwynd, "Splatter-Casting the Sierra Club's Message," *U.S. News & World Report*, March 31, 1997, p. 33.

2. S.J. Breckler, "Empirical Validation of Affect, Behavior, and Cognition as Distinct Components of Attitude," *Journal of Personality and Social Psychology*, May 1984, pp. 1191-1205; and J.M. Olson and M.P. Zanna, "Attitudes and Attitude Change," *Annual Review of Psychology*, 44 (1993), pp. 117–54.

3. P.P. Brooke Jr., D.W. Russell, and J.L. Price, "Discriminant Validation of Measures of Job Satisfaction, Job Involvement, and Organizational Commitment," *Journal of Applied Psychology*, May 1988, pp. 139–45.

4. In the area of job satisfaction, see, for example, A.O. Agho, C.W. Mueller, and J.L. Price, "Determinants of Employee Job Satisfaction: An Empirical Test of a Causal Model," *Human Relations*, August 1993, pp. 1007–27; and J.E. Mathieu, D.A. Hofmann, and J.L. Farr, "Job Perception–Job Satisfaction Relations: An Empirical Comparison of Three Competing Theories," *Organizational Behavior and Human Decision Processes*, December 1993, pp. 370–87. In the area of job involvement, see I.M. Paullay, G.M. Alliger, and E.F. Stone-Romero, "Construct Validation of Two Instruments Designed to Measure Job Involvement and Work Centrality," *Journal of Applied Psychology*, April 1994, pp. 224–28. In the area of organizational commitment, see, D.M. Randall, "Cross-Cultural Research on Organizational Commitment: A Review and Application of Hofstede's Value Survey Module," *Journal of Business Research*, January 1993, pp. 91–110; R.J. Vandenberg and R.M. Self, "Assessing Newcomers' Changing Commitments to the Organization During the First Six Months of Work," *Journal of Applied Psychology*, August 1993, pp. 557–68; and A. Cohen, "Organizational Commitment and Turnover: A Meta-Analysis," *Academy of Management Journal*, October 1993, pp. 1140–57.

5. I. Ajzen and M. Fishbein, *Understanding Attitudes and Predicting Behavior* (Upper Saddle River, NJ: Prentice Hall, 1980).

6. L. Festinger, *A Theory of Cognitive Dissonance* (Stanford, CA: Stanford University Press, 1957).

7. V.H. Vroom, *Work and Motivation* (New York: John Wiley, 1964); M.T. Iaffaldano and P.M. Muchinsky, "Job Satisfaction and Job Performance: A Meta-Analysis," *Psychological Bulletin*, March 1985, pp. 251–73; and C. Ostroff, "The Relationship between Satisfaction, Attitudes, and Performance: An Organizational Level Analysis," *Journal of Applied Psychology*, December 1992, pp. 963–74.

8. See, for example, J.B. Herman, "Are Situational Contingencies Limiting the Job Attitude–Job Performance Relationship?" *Organizational Behavior and Human Performance*, October 1973, pp. 208–24; and M.M. Petty, G.W. McGee, and J.W. Cavender, "A Meta-Analysis of the Relationship between Individual Job Satisfaction and Individual Performance," *Academy of Management Review*, October 1984, pp. 712–21.

9. C.N. Greene, "The Satisfaction-Performance Controversy," *Business Horizons*, February 1972, pp. 31–41; E.E. Lawler III, *Motivation and Organizations* (Monterey, CA: Brooks/Cole, 1973); Petty, McGee, and Cavender, "A Meta-Analysis of the Relationship between Individual Job Satisfaction and Individual Performance"; B.M. Staw and S.G. Barsade, "Affect and Managerial Performance: A Test of the Sadder-but-Wiser vs. Happier-and-Smarter Hypotheses," *Administrative Science Quarterly*, June 1993, pp. 304–28; and S.P. Brown and R.A. Peterson, "The Effect of Effort on Sales Performance and Job Satisfaction," *Journal of Marketing*, April 1994, pp. 70–80.

10. See, for example, E.A. Locke, "The Nature and Causes of Job Satisfaction," in M.D. Dunnette (ed.), *Handbook of Industrial and Organizational Psychology* (Chicago: Rand McNally, 1976) pp. 1297–1350; P.W. Hom, R. Katerberg Jr., and C.L. Hulin, "Comparative Examination of Three Approaches to the Prediction of Turnover," *Journal of Applied Psychology*, June 1979, pp. 280–90; R.P. Tett and J.P. Meyer, "Job Satisfaction, Organizational Commitment, Turnover Intention, and Turnover: Path Analyses Based on Meta-Analytic Findings," *Personnel Psychology*, Summer 1993, pp. 259–93; T.A. Judge, "Does Affective Disposition Moderate the Relationship between Job Satisfaction and Voluntary Turnover?" *Journal of Applied Psychology*, June 1993, pp. 395–401; S.S. Kohler and J.E. Mathieu, "Individual Characteristics, Work Perceptions, and Affective Reactions Influences on Differentiated Absence Criteria," *Journal of Organizational Behavior*, November 1993, pp. 515–30; J.R. Rentsch, "Influence of Cumulation Strategies on the Long-Range Prediction of Absenteeism," *Academy of Management Journal*, December 1995, pp. 1616–34; and T.A. Judge and J.J. Martocchio, "Dispositional Influences on Attributions Concerning Absenteeism," *Journal of Management 22*, No. 6 (1996), pp. 837–61.

11. I. Briggs-Myers, *Introduction to Type* (Palo Alto, CA: Consulting Psychologists Press, 1980); C.K. Coe, "The MBTI: Potential Uses and Misuses in Personnel Administration," *Public Personnel Management*, Winter 1992, pp. 511–22; J. Austin Davey, B.H. Schell, and K. Morrison, "The Myers-Briggs Personality Indicator and Its Usefulness for Problem Solving by Mining Industry Personnel," *Group & Organization Management*, March 1993, pp. 50–65; and W.L. Gardner and M.J. Martinko, "Using the Myers-Briggs Type Indicator to Study Managers: A Literature Review and Research Agenda," *Journal of Management 22*, No. 1 (1996), pp. 45–83.

12. J.M. Digman, "Personality Structure: Emergence of the Five-Factor Model," in M.R. Rosenweig and L.W. Porter (eds.), *Annual Review of Psychology*, vol. 41 (Palo Alto, CA: Annual Review, 1990), pp. 417–40; O.P. John, "The Big Five Factor Taxonomy: Dimensions of Personality in the Natural Language and in Questionnaires," in L.A. Pervin (ed.), *Handbook of Personality Theory and Research* (New York: Guilford Press, 1990), pp. 66–100; M.K. Mount, M.R. Barrick, and J.P. Strauss, "Validity of Observer Ratings of the Big Five Personality Factors," *Journal of Applied Psychology*, April 1996, pp. 272–80; and P.J. Howard and J.M. Howard, "Buddy, Can You Paradigm?" *Training and Development Journal*, September 1995, pp. 28–34.

13. M.R. Barrick and M.K. Mount, "Autonomy as a Moderator of the Relationship between the Big Five Personality Dimensions and Job Performance," *Journal of Applied Psychology*, February 1993, pp. 111–18; see also Barrick and Mount, "The Big Five Personality Dimensions and Job Performance: A Meta-Analysis," *Personnel Psychology 44* (1991), pp. 1–26.

14. J.B. Rotter, "Generalized Expectancies for Internal versus External Control of Reinforcement," *Psychological Monographs 80*, No. 609 (1966).

15. See, for instance, D.W. Organ and C.N. Greene, "Role Ambiguity, Locus of Control, and Work Satisfaction," *Journal of Applied Psychology*, February 1974, pp. 101–02; and T.R. Mitchell, C.M. Smyser, and S.E. Weed, "Locus of Control: Supervision and Work Satisfaction," *Academy of Management Journal*, September 1975, pp. 623–31.

16. R.G. Vleeming, "Machiavellianism: A Preliminary Review," *Psychological Reports*, February 1979, pp. 295–310.

17. Based on J. Brockner, *Self-Esteem at Work* (Lexington, MA: Lexington Books, 1988), chapters 1–4.

18. See M. Snyder, *Public Appearances/Private Realities: The Psychology of Self-Monitoring* (New York: W.H. Freeman, 1987).

19. Snyder, *Public Appearances/Private Realities*; and J.M. Jenkins, "Self-Monitoring and Turnover: The Impact of Personality on Intent to Leave," *Journal of Organizational Behavior*, January 1993, pp. 83–90.

20. N. Kogan and M.A. Wallach, "Group Risk Taking as a Function of Members' Anxiety and Defensiveness," *Journal of Personality*, March 1967, pp. 50–63; and J.M. Howell and C.A. Higgins, "Champions of Technological Innovation," *Administrative Science Quarterly*, June 1990, pp. 317–41.

21. Based on R.H. Brockhaus Sr., "The Psychology of the Entrepreneur," in C.A. Kent, D.L. Sexton, and K.H. Vesper (eds.), *Encyclopedia of Entrepreneurship* (Upper Saddle River, NJ: Prentice Hall, 1982), pp. 41–49; J.A. Hornaday, "Research about Living Entrepreneurs," in Kent, Sexton, and Vesper (eds.), *Encyclopedia of Entrepreneurship*, p. 28; M. Warshaw, "The Entrepreneurial Mind," *Success*, April 1994, pp. 48–51; B. O'Reilly, "The New Face of Small Business," *Fortune*, May 2, 1994, pp. 82–88; R.E. Merrill and H.D. Sedgwick, "To Thine Own Self Be True," *Inc.*, August 1994, pp. 50–56; and J. Chun, "Type E Personality," *Entrepreneur*, January 1997, p. 10.

22. J.L. Holland, *Making Vocational Choices: A Theory of Vocational Personalities and Work Environments*, 2d ed. (Upper Saddle River, NJ: Prentice Hall, 1985).

23. See, for example, A.R. Spokane, "A Review of Research on Person-Environment Congruence in Holland's Theory of Careers," *Journal of Vocational Behavior*, June 1985, pp. 306–43; D. Brown, "The Status of Holland's Theory of Career Choice," *Career Development Journal*, September 1987, pp. 13–23; and T.J. Tracey and J. Rounds, "Evaluating Holland's and Gati's Vocational-Interest Models: A Structural

Meta-Analysis," *Psychological Bulletin*, March 1993, pp. 229–46.

24. H.H. Kelley, "Attribution in Social Interaction," in E. Jones et al. (eds.), *Attribution: Perceiving the Causes of Behavior* (Morristown, NJ: General Learning Press, 1972).

25. See A.G. Miller and T. Lawson, "The Effect of an Informational Option on the Fundamental Attribution Error," *Personality and Social Psychology Bulletin*, June 1989, pp. 194–204.

26. See, for example, S.T. Fiske, "Social Cognition and Social Perception," *Annual Review of Psychology*, 1993, pp. 155–94; and G.N. Powell and Y. Kido, "Managerial Stereotypes in a Global Economy: A Comparative Study of Japanese and American Business Students' Perspectives," *Psychological Reports*, February 1994, pp. 219–26.

27. Based on F.F. Aven Jr., B. Parker, and G.M. McEvoy, "Gender and Attitudinal Commitment to Organizations: A Meta-Analysis," *Journal of Business Research*, January 1993, pp. 63–73; K. Beng Ang, C. Tee Goh, and H. Chye Koh, "The Impact of Age on the Job Satisfaction of Accountants," *Personnel Review*, January 1993, pp. 31–39; B. Mannheim, "Gender and the Effects of Demographics, Status and Work Values on Work Centrality," *Work and Occupations*, February 1993, pp. 3–22; P.V. Marsden, A.L. Kalleberg, and C.R. Cook, "Gender Differences in Organizational Commitment: Influences of Work Positions and Family Roles," *Work and Occupations*, August 1993, pp. 368–90; E.R. Greenglass, "Structural and Social-Psychological Factors Associated with Job Functioning by Women Managers," *Psychological Reports*, December 1993, pp. 979–86; J. Lefkowitz, "Sex-Related Differences in Job Attitudes and Dispositional Variables: Now You See Them...," *Academy of Management Journal*, April 1994, pp. 323–49; C.M. Solomon, "Unlock the Potential of Older Workers," *Personnel Journal*, October 1995, pp. 56–66; and M. Bendick Jr., C.W. Jackson, and J.H. Romero, "Employment Discrimination against Older Workers: An Experimental Study of Hiring Practices," *Journal of Aging* 8 (1996).

28. B.F. Skinner, *Contingencies of Reinforcement* (East Norwalk, CT: Appleton-Century-Crofts, 1971).

29. Based on R.M. Bramson, *Coping with Difficult People* (Garden City, NY: Anchor Press/Doubleday, 1981); J.D. O'Brian, "De-Clawing the Chronic Complainer," *Supervisory Management*, June 1993, pp. 1–2; R. Cooper, "Dealing Effectively with Difficult Peo-

ple," *Nursing*, September 1993, pp. 97–100; and A. Urbaniak, "How to Supervise Problem Employees," *Supervision*, September 1993, pp. 10–13.

Chapter 14

1. S. Sherman, "Secrets of HP's 'Muddled' Team," *Fortune*, March 18, 1996, pp. 116–20.

2. B.W. Tuckman and M.A.C. Jensen, "Stages of Small-Group Development Revisited," *Group and Organizational Studies* 2, No. 3 (1977), pp. 419–27; and P. Buhler, "Group Membership," *Supervision*, May 1994, pp. 8–10.

3. L.N. Jewell and H.J. Reitz, *Group Effectiveness in Organizations* (Glenview, IL: Scott, Foresman, 1981); and M. Kaeter, "Repotting Mature Work Teams," *Training*, April 1994, pp. 54–56.

4. S.E. Asch, "Effects of Group Pressure upon the Modification and Distortion of Judgments," in H. Guetzkow (ed.), *Groups, Leadership and Men* (Pittsburgh: Carnegie Press, 1951), pp. 177–90.

5. See, for instance, E.J. Thomas and C.F. Fink, "Effects of Group Size," *Psychological Bulletin*, July 1963, pp. 371–84; and M.E. Shaw, *Group Dynamics: The Psychology of Small Group Behavior*, 3rd ed. (New York: McGraw-Hill, 1981).

6. See R. Albanese and D.D. Van Fleet, "Rational Behavior in Groups: The Free-Riding Tendency," *Academy of Management Review*, April 1985, pp. 244–55.

7. See, for example, L. Berkowitz, "Group Standards, Cohesiveness, and Productivity," *Human Relations*, November 1954, pp. 509–19; and B. Mullen and C. Copper, "The Relation between Group Cohesiveness and Performance: An Integration," *Psychological Bulletin*, March 1994, pp. 210–27.

8. S.E. Seashore, *Group Cohesiveness in the Industrial Work Group* (Ann Arbor: University of Michigan, Survey Research Center, 1954).

9. This section is adapted from S.P. Robbins, *Managing Organizational Conflict: A Nontraditional Approach* (Upper Saddle River, NJ: Prentice Hall, 1974), pp. 11–14.

10. K.M. Eisenhardt, J.L. Kahwajy, and L.J. Bourgeois III, "How Management Teams Can Have a Good Fight," *Harvard Business Review*, July–August 1997, pp. 77–85.

11. K.W. Thomas, "Conflict and Negotiation Processes in Organizations," in M.D. Dunnette and L.M. Hough (eds.), *Handbook of Industrial and Organizational Psychology*, 2 ed., Vol. 3, (Palo

Alto, CA: Consulting Psychologists Press, 1992), pp. 651–717.

12. This model is substantially based on the work of P.S. Goodman, E. Ravlin, and M. Schminke, "Understanding Groups in Organizations," in L.L. Cummings and B.M. Staw (eds.), *Research in Organizational Behavior*, vol. 9 (Greenwich, CT: JAI Press, 1987), pp. 124–28; and J.R. Hackman, "The Design of Work Teams," in J.W. Lorsch (ed.), *Handbook of Organizational Behavior* (Upper Saddle River, NJ: Prentice Hall, 1987), pp. 315–42.

13. F. Friedlander, "The Ecology of Work Groups," in Lorsch (ed.), *Handbook of Organizational Behavior*, pp. 301–14.

14. M.E. Shaw, *Contemporary Topics in Social Psychology* (Morristown, NJ: General Learning Press, 1976), pp. 350–51.

15. C.B. Gibson, "They Do What They Believe They Can? Group-Efficacy Beliefs and Group Performance across Tasks and Cultures," *Academy of Management Proceedings on Disk*, 1996.

16. Based on L. Copeland, "Making the Most of Cultural Differences at the Workplace," *Personnel*, June 1988, pp. 52–60; C.R. Bantz, "Cultural Diversity and Group Cross-Cultural Team Research," *Journal of Applied Communication Research*, February 1993, pp. 1–19; L. Strach and L. Wicander, "Fitting In: Issues of Tokenism and Conformity for Minority Women," *SAM Advanced Management Journal*, Summer 1993, pp. 22–25; M.L. Maznevski, "Understanding Our Differences: Performance in Decision-Making Groups with Diverse Members," *Human Relations*, May 1994, pp. 531–52; and F. Rice, "How to Make Diversity Pay," *Fortune*, August 8, 1994, pp. 78–86.

17. See, for example, J.R. Hackman and C.G. Morris, "Group Tasks, Group Interaction Process, and Group Performance Effectiveness: A Review and Proposed Integration," in L. Berkowitz (ed.), *Advances in Experimental Social Psychology* (New York: Academic Press, 1975), pp. 45–99; and M.J. Waller, "Multiple-Task Performance in Groups," *Academy of Management Proceedings on Disk*, 1996.

18. "Meaningful Meetings," *Inc.*, September 1994, p. 122.

19. I.L. Janis, *Victims of Groupthink* (Boston: Houghton Mifflin, 1972); R.J. Aldag and S. Riggs Fuller, "Beyond Fiasco: A Reappraisal of the Groupthink Phenomenon and a New Model of Group Decision Processes," *Psychological Bulletin*, May 1993, pp. 533–52; and T. Kameda and S. Sugimori, "Psychological Entrapment in Group Decision Making: An Assigned

Decision Rule and a Groupthink Phenomenon," *Journal of Personality and Social Psychology*, August 1993, pp. 282–92.

20. See, for example, L.K. Michaelson, W.E. Watson, and R.H. Black, "A Realistic Test of Individual vs. Group Consensus Decision Making," *Journal of Applied Psychology* 74, No. 5 (1989), pp. 834–39; R.A. Henry, "Group Judgment Accuracy: Reliability and Validity of Postdiscussion Confidence Judgments," *Organizational Behavior and Human Decision Processes*, October 1993, pp. 11–27; P.W. Paese, M. Bieser, and M.E. Tubbs, "Framing Effects and Choice Shifts in Group Decision Making," *Organizational Behavior and Human Decision Processes*, October 1993, pp. 149–65; N.J. Castellan Jr. (ed.), *Individual and Group Decision Making* (Hillsdale, NJ: Lawrence Erlbaum Associates, 1993); D. Gigone and R. Hastie, "The Common Knowledge Effect: Information Sharing and Group Judgment," *Journal of Personality and Social Psychology*, November 1993, pp. 959–74; and S.G. Straus and J.E. McGrath, "Does the Medium Matter? The Interaction of Task Type and Technology on Group Performance and Member Reactions," *Journal of Applied Psychology*, February 1994, pp. 87–97.

21. A.L. Delbecq, A.H. Van de Ven, and D.H. Gustafson, *Group Techniques for Program Planning* (Glenview, IL: Scott, Foresman, 1975).

22. F.A. Shull, A.L. Delbecq, and L.L. Cummings, *Organizational Decision Making* (New York: McGraw-Hill, 1970), p. 151.

23. A.F. Osborn, *Applied Imagination: Principles and Procedures of Creative Thinking* (New York: Scribners, 1941).

24. See A.R. Dennis, J.F. George, L.F. Jessup, J.F. Nunamaker Jr., and D.R. Vogel, "Information Technology to Support Group Work," *MIS Quarterly*, December 1988, pp. 591–619; D.W. Staub and R.A. Beauclair, "Current and Future Uses of Group Decision Support System Technology: Report on a Recent Empirical Study," *Journal of Management Information Systems*, Summer 1988, pp. 101–16; J. Bartimo, "At These Shouting Matches, No One Says a Word," *Business Week*, June 11, 1990, p. 78; and M.S. Poole, M. Holmes, and G. DeSanctis, "Conflict Management in a Computer-Supported Meeting Environment," *Management Science*, August 1991, pp. 926–53.

25. See W.M. Bulkeley, "Computerizing 'Dull' Meetings Is Touted as an Antidote to the Mouth That Bored," *Wall Street Journal*, January 28, 1992, p. B1; and J.S. Valacich, A.R. Dennis, and T. Connolly, "Idea Generation in Computer-Based Groups: A New Ending to an Old Story," *Organizational Behavior and Human Decision Processes*, March 1994, pp. 448–67.

26. "Teams Become Commonplace in U.S. Companies," *Wall Street Journal*, November 28, 1995, p. A1.

27. B. Dumaine, "The Trouble with Teams," *Fortune*, September 5, 1994, p. 86.

28. Based on C.E. Larson and F.M.J. LaFasto, *TeamWork* (Newbury Park, CA: Sage Publications, 1989); and E. Sundstrom, K.P. DeMeuse, and D. Futrell, "Work Teams," *American Psychologist*, February 1990, p. 120.

29. J. Conkling, "A Team Reaches for and Achieves Excellence," *Workforce*, May 1997, pp. 87–90.

30. G.M. Parker, *Cross-Functional Teams* (San Francisco: Jossey-Bass, 1994), pp. 35–39.

31. H. Rothman, "The Power of Empowerment," *Nation's Business*, June 1993, pp. 49–51.

32. D. Anfuso, "A City's HR Wins with a Corporate Mindset," *Personnel Journal*, December 1995, pp. 38–46.

33. J.A. Byrne, "The Horizontal Corporation," *Business Week*, December 20, 1993, p. 80.

34. L. Grant, "New Jewel in the Crown," *U.S. News & World Report*, February 28, 1994, p. 56.

35. J.R. Katzenbach and D.K. Smith, "The Discipline of Teams," *Harvard Business Review*, March–April 1993, pp. 111–20.

36. See Sundstrom, DeMeuse, and Futrell, "Work Teams"; Larson and LaFasto, *TeamWork*; J.R. Hackman (ed.), *Groups That Work (and Those That Don't)* (San Francisco: Jossey-Bass, 1990); and D.W. Tjosvold and M.M. Tjosvold, *Leading the Team Organization* (New York: Lexington Books, 1991).

37. Larson and LaFasto, *TeamWork*, p. 75.

38. P.E. Brauchle and D.W. Wright, "Fourteen Team Building Tips," *Training & Development*, January 1992, pp. 32–34; R.S. Wellins, "Building a Self-Directed Work Team," *Training & Development*, December 1992, pp. 24–28; S.T. Johnson, "Work Teams: What's Ahead in Work Design and Rewards Management," *Compensation and Benefits Review*, March–April 1993, pp. 35–41; V.A. Hoevemeyer, "How Effective Is Your Team?" *Training & Development*, September 1993, pp. 67–71; S.G. Cohen and G.E. Ledford Jr., "The Effectiveness of Self-Managing Teams: A Quasi-Experiment," *Human Relations*, January 1994, pp. 13–43; and J. Panepinto, "Maximize Teamwork," *Computerworld*, March 21, 1994, p. 119.

39. D.M. Enlen, "Team Goals: Aligning Groups and Management," *Canadian Manager*, Winter 1993, pp. 17–18; and A.M. O'Leary, J.J. Martocchio, and D.D. Frink, "A Review of the Influence of Group Goals on Group Performance," *Academy of Management Journal*, October 1994, pp. 1285–1301.

40. C. Meyer, "How the Right Measures Help Teams Excel," *Harvard Business Review*, May–June 1994, pp. 95–103.

41. T.A. Stewart, "The Great Conundrum—You vs. the Team," *Fortune*, November 25, 1996, pp. 165–66.

42. Parker, *Cross-Functional Teams*, p. 127.

43. P.K. Zingheim and J.R. Schuster, "The Team Pay Research Study," *Compensation & Benefits Review*, November–December 1995, pp. 6–10; G. Flynn, "Teams Won't Push for More Pay," *Personnel Journal*, January 1996, p. 26; J.H. Sheridan, "'Yes' to Team Incentives," *IW*, March 4, 1996, pp. 63–64; V. Frazee, "Recognize Team Success," *Personnel Journal*, September 1996, p. 27; and B. Nelson, "Does One Reward Fit All?" *Workforce*, February 1997, pp. 67–76.

44. B. Krone, "Total Quality Management: An American Odyssey," *The Bureaucrat*, Fall 1990, p. 37.

45. E.E. Adam Jr., "Quality Circle Performance," *Journal of Management*, March 1991, pp. 25–39; G.R. Gray, "Quality Circles: An Update," *SAM Advanced Management Journal*, Spring 1993, pp. 41–47; J. Malone, "Creating an Atmosphere of Complete Employee Involvement in TQM," *Healthcare Financial Management*, June 1993, pp. 126–27; N. Izumi, "The History of the Quality Circle," *Quality Progress*, September 1993, pp. 81–83; and T. Li-Ping Tang, P. Smith Tollison, and H.D. Whiteside, "Differences between Active and Inactive Quality Circles in Attendance and Performance," *Public Personnel Management*, Winter 1993, pp. 579–90.

46. G. Flynn, "Workforce 2000," *Workforce*, May 1997, pp. 78–84.

47. *Profiles in Quality: Blueprints for Action from Leading Companies* (Boston: Allyn and Bacon, 1991), pp. 76–77.

Chapter 15

1. E. Matson, "He Turns Ideas into Companies—At Net Speed," *Fast Company*, December–January 1997, pp. 34–36; J. Useem, "The Start-Up Factory," *Inc.*, February 1997, pp. 40–52; and A. Marsh, "Promiscuous Breeding," *Forbes*, April 7, 1997, pp. 74–77.

2. R. Katerberg and G.J. Blau, "An Examination of Level and Direction of Effort

and Job Performance," *Academy of Management Journal*, June 1983, pp. 249–57.

3. D.C. McClelland, *The Achieving Society* (New York: Van Nostrand Reinhold, 1961); J.W. Atkinson and J.O. Raynor, *Motivation and Achievement* (Washington, DC: Winston, 1974); and McClelland, *Power: The Inner Experience* (New York: Irvington, 1975).

4. McClelland, *The Achieving Society*.

5. D.C. McClelland and D.G. Winter, *Motivating Economic Achievement* (New York: Free Press, 1969).

6. McClelland, *Power*; McClelland and D.H. Burnham, "Power Is the Great Motivator," *Harvard Business Review*, March–April 1976, pp. 100–10.

7. "McClelland: An Advocate of Power," *International Management*, July 1975, pp. 27–29.

8. D. Miron and D.C. McClelland, "The Impact of Achievement Motivation Training on Small Businesses," *California Management Review*, Summer 1979, pp. 13–28.

9. J.C. Naylor and D.R. Ilgen, "Goal Setting: A Theoretical Analysis of a Motivational Technique," in B.M. Staw and L.L. Cummings (eds.), *Research in Organizational Behavior*, vol. 6 (Greenwich, CT: JAI Press, 1984), pp. 95–140; A.R. Pell, "Energize Your People," *Managers Magazine*, December 1992, pp. 28–29; E.A. Locke, "Facts and Fallacies about Goal Theory: Reply to Deci," *Psychological Science*, January 1993, pp. 63–64; M.E. Tubbs, "Commitment as a Moderator of the Goal-Performance Relation: A Case for Clearer Construct Definition," *Journal of Applied Psychology*, February 1993, pp. 86–97; M.P. Collingwood, "Why Don't You Use the Research?" *Management Decision*, May 1993, pp. 48–54; and M.E. Tubbs, D.M. Boehne, and J.S. Dahl, "Expectancy, Valence, and Motivational Force Functions in Goal-Setting Research: An Empirical Test," *Journal of Applied Psychology*, June 1993, pp. 361–73.

10. J.B. Miner, *Theories of Organizational Behavior* (Hinsdale, IL: Dryden Press, 1980), p. 65.

11. J.A. Wagner III, "Participation's Effects on Performance and Satisfaction: A Reconsideration of Research and Evidence," *Academy of Management Review*, April 1994, pp. 312–30; and J. George-Falvey, "Effects of Task Complexity and Learning Stage on the Relationship between Participation in Goal Setting and Task Performance," *Academy of Management Proceedings on Disk*, 1996.

12. J.M. Ivancevich and J.T. McMahon, "The Effects of Goal Setting, External Feedback, and Self-Generated Feedback on Outcome Variables: A Field Experiment," *Academy of Management Journal*, June 1982, pp. 359–72.

13. J.R. Hollenbeck, C.R. Williams, and H.J. Klein, "An Empirical Examination of the Antecedents of Commitment to Difficult Goals," *Journal of Applied Psychology*, February 1989, pp. 18–23; see also J.C. Wofford, V.L. Goodwin, and S. Premack, "Meta-Analysis of the Antecedents of Personal Goal Level and of the Antecedents and Consequences of Goal Commitment," *Journal of Management*, September 1992, pp. 595–615; and Tubbs, "Commitment as a Moderator of the Goal-Performance Relation."

14. A. Bandura, "Self-Efficacy: Toward a Unifying Theory of Behavioral Change," *Psychological Review*, May 1977, pp. 191–215; and M.E. Gist, "Self-Efficacy: Implications for Organizational Behavior and Human Resource Management," *Academy of Management Review*, July 1987, pp. 472–85.

15. E.A. Locke, E. Frederick, C. Lee, and P. Bobko, "Effect of Self-Efficacy, Goals, and Task Strategies on Task Performance," *Journal of Applied Psychology*, May 1984, pp. 241–51; and M.E. Gist and T.R. Mitchell, "Self-Efficacy: A Theoretical Analysis of Its Determinants and Malleability," *Academy of Management Review*, April 1992, pp. 183–211.

16. A. Bandura and D. Cervone, "Differential Engagement in Self-Reactive Influences in Cognitively-Based Motivation," *Organizational Behavior and Human Decision Processes*, August 1986, pp. 92–113.

17. See J.C. Anderson and C.A. O'Reilly, "Effects of an Organizational Control System on Managerial Satisfaction and Performance," *Human Relations*, June 1981, pp. 491–501; and J.P. Meyer, B. Schacht-Cole, and I.R. Gellatly, "An Examination of the Cognitive Mechanisms by Which Assigned Goals Affect Task Performance and Reactions to Performance," *Journal of Applied Social Psychology* 18, No. 5 (1988), pp. 390–408.

18. B.F. Skinner, *Science and Human Behavior* (New York: Free Press, 1953); and Skinner, *Beyond Freedom and Dignity* (New York: Knopf, 1972).

19. The same data, for instance, can be interpreted in either goal-setting or reinforcement terms, as shown in E.A. Locke, "Latham vs. Komaki: A Tale of Two Paradigms," *Journal of Applied Psychology*, February 1980, pp. 16–23.

20. See, for example, R.W. Griffin, "Toward an Integrated Theory of Task Design," in L.L. Cummings and B.M. Staw (eds.), *Research in Organizational Behavior*, vol. 9 (Greenwich, CT: JAI Press, 1987), pp. 79–120; and M. Campion, "Interdisciplinary Approaches to Job Design: A Constructive Replication with Extensions," *Journal of Applied Psychology*, August 1988, pp. 467–81.

21. S. Caudron, "The De-Jobbing of America," *Industry Week*, September 5, 1994, pp. 31–36; W. Bridges, "The End of the Job," *Fortune*, September 19, 1994, pp. 62–74; and K.H. Hammonds, K. Kelly, and K. Thurston, "Rethinking Work," *Business Week*, October 12, 1994, pp. 75–87.

22. M.A. Campion and C.L. McClelland, "Follow-Up and Extension of the Interdisciplinary Costs and Benefits of Enlarged Jobs," *Journal of Applied Psychology*, June 1993, pp. 339–51.

23. See, for example, J.R. Hackman and G.R. Oldham, *Work Redesign* (Reading, MA: Addison-Wesley, 1980); and Miner, *Theories of Organizational Behavior*, pp. 231–66.

24. J.R. Hackman and G.R. Oldham, "Development of the Job Diagnostic Survey," *Journal of Applied Psychology*, April 1975, pp. 159–70.

25. J.R. Hackman, "Work Design," in J.R. Hackman and J.L. Suttle (eds.), *Improving Life at Work* (Glenview, IL: Scott, Foresman, 1977), p. 129.

26. General support for the JCM is reported in Y. Fried and G.R. Ferris, "The Validity of the Job Characteristics Model: A Review and Meta-Analysis," *Personnel Psychology*, Summer 1987, pp. 287–322.

27. "Involve Your Customers," *Success*, October 1995, p. 28.

28. Ibid.

29. J.S. Adams, "Inequity in Social Exchanges," in L. Berkowitz (ed.), *Advances in Experimental Social Psychology*, vol. 2 (New York: Academic Press, 1965), pp. 267–300.

30. P.S. Goodman and A. Friedman, "An Examination of Adams' Theory of Inequity," *Administrative Science Quarterly*, September 1971, pp. 271–88.

31. See, for example, M.R. Carrell, "A Longitudinal Field Assessment of Employee Perceptions of Equitable Treatment," *Organizational Behavior and Human Performance*, February 1978, pp. 108–18; R.G. Lord and J.A. Hohenfeld, "Longitudinal Field Assessment of Equity Effects on the Performance of Major League Baseball Players," *Journal of Applied Psychology*, February 1979, pp. 19–26; and J.E. Dittrich and M.R. Carrell, "Organizational Equity Perceptions, Employee Job Satisfaction, and Departmental Absence and Turnover Rates," *Organizational Behavior and Human Performance*, August 1979, pp. 29–40.

32. P.S. Goodman, "An Examination of Referents Used in the Evaluation of Pay," *Organizational Behavior and Human Performance*, October 1974, pp. 170–95; S. Ronen, "Equity Perception in Multiple Comparisons: A Field Study," *Human Relations*, April 1986, pp. 333–46; R.W. Scholl, E.A. Cooper, and J.F. McKenna, "Referent Selection in Determining Equity Perception: Differential Effects on Behavioral and Attitudinal Outcomes," *Personnel Psychology*, Spring 1987 pp. 113–27; and C.T. Kulik and M.L. Ambrose, "Personal and Situational Determinants of Referent Choice," *Academy of Management Review*, April 1992, pp. 212–37.

33. P.S. Goodman, "Social Comparison Process in Organizations," in B.M. Staw and G.R. Salancik (eds.), *New Directions in Organizational Behavior* (Chicago: St. Clair, 1977), pp. 97–132.

34. V.H. Vroom, *Work and Motivation* (New York: John Wiley, 1964).

35. See, for example, H.G. Heneman III and D.P. Schwab, "Evaluation of Research on Expectancy Theory Prediction of Employee Performance," *Psychological Bulletin*, July 1972, pp. 1–9; and L. Reinharth and M. Wahba, "Expectancy Theory as a Predictor of Work Motivation, Effort Expenditure, and Job Performance," *Academy of Management Journal*, September 1975, pp. 502–37.

36. See, for example, V.H. Vroom, "Organizational Choice: A Study of Pre- and Postdecision Processes," *Organizational Behavior and Human Performance*, April 1966, pp. 212–25; and L.W. Porter and E.E. Lawler III, *Managerial Attitudes and Performance* (Homewood, IL: Richard D. Irwin, 1968).

37. This four-step discussion was adapted from K.F. Taylor, "A Valence-Expectancy Approach to Work Motivation," *Personnel Practice Bulletin*, June 1974, pp. 142–48.

38. See, for instance, M. Siegall, "The Simplistic Five: An Integrative Framework for Teaching Motivation," *The Organizational Behavior Teaching Review* 12, No. 4 (1987–88), pp. 141–43.

39. I. Harpaz, "The Importance of Work Goals: An International Perspective," *Journal of International Business Studies*, First Quarter 1990, pp. 75–93.

40. See, for instance, R.B. Dunham, J.L. Pierce, and M.B. Castaneda, "Alternative Work Schedules: Two Field Quasi-Experiments," *Personnel Psychology*, Summer 1987, pp. 215–42.

41. L.B. Ward, "If It's Friday, This Might Be Your Flex-Time Day Off," *New York Times*, March 31, 1996, p. F11.

42. D. Olson and A.P. Brief, "The Impact of Alternative Workweeks," *Personnel*, January–February 1978, p. 73.

43. N.K. Austin, "How Managers Manage Flexibility," *Working Woman*, July 1994, pp. 19–20.

44. See, for example, J.S. Kim and A.F. Campagna, "Effects of Flextime on Employee Attendance and Performance: A Field Experiment," *Academy of Management Journal*, December 1981, pp. 729–41; and D.R. Ralston, W.P. Anthony, and D.J. Gustafson, "Employees May Love Flextime, But What Does It Do to the Organization's Productivity?" *Journal of Applied Psychology*, May 1985, pp. 272–79.

45. E. Graham, "Flexible Formulas," *Wall Street Journal*, June 4, 1990, p. R34.

46. See, for example, M. Alexander, "Travel-Free Commuting," *Nation's Business*, December 1990, pp. 33–37; L.B. Ward, "The Mixed Blessings of Telecommuting," *New York Times*, September 20, 1992, p. F23; D.C. Churbuck and J.S. Young, "The Virtual Workplace," *Forbes*, November 23, 1992, pp. 184–90; "Telecommute America," *Fortune*, October 30, 1995, pp. 229+; W.R. Pope, "Remote Control," *Inc. Technology* No. 3 (1996), p. 25; and L. Grensing-Pophal, "Employing the Best People from Afar," *Workforce*, March 1997, pp. 30–38.

47. Statistic cited on *NBC Evening News*, July 19, 1997.

48. G. Hofstede, "Motivation, Leadership, and Organizations: Do American Theories Apply Abroad?" *Organizational Dynamics*, Summer 1980, p. 55.

49. D.H.B. Walsh, F. Luthans, and S.M. Sommer, "Organizational Behavior Modification Goes to Russia: Replicating an Experimental Analysis across Cultures and Tasks," *Journal of Organizational Behavior Management*, Fall 1993, pp. 15–35; and J.R. Baum, et al., "Nationality and Work Role Interactions: A Cultural Contrast of Israeli and U.S. Entrepreneurs' versus Managers' Needs," *Journal of Business Venturing*, November 1993, pp. 499–512.

50. A. Ignatius, "Now If Ms. Wong Insults a Customer, She Gets an Award," *Wall Street Journal*, January 24, 1989, p. 1.

51. R.K. Abbott, "Performance-Based Flex: A Tool for Managing Total Compensation Costs," *Compensation and Benefits Review*, March–April 1993, pp. 18–21; J.R. Schuster and P.K. Zingheim, "The New Variable Pay: Key Design Issues," *Compensation and Benefits Review*, March–April 1993, pp. 27–34; C.R. Williams and L.P. Livingstone, "Another Look at the Relationship between Performance and Voluntary Turnover," *Academy of Management Journal*, April 1994, pp.

269–98; and A.M. Dickinson and K.L. Gillette, "A Comparison of the Effects of Two Individual Monetary Incentive Systems on Productivity: Piece Rate Pay versus Base Pay Plus Incentives," *Journal of Organizational Behavior Management*, Spring 1994, pp. 3–82.

52. "Performance-Based Incentives: Four Approaches," *Business Ethics*, January–February 1997, p. 10.

53. V. Frazee, "Variable Compensation Plans Yield Low Return," *Workforce*, April 1997, pp. 21–25.

54. H. Rheem, "Performance Management Programs," *Harvard Business Review*, September–October 1996, pp. 8–9.

55. R.D. Banker, S.-Y. Lee, G. Potter, and D. Srinivasan, "Contextual Analysis of Performance Impacts on Outcome-Based Incentive Compensation," *Academy of Management Journal*, August 1996, pp. 920–48.

56. J. Case, "The Open-Book Revolution," *Inc.*, June 1995, pp. 26–50; A. Kleiner, "The Open-Book Policy," *WorldBusiness*, September–October 1996, pp. 52–53; and J. Case, "Opening the Books," *Harvard Business Review*, March–April 1997, pp. 118–27.

57. R.C. Yafie, "Pass the 10Q, Partner," *Journal of Business Strategy*, January–February 1996, pp. 53–56.

58. J. Fierman, "Winning Ideas from Maverick Managers," *Fortune*, February 6, 1995, pp. 66–80; and J.A. Byrne, "Management Meccas," *Business Week*, September 18, 1995, pp. 126–28.

59. Ibid.

60. P. Weaver, "An ESOP Can Improve a Firm's Performance," *Nation's Business*, September 1996, p. 63; and S. Kaufman, "ESOPs' Appeal on the Increase," *Nation's Business*, June 1997, pp. 43–44.

61. C.M. Rosen and M. Quarrey, "How Well Is Employee Ownership Working?" *Harvard Business Review*, September–October 1987, pp. 126–32.

62. S.C. Kumbhakar and A.E. Dunbar, "The Elusive ESOP-Productivity Link: Evidence from U.S. Firm-Level Data," *The Journal of Public Economics*, September 1993, pp. 273–83; and S.A. Lee, "ESOP Is a Powerful Tool to Align Employees with Corporate Goals," *Pension World*, April 1994, pp. 40–42.

63. J.L. Pierce and C.A. Furo, "Employee Ownership: Implications for Management," *Organizational Dynamics*, Winter 1990, pp. 32–43.

64. Ibid., p. 38.

65. See, for instance, M. Alpert, "The Care and Feeding of Engineers," *Fortune*, September 21, 1992, pp. 86–95; and G. Poole, "How to Manage Your Nerds," *Forbes ASAP*, December 1994, pp. 132–36.

66. G. Fuchsberg, "Parallel Lines," *Wall Street Journal*, April 21, 1993, p. R4; and A. Penzias, "New Paths to Success," *Fortune*, June 12, 1995, pp. 90–94.

67. S.W. Kelley, "Discretion and the Service Employee," *Journal of Retailing*, Spring 1993, pp. 104–26; and S.S. Brooks, "Noncash Ways to Compensate Employees," *HRMagazine*, April 1994, pp. 38–43.

68. C. Yang, A.T. Palmer, S. Browder, and A. Cuneo, "Low-Wage Lessons," *Business Week*, November 11, 1996, pp. 108–16.

69. L.A. Broedling, "Relationship of Internal-External Control to Work Motivation and Performance in Expectancy Model," *Journal of Applied Psychology*, February 1975, pp. 65–70; and T.L. Lied and R.D. Pritchard, "Relationships between Personality Variables and Components of the Expectancy-Valence Model," *Journal of Applied Psychology*, August 1976, pp. 463–67.

70. D.W. Belcher and T.J. Atchison, "Equity Theory and Compensation Policy," *Personnel Administration* 33, No. 3 (1970), pp. 22–33; and Atchison and Belcher, "Equity Rewards and Compensation Administration," *Personnel Administration* 34, No. 2 (1971), pp. 32–36.

71. E.A. Locke, D.B. Feren, V.M. McCaleb, K.N. Shaw, and A.T. Denny, "The Relative Effectiveness of Four Methods of Motivating Employee Performance," in K.D. Duncan, M.M. Gruneberg, and D. Wallis, (eds.), *Changes in Working Life* (London: John Wiley, 1980), pp. 363–83.

Chapter 16

1. S. Caudron, "Create an Empowering Environment," *Personnel Journal*, September 1995, pp. 28–36.

2. J.C. Barrow, "The Variables of Leadership: A Review and Conceptual Framework," *Academy of Management Review*, April 1977, pp. 231–51.

3. F.E. Fiedler, *A Theory of Leadership Effectiveness* (New York: McGraw-Hill, 1967).

4. L.H. Peters, D.D. Hartke, and J.T. Pholmann, "Fiedler's Contingency Theory of Leadership: An Application of the Meta-Analysis Procedures of Schmidt and Hunter," *Psychological Bulletin*, March 1985, pp. 274–85.

5. See, for instance, R.W. Rice, "Psychometric Properties of the Esteem for the Least Preferred Co-Worker (LPC) Scale," *Academy of Management Review*, January 1978, pp. 106–18; and C.A. Schriesheim, B.D. Bannister, and W.H. Money, "Psychometric Properties of the LPC Scale: An Extension of Rice's Review," *Academy of Management Review*, April 1979, pp. 287–90.

6. See E.H. Schein, *Organizational Psychology*, 3rd ed. (Upper Saddle River, NJ: Prentice Hall, 1980), pp. 116–17; and B. Kabanoff, "A Critique of Leader Match and Its Implications for Leadership Research," *Personnel Psychology*, Winter 1981, pp. 749–64.

7. R.J. House, "A Path-Goal Theory of Leader Effectiveness," *Administrative Science Quarterly*, September 1971, pp. 321–38; House and T.R. Mitchell, "Path-Goal Theory of Leadership," *Journal of Contemporary Business*, Autumn 1974, p. 86; and House, "Retrospective Comment," in L.E. Boone and D.D. Bowen (eds.), *The Great Writings in Management and Organizational Behavior*, 2d ed. (New York: Random House, 1987), pp. 354–64.

8. J. Indrik, "Path-Goal Theory of Leadership: A Meta-Analysis," paper presented at the National Academy of Management Conference, Chicago, August 1986; R.T. Keller, "A Test of the Path-Goal Theory of Leadership with Need for Clarity as a Moderator in Research and Development Organizations," *Journal of Applied Psychology*, April 1989, pp. 208–12; J.C. Wofford and L.Z. Liska, "Path-Goal Theories of Leadership: A Meta-Analysis," *Journal of Management*, Winter 1993, pp. 857–76; and A. Sagie, and M. Koslowsky, "Organizational Attitudes and Behaviors as a Function of Participation in Strategic and Tactical Change Decisions: An Application of Path-Goal Theory," *Journal of Organizational Behavior*, January 1994, pp. 37–47.

9. V.H. Vroom and P.W. Yetton, *Leadership and Decision-Making* (Pittsburgh: University of Pittsburgh Press, 1973).

10. V.H. Vroom and A.G. Jago, *The New Leadership: Managing Participation in Organizations* (Upper Saddle River, NJ: Prentice Hall, 1988). See especially chapter 8.

11. See, for example, R.H.G. Field, "A Test of the Vroom-Yetton Normative Model of Leadership," *Journal of Applied Psychology*, October 1982, pp. 523–32; C.R. Leana, "Power Relinquishment versus Power Sharing: Theoretical Clarification and Empirical Comparison of Delegation and Participation," *Journal of Applied Psychology*, May 1987, pp. 228–33; J.T. Ettling and A.G. Jago, "Participation under Conditions of Conflict: More on the Validity of the Vroom-Yetton Model," *Journal of Management Studies*, January 1988, pp. 73–83; and Field and R.J. House, "A Test of the Vroom-Yetton Model Using Manager and Subordinate Reports," *Journal of Applied Psychology*, June 1990, pp. 362–66.

12. See, for instance, J.C. McElroy, "A Typology of Attribution Leadership Research," *Academy of Management Review*, July 1982, pp. 413–17; J.R. Meindl and S.B. Ehrlich, "The Romance of Leadership and the Evaluation of Organizational Performance," *Academy of Management Journal*, March 1987, pp. 91–109; J.C. McElroy and J.D. Hunger, "Leadership Theory as Causal Attribution of Performance," in J.G. Hunt, B.R. Baliga, H.P. Dachler, and C.A. Schriesheim (eds.), *Emerging Leadership Vistas* (Lexington, MA: Lexington Books, 1988); and B. Shami, "Attribution of Influence and Charisma to the Leader: The Romance of Leadership Revisited," *Journal of Applied Social Psychology*, March 1992, pp. 1–15.

13. R.G. Lord, C.L. DeVader, and G.M. Alliger, "A Meta-Analysis of the Relation between Personality Traits and Leadership Perceptions: An Application of Validity Generalization Procedures," *Journal of Applied Psychology*, August 1986, pp. 402–10.

14. G.N. Powell and D.A. Butterfield, "The 'High-High' Leader Rides Again!" *Group and Organization Studies*, December 1984, pp. 437–50.

15. J.R. Meindl, S.B. Ehrlich, and J.M. Dukerich, "The Romance of Leadership," *Administrative Science Quarterly*, March 1985, pp. 78–102.

16. B.M. Staw and J. Ross, "Commitment in an Experimenting Society: A Study of the Attribution of Leadership from Administrative Scenarios," *Journal of Applied Psychology*, June 1980, pp. 249–60.

17. J.A. Conger and R.N. Kanungo, "Behavioral Dimensions of Charismatic Leadership," in Conger, Kanungo, and Associates, *Charismatic Leadership* (San Francisco: Jossey-Bass, 1988), p. 79; and "What's This Thing Called Charisma?" *Personnel Journal*, March 1996, p. 24.

18. R.J. House, "A 1976 Theory of Charismatic Leadership," in J.G. Hunt and L.L. Larson (eds.), *Leadership: The Cutting Edge* (Carbondale: Southern Illinois University Press, 1977), pp. 189–207.

19. W. Bennis, "The Four Competencies of Leadership," *Training and Development Journal*, August 1984, pp. 15–19.

20. Conger and Kanungo, "Behavioral Dimensions of Charismatic Leadership," pp. 78–97.

21. R.J. House, J. Woycke, and E.M. Fodor, "Charismatic and Noncharismatic Leaders: Differences in Behavior and Effectiveness," in Conger and Kanungo et al., *Charismatic Leadership*, pp. 103–04.

22. J.A. Conger and R.N. Kanungo, "Training Charismatic Leadership: A Risky

and Critical Task," in Conger and Kanungo et al., *Charismatic Leadership*, pp. 309–23.

23. J.M. Howell and P.J. Frost, "A Laboratory Study of Charismatic Leadership," *Organizational Behavior and Human Decision Processes*, April 1989, pp. 243–69.

24. House, "A 1976 Theory of Charismatic Leadership."

25. D. Machan, "The Charisma Merchants," *Forbes*, January 23, 1989, pp. 100–01.

26. This definition is based on M. Sashkin, "The Visionary Leader," in Conger and Kanungo et al., *Charismatic Leadership*, pp. 124–25; B. Nanus, *Visionary Leadership* (New York: Free Press, 1992), p. 8; and N.H. Snyder and M. Graves, "Leadership and Vision," *Business Horizons*, January–February 1994, p. 1.

27. Nanus, *Visionary Leadership*, p. 8.

28. P.C. Nutt and R.W. Backoff, "Crafting Vision." Working paper, College of Business, Ohio State University, July 1995, p. 4.

29. Nanus, *Visionary Leadership*, pp. 178–79.

30. Snyder and Graves, "Leadership and Vision," p. 2.

31. Cited in L.B. Korn, "How the Next CEO Will Be Different," *Fortune*, May 22, 1989, p. 157.

32. J.C. Collins and J.I. Porras, *Built to Last: Successful Habits of Visionary Companies* (New York: HarperBusiness, 1994).

33. Nutt and Backoff, "Crafting Vision," pp. 5–7.

34. Based on Sashkin, "The Visionary Leader," pp. 128–30.

35. See, for instance, M. Frohman, "Nothing Kills Teams Like Ill-Prepared Leaders," *IW*, October 2, 1995, pp. 72–76; and Frohman and P. Pascarella, "Don't Abdicate," *IW*, November 6, 1995, pp. 69–73.

36. S. Caminiti, "What Team Leaders Need to Know," *Fortune*, February 20, 1995, pp. 93–100.

37. Ibid., p. 93.

38. Ibid., p. 100.

39. N. Steckler and N. Fondas, "Building Team Leader Effectiveness: A Diagnostic Tool," *Organizational Dynamics*, Winter 1995, p. 20.

40. R.S. Wellins, W.C. Byham, and G.R. Dixon, *Inside Teams* (San Francisco: Jossey-Bass, 1994), p. 318.

41. Steckler and Fondas, "Building Team Leader Effectiveness," p. 21.

42. See J.M. Burns, *Leadership* (New York: Harper & Row, 1978); B.M. Bass, *Leadership and Performance beyond Expectations* (New York: Free Press, 1985); Bass, "From Transactional to Transformational Leadership: Learning

to Share the Vision," *Organizational Dynamics*, Winter 1990, pp. 19–31; D.A. Nadler and M.L. Tushman, "Beyond the Charismatic Leader: Leadership and Organizational Change," *California Management Review*, Winter 1990, pp. 77–97; P.C. Nutt and R.W. Backoff, "Organizational Transformation," *Academy of Management Proceedings on Disk*, 1996; and B.S. Pawar and K.K. Eastman, "The Nature and Implications of Contextual Influences on Transformational Leadership: A Conceptual Examination," *Academy of Management Review*, January 1997, pp. 80–109.

43. B.M. Bass, "Leadership: Good, Better, Best," *Organizational Dynamics*, Winter 1985, pp. 26–40; and J. Seltzer and B.M. Bass, "Transformational Leadership: Beyond Initiation and Consideration," *Journal of Management*, December 1990, pp. 693–703.

44. B.J. Avolio and B.M. Bass, "Transformational Leadership, Charisma, and Beyond." Working paper, School of Management, State University of New York, Binghamton, 1985, p. 14.

45. Cited in B.M. Bass and B.J. Avolio, "Developing Transformational Leadership: 1992 and Beyond," *Journal of European Industrial Training*, January 1990, p. 23.

46. J.J. Hater and B.M. Bass, "Supervisors' Evaluation and Subordinates' Perceptions of Transformational and Transactional Leadership," *Journal of Applied Psychology*, November 1988, pp. 695–702.

47. Bass and Avolio, "Developing Transformational Leadership;" R.T. Keller, "Transformational Leadership and the Performance of Research and Development Project Groups," *Journal of Management*, September 1992, pp. 489–501; J.M. Howell and B.J. Avolio, "Transformational Leadership, Transactional Leadership, Locus of Control, and Support for Innovation: Key Predictors of Consolidated-Business-Unit Performance," *Journal of Applied Psychology*, December 1993, pp. 891–911; and J.P. Schuster, "Transforming Your Leadership Style," *Association Management*, January 1994, pp. 39–43.

48. See J.R.P. French Jr. and B. Raven, "The Bases of Social Power," in D. Cartwright and A.F. Zander (eds.), *Group Dynamics: Research and Theory* (New York: Harper & Row, 1960), pp. 607–23; P.M. Podsakoff and C.A. Schriesheim, "Field Studies of French and Raven's Bases of Power: Critique, Reanalysis, and Suggestions for Future Research," *Psychological Bulletin*, May 1985, pp. 387–411; R.K. Shukla, "Influence of Power Bases in Organi-

zational Decision Making: A Contingency Model," *Decision Sciences*, July 1982, pp. 450–70; D.E. Frost and A.J. Stahelski, "The Systematic Measurement of French and Raven's Bases of Social Power in Workgroups," *Journal of Applied Social Psychology*, April 1988, pp. 375–89; and T.R. Hinkin and C.A. Schriesheim, "Development and Application of New Scales to Measure the French and Raven (1959) Bases of Social Power," *Journal of Applied Psychology*, August 1989, pp. 561–67.

49. T.A. Stewart, "How to Lead A Revolution," *Fortune*, November 28, 1994, pp. 48–61.

50. J.M. Kouzes and B.Z. Posner, *Credibility: How Leaders Gain and Lose It, and Why People Demand It* (San Francisco: Jossey-Bass, 1993), p. 14.

51. Based on L.T. Hosmer, "Trust: The Connecting Link between Organizational Theory and Philosophical Ethics," *Academy of Management Review*, April 1995, p. 393; and R.C. Mayer, J.H. Davis, and F.D. Schoorman, "An Integrative Model of Organizational Trust," *Academy of Management Review*, July 1995, p. 712.

52. P.L. Schindler and C.C. Thomas, "The Structure of Interpersonal Trust in the Workplace," *Psychological Reports*, October 1993, pp. 563–73.

53. J.K. Butler Jr. and R.S. Cantrell, "A Behavioral Decision Theory Approach to Modeling Dyadic Trust in Superiors and Subordinates," *Psychological Reports*, August 1984, pp. 19–28.

54. See Kouzes and Posner, *Credibility*, pp. 278–83.

55. This section is based on F. Bartolome, "Nobody Trusts the Boss Completely—Now What?" *Harvard Business Review*, March–April 1989, pp. 135–42; and J.K. Butler Jr., "Toward Understanding and Measuring Conditions of Trust: Evolution of a Conditions of Trust Inventory," *Journal of Management*, September 1991, pp. 643–63.

56. W.A. Randolph, "Navigating the Journey to Empowerment," *Organizational Dynamics*, Spring 1995, pp. 19–32; R. Hanson, R.I. Porterfield, and K. Ames, "Employee Empowerment at Risk: Effects of Recent NLRB Rulings," *Academy of Management Executive*, April 1995, pp. 45–56; R.C. Ford and M.D. Fottler, "Empowerment: A Matter of Degree," *Academy of Management Executive*, August 1995, pp. 21–31; and J.S. McClenahen, "Empowerment's Downside," *IW*, September 18, 1995, pp. 57–58.

57. See, for instance, M. Billard, "Do Women Make Better Managers?" *Working Woman*, March 1992, pp. 68–71, 106–07; and S.H. Applebaum

and B.T. Shapiro, "Why Can't Men Lead Like Women?" *Leadership & Organization Development Journal*, December 1993, pp. 28–34.

58. Based on D. Tannen, *You Just Don't Understand: Women and Men in Conversation* (New York: Ballentine Books, 1991); D. Tannen, *Talking from 9 to 5* (New York: Morrow, 1994); J.C. Tingley, *Genderflex: Men & Women Speaking Each Other's Language at Work* (New York: American Management Association, 1994); C. Baher, "How to Avoid Communication Clashes," *HR Focus*, April 1994, p. 3; "Communication: Bridging the Gender Gap," *HR Focus*, April 1994, p. 22; and D. Tannen, "The Power of Talk: Who Gets Heard and Why," *Harvard Business Review*, September–October 1995, pp. 138–48.

59. See J. Grant, "Women as Managers: What They Can Offer to Organizations," *Organizational Dynamics*, Winter 1988, pp. 56–63; S. Helgesen, *The Female Advantage: Women's Ways of Leadership* (New York: Doubleday, 1990); A.H. Eagly and B.T. Johnson, "Gender and Leadership Style: A Meta-Analysis," *Psychological Bulletin*, September 1990, pp. 233–56; J.B. Rosener, "Ways Women Lead," *Harvard Business Review*, November–December 1990, pp. 119–25; "Debate: Ways Men and Women Lead," *Harvard Business Review*, January–February 1991, pp. 150–60; A.H. Eagly, S.J. Karau, and B.T. Johnson, "Gender and Leadership Style among School Principals: A Meta-Analysis," *Educational Administration Quarterly*, February 1992, pp. 76–102; H. Collingwood, "Women as Managers: Not Just Different—Better," *Working Woman*, November 1995, p. 14; B.S. Moskal, "Women Make Better Managers," *IW*, February 3, 1997, pp. 17–19; and F.J. Yammarino, A.J. Dubinsky, L.B. Comer, and M.A. Jolson, "Women and Transformational and Contingent Reward Leadership: A Multiple-Levels-of-Analysis Perspective," *Academy of Management Journal*, February 1997, pp. 205–22.

60. S. Helgesen, *The Female Advantage.*

61. P.L. Smith and S.J. Smits, "The Feminization of Leadership?" *Training and Development*, February 1994, pp. 43–46.

62. G.H. Dobbins, W.S. Long, E.J. Dedrick, and T.C. Clemons, "The Role of Self-Monitoring and Gender on Leader Emergence: A Laboratory and Field Study," *Journal of Management*, September 1990, pp. 609–18.

63. F.W. Swierczek, "Leadership and Culture: Comparing Asian Managers,"

Leadership & Organization Development Journal, December 1991, pp. 3–10.

64. G. Hofstede, "Motivation, Leadership, and Organization: Do American Theories Apply Abroad?" *Organizational Dynamics*, Summer 1980, p. 57; and A. Ede, "Leadership and Decision Making: Management Styles and Culture," *Journal of Managerial Psychology*, July 1992, pp. 28–31.

65. G. Hofstede and M.H. Bond, "The Confucius Connection: From Cultural Roots to Economic Growth," *Organizational Dynamics*, Spring 1988, pp. 4–21; C.A. Rodrigues, "The Situation and National Culture as Contingencies for Leadership Behavior: Two Conceptual Models," in S.B. Prasad (ed.), *Advances in International Comparative Management*, vol. 5 (Greenwich, CT: JAI Press, 1990), pp. 51–68.

66. S. Kerr and J.M. Jermier, "Substitutes for Leadership: Their Meaning and Measurement," *Organizational Behavior and Human Performance*, December 1978, pp. 375–403; J.P. Howell and P.W. Dorfman, "Substitutes for Leadership: A Statistical Refinement," paper presented at the 42nd Annual Academy of Management Conference, New York, August 1982; J.P. Howell, P.W. Dorfman, and S. Kerr, "Leadership and Substitutes for Leadership," *Journal of Applied Behavioral Science* 22, No. 1 (1986), pp. 29–46; J.P. Howell, D.E. Bowen, P.W. Dorfman, S. Kerr, and P.M. Podsakoff, "Substitutes for Leadership: Effective Alternatives to Ineffective Leadership," *Organizational Dynamics*, Summer 1990, pp. 21–38; and P.M. Podsakoff, B.P. Niehoff, S.B. MacKenzie, and M.L. Williams, "Do Substitutes for Leadership Really Substitute for Leadership? An Empirical Examination of Kerr and Jermier's Situational Leadership Model," *Organizational Behavior and Human Decision Processes*, February 1993, pp. 1–44.

Chapter 17

1. B.P. Sunoo, "This Employee May Be Loafing: Can You Tell? Should You Care?" *Personnel Journal*, December 1996, pp. 54–62; and "Western Digital Corporation's Internet Access Policy," *Workforce Tools: Supplement to the January 1997 Issue of Workforce*, January 1997, pp. 1–3.

2. K.A. Merchant, "The Control Function of Management," *Sloan Management Review*, Summer 1982, pp. 43–55.

3. E. Flamholtz, "Organizational Control Systems as a Managerial Tool," *California Management Review*, Winter 1979, p. 55.

4. W.G. Ouchi, "A Conceptual Framework for the Design of Organizational Control Mechanisms," *Management Science*, August 1979, pp. 833–38; and Ouchi, "Markets, Bureaucracies, and Clans," *Administrative Science Quarterly*, March 1980, pp. 129–41.

5. S. Kerr, "On the Folly of Rewarding A, While Hoping for B," *Academy of Management Journal*, December 1975, pp. 769–83.

6. H. Koontz and R.W. Bradspies, "Managing through Feedforward Control," *Business Horizons*, June 1972, pp. 25–36.

7. E. MacDonald, "More Accounting Firms Bar Risky Clients," *Wall Street Journal*, April 25, 1997, p. A2.

8. Based on T.J. Peters and R.H. Waterman, *In Search of Excellence* (New York: Harper & Row, 1982); Peters and N. Austin, *A Passion for Excellence: The Leadership Difference* (New York: Random House, 1985); P.R. Monge, L.W. Rothman, E.M. Eisenberg, K.I. Miller, and K.K. Kirste, "The Dynamics of Organizational Proximity," *Management Science* 31 (1985), pp. 1129–41; and A.E. Serwer, "Lessons from America's Fastest-Growing Companies," *Fortune*, August 8, 1994, pp. 59–60.

9. W.H. Newman, *Constructive Control: Design and Use of Control Systems* (Upper Saddle River, NJ: Prentice Hall, 1975), p. 33.

10. See, for instance, Newman, *Constructive Control.*

11. R. Frank, "As UPS Tries to Deliver More to Its Customers, Labor Problems Grow," *Wall Street Journal*, May 23, 1994, p. A1+.

12. See, for instance, B.J. Jaworski and S.M. Young, "Dysfunctional Behavior and Management Control: An Empirical Study of Marketing Managers," *Accounting, Organizations and Society*, January 1992, pp. 17–35.

13. E.E. Lawler III and J.G. Rhode, *Information and Control in Organizations* (Santa Monica, CA: Goodyear, 1976), p. 108.

14. J.D. Thompson, *Organizations in Action* (New York: McGraw-Hill, 1967), p. 124.

15. F. Jossi, "Eavesdropping in Cyberspace," *Business Ethics*, May–June 1994, pp. 22–25.

16. "E-Mail Snooping Is OK in the Eyes of the Law," *Wall Street Journal*, March 19, 1996, p. A1.

17. T.L. Griffith, "Teaching Big Brother to Be a Team Player: Computer Monitoring and Quality," *Academy of Management Executive*, February 1993, pp. 73–80.

18. Griffith, "Teaching Big Brother to be a Team Player"; and "Privacy at Work?

Don't Count on It," *Springfield News Leader*, May 26, 1997, p. 7A.

19. D. Warner, "The Move to Curb Worker Monitoring," *Nation's Business*, December 1993, p. 37.

20. J. Rothfeder, M. Galen, and L. Driscoll, "Is Your Boss Spying on You?" *Business Week*, January 15, 1990, pp. 74–75; and G. Bylinsky, "How Companies Spy on Employees," *Fortune*, November 4, 1991, pp. 131–40.

21. J.I. Rigdon, "Curbing Digital Dillydallying on the Job," *Wall Street Journal*, November 26, 1996, pp. B1+.

22. "Companies Beginning to Monitor Employee 'Cyberloafing'," *CNNfn Web Page*, <http://www.cnnfn.com>, May 20, 1996.

23. Warner, "The Move to Curb Worker Monitoring," p. 38; and S. Greengard, "Privacy: Entitlement or Illusion?" *Personnel Journal*, May 1996, pp. 74–88.

24. "Testing...Testing," *Business Week*, May 2, 1994, p. 6.

25. L. Smith, "What the Boss Knows about You," *Fortune*, August 1993, pp. 88–93.

26. J.E. Bahls, "Checking Up on Workers," *Nation's Business*, December 1990, p. 29; M. Shao, Z. Schiller, and W. Konrad, "If You Light Up on Sunday, Don't Come in on Monday," *Business Week*, August 26, 1991, pp. 68–72; and D.S. Hames and N. Diersen, "The Common Law Right to Privacy: Another Incursion into Employers' Rights to Manage Their Employees," *Labor Law Journal*, November 1991, pp. 757–65.

C h a p t e r   1 8

1. G. Smith and J. Pearson, "Cemex: Solid as Mexico Sinks," *Business Week*, February 27, 1995, pp. 58–59; "Growth Factors," *Chief Executive*, July–August 1995, pp. S10–S13; and D. Dombey, "Well-Built Success," *IW*, May 5, 1997, pp. 32–38.

2. "The Productivity Paradox," *Business Week*, June 6, 1988, p. 101.

3. Ibid., p. 102.

4. M. Magnet, "The Productivity Payoff Arrives," *Fortune*, June 27, 1994, p. 82.

5. "Price Discipline," *U.S. News & World Report*, April 25, 1994, p. 17.

6. K.L. Miller, "The Factory Guru Tinkering with Toyota," *Business Week*, May 17, 1993, pp. 95–97.

7. S.N. Mehta, "Cell Manufacturing Gains Acceptance at Smaller Plants," *Wall Street Journal*, September 15, 1994, p. B2.

8. S.S. Roach, "The Hollow Ring of the Productivity Revival," *Harvard Business Review*, November–December

1996, p. 83; and "Productivity in 1996 up 0.7%, Biggest Rise in 4 Years," *New York Times*, March 12, 1997, p. C4.

9. "Productivity Gap Narrows," *Business Week*, April 1, 1996, p. 8.

10. "U.S. Workers Top Japan's, Germany's, in Productivity," *Los Angeles Times*, October 14, 1992, p. D1.

11. B.B. Auster, "Tending the Troops," *U.S. News & World Report*, November 21, 1994, p. 20.

12. M. Williams, "Some Plants Tear Out Long Assembly Lines, Switch to Craft Work," *Wall Street Journal*, October 24, 1994, p. A1+.

13. T.P. Pare, "A New Tool for Managing Costs," *Fortune*, June 14, 1993, p. 129.

14. L. Zuckerman, "Do Computers Lift Productivity? It's Unclear, But Business Is Sold," *New York Times*, January 2, 1997, p. C15.

15. F.R. Bleakley, "U.S. Economy Can Thank Service Sector," *Wall Street Journal*, February 16, 1996, p. A2.

16. R. Henkoff, "Some Hope for Troubled Cities," *Fortune*, September 9, 1991, pp. 121–28.

17. N. Munk, "Learning from Kodak," *Forbes*, January 22, 1996, p. 37.

18. A.W.H. Grant and L.A. Schlesinger, "Realize Your Customers' Full Profit Potential," *Harvard Business Review*, September–October 1995, pp. 59–72.

19. T.A. Stewart, "A Satisfied Customer Isn't Enough," *Fortune*, July 21, 1997, pp. 112–13.

20. T.A. Stewart, "After All You've Done for Your Customers, Why Are They Still Not Happy?" *Fortune*, December 11, 1995, p. 182.

21. G. Hamel and C.K. Prahalad, *Competing for the Future* (Boston: Harvard Business School Press, 1994); R. McKenna, "Real-Time Marketing," *Harvard Business Review*, July–August 1995, pp. 87–95; S.F. Wiggins, "New Ways to Create Lifetime Bonds with Your Customers," *Fortune*, October 30, 1995, p. 115; S.E. Prokesch, "Competing on Customer Service: An Interview with British Airways' Sir Colin Marshall," *Harvard Business Review*, November–December 1995, pp. 101–12; and A.J. Slywotzky, *Value Migration* (Boston: Harvard Business School Press, 1996).

22. Stewart, "A Satisfied Customer Isn't Enough."

23. T.A. Stewart, "Reengineering—The Hot New Managing Tool," *Fortune*, August 23, 1993, p. 41.

24. Ibid., p. 42.

25. S. Helldorfer and M. Daly, "Reengineering Brings Together Units," *Best's Review*, October 1993, pp. 82–84.

26. J.S. McClenahen, P. Fletcher, and J. Gee, "Europe's Best Practices," *IW*, March 17, 1997, pp. 16–17.

27. "Manufacturing Is in Flower," *Time*, March 26, 1984, pp. 50–52.

28. See, for example, N. Gaither, *Production and Operations Management*, 5th ed. (Orlando, FL: Dryden Press, 1992), chapter 2.

29. See W. Skinner, "Manufacturing—Missing Link in Corporate Strategy," *Harvard Business Review*, May–June 1969, pp. 136–45.

30. G. Bylinsky, "The Digital Factory," *Fortune*, November 14, 1994, p. 94.

31. See, for instance, T.J. Erickson, J.F. Magee, P.A. Roussel, and K.N. Saad, "Managing Technology as a Business Strategy," *Sloan Management Review*, Spring 1990, pp. 73–78; G. Stalk Jr. and T.M. Hout, *Competing against Time: How Time-Based Competition Is Reshaping Global Markets* (New York: Free Press, 1990); and J.W. Dean Jr. and S.A. Snell, "The Strategic Use of Integrated Manufacturing: An Empirical Examination," *Strategic Management Journal* 17 (1996), pp. 459–80.

32. D. McGraw, "Staying Loose in a Tense Tech Market," *U.S. News & World Report*, July 8, 1996, p. 46.

33. See, for instance, B. Render and J. Heizer, *Principles of Operations Management* (Upper Saddle River, NJ: Prentice Hall, 1995), pp. 550–52.

34. N. Rotenier, "Quick Wits, Low Costs," *Forbes*, January 2, 1995, p, 150.

35. R.B. Chase and N.J. Aquilano, *Production and Operations Management: A Life-Cycle Approach*, 3rd ed. (Homewood, IL: Irwin, 1981), pp. 34–41.

36. E.E. Adam Jr. and R.J. Ebert, *Production and Operations Management: Concepts, Models, and Behavior*, 5th ed. (Upper Saddle River, NJ: Prentice Hall, 1992), pp. 53–60.

37. Ibid., pp. 231–33.

38. Ibid., pp. 341–44.

39. Ibid., p. 340; and N.-P. Lin, L. Krajewski, G. Keong Leong, and W.C. Benton, "The Effects of Environmental Factors on the Design of Master Production Scheduling Systems," *Journal of Operations Management*, March 1994, pp. 367–74.

40. D. Bartholomew, "MRP Upstaged," *IW*, February 3, 1997, pp. 39–41.

41. Cited in *Fortune*, October 28, 1985, p. 47.

42. S.E. Barndt and D.W. Carvey, *Essentials of Operations Management* (Upper Saddle River, NJ: Prentice Hall, 1982), p. 112.

43. J. Dreyfuss, "Shaping Up Your Suppliers," *Fortune*, April 10, 1989, pp. 116–22; and T.M. Rohan, "Supplier-

Customer Links Multiplying," *Industry Week*, April 17, 1989, p. 20.

44. Rohan, "Supplier-Customer Links Multiplying."

45. Chase and Aquilano, *Production and Operations Management*; pp. 551–52.

46. J.H. Sheridan, "The CIM Evolution," *Industry Week*, April 20, 1992, pp. 29–51.

47. J. Teresko, "Speeding the Product Development Cycle," *Industry Week*, July 18, 1988, p. 41.

48. L.L. Berry, A. Parasuraman, and V.A. Zeithaml, "Improving Service Quality in America: Lessons Learned," *Academy of Management Executive*, May 1994, p. 35.

49. T.B. Kinni, "Gilbarco," *Industry Week*, October 17, 1994, p. 51.

50. C. Rubel, "Some Colleges Guarantee Their Students Will Succeed at Work," *Marketing News*, October 9, 1995, pp. 1+.

51. J.F. McKenna, "Ohio Votes for TQ Government," *Industry Week*, March 16, 1992, p. 65.

52. J. Hillkirk, "Uncle Sam Begins Push for Quality," *USA Today*, October 7, 1992, p. B1.

53. T.C. Powell, "Total Quality Management as Competitive Advantage: A Review and Empirical Study," *Strategic Management Journal*, January 1995, pp. 15–37.

54. G. Fuchsberg, "Quality Programs Show Shoddy Results," *Wall Street Journal*, May 14, 1992, p. B1; see also Fuchsberg, "'Total Quality' Is Termed Only Partial Success," *Wall Street Journal*, October 1, 1992, p. B1; and "Customer-Driven Strategies: Moving from Talk to Action," *Planning Review*, September–October 1993, pp. 25–29.

55. Fuchsberg, "Quality Programs Show Shoddy Results," and Fuchsberg, "'Total Quality' Is Termed Only Partial Success."

56. This discussion of ISO 9000 is based on D.R. Arter, "Demystifying the ISO 9000/Q90 Series Standards," *Quality Progress*, November 1992, pp. 65–67; A. Marash, "The Future of ISO 9000," *The Corporate Board*, May–June 1994, pp. 20–24; J. Staines, "ISO 9000 Explained," *American Paint and Coatings Journal*, June 6, 1994, pp. 55–59; A. Zuckerman, "The Basics of ISO 9000," *Industrial Engineering*, June 1994, pp. 13–15; T.H. Landelles-Gordon, "ISO 9000: A New Opportunity for CPA Firms," *The CPA Journal*, June 1995, pp. 68–69; and P. Dolack, "ISO 9000 Comes of Age," *CMR Special Report*, April 8, 1996, pp. SR7–SR8.

57. M.V. Uzumeri, "ISO 9000 and Other Metastandards: Principles for Management Practice?" *Academy of Management Executive*, February 1997, pp. 21–36.

58. J.W. Parisher, "ISO 9000 Documentation: A TQM Journey in the Making," *National Productivity Review*, Autumn 1995, pp. 77–88.

59. Reported in the 1996 annual reports of Dow Chemical, Hewlett-Packard, and the Boeing Company.

60. See, for instance, A.T. Sadhwani and M.H. Sarhan, "Putting JIT Manufacturing Systems to Work," *Business*, April–June 1987, pp. 30–37; L. Kuzela, "Efficiency—Just in Time," *Industry Week*, May 2, 1988, p. 63; E.H. Hall Jr., "Just-in-Time Management: A Critical Assessment," *Academy of Management Executive*, November 1989, pp. 315–18; and E. Richman and W.B. Zachary, "Creating Strategies for Successful Materials Management," *Industrial Management*, March–April 1994, pp. 24–27.

61. H. Banks, "Good Bearings," *Forbes*, September 23, 1996, pp. 52–58.

62. S. McCartney, "Compaq Borrows Wal-Mart's Idea to Boost Production," *Wall Street Journal*, June 17, 1994, p. B4.

63. D. Hutchins, "Having a Hard Time with Just-in-Time," *Fortune*, June 9, 1986, pp. 64–66; and A.K. Naj, "Some Manufacturers Drop Efforts to Adopt Japanese Techniques," *Wall Street Journal*, May 7, 1993, pp. A1+.

64. See for example, S. Tully, "You'll Never Guess Who Really Makes...," *Fortune*, October 3, 1994, pp. 124–28; and N. Templin and J. Cole, "Manufacturers Use Suppliers to Help Them Develop New Products," *Wall Street Journal*, December 19, 1994, pp. A1+.

65. Templin and Cole, "Manufacturers Use Suppliers to Help Them Develop New Products."

66. D.J. Schemo, "Is VW's New Plant Lean, or Just Mean?" *New York Times*, November 19, 1996, pp. C1+.

67. P.L. Nemetz and L.W. Fry, "Flexible Manufacturing Organizations: Implications for Strategy Formulation and Organization Design," *Academy of Management Review*, October 1988, pp. 627–38; and A. De Meyer et al., "Flexibility: The Next Competitive Battle the Manufacturing Futures Survey," *Strategic Management Journal*, March–April 1989, pp. 135–44.

68. See, for example, T.A. Stewart, "Brace for Japan's Hot New Strategy," *Fortune*, September 21, 1992, pp. 62–74; and O. Port, "Moving Past the Assembly Line," *Business Week/Reinventing America Special Issue*, November 1992, pp. 177–80.

69. J.S. DeMott, "Look, World, No Hands!" *Nation's Business*, June 1994, p. 41.

70. Bylinsky, "The Digital Factory," p. 94.

71. Ibid., p. 93.

72. S. Moffat, "Japan's New Personalized Production," *Fortune*, October 22, 1990, pp. 132–35.

73. D.L. Boroughs, "Stacking Up the Silver Dollars," *U.S. News & World Report*, April 25, 1994, p. 72.

74. G. Stalk Jr., "Time—The Next Source of Competitive Advantage," *Harvard Business Review*, July–August 1988, pp. 41–51; J.T. Vesey, "The New Competitors: They Think in Terms of 'Speed-to-Market'," *Academy of Management Executive*, May 1991, pp. 23–33; D.E. Vinton, "A New Look at Time, Speed, and the Manager," *Academy of Management Executive*, November 1992, pp. 7–16; J.W. Jones, *High-Speed Management* (San Francisco: Jossey-Bass, 1993); and E.H. Kessler and A.K. Chakrabarti, "Innovation Speed: A Conceptual Model of Context, Antecedents, and Outcomes," *Academy of Management Review* 21, No. 4 (1996), pp. 1143–91.

75. M.B. Grover, "The Odd Couple," *Forbes*, November 18, 1996, pp. 178–81.

76. W.M. Bulkeley, "The Latest Big Thing at Many Companies Is Speed, Speed, Speed," *Wall Street Journal*, December 23, 1994, pp. A1+.

77. J.H. Sheridan, "Creating a 21st-Century Business," *Industry Week*, April 19, 1993, p. 38.

78. J.J. Sieder, "Liz Claiborne Gets Dressed for Success," *U.S. News & World Report*, February 26, 1996, pp. 55–56.

79. Bylinsky, "The Digital Factory," pp. 93–94.

Chapter 19

1. H. Karp, "Managing Well into the Future," *Black Enterprise*, March 1997, p. 60.

2. J.T. Small and W.B. Lee, "In Search of an MIS," *MSU Business Topics*, Autumn 1975, pp. 47–55.

3. H.A. Simon, *Administrative Behavior*, 3rd ed. (New York: Free Press, 1976), p. 294.

4. J.C. Carter and F.N. Silverman, "Establishing an MIS," *Journal of Systems Management*, January 1980, p. 15.

5. L. Hays, "Using Computers to Divine Who Might Buy a Gas Grill," *Wall Street Journal*, August 16, 1994, pp. B1+.

6. See, for example, G.W. Dickson and J.K. Simmons, "The Behavioral Side of MIS," *Business Horizons*, August 1970, pp. 59–71; C. Brod, "Managing Technostress: Optimizing the Use of Computer Technology," *Personnel*

Journal, October 1981, p. 754; and S. Kiesler, J. Siegel, and T.W. McGuire, "Social Psychological Aspects of Computer-Mediated Communication," *American Psychologist*, January 1985, pp. 14–19.

7. B. Ives and M.H. Olson, "User Involvement and MIS Success: A Review of Research," *Management Science*, May 1984, pp. 586–603.

8. See, for instance, G. Bylinsky, "Saving Time with New Technology," *Fortune*, December 30, 1991, pp. 98–104.

9. See, for instance, S.W. Quickel, "Management Joins the Computer Age," *Business Month*, May 1989, pp. 42–46; G.P. Huber, "A Theory of the Effects of Advanced Information Technology on Organizational Design, Intelligence, and Decision Making," *Academy of Management Review*, January 1990, pp. 47–71; and U.G. Gupta, "An Empirical Investigation of the Contribution of Information Systems to Productivity," *Industrial Management*, March–April 1994, pp. 15–18.

10. R. Karlgaard, "*ASAP* Interview with Susan Cramm and John Martin," *Forbes ASAP*, Summer 1994, pp. 67–70.

11. L.M. Applegate, J.I. Cash Jr., and D.Q. Mills, "Information Technology and Tomorrow's Manager," *Harvard Business Review*, November–December 1988, pp. 128–36.

12. J.H. Boyett and H.P. Conn, *Workplace 2000* (New York: Dutton, 1991), p. 25.

13. Ibid.

14. S.P. Robbins, *Organization Theory: Structure, Design, and Applications*, 3rd ed. (Upper Saddle River, NJ: Prentice Hall, 1990), pp. 267–68.

15. J. Pfeffer, *Managing with Power* (Boston: Harvard Business School Press, 1992), pp. 247–65.

16. M. Newman and D. Rosenberg, "Systems Analysts and the Politics of Organizational Control," *Omega* 13, No. 5 (1985), pp. 393–406.

17. See, for example, D.A. DeCenzo and S.P. Robbins, *Human Resource Management*, 4th ed. (New York: Wiley & Sons, 1994), pp. 385–93.

18. BARS have not been without critics. See, for example, L.R. Gomez-Mejia, "Evaluating Employee Performance: Does the Appraisal Instrument Make a Difference?" *Journal of Organizational Behavior Management*, Winter 1988, pp. 155–71.

19. R.D. Bretz Jr., G.T. Milkovich, and W. Read, "The Current State of Performance Appraisal Research and Practice: Concerns, Directions, and Implications," *Journal of Management*, June 1992, p. 331.

20. See, for example, J.S. Lublin, "Turning the Tables: Underlings Evaluate Bosses," *Wall Street Journal*, October 4, 1994, pp. B1+; B. O'Reilly, "360 Feedback Can Change Your Life," *Fortune*, October 17, 1994, pp. 93–100; R. McGarvey, "Rating Game," *Entrepreneur*, December 1996, pp. 83–85; and S. Gruner, "Feedback from Everyone," *Inc.*, February 1997, pp. 102–03.

21. J.F. Milliman, R.A. Zawacki, C. Norman, L. Powell, and J. Kirksey, "Companies Evaluate Employees from All Perspectives," *Personnel Journal*, November 1994, pp. 99–103.

22. R.J. Burke, "Why Performance Appraisal Systems Fail," *Personnel Administration*, June 1972, pp. 32–40.

23. R.B. Peterson (ed.), *Managers and National Culture: A Global Perspective* (Westport, CT: Quorum Books, 1993), pp. 405–29.

24. A.N. Schoonmaker, *Executive Career Strategy* (New York: American Management Association, 1971); A.J. DuBrin, *Fundamentals of Organizational Behavior: An Applied Perspective*, 2d ed. (Elmsford, NY: Pergamon Press, 1978), chapter 5; and E.E. Jennings, "Success Chess," *Management of Personnel Quarterly*, Fall 1980, pp. 2–8.

25. G. Grinstein and W.D. Oliver, "Winning the War against Substance Abuse," *Chief Executive*, January–February 1994, pp. 32–37.

26. "Testing...Testing," *Business Week*, May 2, 1994, p. 6.

27. Grinstein and Oliver, "Winning the War against Substance Abuse," p. 32.

28. D. Elmuti, "Effects of Drug-Testing Programs on Employee Attitudes, Productivity, and Attendance Behaviors," *International Journal of Manpower*, June 1993, pp. 58–69; B. Oliver, "Fight Drugs with Knowledge," *Training and Development*, May 1994, pp. 105–08; E.G. Sorohan, "Making Decisions about Drug Testing," *Training and Development*, May 1994, pp. 111–16; H. LaVan, M. Katz, and J. Suttor, "Litigation of Employer Drug Testing," *Labor Law Journal*, June 1994, pp. 346–51; and R.F. Lisko, "A Manager's Guide to Drug Testing," *Security Management*, August 1994, pp. 92–95.

29. See, for example, B. Caldwell, "EAPs Broaden Their Focus, Evolve from Substance Abuse Genesis," *Employee Benefit Plan Review*, November 1993, pp. 26–28; S.A. Haskins and B.H. Kleiner, "Employee Assistance Programs Take New Directions," *HR Focus*, January 1994, p. 16; and I. St. John-Brooks, "Workplace Counselling to Support Change," *Benefits and Compensation International*, March 1994, p. 32.

30. It has been argued that indirect control mechanisms are most appropriate in organic structures. See S. Kerr and J.W. Slocum Jr., "Controlling the Performance of People in Organizations," in P.C. Nystrom and W.H. Starbuck (eds.), *Handbook of Organizational Design*, vol. 2 (New York: Oxford University Press, 1981), pp. 128–30.

Photo Credits

Frontmatter

p. iv, (top) Laura Ospanik, (bottom) Mary Coulter.

Chapter 1

p. 2, Katherine Lambert; p. 6, Mark Richards/PhotoEdit; p. 6, Courtesy of Hewlett-Packard Company; p. 6, Milton Feinberg/Stock Boston; p. 10, Piki Harralson; p. 12, Jeff Jacobson; p. 21, Mark Richards; p. 24, Jim Lo Scalzo/U.S. News & World Report; p. 29, Provided by Peter Belluschi; p. 29, Provided by Denise Radtke Currier.

Chapter 2

p. 36, Gary T. Collier; p. 38, Raeanne Rubenstein/Index Stock Photography, Inc.; p. 41, Courtesy Stevens Institute of Technology, Hoboken, NJ; p. 43, UPI/Corbis-Bettmann; p. 49, Property of AT&T Archives, Reprinted with permission of AT&T; p. 50, Corbis-Bettmann; p. 56, David Toerge/Black Star; p. 59, Provided by Duke Rohlen; p. 61, B. Kraft/Sygma; p. 62, David Butow/SABA Press Photos, Inc.; p. 68, Provided by Janet Weber; p. 68, Provided by Dave Dayton.

Chapter 3

p. 76, Ideal Steel & Builders' Supplies, Inc.; p. 79, Enrique Gutierrez/Tracy Press; p. 81, Danny Turner Photography; p. 84, Antoine Bootz; p. 85, Action Press/SABA Press Photos, Inc.; p. 88, Mark Peterson/SABA Press Photos, Inc.; p. 92, Courtesy of Mike Dorf; p. 100, Stewart Cohen/Tony Stone Images; p. 103, Provided by Matt Musick.

Chapter 4

p. 110, Jed Share/Westlight; p. 116, Madelyn Gengelbach; 117, Madelyn Gengelbach; 118, Courtesy of Hewlett-Packard Company; p. 122, Mitsuhiro Wasa/Gamma-Liaison, Inc.; p. 123, Ann States/SABA Press Photos, Inc.; p. 128, Karen Kusmauski/Matrix International; p. 133, Provided by Bill Newton; p. 133, Photo provided by W.H. Newton III.

Chapter 5

p. 140, Denise McGill/Springfield News-Leader; p. 144, Tony Cheng/Bank of Hawaii; p. 146, © 1996 Hispanic Business Magazine, Santa Barbara, California; p. 147 Hispanic Business, Inc./© 1996 Hispanic Business Magazine, Santa Barbara, California; p. 148, Trozzo Photography; p. 151, Tom's of Maine; p. 157, Courtesy of José Legaspi; p. 158, Andy Freeberg Photography; p. 162, Doug Thron; p. 163, Boeing Commercial Airplane Group; p. 163, Boeing Commercial Airplane Group; p. 163, Boeing Commercial Airplane Group; p. 173, Provided by Debra Barnhart; p. 173, Provided by Jerry Henry.

Chapter 6

p. 180, William Neumann/William Neumann Photography; p. 185, Churchill & Klehr Photography; p. 192, Fujitsu PC Corporation; p. 198, Graham Jones; p. 202, Provided by Ed Crispin; p. 202, Provided by Kim Scartelli.

Chapter 7

p. 210, Peter Blakely/SABA Press Photos, Inc.; p. 215, Richard Sanders/Sanders PhotoGraphics Inc.; p. 216, Geoffrey Gilpin; p. 219, Mark Duncan/AP/Wide World Photos; p. 225, PBJ Pictures/Liaison Agency, Inc.; p. 227, Provided by Ernie Collette; p. 227, Provided by Keith Smith.

Chapter 8

p. 234, Luxottica Group S.P.A.; p. 238, Anna Clopet; p. 243, Dan Lamont/Matrix International; p. 247, Robert A. Lisak/George C.W. Gatch; p. 249, Jason Reed/Reuters/Archive Photos; p. 250, Kerbs/Monkmeyer Press; p. 253, Hewlett-Packard Company; p. 258, Ed Quinn/SABA Press Photos, Inc.; p. 259, Jeff Sciortino Photography; p. 260, Provided by Joseph Lia; p. 260, Provided by Natalie E. Anderson.

Chapter 9

p. 266, Mojgan Azimi/Outline Press Syndicate Inc.; p. 270, Adrian Bradshaw/SABA Press Photos, Inc.; p. 273, Steven Rubin; p. 277, Robert Brenner/PhotoEdit; p. 278, Provided by Lorraine Cichowski; p. 286, Willie L. Hill Jr./Stock Boston; p. 288, Douglas Levere Photography; p. 289, Mark Richards/PhotoEdit; p. 291, Provided by Peter Babbington; p. 291, Provided by Brad Barnes.

Chapter 10

p. 298, Paul A. Souders; p. 302, James Schnepf Photography, Inc.; p. 306, Holland Productions; p. 311, Scott Montgomery Photography; p. 312, VeriFone, Inc.; p. 316, Sandra Steiner.; p. 318, Courtesy of Bayer AG; p. 321, Barry Fikes/Mercedes-Benz U.S. International; p. 325, Chris Maynard/New York Times Pictures; p. 327, Jessie Hornbuckle; p. 328, Provided by Rebecca Runyon; p. 328, Provided by Lizzi Carol Jones.

Chapter 11

p. 336, Willie Hill/FPG International; p. 338, Will & Deni McIntyre; p. 339, Ed Lallo/Liaison Agency, Inc.; p. 344, Papa John's International; p. 346, Mark Richards/Contact Press Images; p. 349, Provided by Coleman Peterson; p. 355, Provided by Royal Caribbean Cruises Ltd.; p. 361, Jim Judkis; p. 364, Jim Cummins/FPG International; p. 366, Rockwell International Corporation; p. 368, Michael Newman/PhotoEdit; p. 370, Provided by Dennis Alexander; p. 370, Provided by T.J. Owens.

Chapter 12

p. 378, Hispanic Business Inc.; p. 380, Phil Huber/Black Star; p. 381, Pinnacle Brands; p. 382, Joanna B. Pinneo/The Nature Conservancy; p. 385, Chris Corsmeier Photography; p. 387, Provided by Larry Lim; p. 391, Clint Karlsen/AP/Wide World Photos; p. 395, Peter Yates/SABA Press Photos, Inc.; p. 399, Siemens Business Communication Systems, Inc.; p. 400, New York Times Pictures/Fumiko Asahi/NYT Pictures; p. 406, John Abbott Photography; p. 407, John Abbott Photography; p. 408, Provided by Cindy Brewer; p. 408, Provided by Tom Zimmerman.

Chapter 13

p. 416, David Butow/SABA Press Photos, Inc.; p. 419, Robert Holmgren Photography; p. 421, Bozell Worldwide, Inc.; p. 426, Rick Stewart/Allsport Photography; p. 430, Julie Lopez, Habitat for Humanity International/Alphawave Designs; p. 434, Barbara Laing; p. 437, Provided by Samuel W. (Bill) France; p. 440, Provided by Bill Johnston; p. 440, Provided by Ernie Collette.

Krajewski, L., N–27
Kram, K. E., N–11, N–14
Krantz, M., N–11
Kraut, A. I., N–1
Krishnan, R., N–10
Kroll, M., N–9, N–10
Krone, B., N–3, N–21
Kruvent, C., 146
Ksier, K. J., N–3
Kuebler, P., 210–211
Kulik, C. T., N–23
Kumbhakar, S. C., N–23
Kurschner, D., N–6
Kuzela, L., N–28

L

Laabs, J. J., N–15
LaBarre, P., N–5, N–12
Lado, A. A., N–13
LaFasto, F.M.J., N–21
Lamb, R., N–9
Lamont, B. T., N–9, N–12, N–17
Landau, J., N–16
Landelles-Gordon, T. H., N–28
Lane, F. S., N–1
Lane, M., 95
Lang, L., 26
Langley, A., N–7
Lanta, T. K., N–9
Larson, C. R., N–21
Larson, L. L., N–3
Larsson, R., N–14
Latack, J. C., N–17
Lau, A. W., N–1
Laudon, J. P., N–13
Laudon, K. C., N–13
Lauer, S., 509
LaVan, H., N–29
Lavin, D., N–16
Lawler, E. E., III, N–3, N–15, N–19, N–23, N–26
Lawlor, J., N–15
Lawrence, A. T., N–13
Lawrence, P., N–12
Lawson, T., N–20
Lazenby, J., N–18
Leana, C. R., N–24
Ledford, G. E., Jr., N–15, N–21
Lee, C., N–13
Lee, S. A., N–23
Lee, S. M., N–17
Lee, S.-Y., N–23
Lee, W. B., N–28
Lefkowitz, J., N–20
Legaspi, J., 157, SM–6, SM–29
Leger, R., N–15
Lepak, D. P., N–13
Lesin, K., 56, 384
Levy, S., N–4
Lewicki, R. J., N–9
Lewin, K., N–3, N–15
Li, M., N–9
Lia, J., 260
Liden, R. C., N–14

Lieberman, M. A., N–16
Lied, T. L., N–24
Liedtka, J. M., N–12
Lim, L., 387, SM–26, SM–39
Limthongkul, S., 249
Lin, N.-P., N–27
Linden, D. W., N–2
Lindsay, C., N–16
Linowes, R. G., N–2
Li-Ping Tang, T., N–21
Lippitt, R., N–3
Liska, L. Z., N–24
Lisko, R. F., N–29
Litschert, R. J., N–9
Litvan, L. M., N–13
Livingstone, L. P., N–23
Locke, E. A., N–3, N–19, N–22, N–24
Lofton, K. E., 616–618, 639
London, M., N–13
Long, W. S., N–26
Longenecker, J. G., N–12
Longstreet, D., 89
Lord, R. G., N–22, N–24
Lorsch, J. W., N–12, N–20
Loveman, G. W., N–2, N–3
Low, R., 391
Lubin, J. S., N–29
Lumpkin, J. R., N–10
Luthans, F., N–1, N–2, N–5, N–8, N–17, N–23
Lutz, R. A., N–11

M

MacDonald, E., N–26
Machan, D., N–25
MacHardy, S., 95
Machiavelli, N., 427
Mack, A., 574
MacKenzie, S. B., N–26
MacMillan, I. C., N–4
Magee, J. F., N–27
Magnet, M., N–27
Main, J., N–11
Majchrzak, A., N–12
Malone, J., N–21
Mannheim, B., N–20
Manocchio, J. J., N–19
Mao, P., N–6
March, J. G., N–7
Maremont, M., N–5
Marinko, M. J., N–19
Mariotti, J., N–2, N–16
Markels, A., N–4, N–15
Marks, J., N–5
Marline, D., N–9
Marriott, M., N–18
Marsden, P. V., N–20
Marsh, A., N–21
Marshall, M., N–5
Martin, C. L., N–14, N–17
Martin, J., 622, N–11, N–16
Martin, M. H., N–11
Martinez, A., 393
Martinez, N., 379, 408

Martinko, M. J., N–1
Martocchio, J. J., N–21
Maslow, A., 50–51, 62, 65, 485, N–2
Mason, R. O., N–12
Masuda, M., N–17
Matejka, K., N–16
Mathieu, J. E., N–18, N–19
Mathys, N. J., N–10
Matson, E., N–21
Matthews, M. C., N–7
Matusky, G., 489
Maurer, R., N–16
Mausner, B., N–3
Mayer, R. C., N–25
Mayfield, E. C., N–14
Mayo, E., 49, N–2
Maznevski, M. L., N–20
McCaleb, V. M., N–24
McCall, M. W., Jr., N–1, N–7
McCartney, S., N–28
McCaskey, M. B., N–8
McClelland, C. L., N–22
McClelland, D., 485–486
McClelland, D. C., N–22
McClenahen, J. S., N–2, N–5, N–17, N–25, N–27
McElroy, J. C., N–24
McEvoy, G. M., N–20
McGarvey, R., N–29
McGee, G. W., N–19
McGrath, J. E., N–21
McGrath, M. R., N–7
McGrath, R. G., N–13, N–17
McGraw, D., N–27
McGregor, D., 51–52, 484, 485, N–3
McGuire, J. B., N–6
McGuire, J. M., N–5
McGuire, T. W., N–29
McKay, S., N–8
McKenna, D. D., N–1
McKenna, J. F., N–23, N–28
McKenna, R., N–27
McLaughlin, K. J., N–12
McLeod, A., N–16
McMahan, G. C., N–13
McMahon, J. T., N–22
McNamara, R., 47
McQuaid, S. J., N–7
Meadows, D., N–6
Mehta, S. N., N–27
Meindl, J. R., N–4, N–24
Melcher, R. A., N–5, N–10
Merchant, K. A., N–26
Mericle, B., 141, 173
Merrill, R. E., N–19
Mescon, T. S., N–5
Meyer, A. D., N–8
Meyer, C., N–21
Meyer, J. P., N–19, N–22
Meyer, V., N–14
Michaelson, L. K., N–21
Mikovich, G. T., N–29
Milakovich, M. E., N–17
Miles, M. B., N–16

Glindex
(a combination subject index and glossary)

to their superior performance, 273–75

Benefits, 362–65

Big-five model Five-factor model of personality that includes extraversion, agreeableness, conscientiousness, emotional stability, and openness to experience, 425–26

Bona fide occupational qualifications (BFOQs) A criterion such as sex, age, or national origin may be used as a basis for hiring if it can be clearly demonstrated to be job related, 341

Borderless organization A global type of organization in which artificial geographic barriers are eliminated so that the management structure can be more effectively globalized, 121

Boundaryless career, 358

Boundaryless organization An organization whose design is not defined by, or limited to, the horizontal, vertical, or external boundaries imposed by a predefined structure, 320–22

Bounded rationality Behavior that is rational within the parameters of a simplified model that captures the essential features of a problem, 190–91

Brainstorming An idea-generating process that encourages alternatives while withholding criticism, 463

Breakeven analysis A technique for identifying the point at which total revenue is just sufficient to cover total costs, 283–84

Broadbanding compensation An approach to pay systems which reduces the number of job levels or salary grades into a few wide bands, 365

Budget A numerical plan for allocating resources to specific activities, 275–76
as a financial control, 624–25
skill-building activity, SM-7 to SM-9
types of, 276–77
variable versus fixed, 277

Bureaucracy A form of organization marked by division of labor, hierarchy, rules and regulations, and impersonal relationships, 44, 45
organizational design, 314–15, 317

Bureaucratic control An approach to designing control systems which

emphasizes organizational authority and relies on administrative rules, regulations, procedures, policies, standardization of activities, and other administrative mechanisms to ensure that employees exhibit appropriate behaviors and meet performance standards, 554, 555

Business-level strategy Seeks to determine how a corporation should compete in each of its businesses, 237
competitive advantage and, 254
competitive strategies, 255–59
total quality management and, 254–55

C

Calm waters metaphor, 384

Capacity planning Assessing an operating system's ability to produce a desired number of output units for each type of product during a given time period, 590–91

Capital expenditure budget A budget that forecasts investments in property, buildings, and major equipment, 276–77

Career The sequence of positions occupied by a person during the course of a lifetime, 357
development, 357–62

Cash budget A budget that forecasts how much cash an organization will have on hand and how much it will need to meet expenses, 276

Cash cows Businesses that demonstrate low growth but have a high market share, 252

Centralization The degree to which decision making is concentrated in the upper levels of the organization, 308

Certainty A situation in which a manager can make accurate decisions because the outcome of every alternative is known, 195

Chain of command An unbroken line of authority that extends from the upper levels of the organization to the lowest levels and clarifies who reports to whom, 305–6
dual, 318

Change An alteration in people, structure, or technology, 380
external forces for, 380–81
internal forces for, 381–82

issues in, 393–404
managers and, 382
resistance to, 386–88, SM-25 to SM-27
skill-building activity, SM-25 to SM-27
techniques for managing, 389–93
views toward, 383–86

Change agents People who act as catalysts and manage the change process, 382, 383

Charismatic leadership Followers make attributions of heroic or extraordinary leadership abilities when they observe certain behaviors, 528–30

Child Safety Protection Act (1994), 98

Civil Rights Act (1964), 97, 342

Civil Rights Act (1991), 98, 342

Clan control An approach to designing control systems in which employee behaviors are regulated by the shared values, norms, traditions, rituals, beliefs, and other aspects of the organization's culture, 554, 555

Classical theorists The term used to describe early management theorists whose writings established the framework for many of our contemporary ideas on management and organization, 39

Classical view The view that management's only social responsibility is to maximize profits, 142–43

Closed systems Systems that are not influenced by and do not interact with their environment, 19

Coaching, 356, SM-11 to SM-13

Code of ethics A formal statement of an organization's primary values and the ethical rules it expects its employees to follow, 167–69

Coercion, change and, 388

Coercive power Power that rests on the application, or the threat of application, of physical sanctions such as the infliction of pain; the arousal of frustration through restriction of movement; or the controlling by force of basic physiological or safety needs, 535

Cognitive component of an attitude The beliefs, opinions, knowledge, or information held by a person, 419

Cognitive dissonance Any incompatibility between two or more attitudes or between behavior and attitudes, 420–22

Collaboration Resolving conflict by seeking a solution advantageous to all parties, 458

Collectivism A cultural dimension in which people expect others in their group to look after them and protect them when they are in trouble, 127

Combination strategy A corporate-level strategy that pursues two or more of the following strategies–stability, growth, or retrenchment–simultaneously, 251

Command groups, 448

Commitment concept Plans should extend far enough to see through current commitments, 219

Commitments, planning and, 218–19

Communication(s)
affected by technology, 324–26
change and, 387
gender differences, 540
informal, 458
organizational design affected by, 326–27

Compensation and benefits, 362–65

Competitive advantage What sets an organization apart; its competitive edge, 254
flexibility and, 607–8
speed and, 608–9

Competitive strategies, 255–59

Competitor intelligence Environmental scanning activity that seeks to identify who competitors are, what they're doing, and how their actions will affect the organization, 268–69

Competitors, role of, 96–97

Compressed workweek A workweek comprised of four ten-hour days, 502

Compromise An approach to managing conflict in which each party gives up something of value, 458

Computer-integrated manufacturing (CIM) Combines the organization's strategic business plan and manufacturing plan with state-of-the-art computer applications, 603

Computer monitoring, 571–72

Conceptual skills The ability to think and conceptualize about abstract situations, to see the organization as a whole and the relationships among its various subunits, and to visualize how the organization fits into its environment, 17–18

Conceptual style A decision-making style that is characterized by a high tolerance for ambiguity and an intuitive way of thinking, 200

Concurrent control Control that occurs while an activity is in progress, 564

Conditional maintenance Maintenance that calls for an overhaul or repair in response to an inspection, 600

Conflict Perceived incompatible differences that result in interference or opposition, 454
dysfunctional, 456
functional, 456
human relations view of, 455
interactionist view of, 456
managing, 454–58
traditional view of, 455

Conformity, 451–53

Consideration The extent to which a person has job relationships characterized by mutual trust, respect for subordinates' ideas, and regard for their feelings, 55, 57

Consultants, 64

Consumer Product Safety Act (1972), 98

Contingency perspective Recognizing and responding to situational variables as they arise, 21

Contingency variables, 21–22

Contingent workers Nonpermanent workers including temporaries, part-timers, consultants, freelancers, and contract workers, 64–65
motivating, 508

Contract workers, 64

Control Monitoring activities to ensure that they are being accomplished as planned and correcting any significant deviations, 12, 554
bureaucratic, 554, 555
clan, 554, 555
concurrent, 564
cultural differences, 569–70
dysfunctional side of, 568–69
ethics and, 570–73
feedback, 564, 566
feedforward, 563–64
importance of, 555–57
market, 554
of operations, 596–601
process, 557–61
qualities of an effective system, 566–68
types of, 554–55, 563–64, 566

Control charts A management control tool that shows results of measurements over a period of time,

with statistically determined upper and lower limits, 626
skill-building activity, SM-18 to SM-19
total quality management, 626–28

Control process The process of measuring actual performance, comparing it against a standard, and taking managerial action to correct deviations or inadequate standards, 557–61, 563

Control tools and techniques
behavioral controls, 630–38
financial controls, 623–26
information controls, 618–23
operations controls, 626–30

Conventional stage of moral development, 160

Cooptation, change and, 388

Core competencies An organization's major value-creating skills, capabilities, and resources that determine its competitive weapons, 242

Corporate-level strategy Seeks to determine what businesses a corporation should be in, 237
corporate portfolio matrix, 252–54
grand, 248–51
types of, 246

Cost center A unit in which managers are held responsible for all associated costs, 596

Cost control, 596

Cost leadership strategy The strategy an organization follows when it wants to be the lowest-cost producer in its industry, 257

Counseling, stress and, 403

Creativity The ability to combine ideas in a unique way or to make unusual associations between ideas, 404

Credibility Followers perceive someone as honest, competent, and able to inspire, 536–38

Critical incidents A performance appraisal technique in which an evaluator lists key behaviors that separate effective from ineffective job performance, 632

Critical path The longest sequence of activities in a PERT network, 281

Cross-functional team A hybrid grouping of individuals who are experts in various specialties (or functions) and who work together, 305, 448, 466

Culture
See also Organizational culture
assessing cross-cultural differences,

adversely affecting their workplace performance, 637

Employee-oriented leaders, 57

Employee Retirement Income Security Act (1974), 98

Employee stock ownership plan (ESOP) A compensation program in which employees become part owners of the organization by receiving stock as a performance incentive, 506–7

Empowerment Increasing the decision-making discretion of workers, 65
  leading through, 538–39

Entrepreneurs
  as change agents, 383
  global, 129
  how they get their ideas, 95
  managers as, 13, 14
  organizational design and structure and, 315
  personality of, 428
  strategic management and, 241
  versus managers, 26

Entrepreneurship A process by which people pursue opportunities, fulfilling needs and wants through innovation, without regard to the resources they currently control, 26

Environment Outside institutions or forces that potentially affect an organization's performance, 91, 93–94
  See also Global organizations/ globalization
  dynamic, 93
  general, 99–101
  general versus specific, 91
  greening of management, 154–58
  influence of, 90
  managerial decisions affected by, 101–2
  organizations and, 93–94
  specific, 91, 95–98
  stable, 93
  strategic management and, 240–41

Environmental complexity The number of components in an organization's environment and the extent of an organization's knowledge about its environmental components, 93

Environmental scanning The screening of large amounts of information to detect emerging trends and create scenarios, 268–70
  skill-building activity, SM-37 to SM-38

Environmental uncertainty The degree of change and complexity

in an organization's environment, 91, 93, 94
  organizational structure and, 313–14
  planning and, 217–18

Equal Employment Opportunity Act (1972), 98

Equal Pay Act (1963), 342

Equity theory The theory that an employee compares his or job's inputs/outcomes ratio to that of relevant others and then corrects any inequity, 494–96

Esteem needs Internal factors such as self-respect, autonomy, and achievement; and external factors such as status, recognition, and attention, 50

Ethics Rules and principles that define right and wrong conduct, 158
  See also Social responsibility
  audits of, 171
  code of, 167–69
  control and, 570–73
  factors that affect,160–65
  global, 165–66
  how to improve, 166–71
  individual characteristics, 161
  issue intensity and, 164–65
  job goals and, 169
  leadership and, 169
  moral development, stages of, 160–61
  organizational culture and, 162–64
  performance appraisals and, 170
  protective mechanisms, 171
  structural design of organizations and, 162
  training, 170
  views toward, 65–67, 159

Ethnocentric attitude The parochialistic belief that the best work approaches and practices are those of the home country (the country in which the company's headquarters are located), 113–14

European Union (EU) A union of fifteen European nations created to eliminate national barriers to travel, employment, investment, and trade, 115–17

Events End points that represent the completion of major activities in a PERT network, 281

Expectancy theory The theory that an individual tends to act in a certain way based on the expectation that the act will be followed by a given outcome and on the attractiveness of that outcome to the individual, 496–98

Expense budget A budget that lists the primary activities undertaken by a unit and allocates a dollar amount to each, 276

Expert power Influence that results from expertise, special skill, or knowledge, 536

F

Facilities layout planning Assessing and selecting among alternative layout options for equipment and work stations, 593

Facilities location planning The design and location of an operations facility, 591–92

Facsimile (fax) A communication system that allows the transmission of documents containing both text and graphics, 325

Family and Medical Leave Act (1993),98, 342

Family issues, 367–68

Feedback The degree to which carrying out the work activities required by a job results in an individual's obtaining direct and clear information about the effectiveness of his or her performance, 491
  performance appraisals and, 634
  skill-building activity, SM-32 to SM-34
  of survey, 392
  360 degree, 633–34

Feedback control Control imposed after an action has occurred, 564, 566

Feedforward control Control that prevents anticipated problems, 563–64

Fiedler contingency model The theory that effective groups depend on a proper match between a leader's style of interacting with subordinates and the degree to which the situation gives control and influence to the leader, 521–24

Figurehead role, 13, 14

Financial controls, 623–26

Firing employees, 346

First-line managers Supervisors; the lowest level of management, 7

Fixed budget A budget that assumes a fixed level of sales or production, 277

Fixed-interval reordering system A system that uses time as the determining factor for reviewing and reordering inventory items, 599

Policy A guide that establishes parameters for making decisions, 193

Political environment
global, 124–25
influence of, 99

Polycentric attitude The view that the managers in the host country (the foreign country where the organization is doing business) know the best work approaches and practices for running their operations, 113, 114

Polygraph Protection Act (1988), 342

Position power The degree of influence a leader has over power variables such as hiring, firing, discipline, promotions, and salary increases, 522

Power The capacity for a leader to influence work actions or decisions, 535
leaders and, 535–36
skill-building activity, SM-2 to SM-3

Power distance A cultural measure of the extent to which a society accepts the unequal distribution of power in institutions and organizations, 127–28

Preconventional stage of moral development, 160

Pressure groups, role of, 97–98

Preventive maintenance Maintenance performed before a breakdown occurs, 600

Principled stage of moral development, 160

Principles of management Universal truths of management that can be taught in schools, 44, 45

Principles of Scientific Management (Taylor), 40

Privacy Act (1974), 342

Privacy issues, 570

Probability theory The use of statistics to analyze past predictable patterns and to reduce risk in future plans, 287

Problem(s) A discrepancy between an existing and a desired state of affairs, 182
identification of, 182–84
ill-structured, 194
well-structured, 192–94

Problem avoider An approach to problems in which the person avoids or ignores information that points to a problem, 199

Problem seeker An approach to problems in which the person actively seeks out problems to solve or new opportunities to pursue, 199

Problem solver An approach to problems in which the person tries to solve problems as they come up, 199

Problem-solving skills, 355–56, SM-40 to SM-42

Procedure A series of interrelated sequential steps that can be used to respond to a structured problem, 193

Process consultation Help given by an outside consultant to a manager in perceiving, understanding, and acting upon process events, 392

Process control A quality control procedure in which sampling is done during the transformation process to determine whether the process itself is under control, 601

Process departmentalization Grouping jobs on the basis of product or customer flow, 304

Process layout Arranging manufacturing components together according to similarity of function, 593

Process planning Determining how a product or service will be produced, 592–93

Process production Continuous-process production, 313

Product departmentalization Grouping jobs by product line, 303

Product development, technology and, 603

Production-oriented leaders, 57

Productivity The overall output of goods and services produced, divided by the inputs needed to generate that output, 582
managing, 582–85
satisfaction versus, 422–23

Product layout Arranging manufacturing components according to the progressive steps by which a product is made, 593

Professionals, motivating, 507

Profitability test, 625

Profit budget A budget used by separate units of an organization that combines revenue and expense budgets to determine the unit's profit contribution, 276

Program Evaluation and Review Technique (PERT) A technique for scheduling complicated projects comprising many activities, some of which are interdependent, 280–83

Programmed decision A repetitive decision that can be handled by a routine approach, 192–94

Project A one-time-only set of activities that have a definite beginning and ending point in time, 289

Project management The task of getting a project's activities done on time, within budget, and according to specifications, 288–90, 589

Project structure An organization structure in which employees are permanently assigned to projects, 319

Psychological contracts The unwritten commitments and perceived obligations between workers and employers, 65–66

Psychology and Industrial Efficiency (Munsterberg), 48

Purchasing control, 596–99

Q

Qualitative forecasting Uses the judgment and opinions of knowledgeable individuals to predict future outcomes, 271–72

Quality circles Work groups that meet regularly to discuss, investigate, and correct quality problems, 474

Quality control, 600–601

Quality of life A national culture attribute that reflects the emphasis placed upon relationships and concern for others, 128

Quantitative approach The use of quantitative techniques to improve decision making, 46–47

Quantitative forecasting Applies a set of mathematical rules to a series of past data to predict future outcomes, 271, 272

Quantity of life A national culture attribute describing the extent to which societal values are characterized by assertiveness and materialism, 128

Question marks Businesses that demonstrate high growth but have low market share, 252

Queuing theory A technique that balances the cost of having a waiting line against the cost of service to maintain that line, 286–87

R

Range of variation The acceptable parameters of variance between actual performance and the standard, 559

Uncertainty avoidance A cultural measure of the degree to which people tolerate risk and unconventional behavior, 128

Unit production The production of items in units or small batches, 313

Unity of command The management principle that a subordinate should have one and only one superior to whom he or she is directly responsible, 306

Unrelated diversification A way that companies choose to grow that involves merging with or acquiring unrelated firms, or firms that are not directly related to what the company does, 250

Utilitarian view of ethics Decisions are made solely on the basis of their outcomes or consequences, 159

V

Validity The proven relationship that exists between a selection device and some relevant criterion, 348

Values Basic convictions about what is right and wrong, 161
 developing shared, 153–54
 purpose of shared, 151–53

Values-based management An approach to managing in which managers establish, promote, and practice an organization's shared values, 149–54

Variable budget A budget that takes into account those costs that vary with volume, 277

Variable sampling A quality control technique in which a measurement is taken to determine how much an item varies from the standard, 601

Vestibule training Training in which employees learn on the same equipment they will be using but in a simulated work environment, 357

Videoconferencing A communication system that allows a group of people to confer simultaneously and see each other over video screens, 326

Virtual workplaces Offices which are characterized by open spaces, movable furniture, portable phones, laptop computers, and electronic files, 327

Visionary leadership The ability to create and articulate a realistic, credible, attractive vision of the future for an organization or organizational unit that grows out of and improves upon the present, 530–32

Vocational Rehabilitation Act (1973), 342

Voice-mail A communication system that digitizes a spoken message, transmits it over a computer network, and stores the message on disk for the receiver to retrieve later, 325

W

Waiting-line theory, 286
Weak cultures, strong versus, 82–83

Weaknesses Activities the firm doesn't do well or resources it needs but doesn't possess, 242–43

Wealth of Nations, The (Smith), 39

Well-structured problems Straightforward, familiar, easily defined problems, 192–94

White-water rapids metaphor, 384–85
Women's Business Development Act (1991), 98
Worker Adjustment and Retraining Notification Act (1988), 98, 342
Workforce
 aging of, 99–100
 contingent, 64–65
 empowered, 65
 transmittal of organization culture to, 86–87

Workforce diversity Employees in organizations are heterogeneous in terms of gender, race, ethnicity, or other characteristics, 60–61
 managing, 365–66
 motivating, 501–4
 organizational culture and, 89
 planning and, 218
Workplace
 privacy, 570
 safety, 341

Work sampling A personnel selection device in which job applicants are presented with a miniature replica of a job and are asked to perform tasks central to that job, 350

Work specialization The degree to which tasks in the organization are subdivided into separate jobs; also known as division of labor, 301–2

Work teams Formal groups made up of interdependent individuals, responsible for the attainment of a goal, 464
Workweeks
 compressed, 502
 flexible, 502
 reduced, 346
World Wide Web
 job hunting on, 360
 role of, 61

Written essay A performance appraisal technique in which an evaluator writes out a description of an employee's strengths, weaknesses, past performance, and potential, and then makes suggestions for improvement, 632
Written tests, 349–50

LICENSE AGREEMENT

YOU SHOULD CAREFULLY READ THE FOLLOWING TERMS AND CONDITIONS BEFORE BREAKING THE SEAL ON THE PACKAGE. AMONG OTHER THINGS, THIS AGREEMENT LICENSES THE ENCLOSED SOFTWARE TO YOU AND CONTAINS WARRANTY AND LIABILITY DISCLAIMERS. BY BREAKING THE SEAL ON THE PACKAGE, YOU ARE ACCEPTING AND AGREEING TO THE TERMS AND CONDITIONS OF THIS AGREEMENT. IF YOU DO NOT AGREE TO THE TERMS OF THIS AGREEMENT, DO NOT BREAK THE SEAL. YOU SHOULD PROMPTLY RETURN THE PACKAGE UNOPENED.

LICENSE.

Subject to the provisions contained herein, Prentice-Hall, Inc. ("PH") hereby grants to you a non-exclusive, non-transferable license to use the object code version of the computer software product ("Software") contained in the package on a single computer of the type identified on the package.

SOFTWARE AND DOCUMENTATION.

PH shall furnish the Software to you on media in machine-readable object code form and may also provide the standard documentation ("Documentation") containing instructions for operation and use of the Software.

LICENSE TERM AND CHARGES.

The term of this license commences upon delivery of the Software to you and is perpetual unless earlier terminated upon default or as otherwise set forth herein.

TITLE.

Title, and ownership right, and intellectual property rights in and to the Software and Documentation shall remain in PH and/or in suppliers to PH of programs contained in the Software. The Software is provided for your own internal use under this license. This license does not include the right to sublicense and is personal to you and therefore may not be assigned (by operation of law or otherwise) or transferred without the prior written consent of PH. You acknowledge that the Software in source code form remains a confidential trade secret of PH and/or its suppliers and therefore you agree not to attempt to decipher or decompile, modify, disassemble, reverse engineer or prepare derivative works of the Software or develop source code for the Software or knowingly allow others to do so. Further, you may not copy the Documentation or other written materials accompanying the Software.

UPDATES.

This license does not grant you any right, license, or interest in and to any improvements, modifications, enhancements, or updates to the Software and Documentation. Updates, if available, may be obtained by you at PH's then current standard pricing, terms, and conditions.

LIMITED WARRANTY AND DISCLAIMER.

PH warrants that the media containing the Software, if provided by PH, is free from defects in material and workmanship under normal use for a period of sixty (60) days from the date you purchased a license to it.

THIS IS A LIMITED WARRANTY AND IT IS THE ONLY WARRANTY MADE BY PH. THE SOFTWARE IS PROVIDED "AS IS" AND PH SPECIFICALLY DISCLAIMS ALL WARRANTIES OF ANY KIND, EITHER EXPRESS OR IMPLIED, INCLUDING, BUT NOT LIMITED TO, THE IMPLIED WARRANTY OF MERCHANTABILITY AND FITNESS FOR A PARTICULAR PURPOSE. FURTHER, COMPANY DOES NOT WARRANT, GUARANTY OR MAKE ANY REPRESENTATIONS REGARDING THE USE, OR THE RESULTS OF THE USE, OF THE SOFTWARE IN TERMS OF CORRECTNESS, ACCURACY, RELIABILITY, CURRENTNESS, OR OTHERWISE AND DOES NOT WARRANT THAT THE OPERATION OF ANY SOFTWARE WILL BE UNINTERRUPTED OR ERROR FREE. COMPANY EXPRESSLY DISCLAIMS ANY WARRANTIES NOT STATED HEREIN. NO ORAL OR WRITTEN INFORMATION OR ADVICE GIVEN BY PH, OR ANY PH DEALER, AGENT, EMPLOYEE OR OTHERS SHALL CREATE, MODIFY OR EXTEND A WARRANTY OR IN ANY WAY INCREASE THE SCOPE OF THE FOREGOING WARRANTY, AND NEITHER SUBLICENSEE OR PURCHASER MAY RELY ON ANY SUCH INFORMATION OR ADVICE. If the media is subjected to accident, abuse, or improper use; or if you violate the terms of this Agreement, then this warranty shall immediately be terminated. This warranty shall not apply if the Software is used on or in conjunction with hardware or programs other than the unmodified version of hardware and programs with which the Software was designed to be used as described in the Documentation.

LIMITATION OF LIABILITY.

Your sole and exclusive remedies for any damage or loss in any way connected with the Software are set forth below. UNDER NO CIRCUMSTANCES AND UNDER NO LEGAL THEORY, TORT, CONTRACT, OR OTHERWISE, SHALL PH BE LIABLE TO YOU OR ANY OTHER PERSON FOR ANY INDIRECT, SPECIAL, INCIDENTAL, OR CONSEQUENTIAL DAMAGES OF ANY CHARACTER INCLUDING, WITHOUT LIMITATION, DAMAGES FOR LOSS OF GOODWILL, LOSS OF PROFIT, WORK STOPPAGE, COMPUTER FAILURE OR MALFUNCTION, OR ANY AND ALL OTHER COMMERCIAL DAMAGES OR LOSSES, OR FOR ANY OTHER DAMAGES EVEN IF PH SHALL HAVE BEEN INFORMED OF THE POSSIBILITY OF SUCH DAMAGES, OR FOR ANY CLAIM BY ANY OTHER PARTY. PH'S THIRD PARTY PROGRAM SUPPLIERS MAKE NO WARRANTY, AND HAVE NO LIABILITY WHATSOEVER, TO YOU. PH's sole and exclusive obligation and liability and your exclusive remedy shall be: upon PH's election, (i) the replacement of your defective media; or (ii) the repair or correction of your defective media if PH is able, so that it will conform to the above warranty; or (iii) if PH is unable to replace or repair, you may terminate this license by returning the Software. Only if you inform PH of your problem during the applicable warranty period will PH be obligated to honor this warranty. You may contact PH to inform PH of the problem as follows:

SOME STATES OR JURISDICTIONS DO NOT ALLOW THE EXCLUSION OF IMPLIED WARRANTIES OR LIMITATION OR EXCLUSION OF CONSEQUENTIAL DAMAGES, SO THE ABOVE LIMITATIONS OR EXCLUSIONS MAY NOT APPLY TO YOU. THIS WARRANTY GIVES YOU SPECIFIC LEGAL RIGHTS AND YOU MAY ALSO HAVE OTHER RIGHTS WHICH VARY BY STATE OR JURISDICTION.

MISCELLANEOUS.

If any provision of this Agreement is held to be ineffective, unenforceable, or illegal under certain circumstances for any reason, such decision shall not affect the validity or enforceability (i) of such provision under other circumstances or (ii) of the remaining provisions hereof under all circumstances and such provision shall be reformed to and only to the extent necessary to make it effective, enforceable, and legal under such circumstances. All headings are solely for convenience and shall not be considered in interpreting this Agreement. This Agreement shall be governed by and construed under New York law as such law applies to agreements between New York residents entered into and to be performed entirely within New York, except as required by U.S. Government rules and regulations to be governed by Federal law.

YOU ACKNOWLEDGE THAT YOU HAVE READ THIS AGREEMENT, UNDERSTAND IT, AND AGREE TO BE BOUND BY ITS TERMS AND CONDITIONS. YOU FURTHER AGREE THAT IT IS THE COMPLETE AND EXCLUSIVE STATEMENT OF THE AGREEMENT BETWEEN US THAT SUPERSEDES ANY PROPOSAL OR PRIOR AGREEMENT, ORAL OR WRITTEN, AND ANY OTHER COMMUNICATIONS BETWEEN US RELATING TO THE SUBJECT MATTER OF THIS AGREEMENT.

U.S. GOVERNMENT RESTRICTED RIGHTS.

Use, duplication or disclosure by the Government is subject to restrictions set forth in subparagraphs (a) through (d) of the Commercial Computer-Restricted Rights clause at FAR 52.227-19 when applicable, or in subparagraph (c) (1) (ii) of the Rights in Technical Data and Computer Software clause at DFARS 252.227-7013, and in similar clauses in the NASA FAR Supplement.